Baseball america®
PROSPECT
HANDBOOK

BASEBALL AMERICA INC. DURHAM, N.C.

BaseBall america
PROSPECT
HANDBOOK

Editors
MATT EDDY, JOHN MANUEL

Assistant Editors
BEN BADLER, TEDDY CAHILL, J.J. COOPER, KYLE GLASER, MICHAEL LANANNA, VINCENT LARA-CINISOMO, JOSH NORRIS, JIM SHONERD

Database and Application Development
BRENT LEWIS

Contributing Writers
BILL BALLEW, HUDSON BELINSKY, DERRICK GOOLD, TOM HAUDRICOURT, STEVE MELEWSKI, BILL MITCHELL, JOHN PERROTTO, TRACY RINGOLSBY, ALEX SPEIER

Photo Editor
JIM SHONERD

Design & Production
SARA HIATT MCDANIEL, LINWOOD WEBB

Cover Photo
YOAN MONCADA BY LARRY GOREN

ESTABLISHED 1981 • P.O. Box 12877, Durham, NC 27709 • Phone (919) 682-9635

THE TEAM
GENERAL MANAGER Will Lingo @willingo

EDITORIAL
EDITOR IN CHIEF John Manuel @johnmanuelba
MANAGING EDITOR J.J. Cooper @jjcoop36
ASSOCIATE EDITORS Matt Eddy @matteddyba
Kyle Glaser @KyleAGlaser
NEWS EDITOR Josh Norris @jnorris427
WEB EDITOR Vincent Lara-Cinisomo @vincelara
NATIONAL WRITERS Ben Badler @benbadler
Teddy Cahill @tedcahill
ASSISTANT EDITORS Michael Lananna @mlananna
Jim Shonerd @jimshonerdba
EDITORIAL ASSISTANT Hudson Belinsky @hudsonbelinsky

PRODUCTION
DESIGN & PRODUCTION DIRECTOR Sara Hiatt McDaniel
MULTIMEDIA MANAGER Linwood Webb
PRODUCTION MANAGER Inna Cazares

ADVERTISING
ADVERTISING DIRECTOR George Shelton
DIGITAL SALES MANAGER Larry Sarzyniak
MARKETPLACE MANAGER Kristopher M. Lull
ACCOUNT EXECUTIVE Edward Richards
MARKETING MANAGER Abbey Langdon

BUSINESS
CUSTOMER SERVICE Ronnie McCabe, Nicholas Johnson
ACCOUNTING/OFFICE MANAGER Hailey Carpenter
TECHNOLOGY MANAGER Brent Lewis

STATISTICAL SERVICE
MAJOR LEAGUE BASEBALL ADVANCED MEDIA

ACTION/OUTDOOR GROUP
MANAGEMENT
PRODUCTION DIRECTOR Kasey Kelley
VP, FINANCE Matthew Cunningham

SALES & MARKETING
VP, SALES Kristen Ude
SALES ANALYST Mozelle Martinez
SALES & MARKETING SPECIALIST Aaron Santanello

DESIGN
CREATIVE DIRECTOR Marc Hostetter

EVENTS
EVENTS DIRECTOR Scott Desidero
VP/GM, DEW TOUR Adam Cozens
OPERATIONS DIRECTOR, DEW TOUR Anthony Dittman

DIGITAL
DIRECTOR OF ENGINEERING Jeff Kimmel
SENIOR PRODUCT MANAGER Marc Bartell
DIGITAL CONTENT STRATEGIES MANAGER Kristopher Heineman

FACILITIES
MANAGER Randy Ward
IT SUPPORT SPECIALIST James Rodney

THE ENTHUSIAST NETWORK

TEN: THE ENTHUSIAST NETWORK, LLC
CHAIRMAN Peter Englehart
CHIEF EXECUTIVE OFFICER Scott P. Dickey
CHIEF FINANCIAL OFFICER Bill Sutman
PRESIDENT, AUTOMOTIVE Scott Bailey
EVP/GM, SPORTS & ENTERTAINMENT Norb Garrett
CHIEF MARKETING OFFICER Jonathan Anastas
CHIEF COMMERCIAL OFFICER Eric Schwab
GENERAL MANAGER, VIDEO PROGRAMMING Bobby Akin
MANAGING DIRECTOR, STUDIO TEN Jerry Solomon
EVP, OPERATIONS Kevin Mullan
SVP, EDITORIAL & ADVERTISING OPERATIONS Amy Diamond
SVP /GM, PERFORMANCE AFTERMARKET Matt Boice
VP, FINANCIAL PLANNING Mike Cummings
SVP, AUTOMOTIVE DIGITAL Geoff DeFrance
SVP, AFTERMARKET AUTOMOTIVE CONTENT David Freiburger
SVP, IN-MARKET AUTOMOTIVE CONTENT Ed Loh
SVP, DIGITAL, SPORTS & ENTERTAINMENT Greg Morrow
SVP, DIGITAL ADVERTISING OPERATIONS Elisabeth Murray
SVP, MARKETING Ryan Payne

CONSUMER MARKETING, ENTHUSIAST MEDIA SUBSCRIPTION COMPANY, INC.
SVP, CIRCULATION Tom Slater
VP, RETENTION & OPERATIONS FULFILLMENT Donald T. Robinson III

By definition, any prospect ranking is a snapshot in time. Reporters like us at Baseball America find new sources, or seek new data in the numbers or adjust to the changing landscape of the major league game. It's kind of amazing to think about the changes in baseball in the 21st Century. The constant, seemingly endless increase in velocity and strikeouts, the ebb and flow of home run rates and the greater amount of information in the game today have wrought changes not just in how the game is played in the major leagues, but how it's scouted at the amateur level and how players are developed.

Baseball America has done its best to stay abreast of the changes, and BA Grades are a huge part of that. It's the sixth Handbook with our Grades; all 900 players are evaluated with a ceiling Grade (on a 20-80 scale) and a Risk Factor (Low to Extreme). Some teams prefer ceiling while others try to minimize risk with prospects. Some would prefer, for example, Andrew Benintendi, a big league-ready player with a long track record for hitting but a smaller physical frame. Others would prefer Yoan Moncada, a ballplayer in a running back's body with elite athleticism but also more risk due to his more raw offensive approach. One is a 65/Low, the other a 70/High. Whom would you choose? That's one of the fun parts of writing about prospects, and hopefully about reading the Prospect Handbook.

We've continued to be tougher graders every year, and this year, we've eliminated the Safe grade. We have used it sparingly in the past for prospects who we believed already had established themselves at their major league role. But the "Safe" label really doesn't apply to prospects. We cut it, and anticpate trying to further separate out "Extreme" risk prospects in the future as the system keeps evolving, like the game. We've also put a 40 grade on more players than ever this year. As my colleague Ben Badler says, there's nothing wrong with being a 40 if you're a big leaguer. There are plenty of 40s in the major leagues. It's a good point to remember.

Speaking of Ben, he focuses his considerable talents on international players. Matt Eddy, the main editor on the book, also is our most analytically-inclined staffer. Kyle Glaser, our newest staffer, has reporting chops honed while covering college baseball and the minor leagues. J.J. Cooper and I are now BA old hands with lessons learned over prospect rankings gone wrong—and right. The five of us offer our personal Top 50 prospect lists in the pages that follow, hints at what is to come when BA reveals its Top 100 Prospects in February. We bring different approaches and different ways of looking at the game to our lists, with our own unique insights.

In an effort to have more thorough reports, we have limited stat lines for players to the last three years. That gives us more space for scouting information. Complete stats for players are online, for free, in many different places including at www.baseballamerica.com.

One change for 2017 involves our transaction deadline. This year, we waited until after the Rule 5 draft and the end of the Winter Meetings, setting the deadline at Dec. 9. Any changes that happened thereafter—trades, free-agent signings, etc.—are not reflected in this book. But if your team traded for a prospect, you can find him (via the index at the back), read his report and rank him in the appropriate spot in his new organization using his BA Grade.

We tried to combine getting fresh information into the book with giving the book a thorough edit. We hope we succeeded, and we hope you enjoy the 2017 Prospect Handbook.

JOHN MANUEL
EDITOR IN CHIEF, BASEBALL AMERICA

EDITOR'S NOTE: Transactions for this book go through Dec. 8. You can find players even if they have changed organizations by using the handy index in the back.
>> For the purposes of this book, a prospect is any player who has no more than 50 innings pitched, 30 relief appearances or 130 at-bats in the major leagues, regardless of major league service time. Finally, the grades you'll find for each team's drafts are based solely on the quality of the players signed, with no consideration given to the players that draft picks were traded for or how many picks a team might have lost.

TABLE OF CONTENTS

Dansby Swanson got plenty of big league time in 2016, but with 129 major league at-bats, he's still prospect eligible and leading a Braves' farm system loaded with upside and premium arms

DIMAOND IMAGES

For the sixth year in a row, Baseball America has assigned Grades and Risk Factors for each of the 900 prospects in the Prospect Handbook. For the BA Grade, we used a 20-to-80 scale, similar to the scale scouts use, to keep it familiar. However, most major league clubs put an overall numerical grade on players, called the Overall Future Potential or OFP. Often the OFP is merely an average of the player's tools.

The BA Grade is not an OFP. It's a measure of a prospect's value, and it attempts to gauge the player's realistic ceiling. We've continued to adjust our grades to try to be more realistic, and less optimistic, and keep refining the grade vetting process. The majority of the players in this book rest in the 50 High/45 Medium range, because the vast majority of worthwhile prospects in the minors are players who either have a chance to be everyday regulars but are far from that possibility, or players who are closer to the majors but who are likely to be role players and useful contributors. Few future franchise players or perennial all-stars graduate from the minors in any given year. The goal of the Grade/Risk system is to allow readers to take a quick look at how strong their team's farm system is, and how much immediate help the big league club can expect from its prospect. Got a minor leaguer who was traded from one organization to the other after the book went to press? Use the player's Grade/Risk and see where he would rank in his new system.

It also helps with our Organization Rankings, but those will not simply flow, in formulaic fashion, from the Grade/Risk results. Some staff members favor star power in a farm system, while others place more emphasis on depth of talent.

BA GRADE

50 Risk: High

BA Grade Scale

GRADE	HITTER ROLE	PITCHER ROLE	EXAMPLES
75-80	Franchise Player	No. 1 starter	Clayton Kershaw, Kris Bryant, Mike Trout
65-70	Perennial All-Star	No. 2 starter	Robinson Cano, Anthony Rizzo, Johnny Cueto
60	Occasional All-Star	No. 3 starter, Game's best reliever	Starling Marte, Brandon Crawford, Aroldis Chapman
55	First Division Regular	No. 3/No. 4 starter, Elite closer	Rougned Odor, Gio Gonzalez, Zach Britton
50	Solid Average Regular	No. 4 starter, Elite set-up reliever	Mike Leake, Odubel Herrera, Kelvin Herrera,
45	Second-Division Regular/Platoon	No. 5 starter, Lower-leverage reliever	Chris Carter, Tom Milone, Dan Otero
40	Reserve	Fill-in starter, relief specialist	Keyvius Sampson, J.B. Schuck, Jerry Blevins

RISK FACTORS

LOW: Likely to reach realistic ceiling, certain big league career barring injury.

MEDIUM: Still some work to do to turn tools into major league-caliber skills, but fairly polished player.

HIGH: Most draft picks in their first seasons, players with plenty of projection left, players with a significant flaw left to correct or players whose injury history is worrisome.

EXTREME: Teenagers in Rookie ball, players with significant injury histories or players whose struggle with a key skill (especially control for pitchers or strikeout rate for hitters) is a significant barrier to them ever reaching their potential.

Explaining The 20-80 Scouting Scale

None of the authors of this book is a scout, but we all have spoken to plenty of scouts to report on the prospects and scouting reports enclosed in the Prospect Handbook. So we use their lingo, and the 20-80 scouting scale is part of that. Many of these grades are measurable data, such as fastball velocity and speed (usually timed from home to first or in workouts over 60 yards). A fastball grade doesn't stem solely from its velocity—command and life are crucial elements as well—but throwing 100 mph will earn a player an 80 grade. Secondary pitches are graded in a similar fashion. The more swings-and-misses a pitch induces from hitters and the sharper the bite of the movement, the better the grade.

Velocity steadily has increased over the past decade. Many scouts still think of a 88-91 mph fastball as average, but major league Pitch f/x data says it's below-average. Big league starting pitchers sit 91-92 mph. You can reduce the scale by 1 mph for lefthanders as they on average throw with slightly reduced velocity. Fastballs earn their grades based on the average range of the pitch over the course of a typical outing, not touching or bumping the peak velocity on occasion.

A move to the bullpen complicates in another direction. Pitchers airing it out for one inning should throw harder than someone trying to last six or seven innings, so add 1-2 mph for relievers. Yes, nowadays an 80 fastball for a reliever needs to sit at 98-99 mph with some movement and command.

Hitting ability is as much a skill as it is a tool, but the physical elements—hand-eye coordination, swing mechanics, bat speed—are key factors in the hit tool grade. Raw power generally is measured by how far a player can hit the ball, but game power is graded by how many home runs the hitter projects to hit in the majors, preferably an average over the course of a career. Some teams consider the player reaching that level of production as a validation of the power tool grade, while others do not.

Arm strength can be evaluated by observing the velocity and carry of throws, measured in workouts with radar guns or measured in games for catchers with pop times—the time it takes from the pop of the ball in the catcher's mitt to the pop of the ball in the fielder's glove at second base. Defense takes different factors into account by position but starts with proper footwork and technique, incorporates physical attributes such as hands, short-area quickness and fluid actions, then adds subtle skills such as instincts and anticipation as a last layer.

Not every team uses the wording below. Some use a 2-to-8 scale without half-grades, and others use above-average and plus synonymously. But for the Handbook, consider this BA's 20-80 scale.

20: As bad as it gets for a big leaguer. Think Steven Wright's fastball or Michael Martinez's bat.

30: Poor, but not unplayable, such as Coco Crisp's arm or Yunel Escobar' power.

40: Below-average, such as Wilmer Flores' defense, or Mike Fiers' fastball velocity.

45: Fringe-average. Mike Leake's fastball, Trevor Bauer's control and Steven Vogt's defense qualify.

50: Major league average. Jason Hammel's fastball or Melky Cabrera's power.

55: Above-average. Russell Martin's power.

60: Plus. Joe Panik's defense or Jon Lester's control.

70: Plus-Plus. Among the best tools in the game, such as Corey Seager's arm, Felix Hernandez's changeup, Todd Frazier's power or Brandon Crawford's defense.

80: Top of the scale. Some scouts consider only one player's tool in all of the major leagues to be 80. Think Miguel Cabrera's hit tool, Yasiel Puig's arm or Aroldis Chapman's 103 mph fastball.

20-80 Measurables

SPEED 60-Yard Dash Times (In Seconds)	SPEED Home-First (In Secs.) RHH—LHH	POWER Grade Home Runs	FASTBALL Velocity (Starters) Grade Velocity	ARM STRENGTH Catcher: Pop Times To Second Base (In Seconds)
80 .... < 6.44	80 ... 4.00—3.90	80 .... 35+	80 ..... 97+ mph	80 .... < 1.74
70 ..... 6.45-6.64	70 ... 4.10—4.00	70 29-34	70 96	70 ..... 1.75-1.84
60 ..... 6.65-6.84	65 ... 4.15—4.05	65 25-30	65 95	60 ..... 1.85-1.94
50 ..... 6.85-6.99	60 ... 4.20—4.10	60 21-26	60 94	50 ..... 1.95-2.04
40 ..... 7.00-7.24	55 ... 4.25—4.15	55 17-22	55 93	40 ..... 2.05-2.14
30 ..... 7.25-7.44	50 ... 4.30—4.20	50 14-18	50 91-92	30 ..... 2.15-2.24
20 .... > 7.45	45 ... 4.35—4.25	45 11-15	45 90	20 .... > 2.25
	40 ... 4.40—4.30	40 7-12	40 88-89	
	30 ... 4.50—4.40	30 4-8	30 86-87	
	20 ... 4.60—4.50	20 0-5	20 ..... 85 or less	

PARK FACTORS

Our park factors are calculated from 2016 data—100 is neutral—and compare each team's home rates with road rates for: (1) runs per game, (2) home runs per game, and (3) batting average on balls in play.

International (AAA)	Affiliation	Runs	HR	BABIP
Buffalo	Blue Jays	103	95	97
Charlotte	White Sox	108	135	104
Columbus	Indians	120	164	103
Durham	Rays	106	124	102
Gwinnett	Braves	100	104	101
Indianapolis	Pirates	78	65	101
Lehigh Valley	Phillies	107	97	103
Louisville	Reds	98	110	96
Norfolk	Orioles	95	68	97
Pawtucket	Red Sox	97	127	90
Rochester	Twins	103	78	100
Scranton/W-B	Yankees	92	94	100
Syracuse	Nationals	105	81	106
Toledo	Tigers	92	83	100

Pacific Coast (AAA)	Affiliation	Runs	HR	BABIP
Albuquerque	Rockies	132	134	110
Colorado Springs	Brewers	147	89	125
El Paso	Padres	111	125	104
Fresno	Astros	101	102	96
Iowa	Cubs	94	85	97
Las Vegas	Mets	120	121	108
Memphis	Cardinals	81	89	90
Nashville	Athletics	79	64	93
New Orleans	Marlins	78	96	89
Oklahoma City	Dodgers	105	93	103
Omaha	Royals	107	146	100
Reno	D-backs	123	100	109
Round Rock	Rangers	76	79	88
Sacramento	Giants	77	95	90
Salt Lake	Angels	107	112	110
Tacoma	Mariners	78	89	89

Eastern (AA)	Affiliation	Runs	HR	BABIP
Akron	Indians	98	93	100
Altoona	Pirates	109	79	107
Binghamton	Mets	94	94	100
Bowie	Orioles	107	126	100
Erie	Tigers	93	88	103
Harrisburg	Nationals	105	130	98
Hartford	Rockies	87	84	95
New Hampshire	Blue Jays	110	104	107
Portland	Red Sox	113	85	107
Reading	Phillies	108	153	96
Richmond	Giants	88	65	92
Trenton	Yankees	89	96	97

Southern (AA)	Affiliation	Runs	HR	BABIP
Biloxi	Brewers	96	119	96
Birmingham	White Sox	94	88	96
Chattanooga	Twins	119	137	104
Jackson	Mariners	98	83	99
Jacksonville	Marlins	99	120	97
Mississippi	Braves	90	67	104
Mobile	D-backs	106	90	111
Montgomery	Rays	108	100	103
Pensacola	Reds	94	82	97
Tennessee	Cubs	97	123	96

Texas (AA)	Affiliation	Runs	HR	BABIP
Arkansas	Angels	82	56	102
Corpus Christi	Astros	102	145	94
Frisco	Rangers	121	116	112
Midland	Athletics	115	78	106
NW Arkansas	Royals	103	86	107
San Antonio	Padres	77	64	92
Springfield	Cardinals	106	168	92
Tulsa	Dodgers	99	113	97

California (HiA)	Affiliation	Runs	HR	BABIP
Bakersfield	Mariners	106	141	107
High Desert	Rangers	131	152	102
Inland Empire	Angels	84	64	96
Lake Elsinore	Padres	88	67	99
Lancaster	Astros	134	171	109
Modesto	Rockies	82	47	98
R. Cucamonga	Dodgers	103	88	100
San Jose	Giants	84	70	95
Stockton	Athletics	89	108	96
Visalia	D-backs	103	121	100

Carolina (HiA)	Affiliation	Runs	HR	BABIP
Carolina	Braves	79	93	96
Frederick	Orioles	124	196	107
Lynchburg	Indians	105	82	104
Myrtle Beach	Cubs	96	109	94
Potomac	Nationals	89	92	91
Salem	Red Sox	106	53	108
Wilmington	Royals	103	97	104
Winston-Salem	White Sox	101	94	98

Florida State (HiA)	Affiliation	Runs	HR	BABIP
Bradenton	Pirates	100	98	101
Brevard County	Brewers	94	88	103
Charlotte	Rays	106	107	103
Clearwater	Phillies	91	102	93
Daytona	Reds	118	123	105
Dunedin	Blue Jays	108	99	104
Fort Myers	Twins	97	100	98
Jupiter	Marlins	89	58	99
Lakeland	Tigers	99	174	95
Palm Beach	Cardinals	94	47	100
St. Lucie	Mets	103	105	100
Tampa	Yankees	100	80	100

Midwest (LoA)	Affiliation	Runs	HR	BABIP
Beloit	Athletics	103	89	101
Bowling Green	Rays	91	143	94
Burlington	Angels	113	145	96
Cedar Rapids	Twins	107	119	99
Clinton	Mariners	90	87	96
Dayton	Reds	108	120	106
Fort Wayne	Padres	108	59	107
Great Lakes	Dodgers	86	85	96
Kane County	D-backs	94	72	100
Lake County	Indians	103	127	101
Lansing	Blue Jays	110	96	104
Peoria	Cardinals	84	87	95
Quad Cities	Astros	105	92	101
South Bend	Cubs	97	112	99
West Michigan	Tigers	98	62	103
Wisconsin	Brewers	109	131	103

South Atlantic (LoA)	Affiliation	Runs	HR	BABIP
Asheville	Rockies	141	161	116
Augusta	Giants	88	55	103
Charleston	Yankees	84	52	99
Columbia	Mets	89	90	93
Delmarva	Orioles	99	70	100
Greensboro	Marlins	104	206	97
Greenville	Red Sox	100	106	101
Hagerstown	Nationals	95	126	92
Hickory	Rangers	94	116	98
Kannapolis	White Sox	98	75	104
Lakewood	Phillies	87	61	93
Lexington	Royals	104	153	96
Rome	Braves	120	71	105
West Virginia	Pirates	102	116	102

AN OVERVIEW

Another feature of the Prospect Handbook is a depth chart of every organization's minor league talent. This shows you at a glance what kind of talent a system has and provides even more prospects beyond the Top 30.

Players are usually listed on the depth charts where we think they'll ultimately end up. To help you better understand why players are slotted at particular positions, we show you here what scouts look for in the ideal candidate at each spot, with individual tools ranked in descending order.

LF	CF	RF
Power	Fielding	Power
Hitting	Hitting	Hitting
Fielding	Speed	Arm Strength
Arm Strength	Power	Fielding
Speed	Arm Strength	Speed

3B	SS	2B	1B
Power	Fielding	Hitting	Power
Hitting	Arm Strength	Fielding	Hitting
Fielding	Hitting	Power	Fielding
Arm Strength	Speed	Speed	Arm Strength
Speed	Power	Arm Strength	Speed

C
Fielding
Hitting
Arm Strength
Power
Speed

STARTING PITCHERS

No. 1 starter	No. 2 starter	No. 3 starter	No. 4-5 starters
• Two plus pitches	• Two plus pitches	• One plus pitch	• Command of two major
• Average third pitch	• Average third pitch	• Two average pitches	league pitches
• Plus-plus command	• Average command	• Average command	• Average velocity
• Plus makeup	• Average makeup	• Average makeup	• Consistent breaking ball
			• Decent changeup

CLOSER	SETUP MAN
• One dominant pitch	• Plus fastball
• Second plus pitch	• Second above-
• Plus command	average pitch
• Plus-plus makeup	• Average command

When Baseball America ranks prospects, there's almost always a byline attributing the ranking to the person who finally put the players in order, who decided, "OK, this guy's No. 6 and this guy's No. 7." But in truth, all of our rankings are more than one person's opinion. They are most often a reflection of the consensus of sources on the subject—managers, coaches, scouts, front-office personnel, the whole spectrum—filtered through the expertise of our writers and editors.

Except here, really. In this section of the Handbook, we get personal. Sifting through all of the information we've gathered to this point, five of our editors give their own personal takes on the game's top 50 prospects. This helps form the basis of the arguments that shape Baseball America's official Top 100 Prospects list, which is released each February. We consider it the definitive guide to the best talent in the minor leagues, and you can find it in our print edition or online at BaseballAmerica.com.

The rules for these lists are the same for any prospect who appears in the Handbook: no more than 130 at-bats, 50 innings or 30 relief appearances in the major leagues. We do not consider service time in our eligibility requirements. These rankings represent how each person regarded the top minor league talent in the game at a moment in time. Ask us again in a few months (or few weeks) how these prospects stack up, and you'll get a different answer.

Alex Reyes impressed in a late-season stint with the Cardinals

BEN BADLER

1. Andrew Benintendi, of, Red Sox	26. Kyle Lewis, of, Mariners
2. Yoan Moncada, 2b/3b, White Sox	27. Francisco Mejia, c, Indians
3. Victor Robles, of, Nationals	28. Kyle Tucker, of, Astros
4. Dansby Swanson, ss, Braves	29. Triston McKenzie, rhp, Indians
5. Austin Meadows, of, Pirates	30. Cody Reed, lhp, Reds
6. Alex Reyes, rhp, Cardinals	31. Josh Hader, lhp, Brewers
7. Willy Adames, ss, Rays	32. Yadier Alvarez, rhp, Dodgers
8. Cody Bellinger, 1b/of, Dodgers	33. Brendan Rodgers, ss, Rockies
9. Manuel Margot, of, Padres	34. Chance Sisco, c, Orioles
10. Amed Rosario, ss, Mets	35. Clint Frazier, of, Yankees
11. J.P. Crawford, ss, Phillies	36. Vladimir Guerrero Jr., 3b, Blue Jays
12. Gleyber Torres, ss, Yankees	37. Kolby Allard, lhp, Braves
13. Nick Senzel, 3b, Reds	38. Anderson Espinoza, rhp, Padres
14. Ozzie Albies, ss/2b, Braves	39. Lewis Brinson, of, Brewers
15. Rafael Devers, 3b, Red Sox	40. Jose De Leon, rhp, Dodgers
16. Mickey Moniak, of, Phillies	41. Luis Ortiz, rhp, Brewers
17. Eloy Jimenez, of, Cubs	42. Michael Kopech, rhp, White Sox
18. Tyler Glasnow, rhp, Pirates	43. Franklin Perez, rhp, Astros
19. Francis Martes, rhp, Astros	44. German Marquez, rhp, Rockies
20. Josh Bell, 1b/of, Pirates	45. Jeff Hoffman, rhp, Rockies
21. A.J. Reed, 1b, Astros	46. Raimel Tapia, of, Rockies
22. Franklin Barreto, ss/2b, Athletics	47. Alex Verdugo, of, Dodgers
23. Lucas Giolito, rhp, White Sox	48. Tyler O'Neill, of, Mariners
24. Mitch Keller, rhp, Pirates	49. Corey Ray, of, Brewers
25. Jake Bauers, of/1b, Rays	50. Lourdes Gurriel, ss/3b/of, Blue Jays

J.J. COOPER

1. Andrew Benintendi, of, Red Sox
2. Yoan Moncada, 2b/3b, White Sox
3. Dansby Swanson, ss, Braves
4. Alex Reyes, rhp, Cardinals
5. Cody Bellinger, 1b/of, Dodgers
6. Gleyber Torres, ss, Yankees
7. Ozzie Albies, 2b/ss, Braves
8. Francis Martes, rhp, Astros
9. J.P. Crawford, ss, Phillies
10. Austin Meadows, of, Pirates
11. Nick Senzel, 3b, Reds
12. Amed Rosario, ss, Mets
13. Eloy Jimenez, of, Cubs
14. Mitch Keller, rhp, Pirates
15. Brent Honeywell, rhp, Rays
16. Kyle Tucker, of, Astros
17. Reynaldo Lopez, rhp, White Sox
18. Willy Adames, ss, Rays
19. Lucas Giolito, rhp, White Sox
20. Victor Robles, of, Nationals
21. Jose De Leon, rhp, Dodgers
22. Josh Hader, lhp, Brewers
23. Mickey Moniak, of, Phillies
24. Vladimir Guerrero Jr., 3b, Blue Jays
25. Tyler Glasnow, rhp, Pirates
26. Anderson Espinoza, rhp, Padres
27. Brendan Rodgers, ss, Rockies
28. David Paulino, rhp, Astros
29. Rafael Devers, 3b, Red Sox
30. Tyler O'Neill, of, Mariners
31. Manuel Margot, of, Padres
32. Lewis Brinson, of, Brewers
33. Hunter Renfroe, of, Padres
34. Clint Frazier, of, Yankees
35. Ron Acuna, of, Braves
36. Kolby Allard, lhp, Braves
37. Cody Reed, lhp, Reds
38. Francisco Mejia, c, Indians
39. Michael Kopech, rhp, White Sox
40. Luke Weaver, rhp, Cardinals
41. Jorge Alfaro, c, Phillies
42. Riley Pint, rhp, Rockies
43. Josh Bell, 1b/of, Pirates
44. Jeff Hoffman, rhp, Rockies
45. Yadier Alvarez, rhp, Dodgers
46. Mike Soroka, rhp, Braves
47. Kyle Lewis, of, Mariners
48. Franklin Perez, rhp, Astros
49. Sixto Sanchez, rhp, Phillies
50. Jason Groome, lhp, Red Sox

MATT EDDY

1. Yoan Moncada, 2b/3b, White Sox
2. Dansby Swanson, ss, Braves
3. Nick Senzel, 3b, Reds
4. Andrew Benintendi, of, Red Sox
5. Amed Rosario, ss, Mets
6. Ozzie Albies, 2b/ss, Braves
7. Alex Reyes, rhp, Cardinals
8. Gleyber Torres, ss, Yankees
9. Willy Adames, ss, Rays
10. Austin Meadows, of, Pirates
11. Victor Robles, of, Nationals
12. Cody Bellinger, 1b/of, Dodgers
13. Eloy Jimenez, of, Cubs
14. Brendan Rodgers, ss/2b, Rockies
15. J.P. Crawford, ss, Phillies
16. Francis Martes, rhp, Astros
17. Josh Hader, lhp, Brewers
18. Jose De Leon, rhp, Dodgers
19. Tyler Glasnow, rhp, Pirates
20. Brent Honeywell, rhp, Rays
21. Kyle Tucker, of, Astros
22. Mickey Moniak, of, Phillies
23. Anderson Espinoza, rhp, Padres
24. Mitch Keller, rhp, Pirates
25. Francisco Mejia, c, Indians
26. Lucas Giolito, rhp, White Sox
27. Rafael Devers, 3b, Red Sox
28. Vladimir Guerrero Jr., 3b, Blue Jays
29. Michael Kopech, rhp, White Sox
30. Erick Fedde, rhp, Nationals
31. Yadier Alvarez, rhp, Dodgers
32. Lewis Brinson, of, Brewers
33. Zack Collins, c, White Sox
34. Josh Bell, 1b, Pirates
35. Kyle Lewis, of, Mariners
36. Reynaldo Lopez, rhp, White Sox
37. Luke Weaver, rhp, Cardinals
38. Jeff Hoffman, rhp, Rockies
39. Tyler O'Neill, of, Mariners
40. David Paulino, rhp, Astros
41. Manuel Margot, of, Padres
42. Jorge Alfaro, c, Phillies
43. Clint Frazier, of, Yankees
44. Hunter Renfroe, of, Padres
45. Albert Almora, of, Cubs
46. Kolby Allard, lhp, Braves
47. Kevin Newman, ss, Pirates
48. Triston McKenzie, rhp, Indians
49. Sean Reid-Foley, rhp, Blue Jays
50. Matt Manning, rhp, Tigers

TOP 50 PROSPECTS

JOHN MANUEL

1. Alex Reyes, rhp, Cardinals
2. Andrew Benintendi, of, Red Sox
3. Yoan Moncada, 2b/3b, White Sox
4. Gleyber Torres, ss, Yankees
5. Dansby Swanson, ss, Braves
6. Austin Meadows, of, Pirates
7. Cody Bellinger, 1b/of, Dodgers
8. Amed Rosario, ss, Mets
9. Ozzie Albies, 2b/ss, Braves
10. Eloy Jimenez, of, Cubs
11. Vladimir Guerrero Jr., 3b, Blue Jays
12. J.P. Crawford, ss, Phillies
13. Willy Adames, ss, Rays
14. Francis Martes, rhp, Astros
15. Brendan Rodgers, ss, Rockies
16. Brent Honeywell, rhp, Rays
17. Victor Robles, of, Nationals
18. Nick Senzel, 3b, Reds
19. Anderson Espinoza, rhp, Padres
20. Lucas Giolito, rhp, White Sox
21. Yadier Alvarez, rhp, Dodgers
22. Franklin Barreto, ss/2b, Athletics
23. Rafael Devers, 3b, Red Sox
24. Jose De Leon, rhp, Dodgers
25. Clint Frazier, of, Yankees
26. Manuel Margot, of, Padres
27. Josh Hader, lhp, Brewers
28. Kyle Tucker, of, Astros
29. Hunter Renfroe, of Padres
30. Lewis Brinson, of, Brewers
31. Cody Reed, lhp, Reds
32. Corey Ray, of, Brewers
33. Mickey Moniak, of, Phillies
34. Jeff Hoffman, rhp, Rockies
35. Mitch Keller, rhp, Pirates
36. Kolby Allard, lhp, Braves
37. Raimel Tapia, of, Rockies
38. Tyler Glasnow, rhp, Pirates
39. German Marquez, rhp, Rockies
40. Reynaldo Lopez, rhp, Red Sox
41. Jason Groome, lhp, Red Sox
42. Riley Pint, rhp, Rockies
43. Mike Soroka, rhp, Braves
44. Blake Rutherford, of, Yankees
45. Leody Taveras, of, Rangers
46. Jorge Alfaro, c, Phillies
47. Erick Fedde, rhp, Nationals
48. Francisco Mejia, c, Indians
49. Ron Acuna, of, Braves
50. Sixto Sanchez, rhp, Phillies

KYLE GLASER

1. Andrew Benintendi, of, Red Sox
2. Alex Reyes, rhp, Cardinals
3. Dansby Swanson, ss, Braves
4. Yoan Moncada, 2b/3b, White Sox
5. Eloy Jimenez, of, Cubs
6. Tyler Glasnow, rhp, Pirates
7. Brendan Rodgers, ss, Rockies
8. Jose De Leon, rhp, Dodgers
9. Willy Adames, ss, Rays
10. Austin Meadows, of, Pirates
11. Amed Rosario, ss, Mets
12. Anderson Espinoza, rhp, Padres
13. Gleyber Torres, ss, Yankees
14. Victor Robles, of, Nationals
15. Nick Senzel, 3b, Reds
16. J.P. Crawford, ss, Phillies
17. Francisco Mejia, c, Indians
18. Cody Bellinger, 1b, Dodgers
19. Lucas Giolito, rhp, White Sox
20. Ozzie Albies, 2b/ss, Braves
21. Josh Hader, lhp, Brewers
22. Clint Frazier, of, Yankees
23. Mickey Moniak, of, Phillies
24. Yadier Alvarez, rhp, Dodgers
25. Josh Bell, 1b, Pirates
26. Leody Taveras, of, Rangers
27. Riley Pint, rhp, Rockies
28. Lewis Brinson, Brewers
29. Brent Honeywell, rhp, Rays
30. Bradley Zimmer, of, Indians
31. Kyle Lewis, of, Mariners
32. Sean Newcomb, lhp, Braves
33. Nick Gordon, ss, Twins
34. Luis Ortiz, rhp, Brewers
35. Tyler O'Neill, of Mariners
36. Manuel Margot, of, Padres
37. Jeff Hoffman, rhp, Rockies
38. Hunter Renfroe, of, Padres
39. Francis Martes, rhp, Astros
40. Ian Happ, 2b/of, Cubs
41. Jorge Alfaro, c, Phillies
42. Kyle Tucker, of, Astros
43. Vladimir Guerrero Jr., Blue Jays
44. Reynaldo Lopez, rhp, White Sox
45. Corey Ray, of, Brewers
46. Rafael Devers, 3b, Red Sox
47. Amir Garrett, lhp, Reds
48. Franklin Barreto, ss/2b, Athletics
49. Aaron Judge, of, Yankees
50. Mitch Keller, rhp, Pirates

TALENT RANKINGS

Team	2016	2015	2014	2013	2012
1. Atlanta Braves	3	29	26	21	15

The second-worst farm system in baseball two years ago is now the best in the game. The system is built around a deep wave of pitching but has premium middle infielders Dansby Swanson and Ozzie Albies ready to help in 2017, with big draft and international hauls from 2016 boosting the lowest levels of the organization.

| **2. Los Angeles Dodgers** | 1 | 3 | 14 | 19 | 23 |

Even with Corey Seager and Julio Urias graduating to the major leagues, the Dodgers still have one of the game's premier farm systems. It's why the Dodgers are built to win both in the present and the future, especially with a slew of position prospects in the upper levels led by Cody Bellinger, who has star potential.

| **3. New York Yankees** | 16 | 19 | 18 | 11 | 6 |

A pair of midseason trades netted the Yankees huge returns, as general manager Brian Cashman flipped Aroldis Chapman and Andrew Miller to get their top two prospects, Gleyber Torres and Clint Frazier, as well as No. 7 prospect Justus Sheffield. A true commitment to building through young talent has the Yankees' system in the best place it's been in years.

| **4. Houston Astros** | 2 | 10 | 5 | 9 | 17 |

Even with Alex Bregman graduating to the majors one year after the Astros drafted him No. 2 overall, Houston has filled its minor league pipeline with a strong combination of upside and depth. They have done it through all avenues of talent procurement, mixing quality drafts and shrewd trades with a burgeoning Latin American program starting to show results in the lower levels.

| **5. Chicago White Sox** | 23 | 20 | 24 | 29 | 30 |

In less than 48 hours at the Winter Meetings, the White Sox went from one of the game's worst farm systems to one of the best with impact talent to rival anyone. The lack of depth still shows, but with the White Sox only starting to rebuild and holding several valuable major league trade chips, that could change quickly.

| **6. Philadelphia Phillies** | 8 | 22 | 22 | 23 | 27 |

A lineup that needs help should get a boost soon, as seven of the Phillies' top 10 prospects are position players who reached Double-A or higher in 2016. Thanks to a slew of trades and a Latin American program that consistently finds and develops quality pitching prospects at bargain prices, the Phillies have one of the game's deepest farm systems.

| **7. Pittsburgh Pirates** | 11 | 7 | 1 | 8 | 13 |

The upside of the Pirates' top prospects stacks up well against anyone. Austin Meadows is a potential star who should be ready to join a loaded outfield at some point in 2017, while Mitch Keller and Tyler Glasnow could both develop into frontline starters.

| **8. Milwaukee Brewers** | 9 | 21 | 29 | 22 | 25 |

The Brewers have steadily improved a farm system that ranked No. 29 three years ago into a top 10 system. Trades have fueled the rebuild, with four of their top five prospects and 11 of their top 20 entering the organization through that avenue.

| **9. San Diego Padres** | 25 | 14 | 6 | 15 | 8 |

After A.J. Preller's plan to empty the farm system and go for it imploded, the team has turned 180 degrees by bottoming out to amass prospects. A pair of trades with the Red Sox returned their top two prospects (Anderson Espinoza and Manuel Margot), while other deals and spending a fortune on international players in 2016 have helped create one of the game's deepest systems.

| **10. Colorado Rockies** | 6 | 8 | 11 | 20 | 16 |

Colorado's two highest upside prospects—Brendan Rodgers and Riley Pint—are still in the lower minors, but the Rockies are rich in upper-level prospects, with seven of their top 10 prospects having played at Double-A or higher in 2016. Much of that upper-level talent is congregated around starting pitching, with Jeff Hoffman, German Marquez, Kyle Freeland and Antonio Senzatela all candidates to pitch in Colorado this year.

| **11. Tampa Bay Rays** | 13 | 17 | 20 | 4 | 11 |

The Rays have long had had a shrewd eye for other teams' prospects. Three of their top five prospects (including No. 1, shortstop Willy Adames) were acquired through trades and all of their top five prospects played in Double-A or above last year. First-rounder Josh Lowe and Dominican outfielder Jesus Sanchez give them a pair of exciting prospects on the rise in the lower levels.

| **12. St. Louis Cardinals** | 14 | 15 | 7 | 1 | 12 |

Alex Reyes is the game's best pitching prospect. He and Luke Weaver should both boost the major league rotation in 2017, with a good balance of prospects in both the upper and lower levels of the system.

| **13. Cincinnati Reds** | 12 | 16 | 16 | 14 | 7 |

A system built around pitching used the No. 2 overall pick in the 2016 draft to add third baseman Nick Senzel, who could follow the path of recent elite college hitters and reach the major leagues next season. The Reds' three top pitching prospects (Cody Reed, Amir Garrett and Robert Stephenson) should all be big leaguers in 2017.

| **14. Boston Red Sox** | 4 | 5 | 2 | 6 | 10 |

Welcome to the Dave Dombrowski experience. The Red Sox's president has traded Yoan Moncada, Michael Kopech, Anderson Espinoza and Manuel Margot, among others, since arriving in Boston. There's still a strong trio at the top to carry the system, but it's a steep drop in talent beyond them.

15. New York Mets

	15	4	10	26	24

Amed Rosario is the Mets' best position prospect in a decade and their franchise shortstop who could reach New York in 2017. The rest of the farm has a good blend of talent at the upper and lower levels for a middle-tier system.

16. Chicago Cubs

	20	1	4	13	14

With a major league team built around the game's best young nucleus, the Cubs won't need much help from the minors. They won't be picking at the top of the draft for a while, so churning out more international players like Eloy Jimenez will be key.

17. Oakland Athletics

	18	19	23	25	26

The only everyday position player the A's have drafted in the last 10 years is Addison Russell, whom they gave to the Cubs in the Jeff Samardzija trade that still stings. The lack of homegrown hitters still shows, but trades have brought in four of their top six prospects, including No. 1 prospect Franklin Barreto.

18. Cleveland Indians

	17	23	17	24	29

Productive drafts have yielded a strong homegrown core of position players on the major league team, while the Indians used their top prospect, 2013 first-rounder Clint Frazier, to trade for Andrew Miller. Hitters are still the strength of the system, as 12 of their top 15 prospects are position players.

19. Washington Nationals

	5	12	21	16	1

The Nationals cashed in their best pitching prospects (Lucas Giolito and Reynaldo Lopez) for Adam Eaton, but they still have one of the game's most exciting prospects in Victor Robles at No. 1. More high-upside international talent is on the way at the lower levels with players like Juan Soto and Luis Garcia.

20. Toronto Blue Jays

	24	9	15	12	5

For a team that's traded several prospects to add stars to the major league team, the Blue Jays still have a surprising amount of upside in the system with Vladimir Guerrero Jr. and Anthony Alford. Cuban signing Lourdes Gurriel Jr. is an X-factor who could be able to contribute as soon as 2017 and is already locked up long-term at an affordable price.

21. Seattle Mariners

	28	24	25	2	9

Years of squandering high draft picks hurt the Mariners, but in outfielders Kyle Lewis and Tyler O'Neill they have two power bats who could one day hit in the middle of their lineup. GM Jerry Dipoto's front office has emphasized controlling the strike zone, leading to trades for players like Mitch Haniger and Dan Vogelbach.

22. Minnesota Twins

	10	2	3	10	19

With Byron Buxton, Max Kepler, Jorge Polanco and Jose Berrios graduating to the big leagues in 2016, there isn't much star power in the minors. What's left is solid depth but a lot of vanilla from top to bottom.

23. Texas Rangers

	7	11	9	3	2

After trading away a bundle of prospects to add Cole Hamels, Jonathan Lucroy and Yovani Gallardo, the upper-level impact talent has thinned. Still, Leody Taveras is an exciting top prospect and there's surprising depth still thanks in part to a strong international program.

24. San Francisco Giants

	19	26	19	28	21

The Giants reached the playoffs in 2016 behind a homegrown ace and an infield stacked with players the organization has drafted and developed. The next wave of talent doesn't have a Madison Bumgarner or Buster Posey, but while the system is thin, top two prospects Tyler Beede and Christian Arroyo both could help in 2017.

25. Detroit Tigers

	26	30	28	27	22

For the 10th straight year, the Tigers have a bottom-10 system. Some of that is due to trades—Willy Adames sure would look nice at the top—but the Tigers need to find a way to better build a pipeline of homegrown talent.

26. Kansas City Royals

	21	13	8	18	3

The Royals turned one of the best farm systems we've seen into a World Series champion. They haven't been able to keep the pipeline flowing, however, with decent depth but a lack of premium prospects that could make it hard for the Royals to replicate their previous success.

27. Baltimore Orioles

	27	28	12	17	20

Chance Sisco could soon reach Baltimore as an offensive-minded catcher, but the system beyond him is lacking. No team shows less commitment to Latin America than the Orioles.

28. Arizona Diamondbacks

	22	6	13	7	4

The previous front office was a disaster, failing to help the major league team while simultaneously draining the farm system of talent, most notably with its trade of 2015 No. 1 overall pick Dansby Swanson to the Braves. What's left is a system with little upside and few prospects who project as regulars at the major league level.

29. Miami Marlins

	29	25	27	5	28

Years of thin drafts and an underfunded international program have sunk the Marlins' farm system. Beyond 2016 first-rounder Braxton Garrett, there's little upside or depth in the minors to help a mediocre major league team.

30. Los Angeles Angels

	30	27	30	18	16

It's still ugly for the Angels, who repeat as the worst farm system, a ranking they have held three of the last four years. An emaciated prospect inventory leaves the Angels with few options to help the major league club in 2017 through callups or trades, but hey, at least they have Mike Trout.

Arizona Diamondbacks

BY BILL MITCHELL

Shelby Miller ran up a 6.15 ERA after the D-backs paid a steep price to acquire him

The Diamondbacks came out of spring training in 2016 with a Cactus League-best 24-8 record and a huge wave of optimism, largely due to what was expected to be a bolstered rotation after the shocking free-agent signing of Dodgers ace Zack Greinke and the controversial trade to acquire Shelby Miller from the Braves.

With their rotation fortified, Arizona was supposed to thrive in 2016 and catapult into contention for the National League West title.

Instead, everything fell apart.

The D-backs finished 69-93, which was quite the fall from the club's optimistic preseason outlook. They barely squeaked by the Padres to finish one game out of the NL West cellar.

Center fielder A.J. Pollock fractured his elbow in the next-to-last spring training game and missed most of the season. With the outfield depth weakened due to the inclusion of reliable outfielder Ender Inciarte in the Miller trade, the D-backs were forced to put shortstop Chris Owings in center field despite the fact that he hadn't played the outfield since high school.

To compound the shortage, outfielder David Peralta was limited to 48 games with multiple injuries.

Coming off a Cy Young Award runner-up season with the 2015 Dodgers, Greinke didn't live up to expectations. He went 13-7 with a subpar 4.37 ERA, while also missing the entire month of July with an oblique injury. Miller posted some of the worst numbers of any starting pitcher in the game and spent time at Triple-A Reno in an attempt to get his delivery and mechanics back to form.

The trade to acquire Miller had been universally derided in the industry. In addition to giving up Inciarte, the D-backs included shortstop Dansby Swanson, the No. 1 overall pick in the 2015 draft, and top pitching prospect Aaron Blair in the deal.

The front office of chief baseball officer Tony La Russa and general manager Dave Stewart came under fire for the team's performance, but especially for the Miller trade as well as their insistence in following "old school" practices instead of the advanced baseball methodologies practiced by the other 29 organizations.

Ownership finally pulled the plug on their two-year regime, with Stewart, senior vice president of baseball operations De Jon Watson and manager Chip Hale all terminated after the end of the 2016 season. La Russa, the Hall of Fame manager, was retained in a nebulous advisory role with no apparent power.

The organization certainly went in the other

TOP PROSPECTS OF THE DECADE

Year	Player, Pos.	2016 Org
2007	Justin Upton	Tigers
2008	Carlos Gonzalez	Rockies
2009	Jarrod Parker, rhp	Athletics
2010	Jarrod Parker, rhp	Athletics
2011	Jarrod Parker, rhp	Athletics
2012	Trevor Bauer, rhp	Indians
2013	Tyler Skaggs, lhp	Angels
2014	Archie Bradley, rhp	Diamondbacks
2015	Archie Bradley, rhp	Diamondbacks
2016	Braden Shipley, rhp	Diamondbacks

direction for their replacements, bringing in a pair of acclaimed executives from the Red Sox: general manager Mike Hazen and assistant GM Amiel Sawdaye. New manager Torey Lovullo, who had served as Boston bench coach, followed a few weeks later. Another newcomer, Cesar Geronimo Jr., was hired to be the new Latin America scouting director.

The biggest challenge facing Hazen and company is to work within the framework of a projected payroll of around $100 million, especially since one-third of that total is due to Greinke. There's not much help to be expected from the farm system, one of the weakest in baseball.

Arizona is starting from the bottom, but Hazen and the new regime have a blank canvas to work with as they try to get the D-backs back on track.

ORGANIZATION OVERVIEW

General manager: Mike Hazen. **Farm director:** Mike Bell. **Scouting director:** Deric Ladnier.

Class	Team	League	W	L	PCT	Finish	Manager
Majors	Arizona Diamondbacks	National	69	93	.426	12th (15)	Chip Hale
Triple-A	Reno Aces	Pacific Coast	76	68	.528	4th (16)	Phil Nevin
Double-A	Mobile BayBears	Southern	65	73	.471	7th (10)	Robby Hammock
High Class A	Visalia Rawhide	California	81	59	.579	2nd (10)	J.R. House
Low Class A	Kane County Cougars	Midwest	65	75	.464	12th (16)	Mike Benjamin
Short-season	Hillsboro Hops	Northwest	42	33	.560	3rd (8)	Shelley Duncan
Rookie	Missoula Osprey	Pioneer	33	42	.440	7th (8)	Joe Mather
Rookie	AZL Diamondbacks	Arizona	27	29	.482	10th (14)	Darrin Garner
Overall 2016 Minor League Record			389	379	.507	t-13th (30)	

THIS YEAR'S TOP 30

No.	Player, Pos.	Grade/Risk
1.	Anthony Banda, lhp	55/Medium
2.	Dawel Lugo, 3b/ss	50/High
3.	Domingo Leyba, ss/2b	50/High
4.	Socrates Brito, of	45/Medium
5.	Jazz Chisholm, ss	55/Extreme
6.	Anfernee Grier, of	50/High
7.	Taylor Clarke, rhp	50/High
8.	Brad Keller, rhp	50/High
9.	Jon Duplantier, rhp	50/Extreme
10.	Curtis Taylor, rhp	45/High
11.	Alex Young, lhp	45/High
12.	Matt Koch, rhp	40/Medium
13.	Jimmie Sherfy, rhp	45/High
14.	Andy Yerzy, c	50/Extreme
15.	Jack Reinheimer, ss/2b	40/Medium
16.	Mack Lemieux, lhp	50/Extreme
17.	Jhoan Duran, rhp	50/Extreme
18.	Jose Almonte, rhp	50/Extreme
19.	Jared Miller, lhp	45/High
20.	Luis Alejandro Besabe, 2b	45/High
21.	Wei-Chieh Huang, rhp	45/Extreme
22.	Marcus Wilson, of	45/Extreme
23.	Victor Reyes, of	45/Extreme
24.	Jose Herrera, c	45/Extreme
25.	Josh Taylor, lhp	40/High
26.	Steve Hathaway, lhp	40/High
27.	Joey Rose, 3b	45/Extreme
28.	Ildemaro Vargas, 2b/ss	40/High
29.	Ryan January, c	45/Extreme
30.	Tommy Eveld, rhp	40/High

LAST YEAR'S TOP 30

No.	Player, Pos.	Status
1.	Dansby Swanson, ss	(Braves)
2.	Aaron Blair, rhp	(Braves)
3.	Braden Shipley, rhp	Majors
4.	Archie Bradley, rhp	Majors
5.	Brandon Drury,3b	Majors
6.	Yoan Lopez, rhp	Dropped out
7.	Alex Young, lhp	No. 11
8.	Socrates Brito, of	No. 4
9.	Isan Diaz, ss	(Brewers)
10.	Peter O'Brien, c/of	Dropped out
11.	Gabby Guerrero, of	(Reds)
12.	Jack Reinheimer, ss/2b	No. 15
13.	Domingo Leyba, ss	No. 3
14.	Taylor Clarke, rhp	No. 7
15.	Anthony Banda, lhp	No. 1
16.	Wei-Chieh Huang, rhp	No. 21
17.	Brad Keller, rhp	No. 8
18.	Zack Godley, rhp	Majors
19.	Marcus Wilson, of	No. 22
20.	Jose Martinez, rhp	Dropped out
21.	Daniel Gibson, lhp	Dropped out
22.	Oscar Hernandez, c	Dropped out
23.	Adam Miller, rhp	Dropped out
24.	Jake Barrett, rhp	Majors
25.	Jose Herrera, c	No. 24
26.	Victor Reyes, of	No. 23
27.	Ryan Burr, rhp	Dropped out
28.	Sergio Alcantara, ss	Dropped out
29.	Silvino Bracho, rhp	Majors
30.	Jamie Westbrook, 2b	Dropped out

BEST TOOLS

Best Hitter for Average	Dawel Lugo
Best Power Hitter	Kevin Cron
Best Strike-Zone Discipline	Marcus Wilson
Fastest Baserunner	Matt McPhearson
Best Athlete	Gabriel Maciel
Best Fastball	Curtis Taylor
Best Curveball	Mack Lemieux
Best Slider	Tommy Eveld
Best Changeup	Gabriel Moya
Best Control	Matt Koch
Best Defensive Catcher	Oscar Hernandez
Best Defensive Infielder	Jazz Chisholm
Best Infield Arm	Sergio Alcantara
Best Defensive Outfielder	Evan Marzilli
Best Outfield Arm	Socrates Brito

PROJECTED 2020 LINEUP

Catcher	Oscar Hernandez
First Base	Paul Goldschmidt
Second Base	Ketel Marte
Third Base	Jake Lamb
Shortstop	Chris Owings
Left Field	Brandon Drury
Center Field	A.J. Pollock
Right Field	Yasmany Tomas
No. 1 Starter	Zack Greinke
No. 2 Starter	Taijuan Walker
No. 3 Starter	Shelby Miller
No. 4 Starter	Patrick Corbin
No. 5 Starter	Robbie Ray
Closer	Archie Bradley

MINOR LEAGUE DEPTH CHART

ARIZONA DIAMONDBACKS

TOP 2017 ROOKIE: Anthony Banda, lhp. The system's top pitching prospect will get a chance to make the staff out of spring training.
BREAKOUT PROSPECT: Mack Lemieux, lhp. The 2016 sixth-round pick had a nice pro debut and offers projection, arm strength and three average or better pitches.
SLEEPER: Gabriel Maciel, of. The native of Brazil has plus-plus speed and is a solid defender but needs to add strength to become more than a fourth outfielder.

SOURCE OF TOP 30 TALENT			
Homegrown	20	Acquired	10
College	9	Trades	9
Junior college	2	Rule 5 draft	0
High school	4	Independent leagues	1
Nondrafted free agents	0	Free agents/waivers	0
International	5		

LF
Peter O'Brien
Grant Heyman
Jason Heinrich

CF
Anfernee Grier (6)
Marcus Wilson (22)
Gabriel Maciel
Colin Bray
Evan Marzilli

RF
Socrates Brito (4)
Victor Reyes (23)

3B
Dawel Lugo (2)
Joey Rose (27)
Eudy Ramos

SS
Domingo Leyba (3)
Jazz Chisholm (5)
Jack Reinheimer (15)
Ildemaro Vargas (28)
Sergio Alcantara
Yan Sanchez

2B
Luis Alejandro Basabe (20)
Jamie Westbrook
Henry Castillo

1B
Kevin Cron
Francis Martinez
Marty Herum
Austin Byler

C
Andy Yerzy (14)
Jose Herrera (24)
Ryan January (29)
Oscar Hernandez

LHP

LHSP	LHRP
Anthony Banda (1)	Jared Miller (19)
Alex Young (11)	Steve Hathaway (26)
Mack Lemieux (16)	Daniel Gibson
Josh Taylor (25)	Gabe Speier
Cody Reed	Jordan Watson
Junior Garcia	
Anfernee Benitez	

RHP

RHSP	RHRP
Taylor Clarke (7)	Jimmie Sherfy (13)
Brad Keller (8)	Tommy Eveld (30)
Jon Duplantier (9)	Jose Martinez
Curtis Taylor (10)	Miller Diaz
Matt Koch (12)	Drew Muren
Jhoan Duran (17)	Julio Perez
Jose Almonte (18)	Jake Winston
Wei-Chieh Huang (21)	Kevin Ginkel
Tyler Jones	Joey Krehbiel
Joel Payamps	Adam Miller
Justin Donatella	Ryan Burr
Sam McWilliams	
Jake Polancic	

DRAFT ANALYSIS

2016

BEST PURE HITTER: The Diamondbacks were higher than the industry consensus on C Andy Yerzy (2) due to their belief in his bat. He struggled in his debut, batting .216/.240/.265 with 38 strikeouts in 162 at-bats, but improved defensively behind the plate, where he's quite raw.

BEST POWER HITTER: Yerzy has plus raw power and has shown it with wood in showcases. He'll have to prove he can adjust to pro pitching, but the D-backs hope he can follow a similar path to past Canadian catchers who hit their way to the majors such as Justin Morneau and Joey Votto.

FASTEST RUNNER: The Diamondbacks grade OF Anfernee Grier (1) as a 70 runner, which plays more defensively than on the bases at this time. He went just 35-for-53 stealing bases in three seasons at Auburn.

BEST DEFENSIVE PLAYER: Grier has 70 range. He had arm problems after signing, likely incurred during pre-draft workouts, and mostly played DH as a pro. His arm grade as fringe-average before the draft.

BEST FASTBALL: RHP Curtis Taylor (4) reached 96 mph from a low three-quarters angle this spring as a starter and touched 98 in one-inning stints after signing. RHP Kevin Ginkel (22), a local pick who was on Arizona's College World Series finalist team, has reached 97 mph.

BEST SECONDARY PITCH: LHP Jordan Watson (7) led NAIA with 15 strikeouts per nine innings thanks to a plus curveball that could eventually be a 70-grade pitch. Taylor has improved his slider as a pro, adding depth to this power pitch.

BEST PRO DEBUT: SS Mark Karaviotis (19) led the short-season Northwest League in on-base percentage during a .344/.473/.466 season. Taylor struck out 23 in 16 innings with a 2.20 ERA.

BEST ATHLETE: The Diamondbacks considered the 6-foot-1, 180-pound Grier among the best athletes in the draft for his combination of strength, speed and explosiveness.

MOST INTRIGUING BACKGROUND: RHP Tommy Eveld (9) played quarterback at South Florida before knee injuries ended his football career and he became part of the Bulls' bullpen. He told club officials he learned his delivery in part by watching Nolan Ryan videos on YouTube. His brother Bobby, also a former quarterback, signed to pitch with the Blue Jays as a 25-year-old free agent. OF Connor Owings (34), younger brother of the D-backs' Chris, has only one functioning kidney and eventually will need a transplant. He helped lead Coastal Carolina past Ginkel's Wildcats for the CWS championship.

CLOSEST TO THE MAJORS: A reliever, Eveld could get there first thanks to a 94-95 mph fastball and hard cutter, but Taylor would beat him if Arizona moves him to the bullpen. For now, the club intends to start him.

BEST LATE-ROUND PICK: Karaviotis has a good swing and a chance to stick in the infield. In addition to his plus fastball, Ginkel flashes an average curveball and changeup, but his secondary stuff must be more consistent for him to finish off hitters.

THE ONE WHO GOT AWAY: OF Edmong Americann (28), originally from Curacao, has good athleticism and plus speed. He's headed to Chipola (Fla.) JC.

2015

Trading SS Dansby Swanson (1) in the Shelby Miller deal was a colossal mistake by Arizona's old regime. LHP Alex Young (2) and RHP Taylor Clarke (3) should be solid contributors.

GRADE: B

2014

Dealing RHP Touki Toussaint (1) and SS Isan Diaz (2s) has shorn this class of two high-ceiling talents. LHP Zac Curtis (6) reached the majors quickly but was traded to the Mariners, perhaps making way for LHP Jared Miller (11).

GRADE: C

2013

RHPs Braden Shipley (1) reached Arizona in 2016 but had a modest rookie season. Arizona already has traded RHP Aaron Blair (1s), OF Justin Williams (2) and OF Daniel Palka (3).

GRADE: B

TOP DRAFT PICKS OF THE DECADE

Year	Player, Pos.	2016 Org
2007	Jarrod Parker, rhp	Athletics
2008	Daniel Schlereth, lhp	Blue Jays
2009	Bobby Borchering, 3b	Did not play
2010	*Barret Loux, rhp	Atlantic League
2011	Trevor Bauer, rhp	Indians
2012	Stryker Trahan, c	Diamondbacks
2013	Braden Shipley, rhp	Diamondbacks
2014	Touki Toussaint, rhp	Braves
2015	Dansby Swanson, ss	Braves
2016	Anfernee Grier, of (1st round supp.)	D-backs

*Did not sign.

LARGEST BONUSES IN CLUB HISTORY

Yasmany Tomas, 2014	$14,000,000
Travis Lee, 1996	$10,000,000
Yoan Lopez, 2015	$8,270,000
Dansby Swanson, 2015	$6,500,000
Justin Upton, 2005	$6,100,000

1 ANTHONY BANDA, LHP

Born: Aug. 10, 1993. **B-T:** L-L. **Ht.:** 6-2. **Wt.:** 190.
Drafted: San Jacinto (Texas) JC, 2012 (10th round).
Signed by: Brian Sankey (Brewers).

BA GRADE

55 Risk: Medium

SCOUTING GRADES

Fastball: 55.
Curveball: 60
Changeup: 50.
Control: 55.

Based on 20-80 scouting scale and future projection rather than present tools.

Not every trade for prospects works out for the team trading away big league talent, but the Diamondbacks certainly benefited from the deal in which they sent veteran outfielder Gerardo Parra to the Brewers in 2014 in exchange for Banda and outfielder Mitch Haniger. The trade was the D-backs' second attempt to bring Banda into the organization after previously drafting the Texas native in the 33rd round out of high school in 2011. Banda instead played one year at junior college powerhouse San Jacinto, where he went 6-0, 1.95 to help the Gators to a second-place finish at the Division I NJCAA World Series. After his year at San Jacinto, Banda was selected by Milwaukee in the 10th round in 2012 and signed for an over-slot $125,000 bonus. He made it to low Class A with the Brewers by his third season before moving to the D-backs organization. Banda struggled with his command in the early part of his career but started throwing more strikes and increased his velocity not long after joining Arizona. He showed continual improvement in 2015 and 2016. He got a big boost after the 2015 season when he worked with former big league southpaw Mike Gonzalez, a fellow native of the Corpus Christi area and also a one-time San Jacinto pitcher. Shortly after being promoted from Double-A Mobile to Triple-A Reno midway through the 2016 season, Banda was Arizona's lone representative at the Futures Game. By the end of the year, he ranked as the No. 10 prospect in the Double-A Southern League and No. 20 in the Triple-A Pacific Coast League. He led the D-backs system with 152 strikeouts and ranked second with a 2.88 ERA in 150 innings.

Banda uses a four-seam fastball with armside run that has continually ticked up during his pro career. His heater sat 86-89 mph in junior college but now sits 92-95 and touches 96 because to added strength and improved mechanics. The jewel of his arsenal is a slow, mid-70s curveball that flashes plus at times, and he complements the breaking ball with an at least average, firm changeup with down movement. He repeats his smooth, easy delivery and effectively sequences his pitches. Banda consistently records high strikeout totals, with a career rate of 8.8 per nine innings. He has walked just 3.2 per nine since joining Arizona.

One area for improvement is to better control the running game and other small facets of pitching.

Previously cast as a potential No. 5 starter or reliever, Banda is now viewed as a possible mid-rotation arm with one plus pitch and two other average-or-better weapons and above-average control. He will go to big league spring training in 2017 with a chance to break camp on the 25-man roster. More likely he winds up back at Reno for more seasoning. He should make his big league debut at some point in 2017.

Year	Club (League)	Class	W	L	ERA	G	GS	CG	SV	IP	H	HR	BB	SO	K/9	WHIP	AVG
2014	Wisconsin (MWL)	LoA	6	6	3.66	20	14	0	2	84	84	4	38	83	8.9	1.46	.263
	South Bend (MWL)	LoA	3	6	1.54	6	6	0	0	35	32	2	7	34	8.7	1.11	.237
2015	Visalia (CAL)	HiA	8	8	3.32	28	27	1	0	152	150	8	39	152	9.0	1.25	.260
2016	Mobile (SL)	AA	6	2	2.12	13	13	0	0	76	70	4	28	84	9.9	1.28	.241
	Reno (PCL)	AAA	4	4	3.67	13	13	0	0	74	73	6	27	68	8.3	1.36	.257
Minor League Totals			32	27	3.46	108	91	1	2	523	527	34	188	509	8.8	1.37	.262

2 DAWEL LUGO, 3B

Born: Dec. 31, 1994. **B-T:** R-R. **Ht.:** 6-0. **Wt.:** 190. **Signed:** Dominican Republic, 2011. **Signed by:** Marco Paddy/Hilario Soriano (Blue Jays).

Originally signed by the Blue Jays in 2011 for $1.3 million, Lugo was acquired by the Diamondbacks in August 2015 for veteran infielder Cliff Pennington. Lugo dropped 15 pounds at the beginning of 2016, and his better conditioning helped him become a more explosive in all facets of his game. He did everything well at high Class A Visalia and Double-A Mobile before finishing the 2016 season in the Arizona Fall league. Lugo also became more disciplined at the plate by significantly improving his strikeout rate from 17.5 percent in 2015 to 11 percent in 2016. A potentially average hitter with quick hands, Lugo shows excellent hand-eye coordination and has above-average power with strong wrists. Defensively, Lugo came up as a shortstop but has moved to third base, where he has good hands and a plus arm. He will return to Double-A to begin 2017 and has a good chance to reach Triple-A Reno during the summer.

BA GRADE
50 Risk: High

Year	Club (League)	Class	AVG	G	AB	R	H	2B	3B	HR	RBI	BB	SO	SB	CS	OBP	SLG
2014	Lansing (MWL)	LoA	.259	117	474	40	123	17	2	4	53	18	72	3	3	.286	.329
2015	Dunedin (FSL)	HiA	.219	67	260	16	57	9	2	2	21	9	49	1	3	.258	.292
	Lansing (MWL)	LoA	.336	31	122	15	41	6	1	2	23	5	24	3	1	.348	.451
	Kane County (MWL)	LoA	.333	22	81	12	27	1	1	0	3	4	13	2	2	.372	.370
2016	Visalia (CAL)	HiA	.314	79	315	61	99	14	5	13	42	15	41	2	1	.348	.514
	Mobile (SL)	AA	.306	48	173	24	53	9	2	4	20	4	15	1	1	.322	.451
Minor League Totals			.276	478	1856	222	512	73	20	34	226	68	280	18	12	.305	.392

3 DOMINGO LEYBA, SS/2B

Born: Sept. 11, 1995. **B-T:** B-R. **Ht.:** 5-11. **Wt.:** 160. **Signed:** Dominican Republic, 2012. **Signed by:** Miguel Rodriguez/Carlos Santana/Ramon Perez/Miguel Garcia (Tigers).

After struggling at high Class A Visalia in 2015 at age 19, Leyba returned to the California League and produced much better results in 2016. Arizona got him from the Tigers (with lefthander Robbie Ray) after the 2014 season in the three-team deal that sent Didi Gregorius to the Yankees. Leyba boosted his Cal League OPS by nearly 200 points in 2016 to earn a promotion to Double-A Mobile. Overall he hit .296/.355/.429 in 130 games. The key to Leyba's improvement came by becoming more selective at the plate, with his walk total increasing from 26 in 2015 to 46 in 2016. He has a contact-oriented line-drive approach with hands that work well from both sides of the plate and a knack for putting the barrel on the ball. A potentially above-average hitter, Leyba also showed increasing power with 10 home runs in 2016. That exceeded the nine he hit in the first three years of his career. His solid infield instincts and good positioning help to make up for an arm and range that are both a little short for shortstop, but he has shown himself to be an average or better second baseman. His work ethic earns strong reviews across the board from the organization. Leyba is taking the steps forward to become a solid everyday middle infielder. He will return to Double-A to begin 2017.

BA GRADE
50 Risk: High

Year	Club (League)	Class	AVG	G	AB	R	H	2B	3B	HR	RBI	BB	SO	SB	CS	OBP	SLG
2014	Connecticut (NYP)	SS	.264	37	144	20	38	11	1	1	17	8	17	1	2	.303	.375
	West Michigan (MWL)	LoA	.397	30	116	20	46	7	0	1	7	6	13	1	2	.431	.483
2015	Visalia (CAL)	HiA	.237	124	514	60	122	21	5	2	43	26	90	10	6	.277	.309
2016	Visalia (CAL)	HiA	.294	86	340	48	100	25	1	6	40	29	62	5	1	.346	.426
	Mobile (SL)	AA	.301	44	156	21	47	7	1	4	20	17	22	4	2	.374	.436
Minor League Totals			.288	378	1471	220	423	86	16	19	163	120	230	37	21	.343	.407

4 SOCRATES BRITO, OF

Born: Sept, 6, 1992. **B-T:** L-L. **Ht.:** 6-2. **Wt.:** 200. **Signed:** Dominican Republic, 2010. **Signed by:** Junior Noboa.

Injuries to two starting outfielders gave Brito a chance to seize a permanent role with the Diamondbacks in 2016. Instead, he struggled at the plate and spent more than half the season at Triple-A Reno. He also missed time with a fractured toe. Brito still possesses the tools that have tantalized since he first signed with Arizona in 2010. He has upper-body strength with good line-drive power to the gaps, but he hasn't yet developed a good approach at the plate or the feel to hit. He could stand to work counts better. A plus runner with a plus arm, Brito has the ability and range to play all three outfield positions, though some don't believe he's agile enough for

BA GRADE
45 Risk: Medium

center field. He also needs to learn to use his speed better on the bases. Brito fractured his hamate in November while preparing for winter ball in his native Dominican Republic. While he should be healed in time for spring training, the injury is worth watching as he tries to win a big league job out of camp.

Year	Club (League)	Class	AVG	G	AB	R	H	2B	3B	HR	RBI	BB	SO	SB	CS	OBP	SLG
2014	Visalia (CAL)	HiA	.293	128	518	82	152	30	5	10	62	36	109	38	10	.339	.429
2015	Mobile (SL)	AA	.300	129	490	70	147	17	15	9	57	29	84	20	6	.339	.451
	Arizona (NL)	MAJ	.303	18	33	5	10	3	1	0	1	1	7	1	0	.324	.455
2016	Visalia (CAL)	HiA	.111	2	9	1	1	0	0	1	2	0	2	0	0	.111	.444
	Reno (PCL)	AAA	.294	73	303	46	89	10	8	6	39	13	60	7	6	.322	.439
	Arizona (NL)	MAJ	.179	40	95	10	17	3	1	4	12	2	23	2	0	.196	.358
Major League Totals			.211	58	128	15	27	6	2	4	13	3	30	3	0	.229	.383
Minor League Totals			.288	609	2447	347	704	103	50	33	287	158	520	125	54	.331	.411

5 JAZZ CHISHOLM, SS

Born: Feb. 1, 1998. **B-T:** L-R. **Ht.:** 5-11. **Wt.:** 165. **Signed:** Bahamas, 2015. **Signed by:** Craig Shipley.

The Diamondbacks were restricted in 2015 from signing any international player for more than $300,000 because they exceeded their pool amount the previous year, but the organization found a diamond in the rough in Chisholm, who signed for $200,000. The half-brother of Rays prospect Lucius Fox, Chisholm displays a swagger on the field befitting his nickname "Jazz." (He was born Jasrado.) The D-backs assigned the native Bahamian to Rookie-level Missoula in 2016, and he ranked among the Pioneer League's top prospects. Chisholm projects to be an above-average hitter, with good bat speed and the ability to barrel balls and handle

BA GRADE

55 Risk: **Extreme**

velocity. The ball jumps off his bat and he has enough power to project double-digit home run totals each year, though he could use more polish to his plate approach. Chisholm is at least an average runner, perhaps a tick above, and he should get faster as his legs get stronger. Defensively, he is athletic and at times a plus defender with good hands and an average arm, but he needs to learn to slow the game down. Chisholm is very confident on the field, with scouts noting he thinks he's a big leaguer. Chisholm has the highest ceiling of any position player in the system. He should be ready for a move to full-season ball in 2017, with a likely assignment to low Class A Kane County.

Year	Club (League)	Class	AVG	G	AB	R	H	2B	3B	HR	RBI	BB	SO	SB	CS	OBP	SLG
2016	Missoula (PIO)	R	.281	62	249	42	70	12	1	9	37	19	73	13	4	.333	.446
Minor League Totals			.281	62	249	42	70	12	1	9	37	19	73	13	4	.333	.446

6 ANFERNEE GRIER, OF

Born: Oct. 13, 1995. **B-T:** R-R. **Ht.:** 6-0. **Wt.:** 170. **Drafted:** Auburn, 2016 (1st round supplemental). **Signed by:** Kerry Jenkins.

Grier was Arizona's top pick at No. 39 overall in 2016 after the Diamondbacks forfeited their first-round selection by signing Zack Greinke. Grier signed for $1.5 million. A breakout season his sophomore year at Auburn originally put Grier on draft watch lists, and he improved his stock as a junior when he hit .366/.457/.576 with a team-leading 12 home runs. A shoulder injury suffered during a pre-draft workout limited Grier mostly to a DH role in his pro debut. While he struggled at the plate in his pro debut, Grier has a good feel to hit with sneaky power that should come out with more strength, making him a possibly average hitter with average

BA GRADE

50 Risk: **High**

power potential down the road. The ball comes off his bat well, but he struggles with breaking pitches from righthanders. A 28 percent strikeout rate in his pro debut, similar to his college total, raises concerns about Grier's approach at the plate, and he will need to make better contact to use his plus speed. Scouts graded him as a plus defender in college, with his slightly below-average arm being enough for center field. Grier should be fully recovered from his shoulder injury by spring training and ready for a full-season assignment to low Class A Kane County.

Year	Club (League)	Class	AVG	G	AB	R	H	2B	3B	HR	RBI	BB	SO	SB	CS	OBP	SLG
2016	Missoula (PIO)	R	.214	4	14	2	3	1	0	1	2	0	5	0	0	.267	.500
	Hillsboro (NWL)	SS	.240	20	75	8	18	2	0	1	6	3	21	9	2	.278	.307
Minor League Totals			.236	24	89	10	21	3	0	2	8	3	26	9	2	.277	.337

7 TAYLOR CLARKE, RHP

Born: May 13, 1993. **B-T:** R-R. **Ht.:** 6-4. **Wt.:** 200. **Drafted:** College of Charleston, 2015 (3rd round). **Signed by:** George Swain.

Clarke made some impressive moves in 2016, his first full season. After starting at low Class A Kane County he passed through high Class A Visalia and reached Double-A Mobile before the end of May. He pitched well at all three levels, going 12-9, 3.31 with 118 strikeouts and just 33 walks. Clarke sports a solid, muscular frame, with his best attributes on the mound being solid pitchability, command of three pitches and the ability to work up and down in the zone. He gets good downhill plane from a fastball that sits 91-94 mph and touches 96. He gets angle with cut action. Clarke's plus command allows his fastball to play up, and he moves it around to change eye levels. His best secondary pitch is a solid-average slider with downer action that flashes plus. An average changeup rounds out the repertoire. He had Tommy John surgery in college, so the D-backs took it cautiously in his first pro season. His 27 starts in 2016 showed he could take the ball every fifth day. He's very competitive and may be ready for Triple-A Reno in 2017. He profiles as a No. 4 starter.

BA GRADE

50 Risk: High

Year	Club (League)	Class	W	L	ERA	G	GS	CG	SV	IP	H	HR	BB	SO	K/9	WHIP	AVG
2015	Hillsboro (NWL)	SS	0	0	0.00	13	0	0	3	21	8	0	4	27	11.6	0.57	.114
2016	Kane County (MWL)	LoA	3	2	2.83	6	6	0	0	29	24	1	5	24	7.5	1.01	.222
	Visalia (CAL)	HiA	1	1	2.74	4	4	0	0	23	19	3	7	22	8.6	1.13	.221
	Mobile (SL)	AA	8	6	3.59	17	17	0	0	98	99	9	21	72	6.6	1.23	.261
Minor League Totals			12	9	2.91	40	27	0	3	170	150	13	37	145	7.7	1.10	.233

8 BRAD KELLER, RHP

Born: July 27, 1995. **B-T:** R-R. **Ht.:** 6-5. **Wt.:** 230. **Drafted:** HS—Flowery Branch, Ga., 2013 (8th round). **Signed by:** T.R. Lewis.

Keller impressively survived as a 21-year old in the unforgiving Cal League in 2016, throwing strikes and keeping the ball in the park in a productive season at high Class A Visalia. His most impressive attribute was a walk rate of 1.7 per nine innings, and his 1.28 WHIP ranked fifth in the circuit. Keller is a pitch-to-contact type who consistently throws strikes with an advanced feel for pitching. His fastball ranges from 89-93 mph and typically sits 91, and there could be more velocity to come with experience. He commands his heater really well, cuts and sinks it, and pitches to both sides of the plate. Keller shows a good feel for his average secondary pitches, a slider and changeup. Keller keeps the ball down, and more than half of balls in play against him were hit on the ground in 2016. He has also shown himself to be durable and held up over 142 innings in 2015 and 135 in 2016. Keller will open 2017 as a 21-year-old with Arizona's new Double-A Jackson affiliate. He projects as either a No. 3 or 4 starter depending on the development of his offspeed pitches.

BA GRADE

50 Risk: High

Year	Club (League)	Class	W	L	ERA	G	GS	CG	SV	IP	H	HR	BB	SO	K/9	WHIP	AVG
2014	Missoula (PIO)	R	1	4	6.95	8	8	0	0	34	50	6	18	30	8.0	2.02	.347
	Diamondbacks (AZL)	R	4	0	2.30	6	3	0	0	31	30	2	9	20	5.7	1.24	.265
	Hillsboro (NWL)	SS	1	0	0.00	1	1	0	0	6	1	0	1	8	12.0	0.33	.053
2015	Kane County (MWL)	LoA	8	9	2.60	26	25	0	0	142	128	3	37	109	6.9	1.16	.243
2016	Visalia (CAL)	HiA	9	7	4.47	24	24	0	0	135	147	13	26	99	6.6	1.28	.281
Minor League Totals			30	23	3.48	80	74	0	0	411	415	26	121	331	7.3	1.31	.266

9 JON DUPLANTIER, RHP

Born: July 11, 1994. **B-T:** L-R. **Ht.:** 6-3. **Wt.:** 225. **Drafted:** Rice, 2016 (3rd round). **Signed by:** Rusty Pendergrass.

Duplantier is a wild card for the Diamondbacks because he has explosive stuff but a concerning injury record. He missed all of the 2015 college season at Rice with a shoulder injury that did not require surgery, and an elbow issue limited him to only one inning in his pro debut at short-season Hillsboro after he signed for $686,600. Further, he didn't get on the mound in instructional league after he suffered a pulled hamstring during pitcher fielding practice. Duplantier is a strong, physical righthander who struck out 12 batters per nine innings in 2016 at Rice to rank eighth among Division I pitchers and earn third-team All-America honors. Duplantier used a 90-95 mph fastball in college, and he flashed an above-average curveball with some power and a developing changeup that still is a work-in-progress. The control of his pitches suffers when his arm slot wanders, prompted by his shoulder flying open too quickly in his delivery. While he didn't

BA GRADE

50 Risk: Extreme

get into games during instructs, Duplantier threw a few bullpen sessions and reported no issues with his elbow. Months of rest after a customarily heavy Rice workload could do wonders for Duplantier and his health. While he could move quickly as a power reliever relying on his two best pitches, Duplantier will stay in the rotation for now as he makes his full-season debut at low Class A Kane County in 2017.

Year	Club (League)	Class	W	L	ERA	G	GS	CG	SV	IP	H	HR	BB	SO	K/9	WHIP	AVG
2016	Hillsboro (NWL)	SS	0	0	0.00	1	0	0	0	1	0	0	2	3	27.0	2.00	.000
Minor League Totals			0	0	0.00	1	0	0	0	1	0	0	2	3	27.0	2.00	.000

10 CURTIS TAYLOR, RHP

Born: July 25, 1995. **B-T:** R-R. **Ht.:** 6-6. **Wt.:** 215. **Drafted:** British Columbia, 2016 (4th round). **Signed by:** Donnie Reynolds.

Taylor was one of four Canadians drafted by the Diamondbacks in 2016 and comes out of the same college program—University of British Columbia—that produced former big league southpaw Jeff Francis. Taylor was a reliever his first two college seasons before moving to the rotation for his junior year, when he posted a 1.96 ERA with an outstanding 113-to-22 strikeout-to-walk ratio. After signing for $496,700, he pitched effectively out of the short-season Hillboro bullpen, fanning 12.4 batters per nine innings. Taylor's firm fastball sits 93-96 mph with plus sink out of his 6-foot-6 frame. He gets good life on the pitch, with at least one report having him touching 99 mph during the summer. He flashes a plus slider and has emerging feel for his changeup, though the pitch remains fringe-average at best. Taylor has a quick arm with a max-effort delivery that features a three-quarters arm slot and a funky arm action, but he repeats his motion and it adds deception. His delivery and two-pitch mix portend a future bullpen role, but he has the stuff to start and will be developed in that role for now. He will head to full-season ball in 2017, most likely low Class A Kane County as part of the Cougars rotation.

BA GRADE **45** Risk: High

Year	Club (League)	Class	W	L	ERA	G	GS	CG	SV	IP	H	HR	BB	SO	K/9	WHIP	AVG
2016	Hillsboro (NWL)	SS	1	0	2.20	17	0	0	3	16	13	0	5	23	12.7	1.10	.213
Minor League Totals			1	0	2.20	17	0	0	3	16	13	0	5	23	12.7	1.10	.213

11 ALEX YOUNG, LHP

BA GRADE **45** Risk: High

Born: Sept. 9, 1993. **B-T:** L-L. **Ht.:** 6-2. **Wt.:** 205. **Drafted:** Texas Christian, 2015 (2nd round). **Signed by:** J.R. Salinas.

Young pitched sparingly after being drafted 43rd overall in 2015 after his long college season at Texas Christian, but the gloves came off in 2016. He missed about six weeks in April and May 2016 with a forearm sprain but still pitched 118.2 innings and advanced from low Class A Kane County to high Class A Visalia. Young is a pitch-to-contact, command-driven lefty who typically sits 88-90 mph with his fastball and can touch 92. The velocity on Young's heater was down a couple ticks in 2016, but he was still effective with a wider repertoire. His breaking ball is called a true curveball by some observers and a slider by others, explained by the fact that it was not as firm as the previous year. Regardless of what it's called, Young's 76-81 mph breaking ball is an above-average pitch with plus potential. His changeup, which was newer coming out of college, is now a solid-average offering in the mid-80s. Young has good feel for pitching and is a competitor who likes to get the ball in big-game situations. At his best his command is superb, which is exemplified by an 88-pitch complete game he threw against Inland Empire. Keeping his command consistently sharp, though, remains a work in progress for Young and will be key for his development moving forward with no plus offerings in his arsenal. He projects as a back-of-the-rotation starter and is expected to start at Double-A Jackson in 2017.

Year	Club (League)	Class	W	L	ERA	G	GS	CG	SV	IP	H	HR	BB	SO	K/9	WHIP	AVG
2015	Diamondbacks (AZL)	R	0	0	0.00	1	1	0	0	1	0	0	0	1	9.0	0.00	.000
	Hillsboro (NWL)	SS	0	0	1.50	6	1	0	1	6	5	0	1	5	7.5	1.00	.238
2016	Kane County (MWL)	LoA	3	1	2.16	9	9	1	0	50	39	1	16	37	6.7	1.10	.217
	Visalia (CAL)	HiA	2	7	4.59	12	11	1	0	69	79	10	21	56	7.3	1.46	.289
Minor League Totals			5	8	3.44	28	22	2	1	126	123	11	38	99	7.1	1.28	.258

12 MATT KOCH, RHP

BA GRADE **40** Risk: Medium

Born: Nov. 2, 1990. **B-T:** L-R. **Ht.:** 6-3. **Wt.:** 215. **Drafted:** Louisville, 2012 (3rd round). **Signed by:** Jarrett England (Mets).

A closer during his college career at Louisville, Koch (pronounced "cook") has jumped back and forth between the rotation and the bullpen during his five-year pro career. The Diamondbacks acquired him from the Mets in 2015 for big league reliever Addison Reed. After 14 starts for Double-A Mobile and seven for Triple-A Reno in 2016, Koch finished the year with seven big league appearances, including a pair of solid starts in which he gave up just three runs in 11 innings. He is an effective strike-thrower who doesn't miss a lot of bats who uses a four-seam fastball and cutter in the low to mid-90s with sinking action. Koch's average low-80s slider has good depth, and he uses an above-average, firm changeup in the mid-80s. He effectively repeats his three-quarters arm slot. While he pitched effectively as a starter in the minors, Koch is viewed by most observers as a big league bullpen arm with a good chance of earning a job in the D-backs pen out of spring training.

Year	Club (League)	Class	W	L	ERA	G	GS	CG	SV	IP	H	HR	BB	SO	K/9	WHIP	AVG
2014	St. Lucie (FSL)	HiA	10	4	4.64	22	22	0	0	120	141	7	32	63	4.7	1.44	.294
2015	Binghamton (EL)	AA	4	8	3.46	35	8	0	0	88	95	5	15	55	5.6	1.25	.279
	Mobile (SL)	AA	1	0	0.00	1	1	0	0	7	2	0	4	6	7.4	0.82	.083
2016	Mobile (SL)	AA	2	4	4.70	14	14	0	0	75	87	7	13	49	5.9	1.34	.295
	Reno (PCL)	AAA	4	2	3.09	7	7	0	0	47	55	3	6	25	4.8	1.31	.294
	Arizona (NL)	MAJ	1	1	2.00	7	2	0	1	18	9	1	4	10	5.0	0.72	.145
Major League Totals			1	1	2.00	7	2	0	1	18	9	1	4	10	5.0	0.72	.145
Minor League Totals			27	24	4.21	110	69	1	0	443	505	30	81	285	5.8	1.32	.288

13 JIMMIE SHERFY, RHP

BA GRADE

45 Risk: High

Born: Dec. 27, 1991. **B-T:** R-R. **Ht.:** 6-0. **Wt.:** 175. **Drafted:** Oregon, 2013 (10th round). **Signed by:** Donnie Reynolds.

Sherfy appeared to be on the fast track through the Diamondbacks system his first two pro seasons thanks to an electric fastball and two solid offspeed pitches. He struggled mightily at Double-A Mobile in 2015, however, and took a step back to high Class A Visalia to start 2016. Sherfy got back on track both in the Cal League and in a return to Mobile, striking out 52 batters and yielding only one run in 32 innings. A 6.17 ERA in 23.1 innings at Triple-A Reno was inflated by two particularly poor outings. The key for Sherfy in 2016 was improving his focus and developing a better routine off the field, as well as making mechanical changes on the mound that helped him better maintain his stuff. He delivers a fastball in the 95-98 mph range and a plus slider at 87-91. He complements his primary pitches with an 88-92 mph changeup and mid-70s curveball. The D-backs added Sherfy to the 40-man roster after the 2016 season, and he will head to spring training with a shot at being part of the team's rebuilt bullpen. His electric stuff and two potential plus pitches give him closer potential.

Year	Club (League)	Class	W	L	ERA	G	GS	CG	SV	IP	H	HR	BB	SO	K/9	WHIP	AVG
2014	Visalia (CAL)	HiA	2	0	3.27	11	0	0	6	11	6	2	5	23	18.8	1.00	.158
	Mobile (SL)	AA	3	1	4.97	39	0	0	4	38	34	4	18	45	10.7	1.37	.241
2015	Mobile (SL)	AA	1	6	6.52	44	0	0	2	50	50	3	28	50	9.1	1.57	.265
2016	Visalia (CAL)	HiA	0	0	0.00	12	0	0	8	12	5	0	6	21	15.3	0.89	.128
	Mobile (SL)	AA	2	0	0.46	16	0	0	10	20	6	1	5	31	14.2	0.56	.092
	Reno (PCL)	AAA	1	4	6.17	24	0	0	12	23	20	5	13	27	10.4	1.41	.247
Minor League Totals			10	12	4.20	162	0	0	46	171	134	15	79	226	11.9	1.24	.217

14 ANDY YERZY, C

BA GRADE

50 Risk: Extreme

Born: July 5, 1998. **B-T:** L-R. **Ht.:** 6-3. **Wt.:** 215. **Drafted:** HS—Toronto, 2016 (2nd round). **Signed by:** Dennis Sheehan.

The Diamondbacks went for a high school power bat in the second round in 2016, signing Yerzy for $1,214,100 to keep the Canadian high school product from honoring his commitment to Notre Dame. Coming into the draft, Yerzy was regarded as a bat-first catcher with questions about his ability to stay behind the plate because of a slow, stiff body and a fringy arm. He is intelligent with great makeup, and he made good progress at 2016 instructional league, where D-backs coaches worked on Yerzy's defensive technique to try to mold him into an average defender. His fringe-average arm is accurate but his arm action gets long at times. Yerzy had a rough pro debut at the plate, batting just .216/.240/.265 at two Rookie-level stops. He has a calm approach from the left side and started using his legs better at instructs. Yerzy projects to be an above-average hitter with power, but it won't come quickly. He is considered a long-term project who will spend the 2017 season in a short-season league, perhaps short-season Hillsboro.

Year	Club (League)	Class	AVG	G	AB	R	H	2B	3B	HR	RBI	BB	SO	SB	CS	OBP	SLG
2016	Diamondbacks (AZL)	R	.196	27	102	5	20	3	0	1	15	4	22	0	0	.220	.255
	Missoula (PIO)	R	.250	18	60	2	15	2	0	0	1	0	16	0	1	.274	.283
Minor League Totals			.216	45	162	7	35	5	0	1	16	4	38	0	1	.240	.265

15 JACK REINHEIMER, SS/2B

BA GRADE

40 Risk: Medium

Born: July 19, 1992. **B-T:** R-R. **Ht.:** 6-1. **Wt.:** 186. **Drafted:** East Carolina, 2013 (5th round). **Signed by:** Devitt Moore (Mariners).

One of four players acquired from the Mariners in 2015 when Arizona traded Mark Trumbo, Reinheimer completed his first full season in the Diamondbacks organization by being added to the 40-man roster after a solid year at Triple-A Reno. He has a ceiling as a major league utility infielder, but that's also his floor. He projects to have a long career as a capable backup. A hard-nosed, scrappy player, Reinheimer is a below-average hitter with little home run power, though his 37 extra-base hits at Reno indicate he may have enough pop to earn pitchers' respect. He gets in trouble at the plate by expanding his strike zone, which leads to higher-than-desired strikeout totals. An above-average runner, Reinheimer led Reno with 20 stolen bases and has swiped a total of 98 bags over four minor league seasons. Defensively, he plays fast and with great timing and rhythm to his game. His instincts are good, his hands are solid-average and he has an above-average arm. Reinheimer will go to spring training with a shot at a big league role as a reserve infielder but may wind up back at Reno to wait his turn.

Year	Club (League)	Class	AVG	G	AB	R	H	2B	3B	HR	RBI	BB	SO	SB	CS	OBP	SLG
2014	Clinton (MWL)	LoA	.264	110	436	69	115	17	4	2	46	39	76	34	9	.333	.335
	High Desert (CAL)	HiA	.341	20	85	15	29	5	1	1	12	4	12	5	2	.367	.459
2015	Jackson (SL)	AA	.277	48	202	25	56	10	1	1	16	14	39	12	1	.323	.351
	Mobile (SL)	AA	.265	76	283	39	75	14	2	4	26	37	54	9	5	.355	.371
2016	Reno (PCL)	AAA	.288	132	500	64	144	28	7	2	48	48	93	20	11	.353	.384
Minor League Totals			.277	452	1755	251	486	80	16	12	178	174	325	98	33	.346	.361

16 MACK LEMIEUX, LHP

BA GRADE

50 Risk: Extreme

Born: Sept. 6, 1996. **B-T:** L-L. **Ht.:** 6-3. **Wt.:** 205. **Drafted:** Palm Beach State (Fla.) JC, 2016 (6th round). **Signed by:** Frank Damas.

Lemieux, a distant cousin of hockey legend Mario Lemieux, was first drafted in 2015 in the 14th round by the Nationals after finishing his Florida high school career. Instead of signing, he chose to play junior-college ball at Palm Beach State, where he recorded a 2.79 ERA and struck out nearly a batter per inning. Selected by the Diamondbacks in the sixth round in 2016 and signed for $278,500, Lemieux started his pro career with seven strong starts in the Rookie-level Arizona League before heading to short-season Hillsboro. He recorded a 3.03 ERA with 43 strikeouts in 35.2 innings between the two levels. Lemieux has good body control and a quick arm that delivers a fastball that sits 90-91 mph and touches 93. There is room on his frame to add strength, so that velocity should tick up as his body matures. Both his curveball and 82-83 mph changeup project as above-average pitches. He has a loose arm with a simple high three-quarters arm slot that he repeats well. Lemieux projects as a lefthander for the middle or back of a rotation, and he should get to full-season ball in 2017 at low Class A Kane County.

Year	Club (League)	Class	W	L	ERA	G	GS	CG	SV	IP	H	HR	BB	SO	K/9	WHIP	AVG
2016	Diamondbacks (AZL)	R	1	0	1.42	7	4	0	0	13	8	1	3	17	12.1	0.87	.182
	Hillsboro (NWL)	SS	1	2	3.91	7	7	0	0	23	24	1	12	26	10.2	1.57	.270
Minor League Totals			2	2	3.03	14	11	0	0	36	32	2	15	43	10.9	1.32	.241

17 JHOAN DURAN, RHP

BA GRADE

50 Risk: Extreme

Born: Jan. 8, 1998. **B-T:** R-R. **Ht.:** 6-5. **Wt.:** 175. **Signed:** Dominican Republic, 2014. **Signed by:** Junior Noboa.

Duran signed in 2014 for a mere $65,000 and has morphed into one of the most projectable arms in the Diamondbacks system with his 6-foot-5, 175-pound frame and electric fastball. With his very lean but wiry strong frame, he already has a fastball up to 98 mph with good movement. He uses a repeatable, effortless delivery with an easy arm stroke and projects to develop better command of the pitch. His high-80s curveball is still inconsistent, grading sometimes as below-average and at other times flashing as a plus pitch. It plays up because he throws it for strikes. Duran also is developing a feel for a high-80s changeup. It's scary to think how much harder he could throw when he adds strength to his frame, and that projection makes him the sleeper of the system. Duran will likely head to short-season Hillsboro as a teenager after opening the year in extended spring training.

Year	Club (League)	Class	W	L	ERA	G	GS	CG	SV	IP	H	HR	BB	SO	K/9	WHIP	AVG
2015	D-backs (DSL)	R	4	1	3.25	12	12	0	0	64	62	1	22	44	6.2	1.32	.263
2016	Diamondbacks (AZL)	R	1	2	5.85	4	4	0	0	20	24	1	5	13	5.9	1.45	.312
	Missoula (PIO)	R	0	1	3.55	3	3	0	0	13	14	1	5	9	6.4	1.50	.250
Minor League Totals			5	4	3.83	19	19	0	0	96	100	3	32	66	6.2	1.37	.271

18 JOSE ALMONTE, RHP

BA GRADE
50 Risk: Extreme

Born: Sept. 8, 1995. **B-T:** R-R. **Ht.:** 6-2. **Wt.:** 182. **Signed:** Dominican Republic, 2012. **Signed by:** Manny Nanita (Red Sox).

One of the top international signings by the Red Sox in 2012, Almonte signed for $610,000 and worked his way to low Class A in 2016 before being traded to the Diamondbacks (along with second baseman Luis Alejandro Basabe) for veteran reliever Brad Ziegler. Finishing the season at low Class A in Kane County, Almonte combined for a 3.56 ERA and a 104-to-35 strikeout-to-walk ratio in 108.2 innings. With a projectable body and good arm speed, he projects as a starter with good feel for both pitching and spin. He aggressively attacks hitters with his three-pitch mix, highlighted by an above-average fastball coming in at 89-94 mph, and he should be able to add more velocity with more strength. His 74-79 mph curveball projects as an above-average pitch and his average changeup has good fade, though he needs to use it more often. Almonte should be ready for the challenge of the hitter-friendly California League in 2017.

Year	Club (League)	Class	W	L	ERA	G	GS	CG	SV	IP	H	HR	BB	SO	K/9	WHIP	AVG
2014	Red Sox (GCL)	R	2	3	3.02	11	8	0	0	48	46	3	17	33	6.2	1.32	.254
2015	Lowell (NYP)	SS	3	3	3.43	14	14	0	0	66	38	1	38	64	8.8	1.16	.171
2016	Greenville (SAL)	LoA	2	2	3.91	10	10	0	0	53	50	4	13	45	7.6	1.19	.249
	Kane County (MWL)	LoA	2	4	3.23	11	11	0	0	56	48	4	22	59	9.5	1.26	.234
Minor League Totals			12	15	3.24	58	55	0	0	272	220	13	112	244	8.1	1.22	.222

19 JARED MILLER, LHP

BA GRADE
45 Risk: High

Born: Aug. 21, 1993. **B-T:** L-L. **Ht.:** 6-7. **Wt.:** 240. **Drafted:** Vanderbilt, 2014 (11th round). **Signed by:** Nate Birtwell.

Miller was part of the Vanderbilt pitching staff during the Commodores' 2014 College World Series championship season. A college roommate of 2015 Diamondbacks first-rounder Dansby Swanson, he pitched both as a starter and in relief and got the win in the first game of the 2014 CWS Finals. The Diamondbacks took the hulking lefthander in the 11th round that year and signed him for an over-slot $150,000 bonus. Miller's career took off in 2016 after Arizona moved him to the bullpen. He zoomed through four levels of the organization and finished the season at Triple-A Reno before being one of the big surprises of the Arizona Fall League. He allowed no runs and just six hits in 18.1 innings with 30 strikeouts and four walks. Miller's funky, max-effort delivery has him falling to the third-base side but adds deception and doesn't affect his control. He uses a fastball with plus movement in the 92-94 mph range, but the jewel of his arsenal is an 83-88 mph slider with great tilt and depth that flashes plus and gets plenty of swings and misses. Miller's third pitch is a 77-83 mph curveball. While not yet on the 40-man roster, he has a good chance of getting to Chase Field at some point in 2017.

Year	Club (League)	Class	W	L	ERA	G	GS	CG	SV	IP	H	HR	BB	SO	K/9	WHIP	AVG
2014	Hillsboro (NWL)	SS	1	1	3.58	8	5	0	0	28	21	3	9	21	6.8	1.08	.204
2015	Hillsboro (NWL)	SS	7	2	1.81	9	9	1	0	60	42	2	12	57	8.6	0.91	.194
	Kane County (MWL)	LoA	4	5	5.88	13	12	0	0	60	69	5	31	42	6.3	1.68	.291
2016	Kane County (MWL)	LoA	0	0	0.00	9	0	0	2	14	4	0	5	21	13.2	0.63	.085
	Visalia (CAL)	HiA	0	1	1.88	12	0	0	1	14	9	0	3	20	12.6	0.84	.184
	Reno (PCL)	AAA	0	0	6.00	5	0	0	0	6	5	2	2	3	4.5	1.17	.238
	Mobile (SL)	AA	0	1	3.71	19	0	0	2	27	18	1	13	36	12.2	1.16	.188
Minor League Totals			12	10	3.46	75	26	1	5	208	168	13	75	200	8.6	1.17	.218

20 LUIS ALEJANDRO BASABE, 2B

BA GRADE
45 Risk: High

Born: Aug. 26, 1996. **B-T:** B-R. **Ht.:** 5-10. **Wt.:** 170. **Signed:** Venezuela, 2012. **Signed by:** Eddie Romero/Luis Segovia (Red Sox).

When one team signs twins who have the same first and last names, confusion is sure to abound. The Red Sox cleared things up for everyone by trading Luis Alejandro Basabe (known to his teammates as "A.J.") to the Diamondbacks along with Jose Almonte for righthander Brad Ziegler. (Boston later traded also Luis Alexander Basabe to the White Sox in the Chris Sale deal.) A.J. Basabe wasn't even supposed to make the low Class A Greenville roster after spending 2015 in the Gulf Coast League, but he played his way there in spring training, then proved to be a good enough hitter to move to the top of the lineup. Less physically gifted than his brother, Basabe has strong hand-eye coordination and table-setter skills. Basabe is stretched at shortstop because of his iffy footwork, but he's at least an average defender at second base. He lacks his brother's plus speed, but Basabe runs the bases well, has a chance to be an above-average hitter and has enough pop in his bat to survive. He struggled in Kane County after the trade, but as he's shown before, he generally figures out a way to catch up to the level. It's not out of the question that he'll improve enough at shortstop to be a potential utility infielder.

Year	Club (League)	Class	AVG	G	AB	R	H	2B	3B	HR	RBI	BB	SO	SB	CS	OBP	SLG
2014	Red Sox (DSL)	R	.222	30	99	19	22	3	1	0	6	28	25	9	1	.403	.273
2015	Red Sox (GCL)	R	.260	28	100	22	26	5	0	0	6	21	33	8	4	.387	.310
2016	Greenville (SAl.)	LoA	.310	64	229	39	71	16	4	4	25	37	58	14	6	.412	.467
	Kane County (MWL)	LoA	.217	45	161	16	35	4	2	3	13	29	60	3	6	.339	.323
Minor League Totals			.247	225	745	121	184	33	11	8	64	148	224	43	19	.375	.353

21 WEI-CHIEH HUANG, RHP

BA GRADE 45 Risk: Extreme

Born: Sept. 26, 1993. **B-T:** R-R. **Ht.:** 6-1. **Wt.:** 165. **Signed:** Taiwan, 2014. **Signed by:** Tzu Yao Wei.

Huang signed with the Diamondbacks for $450,000 in 2014 after pitching at the National Taiwan University of Physical Education and Sport. Coming off a solid 2015 season at low Class A, Huang's 2016 season got off to a late start because of an offseason military commitment in Taiwan. After six rocky starts at high Class A Visalia he was shut down with shoulder fatigue and soreness. After a couple of months of rest and rehab, Huang finished the season pitching long-relief outings at short-season Hillsboro. His durability has been an ongoing issue and is a red flag moving forward. When he's right, Huang is able to locate his pitches well. He pitches to contact with a plus changeup that he uses to get swings and misses, and his fastball has good angle and sits 87-91 mph. His low-70s curveball is a below-average pitch. The most optimistic projection for Huang is No. 5 starter, but his subpar breaking ball and durability concerns may target him for a bullpen role. He likely will return to Visalia in 2017 to repeat the California League.

Year	Club (League)	Class	W	L	ERA	G	GS	CG	SV	IP	H	HR	BB	SO	K/9	WHIP	AVG
2015	Kane County (MWL)	LoA	7	3	2.00	15	12	0	0	77	58	1	16	68	8.0	0.97	.208
2016	Visalia (CAL)	HiA	1	1	6.49	6	6	0	0	26	33	5	12	25	8.5	1.71	.303
	Diamondbacks (AZL)	R	0	0	6.00	1	1	0	0	3	3	1	0	3	9.0	1.00	.273
	Hillsboro (NWL)	SS	2	2	5.34	9	4	0	0	30	33	4	11	42	12.5	1.45	.277
Minor League Totals			10	6	3.70	31	23	0	0	136	127	11	39	138	9.1	1.22	.245

22 MARCUS WILSON, OF

BA GRADE 45 Risk: Extreme

Born: Aug. 15, 1996. **B-T:** R-R. **Ht.:** 6-3. **Wt.:** 175. **Drafted:** HS—Gardena, Calif., 2014 (2nd round supplemental). **Signed by:** Hal Kurtzman.

Wilson made it to full-season ball in his third year as a pro, which was just about what the organization expected when he was drafted 69th overall in 2014. He has always needed to add strength to his lean frame, and that still holds true, but he has made improvements to his approach at the plate in that time. Wilson began in extended spring training again, then advanced to short-season Hillsboro, where he hit .252/.418/.319. He spent August at low Class A Kane County with similar numbers. Wilson turned in the best walk rate of his career in 2016 (17.5 percent) but also recorded a high strikeout rate (24.7 percent). He was young for his draft class, so he still has time to develop the strength needed to tap into his bat speed. He's a solid defender who covers plenty of ground and has an average arm. A plus runner, Wilson stole 25 bases in 30 attempts in 2016. He will return to Kane County in 2017.

Year	Club (League)	Class	AVG	G	AB	R	H	2B	3B	HR	RBI	BB	SO	SB	CS	OBP	SLG
2014	Diamondbacks (AZL)	R	.206	39	131	15	27	2	2	1	22	16	40	4	2	.297	.275
2015	Missoula (PIO)	R	.258	57	213	42	55	12	1	1	22	33	61	7	4	.357	.338
2016	Hillsboro (NWL)	SS	.252	43	135	24	34	5	2	0	15	38	40	18	3	.418	.319
	Kane County (MWL)	LoA	.253	26	99	11	25	8	1	1	5	13	32	7	2	.357	.384
Minor League Totals			.244	165	578	92	141	27	6	3	64	100	173	36	11	.360	.327

23 VICTOR REYES, OF

BA GRADE 40 Risk: High

Born: Oct. 5, 1994. **B-T:** B-R. **Ht.:** 6-3. **Wt.:** 170. **Signed:** Venezuela, 2011. **Signed by:** Rolando Petit (Braves).

The Diamondbacks acquired Reyes from the Braves in April 2015 as part of a two-part trade that sent Trevor Cahill to Atlanta for salary relief, with the switch-hitting Reyes being swapped for a 2015 supplemental second-round pick. Reyes hit well in his second season with Arizona, batting .303/.349/.416 at high Class A Visalia with significantly better numbers in the second half. The consistent rap on him is that while he makes good contact and can handle velocity, he lacks strength in his swing and hits for very little power. He won't drive many balls over the fence but will hopefully develop more doubles power in time. He showed progress by learning how to hit the ball out in front and elevate the baseball. An at least above-average runner, Reyes legged out 12 triples and stole 20 bases in 2016. He's an above-average defender in the outfield, with his above-average arm being enough for right field. While he hasn't seen much time in center field, he's a competent defender there. Reyes will move to Double-A Jackson in 2017.

Year	Club (League)	Class	AVG	G	AB	R	H	2B	3B	HR	RBI	BB	SO	SB	CS	OBP	SLG
2014	Rome (SAL)	LoA	.259	89	332	32	86	13	0	0	34	24	58	12	7	.309	.298
2015	Kane County (MWL)	LoA	.311	121	424	57	132	17	5	2	59	22	58	13	4	.343	.389
2016	Visalia (CAL)	HiA	.303	124	469	62	142	11	12	6	54	33	78	20	8	.349	.416
Minor League Totals			.300	435	1580	225	474	55	18	8	205	125	262	62	26	.352	.373

24 JOSE HERRERA, C

BA GRADE

45 Risk: Extreme

Born: Feb. 24, 1997. **B-T:** B-R. **Ht.:** 5-10. **Wt.:** 182. **Signed:** Venezuela, 2013. **Signed by:** Marlon Urdaneta.

The Diamondbacks' top international signee in 2013, Herrera has consistently shown solid defensive skills behind the plate and an improving swing. The biggest impediment to the native Venezuelan's development has been an inability to stay healthy. He has been plagued by nagging injuries in both 2015 and 2016. Herrera caught regularly during extended spring training in 2016 but was limited to just 12 games behind the plate at Rookie-level Missoula before shutting down early with a hamate injury. He often batted as DH for the Osprey and showed good patience at the plate (9.7 percent walks). He hit a career-high five home runs. He has the raw power to develop more over-the-fence pop as he gets stronger. Behind the plate, Herrera blocks and throws well, albeit with improvement needed in shifting on pitches. Herrera's mental makeup is strong and he also got himself into better shape in 2016 by losing weight. After three years in short-season ball, Herrera will be ready for low Class A Kane County in 2017.

Year	Club (League)	Class	AVG	G	AB	R	H	2B	3B	HR	RBI	BB	SO	SB	CS	OBP	SLG
2014	Diamondbacks (AZL)	R	.227	43	154	24	35	4	1	0	14	23	37	1	0	.337	.266
	Missoula (PIO)	R	.286	2	7	2	2	1	0	0	1	2	2	0	0	.444	.429
2015	Diamondbacks (AZL)	R	.304	24	79	7	24	3	0	1	9	13	11	0	0	.415	.380
2016	Missoula (PIO)	R	.277	36	137	23	38	5	1	5	18	15	27	1	2	.351	.438
Minor League Totals			.263	105	377	56	99	13	2	6	42	53	77	2	2	.361	.355

25 JOSH TAYLOR, LHP

BA GRADE

40 Risk: High

Born: March 2, 1993. **B-T:** L-L. **Ht.:** 6-5. **Wt.:** 225. **Signed:** Georgia College & State, 2014 (NDFA). **Signed by:** David Seifert (Phillies).

Taylor went undrafted after high school and junior college in the Phoenix area because he was a slender lefthander topping out in the 80s. He also didn't get much attention in his one year at Division II Georgia College & State, where he finished with a 5.62 ERA and 57 strikeouts against 41 walks. Taylor then touched 97 mph at the all-star game in the summer collegiate Northwoods League in 2014, which caught the attention of Phillies scouts, who signed the southpaw for $50,000. The Diamondbacks acquired Taylor about a year later when they unloaded $2.2 million in international bonus pool money in a trade with the Phillies. While he's never put up overwhelming numbers, Taylor jumped up the depth chart late in 2016 with a strong performance in the Arizona Fall League, where he recorded a 3.57 ERA with 20 strikeouts and five walks in 22.2 innings. His fastball sits 91-94 mph with decent cutting action in on righthanded batters and sinking action on lefthanders. None of his three secondary pitches—slider, curveball, changeup—grades as above-average, but deception in his repeatable delivery helps them play up. Taylor projects as a No. 5 starter, though his velocity would likely tick up pitching out of the bullpen.

Year	Club (League)	Class	W	L	ERA	G	GS	CG	SV	IP	H	HR	BB	SO	K/9	WHIP	AVG
2014	Phillies (GCL)	R	2	0	0.00	3	0	0	0	9	5	0	4	13	12.5	0.96	.156
2015	Lakewood (SAL)	LoA	4	5	4.61	13	13	0	0	68	71	6	24	70	9.2	1.39	.265
	Kane County (MWL)	LoA	4	3	3.20	11	11	1	0	59	73	2	20	53	8.1	1.58	.311
2016	Visalia (CAL)	HiA	2	7	5.65	15	13	0	0	78	105	7	24	77	8.9	1.65	.335
	Mobile (SL)	AA	3	4	4.94	11	11	1	0	55	63	4	18	46	7.6	1.48	.289
Minor League Totals			15	19	4.51	53	48	2	0	269	317	19	90	259	8.7	1.51	.297

26 STEVE HATHAWAY, LHP

BA GRADE

40 Risk: High

Born: Sept. 13, 1990. **B-T:** L-L. **Ht.:** 6-1. **Wt.:** 185. **Drafted:** Franklin Pierce (N.H.), 2013 (14th round). **Signed by:** Mike Serbalik.

Hathaway moved steadily through the Diamondbacks system after being drafted out of Franklin Pierce, where he helped the Ravens make it to the Division II College World Series. Hathaway twice had surgery in college and was already 23 when drafted. He made it to the big leagues during his fourth pro season in 2016 after pitching effectively at both Double-A Mobile and Triple-A Reno. While slight of build, Hathaway has a loose, whippy arm and the ball jumps out of his hand from a high three-quarters arm slot. The key to his effectiveness in 2016 was an increase in fastball velocity, and he now sits 92-95 mph with a four-seamer that has natural sinking action with armside run. His high-70s curveball is an above-average pitch, and he also throws a firm mid-80s changeup. With a ceiling of a middle reliever, Hathaway is a strong candidate for a big league bullpen job in 2017.

Year	Club (League)	Class	W	L	ERA	G	GS	CG	SV	IP	H	HR	BB	SO	K/9	WHIP	AVG
2014	South Bend (MWL)	LoA	0	0	3.68	8	0	0	1	15	12	0	6	18	11.0	1.23	.207
2015	Kane County (MWL)	LoA	0	2	4.32	16	0	0	1	17	14	0	6	19	10.3	1.20	.226
	Visalia (CAL)	HiA	5	1	2.00	29	0	0	1	27	21	0	9	29	9.7	1.11	.198
2016	Mobile (SL)	AA	1	1	1.17	13	0	0	0	15	14	0	3	10	5.9	1.11	.250
	Reno (PCL)	AAA	1	2	3.34	28	0	0	1	30	21	2	19	29	8.8	1.35	.210
	Arizona (NL)	MAJ	0	0	4.91	24	0	0	0	15	18	1	6	15	9.2	1.64	.305
Major League Totals			0	0	4.91	24	0	0	0	15	18	1	6	15	9.2	1.64	.305
Minor League Totals			7	7	3.09	97	3	0	4	111	90	4	44	110	8.9	1.21	.218

27 JOEY ROSE, 3B

BA GRADE

45 Risk: Extreme

Born: Jan. 20, 1998. **B-T:** R-R. **Ht.:** 6-1. **Wt.:** 205. **Drafted:** HS—Toms River, N.J., 2016 (5th round). **Signed by:** Rick Matsko.

Coming out of the same town that produced Todd Frazier, Rose is a New Jersey high school product who showed a better swing and defensive skills as the 2016 draft approached. Committed to Oklahoma State, he instead signed with the Diamondbacks for $400,000. Beginning his pro career in the Rookie-level Arizona League, Rose hit a modest .226/.310/.362 with one home run. But he delivered a .796 OPS in August as he learned how to stay inside the ball and use the middle of the field. Rose has a good swing and strength in his hands, with average to above-average power projected as he develops. He showed good actions at the plate and began making better contact during the season. Defensively, he showed surprisingly good lateral agility at third base with at least an above-average arm. He's a below-average runner. Rose will likely need to stay behind in extended spring training in 2017 before reporting to short-season Hillsboro for his second pro season.

Year	Club (League)	Class	AVG	G	AB	R	H	2B	3B	HR	RBI	BB	SO	SB	CS	OBP	SLG
2016	Diamondbacks (AZL)	R	.229	47	153	19	35	10	4	1	9	13	55	2	0	.310	.366
	Hillsboro (NWL)	SS	.000	2	2	0	0	0	0	0	0	1	2	0	0	.333	.000
Minor League Totals			.226	49	155	19	35	10	4	1	9	14	57	2	0	.310	.361

28 ILDEMARO VARGAS, SS/2B

BA GRADE

40 Risk: High

Born: July 16, 1991. **B-T:** B-R. **Ht.:** 6-0. **Wt.:** 170. **Signed:** Venezuela, 2007. **Signed by:** Jobel Jimenez (Cardinals).

The Diamondbacks hit the jackpot last time they dipped into the independent ranks to sign a former Cardinals farmhand from Venezuela. David Peralta eventually became one of Arizona's regular outfielders. Their latest foray netted them Vargas, who began the 2015 season with Bridgeport of the Atlantic League after seven seasons in the St. Louis system. After playing his first season in the D-backs system at low Class A Kane County in 2015, Vargas split 2016 mostly between Double-A Mobile and Triple-A Reno. He hit .305 and struck out just 39 times in 133 games. Vargas is an extreme contact hitter who takes good at-bats but makes mostly soft contact. An average runner, he plays with a lot of energy and is capable of handling multiple positions in a utility role. He has soft hands and is an instinctive defender. The D-backs added Vargas to the 40-man roster after the 2016 season because he would have been eligible for minor league free agency otherwise. He heads back to Reno in 2017 to show his performance wasn't a fluke while waiting for a need to arise in Phoenix.

Year	Club (League)	Class	AVG	G	AB	R	H	2B	3B	HR	RBI	BB	SO	SB	CS	OBP	SLG
2014	Palm Beach (FSL)	HiA	.241	112	431	46	104	17	1	1	40	16	51	1	4	.271	.292
	Springfield, MO (TL)	AA	.000	8	10	1	0	0	0	0	0	0	1	0	0	.000	.000
2015	Bridgeport (ATL)	IND	.273	30	110	17	30	5	0	0	8	6	9	7	1	.316	.318
	Kane County (MWL)	LoA	.321	86	336	62	108	18	3	5	39	35	16	9	6	.385	.438
2016	Mobile (SL)	AA	.276	83	323	41	89	15	2	4	19	24	24	8	0	.325	.372
	Visalia (CAL)	HiA	.250	1	4	0	1	0	0	0	0	0	2	0	0	.250	.250
	Reno (PCL)	AAA	.354	49	198	35	70	13	0	2	18	20	13	13	1	.418	.449
Minor League Totals			.279	664	2414	348	673	121	18	19	235	201	244	63	32	.340	.367

29 RYAN JANUARY, C

BA GRADE

45 Risk: Extreme

Born: May 27, 1997. **B-T:** L-R. **Ht.:** 6-2. **Wt.:** 195. **Drafted:** San Jacinto (Texas) JC, 2016 (8th round). **Signed by:** Rusty Pendergrass.

January had himself re-classified for the 2015 draft a year early so that he could get a jump start on his college career at Louisiana State. Instead he enrolled at San Jacinto (Texas) JC after going undrafted. A broken thumb at San Jac kept him from getting behind the plate in the latter part of the 2016 season, but he was one of the top performers for the Gators' run to second place in the Junior College World Series. January hit 10 home runs in junior college and then 10 more in his pro debut at Rookie-level Missoula after signing with Arizona for an over-slot $350,000. He caught in 38 of the Osprey's 75 games. January owns a live bat from the left side with plus raw power and loft in his swing, though it can get loopy at times. He's still relatively raw behind the plate, but is athletic and shows average or slightly above-average arm strength. There's still a lot of rawness to his game and he may need another year of short-season ball, but the tools and makeup are there.

Year	Club (League)	Class	AVG	G	AB	R	H	2B	3B	HR	RBI	BB	SO	SB	CS	OBP	SLG
2016	Missoula (PIO)	R	.273	51	183	34	50	6	0	10	26	26	63	0	1	.376	.470
Minor League Totals			.273	51	183	34	50	6	0	10	26	26	63	0	1	.376	.470

30 TOMMY EVELD, RHP

BA GRADE

40 Risk: High

Born: Dec. 30, 1993. **B-T:** R-R. **Ht.:** 6-5. **Wt.:** 195. **Drafted:** South Florida, 2016 (9th round). **Signed by:** Luke Wren.

The man known to short-season Hillsboro fans in his pro debut as "Touchdown Tommy" will be 23 in 2017, but he's still relatively new to pitching and owns a fresh arm. Originally a highly-touted football recruit, Eveld went to South Florida as a quarterback, but major knee surgery limited him to the scout team in his first two years on campus. He hadn't played baseball since the eighth grade but studied Nolan Ryan pitching videos on YouTube before joining a men's adult team. He later walked on to the USF baseball team and became the team's closer. He finished with a 2.21 ERA and nine saves. Signing for $125,000 after the Diamondbacks picked him in the ninth round, Eveld turned in an excellent season in the Northwest League. He recorded a 1.86 ERA and an excellent 31-8 strikeout-to-walk ratio in 29 innings. A fan favorite at Hops home games, he took the mound to the "Monday Night Football" theme. Eveld has a fastball that sits 92-95 mph and touches 97, and he complements it with an above-average power slider at 90-91 mph. He also occasionally uses a changeup and curveball, both which need further refinement. Already 23, Eveld will make the jump to full-season ball at low Class A Kane County in 2017.

Year	Club (League)	Class	W	L	ERA	G	GS	CG	SV	IP	H	HR	BB	SO	K/9	WHIP	AVG
2016	Hillsboro (NWL)	SS	2	1	1.86	24	0	0	2	29	17	0	8	31	9.6	0.86	.168
Minor League Totals			2	1	1.86	24	0	0	2	29	17	0	8	31	9.6	0.86	.168

Atlanta Braves

BY BILL BALLEW

At first glance, a 93-loss season would not seem to be cause for celebration.

Yet the air of optimism in the Braves front office and the organization's sense of progress go far beyond the imminent christening of a new ballpark in suburban Cobb County in 2017.

The 2016 campaign started on a sluggish note in Atlanta, and manager Fredi Gonzalez was fired after the Braves opened with a 9-28 record. Noticeable improvements did not happen immediately after Triple-A skipper Brian Snitker was promoted to interim manager on May 17, though baby steps led to bigger strides.

Atlanta finished strong by winning 20 of its final 30 games, beginning Aug. 30, which was 13 days after shortstop Dansby Swanson, the No. 1 overall pick in the 2015 draft, made his big league debut.

Atlanta's solid finish not only earned Snitker a one-year contract with a club option for 2018, it also coincided with a campaign that culminated with a winning atmosphere in the minors. Four of the Braves' six affiliates reached the postseason, with low Class A Rome emerging with the South Atlantic League title and BA Team of the Year honors. Triple-A Gwinnett advanced to the Governors' Cup Finals in the International League.

Such success is a testament to the talent the Braves have stockpiled under their two-year rebuilding project under the direction of president of baseball operations John Hart and general manager John Coppolella. The organization has emerged from a dire situation in which the system lacked talent and depth to one overflowing with prospects, particularly starting pitchers.

Deals with the Padres and Diamondbacks jumpstarted the process—and resulted in the acquisitions of, among others, Swanson, lefthander Max Fried and righthander Touki Toussaint—and relieved Atlanta of some veteran contracts, while a handful of other trades contributed to building a nucleus focused on finding rotation help for homegrown ace Julio Teheran.

While trades account for one-third of the Braves' Top 30 Prospects, the impressive depth in the organization has been accentuated by using the formula incorporated by GM Bobby Cox and scouting director Paul Snyder in the 1980s and maintained under Hall of Fame GM John Schuerholz in the 1990s and 2000s.

Scouting director Brian Bridges has focused on high school pitchers early in both of his draft classes, leading off with lefthander Kolby Allard in 2015 and righthander Ian Anderson in 2016.

Perhaps the boldest moves made by the new

TOMASSO DeROSA

The Braves' rebuilding strategy focused on finding rotation help for ace Julio Teheran

TOP PROSPECTS OF THE DECADE

Year	Player, Pos.	2016 Org
2007	Jarrod Saltalamacchia, c	Tigers
2008	Jordan Schafer, of	Dodgers
2009	Tommy Hanson, rhp	Deceased
2010	Jason Heyward, of	Cubs
2011	Julio Teheran, rhp	Braves
2012	Julio Teheran, rhp	Braves
2013	Julio Teheran, rhp	Braves
2014	Lucas Sims, rhp	Braves
2015	Jose Peraza, 2b	Reds
2016	Dansby Swanson, ss	Braves

regime came in 2016 when the Braves doled out five of the six largest signing bonuses in franchise history while investing more than $22 million between the draft and international market.

After inking Dominican outfielder Cristian Pache and Dominican shortstop Derian Cruz in 2015, the Braves acquired several international bonus slots for 2016 and far exceeded their assigned bonus pool by committing for $4.25 million to sign Venezuelan shortstop Kevin Maitan, the top international prospect of the decade, as well as five other players ranked among the top 41.

Few teams in recent times have been more committed to a complete overhaul than the Braves have executed since late 2014. The overall mold is still forming, but the pieces are on the verge of arriving in a fast and furious manner.

ORGANIZATION OVERVIEW

President: John Hart. **GM:** John Coppolella. **Farm director:** Dave Trembley. **Scouting director:** Brian Bridges.

Class	Team	League	W	L	PCT	Finish	Manager
Majors	Atlanta Braves	National	68	93	.422	13th (15)	F. Gonzalez/B. Snitker
Triple-A	Gwinnett Braves	International	65	78	.455	10th (14)	B. Snitker/J. Moses
Double-A	Mississippi Braves	Southern	73	65	.529	5th (10)	Luis Salazar
High Class A	* Carolina Mudcats	Carolina	52	87	.374	8th (8)	Rocket Wheeler
Low Class A	Rome Braves	South Atlantic	70	69	.504	9th (14)	Randy Ingle
Rookie	Danville Braves	Appalachian	31	36	.4th	7th (10)	Robinson Cancel
Rookie	GCL Braves	Gulf Coast	28	28	.500	8th (17)	Nestor Perez
Overall 2016 Minor League Record			319	363	.468	23rd (30)	

*Affiliate moves to Kissimmee, Fla., to become Florida Fire Frogs (Florida State) 2017

THIS YEAR' TOP 30

No.	Player, Pos.	Grade/Risk
1.	Dansby Swanson, ss	65/Low
2.	Ozzie Albies, 2b/ss	65/Medium
3.	Kolby Allard, lhp	60/High
4.	Mike Soroka, rhp	60/High
5.	Ian Anderson, rhp	65/Extreme
6.	Ronald Acuna, of	60/High
7.	Kevin Maitan, ss	65/Extreme
8.	Sean Newcomb, lhp	55/Medium
9.	Patrick Weigel, rhp	60/High
10.	Max Fried, lhp	55/High
11.	Austin Riley, 3b	55/High
12.	Touki Toussaint, rhp	60/Extreme
13.	Cristian Pache, of	55/Extreme
14.	Lucas Sims, rhp	50/High
15.	Joey Wentz, lhp	55/Extreme
16.	Dustin Peterson, of	50/High
17.	Kyle Muller, lhp	55/Extreme
18.	A.J. Minter, lhp	55/Extreme
19.	Travis Demeritte, 2b	50/High
20.	Rio Ruiz, 3b	45/Medium
21.	Braxton Davidson, of	50/High
22.	Derian Cruz, ss	55/Extreme
23.	Brett Cumberland, c	50/High
24.	Drew Harrington, lhp	50/High
25.	Bryse Wilson, rhp	55/Extreme
26.	Abrahan Gutierrez, c	50/Extreme
27.	Ray-Patrick Didder, of	45/High
28.	Luke Jackson, rhp	45/High
29.	Alex Jackson, of/c	50/Extreme
30.	Lucas Herbert, c	50/Extreme

LAST YEAR'S TOP 30

No.	Player, Pos.	Status
1.	Sean Newcomb, lhp	No. 8
2.	Hector Olivera, 3b/of	Free Agent
3.	Kolby Allard, lhp	No. 3
4.	Ozzie Albies, ss	No. 2
5.	Touki Toussaint, rhp	No. 12
6.	Austin Riley, 3b	No. 11
7.	Max Fried, lhp	No. 10
8.	Mallex Smith, of	Majors
9.	Mike Soroka, rhp	No. 4
10.	Braxton Davidson, of	No. 21
11.	Lucas Sims, rhp	No. 14
12.	Manny Banuelos, lhp	(Angels)
13.	Chris Ellis, rhp	(Cardinals)
14.	Tyrell Jenkins, rhp	(Rangers)
15.	Ricardo Sanchez, lhp	Dropped out
16.	John Gant, rhp	(Cardinals)
17.	Rio Ruiz, 3b	No. 20
18.	Lucas Herbert, c	No. 30
19.	Zack Bird, rhp	(Rangers)
20.	Dustin Peterson, of	No. 16
21.	Jason Hursh, rhp	Dropped out
22.	Shae Simmons, rhp	Majors
23.	Brady Feigl, lhp	(Rangers)
24.	Dan Winkler, rhp	Dropped out
25.	Johan Camargo, ss	Dropped out
26.	Ronald Acuna, of	No. 6
27.	Mauricio Cabrera, rhp	Majors
28.	Andrew Thurman, rhp	Free Agent
29.	Rob Whalen, rhp	(Mariners)
30.	Steve Janas, rhp	Dropped out

BEST TOOLS

Best Hitter for Average	Ozzie Albies
Best Power Hitter	Austin Riley
Best Strike Zone Discipline	Ronald Acuna
Fastest Baserunner	Anfernee Seymour
Best Athlete	Derian Cruz
Best Fastball	Lucas Sims
Best Curveball	Max Fried
Best Slider	A.J. Minter
Best Changeup	Kolby Allard
Best Control	Mike Soroka
Best Defensive Catcher	Lucas Herbert
Best Defensive Infielder	Dansby Swanson
Best Infield Arm	Ozzie Albies
Best Defensive Outfielder	Cristian Pache
Best Outfield Arm	Ray-Patrick Didder

PROJECTED 2020 LINEUP

Catcher	Tyler Flowers
First Base	Freddie Freeman
Second Base	Ozzie Albies
Third Base	Austin Riley
Shortstop	Dansby Swanson
Left Field	Dustin Peterson
Center Field	Ender Inciarte
Right Field	Ronald Acuna
No. 1 Starter	Julio Teheran
No. 2 Starter	Kolby Allard
No. 3 Starter	Mike Soroka
No. 4 Starter	Ian Anderson
No. 5 Starter	Sean Newcomb
Closer	Patrick Weigel

MINOR LEAGUE DEPTH CHART

ATLANTA BRAVES

TOP 2017 ROOKIE: Dansby Swanson, ss. He barely retained his rookie eligibility but is poised to bat toward the top of the Atlanta lineup.
BREAKOUT PROSPECT: Cristian Pache, of. The multi-tooled center fielder has the ability to make an immediate impact in his first full season.
SLEEPER: Corbin Clouse, lhp. Drafted in the 27th round in 2016, he has the makeup to be a closer to go with a mid-90s fastball and curveball that flashes plus.

SOURCE OF TOP 30 TALENT			
Homegrown	14	Acquired	16
College	4	Trades	11
Junior college	0	Rule 5 draft	0
High school	10	Independent leagues	0
Draft-and-follow	0	Free agents/waivers	0
Nondrafted free agents	0	International	5

LF
Dustin Peterson (16)

CF
Ronald Acuna (6)
Cristian Pache (13)
Ray-Patrick Didder (27)
Connor Lien
Keith Curcio
Yoeli Lopez

RF
Braxton Davidson (21)
Alex Jackson (29)
Randy Ventura
Isranel Wilson

3B
Austin Riley (11)
Rio Ruiz (20)

SS
Dansby Swanson (1)
Kevin Maitan (7)
Derian Cruz (22)
Anfernee Seymour
Yunior Severino
Braulio Vasquez
Livan Soto

2B
Ozzie Albies (2)
Travis Demeritte (19)
Luis Ovando
Kevin Josephine
Matt Gonzalez
Omar Obregon

1B
Ramon Osuna
Juan Yepez
Joey Meneses
Carlos Castro

C
Brett Cumberland (23)
Abrahan Gutierrez (26)
Lucas Herbert (30)
Kade Scivicque
Tanner Murphy

LHP

LHSP	LHRP
Kolby Allard (3)	A.J. Minter (18)
Sean Newcomb (8)	Jacob Lindgren
Max Fried (10)	Philip Pfeifer
Joey Wentz (15)	Adam McReery
Kyle Muller (17)	Michael O'Neal
Drew Harrington (24)	Corbin Clouse
Ricardo Sanchez	

RHP

RHSP	RHRP
Mike Soroka (4)	Lucas Sims (14)
Ian Anderson (5)	Bryse Wilson (25)
Patrick Weigel (9)	Luke Jackson (28)
Touki Toussaint (12)	Armando Rivero
Matt Withrow	Jeremy Walker
Luis Mora	Evan Phillips
	Jason Hursh
	Evertz Orozco
	Chad Sobotka
	Jordy Lara
	Devan Watts
	Bladimir Matos

DRAFT ANALYSIS

2016

BEST PURE HITTER: C Brett Cumberland (2) had less-than-stellar numbers in his pro debut, but he was the Pacific 12 Conference player of the year as a draft-eligible sophomore, thanks largely to his .344 batting average. 1B Ramon Osuna (13) was a prolific junior college hitter and batted .276/.342/.423 in his pro debut at Rookie-level Danville.

BEST POWER: Cumberland shows plus raw power in batting practice and can drive the ball out to the opposite field.

FASTEST RUNNER: 2B Matt Gonzalez (6) was a solid senior sign and gets to first base with above-average to plus run times.

BEST DEFENSIVE PLAYER: SS Marcus Mooney (10) was an inexpensive signing, but has smooth hands and long, rangy actions at shortstop.

BEST FASTBALL: RHP Ian Anderson (1) pitches at 92-95 mph and can touch as high as 97 with the ability to command the pitch. RHP Devan Watts (17) and LHP Corbin Clouse (27) can each reach 95 mph, and Clouse shows intriguing fastball life.

BEST SECONDARY PITCH: Anderson's late-breaking curveball and changeup both earn plus grades from some scouts. LHP Joey Wentz (1s) also earns plus grades for his curveball.

BEST PRO DEBUT: The Braves' prep pitchers shoved in their debuts. Anderson allowed two runs or fewer in all but one of his outings. Clouse earned a quick promotion to low Class A Rome; he struck out 53 batters in just 30.1 innings out of the bullpen. Wilson and Muller were unhittable in the Rookie-level Gulf Coast League. Wentz's velocity dipped a bit, but he earned a promotion to Danville. RHP Jeremy Walker (5) saw a jump in stuff and command.

BEST ATHLETE: LHP Kyle Muller (1s) was a prolific two-way player in high school, showing plus raw power and above-average speed in addition to his prowess on the mound. Wilson was a standout prep football player.

MOST INTRIGUING BACKGROUND: Watts is a converted position player, while Wentz originally was more highly regarded as a power-hitting first baseman before a strong start to the spring season. The Braves signed three sons of former major leaguers: RHP Cameron Stanton (30) is the son of ex-Braves and Yankees lefty Mike Stanton; 2B Nick Shumpert (28) is the son of Terry Shumpert; OF Jared James (34) is the son of Dion James, another ex-Brave.

CLOSEST TO THE MAJORS: LHP Drew Harrington (3) has excellent command and could move quickly, either as a potential back-of-the-rotation starter or solid lefthanded middle reliever.

BEST LATE-ROUND PICK: Clouse's excellent fastball and breaking ball made him the Braves' top late-round steal. Watts also has arm strength and a potentially above-average slider. Watts could shoot through the system with a strong fastball-slider repertoire and success at low Class A under his belt. RHP Matt Rowland (11) has upside with his fastball and slider.

THE ONE WHO GOT AWAY: RHP Cameron Jabara (31) has a projectable build and a promising arsenal of offspeed pitches, but he chose to attend Oregon instead.

2015

Atlanta drafted high-ceiling talents in LHPs Kolby Allard (1) and A.J. Minter (2s), RHPs Mike Soroka (1) and Patrick Weigel (7) and 3B Austin Riley (1s). They subsequently acquired the No. 1 overall pick Dansby Swanson from Arizona in the Shelby Miller deal.

GRADE: A

2014

OF Braxton Davidson (1) has shown flashes of being a profile corner bat. RHP Max Povse (3) made progress but was traded to Seattle. RHP Bradley Roney (8) has reached Triple-A.

GRADE: D

2013

RHP Jason Hursh (1) and LHP Matt Marksberry (15) have reached the big leagues in relief roles. Switch-hitting C Victor Caratini (2), the best prospect of the class, was traded to the Cubs in 2014.

GRADE: D

TOP DRAFT PICKS OF THE DECADE

Year	Player, Pos.	2016 Org
2007	Jason Heyward, of	Cubs
2008	Brett DeVall (1st round supp.)	Did not play
2009	Mike Minor, lhp	Royals
2010	Matt Lipka, ss (1st round supp.)	Braves
2011	Sean Gilmartin, lhp	Mets
2012	Lucas Sims, rhp	Braves
2013	Jason Hursh, rhp	Braves
2014	Braxton Davidson, of	Braves
2015	Kolby Allard, lhp	Braves
2016	Ian Anderson, rhp	Braves

LARGEST BONUSES IN CLUB HISTORY

Ian Anderson, 2016	$4,000,000
Kevin Maitan, 2016	$4,000,000
Abrahan Gutierrez, 2016	$3,500,000
Joey Wentz, 2016	$3,050,000
Kolby Allard, 2015	$3,042,400

1 DANSBY SWANSON, SS

Born: Feb. 11, 1994. **B-T:** R-R. **Ht.:** 6-1. **Wt.:** 190.
Drafted: Vanderbilt, 2015 (1st round).
Signed by: Nate Birtwell (Diamondbacks).

BA GRADE
65 Risk: Low

SCOUTING GRADES

Batting: 60.
Power: 50.
Speed: 60.
Defense: 60.
Arm: 60.

Based on 20-80 scouting scale and future projection rather than present tools.

TOMASSO DeROSA

Winning has become synonymous with Swanson since he was a dual-sport athlete at Marietta High in suburban Atlanta. He was part of two state championships in basketball and was a member of the East Cobb Yankees, a team that won the 2012 Perfect Game national championship. After opting to attend Vanderbilt despite being drafted by the Rockies in the 38th round in 2012, Swanson overcame a broken foot and a shoulder injury as a freshman, then led the Commodores to the program's first College World Series national championship as a sophomore in 2014. He earned CWS Most Outstanding Player honors while hitting .323. He moved from second base to shortstop as a junior and helped guide Vandy back to the CWS finals in 2015. That month the Diamondbacks made Swanson the first overall pick in the draft. Hit in the face by a pitch during a simulated game, he bounced back in time to be part of short-season Hillsboro's Northwest League championship in his pro debut. Three months later, Arizona sent Swanson, outfielder Ender Inciarte and righthander Aaron Blair to the Braves for righthander Shelby Miller and low Class A lefthander Gabe Speier. He proceeded to tear up the high Class A Carolina League for a month in 2016 before moving on to the Double-A Southern League, where he ranked as the No. 1 prospect in the circuit. He made his major league debut as Atlanta's starting shortstop on Aug. 17, stroking two hits in four at-bats against the Twins. He batted 129 times, thus retaining his rookie eligibility for 2017 by just two at-bats.

Braves scouting director Brian Bridges got to know Swanson well during the latter's high school career and loved everything the shortstop brought to the table at a young age. Rated by SL managers as the league's best defensive shortstop, Swanson has outstanding quickness with exceptional range, soft and steady hands, and above-average arm strength with excellent accuracy on his throws. He uses his intelligence and superior feel for the game to anticipate plays, which helped him lead all minor league shortstops with an average of 3.27 assists per game in 2016. His cerebral approach is also noticeable on offense, where he uses his above-average speed to take the extra base. An ideal No. 2 hitter, Swanson makes hard and consistent contact with his advanced approach at the plate. His patience and feel for the strike zone allow him to work counts and pile up walks. He also is capable of executing the hit-and-run and driving the ball to all fields, and he should have at least average power once he gains more experience at the game's top level. The biggest question scouts have is how much his power will play to go along with a fairly high strikeout rate going back to his Vanderbilt days.

Swanson looked the part as Atlanta's long-term answer at shortstop over the final seven weeks of the 2016 campaign. While he may not put up the kind of numbers to garner perennial MVP consideration, his steady and consistent performance on the field and his overall makeup and personality off it, while playing his home games in the county where he was born, make Swanson a natural fit for a rebuilding organization. He's positioned to be a face for the franchise as its starting shortstop for years to come.

Year	Club (League)	Class	AVG	G	AB	R	H	2B	3B	HR	RBI	BB	SO	SB	CS	OBP	SLG
2015	Hillsboro (NWL)	SS	.289	22	83	19	24	7	3	1	11	14	14	0	0	.394	.482
2016	Carolina (CAR)	HiA	.333	21	78	14	26	12	0	1	10	15	13	7	1	.441	.526
	Mississippi (SL)	AA	.261	84	333	54	87	13	5	8	45	35	71	6	2	.342	.402
	Atlanta (NL)	MAJ	.302	38	129	20	39	7	1	3	17	13	34	3	0	.361	.442
Major League Totals			.302	38	129	20	39	7	1	3	17	13	34	3	0	.361	.442
Minor League Totals			.277	127	494	87	137	32	8	10	66	64	98	13	3	.367	.435

2 OZZIE ALBIES, 2B/SS

Born: Jan. 7, 1997. **B-T:** B-R. **Ht.:** 5-9. **Wt.:** 160. **Signed:** Curacao, 2013. **Signed by:** Dargello Lodowica.

Albies continued his rapid ascent through the organization in 2016. At age 19, he skipped high Class A and led the Double-A Southern League in average (.321) and on-base percentage (.391). Despite struggling during a two-month stint in Triple-A at midseason, he thrived in a return to Mississippi before breaking the tip of a bone in his right elbow on Sept. 9, keeping him out of the SL playoffs. Strictly a shortstop prior to 2016, Albies shifted to second base when he teamed with Dansby Swanson at Mississippi. The definition of a quick-twitch athlete, Albies' first-step quickness, soft hands, above-average arm strength and baseball instincts make him a plus defender at both middle-infield spots. He has work to do making the pivot on double plays, which should come with experience. His offensive strength is his ability to make hard and consistent contact from both sides of the plate, thanks to his plus bat speed and superior hand-eye coordination. He drives the ball better than advertised, draws walks and uses his plus speed to beat out grounders and steal bases, making him an ideal top-of-the-lineup hitter. Atlanta's long-term second baseman, Albies is headed for Triple-A Gwinnett in 2017 with his first big league callup not far off. .

BA GRADE

65 Risk: Medium

Year	Club (League)	Class	AVG	G	AB	R	H	2B	3B	HR	RBI	BB	SO	SB	CS	OBP	SLG
2014	Braves (GCL)	R	.381	19	63	16	24	3	0	0	5	11	6	7	2	.481	.429
	Danville (APP)	R	.356	38	135	25	48	4	3	1	14	17	17	15	3	.429	.452
2015	Rome (SAL)	LoA	.310	98	394	64	122	21	8	0	37	36	56	29	8	.368	.404
2016	Gwinnett (IL)	AAA	.248	56	222	27	55	11	3	2	20	19	39	9	4	.307	.351
	Mississippi (SL)	AA	.321	82	330	56	106	22	7	4	33	33	57	21	9	.391	.467
Minor League Totals			.310	293	1144	188	355	61	21	7	109	116	175	81	26	.377	.419

3 KOLBY ALLARD, LHP

Born: Aug. 13, 1997. **B-T:** L-L. **Ht.:** 6-1. **Wt.:** 180. **Drafted:** HS—San Clemente, Calif., 2015 (1st round). **Signed by:** Dan Cox.

The Braves selected Allard 14th overall in 2015 after he fell in the draft because of a stress reaction in his back that caused him to miss most of his senior year of high school. He had minor surgery after signing and was held back in extended spring training as a precaution to open 2016. Allard opened at low Class A Rome in June before the Rookie-level Danville season started, then returned to Rome after five starts and got better as the year went on. Allard went 4-0, 1.72 with 37 strikeouts in 31 innings in August before tossing 12 shutout innings in the South Atlantic League playoffs. The lefthander has an excellent feel for pitching and works down in the strike zone. His fastball sits at 90-94 mph and possesses late cutting action. He mixes his heater with a plus hammer curveball with a 1-to-7 drop that may be his best pitch. Allard has made outstanding progress with his changeup that could improve to the point where he winds up with three plus pitches. He throws a lot of strikes and should have above-average command when he matures. Allard has the overall package to be a No. 2 or 3 starter in the big leagues. He should open 2017 at Atlanta's new Florida State League affiliate but could make the jump to Double-A during the campaign.

BA GRADE

60 Risk: High

Year	Club (League)	Class	W	L	ERA	G	GS	CG	SV	IP	H	HR	BB	SO	K/9	WHIP	AVG
2015	Braves (GCL)	R	0	0	0.00	3	3	0	0	6	1	0	0	12	18.0	0.17	.053
2016	Danville (APP)	R	3	0	1.32	5	5	0	0	27	18	0	5	33	10.9	0.84	.186
	Rome (SAL)	LoA	5	3	3.73	11	11	1	0	60	54	5	20	62	9.2	1.23	.244
Minor League Totals			8	3	2.79	19	19	1	0	94	73	5	25	107	10.3	1.05	.217

4 MIKE SOROKA, RHP

Born: August 4, 1997. **B-T:** R-R. **Ht.:** 6-4. **Wt.:** 195. **Drafted:** HS—Calgary, 2015 (1st round). **Signed by:** Brett Evert.

The Braves loved what they saw in Soroka when he pitched on the Canadian Junior National Team and they took the righthander with the 28th overall pick in the 2015 draft. Efficient due to his advanced feel for pitching, Soroka wound up working more innings (143) than any prep first-rounder in his first full season in at least a decade. He served as No. 1 starter in both rounds of the South Atlantic League playoffs for low Class A Rome. Soroka's intelligence is readily apparent on the mound and helped him adjust after lefthanded hitters pounded him in his pro debut. He switched sides of the pitching rubber to locate better to his glove side

BA GRADE

60 Risk: High

and it worked. He limited lefthanders to a .648 OPS in 2016. Soroka mixes three above-average pitches with aplomb and generates lots of groundouts due to his plus control and ability to pound the lower half of the strike zone. His 90-92 mph fastball has excellent sinking action and touches 95 when he guns for a strikeout. His curveball has tight spin, his changeup has solid movement and he reads hitters' swings to attack their weakness. Strong with a solid presence on the bump, Soroka is a former hockey player and a solid all-around athlete who fields his position well. Soroka was one of the youngest players in his draft class and among the youngest pitchers in the SAL in 2016. While his next step will be high Class A, he projects as a mid-rotation starter in the big leagues.

Year	Club (League)	Class	W	L	ERA	G	GS	CG	SV	IP	H	HR	BB	SO	K/9	WHIP	AVG
2015	Braves (GCL)	R	0	0	1.80	4	3	0	0	10	5	0	1	11	9.9	0.60	.143
	Danville (APP)	R	0	2	3.75	6	6	0	0	24	28	0	4	26	9.8	1.33	.283
2016	Rome (SAL)	LoA	9	9	3.02	25	24	1	0	143	130	3	32	125	7.9	1.13	.244
Minor League Totals			9	11	3.05	35	33	1	0	177	163	3	37	162	8.2	1.13	.245

5 IAN ANDERSON, RHP

Born: May 2, 1998. **B-T:** R-R. **Ht.:** 6-3. **Wt.:** 170. **Drafted:** HS—Clifton Park, N.Y., 2016 (1st round). **Signed by:** Greg Morhardt.

Anderson attracted attention in the Metropolitan Baseball Classic prior to his junior year and took off when he pitched against fellow New York state prep and 2015 first-round pick Garrett Whitley the following spring. Despite battling pneumonia and a minor injury during his senior year, Anderson ranked high on the Braves' 2016 draft board, and Atlanta drafted the lanky, projectable righthander third overall and signed him for a below-slot $4 million. He possesses the classic combination of current ability with the potential to become even better with experience and physical development. A cerebral pitcher who was a Vanderbilt

BA GRADE

65 **Risk:** Extreme

commit, he has impressed with his calm, mature approach and ability to dissect the strike zone with his impressive command and ability to work both sides of the plate. He throws all three of his pitches from the same release point, which makes them difficult for hitters to decipher. His fastball sits 92-94 mph and has touched 97. He also throws a late-breaking curveball, with above-average potential and 10-to-4 shape at 79-81 mph and a plus changeup in the mid-80s. After spending his pro debut at Atlanta's two Rookie-level affiliates, Anderson will open 2017 at low Class A Rome. From there he has the ability to move quickly as he develops into a mid-rotation starter at the big league level.

Year	Club (League)	Class	W	L	ERA	G	GS	CG	SV	IP	H	HR	BB	SO	K/9	WHIP	AVG
2016	Braves (GCL)	R	1	0	0.00	5	5	0	0	18	14	0	4	18	9.0	1.00	.222
	Danville (APP)	R	0	2	3.74	5	5	0	0	22	19	1	8	18	7.5	1.25	.244
Minor League Totals			1	2	2.04	10	10	0	0	40	33	1	12	36	8.2	1.13	.234

6 RONALD ACUNA, OF

Born: Dec. 18, 1997. **B-T:** R-R. **Ht.:** 6-0. **Wt.:** 180. **Signed:** Venezuela, 2014. **Signed by:** Rolando Petit.

The Braves have been aggressive in challenging Acuna since he signed for a modest $100,000 in 2014. He performed well in his U.S. debut after bypassing the Dominican Summer League in 2015 and proceeded to get off to a fast start at low Class A Rome in 2016 before a broken thumb sidelined him from mid-May to mid-August. Despite the injury, Acuna displayed his electric tools in all phases of the game. He uses his plus speed to cover center field from gap to gap and has the arm strength to play any position in the garden. He reads balls well, takes good angles and shows impressive anticipation along with excellent first-step quickness. Acuna is

BA GRADE

60 **Risk:** High

aggressive at the plate but has above-average discipline for a teenager. While his body is still developing, he has plus raw power and barrels pitches consistently with his above-average bat speed. Those traits should allow him to hit for average at higher levels. He needs work on stealing bases more consistently but has the speed to make an impact on the basepaths. His shortened season at Rome notwithstanding, Acuna should open the 2017 campaign at high Class A Florida after making up for lost time in the winter Australian Baseball League. Though risky, Acuna has as high a ceiling as any Braves position player.

Year	Club (League)	Class	AVG	G	AB	R	H	2B	3B	HR	RBI	BB	SO	SB	CS	OBP	SLG
2015	Braves (GCL)	R	.258	37	132	31	34	9	2	3	11	18	23	11	3	.376	.424
	Danville (APP)	R	.290	18	69	10	20	5	2	1	7	10	19	5	1	.388	.464
2016	Braves (GCL)	R	.333	2	6	1	2	0	0	0	1	1	1	0	0	.500	.333
	Rome (SAL)	LoA	.311	40	148	27	46	2	2	4	18	18	28	14	7	.387	.432
Minor League Totals			.287	97	355	69	102	16	6	8	37	47	71	30	11	.385	.434

7 KEVIN MAITAN, SS

CLIFF WELCH

Born: Feb. 12, 2000. **B-T:** B-R. **Ht.:** 6-2. **Wt.:** 175. **Signed:** Venezuela, 2016. **Signed by:** Gordon Blakeley/Mike Silvestri/Rolando Petit.

Maitan began to attract the attention of scouts in Venezuela at age 13. Over the next three years, the power-hitting shortstop emerged as the top international prospect and was considered the best foreign amateur to hit the market since Miguel Sano in 2009. Maneuvering their way to make a big splash on the international market in 2016, the Braves made Maitan their primary target and signed him for $4.25 million. He draws comparisons with Chipper Jones for his ability to hit for power and average from both sides of the plate. He gets more loft from the right side but shows an advanced feel for the strike zone and excellent discipline. Like Jones, Maitan is a physical player with solid athleticism and high baseball intelligence. Given his current size, he may move to third base as his body matures, though his easy actions and footwork and strong arm suggest he could remain up the middle. Either way the Braves envision a middle-of-the-lineup hitter thanks his plus raw power. Were Maitan an American player eligible for the draft, he would have been in the 2018 class. He's advanced enough to open his pro career at one of the Braves' Rookie-level affiliates.

BA GRADE
65 Risk: Extreme

Year	Club (League)	Class	AVG	G	AB	R	H	2B	3B	HR	RBI	BB	SO	SB	CS	OBP	SLG
2016	Did not play—Signed 2017 contract																

8 SEAN NEWCOMB, LHP

Born: June 12, 1993. **B-T:** L-L. **Ht.:** 6-5. **Wt.:** 240. **Drafted:** Hartford, 2014 (1st round). **Signed by:** Nick Gorneault (Angels).

The 15th overall pick in the 2014 draft, Newcomb was the centerpiece of the deal that sent Andrelton Simmons to the Angels after the 2015 campaign. A two-sport standout in high school prior to pitching at Hartford, he appeared in the Futures Game during his lone season with the Angels before leading the Double-A Southern League with 152 strikeouts and ranking second with a .224 opponent average in 2016. Newcomb is a power pitcher who improved the consistency of his delivery over the course of the 2016 season. His fastball ranges from 90-95 mph but sits at 92-93 and tends to jump out of his hand due to his ability to hide the ball until he releases it. He records many of his strikeouts with a hard, tight curveball that possesses plus spin and sits at 77-78 mph. Newcomb's mid-80s changeup is at least a solid-average offering but lacks late movement. He tends to lose his rhythm and focus on occasion, helping produce his below-average control, and he needs to get more aggressive with his pitch selection when he's ahead in the count. Newcomb has the broad-shouldered frame and strength to be a workhorse in a big league rotation—if he throws enough strikes. He is ready for Triple-A Gwinnett in 2017 and should make his major league debut at some point during the season.

BA GRADE
55 Risk: Medium

Year	Club (League)	Class	W	L	ERA	G	GS	CG	SV	IP	H	HR	BB	SO	K/9	WHIP	AVG
2014	Angels (AZL)	R	0	0	3.00	2	2	0	0	3	3	1	1	3	9.0	1.33	.273
	Burlington (MWL)	LoA	0	1	6.94	4	4	0	0	12	13	1	5	15	11.6	1.54	.289
2015	Burlington (MWL)	LoA	1	0	1.83	7	7	0	0	34	25	1	19	45	11.8	1.28	.208
	Inland Empire (CAL)	HiA	6	1	2.47	13	13	0	0	66	50	2	33	84	11.5	1.26	.207
	Arkansas (TL)	AA	2	2	2.75	7	7	0	0	36	22	2	24	39	9.8	1.28	.176
2016	Mississippi (SL)	AA	8	7	3.86	27	27	1	0	140	113	4	71	152	9.8	1.31	.224
Minor League Totals			17	11	3.28	60	60	1	0	291	226	11	153	338	10.5	1.30	.216

9 PATRICK WEIGEL, RHP

Born: July 8, 1994. **B-T:** R-R. **Ht.:** 6-6. **Wt.:** 220. **Drafted:** Houston, 2015 (7th round). **Signed by:** Darin Vaughan.

Weigel pitched for three schools in college and was a reliever at Houston when the Braves made him a 2015 seventh-round pick. A mediocre pro debut at Rookie-level Danville that year did little to excite the masses before the righthander displayed the ability to throw four pitches for strikes at low Class A Rome in 2016. He wound up ranking second in the organization in wins (11) and ERA and tying for second in strikeouts (152) while finishing the season at Double-A. Standing 6-foot-6 and possessing a live arm, Weigel has an intimidating presence on the mound. His fastball sits 94-95 mph and touches 98, which is velocity that overpowered most low Class A South Atlantic League hitters. He mixes his heater with a sweeping mid-70s curveball,

BA GRADE
60 Risk: High

a hard mid-80s slider with short, downward action and a changeup that is inconsistent but flashes plus potential when he throws it properly. The development of his changeup could determine whether Weigel starts or relieves at higher levels. He also has ironed out most of the control problems that hampered him in college but needs to fine-tune his command. A classic late bloomer, Weigel will return to Double-A Mississippi to open 2017 and could be knocking on the door to the big leagues by the end of the season.

Year	Club (League)	Class	W	L	ERA	G	GS	CG	SV	IP	H	HR	BB	SO	K/9	WHIP	AVG
2015	Danville (APP)	R	0	3	4.53	14	14	0	0	52	53	2	26	49	8.5	1.53	.256
2016	Rome (SAL)	LoA	10	4	2.51	22	21	1	0	129	92	7	47	135	9.4	1.08	.203
	Mississippi (SL)	AA	1	2	2.18	3	3	0	0	21	9	2	8	17	7.4	0.82	.132
Minor League Totals			11	9	3.00	39	38	1	0	201	154	11	81	201	9.0	1.17	.212

10 MAX FRIED, LHP

Born: Jan. 18, 1994. **B-T:** L-L. **Ht.:** 6-4. **Wt.:** 185. **Drafted:** HS—Los Angeles, 2012 (1st round). **Signed by:** Brent Mayne (Padres).

Atlanta finally had the opportunity to see Fried on the mound after the Braves acquired him from the Padres in December 2014 as part of the Justin Upton trade. The seventh overall pick in the 2012 draft, Fried missed much of 2014 and all of 2015 while recovering from Tommy John surgery. Other than a blister problem that cost him a month at midseason, the lefthander showed few ill effects from the procedure while making 21 appearances at low Class A Rome in 2016. Fried displayed an increase in overall maturity and overcame some early-season rustiness with his fastball command to overpower hitters late in the campaign. He struck out

BA GRADE

55 Risk: High

10 batters in each of his last two starts before notching 11 in his first playoff appearance. Fried showed a plus fastball at 92-95 mph and even touched 97 on several occasions, though his fastball command is below-average. He throws a hard curveball that generated many of his strikeouts. He also throws a slower breaking ball primarily early in counts and became more consistent with both breaking balls as the year progressed. Fried's improving changeup features solid fade and depth and generates swings and misses. He finished the season with 44 strikeouts in his last 25.1 innings, counting the South Atlantic League playoffs. He'll try to maintain that momentum in 2017 at high Class A Florida. With more command, he could pitch toward the front of a big league rotation.

Year	Club (League)	Class	W	L	ERA	G	GS	CG	SV	IP	H	HR	BB	SO	K/9	WHIP	AVG
2014	Padres (AZL)	R	0	0	5.40	3	3	0	0	5	8	0	3	8	14.4	2.20	.348
	Fort Wayne (MWL)	LoA	0	1	4.76	2	2	0	0	6	7	1	2	2	3.2	1.59	.318
2015	Did not play—Injured																
2016	Rome (SAL)	LoA	8	7	3.93	21	20	0	0	103	87	10	47	112	9.8	1.30	.236
Minor League Totals			14	16	3.74	59	57	0	0	250	223	19	114	239	8.6	1.35	.246

11 AUSTIN RILEY, 3B

BA GRADE

55 Risk: High

Born: April 2, 1997. **B-T:** R-R. **Ht.:** 6-2. **Wt.:** 230. **Drafted:** HS—Southaven, Miss., 2015 (1st round supplemental). **Signed by:** Don Thomas.

Riley was a premier two-way player in high school who was considered more of a pitching prospect until the Braves took him 41st overall as a hitter. After a stellar debut in Rookie ball in 2015, Riley overcame a slow start in the South Atlantic League to help lead low Class A Rome to a championship while leading the organization in home runs (20) and ranking second in RBIs (80). His youth and inexperience showed early, when pitchers took advantage of his inability to hit pitches in on his hands, before he made an adjustment with his hitting setup that resulted in a more direct path to inside pitches. Riley barreled the ball consistently and reduced his strikeout rate after the adjustment, allowing him to tap into his double-plus raw power. He has plus arm strength at third base, but his hands are not particularly soft and he needs to improve on balls hit to his left. Some scouts believe he would be better served moving to first base or left field, the latter of which may be a stretch with his below-average speed. The Braves believe Riley can be an impact bat in the middle of the lineup. The primary question centers on which corner position he will play. A promotion to high Class A Florida awaits in 2017.

Year	Club (League)	Class	AVG	G	AB	R	H	2B	3B	HR	RBI	BB	SO	SB	CS	OBP	SLG
2015	Braves (GCL)	R	.255	30	106	18	27	5	0	7	21	12	37	2	1	.331	.500
	Danville (APP)	R	.351	30	111	18	39	9	1	5	19	14	28	0	1	.443	.586
2016	Rome (SAL)	LoA	.271	129	495	68	134	39	2	20	80	39	147	3	3	.324	.479
Minor League Totals			.281	189	712	104	200	53	3	32	120	65	212	5	5	.345	.499

12 TOUKI TOUSSAINT, RHP

BA GRADE

60 Risk: Extreme

Born: June 20, 2016. **B-T:** R-R. **Ht.:** 6-3. **Wt.:** 185. **Drafted:** HS—Coral Springs, Fla., 2014 (1st round). **Signed by:** Frankie Thon Jr. (Diamondbacks).

Toussaint had one of the most electric arms in the 2014 draft and went 16th overall to the Diamondbacks. After a year in the Arizona system, the righthander was traded on his birthday, along with Bronson Arroyo (and his salary), to the Braves for utility infielder Phil Gosselin. The inexplicable move was Atlanta's gain, particularly after Toussaint began to show his previous potential after dropping his arm slot from overhand to three-quarters in 2016 under the tutelage of low Class A Rome pitching coach Dan Meyer. The alteration made Toussaint's delivery more compact and efficient. At the same time, his mid-90s fastball became a swing-and-miss pitch, and his sharp, fall-from-the-sky curveball, which D-backs officials encouraged him not to rely on, returned to its previous status as a plus pitch. As a result, Toussaint's strikeout rate improved from 6.0 per nine innings in the first half to 11.2 in the second. He still is inconsistent with his changeup, though it flashed above-average as an amateur, and he has struggled with his overall control. His progress with his third pitch will determine whether his long-term role is starter or reliever, but better control is mandatory in either situation. He will attempt to improve in those departments in 2017 at high Class A Florida.

Year	Club (League)	Class	W	L	ERA	G	GS	CG	SV	IP	H	HR	BB	SO	K/9	WHIP	AVG
2014	Diamondbacks (AZL)	R	1	1	4.80	7	5	0	0	15	14	0	12	17	10.2	1.73	.237
	Missoula (PIO)	R	1	3	12.51	5	5	0	0	14	24	5	6	15	9.9	2.20	.381
2015	Kane County (MWL)	LoA	2	2	3.69	7	7	0	0	39	31	4	15	29	6.7	1.18	.218
	Rome (SAL)	LoA	3	5	5.73	10	10	1	0	49	40	6	33	38	7.0	1.50	.229
2016	Rome (SAL)	LoA	4	8	3.88	27	24	0	0	132	105	13	71	128	8.7	1.33	.217
Minor League Totals			11	19	4.74	56	51	1	0	249	214	28	137	227	8.2	1.41	.232

13 CRISTIAN PACHE, OF

BA GRADE

55 Risk: Extreme

Born: Nov. 19, 1998. **B-T:** R-R. **Ht.:** 6-2. **Wt.:** 185. **Signed:** Dominican Republic, 2015. **Signed by:** Matias Laureano.

Pache ranked as the No. 21 international prospect in the 2015 class, and the Braves signed the young outfielder for $1.4 million. He progressed rapidly in 2016, starting the season in the Rookie-level Gulf Coast League before moving up the Appalachian League. He ranked among the Top 10 Prospects in both leagues. A lanky, electric player, Pache has an unorthodox swing with a hard stride but manages to make consistent contact because of his superior hand-eye coordination. He rarely swings and misses, and he has the ability to spray line drives from gap to gap. Pache's pitch recognition and feel for the strike zone need work, but he has overcome those shortcomings to this point because he can hit virtually anything he can reach. Pache has double-plus speed he uses on the basepaths as well as in center field, where he could become a Gold Glove defender. He has exceptional range to both sides and outstanding closing speed with above-average arm strength. Pache needs work coming in on balls and taking better angles, but he is advanced for someone who will play the entire 2017 season, most likely at low Class A Rome, at age 18.

Year	Club (League)	Class	AVG	G	AB	R	H	2B	3B	HR	RBI	BB	SO	SB	CS	OBP	SLG
2016	Braves (GCL)	R	.283	27	106	16	30	2	4	0	11	6	11	7	3	.325	.377
	Danville (APP)	R	.333	30	114	12	38	2	3	0	10	7	13	4	2	.372	.404
Minor League Totals			.309	57	220	28	68	4	7	0	21	13	24	11	5	.349	.391

14 LUCAS SIMS, RHP

BA GRADE

50 Risk: High

Born: May 10, 1994. **B-T:** R-R. **Ht.:** 6-2. **Wt.:** 195. **Drafted:** HS—Snellville, Ga., 2012 (1st round). **Signed by:** Brian Bridges.

One of the few remaining prospects from the Frank Wren era, Sims was the 21st overall pick in 2012. After missing two months in 2015 with injuries he suffered in a bus wreck at high Class A Carolina, Sims had a full slate in 2016 that included a disastrous stretch at Triple-A Gwinnett in May and June. However, he regained his dominant form upon his second-half return to Double-A Mississippi and ranked fifth in the minors with 159 strikeouts. A competitive and aggressive righthander with outstanding athleticism, Sims challenges hitters with his plus fastball that sits 93-95 mph and touches 97 with armside run. He mixes it well with his above-average 77-79 mph curveball with a hard, late break. His difficulties have centered the slow development of his changeup and his inability to maintain consistent control and focus, leading to 92 walks, the fourth-highest total in the minors in 2016. He has altered his delivery multiple times with varying degrees of success but has not conquered his wildness. Sims may be headed for a relief role at the major league level, potentially as a closer. The Braves will to give him another shot to gain consistency with his third pitch and remain in the rotation at Triple-A in 2017.

Year	Club (League)	Class	W	L	ERA	G	GS	CG	SV	IP	H	HR	BB	SO	K/9	WHIP	AVG
2014	Lynchburg (CAR)	HiA	8	11	4.19	28	28	0	0	157	146	12	57	107	6.1	1.30	.247
2015	Braves (GCL)	R	0	0	9.00	2	2	0	0	5	7	0	2	7	12.6	1.80	.333
	Carolina (CAR)	HiA	3	4	5.18	9	9	1	0	40	39	2	23	37	8.3	1.55	.260
	Mississippi (SL)	AA	4	2	3.21	9	9	0	0	48	29	1	29	56	10.6	1.22	.180
2016	Gwinnett (IL)	AAA	2	6	7.56	11	10	0	0	50	56	12	37	58	10.4	1.86	.280
	Mississippi (SL)	AA	5	5	2.67	17	17	0	0	91	64	3	55	101	10.0	1.31	.203
Minor League Totals			36	36	3.91	115	104	2	0	541	452	36	262	539	9.0	1.32	.229

15 JOEY WENTZ, LHP

Born: Oct. 6, 1997. **B-T:** L-L. **Ht.:** 6-5. **Wt.:** 210. **Drafted:** HS—Prairie Village, Kan., 2016 (1st round supplemental). **Signed by:** Nate Dion.

A two-way prep standout with a power bat at first base, Wentz overcame a dead arm following his junior season to reemerge as premier pitcher with physical projection remaining. The 40th overall pick in 2016, Wentz signed for an above-slot $3.05 million to forgo a Virginia commitment and earned a promotion to Rookie-level Danville after four dominant Rookie-level Gulf Coast League outings. Scouts love Wentz's tall, lanky build, his easy, repeatable mechanics and his potential as he adds strength and maturity. A decent athlete who repeats his short arm action with consistency, he uses his 6-foot-5 frame to his advantage by pitching downhill and extending toward the plate. Despite struggling with walks at Danville, he has demonstrated at least average control of three pitches. His fastball has good armside run down in the zone and sat at 87-91 mph in pro ball after touching 96 in high school. His upper-70s curveball has late depth, and he shows an advanced feel for a changeup with fade that flashes plus potential. With as much pitching depth as the Braves have in the minors, Wentz can move slowly and spend the entire 2017 season at low Class A Rome. Long-term, he has the ability to be at least a No. 3 starter in the big leagues.

Year	Club (League)	Class	W	L	ERA	G	GS	CG	SV	IP	H	HR	BB	SO	K/9	WHIP	AVG
2016	Braves (GCL)	R	0	0	0.00	4	4	0	0	12	3	0	5	18	13.5	0.67	.083
	Danville (APP)	R	1	4	5.06	8	8	0	0	32	31	0	20	35	9.8	1.59	.265
Minor League Totals			1	4	3.68	12	12	0	0	44	34	0	25	53	10.8	1.34	.222

16 DUSTIN PETERSON, OF

Born: Sept. 10, 1994. **B-T:** R-R. **Ht.:** 6-2. **Wt.:** 185. **Drafted:** HS—Gilbert, Ariz., 2013 (2nd round). **Signed by:** Dave Lottsfeldt (Padres).

Part of the Braves' prospect haul from the Padres in the Justin Upton deal following the 2014 season, Peterson had his best season at Double-A Mississippi in 2016. He led the Southern League with 38 doubles, ranked second in RBIs (88) and third in hits (148). He homered twice in a June series against his brother D.J., a Mariners prospect and 2013 first-round pick. Peterson is an offense-first player with above-average bat speed and the ability to generate backspin with his quick hands and whip-like swing. He has an advanced approach at the plate but tends to accumulate strikeouts due to his tendency to swing and miss. The former third baseman continued to become more comfortable in left field and even saw some time in center in 2016. His glovework, which is fringe-average with his average speed and improving routes, likely limits him to left at higher levels. Peterson has the ability to be a steady contributor but projects as more of a complementary piece at the major league level rather than as a star. He's set for Triple-A Gwinnett in 2017.

Year	Club (League)	Class	AVG	G	AB	R	H	2B	3B	HR	RBI	BB	SO	SB	CS	OBP	SLG
2014	Fort Wayne (MWL)	LoA	.233	126	527	64	123	31	3	10	79	25	137	1	3	.274	.361
2015	Carolina (CAR)	HiA	.251	118	446	58	112	15	2	8	62	44	91	6	3	.317	.348
2016	Mississippi (SL)	AA	.282	132	524	65	148	38	2	12	88	45	100	4	1	.343	.431
Minor League Totals			.259	414	1654	207	429	92	7	30	247	123	361	14	7	.314	.378

17 KYLE MULLER, LHP

Born: Oct. 7, 1997. **B-T:** R-L. **Ht.:** 6-6. **Wt.:** 225. **Drafted:** HS—Dallas, 2016 (2nd round). **Signed by:** Nate Dion.

A stellar senior season from Muller led the Braves to take the lefthander with the 44th overall pick in 2016. His velocity increased from 87-89 mph in the summer of 2015 to sitting in the low 90s and touching 95 mph on a few occasions in 2016. Featuring a heavy swing-and-miss fastball with late action, Muller dominated prep hitters and established a national high school record by fanning 24 consecutive batters over two starts and notched 36 straight outs via the strikeout. An excellent athlete who played first base and the outfield when not pitching, Muller displayed impressive power at the plate and would have been a two-way player at the University of Texas had he not signed an above-slot $2.5 million. The

Braves limited Muller to a maximum of three innings in his 10 Rookie-level Gulf Coast League outings and were impressed with the transition he made to pro ball, even though his velocity fell slightly over the course of the summer. He uses his tall frame to his advantage with a downward plane on his pitches and a strong presence on the mound. Muller consistently repeats his clean delivery despite his 6-foot-6 height, and he does an excellent job of making use of the entire strike zone with his fastball. He showed a solid feel for his slurvy curveball and changeup but needs to hone consistency, break and depth of both pitches in order to emerge as a mid-rotation starter in the big leagues. He has a good shot at opening the 2017 campaign at low Class A Rome.

Year	Club (League)	Class	W	L	ERA	G	GS	CG	SV	IP	H	HR	BB	SO	K/9	WHIP	AVG
2016	Braves (GCL)	R	1	0	0.65	10	9	0	0	28	14	0	12	38	12.4	0.94	.144
Minor League Totals			1	0	0.65	10	9	0	0	28	14	0	12	38	12.4	0.94	.144

18 A.J. MINTER, LHP

Born: Sept. 2, 1993. **B-T:** L-L. **Ht.:** 6-0. **Wt.:** 205. **Drafted:** Texas A&M, 2015. (2nd round supplemental). **Signed by:** Darin Vaughan.

A three-sport star in high school, Minter was drafted in the 38th round by the Tigers in 2012 before attending Texas A&M. He relieved for much of his college career, which included a stint with USA Baseball's Collegiate National Team, then moved to the rotation in 2015 and went 3-0, 0.47 in four starts before succumbing to Tommy John surgery. The Braves selected the rehabbing Minter with the 75th overall pick in 2015 and were rewarded in 2016 when he pitched at three levels during his first taste of pro ball. He recorded a combined 1.30 ERA and 0.84 WHIP with 12.2 strikeouts per nine innings. Minter is a power pitcher who throws from a high three-quarters arm slot and features a fastball-slider combination with improving command. His plus fastball sits 94-96 mph and touches 98 with impressive armside sink and run. His mid-80s slider has horizontal movement and little depth but he keeps it down in the strike zone. He also throws an above-average cutter in the low 90s, giving him three power pitches that miss bats. Minter challenges hitters and has the overall package to be a dominant reliever in the majors if he stays healthy. He probably will open 2017 at Double-A Mississippi.

Year	Club (League)	Class	W	L	ERA	G	GS	CG	SV	IP	H	HR	BB	SO	K/9	WHIP	AVG
2015	Did not play—Injured																
2016	Rome (SAL)	LoA	0	0	0.00	5	0	0	2	7	2	0	1	6	8.1	0.45	.091
	Carolina (CAR)	HiA	0	0	0.00	8	0	0	0	9	3	0	4	10	9.6	0.75	.100
	Mississippi (SL)	AA	1	0	2.41	18	0	0	0	19	13	0	6	31	14.9	1.02	.188
Minor League Totals			1	0	1.30	31	0	0	2	35	18	0	11	47	12.2	0.84	.149

19 TRAVIS DEMERITTE, 2B

BA GRADE 50 Risk: High

Born: Sept. 30, 1994. **B-T:** R-R. **Ht.:** 6-0. **Wt.:** 180. **Drafted:** HS—Winder, Ga., 2013 (1st round). **Signed by:** Derrick Tucker (Rangers).

The Rangers drafted Demeritte 30th overall in 2013 and traded him to the Braves in July 2016 for starter Lucas Harrell and reliever Dario Alvarez. Demeritte finished 2016 tied for 11th in the minors with 28 home runs. While 25 of them came in the hitter-friendly California League, the total demonstrates his power potential. Demeritte also paced the South Atlantic League with 25 homers in 2014 at age 19 before testing positive for Furosemide, a diuretic often used to flush the body of another drug, and received an 80-game suspension in 2015. He possesses quick, strong hands that generate plus bat speed and backspin. His problem comes in making consistent contact. Demeritte struggles with pitch recognition and chases too many pitches outside the strike zone by being overly aggressive, resulting in a strikeout rate pushing 40 percent, which includes a career-high 175 punchouts in 2016. He has made steady improvements at second base after playing shortstop in high school. His hands are not smooth, but he has good arm strength and above-average range and athleticism. He made more contact while still hitting for power in the Arizona Fall League, ranking tied for second with four homers. Demeritte is expected to receive his first taste of Double-A in 2017.

Year	Club (League)	Class	AVG	G	AB	R	H	2B	3B	HR	RBI	BB	SO	SB	CS	OBP	SLG
2014	Hickory (SAL)	LoA	.211	118	398	77	84	16	2	25	66	50	171	6	2	.310	.450
2015	Hickory (SAL)	LoA	.241	48	170	27	41	12	1	5	19	25	69	10	1	.343	.412
	Spokane (NWL)	SS	.150	5	20	0	3	0	0	0	0	2	11	0	2	.227	.150
2016	High Desert (CAL)	HiA	.272	88	331	73	90	20	4	25	59	41	125	13	3	.352	.583
	Carolina (CAR)	HiA	.250	35	124	21	31	9	5	3	11	26	50	4	1	.384	.476
Minor League Totals			.244	333	1187	229	290	62	15	62	175	173	475	38	10	.346	.479

20 RIO RUIZ, 3B

BA GRADE
45 Risk: Medium

Born: May 22, 1994. **B-T:** L-R. **Ht.:** 6-1. **Wt.:** 180. **Drafted:** HS—La Puente, Calif., 2012 (4th round). **Signed by:** Tim Costic (Astros).

Ruiz joined the Braves in January 2015 when he and righthanders Andrew Thurman and Mike Foltynewicz were traded from Houston for Evan Gattis. A heavily-recruited quarterback in high school, Ruiz struggled at the plate throughout most of his first season with the Braves before improving his physique and overall athleticism heading into 2016. He made the jump to Triple-A in 2016 as one of Gwinnett's youngest players and demonstrated excellent plate discipline and pitch recognition. He received his first big league callup at the end of the year. Ruiz has a smooth swing from the left side and makes good contact. He ranked fourth in the organization in RBIs (62) and has shown raw power that produces a steady stream of doubles and could generate more home runs as his body matures. His defense is a tick above-average. His hands are fringe average, but he has improved his range and the accuracy of his throws, leading to just seven errors in 2016 and an International League-leading 31 double plays turned by a third baseman. The Braves believe Ruiz has the ability to develop into a Bill Mueller type of player at the major league level. He will battle for a 25-man roster spot in 2017.

Year	Club (League)	Class	AVG	G	AB	R	H	2B	3B	HR	RBI	BB	SO	SB	CS	OBP	SLG
2014	Lancaster (CAL)	HiA	.293	131	516	76	151	37	2	11	77	82	91	4	4	.387	.436
2015	Mississippi (SL)	AA	.233	127	420	48	98	21	1	5	46	63	94	2	2	.333	.324
2016	Gwinnett (IL)	AAA	.271	133	465	52	126	24	3	10	62	61	116	1	4	.355	.400
	Atlanta (NL)	MAJ	.286	5	7	1	2	0	1	0	2	0	2	1	0	.286	.571
Major League Totals			.286	5	7	1	2	0	1	0	2	0	2	1	0	.286	.571
Minor League Totals			.265	543	1952	243	517	126	10	39	266	272	425	21	13	.353	.400

21 BRAXTON DAVIDSON, OF

BA GRADE
50 Risk: High

Born: June 18, 1996. **B-T:** L-L. **Ht.:** 6-2. **Wt.:** 210. **Drafted:** HS—Asheville, N.C., 2014 (1st round). **Signed by:** Billy Best.

Davidson was drafted 32nd overall in 2014 after displaying impressive power on the high school showcase circuit. Though his raw power is obvious, he has yet to parlay that into run-producing numbers due to a low batting average caused by high strikeout totals. Davidson has feel for the strike zone but is at times too willing to take a walk and relies too often on minor league umpires to make the correct call on close pitches. He also tends to struggle with inside fastballs, which contributed to his 184 strikeouts, the fifth-most in the minors in 2016. While Davidson needs to be more aggressive at the plate, he does have a smooth swing from the left side. Though not blessed with speed, he is an intelligent baserunner. He has developed into a solid right fielder after moving from left early in his pro career and possesses enough arm strength and accuracy to remain at the position. The Braves realize they may have been overaggressive in promoting Davidson to high Class A in 2016 and will probably have him open the 2017 campaign at the same level, with their new Florida State League affiliate.

Year	Club (League)	Class	AVG	G	AB	R	H	2B	3B	HR	RBI	BB	SO	SB	CS	OBP	SLG
2014	Braves (GCL)	R	.243	37	111	23	27	7	1	0	8	22	32	0	0	.400	.324
	Danville (APP)	R	.167	13	36	1	6	2	0	0	3	9	10	0	0	.348	.222
2015	Rome (SAL)	LoA	.242	124	401	51	97	23	0	10	45	84	135	1	6	.381	.374
2016	Carolina (CAR)	HiA	.224	128	428	53	96	24	2	10	63	71	184	4	4	.344	.360
Minor League Totals			.232	302	976	128	226	56	3	20	119	186	361	5	10	.366	.357

22 DERIAN CRUZ, SS

BA GRADE
55 Risk: Extreme

Born: October 3, 1998. **B-T:** B-R. **Ht.:** 6-1. **Wt.:** 180. **Signed:** Dominican Republic, 2015. **Signed by:** Marc Russo.

The Braves signed Cruz for $2 million in 2015, making him their highest-paid player on the international market that year, and he played his way through two Rookie levels in his pro debut in 2016. An impressive athlete with plus-plus speed, Cruz is raw in many facets of the game. He is a natural right-handed hitter learning how to switch-hit. He employs a line-drive approach with solid gap power from the right side, but often is off-balance and struggles to hit with authority from the left side. Cruz is aggressive at the plate with little discipline or strike-zone judgment. Given his speed, some feel he needs to make bunting a bigger part of his game. Defensively he makes the routine plays at shortstop but needs to needs to improve his game awareness. His hands are soft and he has quick feet, but his overall footwork needs improvement. Cruz has shown an above-average arm but can be timid cutting loose on his throws. The Braves are confident Cruz can work through his struggles, particularly given his age. Spring training will determine whether he returns to Rookie-level Danville or moves up to low Class A Rome to open 2017.

Year	Club (League)	Class	AVG	G	AB	R	H	2B	3B	HR	RBI	BB	SO	SB	CS	OBP	SLG
2016	Braves (GCL)	R	.309	26	110	11	34	7	1	2	16	2	16	4	1	.336	.445
	Danville (APP)	R	.183	25	104	10	19	4	3	0	5	3	28	3	2	.204	.279
Minor League Totals			.248	51	214	21	53	11	4	2	21	5	44	7	3	.272	.364

23 BRETT CUMBERLAND, C

BA GRADE
50 Risk: High

Born: June 25, 1995. **B-T:** B-R. **Ht.:** 5-11. **Wt.:** 205. **Drafted:** California, 2016 (2nd round supplemental). **Signed by:** Jim Blueberg.

Cumberland led the Pacific-10 Conference with 16 home runs in 2016, and his power potential and solid swing from both sides of the plate led the Braves to make the draft-eligible sophomore the 76th overall pick. He began his pro career at Rookie-level Danville and failed to impress scouts, though fatigue from catching a full college season played a part. Cumberland showed plus bat speed from both sides as well as raw power to his pull side, but rarely carried it to games. He demonstrated a good approach at the plate and the ability to work counts but needs to hit balls on the outer half with more authority. The Braves knew when drafting Cumberland that his defense needs polish, particularly with his footwork and ability to block balls in the dirt. He has soft hands and catches the ball well. He features average arm strength but needs to quicken his release. Cumberland's stocky build does not exude athleticism and fluidity, which led several scouts to suggest he would be better served moving to first base. The Braves will continue to work with Cumberland behind the plate, starting him at low Class A Rome in 2017.

Year	Club (League)	Class	AVG	G	AB	R	H	2B	3B	HR	RBI	BB	SO	SB	CS	OBP	SLG
2016	Danville (APP)	R	.216	45	162	11	35	11	0	3	30	14	49	0	4	.317	.340
Minor League Totals			.216	45	162	11	35	11	0	3	30	14	49	0	4	.317	.340

24 DREW HARRINGTON, LHP

BA GRADE
50 Risk: High

Born: March 30, 1995. **B-T:** R-L. **Ht.:** 6-2. **Wt.:** 229. **Drafted:** Louisville, 2016 (3rd round). **Signed by:** Rick Sellers.

Harrington worked primarily in relief during his first two seasons at Louisville before moving to the rotation as a junior in 2016 and emerging as the Atlantic Coast Conference's pitcher of the year after going 12-2, 1.95 overall and 8-0, 1.33 in conference play. Drafted 80th overall, Harrington has off-the-charts makeup, work ethic and intelligence to go with a solid-average skill set that has some within the Braves organization believing he could become a Dallas Keuchel-type of hurler at higher levels. Harrington works off an 89-91 mph fastball that touches 93 and an average slider. He has above-average command of both pitches and hides the ball well to create deception. Harrington works both sides of the plate with his fastball and generates late life. He sets up hitters and gets them to chase his slider out of the zone. His long-term role will be determined in large part by the development of his below-average changeup, a pitch he rarely threw in college. Harrington made progress with the depth of the pitch during his pro debut, but he could become a lefty reliever in the big leagues if his third offering does not continue to improve. Spring training will determine which Class A level he joins to open 2017.

Year	Club (League)	Class	W	L	ERA	G	GS	CG	SV	IP	H	HR	BB	SO	K/9	WHIP	AVG
2016	Danville (APP)	R	1	0	2.45	9	1	0	0	15	14	1	5	15	9.2	1.30	.237
Minor League Totals			1	0	2.45	9	1	0	0	15	14	1	5	15	9.2	1.30	.237

25 BRYSE WILSON, RHP

BA GRADE
55 Risk: Extreme

Born: Dec. 20, 1997. **B-T:** R-R. **Ht.:** 6-1. **Wt.:** 225. **Drafted:** HS—Hillsborough, N.C., 2016 (4th round). **Signed by:** Billy Best.

A North Carolina commit, Wilson was a football standout on both sides of the ball and a power pitcher who overwhelmed hitters in high school as well as those in Rookie-level Gulf Coast League in his first taste of pro ball. At Orange High he threw three no-hitters as a senior, including a perfect game in the play-offs, while working with current North Carolina State freshman catcher Brad Debo. Wilson signed for an above-slot $1.2 million as a 2016 fourth-round pick. The uber-athletic righthander brings a football mentality to the mound by challenging hitters without fear. Wilson pounds the strike zone with his 93-95 mph fastball that touches 97 with armside run and a hard slider in the mid-80s. Scouts questioned his ability to spin his breaking ball due to his long arm action, but the Braves were encouraged with Wilson's progress after making minor alterations. He needs a third pitch to remain a starter and has a long way to go for his changeup to be anything more than a show-me offering. His thick, physical frame lacks much projection, but he possesses the arm strength and mentality succeed at higher levels. Wilson is projected to open the 2017 season at low Class A Rome.

Year	Club (League)	Class	W	L	ERA	G	GS	CG	SV	IP	H	HR	BB	SO	K/9	WHIP	AVG
2016	Braves (GCL)	R	1	1	0.68	9	6	0	0	27	16	0	8	29	9.8	0.90	.172
Minor League Totals			1	1	0.68	9	6	0	0	27	16	0	8	29	9.8	0.90	.172

26 ABRAHAN GUTIERREZ, C

BA GRADE
50 Risk: Extreme

Born: Oct. 31, 1999. **B-T:** R-R. **Ht.:** 6-0. **Wt.:** 205. **Signed:** Venezuela, 2016.
Signed by: Gordon Blakeley/Mike Silvestri/Rolando Petit.

Gutierrez has been on scouts' radars since he was an 11-year-old catcher at the 12U World Championship in Taiwan. Three years later, at the age of 14, he was Venezuela's starting catcher at the 15U World Cup in Mexico. He trained at Carlos Guillen's academy and continued to attract attention, though many scouts felt his progress began to level off. The Braves believed otherwise and signed Gutierrez for $3.5 million in 2016 when the international signing period opened on July 2. The thick-bodied receiver does not run well but flashes plus arm strength and raw power potential, and the Braves believe he should develop into at least an average hitter and defender. Gutierrez has good hands and solid catch-and-throw skills with above-average accuracy on his throws. At the plate, his swing tends to get long and he will expand his strike zone. Gutierrez does a good job using the entire field and is projected to be a run producer as he gains experience. He could move quickly once he builds a foundation in pro ball. After a stint in extended spring training, Gutierrez may open the 2017 season in the Rookie-level Gulf Coast League.

Year	Club (League)	Class	AVG	G	AB	R	H	2B	3B	HR	RBI	BB	SO	SB	CS	OBP	SLG
2016	Did not play—Signed 2017 contract																

27 RAY-PATRICK DIDDER, OF

BA GRADE
45 Risk: High

Born: Oct. 1, 1994. **B-T:** R-R. **Ht.:** 6-0. **Wt.:** 170. **Signed:** Aruba, 2013. **Signed by:** Dargello Lodowica.

The Braves tried Didder at second base after they signed him out of Aruba in 2013. After that didn't work, they slid him to right field to take advantage of his double-plus speed and above-average arm. That was going to be the plan for Didder at low Class A Rome in 2016, but when Ronald Acuna went on the disabled list, Didder shifted to center field and wowed Braves officials and scouts with his defense in the middle. He also showed continued refinement at the plate. He has well below-average raw power, but he can line balls in the gaps for doubles and triples. He has a knack for getting hit by pitches (39 in 2016), which plays a significant part in his solid on-base percentage. Didder's defensive versatility makes him a potential fourth outfielder, but his on-base skills could make him a starter. He will head to high Class A Florida in 2017.

Year	Club (League)	Class	AVG	G	AB	R	H	2B	3B	HR	RBI	BB	SO	SB	CS	OBP	SLG
2014	Braves (GCL)	R	.274	45	157	22	43	6	5	0	16	15	33	4	4	.354	.376
2015	Danville (APP)	R	.247	61	223	31	55	5	7	0	16	20	51	10	7	.346	.332
2016	Rome (SAL)	LoA	.274	132	478	95	131	15	9	6	35	50	100	37	12	.387	.381
Minor League Totals			.266	286	993	182	264	28	22	6	79	116	218	59	26	.378	.356

28 LUKE JACKSON, RHP

BA GRADE
45 Risk: High

Born: Aug. 24, 1991. **B-T:** R-R. **Ht.:** 6-2. **Wt.:** 210. **Drafted:** HS—Fort Lauderdale, 2010 (1st round supplemental). **Signed by:** Juan Alvarez (Rangers).

Jackson made his big league debut with the Rangers in 2015 but opened 2016 in the Triple-A Round Rock bullpen before getting called up to Texas in May. After returning to Triple-A a month later and bouncing back up to Texas at the end of June, Jackson allowed six runs in 1.2 innings in a July 2 appearance in Minnesota before the Rangers demoted him to Double-A Frisco, where he spent the rest of the season and continued to struggle with his control. The Braves acquired him at the 2016 Winter Meetings in a trade for righthander Tyrell Jenkins and lefthander Brady Feigl. Jackson still has good stuff but doesn't know where it's going. He throws his fastball 93-97 mph and complements it with a sharp-breaking curveball that grades as a tick above-average. He sprinkles in an occasional fringe-average changeup and slider. What's long plagued Jackson is poor control of all of his pitches, which stems from his inability to control his high-effort delivery or repeat his release point. If Jackson can ever learn to throw more strikes, he can be a middle reliever, but he has to find a delivery that allows him to throw quality strikes before the Braves will trust him at the major league level.

Year	Club (League)	Class	W	L	ERA	G	GS	CG	SV	IP	H	HR	BB	SO	K/9	WHIP	AVG
2014	Frisco (TL)	AA	8	2	3.02	15	14	0	1	83	58	5	24	83	9.0	0.98	.191
	Round Rock (PCL)	AAA	1	3	10.35	11	10	0	0	40	56	9	28	43	9.7	2.10	.333
2015	Round Rock (PCL)	AAA	2	3	4.34	39	5	0	0	66	62	3	35	79	10.7	1.46	.245
	Texas (AL)	MAJ	0	0	4.26	7	0	0	0	6	5	1	2	6	8.5	1.11	.200
2016	Round Rock (PCL)	AAA	1	0	2.45	16	0	0	2	22	13	2	15	27	11.0	1.27	.178
	Texas (AL)	MAJ	0	0	10.80	8	0	0	0	12	22	4	8	3	2.3	2.57	.415
	Frisco (TL)	AA	0	1	4.81	20	0	0	1	24	27	4	17	32	11.8	1.81	.276
Major League Totals			0	0	8.50	15	0	0	0	18	27	5	10	9	4.5	2.06	.346
Minor League Totals			38	26	4.24	171	97	1	4	569	521	44	291	622	9.8	1.43	.244

29 ALEX JACKSON, OF/C

BA GRADE
50 Risk: Extreme

Born: Dec. 25, 1995. **B-T:** R-R. **Ht.:** 6-2. **Wt.:** 215. **Drafted:** HS—San Diego, 2014 (1st round). **Signed by:** Gary Patchett (Mariners).

Jackson was one of the decade's most touted prep players, a three-time high school All-American and the sixth overall pick in 2014 by the Mariners, but his star has since taken a fall in pro ball. The Braves took a flier on him, trading righthanders Max Povse and Rob Whalen for him after the 2016 season. Jackson has 223 strikeouts in 190 career games because of an inefficient bat path, which has raised doubts he'll ever make enough contact to tap into his plus raw power. He still hits the occasional towering home run, but evaluators increasingly grade Jackson as a below-average hitter. The Mariners sent Jackson to extended spring training to begin 2016, the first time this millennium a healthy, non-suspended first-round infielder or outfielder did not begin his second full season assigned to a team. He finally responded to coaching after the move and was bumped to low Class A Clinton in mid-May, but even with improvement in his bat path still struck out in 27 percent of his plate appearances. He has average range in right field and a plus arm, and the Braves have hinted at trying Jackson back at catcher, his primary high school position. Atlanta's roving catching instructor Jeff Datz scouted for the Mariners when they drafted Jackson. He is likely headed for high Class A Florida in 2017.

Year	Club (League)	Class	AVG	G	AB	R	H	2B	3B	HR	RBI	BB	SO	SB	CS	OBP	SLG
2014	Mariners (AZL)	R	.280	23	82	11	23	6	2	2	16	9	24	0	1	.344	.476
2015	Clinton (MWL)	LoA	.157	28	108	10	17	6	0	0	13	6	35	1	1	.240	.213
	Everett (NWL)	SS	.239	48	163	31	39	11	1	8	25	21	61	2	4	.365	.466
2016	Clinton (MWL)	LoA	.243	92	333	43	81	20	1	11	55	34	103	2	1	.332	.408
Minor League Totals			.233	191	686	95	160	43	4	21	109	70	223	5	7	.327	.399

30 LUCAS HERBERT, C

BA GRADE
50 Risk: Extreme

Born: Nov. 28, 1996. **B-T:** R-R. **Ht.:** 6-0. **Wt.:** 200. **Drafted:** HS—San Clemente, Calif., 2015 (2nd round). **Signed by:** Dan Cox.

Since Brian McCann left as a free agent after the 2013 season, the Braves have struggled to develop a homegrown catcher, opting instead for such journeymen as Gerald Laird and A.J. Pierzynski. The likes of Evan Gattis (defense) and Christian Bethancourt (offense) displayed too many weaknesses to stick. Atlanta attempted to address its catcher depth by drafting Herbert with the 54th overall pick in 2015. He played just three games in his pro debut because of a knee injury and then hit .185 at low Class A Rome in 2016 and lost playing time to Jonathan Morales. Herbert lacked consistency with his hitting approach. He has shown raw power on occasion but needs to make adjustments in his setup, swing path and pitch recognition. Conversely, Herbert is the best defensive catcher in the organization, and he started 64 games behind the plate in 2016. He did an outstanding job of working with Rome's talented pitching staff and displayed the necessary leadership skills to call and control a game. He has excellent mobility with plus footwork, and he possesses plus arm strength with good accuracy on his throws. A high school teammate of 2015 first-round lefthander Kolby Allard, Herbert must improve his offensive production to become a top prospect. He will receive that opportunity in 2017 by returning to Rome.

Year	Club (League)	Class	AVG	G	AB	R	H	2B	3B	HR	RBI	BB	SO	SB	CS	OBP	SLG
2015	Braves (GCL)	R	.500	3	4	1	2	0	0	1	1	0	1	0	0	.600	1.250
2016	Rome (SAL)	LoA	.185	96	335	29	62	11	1	6	30	18	96	2	4	.234	.278
Minor League Totals			.189	99	339	30	64	11	1	7	31	18	97	2	4	.239	.289

Baltimore Orioles

BY STEVE MELEWSKI

The Orioles returned to the playoffs for the third time in five seasons in 2016, though their stay there was short. They lost to the Blue Jays in the American League Wild Card Game on Edwin Encarnacion's 11th-inning homer.

It was an abrupt end to an 89-win season, one in which Baltimore led the AL East for 111 days. The Orioles have had five straight .500 seasons or better, and their 444 wins since 2012 are the most in the AL.

While the Orioles are sensitive to organizational prospect rankings that place Baltimore near the bottom of the majors, they point out that several home-grown and developed players contributed to their 2016 playoff season. The team's core players, such as third baseman Manny Machado, second baseman Jonathan Schoop, catcher Matt Wieters, righthander Kevin Gausman and closer Zach Britton, are home-grown.

Moreover, the Orioles had several rookie contributors to their 2016 success, such as five-time No. 1 prospect Dylan Bundy, who stayed healthy and pitched well until tiring late in the season. Rule 5 pick Joey Rickard and Korean import Hyun Soo Kim were outfield starters, while righthander Mychal Givens and lefty Donnie Hart provided key relief innings.

Givens and Hart helped the Orioles lead the AL in reliever ERA at 3.40. Bundy and Gausman led a rotation that was much better in the second half and provides hope for 2017. After years of Orioles pitching prospects not living up to potential—at least until after being traded—could Bundy and/or Gausman be that ace that the club has long been searching for?

Club officials also believe they had a productive draft. Their top three picks—Midwest pitchers Cody Sedlock (Illinois), Keegan Akin (Western Michigan) and Matthias Dietz (Illinois junior college)—all showed instant promise as did their fourth selection, outfielder Austin Hays.

General manager Dan Duquette has shown a willingness to trade prospects for major league help. In recent years, he has dealt righthander Zach Davies (Brewers) and lefties Eduardo Rodriguez (Red Sox), Josh Hader (Astros), Stephen Tarpley (Pirates) and Steven Brault (Pirates). None of the players acquired in return remain with Baltimore.

Those trades have thinned the farm system, and Baltimore didn't have a single affiliate qualify for the minor league playoffs in 2016. Only low Class A Delmarva had a winning record.

Finally healthy, Dylan Bundy showed flashes of being a front-of-the-rotation starter

TOP PROSPECTS OF THE DECADE

Year	Player, Pos.	2016 Org
2007	Billy Rowell, 3b	Did not play
2008	Matt Wieters, c	Orioles
2009	Matt Wieters, c	Orioles
2010	Brian Matusz, lhp	Cubs
2011	Manny Machado, ss	Orioles
2012	Dylan Bundy, rhp	Orioles
2013	Dylan Bundy, rhp	Orioles
2014	Dylan Bundy, rhp	Orioles
2015	Dylan Bundy, rhp	Orioles
2016	Dylan Bundy, rhp	Orioles

But Baltimore brass felt there were individual success stories. Catcher Chance Sisco made strides on defense and ascended to being the No. 1 prospect in the organization. The organization's 2015 minor league player of the year, Trey Mancini, received a September callup and became the third player in history to homer in his first three starts.

The Orioles ended 2016 with a walk-off ending—when manager Buck Showalter used Ubaldo Jimenez instead of Britton in the fateful 11th—but with a hopeful future.

They have a core group of players under team control for at least two more seasons, and Bundy and Gausman will join Chris Tillman to provide a solid trio to lead the 2017 rotation. In other words, the window to keep competing in the AL East remains open.

ORGANIZATION OVERVIEW

General Manager: Dan Duquette. **Farm Director:** Brian Graham. **Scouting Director:** Gary Rajsich.

Class	Team	League	W	L	PCT	Finish	Manager
Majors	Baltimore Orioles	American	89	73	.549	t-4th (15)	Buck Showalter
Triple-A	Norfolk Tides	International	62	82	.431	13th (14)	Ron Johnson
Double-A	Bowie Baysox	Eastern	56	86	.394	12th (12)	Gary Kendall
High Class A	Frederick Keys	Carolina	68	72	.486	5th (8)	Keith Bodie
Low Class A	Delmarva Shorebirds	South Atlantic	73	66	.525	6th (14)	Ryan Minor
Short season	Aberdeen IronBirds	New York-Penn	32	43	.427	11th (14)	Luis Pujols
Rookie	GCL Orioles	Gulf Coast	27	32	.458	11th (17)	Orlando Gomez
Overall 2016 Minor League Record			318	381	.455	25th (30)	

THIS YEAR'S TOP 30

No.	Player, Pos.	Grade/Risk
1.	Chance Sisco, c	55/Medium
2.	Cody Sedlock, rhp	55/High
3.	Ryan Mountcastle, ss	50/High
4.	Hunter Harvey, rhp	55/Extreme
5.	Trey Mancini, 1b	45/Medium
6.	Keegan Akin, lhp	50/High
7.	Austin Hays, of	50/High
8.	Jomar Reyes, 3b	55/Extreme
9.	Anthony Santander, of	50/High
10.	Chris Lee, lhp	50/High
11.	Tanner Scott, rhp	50/Extreme
12.	Ofelky Peralta, rhp	50/Extreme
13.	Jesus Liranzo, rhp	45/High
14.	Matthias Dietz, rhp	50/Extreme
15.	Brian Gonzalez, lhp	45/High
16.	Donnie Hart, rhp	40/Medium
17.	Aneury Tavarez, of	45/High
18.	Adam Brett Walker, rhp	50/Extreme
19.	D.J. Stewart, of	45/High
20.	Joe Gunkel, rhp	40/Medium
21.	Parker Bridwell, rhp	45/High
22.	Jimmy Yacabonis, rhp	45/High
23.	Christian Walker, of/1b	40/Medium
24.	Randolph Gassaway, of	45/High
25.	Alex Wells, lhp	45/High
26.	Cedric Mullens, of	45/High
27.	Stefan Crichton, rhp	45/High
28.	Zack Muckenhirn, lhp	45/High
29.	Jason Garcia, rhp	45/High
30.	Jayson Aquino, lhp	45/High

LAST YEAR'S TOP 30

No.	Player, Pos.	Status
1.	Dylan Bundy, rhp	Majors
2.	Hunter Harvey, rhp	No. 4
3.	Chance Sisco, c	No. 1
4.	Jomar Reyes, 3b	No. 8
5.	Mychal Givens, rhp	Majors
6.	Chris Lee, lhp	No. 10
7.	Ryan Mountcastle, 3b	No. 3
8.	Trey Mancini, 1b	No. 5
9.	D.J. Stewart, of	No. 19
10.	Mike Wright, rhp	Majors
11.	Tanner Scott, lhp	No. 11
12.	Jason Garcia, rhp	No. 29
13.	Dariel Alvarez, of	Dropped out
14.	Christian Walker, 1b	No. 23
15.	Jonah Heim, c	(Rays)
16.	Tim Berry, lhp	Free Agent
17.	Ofelky Peralta, rhp	No. 12
18.	David Hess, rhp	Dropped out
19.	Tyler Wilson, rhp	Majors
20.	Lazaro Leyva, rhp	Dropped out
21.	Oliver Drake, rhp	Dropped out
22.	Parker Bridwell, rhp	No. 21
23.	Ariel Miranda, lhp	(Mariners)
24.	Gray Fenter, rhp	Dropped out
25.	Mike Yastrzemski, of	Dropped out
26.	Garrett Cleavinger, lhp	Dropped out
27.	Alex Murphy, c	Dropped out
28.	Josh Hart, of	Dropped out
29.	Branden Kline, rhp	Dropped out
30.	Glynn Davis, of	Dropped out

BEST TOOLS

Best Hitter For Average	Chance Sisco
Best Power Hitter	Adam Brett Walker
Best Strike-Zone Discipline	Chance Sisco
Fastest Baserunner	Daniel Franco
Best Athlete	Austin Hays
Best Fastball	Tanner Scott
Best Curveball	Hunter Harvey
Best Slider	Cody Sedlock
Best Changeup	Brian Gonzalez
Best Control	Joe Gunkel
Best Defensive Catcher	Austin Wynns
Best Defensive Infielder	Irving Ortega
Best Infield Arm	Jomar Reyes
Best Defensive Outfielder	Cedric Mullins
Best Outfield Arm	Dariel Alvarez

PROJECTED 2020 LINEUP

Catcher	Chance Sisco
First Base	Trey Mancini
Second Base	Jonathan Schoop
Third Base	Jomar Reyes
Shortstop	Manny Machado
Left Field	Ryan Mountcastle
Center Field	Adam Jones
Right Field	Austin Hays
Designated Hitter	Chris Davis
No. 1 Starter	Dylan Bundy
No. 2 Starter	Kevin Gausman
No. 3 Starter	Hunter Harvey
No. 4 Starter	Cody Sedlock
No. 5 Starter	Keegan Akin
Closer	Zach Britton

MINOR LEAGUE DEPTH CHART

BALTIMORE ORIOLES

TOP 2017 ROOKIE: Trey Mancini, 1b. He could have a big role in 2017 if the Orioles lose righthanded power bats Mark Trumbo and Steve Pearce as free agents.
BREAKOUT PROSPECT: Cedric Mullins, of. After filling up the stat sheet in 2016, can he take another step forward?
SLEEPER: Ruben Garcia, rhp. A two-way player in college, he touched 97 mph in the Gulf Coast League.

SOURCE OF TOP 30 TALENT			
Homegrown	22	Acquired	8
College	11	Trades	3
Junior college	2	Rule 5 draft	3
High school	6	Independent leagues	0
Nondrafted free agents	0	Free agents/waivers	2
International	3		

LF
Ryan Mountcastle (3)
Anthony Santander (9)
Adam Brett Walker (18)
D.J. Stewart (19)
Randolph Gassaway (24)

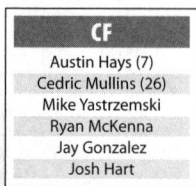
CF
Austin Hays (7)
Cedric Mullins (26)
Mike Yastrzemski
Ryan McKenna
Jay Gonzalez
Josh Hart

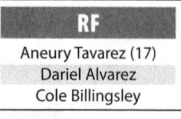
RF
Aneury Tavarez (17)
Dariel Alvarez
Cole Billingsley

3B
Jomar Reyes (8)
Drew Dosch

SS
Irving Ortega
Adrian Marin
Alex Torres
Chris Clare
Erick Salcedo

2B
Drew Turbin

1B
Trey Mancini (5)
Christian Walker (23)
Alex Murphy
Seamus Curran
Preston Palmeiro
Aderlin Rodriguez

C
Chance Sisco (1)
Yermin Mercedes
Audry Perez
Francisco Pena
Austin Wynns

LHP

LHSP	LHRP
Keegan Akin (6)	Tanner Scott (11)
Chris Lee (9)	Donnie Hart (16)
Brian Gonzalez (15)	Garrett Cleavinger
Alex Wells (25)	
Zach Muckenhirn (28)	
Jayson Aquino (30)	
John Means	
Travis Seabrooke	

RHP

RHSP	RHRP
Cody Sedlock (2)	Jesus Liranzo (13)
Hunter Harvey (4)	Parker Bridwell (21)
Ofelky Peralta (12)	Jimmy Yacabonis (22)
Matthias Dietz (14)	Stefan Crichton (27)
Joe Gunkel (20)	Jason Garcia (29)
Alex Wells (25)	Oliver Drake
Branden Kline	Ruben Garcia
David Hess	Jon Keller
Gray Fenter	Ryan Meisinger
Cristian Alvarado	Nick Jobst
Matt Grimes	
Jhon Peluffo	
Brenan Hanifee	
Tobias Myers	

DRAFT ANALYSIS

2016

BEST PURE HITTER: OF Austin Hays (4) was the first position player the Orioles drafted; he broke out with a strong spring at Jacksonville, then continued to hit when in pro ball, batting .336 for short-season Aberdeen. 1B Preston Palmeiro (7) earns praise for his smooth lefthanded stroke.

BEST POWER: Hays has above-average raw power; he posted an isolated slugging percentage over .300 and swatted 16 home runs as a junior at Jacksonville.

FASTEST RUNNER: OF Cole Billingsley (19) can reach first base in four seconds flat, and he grades as a 70-grade runner from the left side. Hays is also a plus runner.

BEST DEFENSIVE PLAYER: Hays is the best defensive player the Orioles selected; he has the speed to play center field and looked natural there during fall instructional league. Hays has elite arm strength to profile well defensively in any outfield spot. SS Alexis Torres (5) also earns high praise for his defense, with smooth hands and above-average arm strength.

BEST ATHLETE: Hays' unique combination of arm strength, speed and power makes him the best athlete in the Orioles' class. RHP Ruben Garcia (14) was primarily an outfielder in junior college; he is a 70 runner and has the body to sell jeans, standing at 6-foot-4 with a chiseled frame.

BEST FASTBALL: RHP Cody Sedlock (1) throws a lively two-seam fastball that has reached as high as 98 and has worked at 94-96. The Orioles believe he could hit triple digits when he learns to throw a four-seam fastball. LHP Keegan Akin (2) can pitch in the mid-90s. LHP Brandon Bonilla (LHP) can hit 98.

BEST SECONDARY PITCH: Baltimore was enamored with Sedlock's two breaking pitches, a curveball and a slider, both of which he can spin tightly and throw for strikes.

BEST PRO DEBUT: Akin and Hays both had success at short-season Aberdeen. Akin pitched to a 1.04 ERA and didn't allow a run in his last six outings. Hays slashed .336/.386/.514.

MOST INTRIGUING BACKGROUND: Bonilla is the son of longtime major leaguer Bobby Bonilla, and Palmeiro is the son of famed slugger Rafael Palmeiro.

CLOSEST TO THE MAJORS: Akin could progress through the system quickly with excellent lefthanded velocity, a strong changeup, a slider that came on strong during instructional league and impressive ability to command his pitches.

BEST LATE ROUND PICK: LHP Zach Muckenhirn's (11) stuff fluctuated throughout the spring, then bounced back strong at the end of the summer. He has four pitches and a low 90s fastball. LHP Willie Rios (16) has impressive lefthanded velocity. LHP Yelin Rodriguez (20) offers upside with an easy delivery, good body and extreme youth, having played the whole summer at 17.

THE ONE WHO GOT AWAY: 3B Daniel Bakst (27) entered the spring as one of the more potent bats from the summer showcase circuit but opted for Stanford instead of signing. LHP Ben Brecht (36) projects well as an athletic 6-foot-7 southpaw.

2015

OF D.J. Stewart (1) had a modest first full season and was surpassed as a prospect by SS Ryan Mountcastle (1). RHP Jonathan Hughes (2) didn't sign, and the pitching class has had modest returns so far.

GRADE: C

2014

Baltimore had no picks in the first two rounds, and RHP Pat Connaughton (4) has chosen basketball to this point over baseball. That leaves LHPs Brian Gonzalez (3) and Tanner Scott (6) carrying the class.

GRADE: D

2013

Injuries have waylaid RHP Hunter Harvey (1), but C Chance Sisco (2) has emerged as the club's top prospect. Traded LHP Steven Brault (11) reached the big leagues, as has 1B Trey Mancini (8), who made a strong debut in 2016.

GRADE: B

TOP DRAFT PICKS OF THE DECADE

Year	Player, Pos.	2016 Org
2007	Matt Wieters, c	Orioles
2008	Brian Matusz, lhp	Cubs
2009	Matt Hobgood, rhp	Did not play
2010	Manny Machado, ss	Orioles
2011	Dylan Bundy, rhp	Orioles
2012	Kevin Gausman, rhp	Orioles
2013	Hunter Harvey, rhp	Orioles
2014	Brian Gonzalez, lhp (3rd round)	Orioles
2015	D.J. Stewart, of	Orioles
2016	Cody Sedlock, rhp	Orioles

LARGEST BONUSES IN CLUB HISTORY

Matt Wieters, 2007	$6,000,000
Manny Machado, 2010	$5,250,000
Kevin Gausman, 2012	$4,320,000
Dylan Bundy, 2011	$4,000,000
Adam Loewen, 2002	$3,200,000

1 CHANCE SISCO, C

Born: Feb. 24, 1995. **B-T:** L-R. **Ht.:** 6-2. **Wt.:** 195.
Drafted: HS—Corona, Calif., 2013 (2nd round).
Signed by: Mark Ralston.

Sisco didn't become a catcher until his senior year in high school, and the Orioles liked his combination of athletic ability, hitting tools and defensive potential to select him 61st overall in 2013. Since signing for $785,000, Sisco just keeps trending up. The 21-year-old always has shown a solid bat, with a career .402 on-base percentage as a pro, but his defense made strides last year. Sisco led the Double-A Eastern League in on-base percentage (.406), ranked fourth in batting (.320) and homered in the Futures Game during a breakout 2016 season. In September, he earned his first promotion to Triple-A Norfolk, where he hit a grand slam in his first game.

Sisco's hit tool is strong, and he has a long track record of success. That success has afforded him the confidence—if not arrogance—required of big league hitters. It starts with excellent hand-eye coordination and a natural feel for hitting that allows him to make consistent hard contact. He has a controlled, line-drive, all-fields approach and solid plate discipline. Showing a solid eye at the plate, he drew a career-best 61 walks. Sisco lets the ball travel deep and improved his ability to pull the ball this year. Pitchers used to try to pound him inside with fastballs, but he has started to adjust, getting his hands to the hitting zone quicker than in the past. He added some strength and showed an increased ability to backspin the ball. His opposite-field home run at the Futures Game in San Diego's cavernous Petco Park hints at his power potential, and he has average raw power. Sisco has shown smarts on the bases but is a well below-average runner. That makes his career .323 average even better because he doesn't get many infield hits. Sisco's defense took steps forward in 2016. It started in big league spring training—he received his first invitation—where he worked with big leaguers Matt Wieters and Caleb Joseph. Pitchers who threw to him at Double-A Bowie said his pitch calling and game management took nice strides. His pop times on throws to second base remain around 2.0 seconds, which is average, but he was over that more often than under it. His arm strength grades a tick below-average, and he needs to continue to improve his footwork and transfer to help him throw out runners. He caught 24

BA GRADE

55 Risk: Medium

SCOUTING GRADES

Batting: 60.
Power: 45.
Speed: 30.
Defense: 50.
Arm: 45.

Based on 20-80 scouting scale and future projection rather than present tools.

percent of base stealers in 136 attempts this year. Sisco's blocking and receiving skills also improved as did his ability to frame pitches. He had just four passed balls in 87 games. When Sisco first got to Double-A in 2015 and began working with older pitchers, he learned from them and grew because of it. It even helped him at the plate because he could understand better how pitchers approach getting hitters out.

Sisco could reach the majors in 2017, but given his youth and lack of Triple-A experience, he probably will not make the Opening Day roster. That holds true even if Wieters leaves via free agency. Sisco should be Wieters' eventual successor, however, and at least a partial season at Norfolk would benefit him.

Year	Club (League)	Class	AVG	G	AB	R	H	2B	3B	HR	RBI	BB	SO	SB	CS	OBP	SLG
2014	Delmarva (SAL)	LoA	.340	114	426	56	145	27	2	5	63	42	79	1	2	.406	.448
2015	Frederick (CAR)	HiA	.308	75	263	30	81	12	3	4	26	33	41	8	1	.387	.422
	Bowie (EL)	AA	.257	20	74	9	19	4	0	2	8	9	14	0	1	.337	.392
2016	Bowie (EL)	AA	.319	111	407	51	130	28	1	4	44	58	82	2	2	.405	.423
	Norfolk (IL)	AAA	.250	4	16	4	4	0	0	2	7	2	5	0	0	.333	.625
Minor League Totals			.323	357	1288	166	416	75	7	18	159	162	244	12	7	.402	.434

2 CODY SEDLOCK, RHP

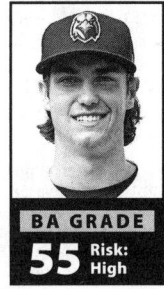

Born: June 19, 1995. **B-T:** R-R. **Ht.:** 6-4. **Wt.:** 205. **Drafted:** Illinois, 2016 (1st round). **Signed by:** Dan Durst.

Sedlock threw just 63 innings in his first two seasons at Illinois but thrived in the Cape Cod League in 2015, when he ranked as its No. 18 prospect. He maintained the momentum in 2016 to become the Big 10 Conference pitcher of the year and Illinois' third-ever first-round pick while setting an school record with 116 strikeouts in 101.1 innings. The Orioles drafted him 27th overall and signed him for a slot bonus of $2,097,200. He ranked as the No. 5 prospect in the short-season New York-Penn League. Sedlock has the build, balanced delivery and repertoire of a workhorse power pitcher. His fastball works in the low 90s and touches 97 mph with strong sink and late life. His curveball and slider flash above-average and show plus potential, but he doesn't always have both working at the same time. His changeup flashes average and ranks as a fourth pitch, behind his fastball, slider and curve. He holds runners well and was timed at 1.2 seconds to the plate. The Orioles loved his athleticism, work ethic and competitiveness and ability to elevate his game when in jams. The Orioles held Sedlock to nine outings of three innings each at short-season Aberdeen. The season workload of around 130 innings, counting college, sets him up well for 2017. He could start at high Class A Frederick in 2017 and will move fast if he performs.

BA GRADE: 55 Risk: High

Year	Club (League)	Class	W	L	ERA	G	GS	CG	SV	IP	H	HR	BB	SO	K/9	WHIP	AVG
2016	Aberdeen (NYP)	SS	0	1	3.00	9	9	0	0	27	16	1	13	25	8.3	1.07	.158
Minor League Totals			0	1	3.00	9	9	0	0	27	16	1	13	25	8.3	1.07	.158

3 RYAN MOUNTCASTLE, SS

Born: Feb. 18, 1997. **B-T:** R-R. **Ht.:** 6-3. **Wt.:** 185. **Drafted:** HS—Oviedo, Fla., 2015 (1st round). **Signed by:** Kelvin Colon.

The Orioles made Mountcastle the 36th overall pick in the 2015 draft and signed him for $1.3 million, which was about $400,000 under slot. He spent his first full season at low Class A Delmarva, where he hit .281 to rank 11th in the South Atlantic League while being one of the SAL's youngest players. Mountcastle has similar hitting skill as top prospect Chance Sisco, but from the right side and with more power potential. He has a mature approach and good understanding of the strike zone. He recognizes offspeed pitches, has a two-strike approach and makes adjustments within games and at times within at-bats. His bat speed is plus, he stays inside the ball well and he showed improved pull power as the season progressed. Club officials expect him to develop at least above-average power eventually. On defense, scouts are convinced he will have to move off shortstop and likely wind up in left field, mostly due to a well below-average arm. He's an average runner with the speed to handle the outfield. The Orioles kept him at short throughout instructional league. Mountcastle is set to move to high Class A Frederick in 2017. The main question he faces, for both 2017 and the future, is his future position. His most likely landing spots, left field and first base, will require his power to develop for him to be a regular.

BA GRADE: 50 Risk: High

Year	Club (League)	Class	AVG	G	AB	R	H	2B	3B	HR	RBI	BB	SO	SB	CS	OBP	SLG
2015	Orioles (GCL)	R	.313	43	163	21	51	7	0	3	14	9	36	10	4	.349	.411
	Aberdeen (NYP)	SS	.212	10	33	2	7	0	0	1	5	0	10	0	1	.206	.303
2016	Delmarva (SAL)	LoA	.281	115	455	53	128	28	4	10	51	25	95	5	4	.319	.426
Minor League Totals			.286	168	651	76	186	35	4	14	70	34	141	15	9	.321	.416

4 HUNTER HARVEY, RHP

Born: Dec. 9, 1994. **B-T:** R-R. **Ht.:** 6-3. **Wt.:** 175. **Drafted:** HS—Catawba, N.C., 2013 (1st round). **Signed by:** Chris Gale.

When the Orioles drafted Harvey 22nd overall in 2013, they probably envisioned him in their rotation by now. The son of former big league closer Bryan Harvey, Hunter showed big-time potential from the outset, but injuries have sidetracked his career. In 2014, he was shut down in late July with a strained right flexor mass. A shin injury and later elbow issues derailed his 2015 season. In May 2016, he had sports hernia surgery. Harvey finally returned to a mound in June 2016, and he managed to make it through just five games before being shut down yet again. He had Tommy John surgery in Charlotte on July 26, with doctors using a tendon from his hamstring to repair his elbow. One scout said a healthy Harvey showed everything you want

BA GRADE: 55 Risk: Extreme

CLIFF WELCH

in a top-of-the-rotation starter—talent, poise and mound presence. Before the injuries, he commanded a fastball that sat between 92-94 mph and touched 97, as well as a plus curveball that overmatched hitters at times. His changeup made solid gains during 2014 and flashed plus. Harvey won't pitch again for 12-18 months after the surgery, though he could resume throwing early in 2017, and his next game action likely will come in 2018. Dylan Bundy's successful return from a similar fallow period gives the Orioles reason for optimism.

Year	Club (League)	Class	W	L	ERA	G	GS	CG	SV	IP	H	HR	BB	SO	K/9	WHIP	AVG
2014	Delmarva (SAL)	LoA	7	5	3.18	17	17	0	0	88	66	5	33	106	10.9	1.13	.209
2015	Did not play—Injured																
2016	Orioles (GCL)	R	0	0	0.00	2	2	0	0	5	3	0	0	11	19.8	0.60	.167
	Aberdeen (NYP)	SS	0	1	3.52	3	3	0	0	8	9	0	6	7	8.2	1.96	.310
Minor League Totals			7	7	2.79	30	30	0	0	126	99	5	45	157	11.2	1.15	.217

5 TREY MANCINI, 1B

Born: March 18, 1992. **B-T:** R-R. **Ht.:** 6-4. **Wt.:** 215. **Drafted:** Notre Dame, 2013 (8th round). **Signed by:** Kirk Fredriksson.

Signed for a slot bonus of $151,900 in 2013 out of Notre Dame, Mancini received his first big league callup in September and became the third player in major league history to homer his first three starts. Mancini hit .359 to win the Double-A Eastern League batting title in 2015 and produced a solid .282/.357/.458 minor league line in 2016, mostly at Triple-A Norfolk. Mancini's bat is solid and scouts believe he could hit at least 20 homers as a regular. He is a solid-average hitter if not a tick above with a swing and bat path that help him keep his hands inside the ball, providing him a chance to get to a good fastball but also stay on offspeed

BA GRADE
45 Risk: Medium

pitches. He uses his hands very well—they come into his body, down and then forward—providing good timing that keeps the bat in the hitting zone a long time. An aggressive hitter, Mancini saw his strikeout rate jump above 20 percent in 2016 for the first time. He is playable at first base, though his lack of athleticism means his defense is seldom smooth. With Chris Davis signed through 2022, the Orioles could try Mancini in the outfield next spring to increase his chances of earning a roster spot in 2017.

Year	Club (League)	Class	AVG	G	AB	R	H	2B	3B	HR	RBI	BB	SO	SB	CS	OBP	SLG
2014	Delmarva (SAL)	LoA	.317	68	268	30	85	13	3	3	42	14	52	1	1	.357	.422
	Frederick (CAR)	HiA	.251	69	275	37	69	19	0	7	41	14	43	0	1	.295	.396
2015	Frederick (CAR)	HiA	.314	52	207	28	65	14	3	8	32	9	35	4	2	.341	.527
	Bowie (EL)	AA	.359	84	326	60	117	29	3	13	57	22	58	2	1	.395	.586
2016	Bowie (EL)	AA	.302	17	63	18	19	4	0	7	14	10	17	0	0	.413	.698
	Norfolk (IL)	AAA	.280	125	483	60	135	22	5	13	54	48	123	2	2	.349	.427
	Baltimore (AL)	MAJ	.357	5	14	3	5	1	0	3	5	0	4	0	0	.400	1.071
Major League Totals			.357	5	14	3	5	1	0	3	5	0	4	0	0	.400	1.071
Minor League Totals			.306	483	1878	276	574	119	16	54	275	137	371	12	8	.357	.472

6 KEEGAN AKIN, LHP

Born: April 1, 1995. **B-T:** L-L. **Ht.:** 6-0. **Wt.:** 200. **Drafted:** Western Michigan, 2016 (2nd round). **Signed by:** Dan Durst.

Akin pitched Western Michigan to its first NCAA tournament appearance since 1989, making two starts in the Mid-American Conference tournament. A third-team All-American, Akin set the Broncos' single-season strikeout record (133 in 109 innings) en route to becoming the Orioles' second pick in the 2016 draft. He signed for $1.177 million and finished his pro debut with 20 consecutive scoreless innings at short-season Aberdeen, retiring 22 of his last 23 batters. Akin's fastball sat mostly at 92-93 mph after signing but touched 97 with solid control. His 82-85 mph slider is his best secondary pitch, and he attacks lefties with it and back-foots

BA GRADE
50 Risk: High

it to righthanded batters. His changeup lags behind and he seldom threw it in college. Akin shows polish and a clean, repeatable delivery with some deception, and Orioles officials believe he could potentially be the fastest mover from their 2016 draft class. While Akin's stocky body gives some evaluators pause, others see a durable pitcher who in college held velocity deep into games and late into his junior season under a heavy workload. Akin should break camp next April in the rotation at either low Class A Delmarva or high Class A Frederick. If his changeup doesn't come around, he could move quickly as a closer.

Year	Club (League)	Class	W	L	ERA	G	GS	CG	SV	IP	H	HR	BB	SO	K/9	WHIP	AVG
2016	Aberdeen (NYP)	SS	0	1	1.04	9	9	0	0	26	15	0	7	29	10.0	0.85	.161
Minor League Totals			0	1	1.04	9	9	0	0	26	15	0	7	29	10.0	0.85	.161

7 AUSTIN HAYS, OF

Born: July 5, 1995. **B-T:** R-R. **Ht.:** 6-1. **Wt.:** 210. **Drafted:** Jacksonville, 2016 (3rd round). **Signed by:** Arthur McConnehead.

Hays' decorated amateur career included helping Spruce Creek High (just south of Daytona Beach, Fla.) to a state 8A championship as a junior and earning the No. 1 ranking on BA's Florida Collegiate Summer League prospects list in 2014. He was MVP of Seminole (Fla.) State JC's team as a freshman in 2014 before transferring to Jacksonville. After a modest sophomore year, he led the Atlantic Sun Conference with 16 homers in 2016 and ranked in the top 25 in Division I in home runs and slugging (.655). In his pro debut, he led short-season Aberdeen with four homers, all after missing a month with a sprained wrist. Hays has a better overall package of tools than former Florida State outfielder D.J. Stewart, the club's 2015 first-round pick. He has a chance to hit for average and power, showing the ability to hit to all fields. Hays shows above-average bat speed, creates leverage with his righthanded swing and is a high-energy player. Ranked as the No. 14 prospect in the short-season New York-Penn League, Hays hit .336 in his pro debut. His speed plays as above-average, and he played solid defense in right field, where he gets good reads and has a plus arm. Some club officials believe he may fit in center field. Hays impressed the Orioles in instructional league with his play in center, and he could play there in 2017 as he embarks on full-season ball.

BA GRADE
50 Risk: High

Year	Club (League)	Class	AVG	G	AB	R	H	2B	3B	HR	RBI	BB	SO	SB	CS	OBP	SLG
2016	Aberdeen (NYP)	SS	.336	38	140	14	47	9	2	4	21	11	32	4	3	.386	.514
Minor League Totals			.336	38	140	14	47	9	2	4	21	11	32	4	3	.386	.514

8 JOMAR REYES, 3B

Born: Feb. 20, 1997. **B-T:** R-R. **Ht.:** 6-3. **Wt.:** 220. **Signed:** Dominican Republic, 2014. **Signed by:** Fred Ferreira/Calvin Maduro/Enrique Constante.

In January 2014, the Orioles signed the then-16-year-old Reyes for $350,000, the club's largest bonus ever for a Dominican amateur. After a strong full-season debut at low Class A Delmarva in 2015, Reyes looked overmatched at high Class A Frederick in 2016, hitting just .228. Reyes struggled as the youngest player in the Carolina League. His batting mechanics got out of synch and it looked like he hit without a plan at times. During some stretches, his swing looked different every night. Recognizing breaking balls was the key to his struggles with righthanders (.213/.264/.293 against them), but during instructional league, a more focused Reyes made gains with his swing mechanics and began to use his hands better. He continues to show raw power to all fields that should eventually be plus power in games. Reyes' defense at third base was also a struggle at times, and one scout felt he took his offensive woes into the field. Reyes has a plus-plus arm, but his footwork needs improvement. He's a below-average runner. Reyes will stay at third base for now but could wind up at first base or an outfield corner. He likely will head back to Frederick to start 2017. He must show the focus, intensity and toughness to bounce back from a poor season.

BA GRADE
55 Risk: Extreme

Year	Club (League)	Class	AVG	G	AB	R	H	2B	3B	HR	RBI	BB	SO	SB	CS	OBP	SLG
2014	Orioles (GCL)	R	.285	53	186	23	53	10	2	4	29	15	38	1	0	.333	.425
2015	Orioles (GCL)	R	.250	5	16	2	4	2	0	0	4	2	5	1	0	.368	.375
	Delmarva (SAL)	LoA	.278	84	309	36	86	27	4	5	44	18	73	1	0	.334	.440
2016	Frederick (CAR)	HiA	.228	126	464	53	106	16	2	10	51	25	102	3	0	.271	.336
Minor League Totals			.255	268	975	114	249	55	8	19	128	60	218	6	0	.305	.387

9 ANTHONY SANTANDER, OF

Born: Oct. 19, 1994. **B-T:** B-R. **Ht.:** 6-2. **Wt.:** 190. **Signed:** Venezuela, 2011. **Signed by:** Ramon Pena/Antonio Caballero (Indians).

The Indians aggressively promoted Santander early in his career by sending him to the Rookie-level Arizona League for his pro debut in 2012 and low Class A Lake County as an 18-year-old the next season. He handled the assignments well but was then slowed by injuries, including an elbow injury that cost him time in both 2013 and 2014. Santander stayed healthy in 2016 and excelled at the plate at high Class A Lynchburg. He had surgery on his right shoulder after the season, so Cleveland decided to risk leaving him exposed to the Rule 5 draft, where the Orioles selected him with their second pick. Santander stands out for his offensive ability as a physical switch-hitter with feel for the barrel and good bat speed. That translates into above-average power,

BA GRADE
50 Risk: High

and his .494 slugging percentage ranked second among all qualified Indians minor leaguers in 2016. Defensively, Santander has primarily been a left fielder since returning from his elbow injury, and he also saw action at first base in 2016. His fringy speed and arm strength limit his impact defensively, but his bat gives him a chance to profile at a corner. Santander would have advanced to Double-A in the Indians system, so he'll be making a three-level jump to Baltimore as a 22-year-old if he can stick.

Year	Club (League)	Class	AVG	G	AB	R	H	2B	3B	HR	RBI	BB	SO	SB	CS	OBP	SLG
2014	Lake County (MWL)	LoA	.184	43	163	16	30	9	1	1	10	17	49	2	0	.260	.270
2015	Mahoning Valley (NYP)	SS	.419	8	31	6	13	6	0	3	9	4	8	0	0	.486	.903
	Lake County (MWL)	LoA	.278	64	248	46	69	16	0	10	42	18	53	4	2	.337	.464
2016	Lynchburg (CAR)	HiA	.290	128	500	90	145	42	0	20	95	54	118	10	5	.368	.494
Minor League Totals			.271	347	1315	212	357	101	2	43	219	119	308	28	13	.343	.449

10   CHRIS LEE, LHP

Born: Aug. 17, 1992. **B-T:** L-L. **Ht.:** 6-3. **Wt.:** 180. **Drafted:** Santa Fe (Fla.) CC, 2011 (4th round). **Signed by:** Larry Pardo (Astros).

The Orioles acquired Lee from the Astros in May 2015 for two international bonus slots worth $655,800. Lee finished 2015 at Double-A Bowie and joined the 40-man roster after the season. He began 5-0, 2.30 in 2016 but didn't pitch after May 23. He went on the disabled list with a lat strain, but when the Orioles shifted him to the 60-day DL in September, they announced he had a shoulder strain. He was shut down for the fall after a visit to Dr. James Andrews. Lee pitches off an above-average fastball, with a sinking fastball that generates ground balls and sits 89-92 mph but jumps into the mid-90s. His slider flashes plus and gets swings and misses from lefties, who he held to a .155 average. He showed a real feel for his changeup at his best, and his changeup is ahead of his slider in terms of consistency. He would get out of his delivery at times, harming his command. Loss of command also seemed to limit Lee's putaway capability and his strikeout rate plummeted. He needs to add some strength for future durability. Had he not gotten hurt, Lee probably would have been called to the majors at some point. The Orioles expect him to be ready for spring training. If healthy, he could start 2017 at Triple-A Norfolk and find his way to Baltimore during the season. His ceiling is back-end starter.

BA GRADE **50** Risk: High

Year	Club (League)	Class	W	L	ERA	G	GS	CG	SV	IP	H	HR	BB	SO	K/9	WHIP	AVG
2014	Quad Cities (MWL)	LoA	8	6	3.66	28	16	0	0	113	120	7	51	75	6.0	1.51	.275
2015	Quad Cities (MWL)	LoA	3	2	4.11	7	6	0	0	31	36	1	10	24	7.0	1.50	.283
	Frederick (CAR)	HiA	3	6	3.07	14	14	0	0	76	76	1	29	48	5.7	1.38	.266
	Bowie (EL)	AA	4	2	3.08	7	7	0	0	38	32	0	20	26	6.2	1.37	.232
2016	Bowie (EL)	AA	5	0	2.98	8	7	0	0	51	41	4	13	19	3.3	1.05	.222
Minor League Totals			27	25	3.72	93	76	0	0	416	408	21	183	302	6.5	1.42	.259

11   TANNER SCOTT, LHP

BA GRADE **50** Risk: Extreme

Born: July 22, 1994. **B-T:** R-L. **Ht.:** 6-2. **Wt.:** 220. **Drafted:** Howard (Texas) JC, 2014 (6th round). **Signed by:** Thom Dreier.

Scott was one of the top arms in the Texas junior-college ranks in 2014 before the Orioles drafted and signed him for an above-slot $650,000 bonus. Club officials were delighted that he finished his second full season in 2016 at Double-A Bowie. He headed to the Arizona Fall League for the second straight year. Scott has the best fastball in the system and also features a slider. He is the rare lefty who reaches triple digits, which he touched just about every game. The Orioles envision a dominant, late-inning bullpen arm if he can harness his control. Pitching from the stretch, his fastball often sat 95-98 mph, and some scouts saw him touch 102. But Scott can't be effective with a career walk rate of 6.9 per nine innings. He must increase his rate of quality strikes, especially with his slider, which sits between 88-92 mph. He needs to stay behind his slider and not get off to the side to maintain the sharpness and depth. Scott needs work on fielding his position and holding runners. The Orioles hope simplifying Scott's delivery from the stretch will help him repeat his motion and throw more strikes. He could follow the lead of bullpen arms Mychal Givens and Donnie Hart and jump straight from the Eastern League to Baltimore in 2017.

Year	Club (League)	Class	W	L	ERA	G	GS	CG	SV	IP	H	HR	BB	SO	K/9	WHIP	AVG
2014	Orioles (GCL)	R	1	5	6.26	10	8	0	0	23	21	0	20	23	9.0	1.78	.236
2015	Aberdeen (NYP)	SS	4	0	3.38	9	1	0	0	21	16	0	12	31	13.1	1.31	.211
	Delmarva (SAL)	LoA	0	3	4.29	9	2	0	2	21	19	0	10	29	12.4	1.38	.247
2016	Frederick (CAR)	HiA	4	2	4.47	29	0	0	5	48	22	1	42	63	11.7	1.32	.133
	Bowie (EL)	AA	1	2	5.63	14	0	0	0	16	18	0	15	18	10.1	2.06	.305
Minor League Totals			10	12	4.72	71	11	0	7	130	96	1	99	164	11.4	1.50	.206

12 OFELKY PERALTA, RHP

BA GRADE

50 Risk: Extreme

Born: April 20, 1997. **B-T:** R-R. **Ht.:** 6-5. **Wt.:** 195. **Signed:** Dominican Republic, 2013. **Signed by:** Fred Ferreira/Enrique Constante/Calvin Maduro/Joel Bradley.

The Orioles signed Peralta for $325,000 on Sept. 7, 2013 at the recommendation of international director Fred Ferreira, who saw the Dominican righthander throw for the first time that day in a showcase in San Pedro de Macoris. A raw pitcher with a live arm, Peralta spent 2014 in the Dominican Summer League and reached low Class A Delmarva in 2016, where he continued to show mid-90s velocity and a solid changeup. He typically pitches at 92-94 mph but shows a wide fastball velocity range, with readings in the high 80s early in games and 97 mph later. Pitching out of a simple, compact delivery, Peralta sometimes gets under the ball and drops his arm slot, which exacerbates his below-average control. His changeup is his bread-and-butter pitch and he throws it in all counts. Held to mostly five-inning outings in 2016, he gave up just three home runs in 103.1 innings, though he also walked 5.2 per nine innings. Peralta will need to decide whether his slider or curve is his third pitch moving forward. Considered very coachable, he should begin 2017 at high Class A Frederick.

Year	Club (League)	Class	W	L	ERA	G	GS	CG	SV	IP	H	HR	BB	SO	K/9	WHIP	AVG
2014	Orioles (DSL)	R	0	4	3.12	11	11	0	0	43	28	0	37	33	6.9	1.50	.187
2015	Orioles (GCL)	R	0	2	5.61	11	10	0	0	26	20	0	19	31	10.9	1.52	.202
2016	Delmarva (SAL)	LoA	8	5	4.01	23	23	1	0	103	87	3	60	101	8.8	1.42	.230
Minor League Totals			8	11	4.02	45	44	1	0	172	135	3	116	165	8.6	1.46	.215

13 JESUS LIRANZO, RHP

BA GRADE

45 Risk: High

Born: March 7, 1995. **B-T:** R-R. **Ht.:** 6-2. **Wt.:** 175. **Signed:** Dominican Republic, 2012. **Signed by:** Matias Laureano Fortunato (Braves).

Liranzo entered 2016 with only 52 pro innings under his belt but ended the season at Double-A Bowie and claimed a 40-man roster spot. The Braves originally signed him out of the Dominican Republic in May 2012 but released him the next season. The Orioles signed Liranzo in July 2013, but that fall he had a screw inserted in his arm to repair a fracture at the tip of his elbow, so he missed all of 2014. Finally healthy, he made his stateside debut in 2016 and flourished. Liranzo struck out 66 and allowed just 20 hits in 53 innings as he jumped from low Class A Delmarva straight to Double-A in late July. Pitching from a three-quarters arm slot, he showed a fastball-slider combination that overpowered hitters. His fastball sat 94-95 mph and touched 97 with sink and run away from lefthanded batters. He can spot his slider for strikes and mixes in a splitter to neutralize lefty batters, but overall his control remains below-average with 5.1 walks per nine innings in his career. Healthy and live-armed, Liranzo could see time in the Orioles bullpen in 2017 as long as he improves his control.

Year	Club (League)	Class	W	L	ERA	G	GS	CG	SV	IP	H	HR	BB	SO	K/9	WHIP	AVG
2014	Did not play—Injured																
2015	Orioles1 (DSL)	R	3	2	2.35	23	0	0	0	38	28	0	19	46	10.8	1.23	.200
2016	Delmarva (SAL)	LoA	0	0	1.05	16	0	0	0	34	12	0	15	46	12.1	0.79	.109
	Bowie (EL)	AA	1	1	3.38	11	0	0	0	19	8	3	12	20	9.6	1.07	.127
Minor League Totals			4	4	3.00	60	3	0	0	105	65	5	60	127	10.9	1.19	.175

14 MATTHIAS DIETZ, RHP

BA GRADE

50 Risk: Extreme

Born: Sept. 20, 1995. **B-T:** R-R. **Ht.:** 6-5. **Wt.:** 220. **Drafted:** John A. Logan (Ill.) JC, 2016 (2nd round). **Signed by:** Dan Durst.

The top junior-college pitcher available in the 2016 draft, Dietz was the Orioles' second-round pick at No. 69 overall and signed for $1.3 million. Dietz grew and added weight between his freshman and sophomore seasons at John A. Logan JC and became the second-highest drafted player in school history. He is a physical, 6-foot-5 righthander who throws a 92-93 mph fastball that touches 97 to go with a slider, changeup and curveball. A high-energy pitcher, he rushed his delivery early in outings for short-season Aberdeen, leading to eight walks in 10.2 innings to start his pro career. Once he gained composure and tempo, he walked just two in his final eight innings. Dietz's mid- to upper-80s slider ranks as his best secondary pitch right now, followed by his curveball and changeup, which he rarely used in college. One scout said Dietz appears animated on the mound and needs to channel that. Another described him as more raw and reported that he needed to better command both sides of the plate with his fastball. Dietz will try to address those concerns when he begins his first full season in 2017 at low Class A Delmarva.

Year	Club (League)	Class	W	L	ERA	G	GS	CG	SV	IP	H	HR	BB	SO	K/9	WHIP	AVG
2016	Aberdeen (NYP)	SS	0	3	4.82	7	7	0	0	19	22	0	10	8	3.9	1.71	.306
Minor League Totals			0	3	4.82	7	7	0	0	19	22	0	10	8	3.9	1.71	.306

15 BRIAN GONZALEZ, LHP

BA GRADE

45 Risk: High

Born: Oct. 25, 1995. **B-T:** R-L. **Ht.:** 6-3. **Wt.:** 230. **Drafted:** HS—Southwest Ranches, Fla., 2014 (3rd round). **Signed by:** Kelvin Colon.

The Orioles' top pick in the 2014 draft as a third-rounder, Gonzalez starred at Archbishop McCarthy High where he played for the Florida powerhouse that won three consecutive state titles. Gonzalez signed for $700,000, nearly $106,000 over slot, to pass up a Miami commitment. After struggling in his first full pro season, Gonzalez made big gains in 2016 as he repeated the low Class A South Atlantic League at age 20. His ERA dropped from 5.71 to 2.50 and his walk rate improved from 5.0 to 3.5 per nine innings. He improved his fastball command by using a cleaner, smoother delivery he streamlined with Delmarva pitching coach Blaine Beatty. Gonzalez pitched more on line to the plate and sat 90-92 mph and touched 94 while also throwing a plus changeup. His changeup features good arm speed with deception and shows late fade, and he is unafraid to use it in any count. His curveball is his third pitch and became more consistent. Gonzalez did a better job holding runners in 2016, but his fielding needs work. He earns raves for his makeup and some feel he could grow into more velocity. He should start 2017 at high Class A Frederick.

Year	Club (League)	Class	W	L	ERA	G	GS	CG	SV	IP	H	HR	BB	SO	K/9	WHIP	AVG
2014	Orioles (GCL)	R	0	0	0.00	8	8	0	0	25	11	0	8	25	9.1	0.77	.134
	Aberdeen (NYP)	SS	0	1	5.00	2	2	0	0	9	10	0	2	11	11.0	1.33	.286
2015	Delmarva (SAL)	LoA	4	9	5.71	23	23	0	0	106	98	8	59	81	6.9	1.49	.249
2016	Delmarva (SAL)	LoA	10	8	2.50	27	27	0	0	148	135	9	58	111	6.8	1.31	.247
Minor League Totals			14	18	3.54	60	60	0	0	287	254	17	127	228	7.1	1.33	.240

16 DONNIE HART, LHP

BA GRADE

40 Risk: Medium

Born: Sept. 6, 1990. **B-T:** L-L. **Ht.:** 5-11. **Wt.:** 180. **Drafted:** Texas State, 2013 (27th round). **Signed by:** Thom Dreier.

Hart saw 818 players drafted ahead of him before the Orioles selected him in 2013. Despite that low profile, Hart made steady progress through the system and began 2016 at Double-A Bowie, where he made the Eastern League all-star team. Days later he made his major league debut and immediately became a key bullpen lefty for the Orioles in the second half. From a sidearm delivery, Hart works with a high-80s fastball with sink and solid command, and he throws a slider that was at times a swing-and-miss pitch. He spotted in a changeup as well. Hart showed poise and was not afraid, according to Baltimore manager Buck Showalter. For example, lefthanded sluggers Bryce Harper and David Ortiz went 0-for-5 against him. His slider, thrown in the high 70s, held hitters to an .050 average. Hart ultimately gave up just one run in 22 appearances over 18.1 innings for the Orioles, holding lefties to a .132 average. In addition to his major league dominance, he was named the Orioles minor league pitcher of the year. Hart sought extensive knowledge and advice from veterans Zach Britton and Darren O'Day, and he's in position to join them as a bullpen stalwart for the long-term in 2017.

Year	Club (League)	Class	W	L	ERA	G	GS	CG	SV	IP	H	HR	BB	SO	K/9	WHIP	AVG
2014	Delmarva (SAL)	LoA	1	3	3.68	24	0	0	4	29	25	2	11	31	9.5	1.23	.227
2015	Delmarva (SAL)	LoA	1	1	2.12	19	0	0	10	17	14	0	4	17	9.0	1.06	.215
	Frederick (CAR)	HiA	5	1	1.03	27	0	0	3	35	26	0	10	29	7.5	1.03	.208
	Bowie (EL)	AA	0	0	3.86	3	0	0	0	2	4	0	2	0	0.0	2.57	.444
2016	Bowie (EL)	AA	3	1	2.72	40	0	0	4	46	41	1	7	50	9.7	1.04	.236
	Baltimore (AL)	MAJ	0	0	0.49	22	0	0	0	18	12	1	6	12	5.9	0.98	.194
Major League Totals			0	0	0.49	22	0	0	0	18	12	1	6	12	5.9	0.98	.194
Minor League Totals			13	7	2.40	132	0	0	26	154	134	3	41	153	8.9	1.14	.233

17 ANEURY TAVAREZ, OF

BA GRADE

45 Risk: High

Born: April 14, 1992. **B-T:** L-R. **Ht.:** 5-9. **Wt.:** 175. **Signed:** Dominican Republic, 2010. **Signed by:** Manny Nanita (Red Sox).

The Red Sox signed Tavarez when he was 18 years old out of the Dominican Republic in October 2010 as a second baseman, and he struggled early in pro ball, shifting to the outfield in 2012 and not reaching full-season ball until 2013. However, he made a significant jump in 2016, when he hit .335 at Double-A Portland to rank second in the Eastern League batting race. He also ranked third in on-base percentage (.379) and fourth in slugging (.506). The Orioles acquired Tavarez as a Rule 5 pick at the Winter Meetings. He's a plus runner but an inefficient basestealer who needs to improve his jumps, both on the base paths and on defense. He's primarily a left fielder due to his below-average routes and reads in center field. Standing 5-foot-9 and owning modest power, Tavaraz is a fine fit as a non-profile left fielder and could enhance the Orioles' recent Rule 5 draft track record, which includes Ryan Flaherty, T.J. McFarland, Jason Garcia and Joey Rickard, all of whom stuck with the organization for more than a year.

Year	Club (League)	Class	AVG	G	AB	R	H	2B	3B	HR	RBI	BB	SO	SB	CS	OBP	SLG
2014	Salem (CAR)	HiA	.250	93	344	52	86	16	5	11	50	17	97	18	5	.298	.422
2015	Salem (CAR)	HiA	.280	39	132	7	37	8	4	2	18	17	28	8	1	.368	.447
	Portland (EL)	AA	.226	67	234	25	53	13	1	5	14	8	64	4	5	.261	.355
	Pawtucket (IL)	AAA	.389	6	18	6	7	2	0	1	5	3	4	2	0	.522	.667
2016	Pawtucket (IL)	AAA	.200	5	15	0	3	0	0	0	0	1	3	2	0	.250	.200
	Portland (EL)	AA	.335	106	385	59	129	19	13	7	47	29	64	18	11	.379	.506
Minor League Totals			.270	536	1920	234	518	96	36	40	221	115	499	90	43	.320	.420

18 ADAM BRETT WALKER, OF

BA GRADE
50 Risk: Extreme

Born: Oct. 18, 1991. **B-T:** R-R. **Ht.:** 6-5. **Wt.:** 225. **Drafted:** Jacksonville, 2012 (3rd round). **Signed by:** Billy Corrigan (Twins).

The Twins signed Walker for $490,400 as a third-rounder in 2012. He has been remarkably consistent as a professional—for better and worse. Though Walker has hit 25 or more home runs at each stop in full-season ball, he's also consistently been a league leader in strikeouts. In 2015 he became the first Twins minor leaguer (dating back to 1961) to lead the minors in strikeouts. In 2016 he did it again, striking out 38 percent of the time. Walker has some of the best raw power in the minors, but his swing-and-miss issues limit his ceiling. As such, the Twins declined to make him a September callup in 2016 despite his presence on the 40-man roster. That changed in November when the Twins designated him for assignment, and he made his way from the Brewers to the Orioles on the waiver wire. The Twins worked with Walker on his approach—and he's proven coachable and eager to learn—but pitch recognition remains a significant issue. He showed defensive growth in left field in 2016, but he grades as well below-average. Primarily a first baseman in college, Walker projects best as a DH, which is what made him attractive to the Orioles. At 25 and after a full season at Triple-A Rochester, he could see time in the majors in 2017. Walker has big league power, but his sky-high strikeout rate could hinder his ability to tap into it.

Year	Club (League)	Class	AVG	G	AB	R	H	2B	3B	HR	RBI	BB	SO	SB	CS	OBP	SLG
2014	Fort Myers (FSL)	HiA	.246	132	505	78	124	19	1	25	94	44	156	9	5	.307	.436
2015	Chattanooga (SL)	AA	.239	133	502	75	120	31	3	31	106	51	195	13	4	.309	.498
2016	Rochester (IL)	AAA	.243	132	478	61	116	22	5	27	75	44	202	7	4	.305	.479
Minor League Totals			.251	584	2225	341	559	110	20	124	429	189	744	43	13	.310	.486

19 D.J. STEWART, OF

BA GRADE
45 Risk: High

Born: Nov. 30, 1993. **B-T:** L-R. **Ht.:** 6-0. **Wt.:** 230. **Drafted:** Florida State, 2015 (1st round). **Signed by:** Arthur McConnehead.

The Orioles made a bold move in 2016 with Stewart, their first-round pick the year before, when they promoted the 22-year-old left fielder from low Class A Delmarva to high Class A Frederick in late June. Baltimore decision-makers debated the promotion because Stewart hit just .218 at short-season Aberdeen in his 2015 debut and .230 at the time of the promotion, but the move seemed to work for Stewart, who hit .279/.389/.448 in 59 games with Frederick. The Orioles finally saw consistency out of the player who produced a brilliant three-year career at Florida State and signed for $2,064,500. Stewart adjusted his stance and stood more upright at the plate to get out of the pronounced low crouch he employed in college. More tweaking saw him eventually switch from an open to a closed stance, providing a more consistent swing path with the bat in the hitting zone longer. Along with those mechanical fixes, Stewart possesses the bat speed, strength and pitch recognition to be at least average in terms of hitting and power. Big bodied but agile for his size, Stewart has fringe-average speed and arm strength and profiles in left field as long as he hits. He may begin 2017 at Double-A Bowie.

Year	Club (League)	Class	AVG	G	AB	R	H	2B	3B	HR	RBI	BB	SO	SB	CS	OBP	SLG
2015	Aberdeen (NYP)	SS	.218	62	238	25	52	8	2	6	24	23	52	4	1	.288	.345
2016	Delmarva (SAL)	LoA	.230	62	213	27	49	12	1	4	25	42	58	16	6	.366	.352
	Frederick (CAR)	HiA	.279	59	201	41	56	12	2	6	30	36	46	10	3	.389	.448
Minor League Totals			.241	183	652	93	157	32	5	16	79	101	156	30	10	.346	.379

20 JOE GUNKEL, RHP

BA GRADE
40 Risk: Medium

Born: Dec. 30, 1991. **B-T:** R-R. **Ht.:** 6-5. **Wt.:** 225. **Drafted:** West Chester (Pa.), 2013 (18th round). **Signed by:** Chris Calciano (Red Sox).

The Orioles traded Alejando De Aza to the Red Sox in June 2015 to acquire Gunkel, an 18th-round selection in 2013 from Division II West Chester (Pa.). He spent most of 2016 starting at Triple-A Norfolk and seemed close to a callup a few times, but it never came. Gunkel recorded a 3.57 ERA through his first 25 starts before being roughed up in his final three. The control specialist has a career walk rate of 1.6 per nine innings, though his strikeout rate dipped to a below-average 6.4 per nine at Double-A and

Triple-A. A sinker-slider pitcher, Gunkel's fastball ranges from 88-92 mph and he mixes in a changeup. He does a good job working in and out and commanding the bottom of the zone with good movement on his pitches. Intelligent and competitive, Gunkel draws comparisons with fellow Orioles control-oriented starter Tyler Wilson, though Wilson has better stuff. The Orioles added Gunkel to the 40-man roster to shield him from the Rule 5 draft, and he will likely provide depth at Triple-A in 2017.

Year	Club (League)	Class	W	L	ERA	G	GS	CG	SV	IP	H	HR	BB	SO	K/9	WHIP	AVG
2014	Greenville (SAL)	LoA	3	0	2.28	17	5	0	2	51	26	3	11	62	10.9	0.72	.149
	Salem (CAR)	HiA	3	5	4.64	10	10	1	0	52	62	3	13	39	6.7	1.43	.294
2015	Salem (CAR)	HiA	1	1	2.05	8	2	0	2	22	16	2	4	22	9.0	0.91	.203
	Portland (EL)	AA	2	1	3.93	4	3	0	0	18	26	1	8	22	10.8	1.85	.347
	Bowie (EL)	AA	8	4	2.59	17	17	0	0	104	85	7	15	69	6.0	0.96	.222
2016	Bowie (EL)	AA	0	3	3.66	4	4	0	0	20	26	2	3	15	6.9	1.47	.310
	Norfolk (IL)	AAA	8	11	4.08	24	24	1	0	141	156	14	18	94	6.0	1.23	.281
Minor League Totals			28	25	3.30	99	65	2	9	430	405	32	75	356	7.4	1.12	.248

21 PARKER BRIDWELL, RHP

BA GRADE
45 Risk: High

Born: Aug. 2, 1991. **B-T:** R-R. **Ht.:** 6-4. **Wt.:** 185. **Drafted:** HS—Hereford, Texas, 2010 (9th round). **Signed by:** Ernie Jacobs.

Bridwell starred in three sports as a prep, and some college programs looked at him as a quarterback. He was committed to Texas Tech before signing with the Orioles for an over-slot $625,000. Bridwell's raw athleticism didn't translate well initially and he advanced slowly as a pro, not advancing past Class A until his sixth season in 2015. After more than 600 innings in the minors and a broken rib that cost him two months in 2016, the Orioles transitioned Bridwell from the Double-A Bowie rotation to a bullpen role. He took to it and zoomed up the system, making his major league debut with two relief appearances in August. Bridwell throws a solid-average fastball that sits in the low 90s and touches the mid-90s, but commanding it has often been an issue. His changeup is a clear plus pitch he throws with good arm speed and movement, and he rounds out his arsenal with a fringe-average slider and a curveball he added in 2016. Bridwell no longer has the mid-rotation upside he once did, but is still an advanced prospect that should begin 2017 at Triple-A Norfolk with a chance to impact the Baltimore bullpen during the year.

Year	Club (League)	Class	W	L	ERA	G	GS	CG	SV	IP	H	HR	BB	SO	K/9	WHIP	AVG
2014	Frederick (CAR)	HiA	7	10	4.45	26	26	1	0	142	123	11	70	142	9.0	1.36	.234
2015	Bowie (EL)	AA	4	5	3.99	18	18	1	0	97	96	7	38	93	8.6	1.38	.257
2016	Orioles (GCL)	R	2	0	0.00	3	0	0	0	6	3	0	3	7	10.5	1.00	.150
	Aberdeen (NYP)	SS	1	1	5.40	2	0	0	0	5	2	1	0	4	7.2	0.40	.118
	Bowie (EL)	AA	1	1	4.53	18	7	0	1	56	56	7	28	38	6.1	1.51	.258
	Baltimore (AL)	MAJ	0	0	13.50	2	0	0	0	3	5	2	1	3	8.1	1.80	.357
	Norfolk (IL)	AAA	1	0	1.80	4	0	0	0	10	4	1	1	14	12.6	0.50	.121
Major League Totals			0	0	13.50	2	0	0	0	3	5	2	1	3	8.1	1.80	.357
Minor League Totals			31	43	4.71	141	117	3	1	653	630	53	301	589	8.1	1.43	.253

22 JIMMY YACABONIS, RHP

BA GRADE
45 Risk: High

Born: March 21, 1992. **B-T:** R-R. **Ht.:** 6-3. **Wt.:** 205. **Drafted:** St. Joseph's, 2013 (13th round). **Signed by:** Dean Albany.

Yacabonis made big strides with his control and command in 2016, which allowed the righthanded reliever to record a 2.03 ERA, 1.08 WHIP and strikeout rate of 9.3 per nine innings in 34 appearances at Double-A Bowie. After walking 90 in 146 innings his first three pro seasons, he shaved that rate to 2.8 per nine innings in 2016, and his opponent average dropped from .296 to .216. Yacabonis flashed plenty of talent during his career by making all-star teams in the New York-Penn (2013) and South Atlantic Leagues (2014) before leading Carolina League relievers with 9.5 strikeouts per nine in 2015. Improvements to his delivery helped Yacabonis sharpen his control. A calmer delivery led to a quieter front leg, and he more consistently got on top of the ball, allowing his arm to be on time more. His fastball sits at 93-95 mph and touches 97, and at times shows sink and cutter action. He throws a heavy dose of fastballs and has a better feel for his slider over his changeup. A fastball-power slider combo would suit him as a middle reliever in the majors. He should start at Triple-A Norfolk in 2017.

Year	Club (League)	Class	W	L	ERA	G	GS	CG	SV	IP	H	HR	BB	SO	K/9	WHIP	AVG
2014	Delmarva (SAL)	LoA	1	1	1.07	21	0	0	14	25	9	0	15	31	11.0	0.95	.113
	Frederick (CAR)	HiA	0	4	8.58	17	0	0	0	28	34	2	28	23	7.3	2.19	.301
2015	Frederick (CAR)	HiA	3	3	4.02	43	0	0	2	63	74	3	33	66	9.5	1.71	.296
2016	Frederick (CAR)	HiA	0	2	3.98	16	0	0	5	20	17	2	6	21	9.3	1.13	.227
	Bowie (EL)	AA	2	2	2.03	34	0	0	6	44	34	2	14	46	9.3	1.08	.211
Minor League Totals			9	13	3.50	149	0	0	31	211	183	9	110	215	9.2	1.39	.235

23 CHRISTIAN WALKER, OF/1B

Born: March 28, 1991. **B-T:** R-R. **Ht.:** 6-0. **Wt.:** 220. **Drafted:** South Carolina, 2012 (4th round). **Signed by:** Chris Gale.

Walker appeared in three consecutive College World Series finals with South Carolina and contributed to winning efforts in 2010 and 2011 and a runner-up finish in 2012. He broke out as a pro in 2014, when he hit 26 home runs combined at Double-A Bowie and Triple-A Norfolk to earn the organization's minor league player of the year award and a September callup. Walker's career has stalled at Triple-A since his 2014 breakthrough, however. In three seasons with Norfolk, he's hit .260/.324/.429 and received scant big league attention. He recognizes pitches well and possesses good bat speed, and he worked himself into better hitter's counts in 2016, but his above-average power is mitigated by a poor contact rate. A natural first baseman, Walker began playing left field in 2016 despite poor speed and athleticism because the Orioles blocked his path when they re-signed Chris Davis for seven years. Walker worked hard to improve defensively in the outfield and eventually became playable. If the Orioles lose righthanded power hitters Mark Trumbo, Steve Pearce and Nolan Reimold to free agency, the focus will shift to Walker and fellow prospect Trey Mancini at 2017 spring training.

Year	Club (League)	Class	AVG	G	AB	R	H	2B	3B	HR	RBI	BB	SO	SB	CS	OBP	SLG
2014	Bowie (EL)	AA	.301	95	366	58	110	15	2	20	77	38	83	2	1	.367	.516
	Norfolk (IL)	AAA	.259	44	166	15	43	10	0	6	19	18	49	0	0	.335	.428
	Baltimore (AL)	MAJ	.167	6	18	1	3	1	0	1	1	1	9	0	0	.211	.389
2015	Norfolk (IL)	AAA	.257	138	534	68	137	33	1	18	74	49	136	1	3	.324	.423
	Baltimore (AL)	MAJ	.111	7	9	0	1	0	0	0	0	3	4	0	0	.333	.111
2016	Norfolk (IL)	AAA	.264	131	504	64	133	29	2	18	64	40	138	1	3	.321	.437
Major League Totals			.148	13	27	1	4	1	0	1	1	4	13	0	0	.258	.296
Minor League Totals			.276	533	2044	268	564	119	5	75	299	189	487	8	11	.342	.449

24 RANDOLPH GASSAWAY, OF

Born: May 23, 1995. **B-T:** R-R. **Ht.:** 6-4. **Wt.:** 210. **Drafted:** HS—Sandy Springs, Ga., 2013 (16th round). **Signed by:** Arthur McConnehead.

Signed for $100,000 as a 16th-round pick out of high school in 2013, Gassaway's production finally started to match his potential in 2016. He played in short-season leagues exclusively during his first three pro seasons, hitting .246 with just two home runs in 451 at-bats. Gassaway began the 2016 season at extended spring training yet again but broke through once he reached low Class A Delmarva by hitting .330/.372/.511 with seven homers in 50 games. He made gains with hitting coach Milt May, and coaches loved working with him because of his strong work ethic. A physical, 6-foot-4 corner outfielder with good bat speed, Gassaway improved his plate approach in 2016 by learning to take the breaking ball to right-center field. He can hit any fastball, showed power to all fields and became much more consistent in the batter's box. He needs to step up his defense in left field because he runs below-average routes and has a below-average arm. The Orioles are excited to see what Gassaway can do with a full year at high Class A Frederick in 2017.

Year	Club (League)	Class	AVG	G	AB	R	H	2B	3B	HR	RBI	BB	SO	SB	CS	OBP	SLG
2014	Orioles (GCL)	R	.167	13	48	5	8	2	0	1	3	1	13	3	0	.184	.271
	Aberdeen (NYP)	SS	.204	17	54	4	11	1	1	1	9	2	18	1	0	.224	.315
2015	Aberdeen (NYP)	SS	.273	60	227	22	62	14	0	0	22	13	48	0	2	.318	.335
2016	Aberdeen (NYP)	SS	.444	5	18	1	8	4	1	0	4	2	4	0	1	.500	.778
	Delmarva (SAL)	LoA	.330	50	182	21	60	12	0	7	17	13	36	2	0	.372	.511
Minor League Totals			.275	181	651	66	179	41	3	9	63	41	138	9	4	.319	.389

25 ALEX WELLS, LHP

Born: Feb. 27, 1997. **B-T:** R-L. **Ht.:** 6-2. **Wt.:** 175. **Signed:** Australia, 2015. **Signed by:** Brett Ward/Mike Snyder.

Wells didn't even discover baseball until he was nine years old growing up in Australia, but Orioles scout Brett Ward saw Wells in an Australian academy and also at the junior national championships and was intrigued. The Orioles signed him at age 18 for $300,000 in Aug. 2015. His twin brother Lachlan, also a lefthander, pitches in the Twins organization after signing in 2014. Wells made his pro debut at short-season Aberdeen in 2016 as the opening-night starter and delivered. His 2.15 ERA ranked third in the New York-Penn League and his 0.91 WHIP topped the circuit. He shows excellent maturity and composure and an advanced feel for pitching, especially for someone who began playing baseball so late in his youth. Wells pounds the strike zone with a fastball that works from 87 -90 mph, and he is not afraid to pitch inside. He changes speeds well with strong command and mixes in his curveball and a solid changeup. One scout noted Wells still needs to gain baseball experience in game situations and learn to read hitters' bats, understandable given his background. Even with that, Wells is in position to advance to low Class A Delmarva in 2017.

Year	Club (League)	Class	W	L	ERA	G	GS	CG	SV	IP	H	HR	BB	SO	K/9	WHIP	AVG
2016	Aberdeen (NYP)	SS	4	5	2.15	13	13	0	0	63	48	1	9	50	7.2	0.91	.216
Minor League Totals			4	5	2.15	13	13	0	0	63	48	1	9	50	7.2	0.91	.216

26 CEDRIC MULLINS, OF

BA GRADE

45 Risk: High

Born: Oct. 1, 1994. **B-T:** B-L. **Ht.:** 5-8. **Wt.:** 175. **Drafted:** Campbell, 2015 (13th round). **Signed by:** Rich Morales.

Mullins is the sort of player who flies under the radar, both because of his short stature at 5-foot-8 and the fact he he was a 13th-round pick from a small college. Still, Mullins was the highest drafted player out of Campbell since 2002 and notably drew praise from Orioles manager Buck Showalter in March 2016 when he went to see Yovani Gallardo pitch at minor league camp. Mullins filled up the stat sheet at low Class A Delmarva in 2016 with 61 extra-base hits—including 14 home runs—79 runs and 30 steals in 124 games. Mullins uses a mature, professional hitting approach with gap-to-gap power and plus speed. He's a good bunter and worked as the leadoff hitter and center fielder for the Shorebirds. He could continue to show doubles pop with fewer homers as he moves up, one scout said. While he doesn't strike out excessively, Mullins will need to make more contact to profile at the top of the order. He is a solid fielder with an arm grading a tick below average. Mullins will start 2017 at high Class A Frederick with a chance to move up to Double-A Bowie during the year.

Year	Club (League)	Class	AVG	G	AB	R	H	2B	3B	HR	RBI	BB	SO	SB	CS	OBP	SLG
2015	Aberdeen (NYP)	SS	.264	68	277	34	73	15	5	2	32	22	33	17	4	.333	.375
2016	Delmarva (SAL)	LoA	.273	124	517	79	141	37	10	14	55	37	101	30	6	.321	.464
Minor League Totals			.270	192	794	113	214	52	15	16	87	59	134	47	10	.325	.433

27 STEFAN CRICHTON, RHP

BA GRADE

45 Risk: High

Born: Feb. 29, 1992. **B-T:** R-R. **Ht.:** 6-3. **Wt.:** 200. **Drafted:** Texas Christian, 2013 (23rd round). **Signed by:** Ken Guthrie.

Crichton worked mostly as a starter as a Texas Christian sophomore and then mostly out of the bullpen, throwing 41 innings, his junior season in 2013. The Orioles made him a 23rd-round pick and kept him working predominately in relief as a pro. Crichton reached Double-A Bowie in 2016 and then ventured to the Arizona Fall League to audition for a 40-man roster spot. He allowed 10 runs in 13 AFL appearances, so Baltimore elected to leave him exposed to the Rule 5 draft. Crichton has a live, easy arm with a fastball that sits 93-95 mph and touches 97 with some armside run and sink. It's an easy plus pitch out of his strong, powerful frame, but his lack of a consistent secondary pitch has proven problematic. Crichton made progress with his slider in 2016 and commanded it better once he began to really believe in his stuff. Some scouts think he needs a changeup to keep hitters off his fastball. Crichton needs to improve his slider so opponents can't just sit on his fastball. If he does, he could fill a middle-relief role in the big leagues or even become a high-leverage arm.

Year	Club (League)	Class	W	L	ERA	G	GS	CG	SV	IP	H	HR	BB	SO	K/9	WHIP	AVG
2014	Aberdeen (NYP)	SS	2	5	4.47	20	1	0	1	44	56	2	7	40	8.1	1.42	.311
2015	Delmarva (SAL)	LoA	4	4	3.27	28	1	0	4	66	64	1	12	50	6.8	1.15	.251
	Frederick (CAR)	HiA	0	0	4.05	7	0	0	2	13	14	0	1	18	12.2	1.13	.286
2016	Bowie (EL)	AA	2	6	3.79	47	4	0	1	71	73	4	26	59	7.4	1.39	.262
Minor League Totals			11	16	3.59	108	10	0	8	218	220	8	49	188	7.8	1.23	.261

28 ZACH MUCKENHIRN, LHP

BA GRADE

45 Risk: High

Born: Feb. 27, 1995. **B-T:** L-L. **Ht.:** 6-1. **Wt.:** 185. **Drafted:** North Dakota, 2016 (11th round). **Signed by:** Scott Thomas.

The Orioles made Muckenhirn the highest-drafted player ever from North Dakota when they selected the Delano, Minn., native in the 11th round in 2016. Since the baseball program was disbanded after the season, he should hold that distinction for a while. Muckenhirn considered transferring to a Southeastern Conference school for his senior year but signed with Baltimore for $100,000 and joined short-season Aberdeen, where sharp control (three walks in 33 innings) helped him record a 2.43 ERA. He pitched at 90-93 mph with his fastball and complemented it with a slider and changeup that both presently grade fringe-average. His slider at times shows plus potential with nice spin and action, and he mixed pitches well enough to strike out 9.2 per nine innings. The Orioles value Muckenhirn's intelligence and athleticism, and he continued to make improvements during instructional league. He could start or relieve at low Class A Delmarva in 2017.

Year	Club (League)	Class	W	L	ERA	G	GS	CG	SV	IP	H	HR	BB	SO	K/9	WHIP	AVG
2016	Aberdeen (NYP)	SS	5	2	2.43	12	3	0	0	33	38	2	3	34	9.2	1.23	.299
Minor League Totals			5	2	2.43	12	3	0	0	33	38	2	3	34	9.2	1.23	.299

29 JASON GARCIA, RHP

BA GRADE

45 Risk: High

Born: Nov. 21, 1992. **B-T:** R-R. **Ht.:** 6-0. **Wt.:** 185. **Drafted:** HS—Land O'Lakes, Fla., 2010 (17th round). **Signed by:** Anthony Turco (Red Sox).

Garcia made a big impression on the Orioles as a Red Sox prospect in 2014 instructional league when he fanned 14 of 18 Orioles hitters, including Chance Sisco, Christian Walker and Chris Davis with mid- to high-90s heat. The Orioles remembered vividly and selected Garcia in the 2015 Rule 5 draft. They carried him on the major league roster for that entire season, knowing he was a long-term bet who would pitch sparingly and return to the minors afterward. Garcia joined Double-A Bowie's rotation in 2016 and went 6-10, 4.73, with a focus more on developing his pitches for a future bullpen role rather than holding up deep into games. Garcia pitched at 92-93 mph as a starter in 2016 but previously touched 97 as a reliever in the big leagues. Garcia's solid-average mid-80s slider is ahead of his changeup right now, and he is gaining confidence to throw his slider when behind in counts. He throws with a free-and-easy delivery and made strides with his command under the tutelage of Bowie pitching coach Alan Mills. Garcia could open 2017 in the Triple-A Norfolk rotation, with a chance to get back to Baltimore as a reliever during the season.

Year	Club (League)	Class	W	L	ERA	G	GS	CG	SV	IP	H	HR	BB	SO	K/9	WHIP	AVG
2014	Lowell (NYP)	SS	1	1	3.48	5	4	0	0	21	19	0	7	22	9.6	1.26	.238
	Greenville (SAL)	LoA	2	1	3.79	9	3	0	3	36	31	0	17	37	9.3	1.35	.242
2015	Bowie (EL)	AA	1	2	4.20	9	0	0	0	15	12	2	9	14	8.4	1.40	.214
	Baltimore (AL)	MAJ	1	0	4.25	21	0	0	0	30	25	3	17	22	6.7	1.42	.223
2016	Bowie (EL)	AA	6	10	4.73	24	24	1	0	124	137	5	54	71	5.2	1.54	.291
Major League Totals			1	0	4.25	21	0	0	0	30	25	3	17	22	6.7	1.42	.223
Minor League Totals			22	28	4.69	106	75	1	6	432	450	19	212	332	6.9	1.53	.271

30 JAYSON AQUINO, LHP

BA GRADE

45 Risk: High

Born: Nov. 22, 1992. **B-T:** L-L. **Ht.:** 6-1. **Wt.:** 225. **Signed:** Dominican Republic, 2009. **Signed by:** Rolando Fernandez/Jonathan Leyba/Frank Roa (Rockies).

Originally signed by the Rockies out of the Dominican Republic in July 2009, Aquino has been a member of six organizations since spring training 2015. The final transaction occurred when the Orioles purchased him from the Cardinals in April 2016 and assigned him to Double-A Bowie. Aquino throws a fastball, a breaking ball with slurve action and a solid changeup. He pitches at 88-93 mph and sits mostly at 89 with average control. He has a loose delivery and good feel for pitching, and he varies the speed on his fastball and above-average changeup. He relies on his changeup as his swing-and-miss pitch. Aquino often pitches backwards and has a strong groundball rate. He went deep into starts at Bowie and one scout said he had a knack for both reading bats and getting out of jams. He projects as a possible No. 5 starter, and he made his big league debut with the Orioles in 2016, tossing 2.1 scoreless innings. He could push for a larger share of innings in 2017 or possibly 2018 as he serves as depth at Triple-A Norfolk.

Year	Club (League)	Class	W	L	ERA	G	GS	CG	SV	IP	H	HR	BB	SO	K/9	WHIP	AVG
2014	Modesto (CAL)	HiA	5	10	5.40	16	16	1	0	95	113	7	30	74	7.0	1.51	.305
	Tulsa (TL)	AA	0	0	3.00	2	2	0	0	12	9	0	8	9	6.8	1.42	.205
2015	Dunedin (FSL)	HiA	2	2	2.81	5	5	0	0	26	27	2	6	16	5.6	1.29	.270
	Bradenton (FSL)	HiA	2	6	3.78	13	13	0	0	79	77	5	19	50	5.7	1.22	.252
	Lynchburg (CAR)	HiA	1	3	2.45	6	6	0	0	33	31	1	5	20	5.5	1.09	.250
2016	Bowie (EL)	AA	5	10	3.90	20	19	1	0	115	130	7	33	77	6.0	1.41	.286
	Norfolk (IL)	AAA	2	0	2.08	5	0	0	0	13	12	0	3	12	8.3	1.15	.250
	Baltimore (AL)	MAJ	0	0	0.00	3	0	0	0	2	1	0	0	3	11.6	0.43	.125
Major League Totals			0	0	0.00	3	0	0	0	2	1	0	0	3	11.6	0.43	.125
Minor League Totals			39	47	3.08	124	117	9	0	719	653	31	181	580	7.3	1.16	.242

Boston Red Sox

BY ALEX SPEIER

After a pair of last-place finishes in 2014 and 2015, the Red Sox regained their footing by winning the American League East in a season that represented a fascinating passing of the baton.

David Ortiz was brilliant in his final season at age 40, matching the middle-of-the-order production that typified his 14-season tenure in Boston. But after he played his final game, with the Red Sox getting dispatched by the Indians in an AL Division Series sweep, Ortiz expressed satisfaction that he was leaving the organization in good hands thanks to an emerging positional core.

As a 23-year-old, Mookie Betts' game crystallized, taking him from that of a potential star to an actual one, his five-tool performance exceeded perhaps only by Mike Trout in 2016. Betts, 23-year-old shortstop Xander Bogaerts and 26-year-old center fielder Jackie Bradley all were all-star starters in 2016, offering an impression of up-the-middle strength in future seasons. Late in the year, they were joined by 2015 first-round outfielder Andrew Benintendi.

At the 2016 trade deadline, Red Sox president of baseball operations Dave Dombrowski underscored his commitment to that emerging core of young talent by shutting down trade talks with the White Sox when Chicago asked for multiple young Red Sox stars. In the offseason, however, the two teams revisited those conversations, this time with the White Sox focusing solely on prospects.

The result was a December 2016 blockbuster that looked like an organizational pivot. Boston acquired ace lefthander Chris Sale from the White Sox while trading away second baseman Yoan Moncada, the 21-year-old Cuban for whom the Red Sox committed $63 million, along with flame-throwing righthander Michael Kopech, shortstop Mauricio Dubon and reliever Victor Diaz.

An organization that had amassed one of the best few farm systems in the game under former GM Ben Cherington had been leveled in just more than a year by Dombrowski. The deal for Sale followed two notable trades with the Padres. The Red Sox surrendered center fielder Manuel Margot and three others to acquire closer Craig Kimbrel in November 2015 and righthander Anderson Espinoza to acquire Drew Pomeranz in July 2016.

On the one hand, Dombrowski's approach highlights a commitment to Boston's current young core, and the clock is ticking now that the Sale is under contract through 2019. On the other hand, Dombrowski has eroded the system depth that seemed likely to perpetuate future depth.

That's not to say the Red Sox system is barren.

Mookie Betts leads a wave of young Red Sox hitters who will operate post-David Ortiz

TOP PROSPECTS OF THE DECADE

Year	Player, Pos.	2016 Org
2007	Daisuke Matsuzaka, rhp	Japan
2008	Clay Buchholz, rhp	Red Sox
2009	Lars Anderson, 1b	Dodgers
2010	Ryan Westmoreland, of	Did not play
2011	Jose Iglesias, ss	Tigers
2012	Will Middlebrooks, 3b	Brewers
2013	Xander Bogaerts, ss	Red Sox
2014	Xander Bogaerts, ss	Red Sox
2015	Blake Swihart, c	Red Sox
2016	Yoan Moncada, 2b	Red Sox

Rafael Devers is one of the best third-base prospects in the minors. Both first baseman Sam Travis (torn ACL in his knee) and catcher Blake Swihart (ankle injury) are expected to be healthy in 2017 and close to the big leagues. Further down the line, the team was elated to land prep lefthander Jason Groome with the No. 12 overall pick in the 2016 draft. He has the potential to be a front-line starter.

The Red Sox won't need to rush Groome as the club evolves from an elite offensive club (they led the AL in runs by more than 100) to a roster anchored by Sale alongside reigning AL Cy Young Award winner Rick Porcello and past winner David Price.

Unquestionably, Dombrowski has fulfilled the mandate that brought him to Boston: Be bold in the pursuit of championships.

ORGANIZATION OVERVIEW

President: Dave Dombrowski. **GM:** Vacant. **Farm Director:** Ben Crockett. **Scouting Director:** Mike Rikard.

Class	Team	League	W	L	PCT	Finish	Manager
Majors	Boston Red Sox	American	93	69	.574	3rd (15)	John Farrell
Triple-A	Pawtucket Red Sox	International	74	68	.521	5th (14)	Kevin Boles
Double-A	Portland Sea Dogs	Eastern	55	84	.396	11th (12)	Carlos Febles
High Class A	Salem Red Sox	Carolina	87	52	.626	1st (8)	Joe Oliver
Low Class A	Greenville Drive	South Atlantic	70	69	.504	t-8th (14)	Darren Fenster
Short season	Lowell Spinners	New York-Penn	47	29	.618	3rd(14)	Iggy Suarez
Rookie	GCL Red Sox	Gulf Coast	33	28	.541	5th (17)	Tom Kotchman
Overall 2016 Minor League Record			366	330	.526	9th (30)	

THIS YEAR'S TOP 30

No.	Player, Pos.	Grade/Risk
1.	Andrew Benintendi, of	65/Low
2.	Rafael Devers, 3b	60/High
3.	Jason Groome, lhp	65/Extreme
4.	Sam Travis, 1b	50/Medium
5.	Bobby Dalbec, 3b	60/Extreme
6.	Roniel Raudes, rhp	50/High
7.	Brian Johnson, lhp	45/Medium
8.	Marco Hernandez, ss/2b	45/Medium
9.	C.J. Chatham, ss	50/High
10.	Josh Ockimey, 1b	50/High
11.	Michael Chavis, 3b	45/High
12.	Mike Shawaryn, rhp	50/High
13.	Travis Lakins, rhp	50/Extreme
14.	Nick Longhi, 1b/of	45/High
15.	Trey Ball, lhp	45/High
16.	Jake Cosart, rhp	45/High
17.	Robby Scott, lhp	40/Low
18.	Kyle Martin, rhp	40/Medium
19.	Yoan Aybar, of	50/Medium
20.	Gerson Bautista, rhp	50/Extreme
21.	Ben Taylor, rhp	40/Medium
22.	Luis Ysla, lhp	45/High
23.	Chandler Shepherd, rhp	40/Medium
24.	Lorenzo Cedrola, of	45/Extreme
25.	Yeison Coca, ss	50/Extreme
26.	Stephen Nogosek, rhp	45/High
27.	Bryan Mata, rhp	50/Extreme
28.	Jamie Callahan, rhp	45/High
29.	Roldani Baldwin, c/3b	45/High
30.	Darwinzon Hernandez, lhp	45/Extreme

LAST YEAR'S TOP 30

No.	Player, Pos.	Status
1.	Yoan Moncada, 2b	(White Sox)
2.	Rafael Devers, 3b	No. 2
3.	Andrew Benintendi, of	No. 1
4.	Anderson Espinoza, rhp	(Padres)
5.	Michael Kopech, rhp	(White Sox)
6.	Brian Johnson, lhp	No. 7
7.	Sam Travis, 1b	No. 4
8.	Deven Marrero, ss	Dropped out
9.	Luis Alexander Basabe, of	(White Sox)
10.	Michael Chavis, 3b	No. 13
11.	Pat Light, rhp	(Twins)
12.	Marco Hernandez, ss	No. 8
13.	Mauricio Dubon, 2b	(Brewers)
14.	Nick Longhi, 1b/of	No. 15
15.	Wendell Rijo, 2b	(Brewers)
16.	Travis Lakins, rhp	No. 14
17.	Trey Ball, lhp	No. 16
18.	Ty Buttrey, rhp	Dropped out
19.	Williams Jerez, lhp	Dropped out
20.	Teddy Stankiewicz, rhp	Dropped out
21.	Kevin McAvoy, rhp	Dropped out
22.	Yoan Aybar, of	No. 19
23.	Josh Ockimey, 1b	No. 10
24.	Roniel Raudes, rhp	No. 6
25.	Luis Ysla, lhp	No. 22
26.	Noe Ramirez, rhp	Dropped out
27.	Jonathan Aro, rhp	(Mariners)
28.	Sean Coyle, 2b	Free agent
29.	Josh Pennington, rhp	(Brewers)
30.	Garin Cecchini, 1b/3b	Free agent

BEST TOOLS

Best Hitter for Average	Andrew Benintendi
Best Power Hitter	Bobby Dalbec
Best Strike-Zone Discipline	Andrew Benintendi
Fastest Baserunner	Nick Hamilton
Best Athlete	Andrew Benintendi
Best Fastball	Gerson Bautista
Best Curveball	Jason Groome
Best Slider	Stephen Nogosek
Best Changeup	Kyle Martin
Best Control	Roniel Raudes
Best Defensive Catcher	Austin Rei
Best Defensive Infielder	Deven Marrero
Best Infield Arm	Rafael Devers
Best Defensive Outfielder	Andrew Benintendi
Best Outfield Arm	Yoan Aybar

PROJECTED 2020 LINEUP

Catcher	Christian Vazquez
First Base	Bobby Dalbec
Second Base	Dustin Pedroia
Third Base	Rafael Devers
Shortstop	Xander Bogaerts
Left Field	Andrew Benintendi
Center Field	Jackie Bradley
Right Field	Mookie Betts
Designated Hitter	Sam Travis
No. 1 Starter	David Price
No. 2 Starter	Chris Sale
No. 3 Starter	Rick Porcello
No. 4 Starter	Eduardo Rodriguez
No. 5 Starter	Jason Groome
Closer	Craig Kimbrel

MINOR LEAGUE DEPTH CHART

BOSTON RED SOX

TOP 2017 ROOKIE: Andrew Benintendi, of. He seems all but certain to have an Opening Day starting job with a chance to make an impact right away.
BREAKOUT PROSPECT: Yeison Coca, ss. The diminutive Coca showed the defensive chops to stay up the middle and hit enough.
SLEEPER: Joan Martinez, rhp. The 20-year-old slipped through the international cracks, but he overpowered DSL opponents with a mid- to high-90s fastball and swing-and-miss slider in 2016.

SOURCE OF TOP 30 TALENT			
Homegrown	27	Acquired	3
College	11	Trades	2
Junior college	1	Rule 5 draft	0
High school	6	Independent leagues	1
Nondrafted free agents	0	Free agents/waivers	0
International	9		

LF
Andrew Benintendi (1)
Nick Longhi (14)
Bryce Brentz
Tyler Hill
Kyri Washington
Aneury Tavarez

CF
Lorenzo Cedrola (24)

RF
Yoan Aybar (19)
Joseph Monge
Tate Matheny
Trent Kemp

3B
Rafael Devers (2)
Bobby Dalbec (5)
Michael Chavis (11)

SS
C.J. Chatham (9)
Yeison Coca (25)
Deven Marrero
Tzu-Wei Lin

2B
Marco Hernandez (8)
Jagger Rusconi

1B
Sam Travis (4)
Josh Ockimey (10)

C
Roldani Baldwin (29)
Jake Romanski
Austin Rei

LHP

LHSP	LHRP
Jason Groome (3)	Trey Ball (15)
Brian Johnson (7)	Robby Scott (17)
	Luis Ysla (22)
	Darwinzon Hernandez (30)
	Jalen Beeks
	Williams Jerez

RHP

RHSP	RHRP
Roniel Raudes (6)	Jake Cosart (16)
Mike Shawaryn (12)	Kyle Martin (18)
Travis Lakins (13)	Gerson Bautista (20)
Bryan Mata (27)	Ben Taylor (21)
Teddy Stankiewicz	Chandler Shepherd (23)
Victor Garcia	Steve Nogosek (26)
	Jamie Callahan (28)
	Joan Martinez
	Noe Ramirez
	Austin Glorious
	Yankory Pimentel
	Shaun Anderson

DRAFT ANALYSIS

2016

BEST PURE HITTER: Senior sign Ryan Scott (7) batted .435 at Arkansas-Little Rock in the spring, then held his own at short-season Lowell in the summer. Scott has a smooth swing and works up the middle with gap power.

BEST POWER: Bobby Dalbec (4) has plus-plus power potential from the right side, and he tapped into that power consistently during his pro debut after an unspectacular spring. Dalbec repeated his swing better and showed better overall consistency in his pro debut and posted a jaw-dropping .288 isolated slugging percentage in nearly 150 plate appearances for short-season Lowell.

FASTEST RUNNER: Boston didn't draft any true game-changing runners, but Santiago Espinal (10) and Chad Hardy (33) are plus runners and C.J. Chatham (2) is an above-average runner who moves particularly well underway.

BEST DEFENSIVE PLAYER: Chatham was arguably the best defensive shortstop available in the 2016 draft; he has a quick first step and shows above-average range in both directions. Chatham has a plus-plus arm that fits well at shortstop.

BEST ATHLETE: Chatham's combination of body control, speed and arm strength makes him the most natural athlete of the class, but Groome and Anderson are very athletic on the mound, and Dalbec has elite physicality and arm strength.

BEST FASTBALL: Groome's fastball has reached the mid-90s from the left side, and Shaun Anderson (3) has reached 96. Reliever Stephen Nogosek (6) has shown the best velocity thus far, reaching 97 mph in short bursts.

BEST SECONDARY PITCH: Anderson's cutter is borderline unhittable and has more consistency than Groome's signature curveball, which flashes plus or better often.

BEST PRO DEBUT: Dalbec's debut is almost unparalleled in the entire class. He slashed a remarkable .386/.427/.674 and played promising defense at third base.

MOST INTRIGUING BACKGROUND: Nick Lovullo is the son of Red Sox bench coach and former interim manager Torey Lovullo.

CLOSEST TO THE MAJORS: Dalbec's rapid recent progress could allow him to move quickly, but Mike Shawaryn's (5) three solid pitches, strike-throwing ability and poise all point toward a quick rise.

BEST LATE-ROUND PICK: Puerto Rican prep catcher Alberto Schmidt (16) earns high praise for his catch and throw skills, as well as his exceptional work ethic and maturity. Schmidt has the defensive skills and aptitude to profile at the highest level if he's able to make offensive improvements.

THE ONE WHO GOT AWAY: Boston had productive talks with Nick Quintana (11) but was not able to sign his potent bat away from his Arizona commitment.

2015

The Red Sox have picked as high as seventh overall on two occasions since 1993, when they took Trot Nixon. OF Andrew Benintendi (1) already has outstripped Trey Ball (2013). He homered in Boston's AL Division Series loss to the Indians. The rest of the class is off to a slow start.

GRADE: A

2014

The Red Sox have traded RHPs Michael Kopech (1) and Josh Pennington (29), who both have reached at least 99 mph. The holdovers with upside are hitters such as 1B Sam Travis (2), 1B Josh Ockimey (5) and top pick 3B Michael Chavis (1).

GRADE: B

2013

LHP Trey Ball (1) has stayed healthy but his stuff hasn't taken a step forward. 2B Carlos Asuaje (11) reached the majors after being dealt to San Diego. RHP Kyle Martin (9) is Boston's best remaining bet. Unsigned C Matt Thaiss (32) became a 2016 first-round pick.

GRADE: D

TOP DRAFT PICKS OF THE DECADE

Year	Player, Pos.	2016 Org
2007	Nick Hagadone, lhp (1st rd supp.)	Did not play
2008	Casey Kelly, rhp	Braves
2009	Reymond Fuentes, of	Royals
2010	Kolbrin Vitek, 3b	Did not play
2011	Matt Barnes, rhp	Red Sox
2012	Deven Marrero, ss	Red Sox
2013	Trey Ball, lhp	Red Sox
2014	Michael Chavis, ss	Red Sox
2015	Andrew Benintendi, of	Red Sox
2016	Jason Groome, lhp	Red Sox

LARGEST BONUSES IN CLUB HISTORY

Yoan Moncada, 2015	$31,500,000
Jose Iglesias, 2009	$6,250,000
Rusney Castillo, 2014	$5,400,000
Dalier Hinojosa, 2013	$4,000,000
Jason Groome, 2016	$3,650,000

1 ANDREW BENINTENDI, OF

Born: July 6, 1994. **B-T:** L-L. **Ht.:** 5-10. **Wt.:** 170.
Drafted: Arkansas, 2015 (1st round).
Signed by: Chris Mears.

BA GRADE

65 Risk: Low

SCOUTING GRADES

Batting: 70.
Power: 60.
Speed: 55.
Defense: 60.
Arm: 50.

Based on 20-80 scouting scale and future projection rather than present tools.

ROB CUNI

Benintendi was one of the top high school hitters in Ohio history and also drafted by the Reds in the 31st round but opted to head to Arkansas. After a modest freshman season with the Razorbacks, Benintendi passed on playing in summer leagues, instead focusing on improving his strength and conditioning. The result was a spectacular 2015 season that saw him lead the country with 20 home runs on the way to winning BA College Player of the Year and vaulted him to top-of-the-first-round status. The Red Sox selected him seventh overall. Benintendi confirmed the expectation that he could take the fast track to the big leagues by flying through high Class A Salem and Double-A Portland—he batted .312/.378/.532 in 97 games—en route to a callup to Boston at the beginning of August. He missed three weeks with a knee injury but returned in September. He homered in his first postseason plate appearance and put together the best at-bats of any Red Sox hitter in their American League Division Series loss to the Indians.

Multiple evaluators believe that Benintendi has a chance to be a perennial all-star who competes for batting titles. "He's a once-in-a-decade hitter," one said. Benintendi combines excellent hand-eye coordination with the pitch recognition to avoid strike zone expansion. His precisely-tuned swing, with his strong forearms and core along with a rare knack for putting the bat on the ball, allow him to drive the ball with surprising authority given his diminutive stature. Another evaluator thought Benintendi's upside was that of a 20-25 home run player with 50 doubles. More conservative views of his abilities still suggest an everyday player with a plus hit tool, which would make him an ideal No. 2 hitter with modest extra-base abilities but whose lack of weakness will minimize slumps. Though he hit just .179 in 28 at-bats against big league lefthanders, his willingness to use the whole field mitigates long-term platoon concerns. Defensively, Benintendi has the ability to play center field at an above-average level, though with Jackie Bradley in center and Mookie Betts in right in Boston, he appears destined for left where his plus range will be barely taxed playing in front of the Green Monster. Benintendi isn't a burner on the bases, but his baserunning impact exceeds his pure speed, which grades as above-average. In short, evaluators see a player who does everything well while displaying phenomenal makeup that could make him a cornerstone for years to come.

Benintendi seems almost certain to open 2017 in the same role he occupied at the end of 2016: a near-everyday outfielder in the big leagues. Depending on how his game evolves—whether to feature more power or take more walks—it would come as little surprise to see him occupying one of the top three spots in the Red Sox lineup for years to come.

Year	Club (League)	Class	AVG	G	AB	R	H	2B	3B	HR	RBI	BB	SO	SB	CS	OBP	SLG
2015	Lowell (NYP)	SS	.290	35	124	19	36	2	4	7	15	25	15	7	1	.408	.540
	Greenville (SAL)	LoA	.351	19	74	17	26	5	0	4	16	10	9	3	2	.430	.581
2016	Salem (CAR)	HiA	.341	34	135	30	46	13	7	1	32	15	9	8	2	.413	.563
	Portland (EL)	AA	.295	63	237	40	70	18	5	8	44	24	30	8	7	.357	.515
	Boston (AL)	MAJ	.295	34	105	16	31	11	1	2	14	10	25	1	0	.359	.476
Major League Totals			.295	34	105	16	31	11	1	2	14	10	25	1	0	.359	.476
Minor League Totals			.312	151	570	106	178	38	16	20	107	74	63	26	12	.392	.540

2 RAFAEL DEVERS, 3B

Born: Oct. 24, 1996. **B-T:** L-R. **Ht.:** 6-0. **Wt.:** 195. **Signed:** Dominican Republic, 2013. **Signed by:** Manny Nanita/Eddie Romero.

BA GRADE

60 Risk: High

The Red Sox felt that Devers was the best international amateur bat available in 2013, viewing him as a future middle-of-the-order slugger. He hasn't disappointed them yet. Devers started slowly at high Class A Salem in 2016, carrying a .195 average into June, but he was one of the best hitters in the Carolina League over the final three months. Devers shows an unusual ability to drive the ball to all fields with loft and backspin that creates the possibility for all-fields power. He's aggressive in a way that likely will cap his on-base percentage but with bat-to-ball skills that suggest solid batting averages and that, to date, have limited his strikeout totals. As a 19-year-old in 2016, his most significant progress came at third base, where evaluators saw a player with above-average to plus range and throwing arm. His wide hips suggest that his weight management and conditioning will always be a focus, but to this point, he's maintained athleticism not only to stay at third but also to surprise as a solid baserunner. That reflects well on his makeup and willingness to work. At this point, Devers looks like the top power-hitting prospect in the system, a future five- or six-hole hitter with plus power and above-average defense. He appears destined for Double-A Portland for most if not all of 2017.

Year	Club (League)	Class	AVG	G	AB	R	H	2B	3B	HR	RBI	BB	SO	SB	CS	OBP	SLG
2014	Red Sox (DSL)	R	.337	28	104	26	35	6	3	3	21	21	20	4	1	.445	.538
	Red Sox (GCL)	R	.312	42	157	21	49	11	2	4	36	14	30	1	0	.374	.484
2015	Greenville (SAL)	LoA	.288	115	469	71	135	38	1	11	70	24	84	3	2	.329	.443
2016	Salem (CAR)	HiA	.282	128	503	64	142	32	8	11	71	40	94	18	6	.335	.443
Minor League Totals			.293	313	1233	182	361	87	14	29	198	99	228	26	9	.348	.457

3 JASON GROOME, LHP

Born: Aug. 23, 1998. **B-T:** L-L. **Ht.:** 6-6. **Wt.:** 220. **Drafted:** HS—Barnegat, N.J., 2016 (1st round). **Signed by:** Ray Fagnant.

BA GRADE

65 Risk: Extreme

The Red Sox considered Groome the best high school pitching prospect in the 2016 draft. His imposing frame and repeatable delivery, along with an easy low- to mid-90s fastball and nasty breaking ball, screamed future big league impact. Though Groome seemed like a possible No. 1 overall pick, questions related to both his signability and off-field concerns left him on the board for the Red Sox at No. 12 overall. He signed for $3.65 million at the July 15 deadline. Groome shows unusual polish for a prep pitcher, his delivery generating easy power in a fashion that reminds some of Jon Lester or Andy Pettitte. Without ratcheting up his effort level, he comfortably dials his fastball from 91-95 mph with a hammer curveball that seems likely to overwhelm lower-levels competition. He didn't need his changeup as an amateur but shows feel for the offering. Feedback about his makeup in his seven-inning pro debut was also universally positive. Groome should open 2017 at low Class A Greenville, and the quality of his stuff suggests he could cruise through the lower levels if he remains healthy and keeps his delivery in order. He shows all the elements of a potential front-of-the-rotation starter.

Year	Club (League)	Class	W	L	ERA	G	GS	CG	SV	IP	H	HR	BB	SO	K/9	WHIP	AVG
2016	Red Sox (GCL)	R	0	0	2.25	2	2	0	0	4	3	0	0	8	18.0	0.75	.200
	Lowell (NYP)	SS	0	0	3.38	1	1	0	0	3	0	0	4	2	6.8	1.50	.000
Minor League Totals			0	0	2.70	3	3	0	0	7	3	0	4	10	13.5	1.05	.125

4 SAM TRAVIS, 1B

Born: Aug. 27, 1993. **B-T:** R-R. **Ht.:** 6-0. **Wt.:** 205. **Drafted:** Indiana, 2014 (2nd round). **Signed by:** Blair Henry.

BA GRADE

50 Risk: Medium

Travis landed on the map as Kyle Schwarber's middle-of-the-order partner in crime at Indiana, but he appeared close to coming into his own both during a strong 2015 and at the start of 2016, when he garnered attention in spring training for the steady thunderous contact he made. A solid if unspectacular start to the 2016 season, however, was derailed when Travis blew out his ACL on the bases. He required season-ending knee surgery but is expected to be at full strength in 2017. One can imagine Travis—who eschews batting gloves—emerging from the womb with bat in hand. Evaluators describe him as a hitting machine whose strength and flat bat path through the strike zone result in resounding collisions of barrel and ball. That same swing plane has, to date, established him as a middle-of-the-field hitter who mostly drives the ball into the gaps, but if he can learn to turn on pitches that are middle-in, he has a chance to develop at least average power. His actions at first base remain inconsistent and sometimes clunky, though his tenacious work ethic convinces some evaluators that he can become average at the position. Despite the lost development time Travis suffered in 2016, his bat is close to big league ready. It wouldn't be a shock to see him contribute at first base and DH in the post-David Ortiz era, or potentially in left field, depending on the rest of the depth chart.

Year	Club (League)	Class	AVG	G	AB	R	H	2B	3B	HR	RBI	BB	SO	SB	CS	OBP	SLG
2014	Lowell (NYP)	SS	.333	40	165	28	55	5	1	4	30	4	18	5	1	.364	.448
	Greenville (SAL)	LoA	.290	27	107	12	31	11	1	3	14	7	14	0	1	.330	.495
2015	Salem (CAR)	HiA	.313	66	246	35	77	15	4	5	40	26	43	10	6	.378	.467
	Portland (EL)	AA	.300	65	243	35	73	17	2	4	38	33	34	9	6	.384	.436
2016	Pawtucket (IL)	AAA	.272	47	173	26	47	10	0	6	29	15	40	1	0	.332	.434
Minor League Totals			.303	245	934	136	283	58	8	22	151	85	149	25	14	.364	.453

5 BOBBY DALBEC, 3B

Born: June 29, 1995. **B-T:** R-R. **Ht.:** 6-4. **Wt.:** 225. **Drafted:** Arizona, 2016 (4th round). **Signed by:** Vaughn Williams.

When Dalbec dominated on the mound at the 2016 College World Series, it led to plenty of questions about why the Red Sox intended to develop him as a third baseman. Once he reported to short-season Lowell, those questions faded, both because the 21-year-old made clear that he wanted to be a full-time position player and because he showed an enormous offensive ceiling, as he had in the 2015 Cape Cod League, when he slugged 12 homers in 27 games. After a junior year in which Dalbec's approach proved inconsistent with varying stances, loads and strides that made it difficult for him to repeat his swing, he relaxed and smoothed out his mechanics in short-season Lowell with dazzling results. The pull-happy approach he showed this year in college was replaced by an up-the-middle emphasis in which Dalbec showed a vastly improved ability to make contact and to drive the ball with prodigious power to all fields. He slugged .674 in the New York-Penn League thanks to impressive bat speed and a power hitter's extension through the ball. He certainly has the arm for third base, with the actions to suggest he can continue to develop at that position. Dalbec's spring will determine whether he opens 2017 at low Class A Greenville or high Class A Salem.

BA GRADE

60 Risk: Extreme

Year	Club (League)	Class	AVG	G	AB	R	H	2B	3B	HR	RBI	BB	SO	SB	CS	OBP	SLG
2016	Lowell (NYP)	SS	.386	34	132	25	51	13	2	7	33	9	33	2	2	.427	.674
Minor League Totals			.386	34	132	25	51	13	2	7	33	9	33	2	2	.427	.674

6 RONIEL RAUDES, RHP

Born: Jan. 16, 1998. **B-T:** R-R. **Ht.:** 6-1. **Wt.:** 160. **Signed:** Nicaragua, 2014. **Signed by:** Eddie Romero/Rafael Mendoza.

When international scouting director Eddie Romero saw Raudes pitch in a tournament in Mexico in 2012, he couldn't help but be mesmerized by a 14-year-old who, despite throwing 78-80 mph, conducted himself like a big leaguer by mixing three pitches and displaying dogged competitiveness. Raudes continues to display fearless strike-throwing ability that has allowed him to hold his own against older competition. Raudes is built like a bird, with long, thin limbs that limit the power of his stuff. He controls and sequences his fastball, curveball and changeup well, however. At 18, none of his pitches grades as plus, but he shows the ability to spin the ball with a quick, whippy arm in a way that has some believing his fastball velocity can tick up from its current 88-91 mph range to be more of a low-90s offering. His fastball is relatively straight right now, but Raudes creates deception with a repeatable delivery, and his ability to command the ball allows him stuff to play up. He limits hard contact against him based on his unpredictably delivery. Raudes will likely be one of the youngest pitchers in the high Class A Carolina League in 2017. Assuming he remains healthy, his control and pitchability suggest the floor of an up-and-down depth starter with a likely ceiling as a No. 4 barring an unexpected jump in his velocity.

BA GRADE

50 Risk: Medium

Year	Club (League)	Class	W	L	ERA	G	GS	CG	SV	IP	H	HR	BB	SO	K/9	WHIP	AVG
2015	Red Sox (DSL)	R	4	3	3.52	11	10	0	0	54	46	3	3	63	10.6	0.91	.228
	Red Sox (GCL)	R	3	0	0.90	4	4	0	0	20	13	0	6	16	7.2	0.95	.191
2016	Greenville (SAL)	LoA	11	6	3.65	24	24	0	0	113	112	8	23	104	8.3	1.19	.260
Minor League Totals			18	9	3.32	39	38	0	0	187	171	11	32	183	8.8	1.09	.244

7 BRIAN JOHNSON, LHP

Born: Dec. 7, 1990. **B-T:** L-L. **Ht.:** 6-3. **Wt.:** 240. **Drafted:** Florida, 2012 (1st round). **Signed by:** Anthony Turco.

The 31st overall pick in the 2012 draft, Johnson reached the majors in 2015 but has had his progression interrupted by multiple ill-timed occurrences. He took a line drive to the face in his 2012 pro debut and then suffered elbow nerve irritation that ended his 2015 season. Johnson struggled early in 2016 with his normally advanced command—22 walks in 33 innings—suggesting more trouble with his elbow. But the lefthander's concerns ran deeper than his mound struggles. Johnson left Triple-A Pawtucket in May to seek treatment for anxiety. After nearly two months in Fort Myers, Fla., and on a rehab assignment, he returned to Triple-A. His control and ability to mix four pitches—fastball, curveball, changeup and cutter—returned, though his stuff was diminished from his dominant 2014 form. His fastball sat in the mid-80s in 2016 rather than his 89-91 mph peak, and his curveball—once a plus pitch—lost bite. Still, the fact Johnson was back on the mound and throwing strikes represented an accomplishment. If his arm strength returns in 2017, he could quickly emerge as a big league depth option.

BA GRADE
45 Risk: Medium

Year	Club (League)	Class	W	L	ERA	G	GS	CG	SV	IP	H	HR	BB	SO	K/9	WHIP	AVG
2014	Salem (CAR)	HiA	3	1	3.86	5	5	0	0	26	23	0	7	33	11.6	1.17	.230
	Portland (EL)	AA	10	2	1.75	20	20	2	0	118	78	6	32	99	7.6	0.93	.189
2015	Boston (AL)	MAJ	0	1	8.31	1	1	0	0	4	3	0	4	3	6.2	1.62	.214
	Pawtucket (IL)	AAA	9	6	2.53	18	18	1	0	96	74	6	32	90	8.4	1.10	.211
2016	Red Sox (GCL)	R	0	1	3.86	2	2	0	0	7	7	0	2	9	11.6	1.29	.259
	Lowell (NYP)	SS	0	0	0.00	2	2	0	0	11	7	0	2	11	9.0	0.82	.184
	Pawtucket (IL)	AAA	5	6	4.09	15	15	0	0	77	74	9	36	54	6.3	1.43	.258
Major League Totals			0	1	8.31	1	1	0	0	4	3	0	4	3	6.2	1.62	.214
Minor League Totals			29	22	2.60	85	85	3	0	425	325	25	147	384	8.1	1.11	.211

8 MARCO HERNANDEZ, SS/2B

Born: Sept. 6, 1992. **B-T:** L-R. **Ht.:** 6-0. **Wt.:** 170. **Signed:** Dominican Republic, 2009. **Signed by:** Jose Serra/Jose Estevez (Cubs).

Hernandez, a former switch-hitter who now bats solely from the left side, continued his ascent in the Red Sox system in 2016. He hit .309 at Triple-A Pawtucket with a .787 OPS that ranked third among International League shortstops and then hit .294/.357/.373 in 40 big league games and made the postseason roster. At Pawtucket, Hernandez hit lefties well (.328) for the first time in his career, but his primary strength is his ability to play shortstop, second base and third base adequately while delivering offensive impact against righthanders. Though his aggressiveness will cap his on-base ability, he shows the potential to hit for solid averages with gap power and speed that is a tick above-average. Hernandez's skill set best fits as a valuable utility infielder, though he could serve as a platoon second baseman.

BA GRADE
45 Risk: Medium

Year	Club (League)	Class	AVG	G	AB	R	H	2B	3B	HR	RBI	BB	SO	SB	CS	OBP	SLG
2014	Daytona (FSL)	HiA	.270	122	441	61	119	13	7	3	55	30	90	22	8	.315	.351
2015	Portland (EL)	AA	.326	68	282	30	92	21	4	5	31	9	49	4	2	.349	.482
	Pawtucket (IL)	AAA	.271	46	181	27	49	9	2	4	22	8	39	1	0	.300	.409
2016	Pawtucket (IL)	AAA	.309	57	223	26	69	7	4	5	29	12	51	4	2	.343	.444
	Boston (AL)	MAJ	.294	40	51	11	15	1	0	1	5	5	10	1	0	.357	.373
Major League Totals			.294	40	51	11	15	1	0	1	5	5	10	1	0	.357	.373
Minor League Totals			.283	634	2435	316	688	118	33	31	284	131	433	93	42	.320	.396

9 C.J. CHATHAM, SS

Born: Dec. 22, 1994. **B-T:** R-R. **Ht.:** 6-4. **Wt.:** 185. **Drafted:** Florida Atlantic, 2016 (2nd round). **Signed by:** Willie Romay.

Many scouts viewed Chatham as a pitching prospect when he played high school ball in Plantation, Fla., but he believed he could play shortstop if he could find a willing college program. He found one in Florida Atlantic. Chatham flourished at FAU, particularly in a junior season in which he hit .357 with eight homers, while showing the glove to convince the Red Sox he could stick at the position. That made him one of the top college shortstop prospects in the 2016 draft, and Boston selected him at the head of that demographic, taking him in the second round, No. 51 overall, and signing him for $1.1 million. Chatham showed rust in his pro debut

BA GRADE
50 Risk: High

at short-season Lowell after he returned from a broken thumb he suffered at the end of the college season, but still he hit .259 with power and above-average contact ability. A merely average runner, he possesses the instincts and body length to show above-average to plus defensive potential at shortstop. While he didn't walk as much in his pro debut as he did in college, Chatham has everyday shortstop potential even with average to below-average hitting potential and fringe power because he plays strong defense at the position. He will likely make the jump to low Class A Greenville in 2017 for his first full season, with the potential to move quickly if there are no lasting effects from his thumb injury.

Year	Club (League)	Class	AVG	G	AB	R	H	2B	3B	HR	RBI	BB	SO	SB	CS	OBP	SLG
2016	Red Sox (GCL)	R	.167	8	24	2	4	2	0	1	2	0	7	0	0	.200	.375
	Lowell (NYP)	SS	.259	27	108	19	28	4	1	4	19	8	20	0	1	.319	.426
Minor League Totals			.242	35	132	21	32	6	1	5	21	8	27	0	1	.299	.417

10 JOSH OCKIMEY, 1B

Born: Oct. 18, 1995. **B-T:** L-L. **Ht.:** 6-1. **Wt.:** 215. **Drafted:** HS—Philadelphia, 2014 (5th round). **Signed by:** Chris Calciano.

The Red Sox were the primary team on Ockimey as he rose late in the 2014 draft process, ultimately taking him in the fifth round and signing him for a $450,000 bonus to pass up an Arkansas commitment. Ockimey appeared to be the organization's breakout player during the first half of 2016, when the powerful first baseman made improvements to his offensive approach to unlock his plus raw power at low Class A Greenville. He hit .297/.435/.531 en route to South Atlantic League all-star recognition, but he faded badly down the stretch, hitting .152 in the second half. Still, Ockimey managed to

BA GRADE

50 Risk: High

rank second among SAL first basemen with 18 home runs and first by a mile with 88 walks. He made plenty of progress compared with 2015 by improving his walk rate from 11 percent to 18 percent and dropping his strikeout rate from 34 percent to 26 percent. At his best, Ockimey displays at least plus power to all fields, though he lost that approach and became pull-heavy down the stretch in a way that resulted in an uptick of whiffs. He will need to make considerable strides against lefties after hitting .192 in 2016 if he is to profile as more than a platoon option. Ockimey has the upside of a middle-of-the-order hitter who is average defensively at first base, and he has shown a strong work ethic and the aptitude to make considerable strides.

Year	Club (League)	Class	AVG	G	AB	R	H	2B	3B	HR	RBI	BB	SO	SB	CS	OBP	SLG
2014	Red Sox (GCL)	R	.188	36	112	17	21	3	1	0	10	14	37	1	0	.292	.232
2015	Lowell (NYP)	SS	.266	56	199	30	53	13	3	4	38	25	78	2	2	.349	.422
2016	Greenville (SAL)	LoA	.226	117	407	60	92	25	1	18	62	88	129	3	1	.367	.425
Minor League Totals			.231	209	718	107	166	41	5	22	110	127	244	6	3	.351	.394

11 MICHAEL CHAVIS, 3B

BA GRADE

45 Risk: High

Born: Aug. 11, 1995. **B-T:** R-R. **Ht.:** 5-10. **Wt.:** 190. **Drafted:** HS—Marietta, Ga., 2014 (1st round). **Signed by:** Brian Moehler.

The Red Sox challenged 2014 first-rounder Chavis with an assignment to low Class A Greenville in 2015. He hit for power but little else, so Boston had him repeat the South Atlantic League in 2016. Initially, the results suggested the possibility of a breakthrough. Chavis showed an ability to stay back on pitches and drive them to all fields with plus power, hitting .356/.415/.576 in his first 15 games of April. However, that early progress stalled when he sprained a thumb ligament that sidelined him for the next two months. When Chavis returned, he was unable to sustain the same approach that had proven so effective early, and he regressed to the pull-heavy, all-or-nothing form he showed in 2015 en route to a .237/.313/.372 season between Greenville and a season-ending seven-game cameo at high Class A Salem. Though his short, compact frame is atypical for third base, Chavis continued to make steady defensive strides to the point where some evaluators can now project him as a potentially average defender with an arm that may grade as a tick above-average, though some wonder if he faces a move to left field. He is likely to return to Salem to start 2017.

Year	Club (League)	Class	AVG	G	AB	R	H	2B	3B	HR	RBI	BB	SO	SB	CS	OBP	SLG
2014	Red Sox (GCL)	R	.269	39	134	21	36	12	3	1	16	15	38	5	3	.347	.425
2015	Greenville (SAL)	LoA	.223	109	435	56	97	29	1	16	58	29	144	8	5	.277	.405
2016	Greenville (SAL)	LoA	.244	74	279	30	68	11	3	8	35	22	74	3	1	.321	.391
	Salem (CAR)	HiA	.160	7	25	5	4	0	0	0	1	2	7	1	0	.222	.160
Minor League Totals			.235	229	873	112	205	52	7	25	110	68	263	17	9	.301	.396

12 MIKE SHAWARYN, RHP

BA GRADE

50 Risk: High

Born: Sept. 17, 1994. **B-T:** R-R. **Ht.:** 6-2. **Wt.:** 200. **Drafted:** Maryland, 2016 (5th round). **Signed by:** Chris Calciano.

Shawaryn entered 2016 as one of the most consistent college performers in the country. He truly shined as a Maryland sophomore by going 13-2, 1.71 with 10.7 strikeouts per nine innings, but the righthander stumbled early in an underwhelming junior year in 2016 and went just 6-4, 3.18 with 8.8 strikeouts per nine. Thus, his draft stock took a hit. The Red Sox saw an unexpected opportunity and selected Shawaryn in the fifth round, signing him for $637,500. They see a potential big league starter with a fastball that sits 92-93 mph and can bump 95 with a curveball—which ticked down from a sharp, true curve in 2015 to a slurve in 2016—and changeup that are roughly average. Shawaryn has untapped potential if his pitch-to-contact emphasis as a junior gives way to a more aggressive arsenal capable of generating swings and misses. With deception creating the possibility that his average arsenal can play up beyond that, Shawaryn looks like a pitcher capable of becoming a possible No. 4 starter. His early college pedigree suggests an advanced pitcher with a chance to move relatively quickly through the Red Sox system.

Year	Club (League)	Class	W	L	ERA	G	GS	CG	SV	IP	H	HR	BB	SO	K/9	WHIP	AVG
2016	Lowell (NYP)	SS	0	1	2.87	6	6	0	0	16	15	0	7	22	12.6	1.40	.254
Minor League Totals			0	1	2.87	6	6	0	0	16	15	0	7	22	12.6	1.40	.254

13 TRAVIS LAKINS, RHP

BA GRADE

50 Risk: Extreme

Born: June 29, 1994. **B-T:** R-R. **Ht.:** 6-1. **Wt.:** 180. **Drafted:** Ohio State, 2015 (6th round). **Signed by:** John Pyle.

Lakins represented something of an unmolded ball of clay when the Red Sox took him out of Ohio State as a draft-eligible sophomore in 2015 and signed him for $320,000. He had been a pitcher who shuttled between the rotation and bullpen while receiving little guidance about how to channel his excellent athleticism and four-pitch mix into consistent results. Lakins showed enough in his pro debut and during spring training to convince the Red Sox to push him to high Class A Salem in 2016, and the initial returns were impressive. He recorded a 2.13 ERA with more than a strikeout per inning in April. However, he proved inconsistent over the next three months with an ERA north of 7.00 before the Red Sox shut him down at the end of July with a stress fracture in the tip of his elbow. The injury may have contributed to his struggles, but his elbow healed enough for him to follow a relatively normal offseason program. At his best, Lakins showed a low- to mid-90s fastball that he mixed with a true 12-to-6 curveball and feel for a potentially average changeup. He paired that repertoire with the athleticism to repeat his delivery, which could lead to average command and a ceiling as a mid-rotation starter. Regardless, his fastball-curveball combination gives him a floor of depth starter or middle reliever.

Year	Club (League)	Class	W	L	ERA	G	GS	CG	SV	IP	H	HR	BB	SO	K/9	WHIP	AVG
2015	Lowell (NYP)	SS	0	0	0.00	1	1	0	0	2	0	0	1	3	13.5	0.50	.000
2016	Salem (CAR)	HiA	6	3	5.93	19	18	0	0	91	111	8	36	79	7.8	1.62	.299
Minor League Totals			6	3	5.81	20	19	0	0	93	111	8	37	82	7.9	1.59	.294

14 NICK LONGHI, 1B/OF

BA GRADE

45 Risk: High

Born: Aug. 16, 1995. **B-T:** R-L. **Ht.:** 6-2. **Wt.:** 205. **Drafted:** HS—Venice, Fla., 2013 (30th round). **Signed by:** Willie Romay.

Longhi surprisingly signed as a 30th-round pick for $440,000 in lieu of attending LSU out of high school and has worked his way into becoming one of the best pure hitters in the Red Sox system. He has an accurate barrel and flat bat plane that allow him to hit line drives to all fields, and those traits make him a doubles machine. One of 11 minor leaguers to hit 40 doubles in 2016, Longhi nonetheless slugged just .393 as a primary first baseman at high Class A Salem. As a lefthanded thrower, he is limited to first base or the outfield, positions that require more thump than he has demonstrated as a pro with his five home runs per 650 plate appearances. Those power questions remain relevant after he hit just two homers in 2016. Some believe he will figure out how to loft the ball as he develops, while others are a bit more skeptical, seeing him as a complementary righthanded-hitting reserve. An answer may start to form in the second half of 2017, when warmer weather at Double-A Portland creates favorable conditions for hitters to drive the ball out of the park.

Year	Club (League)	Class	AVG	G	AB	R	H	2B	3B	HR	RBI	BB	SO	SB	CS	OBP	SLG
2014	Lowell (NYP)	SS	.330	30	109	19	36	10	1	0	10	11	22	0	3	.388	.440
2015	Greenville (SAL)	LoA	.281	115	442	52	124	27	3	7	62	34	88	2	0	.338	.403
2016	Salem (CAR)	HiA	.282	124	471	56	133	40	3	2	77	50	106	2	3	.349	.393
Minor League Totals			.282	285	1067	131	301	82	7	10	153	98	228	5	6	.344	.400

15 TREY BALL, LHP

BA GRADE

45 Risk: High

Born: June 27, 1994. **B-T:** L-L. **Ht.:** 6-6. **Wt.:** 175. **Drafted:** HS—New Castle, Ind., 2013 (1st round). **Signed by:** John Pyle.

Armed with their highest draft pick in 20 years, the Red Sox in 2013 selected Ball with the No. 7 overall pick and signed him for $2.75 million. The team saw a lefthander with tremendous athleticism and arm speed along with a repeatable delivery who already had shown the ability to work into the mid-90s with the potential for a plus curveball and changeup. While that profile suggested an enormous ceiling, Ball's stuff has backed up in pro ball and the former Indiana prep has yet to reach Double-A in four seasons. Despite a strong work ethic and some strength gains, his velocity has slipped to the low 90s, and while he showed the potential to get swings and misses with his slider early in 2016, he didn't sustain that trend. Moreover, hitters appear to track his pitches well, resulting in little separation from his strikeout and walk rates. While he has poor present control, Ball retains an athletic, repeatable delivery, and he can spin the ball enough to keep alive the hope of developing into a back-end starter or reliever. The Red Sox had Ball work as a reliever in the Arizona Fall League, where he allowed 23 baserunners and nine runs in 13 innings.

Year	Club (League)	Class	W	L	ERA	G	GS	CG	SV	IP	H	HR	BB	SO	K/9	WHIP	AVG
2014	Greenville (SAL)	LoA	5	10	4.68	22	22	0	0	100	111	9	39	68	6.1	1.50	.280
2015	Salem (CAR)	HiA	9	13	4.73	25	25	0	0	129	129	16	60	77	5.4	1.46	.263
2016	Salem (CAR)	HiA	8	6	3.84	23	23	0	0	117	121	8	68	86	6.6	1.61	.271
Minor League Totals			22	30	4.45	75	75	0	0	354	371	34	173	236	6.0	1.54	.273

16 JAKE COSART, RHP

BA GRADE

45 Risk: High

Born: Feb. 11, 1994. **B-T:** R-R. **Ht.:** 6-2. **Wt.:** 175. **Drafted:** Seminole State (Fla.) JC, 2014 (3rd round). **Signed by:** Tom Kotchman.

After Cosart struggled to a 5.45 ERA in nine starts at short-season Lowell in 2015, the Red Sox made the decision not to wait on his probable move to the bullpen. As a reliever, he didn't need to hold anything back, and he showed one of the quickest arms in the system while regularly showing 94-99 mph fastballs mixed with an inconsistent curve that flashed plus but was sometimes was thrown too slowly to be effective. He also has been working to add a splitter. Chiefly on the strength of his fastball, Cosart dominated at low Class A Greenville and high Class A Salem in 2016, where he posted a combined 1.78 ERA with 13.2 strikeouts per nine innings. There were times when Cosart made opponents look bad, but in other instances, his rotational, max-effort delivery created struggles with his release point and resulted in the same control problems that plagued him as a starter. His walk rate of 4.6 per nine innings underscores that. On the right day, Cosart has the weapons to out-stuff batters at lower levels, though his mechanics may make it hard to achieve consistent effectiveness. He needs to improve his control and secondary stuff to emerge as a big league option.

Year	Club (League)	Class	W	L	ERA	G	GS	CG	SV	IP	H	HR	BB	SO	K/9	WHIP	AVG
2014	Red Sox (GCL)	R	0	1	2.25	7	7	0	0	16	7	0	11	16	9.0	1.13	.132
2015	Lowell (NYP)	SS	2	2	5.45	9	9	0	0	33	26	3	20	27	7.4	1.39	.215
2016	Greenville (SAL)	LoA	4	1	2.05	29	0	0	2	53	36	2	25	76	13.0	1.16	.193
	Salem (CAR)	HiA	0	0	1.00	8	0	0	0	18	7	0	11	28	14.0	1.00	.111
Minor League Totals			6	4	2.86	53	16	0	2	120	76	5	67	147	11.1	1.19	.179

17 ROBBY SCOTT, LHP

BA GRADE

40 Risk: Low

Born: Aug. 29, 1989. **B-T:** B-L. **Ht.:** 6-3. **Wt.:** 220. **Signed:** Yuma (North American League), 2011. **Signed by:** Jared Porter.

Scott barely pitched in two years at Florida State, so he not surprisingly went undrafted after his senior year in 2011. But he was determined to pursue a pro career, so he ended up pitching for Jose Canseco's team in the independent (and now defunct) North American League. After six relief appearances, Scott showed enough to convince Red Sox scout Al Nipper to sign him after the first inning of his first pro start. Scott thus began the long, deliberate journey up the ladder. The ascent culminated more than five years later with seven scoreless appearances in September 2016. Scott throws strikes using two deliveries—a relatively conventional, over-the-top approach from which he mixes three pitches (85-88 mph fastball, curveball, changeup) against righties and a sidearm delivery from which he uses just fastballs and sliders against lefties. Same-side batters have a difficult time tracking him, creating a clear path to a big league role as a matchup reliever. Scott held Triple-A lefties to a .147 average with 30 percent strikeouts in 2016, and big league lefties looked only marginally better. While he lacks electrifying stuff or a glamorous projected role, he's shown he can be a valuable long-term bullpen piece.

Year	Club (League)	Class	W	L	ERA	G	GS	CG	SV	IP	H	HR	BB	SO	K/9	WHIP	AVG
2014	Portland (EL)	AA	8	2	1.96	35	1	0	3	60	55	3	15	51	7.7	1.17	.249
2015	Portland (EL)	AA	1	1	2.06	25	2	0	0	44	32	3	13	41	8.5	1.03	.198
	Pawtucket (IL)	AAA	1	1	7.67	13	1	0	1	32	47	5	9	27	7.7	1.77	.341
2016	Pawtucket (IL)	AAA	4	3	2.54	32	6	0	0	78	57	9	14	73	8.4	0.91	.202
	Boston (AL)	MAJ	1	0	0.00	7	0	0	0	6	6	0	2	5	7.5	1.33	.273
Major League Totals			1	0	0.00	7	0	0	0	6	6	0	2	5	7.5	1.33	.273
Minor League Totals			19	12	2.75	156	10	0	9	314	261	28	88	275	7.9	1.11	.226

18 KYLE MARTIN, RHP

BA GRADE

40 Risk: Medium

Born: Jan. 18, 1991. **B-T:** R-R. **Ht.:** 6-7. **Wt.:** 230. **Drafted:** Texas A&M, 2013 (9th round). **Signed by:** Jon Adkins.

Martin, a towering, 6-foot-7 righthander, threw sidearm for a time in college, but his return to an over-the-top delivery as a senior clicked in a way that made him an attractive draft candidate as a senior. The Red Sox made him a ninth-round pick because they liked how he could leverage his fastball down in the zone and use his changeup to get chases off of his heater. That view has largely held in a level-by-level progression in the Red Sox system, and it culminated in a strong showing at Triple-A Pawtucket in 2016 in which Martin forged a 3.38 ERA, including a 2.29 mark in his final 35 innings. While he throws his low- to mid-90s fastball for strikes, his lack of precise location results in the offering getting hit hard at times. Still, Martin's willingness to throw his fastball for strikes allows him to sell a plus changeup (while also incorporating a slider) that helped him to punch out 10.5 batters per nine innings in 2016. The Red Sox added Martin to the 40-man roster in November, so he represents an obvious major league depth option in 2017.

Year	Club (League)	Class	W	L	ERA	G	GS	CG	SV	IP	H	HR	BB	SO	K/9	WHIP	AVG
2014	Salem (CAR)	HiA	4	5	4.02	35	0	0	10	81	84	11	16	82	9.1	1.24	.268
2015	Red Sox (GCL)	R	2	0	0.00	3	0	0	0	4	3	0	0	4	9.0	0.75	.200
	Portland (EL)	AA	2	1	4.50	27	0	0	5	42	43	3	16	48	10.3	1.40	.264
2016	Pawtucket (IL)	AAA	3	4	3.38	36	0	0	6	67	58	5	21	78	10.5	1.19	.239
Minor League Totals			15	12	3.41	120	0	0	24	229	207	19	63	242	9.5	1.18	.241

19 YOAN AYBAR, OF

BA GRADE

50 Risk: Extreme

Born: July 3, 1997. **B-T:** L-L. **Ht.:** 6-2. **Wt.:** 165. **Signed:** Dominican Republic, 2013. **Signed by:** Jonathan Cruz/Eddie Romero.

Aybar remains an all-tools exercise in projection. A "colt" in the eyes of one evaluator who, like many others, sees a fantastic athlete who has yet to translate his tools to performance. Aybar hit .207/.247/.315 with a 26 percent strikeout rate at short-season Lowell in 2016. Despite the lack of in-game impact, Aybar is too young to abandon hope—he turned 19 in the middle of the New York-Penn League season. He showed a willingness to work and try to refine his crude tools even through his struggles. He has an elite arm and moves well enough in center field to suggest the possibility of plus defense. If he finds a swing and approach that works, Aybar has a chance to deliver above-average across-the-board impact. If not, he might not make it past Double-A—unless he is converted to the mound.

Year	Club (League)	Class	AVG	G	AB	R	H	2B	3B	HR	RBI	BB	SO	SB	CS	OBP	SLG
2014	Red Sox (DSL)	R	.271	56	214	33	58	12	9	0	26	11	54	7	6	.317	.411
2015	Red Sox (GCL)	R	.268	45	157	19	42	5	3	0	16	7	46	6	6	.298	.338
2016	Lowell (NYP)	SS	.207	60	222	18	46	7	4	3	19	8	61	3	4	.247	.315
Minor League Totals			.246	161	593	70	146	24	16	3	61	26	161	16	16	.286	.356

20 GERSON BAUTISTA, RHP

BA GRADE

50 Risk: Extreme

Born: May 31, 1995. **B-T:** R-R. **Ht.:** 6-2. **Wt.:** 185. **Signed:** Dominican Republic, 2013. **Signed by:** Manny Nanita.

Bautista turned 19 not long after signing with the Red Sox in April 2013 and performed well as a starter in the Dominican Summer League in 2014 and Rookie-level Gulf Coast League in 2015. He showed explosive stuff in his move to the bullpen in 2016, mixing a 95-100 mph fastball with an above-average high-80s slider that has a chance to be a second plus offering. This allowed Bautista to impress evaluators while making the transition from short-season Lowell (where he had a 0.87 ERA) to low Class A Greenville in 2016. He throws with some funk in his stride and delivery, particularly with a dip that occurs with his lower half that can create inconsistency in his ability to throw strikes. But when Bautista is on, he shows the possibility of two plus weapons that creates a potential set-up reliever ceiling. Because of the work he faces in locking in his delivery, Bautista remains far from the big leagues, but he does have more upside than many of the relief prospects in the Red Sox system.

Year	Club (League)	Class	W	L	ERA	G	GS	CG	SV	IP	H	HR	BB	SO	K/9	WHIP	AVG
2014	Red Sox (DSL)	R	2	1	1.03	13	12	0	0	61	37	1	21	32	4.7	0.95	.174
2015	Red Sox (GCL)	R	3	3	2.77	12	11	0	0	52	36	1	27	41	7.1	1.21	.196
2016	Lowell (NYP)	SS	0	0	0.87	8	0	0	5	10	5	0	2	13	11.3	0.68	.143
	Greenville (SAL)	LoA	1	4	3.24	15	0	0	1	25	20	3	11	23	8.3	1.24	.213
Minor League Totals			6	8	2.00	48	23	0	6	148	98	5	61	109	6.6	1.07	.186

21 BEN TAYLOR, RHP

BA GRADE
40 Risk: Medium

Born: Nov. 12, 1992. **B-T:** R-R. **Ht.:** 6-3. **Wt.:** 230. **Drafted:** South Alabama, 2015 (7th round). **Signed by:** Danny Watkins.

Since the Red Sox selected Taylor as a senior sign out of South Alabama in 2015, he has shown that his impressive college strikeout numbers (14.3 per nine innings as a senior) were no fluke. He continues to miss bats with a fastball that peaks at 96 mph with deception, and he complements the pitch with a slider that has shown the potential to miss bats but is inconsistent. Taylor struck out well over a batter per inning at both high Class A Salem and Double-A Portland in 2016, pitching well enough at both levels that he could open 2017 at Triple-A Pawtucket. He has the upside of a Kevin Jepsen-type reliever, a seventh-inning contributor who offers a bit of a different look with the ability to miss bats with his fastball at the top of the strike zone. Taylor receives high marks for his makeup and willingness to work, and he is nearly big league ready.

Year	Club (League)	Class	W	L	ERA	G	GS	CG	SV	IP	H	HR	BB	SO	K/9	WHIP	AVG
2015	Lowell (NYP)	SS	0	0	1.80	4	0	0	0	10	8	0	2	17	15.3	1.00	.222
	Greenville (SAL)	LoA	0	2	3.40	10	10	0	0	45	43	2	15	37	7.4	1.29	.250
2016	Salem (CAR)	HiA	0	2	2.60	15	3	0	3	45	35	0	10	56	11.2	1.00	.213
	Portland (EL)	AA	1	0	3.44	21	0	0	5	34	28	4	12	42	11.1	1.18	.222
Minor League Totals			1	4	3.02	50	13	0	8	134	114	6	39	152	10.2	1.14	.229

22 LUIS YSLA, LHP

BA GRADE
45 Risk: High

Born: April 27, 1992. **B-T:** L-L. **Ht.:** 6-1. **Wt.:** 175. **Signed:** 2012, Venezuela. **Signed by:** Joe Salermo (Giants).

In his first full season in the Red Sox organization, Ysla showed the power lefthanded arm that drew Boston to him in the August 2015 trade that sent Alejandro De Aza to the Giants. Ysla sits in the mid-90s with a two-plane fastball that misses bats. That pitch alone should play in the majors if he can throw it for strikes, though its value is mitigated by the fact that he hasn't developed a consistent secondary pitch as a complement. Given that Ysla's fastball tends to cut to his glove side, he showed significant reverse splits while working as a reliever in 2016. Righthanded batters hit just .225 against him at Double-A Portland (plus one Triple-A appearance) while lefties mashed him at a .321/.404/.523 clip. Still, he struck out 30 percent of the lefties he faced. If he improves his slider and uses it to attack the inner part of the plate, he could emerge as the primary lefthanded bullpen option on the farm, particularly now that the Red Sox have added him to the 40-man roster.

Year	Club (League)	Class	W	L	ERA	G	GS	CG	SV	IP	H	HR	BB	SO	K/9	WHIP	AVG
2014	Augusta (SAL)	LoA	6	7	2.45	24	23	0	0	121	104	8	45	115	8.5	1.23	.231
2015	San Jose (CAL)	HiA	3	6	6.21	33	9	0	0	80	109	9	41	95	10.7	1.88	.329
	Salem (CAR)	HiA	0	0	0.00	2	0	0	0	5	0	0	2	6	10.8	0.40	.000
2016	Portland (EL)	AA	2	5	4.07	39	0	0	3	55	54	4	27	60	9.8	1.46	.262
	Pawtucket (IL)	AAA	0	0	0.00	1	0	0	1	1	1	0	0	2	18.0	1.00	.250
Minor League Totals			15	18	3.68	111	44	0	4	313	306	22	128	330	9.5	1.39	.256

23 CHANDLER SHEPHERD, RHP

BA GRADE
40 Risk: Medium

Born: Aug. 25, 1992. **B-T:** R-R. **Ht:** 6-3. **Wt.:** 205. **Drafted:** Kentucky, 2014 (13th round). **Signed by:** John Pyle.

In his first pro season in 2015, Shepherd showed the sort of strike-throwing ability with a three-pitch mix that allowed him to perform well out of the bullpen at two Class A levels (62-to-10 strikeout-to-walk ratio) and the Arizona Fall League. He carried that success into a dominant start to the 2016 campaign at Double-A Portland, where he posted a 1.80 ERA and held opponents to a .139 average while striking out 11.7 per nine innings. Shepherd's numbers were less impressive after a midyear promotion to Triple-A Pawtucket, with his strikeout rate falling off by roughly a half. Still, he continued to throw strikes with a three-pitch mix of a low-90s fastball, a curveball that has gotten swings and misses and a changeup. Shepherd's command is above-average, and with adjustments to his pitch sequencing, he could have a future as a middle-relief option.

Year	Club (League)	Class	W	L	ERA	G	GS	CG	SV	IP	H	HR	BB	SO	K/9	WHIP	AVG
2014	Lowell (NYP)	SS	4	3	4.05	16	1	0	0	33	33	3	8	35	9.5	1.23	.254
2015	Greenville (SAL)	LoA	3	0	1.23	7	0	0	1	15	16	1	3	16	9.8	1.30	.267
	Salem (CAR)	HiA	0	2	3.61	28	0	0	6	52	48	3	7	46	7.9	1.05	.241
2016	Portland (EL)	AA	1	1	1.80	22	0	0	6	30	14	3	10	39	11.7	0.80	.140
	Pawtucket (IL)	AAA	1	2	3.71	18	1	0	1	34	28	3	8	23	6.1	1.06	.230
Minor League Totals			9	8	3.18	91	2	0	14	164	139	13	36	159	8.7	1.06	.227

24 LORENZO CEDROLA, OF

BA GRADE

40 Risk: High

Born: Jan. 12, 1998. **B-T:** R-R. **Ht.:** 5-11. **Wt.:** 170. **Signed:** Venezuela, 2015.
Signed by: Alex Requena/Eddie Romero.

The Red Sox named Cedrola their Latin American program player of the year in 2015 after he hit .321/.420/.415 in the Dominican Summer League. He followed that performance with another strong showing in the Rookie-level Gulf Coast League in 2016, when he hit .290 and led the GCL with 62 hits and 14 doubles while ranking fourth with 33 runs scored. Though an excellent athlete and plus runner, Cedrola is physically limited. His barrel control allows him to make contact at a high rate (he struck out just 12 percent of the time in 2016), while giving him just enough gap power to sometimes undermine a more sound approach predicated on shooting line drives to all fields. Still, between his contact skills, plus range in center field and average arm, he has a clear path to being at least a reserve outfielder—and possibly a quality fourth outfielder. In games, Cedrola has been a catalyst and a gamer, with two-way impact that has captured the notice of opponents as well as his own organization.

Year	Club (League)	Class	AVG	G	AB	R	H	2B	3B	HR	RBI	BB	SO	SB	CS	OBP	SLG
2015	Red Sox2 (DSL)	R	.321	67	265	61	85	8	7	1	31	23	33	27	7	.420	.415
2016	Red Sox (GCL)	R	.290	53	214	33	62	14	1	2	21	11	28	9	4	.350	.393
Minor League Totals			.307	120	479	94	147	22	8	3	52	34	61	36	11	.390	.405

25 YEISON COCA, SS

BA GRADE

40 Risk: Extreme

Born: May 22, 1999. **B-T:** B-R. **Ht:** 5-10. **Wt.:** 155. **Signed:** Dominican Republic, 2015. **Signed by:** Manny Nanita/Eddie Romero.

In his pro debut in the Dominican Summer League in 2016, Coca impressed by displaying his instincts, athleticism, advanced middle-of-the-field defensive ability and bat-to-ball skills. That combination suggests the possibility of a future everyday shortstop, albeit with a long developmental road in front of him to see if such a ceiling is realistic. Coca's athleticism and footwork allowed him to move well at shortstop, a position where he showed an average arm. Though he has below-average power, he delivered a .308/.372/.408 batting line. The switch-hitter shows the ability to make frequent contact, manage the strike zone and generate liners that found the gap, all while featuring a bit more raw power from the left side of the plate. One evaluator suggested that he has some similarities to a young Starlin Castro.

Year	Club (League)	Class	AVG	G	AB	R	H	2B	3B	HR	RBI	BB	SO	SB	CS	OBP	SLG
2016	Red Sox2 (DSL)	R	.308	63	260	41	80	5	9	1	26	26	42	12	5	.372	.408
Minor League Totals			.308	63	260	41	80	5	9	1	26	26	42	12	5	.372	.408

26 STEVE NOGOSEK, RHP

BA GRADE

45 Risk: High

Born: Jan. 11, 1995. **B-T:** R-R. **Ht.:** 6-2. **Wt.:** 205. **Drafted:** Oregon (6th round), 2016. **Signed by:** Justin Horowitz.

Nogosek concluded three years of dominance at Oregon with a 1.11 ERA and 10.0 strikeouts per nine innings as a junior in 2016, but those numbers told an incomplete story. In the middle of the season, he developed a wicked slider to accompany a fastball that had topped out at 96 mph. In the eyes of Red Sox area scout Justin Horowitz and national pitching cross-checker Chris Mears, Nogosek became a different pitcher down the stretch with that additional weapon, and Boston selected him in the sixth round. His fastball is an impressive offering due both to its velocity and its spin rate that can carry it over the barrel of opponents' bats. Nogosek's plus slider allowed the 21-year-old to hit the ground running in while working as a reliever in his pro debut. He reached low Class A Greenville in August and in 20 combined appearances he recorded a 3.62 ERA with 31 strikeouts and 10 walks in 27 innings. Given his clear development path as a reliever, Nogosek has a chance to move aggressively towards the big leagues in the next two years.

Year	Club (League)	Class	W	L	ERA	G	GS	CG	SV	IP	H	HR	BB	SO	K/9	WHIP	AVG
2016	Lowell (NYP)	SS	1	0	2.03	10	0	0	0	13	9	2	7	19	12.8	1.20	.196
	Greenville (SAL)	LoA	0	2	5.14	10	0	0	2	14	17	1	3	12	7.7	1.43	.293
Minor League Totals			1	2	3.62	20	0	0	2	27	26	3	10	31	10.2	1.32	.250

27 BRYAN MATA, RHP

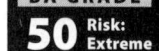

BA GRADE

50 Risk: Extreme

Born: May 3, 1999. **B-T:** R-R. **Ht.:** 6-3. **Wt.:** 160. **Signed:** Venezuela, 2016. **Signed by:** Alex Requena/Eddie Romero.

The Red Sox signed Mata late in the 2015 international signing period, waiting until Jan. 2016 to sign him as a 16-year old out of Venezuela. Physically, Mata looked like a man among boys in his pro debut in the Dominican Summer League in 2016. The 6-foot-3 righthander has both the frame and delivery to suggest the possibility of durability, while his quick arm already has him working up to 94 mph. Mata's performance likewise distinguished the young pitcher. He recorded a 1.55 ERA over his last dozen DSL starts (regular season and playoffs), while his three-pitch mix (fastball, curveball, changeup) is headlined by a heater that projects as a plus offering. His curve and changeup both flash average at times, and their development will determine whether his likelier projection is in the bullpen or as a starter.

Year	Club (League)	Class	W	L	ERA	G	GS	CG	SV	IP	H	HR	BB	SO	K/9	WHIP	AVG
2016	Red Sox2 (DSL)	R	4	4	2.80	14	14	0	0	61	54	2	19	61	9.0	1.20	.242
Minor League Totals			4	4	2.80	14	14	0	0	61	54	2	19	61	9.0	1.20	.242

28 JAMIE CALLAHAN, RHP

BA GRADE

40 Risk: High

Born: Aug. 24, 1994. **B-T:** R-R. **Ht..:** 6-2. **Wt.:** 230. **Drafted:** HS— Dillon, S.C. (2nd round), 2012. **Signed by:** Quincy Boyd.

A second-round pick in 2012, Callahan's career advanced deliberately as a starter and even after his transition to the bullpen in 2015. But after a poor start in 2016 at high Class A Salem, he turned what had been a slurvy breaking ball into a hard slider that became a weapon by midseason. Callahan's numbers reflected the transformative significance of the pitch, both in his arsenal (chiefly that power slider and a fastball that sits at 94-96 mph) as well as his confidence and aggressiveness. After he recorded a 4.32 ERA with 7.9 strikeouts and 5.7 walks per nine innings in the first half of 2016, he dominated in the second half with a 2.23 ERA with 10.0 strikeouts and 4.7 walks per nine. He carried that performance into the Arizona Fall League, posting a 0.75 ERA with 12 strikeouts and three walks in 12 innings while recording a pair of saves. Callahan needs to work on execution with a fastball that gets fewer swings and misses than expected, but if he starts to command that pitch up in the zone, he has a chance to emerge as a big league middle reliever.

Year	Club (League)	Class	W	L	ERA	G	GS	CG	SV	IP	H	HR	BB	SO	K/9	WHIP	AVG
2014	Greenville (SAL)	LoA	3	13	6.96	25	25	0	0	109	137	12	66	89	7.4	1.87	.309
2015	Greenville (SAL)	LoA	7	6	4.53	31	6	0	3	89	94	4	33	94	9.5	1.42	.263
2016	Salem (CAR)	HiA	5	3	3.29	36	0	0	7	66	53	1	38	63	8.6	1.39	.218
Minor League Totals			21	23	4.99	110	47	0	10	332	340	21	157	307	8.3	1.50	.263

29 ROLDANI BALDWIN, C/3B

BA GRADE

45 Risk: High

Born: March 16, 1996. **B-T:** R-R. **Ht.:** 5-11. **Wt.:** 175. **Signed:** Dominican Republic, 2013. **Signed by:** Manny Nanita/Eddie Romero.

Baldwin hasn't found a positional home yet while shuttling between catcher and third base—positions where he did not distinguish himself in 2016—but his bat will keep him progressing up the ladder. He struggled at the outset of 2016 at low Class A Greenville, hitting .235/.275/.382, but when he moved back to the New York-Penn League, he showed the ability to make regular loud contact, pounding the ball at a .305/.358/.442 clip with 10 extra-base hits in 25 games. Even if Baldwin ends up being a below-average defender at catcher, third, and first, that kind of corner versatility in combination with the ability to hit for average with some pop gives him a chance emerge as a valuable reserve, particularly given what he's shown against lefties (.311/.333/.475 in 2016 in Lowell and Greenville). The coming season will be a significant one for Baldwin to prove that he's ready to keep moving up the ladder in full-season ball, but if he cements the impressions that his bat has produced since short-season affiliates, his appeal will grow.

Year	Club (League)	Class	AVG	G	AB	R	H	2B	3B	HR	RBI	BB	SO	SB	CS	OBP	SLG
2014	Red Sox (DSL)	R	.269	65	242	36	65	10	3	4	42	27	41	3	1	.357	.384
2015	Red Sox (GCL)	R	.288	47	156	18	45	8	0	3	25	14	19	1	1	.362	.397
	Lowell (NYP)	SS	.286	3	7	0	2	1	0	0	0	0	1	0	0	.286	.429
2016	Lowell (NYP)	SS	.305	25	95	10	29	8	1	1	14	6	21	0	0	.358	.442
	Greenville (SAL)	LoA	.249	61	225	26	56	12	0	3	23	9	57	1	1	.282	.342
Minor League Totals			.272	201	725	90	197	39	4	11	104	56	139	5	3	.336	.382

30 DARWINZON HERNANDEZ, LHP

Born: Dec. 17, 1996. **B-T:** L-L. **Ht.:** 6-2. **Wt.:** 185. **Signed:** Venezuela, 2013.
Signed by: Rolando Pino/Ramon Mora.

Signed for just $7,500 out of Venezuela in 2013, Hernandez jumped from the Dominican Summer League in 2015 to short-season Lowell for his U.S. debut in 2016. He showed a fastball that featured power up to 96 mph and natural cut that, in concert with the deception in his low three-quarters delivery, generated swings and misses in volume. He struck out 26 percent of batters in in the New York-Penn League in 2016 to rank ninth among pitchers with at least 40 innings. While Hernandez has worked as a starter to date, given the dominance of his fastball and his work-in-progress secondary offerings, it's easier to imagine him in a future relief role. He switched from a curveball to a slider, and he could be taught a split-finger fastball in the future. The cut on his pitches suggests the potential to emerge as a full-inning pitcher as opposed to a left-on-left guy, though in addition to developing a consistent secondary offering, Hernandez will also need to improve his well below-average control. He recorded the highest walk rate (16 percent) in the NYPL in 2016, but that should improve as he continues his physical maturation.

Year	Club (League)	Class	W	L	ERA	G	GS	CG	SV	IP	H	HR	BB	SO	K/9	WHIP	AVG
2014	Red Sox (DSL)	R	1	1	2.89	14	1	0	0	28	24	0	19	15	4.8	1.54	.231
2015	Red Sox2 (DSL)	R	6	1	1.10	16	13	0	0	65	55	0	30	66	9.1	1.30	.227
2016	Lowell (NYP)	SS	3	5	4.10	14	14	0	0	48	39	1	36	58	10.8	1.55	.217
Minor League Totals			10	7	2.48	44	28	0	0	142	118	1	85	139	8.8	1.43	.224

Chicago Cubs

BY JOHN MANUEL

As slogans go, "When it happens" seemed fairly boastful considering the Cubs had not won a World Series since 1908.

That slogan was a mantra throughout the organization since Theo Epstein took over as president of baseball operations and brought general manager Jed Hoyer and assistant GM Jason McLeod from the Padres to rejoin him. The trio had helped end Boston's misery by winning two World Series titles for the Red Sox and stocking the organization with many (though not all) of the pieces that won Boston's 2013 title.

By 2013, the Cubs were in the midst of their rebuild—they drafted Kris Bryant second overall that year—but still in tear-down mode in the big leagues. By 2015, most of the pieces were in place and Chicago won 97 games and advanced to the National League Championship Series.

In 2016, the roster featured Bryant coming off a Rookie of the Year season, a rotation rebuilt through deft trades (Jake Arrieta, Kyle Hendricks) and expensive free agents (Jon Lester, John Lackey) and another year of experience for Anthony Rizzo, Javier Baez and Addison Russell.

The Cubs had built baseball's best team despite a dreadful season by high-priced free agent right fielder Jason Heyward. They ranked second in the NL in runs scored and first in ERA but still moved to fortify the bullpen with two July trades, including a blockbuster with the Yankees in which they surrendered prospect Gleyber Torres to acquire closer Aroldis Chapman. Chicago won 103 games to run away with the NL Central, then won their first NL pennant since 1945.

Then came the World Series, the first for the franchise in the Integration Era. The Cubs rallied from a 3-1 deficit to defeat the Indians in seven games.

When it happened, a reported 5 million fans came out to celebrate in a championship parade that won't soon be forgotten.

What does the BA Organization of the Year do for an encore? The big league core is incredibly young, athletic and dynamic thanks to the growth of rookie catcher Willson Contreras, Baez, Russell and Bryant. Kyle Schwarber returned from a knee injury that cost him most of the season to show truly elite hitting ability in the World Series.

The Cubs cleared room for Schwarber to get at-bats and found a replacement for departing free agent Chapman by trading Jorge Soler after the season for Royals closer Wade Davis.

The farm system's upper levels offer little in the way of help for 2017 other than outfielder Albert

Willson Contreras fits perfectly on a roster filled with versatile, athletic position players

TOP PROSPECTS OF THE DECADE

Year	Player, Pos.	2016 Org
2007	Felix Pie, of	Did not play
2008	Josh Vitters, 3b	Atlantic League
2009	Josh Vitters, 3b	Atlantic League
2010	Starlin Castro, ss	Yankees
2011	Chris Archer, rhp	Rays
2012	Brett Jackson, of	Did not play
2013	Javier Baez, ss	Cubs
2014	Javier Baez, ss	Cubs
2015	Kris Bryant, 3b	Cubs
2016	Gleyber Torres, ss	Yankees

Almora and perhaps some back-end pitching help, such as lefthander Rob Zastryzny.

The lower levels of the Cubs system have talent, which is evident in the rosters at short-season Eugene, low Class A South Bend and high Class A Myrtle Beach, which combined for a .679 winning percentage. Eugene and Myrtle Beach won league championships.

The Cubs have more intriguing arms at the lower levels and stocked up in the 2016 draft by taking 27 pitchers in their 38 picks. But the system has the ammunition for more trades if needed this offseason or during the 2017 season to bolster the rotation or bullpen again.

The new slogan, McLeod says, is "Where it happens," because the Cubs are positioned to win more than one championship.

ORGANIZATION OVERVIEW

President: Theo Epstein **GM:** Jed Hoyer. **Farm director:** Jaron Madison. **Scouting director:** Matt Dorey.

Class	Team	League	W	L	PCT	Finish	Manager
Majors	Chicago Cubs	National	103	58	.640	1st (15)	Joe Maddon
Triple-A	Iowa Cubs	Pacific Coast	67	76	.469	13st (16)	Marty Pevey
Double-A	Tennessee Smokies	Southern	58	81	.417	9th (10)	Mark Johnson
High Class A	Myrtle Beach Pelicans	Carolina	82	57	.590	3rd (8)	Buddy Bailey
Low Class A	South Bend Cubs	Midwest	84	55	.604	3rd (16)	Jimmy Gonzalez
Short-season	Eugene Emeralds	Northwest	54	22	.711	1st (8)	Jesus Feliciano
Rookie	AZL Cubs	Arizona	28	28	.500	9th (14)	Carmelo Martinez
Overall 2016 Minor League Record			373	319	.539	6th (30)	

THIS YEAR'S TOP 30

No.	Player, Pos.	Grade/Risk
1.	Eloy Jimenez, of	65/High
2.	Ian Happ, 2b/of	55/High
3.	Albert Almora, of	50/Low
4.	Dylan Cease, rhp	60/Extreme
5.	Oscar de la Cruz, rhp	55/Extreme
6.	Mark Zagunis, of	50/Medium
7.	Jeimer Candelario, 3b	50/Medium
8.	Trevor Clifton, rhp	50/High
9.	D.J. Wilson, of	55/Extreme
10.	Jose Albertos, rhp	55/Extreme
11.	Eddy Martinez, of	50/High
12.	Donnie Dewees, of	50/High
13.	Thomas Hatch, rhp	50/High
14.	Rob Zastryzny, lhp	45/Medium
15.	Duane Underwoon, rhp	50/Extreme
16.	Chesny Young, 2b/3b	45/Medium
17.	Victor Caratini, c/1b	45/Medium
18.	Wladimir Galindo, 3b	50/Extreme
19.	Pierce Johnson, rhp	45/High
20.	Erling Moreno, rhp	50/Extreme
21.	Jose Paulino, lhp	50/Extreme
22.	P.J. Higgins, c	45/High
23.	Jacob Hannemann, of	45/High
24.	Justin Steele, lhp	50/Extreme
25.	Bryan Hudson, lhp	50/Extreme
26.	David Bote, 3b/2b	45/High
27.	Jack Leathersich, lhp	40/High
28.	Bailey Clark, rhp	50/Extreme
29.	Isaac Paredes, ss	45/Extreme
30.	Chris Pieters, of/1b	45/Extreme

LAST YEAR'S TOP 30

No.	Player, Pos.	Status
1.	Gleyber Torres, ss	(Yankees)
2.	Willson Contreras, c/3b	Majors
3.	Ian Happ, of/2b	No. 2
4.	Duane Underwood, rhp	No. 15
5.	Dylan Cease, rhp	No. 4
6.	Albert Almora, of	No. 3
7.	Billy McKinney, of	(Yankees)
8.	Oscar de la Cruz, rhp	No. 5
9.	Eloy Jimenez, of	No. 1
10.	Jeimer Candelario, 3b	No. 7
11.	Mark Zagunis, of	No. 6
12.	Pierce Johnson, rhp	No. 19
13.	Carl Edwards, rhp	Majors
14.	Justin Steele, lhp	No. 24
15.	Bryan Hudson, lhp	No. 25
16.	D.J. Wilson, of	No. 9
17.	Donnie Dewees, of	No. 12
18.	Trevor Clifton, rhp	No. 8
19.	Paul Blackburn, rhp	(Athletics)
20.	Jen-Ho Tseng, rhp	Dropped out
21.	Jake Stinnett, rhp	Dropped out
22.	Carson Sands, lhp	Dropped out
23.	Brad Markey, rhp	Dropped out
24.	Victor Caratini, c	No. 17
25.	Dan Vogelbach, 1b	(Mariners)
26.	Jacob Hannemann, of	No. 23
27.	Ryan Williams, rhp	Dropped out
28.	Eddy Julio Martinez, of	Dropped out
29.	Andury Acevedo, rhp	Dropped out
30.	David Berg, rhp	Dropped out

BEST TOOLS

Best Hitter for Average	Eloy Jimenez
Best Power Hitter	Eloy Jimenez
Best Strike-Zone Discipline	Mark Zagunis
Fastest Baserunner	D.J. Wilson
Best Athlete	Jacob Hannemann
Best Fastball	Dylan Cease
Best Curveball	Oscar de la Cruz
Best Slider	Thomas Hatch
Best Changeup	Jose Albertos
Best Control	Zach Hedges
Best Defensive Catcher	P.J. Higgins
Best Defensive Infielder	Carlos Penalver
Best Infield Arm	Jeimer Candelario
Best Defensive Outfielder	Albert Almora
Best Outfield Arm	Eddy Martinez

PROJECTED 2020 LINEUP

Catcher	Willson Contreras
First Base	Anthony Rizzo
Second Base	Javier Baez
Third Base	Kris Bryant
Shortstop	Addison Russell
Left Field	Kyle Schwarber
Center Field	Albert Almora
Right Field	Eloy Jimenez
No. 1 Starter	Jon Lester
No. 2 Starter	Kyle Hendricks
No. 3 Starter	Mike Montgomery
No. 4 Starter	Oscar de la Cruz
No. 5 Starter	Trevor Clifton
Closer	Dylan Cease

MINOR LEAGUE DEPTH CHART

CHICAGO CUBS

TOP 2017 ROOKIE: Albert Almora, of. The job won't be handed to him, but Almora has a chance to succeed Dexter Fowler in center field.
BREAKOUT PROSPECT: Thomas Hatch, rhp. The Cubs' top 2016 draftee will start in high Class A and move quickly thereafter.
SLEEPER: James Farris, rhp. A $3,000 signee, he has a plus cutter that could get him to the big league bullpen quickly.

SOURCE OF TOP 30 TALENT			
Homegrown	28	Acquired	2
College	10	Trades	2
Junior college	1	Rule 5 draft	0
High school	7	Independent leagues	0
Nondrafted free agents	0	Free agents/waivers	0
International	10		

LF
Mark Zagunis (6)
Donnie Dewees (12)
Chris Pieters (30)
Bijan Rademacher

CF
Albert Almora (3)
D.J. Wilson (9)
Eddy Martinez (11)
Jacob Hannemann (23)

RF
Eloy Jimenez (1)
Jonathan Sierra

3B
Jeimer Candelario (7)
Wladimir Galindo (18)
David Bote (26)

SS
Isaac Paredes (29)
Aramis Ademan
Carlos Penalver
Delvin Zinn

2B
Ian Happ (2)
Chesney Young (16)
Carlos Sepulvida
Yonathan Perlaza

1B
Yasiel Balaguert

C
Victor Caratini (17)
P.J. Higgins (22)
Michael Cruz
Miguel Amaya

LHP

LHSP	LHRP
Rob Zastryzny (14)	Jack Leathersich (27)
Jose Paulino (21)	Caleb Smith
Justin Steele (24)	Wyatt Short
Bryan Hudson (25)	
Manuel Rondon	
Carson Sands	
Ryan Kellogg	

RHP

RHSP	RHRP
Dylan Cease (4)	Pierce Johnson (19)
Oscar de la Cruz (5)	Felix Pena
Trevor Clifton (8)	Jose Rosario
Jose Albertos (10)	James Farris
Thomas Hatch (13)	Chad Hockin
Duane Underwood (15)	Dakota Mekkes
Erling Moreno (20)	Brad Markey
Bailey Clark (28)	Casey Bloomquist
Ryan Williams	
Tyson Miller	
Adbert Alzolay	
Zach Hedges	
Michael Rucker	

DRAFT ANALYSIS

2016

BEST PURE HITTER: The Cubs signed just six position players in a draft class focused on boosting the organization's pitching. C Michael Cruz (7) had a strong spring at Bethune-Cookman and controlled the strike zone in his debut. He makes a lot of contact.

BEST POWER HITTER: Cruz slugged 16 homers in the spring for Bethune-Cookman, which plays in Jackie Robinson Stadium in Daytona, Fla. The former home of a Cubs high Class A affiliate, the Cubs know it's a tough home run park, especially for lefthanded hitters like Cruz.

FASTEST RUNNER: A part-time player for four years at Texas Tech, OF Zach Davis (32) is a true 80 runner. A hamstring injury ended his pro debut after six games. Fellow OFs Connor Myers (27) and Tolly Filotei (38) are both 70 runners.

BEST DEFENSIVE PLAYER: Myers's speed and reads make him a plus defender in center field if not a tick better.

BEST FASTBALL: RHP Bailey Clark (5) touches 98 mph and can sit 92-96 with some life, though his command is below-average. RHP Chad Hockin (6) hits 97-98 at his best but usually ranges from 91-95. RHP Thomas Hatch (3), the club's top pick, pitches off his fastball better than any Cubs draftee thanks to good velocity (93-94 mph), above-average sink and solid-average fastball command.

BEST SECONDARY PITCH: Hockin's slider outpaces his fastball, earning 70 grades with tilt at up to 87 mph. RHP Duncan Robinson (9) has an above-average curveball that is the best of his four-pitch mix.

BEST PRO DEBUT: LHP Wyatt Short, Mississippi's closer the last two seasons, didn't allow a run for short-season Eugene in 15 regular season innings and 2.1 more in the playoffs for the Northwest League champions.

BEST ATHLETE: SS Delvin Zinn (23), who turned the Cubs down in 2015 as a 28th-rounder, signed this year and brings a loose, lively body at 5-foot-10, 170 pounds. He's raw but has good speed and first-step quickness suited to the infield.

MOST INTRIGUING BACKGROUND: Hockin is the grandson of late Hall of Famer Harmon Killebrew. His brother Grant pitches in the Indians' system. RHP Dakota Mekkes (10) led the nation in strikeouts per nine innings (15.16 K/9) and fewest hits allowed (4.1 H/9) thanks to a fastball with exceptional deception. Even at 92 mph, some scouts say it plays as a 70 grade heater.

CLOSEST TO THE MAJORS: Hatch's command and polish as the ace of Oklahoma State's ace this spring should allow him to debut as high as high Class A Myrtle Beach, putting him on the fast track.

BEST LATE-ROUND PICK: Zinn is the long-term play. RHP Michael Rucker (11), already 22, could move quickly in relief and had an 18-1 strikeout-walk rate in 12.2 innings in his debut. His fastball reaches 95 mph and he showed the ability to spin a breaking ball at altitude in his Brigham Young days.

THE ONE WHO GOT AWAY: The Cubs ran out of money to sign RHP Austin Jones (13), a Tommy John surgery alum. He's back at Wisconsin-Whitewater with a fastball in the mid-90s.

2015

Chicago went hitter-heavy at the top with 2B/OF Ian Happ (1), who's reached Double-A. Other hitters in the Top 30 include OFs D.J. Wilson (4) and Donnie Dewees (2) and C P.J. Higgins (12).
GRADE: B

2014

C/OF Kyle Schwarber (1) helped the Cubs win the World Series (he served as DH in road games). RHP Dylan Cease (6) is the club's top pitching prospect. OF Mark Zagunis (3) and 2B Chesny Young (14) are two of the system's best hitters.
GRADE: A

2013

3B Kris Bryant (1) just keeps living up to expectations in spectacular fashion. RHP Trevor Clifton (12) will be tested in Double-A in 2017. The Cubs went heavy for college arms, and so far the best have been LHP Rob Zastryzny (2) and since-traded Zack Godley (10).
GRADE: A

TOP DRAFT PICKS OF THE DECADE

Year	Player, Pos.	2016 Org
2007	Josh Vitters, 3b	Atlantic League
2008	Andrew Cashner, rhp	Marlins
2009	Brett Jackson, of	Did not play
2010	Hayden Simpson, rhp	Did not play
2011	Javier Baez, ss	Cubs
2012	Albert Almora, of	Cubs
2013	Kris Bryant, 3b	Cubs
2014	Kyle Schwarber, c	Cubs
2015	Ian Happ, of/2b	Cubs
2016	Thomas Hatch, rhp (3rd round)	Cubs

LARGEST BONUSES IN CLUB HISTORY

Kris Bryant, 2013	$6,708,400
Jorge Soler, 2012	$6,000,000
Mark Prior, 2001	$4,000,000
Kosuke Fukudome, 2007	$4,000,000
Albert Almora, 2012	$3,900,000

1 ELOY JIMENEZ, OF

Born: Nov. 27, 1996. **B-T:** R-R. **Ht.:** 6-4. **Wt.:** 205.
Signed: Dominican Republic, 2013.
Signed by: Jose Serra/Carlos Reyes.

BA GRADE

65 Risk: High

SCOUTING GRADES

Batting: 60.
Power: 70.
Speed: 50.
Defense: 50.
Arm: 45.

Based on 20-80 scouting scale and future projection rather than present tools.

ANDREW WOOLLEY

Jimenez's father Luis played and coached basketball in the Dominican Republic, so Jimenez grew up around athletes and some degree of fame. He was ready for the spotlight when his baseball career took off as an amateur and he ranked as the top talent in the 2013 international signing class. The Cubs signed both of the top players that year, Jimenez for $2.8 million and Venezuelan shortstop Gleyber Torres for $1.7 million. They have grown into exactly what the Cubs thought they were, with Torres the savvier, steadier middle infielder and Jimenez the high-risk, high-upside corner bat. When Torres was traded to the Yankees in the Aroldis Chapman deal in July 2016, Jimenez emerged as the Cubs' top prospect with a breakout season at low Class A South Bend. He led the Midwest League in doubles (40) and slugging (.532) while ranking third in batting (.329). He also played in the Futures Game, where he homered and made a highlight-reel over-the-fence catch in foul territory down the right-field line.

Jimenez was signed for his bat and his body— one club official admiringly called him "a physical animal"—and has started to deliver. His body evokes comparisons with former Cub Jorge Soler and Marlins outfielder Giancarlo Stanton, but he is more than just a power-first hitter. Some scouts rate Jimenez's pure hitting ability on par with his power, or put 60 grades on his hitting and 70 on his power (on the 20-80 scouting scale). While his walk rate is modest, Jimenez improved his strike-zone judgment in 2016 by seeing more pitches per at-bat, identifying spin better and applying the Cubs' selective-aggressive mantra. When he turned it loose, he barreled balls and made plenty of hard contact. He added a knee tuck and a bit of a hand pump to his swing, getting less rotational and on time more often, and it aided his ability to drive the ball to right-center field. Some scouts see long levers and a long swing, which could be exploited more by advanced pitchers. However, he has tremendous plate coverage and the aptitude to adjust quickly, and scouts laud his hitting intelligence.

Jimenez is an average runner limited to a corner defensively, and he mostly played left field in 2016. An average defender, he may move to right field if he improves his below-average arm. He must con-tinue to work to improve his throwing mechanics, which remain inconsistent. His throws lack carry, though he has become more accurate He had only one outfield assist in 2016 and has five in his career. He has a chance for an average arm, though, if he dedicates himself to a throwing program. The Cubs are working to keep him lean and athletic physically so he doesn't get too big. Some scouts question Jimenez's ultimate level of athleticism, as he's not graceful, but the Cubs believe he is still growing into his body and will gain body control with natural physical maturity and added strength.

While the Cubs don't need Jimenez soon considering their wealth of outfield options, he may force their hand if his bat continues to progress. He has polish to add against lefthanded pitchers—who handled him with a steady diet of offspeed stuff—and to his defense to be more than just a left fielder. But his bat will play. Jimenez likely will take one step at a time, reporting to high Class A Myrtle Beach for 2017, with a big league ETA of 2019.

Year	Club (League)	Class	AVG	G	AB	R	H	2B	3B	HR	RBI	BB	SO	SB	CS	OBP	SLG
2014	Cubs (AZL)	R	.227	42	150	13	34	8	2	3	27	10	32	3	1	.268	.367
2015	Eugene (NWL)	SS	.284	57	232	36	66	10	0	7	33	15	43	3	2	.328	.418
2016	South Bend (MWL)	LoA	.329	112	432	65	142	40	3	14	81	25	94	8	3	.369	.532
Minor League Totals			.297	211	814	114	242	58	5	24	141	50	169	14	6	.338	.469

2 IAN HAPP, 2B/OF

Born: Aug. 12, 1994. **B-T:** B-R. **Ht.:** 6-0. **Wt.:** 205. **Drafted:** Cincinnati, 2015 (1st round). **Signed by:** Daniel Carte.

Happ prepped at Pittsburgh's Mt. Lebanon High, which also produced big leaguers Don Kelly and Josh Wilson. His college career at Cincinnati featured a star turn in the Cape Cod League in 2014 and he won the American Athletic Conference player of the year award in 2015. He signed for $3 million as the ninth overall pick in 2015 and finished his first full season in Double-A. He ended his 2016 with a 4-for-4, two-homer day—one from each side of the plate—in the Arizona Fall League championship game. Happ combines power and speed offensively. He's an above-average runner and solid basestealer who draws walks and could fit at the top of a lineup. He has present strength and plus bat speed with above-average power from both sides of the plate that plays more with line drives to the gaps for now. Happ goes deep in counts, but doesn't shorten up with two strikes and has a track record of striking out a lot. The Cubs gave him plenty of reps at second base, where scouts see stiff actions, rigid hands and below-average overall defense. His solid-average arm plays in all three outfield spots, which he also played in 2016. Happ hasn't mastered a position yet, mostly because he's not truly average at one. His versatility could help him break into a Cubs roster brimming with young regulars. He should hit enough to earn an everyday lineup spot eventually, just as similarly defensive-challenged players Matt Carpenter and Daniel Murphy did before him.

BA GRADE

55 Risk: High

Year	Club (League)	Class	AVG	G	AB	R	H	2B	3B	HR	RBI	BB	SO	SB	CS	OBP	SLG
2015	Eugene (NWL)	SS	.283	29	106	26	30	8	1	4	11	23	28	9	0	.408	.491
	South Bend (MWL)	LoA	.241	38	145	24	35	9	3	5	22	17	39	1	1	.315	.448
2016	Myrtle Beach (CAR)	HiA	.296	69	240	37	71	16	3	7	42	48	69	10	3	.410	.475
	Tennessee (SL)	AA	.262	65	248	35	65	14	0	8	31	20	60	6	2	.318	.415
Minor League Totals			.272	201	739	122	201	47	7	24	106	108	196	26	6	.362	.452

3 ALBERT ALMORA, OF

Born: April 16, 1994. **B-T:** R-R. **Ht.:** 6-2. **Wt.:** 190. **Drafted:** HS—Hialeah Gardens, Fla., 2012 (1st round). **Signed by:** John Koronka/Laz Llanos.

The sixth overall pick in the 2012 draft, Almora has starred for numerous U.S. national teams as an amateur and professional. He had his best pro season in 2016 when he stayed healthy, playing a career-high 127 games, and he earned his first big league callup in June. Almora made the Cubs postseason roster and, while he went 0-for-10 at the plate, he scored the go-ahead run in Game Seven of the World Series, pinch-running for Kyle Schwarber and alertly tagging up from first base on a Kris Bryant fly ball deep to center field. Scouts long have loved Almora's baseball instincts, evident on the tag-up play, and his defense. While he is a below-average runner out of the batter's box, he is a smart baserunner and has exceptional range in center field thanks to his ability to read hitters' swings, position himself and get tremendous jumps. He's a potential Gold Glove winner in center and has a plus arm that plays in any spot. Almora had his best offensive season in 2016 because he used the whole field and got away from his pull-oriented approach. His over-aggressiveness at the plate tends to short-circuit his solid-average power and may limit his offensive ceiling. With Dexter Fowler leaving Chicago, center field is up for grabs. Almora figures to contend with free agent import Jon Jay and holdover Jason Heyward for the everyday job in 2017, but should at least earn at-bats as a fourth outfielder.

BA GRADE

50 Risk: Low

Year	Club (League)	Class	AVG	G	AB	R	H	2B	3B	HR	RBI	BB	SO	SB	CS	OBP	SLG
2014	Daytona (FSL)	HiA	.283	89	367	55	104	20	2	7	50	12	46	6	3	.306	.406
	Tennessee (SL)	AA	.234	36	141	20	33	7	2	2	10	2	23	0	1	.250	.355
2015	Tennessee (SL)	AA	.272	106	405	69	110	26	4	6	46	32	47	8	4	.327	.400
2016	Iowa (PCL)	AAA	.303	80	320	46	97	18	3	4	43	9	44	10	3	.317	.416
	Chicago (NL)	MAJ	.277	47	112	14	31	9	1	3	14	5	20	0	0	.308	.455
Major League Totals			.277	47	112	14	31	9	1	3	14	5	20	0	0	.308	.455
Minor League Totals			.290	405	1622	256	471	100	16	24	191	74	203	33	17	.322	.416

4 DYLAN CEASE, RHP

PAUL GIERHART

Born: Dec. 28, 1995. **B-T:** R-R. **Ht.:** 6-2. **Wt.:** 190. **Drafted:** HS—Milton, Ga., 2014 (6th round). **Signed by:** Keith Lockhart.

An Under Armour All-American in 2013, Cease already has pitched in Wrigley Field, where the event is held. He also already has had Tommy John surgery, which he had as a high school senior after hitting 98 mph that spring. The Cubs signed him for $1.5 million and have handled him carefully, but they were eager for his short-season Eugene debut in 2016 and he delivered, ranking fourth in the Northwest League in strikeouts (66) even though he didn't pitch enough innings to qualify for its ERA title. Cease fires the best fastball in the Cubs system, with reports of him hitting 103 mph in extended spring training while sitting 93-98 in the NWL. His arm is loose and he has quick hands, which also allow him to throw a power curveball that improved. While his fastball earns 70 grades on the 20-80 scouting scale, Cease's average curve has plus future potential if not better. The Cubs slowly have introduced a changeup to his repertoire, and while it's a fringy pitch at this time, it's serviceable. Hitters' best chance for now is to work walks off Cease, because his fastball command lags behind the pitch's velocity and life. Cease has the athleticism to tame his wild ways and remain a starter. Many scouts see his raw arm strength and power breaking ball and see a closer in the Craig Kimbrel mold. He's an impact arm headed to low Class A South Bend in 2017.

BA GRADE

60 Risk: Extreme

Year	Club (League)	Class	W	L	ERA	G	GS	CG	SV	IP	H	HR	BB	SO	K/9	WHIP	AVG
2015	Cubs (AZL)	R	1	2	2.63	11	8	0	0	24	12	0	16	25	9.4	1.17	.145
2016	Eugene (NWL)	SS	2	0	2.22	12	12	0	0	45	27	1	25	66	13.3	1.16	.175
Minor League Totals			3	2	2.36	23	20	0	0	69	39	1	41	91	11.9	1.17	.165

5 OSCAR DE LA CRUZ, RHP

Born: March 4, 1995. **B-T:** R-R. **Ht.:** 6-4. **Wt.:** 200. **Signed:** Dominican Republic, 2012. **Signed by:** Jose Serra/Marino Encarnacion.

A big-bodied infielder as an amateur, de la Cruz shifted to the mound and signed for $85,000 as a 17-year-old. It took him two years to get to the U.S. because of his lack of pitching experience, but he took off in 2015 at short-season Eugene. His progress was stalled in 2016 by a bout of forearm tenderness, and he didn't pitch in games until July. However, he finished with a flourish at low Class A South Bend, including a six-inning start in the Midwest League playoff opener. His combination of size, stuff and ceiling makes de la Cruz exciting even though he hasn't pitched a full season yet. He uses his size and extension in his delivery to drive his fastball downhill with above-average velocity and life. He pitches with angle at 92-94 mph at his best and touches 97, though he frequently sat 89-92 in 2016 due to his lack of consistent activity. Both of de la Cruz's secondary pitches, a hard curveball and a developing changeup, earn future plus grades, with the curve better at present. He knows how to use his power breaking ball and can throw it for strikes, while he has improved the arm speed on his changeup. De la Cruz has yet to pitch more than 75 innings in a season, but he threw in instructional league and is slated to advance to high Class A Myrtle Beach in 2017.

BA GRADE

55 Risk: Extreme

Year	Club (League)	Class	W	L	ERA	G	GS	CG	SV	IP	H	HR	BB	SO	K/9	WHIP	AVG
2014	Cubs 1 (DSL)	R	8	1	1.80	14	14	0	0	75	56	2	19	64	7.7	1.00	.199
2015	Eugene (NWL)	SS	6	3	2.84	13	13	0	0	73	56	4	17	73	9.0	1.00	.211
2016	Cubs (AZL)	R	0	1	6.00	1	1	0	0	3	3	1	1	2	6.0	1.33	.250
	Eugene (NWL)	SS	0	0	1.08	2	2	0	0	8	5	1	2	14	15.1	0.84	.167
	South Bend (MWL)	LoA	1	2	3.25	6	6	0	0	28	22	0	8	35	11.4	1.08	.218
Minor League Totals			16	7	2.68	40	37	0	0	198	158	10	52	200	9.1	1.06	.216

6 MARK ZAGUNIS, OF

Born: Feb. 5, 1993. **B-T:** R-R. **Ht.:** 6-0. **Wt.:** 205. **Drafted:** Virginia Tech, 2014 (3rd round). **Signed by:** Billy Swope.

Zagunis played catcher and outfield at Virginia Tech and focused on catching as a junior, when the Cubs drafted him with their third selection. After catching in his pro debut, he shifted to an outfield-only role and reached Triple-A Iowa in 2016, a season in which he achieved career bests with 25 doubles, 10 home runs and a .469 slugging percentage. His season ended early when a pitch hit him on the foot in late July, breaking his big toe. Cubs officials have compared Zagunis' strike-zone judgment with Kevin Youkilis. While he still drew walks in 2016, he also became more aggressive on pitches in the zone. His ability to identify pitches early out of

BA GRADE

50 Risk: Medium

the pitcher's hand allows him to lay off tough pitches and attack mistakes more confidently. He has average bat speed but good strength in his hands and wrists, giving him solid-average power potential. He's still learning to stay on time and pull the ball in the air, which would produce more homers. An average runner with an above-average arm, Zagunis still needs reps to be an asset defensively. He's capable in either corner and should make defense more of a focus. The Cubs' big league outfield remains crowded even after trading Jorge Soler, meaning Zagunis is ticketed for a full year at Triple-A. Scouts are split on his potential to become a first-division corner regular, and a club that does would value Zagunis as one of Chicago's better trade chips.

Year	Club (League)	Class	AVG	G	AB	R	H	2B	3B	HR	RBI	BB	SO	SB	CS	OBP	SLG
2014	Cubs (AZL)	R	.125	2	8	1	1	1	0	0	1	1	2	0	0	.222	.250
	Boise (NWL)	SS	.299	41	154	32	46	9	2	2	27	31	31	11	2	.429	.422
	Kane County (MWL)	LoA	.280	14	50	11	14	6	1	0	4	10	9	5	0	.419	.440
2015	Myrtle Beach (CAR)	HiA	.271	115	413	78	112	24	5	8	54	80	86	12	10	.406	.412
2016	Tennessee (SL)	AA	.302	51	179	30	54	13	1	4	24	30	36	1	2	.408	.453
	Iowa (PCL)	AAA	.274	50	179	31	49	12	4	6	25	22	42	4	0	.360	.486
Minor League Totals			.281	273	983	183	276	65	13	20	135	174	206	33	14	.401	.434

7 JEIMER CANDELARIO, 3B

Born: Nov. 24, 1993. **B-T:** B-R. **Ht.:** 6-1. **Wt.:** 210. **Signed:** Dominican Republic, 2010. **Signed by:** Jose Serra/Marino Encarnacion.

In his sixth pro season, Candelario made a strong impression in big league camp in spring training, then struggled to open the season in Double-A. He still was promoted to the big leagues July 3 to replace the injured Chris Coghlan. He got his first hit off Noah Syndergaard, then crushed Triple-A Pacific Coast League pitchers after he was demoted five days later. A switch-hitter who controls the strike zone, Candelario has impressed scouts with a solid swing from both sides of the plate. He set a career high with 72 walks in 2016 and has the strength and plate discipline to get to his average raw power. He's at his best when using the whole field, not when

BA GRADE

50 Risk: Medium

he's trying to pull the ball in an effort to live up to his spring hype. Candelario's pre-pitch anticipation and consistency on routine plays have improved at third base, where he is a solid-average defender despite modest range. Better footwork has sharpened the accuracy of his above-average arm. He's a below-average runner. Candelario doesn't run well enough to try the outfield but added some first-base experience in 2016. His path to playing time in Chicago is as an infield extra backing up Kris Bryant and Anthony Rizzo. Otherwise, he is a trade chip whose value will depend on his 2017 performance.

Year	Club (League)	Class	AVG	G	AB	R	H	2B	3B	HR	RBI	BB	SO	SB	CS	OBP	SLG
2014	Daytona (FSL)	HiA	.193	62	218	24	42	10	2	5	26	23	44	0	3	.275	.326
	Kane County (MWL)	LoA	.250	63	244	32	61	19	3	6	37	18	45	0	1	.300	.426
2015	Myrtle Beach (CAR)	HiA	.270	82	318	42	86	25	3	5	39	20	62	0	1	.318	.415
	Tennessee (SL)	AA	.291	46	158	21	46	10	1	5	25	22	21	0	0	.379	.462
2016	Tennessee (SL)	AA	.219	56	210	30	46	17	1	4	23	32	46	0	0	.324	.367
	Chicago (NL)	MAJ	.091	5	11	0	1	0	0	0	0	2	5	0	0	.286	.091
	Iowa (PCL)	AAA	.333	76	264	44	88	22	3	9	54	38	53	0	2	.417	.542
Major League Totals			.091	5	11	0	1	0	0	0	0	2	5	0	0	.286	.091
Minor League Totals			.270	658	2439	348	659	168	16	56	361	297	456	7	12	.351	.421

8 TREVOR CLIFTON, RHP

Born: May 11, 1995. **B-T:** R-R. **Ht.:** 6-1. **Wt.:** 170. **Drafted:** HS—Maryville, Tenn., 2013 (12th round). **Signed by:** Keith Rymon.

Four of the first 36 players drafted in 2016 were members of the state of Tennessee's prep class of 2013. Clifton was one of just two preps to turn pro out of the Volunteer State that year, signing for $375,000. He had his breakout in 2016, earning high Class A Carolina League pitcher of the year honors while leading Myrtle Beach to the league title. He led the league in ERA (2.72), WHIP (1.16) and opponent average (.225) and won both of his playoff starts. With a body that elicits comparisons to Cubs reliever Justin Grimm, Clifton has filled out physically. Club officials put him closer to 6-foot-4, 220 pounds than his listed weight. With added

BA GRADE

50 Risk: High

strength has come more consistent velocity, namely an above-average fastball that ranges from 90-95 mph. Clifton throws both a slider and a curveball. His solid-average curve is the better pitch, with shape and depth at its best. When his arm slot floats, though, his breaking balls do as well. He has an average to above-average changeup and shackled lefthanded batters (.205/.280/.268) in 2016. He still needs to add polish, such as improving defensively and quickening his time to the plate. Clifton is the best bet the

Cubs have for a homegrown rotation piece, though he's likely no more than a No. 4 starter. He will head to Double-A Tennessee, less than an hour from his hometown, in 2017.

Year	Club (League)	Class	W	L	ERA	G	GS	CG	SV	IP	H	HR	BB	SO	K/9	WHIP	AVG
2014	Boise (NWL)	SS	4	2	3.69	13	13	0	0	61	59	3	30	54	8.0	1.46	.257
2015	South Bend (MWL)	LoA	8	10	3.98	23	22	0	0	109	91	7	47	103	8.5	1.27	.230
2016	Myrtle Beach (CAR)	HiA	7	7	2.72	23	23	0	0	119	97	4	41	129	9.8	1.16	.225
Minor League Totals			19	19	3.52	67	59	0	0	299	260	14	126	301	9.1	1.29	.237

9 D.J. WILSON, OF

Born: Oct. 8, 1996. **B-T:** L-L. **Ht.:** 5-8. **Wt.:** 177. **Drafted:** HS—Canton, Ohio, 2015 (4th round). **Signed by:** Daniel Carte.

Signed away from a Vanderbilt commitment for $1.3 million, Wilson wowed Cubs officials before the draft and in his 2015 pro debut between the Rookie-level Arizona League and instructional league. He got off to a slow start at short-season Eugene in 2016 before making significant progress in the second half, helping the Emeralds win the Northwest League title. Wilson packs power-speed swagger in a smallish frame that evokes Adam Eaton comparisons. He is a dynamic player with bat speed who made adjustments during the season by flattening out what had been a steep bat path. Wilson came to his coaches, took their advice and applied it, lashing line drives to dig out of a 12-for-76 (.158) start. Learning to hit lefthanders (10-for-57, one extra-base hit) will take reps. He has the juice to earn pitchers' respect, though his power will play more to the gaps than over the fence. Defensively, Wilson shines with surprisingly good instincts for a former prep football star, plus speed to run balls down in the gaps and a plus arm. Wilson's aptitude and tools make him a likely future regular, and if he learns to control the strike zone better he could fit the leadoff-hitting center fielder profile. He heads for low Class A South Bend in 2017.

BA GRADE
55 **Risk:** Extreme

Year	Club (League)	Class	AVG	G	AB	R	H	2B	3B	HR	RBI	BB	SO	SB	CS	OBP	SLG
2015	Cubs (AZL)	R	.266	22	79	12	21	3	2	0	6	6	15	5	1	.322	.354
2016	Eugene (NWL)	SS	.257	64	245	37	63	15	2	3	29	20	56	21	8	.320	.371
Minor League Totals			.259	86	324	49	84	18	4	3	35	26	71	26	9	.320	.367

10 JOSE ALBERTOS, RHP

Born: Nov. 7, 1998. **B-T:** R-R. **Ht.:** 6-1. **Wt.:** 190. **Signed:** Mexico, 2015. **Signed by:** Sergio Hernandez/Louie Eljaua.

The Cubs have scouted Mexico aggressively in recent years, with Albertos signing for $1.5 million as part of a package of players the Cubs signed from Tijuana of the Mexican League. He made his pro debut in June 2016 with four electric innings, wowing club officials who were on-hand, but he missed the rest of the season with tightness in his forearm. Albertos was a well-regarded prospect as an amateur, but his extended spring training performance had the Cubs excited. His fastball, previously in the 92-94 mph range, jumped to 94-96 and touched 98. Moreover, Albertos' showed signs of true fastball command when healthy, throwing strikes with his heater to both sides of the plate. His changeup flashes well above-average, overmatching Rookie-level hitters and projecting as a potential 70-grade pitch on the 20-80 scouting scale. His breaking ball was considered ahead of his changeup before he signed, and he has shown the ability to spin a slider. Risk for teen pitchers is always high, and the Cubs handled Albertos extremely carefully, hoping he can gain strength to handle his extreme arm speed and fastball velocity. After pitching in instructional league, Albertos is set for either a repeat of the AZL or potentially short-season Eugene.

BA GRADE
55 **Risk:** Extreme

BILL MITCHELL

Year	Club (League)	Class	W	L	ERA	G	GS	CG	SV	IP	H	HR	BB	SO	K/9	WHIP	AVG
2016	Cubs (AZL)	R	0	0	0.00	1	1	0	0	4	1	0	1	7	15.8	0.50	.077
Minor League Totals			0	0	0.00	1	1	0	0	4	1	0	1	7	15.8	0.50	.077

11 EDDY MARTINEZ, OF

BA GRADE
50 **Risk:** High

Born: Nov. 8, 1995. **B-T:** R-R. **Ht.:** 6-1. **Wt.:** 195. **Signed:** Cuba, 2015. **Signed by:** Louis Eljaua/Jose Serra/Glan Guzman/Alex Suarez.

Martinez, a Cuban outfielder, cost the Cubs a $3 million bonus and $3 million more in overage tax. They knew he had athletic ability and speed, but his hitting track record in Cuba was mixed. Young enough to be age-appropriate for the low Class A Midwest League, Martinez dived into the deep end of the cold, raw Midwestern spring in 2016. He passed the test by getting hot in the summer before tiring and fading late. He did show plus athleticism and the best throwing arm in the system. His arm was plus when he signed, and it's now a premium tool that has garnered 70 grades on the 20-80 scouting scale. A plus runner, Martinez can play center field but fits better in right thanks to his arm. His swing has an exaggerated load that produces a long swing and whiffs at pitches in the strike zone. His hand-eye coordination bails him out at times and allows him to make contact on pitches out of the zone. Martinez started to learn from watching video of his at-bats, and he adopted a wider stance and eliminated some pre-pitch movement to get more under control in the box. He draws walks but needs to polish his plate approach. He's ticketed for high Class A Myrtle Beach in 2017.

Year	Club (League)	Class	AVG	G	AB	R	H	2B	3B	HR	RBI	BB	SO	SB	CS	OBP	SLG
2014	Las Tunas (CNS)	CNS	.273	6	11	2	3	0	0	0	4	0	2	0	0	.273	.273
2015	Did not play																
2016	South Bend (MWL)	LoA	.254	126	460	72	117	24	2	10	67	50	113	8	5	.331	.380
Minor League Totals			.254	126	460	72	117	24	2	10	67	50	113	8	5	.331	.380

12 DONNIE DEWEES, OF

BA GRADE
50 Risk: High

Born: Sept. 29, 1993. **B-T:** L-L. **Ht.:** 5-11. **Wt.:** 180. **Drafted:** North Florida, 2015 (2nd round). **Signed by:** Tom Clark.

Dewees led Division I in slugging (.749), hits (106) and total bases (188) while ranking second in batting (.422) in 2015 at North Florida, which plays in an offensive ballpark. The Cubs often move college picks quickly, but they took it slower with Dewees, who signed for $1.7 million as a second-round pick. Despite his college success, he had to streamline his approach to eliminate pre-swing movement and a toe-tap timing mechanism in favor of a traditional stride. While Dewees may have lost a bit of pop as a result, that's not his game. He is a slasher with double-plus speed who thrives when he's using the whole field and keeping the ball out of the air. His speed played well on the bases with 31 steals in 36 attempts at two Class A levels, and he thrived in the playoffs for high Class A Myrtle Beach. Dewees could stand to walk more to be a true table-setter, and his average defense in center field would improve with refined routes and better jumps. He outruns mistakes now and has a well-below-average arm. Dewees has improvements to make, but is moving along just fine and should reach Double-A Tennessee in 2017.

Year	Club (League)	Class	AVG	G	AB	R	H	2B	3B	HR	RBI	BB	SO	SB	CS	OBP	SLG
2015	Eugene (NWL)	SS	.266	66	282	42	75	14	1	5	30	14	54	19	7	.306	.376
2016	South Bend (MWL)	LoA	.282	94	365	65	103	15	12	3	54	29	51	17	5	.337	.414
	Myrtle Beach (CAR)	HiA	.289	35	149	25	43	10	2	2	19	10	36	14	0	.339	.423
Minor League Totals			.278	195	796	132	221	39	15	10	103	53	141	50	12	.327	.402

13 THOMAS HATCH, RHP

BA GRADE
50 Risk: High

Born: Sept. 29, 1994. **B-T:** R-R. **Ht.:** 6-1. **Wt.:** 190. **Drafted:** Oklahoma State, 2016 (3rd round). **Signed by:** Ty Nichols.

Hatch teamed with White Sox farmhand Trey Michalczewski at Jenks (Okla.) High, the same school that produced Josh Johnson. Hatch ranked No. 128 on the BA 500 draft ranking out of high school but dropped to the 32nd round (Rockies), and an elbow strain caused him to miss the 2015 season. He returned in 2016 with a streamlined delivery engineered by Oklahoma State pitching coach Rob Walton, winning Big 12 Conference pitcher of the year honors and leading the Cowboys to their first College World Series since 1999. Hatch didn't pitch for the Cubs after signing for $573,900 because he tossed 130.1 innings for OSU, though he threw in instructional league. His ability to pitch off his fastball attracted the Cubs the most. It's a plus pitch that sits 93-94 mph at its best with sinking life. He has advanced fastball command for a college pitcher and sets up hitters well by front-dooring lefthanded hitters with two-seam fastballs and back-dooring them with his slider. Nebraska coach Darin Erstad compared Hatch's above-average low-80s slider to that of ex-big leaguer Brad Lidge, and his solid-average changeup plays off his fastball well. Hatch's three-pitch mix and strike-throwing ability give him a chance to move quickly, though his lack of a plus secondary pitch gives him more of a back-of-the-rotation profile.

Year	Club (League)	Class	W	L	ERA	G	GS	CG	SV	IP	H	HR	BB	SO	K/9	WHIP	AVG
2016	Did not play																

14 ROB ZASTRYZNY, LHP

BA GRADE
45 Risk: Medium

Born: March 26, 1992. **B-T:** R-L. **Ht.:** 6-3. **Wt.:** 205. **Drafted:** Missouri, 2014 (3rd round). **Signed by:** Ty Nichols.

The Cubs' second pick in the 2013 draft after Kris Bryant, the Canadian-born Zastryzny endured a difficult 2015 season when he pitched poorly at Double-A Tennessee (6.23 ERA) when healthy and missed two months with a broken left ankle. He didn't get an invitation to big league camp in 2016 but finished the year in Chicago, pitching a career-high 136 innings in the minors despite a bout of shoulder fatigue before making his major league debut in August. Zastryzny has shown solid feel for throwing strikes with three pitches since his days at Missouri, but the improvement of his fourth pitch, a cutter, made a big difference in 2016. He came up with it on his own, showed it to Cubs officials and got the green light. His bread-and-butter remains his solid-average fastball that sits 88-90 mph but bumps up to 94 at its best. His herky-jerky arm action and high glove hand give his delivery needed deception, because his below-average curveball and fringe-average changeup aren't swing-and-miss pitches on their own. A multi-inning relief option in September, Zastryzny has shown the Cubs he can fill a versatile bullpen role. That's his immediate path to major league innings, but as a lefty with four pitches, he's a potential back-end starting option.

Year	Club (League)	Class	W	L	ERA	G	GS	CG	SV	IP	H	HR	BB	SO	K/9	WHIP	AVG
2014	Daytona (FSL)	HiA	4	6	4.66	23	23	0	0	110	121	10	33	108	8.8	1.40	.279
2015	Cubs (AZL)	R	0	0	2.25	1	1	0	0	4	3	0	2	4	9.0	1.25	.200
	Tennessee (SL)	AA	2	5	6.23	14	14	0	0	61	77	9	28	48	7.1	1.73	.310
2016	Tennessee (SL)	AA	3	2	4.28	9	9	0	0	55	50	6	20	42	6.9	1.28	.245
	Iowa (PCL)	AAA	7	3	4.33	15	14	0	0	81	67	7	31	77	8.6	1.21	.229
	Chicago (NL)	MAJ	1	0	1.13	8	1	0	0	16	12	0	5	17	9.6	1.06	.207
Major League Totals			1	0	1.13	8	1	0	0	16	12	0	5	17	9.6	1.06	.207
Minor League Totals			17	16	4.60	73	68	0	0	334	342	32	122	301	8.1	1.39	.266

15 DUANE UNDERWOOD, RHP

BA GRADE
50 Risk: Extreme

Born: July 20, 1994. **B-T:** R-R. **Ht.:** 6-2. **Wt.:** 210. **Drafted:** HS—Marietta, Ga., 2012 (2nd round). **Signed by:** Keith Lockhart.

Underwood remains the pitcher with the highest ceiling in the Cubs system for some club officials, but his likelihood of reaching it keeps diminishing. Signed for $1.05 million in 2012, Underwood hasn't pitched a full season since 2014. Elbow soreness and inflammation interrupted his 2015 season, while similar issues in spring training delayed his 2016 campaign. He made 13 starts at Double-A Tennessee before being sidelined again for over a month with forearm tightness, and he finished the season at low Class A South Bend. He then left the Arizona Fall League after two modest appearances, where his fastball sat around 92 mph. At his best, Underwood sits 93-95 mph with late life on his fastball, though he doesn't hold that velocity deep into games. He flashes plus with his curveball and above-average with his change-up, but he lacks consistency with both pitches. The Cubs added him to the 40-man roster in November, and Underwood stayed in Arizona in the offseason to work on the club's conditioning program. He hopes to shed the "tease" label in a return to Double-A in 2017, but can only do so if his elbow stops barking.

Year	Club (League)	Class	W	L	ERA	G	GS	CG	SV	IP	H	HR	BB	SO	K/9	WHIP	AVG
2014	Kane County (MWL)	LoA	6	4	2.50	22	21	0	0	101	85	10	36	84	7.5	1.20	.231
2015	Cubs (AZL)	R	0	0	0.00	2	2	0	0	5	3	0	0	6	10.8	0.60	.167
	Myrtle Beach (CAR)	HiA	6	3	2.58	14	14	0	0	73	52	6	24	48	5.9	1.04	.202
2016	Tennessee (SL)	AA	0	5	4.91	13	13	1	0	59	66	7	31	46	7.1	1.65	.280
	Cubs (AZL)	R	0	0	0.00	1	1	0	0	1	1	0	0	2	18.0	1.00	.250
	South Bend (MWL)	LoA	0	1	2.08	3	3	0	0	9	5	0	4	12	12.5	1.04	.172
	Myrtle Beach (CAR)	HiA	0	0	1.93	1	1	0	0	5	3	0	0	2	3.9	0.64	.176
Minor League Totals			15	18	3.40	75	71	1	0	315	284	28	128	243	6.9	1.31	.239

16 CHESNY YOUNG, 2B/3B

BA GRADE
45 Risk: Medium

Born: Oct. 6, 1992. **B-T:** R-R. **Ht.:** 6-0. **Wt.:** 170. **Drafted:** Mercer, 2014 (14th round). **Signed by:** Keith Lockhart.

Young ranked second in Division I in hits (105) at Mercer as a sophomore, when he hit .401, but he fell off as a junior and dropped to the 14th round of the 2014 draft. His hitting ability, which is his best asset, re-emerged in pro ball. He won the high Class A Carolina League batting title in 2015 and challenged for the Double-A Southern League batting title in 2016 when he hit .303. A career .314 hitter as a pro, Young has good hands, bat control, feel for the barrel and superior strike-zone judgment. When he gets the pitch he's looking for, he can serve line drives to all fields, though he has well below-average power. Young has improved his chances to be a big leaguer by showing greater defensive ability. He is a solid-average defender at both second base and third (where he played in the Dominican League in winter ball) with a good first step, and he surprised the Cubs in brief looks at shortstop. Despite an average arm, Young played 17 games at short in 2016 and made the routine play. He is a fringy runner but runs better underway, enough to see time in the outfield corners. If Young can continue to handle shortstop, his bat will help him get to the majors. He figures to hit near the top of Triple-A Iowa's lineup in 2017.

Year	Club (League)	Class	AVG	G	AB	R	H	2B	3B	HR	RBI	BB	SO	SB	CS	OBP	SLG
2014	Cubs (AZL)	R	.167	2	6	0	1	0	0	0	0	1	2	0	0	.286	.167
	Boise (NWL)	SS	.354	15	48	13	17	3	0	0	9	8	8	1	0	.466	.417
	Kane County (MWL)	LoA	.324	27	105	14	34	6	2	0	9	5	22	2	1	.348	.419
2015	South Bend (MWL)	LoA	.315	28	108	23	34	5	1	0	14	12	7	9	3	.385	.380
	Myrtle Beach (CAR)	HiA	.321	102	402	65	129	18	3	1	30	45	44	12	5	.394	.388
2016	Tennessee (SL)	AA	.303	126	491	60	149	25	2	4	37	57	64	16	14	.376	.387
Minor League Totals			.314	300	1160	175	364	57	8	5	99	128	147	40	23	.384	.390

17 VICTOR CARATINI, C/1B

BA GRADE

45 Risk: Medium

Born: Aug. 17, 1993. **B-T:** B-R. **Ht.:** 6-1. **Wt.:** 215. **Drafted:** Miami-Dade JC, 2013 (2nd round). **Signed by:** Buddy Hernandez (Braves).

It feels like ancient history when the Cubs were sellers and the Braves buyers, but that's how the Cubs got Caratini. He had only been with the Braves for a year when they traded him for Emilio Bonifacio and James Russell in July 2014. Caratini played catcher and third base as an amateur and mixes in time at first base for the Cubs, but he's taken to the grind of being an everyday catcher. He is a decent athlete with good hands, playable footwork and a fringe-average arm. He threw out 26 percent of basestealers at Double-A Tennessee while consistently turning in 2.05-2.1 second pop times on throws to second base, with 2.0 being average. A poor runner, Caratini nonetheless hits for average and in 2016 ranked second in the Southern League in on-base percentage (.375) and sixth in batting (.291) thanks to a short, repeatable stroke from both sides of the plate. He controls the strike zone well, but the Cubs would like to see more aggressiveness. Club officials worked with him in the Arizona Fall League to try to get to his above-average raw power more often, encouraging him to turn his swing loose and hunt for pitches he can drive. Caratini is headed for Triple-A Iowa in 2017 and currently profiles as a future backup catcher.

Year	Club (League)	Class	AVG	G	AB	R	H	2B	3B	HR	RBI	BB	SO	SB	CS	OBP	SLG
2014	Rome (SAL)	LoA	.279	87	323	42	90	18	4	5	42	34	59	1	1	.352	.406
	Kane County (MWL)	LoA	.264	14	53	7	14	4	1	0	13	4	10	0	0	.310	.377
2015	Myrtle Beach (CAR)	HiA	.257	112	393	39	101	31	1	4	53	49	75	0	0	.342	.372
2016	Tennessee (SL)	AA	.291	115	412	57	120	25	2	6	47	54	80	2	1	.375	.405
Minor League Totals			.277	386	1381	174	383	101	9	16	180	180	273	3	4	.364	.398

18 WLADIMIR GALINDO, 3B

BA GRADE

50 Risk: Extreme

Born: Nov. 6, 1996. **B-T:** R-R. **Ht.:** 6-2. **Wt.:** 190. **Signed:** Venezuela, 2013. **Signed by:** Julio Figueroa/Hector Ortega.

Signed for $50,000 at the end of 2013, Galindo was in the midst of a breakout in 2015 in the Rookie-level Arizona League when a fractured left hand ended his season after just 19 games. At first glance, his short-season Eugene effort in 2016 offers a mixed bag, particularly his strikeout rate of 28.7 percent. Eugene's PK Park depresses offense, and Galindo hit just .172 at home, but on the road he hit .305/.389/.611. His plus raw power and present strength are evident. He is not just a pull-oriented hitter, either, having shown the ability to leave the yard to all fields. Galindo's raw offensive approach can be exploited with soft stuff away, and he has yet to make consistent adjustments. He'll likely never hit for a high average, and scouts also are mixed on his defensive future. His plus arm suits him for third base, where his inconsistent footwork and developing instincts lead to mechanical problems and errant throws. He runs well enough for now for left field to be an option, while some scouts see him as a future first baseman. Galindo's power will earn him development time. He is slated for low Class A South Bend in 2017.

Year	Club (League)	Class	AVG	G	AB	R	H	2B	3B	HR	RBI	BB	SO	SB	CS	OBP	SLG
2014	Cubs (VSL)	R	.278	62	223	29	62	18	1	7	30	20	55	3	2	.356	.462
2015	Cubs (AZL)	R	.358	19	67	15	24	7	2	0	11	4	15	1	1	.400	.522
2016	Eugene (NWL)	SS	.243	66	247	46	60	19	4	9	40	33	81	3	0	.337	.462
Minor League Totals			.272	147	537	90	146	44	7	16	81	57	151	7	3	.353	.469

19 PIERCE JOHNSON, RHP

BA GRADE

45 Risk: High

Born: May 10, 1991. **B-T:** R-R. **Ht.:** 6-3. **Wt.:** 200. **Drafted:** Missouri State, 2012 (1st round supplemental). **Signed by:** Stan Zielinski.

A Colorado prep product and 2012 supplemental first-rounder, Johnson hasn't figured out a way to stay healthy. A partial rundown of injuries include: a forearm strain, blisters, knee and hand injuries from his amateur days, and hamstring, calf and lat muscle strains in the last year. A comebacker to the mound cost him time in 2016 when it struck his pitching arm. In short, Johnson couldn't stay on the mound as a starter, and he had run up a 7.75 ERA in July, when the Cubs pulled the plug on him as a starter. He finished the season in the Triple-A Iowa bullpen, stayed healthy and struck out 35 (while walking 13) in 22.1 innings in that role. Johnson's fastball can still reach 96 mph, and he pared down his repertoire as a reliever, focusing on his fastball and inconsistent, above-average slurvy breaking ball while shelving his changeup and cutter. He still struggles to pitch with conviction to his arm side with his fastball. The Cubs added him to their 40-man roster after the 2016 season, so if he can stay healthy, he could ride the bullpen shuttle to Chicago in 2017.

Year	Club (League)	Class	W	L	ERA	G	GS	CG	SV	IP	H	HR	BB	SO	K/9	WHIP	AVG
2014	Kane County (MWL)	LoA	0	1	2.45	2	2	0	0	11	4	1	3	8	6.5	0.64	.118
	Tennessee (SL)	AA	5	4	2.55	18	17	0	0	92	60	8	54	91	8.9	1.24	.194
2015	Tennessee (SL)	AA	6	2	2.08	16	16	1	0	95	76	4	32	72	6.8	1.14	.223
2016	Iowa (PCL)	AAA	4	6	6.14	22	11	0	0	63	60	8	43	75	10.7	1.63	.256
Minor League Totals			26	19	3.09	87	73	1	0	390	323	26	178	384	8.9	1.28	.231

20 ERLING MORENO, RHP

BA GRADE
50 Risk: Extreme

Born: Jan. 13, 1997. **B-T:** R-R. **Ht.:** 6-3. **Wt.:** 200. **Signed:** Colombia, 2013.
Signed by: Manny Esquivia.

Moreno was a part of the Cubs' international class of 2013, which included No. 1 prospect Eloy Jimenez and now Yankees No. 1 prospect Gleyber Torres. Moreno received a $650,000 bonus but lost a year of development to Tommy John surgery. The longer Moreno pitched in 2016, the harder he threw, and he topped out at 93 mph when he finished the year at short-season Eugene. Some scouts think Moreno has more velocity in the tank, and he hit 94 mph before surgery. Moreno's fastball plays above-average now and has future plus potential due to its heavy, late sinking life, and he got two groundouts for every airout with the Emeralds. His slider has its moments, but his solid-average changeup grades out above his below-average slider. Physical and bigger than his listed 6-foot-3, 200 pounds, Moreno throws a lot of strikes, but his delivery has some stiffness to it. He's part of a glut of Cubs pitchers who could see time in the low Class A South Bend rotation in 2017.

Year	Club (League)	Class	W	L	ERA	G	GS	CG	SV	IP	H	HR	BB	SO	K/9	WHIP	AVG
2014	Cubs (VSL)	R	0	0	0.00	1	0	0	0	3	4	0	0	3	9.0	1.33	.400
	Cubs 1 (DSL)	R	0	1	1.08	4	4	0	0	8	6	0	3	6	6.5	1.08	.194
2015	Cubs (AZL)	R	1	1	1.93	3	0	0	0	5	3	0	2	2	3.9	1.07	.176
2016	Cubs (AZL)	R	2	2	2.78	6	4	0	0	32	31	1	4	33	9.2	1.08	.254
	Eugene (NWL)	SS	2	1	0.90	6	6	0	0	30	16	2	5	22	6.6	0.70	.150
Minor League Totals			5	5	1.72	20	14	0	0	78	60	3	14	66	7.6	0.94	.209

21 JOSE PAULINO, LHP

BA GRADE
50 Risk: Extreme

Born: April 9, 1995. **B-T:** L-L. **Ht.:** 6-2. **Wt.:** 165. **Signed:** Dominican Republic, 2011. **Signed by:** Jose Serra.

Signed in 2011 for $140,000, Paulino finally reached full-season ball in the second half of 2016. He dominated early at short-season Eugene, then after a promotion he started and won low Class A South Bend's only playoff victory. Paulino had struggled with throwing strikes while growing into his listed 6-foot-2, 165-pound frame, but he is considerably bigger than that now. His fastball can touch 95 mph and regularly sits anywhere in the 89-94 range. He has flashed an above-average slider while also flashing a changeup that can be average. Paulino's crossfire delivery helps him pitch inside to righthanded batters, but he may lack the fastball command to start. One area for improvement is he needs to progress with his between-starts routine and mature with his preparation to take advantage of his fast arm and raw arm strength. Paulino may be pushed to high Class A Myrtle Beach in 2017 after his strong South Bend finish.

Year	Club (League)	Class	W	L	ERA	G	GS	CG	SV	IP	H	HR	BB	SO	K/9	WHIP	AVG
2014	Cubs (AZL)	R	3	4	5.98	12	7	0	0	47	55	3	20	42	8.1	1.61	.294
2015	Eugene (NWL)	SS	4	6	4.42	12	6	0	0	55	59	5	21	57	9.3	1.45	.272
2016	Eugene (NWL)	SS	4	2	0.51	6	6	0	0	35	19	0	3	37	9.5	0.63	.156
	South Bend (MWL)	LoA	3	1	3.15	7	7	0	0	40	36	3	10	32	7.2	1.15	.234
Minor League Totals			21	20	3.57	65	43	0	0	295	270	16	86	299	9.1	1.21	.238

22 P.J. HIGGINS, C

BA GRADE
45 Risk: High

Born: May 10, 1993. **B-T:** R-R. **Ht.:** 5-10. **Wt.:** 185. **Drafted:** Old Dominion, 2015 (12th round). **Signed by:** Billy Swoope.

A Connecticut prep product, Higgins started for most of three seasons at Old Dominion, playing mostly second and third base while mixing in time at catcher, his high school position. The Cubs switched Higgins to catcher full-time during instructional league in 2015, and he took to it in 2016, anchoring the low Class A South Bend lineup and defense. Higgins is a good athlete who has the hands and footwork to be an average defender, if not more. He's an above-average thrower with a quick transfer, producing above-average 1.9-2.0-second pop times on throws to second base. He threw out 31 percent of basestealers in 2016. Higgins lacks game-calling experience but is a savvy leader. Pitchers love throwing to him and take to his leadership well. Offensively, Higgins controls the strike zone at an elite level, and he ranked third in the Midwest League with a .389 on-base percentage. He can shoot line drives to the gaps but lacks home run power. His modest size may keep him from ever being a 120-game workhorse catcher, but he has the skills to be a contributor if he keeps developing. His next step is high Class A Myrtle Beach.

Year	Club (League)	Class	AVG	G	AB	R	H	2B	3B	HR	RBI	BB	SO	SB	CS	OBP	SLG
2015	Cubs (AZL)	R	.288	21	80	17	23	4	3	2	10	7	15	3	0	.345	.488
	Eugene (NWL)	SS	.316	15	57	8	18	4	0	0	5	3	11	1	0	.361	.386
2016	South Bend (MWL)	LoA	.283	121	445	57	126	30	1	0	40	72	75	3	1	.389	.355
Minor League Totals			.287	157	582	82	167	38	4	2	55	82	101	7	1	.381	.376

23 JACOB HANNEMANN, OF

BA GRADE
45 Risk: High

Born: April 29, 1991. **B-T:** L-L. **Ht.:** 6-1. **Wt.:** 200. **Drafted:** Brigham Young, 2013 (3rd round). **Signed by:** Steve McFarland.

Hannemann remains the best athlete in the Cubs system. He missed the second half of the 2016 season with a thumb injury, the latest in a long line of injury woes (shoulder, hamstring) due in part to Hannemann's all-out, aggresive style. He's a dynamic speedster with outstanding range in center field who outruns poor jumps to make highlight-reel catches. Scouts never struggle to get good run times on Hannemann because he plays so hard. Some scouts still give him 70 grades on the 20-80 scouting scale for both his defense, despite a fringe-average arm, and speed. He ranked among the Southern League leaders in stolen bases (26) when he got hurt. Hannemann has strength and will flash a good swing path with strength to drive balls to the gaps, and he was just starting to get into his average raw power when he got hurt. Hannemann went to Puerto Rico to play winter ball but was benched after a 9-for-75 start. Added to the 40-man roster after the 2016 season, he faces a probable ceiling as an extra outfielder as he advances to Triple-A Iowa.

Year	Club (League)	Class	AVG	G	AB	R	H	2B	3B	HR	RBI	BB	SO	SB	CS	OBP	SLG
2014	Kane County (MWL)	LoA	.254	88	342	57	87	14	5	6	39	31	77	32	4	.321	.377
	Daytona (FSL)	HiA	.241	36	145	17	35	9	0	2	12	11	34	5	3	.299	.345
2015	Myrtle Beach (CAR)	HiA	.328	16	61	12	20	4	0	0	4	6	15	7	1	.388	.393
	Tennessee (SL)	AA	.233	112	434	60	101	20	9	6	41	32	113	17	1	.291	.362
2016	Tennessee (SL)	AA	.247	74	291	37	72	14	4	10	30	25	55	26	8	.326	.426
Minor League Totals			.249	343	1344	192	334	66	20	25	133	107	306	91	18	.311	.383

24 JUSTIN STEELE, LHP

BA GRADE
50 Risk: Extreme

Born: July 11, 1995. **B-T:** L-L. **Ht.:** 6-2. **Wt.:** 195. **Drafted:** HS—Lucedale, Miss., 2014 (5th round). **Signed by:** Jonathan Davis.

Originally signed for $1 million, Steele is so athletic he can get away with an unorthodox delivery in which his hands, set high, tend to drift. At times his arm doesn't catch up at foot strike and he leaves his 89-91 mph fastball up at belly-button level for hitters to feast upon. When he's on time, though, Steele can reach 95 mph with angle and late life and pound the bottom of the strike zone. That happened less frequently in 2016, though, a year when Steele actually was sent back to Arizona in June to work on his mechanics. He pitched better upon is return by working inside more effectively and challenging hitters with more conviction. His curveball ranks as his best secondary pitch, and he still varies the size and shape of it, but in the second half he threw his below-average changeup more. Due to the Cubs' pitching depth, Steele is likely headed for high Class A Myrtle Beach in 2017.

Year	Club (League)	Class	W	L	ERA	G	GS	CG	SV	IP	H	HR	BB	SO	K/9	WHIP	AVG
2014	Cubs (AZL)	R	0	0	2.89	9	4	0	0	19	15	0	8	25	12.1	1.23	.217
2015	Eugene (NWL)	SS	3	1	2.66	10	10	0	0	41	38	0	15	38	8.4	1.30	.245
2016	South Bend (MWL)	LoA	5	7	5.00	19	19	0	0	77	93	3	39	76	8.8	1.71	.305
Minor League Totals			8	8	4.02	38	33	0	0	137	146	3	62	139	9.2	1.52	.276

25 BRYAN HUDSON, LHP

BA GRADE
50 Risk: Extreme

Born: May 8, 1997. **B-T:** L-L. **Ht.:** 6-8. **Wt.:** 220. **Drafted:** HS—Alton, Ill, 2015 (3rd round). **Signed by:** Stan Zielinski.

The Cubs' hunt for homegrown pitching has hit some bumps, and the 6-foot-8 Hudson hit his share in 2016. He jumped from extended spring training, where he pitched well, to short-season Eugene after just five outings in Rookie ball in 2015, and it was a rough landing. The Cubs fell in love with Hudson's size and plus curveball in the draft, signing him for $1 million. His curve backed up in the Northwest League, where at times it seemed he was pushing the ball, but he found better feel for it in instructional league. He competed with a fastball that backed up into the mid-80s at times as well, though in the past he hit 93 mph. Hudson pitched downhill at times and got plenty of groundball outs. He made progress with his changeup but struggled overall to repeat his delivery and walked as many as he struck out. Tall pitchers often bloom later, and the Cubs may have to push Hudson back to extended spring in 2017.

Year	Club (League)	Class	W	L	ERA	G	GS	CG	SV	IP	H	HR	BB	SO	K/9	WHIP	AVG
2015	Cubs (AZL)	R	0	0	2.70	5	0	0	0	7	6	0	2	5	6.8	1.20	.222
2016	Eugene (NWL)	SS	5	4	5.06	13	13	0	0	59	56	4	41	41	6.3	1.65	.262
Minor League Totals			5	4	4.82	18	13	0	0	65	62	4	43	46	6.3	1.61	.257

26 DAVID BOTE, 3B/2B

BA GRADE
45 Risk: High

Born: April 7, 1993. **B-T:** R-R. **Ht.:** 5-11. **Wt.:** 185. **Drafted:** Neosho County (Kan.) CC, 2012 (18th round). **Signed by:** Rick Schroeder.

Bote hails from a baseball family. His father was a high school coach who coached Cubs farmhand Pierce Johnson in American Legion ball, and his older brother Danny actually coached David as a high school senior. Never a priority prospect, Bote struggled to get playing time and still has yet to receive 400 plate appearances in a season. He opened the 2016 season bouncing between high Class A, Double-A and even Triple-A, filling in for injured infielders, before finally getting regular reps down the stretch at high Class A Myrtle Beach. Bote controlled the strike zone and mashed mistakes to the gaps (he ranked second on the team with 26 doubles in just 72 games), then carried the Pelicans to their second straight Carolina League championship. He went 15-for-26 with five more doubles in seven playoff games. Bote has present strength, got in a hitting rhythm and has enough bat speed to produce solid-average power. He is athletic and has an average arm, with third base his best position. He grades as fringe-average at second base. An average runner, Bote has enough offensive potential and defensive versatility to hit his way into a future super-sub role. He is slated to be the Double-A Tennessee third baseman in 2017.

Year	Club (League)	Class	AVG	G	AB	R	H	2B	3B	HR	RBI	BB	SO	SB	CS	OBP	SLG
2014	Kane County (MWL)	LoA	.210	58	186	19	39	12	0	1	21	21	49	3	4	.323	.290
	Boise (NWL)	SS	.260	37	131	22	34	11	0	2	16	18	24	9	3	.366	.389
	Iowa (PCL)	AAA	.400	4	10	3	4	0	0	1	3	2	1	1	0	.500	.700
2015	South Bend (MWL)	LoA	.253	97	312	45	79	20	2	6	41	28	60	5	3	.329	.388
2016	Iowa (PCL)	AAA	.364	12	22	4	8	0	0	1	3	2	5	0	0	.417	.500
	Tennessee (SL)	AA	.200	7	25	1	5	0	0	0	1	2	6	0	0	.259	.200
	Myrtle Beach (CAR)	HiA	.337	72	276	55	93	26	3	6	41	31	41	6	1	.410	.518
Minor League Totals			.259	415	1382	214	358	87	8	25	178	161	291	35	19	.351	.388

27 JACK LEATHERSICH, LHP

BA GRADE
40 Risk: Medium

Born: July 14, 1990. **B-T:** R-L. **Ht.:** 6-0. **Wt.:** 205. **Drafted:** Massachusetts-Lowell, 2011 (5th round). **Signed by:** Art Pontarelli (Mets).

The Cubs' offseason bullpen makeover opens a door for Leathersich, whom the Cubs claimed off waivers in November 2015 and added to the 40-man roster after the 2016 season. Leathersich was coming off Tommy John surgery, which he had in July 2015. He has big league time with the Mets, and he got back on the mound in June 2016, finishing at Triple-A Iowa and pitching 23 innings overall. Leathersich has never had good control, but he has thrived with deception on a low-90s fastball that tops out at 94 mph. He's wild but gets swing-and-misses at an advanced rate with his high fastball and inconsistent, but at times plus, curveball. That has helped lead to a career mark of 15 strikeouts per nine innings. He will occasionally mix in a below-average changeup. Leathersich will compete with Rule 5 pick Caleb Smith, veteran Brian Duensing and prospect Rob Zastryzny for lefty bullpen innings in 2017.

Year	Club (League)	Class	W	L	ERA	G	GS	CG	SV	IP	H	HR	BB	SO	K/9	WHIP	AVG
2014	Binghamton (EL)	AA	3	3	2.93	37	0	0	1	46	38	1	21	79	15.5	1.28	.221
	Las Vegas (PCL)	AAA	0	0	5.40	11	0	0	0	8	8	2	7	14	15.1	1.80	.242
2015	New York (NL)	MAJ	0	1	2.31	17	0	0	0	12	12	0	7	14	10.8	1.63	.273
	Las Vegas (PCL)	AAA	0	0	5.40	13	0	0	0	13	10	3	7	22	14.9	1.28	.204
2016	Cubs (AZL)	R	1	0	1.13	10	1	0	0	8	4	0	3	16	18.0	0.88	.148
	Tennessee (SL)	AA	0	0	3.48	11	0	0	0	10	11	0	4	12	10.5	1.45	.282
	Iowa (PCL)	AAA	0	0	0.00	5	0	0	0	5	0	0	6	6	10.8	1.20	.000
Major League Totals			0	1	2.31	17	0	0	0	12	12	0	7	14	10.8	1.63	.273
Minor League Totals			10	9	3.38	186	1	0	7	234	179	12	128	390	15.0	1.31	.209

28 BAILEY CLARK, RHP

Born: Dec. 3, 1994. **B-T:** R-R. **Ht.:** 6-4. **Wt.:** 185. **Drafted:** Duke, 2016 (5th round). **Signed by:** Billy Swoope.

BA GRADE

50 Risk: Extreme

The Cubs wound up selecting 27 pitchers among their 38 picks in 2016. The lean Clark, who has a prototypical pitcher's body, was the biggest lottery ticket of the bunch. He opened the season as Duke's Opening Day starter and finished it out of the rotation. Poor command plagued Clark, starting with his long arm action, then was compounded by lost confidence. The Cubs took it slow after signing him for $450,000, building him up before he made his debut in the Rookie-level Arizona League. Clark threw just 11.2 innings after signing but didn't walk a batter, an encouraging sign after he walked 26 in 59 innings while posting a 5.61 ERA at Duke. Clark's fastball touched 98 mph this spring and sits in the 92-95 range with lively late movement. Both his changeup and hard 82-84 mph slider have had their moments, though his arm action makes it hard for him to repeat his release point on his breaking ball. Clark went back to school for the fall instead of attending instructional league, in part because of sports hernia surgery. Cubs coaches can't wait to get their hands on him in spring training.

Year	Club (League)	Class	W	L	ERA	G	GS	CG	SV	IP	H	HR	BB	SO	K/9	WHIP	AVG
2016	Cubs (AZL)	R	0	0	0.00	2	2	0	0	5	3	0	0	4	7.2	0.60	.188
	Eugene (NWL)	SS	0	0	2.70	2	2	0	0	7	8	1	0	9	12.2	1.20	.276
Minor League Totals			0	0	1.54	4	4	0	0	12	11	1	0	13	10.0	0.94	.244

29 ISAAC PAREDES, SS

Born: Feb. 18, 1999. **B-T:** R-R. **Ht.:** 5-11. **Wt.:** 175. **Signed:** Mexico, 2015. **Signed by:** Sergio Hernandez/Louie Eljaua.

BA GRADE

45 Risk: Extreme

The Cubs scout Mexico aggressively, in part because money spent on players there doesn't all count against their bonus pool. Only the portion the players receive counts, while the percentage that goes to the Mexican League club that owns those players' rights doesn't. Chicago signed Paredes away from the Mexico City Red Devils for $800,000, and he was advanced enough to jump to the Rookie-level Arizona League in 2016. There, he hit well enough to earn a late cameo at low Class A South Bend and started all three of its playoff games. He went 1-for-11 with two errors. Paredes is squat and somewhat thick for a shortstop, earning Jhonny Peralta comparisons. But, he has great hands that play at the plate and in the field, and he has surprising agility with nimble, quick feet. An average runner, Paredes has an above-average arm that may work at third base if he has to move. A veteran of Mexico's 15U national team, he is an advanced hitter for his age with an all-field approach, some pop and good plate discipline. He should go back to South Bend for 2017 as a 19-year-old.

Year	Club (League)	Class	AVG	G	AB	R	H	2B	3B	HR	RBI	BB	SO	SB	CS	OBP	SLG
2016	Cubs (AZL)	R	.305	47	167	23	51	14	3	1	26	13	20	4	0	.359	.443
	South Bend (MWL)	LoA	.167	3	12	0	2	0	0	0	0	0	2	0	0	.231	.167
Minor League Totals			.296	50	179	23	53	14	3	1	26	13	22	4	0	.350	.425

30 CHRIS PIETERS, OF/1B

Born: Sept. 21, 1994. **B-T:** L-L. **Ht.:** 6-3. **Wt.:** 185. **Signed:** Curacao, 2011. **Signed by:** Hector Ortega.

BA GRADE

45 Risk: Extreme

The Cubs' pitcher-heavy 2016 draft helped provide plenty of playing time for Pieters, a Curacao native who signed for $350,000 in 2011 as a lefthanded pitcher. Short-season Eugene needed hitters, and he is one now after switching to hitting during Dominican instructional league in 2014. He has made quick strides, helping Eugene win the Northwest League title. Pieters has an athletic frame and the arm strength for any outfield spot, though his routes are so raw that he plays left field when not at first base. He has the bat speed to catch up to good fastballs, some barrel awareness and repeats his flat-planed swing well. He's also an above-average runner who surprised scouts by stealing 20 bags in 23 attempts. He has yet to reach full-season ball and was exposed to the Rule 5 draft in both 2015 and 2016, and it may be harder to hide him if he breaks out at 2017 at low Class A South Bend.

Year	Club (League)	Class	W	L	ERA	G	GS	CG	SV	IP	H	HR	BB	SO	K/9	WHIP	AVG
2014	Cubs (VSL)	R	0	1	18.00	3	0	0	0	4	9	0	5	3	6.8	3.50	.450
	Cubs 1 (DSL)	R	1	0	9.56	15	1	0	0	16	22	1	25	15	8.4	2.94	.328
Minor League Totals			4	11	9.31	51	11	0	0	77	81	2	119	61	7.1	2.59	.280

Year	Club (League)	Class	AVG	G	AB	R	H	2B	3B	HR	RBI	BB	SO	SB	CS	OBP	SLG
2015	Cubs (DSL)	R	.311	53	180	38	56	8	2	3	33	40	32	25	4	.457	.428
	Cubs (AZL)	R	.257	9	35	6	9	5	0	0	6	1	10	0	0	.282	.400
2016	Eugene (NWL)	SS	.246	66	252	36	62	8	3	3	30	28	73	20	3	.324	.337
Minor League Totals			.272	128	467	80	127	21	5	6	69	69	115	45	7	.377	.377

Chicago White Sox

BY HUDSON BELINSKY

The White Sox entered 2016 with some optimism. They were returning a veteran pitching staff with an excellent 1-2 punch of Chris Sale and Jose Quintana. They acquired slugging third baseman Todd Frazier and brought in veterans such as catcher Alex Avila and shortstop Jimmy Rollins. They expected contributions from young cornerstone players like Carlos Rodon and Adam Eaton.

In the beginning of the season, that optimism seemed plausible. Chicago got off to a 24-12 start and appeared to be a contender in the American League Central. But things soured quickly, with a harsh slump in late May.

The team bought low on righthander James Shields in early June, but the righthander's struggles only worsened when he got to Chicago. The White Sox got little production from Avila, Rollins or Austin Jackson, and before long they had settled into mediocrity. As postseason aspirations slipped away, the clubhouse atmosphere deteriorated, culminating in a bizarre incident when ace Chris Sale cut up his uniform in protest of a throwback jersey that made him uncomfortable.

Ultimately, the White Sox had a run-of-the-mill rotation, with the back end failing to produce reliable results to support Sale and Quintana. Chicago's offense produced home runs, with Frazier smashing 40, but the team got on base at a below-average rate and failed to capitalize on many of those home runs.

On the bright side, the White Sox got solid production from shortstop and No. 1 prospect Tim Anderson, who reached the majors and hit .283/.306/.432 in 99 games. He will still need to improve his plate approach to get on base more often, but he had a productive rookie season and appears to factor significantly in the future.

Rodon was inconsistent, but he was also brilliant in flashes and closed out the season with double-digit strikeouts in back-to-back starts.

The White Sox system got a much-needed face lift at the 2016 Winter Meetings, when general manager Rick Hahn completed two franchise-altering trades. First, he traded Sale to the Red Sox for four prospects, including dynamic Cuban second baseman Yoan Moncada and fellow Top 100 Prospect Michael Kopech, a righthander who tops 100 mph. Outfielder Luis Alexander Basabe and reliever Victor Diaz spent most of 2016 at low Class A.

Hahn then shipped center fielder Adam Eaton to the Nationals for three prospects, including big league-ready righthanders Lucas Giolito and Reynaldo Lopez. Chicago also picked up 2016

The White Sox committed to a rebuild when they traded ace Chris Sale for prospects

TOP PROSPECTS OF THE DECADE

Year	Player, Pos.	2016 Org
2007	Ryan Sweeney, of	Did not play
2008	Aaron Poreda, lhp	Yomiuri (Japan)
2009	Gordon Beckham, ss	Giants
2010	Jared Mitchell, of	Yankees
2011	Chris Sale, lhp	White Sox
2012	Addison Reed, rhp	Mets
2013	Courtney Hawkins, of	White Sox
2014	Jose Abreu, 1b	White Sox
2015	Carlos Rodon, lhp	White Sox
2016	Tim Anderson, ss	White Sox

first-round righty Dane Dunning in the deal.

The White Sox effectively acquired three first-round talents in the 2016 draft, when Dunning is combined with catcher Zack Collins and righthander Zack Burdi, Chicago's two first-round selections. All three are likely to advance quickly and could impact the major league roster soon.

Thanks to the prospect acquisitions of 2016, the White Sox could be competitive in the near future if Moncada, Giolito, Lopez and Kopech meet expectations. That's because Chicago's influx of top prospects coincides with what could be a changing of the guard in the AL Central. The Royals and Tigers appear to be downsizing, while the Twins are in the midst of their own rebuild. The only constant in the division should be the Indians, the defending AL champions.

ORGANIZATION OVERVIEW

President: Kenny Williams. **GM:** Rick Hahn. **Farm director:** Chris Getz. **Scouting director:** Nick Hostetler.

Class	Team	League	W	L	PCT	Finish	Manager
Majors	Chicago White Sox	American	78	84	.481	11th (15)	Robin Ventura
Triple-A	Charlotte Knights	International	65	79	.451	11th (14)	Julio Vinas
Double-A	Birmingham Barons	Southern	49	91	.350	10th (10)	Ryan Newman
High Class A	Winston-Salem Dash	Carolina	56	83	.403	6th (8)	Joel Skinner
Low Class A	Kannapolis Intimidators	South Atlantic	58	82	.414	13th (14)	Cole Armstrong
Rookie	Great Falls Voyagers	Pioneer	47	28	.627	1st (8)	Tommy Thompson
Rookie	AZL White Sox	Arizona	21	35	.375	13th (14)	Mike Gellinger
Overall 2016 Minor League Record			296	398	.427	30th (30)	

THIS YEAR'S TOP 30

No.	Player, Pos.	Grade/Risk
1.	Yoan Moncada, 2b/3b	70/Medium
2.	Lucas Giolito, rhp	60/Medium
3.	Reynaldo Lopez, rhp	55/Medium
4.	Zack Collins, c	60/High
5.	Michael Kopech, rhp	60/High
6.	Zack Burdi, rhp	55/High
7.	Carson Fulmer, rhp	55/High
8.	Luis Alexander Basabe, of	55/High
9.	Spencer Adams, rhp	50/High
10.	Alec Hansen, rhp	55/Extreme
11.	Dane Dunning, rhp	50/High
12.	Jordan Stephens, rhp	50/High
13.	Trey Michalczewski, 3b	50/High
14.	Jameson Fisher, of	50/High
15.	Alex Call, of	50/High
16.	Jake Peter, 2b/of	45/Medium
17.	Charlie Tilson, of	45/Medium
18.	Tyler Danish, rhp	45/Medium
19.	Adam Engel, of	45/Medium
20.	Jacob May, of	45/Medium
21.	Aaron Bummer, lhp	50/Extreme
22.	Aaron Schnurbusch, of	50/Extreme
23.	Bernardo Lopez, lhp	50/Extreme
24.	Micker Adolfo, of	50/Extreme
25.	Zach Thompson, rhp	50/High
26.	Victor Diaz, rhp	45/High
27.	Connor Walsh, rhp	45/High
28.	Ian Hamilton, rhp	45/High
29.	Dylan Covey, rhp	40/Medium
30.	Omar Narvaez, c	40/Medium

LAST YEAR'S TOP 30

No.	Player, Pos.	Status
1.	Tim Anderson, ss	Majors
2.	Carson Fulmer, rhp	No. 7
3.	Frankie Montas, rhp	(Athletics)
4.	Spencer Adams, rhp	No. 9
5.	Trayce Thompson, of	(Dodgers)
6.	Trey Michalczewski, 3b	No. 13
7.	Jacob May, of	No. 20
8.	Micah Johnson, 2b	(Dodgers)
9.	Tyler Danish, rhp	No. 18
10.	Adam Engel, of	No. 19
11.	Jordan Guerrero, lhp	Dropped out
12.	Courtney Hawkins, of	Dropped out
13.	Corey Zangari, 1b	Dropped out
14.	Brian Clark, lhp	Dropped out
15.	Jordan Stephens, rhp	No. 12
16.	Micker Adolfo, of	No. 24
17.	Myles Jaye, rhp	(Tigers)
18.	Zack Erwin, lhp	(Athletics)
19.	Chris Beck, rhp	Dropped out
20.	Jason Coats, of	Dropped out
21.	Thad Lowry, rhp	Dropped out
22.	Jake Peter, 2b/ss	No. 16
23.	J.B. Wendelken, rhp	(Athletics)
24.	Robin Leyer, rhp	Dropped out
25.	Brandon Brennan, rhp	Dropped out
26.	Seby Zavala, c	Dropped out
27.	Johan Cruz, 3b/ss	Dropped out
28.	Eddy Alvarez, ss/2b	Dropped out
29.	Danny Hayes, 1b	Dropped out
30.	Matt Davidson, 3b	Dropped out

BEST TOOLS

Best Hitter for Average	Yoan Moncada
Best Power Hitter	Zack Collins
Best Strike-Zone Discipline	Zack Collins
Fastest Baserunner	Yoan Moncada
Best Athlete	Yoan Moncada
Best Fastball	Michael Kopech
Best Curveball	Lucas Giolito
Best Slider	Zack Burdi
Best Changeup	Tyler Danish
Best Control	Spencer Adams
Best Defensive Catcher	Omar Narvaez
Best Defensive Infielder	Mitch Roman
Best Infield Arm	Yoan Moncada
Best Defensive Outfielder	Adam Engel
Best Outfield Arm	Micker Adolfo

PROJECTED 2020 LINEUP

Catcher	Zack Collins
First Base	Jose Abreu
Second Base	Yoan Moncada
Third Base	Trey Michalczewski
Shortstop	Tim Anderson
Left Field	Jameson Fisher
Center Field	Luis Alexander Basabe
Right Field	Alex Call
Designated Hitter	Todd Frazier
No. 1 Starter	Jose Quintana
No. 2 Starter	Carlos Rodon
No. 3 Starter	Lucas Giolito
No. 4 Starter	Reynaldo Lopez
No. 5 Starter	Michael Kopech
Closer	Zack Burdi

MINOR LEAGUE DEPTH CHART

CHICAGO WHITE SOX

TOP 2017 ROOKIE: Yoan Moncada, 2b. The power-speed threat should provide the answer at second base, which has been a revolving door.
BREAKOUT PROSPECT: Aaron Schnurbusch, of. The physical lefthanded-hitting outfielder must prove his explosive debut was more than just a good summer.
SLEEPER: Luis Curbelo, 2b/3b. His promising bat and maturity could propel him forward.

SOURCE OF TOP 30 TALENT			
Homegrown	20	Acquired	10
College	16	Trades	8
Junior college	0	Rule 5 draft	2
High school	3	Independent leagues	0
Nondrafted free agents	0	Free agents/waivers	0
International	1		

LF
Jameson Fisher (14)
Nick Basto
Courtney Hawkins
Landon Lassiter
Hunter Jones
Mason Robbins

CF
Luis Alexander Basabe (8)
Charlie Tilson (17)
Adam Engel (19)
Jacob May (20)
Joel Booker

RF
Alex Call (15)
Aaron Schnurbusch (22)
Micker Adolfo (24)
Josue Guerrero
Luis Mieses

3B
Trey Michalczewski (13)
Luis Curbelo
Zach Remillard

SS
Yoan Moncada (1)
Amado Nunez
Eddy Alvarez
Mitch Roman
Lenyn Sosa

2B
Jake Peter (16)
Toby Thomas

1B
Corey Zangari
Nick Delmonico
K.J. Woods

C
Zack Collins (4)
Omar Narvaez (30)
Carlos Perez
Nate Nolan
Michael Hickman
Seby Zavala
Jhoandro Alfaro

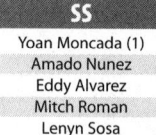

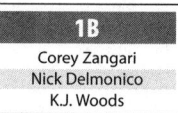

LHP
LHSP
Bernardo Flores (23)
Jordan Guerrero
Alex Katz

LHRP
Aaron Bummer (21)
Brian Clark
Matt Purke
Michael Horejsei

RHP
RHSP
Lucas Giolito (2)
Reynaldo Lopez (3)
Michael Kopech (5)
Carson Fulmer (7)
Spencer Adams (9)
Alec Hansen (10)
Dane Dunning (11)
Jordan Stephens (12)
Tyler Danish (18)
Zach Thompson (25)
Dylan Covey (29)
Blake Hickman
Chris Comito
Nelson Acosta
Yosmer Solorzano

RHRP
Zack Burdi (6)
Victor Diaz (26)
Connor Walsh (27)
Ian Hamilton (28)
Michael Ynoa
Chris Beck
Matt Foster
Danny Dopico
Matt Cooper
Taylore Cherry
Nolan Sanburn

DRAFT ANALYSIS

2016

BEST PURE HITTER: The White Sox see C Zack Collins (1) as a potential on-base machine, gifted with elite strike zone awareness and an uncanny ability to recognize pitches he can do damage with.

BEST POWER: Collins has plus power potential and can hit the ball out of any part of the ballpark. Chicago believes he will hit a lot of doubles in addition to home runs.

FASTEST RUNNER: OF Joel Booker (22) grades as a 70 runner, with the ability to reach first base in 4.1 seconds from the righthanded batter's box. He swiped 41 bags in 65 games in his professional debut this summer.

BEST DEFENSIVE PLAYER: SS Mitch Roman (12) has excellent defensive tools at shortstop, with outstanding hands, lateral quickness and a plus throwing arm. Collins doesn't wow evaluators with athleticism or footwork behind the plate, but he works well with pitchers and shows the soft, quiet hands to develop into a sound pitch framer.

BEST FASTBALL: RHP Zack Burdi (1s) can reach triple digits regularly with some reports of his fastball touching 102 mph. RHP Alec Hansen (2) has plus-plus fastball life and pitches at 92-95, with the ability to hit 98 when he needs. LHP Bernardo Flores (7), whose disastrous spring at Southern California included a 6.70 ERA, has excellent lefthanded velocity with the ability to reach 97.

BEST SECONDARY PITCH: Burdi's slider is a hard, upper 80s frisbee with late sweep. RHP Ian Hamilton (11) also has a hard slider that shows short and late bite. Hansen can spin the ball well at times. LHP Michael Horejsei (21) doesn't have the explosive fastball of his peers, but his slider is a plus pitch.

BEST PRO DEBUT: Hansen's debut was almost unparalleled in the class, especially relative to his performance as at Oklahoma (which included a 5.57 ERA) this spring. In 54.2 innings across rookie ball and low Class A, Hansen struck out 81 and walked just 20. He allowed 24 hits and eight earned runs.

BEST ATHLETE: OF Aaron Schnurbusch (28) is a physical specimen, standing at a listed 6-foot-5 and 235 pounds. The Pittsburgh product has plus bat speed, runs well and throws well. Schnurbusch drew mild football interest from colleges when he was in high school and he was a two-way player in college.

MOST INTRIGUING BACKGROUND: Burdi is the younger brother of Twins' prospect Nick Burdi and former Western Michigan quarterback Drew Burdi. RHP Jimmy Lambert (5) is the brother of Rockies pitching prospect Peter Lambert.

CLOSEST TO THE MAJORS: Burdi cruised through the low minors and reached Triple-A. He is primed to compete for a late-inning relief role for the White Sox in 2017. Collins isn't far behind having already played well at high Class A.

BEST LATE ROUND PICK: Schnurbusch was among many pleasant surprises for the White Sox. He showed an array of tools and performed well at Rookie-level Great Falls to put himself on the map as a legitimate prospect. Booker has long been considered a toolsy prospect and lived up to those expectations with a fine debut in rookie ball.

THE ONE WHO GOT AWAY: The White Sox had productive talks with OF Zach Farrar (26), but he ended up enrolling at Oklahoma as a two-sport athlete playing both football and baseball.

2015

RHP Carson Fulmer (1) was unwisely rushed to the majors and may wind up a reliever. RHP Jordan Stephens (5) is the best of an otherwise disappointing class that lacks upside.

GRADE: D

2014

Somehow, LHP Carlos Rodon (1) slipped to the third pick in the draft, to the White Sox's benefit. RHP Spencer Adams (2) and 2B Jake Peter (7) are the best of the rest of a modest crop.

GRADE: B

2013

SS Tim Anderson (1) ran the gauntlet from junior college to the big leagues in less than three years. The best of the rest includes RHP Tyler Danish (2), 3B Trey Michalczewski (7) and speedy OFs Jacob May (3) and Adam Engel (18).

GRADE: A

TOP DRAFT PICKS OF THE DECADE

Year	Player, Pos.	2016 Org
2007	Aaron Poreda, lhp	Yomiuri (Japan)
2008	Gordon Beckham, ss	Giants
2009	Jared Mitchell, of	Yankees
2010	Chris Sale, lhp	White Sox
2011	Keenyn Walker, of (1st round supp.)	White Sox
2012	Courtney Hawkins, of	White Sox
2013	Tim Anderson, ss	White Sox
2014	Carlos Rodon, lhp	White Sox
2015	Carson Fulmer, rhp	White Sox
2016	Zack Collins, c	White Sox

LARGEST BONUSES IN CLUB HISTORY

Jose Abreu, 2013	$10,000,000
Carlos Rodon, 2014	$6,582,000
Joe Borchard, 2000	$5,300,000
Dayan Viciedo, 2008	$4,000,000
Carson Fulmer, 2015	$3,470,600

1 YOAN MONCADA 2B/3B

Born: May 27, 1995. **B-T:** B-R. **Ht.:** 6-2. **Wt.:** 205.
Signed: Cuba, 2015. **Signed by:** Eddie Romero (Red Sox).

Moncada showed plenty of promise during a transition year in 2015 following his entry into the Red Sox organization for a record-setting $31.5 million bonus. Boston paid a 100 percent penalty tax—$31.5 million—when they signed the young Cuban because they exceeded their allotted international bonus pool. Still, the way in which Moncada's tools coalesced in 2016 proved to be breathtaking at times at high Class A Salem and then Double-A Portland. He hit .294/.407/.511 with 15 home runs and 45 stolen bases in 106 games and also starred at the Futures Game in San Diego, where he earned MVP honors. The Red Sox called up Moncada in September as they sought offensive punch at third base, but it proved to be an anticlimactic final note to the year. He hit just .211 with 12 strikeouts in 19 at-bats. Yet the progress he has made as a professional reinforces the notion that his tools and aptitude could yield a player of rare impact. The White Sox are on board with that projection after trading ace Chris Sale to the Red Sox at the 2016 Winter Meetings for Moncada plus three other prospects: hard-throwing high Class A righthander Michael Kopech, switch-hitting low Class A center fielder Luis Alexander Basabe and low Class A reliever Victor Diaz.

Moncada possesses the size and strength of a linebacker and he runs like a runaway locomotive. Though he typically features a flat bat path that creates screaming line drives, the switch-hitter showed an increasing willingness to drive balls with loft in 2016, resulting in some prodigious home runs on top of doubles. While batting lefthanded, he evokes comparisons with Robinson Cano. On the bases, he possesses elite speed though with still-developing situational awareness, and his enormous stolen base totals are likely to decline as he advances. Moncada showed hickeys in his game even before he struggled in the big leagues. He hit a more modest .243/.371/.379 batting righthanded and striking out 25 percent of the time, both of which raise concerns about this hit tool. Still, many believe that he has the athleticism and aptitude, along with the pitch recognition and strike-zone recognition, to intermingle high averages and on-base percentages with plenty of

BA GRADE

70 Risk: Medium

SCOUTING GRADES

Bat: 60.
Power: 60.
Speed: 70.
Defense: 50.
Arm: 70.

Based on 20-80 scouting scale and future projection rather than present tools.

RODGER WOOD

extra-base power. Moncada spent most of 2016 at second base, where he showed sounder fundamentals and an ability to make standout plays. His late-season move to third base, however, showed off his flexibility. He displayed an enormous arm and quick-twitch actions that could play well at the hot corner, though his footwork and fundamentals suggest a work in progress. Many evaluators believe that he could also handle the outfield, though for now, he will work primarily at second base.

Moncada will be given a chance to compete for a big league job in spring training, but especially given how he struggled after being rushed to the big leagues in 2016, it seems more likely that he'll open the year at Triple-A Charlotte. Still, it wouldn't come as a surprise if he asserted himself as ready to make a substantial big league impact by the middle of 2017. If he makes the adjustments to limit his strikeouts, he could explore a ceiling that may be unrivaled in the minors.

Year	Club (League)	Class	AVG	G	AB	R	H	2B	3B	HR	RBI	BB	SO	SB	CS	OBP	SLG
2014	Did not play																
2015	Greenville (SAL)	LoA	.278	81	306	61	85	19	3	8	38	42	83	49	3	.380	.438
2016	Salem (CAR)	HiA	.307	61	228	57	70	25	3	4	34	45	60	36	8	.427	.496
	Portland (EL)	AA	.277	45	177	37	49	6	3	11	28	27	64	9	4	.379	.531
	Boston (AL)	MAJ	.211	8	19	3	4	1	0	0	1	1	12	0	0	.250	.263
Major League Totals			.211	8	19	3	4	1	0	0	1	1	12	0	0	.250	.263
Minor League Totals			.287	187	711	155	204	50	9	23	100	114	207	94	15	.395	.480

2 LUCAS GIOLITO, RHP

Born: July 14, 1994. **B-T:** R-R. **Ht.:** 6-6. **Wt.:** 255. **Drafted:** HS—Studio City, Calif., 2012 (1st round). **Signed by:** Mark Baca (Nationals).

Giolito has shown incredible promise since his high school days, when he was considered the top prep pitcher in the 2012 draft class until he sprained his ulnar collateral ligament and was shut down early that March. After being drafted by the Nationals 16th overall he had Tommy John surgery later that summer. Washington traded him to the White Sox—along with righthanders Reynaldo Lopez and Dane Dunning—for Adam Eaton at the 2016 Winter Meetings. Giolito made his long-anticipated major league debut in July 2016, completing a closely watched journey through the minors. While he stumbled in Washington, his star remains bright.

BA GRADE
60 **Risk:** **Medium**

Giolito has three above-average offerings and an extra-large frame that allows him to throw from a steep downhill angle. He has touched 100 mph in the past, but his fastball has not typically shown that kind of velocity when he is pitching on a regular schedule. He topped out at 96 mph with his fastball in the major leagues, and sat around 94 mph. He still has a powerful 12-to-6 curveball that can be a plus pitch. His changeup has good sinking action and is effective against lefthanded hitters. Most concerning about Giolito's 2016 performance was his control. After averaging 2.7 walks per nine innings in his first two years of full-season ball, he saw his walk rate spike in 2016, particularly in the big leagues where he averaged 5.1 walks per nine. Giolito often fell behind in the count and will need to get back to consistently throwing quality strikes to get big league hitters out. While Giolito's big league debut was disappointing, he still has incredible upside. He will pitch most of 2017 as a 22-year-old and still has the potential to develop into a front-of-the-rotation starter. He likely will open the season at Triple-A Charlotte.

Year	Club (League)	Class	W	L	ERA	G	GS	CG	SV	IP	H	HR	BB	SO	K/9	WHIP	AVG
2014	Hagerstown (SAL)	LoA	10	2	2.20	20	20	0	0	98	70	7	28	110	10.1	1.00	.197
2015	Potomac (CAR)	HiA	3	5	2.71	13	11	0	0	70	65	1	20	86	11.1	1.22	.244
	Harrisburg (EL)	AA	4	2	3.80	8	8	0	0	47	48	2	17	45	8.6	1.37	.265
2016	Harrisburg (EL)	AA	5	3	3.17	14	14	0	0	71	67	2	34	72	9.1	1.42	.247
	Hagerstown (SAL)	LoA	0	0	5.14	1	1	0	0	7	6	2	0	4	5.1	0.86	.231
	Syracuse (IL)	AAA	1	2	2.17	7	7	0	0	37	31	3	10	40	9.6	1.10	.225
	Washington (NL)	MAJ	0	1	6.75	6	4	0	0	21	26	7	12	11	4.6	1.78	.295
Major League Totals			0	1	6.75	6	4	0	0	21	26	7	12	11	4.6	1.78	.295
Minor League Totals			25	15	2.73	75	73	0	0	369	317	18	123	397	9.7	1.19	.231

3 REYNALDO LOPEZ, RHP

Born: Jan. 4, 1994. **B-T:** R-R. **Ht.:** 6-0. **Wt.:** 185. **Signed:** Dominican Republic, 2012. **Signed by:** Modesto Ulloa (Nationals).

Lopez was an unheralded 18-year-old with a high-80s fastball when the Nationals signed him for $17,000 in 2012. His velocity quickly began to increase, and he took off in 2014. He reached the big leagues two years later, first as a starter before moving to the bullpen down the stretch. His performance as a reliever earned him a spot in the Nationals bullpen during the playoffs. Washington bundled Lopez with first-round righthanders Lucas Giolito and Dane Dunning to acquire Adam Eaton from the White Sox at the 2016 Winter Meeting. Lopez has made incredible strides as a professional, and his fastball now comfortably sits in the mid-90s and touched

BA GRADE
55 **Risk:** **Medium**

100 mph in the big leagues. His improved strength also has helped his curveball, which is a powerful 11-to-5 hammer that is a swing-and-miss offering. Lopez made strides with both his changeup and control in 2016, two areas critical to his chances to remain in the rotation in the big leagues. His changeup has become a third solid pitch for him, giving him a weapon against lefthanded hitters. He also did a better job of repeating his delivery, leading to improved command. That didn't immediately translate to the major leagues, where he averaged 4.5 walks per nine innings. Lopez has shown he is ready to help as a reliever, and he could win a spot in the Chicago bullpen during spring training.

Year	Club (League)	Class	W	L	ERA	G	GS	CG	SV	IP	H	HR	BB	SO	K/9	WHIP	AVG
2014	Auburn (NYP)	SS	3	2	0.75	7	7	0	0	36	15	0	15	31	7.8	0.83	.125
	Hagerstown (SAL)	LoA	4	1	1.33	9	9	0	0	47	27	1	11	39	7.4	0.80	.167
2015	Potomac (CAR)	HiA	6	7	4.09	19	19	1	0	99	93	5	28	94	8.5	1.22	.252
2016	Harrisburg (EL)	AA	3	5	3.18	14	14	0	0	76	69	7	25	100	11.8	1.23	.235
	Syracuse (IL)	AAA	2	2	3.27	5	5	1	0	33	21	6	10	26	7.1	0.94	.179
	Washington (NL)	MAJ	5	3	4.91	11	6	0	0	44	47	4	22	42	8.6	1.57	.272
Major League Totals			5	3	4.91	11	6	0	0	44	47	4	22	42	8.6	1.57	.272
Minor League Totals			19	19	3.16	61	56	2	1	308	252	21	95	303	8.9	1.13	.224

4 ZACK COLLINS, C

Born: Feb. 6, 1995. **B-T:** L-R. **Ht.:** 6-3. **Wt.:** 220. **Drafted:** Miami, 2016 (1st round).
Signed by: Jose Ortega.

Collins claimed the BA college Freshman of the Year award at Miami in 2014 after batting .298 with 11 home runs in a down year for offense in college baseball. In his draft year he batted .363/.544/.668 and drew 78 walks, the most of any Division I player since 2011. He focused on improving as a receiver as his junior year approached, encouraging the White Sox enough to make him the 10th overall pick in 2016. While Collins' calling card will always be his offense, his defensive progress was exceptional his junior year, and he particularly impressed evaluators with his soft hands and framing technique. His footwork is what holds him back from being an average defender. Collins has a thick, muscle-filled lower half and isn't nimble. Regardless of what kind of defensive player he ends up being, his offense will play. He has a rare combination of strength and bat speed, giving him plus power. In his pro debut, he showed the ability to drive the ball out to left-center field or turn on mistake pitches on the inner half. Collins has a patient approach at the plate, with elite strike-zone awareness and an uncanny idea of which pitches he can do damage with. He will look to continue refining his defense as he progresses to the upper minors. He likely will advance to Double-A Birmingham in 2017, and could be on the fast track to Chicago as the club's answer at catcher.

BA GRADE 60 Risk: High

Year	Club (League)	Class	AVG	G	AB	R	H	2B	3B	HR	RBI	BB	SO	SB	CS	OBP	SLG
2016	White Sox (AZL)	R	.091	3	11	1	1	0	0	0	0	0	7	0	0	.091	.091
	Winston-Salem (CAR)HiA		.258	36	120	24	31	7	0	6	18	33	39	0	0	.418	.467
Minor League Totals			.244	39	131	25	32	7	0	6	18	33	46	0	0	.396	.435

5 MICHAEL KOPECH, RHP

Born: April 30, 1996. **B-T:** R-R. **Ht.:** 6-3. **Wt.:** 205. **Drafted:** HS—Mount Pleasant, Texas, 2014 (1st round). **Signed by:** Tim Collinsworth (Red Sox).

The Red Sox viewed Kopech as a power arm when they drafted him out of high school, but no one foresaw his emergence as the hardest-throwing starter in the minors in 2016. Though his innings have been limited by a pair of off-field incidents—a 50-game suspension for testing positive for a banned stimulant in 2015 and a broken right hand from a spring-training fight with a teammate in 2016—he has demonstrated an ability to overpower opponents. The Red Sox traded Kopech, second baseman Yoan Moncada and two other prospects to the White Sox in order to land Chris Sale at the 2016 Winter Meetings. Kopech's fastball sat 95-99 mph and frequently touched triple digits. His 90-92 mph power slider grades average now but projects as plus. Though his changeup is currently below average, Kopech should be able to improve it to near-average. His velocity creates questions of injury risk and limits his command, but he's learned to control his delivery to sustain both power and control. Despite his off-field incidents, most speak highly of Kopech's makeup and ferocious mound demeanor. He should start at Double-A in 2017 and has front-of-the-rotation potential, earning comparisons from scouts to Noah Syndergaard.

BA GRADE 65 Risk: Extreme

Year	Club (League)	Class	W	L	ERA	G	GS	CG	SV	IP	H	HR	BB	SO	K/9	WHIP	AVG
2014	Red Sox (GCL)	R	0	1	4.61	8	8	0	0	14	11	0	9	16	10.5	1.46	.216
2015	Greenville (SAL)	LoA	4	5	2.63	16	15	0	0	65	53	2	27	70	9.7	1.23	.228
2016	Lowell (NYP)	SS	0	0	0.00	1	1	0	0	4	4	0	4	4	8.3	1.85	.250
	Salem (CAR)	HiA	4	1	2.25	11	11	0	0	52	25	1	29	82	14.2	1.04	.147
Minor League Totals			8	7	2.60	36	35	0	0	135	93	3	69	172	11.5	1.20	.198

6 ZACK BURDI, RHP

Born: March 9, 1995. **B-T:** R-R. **Ht.:** 6-3. **Wt.:** 205. **Drafted:** Louisville, 2016 (1st round).
Signed by: Phil Gulley.

Burdi comes from a family of exceptional arm strength. His oldest brother was a Division I quarterback, while his older brother Nick is a hard-throwing prospect in the Twins organization. Nick and Zack are thought to be the only pair of brothers to have thrown 100 mph. Burdi throws really, really hard. His top-of-the-scale fastball is mesmerizing, routinely checking in at 96-100 mph and touching 102. He throws from a lower three-quarters arm slot and works from the third-base side of the rubber, giving him elite deception and allowing him to generate late sinking action on his fastball and changeup, which flashes plus potential. Burdi's plus-plus slider has frisbee-like bend to it, with plus depth and excellent upper-80s velocity. He's still ironing out some

BA GRADE 55 Risk: High

inconsistencies in his delivery that lead to his front shoulder flying open. Burdi can leave his fastball up in the zone, and his slider can sometimes back up when he throws it to his arm side. Burdi could quickly contribute in the White Sox bullpen in 2017. He projects as a closer or setup man.

Year	Club (League)	Class	W	L	ERA	G	GS	CG	SV	IP	H	HR	BB	SO	K/9	WHIP	AVG
2016	White Sox (AZL)	R	0	0	0.00	1	0	0	0	1	1	0	0	1	9.0	1.00	.250
	Winston-Salem (CAR)	HiA	0	0	5.40	4	0	0	0	5	6	1	0	4	7.2	1.20	.316
	Birmingham (SL)	AA	0	0	3.94	12	0	0	0	16	7	2	9	24	13.5	1.13	.132
	Charlotte (IL)	AAA	1	0	2.25	9	0	0	1	16	9	0	11	22	12.4	1.25	.161
Minor League Totals			1	0	3.32	26	0	0	1	38	23	3	20	51	12.1	1.13	.174

7 CARSON FULMER, RHP

Born: Dec. 13, 1993. **B-T:** R-R. **Ht.:** 6-0. **Wt.:** 195. **Drafted:** Vanderbilt, 2015 (1st round). **Signed by:** Phil Gulley.

Fulmer was a three-year mainstay at Vanderbilt, blossoming into the ace of the staff in 2015. He consistently dominated competition that spring. In his first full pro season, he struggled early but earned a month-long cameo in the White Sox bullpen. Fulmer's long-term role remains undefined, but late-season adjustments may allow him to make it as a starter. His plus fastball sat at 92-93 mph and touched 95 out of the bullpen. His above-average curveball showed more consistent top-to-bottom shape, but it lacked the power spin it showed in college. Fulmer showed an improved, potentially above-average changeup in 2016, and he was able to throw it for strikes to both righthanders and lefthanders. He also throws an average short cutter. He struggled to control his pitches for most of the season, so he toned down his exaggerated leg kick out front, keeping his lower leg back along with his knee and hip. This adjustment had him staying more balanced over the rubber and repeating his release point better. Fulmer projects as a No. 3 starter if his late-season progress holds—and a late-inning reliever if it doesn't. He's likely ticketed to start 2017 at Triple-A Charlotte.

BA GRADE **55** **Risk: High**

Year	Club (League)	Class	W	L	ERA	G	GS	CG	SV	IP	H	HR	BB	SO	K/9	WHIP	AVG
2015	White Sox (AZL)	R	0	0	0.00	1	1	0	0	1	1	0	0	1	9.0	1.00	.333
	Winston-Salem (CAR)	HiA	0	0	2.05	8	8	0	0	22	16	2	9	25	10.2	1.14	.205
2016	Birmingham (SL)	AA	4	9	4.76	17	17	0	0	87	82	7	51	90	9.3	1.53	.248
	Chicago (AL)	MAJ	0	2	8.49	8	0	0	0	12	12	2	7	10	7.7	1.63	.273
	Charlotte (IL)	AAA	2	1	3.94	4	4	0	0	16	14	1	5	14	7.9	1.19	.233
Major League Totals			0	2	8.49	8	0	0	0	12	12	2	7	10	7.7	1.63	.273
Minor League Totals			6	10	4.14	30	30	0	0	126	113	10	65	130	9.3	1.41	.239

8 LUIS ALEXANDER BASABE, OF

Born: Aug. 26, 1996. **B-T:** B-R. **Ht.:** 6-0. **Wt.:** 160. **Signed:** Venezuela, 2012. **Signed by:** Luis Segovia/Eddie Romero (Red Sox).

In many ways, Basabe—whom the Red Sox signed along with his twin brother Luis Alejandro—embodies unpredictable world of projecting international amateur talent. While the twins were physically quite similar when they signed, Luis Alexander grew two inches and filled out in a way that distinguished him from his sibling. Boston traded his brother to the Diamondbacks for Brad Ziegler in July, then traded Luis Alexander Basabe to the White Sox at the 2016 Winter Meetings with second baseman Yoan Moncada and righthander Michael Kopech in their blockbuster trade for Chris Sale. Basabe shows solid or better tools across the board, with considerable bat life when batting lefthanded. He strikes out too frequently from both sides of the plate at this stage—including a rate of 32 percent as a righthanded hitter—but when he makes contact, the impact stands out for his age and position. He adjusted his stance in the middle of 2016, becoming more upright to improve his balance and pitch recognition. In center field, he features long strides that produce plus range and also displays excellent arm strength. Basabe's defensive value gives him a high floor of backup outfielder. If his offensive approach continues to make strides, his cluster of tools could make him an above-average regular. He heads to high Class A Winston-Salem in 2017.

BA GRADE **55** **Risk: High**

Year	Club (League)	Class	AVG	G	AB	R	H	2B	3B	HR	RBI	BB	SO	SB	CS	OBP	SLG
2014	Red Sox (DSL)	R	.284	40	148	38	42	7	11	0	26	30	36	13	2	.408	.480
	Red Sox (GCL)	R	.248	32	105	15	26	5	0	1	13	13	23	2	4	.328	.324
2015	Lowell (NYP)	SS	.243	56	222	36	54	8	3	7	23	32	67	15	4	.340	.401
2016	Greenville (SAL)	LoA	.258	105	403	61	104	24	8	12	52	40	116	25	5	.325	.447
	Salem (CAR)	HiA	.364	5	22	5	8	2	1	0	1	1	3	0	0	.391	.545
Minor League Totals			.253	298	1109	204	281	59	25	21	134	165	303	73	20	.353	.408

9 SPENCER ADAMS, RHP

Born: April 13, 1996. **B-T:** R-R. **Ht.:** 6-3. **Wt.:** 171. **Drafted:** HS—Cleveland, Ga., 2014 (2nd round). **Signed by:** Kevin Burrell.

Adams was a standout prep multi-sport athlete who also starred as a basketball player. Ranked 23rd in the 2014 BA 500, he slid to the second round and the White Sox selected him with the 44th overall pick.   Adams got his fastball up to 96 mph in high school and was seen as projectable, but his velocity has settled in at 88-93 as a pro. As Adams continues to add strength to his wide-shouldered, 6-foot-3 frame, the White Sox are hopeful that he can eventually pitch with the plus velocity he showed with longer rest as an amateur. He's shown a heavy reliance on his above-average slider, which shows sharp, two-plane break and late bite. His slider was more consistent in 2016, though it's break will sometimes get wide and long. Adams throws his average changeup with fastball arm speed and generates enough late tumbling action for the pitch to induce poor contact and ground balls. He is an excellent athlete and repeats his mechanics exceptionally well for a pitcher of his age. Adams has the stuff and pitchability to comfortably project as a No. 4 starter, with the ceiling of a No. 3 if he can add a tick more velocity. He's likely to start 2017 at Double-A Birmingham, where he will again be one of the youngest players at the level.

BA GRADE 50 Risk: High

Year	Club (League)	Class	W	L	ERA	G	GS	CG	SV	IP	H	HR	BB	SO	K/9	WHIP	AVG
2014	White Sox (AZL)	R	3	3	3.67	10	9	0	0	42	49	4	4	59	12.7	1.27	.282
2015	Kannapolis (SAL)	LoA	9	5	3.24	19	19	1	0	100	111	7	11	73	6.6	1.22	.275
	Winston-Salem (CAR)	HiA	3	0	2.15	5	5	0	0	29	31	1	7	23	7.1	1.30	.267
2016	Winston-Salem (CAR)	HiA	8	7	4.01	18	18	1	0	108	120	7	21	74	6.2	1.31	.275
	Birmingham (SL)	AA	2	5	3.90	9	9	0	0	55	59	2	10	26	4.2	1.25	.274
Minor League Totals			25	20	3.56	61	60	2	0	334	370	21	53	255	6.9	1.27	.275

10 ALEC HANSEN, RHP

Born: Oct. 10, 1994. **B-T:** R-R. **Ht.:** 6-7. **Wt.:** 235. **Drafted:** Oklahoma, 2016 (2nd round). **Signed by:** Clay Overcash.

Hansen was on the path to being a significant prospect out of high school, but he missed time with arm trouble during his senior year and slipped in the draft. At Oklahoma, Hansen entered his junior year as a candidate to be the No. 1 overall pick, but he pitched poorly enough to lose spot in the weekend rotation for a spell. Hansen has exceptional size and arm strength. His fastball has reached 98 mph and regularly works at 91-95. He generates plus life on his fastball, which shows late finish as it enters the zone. Hansen throws a slider and a curveball, both of which flash plus potential but don't consistently play as plus. His slider is a more usable weapon, with hard 10-to-4 snap and low- to mid-80s velocity, while his curveball shows longer 11-to-5 break. He has also flashed a plus changeup, though it typically plays closer to average. While Hansen's stuff can all flash plus, he'll need to continue making progress timing his delivery and repeating his mechanics because he has a tendency to rush off his back ankle. Hansen likely will start 2017 at low Class A Kannapolis. He will have to significantly refine his delivery and command to reach his front-line starter ceiling.

BRIAN WESTERHOLT

BA GRADE 55 Risk: Extreme

Year	Club (League)	Class	W	L	ERA	G	GS	CG	SV	IP	H	HR	BB	SO	K/9	WHIP	AVG
2016	White Sox (AZL)	R	0	0	0.00	3	3	0	0	7	1	0	4	11	14.1	0.71	.048
	Great Falls (PIO)	R	2	0	1.23	7	7	0	0	37	12	3	12	59	14.5	0.65	.102
	Kannapolis (SAL)	LoA	0	1	2.45	2	2	0	0	11	11	0	4	11	9.0	1.36	.262
Minor League Totals			2	1	1.32	12	12	0	0	55	24	3	20	81	13.3	0.80	.133

11 DANE DUNNING, RHP

BA GRADE 50 Risk: High

Born: Dec. 20, 1994. **B-T:** R-R. **Ht.:** 6-4. **Wt.:** 200. **Drafted:** Florida, 2016 (1st round). **Signed by:** Buddy Hernandez (Nationals).

Dunning was a key piece of Florida's top-ranked recruiting class in 2013, entering with future All-Americans lefthander A.J. Puk and righthander Logan Shore. Dunning mostly worked as a midweek starter and out of the bullpen, but still logged significant innings and helped Florida to back-to-back appearances in the College World Series in 2015 and 2016. The Nationals drafted him 29th overall in 2016, and he made a strong pro debut with short-season Auburn. The Nationals traded him to the White Sox after the 2016 season with righthanders Lucas Giolito and Reynaldo Lopez for Adam Eaton. Dunning throws his fastball in the low 90s as a starter and can reach 95 mph in shorter outings. His slider can be a quality pitch but is inconsistent. His solid-average changeup is his best secondary pitch, and he is comfortable throwing it to batters on both sides of the plate. Dunning's stuff all plays up thanks to his control, and he as a junior ranked sixth in the country in strikeout-to-walk ratio (7.33). He is a good athlete and repeats his easy delivery well. Despite his atypical college career, Dunning has the tools necessary to be a starter. He is advanced enough to handle an assignment to high Class A Winston-Salem in 2017.

Year	Club (League)	Class	W	L	ERA	G	GS	CG	SV	IP	H	HR	BB	SO	K/9	WHIP	AVG
2016	Nationals (GCL)	R	0	0	0.00	1	1	0	0	2	0	0	0	3	13.5	0.00	.000
	Auburn (NYP)	SS	3	2	2.14	7	7	1	0	34	26	1	7	29	7.8	0.98	.208
Minor League Totals			3	2	2.02	8	8	1	0	36	26	1	7	32	8.1	0.93	.198

12 JORDAN STEPHENS, RHP

Born: Sept. 12, 1992. **B-T:** R-L. **Ht.:** 6-3. **Wt.:** 225. **Drafted:** Rice, 2015 (5th round). **Signed by:** Chris Walker.

Stephens served as a rotation stalwart at Rice as a sophomore in 2013, then needed Tommy John surgery early in his junior year. He returned to form as a redshirt junior, and the White Sox selected him in the fifth round in 2015. Stephens has a compact arm action and hides the ball well. He stays balanced over the rubber and coils his front hip with some Asian-style hesitation and gather, giving him deception and allowing the ball to jump on hitters. He typically pitches with average fastball velocity at 91-93 mph, but his velocity will vary by dipping as low as 88 at worst and then running up to 95 on the high end. Stephens has fastball command to both sides of the plate, and he can purposefully elevate to locate his heater above hitters' hands for chase swings. His upper-70s above-average curveball is his best offspeed pitch, consistently showing tight spin and deep three-quarters break. He throws a near-average slider in the low 80s that shows short, horizontal sweeping action and a below-average changeup that needs continued refinement. Stephens will progress to Double-A Birmingham in 2017, where he'll need to continue refining his control and make progress with his changeup. Some evaluators believe he could settle in as a No. 4 starter, while others see him as a quality two-pitch reliever.

Year	Club (League)	Class	W	L	ERA	G	GS	CG	SV	IP	H	HR	BB	SO	K/9	WHIP	AVG
2015	White Sox (AZL)	R	0	0	0.61	9	1	0	0	15	7	0	2	18	11.0	0.61	.140
	Great Falls (PIO)	R	0	0	0.00	2	0	0	0	3	2	0	1	3	9.0	1.00	.182
2016	Winston-Salem (CAR)	HiA	7	10	3.45	27	27	0	0	141	129	12	48	155	9.9	1.26	.243
Minor League Totals			7	10	3.12	38	28	0	0	159	138	12	51	176	10.0	1.19	.234

13 TREY MICHALCZEWSKI, 3B

Born: Feb. 27, 1995. **B-T:** B-R. **Ht.:** 6-3. **Wt.:** 210. **Drafted:** HS—Jenks, Okla., 2013 (7th round). **Signed by:** Clay Overcash.

Michalczewski wasn't a regular on the amateur showcase circuit and didn't have as much exposure to high level competition as some of his peers. He was still valued enough to receive an over-slot bonus of $500,000 as a seventh-round pick in 2013. He tailed off in the second half of 2016, hitting .216/.301/.337 after the all-star break. Michalczewski looks the part, with a lean, athletic build that features a moderately high waist and wide shoulders. He has the footwork and above-average arm strength necessary to be an average defensive third baseman, though some evaluators see him profiling as a corner utility player. He has a loose swing with long levers and swooping motion that prevents his bat from staying in the zone for a long time, but that mechanism also allows him to loft the ball when he's on time. He projects as a fringe-average hitter with average power potential. Upon his jump to Double-A Birmingham, he struggled to execute an approach, often selecting poor pitches to swing at and putting himself into negative counts. He has plus raw power from both sides of the plate, though he has yet to really tap into it. Michalczewski will repeat Double-A in 2017, and he will still be one of the younger players at the level at age 22. He has a chance to develop into an average regular if he can improve his contact rate and continue to settle in defensively.

Year	Club (League)	Class	AVG	G	AB	R	H	2B	3B	HR	RBI	BB	SO	SB	CS	OBP	SLG
2014	Kannapolis (SAL)	LoA	.273	116	432	57	118	25	7	10	70	45	140	6	3	.348	.433
	Winston-Salem (CAR)	HiA	.194	19	72	5	14	2	0	0	5	9	21	1	0	.293	.222
2015	Winston-Salem (CAR)	HiA	.259	127	474	59	123	35	4	7	75	50	114	4	3	.335	.395
2016	Birmingham (SL)	AA	.226	134	487	62	110	24	5	11	59	56	153	4	0	.314	.363
Minor League Totals			.248	452	1660	208	411	91	18	31	230	183	484	17	6	.329	.380

14 JAMESON FISHER, OF

Born: Dec. 18, 1993. **B-T:** L-R. **Ht.:** 6-2. **Wt.:** 200. **Drafted:** Southeastern Louisiana, 2016 (4th round). **Signed by:** Warren Hughes.

Fisher has long intrigued scouts with his impressive offensive upside. He was a third-team All-American catcher in 2012 after batting .554 as a high school senior. He caught for most of his amateur career, but a shoulder injury sidelined him in 2015, and upon his return he played mostly first base as a redshirt junior in 2016. He finished the season with the second-highest batting average in Division I baseball (.424) and led all of D-I with a .558 on-base percentage. He finished in the top 10 in the Pioneer League with his .342 average in his pro debut. Fisher's best tool is his natural hitting ability. He projects to be a plus hitter with a knack for putting barrel on ball and hitting hard line drives. In his pro debut, Fisher showed the ability to drive the ball from foul pole to foul pole. He has a loose, athletic swing and mature strike-zone awareness. Fisher's arm strength has recovered and is near average, and he's an average runner and a graceful athlete. He doesn't have a firm defensive home at present, but the White Sox have tried him at third base and in the outfield, and he has a chance to develop into an adequate defensive player whose offense carries him. Fisher will advance to low Class A in Kannapolis as he continues to adjust to the pro game and gains repetitions against quality competition.

Year	Club (League)	Class	AVG	G	AB	R	H	2B	3B	HR	RBI	BB	SO	SB	CS	OBP	SLG
2016	Great Falls (PIO)	R	.342	50	187	39	64	13	1	4	25	27	43	13	7	.436	.487
Minor League Totals			.342	50	187	39	64	13	1	4	25	27	43	13	7	.436	.487

15 ALEX CALL, OF

BA GRADE
50 Risk: High

Born: Sept. 27, 1994. **B-T:** R-R. **Ht.:** 5-11. **Wt.:** 185. **Drafted:** Ball State, 2016 (3rd round). **Signed by:** Garrett Guest.

Call was a three-year starter at Ball State and began to blossom as a junior in 2016 as he grew into his man strength. He smacked 13 home runs and posted an isolated slugging percentage over .300 in his draft year. While Call doesn't have a bona fide plus tool, he doesn't have any minuses either, and he is universally praised for his work ethic and baseball instincts. He has above-average arm strength and he's an above-average runner, giving him the tools to play any outfield spot, though he doesn't project to be an everyday center fielder. Call has a fluid swing, with loose wrists that allow him to cover the plate well. He has a deep back-elbow swoop that can sometimes prevent him from generating tight backspin, and he cuts up on the ball, but he consistently makes solid contact and has always hit for a high average on balls in play. He has hit everywhere he's gone and projects as an average hitter, though his power production (he has near-average power potential) is a newer development. Call is likely to start 2017 back at low Class A Kannapolis. His polished skill set could allow him to move quickly, but if his offensive production continues to work at the highest level, his bat could separate him.

Year	Club (League)	Class	AVG	G	AB	R	H	2B	3B	HR	RBI	BB	SO	SB	CS	OBP	SLG
2016	Great Falls (PIO)	R	.308	27	107	19	33	3	1	3	17	19	18	4	4	.444	.439
	Kannapolis (SAL)	LoA	.308	46	185	23	57	17	0	3	18	15	40	10	2	.361	.449
Minor League Totals			.308	73	292	42	90	20	1	6	35	34	58	14	6	.394	.445

16 JAKE PETER, 2B/OF

BA GRADE
45 Risk: Medium

Born: April 5, 1993. **B-T:** L-R. **Ht.:** 6-1. **Wt.:** 185. **Drafted:** Creighton, 2014 (7th round). **Signed by:** J.J. Lally.

Peter was a two-way prospect at Creighton, serving as the closer for part of his sophomore year. A seventh-round pick in 2014, Peter has emerged as the organization's top position prospect from that draft class. Advancing to Double-A Birmingham in 2016, he held his own and earned a promotion to Triple-A Charlotte. Now he's knocking on the door of the big leagues. None of Peter's tools is exceptional, but he has excellent defensive value with a good internal clock, fielding instincts and arm strength that plays as above-average or plus at second base or on the outfield corners. Peter's range isn't quite good enough for him to profile as a shortstop, but he could fill in at the position. He has a fluid, contact-oriented swing, and he has consistently put the ball in play as he climbs the ladder. Peter has doubles power and can hit the ball where it's pitched. He has below-average power and can be overmatched against elite velocity, but he makes up for his lack of explosiveness with quality strike zone awareness and solid pitch recognition. Peter has below-average speed. Peter figures to return to Triple-A to start the 2017 season, though he could certainly earn time as a utility player with the major league team.

Year	Club (League)	Class	AVG	G	AB	R	H	2B	3B	HR	RBI	BB	SO	SB	CS	OBP	SLG
2014	Great Falls (PIO)	R	.388	37	152	26	59	11	6	2	21	13	13	1	1	.444	.579
	Winston-Salem (CAR)	HiA	.236	23	89	8	21	4	1	0	5	4	13	1	0	.277	.303
2015	Winston-Salem (CAR)	HiA	.260	130	497	76	129	25	5	3	57	53	89	23	3	.330	.348
2016	Birmingham (SL)	AA	.304	68	253	27	77	14	0	4	29	31	52	5	1	.378	.407
	Charlotte (IL)	AAA	.259	62	228	30	59	13	0	2	24	17	44	3	1	.317	.342
Minor League Totals			.283	320	1219	167	345	67	12	11	136	118	211	33	6	.348	.385

17 CHARLIE TILSON, OF

BA GRADE

45 Risk: Medium

Born: Dec. 2, 1992. **B-T:** L-L. **Ht.:** 5-11. **Wt.:** 195. **Drafted:** HS—Winnetka, Ill., 2011 (2nd round). **Signed by:** Kris Gross (Cardinals).

After forgoing a scholarship at Illinois, Tilson slowly climbed through the Cardinals system. He battled significant injuries, with a labrum tear costing him the 2012 season and a fractured foot costing him a chance to play in the 2014 Arizona Fall League. When healthy, he has been a solid performer in the upper minors, and the White Sox acquired him when they traded Zach Duke to the Cardinals at the 2016 deadline. Tilson immediately went to the big leagues and collected a hit off Anibal Sanchez in his debut before suffering a season-ending hamstring injury that same day. He has a short swing to go with outstanding bat control, and he has struck out in just 14 percent of the time in the minors. Tilson can also impact the game with his speed. He's a plus runner whose speed plays in center field, and he's become a more efficient baserunner as he's progressed through the minors. Tilson's lack of power and injury history hold him back, but he could have a long career as a contact-oriented center fielder or fourth outfielder.

Year	Club (League)	Class	AVG	G	AB	R	H	2B	3B	HR	RBI	BB	SO	SB	CS	OBP	SLG
2014	Palm Beach (FSL)	HiA	.308	89	370	54	114	8	8	5	36	24	76	10	7	.357	.414
	Springfield (TL)	AA	.237	31	139	19	33	4	1	2	17	6	28	2	3	.269	.324
2015	Springfield (TL)	AA	.295	134	539	85	159	20	9	4	32	46	72	46	19	.351	.388
2016	Memphis (PCL)	AAA	.282	100	351	53	99	16	8	4	34	33	51	15	3	.345	.407
	Chicago (AL)	MAJ	.500	1	2	0	1	0	0	0	0	0	0	0	0	.500	.500
Major League Totals			.500	1	2	0	1	0	0	0	0	0	0	0	0	.500	.500
Minor League Totals			.293	471	1836	265	538	59	33	19	154	142	295	89	38	.346	.392

18 TYLER DANISH, RHP

BA GRADE

45 Risk: Medium

Born: Sept. 12, 1994. **B-T:** R-R. **Ht.:** 6-0. **Wt.:** 200. **Drafted:** HS—Plant City, Fla., 2013 (2nd round). **Signed by:** Joe Siers.

The White Sox have a reputation for promoting prospects quickly, and despite being one of the youngest players in each league, Danish has held his own at each step of the way. He earned a quick promotion to high Class A in 2014, his full-season debut, and then logged 142 innings at Double-A Birmingham as a 20-year-old in 2015. Danish pitched well enough at to receive a brief major league stint in the Chicago bullpen in 2016. Evaluators feel Danish is at his best when he's pitching at 87-91 mph with plus sink. He is capable of throwing harder than that, but his fastball doesn't play as well when he's reaching back for extra velocity. His best offspeed pitch is his changeup, an above-average to plus offering with late fade and plus depth. Danish also throws a near-average slider and a shorter cutter in the mid-80s in addition to a get-me-over curveball. His cadre of weapons and pitch-to-contact mentality fit the starting-pitcher prototype. He has enough command and pitchability to profile as a No. 5 starter.

Year	Club (League)	Class	W	L	ERA	G	GS	CG	SV	IP	H	HR	BB	SO	K/9	WHIP	AVG
2014	Kannapolis (SAL)	LoA	3	0	0.71	7	7	0	0	38	28	0	10	25	5.9	1.00	.206
	Winston-Salem (CAR)	HiA	5	3	2.65	18	18	0	0	92	87	7	23	78	7.7	1.20	.249
2015	Birmingham (SL)	AA	8	12	4.50	26	26	2	0	142	175	13	60	90	5.7	1.65	.311
2016	Birmingham (SL)	AA	7	7	4.42	12	12	1	0	75	71	4	16	47	5.6	1.15	.246
	Chicago (AL)	MAJ	0	0	10.80	3	0	0	0	2	6	0	3	0	0.0	5.40	.667
	Charlotte (IL)	AAA	1	3	5.83	7	5	0	0	29	39	0	10	21	6.4	1.67	.320
Major League Totals			0	0	10.80	3	0	0	0	2	6	0	3	0	0.0	5.40	.667
Minor League Totals			21	25	3.57	85	69	3	0	406	417	24	124	289	6.4	1.33	.267

19 ADAM ENGEL, OF

BA GRADE

45 Risk: Medium

Born: Dec. 9, 1991. **B-T:** R-R. **Ht.:** 6-2. **Wt.:** 210. **Drafted:** Louisville, 2013 (19th round). **Signed by:** Phil Gulley.

Engel wasn't a star player in his three seasons at Louisville, struggling to hit consistently, but he was able to impact games with excellent defense and speed. The White Sox took a shot on his athletic ability as a 19th-round pick, and he's made subtle adjustments in pro ball. After finishing 2015 with an exceptional performance in the Arizona Fall League, Engel struggled mightily at Double-A Birmingham in 2016 prior to a May demotion to high Class A Winston-Salem. From that date forward he hit .280/.352/.429 with 33 stolen bases in 103 games as he reached Triple-A Charlotte. Engel is a 70 runner on the 20-80 scouting scale, and some evaluators feel he could be one of the best defensive center fielders in baseball. He flashes above-average raw power, but even those who like him feel that his swing mechanics will always impede his ability to make contact. He starts his swing with a bit of a hand raise, then drops his hands down just before he gets ready to rotate forward. Engel earns comparisons with Peter Bourjos as a plus defensive outfielder with speed and occasional power. He's near big league ready and could reach his ceiling as a fourth outfielder as soon as 2017.

Year	Club (League)	Class	AVG	G	AB	R	H	2B	3B	HR	RBI	BB	SO	SB	CS	OBP	SLG
2014	White Sox (AZL)	R	.364	8	33	6	12	3	3	1	3	3	6	2	0	.447	.727
	Kannapolis (SAL)	LoA	.261	74	307	54	80	14	7	6	30	29	86	28	11	.334	.410
	Winston-Salem (CAR)HiA		.239	21	88	11	21	0	0	0	5	6	21	9	1	.296	.239
2015	Winston-Salem (CAR)HiA		.251	136	529	90	133	23	9	7	43	62	132	65	11	.335	.369
2016	Winston-Salem (CAR)HiA		.327	14	55	15	18	6	1	0	5	7	11	6	0	.413	.473
	Birmingham (SL)	AA	.255	74	306	56	78	18	9	4	25	39	70	31	9	.352	.412
	Charlotte (IL)	AAA	.242	41	149	19	36	6	2	3	16	10	50	8	5	.298	.369
Minor League Totals			.264	424	1706	295	450	82	34	24	157	177	410	180	45	.344	.394

20 JACOB MAY, OF

BA GRADE
45 Risk: Medium

Born: Jan. 23, 1992. **B-T:** B-R. **Ht.:** 5-10. **Wt.:** 180. **Drafted:** Coastal Carolina, 2013 (3rd round). **Signed by:** Kevin Burrell.

May has big league bloodlines. His grandfather is Lee May, while his father Lee Jr. has been a minor league hitting coach. Jacob was a two-year starter at Coastal Carolina and has been a solid-if-unspectacular performer since turning pro. He reached Triple-A in 2016 but a few minor injuries slowed his progression towards Chicago. May does a lot of things well and could profile as an extra outfielder. The switch-hitter makes contact frequently from both sides of the plate but has well below-average power. His best assets are his speed and defense. When May was in college, some evaluators noted his inability to use his plus-plus speed. He has reversed that criticism, and scouts often cite both his pure foot speed and his baserunning technique as strengths. May's outfield route-running and instincts also have improved with experience. His solid all-around skill set could earn him a chance to help the big league team as soon as 2017.

Year	Club (League)	Class	AVG	G	AB	R	H	2B	3B	HR	RBI	BB	SO	SB	CS	OBP	SLG
2014	Winston-Salem (CAR)HiA		.258	109	415	66	107	31	10	2	27	42	71	37	8	.326	.395
2015	White Sox (AZL)	R	.250	3	16	4	4	1	0	0	3	1	3	1	0	.294	.313
	Birmingham (SL)	AA	.275	98	389	47	107	15	1	2	32	29	73	37	17	.329	.334
2016	Charlotte (IL)	AAA	.266	83	301	38	80	19	2	1	24	15	72	19	8	.309	.352
Minor League Totals			.273	359	1372	196	374	73	17	13	121	110	268	118	39	.332	.379

21 AARON BUMMER, LHP

BA GRADE
50 Risk: Extreme

Born: Sept. 21, 1993. **B-T:** L-L. **Ht.:** 6-3. **Wt.:** 200. **Drafted:** Nebraska, 2014 (19th round). **Signed by:** J.J. Lally.

Bummer was a three-year contributor at Nebraska who earned a weekend rotation role as a junior. He pitched to a 3.34 ERA that season, though he struck out fewer than six batters per nine innings. Still, the White Sox selected him in the 19th round of the 2014 draft and shifted him to the bullpen. Bummer succeeded right away by punching out 28 batters in 22 innings at Rookie-level Great Falls in his debut. He missed the entire 2015 season, however, after having Tommy John surgery. He returned to the mound in mid-2016 and quickly and emphatically established himself as a prospect by jumping to high Class A Winston-Salem. Bummer lacked consistency, as do many pitchers recovering from Tommy John surgery, but showed a fastball that grades as at least plus. He reached 99 mph at his best and sat 91-96 on his worst days. Bummer's slurvy breaking ball has been clocked in the upper 80s, giving him a second plus pitch. He is on track to start 2017 at Double-A Birmingham.

Year	Club (League)	Class	W	L	ERA	G	GS	CG	SV	IP	H	HR	BB	SO	K/9	WHIP	AVG
2014	Great Falls (PIO)	R	0	0	2.45	16	0	0	1	22	18	1	6	28	11.5	1.09	.222
2015	Did not play—Injured																
2016	White Sox (AZL)	R	0	0	12.27	4	0	0	0	4	5	0	2	6	14.7	1.91	.313
	Great Falls (PIO)	R	1	1	3.38	7	0	0	0	8	7	0	4	11	12.4	1.38	.233
	Winston-Salem (CAR)	HiA	0	1	1.80	4	0	0	0	5	4	0	1	1	1.8	1.00	.200
Minor League Totals			1	2	3.49	31	0	0	1	39	34	1	13	46	10.7	1.22	.231

22 AARON SCHNURBUSCH, OF

BA GRADE
50 Risk: Extreme

Born: Jan. 21, 1994. **B-T:** L-L. **Ht.:** 6-5. **Wt.:** 235. **Drafted:** Pittsburgh, 2016 (28th round). **Signed by:** Justin Wechsler.

Schnurbusch was a prolific two-way player in junior college before transferring to Pittsburgh in 2015. He continued to play the outfield and pitch as a junior, batting .274 and pitching sporadically. He dropped pitching as a senior in 2016 but batted just .241. White Sox area scout Justin Wechsler stayed on Schnurbusch, though, because he was intrigued by his athleticism and physical 6-foot-5 frame. He convinced the White Sox to work him out before the draft, and Schnurbusch, who bats and throws left, showed off plus raw power. His workout prompted Chicago to take a shot on him in the 28th round, and he signed for just $1,000. Schnurbusch hit .357/.471/.542 at Rookie-level Grand Junction in his debut. He led the Pioneer League with 47 walks while ranking third in the batting race. Schnurbusch made consistent hard contact in his debut, though detractors see his uppercut swing and inconsistent hip rotation as potential barriers to hitting for a high average. He is an above-average runner and projects best as a power-oriented right fielder. He will advance to low Class A Kannapolis to start 2017, and he could establish himself as a late-round steal.

Year	Club (League)	Class	AVG	G	AB	R	H	2B	3B	HR	RBI	BB	SO	SB	CS	OBP	SLG
2016	Great Falls (PIO)	R	.357	66	238	53	85	14	6	6	44	47	69	19	8	.471	.542
Minor League Totals			.357	66	238	53	85	14	6	6	44	47	69	19	8	.471	.542

23 BERNARDO FLORES, LHP

BA GRADE
50 Risk: Extreme

Born: Aug. 25, 1995. **B-T:** L-L. **Ht.:** 6-3. **Wt.:** 170. **Drafted:** Southern California, 2016 (7th round). **Signed by:** Kenny Williams Jr.

Flores made promising progress as a Southern California sophomore, when he pitched to a 3.83 ERA and saw a significant jump in innings. That progress halted as a junior in 2016, when he struggled to throw quality strikes and saw his ERA balloon to 6.70. The White Sox took a shot on Flores because of his arm strength, believing they could correct some of his issues. He found immediate success in pro ball during an 11-start run at Rookie-level Great Falls and then stood out at instructional league. Flores wakes scouts up with an explosive fastball, which can reach 97 mph but typically works at 90-95. He also earns positive reviews for his changeup, which projects as an above-average offering and flashes better than that. Flores hasn't quite figured out how to use his curveball, but he made quick progress with the pitch and shows natural hand speed. As such he generates tight three-quarter rotation when he's on top of the pitch. Flores will begin 2017 in the low Class A Kannapolis rotation.

Year	Club (League)	Class	W	L	ERA	G	GS	CG	SV	IP	H	HR	BB	SO	K/9	WHIP	AVG
2016	White Sox (AZL)	R	0	1	1.50	3	0	0	0	6	4	0	0	7	10.5	0.67	.174
	Great Falls (PIO)	R	6	1	3.66	11	11	0	0	59	63	4	12	45	6.9	1.27	.280
Minor League Totals			6	2	3.46	14	11	0	0	65	67	4	12	52	7.2	1.22	.270

24 MICKER ADOLFO, OF

BA GRADE
50 Risk: Extreme

Born: Sep. 11, 1996. **B-T:** R-R. **Ht.:** 6-3. **Wt.:** 200. **Signed:** Dominican Republic, 2013. **Signed by:** Marco Paddy.

Originally from the U.S. Virgin Islands, Adolfo moved to the Dominican Republic at age 14. He signed with the White Sox for $1.6 million in 2013, demarcating a rebirth of Chicago's international presence. When Adolfo joined the organization he was athletic and wide-shouldered. He has added significant muscle as he has progressed, and scouts who saw him in 2016 noted his physical transition to manhood. In his age-19 season, Adolfo struggled to a .219 average at low Class A Kannapolis. He has plus-plus bat speed and loose wrists, but he has a tendency to trust his hands a little too much. This causes him to over-swing, lose balance and struggle to see the ball into his barrel. He fits the right-field profile with a plus-plus arm and average speed and range in the field. Adolfo will return to Kannapolis to begin 2017, where he'll join a group of older, more mature outfield prospects who could be a positive influence. While Adolfo has yet to perform, he retains his high ceiling, which has been mitigated by even higher risk to this point.

Year	Club (League)	Class	AVG	G	AB	R	H	2B	3B	HR	RBI	BB	SO	SB	CS	OBP	SLG
2014	White Sox (AZL)	R	.218	46	179	27	39	10	2	5	21	14	85	0	0	.279	.380
2015	White Sox (AZL)	R	.253	22	83	14	21	3	1	0	10	6	25	3	2	.323	.313
2016	White Sox (AZL)	R	.250	4	16	2	4	2	0	1	2	1	8	0	0	.333	.563
	Kannapolis (SAL)	LoA	.219	65	247	30	54	13	1	5	21	14	88	0	1	.269	.340
Minor League Totals			.225	137	525	73	118	28	4	11	54	35	206	3	3	.283	.356

25 ZACH THOMPSON, RHP

BA GRADE
45 Risk: High

Born: Oct. 23, 1993. **B-T:** R-R. **Ht.:** 6-7. **Wt.:** 230. **Drafted:** Texas-Arlington, 2014 (5th round). **Signed by:** Keith Staab.

At 6-foot-7, Thompson has an extra-large frame and brings an imposing presence to the mound. As with many tall pitchers, he has been consistently inconsistent. Thompson recorded a 4.71 ERA at Texas-Arlington despite having promising stuff and downhill plane on his pitches. The 2014 draft pick spent the majority of 2015 and 2016 at low Class A Kannapolis, and in his repeat he began to tap into his potential. During one five-start stretch in April and May, Thompson lasted at least six innings and allowed three hits or fewer each time out. He eventually earned a promotion to high Class A Winston-Salem, where his struggles resurfaced. On a good day, Thompson pitches with a plus fastball at 90-95 mph, an average upper-70s curveball and a changeup that registers about 10 mph less than his heater. He pitches downhill and generates ground balls at an above-average rate. In short bursts, such as in the South Atlantic League all-star game, his fastball can reach as high as 97 mph. If he fails to achieve the consistency required for a starter, Thompson could be effective as a two-pitch reliever. He heads back to high Class A in 2017.

Year	Club (League)	Class	W	L	ERA	G	GS	CG	SV	IP	H	HR	BB	SO	K/9	WHIP	AVG
2014	Great Falls (PIO)	R	2	3	3.27	11	11	0	0	44	43	6	14	26	5.3	1.30	.262
2015	Kannapolis (SAL)	LoA	3	8	4.44	16	16	0	0	75	77	2	37	64	7.7	1.52	.270
2016	Kannapolis (SAL)	LoA	6	3	2.62	16	16	0	0	86	58	5	39	88	9.2	1.13	.193
	Winston-Salem (CAR)	HiA	3	5	5.60	10	10	0	0	55	66	7	15	40	6.6	1.48	.292
Minor League Totals			14	19	3.88	53	53	0	0	260	244	20	105	218	7.6	1.34	.250

26 VICTOR DIAZ, RHP

BA GRADE | **45** Risk: High

Born: May 24, 1994. **B-T:** R-R. **Ht.:** 6-3. **Wt.:** 190. **Signed:** Dominican Republic, 2014. **Signed by:** Manny Nanita/Eddie Romero. (Red Sox).

Though Diaz signed with the Red Sox at age 20, much later than when most international prospects are first identified, he quickly demonstrated the sort of power arm that suggests a potential fast track as a bullpen weapon. Boston traded Diaz along with top prospects Yoan Moncada, Michael Kopech and Luis Alexander Basabe to the White Sox for Chris Sale at the 2016 Winter Meetings. Diaz's 6-foot-3 frame is imposing and physically mature, and he comes at hitters with a three-pitch power mix. While Diaz's high-90s fastball—which has touched triple digits—is more of a heavy ball that induces bad contact than a swing-and-miss weapon, his slider and splitter (a pitch he developed in 2016) get plenty of whiffs. He recovered from a slow start at low Class A Greenville in 2016 with complete dominance down the stretch. In his final 39 innings, Diaz recorded a 1.38 ERA with 10.8 strikeouts and 3.5 walks per nine innings, and he concluded the campaign with 23.2 scoreless innings. His delivery keeps his full mix around the strike zone. Diaz should open 2017 at high Class A Winston-Salem and some evaluators feel he has at least a chance to fly through the system, perhaps even pushing for a big league role by the end of the year.

Year	Club (League)	Class	W	L	ERA	G	GS	CG	SV	IP	H	HR	BB	SO	K/9	WHIP	AVG
2015	Red Sox2 (DSL)	R	6	1	1.38	21	0	0	7	33	20	0	16	35	9.6	1.10	.183
2016	Greenville (SAL)	LoA	2	5	3.88	37	0	0	10	60	65	2	25	63	9.4	1.49	.277
Minor League Totals			8	6	3.00	58	0	0	17	93	85	2	41	98	9.5	1.35	.247

27 CONNOR WALSH, RHP

BA GRADE | **45** Risk: High

Born: Oct. 18, 1992. **B-T:** L-R. **Ht.:** 6-2. **Wt.:** 180. **Drafted:** Cincinnati, 2014 (12th round). **Signed by:** Phil Gulley.

Walsh missed his freshman season at Cincinnati after having Tommy John surgery, but he joined the rotation the next year. In his draft year of 2014 he showed excellent stuff but just middling results with a 3.86 ERA and 5.9 strikeouts per nine innings. Walsh moved to the bullpen after the White Sox made him a 12th-round pick. He struggled to limit walks and hard contact in his first couple seasons in the system but made marked progress in 2016 at high Class A Winston-Salem. Rival evaluators note that Walsh is at his best in his first inning, and he tends to struggle when tasked with going multiple innings. He won't have to do that at the big league level. Walsh has a slingshot type of arm action, cocking his right arm as he points his left arm forward. He isn't very balanced on the mound and has a head whack at release, both barriers to command. Walsh does, however, possess elite arm strength. His fastball has reached 98 mph and routinely works at 93-96. He shown flashes of an above-average breaking ball as well. If he can improve his control, Walsh could develop into a set-up reliever.

Year	Club (League)	Class	W	L	ERA	G	GS	CG	SV	IP	H	HR	BB	SO	K/9	WHIP	AVG
2014	Great Falls (PIO)	R	1	1	2.66	15	0	0	2	20	15	0	14	23	10.2	1.43	.200
	Kannapolis (SAL)	LoA	1	0	9.45	4	0	0	0	7	10	0	2	6	8.1	1.80	.357
2015	Kannapolis (SAL)	LoA	2	3	4.92	29	0	0	0	53	39	3	44	79	13.4	1.57	.201
2016	White Sox (AZL)	R	0	0	0.00	1	0	0	0	1	0	0	0	3	27.0	0.00	.000
	Winston-Salem (CAR)	HiA	2	2	3.40	25	0	0	5	40	28	1	19	41	9.3	1.18	.207
	Birmingham (SL)	AA	0	0	4.70	6	0	0	0	8	7	0	5	7	8.2	1.57	.233
Minor League Totals			6	6	4.28	80	0	0	7	128	99	4	84	159	11.2	1.43	.213

28 IAN HAMILTON, RHP

BA GRADE | **45** Risk: High

Born: June 16, 1995. **B-T:** R-R. **Ht.:** 6-0. **Wt.:** 200. **Drafted:** Washington State, 2016 (11th round). **Signed by:** Robbie Cummings.

Hamilton was Washington State's closer in each of his first two seasons on campus. He showed well in the Cape Cod League as a starter as his junior year approached, then took a weekend rotation spot for the Cougars in 2016. Hamilton struggled as a starter and posted a 4.97 ERA, slipping to the 11th round as a result. The righthander went back to the bullpen in pro ball, serving as the closer at low Class A Kannapolis at the end of 2016. He is a bit undersized and has an effortful delivery, with a deep stab in the back of his arm action and an across-body finish. Hamilton's stuff, however, could allow him to excel in a high-leverage relief role and move through the system quickly. His fastball works in the mid-90s out of the bullpen, and his slider is among the best secondary pitches in the system. It features hard sweeping action and registers in the upper 80s. Hamilton could make the jump to high Class A Winston-Salem to start 2017.

Year	Club (League)	Class	W	L	ERA	G	GS	CG	SV	IP	H	HR	BB	SO	K/9	WHIP	AVG
2016	White Sox (AZL)	R	0	0	0.00	1	0	0	0	1	0	0	1	2	18.0	1.00	.000
	Kannapolis (SAL)	LoA	1	1	3.69	21	0	0	8	32	22	3	14	27	7.7	1.14	.202
Minor League Totals			1	1	3.58	22	0	0	8	33	22	3	15	29	8.0	1.13	.196

29 DYLAN COVEY, RHP

BA GRADE
40 Risk: Medium

Born: Aug. 14, 1991. **B-T:** R-R. **Ht.:** 6-2. **Wt.:** 195. **Drafted:** San Diego, 2013 (4th round). **Signed by:** Eric Martins (Athletics).

Covey was drafted 14th overall by the Brewers in 2010, but after a late Type I diabetes diagnosis, he decided to go to college at San Diego so he could better deal with his health. The Athletics drafted him in 2013 in the fourth round, then lost him to the White Sox in the 2016 Rule 5 draft. Covey was off to a solid start to his career before he tore his left oblique at Double-A Midland in May 2016, in the first inning of his sixth start, and missed the remainder of the season. He resumed pitching in the Arizona Fall League, where he recorded a 4.74 ERA and struck out 17 and walked eight in 25 innings. Covey can touch 95 mph with his fastball, but his delivery is not smooth and causes his command to waver. His front knee is stiff and his delivery is difficult to repeat. Covey will make changes to his delivery but then regresses to his previous, comfortable mechanics. With poor command and an inconsistent delivery, Covey relies on keeping the ball low in the zone and is an extreme groundball pitcher. He will have realistic chance with the White Sox to make the pitching staff in 2016, possibly as a No. 5 starter but more likely in a low-leverage relief role.

Year	Club (League)	Class	W	L	ERA	G	GS	CG	SV	IP	H	HR	BB	SO	K/9	WHIP	AVG
2014	Beloit (MWL)	LoA	4	9	4.81	18	17	2	0	101	99	3	26	70	6.2	1.24	.258
	Stockton (CAL)	HiA	3	5	7.15	8	8	0	0	39	49	2	15	22	5.1	1.64	.312
2015	Stockton (CAL)	HiA	8	9	3.59	26	26	0	0	140	135	13	43	100	6.4	1.27	.250
2016	Midland (TL)	AA	2	1	1.84	6	6	0	0	29	21	2	17	26	8.0	1.30	.200
Minor League Totals			18	25	4.20	72	71	2	0	369	377	24	119	264	6.4	1.34	.264

30 OMAR NARVAEZ, C

BA GRADE
40 Risk: Medium

Born: Feb. 10, 1992. **B-T:** L-R. **Ht.:** 5-11. **Wt.:** 215. **Signed:** Venezuela, 2008. **Signed by:** Ronnie Blanco (Rays).

Narvaez slowly navigated the low minors in the Rays system. Tampa Bay saw him as an organizational player because he was a solid defensive catcher whose maturity would make him an asset as a coach on the field. The White Sox liked him too and snagged him in the minor league phase of the 2013 Rule 5 draft. Narvaez had progressed to high Class A Winston-Salem by 2015, and his defensive acumen earned him an invitation to big league camp in 2016. He began the season at Double-A Birmingham, but injuries to big league catchers Dioner Navarro and Alex Avila and Triple-A starter Kevan Smith opened a spot for Narvaez in mid-July. He took advantage of the opportunity. He began his career with an eight-game hitting streak. Narvaez doesn't project as the above-average hitter that his statistics in Chicago would indicate, though he could be enough of an on-base threat to be a quality backup or replacement-level starter. He's an above-average receiver who can handle a major league staff, and he fits in the organization's short-term plans.

Year	Club (League)	Class	AVG	G	AB	R	H	2B	3B	HR	RBI	BB	SO	SB	CS	OBP	SLG
2014	Kannapolis (SAL)	LoA	.291	38	127	7	37	3	0	0	20	9	11	0	0	.331	.315
	Winston-Salem (CAR)	HiA	.279	47	140	18	39	8	0	2	16	27	21	3	2	.393	.379
2015	Winston-Salem (CAR)	HiA	.274	98	339	38	93	10	0	1	27	40	31	1	0	.352	.313
2016	Birmingham (SL)	AA	.222	13	45	4	10	2	0	0	5	4	8	0	0	.286	.267
	Charlotte (IL)	AAA	.245	41	143	14	35	6	0	2	11	9	17	0	0	.292	.329
	Chicago (AL)	MAJ	.267	34	101	13	27	4	0	1	10	14	14	0	0	.350	.337
Major League Totals			.267	34	101	13	27	4	0	1	10	14	14	0	0	.350	.337
Minor League Totals			.277	459	1543	181	427	57	7	7	170	176	168	16	11	.353	.336

Cincinnati Reds

BY J.J. COOPER

The Reds' rebuilding effort hit full speed in 2016. The organization hopes it hit rock bottom with its 94-loss season and can now start the slow climb back to both respectability and contention in the National League Central.

One characteristic of rebuilding teams is opportunity. Teams like the 2016 Reds had a surplus of at-bats and innings available for the taking, and ideally that playing time goes to young players—or at least lesser-noticed players who could turn into valuable big league pieces.

In this context, Cincinnati identified a few possible solutions for the future. Left fielder Adam  Duvall, acquired in the 2015 Mike Leake trade, combined power and surprisingly good defense with plenty of strikeouts. Waiver claim righthander Dan Straily proved to be a surprisingly strong addition as a mid-rotation starter.

Shortstop Jose Peraza, whom the Reds acquired after the 2015 season when they traded Todd Frazier, showed Cincinnati that he needs a spot in the 2017 lineup. The Reds' patience in center fielder Billy Hamilton paid off when his second half at the plate hinted he can get on-base enough to let his best-in-baseball speed play on the bases as well as it does in center field.

The club went 39-43 from July 1 onward. With lefthander Brandon Finnegan and righties Anthony DeSclafani, Homer Bailey and Straily penciled into the rotation and a largely set lineup, the Reds enter 2017 on much firmer footing.

The farm system is deeper as well thanks to holding the No. 2 overall pick in the 2016 draft. The Reds' draft class should pay benefits for years to come, and Cincinnati will choose second overall again in 2017.

But Cincinnati must lament how the system could be even deeper. Cincinnati traded away closer Aroldis Chapman right after news broke that Chapman was being investigated for a domestic violence allegation and faced a possible suspension.

The Reds could have waited until the suspension was announced to trade Chapman. Or they could have held him until he returned from suspension and dealt him at the trade deadline. Instead, they traded him to the Yankees when the uncertainty of his possible suspension had sapped his trade value to its lowest ebb.

Of the four players the Reds acquired from New York for Chapman, none rank among the organization's Top 30 Prospects. For contrast, the Yankees flipped Chapman to the Cubs in July

Jose Peraza may be the best trade acquisition by the Reds during their rebuilding effort

TOP PROSPECTS OF THE DECADE

Year	Player, Pos.	2016 Org
2007	Homer Bailey, rhp	Reds
2008	Jay Bruce, of	Mets
2009	Yonder Alonso, 1b	Athletics
2010	Todd Frazier, 3b/of	White Sox
2011	Aroldis Chapman, lhp	Cubs
2012	Devin Mesoraco, c	Reds
2013	Billy Hamilton, of	Reds
2014	Robert Stephenson, rhp	Reds
2015	Robert Stephenson, rhp	Reds
2016	Robert Stephenson, rhp	Reds

2016 for shortstop Gleyber Torres, one of the top prospects in the game.

The Reds' return from the Mets for right fielder Jay Bruce at the 2016 trade deadline also was modest—Rookie-ball lefthander Max Wotell and Triple-A second baseman Dilson Herrera—and Cincinnati is stuck with 35-year-old second baseman Brandon Phillips for one more season after his 2012 contract extension meant he earned 10-and-5 rights to veto any trade.

All of those missteps can be overcome, but for the Reds to contend before Joey Votto reaches the decline phase of his 10-year extension, they will have to figure out how to turn the team's impressive group of upper-level pitching prospects into solid big leaguers. That will be the biggest challenge in 2017.

ORGANIZATION OVERVIEW

General manager: Dick Williams. **Farm director:** Jeff Graupe. **Scouting director:** Chris Buckley.

Class	Team	League	W	L	PCT	Finish	Manager
Majors	Cincinnati Reds	National	68	94	.420	14th (15)	Bryan Price
Triple-A	Louisville Bats	International	71	73	.493	6th (14)	Delino DeShields
Double-A	Pensacola Blue Wahoos	Southern	81	59	.579	2nd (10)	Pat Kelly
High Class A	Daytona Tortugas	Florida State	76	61	.555	4th (12)	Eli Marrero
Low Class A	Dayton Dragons	Midwest	47	93	.336	16th (16)	Dick Schofield
Rookie	Billings Mustangs	Pioneer	41	34	.547	2nd (8)	Ray Martinez
Rookie	AZL Reds	Arizona	31	24	.564	2nd (14)	Jose Nieves
Overall 2016 Minor League Record			347	344	.502	15th (30)	

THIS YEAR'S TOP 30

No.	Player, Pos.	Grade/Risk
1.	Nick Senzel, 3b	60/Medium
2.	Cody Reed, lhp	60/High
3.	Amir Garrett, lhp	55/Medium
4.	Robert Stephenson, rhp	55/High
5.	Taylor Trammell, of	55/High
6.	Jesse Winker, of	50/Medium
7.	Aristides Aquino, of	55/High
8.	Sal Romano, rhp	50/Medium
9.	Vladimir Gutierrez, rhp	55/High
10.	Tyler Stephenson, c	55/Extreme
11.	Tony Santillan, rhp	55/Extreme
12.	Tyler Mahle, rhp	50/Medium
13.	Jimmy Herget, rhp	50/Medium
14.	Chris Okey, c	50/High
15.	T.J. Freidl, of	50/High
16.	Shed Long, 2b	50/High
17.	Nick Travieso, rhp	40/Low
18.	Phillip Ervin, of	45/Medium
19.	Keury Mella, rhp	50/High
20.	Barrett Astin, rhp	45/Medium
21.	Ariel Hernandez, rhp	50/Extreme
22.	Alfredo Rodriguez, ss	50/Extreme
23.	Michael Beltre, of	50/Extreme
24.	Ryan Hendrix, rhp	45/High
25.	Tanner Rainey, rhp	45/High
26.	Ian Kahaloa, rhp	45/High
27.	Zack Weiss, rhp	45/High
28.	Blake Trahan, ss	40/Medium
29.	Ismael Guillon, lhp	45/High
30.	Nick Hanson, rhp	50/Extreme

LAST YEAR'S TOP 30

No.	Player, Pos.	Status
1.	Robert Stephenson, rhp	No. 4
2.	Cody Reed, lhp	No. 2
3.	Amir Garrett, lhp	No. 3
4.	Tyler Stephenson, c	No. 10
5.	Jesse Winker, of	No. 6
6.	Alex Blandino, 2b	Dropped out
7.	Nick Travieso, rhp	No. 17
8.	Keury Mella, rhp	No. 19
9.	Sal Romano, rhp	No. 8
10.	Tyler Mahle, rhp	No. 12
11.	John Lamb, lhp	(Angels)
12.	Phillip Ervin, of	No. 18
13.	Tony Santillan, rhp	No. 11
14.	Taylor Sparks, 3b	Dropped out
15.	Yorman Rodriguez, of	Free agent
16.	Wyatt Strahan, rhp	Dropped out
17.	Tanner Rainey, rhp	No. 25
18.	Aristides Aquino, of	No. 7
19.	Blake Trahan, ss	No. 28
20.	Ian Kahaloa, rhp	No. 26
21.	Kyle Waldrop, of/1b	Free agent
22.	Zack Weiss, rhp	No. 27
23.	Calten Daal, ss	Dropped out
24.	Gavin LaValley, 3b	Dropped out
25.	Jon Moscot, rhp	Dropped out
26.	Jake Turnbull, c	Dropped out
27.	Tejay Antone, rhp	Dropped out
28.	Narciso Crook, of	Dropped out
29.	Jonathan Crawford, rhp	Dropped out
30.	Nick Howard, rhp	Dropped out

BEST TOOLS

Best Hitter for Average	Nick Senzel
Best Power Hitter	Aristides Aquino
Best Strike-Zone Discipline	Jesse Winker
Fastest Baserunner	Taylor Trammell
Best Athlete	Taylor Trammell
Best Fastball	Tony Santillan
Best Curveball	Ariel Hernandez
Best Slider	Cody Reed
Best Changeup	Ismael Guillon
Best Control	Tyler Mahle
Best Defensive Catcher	Stuart Turner
Best Defensive Infielder	Alfredo Rodriguez
Best Infield Arm	Taylor Sparks
Best Defensive Outfielder	T.J. Friedl
Best Outfield Arm	Aristides Aquino

PROJECTED 2020 LINEUP

Catcher	Devin Mesoraco
First Base	Joey Votto
Second Base	Dilson Herrera
Third Base	Nick Senzel
Shortstop	Jose Peraza
Left Field	Taylor Trammell
Center Field	Billy Hamilton
Right Field	Aristides Aquino
No. 1 Starter	Homer Bailey
No. 2 Starter	Cody Reed
No. 3 Starter	Amir Garrett
No. 4 Starter	Brandon Finnegan
No. 5 Starter	Robert Stephenson
Closer	Raisel Iglesias

MINOR LEAGUE DEPTH CHART

CINCINNATI REDS

TOP 2017 ROOKIE: Cody Reed, lhp. His big league debut went terribly, but the southpaw still has the makings of potentially dominant starter.
BREAKOUT PROSPECT: Ariel Hernandez, rhp. If he can consistently locate his outstanding curveball, he'll be a potentially dominant big league reliever.
SLEEPER: Jose Siri, of. Poor plate discipline is the only thing holding him back from reaching his lofty ceiling.

SOURCE OF TOP 30 TALENT			
Homegrown	26	Acquired	4
College	8	Trades	3
Junior college	0	Rule 5 draft	1
High school	12	Independent leagues	0
Nondrafted free agents	1	Free agents/waivers	0
International	5		

LF
Taylor Trammell (5)
Jesse Winker (6)
Phillip Ervin (20)

CF
T.J. Friedl (15)
Michael Beltre (23)
Miles Gordon

RF
Aristides Aquino (7)
Jose Siri
Gabby Guerrero

3B
Nick Senzel (1)
Brandon Dixon
Hector Vargas

SS
Alfredo Rodriguez (18)
Blake Trahan (28)
Zack Vincej

2B
Shed Long (16)
Tony Renda
Calten Daal
Francis Azcona

1B
Gavin LaValley
Eric Jagielo

C
Tyler Stephenson (10)
Chris Okey (14)
Stuart Turner
Joe Hudson
Cassidy Brown
Chad Wallach
Pabel Manzanero

LHP

LHSP	LHRP
Cody Reed (2)	Ismael Guillon (29)
Amir Garrett (3)	Scott Moss
Max Wotell	Nick Routt
Wennington Romero	

RHP

RHSP	RHRP
Robert Stephenson (4)	Sal Romano (8)
Vladimir Gutierrez (9)	Jimmy Herget (13)
Tony Santillan (11)	Ariel Hernandez (18)
Tyler Mahle (12)	Keury Mella (21)
Nick Travieso (19)	Barrett Astin (22)
Ian Kahaloa (26)	Ryan Hendrix (24)
Nick Hanson (30)	Tanner Rainey (25)
Rookie Davis	Zack Weiss (27)
Jackson Stephens	Evan Mitchell
Tyler Mondile	Joe Kuhnel
Andrew Jordan	Alejandro Chacin
	Jesus Reyes
	Jesse Stallings

DRAFT ANALYSIS

2016

BEST PURE HITTER: 3B Nick Senzel (1) hit .354 in the Southeastern Conference last spring while walking nearly twice as often as he struck out. He is an advanced hitter with excellent plate coverage and rarely gets caught off balance in his swing. He projects as a plus hitter. OF T.J. Freidl (NDFA) hit .401 at Nevada last spring and impressed with USA Baseball this summer with a table-setting approach.

BEST POWER HITTER: It will likely take a while for OF Taylor Trammell (1s) to get to his plus raw power, but he has the frame and developing strength to end up a 20-25 home run hitter. Senzel hits more doubles than home runs right now, but he can be expected to turn some of those doubles to the gap into home runs as he matures physically. C Chris Okey (2) has potentially average power as well.

FASTEST RUNNER: Trammell is a 6.45-6.5 runner over 60 yards, which grades out as a 70 runner on the 20-to-80 scouting scale. He would likely nip Friedl by a nose in a head-to-head race, but Friedl also grades as a 70 runner.

BEST DEFENSIVE PLAYER: Senzel has above-average side-to-side range at third base, but it is his plus arm with plus accuracy that stands out most and makes him a potentially plus defender at third. He is comfortable throwing from many different arm angles.

BEST FASTBALL: RHP Ryan Hendrix (5) was inconsistent this spring and in his pro debut, but the reliever can sit 96-99 mph and touched 100 mph at Texas A&M. Long-term, RHP Nick Hanson (3) could end up with the best fastball of this draft class. He sits 92-93 mph and will touch 96 right now.

BEST SECONDARY PITCH: At his best, Hendrix will pitch with a 70 curveball to go with his 70 fastball. His curveball is hard with an excellent spin rate, but he doesn't command it as consistently as he needs to. LHP Jesse Adams (14) has an above-average changeup.

BEST PRO DEBUT: After a slow start, Senzel hit .305/.398/.514 between Rookie-level Billings and low Class A Dayton with 34 extra-base hits and 18 steals in 68 games. Trammell handled an aggressive assignment to Billings by hitting .303/.374/.421 with 24 steals.

BEST ATHLETE: Trammell was a running back and safety in high school who has size and speed.

MOST INTRIGUING BACKGROUND: Friedl received the largest bonus ever paid to a non-drafted free agent eligible for the draft. He was overlooked by many teams as being draft-eligible, while the ones who did have him turned in did not draft him, allowing the Reds to land a speedy center fielder with on-base skills.

CLOSEST TO THE MAJORS: Senzel should begin next year in high Class A and could reach Cincinnati by the end of 2017. Hendrix could move quickly as a two-pitch reliever.

BEST LATE-ROUND PICK: RHP Joel Kuhnel (11) is a hard-throwing power arm with a lively 92-95 mph fastball and a hard slider.

THE ONE WHO GOT AWAY: C Cooper Johnson (28) impressed scouts with his receiving and his plus arm. He enrolled at Mississippi.

2015

C Tyler Stephenson (1) had a difficult first full season, while hard-throwing RHP Tony Santillan (2) showed flashes amidst his wildness. SS Blake Trahan (3) is on his way to fulfilling his utility infielder projection.

GRADE: C

2014

Top pick RHP Nick Howard (1) has never thrown strikes as a pro, and college bats 2B Alex Blandino (1) and Taylor Sparks (2) had poor 2016 seasons. No one from this draft ranks in the current Top 30.

GRADE: F

2013

RHP Michael Lorenzen (1s) zoomed to the majors as a pitcher after a two-way college career. RHPs Zack Weiss (6) and Tyler Mahle (7), OF Phil Ervin (1) and 2B Shed Long (12) rank in the Top 30, while RHP Ben Lively (4), traded to the Phillies, led the minors in wins in 2016.

GRADE: B

TOP DRAFT PICKS OF THE DECADE

Year	Player, Pos.	2016 Org
2007	Devin Mesoraco, c	Reds
2008	Yonder Alonso, 1b	Athletics
2009	Mike Leake, rhp	Cardinals
2010	Yasmani Grandal, c	Dodgers
2011	Robert Stephenson, rhp	Reds
2012	Nick Travieso, rhp	Reds
2013	Phillip Ervin, of	Reds
2014	Nick Howard, rhp	Reds
2015	Tyler Stephenson, c	Reds
2016	Nick Senzel, 3b	Reds

LARGEST BONUSES IN CLUB HISTORY

Aroldis Chapman, lhp	$16,250,000
Alfredo Rodriguez, ss	$7,000,000
Nick Senzel, 3b	$6,200,000
Rasiel Iglesias, rhp	$5,000,000
Vladimir Gutierrez, rhp	$4,750,000

1 NICK SENZEL, 3B

Born: June 29, 1995. **B-T:** R-R. **Ht.:** 6-1. **Wt.:** 205.
Drafted: Tennessee, 2016 (1st round).
Signed by: Brad Meador.

BA GRADE

60 Risk: Medium

SCOUTING GRADES

Hitting: 60.
Power: 55.
Speed: 50.
Arm: 60.
Defense: 55.

Based on 20-80 scouting scale and future projection rather than present tools.

DAN ARNOLD

All through his prep career at Farragut High in Knoxville, Senzel was never viewed as the star. Teammate Kyle Serrano drew the majority of the scouting attention, though the Reds' reports from that time did note they believed Senzel had a chance to become a very good player. But first, he needed to head to college. After three years at Tennessee, Senzel has now far surpassed Serrano as a prospect. As a junior in 2016, Senzel hit .352/.456/.595 with a Southeastern Conference-best 25 doubles while walking nearly twice as often as he struck out. He even stole 25 bases for the Volunteers. The Reds selected Senzel with the No. 2 overall pick in the 2016 draft and signed him for $6.2 million, the highest signing bonus for any member of the draft class and also the Reds' franchise record for a drafted player. He kept lining doubles as a pro, hitting 23 in 58 games at low Class A Dayton, where he ranked as the No. 1 prospect in the Midwest League.

Senzel was arguably the safest pick in the 2016 draft. Even scouts who aren't sold on him being an impact player see him as a polished college hitter who should move quickly. He has worked hard to develop into an above-average defender at third base, and even held his own in a stint at shortstop with Tennessee. Senzel has above-average short-range quickness thanks to quick hips. His hands are average, while his best asset defensively is his plus arm. Senzel's throws have plenty of carry, but they are even more notable for accuracy. He can throw from a variety of arm angles and doesn't need to set his feet to uncork an accurate throw. At the plate, Senzel is a hitter who sometimes drives the ball for power rather than a slugger who can hit. He stays balanced in his swing and has excellent pitch recognition, laying off tough breaking balls out of the zone while catching up to fastballs. His biggest vulnerability in his pro career has been when pitchers bust him up and in with fastballs, though he will yank the occasional inside pitch. All seven of his pro home runs were pulled to left field. He has average productive power, but he is more comfortable lining the ball from gap to gap. In batting practice he shows plus raw power. Senzel is a heady baserunner who has a knack for basestealing. He will turn singles into doubles by aggressively coming out of the batter's box and reading how outfielders play balls in the gaps.

Senzel's long track record of production—he hit .300 or better in each of his three years at Tennessee and was the Cape Cod League MVP in 2015—makes scouts comfortable he will be a big league regular. The debate is just how much impact he will make. Senzel's excellent work ethic and surprising athleticism give him a chance to exceed some of those expectations. He projects as a .280-.290 hitter with 15-20 home runs, plenty of doubles and solid defense at third base. If he hits the high end of his projection, he is a plus hitter with plus power. Players with Senzel's type of hitting ability and strength sometimes exceed their power projections in the majors. He is ready for high Class A Daytona in 2017 and should reach Double-A Pensacola during the season. If all goes according to plan, Senzel should be competing for a job in Cincinnati by 2018.

Year	Club (League)	Class	AVG	G	AB	R	H	2B	3B	HR	RBI	BB	SO	SB	CS	OBP	SLG
2016	Billings (PIO)	R	.152	10	33	3	5	1	0	0	4	6	5	3	0	.293	.182
	Dayton (MWL)	LoA	.329	58	210	38	69	23	3	7	36	32	49	15	7	.415	.567
Minor League Totals			.305	68	243	41	74	24	3	7	40	38	54	18	7	.398	.514

2 CODY REED, LHP

Born: April 15, 1993. **B-T:** L-L. **Ht.:** 6-5. **Wt.:** 220. **Drafted:** Northwest Mississippi JC, 2013 (2nd round). **Signed by:** Travis Ezi (Royals).

One of three lefthanders the Reds acquired in the 2015 deadline deal that sent Johnny Cueto to the Royals, Reed dominated at Double-A Pensacola in 2015 and impressed at Triple-A Louisville in 2016. That did success did not continue in Cincinnati following his mid-June callup. Reed went 0-7, 7.36 in 10 starts and allowed 67 hits—including 12 home runs—in 48 innings. Reed's big league debut featured many lowlights but also several encouraging signs. He lived in the bottom of the strike zone with a 93-96 mph fastball and a hard 87-89 mph slider that starts on the outer half of the plate and finishes on the hands of righthanded batters. His low three-quarters arm slot gives lefthanded batters a tough look. However, Reed's fastball steadily backed up in the big leagues, in part because he was trying to guide the ball into the strike zone. His slider became less biting and more sweeping. Falling behind in counts, his fringe-average 85-87 mph changeup was effective as a groundball inducer that carries an element of surprise because he throws it so infrequently. Reed's control played as fringe-average in the majors, but his command is a bigger concern after he tended to catch too much of the plate in his debut. Reed still could develop into a frontline starter because he has two potentially plus or better pitches. He will compete for a Reds rotation spot in 2017.

BA GRADE
60 Risk: High

Year	Club (League)	Class	W	L	ERA	G	GS	CG	SV	IP	H	HR	BB	SO	K/9	WHIP	AVG
2014	Lexington (SAL)	LoA	3	9	5.46	19	19	0	0	84	105	5	36	58	6.2	1.68	.312
2015	Wilmington (CAR)	HiA	5	5	2.14	13	10	1	1	67	62	3	18	65	8.7	1.19	.243
	NW Arkansas (TL)	AA	2	2	3.45	5	5	0	0	29	26	3	8	19	6.0	1.19	.239
	Pensacola (SL)	AA	6	2	2.17	8	8	0	0	50	39	1	16	60	10.9	1.11	.220
2016	Cincinnati (NL)	MAJ	0	7	7.36	10	10	0	0	48	67	12	19	43	8.1	1.80	.328
	Louisville (IL)	AAA	6	4	3.08	13	13	0	0	73	71	6	20	65	8.0	1.25	.259
Major League Totals			0	7	7.36	10	10	0	0	48	67	12	19	43	8.1	1.80	.328
Minor League Totals			22	23	3.66	73	61	1	1	332	334	18	121	292	7.9	1.37	.264

3 AMIR GARRETT, LHP

Born: May 3, 1992. **B-T:** L-L. **Ht.:** 6-5. **Wt.:** 225. **Drafted:** HS—Henderson, Nev., 2011 (22nd round). **Signed by:** Clark Crist.

Garrett's dream of becoming an NBA player met reality at St. John's where he was solid but never spectacular in two seasons. Because the Reds signed him for $1 million as a 22nd-round pick in 2011 out of high school, however, Garrett always had a fallback option. He has pursued baseball exclusively since 2014, and in that time the 6-foot-5 southpaw reshaped his body by gaining weight and advanced to Triple-A Louisville. Given his two-sport background, Garrett is one of the most athletic pitchers in the minors. That has allowed him to develop at a rapid rate and catch up with more experienced pitchers. At his best Garrett's plus 90-95 mph fastball and above-average slider keep hitters uncomfortable. His slider is not as consistent as it needs to be, which explains why he had trouble against more advanced hitters in Triple-A. His changeup can be an average pitch when he sells it and locates it, but he has below-average feel for the pitch and below-average command overall. Garrett can be a mid-rotation starter with improved command. Otherwise he could have a lengthy career as a lefthanded reliever relying on his fastball and slider. He heads back to Triple-A in 2017 and is a viable big league callup option at any time.

BA GRADE
55 Risk: Medium

Year	Club (League)	Class	W	L	ERA	G	GS	CG	SV	IP	H	HR	BB	SO	K/9	WHIP	AVG
2014	Dayton (MWL)	LoA	7	8	3.65	27	27	2	0	133	115	11	51	127	8.6	1.25	.231
2015	Daytona (FSL)	HiA	9	7	2.44	26	26	1	0	140	117	4	55	133	8.5	1.23	.230
2016	Pensacola (SL)	AA	5	3	1.75	13	12	0	0	77	51	0	28	78	9.1	1.03	.184
	Louisville (IL)	AAA	2	5	3.46	12	11	0	0	68	48	6	31	54	7.2	1.17	.202
Minor League Totals			25	29	3.18	100	96	3	0	496	411	26	204	442	8.0	1.24	.226

4 ROBERT STEPHENSON, RHP

Born: Feb. 24, 1993. **B-T:** R-R. **Ht.:** 6-2. **Wt.:** 200. **Drafted:** HS—Martinez, Calif., 2011 (1st round). **Signed by:** Rich Bordi.

Stephenson made his big league debut in 2016 and works with as many as three above-average pitches, but his development has been anything but smooth since he reached Double-A Pensacola for the first time in 2013. The 2011 first-rounder cruised through Class A but has shown well below-average control in the upper minors with 4.8 walks per nine innings, and he recorded a similar rate in his first 37 big league innings. The high-90s fastball Stephenson once pitched with has not been present for two years. He generally pitches at 91-94 mph and will bump 96 when needed. He gets downhill plane on both his two- and four-seam fastballs, sticking predominantly with his four-seamer. He can now throw his above-average curveball for strikes and bury it for a chase pitch, but he needs to emphasize staying on top of it. Stephenson's split-changeup is crucial to his outlook but lacks consistency. It flashes above-average with late tumble but just as often lacks deception and movement. A number of Reds officials believe Stephenson has become too reliant on his offspeed pitches rather than pitching off his fastball. Stephenson has struggled in a similar manner as Homer Bailey, a prep first-round righthander drafted by the Reds in 2004. Stephenson can reach a mid-rotation starter ceiling if he sharpens his control, as Bailey did, and he has no glaring delivery flaws to resolve. He should return to the Reds rotation in 2017.

BA GRADE
55 Risk: High

Year	Club (League)	Class	W	L	ERA	G	GS	CG	SV	IP	H	HR	BB	SO	K/9	WHIP	AVG
2014	Pensacola (SL)	AA	7	10	4.74	27	26	0	0	137	114	18	74	140	9.2	1.38	.224
2015	Pensacola (SL)	AA	4	7	3.68	14	14	1	0	78	53	8	43	89	10.2	1.23	.197
	Louisville (IL)	AAA	4	4	4.04	11	11	0	0	56	51	2	27	51	8.2	1.40	.245
2016	Louisville (IL)	AAA	8	9	4.41	24	24	1	0	137	115	17	71	120	7.9	1.36	.228
	Cincinnati (NL)	MAJ	2	3	6.08	8	8	0	0	37	41	9	19	31	7.5	1.62	.279
Major League Totals			2	3	6.08	8	8	0	0	37	41	9	19	31	7.5	1.62	.279
Minor League Totals			33	41	3.94	113	112	2	0	587	479	61	273	608	9.3	1.28	.222

5 TAYLOR TRAMMELL, OF

Born: Sept. 13, 1997. **B-T:** L-L. **Ht.:** 6-2. **Wt.:** 195. **Drafted:** HS—Kennesaw, Ga., 2016 (1st round supplemental). **Signed by:** Jon Poloni.

Even though Trammell was Georgia's high school football player of the year as a senior, he knew his long-term focus would be baseball. He carried a 4.0 grade-point average in high school and his parents are engineers, so teams had to take his Georgia Tech commitment seriously. The Reds had the highest bonus pool in the 2016 draft—nearly $14 million—and flexed that financial advantage to sign Trammell, a supplemental first-rounder taken 35th overall, for $3.2 million. Trammell handled an aggressive assignment to Rookie-level Billings with ease in his pro debut. He hit .303 and ranked third in the Pioneer League with 24 stolen bases. Trammell is a blazing runner who earns 70 grades on the 20-80 scouting scale and hits line drives with modest power. However, scouts won't be surprised to see him grow into a merely above-average runner with plus power as his upper body fills out to match his already developed lower half. Trammell plays center field now but scouts project him to left field based on his instincts and fringe-average arm. For a young hitter, his knowledge of the strike zone and hand-eye coordination are notable and could make him a plus hitter. Trammell impresses the Reds with his work ethic and he is a better-than-even bet to reach his ceiling as an impact left fielder. He will move to low Class A Dayton in 2017.

BA GRADE
55 Risk: High

BILL MITCHELL

Year	Club (League)	Class	AVG	G	AB	R	H	2B	3B	HR	RBI	BB	SO	SB	CS	OBP	SLG
2016	Billings (PIO)	R	.303	61	228	39	69	9	6	2	34	23	57	24	7	.374	.421
Minor League Totals			.303	61	228	39	69	9	6	2	34	23	57	24	7	.374	.421

6 JESSE WINKER, OF

BA GRADE

50 Risk: **Medium**

Born: Aug. 17, 1993. **B-T:** L-L. **Ht.:** 6-3. **Wt.:** 210. **Drafted:** HS—Orlando, 2012 (1st round supplemental). **Signed by:** Greg Zunino.

Winker always has been one of the most advanced hitters in his age group. He was a key member of USA Baseball's 18U team in 2011 and as a pro he has hit .296 in more than 2,000 plate appearances. But wrist injuries have sabotaged his 2015-16 seasons, leading to an evaporation of his power production and questions about his ability to profile in left field. Winker broke his wrist in 2015 diving for a ball in the outfield and missed time in 2016 with a sprained wrist. Most scouts believe Winker will hit for average. He uses the whole field, but his natural lefthanded swing path carries the ball to left-center field and produces more singles than doubles. Winker controls the strike zone, which has contributed to a .398 career on-base percentage. What he doesn't show is power in games, even though he hits for plus power in batting practice. Scouts project him to have average power (about 15 home runs), which combined with his on-base ability could make him an above-average offensive player. Defensively, he's a fringe-average left fielder with an accurate but fringy arm and below-average speed. Scouts who have seen Winker since high school are disappointed he hasn't seemed to get any stronger, but he can really hit. He should make his big league debut at some point in 2017.

Year	Club (League)	Class	AVG	G	AB	R	H	2B	3B	HR	RBI	BB	SO	SB	CS	OBP	SLG
2014	Bakersfield (CAL)	HiA	.317	53	205	42	65	15	0	13	49	40	46	5	1	.426	.580
	Pensacola (SL)	AA	.208	21	77	15	16	5	0	2	8	14	22	0	0	.326	.351
2015	Pensacola (SL)	AA	.282	123	443	69	125	24	2	13	55	74	83	8	4	.390	.433
2016	Reds (AZL)	R	.462	4	13	6	6	0	0	2	6	2	4	0	0	.533	.923
	Louisville (IL)	AAA	.303	106	380	39	115	22	0	3	45	59	59	0	0	.397	.384
Minor League Totals			.296	481	1763	286	521	100	10	54	274	292	339	20	9	.398	.455

7 ARISTIDES AQUINO, OF

BA GRADE

55 Risk: **High**

Born: April 22, 1994. **B-T:** R-R. **Ht.:** 6-4. **Wt.:** 190. **Signed:** Dominican Republic, 2011. **Signed by:** Richard Jimenez.

Heading into 2015, Aquino appeared poised to build on an excellent season at Rookie-level Billings, but instead struggled at low Class A Dayton and returned to Billings. Assigned to high Class A Daytona in 2016, his production caught up to his tools as he ranked second in the Florida State League in home runs (23) and slugging percentage (.531). Aquino always has passed the eye test. He's a tall, broad-shouldered right fielder with athleticism to go with his impressive and still growing strength. He keeps his hands moving, pumping the bat throughout his pre-pitch setup, but he stays controlled in his stance with solid plate coverage. He takes a big rip, but it's a relatively level swing that keeps the bat in the hitting zone for a while. When he gets his arms extended, Aquino pulls the ball for home runs, but he's also comfortable driving the ball to right field for doubles and triples. Because of his power-oriented swing, he often turns in average run times out of the batter's box, but he's a plus runner underway and that speed plays both on the bases and in the outfield. He's an above-average defender in right with a double-plus arm. Aquino has prototype right-field tools, though his plate discipline issues enhance his risk profile. He has impact potential as he heads to Double-A Pensacola in 2017.

Year	Club (League)	Class	AVG	G	AB	R	H	2B	3B	HR	RBI	BB	SO	SB	CS	OBP	SLG
2014	Billings (PIO)	R	.292	71	284	48	83	23	5	16	64	15	66	21	5	.342	.577
2015	Billings (PIO)	R	.308	13	52	7	16	1	3	2	13	2	9	0	1	.333	.558
	Dayton (MWL)	LoA	.234	61	231	25	54	9	3	5	27	11	53	6	1	.281	.364
2016	Daytona (FSL)	HiA	.273	125	484	69	132	26	12	23	79	34	104	11	7	.327	.519
Minor League Totals			.250	456	1752	254	438	90	34	59	278	119	422	52	36	.308	.441

8 SAL ROMANO, RHP

Born: Oct. 12, 1993. **B-T:** L-R. **Ht.:** 6-4. **Wt.:** 220. **Drafted:** HS—Southington, Conn., 2011 (23rd round). **Signed by:** Lee Seras.

The Reds spent $450,000 to lure Romano from a Tennessee commitment as a 23rd-round pick in 2011. As he has filled out his 6-foot-4 frame, he has improved his consistency and stuff and in 2016 at Double-A Pensacola bounced back from a slow start to record strikeout (8.3) and walk (2.0) rates per nine innings that ranked among the best in the Southern League. Romano has started all but one game in his pro career, but scouts project him to the bullpen as a future lock-down closer. This despite his thick frame that suggests durability and above-average control required of starters. Romano's plus 93-98 mph fastball with boring action could top 100 out of the bullpen, and it pairs well with a plus 85-89 mph slider with late tilt. His below-average changeup is too firm and lacks deception, but scouts love Romano's competitiveness, his willingness to throw inside and his high-energy demeanor. Romano is ready to move to Triple-A Louisville as a starter, but a move to the bullpen still looms. As one scout put it, he needs to focus less on missing bats and more on breaking them with his shot-put of a sinker.

BA GRADE
50 Risk: Medium

Year	Club (League)	Class	W	L	ERA	G	GS	CG	SV	IP	H	HR	BB	SO	K/9	WHIP	AVG
2014	Dayton (MWL)	LoA	8	11	4.12	28	28	0	0	149	169	9	42	128	7.7	1.42	.288
2015	Daytona (FSL)	HiA	6	5	3.46	19	18	1	0	104	103	2	33	79	6.8	1.31	.261
	Pensacola (SL)	AA	0	4	10.96	7	7	0	0	23	35	4	12	9	3.5	2.04	.354
2016	Pensacola (SL)	AA	6	11	3.52	27	27	0	0	156	157	10	34	144	8.3	1.22	.260
Minor League Totals			32	48	4.38	121	120	1	0	616	672	36	201	501	7.3	1.42	.280

9 VLADIMIR GUTIERREZ, RHP

CLIFF WELCH

Born: Sept. 18, 1995. **B-T:** R-R. **Ht.:** 6-1. **Wt.:** 172. **Signed:** Cuba, 2016. **Signed by:** Tony Arias/Chris Buckley.

Gutierrez left the Cuban national team at the Caribbean Series in February 2015 after two effective seasons in the Cuban major league at ages 17 and 18. Poor workouts in 2015 kept him from getting the offers he expected, but he eventually signed with the Reds in August 2016 for $4.75 million after he showed an improved fastball. The Reds spent nearly $12 million on Gutierrez and Cuban shortstop Alfredo Rodriguez in 2016 as they blew past their international bonus allotment. At the time of his defection, Gutierrez possessed one of the best combinations of stuff and projection in the rapidly thinning Cuban pitching market. His fastball sat 88-93 mph in Cuba and was 92-96 in a three-inning workout for multiple teams in April 2016. His curveball, the best in Cuba before he came to the U.S., is back after what Gutierrez called an ill-conceived idea to shelve it for a slider. His high-70s curve is a power pitch with tight spin and downer action that could end up being a plus offering. He also still throws a slider as a less-effective but usable breaking ball. Though his changeup was an afterthought in Cuba, Gutierrez has developed an 83-84 mph change with deception and fade that could be average one day. The Reds previously signed athletic Cuban pitchers Aroldis Chapman and Raisel Iglesias, though Gutierrez is further from the big leagues than they were. He was a reliever in Cuba but has a ceiling of mid-rotation starter and will join high Class A Daytona in 2017.

BA GRADE
55 Risk: High

Year	Club (League)	Class	W	L	ERA	G	GS	CG	SV	IP	H	HR	BB	SO	K/9	WHIP	AVG
2014	Pinar del Rio (CNS)	CNS	3	5	2.45	25	0	0	13	51	37	2	19	49	8.6	1.09	—
2015	Did not play																
2016	Did not play																

10 TYLER STEPHENSON, C

Born: Oct. 16, 1996. **B-T:** R-R. **Ht.:** 6-4. **Wt.:** 225. **Drafted:** HS—Kennesaw, Ga., 2015 (1st round). **Signed by:** John Poloni.

The 11th overall pick in the 2015 draft, Stephenson endured an injury-marred full-season debut at low Class A Dayton in 2016. First he sustained a concussion when a ball caromed off a post during a soft-toss drill and hit him in the head. After he returned from the disabled list, he injured his wrist and missed all of June. He tried to return, but his wrist never fully healed, and he had season-ending surgery on his wrist in mid-August. When healthy, Stephenson's natural swing path takes the ball to right and right-center field, and he shows an ability to cover the plate. Scouts like his advanced approach and think he shows at least average hitting potential. Stephenson will have to work on pulling inside pitches to maximize his average power. He shows a plus

BA GRADE
55 Risk: Extreme

arm, but his receiving and blocking seemed to suffer as the accumulation of injuries and struggles at the plate wore him down. Stephenson is big for a catcher and his footwork needs work, but he has the agility to be an average defensive catcher with a strong left hand to frame pitches on the corners. He will have to work hard to maintain flexibility and remain light on his feet. The Reds will give Stephenson a mulligan and he will return to Dayton in 2017 with the hope good health will equal better results.

Year	Club (League)	Class	AVG	G	AB	R	H	2B	3B	HR	RBI	BB	SO	SB	CS	OBP	SLG
2015	Billings (PIO)	R	.268	54	194	28	52	15	0	1	16	22	42	0	2	.352	.361
2016	Reds (AZL)	R	.250	5	20	4	5	1	0	1	2	2	7	0	0	.348	.450
	Dayton (MWL)	LoA	.216	39	139	17	30	4	1	3	16	12	45	0	0	.278	.324
Minor League Totals			.246	98	353	49	87	20	1	5	34	36	94	0	2	.323	.351

11 TONY SANTILLAN, RHP

BA GRADE
55 Risk: Extreme

Born: April 15, 1997. **B-T:** R-R. **Ht.:** 6-3. **Wt.:** 240. **Drafted:** HS—Arlington, Texas, 2015 (2nd round). **Signed by:** Byron Ewing.

Santillan is the classic young power arm, more thrower than pitcher at this stage. He fires a fastball up to 100 mph as a starter, which means he doesn't often have to deal with the subtler aspects of pitching because few can square up his heat. Therefore, his effectiveness wavers from start to start. When Santillan is direct to the plate, he dominates. In a pair of late-season starts at low Class A Dayton in 2016 he struck out 10 and allowed just four baserunners. When he spins off toward first base at the end of his delivery, however, he loses the strike zone and his slider loses its depth. As a young pitcher, Santillan doesn't yet diagnose his own delivery flaws promptly and usually requires visits from the dugout. He has the raw ingredients to succeed, including two pitches that could grade as 70s on the 20-80 scouting scale. Santillan's fastball is overpowering. He sits 95-98 mph, and his 84-87 mph slider also could be a plus pitch or better because of its power and depth. He mixes in a fringy changeup that is making strides. Listed at 240 pounds, Santillan is a thick-bodied pitcher, but that masks athleticism that should help him make adjustments. He will return to Dayton in 2017, but the sky is the limit if he keeps his delivery under control.

Year	Club (League)	Class	W	L	ERA	G	GS	CG	SV	IP	H	HR	BB	SO	K/9	WHIP	AVG
2015	Reds (AZL)	R	0	2	5.03	8	7	0	0	20	15	1	11	19	8.7	1.32	.217
2016	Billings (PIO)	R	1	0	3.92	8	8	0	0	39	32	4	16	46	10.6	1.23	.221
	Dayton (MWL)	LoA	2	3	6.82	7	7	0	0	30	27	3	24	38	11.3	1.68	.245
Minor League Totals			3	5	5.16	23	22	0	0	89	74	8	51	103	10.4	1.40	.228

12 TYLER MAHLE, RHP

BA GRADE
50 Risk: High

Born: Sept. 29, 1994. **B-T:** R-R. **Ht.:** 6-4. **Wt.:** 200. **Drafted:** HS—Westminster, Calif., 2013 (7th round). **Signed by:** Mike Musuraca.

When the Reds drafted Mahle, the younger brother of Angels lefthander Greg Mahle, they bet on his projection. They hoped the athletic but skinny righthander would fill out and turn his fringe-average fastball into an above-average one while improved arm speed would also sharpen his breaking ball. That's exactly what has happened, as Mahle has developed from a starter touching 93 mph to one touching 97. He demonstrated his ability to dominate with his fastball at high Class A Daytona in 2016, when on June 13 he completed a nine-inning no-hitter. He authored the no-no while barely resorting to his near-average changeup, curveball and slider. Mahle manipulates his fastball from 88-96 mph and locates it with precision as he reads hitters' swings. On some nights his slider gives him a second above-average pitch, but most of the time he lives and dies with an above-average fastball. He works quickly and repeats his delivery. Mahle hit his first speed bump at Double-A Pensacola in 2016, and he'll return there in 2017.

Year	Club (League)	Class	W	L	ERA	G	GS	CG	SV	IP	H	HR	BB	SO	K/9	WHIP	AVG
2014	Billings (PIO)	R	5	4	3.87	15	15	2	0	77	80	5	15	71	8.3	1.24	.263
2015	Dayton (MWL)	LoA	13	8	2.43	27	26	0	0	152	145	7	25	135	8.0	1.12	.252
2016	Daytona (FSL)	HiA	8	3	2.50	13	13	1	0	79	58	6	17	76	8.6	0.95	.206
	Pensacola (SL)	AA	6	3	4.92	14	14	0	0	71	78	12	20	65	8.2	1.37	.281
Minor League Totals			33	21	3.13	81	72	3	0	414	393	30	85	377	8.2	1.16	.250

13 JIMMY HERGET, RHP

BA GRADE
50 Risk: High

Born: Sept. 9, 1993. **B-T:** R-R. **Ht.:** 6-3. **Wt.:** 170. **Drafted:** South Florida, 2015 (6th round). **Signed by:** Greg Zunino.

Herget worked as a starter at South Florida but blossomed with a move to the bullpen as a pro. He spent all of 2016 at high Class A Daytona, but many of the scouts and managers who saw him in the Florida State League believe he could jump to the big leagues quickly. Herget's average stuff as a starter turned into plus stuff in shorter outings, but it's his rare combination of funkiness and above-average command that baffles hitters. He fires above-average 94-96 mph fastballs with armside run and occasional sink from a high three-quarters delivery, but every now and then he drops down to sidearm to run a 92-94 mph fastball in on a hitter from a release point he doesn't expect. Herget also quick-pitches at times and does whatever he needs to do to make the hitter uncomfortable. He will back-foot his plus slider with solid late tilt against lefthanded batters or even more effectively use it to get righthanders to roll over in pitcher's counts. Herget is a future setup man who could leap from Double-A Pensacola to Cincinnati by the end of 2017.

Year	Club (League)	Class	W	L	ERA	G	GS	CG	SV	IP	H	HR	BB	SO	K/9	WHIP	AVG
2015	Billings (PIO)	R	3	0	3.20	24	0	0	15	25	16	1	11	26	9.2	1.07	.188
2016	Daytona (FSL)	HiA	4	4	1.78	50	0	0	24	61	47	3	22	83	12.3	1.14	.208
Minor League Totals			7	4	2.20	74	0	0	39	86	63	4	33	109	11.4	1.12	.203

14 CHRIS OKEY, C

BA GRADE
50 Risk: High

Born: Dec. 29. 1994. **B-T:** R-R. **Ht.:** 5-11. **Wt.:** 195. **Drafted:** Clemson, 2016 (2nd round). **Signed by:** Perry Smith.

One of the top players in the 2013 high school class to make it to college, Okey was Clemson's everyday catcher for three years. He caught every game during his sophomore and junior seasons and signed with the Reds for $2 million as a 2016 second-round pick. After carrying such a heavy workload in college, Okey looked worn out by the end of his pro debut at low Class A Dayton. He hit six home runs and slugged .556 in July, but went homerless the rest of the season. When fresh, Okey hit .339/.465/.611 as a Clemson junior. He has average power potential and a fringe-average hit tool, though he needs to work on making more contact. He is an average runner who moves well despite bulking up the past three years. Okey's average arm would play better if he cleans up his balance and consistency of his throwing mechanics. He will box the ball when framing pitches every now and then, but he blocks balls in the dirt well. The Reds were enamored of Okey's leadership skills and his athleticism when scouting him in his amateur days, dating back to high school. He is ready to join what should be a loaded high Class A Daytona club in 2017.

Year	Club (League)	Class	AVG	G	AB	R	H	2B	3B	HR	RBI	BB	SO	SB	CS	OBP	SLG
2016	Billings (PIO)	R	.162	9	37	5	6	1	0	0	1	1	8	0	0	.179	.189
	Dayton (MWL)	LoA	.243	42	148	21	36	8	1	6	21	14	49	5	0	.323	.432
Minor League Totals			.227	51	185	26	42	9	1	6	22	15	57	5	0	.296	.384

15 T.J. FRIEDL, OF

BA GRADE
50 Risk: High

Born: Aug. 14, 1995. **B-T:** L-L. **Ht.:** 5-10. **Wt.:** 170. **Signed:** Nevada, 2016 (NDFA). **Signed by:** Rich Bordi/Sam Grossman.

Very few amateur players truly slip through the cracks today, but Friedl did in 2016. Multiple area scouts didn't realize Friedl, a redshirt sophomore at Nevada, was even eligible to be drafted. Those scouts who did didn't dig too deeply even after he hit .401. (He also ranked among Baseball America's top draft-eligible prospects from the state of Nevada.) After Friedl starred with USA Baseball's Collegiate National Team in 2016, everyone took a second look, and a bidding war ensued among teams that had money left in their draft bonus pools. The Reds won the bidding and signed Freidl for $735,000, the highest bonus ever for a non-drafted free agent. He is an above-average center fielder with 70 speed on the 20-80 scouting scale. Ideally, he becomes a top-of-the-order hitter thanks to his plus hitting ability, albeit with below-average power. Friedl's speed plays well on the bases but he has work to do to learn how to bunt for hits. He probably will begin 2017 at high Class A Daytona and has a floor as a fourth outfielder but at least a chance to be a regular center fielder.

Year	Club (League)	Class	AVG	G	AB	R	H	2B	3B	HR	RBI	BB	SO	SB	CS	OBP	SLG
2016	Billings (PIO)	R	.347	29	121	24	42	11	2	3	17	13	25	7	2	.423	.545
Minor League Totals			.347	29	121	24	42	11	2	3	17	13	25	7	2	.423	.545

16 SHED LONG, 2B

BA GRADE
50 Risk: High

Born: Aug. 22, 1995. **B-T:** L-R. **Ht.:** 5-8. **Wt.:** 180. **Drafted:** HS—Jacksonville, Ala., 2013 (12th round). **Signed by:** Ben Jones.

The Reds drafted Long as a high school catcher in 2013, which makes sense considering his thick, short frame and above-average arm strength. He dropped catching after two years in Rookie ball, however, and moved to second base in 2015. Long has enough range and knocks the ball down well enough to be a fringy defender at the keystone with a slow first step and a bat-first profile. Though he's 5-foot-8, Long takes powerful lefthanded swings and offers yet another reminder that being short isn't an issue for a hitter as long as he has pop in his bat. He has plenty of power for the middle infield and shows average power with a bat path that gives him good extension and carry. He gets into good hitter's counts thanks to a discerning eye. Long hit 15 home runs between two Class A levels in 2016 to rank third most in the organization, and despite average speed he knows how to swipe a base as well. He heads back to high Class A Daytona in 2017 but should reach Double-A soon.

Year	Club (League)	Class	AVG	G	AB	R	H	2B	3B	HR	RBI	BB	SO	SB	CS	OBP	SLG
2014	Billings (PIO)	R	.172	29	87	6	15	3	0	0	6	5	18	2	1	.217	.207
2015	Dayton (MWL)	LoA	.283	42	152	22	43	7	2	6	16	18	31	2	3	.363	.474
2016	Dayton (MWL)	LoA	.281	94	335	47	94	24	1	11	45	44	85	16	3	.371	.457
	Daytona (FSL)	HiA	.322	38	143	22	46	6	4	4	30	10	35	5	1	.371	.503
Minor League Totals			.274	227	795	106	218	42	7	22	105	85	186	26	9	.350	.428

17 NICK TRAVIESO, RHP

BA GRADE
40 Risk: Low

Born: Jan. 31, 1994. **B-T:** R-R. **Ht.:** 6-2. **Wt.:** 215. **Drafted:** HS—Southwest Ranches, 2012 (1st round). **Signed by:** Tony Arias/Miguel Machado.

Signed for a below-slot $2 million as the 14th overall pick in 2012, Travieso has proven to be durable in his pro career. He broke his wrist when hit by a comebacker in 2015 and missed some starts, but he has avoided any significant arm or elbow injuries. However, Travieso has not blossomed into the front-line starter the Reds envisioned. His fastball that touched 97 mph in high school generally sits 91-93 as a pro and his fringe-average slider lacks the bite or depth of an elite pitch. His slider has a chance to become average, while his changeup is below-average. On the plus side, he throws his fastball with good armside run and pitches inside. He also knows how to pitch down in the zone with sink, but he lacks a putaway pitch, which forced him to nibble more than he would liked at Double-A Pensacola in 2016. He showed well below-average control because he refuses to give in to opposing batters, but he must find a way to make hitters uncomfortable if he's going to be more than a No. 5 starter or middle reliever.

Year	Club (League)	Class	W	L	ERA	G	GS	CG	SV	IP	H	HR	BB	SO	K/9	WHIP	AVG
2014	Dayton (MWL)	LoA	14	5	3.03	26	26	1	0	143	123	10	44	114	7.2	1.17	.229
2015	Daytona (FSL)	HiA	6	6	2.70	19	19	0	0	93	82	4	30	76	7.3	1.20	.231
2016	Pensacola (SL)	AA	5	7	3.84	23	23	0	0	117	109	11	53	91	7.0	1.38	.248
Minor League Totals			32	24	3.53	93	93	1	0	456	417	35	159	356	7.0	1.26	.241

18 PHILLIP ERVIN, OF

BA GRADE
45 Risk: Medium

Born: July 15, 1992. **B-T:** R-R. **Ht.:** 5-10. **Wt.:** 207. **Drafted:** Samford, 2013 (1st round). **Signed by:** Ben Jones.

Ervin has moved slowly for a first-round college position player, spending effectively one year at each Class A level and one year at Double-A Pensacola in 2016. Pitchers in the Southern League quickly learned not to challenge him on the inner half of the plate, especially with a fastball. Ervin has the bat speed and strength to make pitchers pay. Opponents also learned, however, that as long as they stayed outside, nibbling at the outer edge of the plate, Ervin could be neutralized. If he can learn to hit the ball to right field every now and then, his natural hand-eye coordination and average power give him a chance to be a solid performer with power. But four seasons into his pro career, Ervin hasn't learned that lesson. His below-average offensive track record—he hit .239 in 2016—stands in the way of an everyday job, especially because he's a fringe-average defender in center field to go with above-average defense in the corners. He fits best in left field because of his fringy arm. Ervin is an average runner out of the box because his pull-heavy swing costs him time, but he turns in better times on the bases. He led the Reds organization with 36 stolen bases and could be on track to be an extra outfielder in the majors.

Year	Club (League)	Class	AVG	G	AB	R	H	2B	3B	HR	RBI	BB	SO	SB	CS	OBP	SLG
2014	Dayton (MWL)	LoA	.237	132	498	68	118	34	7	7	68	46	110	30	5	.305	.376
2015	Daytona (FSL)	HiA	.242	109	405	68	98	18	0	12	63	53	83	30	7	.338	.375
	Pensacola (SL)	AA	.235	17	51	7	12	3	0	2	8	13	15	4	3	.409	.412
2016	Pensacola (SL)	AA	.239	123	419	71	100	22	3	13	45	65	88	36	10	.362	.399
Minor League Totals			.249	427	1545	248	385	88	11	43	219	202	330	114	26	.347	.404

19 KEURY MELLA, RHP

BA GRADE
50 Risk: High

Born: Aug. 2, 1993. **B-T:** R-R. **Ht.:** 6-2. **Wt.:** 200. **Signed:** Dominican Republic, 2011. **Signed by:** Pablo Peguero (Giants).

After an effective season at high Class A San Jose in 2015 that included a midseason trade by the Giants to the Reds in the Mike Leake deal, Mella repeated the high Class A level at Daytona in 2016. He worked on getting more on-line to the plate, which traded some of the deception he got from his crossfire delivery

 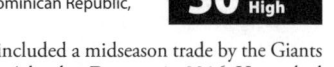

for improved command and control. Mella's numbers seemed to back up in 2016, but scouts still see a future power reliever rather than the starter he is now. Mella's delivery has effort and is difficult to repeat. He gathers over the rubber in a deep coil, then throws into a stiff front side as his arm catches up to his lower half. As a reliever, his above-average 92-95 mph fastball should play up, and his above-average breaking ball also will improve. He won't need his fringy changeup in that role. Mella finished the 2016 season with an effective outing at Triple-A Louisville and could be in the mix for big league innings in 2017.

Year	Club (League)	Class	W	L	ERA	G	GS	CG	SV	IP	H	HR	BB	SO	K/9	WHIP	AVG
2014	Augusta (SAL)	LoA	3	3	3.93	12	12	1	0	66	69	1	13	63	8.5	1.24	.265
	Salem-Keizer (NWL)	SS	1	1	1.83	6	6	0	0	20	16	0	6	20	9.2	1.12	.222
2015	San Jose (CAL)	HiA	5	3	3.31	16	16	0	0	82	66	5	26	83	9.1	1.13	.216
	Daytona (FSL)	HiA	3	1	2.95	4	4	0	0	21	11	2	15	23	9.7	1.22	.151
2016	Daytona (FSL)	HiA	8	9	3.90	25	24	0	0	132	150	7	56	95	6.5	1.56	.290
	Louisville (IL)	AAA	1	0	1.29	1	1	0	0	7	3	1	1	6	7.7	0.57	.130
Minor League Totals			27	22	3.24	88	86	1	0	433	408	19	156	406	8.4	1.30	.248

20 BARRETT ASTIN, RHP

Born: Oct. 22, 1991. **B-T:** R-R. **Ht.:** 6-1. **Wt.:** 200. **Drafted:** Arkansas, 2013 (3rd round). **Signed by:** Tim Collinsworth (Brewers).

BA GRADE
45 Risk: Medium

Astin was a dominating closer for Arkansas' College World Series team as a sophomore in 2012. He moved to the rotation for the Razorbacks in 2013 and spent much of the next three seasons trying ineffectively to start as a pro. After acquiring him in the 2014 trade that sent Jonathan Broxton to the Brewers, the Reds moved him back to the bullpen in 2016 and saw him comfortably slip back into the fireman role he was born to play. Astin's fastball-slider combo plays better out of the pen, and his heavy sinker down in the zone makes him a candidate for a manager looking for a ground ball. In a good outing by Astin, his catcher is going to get dirty because the 6-foot-1 righthander lives at the bottom of the strike zone—and below. His 92-96 mph sinker is extremely hard for righthanded battters to lift, and his hard 88-90 mph cutter-slider has just enough of a wrinkle to get weak contact as well. Added to the 40-man roster after the 2016 season, Astin is a viable bullpen option in 2017.

Year	Club (League)	Class	W	L	ERA	G	GS	CG	SV	IP	H	HR	BB	SO	K/9	WHIP	AVG
2014	Wisconsin (MWL)	LoA	8	7	4.96	27	18	0	4	122	132	12	36	81	6.0	1.38	.277
2015	Daytona (FSL)	HiA	4	3	2.29	16	11	1	0	75	62	0	18	61	7.4	1.07	.222
	Pensacola (SL)	AA	4	6	5.63	14	14	0	0	77	85	9	39	61	7.2	1.62	.290
2016	Pensacola (SL)	AA	9	3	2.26	37	11	0	0	103	74	8	25	96	8.4	0.96	.201
Minor League Totals			26	20	3.87	106	62	1	4	414	394	35	129	330	7.2	1.26	.251

21 ARIEL HERNANDEZ, RHP

Born: July 21, 1994. **B-T:** R-R. **Ht.:** 6-3. **Wt.:** 180. **Signed:** Dominican Republic, 2008. **Signed by:** Felix Peguero (Giants).

BA GRADE
50 Risk: Extreme

Before he ever reached full-season ball, Hernandez had already been released by the Giants, spent time in the independent Frontier League—where he made two appearances in 2015—and resurrected his career with the Diamondbacks. The Reds made him the first pick in the minor league Rule 5 draft in 2015, and a year later the Reds added him to the 40-man roster. Hernandez's well below-average control still gives him issues, but he has one of the best pitch combos in the minors. After working with then-Frontier Greys pitching coach Billy Bryk Jr., Hernandez tweaked his delivery to better transfer his weight. He now pitches with a pair of 70 pitches on the 20-80 scouting scale out of the bullpen, and with better command both could be 80s. His fastball sits 95-97 mph and will touch 100 on some nights, but his power curve is a better pitch. It's a high-spin, hard downer breaking pitch with exceptional velocity at 85-89 mph. Batters hit just .136 against Hernandez at two Class A stops in 2016, when he allowed just four extra-base hits. He will have to keep improving his control, but if he does, he could be a dominating reliever.

Year	Club (League)	Class	W	L	ERA	G	GS	CG	SV	IP	H	HR	BB	SO	K/9	WHIP	AVG
2014	Did not play—Injured																
2015	Frontier (FRN)	IND	0	0	0.00	2	0	0	0	2	0	0	2	5	22.5	1.00	--
	Hillsboro (NWL)	SS	1	1	6.04	22	0	0	2	22	18	1	21	32	12.9	1.75	.212
2016	Dayton (MWL)	LoA	2	1	2.59	18	0	0	2	31	11	0	20	40	11.5	0.99	.107
	Daytona (FSL)	HiA	3	1	1.76	25	0	0	3	31	18	1	19	34	10.0	1.21	.164
Minor League Totals			14	4	3.87	125	15	0	9	205	130	6	150	227	10.0	1.37	.179

22 ALFREDO RODRIGUEZ, SS

BA GRADE
50 Risk: Extreme

Born: June 17, 1994. **B-R:** R-R. **Ht.:** 6-0. **Wt.:** 190. **Signed:** Cuban, 2016. **Signed by:** Tony Arias/Chris Buckley.

In his only full season in the Cuban major league, Rodriguez was voted the top defender at shortstop and the Serie Nacional rookie of the year. The Reds were linked to him almost from the moment he was eligible to sign, but they convinced him to wait to sign for $7 million after the July 2 signing period began in 2016 so they could land him and Cuban righthander Vladimir Gutierrez, whom they signed for $4.75 million. Had the Reds signed Rodriguez as part of the 2015 class, then they would have been ineligible to sign anyone for more than $300,000 in 2016. No one doubts Rodriguez's glove. He immediately becomes the system's best defensive shortstop with outstanding hands, range and feel for the position. He uses his plus arm to make plays deep in the hole, then uses his exceptional hands to barehand balls coming across in front of the second base bag. Rodriguez also is a plus runner, but at the plate he showed no power and no plate discipline in Cuba. The Reds see a line-drive swing with gap power, but scouts from other teams see a Rey Ordonez-style, bottom-of-the-order hitter with bottom-of-the-scale power. Rodriguez showed rust and had to melt away 20 pounds he had gained during his layoff, but he got back on track at instructional league. He will head to high Class A Daytona in 2017.

Year	Club (League)	Class	AVG	G	AB	R	H	2B	3B	HR	RBI	BB	SO	SB	CS	OBP	SLG
2016	Reds (DSL)	R	.234	22	77	12	18	5	0	0	8	9	16	9	0	.333	.299
Minor League Totals			.234	22	77	12	18	5	0	0	8	9	16	9	0	.333	.299

23 MICHAEL BELTRE, OF

BA GRADE
50 Risk: Extreme

Born: July 3, 1995. **B-T:** B-R. **Ht.:** 6-3. **Wt.:** 180. **Signed:** Dominican Republic, 2013. **Signed by:** Richard Jimenez.

Beltre is a late-blooming but very intriguing switch-hitting outfielder who blossomed in part because he avoided the leg injuries that had slowed his development. He isn't as tooled-up as Rookie-level Billings teammate Jose Siri, but he has superior plate discipline that allows him to get better pitches to hit. Beltre is a plus runner who explodes out of the lefthanded batter's box, making any chopper a potential infield hit. He has some strength in his swing that gives him potentially average power. Both of Beltre's swings work best when he focuses on driving the ball to center field, something he did a better job of executing in 2016. Defensively, his arm plays a tick below-average because of a long arm action, but he has the arm strength to eventually become at least average. His speed plays in center field, where his routes and reads are raw. Beltre will attempt to handle a jump to low Class A Dayton in 2017.

Year	Club (League)	Class	AVG	G	AB	R	H	2B	3B	HR	RBI	BB	SO	SB	CS	OBP	SLG
2014	Rojos (DSL)	R	.278	49	162	25	45	7	1	1	9	26	44	12	4	.401	.352
2015	Reds (AZL)	R	.220	28	82	6	18	3	0	1	7	5	27	5	1	.273	.293
2016	Reds (AZL)	R	.292	29	106	23	31	4	6	0	10	11	25	9	0	.380	.443
	Billings (PIO)	R	.309	22	81	14	25	9	0	3	13	15	13	4	1	.423	.531
Minor League Totals			.264	172	557	99	147	28	10	5	50	72	155	36	8	.369	.377

24 RYAN HENDRIX, RHP

BA GRADE
45 Risk: High

Born: Dec. 16, 1994. **B-T:** R-R. **Ht.:** 6-3. **Wt.:** 185. **Drafted:** Texas A&M, 2016 (5th round). **Signed by:** Byron Ewing.

If the 2016 draft had been held at the end of the 2015 summer season, Hendrix would have been a likely second-round pick. He dominated with USA Baseball's Collegiate National Team as its closer and was coming off a sophomore season at Texas A&M where he impressed both as a starter and reliever. But as Hendrix's velocity spiked in his junior year, his control disappeared. He lost his closer job and fell to the Reds in the fifth round. He signed for $410,000. Hendrix can touch 101 mph when needed, and he'll pitch at 96-99 with his four-seamer and supplement it with a 92-95 mph two-seamer. He throws a fringy changeup against lefthanders to keep them honest. But Hendrix's control and the development of his curveball will determine his future success. When he lands his power curve, it's a double-plus pitch with excellent spin. Not only has it become harder to control as he has gained arm speed, it becomes loopier when he dials back to locate it. Given his stuff, Hendrix won't need more than below-average control to succeed as a big league reliever. High Class A Daytona is his probable next step.

Year	Club (League)	Class	W	L	ERA	G	GS	CG	SV	IP	H	HR	BB	SO	K/9	WHIP	AVG
2016	Billings (PIO)	R	0	0	5.19	6	0	0	0	9	11	0	5	5	5.2	1.85	.333
	Dayton (MWL)	LoA	3	1	3.04	15	0	0	0	27	21	0	8	31	10.5	1.09	.212
Minor League Totals			3	1	3.57	21	0	0	0	35	32	0	13	36	9.2	1.27	.242

25 TANNER RAINEY, RHP

BA GRADE 45 Risk: High

Born: Dec. 25, 1992. **B-T:** R-R. **Ht.:** 6-2. **Wt.:** 235. **Drafted:** West Alabama, 2015 (2nd round supplemental). **Signed by:** Ben Jones.

Most pitchers selected with high draft picks begin their pro career in the rotation, whether or not they project to be relievers. This gives them more innings and thus more opportunities to develop their control and secondary offerings. That plan didn't work with Rainey, a 2015 pick from West Alabama. When he started, he was largely a disaster. He mixed three pitches while commanding them well enough to get through five innings. Every now and then it worked, but typically he surrendered too many walks and wild pitches. A late-season move to the bullpen put Rainey back into his natural habitat by allowing him to just rear back and throw. His 95-97 mph fastball became livelier, and he put his ineffective changeup in his back pocket to focus on his slider. His potentially above-average slider got better as well. Rainey didn't allow a run in his final seven appearances out of the pen at low Class A Dayton in 2016, and his arm strength makes him a potentially valuable bullpen option.

Year	Club (League)	Class	W	L	ERA	G	GS	CG	SV	IP	H	HR	BB	SO	K/9	WHIP	AVG
2015	Billings (PIO)	R	2	2	4.27	15	15	0	0	59	58	2	28	57	8.7	1.46	.258
2016	Dayton (MWL)	LoA	5	10	5.57	29	20	0	1	103	109	9	66	113	9.8	1.69	.273
Minor League Totals			7	12	5.10	44	35	0	1	162	167	11	94	170	9.4	1.61	.268

26 IAN KAHALOA, RHP

BA GRADE 45 Risk: High

Born: Oct. 3, 1997. **B-T:** R-R. **Ht.:** 6-1. **Wt.:** 185. **Drafted:** HS—Ewa Beach, Hawaii, 2015 (3rd round). **Signed by:** Rex de la Nuez.

Because he was drafted as a 17-year-old in 2015, Kahaloa was one of the younger players in the Rookie-level Pioneer League in 2016. For example, Kahaloa is less than a month older than Reds 2016 supplemental first-round pick Taylor Trammell. Kahaloa showed impressive feel and command in 2016. He generally worked in the bottom of the strike zone with average stuff that plays up because he hides the ball in his delivery. His fastball will touch 94 mph but generally sits 91-92. His curveball will flash average, and he has good feel for spin for his age. His changeup has improved, but it's still below-average because he needs better location, conviction and deception. Kahaloa's ability to locate his fastball keeps him ahead of hitters, and because he touched 96 mph regularly in high school he may be able to tap into more velocity. Even with his current stuff, Kahaloa could be a back-end starter.

Year	Club (League)	Class	W	L	ERA	G	GS	CG	SV	IP	H	HR	BB	SO	K/9	WHIP	AVG
2015	Reds (AZL)	R	0	0	2.25	8	6	0	0	24	16	1	6	31	11.6	0.92	.184
2016	Reds (AZL)	R	1	0	0.00	2	1	0	0	8	2	0	1	10	11.3	0.38	.077
	Billings (PIO)	R	2	2	2.82	10	10	0	0	45	38	4	13	42	8.5	1.14	.221
Minor League Totals			3	2	2.35	20	17	0	0	77	56	5	20	83	9.7	0.99	.196

27 ZACK WEISS, RHP

BA GRADE 45 Risk: High

Born: June 16, 1992. **B-T:** R-R. **Ht.:** 6-3. **Wt.:** 210. **Drafted:** UCLA, 2013 (6th round). **Signed by:** Rex de la Nuez.

If Weiss had been healthy in 2016 he would have pitched in the big league bullpen, and he could have provided a boost to a porous unit. Instead he never threw an official pitch in 2016, even though his elbow injury never required surgery. Every time Weiss tried to come back, his elbow wasn't ready. He spent the winter after the 2016 season in his normal training program and expects to be ready for spring training. The Reds gambled and left Weiss unprotected in the Rule 5 draft, but because of his health he was not selected. When healthy, he throws three above-average offerings—a 92-95 mph fastball he locates and a slider and curveball that both flash plus. He also has a below-average changeup and solid-average control. That four-pitch mix could work as a starter, but Weiss could excel in the bullpen. After a long layoff, he appears headed for Triple-A Louisville in 2017 to tune up.

Year	Club (League)	Class	W	L	ERA	G	GS	CG	SV	IP	H	HR	BB	SO	K/9	WHIP	AVG
2014	Dayton (MWL)	LoA	2	4	2.42	34	0	0	3	63	50	4	21	80	11.4	1.12	.217
2015	Daytona (FSL)	HiA	0	0	0.00	9	0	0	5	12	2	0	1	22	17.0	0.26	.056
	Pensacola (SL)	AA	1	3	2.42	45	0	0	25	52	40	5	14	68	11.8	1.04	.214
2016	Did not play—Injured																
Minor League Totals			5	11	2.54	100	5	0	33	156	123	16	41	190	11.0	1.05	.216

28 BLAKE TRAHAN, SS

BA GRADE

40 Risk: Medium

Born: Sept. 5, 1993. **B-T:** R-R. **Ht.:** 5-9. **Wt.:** 180. **Drafted:** Louisiana-Lafayette, 2015 (3rd round). **Signed by:** Ben Jones.

In a system filled with a variety of potential second basemen and third basemen, Trahan stands out because of his defensive ability at shortstop. He probably won't play shortstop every day at the big league level, but his average defense there pairs well with his above-average arm. Trahan projects as an above-average glove at second base with good hands and reliable actions, but his versatility makes him a viable utility infield candidate. His above-average speed makes him an option in center field as he works to increase his versatility. At the plate, Trahan has a tendency to try to do too much. He focuses on making contact, driving the ball in the gaps, using the whole field and taking advantage of his speed. But at times his pre-swing load gets big and his swing gets too lengthy for a player with well below-average power. Trahan is a good bunter, which helps him maximize his average hit tool. He will join a crowded infield at Double-A Pensacola in 2017.

Year	Club (League)	Class	AVG	G	AB	R	H	2B	3B	HR	RBI	BB	SO	SB	CS	OBP	SLG
2015	Billings (PIO)	R	.312	47	186	32	58	8	3	1	15	25	19	10	3	.400	.403
	Daytona (FSL)	HiA	.114	11	35	1	4	0	0	0	0	0	5	0	0	.139	.114
2016	Daytona (FSL)	HiA	.263	131	521	90	137	21	9	4	47	49	73	25	8	.325	.361
Minor League Totals			.268	189	742	123	199	29	12	5	62	74	97	35	11	.337	.360

29 ISMAEL GUILLON, LHP

BA GRADE

45 Risk: High

Born: Feb. 13, 1992. **B-T:** L-L. **Ht.:** 6-1. **Wt.:** 222. **Signed:** Venezuela, 2008. **Signed by:** Tony Arias.

Guillon's career with the Reds stretches so far back that when he joined the organization, Edwin Encarnacion was the Cincinnati third baseman. Since then Guillon has missed a season because of Tommy John surgery and another season with a torn lat. But he bounced back in 2016 to show big league-caliber stuff again. Guillon's above-average 92-93 mph fastball will touch 95, but he uses it primarily to set up a plus changeup that earns some plus-plus grades. His control is well below-average, but even that is an improvement on seasons past. He sharpened his curveball to the point where it's a useable below-average pitch. Guillon has yet to reach Double-A and he will be 25 in 2017, so he needs to speed up his development. As a lefty with a plus fastball, a plus changeup and one of the best pickoff moves in the minors, Guillon still has a chance to be a useful reliever.

Year	Club (League)	Class	W	L	ERA	G	GS	CG	SV	IP	H	HR	BB	SO	K/9	WHIP	AVG
2014	Dayton (MWL)	LoA	4	1	3.17	13	12	0	0	65	41	3	27	69	9.5	1.04	.186
	Bakersfield (CAL)	HiA	1	6	6.79	12	11	0	0	58	68	13	28	45	6.9	1.65	.291
2015	Did not play—Injured																
2016	Daytona (FSL)	HiA	7	2	2.41	32	13	0	0	93	50	10	39	116	11.2	0.95	.162
Minor League Totals			31	27	4.10	126	101	0	0	534	432	55	289	588	9.9	1.35	.224

30 NICK HANSON, RHP

BA GRADE

50 Risk: Extreme

Born: June 10, 1998. **B-T:** R-R. **Ht.:** 6-6. **Wt.:** 205. **Drafted:** HS—Savage, Minn., 2016 (5th round). **Signed by:** Andy Stack.

Hanson's future outlook will not come into view for several years because he is a cold-weather high school arm. He appeared destined for Kentucky until his velocity spiked as a senior and the Reds signed the 2016 fifth-rounder for $925,000. With Hanson's massive 6-foot-6 frame and velocity jump, he could develop a fastball that sits in the mid-90s. At this point, though, he struggles to keep his mechanics in sync. Hanson is understandably raw with a loose arm, but he's prone to overthrowing, spiking his curveball in front of the plate or sailing his fastball high out of the zone. His 91-95 mph fastball is excellent and his curveball will show flashes of being an above-average pitch. He has a lot of work to do on developing a changeup. The Reds will take it slow with Hanson, who heads to Rookie-level Billings in 2017.

Year	Club (League)	Class	W	L	ERA	G	GS	CG	SV	IP	H	HR	BB	SO	K/9	WHIP	AVG
2016	Reds (AZL)	R	0	2	9.18	8	8	0	0	17	25	1	15	15	8.1	2.40	.352
Minor League Totals			0	2	9.18	8	8	0	0	17	25	1	15	15	8.1	2.40	.352

Cleveland Indians

BY TEDDY CAHILL

After the Cleveland Cavaliers snapped the city's 52-year championship drought in June with an NBA title, the Indians nearly replicated their neighbor's jubilation. But they came up just short against the Cubs in the World Series, unable to close out a three games to one lead.

The Indians won 94 games in the regular season and captured their first division title since 2007. They kept rolling in the playoffs, overcoming injuries to Carlos Carrasco and Danny Salazar to win their first pennant since 1997. Their World Series appearance ended just as that one 19 years ago did, with a loss in Game 7.

While the Indians' season again ended in dejection, they showed they have found a winning formula, winning 94 regular season games and an American League pennant with their young core deftly managed by the braintrust of team president Chris Antonetti, general manager Mike Chernoff and manager Terry Francona.

Corey Kluber again led the staff, going 18-9, 3.14 and shouldering a hefty burden in the postseason when other key starters went down with injury. Francisco Lindor built on a strong rookie debut and excelled in his first full major league season, earning an appearance in the All-Star Game and hitting .301/.358/.435 to go with his elite defense.

The farm system produced again, as Jose Ramirez and Roberto Perez were pressed into everyday action due to injuries, and Tyler Naquin and Mike Clevinger, both top 10 prospects entering the season, graduated to Cleveland. Naquin, the 15th overall pick in the 2012 draft, became the team's regular center fielder and hit .296/.372/.514 with 14 home runs.

The Indians also showed a willingness to go for it at the trade deadline. To acquire Andrew Miller, who became their biggest weapon out of the bullpen in the playoffs, they dealt outfielder Clint Frazier, their best prospect, and three pitching prospects to the Yankees. On the same day, they nearly dealt four more prospects, headlined by Francisco Mejia, to the Brewers for Jonathan Lucroy, only to see him exercise his no-trade clause.

After years of being on the other side of those kinds of trades, the Indians were ready to capitalize on their window for contention. That window should remain open, as Cleveland can bring its team back almost intact next year. The Indians will have just three free agents, and much of the core will be under control for several years, either through arbitration or long-term contracts. Their

Tyler Naquin became the Indians' regular center fielder as a rookie in 2016

DAVID SEELIG

TOP PROSPECTS OF THE DECADE

Year	Player, Pos.	2016 Org
2007	Adam Miller, rhp	Did not play
2008	Adam Miller, rhp	Did not play
2009	Carlos Santana, c	Indians
2010	Carlos Santana, c	Indians
2011	Lonnie Chisenhall, 3b	Indians
2012	Francisco Lindor, ss	Indians
2013	Francisco Lindor, ss	Indians
2014	Francisco Lindor, ss	Indians
2015	Francisco Lindor, ss	Indians
2016	Bradley Zimmer, of	Indians

oldest pitcher is Josh Tomlin, who turned 32 during the World Series. The lineup is slightly older but is anchored by Lindor, who will play next season as a 23-year-old.

The farm system also remains strong, even after July's trades. Mejia is their top prospect after nearly getting sent to Milwaukee. Bradley Zimmer, who topped the list a year ago, advanced to Triple-A Columbus and is in line to make his major league debut in 2017. Bobby Bradley was MVP of the Carolina League, Triston McKenzie stood out in his first full professional season, and Brady Aiken made his professional debut.

With a stout farm system backing the strong core in the major leagues, the Indians are well positioned for the future to break what is now the sport's longest championship drought.

ORGANIZATION OVERVIEW

President: Chris Antonetti. **GM:** Mike Chernoff. **Farm Director:** Carter Hawkins. **Scouting Director:** Brad Grant.

Class	Team	League	W	L	PCT	Finish	Manager
Majors	Cleveland Indians	American	94	67	.584	2nd (15)	Terry Francona
Triple-A	Columbus Clippers	International	82	62	.569	3rd (14)	Chris Tremie
Double-A	Akron RubberDucks	Eastern	77	64	.546	3rd (12)	Dave Wallace
High Class A	Lynchburg Hillcats	Carolina	84	56	.600	2nd (8)	Mark Budzinski
Low Class A	Lake County Captains	Midwest	72	68	.514	7th (16)	Tony Mansolino
Short season	Mahoning Valley Scrappers	New York-Penn	37	38	.493	9th (14)	Edwin Rodriguez
Rookie	AZL Indians	Arizona	31	25	.554	t-4th (14)	Anthony Medrano
Overall 2016 Minor League Record			383	313	.550	4th (30)	

THIS YEAR'S TOP 30

No.	Player, Pos.	Grade/Risk
1.	Francisco Mejia, c	60/High
2.	Bradley Zimmer, of	60/High
3.	Triston McKenzie, rhp	60/High
4.	Brady Aiken, lhp	60/Extreme
5.	Bobby Bradley, 1b	55/High
6.	Yu-Cheng Chang, ss	50/High
7.	Will Benson, of	55/Extreme
8.	Nolan Jones, 3b	55/Extreme
9.	Erik Gonzalez, ss/2b	45/Medium
10.	Greg Allen, of	50/High
11.	Yandy Diaz, 3b/of	45/Medium
12.	Logan Ice, c	50/High
13.	Mark Mathias, 2b/3b	50/High
14.	Juan Hillman, lhp	50/High
15.	Willi Castro, ss	50/High
16.	Adam Plutko, rhp	45/Medium
17.	Tim Cooney, lhp	50/High
18.	Tyler Krieger, rhp	50/High
19.	Shawn Morimando, lhp	45/Medium
20.	Aaron Civale, rhp	45/High
21.	Shane Bieber, rhp	45/High
22.	Ryan Merritt, lhp	40/Medium
23.	Julian Merryweather, rhp	45/High
24.	Hoby Milner, lhp	40/Medium
25.	Nellie Rodriguez, 1b	45/High
26.	Rob Kaminsky, lhp	45/High
27.	Oscar Gonzalez, of	50/Extreme
28.	Micah Miniard, rhp	50/Extreme
29.	Jose Fermin, ss	50/Extreme
30.	Marcos Gonzalez, ss	50/Extreme

LAST YEAR'S TOP 30

No.	Player, Pos.	Status
1.	Bradley Zimmer, of	No. 2
2.	Clint Frazier, of	(Yankees)
3.	Brady Aiken, lhp	No. 4
4.	Justus Sheffield, lhp	(Yankees)
5.	Bobby Bradley, 1b	No. 5
6.	Tyler Naquin, of	Majors
7.	Mike Clevinger, rhp	Majors
8.	Triston McKenzie, rhp	No. 3
9.	Rob Kaminsky, lhp	No. 26
10.	Francisco Mejia, c	No. 1
11.	Juan Hillman, lhp	No. 14
12.	Erik Gonzalez, ss	No. 9
13.	Mark Mathias, 2b	No. 13
14.	Adam Putko, rhp	No. 16
15.	Yandy Diaz, 3b	No. 11
16.	Yu-Cheng Chang, ss	No. 6
17.	Shawn Morimando, lhp	No. 19
18.	Nellie Rodriguez, 1b	No. 25
19.	Mike Papi, of	Dropped out
20.	Tyler Krieger, ss	No. 18
21.	Shawn Armstrong, rhp	Dropped out
22.	Ryan Merritt, lhp	No. 22
23.	James Ramsey, of	(Mariners)
24.	Dylan Baker, rhp	Dropped out
25.	Luis Lugo, lhp	Dropped out
26.	Willi Castro, ss	No. 15
27.	Luke Wakamatsu, ss	Dropped out
28.	Greg Allen, of	No. 10
29.	Dorssys Paulino, of	Dropped out
30.	Mitch Brown, rhp	Dropped out

BEST TOOLS

Best Hitter for Average	Francisco Mejia
Best Power Hitter	Bobby Bradley
Best Strike-Zone Discipline	Yandy Diaz
Fastest Baserunner	Gabriel Mejia
Best Athlete	Will Benson
Best Fastball	Julian Merryweather
Best Curveball	Triston McKenzie
Best Slider	Shawn Morimando
Best Changeup	Adam Plutko
Best Control	Ryan Merritt
Best Defensive Catcher	Logan Ice
Best Defensive Infielder	Erik Gonzalez
Best Infield Arm	Erik Gonzalez
Best Defensive Outfielder	Greg Allen
Best Outfield Arm	Bradley Zimmer

PROJECTED 2020 LINEUP

Catcher	Yan Gomes
First Base	Bobby Bradley
Second Base	Jason Kipnis
Third Base	Jose Ramirez
Shortstop	Francisco Lindor
Left Field	Tyler Naquin
Center Field	Greg Allen
Right Field	Bradley Zimmer
Designated Hitter	Francisco Mejia
No. 1 Starter	Corey Kluber
No. 2 Starter	Danny Salazar
No. 3 Starter	Trevor Bauer
No. 4 Starter	Carlos Carrasco
No. 5 Starter	Triston McKenzie
Closer	Cody Allen

MINOR LEAGUE DEPTH CHART

CLEVELAND INDIANS

TOP 2017 ROOKIE: Bradley Zimmer, of. The Indians' lack of established outfielders should enable Zimmer to break through to the majors in 2017.

BREAKOUT PROSPECT: Micah Miniard, rhp. With his 6-foot-7 frame and natural cut on his fastball, he is a tough matchup for opponents—all he needs to do is harness his stuff.

SLEEPER: Matt Esparza, rhp. Like many of the college pitchers drafted in recent years by the Indians, Esparza has above-average control and solid stuff.

SOURCE OF TOP 30 TALENT			
Homegrown	27	Acquired	3
College	9	Trades	1
Junior college	2	Rule 5 draft	1
High school	8	Independent leagues	0
Nondrafted free agents	0	Free agents/waivers	1
International	8		

LF
Mike Papi
Todd Isaacs
Dorssys Paulino
Ka'ai Tom

CF
Bradley Zimmer (2)
Greg Allen (10)
Andrew Calica
Conner Capel
Gabriel Mejia

RF
Will Benson (7)
Oscar Gonzalez (27)
Luigi Rodriguez

3B
Nolan Jones (8)
Yandy Diaz (11)
Gavin Collins

SS
Yu-Cheng Chang (6)
Erik Gonzalez (9)
Willi Castro (15)
Jose Fermin (29)
Marcos Gonzalez (30)
Luke Wakamatsu
Eric Stamets

2B
Mark Mathias (13)
Tyler Krieger (18)
Claudio Bautista

1B
Bobby Bradley (5)
Nellie Rodriguez (25)
Jesus Aguilar
Ulysses Cantu

C
Francisco Mejia (1)
Logan Ice (12)
Daniel Salters

LHP

LHSP	LHRP
Brady Aiken (4)	Hoby Milner (24)
Juan Hillman (14)	Edwin Escobar
Tim Cooney (17)	Billy Strode
Shawn Morimando (19)	Thomas Pannone
Ryan Merritt (22)	Luis Lugo
Rob Kaminsky (26)	David Speer
Sam Hentges	
Sean Brady	

RHP

RHSP	RHRP
Triston McKenzie (3)	Shawn Armstrong
Adam Plutko (16)	Perci Garner
Aaron Civale (20)	Leandro Linares
Shane Bieber (21)	Cameron Hill
Julian Merrywather (23)	Joseph Colon
Micah Miniard (28)	Dylan Baker
Matt Esparza	Mitch Brown
Jonas Wyatt	Josh Martin
Grant Hockin	Trevor Frank
Carlos Vargas	Dace Kime

DRAFT ANALYSIS

2016

BEST PURE HITTER: 3B Nolan Jones (2) was considered one of the better pure hitters among high school draftees thanks to consistent contact and an easy, line-drive stroke. OF Andrew Calica (11) was the 2015 Cape Cod League batting champion and hit .382 in his pro debut. He lacks any other plus tools, but Calica is a pure hitter.
BEST POWER HITTER: OF Will Benson (1) doesn't always keep his hands and lower half in sync, but when he does he can hit mammoth home runs. His size, strength and hand speed allow him to drive the ball to the opposite field even when he doesn't properly use his legs in his swing.
FASTEST RUNNER: The Indians drafted very few speedsters, but OF Hosea Nelson (9) is a plus runner. Benson is also a plus runner.
BEST DEFENSIVE PLAYER: C Logan Ice (2s) is a well-rounded catcher who blocks balls well, frames pitches and controls running games with an accurate, average arm.
BEST FASTBALL: RHP Ryder Ryan (30) was a first baseman at North Carolina who made one appearance as a pitcher before the draft. The Indians liked his arm and helped improve his control. He was 94-95 mph in the Arizona League and touched 97, giving the Indians reason to believe he can develop as a starter.
BEST SECONDARY PITCH: RHP Aaron Civale (3) throws a mid-80s slider that varies between having more depth as a slider and a shorter-breaking hard cutter. It grades as an above-average pitch.
BEST PRO DEBUT: Calica hit .382/.474/.556 with 15 steals between short-season Mahoning Valley and low Class A Lake County. The only thing that slowed down righthander Shane Bieber (4) was his innings limit. He was 0-0, 0.38 with 21 strikeouts and 2 walks in 24 innings at Mahoning Valley.
BEST ATHLETE: Benson has a rare combination of size (6-foot-5, 225 pounds) and speed (6.65 in the 60-yard dash). The Duke signee planned to try to walk on to the Duke basketball team if he had not signed to go pro out of high school.
MOST INTRIGUING BACKGROUND: OF Conner Capel's (5) father Mike reached the majors as a righthander with the Cubs and Astros. He was also teammates with Roger Clemens at Texas.
CLOSEST TO THE MAJORS: Bieber and Civale should climb the minor league ladder on an expedited schedule thanks to their advanced control.
BEST LATE-ROUND PICK: Calica had already shown his ability to hit with wood bats in the Cape Cod League. Given the green light to try to get to his power on a more regular basis as a pro, he added some additional thump while still hitting for an extremely high average. His hitting ability could get him to the big leagues.

THE ONE WHO GOT AWAY: Once the Indians signed Jones for $2.25 million, they had no chance to sign RHP Wil Crowe (21). Crowe redshirted 2016 at South Carolina as he recovered from Tommy John surgery. The Indians made a run at signing C Zack Smith (15), a Charlotte signee with some power potential.

2015

RHP Triston McKenzie (1s) has moved ahead of LHPs Brady Aiken (1) and Juan Hillman (2), but all three have upside. 2B Mark Mathias (3) and SS Tyler Krieger (4) have high floors as middle infielders with versatility and a chance to hit.
GRADE: B

2014

OF Bradley Zimmer (1), 1B Bobby Bradley (3) and LHP Justus Sheffield (1), traded with RHP J.P. Feyereisen (16) to the Yankees in the Andrew Miller deal, are quality prospects. OF Greg Allen (6) broke out in 2016, while RHPs Julian Merryweather (5) and Micah Miniard (8) have breakout potential.
GRADE: B+

2013

LHP Kyle Crockett (4) and RHP Adam Plutko (11) sped to the majors, though neither grades as an impact arm. OF Clint Frazier (1), traded to the Yankees in the Andrew Miller along with RHP Ben Heller (22), should be a regular.
GRADE: C

TOP DRAFT PICKS OF THE DECADE

Year	Player, Pos.	2016 Org
2007	Beau Mills, 3b/1b	Did not play
2008	Lonnie Chisenhall, 3b	Indians
2009	Alex White, rhp	Did not play
2010	Drew Pomeranz, lhp	Red Sox
2011	Francisco Lindor, ss	Indians
2012	Tyler Naquin, of	Indians
2013	Clint Frazier, of	Yankees
2014	Bradley Zimmer, of	Indians
2015	Brady Aiken, lhp	Indians
2016	Will Benson, of	Indians

LARGEST BONUSES IN CLUB HISTORY

Danys Baez, 1999	$4,500,000
Clint Frazier, 2013	$3,500,000
Jeremy Guthrie, 2002	$3,000,000
Francisco Lindor, 2011	$2,650,000
Drew Pomeranz, 2010	$2,650,000

1 FRANCISCO MEJIA, C

Born: Oct. 27, 1995. **B-T:** B-R. **Ht.:** 5-10. **Wt.:** 175.
Signed: Dominican Republic, 2012.
Signed by: Ramon Pena.

BA GRADE

60 Risk: High

SCOUTING GRADES

Batting: 60.
Power: 45.
Speed: 40.
Defense: 50.
Arm: 80.

Based on 20-80 scouting scale and future projection rather than present tools.

PAUL GIERHART

The Indians challenged Mejia with aggressive assignments at the outset of his career, and he reached full-season ball as a 19-year old in 2015. That season, he was one of just three teenagers serving as an everyday catcher in the Midwest League. He scuffled at the plate against the older competition (hitting .243/.324/.345), and he returned to low Class A Lake County to start 2016. While repeating the level, Mejia broke out. He authored a historic 50-game hitting streak that is the longest in the modern era of the minor leagues (dating to 1963). Mejia's streak, which began in late May and stretched into August, increased his notoriety, as did a promotion to high Class A Lynchburg and an appearance in the Futures Game, where he started behind the plate for the World team. He was also a popular name as the trade deadline approached, and the Indians nearly dealt him to the Brewers in an attempt to land Jonathan Lucroy at the trade deadline, but Lucroy exercised his no-trade clause to block the move. Mejia kept hitting, even with the off-field distractions, and his .342 average ranked sixth in the minors. He also led all qualified Indians minor leaguers in both slugging percentage (.514) and OPS (.896).

Even before the streak, Mejia has long been known for his hitting ability. The switch-hitter consistently makes hard contact from both sides of the plate. He is a more productive righthanded hitter and has more power from that side of the plate, but can also do damage as a lefthanded hitter. Like many young hitters, he previously had a more pull-oriented approach at the plate. Part of his maturation as a hitter has been to become better at handling pitches on the outer half of the plate and using the opposite field to hit. His bat speed gives him more raw power than his lean, 5-foot-10 frame would suggest, but he more typically drives balls into the gaps than over the fence. He has an aggressive approach and doesn't walk much, but his excellent feel for the barrel prevents him from striking out often and he is comfortable working down in the count. Like most catchers, he is a below-average runner. Mejia has made strides defensively, but his bat is more advanced than his glove. Mejia has elite arm strength and soft hands, but his setup behind the plate still needs work to allow him to block balls and frame pitches more consistently. He is learning how to call games and is comfortable speaking English, a key skill for him to develop a relationship with his pitchers. Mejia often played second base as an amateur and some believe he could handle that position if he moved out from behind the plate. But he is just 21 and has the tools to become a capable defender with some further refinements.

Mejia took a big step forward in 2016, but he will need to continue to improve as he advances to the upper levels of the system. He will likely begin 2017 at Double-A Akron. If he continues to progress, he should be in line to make his major league debut sometime in 2018.

Year	Club (League)	Class	AVG	G	AB	R	H	2B	3B	HR	RBI	BB	SO	SB	CS	OBP	SLG
2014	Mahoning Valley (NYP)	SS	.282	66	248	32	70	17	4	2	36	18	47	2	4	.339	.407
2015	Lake County (MWL)	LoA	.243	109	391	45	95	13	0	9	53	38	78	4	1	.324	.345
2016	Lake County (MWL)	LoA	.347	60	239	41	83	17	3	7	51	15	39	1	0	.384	.531
	Lynchburg (CAR)	HiA	.333	42	168	22	56	12	1	4	29	13	24	1	2	.380	.488
Minor League Totals			.292	307	1151	156	336	68	9	26	193	89	206	11	8	.350	.434

2 BRADLEY ZIMMER, OF

Born: Nov. 27, 1992. **B-T:** L-R. **Ht.:** 6-4. **Wt.:** 185. **Drafted:** San Francisco, 2014 (1st round). **Signed by:** Don Lyle.

Two years after the Royals drafted his older brother Kyle fifth overall, Zimmer became the second first-round pick in the family when the Indians selected him 21st overall. It marked the third straight year the Indians used their top pick on a center fielder. Zimmer had a breakout 2015, as he started in the Futures Game, advanced to Double-A Akron and earned a spot on the BA Minor League All-Star team. While his 2016 wasn't quite on the same level, he reached Triple-A Columbus in late July. Zimmer has the potential to be a five-tool player and is capable of affecting the game in many ways. He has a smooth lefthanded swing and a patient approach at the plate. His strikeout rate spiked in 2016, when he whiffed 30.7 percent of the time, up from 23.8 percent in 2015. At the same time, however, his walk rate also increased, albeit not as dramatically. Zimmer's swing has natural loft to it, and his strength and bat speed give him above-average power. He also has above-average speed, which is further enhanced by his keen instincts on the basepaths and in the outfield. His power-speed combination gives him a chance to be a 20-20 player, while also providing plus defense in the outfield. He has primarily played center field, where his ability to track down balls and above-average arm strength profiles well. The Indians' outfield situation is muddled beyond Michael Brantley, leaving the door open for Zimmer to take over a starting spot sometime during 2017. He appears destined for Columbus, however.

BA GRADE 60 Risk: High

Year	Club (League)	Class	AVG	G	AB	R	H	2B	3B	HR	RBI	BB	SO	SB	CS	OBP	SLG
2014	Mahoning Valley (NYP)	SS	.304	45	168	32	51	11	2	4	30	19	30	11	4	.401	.464
	Lake County (MWL)	LoA	.273	3	11	4	3	1	0	2	2	2	3	1	0	.385	.909
2015	Lynchburg (CAR)	HiA	.310	77	281	60	87	16	3	10	39	37	74	32	5	.406	.495
	Akron (EL)	AA	.219	49	187	24	41	9	1	6	24	18	54	12	2	.313	.374
2016	Akron (EL)	AA	.253	93	340	58	86	20	6	14	53	56	115	13	13	.371	.471
	Columbus (IL)	AAA	.242	37	128	18	31	5	0	1	9	21	56	5	1	.349	.305
Minor League Totals			.268	304	1115	196	299	62	12	37	157	153	332	94	25	.373	.445

3 TRISTON McKENZIE, RHP

Born: Aug. 2, 1997. **B-T:** R-R. **Ht.:** 6-5. **Wt.:** 165. **Drafted:** HS—Palm Beach, Fla., 2015 (1st round supplemental). **Signed by:** Juan Alvarez.

The 2015 draft was a strong one for Florida prep pitchers and McKenzie presented scouts with a difficult assignment that spring. He had an excellent amateur track record and impressive present stuff, but he was listed at a rail-thin 6-foot-5, 165 pounds. While some questioned how much weight his frame will ever carry, the Indians drafted McKenzie 42nd overall and signed him for $2,302,500, the second largest bonus for a player drafted after the first round that year. He rewarded them in 2016 by excelling at short-season Mahoning Valley and then low Class A Lake County. McKenzie stands out as much for his pitchability as for his stuff. He earns praise for his makeup and understanding of his craft. That, along with his control, helps his stuff play up even more. His fastball can get up to 95 mph, but he more typically works in the low 90s. More strength would help him maintain his velocity deeper into games. He uses his height to his advantage and pitches down in the zone. He gets good depth on his curveball, which is a swing-and-miss offering. His changeup lags behind his other two pitches but has the potential to be an above-average offering as he gets more comfortable throwing it Improving his changeup and getting stronger so that he can maintain his velocity deeper into games are his two biggest tasks going forward. McKenzie's combination of upside and advanced pitchability has many excited about his future. He could likely handle starting the 2017 season at high Class A Lynchburg, but he'll pitch nearly the entire season at age 19, giving the Indians time to can bring him along more slowly with an assignment to Lake County.

BA GRADE 60 Risk: High

Year	Club (League)	Class	W	L	ERA	G	GS	CG	SV	IP	H	HR	BB	SO	K/9	WHIP	AVG
2015	Indians (AZL)	R	1	1	0.75	4	3	0	0	12	4	0	3	17	12.8	0.58	.100
2016	Mahoning Valley (NYP)	SS	4	3	0.55	9	9	1	0	49	31	2	16	55	10.0	0.95	.180
	Lake County (MWL)	LoA	2	2	3.18	6	6	0	0	34	27	2	6	49	13.0	0.97	.214
Minor League Totals			7	6	1.51	19	18	1	0	95	62	4	25	121	11.4	0.91	.183

4 BRADY AIKEN, LHP

Born: Aug. 16, 1996. **B-T:** L-L. **Ht.:** 6-4. **Wt.:** 205. **Drafted:** HS—San Diego, 2015 (1st round). **Signed by:** Mike Soper.

Aiken emerged as the best prep player for the 2014 draft, and the Astros made him the No. 1 overall pick. They agreed to sign him for $6.5 million before withdrawing the offer when a post-draft physical revealed an elbow issue. Aiken ultimately turned down a reported $5 million offer and chose to pitch for IMG Academy's postgrad team in 2015. He left his first start of the year and required Tommy John surgery. The Indians selected Aiken 17th overall in 2015, and he finally made his pro debut in 2016. Aiken was slow out of the gate as he returned to playing in competitive games for the first time in more than two years. His fastball velocity, in the upper 80s and reaching 91, was down from what it had been in high school, when he touched 97 mph and sat in the low 90s. But as the summer went on and he got stronger, his velocity ticked up, and he sat in the low 90s at instructional league. His curveball can be a plus offering and his changeup gives him a third promising pitch. At his best, he can locate his fastball well to both sides of the plate and has advanced feel. He has an ideal pitcher's frame, plenty of athleticism and earns praise for his makeup and maturity. After everything Aiken went through, he understandably had some hiccups at the outset of his pro career. After a normal offseason, he should be ready for an assignment to low Class A Lake County.

BA GRADE 60 Risk: Extreme

Year	Club (League)	Class	W	L	ERA	G	GS	CG	SV	IP	H	HR	BB	SO	K/9	WHIP	AVG
2015	Did not play—Injured																
2016	Indians (AZL)	R	0	4	7.13	9	8	0	0	24	32	1	13	35	13.1	1.88	.308
	Mahoning Valley (NYP)	SS	2	1	4.43	5	5	0	0	22	20	3	8	22	8.9	1.25	.233
Minor League Totals			2	5	5.83	14	13	0	0	46	52	4	21	57	11.1	1.58	.274

5 BOBBY BRADLEY, 1B

Born: May 29, 1996. **B-T:** L-R. **Ht.:** 6-1. **Wt.:** 225. **Drafted:** HS—Gulfport, Miss., 2014 (3rd round). **Signed by:** Mike Bradford.

Competition in the Mississippi high school ranks is not as stout as in other parts of the South, but that hasn't held Bradley back. He won the Rookie-level Arizona League triple crown in 2014 by hitting .361 with eight home runs and 50 RBIs. He led the Midwest League with 27 home runs in 2015 and hit 29 more in 2016 to top the Carolina League—he also led in RBIs (102) and walks (75)—to claim the circuit's MVP award. Bradley was one of the younger players in his draft class and he has continued to be among the younger players in his leagues. His inexperience has been exposed at times, but his impressive raw tools shine through more often than not. He creates excellent bat speed that turns into prodigious power. Like most young hitters, he gets pull-happy at times, but he can hit the ball out to all fields. Both his strikeout and walk rates improved a touch last season, though he is still learning how to handle advanced offspeed offerings. He is a well below-average runner. Defensively, Bradley has an average arm and is limited to first base. Bradley will advance to Double-A Akron in 2017 for his first exposure to the upper minors. His power gives him the potential to become a middle-of-the-order hitter in the major leagues in time.

BA GRADE 55 Risk: High

Year	Club (League)	Class	AVG	G	AB	R	H	2B	3B	HR	RBI	BB	SO	SB	CS	OBP	SLG
2014	Indians (AZL)	R	.361	39	155	39	56	13	4	8	50	16	36	3	0	.426	.652
2015	Lake County (MWL)	LoA	.269	108	401	62	108	15	4	27	92	56	148	3	0	.361	.529
	Lynchburg (CAR)	HiA	.000	2	8	0	0	0	0	0	0	1	2	0	0	.111	.000
2016	Lynchburg (CAR)	HiA	.235	131	485	82	114	23	1	29	102	75	170	3	0	.344	.466
Minor League Totals			.265	280	1049	183	278	51	9	64	244	148	356	9	0	.361	.514

6 YU-CHENG CHANG, SS

Born: Aug. 18, 1995. **B-T:** R-R. **Ht.:** 6-1. **Wt.:** 175. **Signed:** Taiwan, 2013. **Signed by:** Allen Lin/Jayson Lynn.

A prominent amateur player in Taiwan, Chang was one of the top amateur free agents to sign out of Asia in 2013. He has made steady progress in the minor leagues and earned all-star honors in the Carolina League in 2016. He reportedly received heavy interest in trade deadline talks and was set to be a part of the deal with the Brewers for Jonathan Lucroy that ultimately fell apart. Instead, he helped high Class A Lynchburg reach the Carolina League finals, going 14-for-28 in the playoffs. A switch-hitter, Chang has solid all-around offensive tools. He hits well from both sides of the plate and exhibits a good feel for the barrel. He has more power than

BA GRADE 55 Risk: High

his lean, 6-foot-1 frame suggests, and he is beginning to learn how to tap into it more often. His swing is more geared for hitting line drives, but he produced 51 extra-base hits in 2016, more than doubling his career total. Chang's arm and speed both grade as above-average. That, combined with his athleticism and infield actions, gives him a chance to stick at shortstop, where the Indians believe he can develop into a capable defender. Some believe he will outgrow the position, which would necessitate a move to second or third base. For now, Chang will continue his development at shortstop. He'll likely move up to Double-A Akron to start the 2017 season.

Year	Club (League)	Class	AVG	G	AB	R	H	2B	3B	HR	RBI	BB	SO	SB	CS	OBP	SLG
2014	Indians (AZL)	R	.346	42	159	39	55	9	4	6	25	18	28	6	1	.420	.566
2015	Lake County (MWL)	LoA	.232	105	393	52	91	16	4	9	52	27	103	5	6	.293	.361
2016	Lynchburg (CAR)	HiA	.259	109	417	78	108	30	8	13	70	45	110	11	3	.332	.463
Minor League Totals			.262	256	969	169	254	55	16	28	147	90	241	22	10	.331	.439

7 WILL BENSON, OF

Born: June 16, 1998. **B-T:** L-L. **Ht.:** 6-5. **Wt.:** 215. **Drafted:** HS—Atlanta, 2016 (1st round). **Signed by:** C.T. Bradford.

Benson began his senior year of high school by helping USA Baseball win the gold medal in the 18U World Cup in Japan. He ended it by being drafted 14th overall by the Indians. His spectacular senior year also included him leading The Westminster Schools to their first baseball state championship since 1975. He was a star basketball player for the Wildcats who earned second-team all-state honors as a forward. On the diamond, Benson stands out most for the elite bat speed his quick hands and strength produce. He turns that bat speed into well above-average lefthanded raw power. He is still learning how to get to that power more consistently and has worked to simplify his swing as a professional. When he struggles, he fails to use his lower half and his bat path gets too steep. He is an excellent athlete and runs well for his size, recording some plus times in the 60-yard dash, but he is slower out of the box and may lose a step as he physically matures. Benson has a plus arm and is a solid defender in right field. As a big, athletic, lefthanded-hitting outfielder from Atlanta, Benson is often compared with Jason Heyward, whom the Braves drafted 14th overall. Benson has a long way to go to reach that ceiling and will likely make his full-season debut at Class A Lake County in 2017.

BILL MITCHELL

BA GRADE
55 **Risk:** **Extreme**

Year	Club (League)	Class	AVG	G	AB	R	H	2B	3B	HR	RBI	BB	SO	SB	CS	OBP	SLG
2016	Indians (AZL)	R	.215	44	158	31	34	10	3	6	27	22	60	10	2	.326	.430
Minor League Totals			.215	44	158	31	34	10	3	6	27	22	60	10	2	.326	.430

8 NOLAN JONES, 3B

Born: May 7, 1998. **B-T:** L-L. **Ht.:** 6-3. **Wt.:** 195. **Drafted:** HS—Bensalem, Pa., 2016 (2nd round). **Signed by:** Mike Kanen.

Jones was regarded as one of the best prep hitters in the 2016 draft class, but he slipped to the second round, where the Indians were happy to be able to take him at No. 55 overall. He signed for $2.25 million, making him one of five players drafted after the first round to sign for more than $2 million. Jones has advanced consistency in his approach and contact skills, especially for a prep hitter from the Northeast. That helped him stand out on the showcase circuit in the summer of 2015, and continued to push him up draft boards in the spring. His easy lefthanded swing generates plus raw power now, but he projects to have more as he physically matures. He has plenty of room to add strength to his lanky frame as he begins to work in a professional training environment. He is an average runner. Jones was a shortstop in high school, but his size made it likely he would soon outgrow the position and profile better at third base. The Indians quickly moved him to the hot corner, and he should be able to develop into an average defender with steady hands and a plus arm at his new position. While he has the defensive tools to develop, it will be up to his bat to carry him through the minor leagues. Jones will join fellow 2016 first-day prep pick Will Benson at low Class A Lake County in 2017.

BILL MITCHELL

BA GRADE
55 **Risk:** **Extreme**

Year	Club (League)	Class	AVG	G	AB	R	H	2B	3B	HR	RBI	BB	SO	SB	CS	OBP	SLG
2016	Indians (AZL)	R	.257	32	109	10	28	5	2	0	9	23	49	3	1	.388	.339
Minor League Totals			.257	32	109	10	28	5	2	0	9	23	49	3	1	.388	.339

9 ERIK GONZALEZ, SS/2B

Born: Aug. 31, 1991. **B-T:** R-R. **Ht.:** 6-3. **Wt.:** 195. **Signed:** Dominican Republic, 2008. **Signed by:** Andres Garcia.

BA GRADE

45 Risk: Medium

Gonzalez played every position but pitcher and catcher at the outset of his career as a result of the infield depth in the Indians system. When Francisco Lindor was promoted from high Class A Carolina in 2013, Gonzalez got a chance to fill the hole left at shortstop. He fared better than expected playing the position full-time and reached the big leagues in 2016. But with Lindor now firmly established as Cleveland's shortstop, Gonzalez returned to his roots as a utility player, and he appeared at four positions in 21 big league games. Gonzalez has made effective adjustments to his offensive game, enabling the righthanded hitter to incorporate his above-average speed and tap into the pop his bat speed and wiry strength produce. He is an aggressive hitter and rarely walks, limiting his chances as a top-of-the-order hitter. Gonzalez has outstanding defensive skills. His quickness and plus arm strength allow him to make highlight-reel plays at shortstop, but he is also prone to making mental mistakes. He's versatile enough to play anywhere in the infield and has gotten some work in the outfield as well. If he can develop more consistency, Gonzalez has the tools to be an everyday shortstop—just not for the Indians. Regardless, his versatility is an ideal fit for the big league roster.

Year	Club (League)	Class	AVG	G	AB	R	H	2B	3B	HR	RBI	BB	SO	SB	CS	OBP	SLG
2014	Carolina (CAR)	HiA	.289	74	308	44	89	14	7	3	46	23	65	15	6	.336	.409
	Akron (EL)	AA	.357	31	129	21	46	6	3	1	16	7	23	6	1	.390	.473
2015	Akron (EL)	AA	.280	72	311	38	87	18	4	6	46	11	56	10	5	.304	.421
	Columbus (IL)	AAA	.223	65	238	32	53	6	3	3	23	15	47	8	2	.277	.311
2016	Columbus (IL)	AAA	.296	104	429	62	127	31	1	11	53	19	88	12	10	.329	.450
	Cleveland (AL)	MAJ	.313	21	16	2	5	0	0	0	0	1	8	0	1	.353	.313
Major League Totals			.313	21	16	2	5	0	0	0	0	1	8	0	1	.353	.313
Minor League Totals			.274	704	2770	401	760	145	38	38	346	156	524	99	38	.316	.395

10 GREG ALLEN, OF

Born: March 15, 1993. **B-T:** B-R. **Ht.:** 6-0. **Wt.:** 175. **Drafted:** San Diego State, 2014 (6th round). **Signed by:** Ryan Thompson.

BA GRADE

50 Risk: High

Allen excelled on the field and in the classroom at San Diego State and was named the school's male student-athlete of the year as a junior. Since the Indians drafted him in the sixth round that year, he has made a smooth transition to pro ball and steadily climbed through the minor leagues, reaching Double-A Akron and ending the year with an assignment to the Arizona Fall League. Allen's game is built around his plus speed. He has good on-base skills, having led the high Class A Carolina League in on-base percentage (.424), and his approach at the plate is geared toward making contact, limiting his power potential. He is a disciplined hitter and walks about as often as he strikes out. He is a good baserunner and has led the Indians system in stolen bases in each of the last two seasons. Allen's speed plays well in the outfield, where he is a plus defender. He takes good routes, has an above-average arm and the speed to cover plenty of ground. Allen came to the organization at the end of a stretch where it had selected a center fielder with its top draft pick for three straight years. While that has made for a crowded organizational depth chart, his defense is a separator. He'll likely begin 2017 back at Akron and could push his way to the big leagues with another strong season.

Year	Club (League)	Class	AVG	G	AB	R	H	2B	3B	HR	RBI	BB	SO	SB	CS	OBP	SLG
2014	Mahoning Valley (NYP)	SS	.244	57	225	46	55	8	2	0	19	27	26	30	5	.361	.298
2015	Lake County (MWL)	LoA	.273	123	479	83	131	27	2	7	45	53	57	43	16	.368	.382
	Lynchburg (CAR)	HiA	.154	3	13	2	2	1	0	0	0	2	3	3	0	.313	.231
2016	Lynchburg (CAR)	HiA	.298	92	346	93	103	16	4	4	31	58	51	38	7	.424	.402
	Akron (EL)	AA	.290	37	145	26	42	7	3	3	13	19	27	7	6	.399	.441
Minor League Totals			.276	312	1208	250	333	59	11	14	108	159	164	121	34	.386	.377

11 YANDY DIAZ, 3B/OF

BA GRADE

45 Risk: Medium

Born: Aug. 8, 1991. **B-T:** R-R. **Ht.:** 6-2. **Wt.:** 185. **Signed:** Cuba, 2013. **Signed by:** Ramon Pena/Juan Alvarez/Felix Nivar.

The Indians haven't been heavy players in the expanding Cuban market, but in 2013 they signed Diaz for $300,000. His feel to hit has stood out in the U.S., as evidenced by a career .307 average with more walks than strikeouts as he climbed quickly to the high minors. Diaz hit .325 at Triple-A Columbus in 2016 to win the International League batting title and was named the circuit's top rookie. He has a good feel for the barrel and a disciplined approach, helping him make contact at a high rate. Diaz's approach comes at the detriment of power numbers, and he is still learning how to drive the ball—his nine home runs in 2016 were a career high. He has raw pop, but his approach is not geared to creating the loft necessary to hit homers. Diaz was primarily a second baseman in Cuba but moved to third base after signing with the Indians. He developed into an above-average defender at his new position, but the Indians began moving him around in 2016 to give him more versatility. He appeared at both second and third base and at all three outfield positions. Diaz's versatility gives him a chance to at least be a super-utility player, a role he could fill in Cleveland as soon as 2017.

Year	Club (League)	Class	AVG	G	AB	R	H	2B	3B	HR	RBI	BB	SO	SB	CS	OBP	SLG
2014	Carolina (CAR)	HiA	.286	76	283	42	81	7	5	2	37	49	35	3	3	.396	.367
2015	Akron (EL)	AA	.315	132	476	61	150	13	5	7	55	78	65	8	7	.412	.408
	Columbus (IL)	AAA	.158	4	19	1	3	2	0	0	1	0	5	0	0	.158	.263
2016	Akron (EL)	AA	.286	26	84	13	24	0	1	2	14	24	16	6	2	.445	.381
	Columbus (IL)	AAA	.325	95	360	53	117	22	3	7	44	47	70	5	1	.399	.461
Minor League Totals			.307	333	1222	170	375	44	14	18	151	198	191	22	13	.403	.410

12 LOGAN ICE, C

BA GRADE
50 Risk: High

Born: May 27, 1995. **B-T:** B-R. **Ht.:** 5-10. **Wt.:** 195. **Drafted:** Oregon State, 2016 (2nd round supplemental). **Signed by:** Conor Glassey.

A three-year starter at Oregon State, Ice broke out offensively as a junior in 2016 and shot up draft boards as a result. The Indians made him a supplemental second-round pick, the highest they have drafted a catcher since they picked Javi Herrera in the second round in 2003. Though Ice improved as a hitter during his college career, defense remains his calling card. He is a good receiver and works with pitchers well, quickly earning praise for his ability to manage a staff in pro ball. He has an accurate, average arm. A switch-hitter, Ice has a patient, disciplined approach at the plate, and he walked more than he struck out at OSU. He also has some juice in his bat but projects as a below-average hitter in the big leagues. Thanks to his defensive ability, Ice won't have to hit much to become a big league contributor. For now, he is advanced enough to handle an assignment to high Class A Lynchburg in 2017.

Year	Club (League)	Class	AVG	G	AB	R	H	2B	3B	HR	RBI	BB	SO	SB	CS	OBP	SLG
2016	Mahoning Valley (NYP)	SS	.198	39	126	13	25	7	0	2	8	23	38	0	0	.329	.302
Minor League Totals			.198	39	126	13	25	7	0	2	8	23	38	0	0	.329	.302

13 MARK MATHIAS, 2B/3B

BA GRADE
50 Risk: High

Born: Aug. 2, 1994. **B-T:** R-R. **Ht.:** 6-0. **Wt.:** 200. **Drafted:** Cal Poly, 2015 (3rd round). **Signed by:** Carlos Muniz.

Mathias won the Big West Conference batting title as a Cal Poly sophomore in 2014 but was limited the following spring by a right shoulder injury that required labrum surgery. Since returning to full health, he has continued to build his reputation for hitting. Mathias rose to Double-A Akron in 2016, the year after being drafted. He has one of the best plate approaches in the organization because he controls the barrel well and is a patient, disciplined hitter. He has below-average power but does a good job of driving balls into the gaps, and he ranked third in the system with 40 doubles in 2016. Mathias has primarily been a second baseman, but he has the versatility to play anywhere in the infield, even playing 19 games at shortstop as a pro. He profiles best at second base, where he is a capable defender with above-average arm strength and speed. After getting a taste of the upper minors late in 2016, Mathias will return to Akron to open the 2017 season.

Year	Club (League)	Class	AVG	G	AB	R	H	2B	3B	HR	RBI	BB	SO	SB	CS	OBP	SLG
2015	Mahoning Valley (NYP)	SS	.282	67	245	38	69	19	3	2	32	35	36	5	4	.382	.408
2016	Lynchburg (CAR)	HiA	.274	115	427	70	117	39	1	5	60	48	87	9	1	.359	.405
	Akron (EL)	AA	.067	5	15	1	1	1	0	0	1	1	6	0	0	.125	.133
Minor League Totals			.272	187	687	109	187	59	4	7	93	84	129	14	5	.363	.400

14 JUAN HILLMAN, LHP

BA GRADE
50 Risk: High

Born: May 15, 1997. **B-T:** L-L. **Ht.:** 6-2. **Wt.:** 185. **Drafted:** HS—Orlando, 2015 (2nd round). **Signed by:** Mike Soper.

Before his sophomore year of high school, Hillman moved in with Tom Gordon, the former all-star righthander and the father of Hillman's prep teammate Nick Gordon. Tom became Hillman's legal guardian and mentor, and the lefthander credits their relationship for many of the strides he made during high school as he developed into a 2015 second-round pick. The Indians took things slowly with Hillman and assigned him to short-season Mahoning Valley in 2016, where he started strong before fading in the final month of the season. Early in the summer, Hillman's fastball sat 90-92 mph but backed up a tick later in the season. His changeup continues to be his best secondary pitch, but his curveball showed improvement and he can throw it for strikes. He has the makings of three average pitches with average control. He has good athleticism, a clean delivery and some projectability, giving evaluators plenty to dream on. Hillman's struggles at the end of the season illustrate his need to improve his stamina to withstand the rigors of a full pro season, as is the case with most teenagers. That will take on greater importance as he advances to low Class A Lake County in 2017.

Year	Club (League)	Class	W	L	ERA	G	GS	CG	SV	IP	H	HR	BB	SO	K/9	WHIP	AVG
2015	Indians (AZL)	R	0	2	4.13	8	6	0	0	24	26	0	5	20	7.5	1.29	.286
2016	Mahoning Valley (NYP)	SS	3	4	4.43	15	15	0	0	63	66	5	24	47	6.7	1.43	.268
Minor League Totals			3	6	4.34	23	21	0	0	87	92	5	29	67	6.9	1.39	.273

15 WILLI CASTRO, SS

BA GRADE
50 Risk: High

Born: April 24, 1997. **B-T:** B-R. **Ht.:** 6-1. **Wt.:** 165. **Signed:** Dominican Republic, 2013. **Signed by:** Ramon Pena/Felix Nivar.

Since signing Castro out of the Dominican Republic in 2013, the Indians have pushed him aggressively. He has been the youngest player on his team at every stop of his pro career, but he has held his own and earned a late-season promotion to high Class A Lynchburg in 2016. A switch-hitter, Castro sprays line drives from both sides of the plate. His power is more doubles pop now, but he projects to develop more as he physically matures. He has above-average speed, which he is still learning to harness. Defensively, he has good hands and infield actions at shortstop. He still needs to work to improve his consistency in the field after making 25 errors in 2016, but his tools give him a chance to stay at shortstop. Castro earns praise for his baseball acumen and confidence. He will return to Lynchburg to start 2017, when he will still be 19 years old.

Year	Club (League)	Class	AVG	G	AB	R	H	2B	3B	HR	RBI	BB	SO	SB	CS	OBP	SLG
2014	Indians (AZL)	R	.239	43	155	31	37	5	3	2	11	6	33	9	4	.285	.348
2015	Mahoning Valley (NYP)	SS	.264	67	273	34	72	9	3	1	25	10	31	20	7	.304	.330
2016	Lake County (MWL)	LoA	.259	123	518	68	134	21	8	7	49	19	96	16	11	.286	.371
	Lynchburg (CAR)	HiA	.222	3	9	0	2	0	0	0	0	0	2	0	1	.222	.222
Minor League Totals			.257	236	955	133	245	35	14	10	85	35	162	45	23	.291	.354

16 ADAM PLUTKO, RHP

BA GRADE
45 Risk: Medium

Born: Oct. 3, 1991. **B-T:** R-R. **Ht.:** 6-3. **Wt.:** 200. **Drafted:** UCLA, 2013 (11th round). **Signed by:** Carlos Muniz.

Plutko pitched behind Gerrit Cole and Trevor Bauer in the UCLA rotation as a freshman, and he eventually succeeded them as the team's ace. He led the Bruins to the 2013 national championship and was named Most Outstanding Player in the College World Series. Plutko made a quick transition to pro ball and reached the major leagues in 2016, where he reunited with Bauer on the Indians' staff. He doesn't have overpowering stuff, succeeding instead with plus control and baseball IQ. Plutko's fastball sits around 90 mph but he can run it up to 94. Even with fringe-average velocity, Plutko's fastball plays up thanks to his ability to throw it for strikes to both sides of the plate. His changeup is his best offspeed offering, and his slider is the better of his two breaking balls. He does a good job of pitch sequencing and understands how to get the most out of his stuff. Plutko can't match the upside of the organization's top pitchers, but his approach gives him a chance to be successful in the big leagues. He will serve as rotation depth at Triple-A Columbus in 2017, in case a need arises in Cleveland.

Year	Club (League)	Class	W	L	ERA	G	GS	CG	SV	IP	H	HR	BB	SO	K/9	WHIP	AVG
2014	Lake County (MWL)	LoA	3	1	3.93	10	10	0	0	53	49	1	12	66	11.3	1.16	.241
	Carolina (CAR)	HiA	4	9	4.08	18	18	0	0	97	99	11	18	78	7.2	1.21	.265
2015	Lynchburg (CAR)	HiA	4	2	1.27	8	8	1	0	50	30	3	5	47	8.5	0.70	.173
	Akron (EL)	AA	5	5	2.86	19	19	1	0	116	96	9	23	90	7.0	1.02	.222
2016	Akron (EL)	AA	3	3	3.27	13	13	0	0	72	64	5	12	63	7.9	1.06	.238
	Columbus (IL)	AAA	6	5	4.10	15	15	0	0	90	87	8	34	67	6.7	1.34	.256
	Cleveland (AL)	MAJ	0	0	7.36	2	0	0	0	4	5	1	2	3	7.4	1.91	.313
Major League Totals			0	0	7.36	2	0	0	0	4	5	1	2	3	7.4	1.91	.313
Minor League Totals			29	25	3.36	83	83	2	0	477	425	37	104	411	7.7	1.11	.237

17 TIM COONEY, LHP

BA GRADE

50 Risk: High

Born: Dec. 19, 1990. **B-T:** L-L. **Ht.:** 6-3. **Wt.:** 195. **Drafted:** Wake Forest, 2012 (3rd round). **Signed by:** Matt Blood (Cardinals).

Cooney made his major league debut in 2015, making six starts for the National League Central-champion Cardinals before an appendectomy in July ended his season. He was poised to play an even bigger role in 2016, but he was sidelined all season after he suffered a shoulder injury during spring training that lingered and eventually required surgery in July to remove a calcium deposit. Cooney missed the remainder of the season and was claimed by the Indians on waivers in November. Before his injury, Cooney's fastball sat around 90 mph and peaked at 92. He gets some late life on the pitch, which he locates well to both sides of the plate. His above-average changeup is his best offering and is capable of being an out pitch. His curveball is the better of his two breaking balls, but his slider is a viable fourth pitch. He pounds the strike zone with his whole arsenal, and has averaged less than 2.0 walks per nine innings as a professional. When he returns to full health, Cooney will add another lefthander to the mix for the Indians. He should be able to help them in the major leagues in 2017, either in the bullpen or as a starter.

Year	Club (League)	Class	W	L	ERA	G	GS	CG	SV	IP	H	HR	BB	SO	K/9	WHIP	AVG
2014	Memphis (PCL)	AAA	14	6	3.47	26	25	1	0	158	158	21	47	119	6.8	1.30	.263
2015	Memphis (PCL)	AAA	6	4	2.74	14	14	1	0	89	61	9	16	63	6.4	0.87	.195
	St. Louis (NL)	MAJ	1	0	3.16	6	6	0	0	31	28	3	10	29	8.3	1.21	.241
2016	Did not play—Injured																
Major League Totals			1	0	3.16	6	6	0	0	31	28	3	10	29	8.3	1.21	.241
Minor League Totals			33	26	3.35	79	76	4	0	457	445	43	93	373	7.4	1.18	.258

18 TYLER KRIEGER, 2B

BA GRADE

50 Risk: High

Born: Jan. 16, 1994. **B-T:** B-R. **Ht.:** 6-2. **Wt.:** 170. **Drafted:** Clemson, 2015 (4th round). **Signed by:** Brad Tyler.

Krieger started the first 101 games of his Clemson career at shortstop before suffering a shoulder injury during his sophomore season. He ultimately required labrum surgery and was limited to second base when he returned to the field midway through his junior season. After drafting him in the fourth round, the Indians shut him down for the rest of the 2015 season to give him more time to recover. That delayed Krieger's pro debut until 2016, when he started at low Class A Lake County and earned a midseason promotion to high Class A Lynchburg. He has above-average feel for the barrel that allows him to hit line drives to all fields. He doesn't provide much in the way of power, but his above-average speed leads to doubles and triples when he drives the ball to the gaps. Krieger's days as a shortstop are likely over, but he is a solid defender at second base, where his infield actions and hands play well. The Indians have enviable middle-infield depth, which could keep Krieger at Lynchburg to start 2017. With another solid showing, he should be in line to reach Double-A Akron later in the season.

Year	Club (League)	Class	AVG	G	AB	R	H	2B	3B	HR	RBI	BB	SO	SB	CS	OBP	SLG
2015	Did not play—Injured																
2016	Lake County (MWL)	LoA	.313	69	262	51	82	13	4	3	35	29	66	15	8	.385	.427
	Lynchburg (CAR)	HiA	.282	59	220	33	62	13	4	2	23	28	52	6	7	.369	.405
Minor League Totals			.299	128	482	84	144	26	8	5	58	57	118	21	15	.377	.417

19 SHAWN MORIMANDO, LHP

BA GRADE

45 Risk: Medium

Born: Nov. 20, 1992. **B-T:** L-L. **Ht.:** 6-0. **Wt.:** 200. **Drafted:** HS—Virginia Beach, 2011 (19th round). **Signed by:** Bob Mayer.

Morimando, a 19th-round pick in 2011, steadily rose through the minors and made his big league debut in 2016. He has been a starter throughout his career but made his first two appearances for Cleveland out of the bullpen. Morimando's fastball sits in the low 90s with running life that makes it tough for hitters to square up. His slider rates as the best in the organization and gives him an out pitch. He also throws both a changeup and a curveball. Though he is slightly undersized, Morimando has proven to be able to handle a hefty workload, throwing more than 150 innings in each of the last three seasons. Whether he can continue in that role in the big leagues depends largely on his ability to improve his below-average control. He has averaged more than 3.0 walks per nine innings from 2014 to 2016. His stuff and makeup would also play well in the bullpen. For now Morimando will return to Triple-A Columbus to open 2017 in the rotation.

Year	Club (League)	Class	W	L	ERA	G	GS	CG	SV	IP	H	HR	BB	SO	K/9	WHIP	AVG
2014	Carolina (CAR)	HiA	8	3	2.99	18	18	0	0	96	72	7	35	65	6.1	1.11	.203
	Akron (EL)	AA	2	6	3.83	10	10	0	0	56	63	2	17	38	6.1	1.42	.281
2015	Akron (EL)	AA	10	12	3.18	28	28	0	0	159	139	9	65	128	7.3	1.29	.240
2016	Akron (EL)	AA	10	3	3.09	16	16	0	0	93	77	5	36	73	7.0	1.21	.225
	Cleveland (AL)	MAJ	0	0	11.57	2	0	0	0	5	9	2	5	5	9.6	3.00	.409
	Columbus (IL)	AAA	5	2	3.51	11	11	0	0	59	64	5	21	46	7.0	1.44	.281
Major League Totals			0	0	11.57	2	0	0	0	5	9	2	5	5	9.6	3.00	.409
Minor League Totals			50	45	3.39	135	132	2	0	715	631	47	304	529	6.7	1.31	.238

20 AARON CIVALE, RHP

BA GRADE
45 Risk: High

Born: June 12, 1995. **B-T:** R-R. **Ht.:** 6-2. **Wt.:** 215. **Drafted:** Northeastern, 2016 (3rd round). **Signed by:** Mike Kanen.

After spending his first two years at Northeastern in the bullpen, Civale moved to the rotation as a junior in 2016 and delivered phenomenal results. He ranked 10th in the country in ERA (1.73), 14th in strikeouts (121) and ninth in WHIP (0.93). The Indians selected him in the third round, making him the highest player drafted from Northeastern since Adam Ottavino went 30th overall to the Cardinals in 2006. Civale continued his impressive year with a strong pro debut at short-season Mahoning Valley. He fills up the zone with his low-90s fastball and is working to develop his changeup after never needing it in college. His hard, tight slider has a chance to be a plus offering, and he also throws a curveball. He repeats his delivery well and works down in the zone. Civale has the stuff and physical frame to continue to develop as a starter. He will probably begin 2017 at high Class A Lynchburg and could advance quickly through the system.

Year	Club (League)	Class	W	L	ERA	G	GS	CG	SV	IP	H	HR	BB	SO	K/9	WHIP	AVG
2016	Mahoning Valley (NYP)	SS	0	2	1.67	13	13	0	0	38	23	0	8	28	6.7	0.82	.180
Minor League Totals			0	2	1.67	13	13	0	0	38	23	0	8	28	6.7	0.82	.180

21 SHANE BIEBER, RHP

BA GRADE
45 Risk: High

Born: May 31, 1995. **B-T:** R-R. **Ht.:** 6-3. **Wt.:** 195. **Drafted:** UC Santa Barbara, 2016 (4th round). **Signed by:** Carlos Muniz.

Bieber succeeded Dillon Tate as UC Santa Barbara's ace in 2016 and led the Gauchos to their first-ever appearance in the College World Series. After the Indians made him a fourth-round pick they limited his workload at short-season Mahoning Valley due to the length of his college season, but he dominated hitters in the New York-Penn League. Bieber does not have overpowering stuff and relies instead on his command and understanding of his craft. His fastball sits around 90 mph, and he can locate it to all four quadrants of the zone, while his slider and changeup give him a pair of average secondary offerings. His stuff all plays up thanks to his above-average control. Bieber repeats his clean, easy delivery and averaged 1.1 walks per nine innings during his college career. He is comparable to fellow Indians prospect Adam Plutko, who also hails from Southern California. Bieber is advanced enough to handle an assignment to high Class A Lynchburg to start 2017 and could move quickly up in the minor leagues.

Year	Club (League)	Class	W	L	ERA	G	GS	CG	SV	IP	H	HR	BB	SO	K/9	WHIP	AVG
2016	Mahoning Valley (NYP)	SS	0	0	0.38	9	8	0	0	24	10	0	2	21	7.9	0.50	.122
Minor League Totals			0	0	0.38	9	8	0	0	24	10	0	2	21	7.9	0.50	.122

22 RYAN MERRITT, LHP

BA GRADE
40 Risk: Medium

Born: Feb. 21, 1992. **B-T:** L-L. **Ht.:** 6-0. **Wt.:** 180. **Drafted:** McLennan (Texas) CC, 2011 (16th round). **Signed by:** Kevin Cullen.

Previously known for his incredible walk rate in the minor leagues and 2014 breakout season at high Class A, Merritt made his major league debut in 2016 and then jumped into the spotlight during the playoffs. After making four appearances in the big leagues (one start) during the regular season, he was pressed into action as the Indians' starter in Game Five of the American League Championship Series at Toronto. He threw 4.1 scoreless innings to help send Cleveland to the World Series for the first time since 1997. Merritt doesn't have overpowering stuff, instead relying on his command and feel for pitching to get outs. His fastball sits in the upper 80s (it peaked at 88 mph in Toronto) and he knows how to add or subtract velocity as necessary. He improved his curveball and added a cutter in 2016, but his above-average changeup remains his best offering. All of his stuff plays up thanks to his plus control. Merritt has issued 1.4 walks per nine innings during his minor league career. His ceiling is as a back-end starter, and he will always have to be fine with his command to succeed. He'll compete for a spot somewhere on the Indians' staff during spring training, with a return to the rotation at Triple-A Columbus likely if he doesn't break camp with the team.

Year	Club (League)	Class	W	L	ERA	G	GS	CG	SV	IP	H	HR	BB	SO	K/9	WHIP	AVG
2014	Carolina (CAR)	HiA	13	3	2.58	25	25	2	0	160	128	12	25	127	7.1	0.95	.216
2015	Akron (EL)	AA	10	7	3.51	22	22	2	0	141	145	8	16	89	5.7	1.14	.269
	Columbus (IL)	AAA	2	0	4.20	5	5	0	0	30	38	1	6	16	4.8	1.47	.309
2016	Columbus (IL)	AAA	11	8	3.70	24	24	2	0	143	156	15	23	92	5.8	1.25	.279
	Cleveland (AL)	MAJ	1	0	1.64	4	1	0	0	11	6	0	0	6	4.9	0.55	.167
Major League Totals			1	0	1.64	4	1	0	0	11	6	0	0	6	4.9	0.55	.167
Minor League Totals			45	31	3.39	120	115	6	1	684	708	50	108	471	6.2	1.19	.267

23 JULIAN MERRYWEATHER, RHP

BA GRADE
45 Risk: High

Born: Oct. 14, 1991. **B-T:** R-R. **Ht.:** 6-4. **Wt.:** 200. **Drafted:** Oklahoma Baptist, 2014 (5th round). **Signed by:** Mark Allen.

Merryweather as a senior helped pitch Oklahoma Baptist to a third-place finish at the 2014 NAIA World Series and then became the highest drafted player in program history when the Indians selected him in the fifth round. After injuries marred his first full season in 2015, he broke out in 2016 by earning all-star honors in the Carolina League and a midseason promotion to Double-A Akron. Merryweather's fastball sits 93-95 mph and regularly touches 97. His changeup, which made significant strides in 2016, and his breaking ball are both above average offerings. In addition to working on his changeup, Merryweather refined his delivery to allow him to repeat it more consistently and better leverage his 6-foot-4 frame. As a result, he threw more strikes and worked well down in the zone more often, helping him create a high number of groundball outs. Merryweather's arsenal gives him a chance to develop into a major league starter, but his stuff would also play well in the bullpen. For now, he'll likely return to the Akron rotation in 2017.

Year	Club (League)	Class	W	L	ERA	G	GS	CG	SV	IP	H	HR	BB	SO	K/9	WHIP	AVG
2014	Mahoning Valley (NYP)	SS	1	2	3.66	13	12	0	0	47	47	2	13	35	6.8	1.29	.260
2015	Lake County (MWL)	LoA	2	3	4.08	21	4	0	1	71	89	6	12	69	8.8	1.43	.299
2016	Lynchburg (CAR)	HiA	8	2	1.03	11	11	0	0	61	47	4	15	58	8.6	1.02	.210
	Akron (EL)	AA	5	4	3.89	13	13	0	0	74	75	6	17	61	7.4	1.24	.255
Minor League Totals			16	11	3.21	58	40	0	1	252	258	18	57	223	8.0	1.25	.259

24 HOBY MILNER, LHP

BA GRADE
40 Risk: Medium

Born: Jan. 13, 1991. **B-T:** L-L. **Ht.:** 6-2. **Wt.:** 165. **Drafted:** Texas, 2012 (7th round). **Signed by:** Steve Cohen (Phillies).

Drafted out of high school by the Nationals, Milner didn't sign and instead excelled at Texas in a swing role from 2010 to 2012, posting a 2.44 ERA in 188 innings. Signed for slot in the seventh round in 2012 by the Phillies, he reached Double-A as a conventional-delivery starter, but the Phillies dropped his arm slot to sidearm in 2015 and made him a reliever. His strikeout rate has spiked in that role, and he's been much more effective. Milner starred in 2016 at Double-A Reading after starting the year in Triple-A, but overall in 65 innings he struck out 76 strikeouts and just 15 walks in 65 innings. He was particularly tough on lefthanded batters in the Eastern League. They hit .230 with no home runs and 27 percent strikeouts against his 88-91 mph fastball and mid-70s curve. The Phillies didn't protect Milner on the 40-man roster and the Indians popped him in the Rule 5 draft, so he must stick on the 25-man roster if healthy or be offered back to Philadelphia. He will compete for a spot in the Cleveland bullpen as a left-on-left reliever.

Year	Club (League)	Class	W	L	ERA	G	GS	CG	SV	IP	H	HR	BB	SO	K/9	WHIP	AVG
2014	Reading (EL)	AA	10	6	4.21	25	25	1	0	143	146	25	56	86	5.4	1.41	.267
2015	Clearwater (FSL)	HiA	0	0	0.00	1	1	0	0	3	2	0	0	3	3.0	0.67	.182
	Reading (EL)	AA	2	1	3.69	29	2	0	0	61	61	6	17	40	5.9	1.28	.268
2016	Reading (EL)	AA	5	3	1.84	38	0	0	5	49	41	3	12	54	9.9	1.08	.224
	Lehigh Valley (IL)	AAA	0	1	4.50	11	0	0	1	16	16	2	3	22	12.4	1.19	.258
Minor League Totals			36	21	3.53	144	66	1	6	484	467	53	151	365	6.8	1.28	.257

25 NELLIE RODRIGUEZ, 1B

BA GRADE
45 Risk: High

Born: June 12, 1994. **B-T:** R-R. **Ht.:** 6-2. **Wt.:** 225. **Drafted:** HS—New York, 2012 (15th round). **Signed by:** Brent Urcheck.

Rodriguez played for Washington High in the Bronx, the same program that produced Manny Ramirez, whom the Indians drafted 21 years before snagging Rodriguez in 2012. He has shown impressive power as a professional, twice leading his league in home runs. He hit 26 at Double-A Akron in 2016, good for third in the Eastern League and among all Indians minor leaguers. Rodriguez produces plenty of raw power and does a good job of getting to it in games. His approach does come with a lot of swing-and-miss and his strikeout rate has gone up for three straight seasons, peaking at 32 percent in 2016. His approach has improved as a professional, however, and he knows how to work a walk. Rodriguez is a bottom-of-the-scale runner and has below-average arm strength, limiting him to first base, where he is an adequate defender. Righthanded-hitting first baseman make for a tough profile, but his power gives him a chance to buck the trend. Rodriguez will advance to Triple-A Columbus in 2016, staying one rung ahead of fast-rising fellow first baseman Bobby Bradley.

Year	Club (League)	Class	AVG	G	AB	R	H	2B	3B	HR	RBI	BB	SO	SB	CS	OBP	SLG
2014	Lake County (MWL)	LoA	.268	130	485	67	130	32	3	22	88	60	142	0	0	.349	.482
2015	Lynchburg (CAR)	HiA	.276	107	391	63	108	32	2	16	82	51	121	1	0	.359	.491
	Akron (EL)	AA	.118	25	93	7	11	2	0	4	14	9	37	0	0	.200	.269
2016	Akron (EL)	AA	.250	132	492	66	123	28	2	26	85	75	186	1	0	.352	.474
Minor League Totals			.253	546	1991	272	503	124	10	82	336	274	641	2	2	.345	.449

26 ROB KAMINSKY, LHP

BA GRADE **45** Risk: High

Born: Sept. 2, 1994. **B-T:** R-L. **Ht.:** 5-11. **Wt.:** 190. **Drafted:** HS—Montvale, N.J., 2013 (1st round). **Signed by:** Sean Moran (Cardinals).

The Cardinals doubled up on lefthanders in the first round of the 2013 draft, selecting Kaminsky nine picks after top choice Marco Gonzales. Kaminsky spent two years with the Cardinals before they dealt him to the Indians at the 2015 trade deadline for Brandon Moss. Kaminsky spent his first full season with Cleveland at Double-A Akron, where he bounced back from an early-season back injury that sidelined him for three weeks in May to finish fourth in the Eastern League with a 3.28 ERA. Kaminsky returned from his injury physically stronger and with a slightly reworked delivery to help him avoid further back problems in the future. His velocity returned as well as he bounced back to his usual 89-92 mph fastball. Kaminsky has lowered his arm slot as a professional, adding deception, but also changing the shape of his breaking ball. Where it once was a 12-to-6 curveball, it is now more of a hard slurve, though he can manipulate the shape well. His changeup gives him a third serviceable pitch. He earns praise for his cerebral approach and does a good job of pounding the strike zone. Kaminsky will look to carry his second-half momentum into 2017 and is on track to advance to Triple-A Columbus.

Year	Club (League)	Class	W	L	ERA	G	GS	CG	SV	IP	H	HR	BB	SO	K/9	WHIP	AVG
2014	Peoria (MWL)	LoA	8	2	1.88	18	18	0	0	101	71	2	31	79	7.1	1.01	.194
2015	Palm Beach (FSL)	HiA	6	5	2.09	17	17	0	0	95	82	0	28	79	7.5	1.16	.228
	Lynchburg (CAR)	HiA	0	1	3.72	2	2	0	0	10	13	0	5	4	3.7	1.86	.342
2016	Akron (EL)	AA	11	7	3.28	25	25	0	0	137	122	7	48	92	6.0	1.24	.241
Minor League Totals			25	18	2.62	70	67	0	0	364	311	10	121	282	7.0	1.19	.229

27 OSCAR GONZALEZ, OF

BA GRADE **50** Risk: Extreme

Born: Jan. 10, 1998. **B-T:** R-R. **Ht.:** 6-2. **Wt.:** 180. **Signed:** Dominican Republic, 2014. **Signed by:** Ramon Pena/Felix Nivar.

The Indians' top target in the 2014 international class, Gonzalez signed for $300,000 that July. He made his U.S. debut in 2016 in the Rookie-level Arizona League and won MVP honors after leading the circuit in home runs (eight) and slugging percentage (.566). His performance earned him a promotion to short-season Mahoning Valley at the end of the season. Gonzalez has both plus power and arm strength. He's more power than pure hitter, and will need to improve both his pitch recognition and his approach at the plate as he faces more advanced pitchers. But he has power to all fields and plenty of bat speed, giving him the tools to develop. His average speed and plus arm give him a chance to play right field, but he primarily played left field in 2016. Wherever Gonzalez ends up defensively, his bat will have to push him through the minor leagues. He will likely advance to full-season ball and low Class A Lake County sometime in 2017 as a 19-year-old.

Year	Club (League)	Class	AVG	G	AB	R	H	2B	3B	HR	RBI	BB	SO	SB	CS	OBP	SLG
2015	Indians (DSL)	R	.203	70	256	25	52	17	1	4	38	19	65	1	3	.262	.324
2016	Indians (AZL)	R	.303	40	145	30	44	10	2	8	26	8	57	4	0	.342	.566
	Mahoning Valley (NYP)	SS	.000	1	3	0	0	0	0	0	0	1	1	0	0	.250	.000
Minor League Totals			.238	111	404	55	96	27	3	12	64	28	123	5	3	.290	.408

28 MICAH MINIARD, RHP

BA GRADE
50 Risk: Extreme

Born: April 12, 1996. **B-T:** R-R. **Ht.:** 6-7. **Wt.:** 195. **Drafted:** HS—Danville, Ky., 2014 (8th round). **Signed by:** Junie Melendez.

Minaird was considered to be the top prep pitcher in Kentucky when the Indians drafted him in the eighth round in 2014. He experienced a breakout in pro ball in 2016 by impressing at short-season Mahoning Valley to earn a promotion to low Class A Lake County for the season's final month. Miniard throws from a three-quarters arm slot, which, along with his 6-foot-7 frame, creates a tough angle for hitters. It also gives cutting action on a fastball that sits 93-94 mph and tops out at 97. He is still learning to harness his fastball and its natural movement to consistently throw quality strikes, but it makes the pitch difficult for hitters to square up. He also throws a low-90s sinker and a breaking ball that is shaped more like a curve but has the velocity of a slider. His changeup remains a work in progress. Miniard has the makings of a starter, but will need to refine his control and develop a viable changeup. He'll return to Lake County in 2017 to work on that.

Year	Club (League)	Class	W	L	ERA	G	GS	CG	SV	IP	H	HR	BB	SO	K/9	WHIP	AVG
2014	Indians (AZL)	R	0	0	5.25	6	0	0	1	12	9	2	5	8	6.0	1.17	.196
2015	Indians (AZL)	R	3	7	3.29	12	10	0	0	63	62	3	16	46	6.6	1.24	.252
	Mahoning Valley (NYP)	SS	0	1	14.29	2	2	0	0	6	11	1	3	1	1.6	2.47	.407
2016	Mahoning Valley (NYP)	SS	1	2	2.38	7	7	0	0	34	34	0	9	28	7.4	1.26	.264
	Lake County (MWL)	LoA	0	2	4.15	8	8	0	0	39	40	2	19	25	5.8	1.51	.263
Minor League Totals			4	12	3.87	35	27	0	1	154	156	8	52	108	6.3	1.35	.260

29 JOSE FERMIN, SS

BA GRADE
50 Risk: Extreme

Born: March 29, 1999. **B-T:** R-R. **Ht.:** 5-11. **Wt.:** 160. **Signed:** Dominican Republic, 2015. **Signed by:** Ramon Pena/Felix Nivar.

Fermin ranked as the No. 28 prospect in the 2015 international signing class, and he stood out for the feel for hitting he showed in the International Prospect League before signing with the Indians for $500,000. He made his pro debut the next year in the Dominican Summer League, though injuries limited his time on the field. Fermin has a mature approach at the plate and good contact skills. He has a good feel for the barrel and hits line drives to all fields. He lacks present strength but doesn't project to hit for much power even as he physically matures. Fermin is a steady defender at shortstop with good instincts. His speed and arm strength are both average to slightly above-average, giving him a chance to stay at shortstop. While Fermin isn't overly flashy, his all-around skill set makes him an intriguing prospect. He will likely make his U.S. debut in the Rookie-level Arizona League as an 18-year-old in 2017.

Year	Club (League)	Class	AVG	G	AB	R	H	2B	3B	HR	RBI	BB	SO	SB	CS	OBP	SLG
2016	Indians (DSL)	R	.224	16	58	5	13	4	2	0	8	7	11	2	2	.303	.362
Minor League Totals			.224	16	58	5	13	4	2	0	8	7	11	2	2	.303	.362

30 MARCOS GONZALEZ, SS

BA GRADE
50 Risk: Extreme

Born: Oct. 22, 1999. **B-T:** R-R. **Ht.:** 6-0. **Wt.:** 160. **Signed:** Dominican Republic, 2016. **Signed by:** Koby Perez/Felix Nivar/Marcelino Vallejo.

The Indians signed Gonzalez for $250,000 in 2016, after he made significant improvements as one of the top performers in the Dominican Prospect League in the year leading up to his signing. He is a steady player with a chance to have about average tools across the board. He has a good feel for the barrel and a short, flat swing geared for hitting line drives. His power is mostly to the gaps now, with the chance to grow into more as he physically matures. He has average speed and arm strength. He already has good defensive instincts and soft hands, giving him a good chance to stick at shortstop. Gonzalez earns praise for his confidence and advanced tool set. He will likely make his pro debut in 2017 in the Dominican Summer League.

Year	Club (League)	Class	AVG	G	AB	R	H	2B	3B	HR	RBI	BB	SO	SB	CS	OBP	SLG
2016	Did not play—Signed 2017 contract																

Colorado Rockies

BY TRACY RINGOLSBY

The transformation has been quick, but virtually unnoticed from afar. With the emergence of a new leadership approach in Colorado two offseasons ago, the Rockies' focus returned to the basics of baseball.

No more gimmicks. No more moaning about altitude. No more attempts to reinvent the wheel.

And look what has happened.

A franchise built on scouting and player development finds itself so confident in the talent it has developed—and the talent that is on the way—that it signed free agent Ian Desmond, not to patch a hole, but to play first base and bring playoff experience.

In other words, the Rockies believe they will be a factor in the National League West in 2017.

It all starts with the homegrown nucleus and confidence in the farm system.

The Rockies will go to spring training with an eight-man lineup in which five of the eight projected regulars will be homegrown: third baseman Nolan Arenado, shortstop Trevor Story, left fielder David Dahl, center fielder Charlie Blackmon and catcher Tom Murphy. At least three members of the rotation will be players originally signed and developed by the Rockies—Jon Gray, Tyler Anderson and Chad Bettis—and the farm system should provide other pieces as well, such as right-hander Jeff Hoffman and lefty Kyle Freeland.

At 27, Bettis—diagnosed in the offseason with testicular cancer but planning to be ready for Opening Day—is the elder statesman. Gray posted a Rockies-record 16 strikeouts in a September shutout, while fellow rookie Anderson, a 2011 first-round pick who didn't even rank among the Top 30 Prospects a year ago, recorded a 3.54 ERA in 19 starts after an injury-plagued tour of the minor leagues.

And there is more on the way.

Scouting director Bill Schmidt, long praised for his ability to uncover young hitting talent, is now also earning respect for the ability of his staff to find quality big league pitchers.

What a difference a change in organizational philosophy can make. With the hiring of Jeff Bridich as general manager and the departure of Bill Geivett from the front office, the Rockies' approach to pitching development changed drastically. For one thing, the Rockies no longer fear pitchers throwing curveballs at altitude. Director of pitching operations Mark Wiley encouraged pitchers throughout the organization to refine the pitch selection they felt most comfortable with.

Pitching coach Steve Foster and bullpen coach

Trevor Story established a National League record for home runs by a rookie shortstop

TOP PROSPECTS OF THE DECADE

Year	Player, Pos.	2016 Org
2007	Ian Stewart, 3b	Did not play
2008	Troy Tulowitzki, ss	Blue Jays
2009	Dexter Fowler, of	Cubs
2010	Tyler Matzek, lhp	Rockies
2011	Tyler Matzek, lhp	Rockies
2012	Drew Pomeranz, lhp	Red Sox
2013	Nolan Arenado, 3b	Rockies
2014	Jon Gray, rhp	Rockies
2015	David Dahl, of	Rockies
2016	Jon Gray, rhp	Rockies

Darren Holmes are heading into the third year of stressing that pitchers go back to basics.

The Rockies are building a pitching staff around power pitchers focused on doing what they do best, regardless of the environment. The 4.79 ERA the rotation compiled in 2016 was the ninth-best in the franchise's 24-year history.

The Rockies, however, now have the type of depth to find rotation help primarily from within. Righthanders German Marquez and Antonio Senzatela should contend for innings in 2017.

The NL West has two mega-franchises at the top—the Dodgers and Giants—but the Rockies have more than enough offense to do the job if the pitching develops. The ingredients for Colorado to contend in 2017 and beyond are in place, and they came primarily from within the organization.

ORGANIZATION OVERVIEW

General manager: Jeff Bridich. **Farm director:** Zach Wilson. **Scouting director:** Bill Schmidt.

Class	Team	League	W	L	PCT	Finish	Manager
Majors	Colorado Rockies	National	75	87	.463	9th (15)	Walt Weiss
Triple-A	Albuquerque Isotopes	Pacific Coast	71	72	.497	7th (16)	Glenallen Hill
Double-A	Hartford Yard Goats	Eastern	74	67	.525	6th (12)	Darin Everson
High Class A	* Modesto Nuts	California	60	80	.429	8th (10)	Fred Ocasio
Low Class A	Asheville Tourists	South Atlantic	66	72	.478	11th (14)	Warren Schaeffer
Short-season	Boise Hawks	Northwest	33	43	.434	5th (8)	Andy Gonzalez
Rookie	Grand Junction Rockies	Pioneer	36	39	.480	6th (8)	Frank Gonzales
Overall 2016 Minor League Record			340	373	.477	21st (30)	

* Affiliate moves to Lancaster (California) in 2017

THIS YEAR'S TOP 30

No.	Player, Pos.	Grade/Risk
1.	Brendan Rodgers, ss	65/High
2.	Riley Pint, rhp	65/Extreme
3.	Jeff Hoffman, rhp	55/Medium
4.	Raimel Tapia, of	55/Medium
5.	German Marquez, rhp	55/Medium
6.	Ryan Castellani, rhp	55/High
7.	Tom Murphy, c	50/Medium
8.	Kyle Freeland, lhp	50/Medium
9.	Ryan McMahon, 3b	50/High
10.	Antonio Senzatela, rhp	50/High
11.	Peter Lambert, rhp	50/High
12.	Dom Nunez, c	50/high
13.	Jordan Patterson, of/1b	45/Medium
14.	Garrett Hampson, ss	45/Medium
15.	Forrest Wall, 2b/of	50/High
16.	Colton Welker, 3b	50/High
17.	Yency Almonte, rhp	45/Medium
18.	Sam Howard, lhp	45/Medium
19.	David Hill, rhp	50/High
20.	Tyler Nevin, 3b	50/Extreme
21.	Mike Nikorak, rhp	50/Extreme
22.	Robert Tyler, rhp	50/Extreme
23.	Ben Bowden, lhp	45/High
24.	Pedro Gonzalez, of	50/Extreme
25.	Parker French, rhp	45/High
26.	Harrison Musgrave, lhp	40/Medium
27.	Sam Moll, lhp	40/Medium
28.	Brian Mundell, 1b	45/High
29.	Manuel Melendez, of	50/Extreme
30.	Jerry Vasto, lhp	40/Medium

LAST YEAR'S TOP 30

No.	Player, Pos.	Status
1.	Jon Gray, rhp	Majors
2.	David Dahl, of	Majors
3.	Brendan Rodgers, ss	No. 1
4.	Jeff Hoffman, rhp	No. 3
5.	Ryan McMahon, 3b	No. 9
6.	Kyle Freeland, lhp	No. 8
7.	Tom Murphy, c	No. 7
8.	Trevor Story, ss	Majors
9.	Antonio Senzatela, rhp	No. 10
10.	Raimel Tapia, of	No. 4
11.	Forrest Wall, 2b	No. 15
12.	Miguel Castro, rhp	Majors
13.	Mike Nikorak, rhp	No. 21
14.	Peter Lambert, rhp	No. 11
15.	Ryan Castellani, rhp	No. 6
16.	Dom Nunez, c	No. 12
17.	Carlos Estevez, rhp	Majors
18.	Kevin Padlo, 3b	(Rays)
19.	Jairo Diaz, rhp	Dropped out
20.	Jordan Patterson, of/1b	No. 13
21.	Jesus Tinoco, rhp	Dropped out
22.	Sam Moll, lhp	No. 27
23.	Tyler Nevin, 3b	No. 20
24.	Yency Almonte, rhp	No. 17
25.	Sam Howard, lhp	No. 18
26.	Cristhian Adames, ss	Majors
27.	Wes Rogers, of	Dropped out
28.	Jonathan Piron, ss/2b	Dropped out
29.	Pedro Gonzalez, ss	No. 24
30.	David Hill, rhp	No. 19

BEST TOOLS

Best Hitter for Average	Raimel Tapia
Best Power Hitter	Brendan Rodgers
Best Strike-Zone Discipline	Garrett Hampson
Fastest Baserunner	Wes Rogers
Best Athlete	Ryan McMahon
Best Fastball	Riley Pint
Best Curveball	Jeff Hoffman
Best Slider	Kyle Freeland
Best Changeup	Riley Pint
Best Control	Kyle Freeland
Best Defensive Catcher	Dom Nunez
Best Defensive Infielder	Garrett Hampson
Best Infield Arm	Jose Gomez
Best Defensive Outfielder	Raimel Tapia
Best Outfield Arm	Sam Hilliard

PROJECTED 2020 LINEUP

Catcher	Tom Murphy
First Base	Ian Desmond
Second Base	Brendan Rogers
Third Base	Nolan Arenado
Shortstop	Trevor Story
Left Field	Charlie Blackmon
Center Field	David Dahl
Right Field	Raimel Tapia
No. 1 Starter	Jon Gray
No. 2 Starter	Riley Pint
No. 3 Starter	Jeff Hoffman
No. 4 Starter	German Marquez
No. 5 Starter	Tyler Anderson
Closer	Antonio Senzatela

MINOR LEAGUE DEPTH CHART

COLORADO ROCKIES

TOP 2017 ROOKIE: Tom Murphy, c. He took a giant step forward in 2016 during the final two months at Triple-A, and the catching job is open.
BREAKOUT PROSPECT: Brian Mundell, 1b. He showed definite power and big-time leadership in his full-season debut.
SLEEPER: Jesus Tinoco, rhp. Picked up in the Troy Tulowtizki deal with the Blue Jays, he has the arm to dazzle after a year of adjusting to new organization.

SOURCE OF TOP 30 TALENT			
Homegrown	27	Acquired	3
College	13	Trades	3
Junior college	0	Rule 5 draft	0
High school	10	Independent leagues	0
Nondrafted free agents	0	Free agents/waivers	0
International	4		

LF
Michael Tacuhman

CF
Ramiel Tapia (4)
Wes Rogers
Omar Carrizales
Yeikel Blandin

RF
Pedro Gonzalez (24)
Manuel Melendez (29)

3B
Ryan McMahon (9)
Colton Welker (16))
Tyler Nevin (20)
Josh Fuentes

SS
Brendan Rogers (1)
Garrett Hampson (14)
Carlos Herrera

2B
Forrest Wall (15)
Jose Gomez
Patrick Valaika
Jonathan Piron

1B
Jordan Patterson (13)
Brian Mundell (28)
Stephen Cardullo

C
Tom Murphy (7)
Dom Nunez (12)

LHP

LHSP	LHRP
Kyle Freeland (8)	Ben Bowden (23)
Sam Howard (18)	Sam Moll (27)
Harrison Musgrave (26)	Jerry Vasto (30)
Jack Wynkoop	
Luis Noguera	

RHP

RHSP	RHRP
Riley Pint (2)	Matt Carasiti
Jeff Hoffman (3)	Salvador Justo
German Marquez (5)	Jairo Diaz
Ryan Castellani (6)	Shane Carle
Antonio Senzatela (10)	Ryan Gonzalez
Peter Lambert (11)	Alexander Guillen
Yency Almonte (17)	Julian Fernandez
David Hill (19)	
Mike Nikorak (21)	
Robert Tyler (22)	
Parker French (25)	
Jesus Tinoco	
Zach Jemiola	
Antonio Santos	
Anderson Amarista	

DRAFT ANALYSIS

2016

BEST PURE HITTER: SS Garrett Hampson (3) hit .303 in three seasons at Long Beach State, which plays at Blair Field, a notorious pitcher's park. He has good hands to go with a solid hitting approach that helped him hit .301 in his pro debut. 3B Colton Welker (4) also has good hands and some present strength.

BEST POWER HITTER: With a sturdy 6-foot-4, 225-pound frame, OF Willie Abreu (6) has plus raw power and no-doubt right field tools.

FASTEST RUNNER: Hampson always had at least plus speed but never stole more than 23 bases in a season at Long Beach State. He stole 36 bags in 40 attempts this summer in his debut and has the speed to play center field if he winds up in a super utility role.

BEST DEFENSIVE PLAYER: Hampson lacks only a true plus arm at shortstop. He has a quick transfer, average arm, soft hands and infield actions. He profiles a bit better at second base than short, where he made 20 errors in his debut.

BEST FASTBALL: RHP Riley Pint (1) has to be on the short list of best fastballs ever by a prep pitcher, hitting 100 mph regularly this spring and sitting in the mid- to upper 90s in his pro debut.

BEST SECONDARY PITCH: Pint's changeup gives him a true plus secondary pitch, and his breaking ball, which the Rockies call a power slurve, gives him a third potential plus pitch. He'll try to hone it into a true curve.

BEST PRO DEBUT: Hampson led the short-season Northwest League in stolen bases (36) and walks (48) while hitting .301/.404/.441. Welker debuted at Rookie-level Grand Junction and hit .329/.366/.490, solid even for the offense-first Pioneer League.

BEST ATHLETE: Hampson has excellent baseball athleticism, lacking only excellent strength. Pint's athleticism stands out for pitchers and helps him throw strikes despite his high-octane stuff and lack of experience.

MOST INTRIGUING BACKGROUND: Rangy 3B/SS Taylor Snyder (13) is the son of ex-big leaguer Cory Snyder, who was the fourth overall pick in the 1984 draft. RHP John Hendry (32), who didn't sign, is the son of ex-Cubs GM and current Yankees special assistant Jim Hendry.

CLOSEST TO THE MAJORS: LHP Ben Bowden (2) made five starts for Vanderbilt in the spring but pitched better out of the bullpen and should move quickly in that role, thanks to his 92-95 mph fastball. He's also a competitor with the toughness needed to put bad outings behind him, a requirement for a future closer.

BEST LATE-ROUND PICK: An Ivy Leaguer drafted out of Columbia, RHP George Thanopoulos (27) has one of the firmer fastballs in the Rockies'

draft class (non-Riley Pint division), sitting at 93-95 mph in shorter bursts this summer.

THE ONE WHO GOT AWAY: RHP Troy Bacon (37), who started his college career at Florida, didn't sign after striking out 53 in 35 innings in the Northwoods League over the summer. He's back at Santa Fe (Fla.) JC. The Rockies also made a run at OF Michael Toglia (35), a switch-hitting, rangy center fielder who went to UCLA.

2015

SS Brendan Rodgers (1) had a strong first full season, as did polished RHP Peter Lambert (2). RHP Mike Nikorak (1) has proven extremely raw. Polished collegians LHP Jack Wynkoop (6) and 1B Brian Mundell (7) have been strong performers.

GRADE: B

2014

LHP Kyle Freeland (1) and RHP Ryan Castellani (2), plus fast-moving LHPs Sam Howard (3) and Harrison Musgrave (8), provide strong pitching depth to the system. 2B Forrest Wall (1s) heads a more modest class of hitters.

GRADE: B

2013

RHP Jon Gray (1) looks primed to be a front-of-the-rotation force. 3B Ryan McMahon (2) found the going tough at Double-A, while intriguing sleeper OF Jordan Patterson (4) and SS Pat Valaika (9) finished the year in Colorado.

GRADE: B

TOP DRAFT PICKS OF THE DECADE

Year	Player, Pos.	2016 Org
2007	Casey Weathers, rhp	Indians
2008	Christian Friedrich, lhp	Padres
2009	Tyler Matzek, lhp	Rockies
2010	Kyle Parker, of	Reds
2011	Tyler Anderson, lhp	Rockies
2012	David Dahl, of	Rockies
2013	Jon Gray, rhp	Rockies
2014	Kyle Freeland, lhp	Rockies
2015	Brendan Rodgers, ss	Rockies
2016	Riley Pint, rhp	Rockies

LARGEST BONUSES IN CLUB HISTORY

Brendan Rodgers, 2015	$5,500,000
Riley Pint, 2016	$4,800,000
Jon Gray, 2013	$4,800,000
Tyler Matzek, 2009	$3,900,000
Greg Reynolds, 2006	$3,200,000

1 BRENDAN RODGERS, SS/2B

Born: Aug. 6, 1996. **B-T:** R-R. **Ht.:** 6-0. **Wt.:** 185.
Drafted: HS—Lake Mary, Fla., 2015 (1st round).
Signed by: John Cedarburg.

Rodgers grew up in a family that had a focus on soccer, but his attention turned to baseball at the age of 5. His best friend's father, Ralph Nema, introduced Rodgers to baseball and coached him a good part of his youth. He was a multi-sport participant during his youth, but in kindergarten he proclaimed that he would be a baseball player when he grew up. He certainly had big league touches to his development. While Nema was his youth coach, former big leaguers Dante Bichette, an original Rockies outfielder, and all-star closer Tom Gordon also coached Rodgers. He was considered the top prospect in the 2015 draft but slipped to the Rockies with the No. 3 pick when the two teams ahead of them opted for college shortstops. The Diamondbacks took Vanderbilt's Dansby Swanson at No. 1 and the Astros selected Louisiana State's Alex Bregman at No. 2, and they both reached the majors in 2016. The Rockies signed Rodgers to a franchise-record $5.5 million bonus. His pro beginning was a challenge. He battled nagging foot, hamstring and hip injuries at Rookie-level Grand Junction in 2015, limiting him to 37 games and leading scouts who hadn't seen him as an amateur to question his attitude and potential. At low Class A Asheville in 2016, Rodgers reaffirmed his elite status. He finished third in the South Atlantic League in home runs (19) and fourth in slugging (.480) despite being one of only 14 players in the SAL who was younger than 20.

Don't be misled by the fact Rodgers saw time at second and third base as well as shortstop in 2016. The Rockies still feel he has a strong future at shortstop, but the front office is trying to create flexibility with its prospects so that they will be able to fill various holes. With Rodgers' athleticism and power potential he could fit anywhere in the infield. He has elite bat speed and good feel for the bat head, and he punished fastballs before SAL pitchers adjusted and fed him a steady diet of offspeed stuff. He made adjustments but will have to do so against quality sliders he rarely saw as an amateur. He has a polished approach for such a young hitter with solid plate discipline. With strength and conditioning in the offseason, he will add strength and durability. He has quality actions at shortstop and a solid, at times plus, arm that will improve in its consistency with added strength. Rodgers does not have the speed of a player who would be considered a basestealing

BA GRADE

65 Risk: High

SCOUTING GRADES

Batting: 60.
Power: 60.
Speed: 50.
Defense: 50.
Arm: 55.

Based on 20-80 scouting scale and future projection rather than present tools.

TONY FARLOW

threat, but his athletic ability and instincts give him surprising range.

The Rockies see Rodgers as an eventual all-star and feel confident he can attain that goal at shortstop if he can stay healthy. A hamstring problem landed him on the disabled list in May 2016, and he went through a dead-arm period in his first full season that he must learn from. The Rockies will allow Rodgers to force the issue when he is ready—they have Trevor Story in Colorado, and he just set an NL record for homers by a rookie shortstop—but the next step is high Class A Modesto.

Year	Club (League)	Class	AVG	G	AB	R	H	2B	3B	HR	RBI	BB	SO	SB	CS	OBP	SLG
2015	Grand Junction (PIO)	R	.273	37	143	22	39	8	2	3	20	15	37	4	3	.340	.420
2016	Asheville (SAL)	LoA	.281	110	442	73	124	31	0	19	73	35	98	6	3	.342	.480
Minor League Totals			.279	147	585	95	163	39	2	22	93	50	135	10	6	.341	.465

2 RILEY PINT, RHP

Born: Nov. 6, 1997. **B-T:** R-R. **Ht.:** 6-4. **Wt.:** 195. **Drafted:** HS—Overland Park, Kan., 2016 (1st round). **Signed by:** Brett Baldwin.

Pint was rated the top prep pitching prospect in the 2016 draft and went fourth overall to the Rockies, who signed him for $4.8 million to forgo a Louisiana State commitment. Working to streamline his mechanics, the Rockies limited Pint's workload at Rookie-level Grand Junction, which led to him never working more than five innings. Athleticism and arm speed give Pint an overpowering fastball that has reached 100 mph and often parks at 97. What makes him special is pairing that with two potential plus offspeed pitches. His breaking pitch, a low-80s power curveball, features natural spin and late break. Once Pint can get a consistent release point, it will be a pitch that can set up his arsenal. His changeup also has plus potential with a lot of action, but he still needs to gain consistency. Command issues are being addressed with subtle adjustments to his delivery. Pint showed his ability to adapt quickly during instructional league, when the Rockies worked to improve his balance and direction to the plate. He fits in well with teammates, keeping a low profile and showing an excellent work ethic. Pint has the type of arm to be a legitimate No. 1 starter, but Colorado will be need to be patient with such a high-risk talent. He will start at low Class A Asheville in 2017.

Year	Club (League)	Class	W	L	ERA	G	GS	CG	SV	IP	H	HR	BB	SO	K/9	WHIP	AVG
2016	Grand Junction (PIO)	R	1	5	5.35	11	11	0	0	37	43	2	23	36	8.8	1.78	.307
Minor League Totals			1	5	5.35	11	11	0	0	37	43	2	23	36	8.8	1.78	.307

3 JEFF HOFFMAN, RHP

Born: Jan. 1, 1993. **B-T:** R-R. **Ht.:** 6-5. **Wt.:** 225. **Drafted:** East Carolina, 2014 (1st round). **Signed by:** Chris Kline (Blue Jays).

The key player among the three prospects the Blue Jays sent to the Rockies for shortstop Troy Tulowitzki in a 2015 deadline deal, Hoffman was Toronto's first pick—ninth overall—in 2014. He had Tommy John surgery shortly before that draft, delaying his pro debut to 2015. He steadily climbed the minor league ladder and made his big league debut in September 2016. Hoffman showed signs of fatigue when he debuted with the Rockies, and he surpassed 150 innings for the first time. During the season he showed a live fastball with sinking life that sits in the 93-96 mph range and reaches 99. Hoffman has an excellent plus curveball but tends to rely on it too much. His slider is a nice secondary breaking pitch, and his changeup is solid. His strikeout rate jumped significantly in the minors, but to keep that up in the big leagues, he has to take better ownership of the inner part of the plate and use any on his four pitches without hesitation. Hoffman has a chance to earn a rotation spot in Denver for 2017. With his power and pitch mix, Hoffman should grow in a solid mid-rotation starter with an inner confidence that bodes well for his success at Coors Field.

Year	Club (League)	Class	W	L	ERA	G	GS	CG	SV	IP	H	HR	BB	SO	K/9	WHIP	AVG
2015	Dunedin (FSL)	HiA	3	3	3.21	11	11	0	0	56	59	4	15	38	6.1	1.32	.284
	New Hampshire (EL)	AA	0	0	1.54	2	2	0	0	12	9	0	2	8	6.2	0.94	.214
	New Britain (EL)	AA	2	2	3.22	7	7	0	0	36	27	3	10	29	7.2	1.02	.209
2016	Albuquerque (PCL)	AAA	6	9	4.02	22	22	0	0	119	117	11	44	124	9.4	1.36	.261
	Colorado (NL)	MAJ	0	4	4.88	8	6	0	0	31	37	7	17	22	6.3	1.72	.287
Major League Totals			0	4	4.88	8	6	0	0	31	37	7	17	22	6.3	1.72	.287
Minor League Totals			11	14	3.56	42	42	0	0	223	212	18	71	199	8.0	1.27	.256

4 RAIMEL TAPIA, OF

Born: Feb. 4, 1994. **B-T:** L-L. **Ht.:** 6-2. **Wt.:** 165. **Signed:** Dominican Republic, 2010. **Signed by:** Rolando Fernandez/Jhonathan Leyba/Hector Roa.

Signed for $175,000 in 2010, Tapia has hit at each level in his development. After taking it one level at a time in his first three pro seasons, he moved from Double-A Hartford to Triple-A Albuquerque to a September callup in 2016 and never slowed down. He hit .328 in the minors in 2016 and owns a career .317 average. Tapia is an offensive threat and run-creator who plays with confidence and backs it up. Don't get caught up in the way he crouches in two-strike situations. He does not have that typical rise before he swings in that situation, instead staying low and maintaining the ability to drive the ball into gaps despite the unique approach. It helps him become more focused on the strike zone in those situations. Tapia has the speed and range to play center field—he earns average grades—and his above-average arm will play on an outfield corner. He has realized the importance of defense and has become more focused on his outfield work, such as hitting the cutoff man, during batting practice. Despite his above-average speed, Tapia is an inefficient basestealer. He should force his way to the big leagues to stay in 2017. His athleticism gives the Rockies options with where to play him in the outfield. They would like to see him adjust to center field, where he is working to get better breaks.

Year	Club (League)	Class	AVG	G	AB	R	H	2B	3B	HR	RBI	BB	SO	SB	CS	OBP	SLG
2014	Asheville (SAL)	LoA	.326	122	481	93	157	32	1	9	72	35	90	33	16	.382	.453
2015	Modesto (CAL)	HiA	.305	131	544	74	166	34	9	12	71	24	105	26	10	.333	.467
2016	Hartford (EL)	AA	.323	104	424	79	137	20	5	8	34	25	49	17	14	.363	.450
	Albuquerque (PCL)	AAA	.346	24	104	14	36	5	5	0	14	2	12	6	3	.355	.490
	Colorado (NL)	MAJ	.263	22	38	4	10	0	0	0	3	2	11	3	0	.293	.263
Major League Totals			.263	22	38	4	10	0	0	0	3	2	11	3	0	.293	.263
Minor League Totals			.317	577	2296	373	728	126	30	37	308	147	363	120	71	.363	.446

5 GERMAN MARQUEZ, RHP

BA GRADE
55 Risk: Medium

Born: Feb. 2, 1995. **B-T:** R-R. **Ht.:** 6-1. **Wt.:** 185. **Drafted:** Venezuela, 2011. **Signed by:** Ronnie Blanco (Rays).

Signed by the Rays in 2011 out of Venezuela for $225,000, Marquez was the prime player the Rockies received after the 2015 season when they traded Corey Dickerson to Tampa Bay. Marquez repaid the Rockies' confidence with a breakout 2016. He made the jump from Double-A Hartford to Triple-A Albuquerque to the big leagues in 2016, beating the Cardinals with five quality innings to win his first start. Marquez has plus velocity and it comes effortlessly at a consistent 94-96 mph and touches 98. The ball comes out of his hand with velocity and never fades. Marquez's solid three-pitch assortment includes a curveball that flashes plus and has good spin. His 2016 focus was to tighten it up, which he did. That allows his curveball to play better at the mile-high altitude of Coors Field. His changeup still needs work but has good velocity differential from his fastball. He has shown an ability to pitch inside and use his changeup even when behind in the count. Most impressively, he reduced his walk rate in 2016 by more than a half walk per nine innings. His command improved with growing confidence in his ability. With his assortment and command, Marquez will challenge Jeff Hoffman to claim the open spot in the big league rotation. He has the stuff to be an upper-tier No. 3 starter.

Year	Club (League)	Class	W	L	ERA	G	GS	CG	SV	IP	H	HR	BB	SO	K/9	WHIP	AVG
2014	Bowling Green (MWL)	LoA	5	7	3.21	22	18	0	0	98	83	5	29	95	8.7	1.14	.228
2015	Charlotte (FSL)	HiA	7	13	3.56	26	23	0	0	139	147	6	29	104	6.7	1.27	.272
2016	Hartford (EL)	AA	9	6	2.85	21	21	0	0	136	124	9	33	126	8.4	1.16	.245
	Albuquerque (PCL)	AAA	2	0	4.35	5	5	0	0	31	30	5	6	29	8.4	1.16	.254
	Colorado (NL)	MAJ	1	1	5.23	6	3	0	0	21	28	2	6	15	6.5	1.65	.326
Major League Totals			1	1	5.23	6	3	0	0	21	28	2	6	15	6.5	1.65	.326
Minor League Totals			25	33	3.63	101	85	0	0	491	473	31	137	421	7.7	1.24	.253

6 RYAN CASTELLANI, RHP

BA GRADE
55 Risk: High

Born: April 1, 1996. **B-T:** R-R. **Ht.:** 6-3. **Wt.:** 190. **Drafted:** HS—Phoenix, 2014 (2nd round). **Signed by:** Chris Forbes.

After drafting Castellani 48th overall in 2014, the Rockies came up with a $1.1 million bonus offer to lure him away from an Arizona State scholarship. They were extremely protective of his workload his first two seasons of pro ball but in 2016 allowed him to work deeper into games. He averaged nearly 6.2 innings per outing over 26 starts at high Class A Modesto en route to being named the California League's No. 1 prospect. Castellani has two prime ingredients in a two-seam fastball with 93-95 mph velocity at its best and good sinking movement and a changeup that mimics his fastball in terms of slot and action. His slider hasn't been as consistent as it needs to be, but it can be plus as well. It gives him that three-pitch mix to succeed as a starter and helped him lead the Cal League in strikeouts while remaining effective the second and third time through batting orders. Castellani has the quick arm action and a clean delivery that limits stress on his shoulder. Managers and scouts appreciate his mound presence and competitive makeup that pushes him that extra step. Castellani can get overlooked by the abundance of quality arms the Rockies have on the verge of the big leagues. He made sure he wouldn't get left behind with his Cal League performance. A potential No. 3 starter, he is headed for Double-A Hartford in 2017.

Year	Club (League)	Class	W	L	ERA	G	GS	CG	SV	IP	H	HR	BB	SO	K/9	WHIP	AVG
2014	Tri-City (NWL)	SS	1	2	3.65	10	10	0	0	37	35	2	9	25	6.1	1.19	.248
2015	Asheville (SAL)	LoA	2	7	4.45	27	27	0	0	113	134	5	29	94	7.5	1.44	.291
2016	Modesto (CAL)	HiA	7	8	3.81	26	26	1	0	168	156	8	50	142	7.6	1.23	.248
Minor League Totals			10	17	4.02	63	63	1	0	318	325	15	88	261	7.4	1.30	.264

7 TOM MURPHY, C

BA GRADE
50 Risk: Medium

Born: April 13, 1991. **B-T:** R-R. **Ht.:** 6-1. **Wt.:** 220. **Drafted:** Buffalo, 2012 (3rd round).
Signed by: Ed Santa.

A September callup in 2015 and 2016, Murphy has impressed with eight homers in 79 at-bats. Healthy since an injury-plagued 2014 that included season-ending shoulder surgery, Murphy earned his 2016 callup with an explosive second half at Triple-A Albuquerque. He raised his average 119 points and hit 11 home runs in the final two months. The Rockies see Murphy as a plus offensive player who can hit in the bottom of the lineup while he adjusts to life in the big leagues. He's a rhythm hitter who can get hot and has above-average power thanks to his great strength. What has the Rockies most excited is the work Murphy has put in to improve his defense. He has softened his hands in his receiving, which helps him frame pitches. He has an above-average arm to slow down the running game. Some scouts worry about a lack of agility behind the plate due to his muscular frame, and that at times slows his pop times on throws to second base as well. He can still fine-tune his defense, and seems eager to do that. The time is now for Murphy, who convinced the Rockies he is ready to compete for the regular big league job with Tony Wolters. If everything comes together, Murphy has the potential to be an offensively potent catcher with above-average defensive ability.

Year	Club (League)	Class	AVG	G	AB	R	H	2B	3B	HR	RBI	BB	SO	SB	CS	OBP	SLG
2014	Tulsa (TL)	AA	.213	27	94	16	20	4	0	5	15	14	27	0	0	.321	.415
2015	New Britain (EL)	AA	.249	72	265	36	66	17	1	13	44	23	80	5	2	.320	.468
	Albuquerque (PCL)	AAA	.271	33	129	19	35	9	2	7	19	5	43	0	1	.301	.535
	Colorado (NL)	MAJ	.257	11	35	5	9	1	0	3	9	4	10	0	0	.333	.543
2016	Albuquerque (PCL)	AAA	.327	80	303	53	99	26	7	19	59	16	78	1	1	.361	.647
	Colorado (NL)	MAJ	.273	21	44	8	12	2	0	5	13	4	19	1	0	.347	.659
Major League Totals			.266	32	79	13	21	3	0	8	22	8	29	1	0	.341	.608
Minor League Totals			.282	367	1360	214	384	100	15	72	258	113	383	11	10	.347	.537

8 KYLE FREELAND, LHP

BA GRADE
50 Risk: Medium

Born: May 14, 1993. **B-T:** L-L. **Ht.:** 6-3. **Wt.:** 170. **Drafted:** Evansville, 2014 (1st round).
Signed by: Scott Corman.

The eighth pick overall in 2014—one spot ahead of Jeff Hoffman—Freeland embraced the idea of pitching in Colorado as a hometown hero. The Denver native was born 39 days after the first regular-season game in Rockies history. Limited in 2015 first by left shoulder fatigue and then surgery to remove a bone chip in his left elbow, Freeland returned fully healthy in 2016 and worked 162 innings between Double-A Hartford and Triple-A Albuquerque. He can pitch to the corners with a fastball that sits in the low 90s and touches 97 mph. His eye-opening pitch is a slider with tilt, which many scouts call a wipeout slider at its best, and he also throws a below-average curveball. The big step for Freeland will be becoming most consistent with his changeup and slider, which at times comes out like a cutter. He took a major step forward in terms of mental maturity in 2016 by learning to focus pitch to pitch and not getting over-amped after a mistake. He commands his pitches well thanks to excellent athleticism that shows up on defense and even at the plate. Freeland will be in the mix for an open spot on the big league staff in 2017 and could also claim a lefty reliever spot to begin his Rockies career. He has the stuff and durability to eventually move into the rotation, but that won't come until he solidifies a third offering.

Year	Club (League)	Class	W	L	ERA	G	GS	CG	SV	IP	H	HR	BB	SO	K/9	WHIP	AVG
2014	Grand Junction (PIO)	R	1	0	1.56	5	5	0	0	17	16	0	2	15	7.8	1.04	.254
	Asheville (SAL)	LoA	2	0	0.83	5	5	0	0	22	14	1	4	18	7.5	0.83	.179
2015	Grand Junction (PIO)	R	0	0	0.00	2	2	0	0	7	2	0	2	9	11.6	0.57	.087
	Modesto (CAL)	HiA	3	2	4.76	7	7	0	0	40	48	5	8	19	4.3	1.41	.308
2016	Hartford (EL)	AA	5	7	3.87	14	14	0	0	88	84	9	25	51	5.2	1.23	.254
	Albuquerque (PCL)	AAA	6	3	3.91	12	12	0	0	74	81	7	19	57	7.0	1.36	.284
Minor League Totals			17	12	3.49	45	45	0	0	248	245	22	60	169	6.1	1.23	.262

9 RYAN McMAHON, 3B/1B

Born: Dec. 14, 1994. **B-T:** L-R. **Ht.:** 6-2. **Wt.:** 185. **Drafted:** HS—Santa Ana, Calif., 2013 (2nd round). **Signed by:** Jon Lukens.

Lured away from a scholarship to Southern California for $1,327,600 as a 2013 second-round pick, McMahon moved off third base and began working at first base in 2016 at Double-A Hartford. It's part of an organizational play to create multiple options for prospects so they don't get blocked at the big league level. A quarterback in high school, McMahon handled the new position well. McMahon struggled offensively for the first time in his life in 2016, which isn't all bad. A competitor, he did show life in the second half, even as Hartford endured a season-long road trip due to construction issues that kept the team from ever playing a true home game.

BA GRADE
50 Risk: High

McMahon will have to adjust at the plate and drive the ball the opposite way, but he does have a bit of a hook in his swing, which makes him susceptible to quality fastballs. He still has average to above-average power. A strong athlete though a below-average runner, he has soft hands and improved footwork at first base. He made 17 errors in 67 games at third. The expectations remain high for McMahon, who dealt with Double-A struggles similar to those experienced by shortstop Trevor Story. McMahon likely will return to Hartford to open 2017, but the Rockies won't hesitate promoting him to Triple-A Albuquerque quickly if he responds.

Year	Club (League)	Class	AVG	G	AB	R	H	2B	3B	HR	RBI	BB	SO	SB	CS	OBP	SLG
2014	Asheville (SAL)	LoA	.282	126	482	93	136	46	3	18	102	54	143	8	5	.358	.502
2015	Modesto (CAL)	HiA	.300	132	496	85	149	43	6	18	75	49	153	6	13	.372	.520
2016	Hartford (EL)	AA	.242	133	466	49	113	27	5	12	75	55	161	11	6	.325	.399
Minor League Totals			.282	450	1662	269	468	134	17	59	304	186	516	29	30	.359	.489

10 ANTONIO SENZATELA, RHP

Born: Jan. 21, 1995. **B-T:** R-R. **Ht.:** 6-1. **Wt.:** 180. **Signed:** Venezuela, 2011. **Signed by:** Rolando Fernandez/Orlando Medina/Carlos Gomez.

Senzatela was limited to seven starts in 2016 because of a recurring right shoulder problem that didn't require surgery but forced him to spend two lengthy stints on the Double-A Hartford disabled list. He showed no ill effects in the offseason, creating the expectation that he will be at full speed in 2017. When he takes the mound he usually wins. Senzatela has gone 41-19 in 88 pro games with a 2.45 ERA and a California League pitcher-of-the-year award in 2015. Everything Senzatela does revolves around a heavy, downhill fastball that sits between 92-95 mph. He can command it to all four quadrants of the strike zone with a tough angle for hitters.

BA GRADE
50 Risk: High

He experimented with a curveball and came up with a hybrid slider that has late tilt and grades average. His curveball is serviceable early in counts but altogether is a below-average offering. There remains work to be done on his changeup, though it has shown flashes of being an average weapon. With three average or better offerings at his disposal and above-average control, Senzatela has excelled at every level. With the limited mound time last year, he will get a look in big league camp, but he would have to shake things up to become a factor in the bid for an Opening Day roster spot. A solid year in the upper minors in 2017 would force the issue.

Year	Club (League)	Class	W	L	ERA	G	GS	CG	SV	IP	H	HR	BB	SO	K/9	WHIP	AVG
2014	Asheville (SAL)	LoA	15	2	3.11	26	26	0	0	145	134	11	36	89	5.5	1.18	.243
2015	Modesto (CAL)	HiA	9	9	2.51	26	26	1	0	154	131	10	33	143	8.4	1.06	.229
2016	Hartford (EL)	AA	4	1	1.82	7	7	0	0	35	27	1	9	27	7.0	1.04	.218
Minor League Totals			41	19	2.45	88	87	2	0	489	412	24	108	360	6.6	1.06	.226

11 PETER LAMBERT, RHP

BA GRADE
50 Risk: High

Born: April 18, 1997. **B-T:** R-R. **Ht.:** 6-2. **Wt.:** 185. **Drafted:** HS—San Dimas, Calif., 2015 (2nd round). **Signed by:** John Lukens.

Lambert, whose brother Jimmy was a fifth-round pick of the White Sox in 2016, was a prime high school prospect who pitched for USA Baseball's 18U national team. He accepted a $1.495 million bonus to sign with the Rockies instead of going to UCLA. A polished product out of Southern California power San Dimas High, where he went 13-0, 0.34 as a senior, Lambert is a command pitcher with some fastball velocity. His fastball sits at a solid 92-93 mph with life, and he has premium command of the pitch for his age and experience level. Many believe he will add velocity as he fills out. He has an excellent changeup to complement his fastball and has the potential for an impact curveball, which is a 79-82 mph offering with depth but at present lacks consistency. With Lambert's feel for pitching, the sum is greater than the whole of the parts. He has sound mechanics and right now would project as a mid-rotation starter, but with added velocity and focus he could exceed expectations. He will head to the challenging environment of high Class A Lancaster in the California League in 2017.

Year	Club (League)	Class	W	L	ERA	G	GS	CG	SV	IP	H	HR	BB	SO	K/9	WHIP	AVG
2015	Grand Junction (PIO)	R	0	4	3.45	8	8	0	0	31	29	3	11	26	7.5	1.28	.227
2016	Asheville (SAL)	LoA	5	8	3.93	26	26	0	0	126	125	7	33	108	7.7	1.25	.264
Minor League Totals			5	12	3.83	34	34	0	0	157	154	10	44	134	7.7	1.26	.256

12 DOM NUNEZ, C

BA GRADE
50 Risk: High

Born: Jan. 17, 1995. **B-T:** L-R. **Ht.:** 6-0. **Wt.:** 175. **Drafted:** HS—Elk Grove, Calif., 2013 (6th round). **Signed by:** Gary Wilson.

A shortstop out of Elk Grove High, a Sacramento-area powerhouse, Nunez played with prospects J.D. Davis (Astros), Derek Hill (Tigers), Rowdy Tellez (Blue Jays) and Dylan Carlson (Cardinals). Nunez played middle infield his first pro season, then tried catcher during instructional league and has been behind the plate ever since. The Rockies knew he had the soft hands to catch, but what got their attention was his feel for the game and the calmness he maintains. Nunez has plus arm strength, and while he is still working on the mechanics for accuracy, he threw out 43 percent of basestealers at high Class A Modesto in 2016 thanks to quicker footwork. His focus has been on defense, so his offensive numbers don't grab attention, but that's not a concern. He has a good feel for the strike zone and focuses on driving the ball to the middle of the field. Over time he will start turning on the ball and projects to have 15-home run potential. A lefthanded-hitting catcher, Nunez profiles well enough for the Rockies to remain patient that he can grow into a future regular. He is on track to move to Double-A Hartford in 2017.

Year	Club (League)	Class	AVG	G	AB	R	H	2B	3B	HR	RBI	BB	SO	SB	CS	OBP	SLG
2014	Grand Junction (PIO)	R	.313	46	176	30	55	12	0	8	40	21	28	5	7	.384	.517
2015	Asheville (SAL)	LoA	.282	104	373	61	105	23	0	13	53	53	55	7	7	.373	.448
2016	Modesto (CAL)	HiA	.241	105	390	44	94	13	2	10	51	49	91	8	1	.321	.362
Minor League Totals			.258	310	1134	159	293	61	3	34	167	141	208	31	23	.339	.407

13 JORDAN PATTERSON, 1B/OF

BA GRADE
45 Risk: Medium

Born: Feb. 12, 1992. **B-T:** L-L. **Ht.:** 6-4. **Wt.:** 215. **Drafted:** South Alabama, 2013 (4th round). **Signed by:** Alan Matthews.

A two-way player at South Alabama, Patterson entered pro ball as a corner outfielder. The Rockies, however, liked what they saw of him as a first baseman when they gave him an extended audition in the second half of 2016 at Triple-A Albuquerque. Patterson moves around the bag well and has the arm to make the 3-6-3 double play. The signing of free agent Ian Desmond after the 2016 season most likely relegates Patterson to Triple-A in 2017, but given Desmond's versatility, he could force the issue with a big first half. He has undergone a complete overhaul of his swing under the guidance of Rockies instructor Marv Foley. Patterson came out of college with a big leg kick and various moving parts, but Foley worked to shorten him up, which allowed him to stay on the ball longer and keep his head still. Patterson drives the ball well to the central part of the field, has a flat swing and has the size and strength to make adjustments to hit more home runs. He's in line to earn a reserve spot if the Rockies have room for an extra lefthanded bat who can play corner outfield and first base.

Year	Club (League)	Class	AVG	G	AB	R	H	2B	3B	HR	RBI	BB	SO	SB	CS	OBP	SLG
2014	Asheville (SAL)	LoA	.278	125	453	69	126	27	0	14	66	46	118	25	8	.359	.430
2015	Modesto (CAL)	HiA	.304	77	303	62	92	26	12	10	43	19	88	9	6	.378	.568
	New Britain (EL)	AA	.286	48	185	26	53	19	0	7	32	11	42	9	4	.342	.503
2016	Albuquerque (PCL)	AAA	.293	119	427	75	125	24	7	14	61	47	118	10	0	.376	.480
	Colorado (NL)	MAJ	.444	10	18	1	8	1	0	0	2	1	1	0	1	.474	.500
Major League Totals			.444	10	18	1	8	1	0	0	2	1	1	0	1	.474	.500
Minor League Totals			.290	429	1574	276	456	108	19	55	239	142	403	63	24	.369	.487

14 GARRETT HAMPSON, SS

BA GRADE
45 Risk: Medium

Born: Oct. 10, 1994. **B-T:** R-R. **Ht.:** 5-11. **Wt.:** 185. **Drafted:** Long Beach State, 2016 (3rd round). **Signed by:** Matt Hattabaugh.

Hampson has been getting attention since he was 10, when he won the competition for his age group at the Pitch, Hit and Run competition at the 2005 All-Star Game. The Rockies drafted Hampson 81st overall in 2016 and signed him for $750,000 after a decorated three-year career as Long Beach State's starting shortstop. Hampson doesn't have the size, power or arm strength of Troy Tulowitzki, Evan Longoria or Danny Espinosa, who preceded him playing shortstop for the Dirtbags, but he has that feel for how to play and for big situations. He earns comparisons with Marco Scutaro as a hitter who pesters pitchers, works the count and gets a mistake he can drive. He is a quality shortstop with good footwork and range as well as an average arm. He has shown the ability to play any infield position, adding to his potential big league value. Pitchers need to be aware with his plus speed and aggressiveness on the basepaths. Hampson had a strong debut at short-season Boise. He led the Northwest League in stolen bases (36) and walks (48). Hampson could move quickly as a utility infielder and potentially more if he keeps getting on base.

Year	Club (League)	Class	AVG	G	AB	R	H	2B	3B	HR	RBI	BB	SO	SB	CS	OBP	SLG
2016	Boise (NWL)	SS	.301	68	256	43	77	14	8	2	44	48	56	36	4	.404	.441
Minor League Totals			.301	68	256	43	77	14	8	2	44	48	56	36	4	.404	.441

15 FORREST WALL, 2B/OF

BA GRADE

50 Risk: High

Born: Nov. 20, 1995. **B-T:** L-R. **Ht.:** 6-0. **Wt.:** 175. **Drafted:** HS—Maitland, Fla. 2014 (1st round supplemental). **Signed by:** John Cedarburg.

The 35th player taken in the 2014 draft—the highest selection of a high school second baseman since the draft moved to one phase in 1987—Wall is getting a chance to show versatility. The Rockies gave him time in center field during 2016 instructional league. Wall has become better at second, particularly in turning the double play, but concentration lapses and a lack of aggressiveness cost him on routine plays, and his 32 errors led the high Class A California League in 2016. Wall, who had surgery for a torn labrum in his right shoulder his junior year in high school, is best suited for the middle of the field due to his athletic ability, though his arm strength remains middling. Also, his offensive game would be a mismatch for a corner position. He is a contact hitter who can drive the ball from gap to gap. As he gets stronger he will hit some home runs, but his offensive game will be putting the ball in play and using plus speed. Wall signed for $2 million because of his bat, which the Rockies hope to see catch fire in 2017.

Year	Club (League)	Class	AVG	G	AB	R	H	2B	3B	HR	RBI	BB	SO	SB	CS	OBP	SLG
2014	Grand Junction (PIO)	R	.318	41	157	48	50	6	6	3	24	27	32	18	5	.416	.490
2015	Boise (NWL)	SS	.500	4	10	4	5	0	0	0	1	6	2	2	2	.647	.500
	Asheville (SAL)	LoA	.280	99	361	57	101	16	10	7	46	41	72	23	9	.355	.438
2016	Modesto (CAL)	HiA	.264	120	459	57	121	16	4	6	56	41	97	22	11	.329	.355
Minor League Totals			.281	264	987	166	277	38	20	16	127	115	203	65	27	.357	.408

16 COLTON WELKER, 3B

BA GRADE

50 Risk: High

Born: Oct. 9, 1997. **B-T:** R-R. **Ht.:** 6-2. **Wt.:** 195. **Drafted:** HS—Parkland, Fla., 2016 (4th round). **Signed by:** Rafael Reyes.

Welker led Douglas High in Parkland, Fla.— Anthony Rizzo's alma mater—to the school's first state championship and No. 1 spot in the Baseball America prep rankings in 2016. A shortstop in high school, he has moved to third base. He is built along the lines of Rockies current third baseman Nolan Arenado and even looks a little like him in the face. Wwlker is not quite as big as the Rockies all-star, but he has similar defensive instincts to the four-time Gold Glove winner. He will need time to adjust to third but has the range, hands and arm strength to be an asset at the hot corner. He debuted at Rookie-level Grand Junction in 2016 and hit .329/.366/.490, even as he was 18 the entire campaign. Welker has the innate ability to recognize pitches and a very good grasp of the strike zone, and his hands work, with good present strength. He uses the entire field, and as he fills out and gets stronger he should grow into plus power. He and Tyler Nevin should compete for playing time at low Class A Asheville, though one also could wind up at short-season Boise.

Year	Club (League)	Class	AVG	G	AB	R	H	2B	3B	HR	RBI	BB	SO	SB	CS	OBP	SLG
2016	Grand Junction (PIO)	R	.329	51	210	38	69	15	2	5	36	13	28	6	4	.366	.490
Minor League Totals			.329	51	210	38	69	15	2	5	36	13	28	6	4	.366	.490

17 YENCY ALMONTE, RHP

BA GRADE

45 Risk: Medium

Born: June 4, 1994. **B-T:** B-R. **Ht.:** 6-3. **Wt.:** 210. **Drafted:** HS—Miami, 2012 (17th round). **Signed by:** Ralph Reyes (Angels).

When the Angels selected the 17-year-old Almonte in 2012, he was considered a raw, projectable pitcher. The Rockies were ready to release reliever Tommy Kahnle after the 2016 season but were able to deal him to the White Sox for Almonte, who after four years in the Angels and White Sox systems was still at the Class A level. Almonte began to physically mature in 2016. He added 25 pounds and saw his fastball move into the 93-96 mph range and touch 98 with movement. He is refining his slider and has the potential for an average changeup, which is a pitch the Rockies stress to their pitchers, especially if they don't throw a curveball. Almonte's breakout season included an organization-best 156 strikeouts and season-ending promotion to Double-A Hartford. Given the Rockies' pitching depth, he could transition to the bullpen, though the club will continue to develop him as a starter. The Rockies view Almonte as an organizational asset because he helps translate for Latin players during instructional league. He should open 2017 back in the Hartford rotation.

Year	Club (League)	Class	W	L	ERA	G	GS	CG	SV	IP	H	HR	BB	SO	K/9	WHIP	AVG
2014	Angels (AZL)	R	0	1	17.18	2	2	0	0	4	7	0	1	5	12.3	2.18	.467
	Burlington (MWL)	LoA	2	5	4.93	9	9	0	0	42	40	5	14	32	6.9	1.29	.252
2015	Kannapolis (SAL)	LoA	8	4	3.88	17	16	0	0	93	92	8	26	71	6.9	1.27	.256
	Winston-Salem (CAR)	HiA	3	3	2.42	7	6	0	0	45	28	1	12	39	7.9	0.90	.179
2016	Modesto (CAL)	HiA	8	9	3.71	22	22	1	0	138	124	14	39	134	8.7	1.18	.237
	Hartford (EL)	AA	3	1	3.00	5	5	1	0	30	22	4	16	22	6.6	1.27	.204
Minor League Totals			27	26	4.24	78	71	2	0	408	384	37	130	338	7.5	1.26	.248

18 SAM HOWARD, LHP

BA GRADE
45 Risk: Medium

Born: March 5, 1993. **B-T:** R-L. **Ht.:** 6-3. **Wt.:** 170. **Drafted:** Georgia Southern, 2014 (3rd round). **Signed by:** Alan Matthews.

Considered a pitchability lefty when he came out of Georgia Southern, Howard has improved his stock since signing with the Rockies for $672,100 as the 82nd overall pick in 2014. The organization worked with him on adding balance to his delivery and that led to him gaining more consistent velocity and command. After leading the low Class A South Atlantic League in strikeouts in 2015, he split the 2016 season between high Class A Modesto and Double-A Hartford and actually improved his strikeout rate to 8.6 per nine innings. Howard's 92-93 mph fastball is a tick above-average and effective because of his ability to work both sides of the plate. Its sinking action creates ground balls. He has downward action on his changeup and has focused on refining a slider for his breaking pitch. His slider can get a bit slurvy at times, but when he stays behind it, it's an effective pitch. Howard has been more effective against righthanders thus far in his career. The Rockies envision him in the rotation, but there are discussions he might better fit in relief, a la the Cubs' Travis Wood. Howard is slated to begin 2017 back in Double-A.

Year	Club (League)	Class	W	L	ERA	G	GS	CG	SV	IP	H	HR	BB	SO	K/9	WHIP	AVG
2014	Grand Junction (PIO)	R	1	3	5.40	14	13	0	0	53	73	6	10	42	7.1	1.56	.333
2015	Asheville (SAL)	LoA	11	9	3.43	25	25	1	0	134	131	8	32	122	8.2	1.22	.252
2016	Modesto (CAL)	HiA	4	3	2.47	11	11	0	0	66	43	3	24	73	10.0	1.02	.184
	Hartford (EL)	AA	5	6	3.99	16	16	0	0	90	113	11	28	67	6.7	1.56	.303
Minor League Totals			21	21	3.70	66	65	1	0	343	360	28	94	304	8.0	1.32	.268

19 DAVID HILL, RHP

BA GRADE
50 Risk: High

Born: May 27, 1994. **B-T:** R-R. **Ht.:** 6-2. **Wt.:** 195. **Drafted:** San Diego, 2015 (4th round). **Signed by:** John Lukens.

Hill was a 17th-round pick of the Phillies out of high school but opted to attend Long Beach State. He said would have signed had he gone in the first five rounds. After pitching one year at LBSU he transferred to Orange Coast (Calif.) JC and then San Diego. He signed for $550,000 as a fourth-rounder with Colorado in 2015. Hill's first pro season was limited to 14 starts at low Class A Asheville before he was sidelined by thoracic outlet syndrome surgery. All went well and he is expected to move at full speed in 2017. When healthy, Hill has the stuff and approach that could allow him to jump to Double-A Hartford by midseason. He has a quick arm and live 90-94 mph fastball but was overly reliant on it last year as he eyed having a major surgical procedure. Hill will focus on developing his plus curveball and making his changeup become a bigger part of his repertoire. His ability to throw strikes was underscored in 2016—he struck out 82 in 82.1 innings and walked just 14 with the Tourists. Hill is slated to start 2017 at high Class A Lancaster.

Year	Club (League)	Class	W	L	ERA	G	GS	CG	SV	IP	H	HR	BB	SO	K/9	WHIP	AVG
2015	Boise (NWL)	SS	0	0	3.09	8	7	0	0	23	20	1	9	23	8.9	1.24	.233
2016	Asheville (SAL)	LoA	4	4	4.48	14	14	0	0	82	95	8	14	82	9.0	1.32	.290
Minor League Totals			4	4	4.17	22	21	0	0	106	115	9	23	105	8.9	1.31	.278

20 TYLER NEVIN, 3B

BA GRADE
50 Risk: Extreme

Born: May 29, 1997. **B-T:** R-R. **Ht.:** 6-4. **Wt.:** 200. **Drafted:** HS—Poway, Calif., 2015 (1st round supplemental). **Signed by:** Jon Lukens.

The son of Phil Nevin, the No. 1 overall pick in 1992 and a 12-year big league veteran, Tyler has a more athletic body than his father, who was two inches shorter and stockier. Taken 37 picks later than his dad,

Nevin signed for $2 million instead of attending UCLA. Nevin held his own in his pro debut at Rookie-level Grand Junction in 2015 but was limited to one at-bat with short-season Boise in 2016 because of a severe hamstring strain he suffered during extended spring training. The hamstring did not tear away from the bone, so he was able to avoid surgery. Nevin grew up at third base, the same position his father played in the majors, and figures to remain at that position, but the Rockies will give him a look at other positions to increase his versatility. He handles third well defensively and has the body that promises to generate offensive power. His approach at the plate is mature, a byproduct of having a former big league player who, after managing in the minor leagues, has been added to the Giants' big league coaching staff. The younger Nevin could return to short-season Boise in 2017, provided he is healthy, but will contend with Colton Welker for the low Class A third-base job.

Year	Club (League)	Class	AVG	G	AB	R	H	2B	3B	HR	RBI	BB	SO	SB	CS	OBP	SLG
2015	Grand Junction (PIO)	R	.265	53.	189	29	50	15	1	2	18	29	42	3	7	.368	.386
2016	Boise (NWL)	SS	1.000	1	1	1	1	1	0	0	0	0	0	0	0	1.000	2.000
Minor League Totals			.268	54	190	30	51	16	1	2	18	29	42	3	7	.371	.395

21 MIKE NIKORAK, RHP

BA GRADE **50** Risk: Extreme

Born: Sept. 16, 1996. **B-T:** R-R. **Ht.:** 6-5. **Wt.:** 220. **Drafted:** HS—Stroudsburg, Pa., 2015 (1st round). **Signed by:** Mike Garlatti.

Nikorak has run up a 6.70 ERA through his first 47 pro innings after signing for $2.3 million as the 27th overall pick in 2015. He passed on a scholarship to Alabama. When Nikorak arrived at extended spring training after being drafted, he was out of whack with his mechanics, and that first summer was spent trying to rectify that issue. He had a breakthrough in instructional league and, with help of pitching coaches Ryan Kibler and Bob Apodaca, appeared ready to move forward in 2016 as he repeated the Pioneer League. But he strained a ligament in his right index finger and was shut down after seven starts. Another strong instructional league, however, gave an indication Nikorak had regained his proper arm action and velocity. His two-seam fastball sits in the low 90s and generates an extreme rate of ground balls. He jumps to 97 mph with his four-seamer that has life. He has the potential for an average low-80s curveball, which will provide separation from his fastball, and shows signs of a changeup, though it is inconsistent. At 6-foot-5, he is taller than most pitchers but is very athletic, having played quarterback in high school. Nikorak needs innings and some confidence in 2017.

Year	Club (League)	Class	W	L	ERA	G	GS	CG	SV	IP	H	HR	BB	SO	K/9	WHIP	AVG
2015	Grand Junction (PIO)	R	0	4	11.72	8	8	0	0	18	26	1	32	14	7.1	3.28	.347
2016	Grand Junction (PIO)	R	1	0	3.68	7	7	0	0	29	33	2	19	20	6.1	1.77	.287
Minor League Totals			1	4	6.70	15	15	0	0	47	59	3	51	34	6.5	2.34	.311

22 ROBERT TYLER, RHP

BA GRADE **50** Risk: Extreme

Born: June 18, 1995. **B-T:** L-R. **Ht.:** 6-5. **Wt.:** 210. **Drafted:** Georgia, 2016 (1st round supplemental). **Signed by:** Sean Gamble.

The Rockies drafted Tyler 38th overall in 2016 and signed him for just over $1.7 million, but he endured a rough pro debut at short-season Boise. He signed late, struggled with control (he walked 16 in seven innings) and then missed most of instructional league with a strained hamstring. Tyler has one of the hardest fastballs in the system at 95-97 mph. He throws a changeup he can command. He rarely threw a breaking pitch in college, in part because he was shut down for three months in 2015 with a forearm strain. He adopted a knuckle-curve as a Georgia junior, with inconsistent but at times encouraging results. The Rockies have made minor adjustments to Tyler's delivery to reduce strain on his forearm. That has led scouts to suggest he will wind up as a late-inning power arm. The Rockies aren't oblivious to that, but they would rather see how his breaking ball develops. That was going to be the focus of instructional league before his hamstring injury. The Rockies would rather have Tyler try to learn that third pitch and give him a chance to start, which will be his focus in 2017.

Year	Club (League)	Class	W	L	ERA	G	GS	CG	SV	IP	H	HR	BB	SO	K/9	WHIP	AVG
2016	Boise (NWL)	SS	0	2	6.43	5	5	0	0	7	2	0	16	5	6.4	2.57	.083
Minor League Totals			0	2	6.43	5	5	0	0	7	2	0	16	5	6.4	2.57	.083

23 BEN BOWDEN, LHP

BA GRADE **45** Risk: High

Born: Oct. 21, 1994. **B-T:** L-L. **Ht.:** 6-4. **Wt.:** 235. **Drafted:** Vanderbilt, 2016 (2nd round). **Signed by:** Scott Corman.

Bowden starred as a Vanderbilt reliever in 2015 and 2016 and was co-MVP of the Cape Cod League in 2015. The Rockies drafted him 45th overall in 2016 and signed him for $1.6 million. Bowden has shown he can handle a bullpen job, but the Rockies are deciding whether to stretch out the well-built lefthander and see how his pitch mix works as starter. Bowden started his junior season at Vandy but moved back into the pen quickly. He hasn't been stretched out since high school but held up over 96.1 innings for the Commodores followed by 23.2 innings in his pro debut at low Class A Asheville. Bowden's fastball sits in the low 90s and hits 95 mph at times, with late life and a steep downhill plane. He showed a solid slider during instructional league and has the makings of a changeup. He has an easy motion despite his solid build, but he the Rockies don't know how his fastball will play if he has to pace himself as a starter. His future role will be determined in spring training, as well as whether he will return to Asheville or move to high Class A Lancaster in 2017.

Year	Club (League)	Class	W	L	ERA	G	GS	CG	SV	IP	H	HR	BB	SO	K/9	WHIP	AVG
2016	Asheville (SAL)	LoA	0	1	3.04	26	0	0	0	24	23	1	15	29	11.0	1.61	.261
Minor League Totals			0	1	3.04	26	0	0	0	24	23	1	15	29	11.0	1.61	.261

24 PEDRO GONZALEZ, OF

BA GRADE
50 Risk: Extreme

Born: Oct. 27, 1997. **B-T:** R-R. **Ht.:** 6-5. **Wt.:** 190. **Signed:** Dominican Republic, 2014. **Signed by:** Rolando Fernandez/Jhonathan Leyba/Martin Cabrera.

The Rockies signed Gonzalez for $1.3 million in 2015, and after one year in the Dominican Summer League they brought him to the U.S. to play at Rookie-level Grand Junction. Gonzalez has a considerable ceiling but is still very raw. A fluent English speaker before he signed, Gonzalez has a high level of intelligence, which allows him to adapt quickly when suggestions are made. He struck out 77 times in 58 games in 2016 but is learning and adjusting. He has excellent bat speed with above-average power potential and also understands the value of using the opposite field. An above-average runner, Gonzalez might lose a step as he fills out. He already has added 25 pounds since signing and could handle another 25 or so. He moved from shortstop to center field in 2016, but with his arm strength he figures to eventually land in right field. Gonzalez is raw enough that he may return to Grand Junction if he doesn't earn a spot at low Class A Asheville.

Year	Club (League)	Class	AVG	G	AB	R	H	2B	3B	HR	RBI	BB	SO	SB	CS	OBP	SLG
2015	Rockies (DSL)	R	.251	63	251	46	63	14	2	8	33	19	81	8	12	.318	.418
2016	Rockies (DSL)	R	.222	7	27	3	6	0	1	0	6	2	4	4	1	.300	.296
	Grand Junction (PIO)	R	.230	58	226	32	52	15	8	2	19	14	77	6	7	.290	.394
Minor League Totals			.240	128	504	81	121	29	11	10	58	35	162	18	20	.305	.401

25 PARKER FRENCH, RHP

BA GRADE
45 Risk: High

Born: March 19, 1993. **B-T:** L-R. **Ht.:** 6-2. **Wt.:** 200. **Drafted:** Texas, 2015 (5th round). **Signed by:** Jeff Edwards.

When French enrolled as a freshman at Texas, he wasn't sure he would play baseball. He wound up playing for four years after spurning the Tigers as a 19th-round pick after his junior season. Since signing with the Rockies for a below-slot $100,000 as a fifth-round senior sign, French has made a quick impression. He threw six shutout innings in three of his first four starts at low Class A Asheville in 2016 and spent the rest of the year at high Class A Modesto, ultimately leading the hitter-friendly California League in ERA (2.85). He's so pitch-efficient that he led the minor leagues with 177.2 innings. French showed few signs of fatigue and tossed five scoreless innings in his final start. He can pitch in and out with his 88-91 mph fastball with big-time sinking action and 90-93 mph with a four-seamer that peaks at 94. His repertoire also includes an average slider and a changeup that mimics his fastball with its action. His knack for pitching and fastball command are both plusses, a key because none of his pitches earns that grade. French will head to Double-A Hartford in 2017.

Year	Club (League)	Class	W	L	ERA	G	GS	CG	SV	IP	H	HR	BB	SO	K/9	WHIP	AVG
2015	Grand Junction (PIO)	R	2	4	3.72	10	10	0	0	48	50	4	2	36	6.7	1.08	.260
2016	Asheville (SAL)	LoA	2	1	1.17	4	4	0	0	23	17	0	4	13	5.1	0.91	.210
	Modesto (CAL)	HiA	8	9	2.85	24	24	1	0	155	136	9	25	109	6.3	1.04	.237
Minor League Totals			12	14	2.87	38	38	1	0	226	203	13	31	158	6.3	1.04	.239

26 HARRISON MUSGRAVE, LHP

BA GRADE
40 Risk: Medium

Born: March 3, 1992. **B-T:** L-L. **Ht.:** 6-1. **Wt.:** 205. **Drafted:** West Virginia, 2014 (8th round). **Signed by:** Ed Santa.

Musgrove doesn't overpower but has a great feel for pitching, plenty of confidence and is on a fast track to the big leagues. After having Tommy John surgery his sophomore year at West Virginia, he came back to win Big 12 Conference pitcher-of-the-year honors and returned for his redshirt junior season after falling to the 33rd round of the 2013 draft. He did not hesitate to sign for slot value ($160,200) after the Rockies made him an eight-round pick in 2014. Musgrave has earned in-season promotions each season and finishing 2016 at Triple-A Albuquerque. His fastball sits 89-90 mph and tops out at 93, but he has good deception in his delivery. His solid-average changeup is his best pitch, and he's not afraid to throw it inside. He is working on a slider for his breaking ball, and it also is average at times. A big asset is his ability to not overreact. Musgrave may never been a high-end starter, but he should get a chance to compete for a rotation spot in Colorado in 2017.

Year	Club (League)	Class	W	L	ERA	G	GS	CG	SV	IP	H	HR	BB	SO	K/9	WHIP	AVG
2014	Grand Junction (PIO)	R	2	4	5.44	13	11	0	0	48	60	10	14	50	9.4	1.54	.303
2015	Modesto (CAL)	HiA	10	1	2.88	16	16	0	0	91	81	7	19	83	8.2	1.10	.240
	New Britain (EL)	AA	3	4	3.18	11	11	0	0	57	55	7	13	53	8.4	1.20	.255
2016	Hartford (EL)	AA	5	1	1.79	6	6	0	0	40	20	1	8	30	6.7	0.69	.145
	Albuquerque (PCL)	AAA	8	7	4.30	19	19	0	0	113	118	17	40	79	6.3	1.40	.271
Minor League Totals			28	17	3.61	65	63	0	0	349	334	42	94	295	7.6	1.23	.252

27 SAM MOLL, LHP

Born: Jan. 3, 1992. **B-T:** L-L. **Ht.:** 5-10. **Wt.:** 185. **Drafted:** Memphis, 2013 (3rd round). **Signed by:** Scott Corman.

BA GRADE
40 Risk: Medium

Moll has the stuff to be a starter, but his slight 5-foot-10, 185-pound frame and injury history have forced him to the bullpen. He hasn't started since his pro debut in Rookie-level Grand Junction in 2013. He broke his toe in his final start that year and bone chips cost him all but nine appearances in 2014. He broke out in 2015 and reached Double-A, but he found the jump to Triple-A and Albuquerque's mile-high altitude in 2016 a bit more challenging. He missed about a month with elbow inflammation, though that didn't keep the Rockies from adding him to the 40-man roster after the season. Moll has life on his 93-96 mph fastball that helps him generate swings and misses and get groundball outs. The same is true of his mid-80 slider. That combo has allowed him to handle lefthanded batters. Moll throws a changeup with promise but doesn't use it much in a relief role. Command and health remain his biggest barriers to success. Given his role as a reliever on the 40-man, Moll could make the jump to the big leagues at some point in 2017.

Year	Club (League)	Class	W	L	ERA	G	GS	CG	SV	IP	H	HR	BB	SO	K/9	WHIP	AVG
2014	Tri-City (NWL)	SS	0	1	4.15	9	0	0	0	13	17	1	4	7	4.8	1.62	.327
2015	Modesto (CAL)	HiA	0	1	3.02	25	0	0	2	54	40	7	12	57	9.6	0.97	.206
	New Britain (EL)	AA	0	0	1.23	13	0	0	0	15	7	0	4	17	10.4	0.75	.140
2016	Grand Junction (PIO)	R	0	0	0.00	2	0	0	0	2	0	0	0	5	22.5	0.00	.000
	Albuquerque (PCL)	AAA	3	5	4.94	42	0	0	2	47	55	5	19	39	7.4	1.56	.296
Minor League Totals			6	8	3.25	101	6	0	4	161	139	13	49	154	8.6	1.17	.232

28 BRIAN MUNDELL, 1B

Born: Feb. 26, 1994. **B-T:** R-R. **Ht.:** 6-2. **Wt.:** 200. **Drafted:** Cal Poly, 2015 (7th round). **Signed by:** Matt Hattabaugh.

BA GRADE
45 Risk: High

Mundell, a seventh-round pick, was the first college player the Rockies selected in the 2015 draft. A catcher as a freshman, he played mostly DH and first base the next two years and has to hit to be a prospect. So far, he has done just that while also improving defensively. After leading all short-season Northwest League first basemen with 11 errors in 2015, he made big strides at low Class A Asheville in 2016. He is such a team leader that the Rockies left him in the South Atlantic League for the entire season, even though his numbers argued for a promotion. Mundell took advantage of the opportunity by hitting 59 doubles, the most by a minor leaguer since the minors reorganized in 1963. He drives the ball to all fields, has a simple, repeatable swing and has above-average power to go with a good feel for hitting. He has a confidence that led him during spring training to mention to farm director Zach Wilson that he liked Wilson's pullover. In late April, he suggested to Wilson that if he won the MVP award in the SAL that he should get one of the pullovers. Wilson agreed and also upped the ante. He would get pullovers for every member of the team. At season's end, after Mundell won the award, he handed Wilson a list with the shirt size of every Tourists player.

Year	Club (League)	Class	AVG	G	AB	R	H	2B	3B	HR	RBI	BB	SO	SB	CS	OBP	SLG
2015	Boise (NWL)	SS	.275	69	244	35	67	19	1	4	36	32	45	7	1	.355	.410
2016	Asheville (SAL)	LoA	.313	136	537	94	168	59	1	14	83	56	83	7	8	.383	.505
Minor League Totals			.301	205	781	129	235	78	2	18	119	88	128	14	9	.374	.475

29 MANUEL MELENDEZ, OF

Born: Jan. 10, 1997. **B-T:** L-L. **Ht.:** 5-11. **Wt.:** 170. **Signed:** Venezuela, 2014.
Signed by: Rolando Fernandez/Orlando Medina.

BA GRADE

50 Risk: Extreme

Melendez is a slender product of the Rockies' Latin American program. The native of Venezuela signed as a 17-year-old and spent two years in the Dominican Summer League before coming to the U.S. and having an impressive debut at Rookie-league Grand Junction in 2016. While the Pioneer League batting average is .286, he batted .294 and ranked third in the league with 24 stolen bases. After playing a lot of center field in the DSL, Melendez played primarily right field for Grand Junction and seemed comfortable in both spots. His above-average arm flashes plus, which suits him in right field and provides a bonus in center. He has line-drive pop but lacks corner-profile power, so the Rockies will push him toward center. Melendez has the plus speed to cover ground—in the field and on the bases. He runs consistently to first base in 4.15 seconds, making him a plus runner. The Rockies were impressed enough by Melendez that they brought him to their offseason workout program at their Arizona training complex and figure to promote him to low Class A Asheville in 2017.

Year	Club (League)	Class	AVG	G	AB	R	H	2B	3B	HR	RBI	BB	SO	SB	CS	OBP	SLG
2014	Rockies (DSL)	R	.227	64	233	25	53	9	2	1	16	18	33	11	7	.295	.296
2015	Rockies (DSL)	R	.267	65	266	37	71	12	7	1	31	23	32	15	13	.343	.376
2016	Grand Junction (PIO)	R	.294	60	265	53	78	10	3	7	33	11	42	24	6	.337	.434
Minor League Totals			.264	189	764	115	202	31	12	9	80	52	107	50	26	.326	.372

30 JERRY VASTO, LHP

Born: Feb. 12, 1992. **B-T:** L-L. **Ht.:** 6-2. **Wt.:** 195. **Drafted:** Felician (N.J.), 2014 (24th round). **Signed by:** Mike Garlatti.

BA GRADE

40 Risk: Medium

As a New Jersey product who attended Hudson High in Highlands and Division II Felician College in Rutherford, Vasto was easy for amateur scouts to miss. In fact the Rockies made him the first Hudson alum to be drafted in 30 years. Vasto finished 2016 at Double-A Hartford and then in the Arizona Fall League and is on the verge of reaching the big leagues. He has added velocity in pro ball and now pitches at 92 mph with his fastball and 86 mph with his hard slider. The two-pitch selection is enough to get by in relief, particularly with the natural deception in his delivery. He has struck out 139 batters in 115 pro innings and is particularly tough on lefthanded batters, who went 27-for-130 (.208) with five extra-base hits in 2015 and 2016. Vasto will compete with Sam Moll for a job as a lefty reliever in the Rockies bullpen both in 2017 and the years to come.

Year	Club (League)	Class	W	L	ERA	G	GS	CG	SV	IP	H	HR	BB	SO	K/9	WHIP	AVG
2014	Tri-City (NWL)	SS	0	0	0.00	1	0	0	0	1	0	0	0	1	9.0	0.00	.000
2015	Asheville (SAL)	LoA	2	4	2.93	46	0	0	3	58	42	3	20	68	10.5	1.06	.199
2016	Modesto (CAL)	HiA	0	1	1.38	23	0	0	10	26	17	0	7	36	12.5	0.92	.181
	Hartford (EL)	AA	4	3	3.03	31	0	0	10	30	28	2	15	34	10.3	1.45	.248
Minor League Totals			6	8	2.58	101	0	0	23	115	87	5	42	139	10.9	1.12	.207

Detroit Tigers

BY JOSH NORRIS

Michael Fulmer graduated from top Tigers prospect to the AL rookie of the year

Tigers owner Mike Ilitch has never been shy about going all out to bring a title to Detroit.

He authorized his general managers, first Dave Dombrowski and now Al Avila, to hand out nine-figure contracts to Prince Fielder, Jordan Zimmermann and Justin Upton in recent years, and he allowed Dombrowski to spin a passel of prospects, including Andrew Miller, to the Marlins for franchise cornerstone Miguel Cabrera back in December 2007.

The Tigers' 2016 payroll checked in at a shade less than $195 million, behind only the Yankees and Dodgers as baseball's most expensive roster. Detroit has ranked among the top five every year since 2013, but after four straight playoff appearances, including two berths in the American League Championship Series, the Tigers missed the postseason for the second straight season in 2016. They missed out on a wild-card berth after losing the final two games of the season at lowly Atlanta.

The Tigers appear headed toward a crossroads. Avila announced in October his intention to move the team toward a younger, less costly roster, telling reporters, "We want to run the organization without having to go over the means of the organization."

The Tigers moved into the offseason with $176 million already committed for 2017, including $28 million each for Cabrera and ace Justin Verlander, who bounced back at age 33 with a Cy Young Award-caliber season. Those players performed, but the previous offseason's big-ticket acquisitions, Upton (six years, $132.75 million) and Zimmermann (five years, $110 million), both proved streaky, and will have to perform better to live up to those deals.

If Avila is to expedite his team's transformation, he and his front office lieutenants will have to get creative in the trade market to supplement a relatively barren farm system. As a blueprint, the team might look to its own deal of outfielder Yoenis Cespedes at the 2015 trade deadline. That trade netted the Tigers righthander Michael Fulmer from the Mets, and he claimed the AL Rookie of the Year award in 2016. The team also flipped ace David Price to the Blue Jays in 2015 for a pair of promising lefthanders in Daniel Norris and Matt Boyd, who combined for 31 starts in 2016, with Norris coming back successfully from a bout with thyroid cancer.

Boyd, Fulmer and Norris should join Verlander and Zimmermann to provide a strong rotation.

Third baseman Nick Castellanos broke out offensively as a 24-year-old, and provides balance behind lineup linchpins Ian Kinsler, Cabrera and Upton.

Help from the farm system, however, is a long way off. Prep righthander Matt Manning, the 2016 first-round pick out of Sacramento, is far and away the organization's top prospect but is years away from the big leagues. Avila will have to be aggressive to find complements to the Tigers' current core.

After years of ruling the roost in the AL Central, the Tigers have seen the Royals—the 2015 World Series champions—and Indians—the 2016 AL pennant winners—surge ahead of them.

They'll have to act fast to return to consistent contention.

TOP PROSPECTS OF THE DECADE

Year	Player, Pos.	2016 Org
2007	Cameron Maybin, of	Tigers
2008	Rick Porcello, rhp	Red Sox
2009	Rick Porcello, rhp	Red Sox
2010	Jacob Turner, rhp	White Sox
2011	Jacob Turner, rhp	White Sox
2012	Jacob Turner, rhp	White Sox
2013	Nick Castellanos, 3b	Tigers
2014	Nick Castellanos, 3b	Tigers
2015	Steven Moya, of	Tigers
2016	Michael Fulmer, rhp	Tigers

ORGANIZATION OVERVIEW

General manager: Al Avila. **Farm director:** Dave Owen. **Scouting director:** Scott Pleis.

Class	Team	League	W	L	PCT	Finish	Manager
Majors	Detroit Tigers	American	86	75	.534	6th (15)	Brad Ausmus
Triple-A	Toledo Mud Hens	International	68	76	.472	9th (14)	Lloyd McClendon
Double-A	Erie SeaWolves	Eastern	62	79	.440	t-9th (12)	Lance Parrish
High Class A	Lakeland Flying Tigers	Florida State	60	72	.455	10th (12)	Dave Huppert
Low Class A	West Michigan Whitecaps	Midwest	71	65	.522	6th (16)	Andrew Graham
Short-season	Connecticut Tigers	New York-Penn	41	35	.539	5th (14)	Mike Rabelo
Rookie	GCL Tigers East	Gulf Coast	21	37	.362	16th (17)	Rafael Gil
Rookie	GCL Tigers West	Gulf Coast	30	28	.517	7th (17)	Rafael Martinez
Overall 2016 Minor League Record			353	392	.474	22nd (30)	

THIS YEAR'S TOP 30

No.	Player, Pos.	Grade/Risk
1.	Matt Manning, rhp	65/Extreme
2.	Christin Stewart, of	50/High
3.	Beau Burrows, rhp	50/High
4.	Tyler Alexander, lhp	45/Medium
5.	Kyle Funkhouser, rhp	50/High
6.	JaCoby Jones, of/3b	50/High
7.	Mike Gerber, of	45/Medium
8.	Adam Ravenelle, rhp	50/High
9.	Steven Moya, of	50/High
10.	Derek Hill, of	50/High
11.	Joe Jimenez, rhp	45/Medium
12.	Jose Azocar, of	50/High
13.	Sandy Baez, rhp	50/High
14.	Dixon Machado, ss	40/Low
15.	Mark Ecker, rhp	45/High
16.	Austin Sodders, lhp	45/High
17.	Myles Jaye, rhp	40/Medium
18.	A.J. Simcox, ss	45/High
19.	Spencer Turnbull, rhp	45/High
20.	Grayson Greiner, c	45/High
21.	Wladimir Pinto, rhp	45/High
22.	Bryan Garcia, rhp	45/High
23.	Zac Houston, rhp	45/High
24.	Drew Smith, rhp	45/High
25.	Jacob Robson, of	45/High
26.	Cristhian Tortosa, lhp	50/Extreme
27.	Arvicent Perez, c	45/High
28.	Matt Hall, lhp	40/High
29.	Jairo Labourt, lhp	45/Extreme
30.	Gregory Soto, lhp	45/Extreme

LAST YEAR'S TOP 30

No.	Player, Pos.	Status
1.	Michael Fulmer, rhp	Majors
2.	Beau Burrows, rhp	No. 3
3.	Mike Gerber, of	No. 7
4.	Christin Stewart, of	No. 2
5.	JaCoby Jones, ss	No. 6
6.	Kevin Ziomek, lhp	Dropped out
7.	Joe Jimenez, rhp	No. 11
8.	Dixon Machado, ss	No. 14
9.	Spencer Turnbull, rhp	No. 19
10.	Derek Hill, of	No. 10
11.	Steven Moya, of	No. 9
12.	Buck Farmer, rhp	Majors
13.	Zach Shepherd, 3b	Dropped out
14.	A.J. Simcox, ss	No. 18
15.	Jose Azocar, of	No. 12
16.	Jairo Labourt, lhp	No. 28
17.	Jefry Marte, 3b	(Angels)
18.	Luis Cessa, rhp	(Yankees)
19.	Drew Smith, rhp	No. 24
20.	Gerson Moreno, rhp	No. 30
21.	Jeff Ferrell, rhp	Dropped out
22.	Drew VerHagen, rhp	Majors
23.	Jose Valdez, rhp	(Angels)
24.	Wynton Bernard, of	(Giants)
25.	Austin Kubitza, rhp	Dropped out
26.	Sandy Baez, rhp	No. 13
27.	Joey Pankake, 2b	Dropped out
28.	Tyler Alexander, lhp	No. 4
29.	Adam Ravenelle, rhp	No. 8
30.	Montreal Robertson, rhp	Dropped out

BEST TOOLS

Best Hitter for Average	Will Maddox
Best Power Hitter	Steven Moya
Best Strike-Zone Discipline	Christin Stewart
Fastest Baserunner	Derek Hill
Best Athlete	Derek Hill
Best Fastball	Matt Manning
Best Curveball	Drew Smith
Best Slider	Joe Jimenez
Best Changeup	Tyler Alexander
Best Control	Tyler Alexander
Best Defensive Catcher	Arvicent Perez
Best Defensive Infielder	Dixon Machado
Best Infield Arm	Dixon Machado
Best Defensive Outfielder	Derek Hill
Best Outfield Arm	Steven Moya

PROJECTED 2020 LINEUP

Catcher	James McCann
First Base	Miguel Cabrera
Second Base	A.J. Simcox
Third Base	Nick Castellanos
Shortstop	Jose Iglesias
Left Field	Justin Upton
Center Field	Derek Hill
Right Field	J.D. Martinez
Designated Hitter	Christin Stewart
No. 1 Starter	Michael Fulmer
No. 2 Starter	Matt Manning
No. 3 Starter	Jordan Zimmermann
No. 4 Starter	Daniel Norris
No. 5 Starter	Matt Boyd
Closer	Adam Ravenelle

MINOR LEAGUE DEPTH CHART

DETROIT TIGERS

TOP 2017 ROOKIE: JaCoby Jones, 3b/of. His power and speed could flourish if he receives an everyday chance.

BREAKOUT PROSPECT: Sandy Baez, rhp. The big-bodied righty can maintain upper-90s gas and throws a pair of changeups.

SLEEPER: Eudis Idrogo, lhp. The southpaw can throw three pitches for strikes but needs to get stronger to unlock potential.

SOURCE OF TOP 30 TALENT

Homegrown	27	Acquired	3
College	15	Trades	3
Junior college	0	Rule 5 draft	0
High school	3	Independent leagues	0
Nondrafted free agents	1	Free agents/waivers	0
International	8		

LF
Christin Stewart (2)
Ignacio Valdez
Cam Gibson
Victor Padron

CF
JaCoby Jones (6)
Derek Hill (10)
Jacob Robson (25)
Daniel Woodrow

RF
Mike Gerber (7)
Steven Moya (9)
Jose Azocar (12)
Jeff McVaney

3B
Joey Pankake
Zac Shepherd

SS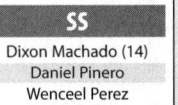
Dixon Machado (14)
Daniel Pinero
Wenceel Perez

2B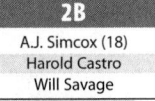
A.J. Simcox (18)
Harold Castro
Will Savage

1B
Dominic Ficociello
Niko Buentello
Will Maddox

C
Grayson Greiner (20)
Arvicent Perez (27)
Austin Athmann
Brady Policelli

LHP

LHSP	LHRP
Tyler Alexander (4)	Matt Hall (28)
Austin Sodders (16)	Jairo Labourt (29)
Cristhian Tortosa (26)	Daniel Stumpf
Gregory Soto (30)	Chad Bell
Kevin Ziomek	
Eudis Idrogo	

RHP

RHSP	RHRP
Matt Manning (1)	Adam Ravenelle (8)
Beau Burrows (3)	Joe Jimenez (11)
Kyle Funkhouser (5)	Marc Ecker (15)
Sandy Baez (13)	Bryan Garcia (22)
Myles Jaye (17)	Zac Houston (23)
Spencer Turnbull (19)	Drew Smith (24)
Wladimir Pinto (21)	Gerson Moreno
Jeff Ferrell	Artie Lewicki
Jeff Thompson	Victor Alcantara
A.J. Ladwig	Paul Voelker
	Ruben Alaniz
	Trey Teakell

DRAFT ANALYSIS

2016

BEST PURE HITTER: OF Jacob Robson (8) batted .321 at Mississippi State last spring as a redshirt junior after hitting .324 as a sophomore, then hit .288 in his pro debut. He has a contact-oriented approach that gives him a shot to be an above-average hitter. Robson was the first hitter the Tigers drafted.

BEST POWER HITTER: In a draft heavy on pitching, the Tigers didn't draft much power. 1B Niko Buentello (18) hit 11 home runs at Auburn and has above-average raw power, but he hit only five home runs in the Gulf Coast League. C Austin Athmann (14) finished second in the Big 10 with a .621 slugging percentage and has average power.

FASTEST RUNNER: Robson is a top-of-the-scale runner, as is OF Daniel Woodrow (12).

BEST DEFENSIVE PLAYER: Robson and Woodrow both are solid center fielders. Daniel Pinero (9) is a tall, rangy infielder who doesn't profile as an everyday shortstop but plays it well enough to serve as a utilityman.

BEST FASTBALL: RHP Matt Manning (1) sits in the mid-90s at his best and has touched 97 mph. RHP Kyle Funkhouser (4) doesn't touch 97 as often, but sits 93-95 at his best. RHP Mark Ecker (5) has touched 100 mph and sits 94-97 in short stints as a reliever.

BEST SECONDARY PITCH: Funkhouser's curveball has flashed above-average, but he needs to improve its consistency. Ecker's changeup has flashed above-average as well.

BEST PRO DEBUT: Ecker struck out 31 and walked only 5 in 28 innings while posting a 0.98 ERA and a 0.76 WHIP between short-season Connecticut and low Class A West Michigan. RHP Zac Houston (11) struck out 15 batters per nine innings and posted a 0.30 ERA in stops at Connecticut and West Michigan.

BEST ATHLETE: Manning had signed to play basketball at Loyola Marymount if he opted not to sign to play pro baseball.

MOST INTRIGUING BACKGROUND: Manning's father Rich played in the NBA for the Vancouver Grizzlies and Los Angeles Clippers. RHP Clate Schmidt (20) beat Hodgkin's lymphoma and been given a clean bill of health.

CLOSEST TO THE MAJORS: Ecker bounced back from a poor junior season to dominate at two levels. As a college reliever with a blazing fastball, he could move very quickly. Funkhouser's inconsistency could slow down his climb, but he is a four-year college starter who should be ready for high Class A in 2017.

BEST LATE-ROUND PICK: The Tigers spent more than $100,000 only twice on picks after the 10th round. Houston was one of them and quickly showed he should easily earn his $190,000 signing bonus. Houston is a big (6-foot-5, 250-pound) reliever with a 92-95 mph fastball and usable secondary offerings. He dominated in his pro debut and proved he can move quickly.

THE ONE WHO GOT AWAY: SS Drew Mendoza (36) was projected as a first- to second-round pick before getting the word out to teams he intended to fulfill his commitment to Florida State. He is one of the top bats of the college freshman class.

2015

OF Christin Stewart (1) and SS A.J. Simcox (14), college teammates at Tennessee, are two of the Tigers' better prospects, as are Dallas-Fort Worth college products LHP Tyler Alexander (2) and RHP Drew Smith (3).

GRADE: C

2014

OF Derek Hill (1) has shown huge defensive ability but also had Tommy John surgery. RHPs Spencer Turnbull (2) and Adam Ravenelle (4) have shown flashes of being impact power arms. OF Mike Gerber (15) and C Grayson Greiner (3) have a chance to be regulars.

GRADE: C

2013

RHP Corey Knebel (1s) reached the majors quickly but already has been traded twice. RHP Jonathon Crawford (1) was dealt to the Reds for Alfredo Simon. RHP Buck Farmer (5) has faltered in several big league callups. Unsigned LHP A.J. Puk (35) went sixth overall in 2016 to Oakland.

GRADE: D

TOP DRAFT PICKS OF THE DECADE

Year	Player, Pos.	2016 Org
2007	Rick Porcello, rhp	Red Sox
2008	Ryan Perry, rhp	Did not play
2009	Jacob Turner, rhp	White Sox
2010	Nick Castellanos, 3b (1st round supp.)	Tigers
2011	James McCann, c (2nd round)	Tigers
2012	Jake Thompson, rhp (2nd round)	Phillies
2013	Jonathon Crawford, rhp	Reds
2014	Derek Hill, of	Tigers
2015	Beau Burrows, rhp	Tigers
2016	Matt Manning, rhp	Tigers

LARGEST BONUSES IN CLUB HISTORY

Jacob Turner, 2009	$4,700,000
Rick Porcello, 2007	$3,580,000
Andrew Miller, 2006	$3,550,000
Matt Manning, 2016	$3,505,800
Eric Munson, 1999	$3,500,000

1 MATT MANNING, RHP

Born: Jan. 28, 1998. **B-T:** R-R. **Ht.:** 6-6. **Wt.:** 190.
Drafted: HS—Sacramento, 2016 (1st round).
Signed by: Scott Cerny.

For the No. 9 overall pick in the 2016 draft, Manning is still relatively green when it comes to baseball. He was a two-sport star at Sheldon High in Sacramento and has basketball in his blood. His father Rich spent parts of two seasons in the NBA and his brother Ryan plays collegiately with Air Force. Matt averaged 19.4 points during his senior season and was committed to play two sports at Loyola Marymount. The Tigers, however, swayed him from that commitment by handing him a bonus of $3,505,800. That number ranks as the fourth-highest in franchise history behind Jacob Turner, Rick Porcello and Andrew Miller. He was hit a little bit in his first taste of pro ball, but also ranked second in the Rookie-level Gulf Coast League with 14.1 strikeouts per nine innings; 46 of his 88 outs came via strikeouts. He ranked as the circuit's No. 2 prospect, behind only Mickey Moniak, whom the Phillies chose as the No. 1 overall pick.

As a basketball standout, Manning comes equipped with long levers and an athletic frame. Those traits help him on the mound, too, where he shows more coordination in his delivery than other pitchers with long arms and legs. His delivery can get a touch across his body at times, but he also creates deception and gets enough extension to the point that one evaluator said it looked like the 6-foot-6 righthander was shaking hands with his catcher. And although the Tigers believe Manning has plenty of projection left in his frame, there are evaluators outside the organization who think his body is nearly maxed out in its present state. Manning's fastball sat at 96-97 mph during the summer but was clocked at 93-94 with hints of the upper 90s and life through the zone during instructional league. He's backs up his fastball with a spike curveball and a changeup that both have potential but also need refinement. Tigers coaches have seen rotation and sharpness from Manning's breaking ball as well as the ability to land it in the zone or bury it for a chase pitch. He will cast his curveball at times and needs to develop overall consistency with it. He had his changeup in high school but, as is the case with a lot of big-time high school arms, didn't need to use it very often because his fastball and curveball were enough to overpower prep hitters. He throws his changeup with the same arm speed and slot as his fastball, but it can get too firm at times and lose effective-

BA GRADE

65 Risk: Extreme

SCOUTING GRADES

Fastball: 70.
Curveball: 55.
Changeup: 50.
Control: 50.

Based on 20-80 scouting scale and future projection rather than present tools.

MIKE JANES

ness. The Tigers believe that once Manning learns to harness his changeup and impart consistent separation from his fastball, it has the potential to be an average to above-average pitch, and Tigers coaches were pleased with its progress toward the end of the instructional league. Team officials also have spoken highly about how teachable Manning is and how well he takes to coaching.

Like 2015 first-rounder Beau Burrows, another high-end prep righthander, Manning probably will begin his first full season at low Class A West Michigan. With the Whitecaps, Manning will continue to gain innings and work on overall refinement. He has a ceiling of a No. 2 starter.

Year	Club (League)	Class	W	L	ERA	G	GS	CG	SV	IP	H	HR	BB	SO	K/9	WHIP	AVG
2016	Tigers West (GCL)	R	0	2	3.99	10	10	0	0	29	27	2	7	46	14.1	1.16	.237
Minor League Totals			0	2	3.99	10	10	0	0	29	27	2	7	46	14.1	1.16	.237

2 CHRISTIN STEWART, OF

Born: Dec. 10, 1993. **B-T:** L-R. **Ht.:** 6-0. **Wt.:** 205. **Drafted:** Tennessee, 2015 (1st round). **Signed by:** Harold Zonder.

Stewart is tied with Micah Owings for the Georgia high school home run record with 69 over his four years. He continued to show big-time power at Tennessee, swatting 23 in three years and 15 in his draft year. The Tigers gave signed him for $1,795,000 in 2015 as the No. 34 overall pick, which they acquired when Max Scherzer signed with the Nationals. His 30 homers in 2016 ranked fifth in the minor leagues. Stewart's calling card is still his above-average power, which plays to all fields in any ballpark. He has shortened his swing a bit as a pro, allowing him to backspin the ball more to his pull side, helping boost his home run power. He runs deep counts consistently, leading to strikeouts but also a system-best 86 walks, sixth-best in the minors. His defense, however, is a greater concern. He gets poor jumps and breaks on balls, his below-average arm limits him to left field and his below-average speed contributes to a lack of range. After a bid in this year's Futures Game and a turn in the Arizona Fall League to continue working on shortening his swing and improving his defense, Stewart likely will return to Double-A Erie to begin 2017.

BA GRADE

50 Risk: High

Year	Club (League)	Class	AVG	G	AB	R	H	2B	3B	HR	RBI	BB	SO	SB	CS	OBP	SLG
2015	Tigers (GCL)	R	.364	6	22	5	8	2	1	1	2	3	5	2	1	.462	.682
	Connecticut (NYP)	SS	.245	14	49	7	12	2	2	2	11	5	18	0	0	.322	.490
	West Michigan (MWL)	LoA	.286	51	185	29	53	9	4	7	31	18	45	3	2	.375	.492
2016	Lakeland (FSL)	HiA	.264	104	356	60	94	22	1	24	68	74	105	3	1	.403	.534
	Erie (EL)	AA	.218	24	87	17	19	2	0	6	19	12	26	0	0	.310	.448
Minor League Totals			.266	199	699	118	186	37	8	40	131	112	199	8	4	.381	.514

3 BEAU BURROWS, RHP

Born: Sept. 18, 1996. **B-T:** R-R. **Ht.:** 6-2. **Wt.:** 200. **Drafted:** HS—Weatherford, Texas, 2015. (1st round). **Signed by:** Chris Wimmer.

Drafted out of the same high school as Orioles all-star closer Zach Britton, Burrows was the 22nd overall pick in 2015. The Tigers signed him for $2,154,200. He got his feet wet in the Rookie-level Gulf Coast League in 2015 and ranked as the No. 8 prospect in the league. He spent all year at low Class A West Michigan in 2016, skipping starts to control his workload. Burrows starts his arsenal with a fastball in the 90-93 mph range that peaks at 94. His heater hit 98 mph as an amateur in short bursts. The pitch has good riding life through the zone, but the Tigers would like Burrows to continue to refine his command. Specifically, they'd like him to focus on getting the ball down more often. His primary offspeed pitch is a 12-to-6 curveball with tight spin that could be a consistently above-average pitch with repetition. He's developing his changeup and already shows conviction and the ability throw it from the same arm slot as the rest of his arsenal. He has a slider as well and used his time at instructional league to refine the pitch to the point that it doesn't blend in with his curveball. Burrows will likely spend 2017 at high Class A Lakeland as a 20-year-old. Improved fastball command would help him fulfill his ceiling as a top-end starter.

BA GRADE

50 Risk: High

Year	Club (League)	Class	W	L	ERA	G	GS	CG	SV	IP	H	HR	BB	SO	K/9	WHIP	AVG
2015	Tigers (GCL)	R	1	0	1.61	10	9	0	0	28	18	0	11	33	10.6	1.04	.184
2016	West Michigan (MWL)	LoA	6	4	3.15	21	20	0	0	97	87	2	30	67	6.2	1.21	.240
Minor League Totals			7	4	2.81	31	29	0	0	125	105	2	41	100	7.2	1.17	.228

4 TYLER ALEXANDER, LHP

Born: July 14, 1994. **B-T:** L-L. **Ht.:** 6-2. **Wt.:** 200. **Drafted:** Texas Christian, 2015 (2nd round). **Signed by:** Matt Lea.

The Tigers drafted Alexander in the 23rd round in 2013, and then again in 2015 after he spent two seasons at Texas Christian. A draft-eligible sophomore, Alexander signed for $1 million in the second round to forgo his junior year. He dominated the short-season New York-Penn League in his pro debut and finished 2016 at Double-A Erie with six scoreless innings in his final start. Alexander won't wow anybody with his stuff, but he uses command and guile to carve up hitters just the same. He parks his fastball in the 89-91 mph range but can reach back to hit 94 when necessary. He is advanced enough to manipulate the break on his slider depending on the situation. He'll throw a looser version early in counts and tighten the pitch for chases late. Both the slider and his changeup earn average grades. His repertoire is enhanced by above-average command

BA GRADE

45 Risk: Medium

and exceptional control that have allowed him to walk just 24 hitters in 168.2 career innings—a rate of 1.3 per nine innings. He also earns praise for his unflappability and maturity on the mound. Alexander will start back at Double-A and could move quickly enough to get a taste of the big leagues at the end of 2017. He has a future as a back-end starter.

Year	Club (League)	Class	W	L	ERA	G	GS	CG	SV	IP	H	HR	BB	SO	K/9	WHIP	AVG
2015	Connecticut (NYP)	SS	0	2	0.97	12	12	0	0	37	17	3	5	33	8.0	0.59	.133
2016	Lakeland (FSL)	HiA	6	7	2.21	19	18	0	0	102	87	7	16	82	7.2	1.01	.226
	Erie (EL)	AA	2	1	3.15	6	6	0	0	34	36	4	4	23	6.0	1.17	.273
Minor League Totals			8	10	2.13	37	36	0	0	173	140	14	25	138	7.2	0.95	.217

5 KYLE FUNKHOUSER, RHP

Born: March 16, 1994. **B-T:** R-R. **Ht.:** 6-2. **Wt.:** 220. **Drafted:** Louisville, 2016 (4th round). **Signed by:** Harold Zonder.

The Dodgers made Funkhouser the No. 35 overall pick in the 2015 draft, at the time the highest ever for a Louisville player. He had been projected as a possible top-10 pick earlier that year, so he returned to school for his senior season. And while Louisville had the best record in the Atlantic Coast Conference for the second straight year, Funkhouser started poorly and fell to the fourth round in 2016. The Tigers were pleased to find Funkhouser available for their second pick. The Tigers limited Funkhouser's workload at short-season Connecticut after he threw 93.1 innings in the spring, but he still showed an impressive arsenal and much-improved control after signing for $750,000. He pitched at 90-95 mph as a pro but peaked at 97 during instructional league. He coupled his fastball with an 82-86 mph slider that scouts project to be an average pitch. His changeup lacks movement but has good separation from his fastball and has average potential. His early-count curveball ranks as a fourth pitch. After walking 4.3 per nine innings in four college seasons, Funkhouser pounded the zone (1.9 BB/9) in his pro debut. If Funkhouser keeps throwing strikes, he has the physicality and fastball to be a mid-rotation innings-eater. He could move quickly, starting 2017 at high Class A Lakeland.

BA GRADE 50 Risk: High

Year	Club (League)	Class	W	L	ERA	G	GS	CG	SV	IP	H	HR	BB	SO	K/9	WHIP	AVG
2016	Connecticut (NYP)	SS	0	2	2.65	13	13	0	0	37	34	0	8	34	8.2	1.13	.246
Minor League Totals			0	2	2.65	13	13	0	0	37	34	0	8	34	8.2	1.13	.246

6 JACOBY JONES, OF/3B

Born: May 10, 1992. **B-T:** R-R. **Ht.:** 6-2. **Wt.:** 205. **Drafted:** Louisiana State, 2013 (3rd round). **Signed by:** Jerome Cochran (Pirates).

Jones was part of the same Mississippi prep class that produced Padres outfielder Hunter Renfroe. The Astros drafted Jones out of high school, but he elected to attend Louisiana State. The Pirates called Jones' name three years later and signed the third-rounder for $612,000. The Tigers acquired Jones at midseason 2015 for closer Joakim Soria, though he served a 50-game suspension at the beginning of 2016. Jones was primarily a second baseman at LSU and played shortstop during his time with the Pirates. He moved to third base early with the Tigers but played mostly center field. He's a plus defender in center with a plus arm, and is a well above-average runner as well. Jones has the above-average power to profile as a regular but has a long swing-and-miss track record, owing to length in his swing, lack of plate discipline and below-average pitch recognition skills. Jones received six extra weeks of reps at the plate and in center field in the Arizona Fall League. He'll have a chance to earn a spot with the Tigers in 2017 if he hits enough, particularly after the trade of Cameron Maybin. If he doesn't win the center field job, his versatility will be an asset.

BA GRADE 50 Risk: High

Year	Club (League)	Class	AVG	G	AB	R	H	2B	3B	HR	RBI	BB	SO	SB	CS	OBP	SLG
2014	West Virginia (SAL)	LoA	.288	117	445	72	128	21	3	23	70	33	132	17	9	.347	.503
2015	Bradenton (FSL)	HiA	.253	93	379	48	96	18	3	10	58	31	113	14	4	.313	.396
	Altoona (EL)	AA	.500	3	10	2	5	0	0	0	2	1	0	1	0	.545	.500
	Erie (EL)	AA	.250	37	136	26	34	7	2	6	20	17	52	10	3	.331	.463
2016	Erie (EL)	AA	.312	20	77	11	24	6	2	4	20	10	23	2	1	.393	.597
	Toledo (IL)	AAA	.243	79	292	33	71	14	5	3	23	25	97	11	4	.309	.356
	Detroit (AL)	MAJ	.214	13	28	3	6	3	0	0	2	0	12	0	0	.214	.321
Major League Totals			.214	13	28	3	6	3	0	0	2	0	12	0	0	.214	.321
Minor League Totals			.269	364	1400	206	377	68	17	47	203	120	431	58	23	.333	.443

7 MIKE GERBER, OF

BA GRADE

45 Risk: Medium

Born: July 8, 1992. **B-T:** L-R. **Ht.:** 6-0. **Wt.:** 190. **Drafted:** Creighton, 2014 (15th round). **Signed by:** Marty Miller.

Gerber was a 40th-round pick out of high school (Yankees) but wasn't drafted after his junior year at Creighton, because he missed part of the season with an appendectomy. He played with his brother David (a righthander) as a senior with the Bluejays before the Tigers drafted him, and he has moved aggressively, playing in the Arizona Fall League last year and finishing 2016 at Double-A Erie. Gerber starts with a swing geared more for line drives than over-the-fence power, but he's got more juice than might be expected. He worked to shorten his swing in 2016 and made strides in his recognition of offspeed pitches. He's not afraid to take a walk, but the deep counts contribute to his strikeout rate, which spiked to 27 percent in 2016, up from 16 percent in 2015. However, he walked and homered more often. He plays all three outfield spots, and his above-average arm strength and average speed fit him best in right field. Gerber is likely ticketed for a return to Double-A. Maintaining improved home run power while making more contact could make him a future regular, though his versatility may allow him to stick in Detroit eventually as a fourth outfielder.

Year	Club (League)	Class	AVG	G	AB	R	H	2B	3B	HR	RBI	BB	SO	SB	CS	OBP	SLG
2014	Connecticut (NYP)	SS	.286	57	217	40	62	16	4	7	37	17	48	8	4	.354	.493
	West Michigan (MWL)	LoA	.387	8	31	4	12	3	0	0	5	4	3	1	0	.457	.484
2015	West Michigan (MWL)	LoA	.292	135	513	74	150	31	10	13	76	49	97	16	4	.355	.468
2016	Lakeland (FSL)	HiA	.282	91	351	52	99	22	3	14	60	32	111	2	3	.343	.481
	Erie (EL)	AA	.261	41	153	17	40	8	3	4	20	20	41	6	0	.349	.431
Minor League Totals			.287	332	1265	187	363	80	20	38	198	122	300	33	11	.353	.472

8 ADAM RAVENELLE, RHP

BA GRADE

50 Risk: High

Born: Oct. 15, 1992. **B-T:** R-R. **Ht.:** 6-3. **Wt.:** 195. **Drafted:** Vanderbilt, 2014 (4th round). **Signed by:** Harold Zonder.

The Yankees chose Ravenelle out of high school in Sudbury, Mass., in 2011, but he chose to spend the next three seasons at Vanderbilt instead. He got the final six outs of the Commodores' 2014 College World Series championship. Ravenelle's hallmarks are his premium pitcher's body and top-end fastball. The pitch took a jump this year, moving from 93-97 mph into triple digits. His fastball also gets excellent sink when his mechanics are in sync and is capable of getting swings and misses. His main secondary offering is a slider that tops out in the low 90s and breaks more vertically than horizontally. Though his fastball can touch 101 mph, the Tigers have reminded Ravenelle that he doesn't need to throw that hard to get outs. His coaches have worked to make his delivery smoother and less rotational. After a second straight assignment to the Arizona Fall League, Ravenelle will likely return to Double-A Erie to start 2017.

Year	Club (League)	Class	W	L	ERA	G	GS	CG	SV	IP	H	HR	BB	SO	K/9	WHIP	AVG
2014	Tigers (GCL)	R	0	0	0.00	1	0	0	0	1	0	0	0	1	9.0	0.00	.000
	West Michigan (MWL)	LoA	0	0	0.00	2	0	0	1	3	0	0	0	5	15.0	0.00	.000
2015	Tigers (GCL)	R	0	0	0.00	2	0	0	0	4	0	0	3	1	2.3	0.75	.000
	West Michigan (MWL)	LoA	2	0	3.93	19	0	0	0	34	31	2	19	40	10.5	1.46	.238
2016	Lakeland (FSL)	HiA	2	1	2.86	23	0	0	3	28	17	3	17	34	10.8	1.20	.168
	Erie (EL)	AA	1	1	4.85	27	0	0	1	30	30	4	16	23	7.0	1.55	.265
Minor League Totals			5	2	3.59	74	0	0	5	100	78	9	55	104	9.3	1.33	.212

9 STEVEN MOYA, OF

BA GRADE

50 Risk: High

Born: Aug. 9, 1991. **B-T:** L-R. **Ht.:** 6-7. **Wt.:** 260. **Signed:** Dominican Republic, 2008. **Signed by:** Miguel Rodriguez/Ramon Perez/Miguel Garcia.

Since his signing eight years ago, Moya has had one of the system's more intriguing skill sets. He's tall, strong and strapped with power. Because he's so tall, however, his ascent through the organization has been slowed by high strikeout totals. He made his big league debut in 2016, where those flaws were writ large with 38 strikeouts in 94 at-bats. Moya owns the best power in the system, but evaluators still question how often he'll get to it. Tigers coaches worked hard with Moya to shorten his swing and hone his pitch recognition, and he cut his strikeout rate to a career-low 22.5 percent at Triple-A Toledo in 2016. His struggles at the major league level suggest there is more work to be done, and his long-levered frame works against him in that regard. He's an adequate defender in right field with an above-average arm. He's a below-average runner, but not so much that he's considered a base-clogger. Moya is out of options, so it's now or never for him to stick in the major leagues. His competition as an extra outfielder, Tyler Collins, also is out of options, so Moya must turn his big-time raw power into a usable skill if he wants to stick in Detroit.

Year	Club (League)	Class	AVG	G	AB	R	H	2B	3B	HR	RBI	BB	SO	SB	CS	OBP	SLG
2014	Erie (EL)	AA	.276	133	515	81	142	33	3	35	105	23	161	16	4	.306	.555
	Detroit (AL)	MAJ	.375	11	8	2	3	0	0	0	0	0	2	0	0	.375	.375
2015	Lakeland (FSL)	HiA	.275	9	40	3	11	3	0	3	8	1	13	0	0	.286	.575
	Toledo (IL)	AAA	.240	126	500	53	120	30	0	20	74	27	162	5	4	.283	.420
	Detroit (AL)	MAJ	.182	9	22	1	4	0	1	0	0	3	10	0	0	.280	.273
2016	Toledo (IL)	AAA	.284	97	409	60	116	23	3	20	66	15	96	3	0	.310	.501
	Detroit (AL)	MAJ	.255	31	94	9	24	4	2	5	11	5	38	0	1	.290	.500
Major League Totals			.250	51	124	12	31	4	3	5	11	8	50	0	1	.293	.452
Minor League Totals			.254	703	2750	363	699	145	17	120	438	146	846	40	14	.295	.450

10 DEREK HILL, OF

BA GRADE

50 Risk: High

Born: Dec. 30, 1995. **B-T:** R-R. **Ht.:** 6-2. **Wt.:** 195. **Drafted:** HS—Elk Grove, Calif., 2014 (1st round). **Signed by:** Scott Cerny.

The Tigers selected Hill out of the same Elk Grove (Calif.) High program that produced 2016 first-rounder Dylan Carlson (Cardinals). The Tigers signed Hill for $2 million, swaying him from his commitment to Oregon. His father Orsino played for 12 pro seasons and is now a scout with the Diamondbacks. The younger Hill, who missed most of 2015 with a quadriceps injury, was healthy for most of 2016 before a ligament tear in his right elbow in August necessitated Tommy John surgery. When on the field, Hill showed the same tantalizing set of skills and got more results in a return to low Class A West Michigan. His best trait is his 70-grade speed on the 20-80 scouting scale, which helps him on the basepaths (he ranked second in the Midwest League with 35 steals) and in center field. He's the system's best defensive outfielder and turned in multiple highlight-reel plays. He also showed above-average arm strength. Before the injury the Tigers were working with Hill to better define what type of hitter he can be in the future. His lack of physicality combined with his speed means he's ideally suited to be a contact hitter who causes havoc on the basepaths. Position players usually come back from Tommy John surgery in about nine months, so Hill could be back by midseason 2017. He should report to high Class A Lakeland when he's ready to hit.

Year	Club (League)	Class	AVG	G	AB	R	H	2B	3B	HR	RBI	BB	SO	SB	CS	OBP	SLG
2014	Tigers (GCL)	R	.212	28	99	12	21	2	2	2	11	16	19	9	1	.331	.333
	Connecticut (NYP)	SS	.203	19	74	8	15	1	1	0	3	2	26	2	1	.244	.243
2015	West Michigan (MWL)	LoA	.238	53	210	33	50	6	5	0	16	20	44	25	7	.305	.314
2016	West Michigan (MWL)	LoA	.266	93	384	66	102	17	6	1	31	24	105	35	6	.312	.349
Minor League Totals			.245	193	767	119	188	26	14	3	61	62	194	71	15	.306	.327

11 JOE JIMENEZ, RHP

BA GRADE

45 Risk: Medium

Born: Jan. 17, 1995. **B-T:** R-R. **Ht.:** 6-3. **Wt.:** 225. **Signed:** HS—Gurabo, P.R., 2013 (NDFA). **Signed by:** Rolando Casanova/German Geigel.

After teams passed on Jimenez out of the Puerto Rico Baseball Academy in 2013, the Tigers decided to take a flyer on him as an undrafted free agent. They were rewarded with a jump in velocity and one of the fastest-moving relievers in their system. Jimenez has pitched in the last two Futures Games, and rose to Triple-A in 2016 after beginning the year in high Class A Lakeland. Jimenez throws from a three-quarters arm slot and can get across his body at times, which leads to command issues the Tigers have worked to clean up. He has primarily been a two-pitch pitcher in his career, coupling a 93-98 mph fastball with a slider he uses to get swings and misses. He worked this year to tighten the break on his slider, which some evaluators described as having slurve-type break. Jimenez has also worked on adding a changeup to his repertoire. The pitch currently gets the fade necessary but Jimenez slows his arm during his delivery, which detracts from its effectiveness. He is likely to return to Triple-A in 2017 to continue working on improving his command and achieving his ceiling as a setup man.

Year	Club (League)	Class	W	L	ERA	G	GS	CG	SV	IP	H	HR	BB	SO	K/9	WHIP	AVG
2014	Connecticut (NYP)	SS	3	2	2.70	23	0	0	4	27	22	1	6	41	13.8	1.05	.218
2015	West Michigan (MWL)	LoA	5	1	1.47	40	0	0	17	43	23	2	11	61	12.8	0.79	.153
2016	Lakeland (FSL)	HiA	0	0	0.00	17	0	0	10	17	5	0	5	28	14.5	0.58	.089
	Erie (EL)	AA	3	2	2.18	21	0	0	12	21	12	0	8	34	14.8	0.97	.171
	Toledo (IL)	AAA	0	1	2.30	17	0	0	8	16	9	1	4	16	9.2	0.83	.164
Minor League Totals			14	6	1.59	126	0	0	52	141	80	4	40	204	13.0	0.85	.163

12 JOSE AZOCAR, OF

BA GRADE

50 Risk: High

Born: May 11, 1996. **B-T:** R-R. **Ht.:** 5-11. **Wt.:** 170. **Signed:** Venezuela, 2012.
Signed by: Pedro Chavez.

Signed for $110,000 in 2012, Azocar has progressed slowly. He spent his first two seasons in the Venezuelan Summer League, moved to the Rookie-level Gulf Coast League in 2015 and made his full-season debut last season with low Class A West Michigan. Along with Derek Hill, Azocar helped form a defensively superb Whitecaps outfield. Azocar has a center fielder's tool set—plus running ability and range to both sides—but was pushed to right because of Hill. Azocar has a plus arm, which further helps him fit in right. He has progressed as a hitter, but at 5-foot-11 and 170 pounds shows almost no power. He has just one home run in 1,173 career at-bats and hasn't gone deep since 2014. He is a quick-twitch athlete with a level swing who can slap balls to all fields, although his power is almost exclusively to the pull side. The Tigers are working with Azocar to cut down his strikeouts (22.5 percent rate in 2016) in the hopes of unlocking more offensive potential. He is ticketed for a move to high Class A Lakeland in 2017.

Year	Club (League)	Class	AVG	G	AB	R	H	2B	3B	HR	RBI	BB	SO	SB	CS	OBP	SLG
2014	Tigers (VSL)	R	.340	65	250	39	85	7	6	1	36	11	48	13	5	.373	.428
2015	Connecticut (NYP)	SS	.087	7	23	1	2	1	0	0	0	1	7	0	0	.125	.130
	Tigers (GCL)	R	.325	51	194	29	63	10	5	0	29	7	31	6	4	.350	.428
2016	West Michigan (MWL)	LoA	.281	129	501	56	141	11	8	0	51	25	119	14	5	.315	.335
Minor League Totals			.289	314	1173	145	339	40	21	1	132	47	248	38	16	.319	.361

13 SANDY BAEZ

BA GRADE

50 Risk: High

Born: Nov. 25, 1993. **B-T:** R-R. **Ht.:** 6-2. **Wt.:** 180. **Signed:** Dominican Republic, 2011. **Signed by:** Carlos Santana/Ramon Perez/Miguel Garcia.

The Tigers gambled $49,000 on Baez's projectability as a 17-year-old throwing in the high-80s. Now 23 and blessed with an ideal pitcher's body, Baez's fastball sits in the mid-90s and has touched 100 mph. He has continued developing his slider, which had slurvy-type break but tightened gradually this year. Baez throws a pair of changeups, one is a traditional circle-changeup and the other is a "fosh," which is thrown harder with a split-fingered grip and bite. Baez's numbers at low Class A West Michigan weren't outstanding—he went 7-9, 3.81 with 88 strikeouts in 113.1 innings—but the Tigers still saw fit to add him to their 40-man roster in advance of the Rule 5 draft. There is still a lot of development remaining, but the Tigers believe they are beginning to see Baez peek at his potential. He will move to high Class A Lakeland in 2017.

Year	Club (League)	Class	W	L	ERA	G	GS	CG	SV	IP	H	HR	BB	SO	K/9	WHIP	AVG
2014	Tigers (GCL)	R	1	2	3.06	12	12	0	0	62	62	3	16	48	7.0	1.26	.258
2015	Connecticut (NYP)	SS	3	4	4.13	14	14	0	0	65	73	4	22	52	7.2	1.45	.289
2016	West Michigan (MWL)	LoA	7	9	3.81	21	21	0	0	113	125	7	28	88	7.0	1.35	.283
Minor League Totals			19	19	3.58	71	66	1	1	340	344	15	94	280	7.4	1.29	.265

14 DIXON MACHADO

BA GRADE

40 Risk: Low

Born: Feb. 22, 1992. **B-T:** R-R. **Ht.:** 6-1. **Wt.:** 170. **Signed:** Venezuela, 2008.
Signed by: German Robles.

After spending three seasons at Rookie-level or short-season ball after signing out of Venezuela in 2008, Machado finally moved to low Class A West Michigan in 2011. He has progressively shortened his swing and gotten more physical since that year, when he managed just three extra-base hits in 124 games, but he is still not big or strong enough to make much of an impact with the bat. Even so, Machado's glove has helped him earn cameos in the big leagues in each of the past two seasons. He is the system's best defensive infielder by a wide margin. He has the arm strength and the chops to stick at shortstop, but he saw time at second base in 2016 and could be most useful in Detroit in a utility role. He is an average runner but not a burner. With Jose Iglesias and Ian Kinsler in Detroit, Machado's likely role will continue to be as an extra infielder who provides depth in the majors and upper minors.

Year	Club (League)	Class	AVG	G	AB	R	H	2B	3B	HR	RBI	BB	SO	SB	CS	OBP	SLG
2014	Lakeland (FSL)	HiA	.252	41	159	30	40	8	1	1	8	23	34	2	1	.348	.333
	Erie (EL)	AA	.305	90	292	45	89	23	1	5	32	40	36	8	5	.391	.442
2015	Toledo (IL)	AAA	.261	127	509	61	133	22	1	4	48	36	85	15	3	.313	.332
	Detroit (AL)	MAJ	.235	24	68	6	16	3	0	0	5	7	14	1	0	.307	.279
2016	Toledo (IL)	AAA	.266	131	492	59	131	28	2	4	48	58	75	17	5	.349	.356
	Detroit (AL)	MAJ	.100	8	10	1	1	0	0	0	0	3	4	0	0	.308	.100
Major League Totals			.218	32	78	7	17	3	0	0	5	10	18	1	0	.307	.256
Minor League Totals			.246	789	2902	390	715	116	14	20	253	314	456	131	35	.323	.317

15 MARK ECKER, RHP

Born: May 27, 1995. **B-T:** R-R. **Ht.:** 6-0. **Wt.:** 180. **Drafted:** Texas A&M, 2016 (5th round). **Signed by:** Matt Lea.

After three seasons in the Texas A&M bullpen, the Tigers liked enough of what they saw out of Ecker to spend their fifth-round pick on him and a $386,500 bonus to sign. Ecker is a relief prospect only, and he spent his first pro season dominating at short-season Connecticut and low Class A West Michigan. Ecker's calling card is his upper-90s fastball, which touched 100 mph in college. He gets armside run and sink, which helps mitigate his short stature. He kept he ball down enough in college to allow just two home runs in three seasons. He couples his fastball with a changeup that improved enough in college to become an average pitch. He throws his changeup with the same arm speed and slot as his fastball and gets effective separation between the two. He also throws a slider that is a clear third pitch at this point. Ecker could start next season at high Class A Lakeland with a chance to move quickly through the system.

Year	Club (League)	Class	W	L	ERA	G	GS	CG	SV	IP	H	HR	BB	SO	K/9	WHIP	AVG
2016	Connecticut (NYP)	SS	2	0	0.50	11	0	0	4	18	7	0	3	21	10.5	0.56	.117
	West Michigan (MWL)	LoA	0	0	1.86	9	0	0	5	10	9	1	2	10	9.3	1.14	.237
Minor League Totals			2	0	0.98	20	0	0	9	28	16	1	5	31	10.1	0.76	.163

16 AUSTIN SODDERS, LHP

Born: April 29, 1995. **B-T:** L-L. **Ht.:** 6-3. **Wt.:** 180. **Drafted:** UC Riverside, 2016 (7th round). **Signed by:** Steve Pack.

Sodders is the son of former Arizona State third baseman and Twins first-rounder Mike Sodders, who was also the recipient of Baseball America's first College Player of the Year award in 1981. The younger Sodders spent two seasons at Riverside CC and was drafted after his sophomore year by the Pirates, but instead transferred to UC Riverside for his junior season. With the Highlanders, Sodders flourished, going 7-4, 2.57 and earning all-Big West honors as the team's No. 1 starter. Sodders doesn't possess a knockout pitch, but instead gets his outs on deception and command of his 88-92 mph fastball with downhill angle and sneaky late life. He has an average changeup as well, and is working on gaining consistency with a slider. Specifically, Sodders is working to add depth to the pitch, which morphs into a small cutter at times. He is likely to begin 2017 at low Class A West Michigan and has the upside of a back-end starter.

Year	Club (League)	Class	W	L	ERA	G	GS	CG	SV	IP	H	HR	BB	SO	K/9	WHIP	AVG
2016	Connecticut (NYP)	SS	0	3	2.29	13	13	0	0	39	35	2	5	33	7.6	1.02	.230
Minor League Totals			0	3	2.29	13	13	0	0	39	35	2	5	33	7.6	1.02	.230

17 MYLES JAYE, RHP

Born: Dec. 28, 1991. **B-T:** B-R. **Ht.:** 6-3. **Wt.:** 170. **Drafted:** HS—Fayetteville, Ga., 2010 (17th round). **Signed by:** Eric McQueen (Blue Jays).

After being drafted by the Blue Jays in 2010, Jaye has been a traveling man. The righthander has been dealt three times in the last six years—to the White Sox in 2012, to the Rangers in 2015 and to the Tigers just before the 2016 season. Jaye split his first season in the Detroit system at Double-A Erie and Triple-A Toledo and put up a 5-12, 3.95 mark. His 135 strikeouts topped the organization. Jaye uses a three-pitch mix, starting with a fastball that sits in the low 90s and tops out at 93 mph. He has good feel for both of his offspeed pitches, including a slider in the 82-86 mph range and a firm changeup that settles in between 80-87 mph. Both of his offspeed pitches project as average, though his slider is ahead of his changeup. Jaye dealt with a strained groin in 2016, though it was never serious enough to land him on the disabled list. He projects as a back-end starter or a swingman in the major leagues and is ready for that role in 2017.

Year	Club (League)	Class	W	L	ERA	G	GS	CG	SV	IP	H	HR	BB	SO	K/9	WHIP	AVG
2014	Winston-Salem (CAR)	HiA	3	0	1.55	4	4	1	0	29	22	2	5	15	4.7	0.93	.200
	Birmingham (SL)	AA	4	12	5.32	24	24	1	0	132	146	10	53	73	5.0	1.51	.287
2015	Birmingham (SL)	AA	12	9	3.29	26	26	0	0	148	135	8	47	104	6.3	1.23	.244
2016	Erie (EL)	AA	4	8	4.04	21	21	1	0	123	127	11	29	104	7.6	1.27	.262
	Toledo (IL)	AAA	1	4	3.69	7	7	0	0	39	30	2	12	31	7.2	1.08	.210
Minor League Totals			44	51	4.11	140	136	5	1	766	776	56	266	570	6.7	1.36	.263

18 A.J. SIMCOX, 2B

Born: June 22, 1994. **B-T:** R-R. **Ht.:** 6-3. **Wt.:** 185. **Drafted:** Tennessee, 2015 (14th round). **Signed by:** Harold Zonder.

The 2015 Tennessee roster featured three future Tigers prospects—outfielder Christin Stewart, first

baseman Will Maddox and Simcox. Simcox ranked No. 1 among Baseball America's Top 10 prospects in the Alaska League in 2013, and his father, Larry, played in the minor leagues and spent 17 years as an assistant coach at Tennessee. The younger Simcox is a fundamentally sound player who won't blow anyone away with any one tool, but is average or near-average across the board. He has a sound hitting approach, stays inside the ball well and has begun to drive the ball with more authority as he's gained strength. He still has a bit of work to do in that strength department, however, in order to round himself into a player with everyday offensive value. He is an average defender with average arm strength, though his accuracy needs improvement. His speed is above-average. If he improves with the bat, Simcox has an outside chance at an everyday role. Otherwise, his future is as a backup or a utility player. He should move to Double-A Erie to begin 2017.

Year	Club (League)	Class	AVG	G	AB	R	H	2B	3B	HR	RBI	BB	SO	SB	CS	OBP	SLG
2015	Tigers (GCL)	R	.333	4	15	4	5	0	0	0	1	1	3	2	0	.375	.333
	Connecticut (NYP)	SS	.270	25	100	14	27	5	1	0	12	5	14	5	2	.306	.340
	West Michigan (MWL)	LoA	.400	20	85	11	34	3	0	1	8	5	11	4	2	.440	.471
2016	Lakeland (FSL)	HiA	.262	127	527	76	138	19	5	5	51	28	108	7	5	.298	.345
Minor League Totals			.281	176	727	105	204	27	6	6	72	39	136	18	9	.317	.359

19 SPENCER TURNBULL, RHP

BA GRADE

45 Risk: High

Born: Sept. 18, 1992. **B-T:** R-R. **Ht.:** 6-3. **Wt.:** 215. **Drafted:** Alabama, 2014 (2nd round). **Signed by:** Bryson Barber.

After three years at Alabama, the Tigers drafted Turnbull and signed him for $900,000 bonus. He had a solid first full season with low Class A West Michigan, where he didn't allow a home run all season long. He pitched just 44.1 innings in the regular season—with half of his starts coming on rehab assignment in the Gulf Coast League—because of recurring stiffness in his throwing shoulder. He was healthy enough to return for a full load in the Arizona Fall League, where he went 1-3, 3.60 with 20 strikeouts in as many innings. More impressively, he got grounders at a 4-to-1 ratio in the AFL and kept the ball in the park. He cranked his fastball up to 96 mph in the Fall League and has touched 99 mph in the past. His fastball features heavy run and sink and he couples it with an average slider and a changeup that has improved to near-average. Getting through the AFL season healthy was an excellent sign for Turnbull, who will try to rebound in 2017 at Double-A Lakeland.

Year	Club (League)	Class	W	L	ERA	G	GS	CG	SV	IP	H	HR	BB	SO	K/9	WHIP	AVG
2014	Tigers (GCL)	R	0	0	3.00	1	1	0	0	3	2	1	1	4	12.0	1.00	.200
	Connecticut (NYP)	SS	0	2	4.45	11	11	0	0	28	31	1	14	19	6.0	1.59	.270
2015	West Michigan (MWL)	LoA	11	3	3.01	22	22	1	0	117	106	0	52	106	8.2	1.35	.242
2016	Tigers East (GCL)	R	0	0	7.36	2	2	0	0	4	4	2	1	5	12.3	1.36	.267
	Tigers West (GCL)	R	0	1	3.38	4	4	0	0	11	3	0	5	7	5.9	0.75	.091
	Lakeland (FSL)	HiA	1	1	3.00	6	6	0	0	30	24	1	10	27	8.1	1.13	.216
Minor League Totals			12	7	3.32	46	46	1	0	192	170	5	83	168	7.9	1.32	.235

20 GRAYSON GREINER, C

45 Risk: High

Born: Oct. 11, 1992. **B-T:** R-R. **Ht.:** 6-6. **Wt.:** 220. **Drafted:** South Carolina, 2014 (3rd round). **Signed by:** Grant Brittain.

Greiner has struggled to stay healthy since signing out of South Carolina for $529,400 as a third-round pick in 2014. He had his first pro season cut short by a broken hamate bone in his left wrist that required surgery and ended his season. He was invited to major league spring training in 2015 but missed a chunk of time after breaking a finger in the first bullpen session he caught. That was followed by a down season at high Class A Lakeland during which he was limited to just 89 games. He bounced back in 2016, hitting .293/.339/.424 with seven home runs mostly at Lakeland and Double-A Erie. Even with his massive frame at 6-foot-6, Greiner earns positive marks for his defensive abilities. He is flexible and able to get into a low crouch, and scouts who saw him this past season give him average marks for blocking and receiving. He's got an above-average, accurate arm and threw out 44 percent of runners trying to steal last season. He finished the year with stint in the Arizona Fall League and will likely return to Triple-A Toledo next season.

Year	Club (League)	Class	AVG	G	AB	R	H	2B	3B	HR	RBI	BB	SO	SB	CS	OBP	SLG
2014	West Michigan (MWL)	LoA	.322	26	90	11	29	5	0	2	16	11	18	0	0	.394	.444
2015	Lakeland (FSL)	HiA	.183	89	312	24	57	12	0	3	21	27	90	0	0	.254	.250
2016	Lakeland (FSL)	HiA	.312	31	109	14	34	6	0	0	12	12	26	0	0	.385	.367
	Erie (EL)	AA	.288	59	208	20	60	9	3	7	30	10	55	1	0	.320	.462
	Toledo (IL)	AAA	.000	1	4	0	0	0	0	0	0	0	2	0	0	.000	.000
Minor League Totals			.249	206	723	69	180	32	3	12	79	60	191	1	0	.310	.351

21 WLADIMIR PINTO, RHP

BA GRADE
45 Risk: High

Born: Feb. 12, 1998. **B-T:** R-R. **Ht.:** 5-11. **Wt.:** 175. **Signed:** Venezuela, 2014.
Signed by: Delvis Pacheco.

Signed out of Venezuela for $30,000 as a 16-year-old in 2014, Pinto has already opened eyes with his combination of arm speed, velocity and flashes of an average or better curveball. He spent his first pro season in the Venezuelan Summer League and made his stateside debut in 2016 with one of the Tigers' two Rookie-level Gulf Coast League teams. Pinto has a short, stocky build that suggests his long-term role is in the bullpen, but there are evaluators who believe he could start if given the chance. Even as a reliever, the Tigers are excited about Pinto's potential. Besides his big fastball, Pinto has shown a potentially above-average curveball and a changeup that could reach the same level with patience and repetitions. Pinto creates good angle on his pitches from a high three-quarters arm slot and gets the most out of his short stature by staying upright during his delivery. There's a lot of refinement to come as control and command are concerned, but Pinto could be the latest in the Tigers' line of high-velocity relief arms moving through the system.

Year	Club (League)	Class	W	L	ERA	G	GS	CG	SV	IP	H	HR	BB	SO	K/9	WHIP	AVG
2015	Tigers (VSL)	R	2	1	3.90	16	0	0	1	28	16	0	28	24	7.8	1.59	.167
2016	Tigers East (GCL)	R	1	1	2.66	16	0	0	1	24	11	0	10	32	12.2	0.89	.134
Minor League Totals			3	2	3.33	32	0	0	2	51	27	0	38	56	9.8	1.27	.152

22 BRYAN GARCIA, RHP

BA GRADE
45 Risk: High

Born: April 19, 1995. **B-T:** R-R. **Ht.:** 6-1. **Wt.:** 205. **Drafted:** Miami, 2016 (6th round). **Signed by:** Nick Avila.

Garcia spent three years in Miami's bullpen and set the school's career record for saves before the Tigers drafted him in sixth round and signed him for $289,400. The Tigers laud Garcia for his makeup, which features the aggression and competitiveness associated with someone who spent three years in a closer's role. Garcia generates plus arm speed from a three-quarters arm slot and starts his arsenal with a sinking fastball that sits in the 92-96 mph range. He complements the pitch with a potentially plus slider in the mid-80s with 10-to-4 break, as well as a changeup that shows fade to both lefthanders and righthanders. He dominated at short-season Connecticut and ended his season in the playoffs with low Class A West Michigan before heading to the instructional league. The Tigers want Garcia to work on commanding all his pitches within the strike zone. If he does that, he could be part of the cadre of Tigers relievers on the fast track to the upper levels. He'll start 2017 at either back at West Michigan or at high Class A Lakeland.

Year	Club (League)	Class	W	L	ERA	G	GS	CG	SV	IP	H	HR	BB	SO	K/9	WHIP	AVG
2016	Connecticut (NYP)	SS	0	1	1.00	16	0	0	6	18	13	1	3	21	10.5	0.89	.194
	West Michigan (MWL)	LoA	0	1	40.50	1	0	0	0	1	3	0	0	1	13.5	4.50	.600
Minor League Totals			0	2	2.41	17	0	0	6	19	16	1	3	22	10.6	1.02	.222

23 ZAC HOUSTON, RHP

BA GRADE
45 Risk: High

Born: Nov. 25, 1994. **B-T:** R-R. **Ht.:** 6-5. **Wt.:** 250. **Drafted:** Mississippi State, 2016 (11th round). **Signed by:** Justin Henry.

Houston was strictly a reliever at Mississippi State until his junior year, when he made six starts. That included the Bulldogs' final win of the season, when Houston spun six innings of two-hit shutout ball against Louisiana Tech in the NCAA Regionals. He reverted back to a relief role in pro ball and made 20 appearances between short-season Connecticut and low Class A West Michigan. Houston has a funky delivery that includes a hook in the back and a jump that reminds some evaluators of Rick Sutcliffe. His fastball sits in the 92-94 mph range and has touched 97 with heavy sink and armside bore. He throws a slider that features hard bite but breaks more horizontally than vertically. He rounds out his arsenal with a fringy curveball and a show-me changeup. The Tigers like the aggressiveness Houston brought with him from college. He is likely to begin the year at high Class A Lakeland and has a ceiling of a middle reliever.

Year	Club (League)	Class	W	L	ERA	G	GS	CG	SV	IP	H	HR	BB	SO	K/9	WHIP	AVG
2016	Connecticut (NYP)	SS	1	0	0.00	7	0	0	0	10	7	0	3	19	17.1	1.00	.189
	West Michigan (MWL)	LoA	1	0	0.46	13	0	0	4	20	5	0	12	30	13.7	0.86	.082
Minor League Totals			2	0	0.30	20	0	0	4	30	12	0	15	49	14.9	0.91	.122

24 DREW SMITH, RHP

BA GRADE
45 Risk: High

Born: Sept. 24, 1993. **B-T:** R-R. **Ht.:** 6-2. **Wt.:** 190. **Drafted:** Dallas Baptist, 2015 (3rd round). **Signed by:** Chris Wimmer.

Though he made 10 starts—including eight in his sophomore year—Smith was primarily a reliever in his three years at Dallas Baptist. He pitched one summer for the Mat-su Miners of the college Alaska League, where he was teammates with fellow Tigers prospects Christin Stewart and A.J. Simcox. Detroit drafted Smith in the third round of 2015 and gave him a $575,800 bonus. His calling card in both college and the professional ranks is his high-powered fastball, which sits in the 92-97 mph range. He also has a 12-to-6 curveball, but had to be convinced to throw it early in the season. He throws the pitch with sufficient arm speed, but early on evaluators said it had a hump that hitters could easily pick up. He also has a changeup, but he throws it very rarely. His delivery is high-effort and features a small collapse on his back leg. Smith has dealt with injuries throughout his career and landed on the disabled list three times since turning pro. This season he dealt with minor injuries to his shoulder, elbow and pectoral muscles. He will head to high Class A Lakeland in 2017.

Year	Club (League)	Class	W	L	ERA	G	GS	CG	SV	IP	H	HR	BB	SO	K/9	WHIP	AVG
2015	Tigers (GCL)	R	0	0	0.00	1	0	0	0	2	1	0	0	3	16.2	0.60	.167
	Connecticut (NYP)	SS	2	0	0.33	11	0	0	2	28	15	0	4	33	10.7	0.69	.155
	West Michigan (MWL)	LoA	1	0	0.00	1	0	0	0	2	1	0	1	2	10.8	1.20	.167
2016	West Michigan (MWL)	LoA	1	2	2.96	35	0	0	4	49	34	0	23	62	11.5	1.17	.205
Minor League Totals			4	2	1.92	48	0	0	6	80	51	0	28	100	11.3	0.99	.185

25 JACOB ROBSON, OF

BA GRADE
45 Risk: High

Born: Nov. 20, 1994. **B-T:** L-R. **Ht.:** 5-10. **Wt.:** 175. **Drafted:** Mississippi State, 2016 (8th round). **Signed by:** Justin Henry.

Robson was drafted out of high school by the Padres in 2012 but chose to attend Mississippi State instead. Four years later, he improved his stock enough to earn an eighth-round selection and a $181,600 signing bonus as a redshirt junior. He missed most of his sophomore season with an elbow injury and missed time his final collegiate season with a broken left pinky. An above-average runner, Robson shows prototypical leadoff skills and proved too advanced for the Rookie-level Gulf Coast League and short-season New York-Penn League, where he hit a combined .301/.407/.405 with nine doubles, a home run and 15 steals in 48 games. The Tigers believe in Robson's ability to play center field, work counts and get on base and laud his makeup as a baseball rat. He doesn't have much in the way of over-the-fence power, so he'll have to stay in center to profile as an everyday player. His college pedigree could put him in line for an aggressive assignment to high Class A, but he is more likely to begin at low Class A West Michigan.

Year	Club (League)	Class	AVG	G	AB	R	H	2B	3B	HR	RBI	BB	SO	SB	CS	OBP	SLG
2016	Tigers West (GCL)	R	.267	28	101	16	27	4	2	0	5	16	22	14	4	.368	.347
	Connecticut (NYP)	SS	.329	21	76	14	25	5	1	1	6	15	20	1	2	.440	.461
Minor League Totals			.294	49	177	30	52	9	3	1	11	31	42	15	6	.399	.395

26 CRISTHIAN TORTOSA, LHP

BA GRADE
50 Risk: Extreme

Born: Oct. 30, 1998. **B-T:** L-L. **Ht.:** 6-4. **Wt.:** 170. **Drafted:** Venezuela, 2015. **Signed by:** Delvis Pacheco.

The Tigers signed Tortosa out of Venezuela in 2015 for $30,000 and under normal circumstances he would have spent his first pro season in the Venezuelan Summer League. The league shuttered after the 2015 season, however, and the Tigers responded by joining the Yankees as clubs with two Gulf Coast League teams. Tortosa pitched all season in the GCL and showed why the Tigers believe in his upside. His fastball sits in the low-90s from a loose, easy delivery. He also showed a slurvy breaking ball and the makings of a changeup as well. The Tigers are particularly intrigued by Tortosa's size and remaining projection, and see him adding velocity and physicality as he gets older. He dealt with two bouts of forearm soreness in 2016—once at midseason and then again during instructional league—but did not have surgery. Tortosa will pitch all of 2017 as an 18-year-old, so he is likely to return to the Gulf Coast League to continue developing in the controlled environment of the Tigers' minor league complex.

Year	Club (League)	Class	W	L	ERA	G	GS	CG	SV	IP	H	HR	BB	SO	K/9	WHIP	AVG
2016	Tigers East (GCL)	R	0	1	4.12	13	0	0	0	20	16	0	10	18	8.2	1.32	.222
Minor League Totals			0	1	4.12	13	0	0	0	20	16	0	10	18	8.2	1.32	.222

27 ARVICENT PEREZ, C

BA GRADE
45 Risk: High

Born: Jan 14, 1994. **B-T:** R-R. **Ht.:** 5-10. **Wt.:** 180. **Signed:** Venezuela, 2011. **Signed by:** Alejandro Rodriguez.

The Tigers signed Perez out of Venezuela as a defensive backstop with the hopes that he might grow into enough offense to find a spot in the majors. He has moved slowly throughout his career, spending two years in the Venezuelan Summer League before coming stateside. Since then, he has spent parts of three seasons at low Class A West Michigan before finally showing signs with the bat this season, hitting .303/.320/.391. The Tigers like his strong build and compact swing, although they don't expect much in the way of power. As a defender, Perez's calling card is his plus arm. He threw out 43 percent (26-of-60) of potential basestealers in 2016, which would have ranked third in the Midwest League if he hadn't been limited to just 74 games while splitting time with Shane Zeile. He needs to continue sharpening his receiving skills and has gotten better at game-calling as well. Perez ranks as the system's best defensive catcher, and is likely to move up to the high Class A Florida State League this year to keep working on his overall game.

Year	Club (League)	Class	AVG	G	AB	R	H	2B	3B	HR	RBI	BB	SO	SB	CS	OBP	SLG
2014	Tigers (GCL)	R	.309	27	81	14	25	6	1	3	20	1	7	3	0	.310	.519
	West Michigan (MWL)	LoA	.348	14	46	7	16	2	0	0	6	1	5	1	1	.375	.391
2015	Connecticut (NYP)	SS	.263	5	19	3	5	1	0	0	1	0	2	0	1	.263	.316
	West Michigan (MWL)	LoA	.229	33	118	7	27	4	0	0	5	3	20	1	0	.252	.263
2016	West Michigan (MWL)	LoA	.303	74	271	28	82	16	4	0	30	7	36	1	0	.320	.391
Minor League Totals			.291	235	780	81	227	39	8	5	103	25	95	12	4	.316	.381

28 MATT HALL, LHP

Born: July 23, 1993. **B-T:** L-L. **Ht.:** 6-0. **Wt.:** 200. **Drafted:** Missouri State, 2015 (6th round). **Signed by:** Marty Malloy.

BA GRADE
40 Risk: High

Hall busted out in a big way his junior year at Missouri State when led the NCAA with 171 strikeouts in 125 innings. He capped off his brilliant season when he spun a one-hitter with eight strikeouts against Arkansas in the Super Regionals in what turned out to be his final outing. The Tigers popped Hall in the sixth round and gave him a $239,400 signing bonus. Hall's primary weapon is a slow, sweeping curveball thrown in the 69-73 mph range that gives lefthanders fits. His fastball is below-average at 86-88 mph, and his changeup is in the developmental stages and a clear third pitch at this point. He dominated at low Class A West Michigan, going 8-0, 1.09 with 72 strikeouts in 66.1 innings but ran into more trouble at high Class A Lakeland. He walked more than four hitters per nine innings at that level, and surrendered nearly a hit per inning. He was effective against lefties at both levels, however, allowing just seven extra-base hits—no home runs—in 145 plate appearances all season. That role as a lefthanded specialist is Hall's most likely path to the majors.

Year	Club (League)	Class	W	L	ERA	G	GS	CG	SV	IP	H	HR	BB	SO	K/9	WHIP	AVG
2015	Tigers (GCL)	R	0	0	3.00	1	1	0	0	3	4	0	1	4	12.0	1.67	.308
	Connecticut (NYP)	SS	0	1	2.90	10	10	0	0	31	29	3	7	30	8.7	1.16	.246
2016	West Michigan (MWL)	LoA	8	0	1.09	12	12	0	0	66	49	0	21	72	9.8	1.06	.202
	Lakeland (FSL)	HiA	3	2	4.15	12	11	1	0	61	61	6	28	54	8.0	1.47	.264
Minor League Totals			11	3	2.63	35	34	1	0	161	143	9	57	160	8.9	1.24	.237

29 JAIRO LABOURT, LHP

Born: March 7, 1994. **B-T:** L-L. **Ht.:** 6-4. **Wt.:** 205. **Signed:** Dominican Republic, 2011. **Signed by:** Marco Paddy/Hilario Soriano (Blue Jays).

BA GRADE
45 Risk: Extreme

The Blue Jays traded nearly everything not nailed down during their push to the playoffs in 2015, and Labourt went to the Tigers with fellow lefthanders Daniel Norris and Matt Boyd in exchange for ace David Price, who was brilliant for the Blue Jays before signing a megadeal with the Red Sox in the offseason. Labourt earned a spot in the 2015 Futures Game with the Blue Jays but has struggled since changing organizations. He still throws his fastball in the low-to-mid-90s with sinking life and couples it with a slider that gets swings and misses, but an exaggerated arm swing hampered his command and control greatly with high Class A Lakeland. He issued 70 walks in 87.1 innings while striking out 81, and was moved to the bullpen in an attempt to rebuild his confidence. There still might be hope for Labourt if he can harness his arsenal—he still held hitters to a .202 average—and the Tigers still believe he has an outside chance at returning to the rotation. He is likely to return to Lakeland in 2017 to work on re-establishing himself and rebuilding confidence.

Year	Club (League)	Class	W	L	ERA	G	GS	CG	SV	IP	H	HR	BB	SO	K/9	WHIP	AVG
2011	Blue Jays (DSL)	R	0	4	2.23	12	12	0	0	36	29	0	14	29	7.2	1.18	.220
2012	Blue Jays (GCL)	R	0	3	3.79	12	12	0	0	38	38	2	23	39	9.2	1.61	.253
2013	Bluefield (APP)	R	2	2	1.92	12	8	0	0	52	39	3	14	45	7.8	1.03	.204
2014	Lansing (MWL)	LoA	0	0	6.43	6	3	0	0	14	15	1	20	11	7.1	2.50	.300
	Vancouver (NWL)	SS	5	3	1.77	15	15	0	0	71	47	0	37	82	10.3	1.18	.188
2015	Dunedin (FSL)	HiA	2	7	4.59	18	18	0	0	80	83	6	44	70	7.8	1.58	.263
	Lakeland (FSL)	HiA	1	5	6.31	7	7	0	0	36	45	3	15	34	8.6	1.68	.319
2016	Lakeland (FSL)	HiA	7	9	5.26	30	12	0	1	87	65	3	70	81	8.3	1.55	.202
Minor League Totals			17	33	3.84	112	87	0	1	415	361	18	237	391	8.5	1.44	.233

30 GREGORY SOTO, LHP

BA GRADE

45 Risk: Extreme

Born: Feb. 11, 1995. **B-T:** L-L. **Ht.:** 6-1. **Wt.:** 180. **Signed:** Dominican Republic, 2012. **Signed by:** Carlos Santana/Ramon Perez.

The Tigers signed Soto out of the Dominican Republic in 2012 and has slowly matured into an impressive young lefthander with potential waiting to be harnessed. Pitching at short-season Connecticut this year, Soto showed a lively fastball in the low-90s that peaked at 95-96 at times. Particularly, the Tigers are impressed with the way Soto can spin a breaking ball. He throws two types of curveballs—one with traditional deep break and a harder, shorter version that looks like a slider. The Tigers believe his breaking balls can be plus with repetition and consistency. They also were particularly pleased with the way Soto improved his pitchability this season. When he struggled in the middle of games he was able to make adjustments without letting things snowball on him. Scouts who saw him in the New York-Penn League would like to see him trust his stuff instead of aiming it, and they noticed that he has a tendency to slow down his arm when throwing the curveball. Soto has a chance as a starter if he continues making strides with his overall game. He will start 2017 with low Class A West Michigan.

Year	Club (League)	Class	W	L	ERA	G	GS	CG	SV	IP	H	HR	BB	SO	K/9	WHIP	AVG
2014	Tigers (DSL)	R	5	3	3.20	16	10	0	0	51	41	0	25	57	10.1	1.30	.224
2015	Connecticut (NYP)	SS	0	1	22.50	2	1	0	0	2	1	0	6	5	22.5	3.50	.143
	Tigers (GCL)	R	2	4	2.19	9	5	0	0	37	34	0	25	40	9.7	1.59	.250
2016	Connecticut (NYP)	SS	3	2	3.03	15	15	0	0	71	68	1	34	62	7.8	1.43	.256
Minor League Totals			11	12	3.45	58	43	0	0	198	173	2	126	215	9.8	1.51	.240

Houston Astros

BY J.J. COOPER

In the past two seasons, trusting the process and being patient has paid off for two long-suffering fan bases. Dayton Moore and Royals, the doorstop of the American League since the 1994 strike, finished off a seven-year rebuild with a World Series title in 2015. A year later, Theo Epstein, Jed Hoyer and the Cubs guided the Cubs to their first World Series victory in more than a century.

And that leaves the Astros. Like the Cubs, the Astros have a title drought that is better described in decades than years. Houston's 55 years in baseball without a  title now counts as the third-longest in the game, behind only the Indians and Rangers franchises.

Like the Cubs and the Royals, the Astros are now bearing fruit from a complete teardown. General manager Jeff Luhnow and his staff took over the same offseason as Epstein took over the Cubs. Houston had further to go because of a thinner farm system and less big league talent. Like Chicago, Houston signaled the long rebuild had reached a new stage with a playoff appearance in 2015.

But while the Cubs took a step forward in 2016, leaping from wild card team to World Series champions, the Astros took a step back. After winning 86 games in 2015, Houston slid back to 84 wins. A full season from shortstop Carlos Correa and an outstanding year by second baseman Jose Altuve were not enough to make up for a nearly complete collapse by Astros outfielders, a revolving door of ineffective first basemen and a rotation that regressed dramatically.

That leaves the Astros with opportunities but also significant challenges heading into 2017. The strength of the organization's system is its pitching, even after graduating righthanders Chris Devenski, Joe Musgrove and Michael Feliz in 2016. Houston used that pitching depth to trade hard-throwing righties Albert Abreu and Jorge Guzman for Yankees catcher Brian McCann in mid-November.

The Astros also have shown a willingness to spend money. Houston blew up their outfield, bringing in Josh Reddick and Carlos Beltran to try to fix the lack of production from that unit.

That pitching depth means even after acquiring McCann, Reddick and Beltran, the Astros could make further moves. Francis Martes, David Paulino and fellow righties Forrest Whitley, the club's first-round pick in 2016, and Franklin Perez, a breakout prospect at low Class A, would be in high demand if offered in the right deal.

The Astros have depth in the lineup now

The Astros received contributions from rookie pitchers in 2016, including Chris Devenski

TOP PROSPECTS OF THE DECADE

Year	Player, Pos.	2016 Org
2007	Hunter Pence, of	Giants
2008	J.R. Towles, c	Did not play
2009	Jason Castro, c	Astros
2010	Jason Castro, c	Astros
2011	Jordan Lyles, rhp	Rockies
2012	Jon Singleton, 1b/of	Astros
2013	Carlos Correa, ss	Astros
2014	Carlos Correa, ss	Astros
2015	Carlos Correa, ss	Astros
2016	A.J. Reed, 1b	Astros

because of Alex Bregman and Yulieski Gurriel's defensive versatility and the team's ability to move Marwin Gonzalez back to a utility role. Houston is well-equipped to handle injuries in the lineup in 2017. The rotation's depth must come from the farm system.

Houston's window to contend still is wide open. Altuve is under contract through 2019, while Correa and righthander Lance McCullers Jr. won't even reach arbitration until after 2019. But, the time to rely on building from within is over.

The Astros did not spend significantly on the free agent market coming into 2016, and they were relatively quiet at the trade deadline, too. That won't be the case anymore. Houston has signalled that it's going to be aggressive.

The time to win is now.

ORGANIZATION OVERVIEW

General manager: Jeff Luhnow. **Farm director:** Pete Putila. **Scouting director:** Mike Elias.

Class	Team	League	W	L	PCT	Finish	Manager
Majors	Houston Astros	American	84	78	.519	t-8th (15)	A.J. Hinch
Triple-A	Fresno Grizzlies	Pacific Coast	73	70	.510	t-5th (16)	Tony DeFrancesco
Double-A	Corpus Christi Hooks	Texas	85	55	.607	1st (8)	Rodney Linares
High Class A	* Lancaster JetHawks	California	77	63	.550	4th (10)	Ramon Vazquez
Low Class A	Quad Cities River Bandits	Midwest	61	78	.439	14th (16)	Omar Lopez
Short-season	Tri-City ValleyCats	New York-Penn	38	38	.500	t-7th (14)	Lamarr Rogers
Rookie	Greeneville Astros	Appalachian	33	34	.493	6th (10)	Josh Bonifay
Rookie	GCL Astros	Gulf Coast	22	31	.415	14th (17)	Marty Malloy
Overall 2016 Minor League Record			389	369	.513	11th (30)	

* Affiliate moves to Buies Creek, N.C., to become Buies Creek Astros (Carolina) 2017

THIS YEAR'S TOP 30

No.	Player, Pos.	Grade/Risk
1.	Francis Martes, rhp	65/Medium
2.	Kyle Tucker, of	60/Medium
3.	David Paulino, rhp	60/High
4.	Franklin Perez, rhp	60/High
5.	A.J. Reed, 1b	55/High
6.	Forrest Whitley, rhp	60/Extreme
7.	Teoscar Hernandez, of	55/High
8.	Yulieski Gurriel, 3b/1b	50/Medium
9.	Derek Fisher, of	50/Medium
10.	Garrett Stubbs, c	50/High
11.	Miguelangel Sierra, ss/2b	55/Extreme
12.	J.D. Davis, 3b	45/Medium
13.	Ramon Laureano, of	50/High
14.	Daz Cameron, of	50/High
15.	Ronnie Dawson, of	50/High
16.	Hector Perez, rhp	55/Extreme
17.	Jonathan Arauz, ss/2b	50/High
18.	Jandel Gustave, rhp	50/High
19.	Gilberto Celestino, of	50/High
20.	Jake Rogers, c	45/High
21.	Trent Thornton, rhp	45/High
22.	Brady Rodgers, rhp	40/Medium
23.	James Hoyt, rhp	40/Medium
24.	Rogelio Armenteros, rhp	40/Medium
25.	Lupe Chavez, rhp	45/High
26.	Freudis Nova, ss	50/Extreme
27.	Tony Kemp, 2b/of	40/Medium
28.	Yordan Alvarez, 1b	45/Extreme
29.	Jose Luis Hernandez, rhp	40/Medium
30.	Colin Moran, 3b	40/Medium

LAST YEAR'S TOP 30

No.	Player, Pos.	Status
1.	A.J. Reed, 1b	No. 5
2.	Francis Martes, rhp	No. 1
3.	Alex Bregman, ss	Majors
4.	Kyle Tucker, of	No. 2
5.	Daz Cameron, of	No. 14
6.	Joe Musgrove, rhp	Majors
7.	David Paulino, rhp	No. 3
8.	Mark Appel, rhp	(Phillies)
9.	Colin Moran, 3b	No. 30
10.	Derek Fisher, of	No. 9
11.	Michael Feliz, rhp	Majors
12.	Albert Abreu, rhp	(Yankees)
13.	Jon Kemmer, of	Dropped out
14.	J.D. Davis, 3b	No. 12
15.	Tony Kemp, 2b/of	No. 27
16.	Tyler White, 3b	Majors
17.	Thomas Eshelman, rhp	(Phillies)
18.	Jandel Gustave, rhp	No. 18
19.	Max Stassi, c	Dropped out
20.	Riley Ferrell, rhp	Dropped out
21.	Franklin Perez, rhp	No. 4
22.	Wander Franco, 3b	Dropped out
23.	Andrew Aplin, of	Dropped out
24.	Gilberto Celestino, of	No. 19
25.	Miguelangel Sierra, ss	No. 11
26.	Alfredo Gonzalez, c	(White Sox)
27.	James Hoyt, rhp	No. 23
28.	Matt Duffy, 3b	(Japan)
29.	Nolan Fontana, ss	(Angels)
30.	Michael Freeman, lhp	Dropped out

BEST TOOLS

Best Hitter for Average	Kyle Tucker
Best Power Hitter	A.J. Reed
Best Strike-Zone Discipline	Yulieski Gurriel
Fastest Baserunner	Myles Straw
Best Athlete	Daz Cameron
Best Fastball	Francis Martes
Best Curveball	Francis Martes
Best Slider	Hector Perez
Best Changeup	Francis Martes
Best Control	Brady Rodgers
Best Defensive Catcher	Garrett Stubbs
Best Defensive Infielder	Miguelangel Sierra
Best Infield Arm	J.D. Davis
Best Defensive Outfielder	Gilberto Celestino
Best Outfield Arm	Teoscar Hernandez

PROJECTED 2020 LINEUP

Catcher	Garrett Stubbs
First Base	A.J. Reed
Second Base	Jose Altuve
Third Base	Alex Bregman
Shortstop	Carlos Correa
Left Field	Kyle Tucker
Center Field	Teoscar Hernandez
Right Field	George Springer
Designated Hitter	Josh Reddick
No. 1 Starter	Francis Martes
No. 2 Starter	Dallas Keuchel
No. 3 Starter	Lance McCullers Jr.
No. 4 Starter	Joe Musgrove
No. 5 Starter	Franklin Perez
Closer	David Paulino

MINOR LEAGUE DEPTH CHART

HOUSTON ASTROS

TOP 2017 ROOKIE: Francis Martes, rhp. He could join Lance McCullers Jr. in the rotation to give the Astros a pair of hard-throwing right-handers with filthy breaking balls.

BREAKOUT PROSPECT: Hector Perez, rhp. The Astros have built an assembly line of young, hard-throwing Latin pitchers who blossom with arm strength and feel. Perez is the next man up.

SOURCE OF TOP 30 TALENT			
Homegrown	23	Acquired	7
College	9	Trades	7
Junior college	1	Rule 5 draft	0
High school	3	Independent leagues	0
Nondrafted free agents	0	Free agents/waivers	0
International	10		

SLEEPER: Angel Macuare, rhp: One of Houston's top international targets in 2016, he has present stuff and feel for his secondary pitches, giving him a chance to develop as a starter.

LF
Derek Fisher (9)
Ronnie Dawson (15)
Jon Kemmer
Jason Martin
Bobby Boyd
Alejandro Garcia

CF
Teoscar Hernandez (7)
Ramon Laureano (13)
Daz Cameron (14)
Gilberto Celestino (19)
Stephen Wrenn
Osvaldo Duarte
Myles Straw

RF
Kyle Tucker (2)
Carmen Benedetti
Bryan de la Cruz
Carlos Machado

3B
J.D. Davis (12)
Colin Moran (30)
Abraham Toro
Wander Franco

SS
Miguelangel Sierra (12)
Jonathan Arauz (17)
Freudis Nova (26)
Anibal Sierra
Yorbin Ceuta
Stijn van der Meer
Deurys Carrasco
Yeuris Ramirez

2B
Tony Kemp (27)
Ryne Birk
Nick Tanielu
Enmanuel Valdez

1B
A.J. Reed (5)
Yuliesky Gurriel (8)
Yordan Alvarez (28)
Spencer Johnson

C
Garrett Stubbs (10)
Jake Rogers (20)
Anthony Hermelyn
Tyler Heineman
Ruben Castro
Chuckie Robinson
Nerio Rodriguez
Gabriel Bracamonte

LHP

LHSP	LHRP
Brett Adcock	Reymin Guduan
Kent Emanuel	Ashur Tolliver
Patrick Sandoval	Framber Valdez
	Michael Freeman
	Javier Navas

RHP

RHSP	RHRP
Francis Martes (1)	Jandel Gustave (18)
David Paulino (3)	James Hoyt (23)
Franklin Perez (4)	Riley Ferrell
Forrest Whitley (6)	Brendan McCurry
Hector Perez (16)	Cy Sneed
Trent Thornton (21)	Jairo Solis
Brady Rodgers (22)	Nick Hernandez
Lupe Chavez (25)	Akeem Bostick
Rogelio Armenteros (24)	Deen Deetz
Jose Luis Hernandez (29)	Carson LaRue
Jorge Alcala	Yoanis Quiala
Angel Macuare	
Brock Dykxhorn	
Kevin McCanna	

DRAFT ANALYSIS

2016

BEST PURE HITTER: OF Ronnie Dawson (2) didn't hit in his pro debut, as he turned in a .225/.351/.373 line for short-season Tri-City, but he hit .331 at Ohio State and projects as a potentially average to above-average hitter thanks to his bat speed, strength and speed. 2B Ryne Birk (13) is a lefthanded hitter who can spray the ball to all fields.

BEST POWER HITTER: Dawson has plus raw power with plenty of strength and a thick, muscular frame although he's yet to fully tap into that power. 1B/LF Spencer Johnson (16) hit 24 home runs this spring at Missouri State to lead NCAA Division I and added 10 more in his pro debut. He has a lot of swing and miss, but he could hit 25-30 home runs a year.

FASTEST RUNNER: OF Stephen Wrenn (6) will turn in 4.1s to first from the right side which earns 70 grades on the 20-to-80 scouting scale.

BEST DEFENSIVE PLAYER: C Jake Rogers (3) was considered the top defensive catcher in college baseball in 2016 by near unanimous acclamation. He moves well behind the plate, has soft hands, blocks pitches in the dirt and has a plus-plus arm that shuts down running games.

BEST FASTBALL: RHP Forrest Whitley (1) sat 92-94 mph and touched 97 mph this spring and summer. His fastball gets on hitters quickly and it has excellent life.

BEST SECONDARY PITCH: Whitley's main off-speed offering right now is a plus curveball with depth. Whitley can throw it for strikes, or bury it through the bottom of the strike zone for late-count swings and misses. He doesn't throw his 86-88 mph slider very often yet, but when he does, it flashes plus and could end up as a better pitch than the curveball.

BEST PRO DEBUT: Birk played his way out of the New York-Penn League by showing an advanced approach at the plate. He hit .323 in a promotion to low Class A Quad Cities for the final week.

BEST ATHLETE: Wrenn is a speedy outfielder who can stay in center field. Dawson is a power-speed outfielder who runs well for a big man. 3B Abraham Toro (5) is a strong, well-built 6-footer who has average speed to go with his strength.

MOST INTRIGUING BACKGROUND: SS Stijn Van Der Meer (32) grew up in the Netherlands and is the shortstop for the Dutch national team that won the European Baseball Championship in September. Van Der Meer came to the U.S. to play at Lamar.

CLOSEST TO THE MAJORS: Catchers don't usually move quickly, but Rogers extremely advanced defensive ability should get him to high Class A in 2017 and could allow him to move quickly. For a high school pitcher, Whitley's advanced assortment will make him a quick mover.

BEST LATE-ROUND PICK: Birk faced questions about his defense when he was at Texas A&M, but his bat and his willingness to work to alleviate some of his defensive issues could make him a potential big leaguer.

THE ONE WHO GOT AWAY: The Astros were one of only two teams to fail to sign a top-10 rounds pick. RHP Tyler Buffett (7) decided to head back to Oklahoma State.

2015

Getting SS Alex Bregman (1) with the compensation pick for not signing 2014 No. 1 Brady Aiken worked out in stellar fashion, and OF Kyle Tucker (1) is off to a great start. C Garrett Stubbs (8) has been a nice find, and OF Myles Straw (12) won the 2016 minor league batting title.

GRADE: A

2014

Houston didn't sign No. 1 overall pick Brady Aiken (1) or RHP Jacob Nix (5), and 1B A.J. Reed (2) flopped in his first big league trial, as did since-traded RHP Daniel Mengden (4). The Astros like OF Derek Fisher (1s) and 3B J.D. Davis (3).

GRADE: C

2013

The Astros cut bait on No. 1 overall pick Mark Appel (1) in the Ken Giles deal. While 2B Tony Kemp (5) and 1B Tyler White (33) have reached the majors, since-traded C Jacob Nottingham (6), now with Milwaukee, may have the biggest upside.

GRADE: D

TOP DRAFT PICKS OF THE DECADE

Year	Player, Pos.	2016 Org
2007	*Derek Dietrich, 3b (3rd round)	Marlins
2008	Jason Castro, c	Astros
2009	Jio Mier, ss	Blue Jays
2010	Delino DeShields Jr., 2b	Rangers
2011	George Springer, of	Astros
2012	Carlos Correa, ss	Astros
2013	Mark Appel, rhp	Phillies
2014	*Brady Aiken, lhp	Indians
2015	Alex Bregman, ss	Astros
2016	Forrest Whitley, rhp	Astros

*Did not sign.

LARGEST BONUSES IN CLUB HISTORY

Mark Appel, 2013	$6,350,000
Alex Bregman, 2015	$5,900,000
Carlos Correa, 2012	$4,800,000
Kyle Tucker, 2015	$4,000,000
Daz Cameron, 2015	$4,000,000

1 FRANCIS MARTES, RHP

Born: Nov. 24, 1995. **B-T:** R-R. **Ht.:** 6-0. **Wt.:** 232.
Signed: Dominican Republic, 2012. **Signed by:** Albert Gonzalez/Sandy Nin/Domingo Ortega (Marlins).

BA GRADE

65 Risk: Medium

SCOUTING GRADES

Fastball: 70.
Curveball: 70.
Changeup: 55.
Control: 55.

Based on 20-80 scouting scale and future projection rather than present tools.

BILL MITCHELL

The Marlins don't spend much money internationally, but they have done a great job of finding bargains on the international market. Miami signed Martes for just $78,000 in 2012 and watched him quickly develop from a pitcher with a high-80s fastball and some feel into a low- to mid-90s fireballer. He stood out in the Dominican Summer League in 2013 before he ever pitched in the U.S. Impressed with Martes' ability to mix a plus fastball and plus curveball in the Rookie-level Gulf Coast League in 2014, the Astros ensured he was included in the Jarred Cosart trade that July, even though Martes was struggling to get outs and throw strikes in a complex league. He has made dramatic leaps since then as he has filled out and developed a changeup. Once considered a likely power reliever, Martes has developed into one of the fastest-moving starting pitchers in the minors. For example, he was the youngest pitcher in Double-A when the 2016 season began. Martes started slowly at Corpus Christi and had a 5.03 ERA in early June, but he went 5-4, 2.67 in the second half with 81 strikeouts and 20 walks in 71 innings.

Few minor league pitchers can match Martes in terms of raw stuff, and the same is true for major leaguers. He has touched 100 mph with his fastball and generally sits 93-97. His plus-plus four-seamer doesn't have exceptional run, but it still generates plenty of swings and misses thanks to its extreme velocity and his ability to work in and out and up and down. Scouts debate whether Martes' ability to work all four quadrants is by design or by good fortune, because he sometimes misses his target significantly but still manages to be around the strike zone. Even though he's short for a righthander—he is officially listed at 6-foot-1 but probably is closer to 6 feet—Martes gets some downhill plane when he works down in the zone. His hard downer curveball at 85-87 mph gives him a second potential 70-grade pitch on the 20-80 scouting scale. It has power and downward break reminiscent of that of fellow Astros righthander Lance McCullers Jr. Martes' curve comes in at slider speed, but it has true 12-to-6 or 11-to-5 break rather than the sweep of a slider. Unlike

McCullers, Martes uses his fastball as his main weapon, which sets up his curve. His changeup is less consistent, but it generates plus grades from some and it improved as 2016 wore on. He throws it harder than most changeups, but it generates whiffs thanks to its late drop. It will show some late fade at times, though more by accident than design. The fade generally happens when he spins out of his delivery instead of staying direct to the plate. Martes has also toyed with using a cutter against lefthanders.

Martes has the raw profile of an ace with two pitches that grade near the top of the scale, a changeup that is at least average and at least average control. He has filled out into a thick-chested, meaty righthander who evokes comparisons with Johnny Cueto because of his short stature and big stuff. After six starts in the Arizona Fall League, Martes is ready for Triple-A Fresno and could reach the big leagues at some point in 2017.

Year	Club (League)	Class	W	L	ERA	G	GS	CG	SV	IP	H	HR	BB	SO	K/9	WHIP	AVG
2014	Marlins (GCL)	R	2	2	5.18	8	6	0	0	33	29	0	20	33	9.0	1.48	.232
	Astros (GCL)	R	1	1	0.82	4	3	0	0	11	5	0	3	12	9.8	0.73	.132
2015	Quad Cities (MWL)	LoA	3	2	1.04	10	8	1	2	52	33	1	13	45	7.8	0.88	.181
	Lancaster (CAL)	HiA	4	1	2.31	6	5	0	0	35	31	1	8	37	9.5	1.11	.230
	Corpus Christi (TL)	AA	1	0	4.91	3	3	0	0	15	19	2	7	16	9.8	1.77	.311
2016	Corpus Christi (TL)	AA	9	6	3.30	25	22	0	0	125	104	4	47	131	9.4	1.20	.222
Minor League Totals			23	15	2.97	68	53	1	2	321	272	9	112	307	8.6	1.20	.227

2 KYLE TUCKER, OF

Born: Jan. 17, 1997. **B-T:** L-R. **Ht.:** 6-4. **Wt.:** 189. **Drafted:** HS—Tampa, 2015 (1st round). **Signed by:** John Martin.

The younger brother of Astros big league outfielder Preston Tucker, Kyle was the BA High School Player of the Year in 2015, when he hit .484 with 10 home runs and 10 stolen bases. The fifth overall pick that year, he stood out in a pair of Rookie-level stops in his pro debut then jumped to low Class A Quad Cities in 2016. Tucker's advanced bat gives him a shot to be a plus hitter with plus power. Even though he is lean with long levers, he actually prefers hitting balls on the inner half, which helps explain why he has handled lefthanders well. He can pull his hands in on the inside pitch, and his hands and wrists work well to make his pull-oriented approach work. His swing generates excellent loft. But that projected power won't arrive until Tucker adds some more good weight to add strength in his trunk and legs. The Astros have worked him in all three outfield spots, but he projects as an above-average right fielder with an above-average arm. He's an average runner but does a great job reading pitchers and timing his jumps. Tucker handled a late-season cameo at high Class A Lancaster with no issues. He will return to high Class A in 2017—at the Astros' new Carolina League affiliate—and could reach Double-A before he turns 21.

BA GRADE
60 Risk: Medium

Year	Club (League)	Class	AVG	G	AB	R	H	2B	3B	HR	RBI	BB	SO	SB	CS	OBP	SLG
2015	Astros (GCL)	R	.208	33	120	19	25	3	2	2	13	9	14	4	2	.267	.317
	Greeneville (APP)	R	.286	30	112	11	32	9	0	1	20	7	15	14	2	.322	.393
2016	Quad Cities (MWL)	LoA	.276	101	373	43	103	19	5	6	56	40	75	31	9	.348	.402
	Lancaster (CAL)	HiA	.339	16	59	13	20	6	2	3	13	10	6	1	3	.435	.661
Minor League Totals			.271	180	664	86	180	37	9	12	102	66	110	50	16	.338	.408

3 DAVID PAULINO, RHP

Born: Feb. 6, 1994. **B-T:** R-R. **Ht.:** 6-7. **Wt.:** 214. **Signed:** Dominican Republic, 2010. **Signed by:** Carlos Santana/Ramon Perez/Miguel Garcia (Tigers).

As well as Francis Martes has panned out, Paulino has a better frame and equal stuff. The Astros acquired him from the Tigers for reliever Jose Veras in July 2013. Paulino had Tommy John surgery in 2014 and never has pitched 100 innings in a season. Paulino is 6-foot-7 but unlike many young, long-limbed pitchers he has a knack for duplicating his simple, low-effort delivery. He already has above-average control, and he walked two batters or fewer in each 2016 outing. Paulino's plus fastball sits 91-96 mph with good downhill plane and adequate run and life, though it sometimes takes a while to build velocity. In some starts he'll pitch at 90-92 mph early, then touch 98 a couple of innings later. He uses both a plus 78-81 mph curveball with 12-to-6 action and depth and a fringe-average slider. His mid-80s changeup flashes plus as well. Paulino missed time in 2016 both for elbow tendinitis and a minor disciplinary issue. He should contend for a big league role—either starting or relieving—at some point in 2017, and he has frontline potential if he can prove his durability.

BA GRADE
60 Risk: High

Year	Club (League)	Class	W	L	ERA	G	GS	CG	SV	IP	H	HR	BB	SO	K/9	WHIP	AVG
2014	Did not play—Injured																
2015	Tri-City (NYP)	SS	1	0	0.00	2	2	0	0	9	4	0	2	10	9.6	0.64	.125
	Quad Cities (MWL)	LoA	3	2	1.57	5	5	0	0	29	21	0	7	32	10.0	0.98	.202
	Lancaster (CAL)	HiA	1	1	4.91	6	5	0	1	29	24	1	10	30	9.2	1.16	.220
2016	Astros (GCL)	R	0	0	0.75	3	3	0	0	12	9	0	2	14	10.5	0.92	.196
	Corpus Christi (TL)	AA	5	2	1.83	14	9	0	1	64	47	3	11	72	10.1	0.91	.204
	Fresno (PCL)	AAA	0	2	3.86	3	3	0	0	14	16	1	6	20	12.9	1.57	.267
	Houston (AL)	MAJ	0	1	5.14	3	1	0	0	7	6	0	3	2	2.6	1.29	.240
Major League Totals			0	1	5.14	3	1	0	0	7	6	0	3	2	2.6	1.29	.240
Minor League Totals			13	9	2.20	48	39	0	2	196	146	6	50	219	10.0	1.00	.205

4 FRANKLIN PEREZ, RHP

BA GRADE

60 Risk: High

Born: Dec. 6, 1997. **B-T:** R-R. **Ht.:** 6-3. **Wt.:** 222. **Signed:** Venezuela, 2014. **Signed by:** Oz Ocampo/Oscar Alvarado.

Perez was a big, reasonably athletic third baseman in Carlos Guillen's program in Venezuela, but it was his throwing arm that stood out more than his power, so he wisely moved to the mound and signed for $1 million. He was one of the younger players in the low Class A Midwest League in 2016. The Astros saw Perez as one of the best arms in the 2014 international class (which included Anderson Espinoza), and so far he's lived up to those expectations. Perez's present size and stuff give him an excellent chance to develop as a starter. He pitched at 87-91 mph when he signed, but he's now sitting 92-94 and touching 96 with a plus fastball, and he does it with little effort. Perez's high-70s curveball has good shape and bite, and his changeup has fade and late sink along with good deception. He also toys with a low-80s slider that has potential as a right-on-right weapon. His control is advanced for his age, and 66 percent of his pitches he threw in Quad Cities were strikes. With a strong 2017, Perez could leap into the top tier of pitching prospects. With his feel and control he's ready to pitch in high Class A as a 19-year-old. He has a chance to have three plus pitches with at least average control, and he has the frame and ease of delivery that indicates he could be durable.

Year	Club (League)	Class	W	L	ERA	G	GS	CG	SV	IP	H	HR	BB	SO	K/9	WHIP	AVG
2015	Astros Orange (DSL)	R	1	2	4.37	11	9	0	0	35	34	1	11	44	11.3	1.29	.250
	Astros (GCL)	R	0	2	4.80	5	1	0	0	15	19	0	3	17	10.2	1.47	.292
2016	Quad Cities (MWL)	LoA	3	3	2.84	15	10	0	1	67	63	1	19	75	10.1	1.23	.250
Minor League Totals			4	7	3.55	31	20	0	1	117	116	2	33	136	10.5	1.28	.256

5 A.J. REED, 1B

BA GRADE

55 Risk: High

Born: May 10, 1993. **B-T:** L-L. **Ht.:** 6-4. **Wt.:** 275. **Drafted:** Kentucky, 2014 (2nd round). **Signed by:** Nick Venuto.

One of the best hitters in the minors in 2015 and the BA College Player of the Year in 2014, Reed produced at Triple-A Fresno in 2016, hitting .291/.368/.556 in 70 games. But in 45 games with the big league club, he looked helpless against good breaking balls, showing very little of his trademark power. Reed failed in 2016 for the first time in years. He still showed patience and plus power in the Pacific Coast League, but with Houston he was too pull-happy and must prove he can lay off sliders out of the strike zone. Reed has adequate but not exceptional bat speed, so he has to show he can make adjustments to translate his exceptional minor league performance to the big leagues. For a second straight season, he reported to camp about 20-30 pounds beyond his ideal weight, which did not help his bat speed or his nimbleness at first base. Reed scoops balls well at first and, as a former pitcher, has a plus arm. Slow-footed, slugging first basemen face plenty of skepticism until they hit at the big league level. Because they are aiming to win, the Astros aren't in a position to give Reed an extended trial, so he'll have to fight for an opportunity. His ceiling is still that of a plus hitter with plus power, but he now faces healthy skepticism in the industry.

Year	Club (League)	Class	AVG	G	AB	R	H	2B	3B	HR	RBI	BB	SO	SB	CS	OBP	SLG
2014	Tri-City (NYP)	SS	.306	34	124	22	38	11	0	5	30	22	22	2	0	.420	.516
	Quad Cities (MWL)	LoA	.272	34	125	21	34	9	1	7	24	8	32	0	0	.326	.528
2015	Lancaster (CAL)	HiA	.346	82	318	75	110	16	4	23	81	59	73	0	0	.449	.638
	Corpus Christi (TL)	AA	.332	53	205	38	68	14	1	11	46	27	49	0	0	.405	.571
2016	Fresno (PCL)	AAA	.291	70	261	42	76	22	1	15	50	32	67	0	0	.368	.556
	Houston (AL)	MAJ	.164	45	122	11	20	3	0	3	8	18	48	0	0	.270	.262
Major League Totals			.164	45	122	11	20	3	0	3	8	18	48	0	0	.270	.262
Minor League Totals			.316	273	1033	198	326	72	7	61	231	148	243	2	0	.403	.576

6 FORREST WHITLEY, RHP

MIKE JANES

Born: Sept. 15, 1997. **B-T:** R-R. **Ht.:** 6-7. **Wt.:** 240. **Drafted:** HS—San Antonio, 2016 (1st round). **Signed by:** Noel Gonzales

Like many top high school pitching prospects, Whitley went from nothing to something after a growth spurt. A sub-six-feet freshman, he gained six inches and 15 mph before his sophomore year, but it wasn't until he shed baby fat that he emerged as a potential first-rounder. Whitley went to the Astros 17th overall in the 2016 draft. Whitley has the plus-plus fastball you expect from a first-round prep pitching prospect. He sits 92-94 mph and touches 97, and his fastball generates swings and misses due to its excellent life. But unlike many young power pitches, Whitley has three secondary pitches that he has confidence in. His curveball is a plus downer and was the pitch he focused on in his pro debut, but some scouts believe his high-80s power slider could end up being even better. He threw it only once or twice a game as a pro, but it was his go-to weapon in high school. It lacks massive depth, but Whitley makes up for it with velocity and late movement. His changeup is advanced for a power pitcher his age. The path from the draft to the big leagues for high school righthanders is rarely a straight road, but Whitley's plus stuff and advanced control give him the building blocks to be a front-of-the-rotation starter. He should pitch at low Class A Quad Cities in 2017.

BA GRADE
60 Risk: Extreme

Year	Club (League)	Class	W	L	ERA	G	GS	CG	SV	IP	H	HR	BB	SO	K/9	WHIP	AVG
2016	Astros (GCL)	R	1	1	7.36	4	2	0	0	7	8	0	3	13	16.0	1.50	.267
	Greeneville (APP)	R	0	1	3.18	4	4	0	0	11	11	0	3	13	10.3	1.24	.244
Minor League Totals			1	2	4.82	8	6	0	0	19	19	0	6	26	12.5	1.34	.253

7 TEOSCAR HERNANDEZ, OF

Born: Oct. 15, 1992. **B-T:** R-R. **Ht.:** 6-2. **Wt.:** 198. **Signed:** Dominican Republic, 2011. **Signed by:** Felix Francisco/Rafael Belen/Francis Mojica.

The Astros signed Hernandez for a bargain $20,000 in 2011 and saw him quickly climb on the prospect radar. He regressed with a disastrous 2015 season, after which the Astros left him off the 40-man roster—but he went unselected in the Rule 5 draft. Hernandez went to the Astros' Dominican complex to focus on tracking breaking-ball spin and it paid off in 2016, when he slashed his strikeout rate from 25 percent to 17 percent. Hernandez went from being an easy out to an above-average hitter because he adopted a two-strike approach. He now takes or spoils tough, two-strike pitches he chased in the past. The improved approach did dilute his power slightly, but he still has above-average power to go with his much-improved hit tool. He is an above-average defender in center field and plus in the corners with an above-average arm, though he needs to improve his accuracy. With Houston aiming to win the American League West, it probably won't hand Hernandez a full-time job out of spring training. But with his ability to play all three outfield spots, he could fit as a useful extra outfielder who plays his way into a larger role.

BA GRADE
55 Risk: High

Year	Club (League)	Class	AVG	G	AB	R	H	2B	3B	HR	RBI	BB	SO	SB	CS	OBP	SLG
2014	Lancaster (CAL)	HiA	.294	96	391	72	115	33	8	17	75	49	117	31	6	.376	.550
	Corpus Christi (TL)	AA	.284	23	95	12	27	4	1	4	10	2	36	2	3	.299	.474
2015	Corpus Christi (TL)	AA	.219	121	470	92	103	12	2	17	48	33	126	33	7	.275	.362
2016	Corpus Christi (TL)	AA	.305	69	279	53	85	19	0	6	30	32	55	29	11	.384	.437
	Fresno (PCL)	AAA	.313	38	144	20	45	9	3	4	23	13	25	5	4	.365	.500
	Houston (AL)	MAJ	.230	41	100	15	23	7	0	4	11	11	28	0	2	.304	.420
Major League Totals			.230	41	100	15	23	7	0	4	11	11	28	0	2	.304	.420
Minor League Totals			.269	594	2306	414	621	128	32	73	299	220	602	151	47	.337	.448

8 YULIESKI GURRIEL, 3B/1B

Born: June 9, 1984. **B-T:** R-R. **Ht.:** 6-0. **Wt.:** 190. **Signed:** Cuba, 2016. **Signed by:** Charlie Gonzalez.

A teammate of Kendrys Morales on dominant Cuban junior national teams, Gurriel was long considered one of the best players in the world to not play in the U.S. majors. He bolted Cuba at the Caribbean Series in February 2016 and signed a five-year, $47.5 million deal with the Astros. Wherever Gurriel ends up on the diamond, the Astros paid him to hit. He looked rusty in his big league debut and has to adjust to seeing better breaking balls, but scouts see an above-average hitter with above-average power. Gurriel understandably isn't as nimble as he once was, but he's still capable of playing average or better defense at first and third base,

BA GRADE
50 Risk: Medium

and he's fringe-average in left field. He has quick hands and good body control with a plus arm. He is a fringe-average runner. The future is now with Gurriel because he turns 33 during the 2017 season. His versatility gives him a chance to play multiple positions for Houston, but his most logical everyday spot for now appears to be first base, where rookies A.J. Reed and Tyler White failed to hit in 2016. Gurriel plays on a front-loaded contract that will earn him $14 million in 2017.

Year	Club (League)	Class	AVG	G	AB	R	H	2B	3B	HR	RBI	BB	SO	SB	CS	OBP	SLG
2014	Yokohama (NPB)	NPB	.305	62	239	46	73	22	0	11	30	15	40	3	0	.349	.536
	Industriales (CNS)	CNS	.343	49	175	40	60	18	1	7	35	27	18	11	2	.343	.577
2015	Industriales (CNS)	CNS	.500	49	174	55	87	20	0	15	51	38	3	3	0	.589	.874
2016	Astros (GCL)	R	.286	2	7	0	2	1	0	0	0	0	2	0	0	.286	.429
	Lancaster (CAL)	HiA	.429	4	14	2	6	2	0	1	9	0	3	0	0	.375	.786
	Corpus Christi (TL)	AA	.118	5	17	0	2	0	0	0	3	1	6	0	0	.158	.118
	Fresno (PCL)	AAA	.222	4	18	3	4	1	0	1	2	1	4	0	0	.263	.444
	Houston (AL)	MAJ	.262	36	130	13	34	7	0	3	15	5	12	1	1	.292	.385
Major League Totals			.262	36	130	13	34	7	0	3	15	5	12	1	1	.292	.385
Minor League Totals			.250	15	56	5	14	4	0	2	14	2	15	0	0	.262	.429

9 DEREK FISHER, OF

Born: Aug. 21, 1993. **B-T:** L-R. **Ht.:** 6-3. **Wt.:** 205. **Drafted:** Virginia, 2014 (1st round supplemental). **Signed by:** Tim Bittner.

BA GRADE
50 Risk: Medium

Scouts have been dreaming on Fisher's combination of speed and power for years. Out of high school he fell to the sixth round after a poor senior season where he struggled at the plate. He largely continued to struggle in three years at Virginia. The Astros have seen him blossom as a pro after making him a 2014 sandwich pick. Fisher is the only minor league player to hit 20 homers and steal 20 bases in both 2015 and 2016. Fisher's impressive athleticism helps him maximize his tools. He has plus-plus raw power and has developed the ability to draw walks and get on base at a high rate. His swing is smooth, and he has plenty of bat speed, and he unleashes it with a significant load that emphasizes power over contact. He's always going to swing and miss a lot, making him more of a .240-type hitter, but his above-average power will produce plenty of extra-base hits. Defensively, Fisher has improved to the point where he's a fringe-average left fielder and a below-average center fielder with a below-average arm. His power, speed and on-base ability make him a potentially valuable regular even with a below-average hit tool. The Astros' lineup leans heavily toward the right side, which opens an opportunity for the lefthanded-hitting Fisher. He heads back to Triple-A Fresno in 2017.

Year	Club (League)	Class	AVG	G	AB	R	H	2B	3B	HR	RBI	BB	SO	SB	CS	OBP	SLG
2014	Astros (GCL)	R	.667	1	3	0	2	1	0	0	0	1	0	0	0	.750	1.000
	Tri-City (NYP)	SS	.303	41	152	31	46	4	3	2	18	16	35	17	4	.378	.408
2015	Quad Cities (MWL)	LoA	.305	39	151	32	46	11	1	6	24	19	37	8	2	.386	.510
	Lancaster (CAL)	HiA	.262	84	344	74	90	10	7	16	63	47	95	23	5	.354	.471
2016	Corpus Christi (TL)	AA	.245	102	371	54	91	13	4	16	59	74	128	23	7	.373	.471
	Fresno (PCL)	AAA	.290	27	107	17	31	8	0	5	17	9	26	5	0	.347	.505
Minor League Totals			.271	294	1128	208	306	47	15	45	181	166	321	76	18	.368	.459

10 GARRETT STUBBS, C

Born: May 26, 1993. **B-T:** L-R. **Ht.:** 5-10. **Wt.:** 161. **Drafted:** Southern California, 2015 (8th round). **Signed by:** Tim Costic.

BA GRADE
50 Risk: High

Stubbs played center field, left field, second base and catcher at Southern California before he became too valuable behind the plate to play elsewhere. A first-team All-American as a senior, he still slid to the eighth round because of his size. Stubbs' skinny, 5-foot-10 frame raises durability questions but also is one of his greatest assets. He is an outstanding pitch-framer in part because he can get lower than most catchers, allowing him to get his hand under balls other catchers have to flip their mitts to snag. His agility also pays off in blocking balls in the dirt and helps his above-average arm play up thanks to excellent footwork. He threw out 51 percent of basestealers in 2016. Though he called pitches in college, it remains the weakest part of his catching. At the plate, Stubbs has a pretty straightforward lefthanded stroke geared more for contact than power. He can square up a good fastball and has some pull power. He projects as a near-average hitter with well below-average power. He runs well for a catcher and is an average runner. Stubbs' size is the biggest impediment to him becoming a big league regular. No regular backstop today weighs as little as Stubbs, but he could be a solid contributor even if limited to a part-time role behind the plate.

Year	Club (League)	Class	AVG	G	AB	R	H	2B	3B	HR	RBI	BB	SO	SB	CS	OBP	SLG
2015	Tri-City (NYP)	SS	.235	11	34	5	8	0	0	0	2	7	3	2	0	.366	.235
	Quad Cities (MWL)	LoA	.274	25	84	15	23	5	0	0	5	14	2	1	0	.370	.333
2016	Lancaster (CAL)	HiA	.291	55	206	35	60	13	0	6	38	29	37	10	3	.385	.442
	Corpus Christi (TL)	AA	.325	31	120	23	39	9	1	4	16	14	11	5	0	.401	.517
Minor League Totals			.293	122	444	78	130	27	1	10	61	64	53	18	3	.385	.426

11 MIGUELANGEL SIERRA, SS/2B

BA GRADE
55 Risk: Extreme

Born: Dec. 2, 1997. **B-T:** R-R. **Ht.:** 5-11. **Wt.:** 176. **Signed:** Venezuela, 2014.
Signed by: Oz Ocampo/Oscar Alvarado/Jose Palacios.

When the Astros signed Sierra on the first day of the 2014 international signing period they knew they were getting a polished shortstop for the $1 million they were spending. What they didn't expect was he would turn into a top slugger in the Rookie-level Appalachian League in 2016. Scouts see Sierra as having fringe-average power potential, but he hit 11 home runs in 31 games at Greeneville while posting an unfathomable .331 isolated slugging percentage. As might have been expected, the power spike led to some bad habits as he morphed his swing from line drive-oriented to pull-heavy with a load-and-lift approach. Those poor habits were exposed in a late-season stint at short-season Tri-City. Power won't be what gets Sierra to the big leagues, but he has the bat speed to be an average hitter. Shortstop defense is his calling card. Sierra has gotten significantly bigger since signing, but he still shows plus hands and an above-average arm with excellent body control and feel for the position. He's not particularly quick-twitch and is an average runner. Sierra has the tools to be an everyday shortstop, but he'll need to go back to lining balls all over the field at low Class A Quad Cities in 2017.

Year	Club (League)	Class	AVG	G	AB	R	H	2B	3B	HR	RBI	BB	SO	SB	CS	OBP	SLG
2015	Astros Orange (DSL)	R	.302	45	169	31	51	17	2	3	19	20	48	8	5	.406	.479
	Astros (GCL)	R	.160	24	75	6	12	2	1	0	1	8	33	4	3	.267	.213
2016	Greeneville (APP)	R	.289	31	121	23	35	3	2	11	19	12	40	6	6	.386	.620
	Tri-City (NYP)	SS	.140	25	93	6	13	2	1	0	5	7	34	0	3	.216	.183
Minor League Totals			.242	125	458	66	111	24	6	14	44	47	155	18	17	.342	.413

12 J.D. DAVIS, 3B

BA GRADE
45 Risk: Medium

Born: April 27, 1993. **B-T:** R-R. **Ht.:** 6-3. **Wt.:** 223. **Drafted:** Cal State Fullerton, 2014 (3rd round). **Signed by:** Brad Budzinski.

No college team of recent memory had a better collection of position-player arms than Cal State Fullerton in 2013 and 2014. Davis has a 70 arm on the 20-80 scouting scale that is one of the better throwing arms in the minors, but it ranked third-best on his college team because he shared the field with a pair of 80 throwers: third baseman Matt Chapman (now in the Athletics system) and center fielder Michael Lorenzen (now a Reds righthander). Davis played mostly DH and right field in college because of Chapman, but the Astros have focused on developing him at third base. His arm compensates for a lack of speed and agility, but scouts don't see him developing into better than a below-average defender because of limited range and below-average footwork, though his hands work well. He's a well below-average runner, which limits him to first base if he changes positions. Davis' plus-plus raw power is as impressive as his arm, but is more strength-based than generated from bat speed, and he strikes out frequently. That and his pull-heavy approach make it hard for scouts to project him as more than a fringe-average hitter. Davis is blocked by Alex Bregman and Yulieski Gurriel, so he will head to Triple-A Fresno in 2017 to wait for an opportunity somewhere.

Year	Club (League)	Class	AVG	G	AB	R	H	2B	3B	HR	RBI	BB	SO	SB	CS	OBP	SLG
2014	Tri-City (NYP)	SS	.279	30	111	18	31	7	1	5	20	15	25	1	0	.382	.495
	Quad Cities (MWL)	LoA	.303	43	155	20	47	9	0	8	32	13	41	4	0	.363	.516
2015	Lancaster (CAL)	HiA	.289	120	485	93	140	28	3	26	101	54	157	5	2	.370	.520
2016	Corpus Christi (TL)	AA	.270	125	482	61	130	34	1	23	80	45	142	1	3	.336	.488
Minor League Totals			.282	318	1233	192	348	78	5	62	233	127	365	11	5	.357	.504

13 RAMON LAUREANO, OF

BA GRADE
50 Risk: High

Born: July 15, 1994. **B-T:** R-R. **Ht.:** 5-11. **Wt.:** 194. **Drafted:** Northeast Oklahoma A&M JC, 2014 (16th round). **Signed by:** Jim Stevenson.

The Astros consistently turn late-round draft picks into productive minor league players, and every now and then they find a Tyler White, who was a 33rd-round pick in 2013 who reached the majors. Laureano, a Dominican Republic native who played high school ball on Long Island and junior college ball in Oklahoma, has the hitting ability the Astros covet in later-round college players, but he also has impressive athleticism. He has baseball intelligence, effort level and desire to learn and marries that with plus speed and solid defense. Laureano can play all three outfield spots. He's an above-average defender in either corner-outfield spot and average in center, with a plus arm and knack for making highlight-reel catches. He has a quiet setup at the plate and a simple, line-drive stroke, but he has the strength to produce average power in addition to his above-average hitting ability. He improved his pitch selection dramatically in 2016, which helped him lead the minors with a .428 on-base percentage.

Year	Club (League)	Class	AVG	G	AB	R	H	2B	3B	HR	RBI	BB	SO	SB	CS	OBP	SLG
2014	Greeneville (APP)	R	.189	16	53	8	10	0	0	1	2	7	16	4	0	.283	.245
2015	Quad Cities (MWL)	LoA	.265	76	287	43	76	15	8	4	34	21	83	18	3	.323	.415
2016	Lancaster (CAL)	HiA	.317	80	293	69	93	19	5	10	60	50	86	33	11	.426	.519
	Corpus Christi (TL)	AA	.323	36	124	20	40	9	2	5	13	20	33	10	3	.432	.548
Minor League Totals			.289	208	757	140	219	43	15	20	109	98	218	65	17	.380	.465

14 DAZ CAMERON, OF

BA GRADE

50 Risk: High

Born: Jan. 15, 1997. **B-T:** R-R. **Ht.:** 6-2. **Wt.:** 189. **Drafted:** HS—McDonough, Ga., 2015 (1st round supplemental). **Signed by:** Gavin Dickey.

Though he fell to 37th overall in the 2015 draft, the son of former All-Star Mike Cameron landed a $4 million bonus that tied with fellow Astros pick Kyle Tucker for fifth-highest in his class. While Tucker sped to the high Class A California League, Cameron hit just .143 during his full-season debut at low Class A Quad Cities in 2016. The Astros demoted him to short-season Tri-City, where his struggles continued initially. Just when Cameron appeared to turn a corner, he broke his left index finger and missed the final two months.. He has well-rounded, but not plus, tools. Cameron is a solid-average defender in center field with above-average speed that plays better underway, but none of that will matter if he doesn't hit, and so far he looks like a below-average hitter. Cameron's worked on retooling his swing in extended spring training to improve his bat path and use his lower half better. Still, he struck out 33 percent of the time in 2016 and has just average power. Cameron will get a second chance at low A in 2017.

Year	Club (League)	Class	AVG	G	AB	R	H	2B	3B	HR	RBI	BB	SO	SB	CS	OBP	SLG
2015	Astros (GCL)	R	.222	21	72	14	16	2	0	0	6	9	18	13	4	.326	.250
	Greeneville (APP)	R	.272	30	103	20	28	2	3	0	11	16	31	11	6	.372	.350
2016	Quad Cities (MWL)	LoA	.143	21	77	5	11	2	2	0	6	8	33	4	3	.221	.221
	Tri-City (NYP)	SS	.278	19	79	13	22	3	1	2	14	6	26	8	2	.352	.418
Minor League Totals			.233	91	331	52	77	9	6	2	37	39	108	36	15	.323	.314

15 RONNIE DAWSON, OF

BA GRADE

50 Risk: High

Born: May 19, 1995. **B-T:** L-R. **Ht.:** 6-2. **Wt.:** 225. **Drafted:** Ohio State, 2016 (2nd round). **Signed by:** Nick Venuto.

Dawson wrapped his career at Ohio State with a bang by winning the MVP award at the Big Ten Conference tournament, where he hit .577 with six doubles, a home run and four steals to lead the Buckeyes to victory. He became the highest drafted OSU position player since the Tigers made Ronnie Bourquin a second-round pick in 2006. Dawson's introduction to pro ball at short-season Tri-City did not go smoothly. He projects as a power-speed left fielder with the chance to hit 15-20 home runs and steal 15-20 bags, but for that to happen, he has to be an average hitter, and that remains in question. Dawson starred in football as well as baseball in high school, so the Astros believe he still is catching up with pitchers as he focuses on baseball exclusively. He is an average runner out of the batter's box but an above-average runner underway. Defensively he is limited to left field. Dawson will join a prospect-laden outfield at low Class A Quad Cities in 2017.

Year	Club (League)	Class	AVG	G	AB	R	H	2B	3B	HR	RBI	BB	SO	SB	CS	OBP	SLG
2015	Astros (GCL)	R	.222	21	72	14	16	2	0	0	6	9	18	13	4	.326	.250
	Greeneville (APP)	R	.272	30	103	20	28	2	3	0	11	16	31	11	6	.372	.350
2016	Quad Cities (MWL)	LoA	.143	21	77	5	11	2	2	0	6	8	33	4	3	.221	.221
	Tri-City (NYP)	SS	.278	19	79	13	22	3	1	2	14	6	26	8	2	.352	.418
Minor League Totals			.233	91	331	52	77	9	6	2	37	39	108	36	15	.323	.314

16 HECTOR PEREZ, RHP

BA GRADE

55 Risk: Extreme

Born: June 6, 1996. **B-T:** R-R. **Ht.:** 6-3. **Wt.:** 190. **Signed:** Dominican Republic, 2014. **Signed by:** Oz Ocampo/Roman Ocumarez/Leocadio Guevara.

Perez spent most of 2015 in the Dominican Summer League but finished 2016 with seven starts at low Class A Quad Cities. When he takes the mound, hitters know what to expect. They better gear up for velocity, because almost everything he throws is hard. They can't get too comfortable in the batter's box, either, because he often misses out of the strike zone. Perez can dominate with a plus 92-94 mph fastball that touches 96. His fastball sets up a wipeout slider that also earns plus grades at its best. He will mix in a bigger, slower high-70s curveball with 11-to-5 action early in counts, and he's working on a split-finger fastball in lieu of a changeup. It flashes average. Perez's control is below-average, and he will struggle to find the strike zone at some point in most every outing. His delivery, though, has no glaring long-term issues to suggest he can't find the strike zone. Perez's all-power approach would work as a high-leverage reliever, but he will be given plenty of opportunities to work through his control issues.

Year	Club (League)	Class	W	L	ERA	G	GS	CG	SV	IP	H	HR	BB	SO	K/9	WHIP	AVG
2015	Astros Blue (DSL)	R	1	0	2.12	7	7	0	0	30	20	0	6	32	9.7	0.88	.185
	Astros (GCL)	R	1	0	1.16	9	3	0	1	23	10	0	16	16	6.2	1.11	.135
	Greeneville (APP)	R	0	0	0.00	1	0	0	0	2	0	0	1	2	9.0	0.50	.000
2016	Tri-City (NYP)	SS	2	0	1.57	7	3	0	0	29	19	0	12	36	11.3	1.08	.181
	Quad Cities (MWL)	LoA	2	1	4.60	7	7	0	0	31	28	1	22	44	12.6	1.60	.246
Minor League Totals			6	1	2.43	31	20	0	1	115	77	1	57	130	10.2	1.17	.190

17 JONATHAN ARAUZ, SS/2B

BA GRADE **50** Risk: High

Born: Aug. 3, 1998. **B-T:** B-R. **Ht.:** 6-0. **Wt.:** 150. **Signed:** Panama, 2014. **Signed by:** Norman Anciani (Phillies).

The Phillies signed Arauz for $600,000, then bundled him with closer Ken Giles after the 2015 season in a trade with the Astros that sent Vince Velasquez, Mark Appel and three others to Philadelphia. Arauz held his own at Rookie-level Greeneville in 2016 as one of the younger players in the Appalachian League. He lacks a clear plus tool, though his arm is above-average, but his well-rounded skill set gives him a chance to be an average hitter with gap power and a solid if unspectacular up-the-middle defender. There's nothing flashy about Arauz, and he is not as quick-twitch as many shortstops. That said, he shows good instincts, a solid internal clock and good hands at shortstop, giving him a chance to be an average defender. At the plate his lefthanded swing is a little better than his righthanded swing, but both are similar and straightforward. He's an average runner. Arauz will play most of the 2017 season as an 18-year-old, possibly at short-season Tri-City if the Astros don't want him to double up with Miguelangel Sierra.

Year	Club (League)	Class	AVG	G	AB	R	H	2B	3B	HR	RBI	BB	SO	SB	CS	OBP	SLG
2015	Phillies (GCL)	R	.254	44	173	21	44	10	2	2	18	13	29	2	0	.309	.370
2016	Greeneville (APP)	R	.249	53	201	26	50	10	1	2	18	19	45	1	3	.323	.338
Minor League Totals			.251	97	374	47	94	20	3	4	36	32	74	3	3	.316	.353

18 JANDEL GUSTAVE, RHP

BA GRADE **50** Risk: High

Born: Oct. 12, 1992. **B-T:** R-R. **Ht.:** 6-2. **Wt.:** 209. **Signed:** Dominican Republic, 2010. **Signed by:** Felix Francisco/Rafael Belen.

When the Astros signed Gustave, they knew they were getting a great arm with a near complete lack of control. It took him five seasons to make it to full-season ball, at a point where he was just becoming Rule 5 draft eligible. In the two seasons since, he's made massive strides with his control, which now grades as fringe-average, and he reached the majors as a reliever in 2016. He has scrapped the full windup he used to use, replacing it with a much-simplified motion. Gustave's 97.1 mph average fastball velocity ranked 13th among all major league pitchers in 2016. He throws from a low three-quarters arm slot, which helps generate excellent sink on his fastball. His high-80s slider is also a plus pitch with cutter action and late, tight movement. Those two pitches give Gustave a chance to be an impact reliever if he can throw enough strikes.

Year	Club (League)	Class	W	L	ERA	G	GS	CG	SV	IP	H	HR	BB	SO	K/9	WHIP	AVG
2014	Quad Cities (MWL)	LoA	5	5	5.01	23	14	0	2	79	94	3	29	82	9.3	1.56	.289
2015	Corpus Christi (TL)	AA	5	2	2.15	46	0	0	20	59	51	2	25	49	7.5	1.30	.235
2016	Fresno (PCL)	AAA	3	3	3.79	47	0	0	3	57	46	1	23	55	8.7	1.21	.219
	Houston (AL)	MAJ	1	0	3.52	14	0	0	0	15	13	2	4	16	9.4	1.11	.232
Major League Totals			1	0	3.52	14	0	0	0	15	13	2	4	16	9.4	1.11	.232
Minor League Totals			17	23	4.70	164	34	0	25	312	301	10	194	303	8.7	1.59	.252

19 GILBERTO CELESTINO, OF

BA GRADE **50** Risk: High

Born: Feb. 13, 1999. **B-T:** R-L. **Ht.:** 6-0. **Wt.:** 170. **Signed:** Dominican Republic, 2015. **Signed by:** Oz Ocampo/Roman Ocumarez.

Unlike many signees from the Dominican Republic who are first spotted at workouts, Celestino had a long history of playing internationally, which gave scouts multiple chances to see him against top-level competition. He played in the Cal Ripken World Series as a 12-year-old, the COPABE 15U tournament

and with an international team at the National High School Invitational. The Astros liked what they saw in all their different looks and signed him for $2.25 million during the 2015 international signing period. Celestino's hard-earned baseball savvy was apparent in his pro debut in the Dominican Summer League in 2016. He walked more than he struck out, demonstrated a knack for contact and showed more pop than the average 17-year-old in the DSL. He has solid bat speed and reads pitches well for his age, but whatever he does offensively pales in comparison with his defense in center field. Celestino is an average runner, but he reads the ball off the bat exceptionally well and takes outstanding routes. He's at least a plus defender with an above-average, accurate arm. Scouts can't help but compare Celestino with Cubs outfielder Albert Almora, another hit-over-power center fielder with exceptional defense despite modest speed.

Year	Club (League)	Class	AVG	G	AB	R	H	2B	3B	HR	RBI	BB	SO	SB	CS	OBP	SLG
2016	Astros Orange (DSL)	R	.279	38	136	22	38	9	3	2	17	25	23	9	2	.388	.434
	Astros (GCL)	R	.200	18	55	7	11	3	1	0	2	8	16	6	1	.308	.291
Minor League Totals			.257	56	191	29	49	12	4	2	19	33	39	15	3	.365	.393

20 JAKE ROGERS, C

BA GRADE **45** Risk: High

Born: April 15, 1995. **B-T:** R-R. **Ht.:** 6-1. **Wt.:** 190. **Drafted:** Tulane, 2016 (3rd round). **Signed by:** Justin Cryer.

From the moment Rogers arrived at Tulane, he was the team's anchor behind the plate. His catch-and-throw skills quickly taught Green Wave opponents to stay put at first base and he ultimately threw out 57 percent of basestealers in his college career. Scouts regularly gave his arm 70 grades on the 20-to-80 scouting scale. That reputation is why the Astros in 2016 made Rogers the highest-drafted player out of Tulane since 2008 sandwich pick Shooter Hunt. Rogers is athletic, loose and limber behind the plate with a soft left hand that should make him an excellent framer. He picked off seven baserunners in just 43 games behind the plate in his pro debut, which he finished at low Class A Quad Cities. Rogers has work to do offensively. Since high school, he has had a very power-oriented swing with an exaggerated leg kick and weight transfer, but it's never really worked for him. Rogers has shown average power, but the tradeoff is a struggle to regularly make solid contact. A career .233 hitter at Tulane, he matched that average exactly in his pro debut, so his ability to hit will determine whether he profiles as a big league starter or backup.

Year	Club (League)	Class	AVG	G	AB	R	H	2B	3B	HR	RBI	BB	SO	SB	CS	OBP	SLG
2016	Tri-City (NYP)	SS	.253	25	87	11	22	7	1	2	12	13	18	0	2	.369	.425
	Quad Cities (MWL)	LoA	.208	21	72	7	15	3	1	1	4	8	25	1	0	.305	.319
Minor League Totals			.233	46	159	18	37	10	2	3	16	21	43	1	2	.341	.377

21 TRENT THORNTON, RHP

BA GRADE **45** Risk: High

Born: Sept. 30, 1993. **Ht.:** 6-0. **Wt.:** 182. **B-T:** R-R. **Drafted:** North Carolina, 2015 (5th round). **Signed by:** Tim Bittner.

After two outstanding seasons at North Carolina—he went 12-1, 1.37 as a freshman—Thornton inopportunely fell apart as a junior. His first two pro seasons have been more reminiscent of his first two years as a Tar Heel, however. Thornton reached Double-A Corpus Christi in the second half of 2016 while impressing with a solid four-pitch mix. His 6-foot stature and delivery have led some scouts to project him to the bullpen. His windup involves a deep plunge with both hands, followed by an exaggerated two-handed windup that ends up with a hand break above and behind his right ear and a stab in the back. While his delivery features a lot of moving parts, Thornton has shown plus control as a pro with a walk rate of 1.5 per nine innings—and he maintains the quality of his stuff through the entire outing. Thornton can touch 95 mph at his peak, but he generally sits 90-91 with a fastball that grades as average thanks in part to its riding action. His 12-to-6 curveball is an above-average offering at its best, and he mixes in a fringe-average slider and below-average changeup. Thornton projects as a back-end starter.

Year	Club (League)	Class	W	L	ERA	G	GS	CG	SV	IP	H	HR	BB	SO	K/9	WHIP	AVG
2015	Tri-City (NYP)	SS	4	0	3.27	15	12	0	0	55	62	2	10	48	7.9	1.31	.286
2016	Lancaster (CAL)	HiA	7	4	4.12	17	14	1	0	90	91	14	16	89	8.9	1.19	.265
	Corpus Christi (TL)	AA	3	1	2.35	7	7	0	0	46	42	5	5	35	6.8	1.02	.243
Minor League Totals			14	5	3.45	39	33	1	0	191	195	21	31	172	8.1	1.19	.266

22 BRADY RODGERS, RHP

BA GRADE **40** Risk: Medium

Born: Sept. 17, 1990. **B-T:** R-R. **Ht.:** 6-2. **Wt.:** 212. **Drafted:** Arizona State, 2012 (3rd round). **Signed by:** Mike Brown.

High school teammates with Cardinals outfielder Randal Grichuk and one of the most successful pitchers in Arizona State history, Rodgers had a breakthrough minor league season in 2016 and a dud of a big league debut. He changed the grip on his slider with help from Astros reliever Luke Gregerson, which helped him make a big step forward in his second try at Triple-A Fresno. Houston had left Rodgers unprotected for 2015 Rule 5 draft, but by the end of the 2016 season, he had earned a spot on the 40-man roster and the pitcher-of-the-year award in the Pacific Coast League. Unfortunately for him, his season didn't end on Sept. 1. He allowed 10 earned runs in 1.2 innings in his first two major league appearances. When Rodgers is effective it is because his average across-the-board stuff plays up because of plus control and command, but he has very little margin for error. He can overwhelm hitters by throwing five different pitches—a fastball, cutter, slider, curveball and changeup—but his above-average slider is the only one that grades out as better than average. For now, Rodgers projects as a Triple-A depth starter.

Year	Club (League)	Class	W	L	ERA	G	GS	CG	SV	IP	H	HR	BB	SO	K/9	WHIP	AVG
2014	Oklahoma City (PCL)	AAA	1	0	0.00	1	1	0	0	6	2	0	1	4	6.0	0.50	.111
	Corpus Christi (TL)	AA	5	12	4.77	26	17	0	2	121	135	15	19	87	6.5	1.28	.287
2015	Fresno (PCL)	AAA	9	7	4.51	21	21	0	0	116	136	13	25	89	6.9	1.39	.289
2016	Fresno (PCL)	AAA	12	4	2.86	22	22	2	0	132	129	7	23	116	7.9	1.15	.257
	Houston (AL)	MAJ	0	1	15.12	5	1	0	0	8	15	0	7	3	3.2	2.64	.385
Major League Totals			0	1	15.12	5	1	0	0	8	15	0	7	3	3.2	2.64	.385
Minor League Totals			45	33	4.06	111	93	2	3	559	607	54	102	459	7.4	1.27	.277

23 JAMES HOYT, RHP

BA GRADE
40 Risk: Medium

Born: Sept. 30, 1986. **B-T:** R-R. **Ht.:** 6-6. **Wt.:** 229. **Signed:** Tabasco (Mexican League), 2012. **Signed by:** Manuel Samaniego (Braves).

Centenary College in Shreveport, La., went out with a bang. In its second-to-last year in Division I before moving to D-III, the program had a pair of future big league pitchers on its roster. Seth Lugo, now with the Mets, was a solid swingman, while Hoyt battled a knee injury and posted an 18.82 ERA in nine appearances. Hoyt pitched in the independent (and now-defunct) North American Baseball League, graduated to the American Association and eventually the Mexican League. Along the way his stuff just kept getting better. Hoyt's once high-80s fastball became a 93-96 mph heater, and his fastball now earns at least plus grades and has earned 70s on the 20-to-80 scale from some scouts. It sets up a plus mid-80s slider that is a true out pitch. His fringe-average control is the only thing keeping him from a being a high-leverage reliever. Hoyt's stuff wasn't as firm in the second half of 2016 as it was in the first, which was poor timing for a pitcher who made his big league debut in July. Already 30, he'll compete for a job in the Houston bullpen in 2017.

Year	Club (League)	Class	W	L	ERA	G	GS	CG	SV	IP	H	HR	BB	SO	K/9	WHIP	AVG
2014	Gwinnett (IL)	AAA	1	1	5.46	24	0	0	1	28	38	4	14	34	10.9	1.86	.314
	Mississippi (SL)	AA	2	1	1.14	28	0	0	6	32	19	1	10	43	12.2	0.92	.170
2015	Fresno (PCL)	AAA	0	1	3.49	47	0	0	9	49	48	1	11	66	12.1	1.20	.246
2016	Fresno (PCL)	AAA	4	3	1.64	49	0	0	29	55	29	2	19	93	15.2	0.87	.154
	Houston (AL)	MAJ	1	1	4.50	22	0	0	0	22	16	5	9	28	11.5	1.14	.203
Major League Totals			1	1	4.50	22	0	0	0	22	16	5	9	28	11.5	1.14	.203
Minor League Totals			10	12	3.09	198	3	0	47	259	202	13	99	361	12.5	1.16	.209

24 ROGELIO ARMENTEROS, RHP

BA GRADE
40 Risk: Medium

Born: June 30, 1994. **B-T:** R-R. **Ht.:** 6-1. **Wt.:** 215. **Signed:** Cuba, 2014. **Signed by:** Alex Jacobs.

Armenteros posted a 9.45 ERA as a 17-year-old in his lone year in Cuba's top league, Serie Nacional, and he was not a significant name on the showcase circuit as a Cuban looking for a contract. But he pitched well enough in workouts facing Rusney Castillo and other notable names that the Astros signed him for $40,000. In the two seasons since, he has impressed the Astros with feel, deception and better-than-expected stuff. Armenteros gets swings-and-misses up in the zone with an 88-93 mph fastball, and he can sink a heavy fastball down in the zone that is hard to lift. But hitters struggle to sit on his fastball because he likes to mix in his cutter, curveball, changeup and slider. None is plus, but all are fringe-average to average. Armenteros' 76-78 mph curve is a deep 12-to-6 breaker. His 80-81 mph slider is a little sweepy, while his 81-83 mph changeup has good deception and angle. Armenteros finished 2016 as a starter at Double-A Corpus Christi, and he should open there in 2017.

Year	Club (League)	Class	W	L	ERA	G	GS	CG	SV	IP	H	HR	BB	SO	K/9	WHIP	AVG
2015	Tri-City (NYP)	SS	2	2	4.09	12	9	0	0	44	44	3	17	40	8.2	1.39	.262
	Quad Cities (MWL)	LoA	1	0	2.65	3	3	0	0	17	9	1	7	21	11.1	0.94	.150
2016	Quad Cities (MWL)	LoA	0	2	1.93	4	3	0	0	19	12	0	3	20	9.6	0.80	.179
	Lancaster (CAL)	HiA	6	4	4.18	19	16	0	1	90	87	13	37	107	10.7	1.37	.251
	Corpus Christi (TL)	AA	2	0	1.96	3	3	0	0	18	17	1	4	13	6.4	1.15	.262
Minor League Totals			11	8	3.58	41	34	0	1	188	169	18	68	201	9.6	1.26	.239

25 LUPE CHAVEZ, RHP

Born: Dec. 3, 1997. **B-T:** R-R. **Ht.:** 6-2. **Wt.:** 170. **Signed:** Mexico, 2014. **Signed by:** Ismael Cruz/Luis Marquez (Blue Jays).

BA GRADE

45 Risk: High

Chavez has changed organizations frequently at a young age. The Blue Jays purchased his rights from the Quintana Roo of the Mexican League, and then the Astros acquired him for Scott Feldman at the 2016 trade deadline. Chavez actually grew up playing the outfield, but he pitches like a veteran with years of experience on the mound. He has a plus changeup right now, but his ceiling depends on projecting strength and velocity gains. He's got a sturdy lower half already, but his shoulders, chest and arms haven't filled out yet. If he adds some upper-body strength, his present 88-92 mph fastball could tick up a grade. He already locates it well and does a good job of adding and subtracting velocity with it. Similarly, his curveball already has good shape, but it needs more power. If he can find a way to throw it harder, it can be a plus pitch. Chavez's understanding of how to set up hitters means he could make a case to jump to low Class A Quad Cities in 2017.

Year	Club (League)	Class	W	L	ERA	G	GS	CG	SV	IP	H	HR	BB	SO	K/9	WHIP	AVG
2015	Blue Jays (DSL)	R	4	1	2.98	10	10	0	0	42	40	0	14	45	9.6	1.28	.250
	Blue Jays (GCL)	R	3	1	2.37	4	3	0	0	19	16	0	6	14	6.6	1.16	.225
2016	Blue Jays (GCL)	R	4	1	1.69	6	6	0	0	32	29	1	4	26	7.3	1.03	.248
	Astros (GCL)	R	0	0	0.00	3	1	0	0	6	3	0	1	5	7.5	0.67	.150
	Greeneville (APP)	R	0	0	1.17	2	1	0	0	8	4	0	5	10	11.7	1.17	.154
Minor League Totals			11	3	2.19	25	21	0	0	107	92	1	30	100	8.4	1.14	.234

26 FREUDIS NOVA, SS

Born: Jan. 12, 2000. **B-T:** R-R. **Ht.:** 6-1. **Wt.:** 170. **Signed:** Dominican Republic, 2016. **Signed by:** Oz Ocampo/Roman Ocumarez/Jose Lima.

BA GRADE

50 Risk: Extreme

Nova was expected to land one of the top bonuses in the 2016 international signing class, but his rumored $2.6 million deal to the Marlins fell apart after he tested positive in February for a performance-enhancing substance. He passed multiple drug tests since then and landed on his feet when the Astros swept in to sign him for $1.2 million in July 2016. Arguably the best athlete available in his signing class, Nova is a twitchy, rangy athlete with fast hands, plenty of bat speed, a plus arm and plus speed. He has even flashed above-average raw power in workouts. With a long and lean frame, Nova isn't much of a risk to thicken and outgrow shortstop. He can play a little too fast defensively at times, rushing throws and struggling with accuracy when he doesn't set his feet, but his defensive issues are ones that usually are rectified by repetition. Nova is a long way from Houston, but his raw tools stand above the other talented shortstops in the system.

Year	Club (League)	Class	W	L	ERA	G	GS	CG	SV	IP	H	HR	BB	SO	K/9	WHIP	AVG
2016	Did not play—Signed 2017 contract																

27 TONY KEMP, 2B/OF

Born: Oct. 31, 1991. **B-T:** L-R. **Ht.:** 5-6. **Wt.:** 163. **Drafted:** Vanderbilt, 2013 (5th round). **Signed by:** Nick Venuto.

BA GRADE

40 Risk: Medium

Astros second baseman Jose Altuve has proven that a 5-foot-6 hitter can be a star. Now the 5-foot-6 Kemp, the 2013 Southeastern Conference Player of the Year while at Vanderbilt, is trying to follow in his footsteps. Altuve looms over any chance Kemp has to be a regular. That's because Kemp's best bet for regular play would be as a fringe defensive second baseman who hits enough for a team to live with his defense. In the outfield, his below-average range in center field and his below-average arm in right limits him to left field. Because of that, Kemp served largely as a pinch-hitter, pinch-runner and occasional left fielder in Houston. He has the short stroke from the left side and bat control to be an above-average or even plus hitter, albeit with well below-average power. He is a plus runner, though he's not fast enough to be an elite basestealer. Kemp is likely to begin 2017 at Triple-A Fresno.

Year	Club (League)	Class	AVG	G	AB	R	H	2B	3B	HR	RBI	BB	SO	SB	CS	OBP	SLG
2014	Lancaster (CAL)	HiA	.336	72	295	79	99	19	4	4	37	45	35	28	7	.433	.468
	Corpus Christi (TL)	AA	.292	59	233	42	68	11	4	4	21	28	32	13	6	.381	.425
2015	Corpus Christi (TL)	AA	.358	50	193	36	69	10	1	0	19	35	28	15	8	.457	.420
	Fresno (PCL)	AAA	.273	71	271	42	74	9	3	3	29	21	37	20	6	.334	.362
2016	Fresno (PCL)	AAA	.306	69	255	36	78	9	4	2	24	34	34	10	8	.389	.396
	Houston (AL)	MAJ	.217	59	120	15	26	4	3	1	7	14	27	2	1	.296	.325
Major League Totals			.217	59	120	15	26	4	3	1	7	14	27	2	1	.296	.325
Minor League Totals			.304	396	1522	281	463	66	19	15	152	203	213	107	46	.392	.402

28 YORDAN ALVAREZ, 1B

Born: June 27, 1997. **B-T:** L-L. **Ht.:** 6-5. **Wt.:** 225. **Signed:** Cuba, 2016. **Signed** by: Ismael Cruz/Mike Tosar (Dodgers).

The Astros were one of the teams intrigued by Alvarez after he emigrated with the Cuban government's assent, but it's hard to compete with the Dodgers' checkbook. Los Angeles signed Alvarez for $2 million in June 2016 on a deal that included a $2 million penalty for exceeding its international bonus pool. The Dodgers then traded Alvarez to the Astros just a month and a half later for reliever Josh Fields. Alvarez never played a game in the Dodgers system. He first demonstrated his advanced understanding of hitting when he batted .351/.402/.387 as a 17-year-old in Cuba's top league, Serie Nacional, in 2014. Alvarez's calling card is his bat control and picturesque lefthanded swing. He has a discerning batting eye and a knack for contact. If the plus raw power he has demonstrated in workouts translates to games—he's working on elevating the ball more—he checks the boxes teams look for in a first baseman. He is below-average defensively and played left field sporadically in Cuba. Alvarez is ready for full-season ball.

Year	Club (League)	Class	AVG	G	AB	R	H	2B	3B	HR	RBI	BB	SO	SB	CS	OBP	SLG
2014	Las Tunas (CNS)	CNS	.351	40	111	14	39	1	0	1	17	8	10	2	2	.402	.387
2015	Did not play																
2016	Astros Orange (DSL)	R	.341	16	44	7	15	2	1	1	4	12	7	2	1	.474	.500
Minor League Totals			.341	16	44	7	15	2	1	1	4	12	7	2	1	.474	.500

29 JOSE LUIS HERNANDEZ, RHP

Born: May 1, 1995. **B-T:** R-R. **Ht.:** 6-0. **Wt.:** 210. **Signed:** Mexico, 2015. **Signed** by: Oz Ocampo/Carlos Alfonso/Raul Lopez.

The Hangar, home field for high Class A Lancaster, can destroy the psyche of even the best young pitcher. The degree of difficulty, however, barely raised Hernandez's blood pressure. In seven California League starts in 2016 he recorded a 3.48 ERA, which ranked significantly above league average once park-adjusted. Much like teammate Rogelio Armenteros, Hernandez stands out more for the consistency of his stuff. A thick-bodied, 6-foot righthander with a simple delivery, Hernandez can locate to the arm side or glove side with above-average control. He has outstanding feel for his secondary stuff, of which he has many offerings for hitters to consider. He throws cutters, curveballs, changeups and splitters to go with a fringe-average 88-92 mph fastball. Hernandez's plus changeup is his best pitch, but both his curveball and slider earn fringe-average to average grades. Hernandez will start at high Class A Buies Creek in 2017.

Year	Club (League)	Class	W	L	ERA	G	GS	CG	SV	IP	H	HR	BB	SO	K/9	WHIP	AVG
2015	Greeneville (APP)	R	1	1	2.11	6	3	0	1	21	16	0	4	25	10.5	0.94	.211
	Tri-City (NYP)	SS	1	0	4.96	5	2	0	0	16	18	1	5	17	9.4	1.41	.290
2016	Quad Cities (MWL)	LoA	3	2	2.66	17	14	0	1	81	78	4	15	84	9.3	1.14	.248
	Lancaster (CAL)	HiA	3	3	3.48	7	7	2	0	44	47	5	9	43	8.8	1.27	.269
Minor League Totals			8	6	3.04	35	26	2	2	163	159	10	33	169	9.3	1.18	.254

30 COLIN MORAN, 3B

Born: Oct. 1, 1992. **B-T:** L-R. **Ht.:** 6-4. **Wt.:** 203. **Drafted:** North Carolina, 2013 (1st round). **Signed:** Joel Matthews (Marlins).

Moran was one of the most productive college hitters in the 2013 draft coming out of North Carolina, but the Marlins soured on their first-round pick after only a year. Miami traded him to the Astros after they decided his low-energy approach and below-average power didn't fit their plans at third base. Houston focused on what Moran could do: hit for average, make plenty of contact and throw. He has made defensive improvements at third base, where he now grades as fringe-average with a plus arm, but that won't matter if he is as punchless as he was at Triple-A Fresno in 2016. He hit .259 with 10 home runs and a below-average .697 OPS for the Pacific Coast League, and his strikeout rate jumped without a corresponding bump in his power. At his best, Moran has shown himself to be an above-average hitter with the power to hit 10-12 home runs. He still is young enough to bounce back, but the Astros' days of playing a second-division caliber player at third base are over, so Moran will head back to Triple-A.

Year	Club (League)	Class	AVG	G	AB	R	H	2B	3B	HR	RBI	BB	SO	SB	CS	OBP	SLG
2014	Jupiter (FSL)	HiA	.294	89	361	34	106	21	0	5	33	28	53	1	2	.342	.393
	Corpus Christi (TL)	AA	.304	28	112	12	34	6	0	2	22	9	23	0	1	.350	.411
2015	Corpus Christi (TL)	AA	.306	96	366	47	112	25	2	9	67	43	79	1	0	.381	.459
2016	Fresno (PCL)	AAA	.259	117	459	50	119	18	1	10	69	47	124	3	2	.329	.368
	Houston (AL)	MAJ	.130	9	23	1	3	1	0	0	2	1	8	0	0	.200	.174
Major League Totals			.130	9	23	1	3	1	0	0	2	1	8	0	0	.200	.174
Minor League Totals			.287	372	1452	162	417	78	4	30	214	142	304	6	5	.350	.408

Kansas City Royals

BY J.J. COOPER

The bill for the Royals' back-to-back World Series appearances and its 2015 title started to come due in 2016, but the balloon payment is looming in 2018.

Understandably, the defending World Series champs tried to keep the team together to attempt a repeat. Free agent Alex Gordon was re-signed, ensuring the Royals began 2016 with largely the same lineup that won it all in 2015.

The dominant bullpen was largely kept intact (closer Greg Holland was allowed to reach free agency as he rehabbed from Tommy John surgery) while free agent righthander Ian Kennedy was signed to try to fill some of the innings lost when trade pickup Johnny Cueto signed with the Giants as a free agent.

It didn't work. A knee injury cost Mike Moustakas all but a month of the season. Lorenzo Cain missed time. Gordon hit a baffling .220/.312/.380 as the offense cratered.

And the Royals' bullpen, the most-feared in baseball in 2014-15, became merely mildly intimidating in 2016 thanks to an injury to Wade Davis and the struggles of free agent signee Joakim Soria.

The emergence of Duffy as an ace and a still-impressive defense allowed the Royals to hang around the periphery of the wild-card race until the start of September. But when the bullpen blew two saves as part of four one-run losses in a five-game span, Kansas City's season was effectively over.

The result was an 81-81 record. Now Kansas City has one more shot at the postseason before this group largely heads elsewhere.

Six members of the lineup—Cain, Moustakas, Eric Hosmer, Kendrys Morales, Jarrod Dyson and Alcides Escobar—will be free agents after 2017. So will lefthander Danny Duffy. Even a large-revenue team would have trouble keeping that group together. For the Royals, it will be tough enough to find the payroll room to keep them this year when the majority head to arbitration.

So Kansas City heads into 2017 knowing this is the final bid for postseason glory before a likely lengthy rebuilding process.

It's a worthwhile tradeoff to trade off future success to win a World Series, and that's exactly what the Royals did. Lefthanders Sean Manaea, Cody Reed and Brandon Finnegan would likely all fit in the Kansas City rotation in 2017 as young, hard-throwing and cost-controlled starting pitchers. All three were traded away to help fuel the successful 2015 World Series run.

Kansas City lost its first-round pick in the 2016 draft to sign Kennedy as a free agent,

Danny Duffy emerged as the Royals' best starting pitcher after a spell in the bullpen

TOP PROSPECTS OF THE DECADE

Year	Player, Pos.	2016 Org
2007	Alex Gordon, 3b	Royals
2008	Mike Moustakas, 3b	Royals
2009	Mike Moustakas, 3b	Royals
2010	Mike Montgomery, lhp	Cubs
2011	Eric Hosmer, 1b	Royals
2012	Mike Montgomery, lhp	Cubs
2013	Kyle Zimmer, rhp	Royals
2014	Kyle Zimmer, rhp	Royals
2015	Raul A. Mondesi, ss	Royals
2016	Raul A. Mondesi, ss	Royals

giving the club the second smallest draft pool in 2016. The farm system is the thinnest it has been since before Dayton Moore's rebuilding process hit full speed in 2009-10.

The Royals have already traded one pending free agent as Wade Davis went to the Cubs for Jorge Soler, now penciled in as Kansas City's starting right fielder.

Whether that's the only trade will likely depend on how the season goes. The Royals are too close to their back-to-back World Series appearances to undergo a massive selloff just yet.

But if Kansas City falls out of the playoff race by the July trade deadline, it could dominate the trade market with a slew of desirable talents that could speed up the rebuilding process. Whatever happens, 2018 will likely be a difficult year.

ORGANIZATION OVERVIEW

General manager: Dayton Moore. **Farm director:** Ronnie Richardson. **Scouting director:** Lonnie Goldberg.

Class	Team	League	W	L	PCT	Finish	Manager
Majors	Kansas City Royals	American	81	81	.500	10th (15)	Ned Yost
Triple-A	Omaha Storm Chasers	Pacific Coast	58	82	.414	16th (16)	Brian Poldberg
Double-A	NW Arkansas Naturals	Texas	65	75	.464	6th (8)	Vance Wilson
High Class A	Wilmington Blue Rocks	Carolina	54	84	.391	7th (8)	Jamie Quirk
Low Class A	Lexington Legends	South Atlantic	52	87	.374	14th (14)	Omar Ramirez
Rookie	Idaho Falls Chukars	Pioneer	40	36	.526	3rd (8)	Justin Gemoll
Rookie	Burlington Royals	Appalachian	42	26	.618	1st (10)	Scott Thorman
Rookie	AZL Royals	Arizona	31	24	.564	t-2nd (14)	Darryl Kennedy
Overall 2016 Minor League Record			342	414	.452	27th (30)	

THIS YEAR'S TOP 30

No.	Player, Pos.	Grade/Risk
1.	Josh Staumont, rhp	60/Extreme
2.	Matt Strahm, lhp	55/Medium
3.	Hunter Dozier, 3b/of	50/Medium
4.	Eric Skoglund, lhp	50/Medium
5.	A.J. Puckett, rhp	50/High
6.	Scott Blewett, rhp	50/High
7.	Chase Vallot, c	50/High
8.	Ryan O'Hearn, 1b	45/Medium
9.	Jorge Bonifacio, of	45/Medium
10.	Kyle Zimmer, rhp	55/Extreme
11.	Seuly Matias, of	55/Extreme
12.	Khalil Lee, of	50/High
13.	Nicky Lopez, ss	50/High
14.	Alec Mills, rhp	45/Medium
15.	Jake Junis, rhp	45/Medium
16.	Nolan Watson, rhp	50/Extreme
17.	Cam Gallagher, c	40/Medium
18.	Meibrys Viloria, c	50/Extreme
19.	Samir Duenez, 1b	45/High
20.	Andrew Edwards, rhp	45/High
21.	Gerson Garabito, rhp	45/High
22.	Marten Gasparini, ss	50/Extreme
23.	Ashe Russell, rhp	50/Extreme
24.	Ramon Torres, ss/2b	40/Low
25.	Miguel Almonte, rhp	45/High
26.	Sebastian Rivero, c	50/Extreme
27.	Jeison Guzman, ss	50/Extreme
28.	Kevin McCarthy, rhp	40/Medium
29.	Foster Griffin, lhp	45/High
30.	Bubba Starling, of	40/High

LAST YEAR'S TOP 30

No.	Player, Pos.	Status
1.	Raul A. Mondesi, ss	Majors
2.	Kyle Zimmer, rhp	No. 10
3.	Bubba Starling, of	No. 30
4.	Miguel Almonte, rhp	No. 25
5.	Nolan Watson, rhp	No. 16
6.	Ashe Russell, rhp	No. 23
7.	Marten Gasparini, ss	No. 22
8.	Matt Strahm, lhp	No. 2
9.	Scott Blewett, rhp	No. 6
10.	Cheslor Cuthbert, 3b	Majors
11.	Jorge Bonifacio, of	No. 9
12.	Alec Mills, rhp	No. 14
13.	Foster Griffin, lhp	No. 29
14.	Ryan O'Hearn, 1b	No. 8
15.	Josh Staumont, rhp	No. 1
16.	Chase Vallot, c	No. 7
17.	Brett Eibner, of	(Athletics)
18.	Pedro Fernandez, rhp	Dropped out
19.	Gerson Garabito, rhp	No. 21
20.	Ramon Torres, ss/2b	No. 24
21.	Amalani Fukofuka, of	Dropped out
22.	Cam Gallagher, c	No. 17
23.	Brian Flynn, lhp	Majors
24.	Jose Martinez, of	(Cardinals)
25.	Alfredo Escalera, of	Dropped out
26.	Elier Hernandez, of	Dropped out
27.	Ricky Aracena, ss	Dropped out
28.	Seuly Matias, of	No. 11
29.	Jeison Guzman, ss	No. 27
30.	Hunter Dozier, 3b	No. 3

BEST TOOLS

Best Hitter for Average	Hunter Dozier
Best Power Hitter	Ryan O'Hearn
Best Strike-Zone Discipline	Nicky Lopez
Fastest Baserunner	Terrance Gore
Best Athlete	Khalil Lee
Best Fastball	Josh Staumont
Best Curveball	Jake Junis
Best Slider	Andrew Edwards
Best Changeup	A.J. Puckett
Best Control	Eric Skoglund
Best Defensive Catcher	Cam Gallagher
Best Defensive Infielder	Humberto Arteaga
Best Infield Arm	Emmanuel Rivera
Best Defensive Outfielder	Bubba Starling
Best Outfield Arm	Seuly Matias

PROJECTED 2020 LINEUP

Catcher	Salvador Perez
First Base	Eric Hosmer
Second Base	Raul A. Mondesi
Third Base	Mike Moustakas
Shortstop	Alcides Escobar
Left Field	Hunter Dozier
Center Field	Lorenzo Cain
Right Field	Jorge Soler
Designated Hitter	Cheslor Cuthbert
No. 1 Starter	Danny Duffy
No. 2 Starter	Yordano Ventura
No. 3 Starter	Josh Staumont
No. 4 Starter	Matt Strahm
No. 5 Starter	A.J. Puckett
Closer	Kelvin Herrera

MINOR LEAGUE DEPTH CHART

KANSAS CITY ROYALS

TOP 2017 ROOKIE: Matt Strahm, lhp. Starter or reliever, Strahm has the stuff to play a role in Kansas City.

BREAKOUT PROSPECT: Nicky Lopez, ss. The Royals are intrigued by the 2016 fifth-rounder's athleticism and defensive acumen.

SLEEPER: Kort Peterson, of. He struggled at UCLA but showed improved feel at the plate in his pro debut to go with solid defense and plus raw power.

SOURCE OF TOP 30 TALENT			
Homegrown	30	Acquired	0
College	11	Trades	0
Junior college	0	Rule 5 draft	0
High school	9	Independent leagues	0
Nondrafted free agents	0	Free agents/waivers	0
International	10		

LF
Khalil Lee (12)
Terrance Gore
Kort Peterson
Alfredo Escalera
Anderson Miller

CF
Bubba Starling (30)
Cal Jones
Rudy Martin

RF
Hunter Dozier (3)
Jorge Bonifacio (9)
Seuly Matias (11)
Jeison Guzman (27)
Yeison Melo
Amalani Fukofuka

3B
Emanuel Rivera
Travis Maezes
Mauricio Ramos

SS
Nicky Lopez (13)
Marten Gasparino (22)
Ricky Aracena

2B
Ramon Torres (24)
Corey Toups
D.J. Burt
Gabriel Cancel
Angelo Castellano

1B
Ryan O'Hearn (7)
Samir Duenez (19)

C
Chase Vallot (6)
Cam Gallagher (17)
Meibrys Viloria (18)
Sebastian Rivero (26)
Xavier Fernandez

LHP

LHSP	LHRP
Matt Strahm (2)	Scott Alexander
Eric Skoglund (8)	Andre Davis
Foster Griffin (29)	Daniel Stumpf
Garrett Davila	Richard Lovelady
Cristian Castillo	

RHP

RHSP	RHRP
Josh Staumont (1)	Andrew Edwards (20)
Scott Blewett (4)	Miguel Almonte (25)
A.J. Puckett (5)	Kevin McCarthy (28)
Kyle Zimmer (10)	Mark Peterson
Alec Mills (14)	Andres Machado
Jake Junis (15)	Dillon Drabble
Nolan Watson (16)	Jace Vines
Gerson Garabito (21)	Walker Sheller
Ashe Russell (23)	
Pedro Fernandez	
Janser Lara	

DRAFT ANALYSIS

2016

BEST PURE HITTER: Some teams liked OF Khalil Lee (3) more as a lefthanded pitcher, but he impressed the Royals scouts with his bat speed and feel to hit. SS Nicky Lopez (5) showed excellent ability to put the bat on the ball at Creighton. He doesn't drive the ball with much authority butrarely strikes out.

BEST POWER HITTER: 1B Chris DeVito (8) hit 16 home runs for New Mexico last spring and added nine more for Rookie-level Burlington to lead the B-Royals this summer. He has plus raw power with strength and leverage but faces questions about his bat speed.

FASTEST RUNNER: OF Nick Heath (16) is a 70 runner on the 20-to-80 scouting scale. OF Cal Jones (6) is a plus runner.

BEST DEFENSIVE PLAYER: Lopez was more notable at Creighton for his glove than his bat. He is an athletic shortstop who has a shot to remain at the position long-term as an average defender.

BEST FASTBALL: RHP A.J. Puckett's (2) low-90s fastball that touches 94 plays a little better than its average grades because he locates it well. RHP Anthony Bender (20) has a more pure arm strength than Puckett with a fastball that touches 95 mph regularly. LHP Richard Lovelady (10) earns above-average grades with his 92-94 mph fastball.

BEST SECONDARY PITCH: Puckett's changeup flashes above-average. RHP Dillon Drabble (17) flashes an above-average slider and RHP Grant Gavin (29) shows an above-average curveball at times.

BEST PRO DEBUT: OF Kort Peterson (23) hit .347/.437/.545 for Rookie-level Burlington. Lopez hit .281/.393/.429 while playing a solid shortstop for that same Burlington club, helping lead them to a playoff spot.

BEST ATHLETE: Lee was a two-way option out of high school as a lefthanded pitcher with a 91-93 mph fastball in addition to above-average speed and good burst. Jones (6) was his school's high school quarterback in addition to being a speedy center fielder.

MOST INTRIGUING BACKGROUND: Puckett survived a serious car accident during high school that left him in a medically-induced coma for two weeks. He pitches with metal plates in his skull.

CLOSEST TO THE MAJORS: Puckett doesn't project as more than a No. 4 starter, but he has already spent significant time in low Class A and should head to high Class A to start his first full season.

BEST LATE-ROUND PICK: Peterson is an excellent athlete with plus raw power, but he struck out too much to ever get to his impressive tools in college. Peterson's tools are that of a potential regular, so if the Royals are able to fix his swing-and-miss

issues, they could have a steal.

THE ONE WHO GOT AWAY: The Royals signed all but three of their picks. OF Luke Bandy (32) is a speedy outfielder who signed with Dallas Baptist. OF Kameron Misner (33) is a projectable outfielder who is attending Missouri.

2015

In a volatile pitching-heavy class, RHP Josh Staumont (2) finished 2016 with a flourish and ranks as the Royals' top prospect. Indiana prep RHPs Ashe Russell (1) and Nolan Watson (1) had disastrous 2016 seasons. LHP Garrett Davila (4) shined for Rookie-level Burlington.

GRADE: C

2014

LHP Brandon Finnegan (1) pitched in the College and major league World Series in 2014, and then was used in the Johnny Cueto trade. C Chase Vallot (1s) and 1B Ryan O'Hearn (8) provide power, while LHP Eric Skoglund (3) took a big step forward in 2016.

GRADE: C

2013

Power-armed LHPs Sean Manaea (1s) and Cody Reed (2) were packaged in two trades for Ben Zobrist and Johnny Cueto for the 2015 World Series run. 3B Hunter Dozier (1) bounced back in 2016.

GRADE: B+

TOP DRAFT PICKS OF THE DECADE

Year	Player, Pos.	2016 Org
2007	Mike Moustakas, 3b	Royals
2008	Eric Hosmer, 1b	Royals
2009	Aaron Crow, rhp	Cubs
2010	Christian Colon, ss	Royals
2011	Bubba Starling, of	Royals
2012	Kyle Zimmer, rhp	Royals
2013	Hunter Dozier, 3b	Royals
2014	Brandon Finnegan, lhp	Reds
2015	Ashe Russell, rhp	Royals
2016	A.J. Puckett, rhp (2nd round)	Royals

LARGEST BONUSES IN CLUB HISTORY

Bubba Starling, 2011	$7,500,000
Eric Hosmer, 2008	$6,000,000
Alex Gordon, 2005	$4,000,000
Mike Moustakas, 2007	$4,000,000
Sean Manaea, 2013	$3,550,000

1 JOSH STAUMONT, RHP

Born: Dec. 21, 1993. **B-T:** R-R. **Ht.:** 6-3. **Wt.:** 200.
Drafted: Azusa Pacific (Calif), 2015 (2nd round).
Signed by: Colin Gonzalez.

A little-noticed high school arm who grew from being a short and thick underclassman to a tall-and-lean senior at La Habra (Calif.) High, Staumont earned a spot in NAIA Biola (Calif.) University's rotation as a freshman (he worked 10.2 innings in one marathon outing), but he transferred to Division II Azusa (Calif.) Pacific to follow coach John Verhoeven. It says something about Staumont's stuff that he posted a 3.67 ERA in his junior season at Azusa Pacific despite walking more than seven batters per nine innings. It says even more that he was a second-round pick despite his wildness. And in his first full season as a pro, Staumont led the minors with 104 walks, but he also ranked second in strikeouts (167) and first among full-season starters with 12.2 strikeouts per nine innings. He went 2-0, 1.57 with 53 strikeouts and 12 walks in his final 40 innings between the regular season and playoffs and was effective as a starter in the Arizona Fall League.

Staumont creates extremely easy top-of-the-scale velocity. He's touched triple digits with a delivery that looks almost effortless. Staumont's right arm has allowed him to pitch successfully at a level beyond his current understanding of the craft. This year his understanding of pitching started to catch up to his stuff, though it still has a ways to go before he's consistently setting up hitters. His plus-plus four-seamer sits anywhere from 92-98 as a starter and has touched 102 when working out of the bullpen. It is a rather true pitch without much life. The only thing keeping it from an 80 grade is its lack of life. He also throws a two-seamer with sink, but the Royals have had him focus on commanding the four-seamer first before letting him rely on the harder-to-control two-seamer. His 11-to-5 curveball isn't consistent but is a plus pitch at some point in most every outing and will flash plus-plus at its best. His changeup is below-average and he uses it more at this point because he knows he needs to rather than because it's a reliable weapon. Staumont's control improved as the season progressed in part because of a mechanical tweak. He now brings his hands above his head in his windup instead of the simple hand break he used earlier. It improved his timing. He is focused on using his legs in his delivery more instead of the "tall and fall" delivery he used in college. He is somewhat

BA GRADE

60 Risk: Extreme

SCOUTING GRADES

Fastball: 70.
Curveball: 60.
Changeup: 40.
Control: 45.

Based on 20-80 scouting scale and future projection rather than present tools.

stiff, which limits his below-average control and command and his ability to diagnose and correct delivery issues quickly as they crop up. Staumont has work to do on holding runners. He was easy to steal on and four of his five errors in 2016 came on errant pickoff throws.

Staumont's rapid improvement has raised Royals' hopes that he could stay in the rotation, although his feel doesn't always match his stuff. Staumont's ceiling is that of a front-end starter if he can improve his control with a fallback option of serving as an impact reliever. His strong finish in Double-A in 2016 has him positioned to challenge for a spot in Triple-A to start 2017.

Year	Club (League)	Class	W	L	ERA	G	GS	CG	SV	IP	H	HR	BB	SO	K/9	WHIP	AVG
2015	Royals (AZL)	R	0	0	0.00	4	3	0	0	9	3	0	8	7	7.3	1.27	.103
	Idaho Falls (PIO)	R	3	1	3.16	14	1	0	1	31	18	0	24	51	14.6	1.34	.168
2016	Wilmington (CAR)	HiA	2	10	5.05	18	15	0	0	73	62	3	67	94	11.6	1.77	.230
	NW Arkansas (TL)	AA	2	1	3.04	11	11	0	0	50	42	2	37	73	13.1	1.57	.232
Minor League Totals			7	12	3.80	47	30	0	1	163	125	5	136	225	12.4	1.60	.213

2 MATT STRAHM, LHP

BA GRADE

55 Risk: Medium

Born: Nov. 12, 1991. **B-T:** R-L. **Ht.:** 6-3. **Wt.:** 185. **Drafted:** Neosho County (Kan.) CC, 2012 (21st round). **Signed by:** Matt Price.

Strahm went from a little-noticed string bean throwing 82 mph to the ace of the Neosho County (Kan.) CC staff. He spent all of 2013 and much of 2014 recovering from Tommy John surgery, but he moved fast once he was healthy. He made it to the big leagues after less than 250 minor league innings, then struck out 19 of his first 40 big league batters. Strahm's arsenal is that of a starter, but it plays up even more as a reliever. His 90-93 mph fastball (which sits 92-96 mph as a reliever) is a plus pitch with swing-and-miss capabilities thanks to its late-riding life, his mid-80s changeup is an average pitch and his now-harder curveball is also average. He worked in 2016 to stop collapsing his front shoulder in his delivery. That helped him firm up his slurvy curveball (it bumped up from 68-72 mph to 75-78 mph) and gave it more depth and less sweep. It also helped Strahm get more consistently down in the zone–he's always been comfortable elevating his fastball. He has a no-fear mentality and average control. Strahm has starter stuff, but he may fit better on the Royals' 2017 roster as a reliever. A stint as a reliever that eventually morphs into a starting role, a la Danny Duffy, is a likely result. Long-term, he projects as a No. 3 starter.

Year	Club (League)	Class	W	L	ERA	G	GS	CG	SV	IP	H	HR	BB	SO	K/9	WHIP	AVG
2014	Idaho Falls (PIO)	R	1	0	2.29	10	1	0	1	20	10	1	10	27	12.4	1.02	.149
2015	Lexington (SAL)	LoA	2	1	2.08	14	0	0	4	26	12	1	12	38	13.2	0.92	.140
	Wilmington (CAR)	HiA	1	6	2.78	15	11	0	1	68	48	7	19	83	11.0	0.99	.194
2016	NW Arkansas (TL)	AA	3	8	3.43	22	18	0	0	102	102	14	23	107	9.4	1.22	.260
	Kansas City (AL)	MAJ	2	2	1.23	21	0	0	0	22	13	0	11	30	12.3	1.09	.173
Major League Totals			2	2	1.23	21	0	0	0	22	13	0	11	30	12.3	1.09	.173
Minor League Totals			8	18	3.29	80	30	0	6	246	206	24	81	297	10.9	1.17	.224

3 HUNTER DOZIER, 3B/OF

BA GRADE

50 Risk: Medium

Born: Aug. 22, 1991. **B-T:** R-R. **Ht.:** 6-4. **Wt.:** 220. **Drafted:** Stephen F. Austin, 2013 (1st round). **Signed by:** Mitch Thompson.

After a fast start to his career, Dozier struggled after a promotion to Double-A to finish the 2014 season. He regressed more in 2015 He bounced back in dramatic fashion in 2016, finishing second in the Pacific Coast League in doubles (36) while posting 68 extra base hits between Double-A and Triple-A. Dozier's problems all started with poor timing and an inability to get into a rhythm. At instructional league in 2015 Dozier focused on shortening his swing and improving his bat path. He reworked his load, eliminating a drift in his hands that cocked his bat for his swing and replacing it with a shorter, more fluid load. Dozier cut his strikeout rate, hit for the best power of his career and did a better job of using the whole field. If he can stick with his newfound approach, he again projects to be an above-average hitter with average power. Defensively, Dozier is fringe-average at third base with an average arm. He's currently a below-average defender in the outfield due to inexperience, but as an average runner, he has room for improvement. Dozier's rebound gives hope that he can be an everyday regular. Cheslor Cuthbert's superior defense means Dozier likely ends up in the outfield.

Year	Club (League)	Class	AVG	G	AB	R	H	2B	3B	HR	RBI	BB	SO	SB	CS	OBP	SLG
2014	Wilmington (CAR)	HiA	.295	66	224	36	66	18	0	4	39	35	56	7	3	.397	.429
	NW Arkansas (TL)	AA	.209	64	234	33	49	12	0	4	21	31	70	3	2	.303	.312
2015	NW Arkansas (TL)	AA	.213	128	475	65	101	27	1	12	53	45	151	6	2	.281	.349
2016	NW Arkansas (TL)	AA	.305	26	95	14	29	8	0	8	21	14	23	4	0	.400	.642
	Omaha (PCL)	AAA	.294	103	391	65	115	36	1	15	54	40	100	3	1	.357	.506
	Kansas City (AL)	MAJ	.211	8	19	4	4	1	0	0	1	2	8	0	0	.286	.263
Major League Totals			.211	8	19	4	4	1	0	0	1	2	8	0	0	.286	.263
Minor League Totals			.262	456	1692	262	444	131	2	50	240	203	437	26	9	.344	.431

4 ERIC SKOGLUND, LHP

Born: Oct. 26, 1992. **B-T:** L-L. **Ht.:** 6-7. **Wt.:** 200. **Drafted:** Central Florida, 2014 (3rd round). **Signed by:** Jim Buckley/Gregg Kilby.

An accomplished skinny lefthander at Sarasota (Fla.) High, Skoglund became the ace of his Central Florida staff before signing with the Royals for $576,100. Skoglund missed the second half of the 2015 season with elbow soreness but avoided surgery, and he showed no ill effects in 2016 He led the Texas League in innings pitched (156) and strikeouts (134), was second-best in the league in walk rate among starters and finished third average against (.230). Though he's 6-foot-7, Skoglund generally works side to side, going in and out on hitters, rather than working up and down in the strike zone with downhill plane. He succeeds with his average 90-92 mph fastball because he has above-average command and control. Skoglund did a good job of tightening up his once-slurvy breaking ball into an average curveball with 2-to-7 shape. He locates it well, but it lacks the late-break or depth to be a plus pitch. He's also tinkered with a below-average slider. His changeup is fringe-average as well. As a lefthander with three average pitches and excellent control but no plus offering, Skoglund is the epitome of a back-of-the-rotation starter. He's ready for Triple-A and could see some big league time in 2017 With a rebuild looming, Skoglund should be a significant part of the 2018 rotation plans.

BA GRADE
50 Risk: Medium

Year	Club (League)	Class	W	L	ERA	G	GS	CG	SV	IP	H	HR	BB	SO	K/9	WHIP	AVG
2014	Idaho Falls (PIO)	R	0	2	5.09	9	8	0	0	23	30	2	9	25	9.8	1.70	.316
2015	Wilmington (CAR)	HiA	6	3	3.52	15	15	1	0	84	83	2	11	66	7.0	1.11	.260
2016	NW Arkansas (TL)	AA	7	10	3.45	27	27	0	0	156	135	19	38	134	7.7	1.11	.230
Minor League Totals			13	15	3.62	51	50	1	0	264	248	23	58	225	7.7	1.16	.248

5 A.J. PUCKETT, RHP

Born: May 27, 1995. **B-T:** R-R. **Ht.:** 6-4. **Wt.:** 200. **Drafted:** Pepperdine, 2016 (2nd round). **Signed by:** Rich Amaral.

A promising athlete at De La Salle High in San Francisco's East Bay area, Puckett gave up football and focused full-time on baseball after a car accident left him in a medically induced coma for two weeks; surgery left him with plates in his skull. After a middling sophomore season, Puckett emerged as Pepperdine's ace as a junior, putting together a 45.2-inning scoreless streak and finishing among the Top 10 in Division I in ERA (1.27) and WHIP (0.92). The Royals let Puckett throw another 59 innings as a pro on top of his 99 innings for Pepperdine because he

BA GRADE
50 Risk: High

was very pitch-efficient—he topped 80 pitches only once in 13 pro appearances. Puckett does an excellent job locating his 91-93 mph average fastball to both sides of the plate and changes hitters' eye levels by working down and then elevating, with the potential to have above-average control. His changeup is a plus offering with excellent deception. His fringe-average curveball is loopier than scouts would like, although he'll occasionally flash a tighter breaker. Puckett's ultimate ceiling will depend on how his breaking ball develops. His fastball and changeup are big league caliber, and his curveball has shown signs of developing into an average pitch as well. If the curve improves, he could be a No. 3 starter. He should move quickly through the minors, but will likely start in high Class A Wilmington.

Year	Club (League)	Class	W	L	ERA	G	GS	CG	SV	IP	H	HR	BB	SO	K/9	WHIP	AVG
2016	Royals (AZL)	R	0	1	3.86	2	2	0	0	7	8	1	0	8	10.3	1.14	.258
	Lexington (SAL)	LoA	2	3	3.66	11	11	0	0	52	42	4	15	37	6.4	1.10	.227
Minor League Totals			2	4	3.68	13	13	0	0	59	50	5	15	45	6.9	1.11	.231

6 SCOTT BLEWETT, RHP

Born: Aug. 10, 1996. **B-T:** R-R. **Ht.:** 6-6. **Wt.:** 210. **Drafted:** HS—Baldwinsville, N.Y., 2014 (2nd round). **Signed by:** Bobby Gandolfo.

High school pitchers from New York usually go to college or they go much later in the draft. But Blewett's size and arm strength convinced the Royals to make him the first New York high school righthander to be picked in the top two rounds in 15 years. Blewett had an excellent first half in 2015 but tailed off badly down the stretch. Repeating low Class A Lexington in 2016, he struggled early (3-6, 5.12) and but was much better in the second half (5-5, 3.55). Blewett's turnaround began when he figured out how to regain some of the fluidity in his delivery he had lost in his attempts to stay direct to the plate. He had become too mechanical and

BA GRADE
50 Risk: High

segmented in his motion. Once he fixed that, his fastball ticked back up from the 90-92 mph it was in the first half to a plus 93-95 mph heater with angle. His curveball sharpened up as well. It flashes average now and should become a solid-average offering. His inconsistent changeup generally is below-average (lefthanded hitters posted an .837 OPS against him), but will flash fringe-average every now and then. Blewett is yet to put together a full season of success as a professional, but he has the building blocks to be a durable mid-rotation starter if he continues to refine his secondary stuff.

Year	Club (League)	Class	W	L	ERA	G	GS	CG	SV	IP	H	HR	BB	SO	K/9	WHIP	AVG
2014	Burlington (APP)	R	1	2	4.82	8	7	0	0	28	27	3	15	29	9.3	1.50	.262
2015	Lexington (SAL)	LoA	3	5	5.20	18	18	0	0	81	88	6	24	60	6.6	1.38	.272
2016	Lexington (SAL)	LoA	8	11	4.31	25	25	2	0	129	138	10	51	121	8.4	1.46	.275
Minor League Totals			12	18	4.68	51	50	2	0	239	253	19	90	210	7.9	1.44	.273

7 CHASE VALLOT, C

Born: Aug. 21, 1996 **B-T:** R-R. **Ht.:** 6-0. **Wt.:** 215. **Drafted:** HS—Lafayette, La., 2014 (1st round supplemental). **Signed by:** Travis Ezi.

Low Class A Lexington has an auxiliary video board in left center field that proved to be a useful target for Vallot. Many of his 13 home runs (in only 82 games) landed around the board and one actually destroyed part of it. It was a highlight of a season that had plenty of bumps and some broken bones. A 93-mph Gage Hinsz fastball to the face was the worst injury, as Vallot missed a month recovering. He also missed time with a back injury. In between his injuries, Vallot showed some of the best power in the South Atlantic League. He was repeating the league, but was still among its younger catchers. Vallot can square up velocity and has started to show signs of recognizing spin. He projects as a below-average hitter with above-average power. Vallot is a well-below-average defensive catcher at this point with inconsistent footwork. He has to continue to work to stay nimble enough to have a chance to stay behind the plate. He struggles with throwing accuracy–all 17 errors he committed behind the plate came on wild throws. In a perfect world, Vallot is a Mike Napoli-type slugging catcher whose ability to catch gives his bat time to adjust to the big leagues. High Class A Wilmington is not a friendly place for power hitters, but it is Vallot's next step.

BA GRADE

50 Risk: High

Year	Club (League)	Class	AVG	G	AB	R	H	2B	3B	HR	RBI	BB	SO	SB	CS	OBP	SLG
2014	Burlington (APP)	R	.215	53	186	29	40	14	0	7	27	26	81	0	1	.329	.403
2015	Lexington (SAL)	LoA	.219	80	279	46	61	13	3	13	40	41	105	1	0	.331	.427
2016	Royals (AZL)	R	.133	10	30	5	4	1	0	2	2	3	14	0	0	.257	.367
	Lexington (SAL)	LoA	.246	82	272	37	67	20	0	13	44	39	118	0	0	.367	.463
Minor League Totals			.224	225	767	117	172	48	3	35	113	109	318	1	1	.341	.432

8 RYAN O'HEARN, 1B

Born: July 26, 1993. **B-T:** L-L. **Ht.:** 6-3. **Wt.:** 200. **Drafted:** Sam Houston State, 2014 (8th round). **Signed by:** Justin Lehr.

Scouts frequently complain that college baseball encourages hitters to focus too much on contact and not enough on driving the ball. O'Hearn is one of their prime examples, as he went from a singles hitter at Sam Houston State to a slugger in pro ball. He hit a home run every 60 at-bats in college but one every 20 at-bats as a pro. O'Hearn's power comes from strength and leverage. His bat speed is average at best, which leads to some concerns. His plus raw power plays in games though, giving him a chance to hit 25 home runs in an everyday big league role. The Royals have emphasized getting O'Hearn to use the entire field and he responded. After hitting two home runs the opposite way to left field in 2015, he hit nine to left in 2016 O'Hearn is an average defender at first base. He does a good job of scooping low throws, though his range is limited. The Royals have worked to get him time in left field as well, but he's well below-average in the outfield largely because he is a well below-average runner. With Eric Hosmer heading into his final year before free agency, O'Hearn is the best homegrown option to earn to a starting job in Kansas City in 2018 He still has work to do in Triple-A this year to prove he is more than a minor league slugger.

BA GRADE

45 Risk: Medium

Year	Club (League)	Class	AVG	G	AB	R	H	2B	3B	HR	RBI	BB	SO	SB	CS	OBP	SLG
2014	Idaho Falls (PIO)	R	.361	64	249	61	90	16	1	13	54	39	59	3	2	.444	.590
2015	Lexington (SAL)	LoA	.277	81	314	44	87	11	0	19	56	36	87	7	2	.351	.494
	Wilmington (CAR)	HiA	.236	46	161	14	38	10	0	8	21	19	54	0	0	.315	.447
2016	Wilmington (CAR)	HiA	.352	22	88	13	31	7	0	7	18	8	27	0	0	.408	.670
	NW Arkansas (TL)	AA	.258	112	414	49	107	25	2	15	60	48	131	3	5	.339	.437
Minor League Totals			.288	325	1226	181	353	69	3	62	209	150	358	13	9	.366	.501

9 JORGE BONIFACIO, OF

Born: June 4, 1993. **B-T:** R-R. **Ht.:** 6-1. **Wt.:** 220. **Signed:** Dominican Republic, 2009. **Signed by:** Edis Perez.

The younger brother of veteran big leaguer Emilio Bonifacio, Jorge Bonifacio began his pro career as a hitter who liked to use the opposite field. He morphed into a pull-heavy slugger whose batting average plunged in response. Now he's trying to find a balance. Bonifacio has spent years working to balance his power and hitting tools, trying to get to his raw power without gutting his ability to use the whole field and hit for average. Early in his pro career, his inside out swing kept him from driving the ball but led to plenty of singles and doubles. His attempt to pull the ball led to his average cratering after he reached Double-A. In 2016, he finally started to find a happy medium. He improved his selectivity and started to drive the ball from gap to gap, but his power tailed off badly in the second half. Bonifacio projects as an average hitter with average power. He is an above-average arm that fits in right field but his below-average speed limits his fringe-average range. Bonifacio doesn't fit in as an extra outfielder because of his defense. If he gets to his power, he profiles as a second-division regular. If not, he'll be a long-time Triple-A/up-and-down player. With Paulo Orlando and Hunter Dozier ahead of him, he returns to Triple-A in 2017.

BA GRADE
45 Risk: Medium

Year	Club (League)	Class	AVG	G	AB	R	H	2B	3B	HR	RBI	BB	SO	SB	CS	OBP	SLG
2014	NW Arkansas (TL)	AA	.230	132	505	49	116	20	4	4	51	50	127	8	3	.302	.309
2015	NW Arkansas (TL)	AA	.240	125	483	60	116	30	2	17	64	42	126	3	2	.305	.416
2016	Omaha (PCL)	AAA	.277	134	495	82	137	22	6	19	86	51	130	6	2	.351	.461
Minor League Totals			.267	715	2700	353	721	149	34	62	380	259	652	45	26	.335	.416

10 KYLE ZIMMER, RHP

Born: Sept. 13, 1991. **B-T:** R-R. **Ht.:** 6-3. **Wt.:** 230. **Drafted:** San Francisco, 2012 (1st round). **Signed by:** Max Valencia.

At this point, Zimmer seems as much a legend as an actual flesh-and-blood pitcher. He and the Royals hoped a labrum cleanup in 2015 would give him a chance to pitch significant innings in 2016, but he was instead shut down once again. He was diagnosed with thoracic outlet syndrome, a condition that causes numbness and weakness in the shoulder and arm. He had surgery to correct the issue and expects to be ready for spring training. The hope for everyone involved is that the thoracic outlet syndrome explains why Zimmer sometimes felt great with plus stuff and at other times struggled to break 90 mph. Zimmer has not been healthy for a full season at any point since he was the fifth overall pick in 2012, but he can still sit 92-94 mph with a plus fastball that has late life and his curveball that is at least plus. Zimmer has never had trouble generating swings and misses. His slider and changeup have atrophied, but both have been average or better in the past. The successful returns of Dylan Bundy and Jameson Taillon are reminders that pitchers can bounce back from lengthy injury layoffs. If Zimmer is healthy, he still has better stuff than almost anyone in the Royals' system and could pitch in the big leagues in 2017.

BA GRADE
55 Risk: Extreme

Year	Club (League)	Class	W	L	ERA	G	GS	CG	SV	IP	H	HR	BB	SO	K/9	WHIP	AVG
2014	Idaho Falls (PIO)	R	0	0	1.93	6	5	0	0	5	5	0	4	5	9.6	1.93	.263
2015	Lexington (SAL)	LoA	1	0	1.13	9	0	0	0	16	11	1	6	21	11.8	1.06	.190
	NW Arkansas (TL)	AA	2	5	2.81	15	7	0	3	48	42	4	14	51	9.6	1.17	.235
2016	Wilmington (CAR)	HiA	0	1	1.93	2	2	0	0	5	3	0	4	9	17.4	1.50	.176
	NW Arkansas (TL)	AA	0	1	0.00	1	1	0	0	1	1	0	2	2	18.0	3.00	.250
Minor League Totals			12	19	3.24	64	46	2	3	222	192	17	74	270	10.9	1.20	.232

11 SEULY MATIAS, OF

BA GRADE
55 Risk: Extreme

Born: Sept. 9, 1998. **B-T:** R-R. **Ht.:** 6-3. **Wt.:** 198. **Signed:** Dominican Republic, 2015. **Signed by:** Fausto Morel.

The Royals spent big $2.2 million to land Matias in 2015 by handing out the second-largest bonus awarded to an international amateur in franchise history. He had some of the best power in his international class and easily possessed the best outfield arm. He made a point of throwing from the warning track to make sure scouts saw the power of his arm, which easily grades as a 70 on the 20-to-80 scouting scale. Matias also draws 70 grades on his raw power that already pays off in towering home runs during games. He led the Rookie-level Arizona League with eight homers and ranked second with 21 extra-base hits in 2016, impressive feats for a 17-year-old. His eyes light up when he gets a fastball to drive. Matias doesn't recognize spin well, and he can be induced to chase, but he has exceptional bat speed that generates power. He drew a high volume of walks (11.1 percent of plate appearances) to go with an extreme strikeout rate (36.9 percent). Matias has as much potential as any hitter in the system. If he develops into even a fringe-average hitter he will profile as a prototypical right fielder. He plays center field occasionally but his above-average speed will likely wane as he matures. He heads to spring training in 2017 trying to prove he can handle low Class A Lexington as an 18-year-old.

Year	Club (League)	Class	AVG	G	AB	R	H	2B	3B	HR	RBI	BB	SO	SB	CS	OBP	SLG
2016	Royals (DSL)	R	.125	7	24	2	3	1	0	0	2	2	13	0	0	.222	.167
	Royals (AZL)	R	.250	46	172	32	43	11	2	8	29	22	73	2	4	.348	.477
Minor League Totals			.235	53	196	34	46	12	2	8	31	24	86	2	4	.333	.439

12 KHALIL LEE, OF

BA GRADE
50 Risk: High

Born: June 26, 1998. **B-T:** L-L. **Ht.:** 5-10. **Wt.:** 170. **Drafted:** HS—Oakton, Va., 2016 (3rd round). **Signed by:** Jim Farr.

Many scouts saw Lee as a more promising lefthanded pitcher than outfielder, and if he had headed to Liberty, he would have been a two-way contributor. The Royals made him a 2016 third-round pick because of his bat, and he paid off their belief by finishing among the Rookie-level Arizona League leaders in many categories, including on-base percentage (.396) and slugging (.484). Lee stands out because of his athleticism, body control and plus bat speed. In his pro debut, he showed better-than-expected barrel control as well. Unlike many young hitters, he's comfortable hitting with two strikes and showed an ability to string together good takes on breaking balls out of the zone. Lee is small for an outfielder but has surprising strength and above-average raw power. Despite a high strikeout rate, he draws frequent walks and drives the ball enough to project as an average hitter. Lee played all three outfield spots in the AZL, but he is an average runner without the exceptional first step or reads required to play center field. His above-average arm (he sat 91-93 mph as a pitcher) fits in right field. Lee is ready for full-season ball with a jump to low Class A Lexington in 2017.

Year	Club (League)	Class	AVG	G	AB	R	H	2B	3B	HR	RBI	BB	SO	SB	CS	OBP	SLG
2016	Royals (AZL)	R	.269	49	182	43	49	9	6	6	29	33	57	8	4	.396	.484
Minor League Totals			.269	49	182	43	49	9	6	6	29	33	57	8	4	.396	.484

13 NICKY LOPEZ, SS

BA GRADE
50 Risk: High

Born: March 13, 1995. **B-T:** L-R. **Ht.:** 5-11. **Wt.:** 175. **Drafted:** Creighton, 2016 (5th round). **Signed by:** Matt Price.

If the 2015 draft was notable for college shortstops at the head of the class—Dansby Swanson went No. 1 and Alex Bregman No. 2— the 2016 class was notable for its lack of first-round shortstops. The Royals were thrilled to find Lopez still available in the fifth round, since they had him near the top of their college-shortstop board. A lefthanded hitter, he has a plus arm and enough athleticism to stay at the position, thanks to soft hands and excellent body control. Lopez hit two home runs in three college seasons, but freed from power-sapping TD Ameritrade Park in Omaha, he hit six home runs at Rookie-level Burlington. He projects as a below-average power hitter, but he can catch up to fastballs and has a solid feel for the strike zone, which gives him a shot to be a top-of-the-order hitter with an average hit tool and plus speed on the bases. The Royals are thrilled with his makeup and grinder mentality. Lopez has enough experience for the Royals to contemplate sending him to high Class A Wilmington in 2017.

Year	Club (League)	Class	AVG	G	AB	R	H	2B	3B	HR	RBI	BB	SO	SB	CS	OBP	SLG
2016	Burlington (APP)	R	.281	62	231	54	65	6	5	6	29	35	30	24	4	.393	.429
Minor League Totals			.281	62	231	54	65	6	5	6	29	35	30	24	4	.393	.429

14 ALEC MILLS, RHP

BA GRADE
45 Risk: Medium

Born: Nov. 30, 1991. **B-T:** R-R. **Ht.:** 6-4. **Wt.:** 190. **Drafted:** Tennessee-Martin, 2012 (22nd round). **Signed by:** Sean Gibbs.

Mills has spent his career proving people wrong. A walk-on at Tennessee-Martin, he gained velocity as he matured and grew to be staff ace. Even then, Mills operated in the high 80s, so he fell to the 22nd round. He got back to work in pro ball by adding more velocity, and he turned himself into a big leaguer when the Royals called him up in May 2016. Scouts generally don't get excited when they see a pitcher like Mills, who throws an average 90-93 mph fastball with sink and bore, an above-average changeup and a fringe-average curveball and slider. What makes it all work is Mills' ability to stay away from the middle of the strike zone and the sweet spot of bats with above-average control. He's a fast worker who pitches down in the zone and on the corners. His lack of an out pitch requires him to hit his spots, but when

Mills is on, his fastball rarely arrives above the knees. Mills is a No. 5 starter or low-leverage reliever who could pitch in the big leagues in 2017.

Year	Club (League)	Class	W	L	ERA	G	GS	CG	SV	IP	H	HR	BB	SO	K/9	WHIP	AVG
2014	Idaho Falls (PIO)	R	2	2	4.66	7	6	0	0	19	20	0	4	14	6.5	1.24	.278
	Lexington (SAL)	LoA	2	1	1.18	7	7	0	0	38	25	0	10	33	7.8	0.92	.198
2015	Wilmington (CAR)	HiA	7	7	3.02	21	21	1	0	113	122	3	14	111	8.8	1.20	.271
2016	NW Arkansas (TL)	AA	1	2	2.39	12	12	0	0	68	57	2	12	68	9.0	1.02	.234
	Omaha (PCL)	AAA	4	3	4.19	12	11	0	0	58	62	8	19	54	8.4	1.40	.272
	Kansas City (AL)	MAJ	0	0	13.50	3	0	0	0	3	3	0	5	4	10.8	2.40	.231
Major League Totals			0	0	13.50	3	0	0	0	3	3	0	5	4	10.8	2.40	.231
Minor League Totals			19	22	3.03	94	67	1	9	392	372	21	85	377	8.6	1.16	.249

15 JAKE JUNIS, RHP

BA GRADE

45 Risk: Medium

Born: Sept. 16, 1992. **B-T:** R-R. **Ht.:** 6-2. **Wt.:** 225. **Drafted:** HS—Rock Falls, Ill., 2011 (29th round). **Signed by:** Scott Melvin.

The Royals spent big in the late rounds of the 2011 draft because the new Collective Bargaining Agreement for 2012 threatened to restrict draft spending. Junis, a 29th-round pick, was one of the beneficiaries, turning down North Carolina State after the Royals offered $675,000. Junis cleaned up the timing of his delivery, found more arm speed and pitched more aggressively in 2016 It paid off, mainly because a righthander who ranges from 89-95 mph makes hitters much less comfortable than one who sits at 87-92 mph, like Junis did in 2015 He always has had above-average control and excellent durability, but thanks to the better arm speed, his curveball, slider and changeup all got sharper as well. Nothing in Junis' repertoire grades as plus, but with an average fastball and curve, fringe-average change and improved deception, he has a shot to be a No. 5 starter. After a rough finish at Triple-A Omaha in 2016, he will return there in 2017 with a chance to be an emergency big league option.

Year	Club (League)	Class	W	L	ERA	G	GS	CG	SV	IP	H	HR	BB	SO	K/9	WHIP	AVG
2014	Lexington (SAL)	LoA	9	8	4.30	26	22	0	0	136	136	16	38	109	7.2	1.28	.262
2015	NW Arkansas (TL)	AA	0	1	9.00	1	1	0	0	4	7	0	1	3	6.8	2.00	.412
	Wilmington (CAR)	HiA	5	10	3.73	25	25	0	0	150	140	11	26	119	7.2	1.11	.251
2016	NW Arkansas (TL)	AA	9	7	3.25	21	21	0	0	119	110	12	27	117	8.8	1.15	.246
	Omaha (PCL)	AAA	1	3	7.20	6	6	0	0	30	39	6	7	26	7.8	1.53	.320
Minor League Totals			28	37	4.44	99	94	0	0	533	556	60	121	451	7.6	1.27	.270

16 NOLAN WATSON, RHP

BA GRADE

50 Risk: Extreme

Born: Jan. 25, 1997. **B-T:** R-R. **Ht.:** 6-2. **Wt.:** 195. **Drafted:** HS—Indianapolis, 2015 (1st round). **Signed by:** Mike Farrell.

The Royals emphasized high school pitchers at the top of the 2014 and 2015 drafts, but the strategy has not borne fruit in the early going. Foster Griffin (first round) and Scott Blewett (second) from the 2014 draft have career ERAs hovering near 5.00, while 2015 first-round righties Watson (3-11, 7.57 at low Class A Lexington) and Ashe Russell (just two innings) endured tough 2016 seasons. However, scouts who saw Watson reported fine velocity with a solid-average 92-93 mph fastball that peaked at 95 He struggled to command the pitch and left it elevated too often, leading to a .314 opponent average. Watson also showed a plus slider that he could throw to righties and lefties. One problem is the Royals encourage young pitchers to throw curveballs, so Watson's slider laid mostly dormant. Instead he tried to keep hitters off balance with a curveball and changeup that both graded well below-average. His changeup lacks deception and his curve lacks shape or depth, necessitating Watson to throw many fastballs in fastball counts. Unless Watson dominates in spring training, he seems destined to repeat the South Atlantic League in 2017.

Year	Club (League)	Class	W	L	ERA	G	GS	CG	SV	IP	H	HR	BB	SO	K/9	WHIP	AVG
2015	Burlington (APP)	R	0	3	4.91	11	11	0	0	29	39	2	11	16	4.9	1.70	.320
2016	Lexington (SAL)	LoA	3	11	7.57	24	24	0	0	96	125	19	44	60	5.6	1.75	.314
Minor League Totals			3	14	6.95	35	35	0	0	126	164	21	55	76	5.4	1.74	.315

17 CAM GALLAGHER, C

BA GRADE

40 Risk: Medium

Born: Dec. 6, 1992. **B-T:** R-R. **Ht.:** 6-3. **Wt.:** 230. **Drafted:** HS—Lancaster, Pa., 2011 (2nd round). **Signed by:** Jim Farr.

The best defensive catcher in the Royals system, Gallagher led Double-A Texas League catchers in most defensive categories in 2016. He committed just three errors all season and led the league by throwing out 48 percent of basestealers. Gallagher's arm grades as above-average, but it's the consistency of his throwing mechanics and accuracy that helps him shut down running games. He is a quiet receiver who presents pitches well. Gallagher's glove will get him to the big leagues and explains why the Royals added him to the 40-man roster in November. His bat, however, will likely prevent him from ever being a big league regular. Gallagher projects as a 30 hitter on the 20-to-80 scouting scale with modest bat speed, but he does draw enough walks to post reasonable on-base percentages. He will show average raw power in batting practice, but that rarely translates to games. Scouts project him to hit 6-10 home runs at most. Gallagher moves to Triple-A Omaha in 2017, where he will be only a call away from Kansas City.

Year	Club (League)	Class	AVG	G	AB	R	H	2B	3B	HR	RBI	BB	SO	SB	CS	OBP	SLG
2014	Wilmington (CAR)	HiA	.228	96	312	24	71	18	0	5	34	37	38	1	0	.306	.333
2015	Wilmington (CAR)	HiA	.245	76	249	24	61	15	0	5	22	28	34	0	0	.324	.365
2016	NW Arkansas (TL)	AA	.259	91	301	23	78	16	1	4	24	37	52	2	2	.348	.359
Minor League Totals			.234	393	1319	111	309	74	1	21	122	146	187	4	5	.314	.340

18 MEIBRYS VILORIA, C

BA GRADE
50 Risk: Extreme

Born: Feb. 15, 1997. **B-T:** L-R. **Ht.:** 5-11. **Wt.:** 175. **Signed:** Colombia, 2013.
Signed by: Rafael Miranda.

Viloria didn't strike a single extra-base hit in 150 at-bats in 2015, but he came a long way in 2016, when he led the Rookie-level Pioneer League with 28 doubles and claimed the circuit's batting title at .376 He also added an MVP award for his time at Idaho Falls. Viloria offers aggressively at pitches in the zone, but showed an ability lay off pitches out of the zone in 2016 He likes to jump on mistakes with average power. Viloria's lefthanded bat should be plenty potent if he can stay behind the plate, but that's still a question. He is a high-energy presence at catcher with an average throwing arm. He led the Pioneer League by throwing out 34 percent of basestealers and likes to back-pick runners at first base. His blocking and game-calling have improved, but he still has work to do. Some scouts worry he may end up getting too big to stay at catcher, but he moves well enough if he can watch his weight. He's ready for low Class A Lexington and projects as a bat-first catcher.

Year	Club (League)	Class	AVG	G	AB	R	H	2B	3B	HR	RBI	BB	SO	SB	CS	OBP	SLG
2014	Burlington (APP)	R	.200	13	40	4	8	2	0	1	5	10	10	0	0	.373	.325
	Royals (DSL)	R	.306	33	111	16	34	8	1	2	20	14	18	1	1	.383	.450
2015	Burlington (APP)	R	.260	45	150	20	39	0	0	0	16	17	23	0	0	.335	.260
2016	Idaho Falls (PIO)	R	.376	58	226	54	85	28	3	6	55	20	36	1	1	.436	.606
Minor League Totals			.315	149	527	94	166	38	4	9	96	61	87	2	2	.391	.454

19 SAMIR DUENEZ, 1B

BA GRADE
45 Risk: High

Born: June 11, 1996. **B-T:** L-R. **Ht.:** 6-1. **Wt.:** 195. **Signed:** Venezuela, 2012.
Signed by: Alberto Garcia/Richard Castro/Orlando Estevez.

Duenez moved more quickly than any other position player in the Royals system in 2016. He started the season at low Class A Lexington but jumped to high Class A Wilmington in June and joined Double-A Northwest Arkansas before the season ended, making him one of the youngest players in Double-A. Along the way, Duenez became the first Royals minor leaguer to compile 100 RBIs in a season since Wil Myers in 2012, when he won the BA Minor League Player of the Year award. Duenez is a pure hitter. His sweet lefty swing keeps the bat in the hitting zone for a long time, he uses the entire field and he catches up to good velocity. He projects as a plus hitter, but his power potential is in question because he prioritizes contact above all and is a hit-over-power corner bat. Defensively, he fits best at first base, where he's average, but he has tried left field in the past. Duenez stole 24 bases in 2016 because of savvy, but he's a tick below-average runner. Added to the 40-man roster in November, he heads back to Double-A in 2017 as a 20-year-old.

Year	Club (League)	Class	AVG	G	AB	R	H	2B	3B	HR	RBI	BB	SO	SB	CS	OBP	SLG
2014	Lexington (SAL)	LoA	.232	41	142	12	33	9	2	0	9	7	19	2	1	.268	.324
	Idaho Falls (PIO)	R	.304	39	135	16	41	7	1	1	27	10	20	4	2	.347	.393
2015	Lexington (SAL)	LoA	.266	101	361	47	96	13	4	1	37	24	33	11	5	.314	.332
2016	Lexington (SAL)	LoA	.272	68	265	30	72	15	3	6	49	15	40	14	2	.312	.419
	Wilmington (CAR)	HiA	.300	56	213	30	64	13	2	7	42	19	34	10	2	.363	.479
	NW Arkansas (TL)	AA	.278	14	54	4	15	5	0	0	9	5	12	2	0	.339	.370
Minor League Totals			.277	366	1357	165	376	74	14	15	192	92	185	49	16	.324	.385

20 ANDREW EDWARDS, RHP

BA GRADE

45 Risk: High

Born: Oct. 7, 1991. **B-T:** R-R. **Ht.:** 6-6. **Wt.:** 265. **Drafted:** Western Kentucky, 2013 (19th round). **Signed by:** Jason Bryans.

Edwards has always shown arm strength, but until 2016 hitters caught up to his mid-90s velocity all too often. The former Western Kentucky weekend starter cleaned up his mechanics in 2016, largely by focusing on firming up the front side in his delivery, en route to a spot on the 40-man roster in November. Once he did that, the quality of his slider improved significantly because he started to generate more bite and less sweep. It didn't hurt that his velocity ticked up as well. Edwards sits 96-97 mph and has touched 100, and his slider now earns some above-average grades. Edwards is an imposing 6-foot-6 presence on the mound, and his three-quarters arm slot helps him generate sink. His control still wavers, but he has made big strides in that department. Edwards heads to spring training with a shot at winning a job in the Royals bullpen in 2017, with middle reliever his most likely future role.

Year	Club (League)	Class	W	L	ERA	G	GS	CG	SV	IP	H	HR	BB	SO	K/9	WHIP	AVG
2014	Lexington (SAL)	LoA	3	5	4.76	22	6	0	1	68	87	2	29	48	6.4	1.71	.311
	Wilmington (CAR)	HiA	0	4	5.79	11	0	0	1	19	22	1	7	15	7.2	1.55	.297
2015	Wilmington (CAR)	HiA	0	2	3.86	29	0	0	2	42	33	2	19	30	6.4	1.24	.223
2016	NW Arkansas (TL)	AA	0	0	0.50	10	0	0	2	18	14	0	4	23	11.5	1.00	.222
	Omaha (PCL)	AAA	0	1	5.40	32	0	0	5	43	44	7	29	51	10.6	1.68	.267
Minor League Totals			5	13	4.05	122	6	0	20	213	213	12	101	184	7.8	1.47	.264

21 GERSON GARABITO, RHP

BA GRADE

45 Risk: High

Born: August 19, 1995. **B-T:** R-R. **Ht.:** 6-0. **Wt.:** 160. **Signed:** Dominican Republic, 2012. **Signed by:** Edis Perez.

The low Class A Lexington rotation faced a rough assignment in 2016 because it played in front of a generally rocky defense. Legends defenders ranked last in the South Atlantic League with a .966 fielding percentage and near the bottom in double plays and passed balls. Additionally, most of the Lexington starters worked on strict limits of 75-80 pitches. That helps explain Garabito's 2-11 record in 2016, his fourth pro season but first in full-season ball. He worked through five innings in just six of his 18 starts, ruling out the potential for a win in the majority of appearances. Garabito's fastball-curveball combo gives him at least a chance to be a useful reliever, and he flashes enough fade and deception with his changeup in bullpen sessions to show signs he'll have three pitches to remain a starter. He shows very little confidence in his change in games, however, so he doesn't sell in convincingly. He sits 90-93 mph and touches 95 with his average fastball. He also has long shown the ability to spin his curveball. It has good depth and projects as a future plus pitch. Garabito heads to high Class A Wilmington in 2017 as he continues to acquire feel for his changeup.

Year	Club (League)	Class	W	L	ERA	G	GS	CG	SV	IP	H	HR	BB	SO	K/9	WHIP	AVG
2014	Royals (DSL)	R	2	1	1.28	13	13	0	0	49	24	1	27	61	11.1	1.03	.143
2015	Royals (AZL)	R	3	2	4.11	14	11	0	0	57	52	2	19	42	6.6	1.25	.242
2016	Lexington (SAL)	LoA	2	11	4.80	18	18	0	0	81	78	9	35	61	6.8	1.40	.256
Minor League Totals			8	14	3.58	57	44	0	0	214	177	12	98	181	7.6	1.29	.227

22 MARTEN GASPARINI, SS

BA GRADE

50 Risk: Extreme

Born: May 24, 1997. **B-T:** B-R. **Ht.:** 6-0. **Wt.:** 165. **Signed:** Italy, 2013. **Signed by:** Nick Leto.

Signed for a European-record $1.3 million in 2013, Gasparini's development path has been understandably rocky. A native Italian, he still is trying to catch up to the speed of the game and owns a career .219 average through three pro seasons. Gasparini's 2016 effort at low Class A Lexington was particularly disappointing. His pitch recognition and plate approach are so raw that he looks fastball regardless of count. Therefore, he tends to pull off even ordinary breaking balls and changeups. A switch-hitter, Gasparini has plenty of bat speed and the raw ingredients to hit for average. He shows gap power now that projects to potentially average power. Working with Lexington coach Glenn Hubbard, Gasparini showed improvements defensively but still a lot work to do. His internal clock at shortstop still needs fine-tuning and his throwing motion is longer than scouts would like to see. He stabs with his arm action as he pulls the ball from his glove, creating a slower-than-desired release, not to mention accuracy issues. Gasparini has above-average arm strength, is a plus runner and is twitchy enough to cover enough ground at shortstop, but there are concerns about his hands. He committed 48 errors in 2016, including 31 fielding miscues, which led to a putrid .885 fielding percentage and speculation as to whether he his speed would play in center field. Gasparini is slated to return to Lexington in 2017.

Year	Club (League)	Class	AVG	G	AB	R	H	2B	3B	HR	RBI	BB	SO	SB	CS	OBP	SLG
2014	Burlington (APP)	R	.191	19	68	11	13	2	1	0	1	3	32	4	1	.225	.250
	Idaho Falls (PIO)	R	.455	4	11	4	5	0	0	1	3	1	2	2	0	.500	.727
2015	Idaho Falls (PIO)	R	.259	54	197	36	51	4	10	2	25	25	80	26	9	.341	.411
2016	Lexington (SAL)	LoA	.196	111	382	35	75	12	2	7	42	31	134	14	10	.256	.293
Minor League Totals			.219	188	658	86	144	18	13	10	71	60	248	46	20	.284	.331

23 ASHE RUSSELL, RHP

BA GRADE
50 Risk: Extreme

Born: Aug. 26, 1996. **B-T:** R-R. **Ht.:** 6-4. **Wt.:** 201. **Drafted:** HS—Indianapolis, 2015 (1st round). **Signed by:** Mike Farrell.

Much like oft-injured 2012 top pick Kyle Zimmer, Russell is a Royals first-round pitcher whose value fluctuates wildly from year to year. The first prep righthander off the board in 2015, Russell threw just two innings in two outings in 2016 as his mechanics completely broke down and he lost the ability to throw strikes. Things got so bad the Royals were not comfortable putting him back on the mound in instructional league. Kansas City expected Russell to head to low Class A Lexington at some point in 2016, but she showed up to spring training bigger and wider in the shoulders with a resulting loss of flexibility and looseness. His velocity backed up to the high 80s, his control wavered and he lacked the fluidity and consistency of his delivery. Even as he reworked his training program, he never rediscovered his delivery or arm speed during side work. Prior to his lost year, Russell had shown a plus 92-94 mph fastball and a hard slider that flashed plus, though his high-energy delivery, timing issues and stabbing arm action led a number of evaluators to project him to the bullpen. Now he's a wild card who will be starting over in 2017.

Year	Club (League)	Class	W	L	ERA	G	GS	CG	SV	IP	H	HR	BB	SO	K/9	WHIP	AVG
2015	Burlington (APP)	R	0	3	4.21	11	11	0	0	36	32	8	13	24	5.9	1.24	.235
2016	Royals (AZL)	R	0	1	9.00	2	2	0	0	2	1	0	2	1	4.5	1.50	.200
Minor League Totals			0	4	4.46	13	13	0	0	38	33	8	15	25	5.9	1.25	.234

24 RAMON TORRES, SS/2B

BA GRADE
40 Risk: Low

Born: Jan. 22, 1993. **B-T:** B-R. **Ht.:** 5-11. **Wt.:** 170. **Signed:** Dominican Republic, 2009. **Signed by:** Fausto Morel.

From 2009 to 2011, the Royals signed Torres, Humberto Arteaga, Orlando Calixte and Raul A. Mondesi internationally and drafted Christian Colon and Jack Lopez in an attempt to find a long-term shortstop. While Mondesi appears to be Alcides Escobar's heir apparent for 2018, and Colon—the fourth overall pick in 2010—fills a utility infielder role in Kansas City, none of the others have developed for the Royals. Torres, a member of the 40-man roster, presents them with a viable utilityman option. He doesn't have Mondesi's speed or power or Arteaga's pure range, but he's a well-rounded and versatile middle infielder. He has played a lot of second base in deference to Mondesi and is a plus defender, but he's also above-average at shortstop thanks in part to his plus arm. He plays third base as well. A switch-hitter, Torres doesn't project to hit enough from either side to be more than a backup. He's a 40 hitter with 20 power on the 20-to-80 scouting scale, but his defensive acumen and put-it-in-play approach could make him a bench candidate. Torres will return to Triple-A Omaha in 2017.

Year	Club (League)	Class	AVG	G	AB	R	H	2B	3B	HR	RBI	BB	SO	SB	CS	OBP	SLG
2014	Lexington (SAL)	LoA	.304	73	276	46	84	15	2	5	26	16	40	15	5	.346	.428
	Wilmington (CAR)	HiA	.248	44	149	14	37	5	3	0	8	10	16	5	2	.298	.322
2015	Wilmington (CAR)	HiA	.261	70	283	29	74	10	3	1	18	11	32	14	7	.292	.329
	NW Arkansas (TL)	AA	.275	51	189	23	52	10	1	4	13	17	23	4	8	.338	.402
2016	NW Arkansas (TL)	AA	.268	41	164	20	44	5	1	1	8	18	18	9	4	.339	.329
	Omaha (PCL)	AAA	.259	73	297	35	77	12	1	2	21	15	61	12	3	.295	.327
Minor League Totals			.269	585	2183	307	587	98	21	22	190	171	306	111	57	.324	.363

25 MIGUEL ALMONTE, RHP

BA GRADE
45 Risk: High

Born: April 4, 1993. **B-T:** R-R. **Ht.:** 6-2. **Wt.:** 210. **Signed:** Dominican Republic, 2009. **Signed by:** Fausto Morel.

A Top 10 Prospect for the Royals for four straight seasons, Almonte's development has gone backwards the past two years. After making his major league debut in 2015, he ended up back in Double-A Northwest Arkansas in 2016 to try to fix significant delivery issues that have sapped his once-impressive control. Almonte consistently opened up in his delivery too early, causing his elbow and arm slot to drop, which cost him control. He left his fastball and changeup elevated, while his curveball got sweepier. The result was too many walks and too many hittable pitches up in the zone. Almonte's fastball varied from 92-98 mph depending on how well he was maintaining his delivery. At his best, he still has

70 fastball and a 60 changeup on the 20-to-80 scouting scale, with a below-average curveball. Opposing scouts have long thought Almonte would be better served by throwing a slider or a cutter because his lower arm slot makes it hard to stay on top of his curve. He still has the stuff to be a high-leverage reliever, but his last two seasons have not been encouraging. Almonte has to prove he can handle Triple-A Omaha before getting another shot in Kansas City.

Year	Club (League)	Class	W	L	ERA	G	GS	CG	SV	IP	H	HR	BB	SO	K/9	WHIP	AVG
2014	Wilmington (CAR)	HiA	6	8	4.49	23	22	0	0	110	107	9	32	101	8.2	1.26	.259
2015	NW Arkansas (TL)	AA	4	4	4.03	17	17	0	0	67	65	4	27	55	7.4	1.37	.255
	Omaha (PCL)	AAA	2	2	5.40	11	6	0	0	37	33	3	15	41	10.1	1.31	.244
	Kansas City (AL)	MAJ	0	2	6.23	9	0	0	0	9	7	4	7	10	10.4	1.62	.212
2016	Omaha (PCL)	AAA	3	7	5.55	21	12	0	0	60	63	5	42	57	8.6	1.75	.274
	NW Arkansas (TL)	AA	2	1	7.31	11	0	0	0	16	24	4	4	15	8.4	1.75	.348
Major League Totals			0	2	6.23	9	0	0	0	9	7	4	7	10	10.4	1.62	.212
Minor League Totals			31	33	3.96	129	95	1	0	509	474	33	176	484	8.6	1.28	.248

26 SEBASTIAN RIVERO, C

BA GRADE

50 Risk: Extreme

Born: Jan. 16, 1998. **B-T:** R-R. **Ht.:** 6-1. **Wt.:** 180. **Signed:** Venezuela, 2015.
Signed by: Richard Castro/Alberto Garcia/Orlando Estevez

Rivero has just 46 pro games under his belt, most of them in the Rookie-level Arizona League. He has yet to hit a pro home run, and he's many years from the big leagues. But when Royals officials watch Rivero, they can't help but recall a young Salvador Perez. The comparison comes as much from Rivero's mindset, determination and personality as his tools. He responds to instruction and quickly carries the lessons into games. He got dramatically better at the plate in 2016 as the season progressed. He improved his pitch selection, allowing his short, simple swing to play. He hit .345 in August and scouts think highly of his offensive potential. Defensively, Rivero is a potentially plus defender with a good body, in particular a strong lower half. He has excellent blocking ability, a potentially above-average arm and he receives well. He has just started working on game-calling. With Rivero's work ethic, the Royals are excited to see how he'll develop, though he probably will require another year of short-season ball in 2017.

Year	Club (League)	Class	AVG	G	AB	R	H	2B	3B	HR	RBI	BB	SO	SB	CS	OBP	SLG
2016	Royals (DSL)	R	.333	8	27	3	9	0	0	0	4	1	1	0	0	.357	.333
	Royals (AZL)	R	.269	38	134	15	36	10	0	0	20	6	28	0	0	.303	.343
Minor League Totals			.280	46	161	18	45	10	0	0	24	7	29	0	0	.312	.342

27 JEISON GUZMAN, SS

BA GRADE

50 Risk: Extreme

Born: Oct. 8, 1998. **B-T:** B-R. **Ht.:** 6-2. **Wt.:** 180. **Signed:** Dominican Republic, 2015. **Signed by:** Edis Perez.

The Royals spent lavishly on the international market in 2015, signing outfielder Seuly Matias for $2.25 million and Guzman for $1.5 million. They knew the outlay would put them in the penalty box and restrict their international spending limits—no player could sign for more than $300,000—in 2016 and 2017. The early returns are encouraging, however. Guzman, like Matias, skipped straight to the Rookie-level Arizona League for his pro debut in 2016. Guzman is a promising shortstop with potentially average power down the road. His line-drive, all-fields approach already gives him the ability to find the gaps. A switch-hitter, his swings show promise from both sides of the plate, and his pitch recognition is reasonably advanced for his age. Some question whether Guzman is twitchy enough to stay at shortstop. He's a smooth athlete with fluid actions, but his range may be limited by his lack of burst, and his arm is merely average, not the plus cannon teams desire. He's a tick below-average runner.

Year	Club (League)	Class	AVG	G	AB	R	H	2B	3B	HR	RBI	BB	SO	SB	CS	OBP	SLG
2016	Royals (DSL)	R	.171	9	35	4	6	2	0	0	0	3	6	2	0	.237	.229
	Royals (AZL)	R	.261	45	188	35	49	9	5	1	19	18	44	5	3	.329	.378
Minor League Totals			.247	54	223	39	55	11	5	1	19	21	50	7	3	.314	.354

28 KEVIN McCARTHY, RHP

BA GRADE

40 Risk: Medium

Born: Feb. 22, 1992. **B-T:** R-R. **Ht.:** 6-3. **Wt.:** 200. **Drafted:** Marist, 2013 (16th round). **Signed by:** Keith Connolly.

McCarthy became the first player in Marist history to play in the major leagues when the Royals called him up in September. He made a quick trip to the majors, all things considered. McCarthy missed time in college and then again in 2013 with a pair of knee surgeries. A partially torn elbow ligament cost him time in 2014 as well, though he was able to rehab the injury without surgery. Since returning to health in 2015, McCarthy has moved quickly. He jumped three levels in 2015 and did it again in 2016.

His hard slider has improved to the point where it's a fringe-average pitch. It lacks the two-plane movement to grade as average, but he still makes his living working down in the zone with plenty of two-seam fastballs. McCarthy's 92-95 mph sinker generates plenty of ground balls and can grade as an above-average pitch on good days. He also mixes in a fringy changeup. McCarthy's control is the biggest thing standing between him and a big league role. He showed some improvement early in 2016, but he still needs to work to throw more strikes.

Year	Club (League)	Class	W	L	ERA	G	GS	CG	SV	IP	H	HR	BB	SO	K/9	WHIP	AVG
2014	Lexington (SAL)	LoA	1	0	0.00	2	0	0	0	4	2	0	2	1	2.3	1.00	.182
2015	Lexington (SAL)	LoA	1	1	1.50	6	0	0	2	12	10	0	1	8	6.0	0.92	.222
	Wilmington (CAR)	HiA	3	3	1.64	16	0	0	4	33	24	2	5	23	6.3	0.88	.205
	NW Arkansas (TL)	AA	1	0	5.71	11	0	0	0	17	24	1	8	9	4.7	1.85	.329
2016	NW Arkansas (TL)	AA	3	2	3.12	22	0	0	11	35	26	3	8	29	7.5	0.98	.208
	Omaha (PCL)	AAA	2	4	2.97	25	0	0	5	33	28	4	16	30	8.1	1.32	.230
	Kansas City (AL)	MAJ	1	0	6.48	10	0	0	0	8	11	1	5	7	7.6	1.92	.314
Major League Totals			1	0	6.48	10	0	0	0	8	11	1	5	7	7.6	1.92	.314
Minor League Totals			15	12	2.95	92	5	0	22	177	163	12	45	132	6.7	1.18	.247

29 FOSTER GRIFFIN, LHP

Born: July 27, 1995. **B-T:** R-L. **Ht.:** 6-3. **Wt.:** 200. **Drafted:** HS—Orlando, 2014 (1st round). **Signed by:** Jim Buckley.

BA GRADE 45 Risk: High

Considered one of the top high school arms in the 2014 draft, Griffin impressed scouts with a strong track record of success, solid stuff and an excellent ability to locate three pitches. He was a projection pick in many ways, because scouts saw his long limbs and solid frame and figured as he matured he would add a tick to his 88-92 mph fastball. Instead, Griffin has struggled to maintain even his prep velocity while starting every fifth day. With a fringe-average fastball at best and a fringe-average curveball and changeup, he lacks an out pitch. So far, hitters have been quite comfortable facing Griffin—he allowed a career .291 opponent average before high Class A Carolina League batters hit .330 against him in 2016. Griffin tinkers with his delivery too much during and between starts, but he has the potential for average control. If he can find a little more velocity, he could still be a back-end starter thanks to his ability to locate, but the projections of a future mid-rotation innings-eater now seem unrealistic.

Year	Club (League)	Class	W	L	ERA	G	GS	CG	SV	IP	H	HR	BB	SO	K/9	WHIP	AVG
2014	Burlington (APP)	R	0	2	3.21	11	11	0	0	28	19	2	12	19	6.1	1.11	.186
2015	Lexington (SAL)	LoA	4	6	5.44	22	22	0	0	103	123	8	35	71	6.2	1.54	.296
2016	Lexington (SAL)	LoA	1	4	3.38	7	7	0	0	37	35	3	9	29	7.0	1.18	.243
	Wilmington (CAR)	HiA	5	10	6.23	20	20	0	0	95	130	9	43	76	7.2	1.81	.330
Minor League Totals			10	22	5.19	60	60	0	0	263	307	22	99	195	6.7	1.54	.291

30 BUBBA STARLING, OF

Born: Aug. 3, 1992. **B-T:** R-R. **Ht.:** 6-4. **Wt.:** 210. **Drafted:** HS—Gardner, Kan., 2011 (1st round). **Signed by:** Blake Davis/Lonnie Goldberg/Mitch Webster.

BA GRADE 40 Risk: High

The 2011 draft already has produced five players among the top 20 selections who have either made an all-star team or earned MVP votes. That list includes Gerrit Cole, Sonny Gray, Francisco Lindor, Anthony Rendon and the late Jose Fernandez. Starling, selected fifth overall in 2011, is one of two players taken among the top 20 who has not reached the big leagues. Making consistent, solid contact has been a struggle for Starling, in part because he has never figured out how to lay off sliders out of the zone. His 2015 season seemed to indicate that he was finally catching up to his peers—he reached career highs by hitting .269 with 12 home runs—but in 2016 he looked more lost at the plate than ever before, hitting an abysmal .183/.235/.298 in 109 games at Double-A and Triple-A. His on-base percentage ranked worst in the full-season minors. Starling consistently took defensive swings in which he appeared to be guessing at pitches. The Royals promoted him to Triple-A Omaha in July in a change-of-scenery gambit, but he hit just .181 in the Pacific Coast League. Starling's above-average raw power evaporated as he seemed to lack the confidence or ability to get into hitter's counts. A plus-plus defender in center field with an above-average arm and above-average speed, he has no chance to claim even a bench role unless he can up his average to .240.

Year	Club (League)	Class	AVG	G	AB	R	H	2B	3B	HR	RBI	BB	SO	SB	CS	OBP	SLG
2014	Wilmington (CAR)	HiA	.218	132	482	67	105	23	4	9	54	49	150	17	2	.304	.338
2015	Wilmington (CAR)	HiA	.386	12	44	6	17	4	0	2	12	7	17	2	1	.471	.614
	NW Arkansas (TL)	AA	.254	91	331	51	84	19	4	10	32	30	91	4	5	.318	.426
2016	NW Arkansas (TL)	AA	.185	62	233	28	43	15	1	5	23	15	81	10	1	.251	.322
	Omaha (PCL)	AAA	.181	47	166	14	30	8	0	2	17	7	64	1	0	.213	.265
Minor League Totals			.232	522	1891	252	439	98	15	51	234	189	601	66	13	.310	.381

Los Angeles Angels

BY BILL MITCHELL

I t was a disheartening year in Anaheim.

The Angels couldn't overcome a slow start to the 2016 season, in part due to key injuries in the rotation, and the franchise recorded just its second losing season (74-88) in the last 13 years.

An 8-19 record for June put the Angels far behind the pack at the season's midpoint, and a 37-36 record after the all-star break wasn't nearly good enough to get them anywhere close in the American League West race.

With large contract obligations to Albert Pujols, C.J. Wilson, Jered Weaver and the long-departed Josh Hamilton already on the books, the Angels were not able to spend big in the free agent market heading into 2016. With the worst farm system in baseball and the organization's most talented prospects at the lower levels, there was no real help coming from Triple-A Salt Lake or Double-A Arkansas during the season.

And so the Angels had a gaping hole in left field, and lacked the depth to overcome injuries to starters Garrett Richards, Nick Tropeano and Andrew Heaney. (A failed comeback bid by Tim Lincecum was particularly painful to watch.) The pitching staff as a whole ranked near the bottom of the AL in most key statistics. Even the big offseason trade to acquire shortstop Andrelton Simmons from the Braves didn't help as much as expected, especially when he missed more than a month to a thumb injury.

The Angels also experienced a down year on the farm. The organization's six domestic affiliates compiled a .451 winning percentage that ranked 28th out of 30 organizations. However, both Rookie-level teams made their league playoffs, with Orem capturing the Pioneer League crown.

What talent is in the Angels system is at the lower levels. Salt Lake and high Class A Inland Empire both finished in last place in their respective leagues, with the latter going 48-92, second worst among all full-season teams.

On the bright side, the Angels possess the best player in the game in center fielder Mike Trout. Still just 25, Trout put together his usual outstanding season, winning his third Baseball America Major League Player of the Year Award in five seasons while batting .315/.441/.550 with 29 homers and 30 stolen bases. He also claimed his second AL MVP award.

Looking ahead to 2017, the Angels will gain around $40 million in salary relief just from the expiring contracts of Weaver and Wilson. General manager Billy Eppler begins his second year at the helm and started reshaping the front office. In

The Angels have made the playoffs only once during Mike Trout's historic five-year run

TOP PROSPECTS OF THE DECADE

Year	Player, Pos.	2016 Org
2007	Brandon Wood, ss	Did not play
2008	Brandon Wood, ss	Did not play
2009	Nick Adenhart, rhp	Deceased
2010	Hank Conger, c	Rays
2011	Mike Trout, of	Angels
2012	Mike Trout, of	Angels
2013	Kaleb Cowart, 3b	Angels
2014	Taylor Lindsey, 2b	Padres
2015	Andrew Heaney, lhp	Angels
2016	Taylor Ward, c	Angels

August, he replaced scouting director Ric Wilson, who had been with the organization since 2003, with former Cardinals crosschecker Matt Swanson.

Eppler had already put his stamp on the Angels' 2016 draft, bringing more analytics to the process. He also used four of the club's top 10 to select projectable high school athletes, a departure from previous years that saw more college players taken early.

Performance analysis helped make Virginia catcher Matt Thaiss, one of the top college bats available, the No. 16 overall pick. He quickly reached low Class A Burlington in his pro debut, though he switched positions to first base.

The Angels will pick 10th in Swanson's first draft in 2017, their highest draft position since 2000, when they also picked 10th.

DAVID SEELIG

ORGANIZATION OVERVIEW

General manager: Billy Eppler. **Farm director:** Mike LaCassa. **Scouting director:** Matt Swanson.

Class	Team	League	W	L	PCT	Finish	Manager
Majors	Los Angeles Angels	American	74	88	.457	12th (15)	Mike Scioscia
Triple-A	Salt Lake Bees	Pacific Coast	63	79	.444	15th (16)	Keith Johnson
Double-A	* Arkansas Travelers	Texas	67	73	.479	5th (8)	Mark Parent
High Class A	Inland Empire 66ers	California	48	92	.343	10th (10)	Chad Tracy
Low Class A	Burlington Bees	Midwest	68	72	.486	10th (16)	Adam Melhuse
Rookie	Orem Owlz	Pioneer	38	38	.500	t-4th (8)	Dave Stapleton
Rookie	AZL Angels	Arizona	29	27	.518	7th (14)	Elio Sarmiento
Overall 2016 Minor League Record			313	381	.451	28th (30)	

* Affiliate moves to Mobile (Southern) for 2017

THIS YEAR'S TOP 30

No.	Player, Pos.	Grade/Risk
1.	Jahmai Jones, of	55/High
2.	Matt Thaiss, 1b	50/High
3.	Alex Meyer, rhp	50/High
4.	Brandon Marsh, of	55/Extreme
5.	Nate Smith, lhp	45/Medium
6.	Taylor Ward, c	45/Medium
7.	Grayson Long, rhp	50/High
8.	Chris Rodriguez, rhp	55/Extreme
9.	Keynan Middleton, rhp	45/Medium
10.	Jaime Barria, rhp	45/High
11.	Nonie Williams, ss	50/Extreme
12.	David Fletcher, 2b/ss	45/High
13.	Vicente Campos, rhp	50/Extreme
14.	Connor Justus, ss	45/High
15.	Jose Suarez, lhp	50/Extreme
16.	Michael Hermosillo, of	45/High
17.	Sam Pastrone, rhp	50/Extreme
18.	Jared Foster, of	45/High
19.	Cole Duensing, rhp	50/Extreme
20.	Brooks Pounders, rhp	40/Medium
21.	Adam Hofacket, rhp	45/High
22.	Kyle McGowin, rhp	40/Medium
23.	Jesus Castillo, rhp	50/Extreme
24.	Jordan Zimmerman, 2b	45/High
25.	Austin Adams, rhp	40/Medium
26.	Justin Anderson, rhp	40/High
27.	Tyler Carpenter, rhp	40/High
28.	Brennon Lund, of	40/High
29.	Jake Jewell, rhp	40/High
30.	Joe Gatto, rhp	45/Extreme

LAST YEAR'S TOP 30

	Player, Pos.	Status
1.	Taylor Ward, c	No. 6
2.	Jahmai Jones, of	No. 1
3.	Nate Smith, lhp	No. 5
4.	Victor Alcantara, rhp	(Tigers)
5.	Jake Jewell, rhp	No. 29
6.	Grayson Long, rhp	No.7
7.	Joe Gatto, rhp	No. 30
8.	Kaleb Cowart, 3b	Majors
9.	Jaime Barria, rhp	No. 10
10.	Chad Hinshaw, of	Dropped out
11.	David Fletcher, ss	No. 12
12.	Roberto Baldoquin, ss	Dropped out
13.	Greg Mahle, lhp	Dropped out
14.	Julio Garcia, ss	Dropped out
15.	Brendon Sanger, of	Dropped out
16.	Kyle Kubitza, 3b	(Braves)
17.	Kyle McGowin, rhp	No. 22
18.	Rafael Ortega, of	Majors
19.	Austin Adams, rhp	No. 25
20.	Jared Foster, of	No. 18
21.	Jeremy Rhoades, rhp	Dropped out
22.	Justin Anderson, rhp	No. 26
23.	Jose Suarez, lhp	No. 15
24.	Adam Hofacket, rhp	No. 21
25.	Sam Pastrone, rhp	No. 17
26.	Todd Cunningham, of	Dropped out
27.	Jett Bandy, c	Majors
28.	Jake Yacinich, ss	Dropped out
29.	Natanael Delgado, of	Dropped out
30.	Hunter Green, lhp	Retired

BEST TOOLS

Best Hitter for Average	Jahmai Jones
Best Power Hitter	Matt Thaiss
Best Strike-Zone Discipline	Matt Thaiss
Fastest Baserunner	Leonardo Rivas
Best Athlete	Brandon Marsh
Best Fastball	Keynan Middleton
Best Curveball	Joe Gatto
Best Slider	Austin Adams
Best Changeup	Jose Suarez
Best Control	Jaime Barria
Best Defensive Catcher	Taylor Ward
Best Defensive Infielder	Connor Justus
Best Infield Arm	Connor Justus
Best Outfield Arm	Jared Foster

PROJECTED 2020 LINEUP

Catcher	Taylor Ward
First Base	Matt Thaiss
Second Base	David Fletcher
Third Base	Jefry Marte
Shortstop	Andrelton Simmons
Left Field	Jahmai Jones
Center Field	Mike Trout
Right Field	Kole Calhoun
Designated Hitter	Albert Pujols
No. 1 Starter	Garrett Richards
No. 2 Starter	Tyler Skaggs
No. 3 Starter	Andrew Heaney
No. 4 Starter	Alex Meyer
No. 5 Starter	Matt Shoemaker
Closer	Cam Bedrosian

MINOR LEAGUE DEPTH CHART

LOS ANGELES ANGELS

TOP 2017 ROOKIE: Alex Meyer, rhp. The Angels worked on correcting the 6-foot-9 righty's delivery after acquiring him and will give him a shot to earn a rotation spot.

BREAKOUT PROSPECT: Cole Duensing, rhp. The Kansas prep product flashed outstanding stuff in his limited debut and could make progress as he adds strength to a lean, lanky frame.

SOURCE OF TOP 30 TALENT			
Homegrown	27	Acquired	3
College	14	Trades	2
Junior college	2	Rule 5 draft	0
High school	8	Independent leagues	0
Draft-and-follow	0	Free agents/waivers	1
Nondrafted free agents	0	International	3

SLEEPER: Leonardo Rivas, ss/2b. The 19-year-old Venezuelan impressed scouts after moving stateside and is the fastest runner in the organization but needs to add strength.

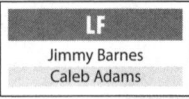

LF
Jimmy Barnes
Caleb Adams

CF
Jahmai Jones (1)
Jared Foster (18)
Michael Hermosillo (16)
Brennon Lund (28)
Troy Montgomery
Chad Hinshaw

RF
Brandon Marsh (4)
Brendon Sanger
Cal Towey

3B
Andrew Daniel
Zach Houchins

SS
Nonie Williams (11)
Connor Justus (14)
Nolan Fontana
Julio Garcia

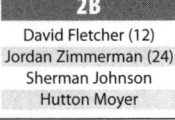

2B
David Fletcher (12)
Jordan Zimmerman (24)
Sherman Johnson
Hutton Moyer

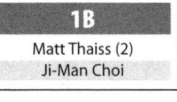

1B
Matt Thaiss (2)
Ji-Man Choi

C
Taylor Ward (6)
Keinner Pina

LHP

LHSP	LHRP
Nate Smith (5)	Greg Mahle
Jose Suarez (15)	Kevin Grendell
Manny Banuelos	Cody Ege
Tyler DeLoach	Chris O'Grady

RHP

RHSP	RHRP
Alex Meyer (3)	Keynan Middleton (9)
Grayson Long (7)	Brooks Pounders (20)
Chris Rodriguez (8)	Adam Hofacket (21)
Jaime Barria (10)	Austin Adams (25)
Vicente Campos (13)	Justin Anderson (26)
Sam Pastrone (17)	Jake Jewell (29)
Cole Duensing (19)	Eduardo Paredes
Kyle McGowin (22)	Luis Pena
Jesus Castillo (23)	
Tyler Carpenter (27)	
Joe Gatto (30)	
Jose D. Rodriguez	
Travis Herrin	
Oliver Ortega	
Elvin Rodriguez	

DRAFT ANALYSIS

2016

BEST PURE HITTER: Angels scouts didn't have C/1B Matt Thaiss (1) shoved up their boards, but the club's analytics had him as one of the best hitters available in the draft class. He hit .348 with 20 homers over his final two seasons at Virginia with more walks (72) than strikeouts (42) thanks to pitch recognition, bat speed and strength that are all above-average. 2B Jordan Zimmerman (7) also has above-average hitting potential thanks to a simple, direct righthanded swing and plate discipline.
BEST POWER HITTER: Thaiss has above-average power potential. Early pro reports on his power were mixed, but his amateur track record, with wood and metal, speaks to 18-22 home run potential.
FASTEST RUNNER: OF Brandon Marsh (2) and SS Nonie Williams (3) both are plus runners, as is OF Brennan Lund (11). Lund, a potential above-average hitter as well, knows how to use his speed more at this time.
BEST DEFENSIVE PLAYER: SS Connor Justus (5) and C Michael Barash (9) were college players with polished defensive tools who just enough to get into the top 10 rounds. Barash's blocking, receiving and pitch presentation are ahead of his fringy throwing arm. Justus has steady rather than flashy shortstop actions and tools.
BEST FASTBALL: RHP Chris Rodriguez (4) pitched his way into the top five rounds with a strong performance at Florida's high school all-star weekend, showing a 93-95 mph fastball. His fastball has a bit more life and plane than that of 5-foot-9 RHP Mike Kaelin (15), who can reach the mid-90s. RHP Blake Smith (29) also has reached touched 95 in short relief outings.
BEST SECONDARY PITCH: Rodriguez has a hard slider that resembles a cutter with short, late break and power. With refinement, it projects as a second plus pitch for him, though his delivery has effort in it.
BEST PRO DEBUT: Thaiss hit .292/.361/.462 in 264 at-bats, most of them coming at low Class A Burlington, while shifting full time to first base. SS/2B Keith Grieshaber (16) has an aggressive approach but hit .317/.362/.405 between two Rookie-level stops.
BEST ATHLETE: Williams gets a slight edge over Marsh, but both provide the kind of athleticism the Angels' organization and big league team lack. Williams is raw but has a lively 6-foot-2, 200-pound body and could stick at shortstop with refinement, though he'll need time. Marsh has more power, earning Colby Rasmus comparisons.
MOST INTRIGUING BACKGROUND: OF Torii Hunter (23), son of the retired big leaguer and ex-Angel, plays more wide receiver at Notre Dame than baseball. He signed for $100,000 but didn't play this summer for the Angels.
CLOSEST TO THE MAJORS: Thaiss fits the John Jaso profile as an OBP-oriented first baseman.
BEST LATE-ROUND PICK: The Angels bought C Jack Kruger (20) out of another year at Mississippi State with a $395,000 bonus. His bat's ahead of his glove and he was more of a DH for the Bulldogs. Lund was one of the better college outfielders available but slipped in the 11th round.
THE ONE WHO GOT AWAY: SS David Hamilton (28), another plus athlete, was a star prep quarterback who headed to Texas to play baseball.

2015

OF Jahmai Jones (2) has emerged as the club's No. 1 prospect. College picks such as C Taylor Ward (1), RHPs Grayson Long (3) and Adam Hofacket (10), OF Jared Foster (5) and SS David Fletcher have a chance to contribute.
GRADE: C

2014

The Angels traded LHP Sean Newcomb (1) and RHP Chris Ellis (3) to Atlanta in the Andrelton Simmons deal. RHP Joe Gatto (2) flopped badly in 2016.
GRADE: D

2013

Top pick LHP Hunter Green (2) retired after 17 career innings. LHP Nate Smith (8) has become the class' top prospect, while RHP Keynan Middleton (3) offers hope and RHP Kyle McGowin (5) was used in the Danny Espinosa trade.
GRADE: D

TOP DRAFT PICKS OF THE DECADE

Year	Player, Pos.	2016 Org
2007	Jon Bachanov, rhp (1st round supp.)	Did not play
2008	Tyler Chatwood, rhp (2nd round)	Rockies
2009	Randal Grichuk, of	Cardinals
2010	Kaleb Cowart, 3b	Angels
2011	C.J. Cron, 1b	Angels
2012	R.J. Alvarez, rhp (3rd round)	Rangers
2013	Hunter Green, lhp (2nd round)	Did not play
2014	Sean Newcomb, lhp	Braves
2015	Taylor Ward, c	Angels
2016	Matt Thaiss, 1b	Angels

LARGEST BONUSES IN CLUB HISTORY

Roberto Baldoquin, 2015	$8,000,000
Jered Weaver, 2004	$4,000,000
Kendrys Morales, 2004	$3,000,000
Sean Newcomb, 2014	$2,518,400
Kaleb Cowart, 2010	$2,300,000

1 JAHMAI JONES, OF

Born: Aug. 4, 1997. **B-T:** R-R. **Ht.:** 6-0. **Wt.:** 215.
Drafted: HS—Norcross, Ga., 2015 (2nd round).
Signed by: Todd Hogan.

BILL MITCHELL

Jones, who hails from a rich football background, comes by his athleticism naturally. His late father Andre played for Lou Holtz at Notre Dame and in the NFL, while brother T.J. played wide receiver for the Detroit Lions in 2015. Another brother, Malachi, played collegiately at Appalachian State. Jahmai was a star wide receiver as a high school sophomore before giving up the gridiron to focus on baseball. He passed on a baseball scholarship to North Carolina to join the Angels organization, signing for $1.1 million as a second-round pick in 2015. Jones ranked as the organization's No. 2 prospect last year, behind first-rounder Taylor Ward, but jumped to the top of the list in 2017 as a supreme athlete who has started to add polish. He showed significant improvement at 2016 extended spring training, both in his baseball instincts and with an improved physique better suited for baseball than football. Those gains carried through to his outstanding season at Rookie-level Orem, and he earned a late promotion to low Class A Burlington.

Jones stands out most for top-of-the-scale makeup that will consistently allow him to play above his tools. He took on more of a leadership role in his second pro season, helping to position other outfielders during his time at Orem. His baseball smarts, quick-twitch athleticism and above-average to plus speed should allow him to stay in center field, though some observers are concerned that his body is maxed out and that he may slow down with age. He takes good routes in the outfield and consistently re-positions himself based on hitter tendencies. His average arm should be sufficient for a corner spot if he moves out of center, a likely possibility with the Angels having Mike Trout entrenched at the position. At the plate, Jones has a short stroke with plus bat speed that indicates he could be an above-average hitter in time. He hits mostly line drives with gap-to-gap power, but shows average raw power with a good swing path and likely will hit for more power as he progresses. Jones has controlled the strike zone well against lower-level pitchers and makes a lot of contact—he struck out less than 13 percent of the time at Orem. He has the ability to make adjustments quickly but needs to work on the short game to round out his skill set. Jones is an instinctual runner who stole 20 bases in 26 attempts in 2016.

BA GRADE
55 Risk: High

SCOUTING GRADES

Batting: 55.
Power: 50.
Speed: 60.
Defense: 55.
Arm: 50.

Based on 20-80 scouting scale and future projection rather than present tools.

He's a good teammate and clubhouse leader with an advanced mix of smarts, skills and effort that earns everyone's respect.

Jones was young for his high school class and just turned 19 in August. After getting a brief taste of full-season ball at the end of 2016, he likely will return to low Class A to start 2017, but he could earn a bump to high Class A Inland Empire by midseason. One Angels official called Jones the most likely prospect in the organization to contribute at the big league level, making him even more valuable to a farm system lacking potential impact talent.

Year	Club (League)	Class	AVG	G	AB	R	H	2B	3B	HR	RBI	BB	SO	SB	CS	OBP	SLG
2015	Angels (AZL)	R	.244	40	160	28	39	6	2	2	20	17	33	16	7	.330	.344
2016	Orem (PIO)	R	.321	48	196	49	63	12	3	3	20	21	29	19	6	.404	.459
	Burlington (MWL)	LoA	.242	16	62	8	15	1	0	1	10	5	13	1	0	.294	.306
Minor League Totals			.280	104	418	85	117	19	5	6	50	43	75	36	13	.360	.392

2 MATT THAISS, 1B

Born: May 6, 1995. **B-T:** L-R. **Ht.:** 6-0. **Wt.:** 195. **Drafted:** Virginia, 2016 (1st round). **Signed by:** Nick Gorneault.

The Angels used their first-round pick to select a college catcher for the second straight year, but unlike 2015 pick Taylor Ward, Thaiss probably won't don catcher's gear as a pro. The Angels coveted his advanced hitting ability and played him at first base in his pro debut. There's little doubt Thaiss is a plus hitter. He takes excellent at-bats, knows his plan, doesn't chase bad pitches and isn't afraid to take a walk. He walked nearly as often as he struck out in pro ball after compiling a 55-to-74 strikeout-to-walk ratio in three college seasons. With plus bat speed and a strong swing with leverage, Thaiss has above-average to plus raw power. While some scouts project he'll hit 10-15 home runs per season, his plate discipline should help him translate his raw power to game power. He's a below-average runner. The biggest question about Thaiss is where he'll play on the field. He is still inexperienced at first base, with stiff hands and uncertain actions around the bag. Thaiss' polished bat could move very quickly. He will head to high Class A Inland Empire in 2017, but if he hits could shoot through the system to a big league roster shy on lefthanded bats.

BA GRADE 50 Risk: High

Year	Club (League)	Class	AVG	G	AB	R	H	2B	3B	HR	RBI	BB	SO	SB	CS	OBP	SLG
2016	Orem (PIO)	R	.338	15	65	16	22	7	1	2	12	4	4	2	4	.394	.569
	Burlington (MWL)	LoA	.276	52	199	24	55	12	3	4	31	22	28	1	0	.351	.427
Minor League Totals			.292	67	264	40	77	19	4	6	43	26	32	3	4	.361	.462

3 ALEX MEYER, RHP

Born: Jan. 3, 1990. **B-T:** R-R. **Ht.:** 6-9. **Wt.:** 225. **Drafted:** Kentucky, 2011 (1st round). **Signed by:** Reed Dunn (Nationals).

The 23rd overall pick in the 2011 draft, Meyer has battled injuries and control issues and been traded twice, first by the Nationals to the Twins for Denard Span, and then to the Angels in the Ricky Nolasco-Hector Santiago swap in August 2016. He pitched a total of just 54 innings in 2016 because of recurring shoulder issues. Meyer lowered his arm slot as a pro due to a biceps injury, so the Angels worked to get his release point back to the higher slot he used in college. They also helped the 6-foot-9 righty refine his mechanics to help his fastball control and keep him from pulling off on his front side. Meyer's best pitch is a sinking four-seam fastball with tail that averages 95-96 mph and in the past touched triple digits. He complements it with a hard mid-80s knuckle curveball that gets swings and misses. Meyer's circle changeup with armside fade is a hard pitch around 90 mph, while a sinker with tail generates plenty of ground balls. If Meyer can stay healthy and improve his mechanics, he will be in the Angels' rotation in 2017 and beyond.

BA GRADE 50 Risk: High

Year	Club (League)	Class	W	L	ERA	G	GS	CG	SV	IP	H	HR	BB	SO	K/9	WHIP	AVG
2014	Rochester (IL)	AAA	7	7	3.52	27	27	0	0	130	116	10	64	153	10.6	1.38	.241
2015	Minnesota (AL)	MAJ	0	0	16.88	2	0	0	0	3	4	2	3	3	10.1	2.63	.364
	Rochester (IL)	AAA	4	5	4.79	38	8	0	0	92	101	4	48	100	9.8	1.62	.281
2016	Rochester (IL)	AAA	1	1	1.04	3	2	0	1	17	11	0	4	19	9.9	0.87	.183
	Minnesota (AL)	MAJ	0	1	12.27	2	1	0	0	4	8	1	4	5	12.3	3.27	.421
	Angels (AZL)	R	0	0	1.69	3	3	0	0	5	6	0	1	12	20.3	1.31	.273
	Inland Empire (CAL)	HiA	0	0	11.57	1	1	0	0	2	3	0	1	3	11.6	1.71	.273
	Salt Lake (PCL)	AAA	0	0	0.00	1	1	0	0	4	2	0	0	6	13.5	0.50	.143
	Los Angeles (AL)	MAJ	1	2	4.57	5	5	0	0	22	17	2	13	24	10.0	1.38	.215
Major League Totals			1	3	6.75	9	6	0	0	28	29	5	20	32	10.3	1.75	.266
Minor League Totals			26	22	3.39	114	83	1	1	459	403	23	195	532	10.4	1.30	.237

4 BRANDON MARSH, OF

BILL MITCHELL

Born: Dec. 18, 1997. **B-T:** L-R. **Ht.:** 6-2. **Wt.:** 190. **Drafted:** HS—Buford, Ga., 2016 (2nd round). **Signed by:** Todd Hogan.

After drafting Jahmai Jones in 2015, the Angels again used a second-round pick in 2016 to take another physically-talented Georgia prep outfielder. The Angels found a back issue in Marsh's post-draft physical that delayed his signing, but he wound up signing for slot value of $1,073,300. He missed all of the Rookie-level Arizona League and instructional league seasons with a stress reaction in his back but spent that time working out at the Angels' facility in Arizona. A two-sport athlete whose football career limited his showcase exposure as a prep, Marsh showed scouts a loud set of tools during his scholastic career, with both plus speed and a plus arm. He has a

BA GRADE 55 Risk: Extreme

strong, athletic frame, and scouts who saw him take batting practice during instructional league noted the raw power and good loft in his swing as well as an ability to make adjustments from one session to the next. He's a bit raw offensively, however, and the lost development time won't help. The Angels expect a complete recovery for Marsh, and he will be ready to begin his career in 2017. Some scouts have likened him physically and tools-wise to Colby Rasmus, though he's less polished at a similar age. Marsh will start 2017 in extended spring training, then likely make his pro debut at Rookie-level Orem.

Year	Club (League)	Class	AVG	G	AB	R	H	2B	3B	HR	RBI	BB	SO	SB	CS	OBP	SLG
2016	Did not play—Injured																

5 NATE SMITH, LHP

Born: Aug. 28, 1991. **B-T:** L-L. **Ht.:** 6-3. **Wt.:** 205. **Drafted:** Furman, 2013 (8th round). **Signed by:** Todd Hogan.

A 2016 Futures Game participant, Smith originally signed for a bargain price of $12,000 after being Furman's highest draft pick since 1972. Smith is the closest of the organization's top prospects to making it to the big leagues. In fact, he likely would have made his debut in 2016, especially considering the pitching woes on the big league club, had it not been for some minor elbow tendinitis toward the end of the year. Smith survived his first Triple-A Pacific Coast League season with diminished fastball velocity. His fastball typically sat in the upper 80s while touching 92 mph and comes out of a somewhat funky arm action and high three-quarters

BA GRADE
45 Risk: Medium

arm slot. The plus changeup that he throws 75-77 mph and commands well is the difference-maker for Smith. It's a pitch that he uses to get swings-and-misses, but his reduced fastball velocity seemed to make him more reliant on the changeup, according to some observers. He added an 80 mph slider in 2015 and now uses it more than his mid-70s curveball, and it has become his bat-missing pitch. Smith has to be fine but has above-average control. Smith will go to spring training in 2017 with a decent chance of making the Opening Day roster, possibly as a long reliever. He has the pitching smarts and mound presence to handle a big league role, assuming his elbow woes are behind him.

Year	Club (League)	Class	W	L	ERA	G	GS	CG	SV	IP	H	HR	BB	SO	K/9	WHIP	AVG
2014	Inland Empire (CAL)	HiA	6	3	3.07	10	10	0	0	56	41	3	14	51	8.2	0.99	.201
	Arkansas (TL)	AA	5	3	2.89	11	11	0	0	62	48	3	30	67	9.7	1.25	.218
2015	Arkansas (TL)	AA	8	4	2.48	17	17	1	0	102	82	10	28	81	7.2	1.08	.216
	Salt Lake (PCL)	AAA	2	4	7.75	7	7	0	0	36	48	7	15	23	5.8	1.75	.308
2016	Salt Lake (PCL)	AAA	8	9	4.61	26	26	0	0	150	166	18	44	122	7.3	1.40	.283
Minor League Totals			31	25	3.88	86	80	1	0	441	419	45	138	375	7.7	1.26	.250

6 TAYLOR WARD, C

Born: Dec. 14, 1993. **B-T:** R-R. **Ht.:** 6-1. **Wt.:** 190. **Drafted:** Fresno State, 2015 (1st round). **Signed by:** Scott Richardson.

Ward was the full-time catcher for two seasons at Fresno State in addition to spending a summer with USA Baseball's Collegiate National Team. While projected as more of a third-round pick, Ward went to the Angels with the 26th overall pick in 2015. He spent the entire 2016 season at high Class A Inland Empire, improving his OPS from .541 in the first half to .774 in the second. Scouts have generally been skeptical of Ward's offensive potential, but his improvement included nine of his 10 home runs coming in the second half. He was too aggressive early in the season and had to make adjustments by getting his hands higher. He doesn't always have a

BA GRADE
45 Risk: Medium

consistent approach at the plate or get enough load in his swing. Ward stands out as a potentially above-average or better defender behind the plate, with a plus arm that allowed him to throw out 38 percent of basestealers in 2016. He wasn't receiving the ball well early in the year, especially in catching strikes to his glove side, and his 19 passed balls tied for most in the California League, but he improved his glove positioning. He is a below-average runner but not a base-clogger. Ward will move up to Double-A Mobile in 2017 and could get Triple-A time before the end of the summer. Barring a future catcher acquisition, he doesn't face much competition to be the club's backstop of the future.

Year	Club (League)	Class	AVG	G	AB	R	H	2B	3B	HR	RBI	BB	SO	SB	CS	OBP	SLG
2015	Orem (PIO)	R	.349	32	109	20	38	4	1	2	19	29	8	5	2	.489	.459
	Burlington (MWL)	LoA	.348	24	92	10	32	3	0	1	12	10	15	1	1	.412	.413
2016	Inland Empire (CAL)	HiA	.249	123	466	61	116	11	0	10	56	48	81	0	0	.323	.337
Minor League Totals			.279	179	667	91	186	18	1	13	87	87	104	6	3	.365	.367

7 GRAYSON LONG, RHP

Born: May 27, 1994. **B-T:** R-R. **Ht.:** 6-5. **Wt.:** 230. **Drafted:** Texas A&M, 2015 (3rd round). **Signed by:** Rudy Vasquez.

Long threw 96 innings at Texas A&M in 2015, so the Angels limited him to 20 innings in his pro debut after signing him for $548,600. He turned in eight productive starts at low Class A Burlington in 2016 before general fatigue and soreness warranted a couple of months on the sidelines. After four rehab outings in the Rookie-level Arizona League, Long finished his regular season with three starts at high Class A Inland Empire before being assigned to the Arizona Fall League. Big and physical, Long uses a low-maintenance, high three-quarters arm slot that keeps his pitches down in the zone, while allowing his heater to play up. His fast-

BA GRADE

50 Risk: High

ball comes out of his hand well with good movement and sits 88-92 mph. He touches 95 mph with late life that allows him to get some swings and misses. His slider-cutter hybrid, a solid-average pitch, shows quality depth and late action. His changeup flashes firm, late, sinking depth and projects as an average offering. Long has the 6-foot-5 frame and easy delivery for an innings-eater type of starter, but he needs to show he can hold up over a full season. He should begin 2017 back at Inland Empire, with a move to Double-A during the season.

Year	Club (League)	Class	W	L	ERA	G	GS	CG	SV	IP	H	HR	BB	SO	K/9	WHIP	AVG
2015	Orem (PIO)	R	0	0	5.03	13	12	0	0	20	19	1	10	22	10.1	1.47	.253
2016	Burlington (MWL)	LoA	3	3	1.58	8	8	0	0	40	27	2	16	45	10.1	1.08	.190
	Angels (AZL)	R	0	1	6.55	4	4	0	0	11	13	0	5	10	8.2	1.64	.295
	Inland Empire (CAL)	HiA	2	1	5.14	3	3	0	0	14	14	5	4	15	9.6	1.29	.269
Minor League Totals			5	5	3.61	28	27	0	0	85	73	8	35	92	9.8	1.28	.233

8 CHRIS RODRIGUEZ, RHP

Born: Jul. 20 1998. **B-T:** R-R. **Ht.:** 6-2. **Wt.:** 185. **Drafted:** HS—Miami, 2016 (4th round). **Signed by:** Ralph Reyes.

Rodriguez raised his draft stock in 2016 with a strong spring, including a seven-inning, 85-pitch, two-hit shutout in the state 5A semifinal for Miami's Pace High. He passed on a Jacksonville commitment to sign with the Angels for a well over-slot $850,000 and made his pro debut with seven Rookie-level Arizona League outings before being shut down for the year. Rodriguez has a lean, athletic build and delivers his fastball in the 92-94 mph range and tops out at 96. His breaking ball, which sits 78-80 mph, was called a two-plane slider by some scouts while others pegged it as a curveball. Rounding out his arsenal is a mid-80s changeup, with both of

BA GRADE

50 Risk: Extreme

his secondary pitches grading as average right now. Rodriguez also works in a sinking two-seamer that moves like a slider. He has a quick arm and his pitches get good running movement. There's effort to his delivery, which he finishes with a big head whack, but he repeats it well and has good rhythm. At this point, Rodriguez is the best homegrown arm the Angels have, though lefthander Nate Smith is much more polished. He may profile better as a reliever down the road, but for now he'll continue to work as a starter. He's mature, a good worker and a leader on the field, with a chance to jump to low Class A Burlington in 2017.

Year	Club (League)	Class	W	L	ERA	G	GS	CG	SV	IP	H	HR	BB	SO	K/9	WHIP	AVG
2016	Angels (AZL)	R	0	0	1.59	7	5	0	0	11	6	0	3	17	13.5	0.79	.154
Minor League Totals			0	0	1.59	7	5	0	0	11	6	0	3	17	13.5	0.79	.154

9 KEYNAN MIDDLETON, RHP

Born: Sep. 12, 1993. **B-T:** R-R. **Ht.:** 6-2. **Wt.:** 185. **Drafted:** Lane (Ore.) CC, 2013 (3rd round). **Signed by:** Jason Ellison.

The former basketball star struggled to translate his athleticism into production as a starter, and the Angels moved him to the bullpen at high Class A Inland Empire in 2016 and told him to stop overthinking and just throw the ball. He took to the relief role quickly, shooting up the system and finishing 2016 at Triple-A Salt Lake. Middleton's lively fastball jumped a few ticks in relief and now sits in the upper 90s and touches triple digits. He pitched off his heater with a low-90s wipeout slider to generate a lot of strikeouts and weak contacts and showed an occasional below-average mid-80s changeup. With improved stuff and a better plan of attack

BA GRADE

45 Risk: High

to the mound, Middleton averaged 12 strikeouts per nine innings and significantly cut his walk rate in the second half. His high-three-quarters arm slot can be a little stiff, and his delivery features some effort, but both work well enough in a relief role. The Angels added Middleton to the 40-man roster to shield him from the Rule 5 draft. With his big step forward in 2016, he will go to spring training in 2017 with a shot at earning a role in the Angels' bullpen

Year	Club (League)	Class	W	L	ERA	G	GS	CG	SV	IP	H	HR	BB	SO	K/9	WHIP	AVG
2014	Orem (PIO)	R	5	4	6.45	14	14	0	0	67	69	9	30	53	7.1	1.48	.260
2015	Burlington (MWL)	LoA	6	11	5.30	26	26	0	0	126	148	15	47	88	6.3	1.55	.306
2016	Inland Empire (CAL)	HiA	1	1	3.72	25	0	0	0	36	22	7	20	56	13.9	1.16	.172
	Arkansas (TL)	AA	0	0	1.20	13	0	0	6	15	11	1	4	18	10.8	1.00	.196
	Salt Lake (PCL)	AAA	0	1	4.91	8	0	0	2	15	14	1	4	14	8.6	1.23	.250
Minor League Totals			13	20	5.38	96	47	0	8	288	296	37	123	249	7.8	1.46	.269

10 JAIME BARRIA, RHP

Born: July 18, 1996. **B-T:** R-R. **Ht.:** 6-1. **Wt.:** 205. **Signed:** Panama, 2013. **Signed by:** Roman Ocumarez.

The Angels appear to have gotten good value in signing Barria in 2013 for $60,000. The Panamanian made his full-season debut in 2016, earning midseason Midwest League all-star honors and pitching a full workload at low Class A Burlington despite not turning 20 until midseason. Barria's game is all about pitchability and racking up early-count outs, and he gets the most out of a limited repertoire. A fastball that he consistently throws for strikes sits in the low 90s with movement, and he commands it well despite its life. The combination of factors helps it play as a solid-average pitch. Barria's best pitch is a solid-average changeup

BA GRADE
45 Risk: High

with good fade at 77-80 mph that projects to be at least an above-average offering. He rounds out his repertoire with a curveball that flashes average at times. With a clean, repeatable, high three-quarters arm slot that allows him to throw his two-seamer, Barria uses the same arm speed to deliver his fastball and curveball. He projects to add velocity as his well-conditioned body matures. He controls the running game well, allowing just four stolen bases in 10 attempts in 2016. With his first full season behind him, Barria is ready for the challenge of the hitter-friendly California League in 2017. He commands his pitches well enough to project as a reliable back-of-the-rotation starter.

Year	Club (League)	Class	W	L	ERA	G	GS	CG	SV	IP	H	HR	BB	SO	K/9	WHIP	AVG
2014	Angels (DSL)	R	4	4	3.03	16	8	0	1	59	57	1	11	55	8.3	1.15	.252
2015	Angels (AZL)	R	3	0	2.00	7	6	0	0	36	40	0	3	31	7.8	1.19	.280
	Orem (PIO)	R	2	4	6.21	8	8	0	0	33	45	4	7	30	8.1	1.56	.324
2016	Burlington (MWL)	LoA	8	6	3.85	25	25	0	0	117	133	6	21	78	6.0	1.32	.282
Minor League Totals			17	15	3.84	60	47	0	1	251	288	11	43	198	7.1	1.32	.286

11 NONIE WILLIAMS, SS

BA GRADE
50 Risk: Extreme

Born: May 22, 1998. **B-T:** L-R. **Ht.:** 6-2. **Wt.:** 200. **Drafted:** HS—Kansas City, Kan., 2016 (3rd round). **Signed by:** Drew Chadd.

Williams, whose given name is Nolan, was home-schooled in his native Kansas City but took one class at Turner High, and thus was allowed to play baseball for them. He hit .533 as a senior and was committed to Louisiana State before the Angels drafted him in the third round, No. 96 overall, and signed him for $950,000. Considered one of the better athletes in the 2016 class after being reclassified from the 2017 draft, Williams started slowly in his first pro season in the Rookie-level Arizona League. He finished strong when he started barreling up more balls, ending with a 9-for-24 stretch. Williams possesses a lot of raw tools, but scouts consider the switch-hitting infielder a long way off from turning them into baseball skills. He is a disciplined, gap-to-gap hitter currently more comfortable from the right side of the plate, which is not surprising because he's been switch-hitting for less than two years. An average runner, he is sneaky fast and handles himself well on the bases. Early reviews on Williams said he is not likely to stay at shortstop long-term, with the athleticism for the position but not the actions. His strong arm should allow him to move to either third base or an outfield corner. Williams is raw enough that he'll need another year of short-season ball. He will start 2017 in extended spring training with a likely assignment to Rookie-level Orem.

Year	Club (League)	Class	AVG	G	AB	R	H	2B	3B	HR	RBI	BB	SO	SB	CS	OBP	SLG
2016	Angels (AZL)	R	.244	38	156	23	38	4	1	0	11	8	40	9	3	.280	.282
Minor League Totals			.244	38	156	23	38	4	1	0	11	8	40	9	3	.280	.282

12 DAVID FLETCHER, 2B/SS

BA GRADE
45 Risk: High

Born: May 31, 1994. **B-T:** R-R. **Ht.:** 5-10. **Wt.:** 175. **Drafted:** Loyola Marymount, 2015 (6th round). **Signed by:** Ben Diggins.

After being picked as a draft-eligible sophomore from Loyola Marymount in 2015, Fletcher made it to Double-A Arkansas before the end of his first full season and wrapped up 2016 with an assignment to the Arizona Fall League. He missed time early in the year with wrist tendinitis, but returned to hit .308/.346/.389 across two levels after the injury. The label typically put on Fletcher is a "gamer" or "grinder" who will consistently play above his tools. Fletcher is solid at both middle infield positions, using excellent instincts to compensate for limited physical tools. He quickly reads balls off the bat and positions himself well, helping his arm play up because of his positioning and excellent footwork. Fletcher doesn't pack much power at the plate but grinds out at-bats and has a solid approach with a line-drive stroke. He is an average runner but with advanced instincts that help him steal bases efficiently. Fletcher will return to the Double-A Texas League to pick up where he left off last year. With a lack of depth in the upper levels of the system, he should get a chance at Triple-A before the end of 2017.

Year	Club (League)	Class	AVG	G	AB	R	H	2B	3B	HR	RBI	BB	SO	SB	CS	OBP	SLG
2015	Burlington (MWL)	LoA	.283	32	120	18	34	4	1	1	10	12	13	6	1	.358	.358
	Orem (PIO)	R	.331	37	160	28	53	12	4	0	30	16	9	11	4	.391	.456
2016	Inland Empire (CAL)	HiA	.275	78	324	42	89	12	1	3	31	22	43	15	3	.321	.346
	Arkansas (TL)	AA	.300	20	80	10	24	6	0	0	6	3	13	1	0	.325	.375
Minor League Totals			.292	167	684	98	200	34	6	4	77	53	78	33	8	.345	.377

13 VICENTE CAMPOS, RHP

BA GRADE
50 Risk: Extreme

Born: July 27, 1992. **B-T:** R-R. **Ht.:** 6-3. **Wt.:** 230. **Signed:** Venezuela, 2009.
Signed by: Emilio Carrasquel/Patrick Guerrero (Mariners).

Campos joins his fourth organization, continually tantalizing with a premier repertoire but frustrating with an inability to stay healthy. The Angels claimed the native Venezuelan off waivers in the offseason from the Diamondbacks, who had acquired Campos in a trade deadline deal for reliever Tyler Clippard in July. Arizona waived Campos after he underwent surgery to repair an ulnar fracture in his right arm, and he's expected to miss the beginning of the 2017 season. After missing 2014 with Tommy John surgery and still on the comeback trail in 2015, Campos was healthy and productive for most of 2016, with a 10-5, 3.22 combined record spread over five different minor league teams. He finally made his big league debut for Arizona with a 5.2 inning relief stint in late August before the fracture occurred in early September. When healthy, Campos delivers an above-average four-seam fastball in the mid-90s, but he averaged 90 mph in his lone big league game. He also uses a mid-80s changeup with good movement and a mid-70s curveball, both of which flash plus at times. Campos expected recovery time from his surgery is eight months, meaning he won't get any meaningful time on the mound until midseason.

Year	Club (League)	Class	W	L	ERA	G	GS	CG	SV	IP	H	HR	BB	SO	K/9	WHIP	AVG
2014	Did not play—Injured																
2015	Yankees1 (GCL)	R	0	1	5.79	1	1	0	0	5	8	1	0	5	9.6	1.71	.364
	Yankees2 (GCL)	R	0	0	0.00	1	1	0	0	5	2	0	0	9	16.2	0.40	.118
	Tampa (FSL)	HiA	3	7	7.05	11	11	0	0	45	54	5	10	31	6.2	1.43	.297
2016	Tampa (FSL)	HiA	4	2	3.49	10	10	0	0	59	50	3	23	56	8.5	1.23	.235
	Trenton (EL)	AA	5	1	3.02	9	9	1	0	57	45	1	14	48	7.6	1.04	.220
	Scranton/W-B (IL)	AAA	0	0	1.80	1	1	0	0	5	8	0	1	1	1.8	1.80	.400
	Mobile (SL)	AA	1	2	3.60	4	4	0	0	20	22	0	5	15	6.8	1.35	.289
	Arizona (NL)	MAJ	0	0	3.18	1	0	0	0	6	4	2	2	4	6.4	1.06	.182
	Reno (PCL)	AAA	0	0	0.00	1	1	0	0	2	0	0	0	0	0.0	0.00	.000
Major League Totals			0	0	3.18	1	0	0	0	6	4	2	2	4	6.4	1.06	.182
Minor League Totals			34	25	3.66	109	92	2	3	480	444	24	125	435	8.2	1.19	.245

14 CONNOR JUSTUS, SS

BA GRADE
45 Risk: High

Born: Nov. 2, 1994. **B-T:** R-R. **Ht.:** 6-0. **Wt.:** 195. **Drafted:** Georgia Tech, 2016 (5th round). **Signed by:** Todd Hogan.

Justus was best known for his defense at Georgia Tech before his bat emerged in his junior season, breaking out with a .324/.442/.486 line and a 38-to-41 strikeout-to-walk ratio. The improved offense to go with solid shortstop play earned Justus a fifth-round selection by the Angels and a $250,000 signing bonus. He moved quickly after signing, beginning his career at Rookie-level Orem before finishing at low Class A Burlington. Justus' best tool is his defense, where his athleticism makes him above-average at shortstop with good range, smooth actions and quick hands. His average arm plays up because he gets the ball out of his glove quickly. A gap-to-gap hitter, Justus' bat is well behind his glove, as he swings hard but doesn't make consistent hard contact. He draws a fair share of walks and is an average runner with good instincts on the bases. Justus' development as a hitter will determine whether he becomes an everyday player or utilityman, but his shortstop defense is enough to keep him ascending in some capacity. He will return to Burlington to start 2017 with a likely promotion to high Class A Inland Empire by midseason.

Year	Club (League)	Class	AVG	G	AB	R	H	2B	3B	HR	RBI	BB	SO	SB	CS	OBP	SLG
2016	Orem (PIO)	R	.344	26	93	19	32	6	1	0	23	18	19	0	2	.465	.430
	Burlington (MWL)	LoA	.230	42	139	19	32	3	1	2	9	14	34	1	2	.345	.309
Minor League Totals			.276	68	232	38	64	9	2	2	32	32	53	1	4	.394	.358

15 JOSE SUAREZ, LHP

BA GRADE

50 Risk: Extreme

Born: Jan. 3, 1998. **B-T:** L-L. **Ht.:** 5-10 **Wt.:** 195 **Signed:** Venezuela, 2014. **Signed by:** Lebi Ochoa/Carlos Ramirez.

The Angels signed Suarez as a 16-year old out of Venezuela for $300,000 in 2014, and the southpaw quickly impressed when showed up in instructional league that fall with an already advanced feel for pitching. He began his second pro season in the Arizona League before joining Rookie-level Orem to aid their postseason run to the Pioneer League championship in 2016. He started the title-clinching game against Billings, pitching five innings and giving up only two hits and one run. Suarez has above-average pitchability and uses an easy, repeatable high-three-quarters delivery with good direction to the plate. His changeup is a potential plus pitch he can throw in any count, and he mixes it well with his 88-92 mph fastball that projects to average as he develops more physically. He is still developing his below-average breaking ball but still significantly increased his strikeout rate, fanning 10.7 batters per nine innings in 2016 compared to 6.1 in 2015. With advanced pitching smarts and above-average control, Suarez may be able to head to low Class A in 2017 at age 19.

Year	Club (League)	Class	W	L	ERA	G	GS	CG	SV	IP	H	HR	BB	SO	K/9	WHIP	AVG
2015	Angels (DSL)	R	2	2	2.13	11	11	0	0	55	43	0	8	34	5.6	0.93	.215
	Angels (AZL)	R	1	1	5.60	4	2	0	0	18	28	0	4	12	6.1	1.81	.364
2016	Angels (AZL)	R	1	3	5.36	11	5	0	0	40	48	1	13	46	10.3	1.51	.296
	Orem (PIO)	R	0	1	0.00	1	1	0	0	4	6	0	1	7	14.5	1.62	.300
Minor League Totals			4	7	3.68	27	19	0	0	117	125	1	26	99	7.6	1.29	.272

16 MICHAEL HERMOSILLO, OF

BA GRADE

45 Risk: High

Born: Jan. 17, 1995. **B-T:** R-R. **Ht.:** 5-11. **Wt.:** 190. **Drafted:** HS—Ottawa, Ill., 2013 (28th round). **Signed by:** Joel Murrie.

Hermosillo was an outstanding high school football player in suburban Chicago who signed with Illinois as a three-star football recruit, but the Angels diverted the running back/defensive back to a baseball career with a $100,000 bonus after drafting him in the 28th round in 2013. Hermosillo was more of a raw athlete than baseball player the first three years of his career before blossoming in 2016. He split the year between low Class A Burlington and high Class A Inland Empire, batting a career-best .317/.402/.467 between the two levels. Hermosillo makes good contact and has surprising plate discipline for a player still relatively raw in baseball skills. While some power began to emerge, he is going to need to hit for a high average to continue to move through the system. Hermosillo has a tick above-average speed and an average arm, allowing him to handle all three outfield positions. He struggles at times in center field, having to play deep because he doesn't go back on balls well. Hermosillo got some added development time in the Arizona Fall League before a wrist injury ended his time there. He will get more seasoning back in the California League in 2017 before moving up to Double-A.

Year	Club (League)	Class	AVG	G	AB	R	H	2B	3B	HR	RBI	BB	SO	SB	CS	OBP	SLG
2014	Orem (PIO)	R	.244	54	180	36	44	10	4	3	23	29	48	10	4	.358	.394
2015	Burlington (MWL)	LoA	.218	79	261	33	57	7	0	0	23	45	49	19	13	.340	.245
	Orem (PIO)	R	.294	14	51	9	15	3	0	0	2	6	10	5	3	.368	.353
2016	Burlington (MWL)	LoA	.326	37	138	22	45	8	1	2	22	18	22	4	3	.411	.442
	Inland Empire (CAL)	HiA	.309	40	149	36	46	7	4	4	17	16	30	6	7	.393	.490
Minor League Totals			.268	235	795	139	213	35	9	9	87	115	162	45	30	.370	.369

17 SAM PASTRONE, RHP

BA GRADE

50 Risk: Extreme

Born: June 28, 1997. **B-T:** R-R. **Ht.:** 6-0. **Wt.:** 175. **Drafted:** HS—Las Vegas, 2015 (17th round). **Signed by:** Chad Hermansen.

The Angels bought Pastrone out of a Nevada-Las Vegas commitment with a $250,000 bonus after taking the Las Vegas high school product in the 17th round in 2015. After pitching in the Arizona League for his pro debut, the athletic righthander turned in a solid growth season at Rookie-level Orem in 2016. While he struggled at times with the more advanced hitters and tough pitching environments of the Pioneer League, Pastrone finished strong at the end of the season and in the playoffs, including six perfect innings against Billings to win Game One of the league championship series. Pastrone has arm strength and a quick arm that helps him get his fastball up to 96 mph, sitting 90-94. His separator pitch is a curveball, rated as one of the best in the organization, that he consistently drops in for strikes. He also has good feel for an improving changeup. While his delivery has some effort to it, it is clean and repeatable, and he works hard at his craft. Pastrone should be ready for his first taste of full-season ball with low Class A Burlington in 2017.

Year	Club (League)	Class	W	L	ERA	G	GS	CG	SV	IP	H	HR	BB	SO	K/9	WHIP	AVG
2015	Angels (AZL)	R	0	2	3.26	10	10	0	0	30	30	0	8	22	6.5	1.25	.265
2016	Orem (PIO)	R	3	4	6.00	14	13	0	0	57	77	4	21	45	7.1	1.72	.322
Minor League Totals			3	6	5.05	24	23	0	0	87	107	4	29	67	6.9	1.56	.304

18 JARED FOSTER, OF

BA GRADE

45 Risk: High

Born: Nov. 2, 1992. **B-T:** R-R. **Ht.:** 6-1. **Wt.:** 200. **Drafted:** Louisiana State, 2015 (5th round). **Signed by:** J.T. Zink.

Foster was a two-sport athlete at Louisiana State, playing four years on the baseball team and doubling as the backup quarterback on the 2011 national championship football team. While still plenty raw in baseball skills, the Angels gambled on Foster's athleticism and powerful arm, taking him in the fifth round in 2015 and signing him for a below-slot $100,000 bonus. He spent the first half of 2016 with low Class A Burlington before finishing the year at high Class A Inland Empire, putting up similar numbers at both levels. Foster possesses plenty of tools, but scouts worry he won't develop the necessary pitch recognition to hit at higher levels. He shows plus bat speed in batting practice and is aggressive at the plate but hasn't tapped into his plus raw power and gets himself out by swinging at bad pitches. He also needs to learn to better use his speed on the bases after going just 9-for-19 in stolen bases. Possessing a borderline plus arm and at least average speed, Foster improved his routes in the outfield and was a solid defender in 2016 With not a lot of organizational depth ahead of him, Foster may head right to Double-A Mobile in 2017.

Year	Club (League)	Class	AVG	G	AB	R	H	2B	3B	HR	RBI	BB	SO	SB	CS	OBP	SLG
2015	Orem (PIO)	R	.259	57	232	36	60	11	1	6	38	16	42	13	5	.307	.392
2016	Burlington (MWL)	LoA	.266	69	267	26	71	20	2	5	33	20	48	3	8	.315	.412
	Inland Empire (CAL)	HiA	.294	40	160	23	47	7	2	4	23	4	33	6	2	.320	.438
Minor League Totals			.270	166	659	85	178	38	5	15	94	40	123	22	15	.313	.411

19 COLE DUENSING, RHP

BA GRADE

50 Risk: Extreme

Born: June 16, 1998. **B-T:** L-R. **Ht.:** 6-2 **Wt.:** 180. **Drafted:** HS—Overland Park, Kan., 2016 (6th round). **Signed by:** Drew Chadd.

The cousin of big league lefthander Brian Duensing, Cole suffered through an inconsistent senior season and looked like he would be honoring his commitment to Kansas State. Instead, the Angels went over slot to sign the lanky, projectable righthander to a $501,300 bonus, and the Kansas City-area native was impressive in eight short outings in the Rookie-level Arizona League. Duensing has a quick arm and a quick-twitch body, and his low-90s fastball with sink should tick up with physical maturity. It's a solid foundation, but the rest of his game needs polish. Duensing's slurvy breaking ball is inconsistent, sometimes delivered with depth and at other times with too much sweep. He doesn't yet have a lot of feel for a changeup. He pitches with a lot of energy, causing him to rush his three-quarters delivery at times and use too much effort. Still, Duensing will be only 18 next spring and has plenty of time to develop. He'll start in extended spring training with an expected assignment to Rookie-level Orem when Pioneer League play begins.

Year	Club (League)	Class	W	L	ERA	G	GS	CG	SV	IP	H	HR	BB	SO	K/9	WHIP	AVG
2016	Angels (AZL)	R	2	0	1.38	8	4	0	0	13	13	0	5	11	7.6	1.38	.250
Minor League Totals			2	0	1.38	8	4	0	0	13	13	0	5	11	7.6	1.38	.250

20 BROOKS POUNDERS, RHP

BA GRADE

40 Risk: Medium

Born: Sept. 26, 1990. **B-T:** R-R. **Ht.:** 6-5. **Wt.:** 265 **Drafted:** HS—Temecula, Calif., 2009 (2nd round). **Signed by:** Sean Campbell (Pirates).

Pounders starred at Southern California prep power Temecula Valley High before the Pirates drafted him 53rd overall in 2009 and signed him for $670,000. The Pirates traded him two years later to the Royals in a deal for infielder Yamaico Navarro, and the Angels brought him back to his native southern California after the 2016 season in exchange for minor league righthander Jared Ruxer. Pounders has the size of a power pitcher, but he's long succeeded more with feel and the ability to mix pitches and locate. The son of former UC Riverside and Padres minor league pitcher Brad Pounders, Brooks missed much of 2014 and 2015 recovering from Tommy John surgery and a strained oblique but has gained a small bump in velocity since returning to health, with his once 88-91 mph fastball now sitting 91-93. Pounders' slider is his best secondary offering, but like his fastball, it's average. He will mix in a changeup that flashes average but isn't consistent and a fringy early-count curveball. Pounders made his big league debut in 2016 after seven seasons in the minors. He's an emergency starter/low-leverage reliever, but he's ready to handle that role right now.

Year	Club (League)	Class	W	L	ERA	G	GS	CG	SV	IP	H	HR	BB	SO	K/9	WHIP	AVG
2014	Idaho Falls (PIO)	R	0	1	4.80	6	5	0	0	15	13	0	5	19	11.4	1.20	.241
	Wilmington (CAR)	HiA	0	1	4.02	3	3	0	0	16	16	0	7	18	10.3	1.47	.262
2015	Royals (AZL)	R	0	0	1.50	4	4	0	0	6	5	0	0	5	7.5	0.83	.217
	Idaho Falls (PIO)	R	0	0	0.00	1	1	0	0	3	1	0	3	4	12.0	1.33	.100
	Wilmington (CAR)	HiA	0	1	5.40	2	2	0	0	10	12	1	1	10	9.0	1.30	.316
	NW Arkansas (TL)	AA	3	4	2.19	8	8	0	0	49	39	3	19	32	5.8	1.18	.223
2016	Omaha (PCL)	AAA	5	3	3.14	31	7	0	0	80	67	5	37	90	10.1	1.29	.226
	Kansas City (AL)	MAJ	2	1	9.24	13	0	0	0	13	19	6	3	13	9.2	1.74	.352
Major League Totals			2	1	9.24	13	0	0	0	13	19	6	3	13	9.2	1.74	.352
Minor League Totals			32	33	3.77	171	81	1	5	561	519	43	198	531	8.5	1.28	.245

21 ADAM HOFACKET, RHP

BA GRADE

45 Risk: High

Born: Feb. 18, 1994. **B-T:** R-R. **Ht.:** 6-1. **Wt.:** 195. **Drafted:** California Baptist, 2015 (10th round). **Signed by:** Tim Corcoran.

A starter in college at Division II California Baptist, Hofacket converted to the bullpen after the Angels took him in the 10th round in 2015 and turned out to be one of the organization's more pleasant surprises from that draft. Hofacket owns a decent four-pitch mix but is better suited to a relief role because of his delivery and arm action, coming across his body with a three-quarters delivery that provides some deception. He has a good feel for his pitches, with the fastball and slider both being potential plus offerings, and he attacks hitters with a max-effort but simple delivery. Hofacket commands his 92-96 mph four-seamer with tailing life and gets sharp late spin on the 84-88 mph slider. He has good feel for both breaking balls and a changeup. Overall he averaged 9.9 strikeouts-per-nine innings for the season, splitting time between low Class A Burlington and high Class A Inland Empire. After getting in a few more games in the Arizona Fall League, Hofacket should be ready to jump to Double-A to start 2017 with an outside shot to join the Angels bullpen during the year.

Year	Club (League)	Class	W	L	ERA	G	GS	CG	SV	IP	H	HR	BB	SO	K/9	WHIP	AVG
2015	Orem (PIO)	R	4	0	3.77	26	0	0	8	31	32	5	3	23	6.7	1.13	.269
2016	Burlington (MWL)	LoA	1	1	2.53	15	0	0	7	21	20	2	2	24	10.1	1.03	.238
	Inland Empire (CAL)	HiA	1	2	6.03	26	0	0	2	34	38	4	13	37	9.7	1.49	.275
Minor League Totals			6	3	4.36	67	0	0	17	87	90	11	18	84	8.7	1.25	.264

22 KYLE McGOWIN, RHP

BA GRADE

40 Risk: Medium

Born: Nov. 27, 1991. **B-T:** R-R. **Ht.:** 6-3. **Wt.:** 195. **Drafted:** Savannah State, 2013 (5th round). **Signed by:** Todd Hogan.

McGowin was able to take the mound for 27 starts for the second year in a row in 2016, erasing memories of early-career injury issues that limited him to just 20 games over his first two pro seasons. He split the year between Double-A Arkansas and Triple-A Salt Lake, going 9-14, 5.83, marked by the usual adjustment period when pitching in hitter-friendly Salt Lake for the first time. The positive signs were there as McGowin regained some fastball velocity, sitting 89-93 mph, and improved both of his off-speed pitches. McGowin's slider is an average pitch with plenty of depth at 79-82 mph, and his low-80s changeup projects to be an average offering. McGowin doesn't have a real physical frame, so long-term he may be better suited to a bullpen role. He'll head back to Salt Lake for another crack at PCL hitters unless he is taken in the Rule 5 draft after the Angels chose to leave him unprotected off the 40-man roster.

Year	Club (League)	Class	W	L	ERA	G	GS	CG	SV	IP	H	HR	BB	SO	K/9	WHIP	AVG
2014	Inland Empire (CAL)	HiA	1	5	2.93	10	10	0	0	58	51	4	16	48	7.4	1.15	.236
	Arkansas (TL)	AA	0	1	5.40	1	1	0	0	5	6	1	0	3	5.4	1.20	.286
	Angels (AZL)	R	0	0	0.00	1	1	0	0	2	2	0	1	2	9.0	1.50	.250
2015	Arkansas (TL)	AA	9	9	4.38	27	27	0	0	154	148	16	50	125	7.3	1.29	.255
2016	Arkansas (TL)	AA	3	2	4.56	5	5	1	0	26	22	4	9	32	11.2	1.21	.227
	Salt Lake (PCL)	AAA	6	12	6.11	22	22	0	0	116	144	16	46	98	7.6	1.63	.308
Minor League Totals			20	30	4.77	75	67	1	0	376	385	43	127	320	7.7	1.36	.267

23 JESUS CASTILLO, RHP

BA GRADE
50 Risk: Extreme

Born: Aug. 23, 1995. **B-T:** R-R. **Ht.:** 6-2. **Wt.:** 180. **Signed:** Venezuela, 2011.
Signed by: Marlon Urdaneta (Diamondbacks).

Castillo was one of the Diamondbacks' top international signees in 2011, receiving a $250,000 bonus. The native Venezuelan was included in two trades for major leaguers before ever making it to full-season ball, first being swapped by the D-backs to the Cubs in 2013 for outfielder Tony Campana and then sent by the Cubs to the Angels at the 2016 trade deadline for reliever Joe Smith. Castillo began 2016 at short-season and excelled, so the Angels bumped him to low Class A after the trade. He made a positive first impression in the system by going 3-2, 2.43 over six starts at Burlington. Castillo stands out for his feel for pitching and is an efficient, projectable strike thrower with a very loose arm who regularly repeats his high-three-quarters delivery. Castillo uses a fastball that sits 89-93 mph and plays up because of the good extension he gets on his pitches. His plus changeup shows good action, but his curveball is still inconsistent. Castillo is expected to return to Burlington for more seasoning, with a chance to reach high Class A Inland Empire later in the year.

Year	Club (League)	Class	W	L	ERA	G	GS	CG	SV	IP	H	HR	BB	SO	K/9	WHIP	AVG
2014	Cubs (AZL)	R	1	0	2.67	11	4	0	0	30	28	0	16	23	6.8	1.45	.252
2015	Cubs (AZL)	R	1	2	4.58	11	0	0	0	20	26	1	9	17	7.8	1.78	.306
2016	Eugene (NWL)	SS	2	3	3.27	7	7	0	0	33	28	1	11	38	10.4	1.18	.224
	Burlington (MWL)	LoA	3	2	2.43	6	6	0	0	30	33	1	7	23	7.0	1.35	.295
Minor League Totals			9	13	3.84	54	29	0	0	178	192	8	63	156	7.9	1.43	.278

24 AUSTIN ADAMS, RHP

BA GRADE
40 Risk: Medium

Born: May 5, 1991. **B-T:** R-R. **Ht.:** 6-2. **Wt.:** 220. **Drafted:** South Florida, 2012 (8th round). **Signed by:** Tom Kotchman.

Adams continued to show some of the best stuff in the system in his return to Double-A Arkansas, recording 13.3 strikeouts per nine innings, posting a 3.05 ERA and converting four of five save opportunities while cutting his walk rate from 7.7 to 5.2 per nine. He was shut down for about a month late in the season due to fatigue before returning with six scoreless, hitless appearances to finish the year. Adams has a plus fastball averaging 94 mph and getting up to 97, while his slider is a wipeout pitch when he gets ahead in the count, flashing as a plus offering. Adams is aggressive on the mound with a max-effort delivery and an arm action that's a bit slingy, resulting in poor control. He was left off the 40-man roster last year and was a possibility for the Rule 5 draft but wound up staying with the Angels. The Angels added him to the 40-man after 2016, though, impressed by the strides he made. Adams could be a force at the back end of the bullpen with better control, but at 25 years old needs to take that next step forward soon.

Year	Club (League)	Class	W	L	ERA	G	GS	CG	SV	IP	H	HR	BB	SO	K/9	WHIP	AVG
2014	Inland Empire (CAL)	HiA	3	2	3.79	42	0	0	1	59	27	3	53	80	12.1	1.35	.141
2015	Inland Empire (CAL)	HiA	2	1	2.45	9	0	0	0	15	10	0	7	21	12.9	1.16	.189
	Arkansas (TL)	AA	1	1	2.95	27	0	0	1	37	22	0	31	49	12.0	1.45	.183
	Salt Lake (PCL)	AAA	0	0	9.82	2	0	0	0	4	1	0	9	1	2.5	2.73	.091
2016	Angels (AZL)	R	0	0	3.00	2	0	0	0	3	1	0	0	2	6.0	0.33	.100
	Arkansas (TL)	AA	0	1	3.05	32	0	0	4	41	29	2	24	61	13.3	1.28	.199
Minor League Totals			8	7	3.75	166	0	0	11	218	137	9	156	281	11.6	1.34	.183

25 JUSTIN ANDERSON, RHP

BA GRADE
45 Risk: High

Born: Sept. 28, 1992. **B-T:** L-R. **Ht.:** 6-3. **Wt.:** 220. **Drafted:** Texas-San Antonio, 2014 (14th round). **Signed by:** Rudy Vasquez.

Already 24 and coming off a difficult season at high Class A Inland Empire, Anderson nonetheless remains an intriguing prospect. He is still relatively inexperienced at pitching, having been a two-way player at Texas-San Antonio and pitching sparingly until his junior year with the Roadrunners. Anderson saw relatively little action in his first summer as a pro before working mostly as a starter in 2015 with low Class A Burlington. He struggled with the difficult jump to the California League, posting a 5.70 ERA with a .322 opponent average. His main problem was leaving balls up too much, and he had to work on landing his offspeed pitches down in the zone for strikes. Anderson has plenty of arm strength, delivering a fastball with arm side tail sitting 90-95 mph and touching 98. He added more depth to his 82-86 mph slider during the season, which contributed to his 83-86 mph changeup becoming a more useful weapon. Observers believe Anderson's arsenal would play up out of the bullpen, especially considering his rough delivery. He worked as a reliever in the Arizona Fall League and could jump to Double-A in Mobile's bullpen in 2017.

Year	Club (League)	Class	W	L	ERA	G	GS	CG	SV	IP	H	HR	BB	SO	K/9	WHIP	AVG
2014	Orem (PIO)	R	1	4	9.00	11	5	0	0	22	31	1	12	13	5.3	1.95	.316
	Angels (AZL)	R	0	0	5.14	2	2	0	0	7	9	0	3	6	7.7	1.71	.310
2015	Burlington (MWL)	LoA	9	9	3.41	28	22	0	0	143	148	4	51	112	7.1	1.39	.273
2016	Inland Empire (CAL)	HiA	8	12	5.70	28	27	0	0	145	193	15	48	107	6.6	1.66	.322
Minor League Totals			18	25	4.88	69	56	0	0	317	381	20	114	238	6.8	1.56	.300

26 JORDAN ZIMMERMAN, 2B

BA GRADE
45 Risk: High

Born: Nov. 11, 1994. **B-T:** R-R. **Ht.:** 6-0. **Wt.:** 195. **Drafted:** Michigan State, 2016 (7th round). **Signed by:** Jared Barnes.

Zimmerman went undrafted out of high school in the Phoenix area and two seasons at Mesa (Ariz.) CC. After not drawing interest from the major college programs in Arizona, Zimmerman headed off to Michigan State and posted a .373/.461/.594 slash line, leading the Spartans in batting average, home runs and slugging percentage. The Angels subsequently drafted him in the seventh round and signed for a $175,000 bonus. Zimmerman continued to rake with a .422/.478/.639 line at Rookie-level Orem but struggled after a promotion to the low Class A Midwest League, hitting only .154/.236/.208 while he adjusted to better-caliber pitching. Scouts were impressed with the strides Zimmerman made in instructional league, where he consistently found the barrel and was better defensively at second base than expected. He has a strong body with plus raw power, using a swing that's a bit linear and has some length to it. He's a fringe-average runner. Zimmerman played some first base at Michigan State out of need and scouts believe he's athletic enough to handle a corner outfield spot, so he could ultimately fit a utility profile. He'll return to Burlington to start 2017 for another shot at the Midwest League.

Year	Club (League)	Class	AVG	G	AB	R	H	2B	3B	HR	RBI	BB	SO	SB	CS	OBP	SLG
2016	Orem (PIO)	R	.422	19	83	22	35	4	1	4	22	6	12	4	1	.478	.639
	Burlington (MWL)	LoA	.154	37	130	15	20	5	1	0	13	13	34	0	3	.236	.208
Minor League Totals			.258	56	213	37	55	9	2	4	35	19	46	4	4	.329	.376

27 TYLER CARPENTER, RHP

BA GRADE
45 Risk: High

Born: Feb. 5, 1992. **B-T:** R-R. **Ht.:** 6-5. **Wt.:** 225. **Drafted:** Georgia-Gwinnett, 2014 (25th round). **Signed by:** Todd Hogan.

The Angels pop-up prospect for 2016 turned out to be their 2014 25th-round pick from NAIA program Georgia Gwinnett. Carpenter improved his nutrition after 2015 and dropped 20 pounds, gaining the confidence he needed to put himself on the prospect map. Strictly a reliever coming into 2016, Carpenter took advantage of an early season injury to one of high Class A Inland Empire's starters and threw five scoreless innings in his first career start. He ran with the opportunity and got a promotion to Double-A Arkansas after five Cal League outings. Carpenter's stuff was better across the board in 2016, and he consistently threw it for strikes. His fastball sat 90-94 mph, and he showed that he could hold the velocity deeper into games with his starts with his improved physique. His slider flashes average, and his changeup could turn into a useable third pitch. Profiling now as a potential back-end starter, Carpenter will begin 2017 back in Double-A with a chance to rise to Triple-A Salt Lake sooner rather than later.

Year	Club (League)	Class	W	L	ERA	G	GS	CG	SV	IP	H	HR	BB	SO	K/9	WHIP	AVG
2014	Angels (AZL)	R	1	0	0.00	2	0	0	0	3	1	0	0	3	9.0	0.33	.100
	Orem (PIO)	R	0	0	3.74	10	0	0	1	22	26	2	2	15	6.2	1.29	.289
2015	Burlington (MWL)	LoA	1	1	2.97	20	0	0	0	30	33	0	11	21	6.2	1.45	.275
	Inland Empire (CAL)	HiA	0	0	6.91	16	0	0	0	27	36	4	7	31	10.2	1.57	.310
2016	Inland Empire (CAL)	HiA	2	0	0.82	5	5	0	0	33	19	1	3	27	7.4	0.67	.176
	Arkansas (TL)	AA	4	9	5.58	15	15	0	0	71	93	6	17	50	6.3	1.55	.323
Minor League Totals			8	10	4.20	68	20	0	1	186	208	13	40	147	7.1	1.33	.284

28 BRENNON LUND, OF

BA GRADE
45 Risk: High

Born: Nov. 27, 1994. **B-T:** L-R. **Ht.:** 5-9. **Wt.:** 180. **Drafted:** Brigham Young, 2016 (11th round). **Signed by:** Chad Hermansen.

Lund, a Utah native, was a hometown hero at Brigham Young as a consistent force in the Cougars outfield for three years. Projected as a fifth-rounder, Lund lasted until the 11th round and signed with the Angels for $100,000. Lund is extremely athletic, is strong for his size and plays the game hard. He is a prototypical leadoff hitter with above-average speed, good on-base skills and the ability to bunt. With strong, quick hands, he has good bat speed and feel for the barrel. Lund is an instinctual defender with a slightly below-average arm that's enough to keep him in the center of the diamond. He spent most of his first pro season at low Class A Burlington, and with his baseball smarts should be able to head to high Class A Inland Empire in 2017 He projects as an extra outfielder who can consistently play above his tools.

Year	Club (League)	Class	AVG	G	AB	R	H	2B	3B	HR	RBI	BB	SO	SB	CS	OBP	SLG
2016	Orem (PIO)	R	.397	18	73	15	29	3	0	2	11	7	11	7	2	.463	.521
	Burlington (MWL)	LoA	.271	45	181	19	49	9	2	1	19	12	33	8	1	.316	.359
Minor League Totals			.307	63	254	34	78	12	2	3	30	19	44	15	3	.360	.406

29 JAKE JEWELL, RHP

BA GRADE
45 Risk: High

Born: May 16, 1993. **B-T:** R-R. **Ht.:** 6-3. **Wt.:** 215. **Drafted:** Northeastern Oklahoma A&M JC, 2014 (5th round). **Signed by:** Drew Chadd.

Jewell was the Angels' breakout candidate for 2016, ranking as the fifth-best prospect after a strong growth season in 2015 with low Class A Burlington. Instead, he struggled mightily at high Class A Inland Empire, turning in a 2-15, 6.31 record. The biggest issue for Jewell was an inconsistent arm slot and mechanics, with a tendency to drop his arm slot down and leave pitches in the upper part of the zone, where they were crushed. At present, he is a four-pitch righthander with little feel for any of his offerings. Jewell attacks the zone with a lively 92-95 mph fastball but struggles to command it. An average changeup is Jewell's best secondary pitch, while his curveball and slider are both below-average pitches. Jewell also added an 86-90 mph two-seamer during the season that would cut in under the hands of righthanded hitters. His ability to mentally handle adversity came under criticism during the year, as did his competitiveness on the mound. Jewell is a project at this point, with the hope that getting him in the right frame of mind and improving his mechanics could help him get back on track. He'll get a second try at Inland Empire in 2017.

Year	Club (League)	Class	W	L	ERA	G	GS	CG	SV	IP	H	HR	BB	SO	K/9	WHIP	AVG
2014	Angels (AZL)	R	1	0	1.48	9	6	0	0	30	23	0	12	26	7.7	1.15	.213
	Orem (PIO)	R	0	2	8.76	3	3	0	0	12	22	1	4	9	6.6	2.11	.386
2015	Burlington (MWL)	LoA	6	8	4.77	31	15	0	2	111	110	8	31	110	8.9	1.27	.263
2016	Inland Empire (CAL)	HiA	2	15	6.31	28	27	0	0	137	191	10	65	104	6.8	1.87	.334
Minor League Totals			9	25	5.32	71	51	0	2	291	346	19	112	249	7.7	1.57	.299

30 JOE GATTO, RHP

BA GRADE
45 Risk: Extreme

Born: June 14, 1995. **B-T:** R-R. **Ht.:** 6-3. **Wt.:** 225. **Drafted:** HS—Richland, N.J., 2014 (2nd round). **Signed by:** Nick Gorneault.

The 2016 season was nothing short of a disaster for Gatto, who previously ranked in the top 10 in the organization every year since being taken by the Angels in the second round in 2014. Gatto made his full-season debut in 2016 at low Class A Burlington and posted a horrific 7.03 ERA in 15 starts. He struggled to command any of his pitches and in June was pulled out and sent to the Angels' minor league complex in Arizona to rebuild his mechanics and delivery from scratch. He worked strictly in side sessions as the coaching staff in Arizona made tweaks to his delivery to get it more athletic and give his offerings more downhill plane. Gatto returned to games during instructional league, pitching every five days. He still flashes the best curveball in the system and has a fastball sitting 92-95 mph. His changeup got better and he used it to get swings-and-misses in instructs. Gatto will likely return to Burlington to start the 2017 season, hoping to build on the strides he made during instructional league. He remains a starter for now, although some evaluators believe he'll ultimately be more effective pitching out of the bullpen.

Year	Club (League)	Class	W	L	ERA	G	GS	CG	SV	IP	H	HR	BB	SO	K/9	WHIP	AVG
2014	Angels (AZL)	R	2	1	5.40	10	6	0	0	25	33	1	9	15	5.4	1.68	.320
	Orem (PIO)	R	0	0	4.50	1	1	0	0	2	3	1	0	1	4.5	1.50	.375
2015	Orem (PIO)	R	2	3	4.31	12	12	0	0	54	73	4	17	38	6.3	1.66	.340
2016	Burlington (MWL)	LoA	3	8	7.03	15	15	0	0	64	88	5	33	54	7.6	1.89	.321
Minor League Totals			7	12	5.70	38	34	0	0	145	197	11	59	108	6.7	1.76	.328

Los Angeles Dodgers

BY BEN BADLER

Not only has a World Series title eluded the Dodgers, owners of the highest payroll in baseball, but all four of their National League West rivals have played in the World Series since Los Angeles last appeared in 1988.

But the Dodgers have been able to accomplish a universal goal among front offices. They have constructed a team that's built to win both in the present and the future.

With their fourth straight NL West division title in 2016, the Dodgers rank second in the league in wins in the past four seasons, trailing only the Cardinals. Homegrown ace Clayton Kershaw is on a Hall of Fame trajectory and remains the centerpiece of the team's success, but the rest of the club is built around young talent, with more help on the way from the farm system.

Shortstop Corey Seager led the offensive charge in 2016, not only running away with the Baseball America Rookie of the Year award but also becoming one of the game's stars at just 22 years old. Seager, the No. 1 prospect in baseball entering the 2016 season, is an elite offensive player who has defied expectations about his defense by sticking at shortstop.

Lefthander Julio Urias made his major league debut as a 19-year-old in 2016 and showed a calm, easy delivery with three plus pitches and feel for pitching far beyond his years during his rookie season. He projects as a top-of-the-rotation starter. With Yasmani Grandal locked in at catcher and Joc Pederson in center field, the Dodgers are young and strong up the middle.

More young talent is headed to Los Angeles soon. The team's top prospect is Cody Bellinger, the rare first-base prospect with a chance for five average or better tools. Coming off a big year at Double-A Tulsa, he has a chance to hit in the middle of the lineup and play Gold Glove defense. With veteran Adrian Gonzalez under contract for two more seasons, though, Bellinger's ability to play the outfield could come in handy.

Bellinger was part of a talented Double-A lineup that included center fielder Alex Verdugo and second baseman Willie Calhoun, both of whom will head to Triple-A Oklahoma City in 2017 with a chance to be called up in the second half. Outfielder Andrew Toles went from out of baseball in 2015 to rising four levels in 2016 and playing for the Dodgers in the postseason.

On the pitching side, righthander Jose De Leon must prove he can handle a starter's workload after running into durability issues the last two seasons—but he has mid-rotation starter potential.

Corey Seager graduated from top prospect in baseball to BA Rookie of the Year in 2016

ED WOLFSTEIN

TOP PROSPECTS OF THE DECADE

Year	Player, Pos.	2016 Org
2007	Andy LaRoche, 3b	Atlantic League
2008	Clayton Kershaw, lhp	Dodgers
2009	Andrew Lambo, of	Athletics
2010	Dee Gordon, ss	Marlins
2011	Dee Gordon, ss	Marlins
2012	Zach Lee, rhp	Mariners
2013	Hyun-Jin Ryu, lhp	Dodgers
2014	Joc Pederson	Dodgers
2015	Corey Seager, ss	Dodgers
2016	Cody Bellinger, 1b/of	Dodgers

De Leon, Brock Stewart and Trevor Oaks are all righthanded starters who should figure into the Dodgers' injury-prone rotation. The team's best pitching prospect is Cuban righty Yadier Alvarez, who carries extreme risk but looked superb in his pro debut, showing the electric stuff of a frontline starter.

The Dodgers have enormous financial advantages over their rivals, but the majority of these young players are a testament to the team's scouting and player development system. The organization has burned through a lot of money on bad investments in Cuban signings, but the core young talent in the major leagues and the next wave coming from one of the better farm systems in baseball has more to do with smart evaluations and good development than having a big bankroll.

ORGANIZATION OVERVIEW

President: Andrew Friedman. **GM:** Farhan Zaidi. **Farm director:** Gabe Kapler. **Scouting director:** Billy Gasparino.

Class	Team	League	W	L	PCT	Finish	Manager
Majors	Los Angeles Dodgers	National	91	71	.562	3rd (15)	Dave Roberts
Triple-A	Oklahoma City Dodgers	Pacific Coast	81	60	.574	2nd (16)	Bill Haselman
Double-A	Tulsa Drillers	Texas	68	71	.489	4th (8)	Ryan Garko
High Class A	Rancho Cucamonga Quakes	California	79	61	.564	3rd (10)	Drew Saylor
Low Class A	Great Lakes Loons	Midwest	65	75	.464	11th (16)	Gil Velazquez
Rookie	Ogden Raptors	Pioneer	38	38	.500	4th (8)	Shaun Larkin
Rookie	AZL Dodgers	Arizona	33	22	.600	1st (14)	John Shoemaker
Overall 2016 Minor League Record			364	327	.527	8th (30)	

THIS YEAR'S TOP 30

No.	Player, Pos.	Grade
1.	Cody Bellinger, 1b/of	70/Medium
2.	Yadier Alvarez, rhp	65/Extreme
3.	Jose De Leon, rhp	60/High
4.	Alex Verdugo, of	55/Medium
5.	Willie Calhoun, 2b	55/Medium
6.	Andrew Toles, of	50/Medium
7.	Yusniel Diaz, of	55/High
8.	Brock Stewart, rhp	45/Low
9.	Gavin Lux, ss	55/Extreme
10.	Austin Barnes, c	45/Low
11.	Walker Buehler, rhp	55/Extreme
12.	Jordan Sheffield, rhp	50/High
13.	Dustin May, rhp	55/Extreme
14.	Trevor Oaks, rhp	45/Medium
15.	Johan Mieses, of	50/Extreme
16.	Will Smith, c	45/High
17.	Grant Dayton, lhp	40/Low
18.	Josh Sborz, rhp	45/High
19.	Mitchell White, rhp	50/Extreme
20.	Keibert Ruiz, c	45/High
21.	D.J. Peters, of	50/Extreme
22.	Yaisel Sierra, rhp	45/High
23.	Micah Johnson, 2b/of	40/Medium
24.	Omar Estevez, 2b	45/High
25.	Chase De Jong, rhp	40/High
26.	Andrew Sopko, rhp	40/High
27.	Oneil Cruz, ss/3b	50/Extreme
28.	Mitch Hansen, of	45/Extreme
29.	Cody Thomas, of	45/Extreme
30.	Jacob Scavuzzo, of	40/High

LAST YEAR'S TOP 30

No.	Player, Pos.	Status
1.	Corey Seager, ss	Majors
2.	Julio Urias, lhp	Majors
3.	Jose De Leon, rhp	No. 3
4.	Jose Peraza, 2b	(Reds)
5.	Cody Bellinger, 1b/of	No. 1
6.	Grant Holmes, rhp	(Athletics)
7.	Alex Verdugo, of	No. 4
8.	Austin Barnes, c	No. 10
9.	Jharel Cotton, rhp	(Athletics)
10.	Yadier Alvarez, rhp	No. 2
11.	Walker Buehler, rhp	No. 11
12.	Johan Mieses, of	No. 15
13.	Willie Calhoun, 2b	No. 5
14.	Scott Schebler, of	(Reds)
15.	Zach Lee, rhp	(Mariners)
16.	Chase DeJong, rhp	No. 25
17.	Josh Sborz, rhp	No. 18
18.	Jacob Scavuzzo, of	No. 30
19.	Mitch Hansen, of	No. 28
20.	Jacob Rhame, rhp	Dropped out
21.	Chris Anderson, rhp	Dropped out
22.	Starling Heredia, of	Dropped out
23.	Ross Stripling, rhp	Majors
24.	Joe Wieland, rhp	(Braves)
25.	Brendon Davis, ss	Dropped out
26.	Ronald Torreyes, 2b	(Yankees)
27.	Angel German, rhp	Dropped out
28.	Ariel Sandoval, of	Dropped out
29.	Kyle Farmer, c	Dropped out
30.	Jordan Paroubeck, of	Dropped out

BEST TOOLS

Best Hitter for Average	Willie Calhoun
Best Power Hitter	Cody Bellinger
Best Strike-Zone Discipline	Austin Barnes
Fastest Baserunner	Andrew Toles
Best Athlete	Andrew Toles
Best Fastball	Yadier Alvarez
Best Curveball	Yadier Alvarez
Best Slider	Dustin May
Best Changeup	Jose De Leon
Best Control	Trevor Oaks
Best Defensive Catcher	Austin Barnes
Best Defensive Infielder	Cody Bellinger
Best Infield Arm	Ronny Brito
Best Defensive Outfielder	Andrew Toles
Best Outfield Arm	Alex Verdugo

PROJECTED 2020 LINEUP

Catcher	Yasmani Grandal
First Base	Cody Bellinger
Second Base	Willie Calhoun
Third Base	Justin Turner
Shortstop	Corey Seager
Left Field	Andrew Toles
Center Field	Joc Pederson
Right Field	Yasiel Puig
No. 1 Starter	Clayton Kershaw
No. 2 Starter	Julio Urias
No. 3 Starter	Yadier Alvarez
No. 4 Starter	Jose De Leon
No. 5 Starter	Kenta Maeda
Closer	Kenley Jansen

MINOR LEAGUE DEPTH CHART

LOS ANGELES DODGERS

TOP 2017 ROOKIE: Jose De Leon, rhp. If he can shoulder a starter's workload, he has the swing-and-miss stuff to immediately become a mid-rotation starter.

BREAKOUT PROSPECT: Dustin May, rhp. A strike-thrower with excellent feel to spin his breaking ball, he has physical projection remaining.

SLEEPER: Albert Suarez, ss. Signed as a 16-year-old from the Dominican Republic for $300,000 in 2016, he is a true shortstop with smooth defense and a contact-oriented bat.

SOURCE OF TOP 30 TALENT			
Homegrown	26	Acquired	4
College	11	Trades	3
Junior college	2	Rule 5 draft	0
High school	6	Independent leagues	0
Nondrafted free agents	0	Free agents/waivers	1
International	7		

LF
Mitch Hansen (28)
Cody Tomas (29)
Jacob Scavuzzo (30)
Jordan Paroubeck

CF
Alex Verdugo (4)
Andrew Toles (6)
Yusniel Diaz (7)

RF
Johan Mieses (15)
D.J. Peters (21)
Starling Heredia
Carlos Rincon
Ariel Sandoval

3B
Oneil Cruz (27)
Brendon Davis
Edwin Rios
Mike Ahmed
Cristian Santana

SS
Gavin Lux (8)
Ronny Brito
Erick Mejia
Errol Robinson

2B
Willie Calhoun (5)
Micah Johnson (23)
Omar Estevez (24)
Tim Locastro
Brandon Montgomery

1B
Cody Bellinger (1)
Ibandel Isabel
Rob Segedin

C
Austin Barnes (9)
Will Smith (16)
Keibert Ruiz (20)
Kyle Farmer
Julian Leon

LHP	
LHSP	**LHRP**
Caleb Ferguson	Grant Dayton (17)
Devin Smeltzer	Michael Johnson
Victor Gonzalez	

RHP	
RHSP	**RHRP**
Yadier Alvarez (2)	Josh Sborz (18)
Jose De Leon (3)	Yaisel Sierra (22)
Brock Stewart (10)	Jacob Rhame
Walker Buehler (11)	Dennis Santana
Jordan Sheffield (12)	Ralston Cash
Dustin May (13)	Chris Anderson
Trevor Oaks (14)	Angel German
Mitchell White (19)	
Chase De Jong (25)	
Andrew Sopko (26)	
Imani Abdullah	
A.J. Alexy	
Oscar Arzaga	

DRAFT ANALYSIS

2016

BEST PURE HITTER: SS Gavin Lux (1), the Dodgers' top pick, has a pretty swing from the left side and showed enough speed, barrel awareness and pop to project as an above-average hitter. The Wisconsin prep product has to continue to show he can handle advanced pitching.
BEST POWER: OFs D.J. Peters (4) and Cody Thomas (13) both flirt with 70-grade power. Peters' track record is much longer, as Thomas has played a lot of football as an amateur, and they combined for 29 homers with Rookie-level Ogden this summer.
FASTEST RUNNER: Speed was a feature of this draft class, with OF Bryan Morales (15) the fastest of a group of 70 runners that includes SS Kevin Lachance (10) and OFs Saige Jenco (24) and Darien Tubbs (16).
BEST DEFENSIVE PLAYER: The Dodgers thought highly of C Will Smith (1) for his job handling Louisville's high-octane, diverse staff in the spring, but Smith still impressed them after signing with both his receiving and throwing. He's a plus athlete and above-average runner, rare for a catcher.
BEST FASTBALL: While RHP Jordan Sheffield (1s) throws hard, up to 97-98, RHP Mitchell White (2) has the better fastball. It sits 91-96, with spikes of 97, with excellent finish and life. White locates his fastball well and has a chance to pitch with a 70 fastball as a starter.
BEST SECONDARY PITCH: RHP Dustin May (3) stands out for his long reddish hair and plus slider. When he repeats his delivery, it's a consistent swing-and-miss pitch. White has flashed plus with both his curveball and cutter-like slider, with the curve the better pitch as a pro so far. He throws both breaking balls with power.
BEST PRO DEBUT: White roared out of the gate with 30 strikeouts in 22 innings without giving up an earned run over three stops, finishing at high Class A Rancho Cucamonga. Thomas hit 19 homers overall in two Rookie-ball stops, batting .297/.382/.621 in 232 at-bats, though he struck out 87 times.
BEST ATHLETE: Drafted twice before this year, Peters moves well and has power-speed potential at 6-foot-6, 225 pounds.
BACKGROUND: LHP Devin Smeltzer (5) survived a bout with cancer in his abdomen when he was just 9, though he's been in remission since 2012. He remains active in cancer charities. Thomas played in 10 games as an Oklahoma quarterback, accounting for nearly 500 total yards and throwing two touchdown passes. Sheffield's brother Justus pitches for the Yankees after being traded for Andrew Miller.
CLOSEST TO THE MAJORS: White signed for a below-slot bonus, giving the Dodgers flexibility, but has jumped on the fast track.
BEST LATE-ROUND PICK: Thomas edges out 2B/3B Brandon Montgomery (26), a scrappy but athletic infielder who hit .329/.377/.636 with Ogden.
THE ONE WHO GOT AWAY: RHP Graham Ashcraft (12) has hit 99 mph and led the state of Alabama with 16 homers as a prep junior. His raw tools could make him a first-rounder after three seasons at Mississippi State.

2015

RHP Walker Buehler (1) had Tommy John surgery, but RHP Josh Sborz (2s) had a huge first full season, as did 2B Willie Calhoun (4) and 1B/3B Edwin Rios (6), who each hit 27 homers.
GRADE: B

2014

The Dodgers have traded RHPs Grant Holmes (1, Oakland), John Richy (3, Philadelphia) and Jeff Brigham (4, Miami), but RHPs Brock Stewart (6) and Trevor Oaks (7) took steps forward to help replace them. OF Alex Verdugo (2) has star potential.
GRADE: B

2013

1B/OF Cody Bellinger (4) is the club's top prospect, and RHP Jose De Leon (23) isn't far behind after getting into much better shape as a pro. OF Chris Anderson (1) has disappointed. RHP Greg Harris (17) has emerged since a trade to the Rays.
GRADE: B

TOP DRAFT PICKS OF THE DECADE

Year	Player, Pos.	2016 Org
2007	Chris Withrow, rhp	Braves
2008	Ethan Martin, rhp	Did not play
2009	Aaron Miller, lhp (1st round supp.)	Did not play
2010	Zach Lee, rhp	Mariners
2011	Chris Reed, lhp	Marlins
2012	Corey Seager, ss	Dodgers
2013	Chris Anderson, rhp	Dodgers
2014	Grant Holmes, rhp	Athletics
2015	Walker Buehler, rhp	Dodgers
2016	Gavin Lux, ss	Dodgers

LARGEST BONUSES IN CLUB HISTORY

Hector Olivera, 2015	$28,000,000
Yadier Alvarez, 2015	$16,000,000
Yusniel Diaz, 2015	$15,500,000
Yasiel Puig, 2012	$12,000,000
Alex Guerrero, 2013	$10,000,000

1 CODY BELLINGER, 1B/OF

Born: July 13, 1995. **B-T:** L-L. **Ht.:** 6-4. **Wt.:** 210.
Drafted: HS—Chandler, Ariz., 2013 (4th round).
Signed by: Dustin Yount.

BA GRADE
65 Risk: Medium

SCOUTING GRADES
Batting: 60.
Power: 70.
Speed: 50.
Defense: 70.
Arm: 60.

Based on 20-80 scouting scale and future projection rather than present tools.

JOHN WILLIAMSON

Bellinger's father Clay played three seasons with the Yankees from 1999-2001 and two games with the Angels in 2002, batting .193 over 311 career at-bats. While Clay's major league career was brief, his son Cody has a chance to develop into one of the game's stars. Bellinger was 17 when the Dodgers drafted him in the fourth round of the 2013 draft and signed him for $700,000. His first two years in the system, Bellinger showed impressive pure hitting ability but mostly gap power as a first baseman. In 2015, Bellinger transformed himself into slugger who hit 30 home runs at high Class A Rancho Cucamonga despite skipping a level. In 2016, after missing most of April with a strained left hip, he put himself among baseball's elite prospects with a terrific season in the Double-A Texas League. In September, he joined Triple-A Oklahoma City, hit three home runs in three games, then went to the Arizona Fall League and batted .314/.424/.557 in 85 plate appearances. Cody's younger brother, Cole Bellinger, played in the 2016 Area Code Games and is committed to play baseball at Grand Canyon.

While most first base prospects tend to be one-dimensional sluggers, Cody is a dynamic all-around player in both the batter's box and with his glove. He made an adjustment in 2015 to load his hands to create better torque instead of relying more on his body in his swing. That change increased his power production, but also created a more uphill swing plane, leaving him with a bigger strikeout rate. Toward the end of 2015, Bellinger condensed his hand trigger slightly and became more studious of opposing pitchers and his own strengths and weaknesses, which allowed him to cut his strikeout rate. Those changes carried over into 2016, as he lowered his strikeout rate from 27 percent at high Class A in 2015 to 20 percent in Double-A in 2016 without sacrificing his power. Bellinger has a balanced lefthanded swing with plus bat speed, good leverage and use of his lower half, generating the potential to hit 30 home runs at the next level. He has good hand-eye coordination and a disciplined feel for the strike zone and he hangs in well against lefties. Bellinger is a supreme athlete for a first baseman and a gifted fielder who earns 70 grades on the 20-80 scouting scale for his defense. He's a potential Gold Glove winner with excellent range, smooth actions, clean footwork and soft hands to go along with a plus lefthanded arm. Bellinger is even an average runner, so the Dodgers have had him play the outfield as well. He's stretched thin in center field but is playable at both corners.

Bellinger has a chance to be a foundational hitter in the middle of a lineup who can also save runs with his fielding at first base. The Dodgers have first baseman Adrian Gonzalez signed through the 2018 season, but Bellinger will be ready before then, so Bellinger's versatility and athleticism in the outfield could come in handy soon. Bellinger should start 2017 in Oklahoma City, but he could make his major league debut in the second half of the year.

Year	Club (League)	Class	AVG	G	AB	R	H	2B	3B	HR	RBI	BB	SO	SB	CS	OBP	SLG
2014	Dodgers (AZL)	R	.150	5	20	2	3	1	0	0	0	1	5	0	0	.190	.200
	Ogden (PIO)	R	.328	46	195	49	64	13	6	3	34	14	35	8	0	.368	.503
2015	R. Cucamonga (CAL)	HiA	.264	128	478	97	126	33	4	30	103	52	150	10	2	.336	.538
2016	Tulsa (TL)	AA	.263	114	399	61	105	17	1	23	65	59	94	8	2	.359	.484
	Oklahoma City (PCL)	AAA	.545	3	11	5	6	0	0	3	6	1	0	0	0	.583	1.364
Minor League Totals			.267	343	1265	239	338	73	17	60	238	158	330	29	7	.349	.494

2 YADIER ALVAREZ, RHP

AMANDA RAY – GREAT LAKES LOONS

Born: March 7, 1996. **B-T:** R-R. **Ht.:** 6-3. **Wt.:** 175. **Signed:** Cuba, 2015. **Signed by:** Mike Tosar/Patrick Guerrero/Bob Engle.

In 2014, Alvarez couldn't make Cuba's 18U junior national team in 2014, as he walked 35 in 31 innings in the country's 18U youth league. Yet when Alvarez popped up in the Dominican Republic, his fastball skyrocketed and the Dodgers signed him for $16 million. Alvarez is a good athlete who fires explosive stuff with remarkably little effort. With a free-and-easy delivery, Alvarez's electric fastball explodes on hitters, sitting at 94-97 mph and reaching 101. He has shortened his loose arm action as a pro to add deception and create a more repeatable arc, which helped his control. Fastball command, however, is still a focal point. Beyond a lively, overpowering fastball, Alvarez has a plus curveball that, when it's on, is a true putaway pitch. He hasn't thrown his changeup much, so it's inconsistent, but it flashes plus with late tail and could become a plus pitch once he uses it more. Alvarez only threw 59 innings and his longest outing was five innings—something he did in just five of his 14 starts—so his durability is still unknown. Alvarez is a tantalizing mix of immense potential with high risk and minimal track record. If he can maintain his stuff over a full season's workload, he can develop into a frontline starter.

BA GRADE
65 Risk: Extreme

Year	Club (League)	Class	W	L	ERA	G	GS	CG	SV	IP	H	HR	BB	SO	K/9	WHIP	AVG
2016	Dodgers (AZL)	R	1	1	1.80	5	5	0	0	20	9	0	10	26	11.7	0.95	.127
	Great Lakes (MWL)	LoA	3	2	2.29	9	9	0	0	39	31	1	11	55	12.6	1.07	.214
Minor League Totals			4	3	2.12	14	14	0	0	59	40	1	21	81	12.3	1.03	.185

3 JOSE DE LEON, RHP

Born: Aug. 7, 1992. **B-T:** R-R. **Ht.:** 6-2. **Wt.:** 190. **Drafted:** Southern, 2013 (24th round). **Signed by:** Matthew Paul.

De Leon quickly turned into a late-round gem for the Dodgers by improving his conditioning after signing and seeing his stuff spike in turn. He missed time with shoulder inflammation in 2016 but dominated when healthy with Triple-A Oklahoma City. He made his major league debut in September. De Leon pitches off a fastball that sits 90-94 mph and touches 96. It's not overpowering velocity, but it has late life and he hides the ball well behind his body in his delivery, so the ball jumps on hitters faster than they expect, leading to empty swings in the strike zone. His go-to weapon is an 80-84 mph changeup. It's a plus pitch with good speed differential off his fastball and is effective against both lefties and righties. De Leon's third pitch is an average slider, a pitch some evaluators would like to see him use more frequently. They'd also like to see more of him; he's yet to top 115 innings in a season. With a delivery that will require some maintenance, durability is still a question mark. If De Leon can maintain the stuff he showed at the end of 2016 over a full season's workload, he can be a No. 2 starter. He has a chance to realize that potential immediately in 2017.

BA GRADE
60 Risk: High

Year	Club (League)	Class	W	L	ERA	G	GS	CG	SV	IP	H	HR	BB	SO	K/9	WHIP	AVG
2014	Ogden (PIO)	R	5	0	2.65	10	8	0	0	54	44	2	19	77	12.8	1.16	.217
	Great Lakes (MWL)	LoA	4	0	1.19	4	4	0	0	23	14	1	2	42	16.7	0.71	.171
2015	R. Cucamonga (CAL)	HiA	4	1	1.67	7	7	0	0	38	26	1	8	58	13.9	0.90	.193
	Tulsa (TL)	AA	2	6	3.64	16	16	1	0	77	61	11	29	105	12.3	1.17	.216
2016	Oklahoma City (PCL)	AAA	7	1	2.61	16	16	0	0	86	61	9	20	111	11.6	0.94	.194
	Los Angeles (NL)	MAJ	2	0	6.35	4	4	0	0	17	19	5	7	15	7.9	1.53	.288
Major League Totals			2	0	6.35	4	4	0	0	17	19	5	7	15	7.9	1.53	.288
Minor League Totals			23	13	3.35	67	64	1	0	331	273	30	99	446	12.1	1.13	.221

4 ALEX VERDUGO, OF

Born: May 15, 1996. **B-T:** L-L. **Ht.:** 6-0. **Wt.:** 205. **Drafted:** HS—Tucson, 2014 (2nd round). **Signed by:** Dustin Yount.

Other teams preferred Verdugo as a pitcher when he was a two-way player in high school, but the Dodgers' belief in his hitting ability has proven justified. Verdugo was pushed aggressively to Double-A in 2016, and he responded with a solid season as one of the youngest players in the Texas League. Verdugo has good rhythm and body control in the box, with some unorthodox elements to his swing but good plate coverage thanks to superb hand-eye coordination. He sets up with his hands close to his body and stays inside the ball well, shooting line drives to all fields. Verdugo recognizes offspeed pitches well and doesn't chase much. He

BA GRADE
55 Risk: Medium

has a strong build and good bat speed, though his swing lacks leverage for big power, and he projects to hit 15-20 home runs. Verdugo's fringe-average speed isn't ideal for center field, which is part of why his defense draws mixed reviews. There's universal praise for Verudgo's arm, which earns plus-plus grades for its strength and accuracy. Some scouts are concerned with his inconsistent motor, a complaint dating back to his prep days. With similarities to Melky Cabrera, Verdugo could develop into a solid-average regular. His next stop is Triple-A Oklahoma City with a chance to get to the big leagues after the all-star break.

Year	Club (League)	Class	AVG	G	AB	R	H	2B	3B	HR	RBI	BB	SO	SB	CS	OBP	SLG
2014	Dodgers (AZL)	R	.347	49	170	28	59	14	3	3	33	20	14	8	0	.423	.518
	Ogden (PIO)	R	.400	5	20	3	8	1	0	0	8	0	4	3	0	.400	.450
2015	Great Lakes (MWL)	LoA	.295	101	421	50	124	23	2	5	42	17	53	13	5	.325	.394
	R. Cucamonga (CAL)	HiA	.385	23	91	20	35	9	2	4	19	4	12	1	0	.406	.659
2016	Tulsa (TL)	AA	.273	126	477	58	130	23	1	13	63	44	67	2	6	.336	.407
Minor League Totals			.302	304	1179	159	356	70	8	25	165	85	150	27	11	.352	.439

5 WILLIE CALHOUN, 2B

Born: Nov. 4, 1994. **B-T:** L-R. **Ht.:** 5-8. **Wt.:** 187. **Drafted:** Yavapai (Ariz.) JC, 2015 (4th round). **Signed by:** Dustin Yount.

After a season at Arizona, Calhoun transferred to Yavapai (Ariz.) JC in 2015 and led the nation's jucos with 31 home runs in 61 games. The Dodgers pushed him to Double-A Tulsa for his first full season and he ranked second in the league in homers (27) with the second-lowest strikeout rate among qualified hitters. Small and stocky, Calhoun is built like a fire hydrant. He has a sweet, balanced lefty stroke that's quick, compact and stays through the hitting zone for a long time. He has excellent barrel control and good plate coverage, leading to a high contact rate, with a sharp eye at the plate. Calhoun is no small slap hitter. He has above-average

BA GRADE

55 Risk: Medium

power and gets to it frequently because of his contact frequency, making him a threat to hit 25-30 home runs. As gifted as Calhoun is at the plate, he's a long way from being an adequate defender at second base. He's a well below-average runner with limited range and first-step quickness and a below-average arm. He also boots too many routine plays with hard hands and awkward defensive actions. Calhoun could be the Dodgers' second baseman of the future, but his fielding has to take a big step forward to avoid a move to left field.

Year	Club (League)	Class	AVG	G	AB	R	H	2B	3B	HR	RBI	BB	SO	SB	CS	OBP	SLG
2015	Ogden (PIO)	R	.278	38	151	28	42	13	1	7	26	23	18	2	1	.371	.517
	Great Lakes (MWL)	LoA	.393	15	61	9	24	3	0	1	8	5	7	0	0	.439	.492
	R. Cucamonga (CAL)	HiA	.329	20	73	11	24	7	0	3	14	7	13	0	0	.390	.548
2016	Tulsa (TL)	AA	.254	132	503	75	128	25	1	27	88	45	65	0	0	.318	.469
Minor League Totals			.277	205	788	123	218	48	2	38	136	80	103	2	1	.345	.487

6 ANDREW TOLES, OF

Born: May 24, 1992. **B-T:** L-R. **Ht.:** 5-10. **Wt.:** 185. **Drafted:** Chipola (Fla.) JC, 2012 (3rd round). **Signed by:** Milt Hill (Rays).

Toles was the Rays' No. 6 prospect after the 2013 season, but he dealt with anxiety and related behavioral effects, and the Rays released him just before the 2015 season. Out of baseball and working in the frozen foods section at a Kroger grocery store, the Dodgers gave Toles a chance and signed him to a minor league deal in time for instructional league in 2015. He embarked on a four-level rise in 2016 to make his major league debut, including starting for the Dodgers in the postseason. Toles, whose father Alvin was a first-round NFL draft pick, has long stood out for his quick-twitch athleticism. He starts his lefthanded swing with a leg kick, then

BA GRADE

50 Risk: Medium

unleashes quick hands to stay short and direct to the ball. He is an aggressive hitter but doesn't strike out much. He has a line-drive approach with enough power to hit 10-15 home runs. Toles is a double-plus runner who plays all three outfield spots, fitting in center and playing above-average defense for a corner outfielder. His plus arm is another asset. Toles could be an everyday center fielder but not with Joc Pederson in Los Angeles. He is likely to see playing time in left field in 2017 and rotate around the outfield as needed.

Year	Club (League)	Class	AVG	G	AB	R	H	2B	3B	HR	RBI	BB	SO	SB	CS	OBP	SLG
2014	Charlotte (FSL)	HiA	.261	46	199	28	52	10	1	1	13	12	31	18	10	.302	.337
	Rays (GCL)	R	.292	6	24	4	7	0	1	0	2	0	6	6	0	.320	.375
2015	Did not play																
2016	R. Cucamonga (CAL)	HiA	.370	22	92	22	34	8	2	0	9	6	13	9	3	.414	.500
	Tulsa (TL)	AA	.314	43	175	27	55	14	3	5	22	12	30	13	3	.363	.514
	Oklahoma City (PCL)	AAA	.321	17	56	6	18	5	0	2	7	2	8	1	5	.339	.518
	Los Angeles (NL)	MAJ	.314	48	105	19	33	9	1	3	16	8	25	1	1	.365	.505
Major League Totals			.314	48	105	19	33	9	1	3	16	8	25	1	1	.365	.505
Minor League Totals			.309	306	1264	197	391	85	26	17	143	66	229	123	43	.348	.458

7 YUSNIEL DIAZ, OF

Born: Oct. 7, 1996. **B-T:** R-R. **Ht.:** 6-1. **Wt.:** 195. **Signed:** Cuba, 2015.

Diaz was a standout player in Cuba's junior national leagues and excelled during his rookie year in Serie Nacional before leaving the country in 2015. He went to the Dominican Republic and signed with the Dodgers after the 2015 season for $15.5 million. In an aggressive assignment to the high Class A California League, Diaz held his own as one of the league's youngest players but missed time due to shoulder fatigue. Diaz has an exciting combination of athleticism, tools and performance record, though he's still learning to sync everything at the plate. He has plus bat speed and good hand-eye coordination to put the bat to the ball consistently, but he is considered to have average raw power at best. He doesn't show power in games— five of his eight Cal League home runs came in extreme hitters' parks in Lancaster and High Desert—as he doesn't use his lower half well. Diaz gears his swing more for low line drives, often shooting the ball the opposite way. He's a plus runner but doesn't get good jumps stealing bases. He played all three outfield spots with the speed and above-average arm to fit in center. Diaz has the upside to develop into an everyday center fielder but has to make adjustments to handle better pitching. He'll head to Double-A in 2017.

BA GRADE
55 Risk: High

Year	Club (League)	Class	AVG	G	AB	R	H	2B	3B	HR	RBI	BB	SO	SB	CS	OBP	SLG
2016	Dodgers (AZL)	R	.143	3	14	2	2	0	0	1	3	0	3	0	0	.143	.357
	R. Cucamonga (CAL)	HiA	.272	82	316	47	86	8	7	8	54	29	71	7	8	.333	.418
Minor League Totals			.267	85	330	49	88	8	7	9	57	29	74	7	8	.326	.415

8 BROCK STEWART, RHP

Born: Oct. 3, 1991. **B-T:** L-R. **Ht.:** 6-3. **Wt.:** 210. **Drafted:** Illinois State, 2014 (6th round). **Signed by:** Chet Sergo.

Stewart was a third baseman at Illinois State, where his father Jeff—who now scouts for the Rays—was a longtime coach. He pitched a little out of the bullpen, signed with the Dodgers as a reliever, then converted to starting in 2015. He took off in 2016, flying through four levels to make his major league debut on June 29. He spent most of August and September with the big league club. Stewart's best pitch is his high-spin fastball, which sits 91-95 mph and can scrape 96. He has tremendous confidence in his fastball and pounds the zone with plus control. Moving to the first-base side of the rubber helped him locate the pitch down and away against righthanded hitters. Stewart's low-80s changeup improved to become an average offering, though when he got to the majors it flattened out and he had trouble landing it in the zone. He throws a hard 85-88 mph slider that's fringy but flashes average with short, late break. His slider gets swings and misses as a chase pitch despite its lack of depth, though it's sometimes easy to detect out of his hand. Stewart projects as a back-end starter. He might open 2017 in Triple-A but should be a factor in the Dodgers' rotation.

BA GRADE
50 Risk: Medium

Year	Club (League)	Class	W	L	ERA	G	GS	CG	SV	IP	H	HR	BB	SO	K/9	WHIP	AVG
2014	Ogden (PIO)	R	3	2	3.41	17	1	0	3	34	36	1	17	45	11.8	1.54	.259
2015	Great Lakes (MWL)	LoA	2	2	2.84	7	7	0	0	38	38	4	6	38	9.0	1.16	.262
	R. Cucamonga (CAL)	HiA	2	4	5.43	18	12	0	0	63	75	6	18	65	9.3	1.48	.291
2016	R. Cucamonga (CAL)	HiA	2	0	0.82	2	2	0	0	11	5	0	2	10	8.2	0.64	.135
	Oklahoma City (PCL)	AAA	4	0	2.49	9	9	0	0	51	41	4	6	54	9.6	0.93	.217
	Tulsa (TL)	AA	3	4	1.37	10	10	1	0	59	41	0	11	65	9.9	0.88	.196
	Los Angeles (NL)	MAJ	2	2	5.79	7	5	0	0	28	33	7	12	25	8.0	1.61	.292
Major League Totals			2	2	5.79	7	5	0	0	28	33	7	12	25	8.0	1.61	.292
Minor League Totals			16	12	3.05	63	41	1	3	256	236	15	60	277	9.7	1.15	.242

9 GAVIN LUX, SS

BILL MITCHELL

Born: Nov. 23, 1997. **B-T:** L-R. **Ht.:** 6-2. **Wt.:** 190. **Drafted:** HS—Kenosha, Wis., 2016 (1st round). **Signed by:** Trey Magnuson.

Lux is a nephew of Augie Schmidt, who won the Golden Spikes Award as the nation's top college player in 1982 for New Orleans and was the No. 2 overall pick in the draft that year. Lux emerged from cold-weather Wisconsin and went 20th overall in the 2016 draft, signing with the Dodgers for $2,314,500 to forgo an Arizona State commitment. Lux is a steady player whose best asset is he should be able stick at shortstop, though he also has a chance to be a solid hitter. He has a smooth, low-maintenance swing from the left side with good bat speed, a line-drive approach and the ability to use the whole field. He is a patient hitter who works deep counts. Improved strength helped him his senior year, but he doesn't have much power yet and projects as more of a doubles hitter than a home run threat. Lux is a good athlete with above-average speed despite an awkward gait, quick feet, smooth actions and a solid-average arm with a quick exchange at shortstop. Coming out of a Wisconsin high school, Lux hasn't faced much quality competition yet, though he had a sound debut in the Rookie-level Arizona League. He should be comfortable going to the cold weather of low Class A Great Lakes to begin his first full season.

BA GRADE
55 Risk: **Extreme**

Year	Club (League)	Class	AVG	G	AB	R	H	2B	3B	HR	RBI	BB	SO	SB	CS	OBP	SLG
2016	Dodgers (AZL)	R	.281	48	192	34	54	10	5	0	18	25	43	1	0	.365	.385
	Ogden (PIO)	R	.387	8	31	7	12	3	0	0	3	3	8	1	0	.441	.484
Minor League Totals			.296	56	223	41	66	13	5	0	21	28	51	2	0	.375	.399

10 AUSTIN BARNES, C/2B

Born: Dec. 28, 1989. **B-T:** R-R. **Ht.:** 5-10. **Wt.:** 195. **Drafted:** Arizona State, 2011 (9th round). **Signed by:** Scott Stanley (Marlins).

Barnes is the rare 27-year-old who is a legitimate prospect. The Marlins moved Barnes slowly through their system, then traded him to the Dodgers after the 2014 season in the six-player deal that brought Dee Gordon to Miami. He continued to be an on-base machine in Triple-A Oklahoma City but was blocked on the depth chart from getting much playing time in Los Angeles. Barnes does a stellar job of controlling the strike zone. He detects spin early and doesn't chase bad pitches. He's a calm, balanced hitter with a simple, direct stroke to make contact at a high clip and stays through the middle of the field with mostly doubles power. Barnes has just

BA GRADE
45 Risk: **Medium**

fringe-average raw speed but runs the bases well, stealing 18 bags in 21 attempts. Above-average behind the plate, Barnes excels at blocking and receiving with soft hands and highly-regarded pitch framing skills. His arm strength is average, and he threw out 25 percent of basestealers last year. He also has the versatility and athleticism to play second and third base when necessary. With the Dodgers trading Carlos Ruiz to the Mariners, Barnes should be Yasmani Grandal's full-time backup in 2017 while also seeing time at second and third base. In another organization, he would be a starter.

Year	Club (League)	Class	AVG	G	AB	R	H	2B	3B	HR	RBI	BB	SO	SB	CS	OBP	SLG
2014	Jupiter (FSL)	HiA	.317	44	180	24	57	11	2	1	14	19	25	3	3	.385	.417
	Jacksonville (SL)	AA	.296	78	284	56	84	20	2	12	43	50	36	8	0	.406	.507
2015	Oklahoma City (PCL)	AAA	.315	81	292	40	92	17	2	9	42	35	36	12	2	.389	.479
	Los Angeles (NL)	MAJ	.207	20	29	4	6	2	0	0	1	6	6	1	0	.361	.276
2016	Oklahoma City (PCL)	AAA	.295	85	336	59	99	22	5	6	39	43	53	18	3	.380	.443
	Los Angeles (NL)	MAJ	.156	21	32	3	5	1	0	0	2	5	9	0	0	.270	.188
Major League Totals			.180	41	61	7	11	3	0	0	3	11	15	1	0	.315	.230
Minor League Totals			.299	585	2201	340	659	136	17	46	267	295	302	61	13	.388	.439

11 WALKER BUEHLER, RHP

BA GRADE
55 Risk: **Extreme**

Born: July 28, 1994. **B-T:** R-R. **Ht.:** 6-2. **Wt.:** 175. **Drafted:** Vanderbilt, 2015 (1st round). **Signed by:** Marty Lamb.

Buehler never felt quite right during his junior season at Vanderbilt in 2015. The Dodgers drafted him with the 24th overall pick that year, with an MRI revealing he would need Tommy John surgery. After signing for $1,77,500, Buehler had the operation that August and was back on the mound 11 months later. Despite missing most of 2016 to rehab, Buehler still won a ring as he pitched five scoreless innings over two playoff starts for low Class A Great Lakes, which won the Midwest League championship. Buehler's progress has been encouraging so far, especially since he was throwing 91-96 mph before surgery but upon his return was touching 98. It's difficult to judge Buehler's other pitches since his return, but before the operation he threw a curveball and slider with tight spin, though they had a tendency to run together. He also throws a changeup with late fade that flashes as an above-average offering. It's not the cleanest arm action, but Buehler is a solid strike-thrower who has the athleticism to repeat his high-intensity mechanics. Durability is a question mark for the thin-framed Buehler, but he has the stuff to pitch in the middle of a rotation.

Year	Club (League)	Class	W	L	ERA	G	GS	CG	SV	IP	H	HR	BB	SO	K/9	WHIP	AVG
2015	Did not play—Injured																
2016	Dodgers (AZL)	R	1	0	0.00	1	0	0	0	2	0	0	0	3	13.5	0.00	.000
	Great Lakes (MWL)	LoA	0	0	0.00	2	1	0	0	3	0	0	3	3	9.0	1.00	.000
Minor League Totals			1	0	0.00	3	1	0	0	5	0	0	3	6	10.8	0.60	.000

12 JORDAN SHEFFIELD, RHP

BA GRADE

50 Risk: High

Born: June 1, 1995. **B-T:** R-R. **Ht.:** 6-0. **Wt.:** 185. **Drafted:** Vanderbilt, 2016 (1st round supp,) **Signed by:** Marty Lamb.

The Dodgers have been raiding the Vanderbilt pitching staff in recent years. They drafted Walker Buehler and Phil Pfeifer in 2015, then used their 2016 supplemental first-round pick (No. 36 overall) on Sheffield, who signed for $1,847,500. His younger brother, Justus, is a pitching prospect in the Yankees organization. Sheffield, who had Tommy John surgery in 2013, has outstanding arm speed on a fastball that sits at 93-96 mph and can reach 98, with the ability to carry that velocity deep into his starts. Sheffield's hard curveball and changeup are both 55-grade pitches that flash plus. He has more confidence in his curveball, which has sharp bite but is inconsistent, while his mid-80s changeup gets excellent arm-side run. With a high-effort delivery, Sheffield struggles to repeat his release point. While he improved his control in 2016, it's still scattered. Sheffield has the repertoire to start, but his command, mechanics and medical track record create reliever risk.

Year	Club (League)	Class	W	L	ERA	G	GS	CG	SV	IP	H	HR	BB	SO	K/9	WHIP	AVG
2016	Dodgers (AZL)	R	0	0	0.00	1	1	0	0	1	0	0	0	0	0.00	0.00	.000
	Great Lakes (MWL)	LoA	0	1	4.09	7	7	0	0	11	11	2	6	13	10.6	1.55	.275
Minor League Totals			0	1	3.75	8	8	0	0	12	11	2	6	13	9.8	1.42	.256

13 DUSTIN MAY, RHP

BA GRADE

55 Risk: Extreme

Born: Sept. 6, 1997. **B-T:** R-R. **Ht.:** 6-6. **Wt.:** 180. **Drafted:** HS—Justin, Texas, 2016 (3rd round). **Signed by:** Josh Herzenberg.

It's hard to miss May, between his gangly 6-foot-6 frame and bushy red hair. After the Dodgers signed him for $997,500 as a third-round pick in 2016, his numbers stood out as well, with a 34-4 strikeout-to-walk mark in 30.1 innings in the Rookie-level Arizona League. May has strong hands with a skinny, underdeveloped frame that's oozing with physical projection. Once he gains weight and strength, that should allow him to add to a high-spin fastball that ranges from 88-94 mph with late movement. May's slider is his out pitch, flashing plus to get swings-and-misses, while his changeup is firm and still raw. For such a thin pitcher with long arms and legs, May does a solid job of keeping his delivery in sync. He's a good athlete who pounded the strike zone in the AZL and should only continue to make improvements to being able to repeat his mechanics once he gets stronger. May's future still involves a high dose of physical projection coming to fruition, but if that comes, he has a chance to develop into a mid-rotation starter at the next level.

Year	Club (League)	Class	W	L	ERA	G	GS	CG	SV	IP	H	HR	BB	SO	K/9	WHIP	AVG
2016	Dodgers (AZL)	R	0	1	3.86	10	6	0	1	30	37	0	4	34	10.1	1.35	.291
Minor League Totals			0	1	3.86	10	6	0	1	30	37	0	4	34	10.1	1.35	.291

14 TREVOR OAKS, RHP

BA GRADE

45 Risk: Medium

Born: March 26, 1993. **B-T:** R-R. **Ht.:** 6-3. **Wt.:** 220. **Drafted:** California Baptist, 2014 (7th round). **Signed by:** Bobby Darwin.

Oaks had Tommy John surgery in high school, played his freshman year at NAIA Biola (Calif.), then transferred to Division II Cal Baptist, where he became the team's ace as a draft-eligible sophomore. The Dodgers drafted Oaks in the seventh round and signed him for $161,600. He was steady in his first full season in 2015, then zipped through three levels in 2016 as he added velocity and continued to display excellent control, though a strained groin ended his season in August. With strong, broad shoulders, Oaks' best pitch is his heavy sinker, which gained steam in 2016 to sit at 90-94 mph and touch 96. He generates downhill plane and the sinker dives as it gets near home plate, making Oaks one of the most prolific groundball pitchers in the minors. Oaks showed plus control by walking just 1.3 batters per nine innings between three levels in 2016. Oaks doesn't have the secondary pitches to miss many bats, so he relies on throwing strikes and avoiding barrels to generate weak contact with his sinker and cutter. He added the cutter in 2016, and it flashes as an average pitch in the upper-80s. His changeup is fringe-average and his short slider is below-average, with an occasional show-me curveball mixed in, too. Oaks pitched eight innings or more in four starts, a testament to his efficiency. Oaks should start 2017 back in Triple-A, but he should make his major league debut at some point during the season with the upside of a back-end starter.

Year	Club (League)	Class	W	L	ERA	G	GS	CG	SV	IP	H	HR	BB	SO	K/9	WHIP	AVG
2014	Ogden (PIO)	R	5	2	6.31	14	3	0	0	36	41	2	13	29	7.3	1.51	.283
2015	Great Lakes (MWL)	LoA	5	5	2.56	18	16	2	0	102	84	3	14	58	5.1	0.96	.221
	R. Cucamonga (CAL)	HiA	3	0	3.04	5	5	0	0	24	28	2	5	16	6.1	1.39	.292
2016	R. Cucamonga (CAL)	HiA	1	1	3.60	4	4	0	0	25	26	1	3	22	7.9	1.16	.280
	Tulsa (TL)	AA	8	1	2.14	10	10	0	0	63	56	1	9	38	5.4	1.03	.239
	Oklahoma City (PCL)	AAA	5	1	3.00	10	10	1	0	63	64	7	9	48	6.9	1.16	.262
Minor League Totals			27	10	3.11	61	48	3	0	312	299	16	53	211	6.1	1.13	.251

15 JOHAN MIESES, OF

BA GRADE
50 Risk: Extreme

Born: July 13, 1995. **B-T:** R-R. **Ht.:** 6-2. **Wt.:** 200. **Signed:** Dominican Republic, 2013. **Signed by:** Patrick Guerrero.

Mieses signed for $40,000 out of the Dominican Republic in 2013 and has moved quickly through the farm system, though he's far from a polished product. With a strong, powerful frame, Mieses generates plus raw power and led the high Class A California League with 28 home runs in 2016, though his free-swinging approach remains a concern. Mieses has strong hands, quick bat speed and the power to hit the ball out to any part of the park when he connects, even driving the ball with authority when he mis-hits the ball. Mieses will have to overhaul his swing and approach to have success at higher levels. His swing has a lot of head movement, which hurts his ability to recognize pitches, with a frequent habit of chasing pitches outside the strike zone. He sells out for power on nearly every swing, getting underneath a lot of pitches with a max-effort, uphill stroke and pull-conscious approach. The barrel doesn't stay in the hitting zone very long, so he will have to flatten his swing and develop better strike-zone judgment to close his offensive holes. Mieses is a good athlete with average speed and a plus arm to collect 14 assists. He has spent most of his time in center field and might be able to stay there, though a lot of scouts prefer him in right field.

Year	Club (League)	Class	AVG	G	AB	R	H	2B	3B	HR	RBI	BB	SO	SB	CS	OBP	SLG
2014	Dodgers (DSL)	R	.299	59	204	31	61	11	8	5	24	21	40	29	3	.371	.505
2015	Great Lakes (MWL)	LoA	.277	45	166	16	46	10	1	5	20	11	31	7	4	.320	.440
	R. Cucamonga (CAL)	HiA	.245	51	196	35	48	18	1	6	19	13	57	3	1	.299	.439
2016	R. Cucamonga (CAL)	HiA	.247	122	461	72	114	31	3	28	78	36	147	3	7	.314	.510
Minor League Totals			.260	293	1081	162	281	72	13	44	144	88	288	45	18	.324	.473

16 WILL SMITH, C

BA GRADE
45 Risk: High

Born: March 28, 1995. **B-T:** R-R. **Ht.:** 6-0. **Wt.:** 195. **Drafted:** Louisville, 2016 (1st round). **Signed by:** Marty Lamb.

With the No. 35 overall pick in the 2015 draft, the Dodgers drafted but were unable to sign Louisville ace righthander Kyle Funkhouser. The next year, they drafted Funkhouser's catcher, Smith, with the No. 32 overall pick in the first round and signed him for $1,772,500. The Dodgers pushed Smith quickly after he signed, putting him in the high Class A California League the final month of the season. A high school shortstop who converted to catching in college, Smith is extremely athletic for a backstop and a legitimate above-average runner. He has experience handling power arms on the deep Louisville pitching staff and stands out for his receiving and blocking skills. He has an average arm that plays up due to his fast exchange, throwing out 42 percent of baserunners in his pro debut. Smith has solid bat-to-ball skills with a short, flat stroke, the ability to hit to all fields and sound command of the strike zone. Smith doesn't project to hit for power but has some pull pop, enough to get to 8-12 home runs.

Year	Club (League)	Class	AVG	G	AB	R	H	2B	3B	HR	RBI	BB	SO	SB	CS	OBP	SLG
2016	Ogden (PIO)	R	.321	7	28	4	9	0	0	1	5	4	1	0	0	.394	.429
	Great Lakes (MWL)	LoA	.256	23	82	12	21	1	0	1	7	11	18	2	1	.371	.305
	R. Cucamonga (CAL)	HiA	.216	25	97	13	21	4	0	2	12	14	31	1	0	.330	.320
Minor League Totals			.246	55	207	29	51	5	0	4	24	29	50	3	1	.355	.329

17 GRANT DAYTON, LHP

BA GRADE
40 Risk: Low

Born: Nov. 5, 1987. **B-T:** L-L. **Ht.:** 6-2. **Wt.:** 195. **Signed:** Auburn, 2010 (11th round). **Signed by:** Mark Willoughby (Marlins).

At 29, Dayton is one of the oldest players in the Prospect Handbook, but he should play a key role in the Dodgers' 2017 bullpen. A starter at Auburn, Dayton immediately moved to the bullpen when the Marlins drafted him in 2010 and slowly climbed through their farm system before Miami traded him to the Dodgers in July 2015 for lefthander Chris Reed. He pounded the strike zone and struck out 15.8 batters per nine innings between Double-A and Triple-A in 2016, then continued to flourish the last two months of the season and in the playoffs. Dayton's fastball sits at 91-94 mph and can touch 95, with late riding life and deception that gets hitters to swing-and-miss through that pitch at a high clip. Dayton pitches aggressively off his fastball with sharp command of the pitch to both sides of the plate and the ability to work up in the zone to get empty swings. While Dayton's changeup was his go-to secondary pitch earlier in his career, he rarely threw it once he got to the major leagues, instead relying more on a curveball. It's a fringe-average pitch at best, an offering he adds and subtracts from depending on the situation anywhere from 71-79 mph. Dayton he should be a key set-up man for the Dodgers in 2017.

Year	Club (League)	Class	W	L	ERA	G	GS	CG	SV	IP	H	HR	BB	SO	K/9	WHIP	AVG
2014	Jacksonville (SL)	AA	0	1	1.10	11	0	0	3	16	17	0	4	18	9.9	1.29	.262
	New Orleans (PCL)	AAA	2	2	3.72	39	0	0	1	56	53	10	22	61	9.9	1.35	.249
2015	New Orleans (PCL)	AAA	2	1	2.83	25	0	0	0	35	25	1	5	35	9.0	0.86	.207
	Oklahoma City (PCL)	AAA	1	1	9.26	9	0	0	0	12	16	1	3	13	10.0	1.63	.327
	Tulsa (TL)	AA	0	2	2.53	8	0	0	1	11	9	0	7	17	14.3	1.50	.231
2016	Tulsa (TL)	AA	3	0	2.30	12	0	0	1	16	8	0	3	28	16.1	0.70	.148
	Oklahoma City (PCL)	AAA	2	2	2.48	26	0	0	4	36	22	2	8	63	15.6	0.83	.169
	Los Angeles (NL)	MAJ	0	1	2.05	25	0	0	0	26	14	4	6	39	13.3	0.76	.149
Major League Totals			0	1	2.05	25	0	0	0	26	14	4	6	39	13.3	0.76	.149
Minor League Totals			26	21	2.79	265	6	0	20	394	320	26	125	504	11.5	1.13	.220

18 JOSH SBORZ, RHP

BA GRADE
45 Risk: High

Born: Dec. 17, 1993. **B-T:** R-R. **Ht.:** 6-3. **Wt.:** 225. **Drafted:** Virginia, 2015 (2nd round supplemental). **Signed by:** Clair Rierson.

Sborz won the won the 2015 College World Series Most Outstanding Player award, then signed with the Dodgers for $772,500 as the No. 74 overall pick in the draft. Sborz, whose brother Jay pitched in one major league game for the Tigers in 2010, was mostly a reliever at Virginia, but the Dodgers developed him as a starter with high Class A Rancho Cucamonga in 2016. However, when the Dodgers promoted Sborz to Double-A Tulsa in August, they moved him back to the bullpen to curb his workload. A relief role may ultimately suit Sborz best. As a starter he sits at 91-94 mph with good armside run, though in short bursts out of the bullpen he can crank it up to 97 mph. His out pitch is an above-average slider with good depth and late break. Sborz has a four-pitch mix, but his fringe-average curveball and below-average changeup don't grade out as well as his fastball and slider. There's some violence to Sborz's arm action and effort in his delivery. He throws strikes but needs to tighten his fastball command. Sborz could fit well in a middle relief role, with a chance he could get to Los Angeles by the end of the 2017 season.

Year	Club (League)	Class	W	L	ERA	G	GS	CG	SV	IP	H	HR	BB	SO	K/9	WHIP	AVG
2015	Ogden (PIO)	R	0	1	4.50	2	1	0	0	4	2	0	4	4	9.0	1.50	.167
	Great Lakes (MWL)	LoA	0	1	2.84	2	2	0	0	6	5	2	2	9	12.8	1.11	.185
	R. Cucamonga (CAL)	HiA	0	0	1.50	9	0	0	2	12	12	1	3	12	9.0	1.25	.255
2016	R. Cucamonga (CAL)	HiA	8	4	2.66	20	19	0	0	108	82	8	30	108	9.0	1.03	.207
	Tulsa (TL)	AA	0	1	3.78	10	0	0	1	17	17	2	6	17	9.2	1.38	.258
Minor League Totals			8	7	2.75	43	22	0	3	147	118	13	45	150	9.2	1.11	.215

19 MITCHELL WHITE, RHP

BA GRADE
50 Risk: Extreme

Born: Dec. 28, 1994. **B-T:** R-R. **Ht.:** 6-4. **Wt.:** 207. **Drafted:** Santa Clara, 2016 (2nd round). **Signed by:** Tom Kunis.

Few players in the 2016 draft had as much late helium as White. He didn't pitch much in high school—he had Tommy John surgery his senior year—and pitched just 32 innings out of Santa Clara's bullpen in 2015. Moved to the rotation in 2016, White's fastball velocity spiked and the Dodgers took notice, popping him in the second round and cutting an under-slot deal with him for $588,300. While the Dodgers kept him on a tight leash of no more than two innings per outing after he signed, White excelled in his pro debut by allowing only one run (unearned) in 22 innings. The Dodgers want to develop White as a starter, and he has a chance to stick in that role. White's fastball sat at 89-93 mph early in his final college season, but by the end he was cruising at 91-96 mph and tickling 97 with good fastball command. His curveball and cutter-esque slider are both solid-average offerings with the curveball flashing plus and the more effective pitch early in his pro career. He has a changeup, but it's still in its nascent stages since he just started throwing it in March. White is a late bloomer with a limited track record, but he has the stuff to be a solid starter or a high-leverage reliever with a chance to move quickly.

Year	Club (League)	Class	W	L	ERA	G	GS	CG	SV	IP	H	HR	BB	SO	K/9	WHIP	AVG
2016	Dodgers (AZL)	R	0	0	0.00	2	2	0	0	4	3	0	0	8	18.0	0.75	.200
	Great Lakes (MWL)	LoA	0	0	0.00	8	4	0	0	16	3	0	6	20	11.3	0.56	.058
	R. Cucamonga (CAL)	HiA	1	0	0.00	1	0	0	0	2	1	0	0	2	9.0	0.50	.167
Minor League Totals			1	0	0.00	11	6	0	0	22	7	0	6	30	12.3	0.59	.096

20 KEIBERT RUIZ, C

BA GRADE

45 Risk: High

Born: July 20, 1998. **B-T:** B-R. **Ht.:** 6-0. **Wt.:** 165. **Signed:** Venezuela, 2014. **Signed by:** Francisco Cartaya/Pedro Avila.

As an amateur in Venezuela, Ruiz trained in the program run by former major league shortstop Carlos Guillen. The Dodgers were drawn to his advanced defensive skills behind the plate for his age and signed him for $140,000 when he turned 16 on July 20, 2014. Ruiz was 17 most of the 2016 season, making him one of the youngest players in the Rookie-level Pioneer League, but he still thrived during his time there. Ruiz projects to stick at catcher because he is an excellent receiver with good hands and quick footwork, though he does need to get better at blocking balls in the dirt. He has an average arm with a quick release, though he threw out just 20 percent of runners last season. Ruiz is a switch-hitter with a contact-oriented approach. His hands work well at the plate, though some scouts had concerns that he was late on too many hittable pitches. Ruiz doesn't bring much power, mostly working gap to gap. The Pioneer League is extremely kind toward hitters, so Ruiz will face a big test in 2017 in low Class A Great Lakes.

Year	Club (League)	Class	AVG	G	AB	R	H	2B	3B	HR	RBI	BB	SO	SB	CS	OBP	SLG
2015	Dodgers (DSL)	R	.300	44	150	14	45	8	1	1	19	8	15	4	2	.340	.387
2016	Dodgers (AZL)	R	.485	8	33	5	16	4	1	0	15	3	4	0	0	.513	.667
	Ogden (PIO)	R	.354	48	189	28	67	18	2	2	33	12	23	0	0	.393	.503
Minor League Totals			.344	100	372	47	128	30	4	3	67	23	42	4	2	.384	.470

21 D.J. PETERS, OF

BA GRADE

50 Risk: Extreme

Born: Dec. 12, 1995. **B-T:** R-R. **Ht.:** 6-6. **Wt.:** 225. **Drafted:** Western Nevada JC, 2016 (4th round). **Signed by:** Tom Kunis.

Peters signed for $247,500 as the No. 131 overall pick in the 2016 draft, then proceeded to the Rookie-level Pioneer League, where he ranked third in OBP (.437) and second in slugging (.615). At 6-foot-6, Peters has a promising combination of size, athleticism and power. His raw power earns plus or better grades, with the ability to drive the ball out to any part of the park with his strength and leverage. He's an aggressive hitter who showed more patience in pro ball as he got pitched around. He kept his strikeout rate to a manageable 22 percent, though with a longer swing that is a concern going forward. Peters doesn't have a quick first step so it takes him a bit to get going, but he's an average runner underway. Peters split time between center and right field with Ogden. He has a plus arm and fits best in right field. If Peters can maintain control of the strike zone, he has a chance to become an everyday right fielder.

Year	Club (League)	Class	AVG	G	AB	R	H	2B	3B	HR	RBI	BB	SO	SB	CS	OBP	SLG
2016	Ogden (PIO)	R	.351	66	262	63	92	24	3	13	48	35	66	5	3	.437	.615
Minor League Totals			.351	66	262	63	92	24	3	13	48	35	66	5	3	.437	.615

22 YAISEL SIERRA, RHP

BA GRADE

45 Risk: High

Born: June 5, 1991. **B-T:** R-R. **Ht.:** 6-1. **Wt.:** 180. **Signed:** Cuba, 2016.

Sierra was one of the better pitching prospects in Cuba, though the results never matched his potential. During Sierra's final season in Serie Nacional in Cuba, he posted a 6.10 ERA with a 55-31 strikeout-to-walk mark in 70 innings and led the league with 11 wild pitches despite pitching as a reliever. The Dodgers' made a bet that Sierra's stuff would translate into better performance, signing him to a six-year, $30 million major league deal that included a $6 million signing bonus in February 2016. They sent Sierra to high Class A Rancho Cucamonga as a starter and he struggled, with the Dodgers removing him from the 40-man roster on July 3 and putting him in the bullpen two weeks later. Sierra is already 25, but the stuff is still there. He has an athletic frame to go with clean, easy arm action and quick arm speed, delivering lively fastballs that sit 93-95 mph in relief and can touch 97. His slider flashes above-average with tight spin and late tilt to miss bats. At one point, Sierra was using his slider so frequently that the Dodgers told him he couldn't throw his slider any more until he got into a two-strike count in an attempt to get him to work more off his fastball. Sierra threw a splitter in Cuba but scrapped that for a changeup, though it's below-average. Sierra's undoing is his command. Despite an easy delivery, he misses his location and tends to leave the ball up, allowing hitters to punish his mistakes. While starting no longer appears to be in Sierra's future, he can develop into a quality middle reliever if he can figure out his command.

Year	Club (League)	Class	W	L	ERA	G	GS	CG	SV	IP	H	HR	BB	SO	K/9	WHIP	AVG
2014	Holguin (CNS)	CNS	6	6	3.92	25	18	0	3	101	79	3	64	79	7.0	1.42	—
2015	Did not play																
2016	R. Cucamonga (CAL)	HiA	5	5	6.20	20	13	0	0	74	87	9	25	65	7.9	1.51	.293
	Tulsa (TL)	AA	1	2	4.30	10	0	0	0	15	14	0	5	21	12.9	1.30	.237
Minor League Totals			6	7	5.89	30	13	0	0	89	101	9	30	86	8.7	1.48	.284

23 MICAH JOHNSON, 2B/OF

BA GRADE
40 Risk: Medium

Born: Dec. 18, 1990. **B-T:** L-R. **Ht.:** 6-0. **Wt.:** 210. **Drafted:** Indiana, 2012 (9th round). **Signed by:** Mike Shirley (White Sox).

Johnson used his quick-twitch athleticism and speed to great effect with the White Sox, performing well up to Triple-A in 2015. After the 2015 season, the White Sox sent Johnson, outfielder Trayce Thompson and righthander Frankie Montas to the Dodgers in the three-team deal in which the Dodgers sent infielders Jose Peraza and Brandon Dixon and outfielder Scott Schebler to the Reds, who sent Todd Frazier to the White Sox. Staying in Triple-A but switching to the Pacific Coast League in 2016, Johnson scuffled. Johnson is a plus-plus runner whose hitting style is to put the ball on the ground and try to beat out hits. It leaves him with minimal impact in his bat or power due to his frequent grounders and many balls not leaving the infield. His contact skills and plate discipline are solid but not above-average. Johnson doesn't have soft hands or clean actions at second base, though he gets to balls others can't because of his range. The Dodgers also had him spend time in center and left field to increase his versatility. Entering his age-26 season, Johnson will have to perform better offensively to break through in a reserve role.

Year	Club (League)	Class	AVG	G	AB	R	H	2B	3B	HR	RBI	BB	SO	SB	CS	OBP	SLG
2014	Birmingham (SL)	AA	.329	37	146	18	48	9	1	3	16	21	27	10	7	.414	.466
	Charlotte (IL)	AAA	.275	65	273	30	75	10	5	2	28	16	42	12	6	.314	.370
2015	White Sox (AZL)	R	.333	5	15	4	5	2	0	0	0	2	2	0	0	.412	.467
	Charlotte (IL)	AAA	.315	78	311	54	98	17	3	8	36	32	63	28	7	.375	.466
	Chicago (AL)	MAJ	.230	36	100	10	23	4	0	0	4	9	30	3	2	.306	.270
2016	Oklahoma City (PCL)	AAA	.261	120	464	72	121	23	3	5	37	41	105	26	11	.321	.356
	Los Angeles (NL)	MAJ	.167	7	6	1	1	0	0	0	0	0	1	0	0	.167	.167
Major League Totals			.226	43	106	11	24	4	0	0	4	9	31	3	2	.299	.264
Minor League Totals			.292	505	2016	333	588	95	32	29	200	205	411	179	63	.357	.414

24 OMAR ESTEVEZ, 2B

BA GRADE
45 Risk: High

Born: Feb. 25, 1998. **B-T:** R-R. **Ht.:** 5-11. **Wt.:** 185. **Signed:** Cuba, 2015..

Estevez was one of the better hitters in Cuba's junior national leagues. Estevez played for Cuba as a 16-year-old in the COPABE 18U Pan American Championship in Mexico in 2014, then made his Serie Nacional debut at 16 during the 2014-15 season in Cuba. While Estevez played against older competition from a young age, he was regarded as more of a steady prospect than a premium player. Yet when he became eligible to sign after the 2016 season, the Dodgers gave him a $6 million bonus, with the team's total tab coming to $12 million including the 100 percent overage tax for having already exceeded their international bonus pool. The Dodgers aggressively pushed Estevez as an 18-year-old to the low Class A Midwest League, where he hit just .212/.252/.311 in the first half. He turned things around in the second half by batting .293/.340/.458 with eight of his nine home runs. There's nothing plus on Estevez, who isn't athletic or flashy. His bat speed is just fair, but he does have a simple, balanced swing. He can pull an occasional home run, but his power is mostly to the gaps. Estevez is a well below-average runner without great range or agility at second base and a below-average arm.

Year	Club (League)	Class	AVG	G	AB	R	H	2B	3B	HR	RBI	BB	SO	SB	CS	OBP	SLG
2016	Great Lakes (MWL)	LoA	.255	122	471	46	120	32	2	9	61	26	121	3	6	.298	.389
Minor League Totals			.255	122	471	46	120	32	2	9	61	26	121	3	6	.298	.389

25 CHASE DE JONG, RHP

BA GRADE
40 Risk: High

Born: Dec. 29, 1993. **B-T:** L-R. **Ht.:** 6-4. **Wt.:** 205. **Drafted:** HS—Long Beach, 2012 (2nd round). **Signed by:** Joe Aversa (Blue Jays).

When the Dodgers blasted through their 2015-16 international bonus pool, they decided it would be better to trade away their international slot values, even if it meant paying a higher overage tax as a result. When the Blue Jays were looking to sign Vladimir Guerrero Jr. but wanted to trade for enough pool space to only take one year of signing penalties instead of two, the Dodgers shipped three slots to Toronto in exchange for De Jong and second baseman Tim Locastro. After De Jong tamed the Double-A Texas League in 2016, the Dodgers put him on the 40-man roster. There's nothing better than average in De Jong's repertoire, but he's a smart pitcher who understands how to attack hitters. His fastball sits at 88-92 mph and touches 93 and his curveball is an average pitch. His changeup, slider and cutter are all below-average to fringy, but he's been able to have success by using an efficient delivery to throw strikes, change speeds and move the ball around to keep hitters off balance. De Jong's stuff leaves him with little margin for error, but he will go to Triple-A in 2017 with a chance to become a starter in the back of a rotation.

Year	Club (League)	Class	W	L	ERA	G	GS	CG	SV	IP	H	HR	BB	SO	K/9	WHIP	AVG
2014	Lansing (MWL)	LoA	1	6	4.82	23	21	0	0	97	113	12	22	73	6.8	1.39	.290
2015	Lansing (MWL)	LoA	7	4	3.13	14	14	1	0	86	75	9	18	77	8.0	1.08	.231
	R. Cucamonga (CAL)	HiA	4	3	3.96	11	10	0	0	50	44	6	15	52	9.4	1.18	.228
2016	Tulsa (TL)	AA	14	5	2.86	25	25	2	0	142	106	15	39	125	7.9	1.02	.207
	Oklahoma City (PCL)	AAA	1	0	1.69	1	1	0	0	5	6	0	1	8	13.5	1.31	.273
Minor League Totals			30	21	3.43	93	81	4	0	448	409	44	106	416	8.4	1.15	.240

26 ANDREW SOPKO, RHP

BA GRADE
40 Risk: High

Born: Aug. 7, 1994. **B-T:** R-R. **Ht.:** 6-2. **Wt.:** 205. **Drafted:** Gonzaga, 2015 (7th round). **Signed by:** Hank Jones.

Sopko arrived at Gonzaga from a Montana high school and eventually developed into one of the better starters in the West Coast Conference. He signed with the Dodgers for $147,500 as a seventh-round pick in 2015, then caught the attention of scouts with his feel for pitching in his first full season of pro ball. Like fellow Dodgers righthander Chase De Jong, Sopko stands out more for his pitchability than his pure stuff. Sopko lacks a plus pitch, but he's able to command his arsenal, hit his spots, moves the ball around the zone and change speeds. He works off a fastball that sits at 89-92 mph and can hit 94. It's not over-powering, but he pounds the zone and attacks hitters on the inner third. Sopko is able to land his curve-ball, slider and changeup for strikes, though without a true out pitch, Double-A hitters made him pay for mistakes he was able to get away with at high Class A Rancho Cucamonga. They're all fringe-average pitches, with his slider his best weapon against righties, while he uses the changeup and curveball more to attack lefties. Sopko, who likely returns to Double-A Tulsa in 2017, has the upside of a back-end starter.

Year	Club (League)	Class	W	L	ERA	G	GS	CG	SV	IP	H	HR	BB	SO	K/9	WHIP	AVG
2015	Ogden (PIO)	R	0	0	2.57	6	1	0	0	14	14	1	1	18	11.6	1.07	.264
	Great Lakes (MWL)	LoA	3	1	2.74	5	5	0	0	23	18	2	4	18	7.0	0.96	.212
2016	Great Lakes (MWL)	LoA	0	0	0.00	1	1	0	0	5	4	0	0	8	15.4	0.86	.235
	R. Cucamonga (CAL)	HiA	11	2	3.26	18	17	0	0	99	100	5	24	99	9.0	1.25	.264
	Tulsa (TL)	AA	2	2	4.94	6	6	0	0	31	35	4	11	25	7.3	1.48	.287
Minor League Totals			16	5	3.35	36	30	0	0	172	171	12	40	168	8.8	1.23	.261

27 ONEIL CRUZ, SS/3B

BA GRADE
50 Risk: Extreme

Born: Oct. 4, 1998. **B-T:** L-R. **Ht.:** 6-6. **Wt.:** 175. **Signed:** Dominican Republic, 2015. **Signed by:** Patrick Guerrero/Franklin Taveras/Bob Engle.

Cruz is a great example of the challenges unique to international scouting. As a 15-year-old working out for clubs in the Dominican Republic, Cruz was a 6-foot-1 shortstop. By the time he signed with the Dodgers for $950,000 as a 16-year-old, Cruz had shot up to 6-foot-4. He grew taller after signing, and by the time the 2016 Dominican Summer League season began, he was pushing 6-foot-6. Cruz spent time at shortstop but was mostly a third baseman in the DSL. Cruz is a good athlete for his size and has natural feel for hitting with a loose, handsy swing and good barrel control for a lanky, long-armed hitter. In batting practice, Cruz shows plus raw power with loft and leverage. In games, he mostly hits groundballs because he's still learning to sync up his swing with his new long levers. That should come with experience, with the power potential to hit 20-plus home runs. He's an average runner who might slow down, though getting stronger should help his coordination. He's too big for short, and while he has a plus arm and plays under control at third, he might end up too big for the infield. If he moves to the outfield, his tools would fit right in. Cruz will make his U.S. debut at one of the Dodgers' Rookie-level affiliates in 2017.

Year	Club (League)	Class	AVG	G	AB	R	H	2B	3B	HR	RBI	BB	SO	SB	CS	OBP	SLG
2016	Dodgers (DSL)	R	.294	55	187	28	55	18	5	0	23	22	44	11	5	.367	.444
Minor League Totals			.294	55	187	28	55	18	5	0	23	22	44	11	5	.367	.444

28 MITCH HANSEN, OF

Born: May 1, 1996. **B-T:** L-L **Ht.:** 6-4. **Wt.:** 195. **Drafted:** HS—Plano, Texas, 2015
(2nd round). **Signed by:** Josh Herzenberg.

In high school, Hansen was a standout baseball player and football player as a quarterback and wide receiver. After he signed with the Dodgers as a second-round pick in 2015, he looked raw in his pro debut in the Rookie-level Arizona League, so the Dodgers held him back from full-season ball in 2016 and assigned him instead to the Rookie-level Pioneer League, where he had a solid season. Hansen has a loose lefty swing with good leverage. There is length that leads to strikeouts, though he cut his strikeout rate from 31 percent in 2015 to 21 percent last season. Hansen has a tall frame, good bat speed and average raw power. He runs well for his size with above-average speed once he's underway, though he might slow down as he fills out. He has played all three outfield spots but mostly the corners, with his below-average arm fitting best in left field. Hansen will get his first full-season test in low Class A Great Lakes in 2017.

Year	Club (League)	Class	AVG	G	AB	R	H	2B	3B	HR	RBI	BB	SO	SB	CS	OBP	SLG
2015	Dodgers (AZL)	R	.201	44	149	23	30	6	3	0	17	15	51	6	1	.281	.282
2016	Ogden (PIO)	R	.311	70	293	55	91	8	6	11	50	22	70	11	4	.356	.491
Minor League Totals			.274	114	442	78	121	14	9	11	67	37	121	17	5	.331	.421

29 CODY THOMAS, OF

Born: Oct. 8, 1994. **B-T:** L-R. **Ht.:** 6-4. **Wt.:** 211. **Drafted:** Oklahoma, 2016 (13th round). **Signed by:** Josh Herzenberg.

Thomas spent more time playing football than baseball at Oklahoma, where he was a backup quarterback who played just one season of baseball. The Dodgers took a chance on him in the 13th round of the 2016 draft, signing him for an above-slot $297,500. They sent him to the Rookie-level Pioneer League, where he immediately hit for power (his 16 home runs ranked second in the league) but showed the expected lack of polish for a player who hasn't focused much on baseball. While Thomas is raw for his age, the athleticism, physicality and tool set are all intriguing. He's strong with plus raw power that showed up in games with some help from the hitter-friendly Pioneer League. His pure hitting ability lags behind his power, with length and stiffness to his stroke and trouble recognizing spin, which led to a 33 percent strikeout rate. Thomas' speed and arm strength are both average. He rotated among all three outfield spots in 2016 and is best suited for one of the corners. Despite being a college draft pick, Thomas is unlikely to move quickly given his background. He should start 2017 in the low Class A Midwest League.

Year	Club (League)	Class	AVG	G	AB	R	H	2B	3B	HR	RBI	BB	SO	SB	CS	OBP	SLG
2016	Dodgers (AZL)	R	.500	7	22	10	11	1	1	3	6	3	3	1	0	.571	1.045
	Ogden (PIO)	R	.276	52	210	41	58	9	3	16	44	18	84	9	3	.360	.576
Minor League Totals			.297	59	232	51	69	10	4	19	50	21	87	10	3	.382	.621

30 JACOB SCAVUZZO, OF

Born: Jan. 15, 1994. **B-T:** R-R. **Ht.:** 6-4. **Wt.:** 210. **Drafted:** HS—Villa Park, Calif., 2012 (21st round). **Signed by:** Jeffrey Lachman.

Scavuzzo's combination of athleticism and physicality drew the Dodgers to draft him out of high school in 2012, taking the chance that his raw hitting approach would come around. He appeared to progress in 2015 once he got promoted to high Class A Rancho Cucamonga and performed well after the season in the Arizona Fall League, but his offensive output leveled off in 2016 when he got to Double-A Tulsa. Scavuzzo has quick hands, strong wrists and generates above-average raw power, which is now his best tool. He has overhauled his hitting mechanics, loading his swing with a big leg lift and staying compact for a big man. He isn't a free-swinger, but he's also not a pure hitter, with his pitch recognition and plate discipline holding him back from fully tapping into his power. Scavuzzo's speed and arm strength are both fringe-average, so he's limited to left field. He should head to Triple-A Oklahoma City in 2017.

Year	Club (League)	Class	AVG	G	AB	R	H	2B	3B	HR	RBI	BB	SO	SB	CS	OBP	SLG
2014	Great Lakes (MWL)	LoA	.209	108	402	46	84	18	4	5	35	32	126	17	4	.277	.311
	Ogden (PIO)	R	.289	14	45	6	13	6	0	1	5	3	10	2	0	.333	.489
2015	Great Lakes (MWL)	LoA	.263	58	213	30	56	14	3	5	20	7	44	4	1	.292	.427
	R. Cucamonga (CAL)	HiA	.308	61	227	47	70	18	1	13	49	21	54	3	4	.376	.568
2016	Tulsa (TL)	AA	.266	112	421	59	112	21	2	10	39	28	100	4	2	.318	.397
Minor League Totals			.262	440	1634	248	428	98	14	49	195	113	408	40	18	.316	.429

Miami Marlins

BY VINCE LARA-CINISOMO

Jose Fernandez's death overshadowed the Marlins' season and clouded their future

The Marlins' season of promise and progress came to an abrupt end in the early morning of Sunday, Sept. 25.

The awful news that morning—that ace righthander Jose Fernandez and two friends were killed in a boating accident off Miami Beach—rocked all of baseball. It cast a pall over a season in which the Marlins remained in the wild-card chase until August and clouded the future of the franchise.

Fernandez was in the midst of a terrific season after Tommy John surgery cost him parts of 2014 and 2015. In 29 starts, he went 16-8, 2.86 with 253 strikeouts and led the majors with 12.5 whiffs per nine innings. He was proud of a revamped changeup and struck out 12 Nationals hitters in what ended up being his final start on Sept. 20.

The Marlins were building around Fernandez and $325 million slugging right fielder Giancarlo Stanton.

Where they go next is unknown.

"When you talk about a tragedy like this, there are no words," team president David Samson told reporters that day. "There is no playbook."

Before a late-season swoon—and the tragedy—the Marlins had compiled winning records in April, May, June and July and were 47-41 at the all-star break. As expected, the team's outfield led the way. Stanton, despite a groin strain, hit 27 homers, but he was the third-most productive member of the crew. Center fielder Marcell Ozuna (23 homers, .778 OPS) bounced back and left fielder Christian Yelich broke out with a career-best 21 homers and .298/.376/.483 season.

There were also encouraging signs from young players, such as lefthander Adam Conley, 26, now the club's best homegrown arm. Rookie righthanders Kyle Barraclough, Nick Wittgren and Brian Ellington buoyed a powerful bullpen that ranked in the top half of the National League in strikeout rate.

The optimism did not trickle down to the farm system. The organization ranked 26th in baseball in domestic winning percentage at .454. That, however, was an improvement over 2015, when Miami ranked last at .427, which was part of the reason the Marlins fired farm director Marty Scott and replaced him with former organization stalwart Marc DelPiano, who served in that role in 2003-04.

Big righthander Tyler Kolek, the No. 2 overall pick in 2014, needed Tommy John surgery after an uneven full-season debut in 2015, but he's expected to be healthy for spring training. First baseman Josh Naylor, the No. 12 overall pick

TOP PROSPECTS OF THE DECADE

Year	Player, Pos.	2016 Org
2006	Jeremy Hermida, of	Did not play
2007	Chris Volstad, rhp	White Sox
2008	Cameron Maybin, of	Tigers
2009	Cameron Maybin, of	Tigers
2010	Giancarlo Stanton, of	Marlins
2011	Matt Dominguez, 3b	Blue Jays
2012	Christian Yelich, of	Marlins
2013	Jose Fernandez, rhp	Deceased
2014	Andrew Heaney, lhp	Angels
2015	Tyler Kolek, rhp	Marlins
2016	Braxton Garrett, lhp	Marlins

in 2015, was suspended after a knife incident in which he injured teammate Stone Garrett, then was traded to the Padres in a deal that netted righthander Andrew Cashner, a pending free agent, and wild 6-foot-8 reliever Tayron Guerrero.

Miami's wild-card chase also prompted the club to trade for Padres closer Fernando Rodney, which cost them their No. 5 prospect at midseason, righthander Chris Paddack. The deals thinned an already shallow farm system, but the 2016 draft provides some promise, led by prep lefthander Braxton Garrett, the seventh overall pick, who finally got on a mound during instructional league.

But the Marlins face large obstacles in trying to contend in 2017, most notably the loss of their ace—and franchise face.

ORGANIZATION OVERVIEW

General Manager: Michael Hill. **Farm Director:** Marc DelPiano. **Scouting Director:** Stan Meek.

Class	Team	League	W	L	PCT	Finish	Manager
Majors	Miami Marlins	National	79	82	.491	7th (15)	Don Mattingly
Triple-A	New Orleans Zephyrs	Pacific Coast	69	70	.496	9th (16)	Arnie Beyeler
Double-A	Jacksonville Suns	Southern	63	76	.453	8th (10)	Dave Berg
High Class A	Jupiter Hammerheads	Florida State	68	69	.496	8th (12)	Randy Ready
Low Class A	Greensboro Grasshoppers	South Atlantic	65	75	.464	12th (14)	Kevin Randel
Short-season	Batavia Muckdogs	New York-Penn	22	53	.293	14th (14)	Angel Espada
Rookie	GCL Marlins	Gulf Coast	24	31	.436	12th (17)	Julio Bruno
Overall 2016 Minor League Record			311	374	.454	26th (30)	

THIS YEAR'S TOP 30

No.	Player, Pos.	Grade/Risk
1.	Braxton Garrett, lhp	60/Extreme
2.	Luis Castillo, rhp	50/High
3.	Tyler Kolek, rhp	55/Extreme
4.	Brian Anderson, 3b	50/High
5.	Dillon Peters, lhp	50/High
6.	Jarlin Garcia, lhp	50/High
7.	Edward Cabrera, rhp	50/Extreme
8.	Austin Dean, of	45/High
9.	Stone Garrett, of	50/Extreme
10.	Thomas Jones, of	50/Extreme
11.	Isael Soto, of	50/Extreme
12.	Jake Esch, rhp	40/Medium
13.	Austin Brice, rhp	40/Medium
14.	Cody Poteet, rhp	45/High
15.	Jordan Holloway, rhp	45/Extreme
16.	Tayron Guerrero, rhp	45/Extreme
17.	Albert Guaimaro, of	45/Extreme
18.	James Nelson, 3b	45/Extreme
19.	Jeff Brigham, rhp	40/High
20.	Roy Morales, c	40/High
21.	J.T. Riddle, ss	40/High
22.	Isaiah White, of	45/Extreme
23.	Sam Perez, rhp	40/High
24.	Drew Steckenrider, rhp	40/High
25.	Brett Lilek, lhp	45/Extreme
26.	Remey Reed, rhp	40/High
27.	Andy Beltre, rhp	45/Extreme
28.	Justin Twine, 2b	45/Extreme
29.	John Norwood, of	40/High
30.	Yefri Perez, of	40/High

LAST YEAR'S TOP 30

No.	Player, Pos.	Status
1.	Tyler Kolek, rhp	No. 3
2.	Josh Naylor, 1b	(Padres)
3.	Jarlin Garcia, lhp	No. 6
4.	Stone Garrett, of	No. 9
5.	Kendry Flores, rhp	(Cardinals)
6.	Brian Anderson, 3b	No. 4
7.	Austin Dean, of	No. 8
8.	Isaiah White, of	No. 22
9.	Isael Soto, of	No. 11
10.	Jordan Holloway, rhp	No. 15
11.	Anfernee Seymour, ss	(Braves)
12.	Kyle Barraclough, rhp	Majors
13.	Jake Esch, rhp	No. 12
14.	Austin Brice, rhp	No. 13
15.	K.J. Woods, of	(White Sox)
16.	Garvis Lara, ss	Dropped out
17.	Chris Paddack, rhp	(Padres)
18.	Tomas Telis, c	Dropped out
19.	Cody Poteet, rhp	No. 14
20.	Brett Lilek, lhp	No. 25
21.	Justin Jacome, lhp	Dropped out
22.	J.T. Riddle, ss	No. 21
23.	Avery Romero, 2b	Dropped out
24.	Michael Mader, lhp	(Braves)
25.	Brian Ellington, rhp	Majors
26.	Nick Wittgren, rhp	Majors
27.	Xavier Scruggs, 1b/of	Free agent
28.	Jhonny Santos, of	Dropped out
29.	Justin Twine, ss	No. 28
30.	Jose Adames, rhp	Dropped out

BEST TOOLS

Best Hitter for Average	Brian Anderson
Best Power Hitter	Isael Soto
Best Strike-Zone Discipline	Brian Anderson
Fastest Baserunner	Yefri Perez
Best Athlete	Thomas Jones
Best Fastball	Luis Castillo
Best Curveball	Braxton Garrett
Best Slider	Edward Cabrera
Best Changeup	Jarlin Garcia
Best Control	Dillon Peters
Best Defensive Catcher	Roy Morales
Best Defensive Infielder	Brian Anderson
Best Infield Arm	Brian Anderson
Best Defensive Outfielder	Aaron Knapp
Best Outfield Arm	Isael Soto

PROJECTED 2020 LINEUP

Catcher	J.T. Realmuto
First Base	Justin Bour
Second Base	Dee Gordon
Third Base	Brian Anderson
Shortstop	Adeiny Hechavarria
Left Field	Christian Yelich
Center Field	Marcell Ozuna
Right Field	Giancarlo Stanton
No. 1 Starter	Braxton Garrett
No. 2 Starter	Luis Castillo
No. 3 Starter	Adam Conley
No. 4 Starter	Tom Koehler
No. 5 Starter	Justin Nicolino
Closer	Kyle Barraclough

MINOR LEAGUE DEPTH CHART

MIAMI MARLINS

TOP 2017 ROOKIE: Austin Brice, rhp. Moved to the bullpen midway through 2016, he started mixing a four-seamer and a power slider.
BREAKOUT PROSPECT: Remey Reed, rhp. The 2016 sixth-rounder from Oklahoma State has been up to 97 mph and pairs it with a slider.
SLEEPER: J.J. Gould, 3b. A 24th-round pick from Jacksonville, he has good bat control and sneaky pop and plays second base, shortstop and third base.

SOURCE OF TOP 30 TALENT			
Homegrown	26	Acquired	4
College	9	Trades	4
Junior college	1	Rule 5 draft	0
High school	11	Independent leagues	0
Nondrafted free agents	1	Free agents/waivers	0
International	4		

LF
Austin Dean (8)
Thomas Jones (10)
Destin Hood
Zach Sullivan
Dalton Wheat

CF
Stone Garrett (9)
Isaiah White (22)
John Norwood (29)
Yefri Perez (30)
Aaron Knapp
Corey Bird
Casey Soltis

RF
Isael Soto (11)
Albert Guaimaro (17)
Sean Reynolds

3B
Brian Anderson (4)
James Nelson (18)
Brian Schales

SS
J.T. Riddle (21)
Sam Castro)
Austin Nola
Justin Bohn
Garvis Lara
J.J. Gould
Luis Pintor

2B
Justin Twine (28)
Avery Romero
Mike Garzillo

1B
Eric Gutierrez
Colby Lusignan

C
Roy Morales (20)
Tomas Telis
Cam Maron
Justin Cohen
Jarett Rindfleisch
Blake Anderson

LHP

RHSP	RHRP
Luis Castillo (2)	Austin Brice (13)
Tyler Kolek (3)	Tayron Guerrero (16)
Edward Cabrera (7)	Sam Perez (23)
Jake Esch (12)	Drew Steckenrider (24)
Cody Poteet (14)	Andy Beltre (27)
Jordan Holloway (15)	Remey Reed (30)
Jeff Brigham (17)	Juancito Martinez
Reilly Hovis	Steven Farnworth
Jorgan Cavanerio	Chuck Weaver
R.J. Peace	Parker Bugg
	Humberto Mejia

RHP

LHSP	LHRP
Braxton Garrett (1)	Raudel Lazo
Dillon Peters (5)	Ben Holmes
Jarlin Garcia (6)	Jose Quijada
Brett Lilek (25)	Chris Sadberry
Justin Jacome	Matt Tomshaw
Gabe Castellanos	Dylan Lee
Matt Tracy	

DRAFT ANALYSIS

2016

BEST PURE HITTER: OF Thomas Jones (3) got off to a slow start after a long layoff between his high school season and signing, but he has a loose swing and showed very promising pitch recognition skills and a sound approach in fall instructional league. 3B James Nelson (15) also impressed the Marlins with his simple swing and ability to square balls up.

BEST POWER: Jones has plus raw power, with a quick bat and a wide-shouldered frame that gives him the leverage and torque to drive the ball. 1B Colby Lusignan (28) has elite raw power and can send a fastball a mile, though he strikes out at a high rate and may have more difficulty getting to his power than Jones.

FASTEST RUNNER: OF Andrew Knapp (8) and OF Corey Bird (7) can both impact the game with their speed, both grading as at least 70 runners. They know how to use their speed, showing the ability to bunt for hits, steal bases, and close gaps in the outfield. Jones is also a plus runner.

BEST DEFENSIVE PLAYER: The Marlins like the defensive upside of Knapp, Bird and Jones, but one standout from their class was C David Gauntt (18), who shows plus arm strength and sound receiving ability behind the plate.

BEST FASTBALL: Garrett doesn't hit the upper 90s, but his fastball plays very well and has reached as high as 94. RHP Chad Smith (11) can reach 96. RHP Mike King (12) showed improved velocity in pro ball, reaching 95 at his best. RHP Remey Reed (7) can touch 95.

BEST SECONDARY PITCH: The Marlins see Garrett's curveball as a plus-plus offering. He can command the pitch and it shows hard, late 1-to-7 snapping action and powerful low 80s velocity. RHP Michael Mertz (14) has a strong slider.

BEST PRO DEBUT: No player came out and dominated at an age-appropriate level, but Nelson held his own as an 18-year-old in the Gulf Coast League, batting .284 and drawing praise for his defense and athleticism.

BEST ATHLETE: Jones has speed, arm strength and looseness to his actions, in addition to a sculpted body. He was a significant football recruit, and had been recruited to play wide receiver by Notre Dame and South Carolina. LHP Braxton Garrett (1) is incredibly athletic on the mound, with looseness, balance and flexibility.

MOST INTRIGUING BACKGROUND: Nelson is the younger brother of 2004 first-round pick Chris Nelson, who has played in parts of five major league seasons. Knapp is the brother of Phillies prospect Andrew Knapp.

CLOSEST TO THE MAJORS: Garrett's poise, pitchability and robust three-pitch mix could allow him to move quickly. He is not the standard prep pitching prospect who has a long way to go, and the Marlins have promoted prospects of his caliber and polish aggressively in the past.

BEST LATE ROUND PICK: Nelson's athleticism and chance to hit make him a very nice value in the 15th round.

THE ONE WHO GOT AWAY: The Marlins tried to sign RHP Nick Eichholtz (13), but they ended up using up their pool money to sign Garrett just before the deadline. Eichholtz's fastball/curveball combo will have him scouted again as a senior at Alabama.

2015

1B Josh Naylor (1) knifed a teammate, then was traded to the Padres; so was emerging RHP Chris Paddack (8). RHP Cody Poteet (4) leads the rest of a modest pack that includes raw OF Isaiah White (3) and LHP Brett Lilek (2).

GRADE: D

2014

Drafting RHP Tyler Kolek (1) ahead of Miami-born Carlos Rodon hasn't worked out; Kolek missed 2016 after Tommy John surgery. Most of the rest of this class has disappointed or been traded. 3B Brian Anderson (3) and LHP Dillon Peters (10) stand out otherwise.

GRADE: D

2013

The Marlins have traded, released or failed to sign every pick in the first six rounds of this class. INF J.T. Riddle (13) is the best remaining prospect in the class.

GRADE: F

TOP DRAFT PICKS OF THE DECADE

Year	Player, Pos.	2016 Org
2007	Matt Dominguez, 3b	Blue Jays
2008	Kyle Skipworth, c	Reds
2009	Chad James, lhp	Did not play
2010	Christian Yelich, of	Marlins
2011	Jose Fernandez, rhp	Deceased
2012	Andrew Heaney, lhp	Angels
2013	Colin Moran, 3b	Astros
2014	Tyler Kolek, rhp	Marlins
2015	Josh Naylor, 1b	Padres
2016	Braxton Garrett, lhp	Marlins

LARGEST BONUSES IN CLUB HISTORY

Tyler Kolek, 2014	$6,000,000
Braxton Garrett, 2016	$4,145,900
Josh Beckett, 1999	$3,625,000
Colin Moran, 2013	$3,516,500
Adrian Gonzalez, 2000	$3,000,000

1 BRAXTON GARRETT, LHP

Born: Aug. 5, 1997. **B-T:** L-L. **Ht.:** 6-3. **Wt.:** 190.
Drafted: HS—Florence, Ala., 2016 (1st round).
Signed by: Mark Willoughby.

For the second time in three years, the Marlins drafted a high school pitcher with their first-round pick. But unlike burly righthanded Texan Tyler Kolek—the No. 2 overall pick in 2014—the Alabama prep lefthander does not light up radar guns. His fastball sits in the low 90s compared with the high 90s where Kolek resides. Garrett has big-game experience, having helped USA Baseball's 18U team win the gold medal at the 2015 World Cup—which he called his favorite baseball experience—and then throwing a four-hit shutout at USA Baseball's National High School Invitational in March 2016. At No. 7 overall, Garrett was the highest-drafted Alabama prep player since shortstop Condredge Holloway of Lee High in Huntsville went fourth overall to the Expos in 1971 He was the highest-drafted Alabama prep pitcher since righty Rick James, drafted sixth overall in the first draft in 1965. Garrett, a Vanderbilt commit with a 3.8 grade-point average, was considered a tough sign and cost the Marlins $4,145,900, well above the $3,756,300 slot value.

Garrett's pitch best is his 11-to-5 curveball, which has earned future plus grades for its tight spin and break. He also commands the pitch well by throwing it for strikes and as a chase pitch. He had just 15 walks in 65.1 innings with a 0.53 ERA and 131 strikeouts as a senior at Florence (Ala.) High, which earned him Gatorade player-of-the-year honors for the state of Alabama. Garrett's father Steve, who coached him in high school, taught him his curveball at age 13. Scouts said his curve was one of the best in the 2016 draft—just behind New Jersey prep lefthander Jason Groome, a Red Sox first-round pick—and rated him as having the best control of any pitcher in the class. Garrett's fastball sits 91-93 mph with late life. At 6-foot-3, he has the frame to add good weight, which could enable him to add velocity. He has worked the most on improving the arm speed on his changeup, and it shows some fade. He has a balanced, easy delivery that he repeats extremely well, allowing him to fill the zone with quality strikes. Garrett has worked with Marlins coaches on developing a between-starts routine for the more demanding pro throwing schedule.

Garrett did not sign until the signing deadline on July 15. His late signing, combined with the Marlins' cautious approach, prevented the 19-year-old from taking a mound as a pro until instructional league, when he had three abbreviated outings. The Marlins say Garrett was not injured. Rather they were being cautious after his spring workload. He did travel with the Rookie-level Gulf Coast League team. Evaluators believe Garrett could have three above-average pitches to go with at above-average command. Given his pitchability and age (he was old for the draft class), the Marlins could skip Garrett to full-season ball in 2017.

BA GRADE

60 Risk: Extreme

SCOUTING GRADES

Fastball: 55.
Curveball: 60.
Changeup: 55
Control: 55

Based on 20-80 scouting scale and future projection rather than present tools.

TOM DIPACE

Year	Club (League)	Class	W	L	ERA	G	GS	CG	SV	IP	H	HR	BB	SO	K/9	WHIP	AVG
2016	Did not play																

2 LUIS CASTILLO, RHP

Born: Dec. 12, 1992. **B-T:** R-R. **Ht.:** 6-2. **Wt.:** 170. **Signed:** Dominican Republic, 2011. **Signed by:** Felix Peguero (Giants).

The Giants kept Castillo in the Dominican Summer League for two years before jumping him to low Class A Augusta in 2014. The Marlins, who also have an affiliate in the South Atlantic League, acquired him (and righty Kendry Flores) in a December 2014 trade for veteran Casey McGehee. The Marlins traded Castillo in the Andrew Cashner-headlined deal with the Padres in July 2016, only to have Castillo returned because Colin Rea reported to Miami with a bad elbow and later had Tommy John surgery. Castillo first joined the rotation in July 2015 but maintains elite fastball velocity thanks to outstanding arm strength. He hit 101 mph in 2016 and sat consistently at 96-97. He has easy velocity, with a smooth delivery that helps his fastball jump on hitters, though it can be straight at times. Castillo throws from a three-quarters arm angle, which helps give his slider depth and some curveball-like action. It projects as an above-average pitch. Castillo has feel for a power changeup, but he's still finding the right grip. It has potential to be an average pitch as well. He has shown great makeup and the ability to overcome in-game adversity. With an overpowering fastball and the potential for two at-least-average secondary pitches, Castillo has moved from bullpen arm to potential mid-rotation starter. He should begin 2017 at Double-A Jacksonville.

BA GRADE
50 Risk: High

Year	Club (League)	Class	W	L	ERA	G	GS	CG	SV	IP	H	HR	BB	SO	K/9	WHIP	AVG
2014	Augusta (SAL)	LoA	2	2	3.07	48	0	0	10	59	56	6	25	66	10.1	1.38	.247
2015	Greensboro (SAL)	LoA	4	3	2.98	25	7	0	4	63	59	1	19	63	9.0	1.23	.246
	Jupiter (FSL)	HiA	2	3	3.50	10	9	0	0	44	44	3	14	31	6.4	1.33	.263
2016	Jupiter (FSL)	HiA	8	4	2.07	23	21	1	0	118	95	2	18	91	7.0	0.96	.219
	Jacksonville (SL)	AA	0	2	3.86	3	3	0	0	14	12	1	7	12	7.7	1.36	.218
Minor League Totals			17	18	2.68	155	40	1	36	380	328	14	108	344	8.1	1.15	.231

3 TYLER KOLEK, RHP

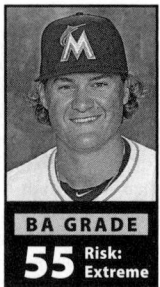

Born: Dec. 15, 1995. **B-T:** R-R. **Ht.:** 6-5. **Wt.:** 260. **Drafted:** HS—Shepherd, Texas, 2014 (1st round). **Signed by:** Ryan Wardinsky.

The No. 2 overall pick in 2014, Kolek signed for a franchise-record $6 million but hasn't shown the Marlins the 100 mph velocity he had in high school. After struggling through a 2015 season in which his stuff backed up at low Class A Greensboro, Kolek missed the 2016 season following Tommy John surgery in April. At 6-foot-5 and 260 pounds, Kolek counts size and physicality among his biggest strengths. He has a bulky torso and lower half with great arm strength and surprising quickness when he's healthy. He powers the ball to the plate with a long stride and can drive his fastball down in the zone with heavy sink. Despite his 2015 struggles, Kolek has allowed just seven homers in 130.2 pro innings, evidence his pitches are difficult to hit squarely. However, his slider and changeup played as well below-average, making it easy for batters to wait on his fastball, and his command also was below-average. Prior to his injury, Kolek struggled to have a consistent direct path to the plate and tended to get side-to-side with a crossfire delivery. Despite his draft pedigree, he competes and has the makeup of a grinder. The Marlins plan to rebuild Kolek's delivery and attempt to sharpen his offspeed pitches in spring training. His performance there will determine where and when he opens 2017, but he's unlikely to be ready by Opening Day.

BA GRADE
55 Risk: Extreme

Year	Club (League)	Class	W	L	ERA	G	GS	CG	SV	IP	H	HR	BB	SO	K/9	WHIP	AVG
2014	Marlins (GCL)	R	0	3	4.50	9	8	0	0	22	22	0	13	18	7.4	1.59	.275
2015	Greensboro (SAL)	LoA	4	10	4.56	25	25	0	0	109	108	7	61	81	6.7	1.56	.258
2016	Did not play—Injured																
Minor League Totals			4	13	4.55	34	33	0	0	131	130	7	74	99	6.8	1.56	.261

4 BRIAN ANDERSON, 3B

Born: May 19, 1993. **B-T:** R-R Ht: 6-3. **Wt.:** 185. **Drafted:** Arkansas, 2014 (3rd round).
Signed by: Brian Kraft.

Anderson's prep roots in Oklahoma helped get him on the Marlins' radar. Scouting director Stan Meek is a former OU pitcher and assistant coach and long-time Norman resident. Miami made him a 2014 third-round pick out of Arkansas because they admired his versatility and strong, righthanded bat. Anderson began 2016 at high Class A Jupiter but hit his way to Double-A Jacksonville, then led the Arizona Fall League with five home runs. Anderson identifies pitches early and is selective, and his feel for hitting helps his above-average raw power play more and more as he gains experience. Scouts believe he could hit 15-20 homers or more at his peak. At 6-foot-3, 185 pounds, Anderson has projection left in his wiry, athletic frame. At third base, he has above-average defensive tools with good footwork and range and a plus throwing arm capable of easily making throws from deep third. While he slumped defensively with a career-worst 27 errors in 2016, one evaluator called him the best defensive player in the organization. Anderson added time at first base in the AFL, played some second base in 2014 and played outfield in college at Arkansas. He has a floor as a utility player with power, in the Ryan Raburn mold, but the Marlins see him as a future regular at third. He probably will return to Jacksonville to start 2017 with an eye on Triple-A New Orleans by midseason.

BA GRADE
50 Risk: High

Year	Club (League)	Class	AVG	G	AB	R	H	2B	3B	HR	RBI	BB	SO	SB	CS	OBP	SLG
2014	Batavia (NYP)	SS	.273	20	77	11	21	3	1	3	12	6	11	1	1	.333	.455
	Greensboro (SAL)	LoA	.314	39	153	27	48	7	0	8	37	13	28	0	0	.378	.516
2015	Jupiter (FSL)	HiA	.235	132	477	50	112	22	2	8	62	40	109	2	2	.304	.340
2016	Jupiter (FSL)	HiA	.302	49	182	27	55	12	2	3	25	22	38	3	0	.377	.440
	Jacksonville (SL)	AA	.243	86	301	38	73	9	1	8	40	36	59	0	0	.330	.359
Minor League Totals			.260	326	1190	153	309	53	6	30	176	117	245	6	3	.334	.390

5 DILLON PETERS, LHP

Born: Aug. 31, 1992. **B-T:** L-L. **Ht.:** 5-9. **Wt.:** 195. **Drafted:** Texas, 2014 (10th round).
Signed by: Ryan Wardinsky.

The "p" in the Peters family stands for pitching. His grandfather pitched semipro ball, and his father Mark pitched in college and coached Dillon in travel ball. A prep star in Indianapolis, Peters turned down big offers out of high school (the Indians drafted him in the 20th round in 2011) to go to Texas. He thrived there (17-7, 2.26) until hurting his elbow in May 2014. The Marlins drafted him that year knowing he needed Tommy John surgery and signed him for $175,000. He finished 2016 at Double-A Jacksonville. After touching 96 mph in high school, Peters' velocity stepped back in college to the 88-92 range. But following surgery, recovery and rehabilitation, his velocity ticked back up in 2016 to where he was touching 96 mph and sitting 93-94 with sink. More impressively, the smallish lefty maintained his velocity late into games with the above-average command he had as an amateur. His curveball has tight spin and is at least an average pitch and flashes above-average. His changeup is solid-average as well. In addition, Peters has a bulldog mentality that helps his stuff play up. Even at 5-foot-9, Peters has big league stuff and command, and he has positioned himself to help in Miami as soon as 2017. He should return to Jacksonville to begin 2017, but with his poise and makeup, could jump right to the majors if the need arises. He projects as a No. 4 starter.

BA GRADE
50 Risk: High

Year	Club (League)	Class	W	L	ERA	G	GS	CG	SV	IP	H	HR	BB	SO	K/9	WHIP	AVG
2014	Did not play—Injured																
2015	Marlins (GCL)	R	1	1	0.68	4	4	0	0	13	10	0	3	13	8.8	0.98	.217
	Batavia (NYP)	SS	0	3	4.83	7	7	0	0	32	40	2	10	27	7.7	1.58	.299
2016	Jupiter (FSL)	HiA	11	6	2.46	20	20	0	0	106	102	2	16	89	7.6	1.11	.253
	Jacksonville (SL)	AA	3	0	1.99	4	4	0	0	23	17	2	4	16	6.4	0.93	.205
Minor League Totals			15	10	2.69	35	35	0	0	174	169	6	33	145	7.5	1.16	.254

6 JARLIN GARCIA, LHP

Born: Jan. 18, 1993. **B-T:** L-L. **Ht.:** 6-3. **Wt.:** 215. **Signed:** Dominican Republic, 2010. **Signed by:** Albert Gonzalez/Sandy Nin.

Garcia grew up playing soccer and didn't play baseball until he was 15, when his friends and a coach in the Dominican Republic convinced him to try the game. He was just 5-foot-7 at the time but grew seven inches before signing with the Marlins. It took Garcia three seasons to reach full-season ball, and he missed more than two months in 2016 with a triceps strain. He returned to the field as a reliever, which he also filled in the Arizona Fall League and in winter ball in the Dominican. Garcia has some of the best pure stuff in the system, with a fastball that touches 96 mph, a curveball that can be a strikeout pitch and a slider and changeup, both of which grade presently as fringe-average offerings. The lithe lefthander is athletic, with a clean delivery that helps give him above-average control. He has averaged just 2.2 walks per nine innings as a pro. Because he doesn't have a consistent swing-and-miss secondary pitch, he will have to improve his fastball command or sharpen his curveball to remain a starter. Garcia received a brief callup to the majors in July 2016—he was not used in his four-day stay—but he could see Marlins Park again in 2017 if he stays healthy. He has a No. 4 starter ceiling but may wind up in the bullpen.

BA GRADE
50 Risk: High

Year	Club (League)	Class	W	L	ERA	G	GS	CG	SV	IP	H	HR	BB	SO	K/9	WHIP	AVG
2014	Greensboro (SAL)	LoA	10	5	4.38	25	25	0	0	134	152	13	21	111	7.5	1.29	.286
2015	Jupiter (FSL)	HiA	3	5	3.06	18	18	1	0	97	96	4	23	69	6.4	1.23	.257
	Jacksonville (SL)	AA	1	3	4.91	7	7	0	0	37	38	4	17	35	8.6	1.50	.273
2016	Jacksonville (SL)	AA	1	3	4.54	9	9	0	0	40	38	4	11	27	6.1	1.24	.253
	Marlins (GCL)	R	0	0	0.00	3	3	0	0	4	1	0	0	6	13.5	0.25	.077
	Jupiter (FSL)	HiA	0	0	1.29	5	0	0	0	7	4	1	1	5	6.4	0.71	.154
Minor League Totals			23	27	3.72	108	89	1	1	480	472	38	117	405	7.6	1.23	.256

7 EDWARD CABRERA, RHP

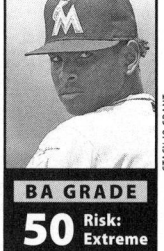

STACY JO GRANT

Born: April 13, 1998. **B-T:** R-R. **Ht.:** 6-4. **Wt.:** 175. **Signed:** Dominican Republic, 2015. **Signed by:** Albert Gonzalez/Sandy Nin/Domingo Ortega.

Cabrera was one of five players the Marlins signed for $100,000 in July 2015. He trained with Ramon Genao, who also trained the Marlins' most expensive signee of that class, outfielder Mario Prenza, who received $550,000. While Prenza reported to the Dominican Summer League and hit .136 in 2016, Cabrera followed an impressive showing at instructional league with a jump to the Rookie-level Gulf Coast League for his pro debut. Cabrera has a tall, projectable frame and has already seen his stuff tick up since he signed. He touched 94 mph in 2016 and sat 92-93 with his fastball, and he can cut and run it in to righthanded batters. Evaluators project he could add more velocity to his fastball as he fills out physically. His slider flashes plus with good tilt, and his firm changeup, while currently below-average, flashes promise. As with most teenagers, Cabrera has some mechanical adjustments to make. For instance, he doesn't get enough extension over his front leg. Cabrera was one of the most sought-after players in the Marlins system as the organization went shopping for pitching help at the 2016 trade deadline. He shows uncommon poise for his age, and one evaluator said his stuff compares favorably with former Marlins farmhand (and current Astros No. 1 prospect) Francis Martes at the same age. Cabrera projects as a midrotation starter and should make his full-season debut in 2017.

BA GRADE
50 Risk: Extreme

Year	Club (League)	Class	W	L	ERA	G	GS	CG	SV	IP	H	HR	BB	SO	K/9	WHIP	AVG
2016	Marlins (GCL)	R	2	6	4.21	11	7	0	0	47	54	1	10	28	5.4	1.36	.289
Minor League Totals			2	6	4.21	11	7	0	0	47	54	1	10	28	5.4	1.36	.289

8 AUSTIN DEAN, OF

Born: Oct. 14, 1993. **B-T:** R-R. **Ht.:** 6-1. **Wt.:** 190. **Drafted:** HS—Spring, Texas, 2012 (4th round). **Signed by:** Ryan Wardinsky.

Dean played first and second base at Klein Collins High, but the Marlins drafted him as an outfielder because of his slow footwork and because they believed his raw power would profile in left field. He turned down a chance to play at Texas with prep teammate C.J. Hinojosa (now with the Giants) when he signed for $367,200 as a 2012 fourth-round pick. Dean has a feel for the barrel, so the Marlins believed the raw power he shows in batting practice would play in games once he got out of the power-suppressing Florida State League. He hit a career-high 11 homers at Double-A Jacksonville in 2016 but appeared to sell out for the improved power production, striking out a career-worst 110 times. Pitchers got wise to Dean's approach, or lack thereof, in the second half, when he hit .212/.262/.320 with just three homers. He has average to a tick above-average speed but attempted just three steals in 2016 after swiping 18 of 28 in 2015. He's an average outfield defender with a below-average arm, limiting him to left field. Dean still has time to develop, but as a left fielder, he's going to have to get to his power more often. The Marlins have a young, talented big league outfield, so they didn't shield Dean from the Rule 5 draft. He will be ticketed for Triple-A New Orleans in 2017.

BA GRADE
45 Risk: High

Year	Club (League)	Class	AVG	G	AB	R	H	2B	3B	HR	RBI	BB	SO	SB	CS	OBP	SLG
2014	Greensboro (SAL)	LoA	.308	99	403	67	124	20	4	9	58	38	72	4	4	.371	.444
2015	Jupiter (FSL)	HiA	.268	136	519	67	139	32	2	5	52	39	76	18	10	.318	.366
2016	Jacksonville (SL)	AA	.238	130	480	60	114	23	5	11	67	48	110	1	2	.307	.375
Minor League Totals			.264	475	1783	241	471	99	18	30	214	170	345	25	20	.330	.390

9 STONE GARRETT, OF

Born: Nov. 22, 1995. **B-T:** R-R. **Ht.:** 6-2. **Wt.:** 195. **Drafted:** HS—Richmond, Texas, 2014 (8th round). **Signed by:** Ryan Wardinsky.

Garrett passed on a Rice commitment to sign with the Marlins in 2014 for $162,400. He missed more than two months in 2016 after injuring his hand in an incident with 2015 first-rounder Josh Naylor that involved a knife. The Marlins termed it a "prank gone bad," but Miami subsequently traded Naylor in July, while Garrett's agent, Larry Reynolds, told reporters the incident was not just horseplay gone awry. Garrett needed three stitches and sustained some nerve damage to his right thumb, which necessitated surgery. Garrett has above-average strength, speed and power potential, with a premium pro body, but his raw tools need a lot of refinement. It's difficult to gauge how much the rehab and injury factored into Garrett's struggles upon his return—he went 10-for-76 with 24 strikeouts. Well-regarded for his self-motivating makeup, he has a lot of work to do on his offensive approach. He needs to use his lower half in his swing better to tap into his raw power. He may wind up in left field rather than center, putting further pressure on his bat. Garrett went to instructional league before getting some extra reps in the Australian Baseball League. He's raw enough that he could repeat low Class A Greensboro in 2017.

BA GRADE
50 Risk: Extreme

Year	Club (League)	Class	AVG	G	AB	R	H	2B	3B	HR	RBI	BB	SO	SB	CS	OBP	SLG
2014	Marlins (GCL)	R	.236	40	148	17	35	3	1	0	11	7	31	4	1	.269	.270
2015	Batavia (NYP)	SS	.297	58	222	36	66	18	6	11	46	19	60	8	5	.352	.581
2016	Marlins (GCL)	R	.143	3	7	1	1	0	0	0	0	2	3	1	0	.333	.143
	Greensboro (SAL)	LoA	.213	52	197	21	42	9	2	6	16	11	71	1	2	.265	.371
Minor League Totals			.251	153	574	75	144	30	9	17	73	39	165	14	8	.302	.423

10 THOMAS JONES, OF

Born: Dec. 9, 1997. **B-T:** R-R. **Ht.:** 6-4. **Wt.:** 195. **Drafted:** HS—Laurens, S.C., 2016 (2nd round). **Signed by:** Blake Newsome.

A two-sport star in high school, Jones drew interest from high-profile college football programs such as Notre Dame, Clemson and South Carolina. Ultimately, he chose to pass on football, as well as his college baseball commitment to Vanderbilt, to sign with the Marlins as a 2016 second-round pick for $1 million. At 6-foot-4, 195 pounds, Jones is a physical specimen and the kind of "off-the-bus" guy scouts fall in love with. He has five-tool potential, but he's super raw. Some evaluators see natural talent and athleticism to dream on. Others cite a lack of polish and lack of focus at times that make an already high-risk player even more risky. One evaluator

BA GRADE
50 Risk: Extreme

MIKE JANES

said Jones has plus bat speed but lacks bat control. Another said he looks bored in the outfield and lacks the defensive chops and arm to play anywhere but left field, though his below-average power would be stretched there. He is a plus runner. Jones is all about projection, not present ability. If he develops, he could make an impact in several aspects of the game, but the Marlins will need to take the long view. Jones will likely begin 2017 in extended spring training then head back to the Rookie-level Gulf Coast League.

Year	Club (League)	Class	AVG	G	AB	R	H	2B	3B	HR	RBI	BB	SO	SB	CS	OBP	SLG
2016	Marlins (GCL)	R	.234	19	64	11	15	3	1	0	6	11	20	6	2	.380	.313
Minor League Totals			.234	19	64	11	15	3	1	0	6	11	20	6	2	.380	.313

11 ISAEL SOTO, OF

BA GRADE
50 Risk: Extreme

Born: Nov. 2, 1996. **B-T:** L-L. **Ht.:** 6-0. **Wt.:** 190. **Signed:** Dominican Republic, 2013. **Signed by:** Albert Gonzalez/Sandy Nin/Domingo Ortega.

Soto's $310,000 bonus was the second-highest payout behind Jhonny Santos among Miami's 2013 international signings. The Marlins were comfortable enough with his makeup to jump him straight to the U.S. The stocky Soto has short arms that produce above-average bat speed and he consistently puts the barrel to fastballs. His full-season debut showed promise, especially against righthanders. But he struggled against lefthanders (.211/.280/.316), with one evaluator saying Soto did not make the adjustments to seeing more spin than he had previously. He has plus raw power to the gaps, more doubles power than over-the fence pop because of his line-drive bat path. Soto was a center fielder when he signed but has played primarily right field as a pro. He's an average defender in the corner with a slightly above-average arm. He's an average runner for now who could slow with age. One of the Marlins' better low-minors bats, Soto will reach high Class A Jupiter at some point in 2017.

Year	Club (League)	Class	AVG	G	AB	R	H	2B	3B	HR	RBI	BB	SO	SB	CS	OBP	SLG
2014	Marlins (GCL)	R	.251	50	183	26	46	9	1	7	23	10	47	1	2	.302	.426
2015	Greensboro (SAL)	LoA	.125	17	64	2	8	1	0	0	1	3	27	0	0	.164	.141
	Marlins (GCL)	R	.346	7	26	3	9	2	1	1	5	5	6	0	1	.438	.615
	Batavia (NYP)	SS	.095	5	21	1	2	0	0	0	0	1	10	0	0	.136	.095
2016	Greensboro (SAL)	LoA	.247	113	401	51	99	24	5	9	38	43	115	3	0	.320	.399
Minor League Totals			.236	192	695	83	164	36	7	17	67	62	205	4	3	.301	.381

12 JAKE ESCH, RHP

BA GRADE
45 Risk: High

Born: March 27, 1990. **B-T:** R-R. **Ht.:** 6-4. **Wt.:** 190. **Drafted:** Georgia Tech, 2011 (11th round). **Signed by:** Carmen Carcone

A prep shortstop in Minnesota, Esch was mostly a middle infielder at Georgia Tech, but scouts believed his pro future would be on the mound even though he pitched just five innings as a junior. The Marlins liked his arm strength and grabbed him in the 11th round. Esch finally got to Double-A in 2015 and took a big step forward, executing his pitches down in the zone and showing improvements across the board. The Marlins put him on the 40-man roster last December, paving his way to make his big league debut in 2016. As expected of a former position player, Esch is athletic, with a smooth arm action and clean delivery. He has a two-seam and four-seam fastball at 90-94 mph, a slider that ranges 82-86 that flashes average to tick above and a changeup with fade that can be too firm at times. The 26-year-old Esch profiles as a back-end starter, and with the untimely death of Jose Fernandez, is likely to push for a big league job in 2017.

Year	Club (League)	Class	W	L	ERA	G	GS	CG	SV	IP	H	HR	BB	SO	K/9	WHIP	AVG
2014	Jupiter (FSL)	HiA	6	6	4.05	25	24	1	0	136	147	7	34	105	7.0	1.33	.276
2015	Jacksonville (SL)	AA	6	5	3.48	15	15	0	0	85	69	5	33	68	7.2	1.20	.223
	Marlins (GCL)	R	1	0	0.00	2	2	0	0	8	2	0	1	7	7.9	0.38	.074
	New Orleans (PCL)	AAA	1	3	5.40	6	6	0	0	30	41	3	9	20	6.0	1.67	.331
2016	Jacksonville (SL)	AA	10	9	4.03	22	22	0	0	118	117	8	37	82	6.2	1.30	.264
	New Orleans (PCL)	AAA	2	1	5.70	4	4	1	0	24	26	2	9	14	5.3	1.48	.299
	Miami (NL)	MAJ	0	1	5.54	3	3	0	0	13	17	4	6	10	6.9	1.77	.327
Major League Totals			0	1	5.54	3	3	0	0	13	17	4	6	10	6.9	1.77	.327
Minor League Totals			35	38	4.02	125	98	2	1	582	576	34	193	423	6.5	1.32	.261

13 AUSTIN BRICE, RHP

BA GRADE
40 Risk: Medium

Born: June 19, 1992. **B-T:** R-R. **Ht.:** 6-4. **Wt.:** 205. **Drafted:** HS—Pittsboro, N.C., 2010 (9th round). **Signed by:** Joel Matthews.

Brice passed on Appalachian State to sign for $205,000 in 2010, and this is his sixth appearance in the Marlins' Top 30. He's made upward progress the past four. It took six seasons for Brice to get onto the

40-man roster, and in the seventh year, he got to the majors. Brice always has had swing-and-miss stuff, but he started mixing a two-seam fastball at 90-94 mph for ground balls along with a power, downer slider that helps him dominate righthanded hitters (.203 average). He lacked a third pitch to keep lefthanders at bay, although he showed improvement from his career norms (.267 vs. .319 opponent average in 2015). A move to the bullpen midway through the season accelerated his development. His control improved, largely because he stopped nibbling as he did as a starter, while his strikeout rate remained in line with career norms. He's likely in 2017 to be a part of a young Marlins bullpen.

Year	Club (League)	Class	W	L	ERA	G	GS	CG	SV	IP	H	HR	BB	SO	K/9	WHIP	AVG
2014	Jupiter (FSL)	HiA	8	9	3.60	25	24	0	0	127	114	5	55	109	7.7	1.33	.241
2015	Jacksonville (SL)	AA	6	9	4.67	25	25	0	0	125	114	11	69	127	9.1	1.46	.245
2016	Jacksonville (SL)	AA	4	7	2.89	27	13	0	2	93	79	5	29	79	7.6	1.16	.231
	New Orleans (PCL)	AAA	0	0	1.04	5	0	0	2	9	3	1	1	10	10.4	0.46	.111
	Miami (NL)	MAJ	0	1	7.07	15	0	0	0	14	9	2	5	14	9.0	1.00	.173
Major League Totals			0	1	7.07	15	0	0	0	14	9	2	5	14	9.0	1.00	.173
Minor League Totals			40	43	4.14	150	113	0	7	634	563	48	344	621	8.8	1.43	.239

14 CODY POTEET, RHP

Born: July 30, 1994. **B-T:** R-R. **Ht.:** 6-1. **Wt.:** 190. **Drafted:** UCLA, 2015 (4th round). **Signed by:** Tim McDonnell.

BA GRADE
45 Risk: High

Poteet pitched in multiple roles for deep Bruins staffs that included 2015 first-rounder James Kaprelian, making 39 starts and 34 relief appearances in three seasons. The Marlins placed him in the rotation upon drafting him and signing him for a slot bonus of $488,700 in the fourth round in 2015. Poteet's velocity ticks up out of the bullpen to about 94 mph, but as a starter he sits 88-92 mph with his fastball with running action to the arm side. He generates a fair amount of ground balls thanks to the pitch's boring action. His slider flashes above-average with some tilt and his curveball shows average, although it can get loopy. His changeup needs more repetitions to become useful. Poteet profiles as a back-end starter and has been compared to Tom Koehler, albeit with less velocity, and Mike Leake. If he can't clean up his changeup, he could be a solid middle relief option who relies primarily on a fastball and slider.

Year	Club (League)	Class	W	L	ERA	G	GS	CG	SV	IP	H	HR	BB	SO	K/9	WHIP	AVG
2015	Batavia (NYP)	SS	0	1	2.13	5	4	0	0	13	9	1	2	12	8.5	0.87	.188
2016	Greensboro (SAL)	LoA	4	9	2.91	24	24	0	0	117	108	5	44	106	8.1	1.30	.246
Minor League Totals			4	10	2.84	29	28	0	0	130	117	6	46	118	8.2	1.25	.240

15 JORDAN HOLLOWAY, RHP

Born: June 13, 1996. **B-T:** R-R. **Ht.:** 6-5. **Wt.:** 210. **Drafted:** HS—Arvada, Colo., 2014 (20th round). **Signed by:** Scott Stanley.

BA GRADE
45 Risk: Extreme

As a junior in high school in Colorado, Holloway was 5-foot-9, 135 pounds. Now he stands 6-5, 210 pounds with perhaps the best pure stuff in the organization beside Luis Castillo. The projectable righthander has athletic lineage. His father pitched in college; his mother was a high school hurdler who now runs marathons; and his younger sister plays volleyball. But after a breakout 2015, Holloway struggled in 2016. In addition to minor triceps and biceps issues, Holloway battled his emotions, getting too amped up on the mound. His fastball velocity is plus—he touched 98 mph this season—and his curveball flashes plus. His changeup is a work in progress. Evaluators expect his current below-average command will improve as he gets used to his still-growing body and the subsequent impact on his mechanics. Holloway is raw but has plenty of ability, with athleticism and two potentially plus pitches. The Marlins say the injuries were not a long-term concern and he'll probably get another shot at start at low Class A in 2017.

Year	Club (League)	Class	W	L	ERA	G	GS	CG	SV	IP	H	HR	BB	SO	K/9	WHIP	AVG
2014	Marlins (GCL)	R	1	3	6.41	10	6	0	0	27	38	0	8	8	2.7	1.73	.352
2015	Greensboro (SAL)	LoA	0	1	7.00	2	2	0	0	9	8	0	6	4	4.0	1.56	.250
	Batavia (NYP)	SS	5	6	2.91	14	14	0	0	68	60	0	36	40	5.3	1.41	.234
2016	Greensboro (SAL)	LoA	2	4	6.16	8	8	0	0	31	31	8	15	24	7.0	1.50	.261
	Batavia (NYP)	SS	0	3	6.23	5	5	0	0	17	21	0	13	17	8.8	1.96	.280
Minor League Totals			8	17	4.81	39	35	0	0	152	158	8	78	93	5.5	1.56	.268

16 TAYRON GUERRERO, RHP

Born: Jan. 9, 1991. **B-T:** R-R. **Ht.:** 6-7. **Wt.:** 215. **Signed:** Colombia, 2009. **Signed by:** Robert Rowley/Felix Feliz/Marcial Del Valle (Padres).

A 170-pound beanpole when he signed out of Boca Chica in 2009, Guerrero put on 45 pounds and started setting off radar guns. The towering Colombian reliever routinely touched 100 mph in 2016 and earned his first big league callup with the Padres before being traded to the Marlins in July in the deal that sent Josh Naylor to San Diego. The swing-and-miss stuff is there for Guerrero to be a back-end reliever in the majors with upper-90s velocity and a slider that flashes plus at times. But like many pitchers his size, Guerrero has trouble keeping his delivery in sync. his delivery isn't violent but lacks efficiency; one evaluator likened it to an angry stork. Coordination and general mechanics will need a lot of work for him to have enough control to be effective. But if he can curtail his wildness, as he did at times at Double-A Jacksonville, he can be a neffective, late-inning reliever.

Year	Club (League)	Class	W	L	ERA	G	GS	CG	SV	IP	H	HR	BB	SO	K/9	WHIP	AVG
2014	Fort Wayne (MWL)	LoA	6	1	1.00	25	0	0	1	36	22	2	12	42	10.5	0.94	.169
	Lake Elsinore (CAL)	HiA	0	0	2.63	14	0	0	3	14	10	1	8	14	9.2	1.32	.200
2015	San Antonio (TL)	AA	1	5	2.76	37	0	0	13	42	33	3	20	46	9.8	1.25	.205
	El Paso (PCL)	AAA	0	0	3.95	11	0	0	1	14	8	0	11	15	9.9	1.39	.178
2016	San Diego (NL)	MAJ	0	0	4.50	1	0	0	0	2	3	0	1	0	0.0	2.00	.375
	El Paso (PCL)	AAA	0	0	6.00	13	0	0	0	12	12	2	9	11	8.3	1.75	.250
	San Antonio (TL)	AA	0	3	4.94	19	0	0	0	24	20	2	10	25	9.5	1.27	.235
	Jacksonville (SL)	AA	1	1	1.93	12	0	0	4	14	11	0	3	15	9.6	1.00	.212
Major League Totals			0	0	4.50	1	0	0	0	2	3	0	1	0	0.0	2.00	.375
Minor League Totals			14	22	3.99	194	20	0	23	302	253	11	193	303	9.0	1.48	.228

17 ALBERT GUAIMARO, OF

BA GRADE
45 Risk: Extreme

Born: Jan. 17, 1999. **B-T:** R-R. **Ht.:** 6-0. **Wt.:** 180. **Signed:** Venezuela, 2016. **Signed by:** Albert Gonzalez and Wilmer Castillo.

Guaimaro is one of five Venezuelan prospects removed from the Red Sox in 2016 after the organization, according to the office of the commissioner, engaged in circumvention of the international bonus pools by signing several Venezuelan players in "package deals." The Marlins signed Guaimaro in July. He has a compact frame and a short stroke from the right side with good bat speed. He's an aggressive hitter with a line-drive approach, he hits to all fields and the ball already jumps off his bat well. Guaimaro is a good athlete who had been playing center field for the Red Sox, though with his body type, he projects to slow down from his tick above-average speed and would likely end up in right field if he stayed in the outfield. The Marlins had discussed converting Guaimaro to catcher, as he has an above-average throwing arm. Guaimaro has a high baseball IQ and gets high marks for makeup and his love for the game. He should make his U.S. debut in 2017 in the Rookie-level Gulf Coast League.

Year	Club (League)	Class	AVG	G	AB	R	H	2B	3B	HR	RBI	BB	SO	SB	CS	OBP	SLG
2016	Red Sox2 (DSL)	R	.250	23	88	9	22	10	1	1	13	6	11	4	4	.302	.420
	Marlins (DSL)	R	.194	19	72	3	14	2	0	0	9	6	13	2	0	.256	.222
Minor League Totals			.225	42	160	12	36	12	1	1	22	12	24	6	4	.282	.331

18 JAMES NELSON, 3B

BA GRADE
45 Risk: Extreme

Born: Oct. 18, 1997. **B-T:** R-R. **Ht.:** 6-2. **Wt.:** 180. **Drafted:** Cisco (Texas) JC, 2016 (15th round). **Signed by:** Ryan Wardinsky.

The Red Sox drafted Nelson in the 18th round out of a Georgia high school but the sides couldn't match up, so he headed to Cisco (Texas) JC for a season. The Marlins signed the nephew of 2004 first-rounder and ex-big leaguer Chris Nelson for $75,000 in June. A shortstop in high school, the Marlins placed Nelson at third base and saw him make 12 errors in 40 games. A scout who saw him said despite the errors, Nelson looked comfortable at the hot corner and settled in as the season went on. Nelson has the plus arm strength to play third but does short-arm the ball on occasion. Nelson has an athletic frame with plenty of room for strength gains. He has an upper-cut swing and just average bat speed, but still manages to put together solid at-bats and doesn't show much swing and miss, although he'll occasionally chase. Scouts, however, note his aptitude that after he chases, if the pitcher doubles up, Nelson can do damage. As he grows into man strength, Nelson projects to have average power and he has some feel to hit. He's an average runner who may be challenged with a jump to low Class A Greensboro in 2017.

Year	Club (League)	Class	AVG	G	AB	R	H	2B	3B	HR	RBI	BB	SO	SB	CS	OBP	SLG
2016	Marlins (GCL)	R	.284	43	162	26	46	10	0	1	24	14	30	7	3	.344	.364
Minor League Totals			.284	43	162	26	46	10	0	1	24	14	30	7	3	.344	.364

19 JEFF BRIGHAM, RHP

BA GRADE
40 Risk: High

Born: Feb. 16, 1992. **B-T:** R-R. **Ht.:** 6-0. **Wt.:** 200. **Drafted:** Washington, 2014 (4th round). **Signed by:** Henry Jones (Dodgers).

The righthander missed his junior year at Washington with Tommy John surgery but bounced back as a redshirt junior in 2014, which prompted the Dodgers to pop him in the fourth round. The Marlins acquired Brigham at the 2015 trade deadline for Mat Latos, and his velocity has come back. Brigham was touching 98 mph this season and mostly sitting 90-94. Brigham combines easy plus velocity with an attack mentality and has late movement on his fastball. His biggest development has been sharpening his slider from sweepy to hard and slicing, flashing plus. That led to more strikeouts in 2016, though his groundball rate plummeted. His below-average changeup has significant room to improve. Brigham is a good athlete and fields his position well. He's ultra competitive to the point of losing composure at times. His most likely role in the long-term is as a power reliever. He's headed for Double-A in 2017.

Year	Club (League)	Class	W	L	ERA	G	GS	CG	SV	IP	H	HR	BB	SO	K/9	WHIP	AVG
2014	Ogden (PIO)	R	0	3	3.58	11	10	0	0	33	32	2	16	33	9.1	1.47	.267
2015	Great Lakes (MWL)	LoA	2	0	1.29	2	0	0	0	7	3	0	2	11	14.1	0.71	.125
	R. Cucamonga (CAL)	HiA	4	5	5.96	17	14	0	0	68	78	8	36	64	8.5	1.68	.286
	Jupiter (FSL)	HiA	2	2	1.87	6	5	0	0	34	34	0	9	22	5.9	1.28	.276
2016	Jupiter (FSL)	HiA	7	8	4.04	27	23	0	1	123	115	6	47	112	8.2	1.32	.246
Minor League Totals			15	18	4.13	63	52	0	1	264	262	16	110	242	8.3	1.41	.260

20 ROY MORALES, C

BA GRADE
40 Risk: High

Born: June 25, 1995. **B-T:** R-R. **Ht.:** 6-2. **Wt.:** 195. **Drafted:** HS—San Juan, P.R., 2014 (12th round). **Signed by:** Lazaro Llanes.

Morales was eligible for the 2013 draft but was not selected and ended up repeating his senior year after breaking his right wrist. Morales fits the profile for Puerto Rican catchers, with a strong arm as his carrying tool. His receiving and blocking skills have improved to earn average grades, if not a tick above. His plus arm strength is good enough for the Marlins to consider pitching a fallback option. But one evaluator called Morales the Marlins' best catching prospect. The 6-foot-2, 195-pounder has a strong, durable body and a bushel of intangibles. Morales has average bat speed, giving him potential for average power, but he has not tapped into it in games. Morales has some feel to hit and grinds at-bats. His poor speed helped result in 10 double plays in just 60 games. He missed the last month of the season and instructional league with a right wrist issue but should return to Greensboro as the full-time starter to start 2017.

Year	Club (League)	Class	AVG	G	AB	R	H	2B	3B	HR	RBI	BB	SO	SB	CS	OBP	SLG
2014	Marlins (GCL)	R	.224	25	76	11	17	3	0	0	7	6	2	0	2	.307	.263
2015	Greensboro (SAL)	LoA	.182	14	44	2	8	2	0	0	0	3	5	0	0	.294	.227
	Batavia (NYP)	SS	.311	33	122	7	38	3	1	0	14	10	13	0	1	.360	.352
2016	Greensboro (SAL)	LoA	.288	60	205	26	59	8	0	1	21	22	23	2	0	.374	.341
Minor League Totals			.273	132	447	46	122	16	1	1	42	41	43	2	3	.351	.320

21 J.T. RIDDLE, SS

BA GRADE
40 Risk: High

Born: Oct. 12, 1991. **B-T:** L-R. **Ht.:** 6-3. **Wt.:** 175. **Drafted:** Kentucky, 2013 (13th round). **Signed by:** Matt Gaski

Kentucky's Mr. Baseball in 2010 turned down the Red Sox, who drafted him in the 35th round, to attend UK. He played all over the infield for Kentucky, though primarily at second base, and has primarily played shortstop as a pro. He shows a plus arm and good-enough hands to stay at the position, which helps him profile well as a future utility man with a lefthanded bat. He committed just six errors in 84 games at short in 2016 and had a .982 fielding percentage. Despite his aggressive offensive approach, Riddle limits his strikeouts (13.7 percent for his career) because of a compact swing and level bat path. Riddle has gap power and some ability to pop the ball out of the park but produces below-average power. He's an average runner but doesn't try to steal much. His ability to play multiple positions and propensity for contact portend a useful utility career. Riddle receives high marks for leadership and makeup.

Year	Club (League)	Class	AVG	G	AB	R	H	2B	3B	HR	RBI	BB	SO	SB	CS	OBP	SLG
2014	Greensboro (SAL)	LoA	.280	103	435	65	122	17	4	9	60	26	55	5	1	.323	.400
2015	Jupiter (FSL)	HiA	.270	45	185	30	50	6	1	0	9	11	29	7	3	.311	.314
	New Orleans (PCL)	AAA	.667	1	3	2	2	0	0	0	0	2	0	0	0	.800	.667
	Jacksonville (SL)	AA	.289	44	173	26	50	6	1	5	20	8	24	0	0	.323	.422
2016	Jacksonville (SL)	AA	.278	101	389	49	108	18	4	3	51	33	72	5	1	.332	.368
	New Orleans (PCL)	AAA	.268	15	56	4	15	2	0	1	2	1	9	1	0	.281	.357
Minor League Totals			.274	368	1463	214	401	59	10	20	160	91	217	24	6	.318	.369

22 ISAIAH WHITE, OF

BA GRADE
45 Risk: Extreme

Born: Jan. 7, 1997. **B-T:** R-R. **Ht.:** 6-0. **Wt.:** 170. **Drafted:** HS—Wilson, N.C., 2015 (3rd round). **Signed by:** Joel Matthews.

White was drafted out of tiny Greenfield School—which had never had a player drafted and then had two popped in 2015. He is a super athletic player with plus-plus speed. One scout compared him to Royals burner Terrence Gore. But White is very raw as a ballplayer. He lacks polish and will need plenty of at-bats to stabilize his approach. He was not accustomed to facing top-notch pitching as an amateur and will have to continue to make adjustments at the plate. White does not recognize pitches well and generally needs a hitting approach. Scouts are split on his bat speed, with one rating it as top-of-the-scale but another saying it was just average. He has the raw speed to outrun mistakes in the outfield but doesn't take charge in center field. Still, White earns good marks for his makeup and coachability, leading scouts to believe patience is necessary for him to reach his projection.

Year	Club (League)	Class	AVG	G	AB	R	H	2B	3B	HR	RBI	BB	SO	SB	CS	OBP	SLG
2015	Marlins (GCL)	R	.294	35	126	19	37	7	2	0	8	3	44	13	0	.321	.381
2016	Batavia (NYP)	SS	.214	51	173	23	37	6	3	1	17	22	60	5	4	.306	.301
Minor League Totals			.247	86	299	42	74	13	5	1	25	25	104	18	4	.312	.334

23 SAM PEREZ, RHP

BA GRADE
40 Risk: High

Born: Aug. 17, 1994. **B-T:** R-R. **Ht.:** 6-3. **Wt.:** 210. **Drafted:** Missouri State, 2016 (5th round). **Signed by:** Brian Kraft.

Perez was a fireman for Missouri State in the old-school, Rollie Fingers sense of the word. He threw 91 innings in 36 appearances. Some teams might have been concerned about how frequently he pitched and how many innings he threw, but the Marlins were impressed with his durability and intelligence, and the fact that he would sign for just $20,000, allowing them to allocate more of their bonus pool to sign top pick Braxton Garrett. They also used him heavily in his pro debut, as he tossed 48.1 more innings. He has a strong body and his velocity zoomed when he had proper rest. He was flashing 96 mph, and he throws a slider and changeup as well with good deception as the ball appears to come out of his shirt. He's lean and athletic and draws comparisons to former Marlins draft pick Anthony DeSclafani. His delivery makes it seem as though he jumps at the batter, but it is not a maximum effort delivery. Tall and physical, Perez is an aggressive strike-thrower who has the poise to move quickly as a reliever, but the Marlins intend to see what he can do as a starter. His ultimate role, however, is probably back in the bullpen.

Year	Club (League)	Class	W	L	ERA	G	GS	CG	SV	IP	H	HR	BB	SO	K/9	WHIP	AVG
2016	Batavia (NYP)	SS	1	1	3.54	16	8	0	0	48	41	4	15	36	6.7	1.16	.234
Minor League Totals			1	1	3.54	16	8	0	0	48	41	4	15	36	6.7	1.16	.234

24 DREW STECKENRIDER, RHP

BA GRADE
40 Risk: High

Born: Jan. 10, 1991. **B-T:** R-R. **Ht.:** 6-5. **Wt.:** 215. **Drafted:** Tennessee, 2012 (8th round). **Signed by:** Carmen Carcone.

Steckenrider only teased tools as a two-way player in high school, and it took a while for the package to come together at Tennessee. But as a junior for then-new Volunteers coach Dave Serrano, Steckenrider was terrific out of the 'pen and got drafted in the eighth round by the Marlins. After a solid debut, he felt pain in his elbow and needed Tommy John surgery in 2013. He lost 18 months to rehab before returning in 2015. Steckenrider was finally healthy in 2016 and put himself squarely on the Marlins' radar, reaching Triple-A. After bouncing between the rotation and bullpen, Steckenrider thrived in a bullpen-only role in 2016 as he held opponents to a .141 average across the three levels, using a fastball that touches the mid-90s and a slider that flashes above-average. He throws in the occasional low-90s cutter and firm mid-80s changeup as well. He struck out 71 in 52 innings this season, including a brief-but-dominant high Class A stint in which he struck out more than half the batters he faced. He then went 2-1, 3.46 with 15 strikeouts in 13 innings in the Arizona Fall League, and was part of the first no-hitter in the AFL in 15 years. He should be in the mix for a major league bullpen role in 2017.

Year	Club (League)	Class	W	L	ERA	G	GS	CG	SV	IP	H	HR	BB	SO	K/9	WHIP	AVG
2014	Marlins (GCL)	R	0	0	0.00	1	0	0	0	1	0	0	1	0	0.0	1.00	.000
2015	Greensboro (SAL)	LoA	1	3	2.75	10	5	0	0	39	38	2	17	34	7.8	1.40	.260
	Jupiter (FSL)	HiA	4	3	3.18	15	8	1	1	57	59	2	25	44	7.0	1.48	.266
2016	Jupiter (FSL)	HiA	0	0	0.00	6	0	0	1	10	2	0	2	17	15.3	0.40	.065
	Jacksonville (SL)	AA	1	0	1.48	24	0	0	6	30	12	0	10	39	11.6	0.73	.120
	New Orleans (PCL)	AAA	0	1	5.40	10	0	0	7	12	11	1	7	15	11.6	1.54	.239
Minor League Totals			8	10	3.03	81	25	1	15	205	165	7	97	215	9.4	1.28	.220

25 BRETT LILEK, LHP

BA GRADE

45 Risk: Extreme

Born: Aug. 10, 1993. **B-T:** L-L. **Ht.:** 6-4. **Wt.:** 220. **Drafted:** Arizona State, 2015 (2nd round). **Signed by:** Scott Stanley

Lilek was originally drafted in the 37th round in 2012 by Seattle but had his heart set on Arizona State. After an excellent sophomore season, inconsistency as a junior cost Lilek his Friday starting slot in 2015, and cost him in the draft. He didn't fall far, though, and the Marlins made him a second-round pick, signing him for $1 million. Lilek battled left biceps tendinitis and arm fatigue and made just seven appearances in 2016, and he's thrown just 51 pro innings thus far. He rehabbed in instructional league and was expected to be ready for 2017. While Lilek lacks a true plus pitch, he pitches to his strengths and his arm slot gives him deception that helps his offerings play up. His fastball sits 90-94 mph at his best, and his curveball shows above average with tilt, but is not consistent. His changeup flashes average potential. He has the size, polish and stuff to project as a back-end starter, though health now is a factor as Lilek also battled shoulder tenderness in 2015.

Year	Club (League)	Class	W	L	ERA	G	GS	CG	SV	IP	H	HR	BB	SO	K/9	WHIP	AVG
2015	Batavia (NYP)	SS	1	2	3.34	11	10	0	0	35	30	1	7	43	11.1	1.06	.231
2016	Greensboro (SAL)	LoA	0	1	5.06	7	5	0	0	16	19	1	16	13	7.3	2.19	.311
Minor League Totals			1	3	3.88	18	15	0	0	51	49	2	23	56	9.9	1.41	.257

26 REMEY REED, RHP

BA GRADE

40 Risk: High

Born: May 5, 1995. **B-T:** R-R. **Ht.:** 6-5. **Wt.:** 230. **Drafted:** Oklahoma State, 2016 (6th round). **Signed by:** Brian Kraft.

Undrafted out of his Texas high school, Reed spent a year at Navarro (Texas) JC before enrolling at Oklahoma State. Reed made just five starts in 63 appearances as a collegian but his future could be in a rotation. A versatile part of the Cowboys' bullpen—he helped set up for closer Koda Glover in 2015—Reed struck out 44 in 35 innings in 2016. OSU coaches leaned on Reed early in the season, which caused his velocity to drop a tick during the season, when he was sitting 90-92 with his fastball and touching 94. But after he was drafted by the Marlins, the big-bodied righthander was up to 97 mph at short-season Batavia. The country-strong Texan also has pitchability with a four-pitch mix that makes starting him a possibility. He was primarily a fastball/slider pitcher, but he just began throwing a curveball last year and it might already be his best pitch. His changeup needs more repetitions to be usable. Even at 6-foot-5, 230 pounds, Reed has room to grow. He's a strike-thrower who always wants the ball with a loose, easy and clean arm action and delivery. Expect him to earn a spot in low Class A Greensboro's rotation.

Year	Club (League)	Class	W	L	ERA	G	GS	CG	SV	IP	H	HR	BB	SO	K/9	WHIP	AVG
2016	Marlins (GCL)	R	1	0	5.79	3	0	0	0	5	7	1	1	2	3.9	1.71	.350
	Batavia (NYP)	SS	0	0	0.00	1	0	0	0	1	0	0	1	2	13.5	0.75	.000
Minor League Totals			1	0	4.50	4	0	0	0	6	7	1	2	4	6.0	1.50	.292

27 ANDY BELTRE, RHP

BA GRADE

45 Risk: Extreme

Born: July 6, 1993. **B-T:** R-R. **Ht.:** 6-4. **Wt.:** 195. **Signed:** Dominican Republic, 2010. **Signed by:** Albert Gonzalez and Sandy Nin.

Beltre was signed as part of the 2010 international class, which also brought Jarlin Garcia. Beltre's talent has intrigued the organization for years, but injuries—including Tommy John surgery, which wiped out 2015—had slowed his progress. Healthy (for the most part) in 2016, Beltre showed his plus arm strength, hitting 100 mph in his final outing of the season and sitting 95-97 mph most of the season. In addition to his plus velocity, Beltre can command his three pitches—breaking ball and changeup–and profiles as a high-leverage reliever, one who could potentially ascend quickly if healthy. But his injuries are a major red flag, and he missed a month in 2016 as well. The Marlins decided not to protect him in the Rule 5 draft, even after re-signing him once he became a six-year free agent. After passing through the draft unselected, he gets to be a Jumbo Shrimp, as he should open 2017 at Double-A Jacksonville.

Year	Club (League)	Class	W	L	ERA	G	GS	CG	SV	IP	H	HR	BB	SO	K/9	WHIP	AVG
2014	Batavia (NYP)	SS	1	1	6.00	3	3	0	0	12	14	2	4	15	11.3	1.50	.286
2015	Did not play—Injured																
2016	Greensboro (SAL)	LoA	0	0	1.37	13	0	0	1	20	15	1	5	23	10.5	1.02	.205
	Jupiter (FSL)	HiA	0	1	2.00	19	0	0	4	27	15	0	11	31	10.3	0.96	.156
Minor League Totals			3	12	3.72	69	20	0	5	172	159	6	69	180	9.4	1.33	.239

28 JUSTIN TWINE, 2B

BA GRADE
45 Risk: Extreme

Born: Oct. 7, 1995. **B-T:** R-R. **Ht.:** 5-11. **Wt.:** 205. **Drafted:** HS—Falls City, Texas, 2014 (2nd round). **Signed by:** Ryan Wardinsky.

A track and football star in high school, Twine has plus athleticism but his baseball skills remain somewhat rudimentary. His best tool presently is double-plus speed. Scouts believe he has above-average raw power, but his aggressive approach negates that during games because he chases too often. He embraced a change in his swing, a leg tuck that the Marlins hope can lead to more consistent contact. When he does hit the ball, his exit velocity was among the best on the Greensboro club. He also took on a new position, second base, where evaluators said he looked natural and comfortable. He made just seven errors there (.985 fielding percentage) after making 29 (.940 FP) in 2015 at shortstop. His has plenty of arm strength for the position and cleaned up his arm stroke, now throwing three-quarters instead of sidearm. Twine gets plus marks for his work ethic, desire and competitiveness.

Year	Club (League)	Class	AVG	G	AB	R	H	2B	3B	HR	RBI	BB	SO	SB	CS	OBP	SLG
2014	Marlins (GCL)	R	.229	44	166	19	38	8	5	1	16	6	52	5	1	.285	.355
2015	Greensboro (SAL)	LoA	.206	117	451	44	93	20	3	7	33	6	108	8	4	.235	.310
2016	Greensboro (SAL)	LoA	.249	99	353	42	88	17	2	3	33	19	116	8	6	.308	.334
Minor League Totals			.226	260	970	105	219	45	10	11	88	31	276	21	11	.271	.327

29 JOHN NORWOOD, CF

BA GRADE
40 Risk: High

Born: Sept. 24, 1992. **B-T:** R-R. **Ht.:** 6-1. **Wt.:** 185. **Signed:** Vanderbilt, 2014 (NDFA). **Signed by:** Mark Willoughby.

The 2014 College World Series hero was not drafted that June, even after hitting .400 and leading the Commodores to their first national championship with the game-winning home run in the '14 CWS Finals clincher. But Norwood didn't escape the Marlins' notice. They liked his Vanderbilt pedigree and the fact that he wanted to be a Marlin. They followed him in the Cape Cod League, where he hit .324 for Cotuit, and signed him shortly after for $275,000. Norwood is a quick-twitch athlete who can play all three outfield spots, but is better in a corner. His .397 slugging percentage at Jupiter was well above the .356 average in the high Class A Florida State League. He shows plus raw power to the pull side and has to get to it enough to profile as a regular. His pitch recognition and feel to hit trail behind his power. He's a solid average defender with solid average speed. The Marlins hope he's a late bloomer who takes off at Double-A Jacksonville.

Year	Club (League)	Class	AVG	G	AB	R	H	2B	3B	HR	RBI	BB	SO	SB	CS	OBP	SLG
2014	Batavia (NYP)	SS	.256	20	78	4	20	1	1	0	6	3	25	0	0	.284	.295
2015	Greensboro (SAL)	LoA	.233	120	446	53	104	19	2	16	55	42	113	34	14	.304	.392
2016	Jupiter (FSL)	HiA	.271	127	469	68	127	24	4	9	50	49	116	14	12	.347	.397
Minor League Totals			.253	267	993	125	251	44	7	25	111	94	254	48	26	.323	.387

30 YEFRI PEREZ, OF/2B

BA GRADE
40 Risk: High

Born: February 24, 1991. **B-T:** B-R. **Ht.:** 5-11. **Wt.:** 170. **Signed:** Dominican Republic, 2014. **Signed by:** Albert Gonzalez,/Sandy Nin.

Perez signed in 2008 but had a largely unremarkable pro career until 2014, when he led the organization's minor leaguers with 30 steals at low Class A. In 2015, he was second in the minors with 71 steals, just short of the record for a Marlins' farmhand (Quincey Foster, 73 in 1998 for high Class A Kane County). He got his first big league promotion in July, used as a pinch-runner. A shortstop when he signed, the Marlins have tried to exploit his one above-average tool—speed, for which he grades an 80 on the 20-80 scout scale—by expanding upon his versatility. Scouts say his speed makes him an asset in center field, and he can also play short, second and third base, with his solid-average arm serving well at those spots. He played center, short and second in the Arizona Fall League. He's an average defender who can outrun misreads in the outfield. At bat, Perez has little power impact, with an occasional double, but he uses his speed well. Perez has a good short game, with a quick, downward-slashing swing that he uses to lash singles around the field. He's also a good bunter. Perez profiles as a utility man or pinch-runner.

Year	Club (League)	Class	AVG	G	AB	R	H	2B	3B	HR	RBI	BB	SO	SB	CS	OBP	SLG
2014	Greensboro (SAL)	LoA	.287	118	421	65	121	17	0	1	29	26	54	30	9	.335	.335
2015	Jupiter (FSL)	HiA	.240	135	517	74	124	10	1	1	22	31	95	71	21	.286	.269
2016	Jacksonville (SL)	AA	.259	84	328	49	85	7	3	1	28	39	66	39	11	.334	.308
2016	Miami (NL)	MLB	.667	12	3	5	2	1	0	0	0	0	1	4	2	.667	1.000
Minor League Totals			.253	267	993	125	251	44	7	25	111	94	254	48	26	.323	.387
Major League Totals			.667	12	3	5	2	1	0	0	0	0	1	4	2	.667	1.000

Milwaukee Brewers

BY TOM HAUDRICOURT

In the first full year of their large-scale rebuild, the Brewers had two primary goals for the 2016 season.

First, they wanted to be as competitive as possible under the circumstances and ignore all the preseason chatter about tanking. Considering how few experienced players were on the transitional 2016 squad and how many players (50) were used, the Brewers exceeded most expectations with a 73-89 record.

The second objective was to identify as many keepers as possible who could be part of the equation moving forward. Much of the rebuilding plan revolves around the vastly improved farm system, but the Brewers hoped to find others at the big league level who could be contributors as well.

Beyond Ryan Braun—the last man standing from the 2011 National League Central champs—manager Craig Counsell and his staff found players to take into next season.

Shrewd offseason trade pickup Jonathan Villar, who moved from shortstop to third base during the season, led the majors with 62 stolen bases and led Milwaukee with a .369 on-base percentage, 168 hits, 79 walks and 92 runs scored. Infield rover Hernan Perez and center fielder Keon Broxton carved out roles for 2017.

Rookie righthanders Zach Davies and Junior Guerra made such an impact that they are penciled into the Milwaukee rotation for the future.

While a rumored in-season Braun trade to the Dodgers fell through, the Brewers successfully executed a pair of other trades on Aug. 1 that reshaped the top of the system's prospect list.

Milwaukee shipped all-star catcher Jonathan Lucroy and closer Jeremy Jeffress to the Rangers for outfielder Lewis Brinson and righthander Luis Oriz, a pair of first-round picks from 2012 and 2014. The Brewers also snagged 2015 first-round righthander Phil Bickford plus catcher Andrew Susac from the Giants for reliever Will Smith on the same day.

The Brewers will look to keep the rebuilding process on track in 2017, but they were satisfied with progress made in 2016.

"At this stage, you have to set incremental goals for yourself, for your organization," first-year general manager David Stearns said. "We've achieved some of those goals, and so we should feel proud of that.

"But we recognize we have a lot of work to do to get to the ultimate stage of . . . competing for a division championship every single year."

The success of the rebuild will depend on how

Trade acquisition Zach Davies emerged as a surprising staff leader as a 23-year-old rookie

TOP PROSPECTS OF THE DECADE

Year	Player, Pos.	2016 Org
2007	Yovani Gallardo, rhp	Orioles
2008	Matt LaPorta, of	Did not play
2009	Alcides Escobar, ss	Royals
2010	Alcides Escobar, ss	Royals
2011	Mark Rogers, rhp	Did not play
2012	Wily Peralta, rhp	Brewers
2013	Wily Peralta, rhp	Brewers
2014	Jimmy Nelson, rhp	Brewers
2015	Tyrone Taylor, of	Brewers
2016	Orlando Arcia, ss	Brewers

many prospects develop into big league regulars. Shortstop Orlando Arcia, the system's preseason No. 1 prospect, received the first callup among the touted prospects when he debuted in August. The Brewers expect others to follow suit in 2017.

Beyond the many prospects acquired in trades, the Brewers also used the fifth pick in the 2016 draft to select Louisville outfielder Corey Ray, who jumped straight to high Class A Brevard County. He suffered a minor knee injury in instructional league that required surgery but presents no issues for 2017.

After the season, the Brewers announced a reorganization of their scouting department. Tod Johnson moves up to scouting director, replacing Ray Montgomery, who becomes vice president of scouting.

ORGANIZATION OVERVIEW

General manager: David Stearns. **Farm director:** Tom Flanagan. **Scouting director:** Tod Johnson.

Class	Team	League	W	L	PCT	Finish	Manager
Majors	Milwaukee Brewers	National	73	89	.451	10th (15)	Craig Counsell
Triple-A	Colorado Springs Sky Sox	Pacific Coast	67	71	.486	11th (16)	Rick Sweet
Double-A	Biloxi Shuckers	Southern	72	67	.518	6th (10)	Mike Guerrero
High Class A	* Brevard County Manatees	Florida State	40	97	.292	12th (12)	Joe Ayrault
Low Class A	Wisconsin Timber Rattlers	Midwest	71	69	.507	8th (16)	Matt Erickson
Rookie	Helena Brewers	Pioneer	28	46	.378	8th (8)	Nestor Corredor
Rookie	AZL Brewers	Arizona	24	29	.453	12th (14)	Tony Diggs
Overall 2016 Minor League Record			302	379	.443	29th (30)	

* Affiliate moves to Carolina (Carolina) in 2017

THIS YEAR'S TOP 30

No.	Player, Pos.	Grade/Risk
1.	Lewis Brinson, of	55/Medium
2.	Josh Hader, lhp	55/Medium
3.	Luis Ortiz, rhp	60/High
4.	Corey Ray, of	60/High
5.	Isan Diaz, ss/2b	55/High
6.	Trent Clark, of	60/Extreme
7.	Brandon Woodruff, rhp	55/High
8.	Phil Bickford, rhp	55/High
9.	Lucas Erceg, 3b	55/High
10.	Marcos Diplan, rhp	55/High
11.	Mauricio Dubon, ss	50/Medium
12.	Brett Phillips, of	55/High
13.	Gilbert Lara, ss	55/Extreme
14.	Jacob Nottingham, c	50/High
15.	Jorge Lopez, rhp	55/Extreme
16.	Cody Ponce, rhp	50/High
17.	Kodi Medeiros, lhp	50/High
18.	Ryan Cordell, of	50/High
19.	Josh Pennington, rhp	50/High
20.	Monte Harrison, of	55/Extreme
21.	Freddy Peralta, rhp	50/High
22.	Jacob Barnes, rhp	45/Medium
23.	Jake Gatewood, 3b/1b	55/Extreme
24.	Corbin Burnes, rhp	50/High
25.	Devin Williams, rhp	55/Extreme
26.	Nathan Kirby, lhp	55/Extreme
27.	Demi Orimoloye, of	55/Extreme
28.	Mariano Feliciano, c	50/Extreme
29.	Chad McClanahan, 3b	50/Extreme
30.	Michael Reed, of	45/High

LAST YEAR'S TOP 30

No.	Player, Pos.	Status
1.	Orlando Arcia, ss	Majors
2.	Jorge Lopez, rhp	No. 15
3.	Trent Clark, of	No. 6
4.	Brett Phillips, of	No. 12
5.	Gilbert Lara, ss	No. 13
6.	Kodi Medeiros, lhp	No. 17
7.	Tyrone Taylor, of	Dropped out
8.	Clint Coulter, of	Dropped out
9.	Cody Ponce, rhp	No. 16
10.	Devin Williams, rhp	No. 25
11.	Josh Hader, lhp	No. 2
12.	Zach Davies, rhp	Majors
13.	Demi Orimoloye, of	No. 27
14.	Monte Harrison, of	No. 20
15.	Nathan Kirby, rhp	No. 26
16.	Jake Gatewood, 3b/1b	No. 23
17.	Michael Reed, of	No. 30
18.	Marcos Diplan, rhp	No. 10
19.	Tyler Wagner, rhp	(Rangers)
20.	Adrian Houser, rhp	Dropped out
21.	Yadiel Rivera, ss/2b	Dropped out
22.	Taylor Williams, rhp	Dropped out
23.	Ramon Flores, of	(Angels)
24.	Victor Roache, of	Dropped out
25.	Miguel Diaz, rhp	(Padres)
26.	Hobbs Johnson, lhp	Free agent
27.	Ariel Pena, rhp	Free agent
28.	Kyle Wren, of	Dropped out
29.	Yhonathan Barrios, rhp	Dropped out
30.	Damien Magnifico, rhp	Dropped out

BEST TOOLS

Best Hitter for Average	Trent Clark
Best Power Hitter	Lucas Erceg
Best Strike-Zone Discipline	Trent Clark
Fastest Baserunner	Johnny Davis
Best Athlete	Corey Ray
Best Fastball	Brandon Woodruff
Best Curveball	Corbin Burnes
Best Slider	Kodi Medeiros
Best Changeup	Devin Williams
Best Control	Jon Perrin
Best Defensive Catcher	Dustin Houle
Best Defensive Infielder	Angel Ortega
Best Infield Arm	Lucas Erceg
Best Defensive Outfielder	Tyrone Taylor
Best Outfield Arm	Clint Coulter

PROJECTED 2020 LINEUP

Catcher	Andrew Susac
First Base	Lucas Erceg
Second Base	Isan Diaz
Third Base	Jonathan Villar
Shortstop	Orlando Arcia
Left Field	Corey Ray
Center Field	Lewis Brinson
Right Field	Trent Clark
No. 1 Starter	Josh Hader
No. 2 Starter	Luis Ortiz
No. 3 Starter	Brandon Woodruff
No. 4 Starter	Marcos Diplan
No. 5 Starter	Zach Davies
Closer	Phil Bickford

MINOR LEAGUE DEPTH CHART

MILWAUKEE BREWERS

TOP 2017 ROOKIE: Josh Hader, lhp. One of the most dominant strikeout pitchers in the minors should be ready to help the Brewers in some capacity.
BREAKOUT PROSPECT: Demi Orimoloye, of. He struggled in Rookie ball in 2016 but has the skill set to do big things.
SLEEPER: Wei-Chung Wang, lhp. A double-plus changeup and feel for spin could make him a depth option for the big league staff.

SOURCE OF TOP 30 TALENT			
Homegrown	18	Acquired	12
College	7	Trades	12
Junior college	0	Rule 5 draft	0
High school	10	Independent leagues	0
Nondrafted free agents	0	Free agents/waivers	0
International	1		

LF
Ryan Cordell (18)
Victor Roache
Malik Collymore
Brandon Diaz

CF
Lewis Brinson (1)
Corey Ray (4)
Trent Clark (6)
Monte Harrison (20)
Tyrone Taylor
Kyle Wren
Johnny Davis
Omar Garcia

RF
Brett Phillips (12)
Demi Orimoloye (27)
Michael Reed (30)
Clint Coulter
David Denson

3B
Lucas Erceg (9)
Jake Gatewood (23)
Chad McClanahan (29)
Jose Cuas

SS
Mauricio Dubon (11)
Gilbert Lara (13)
Angel Ortega
Yadiel Rivera
Luis Aviles
Trever Morrison
Francisco Thomas

2B
Isan Diaz (5)
Nate Orf
Javier Betancourt
Blake Allemand
Tucker Neuhaus

1B
Garrett Cooper
Dustin DeMuth
Gabriel Garcia
Ronnie Gideon

C
Jacob Nottingham (14)
Mario Feliciano (28)
Adam Weisenburger
Dustin Houle
Mitch Ghelfi
Max McDowell

LHP

LHSP	LHRP
Josh Hader (2)	Brent Suter
Kodi Medeiros (17)	Mitch Lambson
Nathan Kirby (26)	Nick Ramirez
Wei-Chung Wang	Stephen Peterson
Jake Drossner	Zach Hirsch
Drake Owenby	Brad Kuntz
Daniel Brown	
Blake Fox	

RHP

RHSP	RHRP
Luis Ortiz (3)	Jacob Barnes (22)
Brandon Woodruff (7)	Damien Magnifico
Phil Bickford (8)	Adrian Houser
Marcos Diplan (10)	Drew Gagnon
Jorge Lopez (15)	Stephen Kohlscreen
Cody Ponce (16)	Tyler Spurlin
Josh Pennington (19)	Tayler Scott
Freddy Peralta (21)	Nate Griep
Corbin Burnes (24)	Tristan Archer
Devin Williams (25)	Junior Rincon
Taylor Williams	Gage Smith
Trey Supak	
Braden Webb	
Aaron Wilkerson	
Jorge Ortega	
Jon Perrin	
Javier Salas	
David Burkhalter	
Bubba Derby	
Jordan Yamamoto	

DRAFT ANALYSIS

2016

BEST PURE HITTER: 3B Lucas Erceg (2) was seen as an advanced hitter and lived up to those expectations with a .327/.376/.518 debut between Rookie-level Helena and low Class A Wisconsin. OF Corey Ray (1) projects as at least an average hitter, and his short stroke gives him a chance to be more than that depending on how much he focuses on getting to his power.

BEST POWER HITTER: Ray has above-average power potential and has shown plus raw power. 1B Ronnie Gideon (23) didn't get much chance to tap into his plus raw power in college, hitting 13 home runs in three years at Texas A&M, but hit 17 home runs in the Pioneer League given almost as many at-bats at Helena as he had in college.

FASTEST RUNNER: Zach Clark (19) is a 70 runner on the 20-to-80 scouting scale underway, although a big swing kslows him coming out of the batter's box. Ray is a plus runner with a better feel for stealing bases than Clark.

BEST DEFENSIVE PLAYER: Erceg has a 70 arm that helped him touch 97 mph on the mound. He also has excellent short-range agility and good hands. He is a plus third baseman who impressed the Brewers enough they worked on playing him at shortstop in instructional league.

BEST FASTBALL: The Brewers worked on helping RHP Zack Brown (5) get more extension. It paid off as he controlled his 91-94 mph fastball better this summer then he did in an up-and-down spring at Kentucky.

BEST SECONDARY PITCH: RHP Corbin Burnes (4) has a power curveball that flashes plus. a big reason he struck out more than 10 batters per nine innings in his debut.

BEST PRO DEBUT: Erceg hit for average and had 30 extra-base hits in 68 games in his pro debut.

BEST ATHLETE: Ray has power and speed and showed better defense in center field than the Brewers expected. Clark may have the best all-around tools as anyone the Brewers picked in the draft, but he is much further away from utilizing those tools than Ray.

MOST INTRIGUING BACKGROUND: LHP Blake Fox (10) earned Internet fame with a pickoff move where he stood off the rubber removing his cap with his right hand, hid the ball in his left hand and tossed aside his glove to make the pickoff. Gideon's father Ron has coached and managed in the Rockies system for more than 20 years. Unsigned RHP Kyle Serrano (40) is the son of Tennessee coach Dave Serrano.

CLOSEST TO THE MAJORS: Ray spent of most of his pro debut at high Class A Brevard County. Even if he returns to high Class A to start 2017 he should spend much of next year at Double-A and isn't far from Milwaukee.

BEST LATE-ROUND PICK: 3B Chad McClanahan (11) signed for $1.2 million. He has the size and power to fit the third base profile, although he has a lot of work to do defensively to get to that point. 3B Weston Wilson (17) lacks a plus tool but is a very well-rounded player.

THE ONE WHO GOT AWAY: RHP Jared Horn (20) was considered a potential first-round pick. The California signee ranked No. 1 on Baseball America's West Coast League Top 10 Prospects list this summer thanks to his mid-90s fastball an above-average curveball.

2015

OFs Trent Clark (1) and Demi Orimoloye (4) have flashed tools but are far away, while LHP Nathan Kirby (1s) missed 2016 recovering from Tommy John surgery. The Brewers still have high hopes for RHP Cody Ponce (2) as well.

GRADE: C

2014

Scouting director Bruce Seid died unexpectedly after a high-risk, high-reward class. LHP Kodi Medeiros (1), 3B Jake Gatewood (1s) and OF Monte Harrison (2) all have been passed by RHP Brandon Woodruff (11), who leapt to Double-A.

GRADE: C

2013

RHP Devin Williams (2) has a live arm. Speedy OF Johnny Davis (22), who has reached Double-A, could be another Terrance Gore.

GRADE: F

TOP DRAFT PICKS OF THE DECADE

Year	Player, Pos.	2016 Org
2007	Matt LaPorta, of	Did not play
2008	Brett Lawrie, c/3b	White Sox
2009	Eric Arnett, rhp	Did not play
2010	*Dylan Covey, rhp	Athletics
2011	Taylor Jungmann, rhp	Brewers
2012	Clint Coulter, c	Brewers
2013	Devin Williams, rhp (2nd round)	Brewers
2014	Kodi Medeiros, lhp	Brewers
2015	Trent Clark, of	Brewers
2016	Corey Ray, of	Brewers

*Did not sign.

LARGEST BONUSES IN CLUB HISTORY

Corey Ray, 2016	$4,125,000
Rickie Weeks, 2003	$3,600,000
Gilbert Lara, 2014	$3,097,500
Trent Clark, 2015	$2,700,000
Taylor Jungmann, 2011	$2,525,000

1 LEWIS BRINSON, OF

Born: May 8, 1994. **B-T:** R-R. **Ht.:** 6-4. **Wt.:** 205.
Drafted: HS—Coral Springs, Fla., 2012 (1st round).
Signed by: Frankie Thon (Rangers).

BA GRADE

55 Risk: Medium

SCOUTING GRADES

Batting: 50.
Power: 60.
Speed: 60.
Defense: 55.
Arm: 60.

Based on 20-80 scouting scale and future projection rather than present tools.

JOHN WILLIAMSON

The Rangers selected Brinson with the next-to-last pick in the first round of the 2012 draft, and he broadcast his power-speed ability in five years in the Texas system. He had scuffled at Double-A Frisco in 2016, however, before the Brewers acquired him (and Luis Ortiz) from the Rangers at the trade deadline for Jonathan Lucroy and Jeremy Jeffress. Some of Brinson's struggles were related to a shoulder issue that forced him to the disabled list for a month in June. The Brewers opted to elevate him to the hitter-friendly environment at Triple-A Colorado Springs, and he thrived more than anyone could have anticipated by recording a 1.005 OPS in 23 games. High altitude or not, that showing was a huge confidence boost for both Brinson and the organization, and it put him in position to challenge for a spot on the major league roster sometime in 2017. He quickly inherited No. 1 prospect status in the Brewers system after the promotion of shortstop Orlando Arcia to Milwaukee, which coincided with the trade.

Brinson has worked hard to reduce his strikeout rate since whiffing 38 percent of the time in his full-season debut at low Class A Hickory in 2013. He trimmed that rate to 20 percent in 2016. Brinson has the coveted combination of speed and power, and he projects to be at least an average hitter. It is difficult for pitchers to get a fastball past Brinson, who has great bat speed, but he has trouble laying off breaking balls out of the zone and continues to work on plate discipline. He still needs plenty of work in patience, as evidenced by his two walks in 93 plate appearances at Colorado Springs. He has learned to use the whole field and is not as pull-conscious as he was earlier in his career. Some scouts question whether Brinson will be able to remain in center field, where he continues to work on improving his routes and throwing accuracy. He has good gap-to-gap range and arm strength, and the Brewers prefer to keep him in center until proven he needs to move to a corner. He would likely fit well in right field, if he does need to eventually change positions. Brinson clearly has the raw tools to be an impact player, but it's up to him to make the most of them, especially on offense. His overall skill set will serve him well in the outfield, but he might not be cut out to bat near the top of the order unless he improves his walk rate.

While Keon Broxton got a foot in the door in center field for the Brewers over the final two months of 2016, Brinson is guaranteed to get a good look in spring training. The Brewers have stockpiled young center fielders in recent years—whether they be draft picks Trent Clark and Corey Ray or trade pickups Brinson and Brett Phillips—but only one can play there at a time. Brinson has the most experience of the group, but his arm strength and power potential also would play in a corner.

Year	Club (League)	Class	AVG	G	AB	R	H	2B	3B	HR	RBI	BB	SO	SB	CS	OBP	SLG
2014	Hickory (SAL)	LoA	.335	43	164	36	55	8	1	10	28	18	46	7	4	.405	.579
	Myrtle Beach (CAR)	HiA	.246	46	183	17	45	8	1	3	22	15	50	5	5	.307	.350
2015	High Desert (CAL)	HiA	.337	64	258	51	87	22	7	13	42	31	64	13	6	.416	.628
	Frisco (TL)	AA	.291	28	110	14	32	8	1	6	23	6	28	2	1	.328	.545
	Round Rock (PCL)	AAA	.433	8	30	9	13	1	0	1	4	7	6	3	0	.541	.567
2016	Rangers (AZL)	R	.231	4	13	3	3	1	0	0	1	2	2	2	0	.333	.308
	Frisco (TL)	AA	.237	77	304	46	72	14	6	11	40	17	64	11	4	.280	.431
	Colorado Springs (PCL)	AAA	.382	23	89	14	34	9	0	4	20	2	21	4	2	.387	.618
Minor League Totals			.280	469	1835	308	514	111	25	76	274	167	546	85	31	.345	.492

2 JOSH HADER, LHP

BA GRADE

55 Risk: Medium

Born: April 7, 1994. **B-T:** L-L. **Ht.:** 6-3. **Wt.:** 172. **Drafted:** HS—Millersville, Md., 2012 (19th round). **Signed by:** Dean Albany (Orioles).

One of four players acquired from the Astros in the July 2015 trade that sent Carlos Gomez and Mike Fiers to Houston, Hader drew raves from scouts with a sensational showing in that year's Arizona Fall League. He breezed through 11 starts at Double-A Biloxi in 2016 before encountering trouble at Triple-A Colorado Springs, a hitter's haven. Still, he struck out 161 batters to rank fourth in the minors. Hader has no trouble striking out batters from both sides of the plate with a live fastball in the 92-97 mph range and a filthy, sharp-breaking slider he throws from a low three-quarters arm slot. With the low arm angle and funky delivery, deception is a big part of his game. Hader made it even harder to track his pitches by moving to the first-base side of the rubber, and he changed the grip on his slider to give him more command of the high-80s breaking ball. If Hader ever finds consistency with his changeup, he'll be almost completely unhittable, but he has struggled to stay on top of the pitch. Because he is not afraid to pitch inside, righties cannot dig in on him. He still has bouts of wildness and must concentrate on his mechanics to avoid having those issues elevate his pitch counts. Hader has front-line starter's stuff but must improve his changeup and control to reach his ceiling. Now that the Brewers have added him to the 40-man roster, he will compete for a big league job in spring training.

Year	Club (League)	Class	W	L	ERA	G	GS	CG	SV	IP	H	HR	BB	SO	K/9	WHIP	AVG
2014	Lancaster (CAL)	HiA	9	2	2.70	22	15	0	2	103	76	9	38	112	9.8	1.10	.206
	Corpus Christi (TL)	AA	1	1	6.30	5	4	0	0	20	16	2	16	24	10.8	1.60	.216
2015	Corpus Christi (TL)	AA	3	3	3.17	17	10	0	1	65	60	5	24	69	9.5	1.29	.237
	Biloxi (SL)	AA	1	4	2.79	7	7	0	0	39	27	3	11	50	11.6	0.98	.200
2016	Biloxi (SL)	AA	2	1	0.95	11	11	0	0	57	38	1	19	73	11.5	1.00	.194
	Colorado Springs (PCL)	AAA	1	7	5.22	14	14	0	0	69	63	5	36	88	11.5	1.43	.245
Minor League Totals			24	24	3.03	115	83	0	5	489	375	31	207	559	10.3	1.19	.212

3 LUIS ORTIZ, RHP

BA GRADE

60 Risk: High

Born: Sept. 22, 1995. **B-T:** R-R. **Ht.:** 6-3. **Wt.:** 230. **Drafted:** HS—Sanger, Calif., 2014 (1st round). **Signed by:** Butch Metzger (Rangers).

Ortiz dealt with a forearm injury as a high school senior that forced him down the board to the Rangers at No. 30 overall in the 2014 draft. Texas dealt him along with 2012 first-rounder Lewis Brinson to the Brewers in the Jonathan Lucroy deal at the 2016 trade deadline. Milwaukee assigned Ortiz to Double-A Biloxi, where he recorded a 1.93 ERA in six starts while working on strict pitch counts. With a large, physical frame, Ortiz maintains his mid-90s velocity throughout his outings and also throws an above-average low-80s slider that has tight, late break. He has tried to incorporate his changeup more often, and it is an improving pitch with average potential. Using a smooth, three-quarters delivery that he repeats consistently, Ortiz pounds the bottom of the strike zone and has at least average control. He has shown a feel for working both sides of the plate and keeps the ball in the park. Durability is the obvious concern because of his history of health issues, including a strained flexor muscle that cost him two months in 2015 and a strained groin in 2016 that cost him a couple starts. Ortiz has the stuff and touch to be mid-rotation starter, but he has to commit more to conditioning and stay off the disabled list. He still is young and already has pitched at Double-A, and he could reach Milwaukee later in 2017 with a big year.

Year	Club (League)	Class	W	L	ERA	G	GS	CG	SV	IP	H	HR	BB	SO	K/9	WHIP	AVG
2014	Rangers (AZL)	R	1	1	2.03	6	5	0	0	13	12	0	3	15	10.1	1.13	.240
	Hickory (SAL)	LoA	0	0	1.29	3	1	0	1	7	4	1	3	4	5.1	1.00	.154
2015	Hickory (SAL)	LoA	4	1	1.80	13	13	0	0	50	45	1	9	46	8.3	1.08	.238
2016	High Desert (CAL)	HiA	3	2	2.60	7	6	0	0	28	23	4	6	28	9.1	1.05	.221
	Frisco (TL)	AA	1	4	4.08	9	8	0	1	40	47	3	7	34	7.7	1.36	.296
	Biloxi (SL)	AA	2	2	1.93	6	6	0	0	23	26	2	10	16	6.2	1.54	.280
Minor League Totals			11	10	2.52	44	39	0	2	161	157	11	38	143	8.0	1.21	.253

4 COREY RAY, OF

Born: Sept. 22, 1994. **B-T:** L-L. **Ht.:** 5-11. **Wt.:** 185. **Drafted:** Louisville, 2016 (1st round). **Signed by:** Jeff Simpson.

The Brewers selected Ray with the No. 5 overall pick in 2016 and signed him for $4.125 million, the largest bonus in club history. He put his combination of power and speed on display at Louisville with 15 home runs and 44 stolen bases. The Brewers aggressively assigned him to high Class A Brevard County, a brutal hitter's park, and while he hit just .247 in 57 games, he showed above-average power. He joined low Class A Wisconsin late in the year for its playoff run. Ray has tremen-dous bat speed and makes hard contact consistently, which is why he hit for both average and power at Louisville. He uses the entire field and has shown improved plate discipline and pitch recognition, though he still chases breaking balls off the plate. He has plus speed and uses it well on the bases, stealing with abandon. Ray played mostly right field in college, but the Brewers believe he has center-field tools and played him there in his pro debut. He has average arm strength and at least solid-average range. Ray ended 2016 on a down note by having arthroscopic surgery on his left knee after tearing his meniscus in instructional league. He should be ready to go in spring training and faces a probable return to high Class A and in-season move to Double-A Biloxi. The Brewers view him as an impact outfielder who could be big league ready at some point in 2018.

BA GRADE
60 Risk: High

Year	Club (League)	Class	AVG	G	AB	R	H	2B	3B	HR	RBI	BB	SO	SB	CS	OBP	SLG
2016	Brevard County (FSL)	HiA	.247	57	231	24	57	13	2	5	17	20	54	9	5	.307	.385
	Wisconsin (MWL)	LoA	.083	3	12	2	1	0	0	0	0	3	4	1	1	.313	.083
Minor League Totals			.239	60	243	26	58	13	2	5	17	23	58	10	6	.307	.370

5 ISAN DIAZ, SS/2B

Born: May 27, 1996. **B-T:** L-R. **Ht.:** 5-10. **Wt.:** 185. **Drafted:** HS—Springfield, Mass., 2014 (2nd round supplemental). **Signed by:** Mike Serbalik (Diamondbacks).

The Brewers made Diaz their primary target when they traded Jean Segura to the Diamondbacks after the 2015 season. Diaz was coming off an MVP performance in the Rookie-level Pioneer League in which the 5-foot-10 shortstop led the circuit with a .640 slugging percentage. Milwaukee assigned him to low Class A Wisconsin in 2016 and he mashed 20 home runs to lead the Midwest League as a 20-year-old. The lefthanded-hitting Diaz has plus bat speed and great hand-eye coordination, resulting in lots of hard contact and the ability to drive the ball to all parts of the field. He has an advanced offensive approach (he ranked second in the MWL with 72 walks) but is learning to find a middle ground between discipline and natural aggression (he also ranked second with 148 strikeouts). A fringe-average runner, Diaz has good instincts on the bases and gets good jumps to compensate. With merely average range and arm strength, he began playing second base more frequently in the second half of 2016, and that's the position where he profiles best. Already one of the Brewers top position prospects, Diaz might be two years away form forming a double-play combina-tion with shortstop Orlando Arcia. First, Diaz must contend with the high Class A Carolina League.

BA GRADE
55 Risk: High

Year	Club (League)	Class	AVG	G	AB	R	H	2B	3B	HR	RBI	BB	SO	SB	CS	OBP	SLG
2014	Diamondbacks (AZL)	R	.187	49	182	22	34	7	5	3	21	25	56	6	5	.289	.330
2015	Missoula (PIO)	R	.360	68	272	58	98	25	6	13	51	34	65	12	7	.436	.640
2016	Wisconsin (MWL)	LoA	.264	135	507	71	134	34	5	20	75	72	148	11	8	.358	.469
Minor League Totals			.277	252	961	151	266	66	16	36	147	131	269	29	20	.367	.491

6 TRENT CLARK, OF

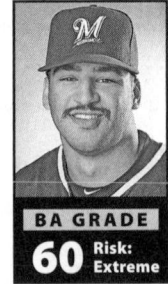

Born: Nov. 1, 1996. **B-T:** L-L. **Ht.:** 6-0. **Wt.:** 205. **Drafted:** HS—North Richland Hills, Texas, 2015 (1st round). **Signed by:** K.J. Hendricks.

The Brewers regarded Clark as a steal when they selected the prep center fielder 15th overall in 2015, and after signing for $2.7 million he hit .309/.424/.430 at two Rookie-level stops. Assigned to low Class A Wisconsin in 2016, he failed to build on that success because he couldn't stay healthy. Clark suffered strained hamstrings twice and spent extensive time on the disabled list, curtailing his action to 59 games. Clark entered pro ball with an unorthodox golf-style batting grip in which he positions his thumbs along the bat, and after experimenting with a traditional grip he stuck with what works. That's because his short lefthanded swing produces consistent hard contact. He keeps his bat in the zone a long time and should develop average power with more experience. A good athlete who possesses above-average speed, Clark shows instincts on the bases

BA GRADE
60 Risk: Extreme

and in center field, though hamstring issues had an obvious effect on his range. If he moves to a corner, his fringe-average arm would fit better in left field. Not only is he an advanced young hitter but Clark also shows leadership skills at a young age. Because Clark spent so much time on the DL in 2016, he might have to repeat the Midwest League. With so many center fielders ahead of Clark on the depth chart, the Brewers can afford to be patient. He has the potential for five average or better tools.

Year	Club (League)	Class	AVG	G	AB	R	H	2B	3B	HR	RBI	BB	SO	SB	CS	OBP	SLG
2015	Brewers (AZL)	R	.309	43	165	34	51	7	6	1	16	30	36	20	5	.422	.442
	Helena (PIO)	R	.310	12	42	5	13	0	0	1	5	9	8	5	3	.431	.381
2016	Wisconsin (MWL)	LoA	.231	59	221	27	51	15	2	2	24	37	68	5	10	.346	.344
Minor League Totals			.269	114	428	66	115	22	8	4	45	76	112	30	18	.384	.386

7 BRANDON WOODRUFF, RHP

Born: Feb. **10, 1993. B-T:** R-R. **Ht.:** 6-2. **Wt.:** 225. **Drafted:** Mississippi State, 2014 (11th round). **Signed by:** Scott Nichols.

Beset by injuries at Mississippi State, Woodruff fell to the Brewers in the 11th round of the 2014 draft, then produced modest results in two pro seasons before breaking out in his third. After earning midseason all-star honors in the Florida State League in 2016, he climbed to Double-A Biloxi and continued to excel, even overcoming the July death of his older brother in an ATV accident back in Mississippi. He went 14-9, 2.68 overall and led the minors with 173 strikeouts to earn the organization's minor league pitcher of the year award. Woodruff pitched in the low 90s early in his career but cleaned up his mechanics and pitched regularly

BA GRADE

55 Risk: High

at 93-94 mph in 2016 with good movement and sink. He benefitted greatly by increasing his tempo and rhythm, which allowed him to repeat his delivery more consistently. Woodruff also features an above-average slider and an average changeup to round out a starter's repertoire. He had control issues in college but has thrown strikes as a pro. With a bulldog approach and groundball tendencies he has a floor as high-leverage reliever. Woodruff has a No. 3 starter ceiling and is ready for Triple-A Colorado Springs, which presents the Brewers with a conundrum. The harsh pitching conditions there have sidetracked prospects such as Josh Hader, Jorge Lopez and Taylor Jungmann, so a return to Biloxi is possible.

Year	Club (League)	Class	W	L	ERA	G	GS	CG	SV	IP	H	HR	BB	SO	K/9	WHIP	AVG
2014	Helena (PIO)	R	1	2	3.28	14	8	0	0	47	48	2	16	37	7.1	1.37	.262
2015	Brevard County (FSL)	HiA	4	7	3.45	21	19	0	0	110	112	2	33	71	5.8	1.32	.270
2016	Brevard County (FSL)	HiA	4	1	1.83	8	8	0	0	44	33	2	10	49	9.9	0.97	.205
	Biloxi (SL)	AA	10	8	3.01	20	20	1	0	114	88	4	30	124	9.8	1.04	.211
Minor League Totals			19	18	3.03	63	55	1	0	314	281	10	89	281	8.0	1.18	.239

8 PHIL BICKFORD, RHP

Born: July 10, 1995. **B-T:** R-R. **Ht.:** 6-4. **Wt.:** 200. **Drafted:** JC of Southern Nevada, 2015 (1st round). **Signed by:** Chuck Fick (Giants).

Drafted 10th overall by the Blue Jays in 2013, Bickford didn't sign and went to Cal State Fullerton. After a big summer in the Cape Cod League, he transferred to the JC of Southern Nevada for 2015, then went to the Giants at No. 18 overall in that year's draft. The Brewers acquired Bickford plus catcher Andrew Susac when they sent reliever Will Smith to San Francisco at the 2016 trade deadline. Bickford recorded a 2.69 ERA through 17 starts at two Class A stops in the Giants system prior to the trade, but he struggled to throw strikes at high Class A Brevard County. A power pitcher, he can reach 95 mph with his high-spin, four-seam fastball and

BA GRADE

55 Risk: High

sits comfortably in the low 90s with a two-seamer that has good sink. His slider is an above-average pitch when he stays on top of it, but at times it becomes too slurvy. He made progress with his changeup and it can become a near-average pitch. Bickford's main issue is maintaining his release point because he tends to drop his elbow and lose tilt on his slider. Coaches have worked with him to dial back his velocity in order to command his pitches. Because Bickford can be electric in short bursts, some project him as a reliever, perhaps even a closer. The Brewers plan to keep him in the rotation until he shows he can't handle it. He'll start 2017 serving a 50-game suspension following his second positive test for a drug of a abuse.

Year	Club (League)	Class	W	L	ERA	G	GS	CG	SV	IP	H	HR	BB	SO	K/9	WHIP	AVG
2015	Giants (AZL)	R	0	1	2.01	10	10	0	0	22	13	0	6	32	12.9	0.85	.169
2016	Augusta (SAL)	LoA	3	4	2.70	11	11	1	0	60	49	2	15	69	10.4	1.07	.220
	San Jose (CAL)	HiA	2	2	2.73	6	6	1	0	33	21	3	12	36	9.8	1.00	.186
	Brevard County (FSL)	HiA	2	1	3.67	6	5	0	0	27	26	1	15	30	10.0	1.52	.252
Minor League Totals			7	8	2.78	33	32	2	0	142	109	6	48	167	10.6	1.10	.211

9 LUCAS ERCEG, 3B

Born: May 1, 1995. **B-T:** L-R. **Ht.:** 6-3. **Wt.:** 200. **Drafted:** Menlo (Calif.), 2016 (2nd round). **Signed by:** Joe Graham.

The Brewers viewed Erceg as a steal in the second round of the 2016 draft and quickly signed him for $1.15 million. He was firmly on Milwaukee's radar after a strong sophomore season at California, and he remained there even after he became academically ineligible and enrolled at NAIA Menlo College near his home in San Jose. The competition obviously wasn't as strong at Menlo, but the Brewers focused on Erceg's solid offensive and defensive tools. He did not disappoint in pro ball by hitting .400/.452/.552 in 26 games at Rookie-level Helena to earn a promotion to low Class A Wisconsin. He hit for average and power in his debut and should grade as at least average in both departments. Erceg doubled as a reliever in college, even closing at Menlo, and has the arm to show for it, helping his case to remain at third base. He is athletic with good hands. In an organization lacking in blue-chip third-base prospects, Erceg already stands out and is expected to move steadily up the ladder. One scout who saw him compared him with the Cardinals' Matt Carpenter in terms of body type, athleticism and a lefthanded bat with some pop. He will tackle high Class A Brevard County in 2017.

BA GRADE
55 Risk: High

Year	Club (League)	Class	AVG	G	AB	R	H	2B	3B	HR	RBI	BB	SO	SB	CS	OBP	SLG
2016	Helena (PIO)	R	.400	26	105	17	42	8	1	2	22	8	16	8	1	.452	.552
	Wisconsin (MWL)	LoA	.281	42	167	17	47	9	3	7	29	12	38	1	3	.328	.497
Minor League Totals			.327	68	272	34	89	17	4	9	51	20	54	9	4	.376	.518

10 MARCOS DIPLAN, RHP

Born: Sept. 18, 1996. **B-T:** R-R. **Ht.:** 6-0. **Wt.:** 170. **Signed:** Dominican Republic, 2013. **Signed by:** Willie Espinal/Mike Daly (Rangers).

The Rangers ponied up $1.3 million to sign Diplan out of the Dominican Republic in 2013, then bundled him with two other prospects to acquire Yovani Gallardo after the 2014 season. Diplan pitched at two Class A levels for the Brewers in 2016 at age 19 and would have claimed the low Class A Midwest League ERA title (1.80) had he the required number of innings. Though 6-feet and a bit undersized, Diplan has a big arm and great feel for pitching for such a young player. He ranges from 92-96 mph with late life on his fastball and also features a slider that has been a plus pitch for him. Diplan continues to work on a changeup that will be important in remaining in a starting role. He needs to reduce his walk rate but otherwise excels at missing bats, limiting hard contact and keeping the ball on the ground. Command should come because he maintains consistency in his delivery. Diplan shows poise and mound presence not often seen in such an inexperienced pitcher. Reaching high Class A Brevard County as a teenager is a good sign for Diplan's future, and he should reach Double-A at age 20. He could be a No. 3 starter if everything breaks right.

BA GRADE
55 Risk: High

Year	Club (League)	Class	W	L	ERA	G	GS	CG	SV	IP	H	HR	BB	SO	K/9	WHIP	AVG
2014	Rangers (DSL)	R	7	2	1.54	13	13	0	0	64	32	2	36	57	8.0	1.06	.155
2015	Helena (PIO)	R	2	2	3.75	13	7	0	2	50	47	4	21	54	9.7	1.35	.257
2016	Wisconsin (MWL)	LoA	6	2	1.80	17	11	0	1	70	49	3	32	89	11.4	1.16	.191
	Brevard County (FSL)	HiA	1	2	4.98	10	6	1	0	43	47	4	18	40	8.3	1.50	.276
Minor League Totals			16	8	2.76	53	37	1	3	228	175	13	107	240	9.5	1.24	.214

11 MAURICIO DUBON, SS

BA GRADE
50 Risk: Medium

Born: July 19, 1994. **B-T:** R-R. **Ht.:** 6-0. **Wt.:** 165. **Drafted:** HS—Sacramento, 2013 (26th round). **Signed by:** Demond Smith (Red Sox).

Dubon, a native of Honduras who moved to the U.S. in high school in hopes of pursuing a baseball career, has elevated the view of his ceiling and floor in each year of his pro career. The Brewers acquired him along with third baseman Travis Shaw and righthander Josh Pennington when they sent reliever Tyler Thornburg to the Red Sox at the 2016 Winter Meetings. Dubon lacks a single plus tool, but the sum of his parts suggests a valuable player. He has long showed an unusual ability to put the bat on the ball, with low strikeouts contributing to consistently high averages. More experience along with a solidifying frame have permitted him a growing ability to drive the ball, most strikingly when he demonstrated steady doubles power in Double-A Portland in 2016 after a mid-year promotion from high Class A Salem. His fundamentally sound approach in the field permitted him to play average to plus defense at shortstop, though his versatility (which has already seen him spend time at second and third base) will be cultivated, and he played center field in the Arizona Fall League. Dubon seems likely to open 2017 at Triple-A

Colorado Springs, where his versatility will put him on the radar as a big league depth option.

Year	Club (League)	Class	AVG	G	AB	R	H	2B	3B	HR	RBI	BB	SO	SB	CS	OBP	SLG
2014	Lowell (NYP)	SS	.320	66	256	40	82	8	1	3	34	9	26	7	8	.337	.395
2015	Greenville (SAL)	LoA	.301	58	236	43	71	12	3	4	29	18	34	18	4	.354	.428
	Salem (CAR)	HiA	.274	62	237	27	65	9	0	1	18	23	38	12	3	.343	.325
2016	Salem (CAR)	HiA	.306	62	235	53	72	11	3	0	29	33	25	24	4	.387	.379
	Portland (EL)	AA	.339	62	251	48	85	20	6	6	40	11	36	6	3	.371	.538
Minor League Totals			.306	330	1268	219	388	63	13	14	154	95	171	73	24	.356	.409

12 BRETT PHILLIPS, OF

BA GRADE
55 Risk: High

Born: May 30, 1994. **B-T:** L-R. **Ht.:** 6-0. **Wt.:** 175. **Drafted:** HS—Seminole, Fla., 2012 (6th round). **Signed by:** John Martin (Astros).

The Brewers picked up Phillips, lefthander Josh Hader and two others in July 2015 when they traded Carlos Gomez and Mike Fiers to the Astros. Phillips suffered an oblique strain that forced him to miss much of 2016 spring training, and he started slowly at Double-A Biloxi and never recovered. His strikeout rate climbed to an out-of-character 30 percent and sent his average into a tailspin (.229), and the same problems manifested in the Arizona Fall League after the season. Though Phillips led the Southern League with 154 strikeouts in 2016, he also ranked among the league leaders with 16 home runs (fourth) and 67 walks (third). Previously known for his short, compact stroke, he got pull-happy and showed why an all-fields approach would probably better suit him. Defensively, Phillips grades as above-average in center field, with a cannon arm that profiles in right and discourages runners from taking liberties. If he can achieve better balance between his hit and power tools, he would profile as a table-setting corner outfielder with above-average speed and patience. He profiles as more of a fourth outfielder for some scouts because he lacks a carrying offensive tool. Had Phillips produced at Biloxi, he would have been a cinch to open 2017 at Triple-A Colorado Springs, but particularly after his AFL showing he faces a probable Double-A repeat. The Brewers believe he has too much talent and determination to fall out of favor.

Year	Club (League)	Class	AVG	G	AB	R	H	2B	3B	HR	RBI	BB	SO	SB	CS	OBP	SLG
2014	Quad Cities (MWL)	LoA	.302	103	384	68	116	21	12	13	58	36	76	18	10	.362	.521
	Lancaster (CAL)	HiA	.339	27	109	19	37	8	2	4	10	14	20	5	4	.421	.560
2015	Lancaster (CAL)	HiA	.320	66	291	68	93	19	7	15	53	22	64	8	6	.379	.588
	Corpus Christi (TL)	AA	.321	31	134	22	43	8	4	1	18	8	26	7	2	.372	.463
	Biloxi (SL)	AA	.250	23	80	14	20	7	3	0	6	14	30	2	1	.361	.413
2016	Biloxi (SL)	AA	.229	124	441	60	101	14	6	16	62	67	154	12	7	.332	.397
Minor League Totals			.278	469	1738	290	484	93	41	49	232	209	449	64	39	.360	.464

13 GILBERT LARA, SS

BA GRADE
55 Risk: Extreme

Born: Oct. 30, 1997. **B-T:** R-R. **Ht.:** 6-3. **Wt.:** 205. **Signed:** Dominican Republic, 2014. **Signed by:** Eduardo Brizuela.

The Brewers thought enough of Lara's offensive potential at age 16 to sign the Dominican shortstop for $3,097,500. In two years of Rookie ball, he has compiled a light .609 OPS with three home runs in the extremely hitter-friendly Arizona and Pioneer leagues. With below-average speed, Lara needs to drive the ball to have real impact. Big and strong, he has yet to translate his raw power to games because he hasn't gotten his swing mechanics together. Specifically, he lacks balance and plate discipline. The Brewers have worked with Lara to use his hands more, which could be the answer to tapping into his natural power. He has exceeded defensive expectations at shortstop, however, and has shown good range and arm strength, putting off thoughts of a shift to third base for now. Lara is going to take time to develop, obviously, but scouts believe he has too many physical tools not to break through at some point. He will need a big spring training to make the jump to low Class A Wisconsin.

Year	Club (League)	Class	AVG	G	AB	R	H	2B	3B	HR	RBI	BB	SO	SB	CS	OBP	SLG
2015	Brewers (AZL)	R	.248	51	202	29	50	4	5	1	25	9	41	3	3	.285	.332
	Helena (PIO)	R	.205	12	44	2	9	3	0	0	5	5	12	0	0	.286	.273
2016	Helena (PIO)	R	.250	59	228	30	57	10	0	2	28	12	59	2	1	.293	.320
Minor League Totals			.245	122	474	61	116	17	5	3	58	26	112	5	4	.289	.321

14 JACOB NOTTINGHAM, C

BA GRADE
50 Risk: High

Born: April 3, 1995. **B-T:** R-R. **Ht.:** 6-3. **Wt.:** 230. **Drafted:** HS—Redlands, Calif., 2013 (6th round). **Signed by:** Brad Budzinski (Astros).

The rebuilding Brewers went into 2016 knowing they would probably trade veteran catcher Jonathan Lucroy, a free agent after the 2017 season. Milwaukee did in fact end up dealing Lucroy to the Rangers at the trade deadline in a deal that fetched top prospects Lewis Brinson and Luis Ortiz. With the pending vacancy at catcher, they realized they had no young catcher on standby to replace Lucory, so they made a preemptive trade with the Athletics that sent slugger Khris Davis to Oakland for Nottingham and right-hander Bubba Derby. The Brewers then aggressively assigned the 21-year-old Nottingham to Double-A Biloxi, where he had his hands full in the Southern League, one of the most unforgiving environments for catchers. He caught 98 games, one of the highest totals in the minors, and threw out a league-average 29 percent of basestealers. The Brewers believe Nottingham will develop into a home-run hitter because of his combination of physical strength and bat speed. He already is learning to drive the ball to all parts of the park. Overmatched at times in the SL, he struck out 30 percent of the time while drawing just 29 walks. Nottingham faces defensive questions because despite obvious arm strength, he still is raw in terms of receiving and blocking balls in the dirt. He might simply outgrow the position as well, which raises the possibility of a move to first base. Given Nottingham's youth, a return to Biloxi seems likely.

Year	Club (League)	Class	AVG	G	AB	R	H	2B	3B	HR	RBI	BB	SO	SB	CS	OBP	SLG
2014	Greeneville (APP)	R	.230	48	174	25	40	10	1	5	28	18	54	3	2	.307	.385
2015	Quad Cities (MWL)	LoA	.326	59	230	34	75	18	1	10	46	18	51	1	2	.387	.543
	Lancaster (CAL)	HiA	.324	17	71	14	23	6	1	4	14	3	10	0	0	.368	.606
	Stockton (CAL)	HiA	.299	43	164	25	49	9	0	3	22	12	38	1	0	.352	.409
2016	Biloxi (SL)	AA	.234	112	415	46	97	14	0	11	37	29	138	9	2	.295	.347
Minor League Totals			.267	323	1200	167	320	67	5	34	167	101	329	18	8	.333	.416

15   JORGE LOPEZ, RHP

BA GRADE
55 Risk: Extreme

Born: Feb. 10, 1993. **B-T:** R-R. **Ht.:** 6-4. **Wt.:** 185. **Drafted:** HS—Gurabo, P.R., 2011 (2nd round). **Signed by:** Charlie Sullivan/Manolo Hernandez.

No prospect in the organization went backwards as much as Lopez did in 2016, and it was difficult to assign blame. Was it solely his fault or did the hitter-friendly conditions at Triple-A Colorado Springs do him in? Lopez's best pitch is a knee-bending curveball, and when he couldn't get it to break as much at high altitude in the Pacific Coast League, he failed to adjust and went into a deep funk. His command completely deserted him to the point that he issued an incredible 55 walks in 79.1 innings in Triple-A. It got so bad that the Brewers eventually removed him from that club, sent him to their training complex in Phoenix to regroup and then downward to Double-A Biloxi, where Lopez had been the Southern League pitcher of the year in 2015. Now, it remains to be seen if he can re-gather his mechanics and move forward again. When on top of his game, he features an explosive fastball at 92-95 mph and the aforementioned curveball with strong downward tilt. Lopez needs to work more on his changeup to gain more consistency and keep hitters off his fastball. It remains to be seen if 2015 was a season that Lopez never will be able to repeat, or if he can survive if sent back to Colorado Springs. The 2017 season will be telling.

Year	Club (League)	Class	W	L	ERA	G	GS	CG	SV	IP	H	HR	BB	SO	K/9	WHIP	AVG
2014	Brevard County (FSL)	HiA	10	10	4.58	25	25	1	0	138	144	12	46	119	7.8	1.38	.273
2015	Biloxi (SL)	AA	12	5	2.26	24	24	0	0	143	105	9	52	137	8.6	1.10	.205
	Milwaukee (NL)	MAJ	1	1	5.40	2	2	0	0	10	14	0	5	10	9.0	1.90	.350
2016	Colorado Springs (PCL)	AAA	1	7	6.81	17	16	0	0	79	101	12	55	66	7.5	1.97	.312
	Biloxi (SL)	AA	2	4	3.97	8	8	0	0	45	45	5	16	47	9.3	1.35	.260
Major League Totals			1	1	5.40	2	2	0	0	10	14	0	5	10	9.0	1.90	.350
Minor League Totals			33	38	4.39	115	105	1	4	583	577	53	242	517	8.0	1.41	.259

16   CODY PONCE, RHP

BA GRADE
50 Risk: High

Born: April 25, 1994. **B-T:** R-R. **Ht.:** 6-6. **Wt.:** 240. **Drafted:** Cal Poly Pomona, 2015 (2nd round). **Signed by:** Josh Belovsky.

The Brewers had high hopes for Ponce after a strong pro debut in 2015, when he was taken in the second round and signed for $1.1 million. But he developed arm issues in 2016 spring training and was held back in Phoenix for two months, then spent the rest of the season trying to catch up. Ponce's stuff backed up once he was assigned to high Class A Brevard County, which slowed his progress through the system. When healthy, the big-bodied, 6-foot-6 righthander has the stuff to succeed as a bulldog starter in the majors. His fastball sits in the mid-90s and he can reach 98 mph at times, with an effective cutter in the upper 80s he uses to battle lefthanded batters. Ponce needs to work on a changeup that he often throws too firmly, and he needs to find more consistency with his curveball. He uses his size to throw his fastball on a downward plan and induce groundballs and shows good command of all his pitches when in good health. Ponce has more athleticism than might be expected of a pitcher of his size and has an aggressive approach to pitching. The Brewers think he has the durability and stuff to remain a starter and advance to the big leagues in that role.

Year	Club (League)	Class	W	L	ERA	G	GS	CG	SV	IP	H	HR	BB	SO	K/9	WHIP	AVG
2015	Helena (PIO)	R	0	0	3.60	2	2	0	0	5	4	0	0	4	7.2	0.80	.222
	Wisconsin (MWL)	LoA	2	1	2.15	12	7	0	3	46	43	1	9	36	7.0	1.13	.246
2016	Brevard County (FSL)	HiA	2	8	5.25	17	17	0	0	72	84	6	17	69	8.6	1.40	.285
Minor League Totals			4	9	4.02	31	26	0	3	123	131	7	26	109	8.0	1.28	.268

17 KODI MEDEIROS, LHP

BA GRADE

50 Risk: High

Born: May 25, 1996. **B-T:** L-L. **Ht.:** 6-2. **Wt.:** 180. **Drafted:** HS—Hilo, Hawaii, 2014 (1st round). **Signed by:** Josh Belovsky.

Medeiros pitched so well as a teenager in his first full season at low Class A Wisconsin in 2015 that the Brewers assumed he would do likewise at high Class A Brevard County in 2016. Instead he struggled with his control (63 walks in 85 innings), ran up high pitch counts, exited games early and finished with a 1.94 WHIP. It was not the step forward the Brewers envisioned for the 12th overall pick in the 2014 draft, but Medeiros didn't turn 20 until late May. When he has his mechanics together, he delivers pitches from a low three-quarters angle with a fastball in the 92-95 mph range with late movement and sinking action that results in lots of groundballs. He mixes in a plus slider that is death on lefthanded batters with tremendous lateral movement. Medeiros has worked to improve his changeup, which he also keeps down in the strike zone when on top of his game. He is athletic and mature for his age, and the Brewers believe he will continue to improve and remain a starter despite concern over his low arm slot. He will receive another run at high Class A in 2017 to prove his future is in the rotation and not the bullpen.

Year	Club (League)	Class	W	L	ERA	G	GS	CG	SV	IP	H	HR	BB	SO	K/9	WHIP	AVG
2014	Brewers (AZL)	R	0	2	7.13	9	4	0	1	18	24	2	13	26	13.2	2.09	.308
2015	Wisconsin (MWL)	LoA	4	5	4.44	25	16	0	1	93	79	0	40	94	9.1	1.28	.228
2016	Brevard County (FSL)	HiA	4	12	5.93	23	22	0	0	85	102	4	63	64	6.8	1.94	.300
Minor League Totals			8	19	5.33	57	42	0	2	196	205	6	116	184	8.4	1.64	.268

18 RYAN CORDELL, OF

BA GRADE

50 Risk: High

Born: March 31, 1992. **B-T:** R-R. **Ht.:** 6-4. **Wt.:** 205. **Drafted:** Liberty, 2011 (11th round). **Signed by:** Jonathan George (Rangers).

An athletic outfielder who toyed around at third base and shortstop at times while in the Rangers system, Cordell joined the Brewers after the 2016 minor league season as the player to be named in the Jonathan Lucroy deal. Milwaukee also picked up outfielder Lewis Brinson and righthander Luis Ortiz in that transaction. The Brewers plan to play Cordell exclusively in the outfield. They selected him off a short list even though he had suffered a high ankle sprain crashing into a wall the day after the Lurcroy trade was consummated and didn't play again. Cordell has good bat speed and developing power and made adjustments as he moved through the Rangers system. Though he hit just .264 at Double-A Frisco, he slammed 46 extra-base hits and ranked third in the Texas League with a .220 isolated slugging percentage. Cordell's strikeout rate rose accordingly and he won't be a huge source of on-base percentage. In addition to above-average power, he also possesses plus speed that makes him a threat on the bases and a gap-to-gap fly chaser in center field. He split his time at all three outfield spots at Frisco and has the arm to fill any of the positions. He is ready for Triple-A Colorado Springs in 2017.

Year	Club (League)	Class	AVG	G	AB	R	H	2B	3B	HR	RBI	BB	SO	SB	CS	OBP	SLG
2014	Hickory (SAL)	LoA	.321	73	274	53	88	18	4	8	40	27	53	18	3	.388	.504
	Myrtle Beach (CAR)	HiA	.306	16	62	12	19	2	2	5	19	7	13	3	1	.371	.645
2015	High Desert (CAL)	HiA	.311	68	286	58	89	13	5	13	57	28	53	10	5	.376	.528
	Frisco (TL)	AA	.217	56	221	26	48	5	3	5	18	12	73	10	1	.263	.335
2016	Frisco (TL)	AA	.264	107	405	69	107	22	5	19	70	32	97	12	4	.319	.484
Minor League Totals			.275	384	1480	252	407	72	19	55	227	129	342	72	18	.337	.461

19 JOSH PENNINGTON, RHP

BA GRADE

55 Risk: Extreme

Born: July 6, 1995. **B-T:** R-R. **Ht.:** 6-0. **Wt.:** 175. **Drafted:** HS—Cape May, N.J., 2014 (29th round). **Signed by:** Ray Fagnant (Red Sox).

Pennington represented one of the more intriguing Northeastern prep arms entering the 2014 season because of his 89-92 mph fastball that produced plenty of swings and misses. However, he blew out his elbow in the third start of his senior year, resulting in his availability in the 29th round. Pennington signed with the Red Sox for $90,000 and spent the 2014 season rehabbing from Tommy John surgery. Boston traded him to the Brewers along with shortstop Mauricio Dubon and third baseman Travis Shaw at the 2016 Winter Meetings for reliever Tyler Thornburg. When Pennington returned to the mound in 2015, he did so featuring premium arm strength. He typically pitched at 94-99 mph in 2016 while dominating at times at short-season Lowell, where he recorded a 2.86 ERA with 7.8 strikeouts per nine innings. His secondary pitches remain raw and inconsistent, but the righthander shows the potential for an above-average curveball and average changeup, offering starter potential if he can harness those weapons and more consistently throw strikes. He walked 4.3 per nine in 2016. Pennington's delivery is sufficiently clean and repeatable, though he had surgery after the 2016 season to remove a bone chip from his elbow. If everything clicks, he has mid-rotation starter potential and a floor as a possible power reliever.

Year	Club (League)	Class	W	L	ERA	G	GS	CG	SV	IP	H	HR	BB	SO	K/9	WHIP	AVG
2014	Did not play—Injured																
2015	Red Sox (GCL)	R	2	1	0.82	7	6	0	0	22	17	0	13	22	9.0	1.36	.218
2016	Lowell (NYP)	SS	5	3	2.86	13	13	0	0	57	39	2	27	49	7.8	1.16	.200
Minor League Totals			7	4	2.29	20	19	0	0	79	56	2	40	71	8.1	1.22	.205

20 MONTE HARRISON, OF

BA GRADE
55 Risk: Extreme

Born: Aug. 10, 1995. **B-T:** R-R. **Ht.:** 6-3. **Wt.:** 220. **Drafted:** HS—Lee's Summit, Mo., 2014 (2nd round). **Signed by:** Drew Anderson.

No one will ever know what Harrison would have accomplished in his first pro seasons had he stayed healthy. The 2014 second-round pick played just 74 games in 2015 because he slipped rounding third base at Rookie-level Helena and broke his left tibia and ankle. It took a metal plate and screws to repair but Harrison worked hard on his rehab and got ready for 2016. Playing at low Class A Wisconsin, Harrison suffered a broken hamate bone in his left wrist that sidelined him for two months. So one of the best athletes in the system had his development stalled twice, making 2017 a big year for him. When healthy, Harrison has excellent bat speed that should allow him to develop at least average power because of his physical strength. He has plus speed that makes him a threat on the bases and a powerful arm that plays at any outfield spot. Harrison does get long with his swing and has piled up too many strikeouts, but he merely needs to get at-bats and make adjustments. Harrison shined at 2016 instructional league and can develop into an impact player on both offense and defense if he can just stay on the field.

Year	Club (League)	Class	AVG	G	AB	R	H	2B	3B	HR	RBI	BB	SO	SB	CS	OBP	SLG
2014	Brewers (AZL)	R	.261	50	180	37	47	7	2	1	20	31	48	32	2	.402	.339
2015	Wisconsin (MWL)	LoA	.148	46	162	18	24	6	2	2	11	14	77	6	4	.246	.247
	Helena (PIO)	R	.299	28	97	20	29	4	2	3	13	14	23	14	2	.410	.474
2016	Brewers (AZL)	R	.211	5	19	4	4	1	1	0	1	4	4	0	0	.375	.368
	Wisconsin (MWL)	LoA	.221	75	267	34	59	11	1	6	37	20	97	8	3	.294	.337
Minor League Totals			.225	204	725	113	163	29	8	12	82	83	249	60	11	.331	.337

21 FREDDY PERALTA, RHP

BA GRADE
50 Risk: High

Born: June 4, 1996. **B-T:** R-R. **Ht.:** 5-11. **Wt.:** 175. **Signed:** Dominican Republic, 2013. **Signed by:** Tim Kissner/Eddy Toledo/Kelvin Dominguez (Mariners).

When the Brewers traded first baseman Adam Lind to the Mariners after the 2015 season they did so with an eye toward the future. They acquired three pitchers, all 19 years old at the time, in Peralta, Carlos Herrera and Daniel Missaki. Peralta was considered the most advanced of the three and went out and proved it in 2016 with an all-star showing at low Class A Wisconsin that earned him a bump to high Class A Brevard County. The epitome of an undersized righthander, he makes up for it with a repertoire and presence on the mound to still project as a starter. Peralta shows a fastball in the low 90s that tops out at 94 mph with a smooth, clean and repeatable delivery. He mixes in a slider and changeup that have a chance to be at least average in the majors—the change could be above-average—and throws strikes with all three. Peralta's changeup has deceptive arm speed and keeps hitters off his hard stuff. He struck out batters at an elite rate in the Midwest League—77 in 60 innings—but still issues too many walks. Because of Peralta's youth, the Brewers have plenty of time to develop him as a starter. He faces a return to high Class A.

Year	Club (League)	Class	W	L	ERA	G	GS	CG	SV	IP	H	HR	BB	SO	K/9	WHIP	AVG
2014	Mariners (AZL)	R	1	6	5.29	12	12	0	0	51	55	3	24	42	7.4	1.55	.275
2015	Mariners (AZL)	R	2	3	4.11	11	9	0	0	57	52	1	8	67	10.6	1.05	.242
2016	Wisconsin (MWL)	LoA	4	1	2.85	16	8	0	2	60	45	3	24	77	11.6	1.15	.202
	Brevard County (FSL)	HiA	0	3	5.73	8	2	0	0	22	27	4	12	20	8.2	1.77	.321
Minor League Totals			10	16	3.60	60	41	1	2	245	217	11	83	255	9.4	1.22	.237

22 JACOB BARNES, RHP

BA GRADE
45 Risk: Medium

Born: April 14, 1990. **B-T:** R-R. **Ht.:** 6-2. **Wt.:** 220. **Drafted:** Florida Gulf Coast, 2011 (14th round). **Signed by:** Tim McIlvaine.

While many pitching prospects struggled in the hitter-friendly conditions at Triple-A Colorado Springs, Barnes prospered in 2016. That's because a pitcher with a devastating sinker with great movement and a sharp-breaking slider can succeed at high altitude by inducing ground balls and piling up strikeouts. Barnes recorded a 1.21 ERA in 17 relief appearances, forcing the Brewers to call him up in early June. He went on the disabled list in late July with an elbow issue and did not return until September, but he made a favorable impression. Barnes sits in the mid-90s with his fastball while reaching 97 mph at times. He also relies on a high-80s cutter, the pitch that allowed him to elevate his game. Barnes uses a sharp-breaking slider in the mid-80s effectively against righthanded batters when ahead in the count. He is a bulldog type with great lower body strength who throws strikes consistently enough to be used in high-leverage situations. Barnes flourished after moving to the bullpen at Double-A Biloxi in 2015. He gained the confidence of Brewers manager Craig Counsell in 2016 and will be a member of the bullpen in 2017.

Year	Club (League)	Class	W	L	ERA	G	GS	CG	SV	IP	H	HR	BB	SO	K/9	WHIP	AVG
2014	Brevard County (FSL)	HiA	0	0	1.23	3	0	0	0	7	3	1	0	8	9.8	0.41	.125
	Huntsville (SL)	AA	2	6	4.26	23	21	0	0	106	94	9	38	75	6.4	1.25	.244
2015	Biloxi (SL)	AA	4	5	3.36	39	6	0	0	75	74	2	30	84	10.1	1.39	.262
2016	Colorado Springs (PCL)	AAA	2	1	1.21	17	0	0	1	22	14	1	7	23	9.3	0.94	.184
	Biloxi (SL)	AA	0	0	0.00	3	0	0	0	3	2	0	0	4	13.5	0.75	.182
	Milwaukee (NL)	MAJ	0	1	2.70	27	0	0	1	27	24	1	6	26	8.8	1.13	.245
Major League Totals			0	1	2.70	27	0	0	1	27	24	1	6	26	8.8	1.13	.245
Minor League Totals			23	26	3.36	149	48	1	6	442	397	32	163	386	7.9	1.27	.244

23 JAKE GATEWOOD, 3B/1B

BA GRADE
55 Risk: Extreme

Born: Sept. 25, 1995. **B-T:** R-R. **Ht.:** 6-6. **Wt.:** 210. **Drafted:** HS—Clovis, Calif., 2014 (1st round supplemental). **Signed by:** Dan Huston.

The Brewers knew that because of his swing-and-miss tendencies, Gatewood would be a high-risk prospect when they drafted him in 2014. He wowed amateur scouts with his power displays, but has struggled to make contact as a pro, whiffing 345 times in 285 games for a 30 percent rate. The Brewers also figured the 6-foot-6 Gatewood would grow out of the shortstop position, and that happened quickly as he physically matured. At low Class A Wisconsin in 2016 he played third base and first base, and the latter might be his position for the future. Gatewood stumbled badly in the Midwest League in 2015 but rebounded to hit for above-average power with 14 home runs and 33 doubles in 2016. He showed a free-swinging plate approach, however, with few walks and many strikeouts contributing to a .240 average and below-average hit tool. Gatewood has tremendous bat speed and plus power potential. He has good athleticism for his size and a strong-enough arm to play third base but is going to need time to develop his skills at the hot corner. He must find a way to be more selective at the plate and shorter to the ball to keep his strikeouts within an acceptable range. He will head to high Class A Brevard County in 2017.

Year	Club (League)	Class	AVG	G	AB	R	H	2B	3B	HR	RBI	BB	SO	SB	CS	OBP	SLG
2014	Brewers (AZL)	R	.206	50	204	19	42	6	0	3	32	13	71	7	8	.249	.279
2015	Helena (PIO)	R	.274	54	212	38	58	23	1	6	41	18	68	3	5	.331	.476
	Wisconsin (MWL)	LoA	.209	55	177	16	37	5	1	4	16	14	65	5	0	.275	.316
2016	Wisconsin (MWL)	LoA	.240	126	496	70	119	33	0	14	64	18	141	3	2	.268	.391
Minor League Totals			.235	285	1089	143	256	67	2	27	153	63	345	18	15	.278	.375

24 CORBIN BURNES, RHP

BA GRADE
50 Risk: High

Born: Oct. 22, 1994. **B-T:** R-R. **Ht.:** 6-3. **Wt.:** 205. **Drafted:** St. Mary's, 2016 (4th round). **Signed by:** Joe Graham.

Burnes was not highly recruited and ended up at St. Mary's, where he prospered under head coach Eric Valenzuela, a mentor to such future major leaguers as Brian Matusz, A.J. Griffin and Sammy Solis. Burnes got better each year and picked up velocity on his fastball, which reached 97 mph in the Cape Cod League in 2015. He served as St. Mary's ace as a junior and the Brewers stayed on him until the 2016 draft and popped him in the fourth round. Burnes throws his fastball in the 91-93 mph range and touches 95 when he needs it. He still needs work on his secondary pitches but has a promising slider and also mixes in a curveball and changeup. Some worry that Burnes throws with maximum effort and that his arm action is too quick, which could land him in the bullpen at some point. But he has maintained his velocity deep into starts, and as long as he holds his mechanics together the Brewers believe he has a future as a starter. Burnes certainly has the frame to handle a solid workload. After three outings in the Rookie-level Arizona League he joined low Class A Wisconsin and held opponents to a .200 average with a 1.26 WHIP at that level. The Brewers think he will only get better with experience and move steadily through the system.

Year	Club (League)	Class	W	L	ERA	G	GS	CG	SV	IP	H	HR	BB	SO	K/9	WHIP	AVG
2016	Brewers (AZL)	R	0	0	1.29	3	1	0	0	7	3	0	2	10	12.9	0.71	.125
	Wisconsin (MWL)	LoA	3	0	2.20	9	5	0	0	29	20	1	16	31	9.7	1.26	.200
Minor League Totals			3	0	2.02	12	6	0	0	36	23	1	18	41	10.3	1.15	.185

25 DEVIN WILLIAMS, RHP

BA GRADE
55 Risk: Extreme

Born: Sept. 21, 1994. **B-T:** R-R. **Ht.:** 6-3. **Wt.:** 180. **Drafted:** HS—Hazelwood, Mo., 2013 (2nd round). **Signed by:** Harvey Kuenn Jr.

Though taken in the second round in 2013, the Brewers always have thought Williams had first-round talent. Because of maturity issues and a few health setbacks, it has taken him a while to deliver on that projection. Williams spent two seasons in Rookie ball before his full-season debut in 2015. He returned to low Class A Wisconsin in 2016 after staying behind in extended spring training to work through a shoulder issue. Williams still has the potential to be a solid major league starter, but he's on a slower than average development track. His fastball sits in the low 90s with good life and touches 95 mph at times. As Williams matures and his lanky 6-foot-3 frame fills out, the Brewers believe his velocity will sit in the mid-90s. He has a mid-80s slider that he sometimes gets under but has a chance to be an average pitch, along with an improving changeup. Williams focused on better command after issuing too many walks in 2015 and leading the Midwest League with 19 wild pitches. He is very athletic and should improve at repeating his delivery. The Brewers still think Williams has the talent to make a big leap at some point.

Year	Club (League)	Class	W	L	ERA	G	GS	CG	SV	IP	H	HR	BB	SO	K/9	WHIP	AVG
2014	Helena (PIO)	R	4	7	4.48	15	8	0	0	66	74	5	20	66	9.0	1.42	.282
2015	Wisconsin (MWL)	LoA	3	9	3.44	22	13	0	0	89	75	3	36	89	9.0	1.25	.226
2016	Wisconsin (MWL)	LoA	6	3	3.61	17	10	0	2	72	64	4	34	74	9.2	1.35	.240
	Brevard County (FSL)	HiA	1	2	4.32	5	2	0	0	25	27	2	12	20	7.2	1.56	.278
Minor League Totals			15	24	3.79	72	39	0	3	287	268	14	124	288	9.0	1.36	.246

26 NATHAN KIRBY, LHP

BA GRADE
55 Risk: Extreme

Born: Nov. 23, 1993. **B-T:** L-L. **Ht.:** 6-2. **Wt.:** 200. **Drafted:** Virginia, 2015 (1st round supplemental). **Signed by:** Dan Nellum.

It didn't shock the Brewers when Kirby needed Tommy John surgery after throwing just 13 innings in his pro debut in 2015. He missed much of his junior year at Virginia with a strained lat, and then a post-draft physical turned up elbow issues that reduced Kirby's bonus to $1.25 million. The Brewers planned for him to pitch at low Class A Wisconsin until his elbow forced him to stop, which happened sooner than later. Tommy John surgery forced him to miss the entire 2016 season. Kirby still wasn't ready to face hitters in game action in instructional league but is expected to be ready to go at the outset of 2017. When healthy, he pitches in the low 90s with his fastball, but it has good action and plays better because of his arm angle and ability to pitch to both sides of the plate. His mid-80s slider is a strong secondary pitch, though some wondered if using it so often in college led to the arm issues. Kirby also features an above-average changeup with good deception, giving him a solid three-pitch mix that should allow him to remain a starter. His combination of athleticism and stuff should allow him to move quickly once healthy and make it to the majors as a mid-rotation starter.

Year	Club (League)	Class	W	L	ERA	G	GS	CG	SV	IP	H	HR	BB	SO	K/9	WHIP	AVG
2015	Wisconsin (MWL)	LoA	0	1	5.68	5	2	0	0	13	15	0	7	7	5.0	1.74	.313
2016	Did not play—Injured																
Minor League Totals			0	1	5.68	5	2	0	0	13	15	0	7	7	5.0	1.74	.313

27 DEMI ORIMOLOYE, OF

BA GRADE
55 Risk: Extreme

Born: Jan. 6, 1997. **B-T:** R-R. **Ht.:** 6-4. **Wt.:** 225. **Drafted:** HS—Orleans, Ont., 2015 (4th round). **Signed by:** Jay Lapp.

Because of Orimoloye's impressive skill set and growth potential when drafted at age 18, the Brewers thought he was a steal in the fourth round of the 2015 draft. A native of Nigeria whose family moved to Toronto when he was 10 months old, Orimoloye made the Brewers feel even better about the pick when he posted an .838 OPS in the Rookie-level Arizona League. Things didn't go nearly as well in 2016 when Orimoloye recorded a .617 OPS at Rookie-level Helena in the hitter-friendly Pioneer League. He has tremendous raw tools, including power, arm strength and speed, but he needs experience, both at the plate and in the field. He lacks polish in all areas of the game because he just hasn't played that much baseball, but he did show a patient approach and stole 18 bases in 22 tries in the PL. As with most young hitters, Orimoloye needs to strike a balance between passivity and aggression at the plate. Once his game comes together, Orimoloye projects to be an impact player in right field. The Brewers believe he has untapped potential and hope he can handle the jump to low Class A Wisconsin in 2017.

Year	Club (League)	Class	AVG	G	AB	R	H	2B	3B	HR	RBI	BB	SO	SB	CS	OBP	SLG
2015	Brewers (AZL)	R	.292	33	137	23	40	9	2	6	26	3	39	19	6	.319	.518
2016	Helena (PIO)	R	.205	61	219	26	45	5	3	5	17	23	57	18	5	.293	.324
Minor League Totals			.239	94	356	49	85	14	5	11	43	26	96	37	11	.303	.399

28 MARIANO FELICIANO, C

BA GRADE

50 Risk: Extreme

Born: Nov. 20, 1998. **B-T:** R-R. **Ht.:** 6-1. **Wt.:** 195. **Drafted:** HS—Florida, P.R., 2016 (2nd round supplemental). **Signed by:** Charlie Sullivan.

Catching has been a positional weakness in the Brewers organization for years, so the new front office regime put an emphasis on building backstop inventory in the 2016 draft. The Brewers made Feliciano one of their first picks. An offensive-minded catcher, he showed a good feel for hitting at the young age of 17 with budding power and good hands. Feliciano didn't draw many walks in his pro debut in the Rookie-level Arizona League, but he didn't strike out much either and certainly did not look overmatched at the plate. He is very athletic and moves well behind the plate and on the bases. Feliciano has above-average arm strength and the tools to develop into a solid defender with more work and experience. Some scouts question Feliciano's long-term future behind the plate, but the Brewers intend to give him the development time to stick there because of his potential for at least average hit and power ability.

Year	Club (League)	Class	AVG	G	AB	R	H	2B	3B	HR	RBI	BB	SO	SB	CS	OBP	SLG
2016	Brewers (AZL)	R	.265	29	117	16	31	5	3	0	16	7	19	2	2	.307	.359
Minor League Totals			.265	29	117	16	31	5	3	0	16	7	19	2	2	.307	.359

29 CHAD McCLANAHAN, 3B

BA GRADE

50 Risk: Extreme

Born: Dec. 22, 1997. **B-T:** L-R. **Ht.:** 6-5. **Wt.:** 200. **Drafted:** HS—Phoenix, 2016 (11th round). **Signed by:** Jeff Scholzen.

The Brewers knew signability could be an issue with McClanahan, who let it be known that he planned to attend Arizona State if his bonus demand was not met. The Brewers selected him in the 11th round and moved on to signing other players but kept money in reserve for a late run at him. Even though they paid a substantial penalty, Milwaukee went over their bonus pool to sign McClanahan for $1.2 million, which is second-round money. A physical specimen who might still grow some, McClanahan has tremendous upside and certainly didn't lower the bar when he homered in his first pro at-bat in the Rookie-level Arizona League. He struck out frequently in his debut and lacked plate discipline, but he hit for above-average power. He projects as a slightly below-average runner. While his offense shows considerable promise, McClanahan is not a lock to remain at third base. His arm is strong enough but some believe he'll move to first base or possibly the outfield, where his athleticism could play. However it plays out position-wise for McClanahan, his offensive potential excites the Brewers.

Year	Club (League)	Class	AVG	G	AB	R	H	2B	3B	HR	RBI	BB	SO	SB	CS	OBP	SLG
2016	Brewers (AZL)	R	.208	35	144	22	30	7	1	3	14	11	45	1	2	.277	.333
Minor League Totals			.208	35	144	22	30	7	1	3	14	11	45	1	2	.277	.333

30 MICHAEL REED, OF

BA GRADE

45 Risk: High

Born: Nov. 18, 1992. **B-T:** R-R. **Ht.:** 6-0. **Wt.:** 210. **Drafted:** HS—Leander, Texas, 2011 (5th round). **Signed by:** Jeremy Booth.

The Brewers weathered injuries to the major league outfield in 2016, presenting an opportunity for Reed to move up and seize the day—but he seemed to be struggling at Triple-A Colorado Spring every time a chance arose. He remained in the Pacific Coast League all season before finally receiving a late-September callup when center fielder Keon Broxton was lost with a broken wrist. Reed is a physical player with a football background who approaches the game with the aggressiveness and intensity of the other sport. Known for a good eye at the plate and plus patience, he ranked fourth in the PCL with 74 walks in 2016, though he hit just .248 with well below-average power. He also struck out about a quarter of the time. Reed is an above-average runner who shows good instincts on the bases. That speed serves him well in center field, but he mostly played right field in 2016, where his arm strength is an asset. At this point, Reed's ceiling appears to be extra outfielder with on-base ability and speed, though as a righthanded hitter, he will need to shine in those areas to elevate himself above lefthanded candidates for the bench.

Year	Club (League)	Class	AVG	G	AB	R	H	2B	3B	HR	RBI	BB	SO	SB	CS	OBP	SLG
2014	Brevard County (FSL)	HiA	.255	110	365	50	93	20	5	5	47	78	79	33	13	.396	.378
2015	Biloxi (SL)	AA	.278	93	313	43	87	20	5	5	49	53	80	25	7	.379	.422
	Colorado Springs (PCL)	AAA	.246	38	126	19	31	13	2	0	21	20	31	1	0	.351	.381
	Milwaukee (NL)	MAJ	.333	7	6	2	2	1	0	0	0	0	3	0	0	.333	.500
2016	Colorado Springs (PCL)	AAA	.248	121	411	68	102	20	2	8	45	74	124	20	8	.366	.365
	Milwaukee (NL)	MAJ	.182	8	22	3	4	0	0	0	0	2	7	1	0	.250	.182
Major League Totals			.214	15	28	5	6	1	0	0	0	2	10	1	0	.267	.250
Minor League Totals			.262	556	1944	293	509	105	30	20	232	333	508	120	39	.373	.378

Minnesota Twins

BY MICHAEL LANANNA

The signs all seemed to point in a positive direction.

After four straight years of 92 or more losses, the 2015 Twins won 83 games under first-year manager Paul Molitor. They competed for a postseason berth. A wave of top prospects, led by outfielder Byron Buxton, seemed ready to seize big league roles.

Then the 2016 season rolled in, and those good feelings quickly evaporated. The Twins started the season 0-9 and were 33-58 at midseason (the second-worst midseason mark in franchise history), so owner Jim Pohlad fired longtime general manager Terry Ryan in mid-July.

Ryan was in his second stint as GM. His first ended with a flourish, when the Twins finished first in the American League Central four times between 2002-06. His second stint ended in failure, as he was unable to get the franchise back on track. The Twins finished the 2016 season 59-103—worst in franchise history.

Obviously, little went right for Minnesota in 2016. Byung Ho Park, a 29-year-old Korean first baseman signed to be the primary DH, struggled to adjust to American baseball, batting .191/.274/.409 before being demoted to Triple-A Rochester. Righthander Phil Hughes had season-ending surgery in early July after an ineffective first two months of the season. Righthanders Tyler Duffey (9-12, 6.43) and Kyle Gibson (6-11, 5.07) took steps back from their strong 2015 seasons. Powerful Miguel Sano—the team's No. 2 prospect in 2015—missed all of June with a hamstring strain after an ill-fated attempt to play him in right field. Injury limited veteran Trevor Plouffe to just 84 games.

The Twins graduated five of their Top 10 Prospects, with varying levels of success. Buxton, sent down twice during the season, finally clicked in September, hitting nine home runs in 101 at-bats. Righthander Jose Berrios went 3-7, 8.02 in the first 14 starts of his big league career, walking 5.4 per nine. Shuttled between Rochester and Minnesota, both outfielder Max Kepler and shortstop Jorge Polanco seemingly solidified major league roles by season's end.

The Twins decided to make two hires to replace Ryan. First came Indians assistant GM Derek Falvey, whose title is chief baseball officer, and right after the World Series they hired Thad Levine from the Rangers as GM. They inherit a major league roster in transition and a farm system thinned by prospect graduations.

The Twins' Top 10 might have more questions

Rookie outfielder Max Kepler hit 17 home runs after ranking as the Twins' No. 3 prospect

TOP PROSPECTS OF THE DECADE

Year	Player, Pos.	2016 Org
2007	Matt Garza, rhp	Brewers
2008	Nick Blackburn, rhp	Did not play
2009	Aaron Hicks, of	Yankees
2010	Aaron Hicks, of	Yankees
2011	Kyle Gibson, rhp	Twins
2012	Miguel Sano, 3b	Twins
2013	Miguel Sano, 3b	Twins
2014	Byron Buxton, of	Twins
2015	Byron Buxton, of	Twins
2016	Byron Buxton, of	Twins

than answers. Does top prospect Nick Gordon have the athleticism to stick at shortstop? Will he hit for enough power? Can lefthander Tyler Jay, the No. 6 overall pick in 2015, make a successful transition from reliever to starter? Can righthander Kohl Stewart, the No. 4 overall pick in 2013, find a way to miss bats with his power stuff? The answers to those questions could define the Twins' immediate future.

The Twins drafted high schoolers in the first four rounds in 2016, and while those picks—led by outfielder Alex Kirilloff—offer plenty of upside, they are far from helping the big league club.

If there's a silver lining from a disastrous 2016 season, it's that the 2017 draft will give them an opportunity to restock, starting with the No. 1 overall pick.

ORGANIZATION OVERVIEW

Chief Baseball Officer: Derek Falvey. **GM:** Thad Levine. **Farm director:** Brad Steil. **Scouting director:** Sean Johnson.

Class	Team	League	W	L	PCT	Finish	Manager
Majors	Minnesota Twins	American	59	103	.364	15th (15)	Paul Molitor
Triple-A	Rochester Red Wings	International	81	63	.563	4th (14)	Mike Quade
Double-A	Chattanooga Lookouts	Southern	75	65	.536	4th (10)	Doug Mientkiewicz
High Class A	Fort Myers Miracle	Florida State	70	68	.507	7th (12)	Jeff Smith
Low Class A	Cedar Rapids Kernels	Midwest	78	61	.561	4th (16)	Jake Mauer
Rookie	Elizabethton Twins	Appalachian	36	31	.537	5th (10)	Ray Smith
Rookie	GCL Twins	Gulf Coast	32	29	.525	6th (17)	Ramon Borrego
Overall 2016 Minor League Record			372	317	.540	5th (30)	

THIS YEAR'S TOP 30

No.	Player, Pos.	Grade/Risk
1	Nick Gordon, ss	55/High
2	Stephen Gonsalves, lhp	50/Medium
3	Alex Kirilloff, of/1b	60/Extreme
4	Fernando Romero, rhp	60/Extreme
5	Tyler Jay, lhp	55/High
6	Adalberto Mejia, lhp	45/Low
7	Kohl Stewart, rhp	50/High
8	Felix Jorge, rhp	50/High
9	Daniel Palka, of	50/High
10	Travis Blankenhorn, 3b/2b	50/High
11	J.T. Chargois, rhp	45/Medium
12	Luis Arraez, 2b	50/High
13	Wander Javier, ss	55/Extreme
14	Pat Light, rhp	45/Medium
15	Nick Burdi, rhp	50/Extreme
16	Akil Baddoo, of	50/Extreme
17	Mitch Garver, c	45/Medium
18	Zack Granite, of	45/Medium
19	Lewis Thorpe, lhp	50/Extreme
20	Justin Haley, rhp	40/Medium
21	LaMonte Wade, of	45/High
22	Griffin Jax, rhp	50/Extreme
23	Ben Rortvedt, c	50/Extreme
24	Jose Miranda, ss/3b	50/Extreme
25	Engelb Vielma, ss	40/Medium
26	Lewin Diaz, 1b	50/Extreme
27	Trevor Hildenberger, rhp	40/Medium
28	Jake Reed, rhp	45/High
29	Huascar Ynoa, rhp	50/Extreme
30	Mason Melotakis, lhp	45/High

LAST YEAR'S TOP 30

No.	Player, Pos.	Status
1.	Byron Buxton, of	Majors
2.	Jose Berrios, rhp	Majors
3.	Max Kepler, of	Majors
4.	Nick Gordon, ss	No. 1
5.	Tyler Jay, lhp	No. 5
6.	Jorge Polanco, ss	Majors
7.	Byung Ho Park, 1b	Majors
8.	Kohl Stewart, rhp	No. 7
9.	Stephen Gonsalves, lhp	No. 2
10.	Nick Burdi, rhp	No. 15
11.	Wander Javier, ss	No. 13
12.	Alex Meyer, rhp	(Angels)
13.	Lewis Thorpe, lhp	No. 19
14.	Taylor Rogers, lhp	Majors
15.	J.T. Chargois, rhp	No. 11
16.	Stuart Turner, c	Dropped out
17.	Adam Brett Walker, of	(Orioles)
18.	Engelb Vielma, ss	No. 25
19.	Jermaine Palacios, ss	Dropped out
20.	Jake Reed, rhp	No. 28
21.	Lewin Diaz, 1b	No. 26
22.	Randy Rosario, lhp	Dropped out
23.	Yorman Landa, rhp	Deceased
24.	Felix Jorge, rhp	No. 8
25.	Huascar Ynoa, rhp	No. 29
26.	Travis Blankenhorn, 3b	No. 10
27.	Trevor Hildenberger, rhp	No. 27
28.	Mason Melotakis, lhp	No. 30
29.	Fernando Romero, rhp	No. 4
30.	Amaurys Minier, 1b	Dropped out

BEST TOOLS

Best Hitter for Average	Luis Arraez
Best Power Hitter	Daniel Palka
Best Strike-Zone Discipline	Luis Arraez
Fastest Baserunner	Zach Granite
Best Athlete	LaMonte Wade
Best Fastball	Fernando Romero
Best Curveball	Sam Clay
Best Slider	Tyler Jay
Best Changeup	Stephen Gonsalves
Best Control	Adalberto Mejia
Best Defensive Catcher	Stuart Turner
Best Defensive Infielder	Engelb Vielma
Best Infield Arm	Engelb Vielma
Best Defensive Outfielder	Zach Granite
Best Outfield Arm	Tanner English

PROJECTED 2020 LINEUP

Catcher	Mitch Garver
First Base	Kennys Vargas
Second Base	Brian Dozier
Third Base	Travis Blankenhorn
Shortstop	Nick Gordon
Left Field	Max Kepler
Center Field	Byron Buxton
Right Field	Alex Kirilloff
Designated Hitter	Miguel Sano
No. 1 Starter	Jose Berrios
No. 2 Starter	Stephen Gonsalves
No. 3 Starter	Fernando Romero
No. 4 Starter	Tyler Jay
No. 5 Starter	Kohl Stewart
Closer	Nick Burdi

MINOR LEAGUE DEPTH CHART

MINNESOTA TWINS

TOP 2017 ROOKIE: Adalberto Mejia, lhp. Acquired from the Giants late last season, Mejia has the chance to open the year in the big league rotation.

BREAKOUT PROSPECT: Luis Arraez, 2b. Though undersized, Arraez has done nothing but hit since the Twins signed him and has an uncanny ability to make contact.

SOURCE OF TOP 30 TALENT			
Homegrown	26	Acquired	4
College	10	Trades	3
Junior college	0	Rule 5 draft	1
High school	8	Independent leagues	0
Nondrafted free agents	0	Free agents/waivers	0
International	8		

SLEEPER: Miguel De Jesus, rhp. The Dominican starter experienced a velocity jump in 2016, touching the upper 90s. A three-pitch mix gives him the chance to start.

LF	CF	RF
Akil Baddoo (16)	Zach Granite (18)	Alex Kirilloff (3)
LaMonte Wade (21)	Tanner English	Daniel Palka (9)
Jaylin Davis	Aaron Whitefield	Max Murphy
Shane Carrier	Jean Carlos Arias	

3B	SS	2B	1B
Travis Blankenhorn (10)	Nick Gordon (1)	Luis Arraez (12)	Lewin Diaz (26)
Jose Miranda (24)	Wander Javier (13)	Levi Michael	Amaurys Minier
Niko Goodrum	Engelb Vielma (25)	Andre Jernigan	Zander Wiel
Trey Cabbage	Jermaine Palacios		D.J. Hicks
Chris Paul	Brandon Lopez		Kolton Kendrick
	Gorge Munoz		

C
Mitch Garver (17)
Ben Rortvedt (23)
Brian Navarreto
A.J. Murray
Rainis Silva

LHP		RHP	
LHSP	**LHRP**	**RHSP**	**RHRP**
Stephen Gonsalves (2)	Mason Melotakis (30)	Fernando Romero (4)	J.T. Chargois (11)
Tyler Jay (5)	Randy Rosario	Kohl Stewart (7)	Pat Light (14)
Adalberto Mejia (6)	Alex Robinson	Felix Jorge (8)	Nick Burdi (15)
Lewis Thorpe (19)	Corey Williams	Justin Haley (20)	Trevor Hildenberger (27)
Lachlan Wells	Michael Theofanopoulos	Griffin Jax (22)	Jake Reed (28)
Taylor Clemensia	Andrew Vasquez	Huascar Ynoa (29)	John Curtiss
Sam Clay		Miguel De Jesus	Zack Jones
Domenick Carlini		Jordan Balazovic	Tom Hackimer
		Brusdar Graterol	Alex Schick
		Aaron Slegers	Ryan Eades
		Cody Stashak	Luke Bard
		Keaton Steele	Michael Cederoth
		Jose Martinez	Kuo Hua Lo
		Eddie Del Rosario	Johan Quezada
		Tyler Wells	

DRAFT ANALYSIS

2016

BEST PURE HITTER: The son of a hitting coach, OF Alex Kirilloff (1) had a batting cage at his house and it shows in his advanced feel for hitting. Kirilloff stays balanced at the plate, uses the entire field and has a bat that stays in the zone for quite a while. SS Jose Miranda (2s) has an advanced approach and good feel for controlling the barrel, although he struggled in the Gulf Coast League.

BEST POWER HITTER: Kirilloff hasn't grown into his strength yet, but with his size (6-foot-2, 195 pounds) and strength the Twins believe he could end up a 20-25 home run hitter in his prime. OF Shane Carrier (8) has plus raw power.

FASTEST RUNNER: OF Akil Baddoo (2s) is a plus runner who turns in times between 4.0 and 4.1 seconds to first from the left side. OF Matt Albanese (7) doesn't run as well as Baddoo, but runs very well for his 6-foot-2, 200-pound frame.

BEST DEFENSIVE PLAYER: C Ben Rortvedt (2) was drafted as a well-rounded high school catcher with power potential to go with solid defense. He moves well and his arm produces average to slightly above-average pop times.

BEST FASTBALL: RHP Griffin Jax (3) sat at 92-93 mph and touched 95 in the spring for Air Force. He threw only 8.2 innings this summer as a pro as the Twins let him rest after he threw 105 innings for the Falcons this spring.

BEST SECONDARY PITCH: Jax's changeup earns plus grades from some scouts, although others see it as consistently average. RHP Tyler Benninghoff (11) showed a potentially plus curveball but has to regain the feel for it post-Tommy John surgery.

BEST PRO DEBUT: Kirilloff was named the Appalachian League's player of the year. He was hitting .361 as late as Aug. 10 before a late slump cut more than 50 points from his batting average.

BEST ATHLETE: Baddoo has grown nearly two inches over the past year, offering a hint that the now 6-foot-2 outfielder could end up as a power/speed left fielder. With his plus speed, though, there is reason to see if he can improve his routes to stick in center field.

MOST INTRIGUING BACKGROUND: Jax's father Garth played seven years in the NFL, primarily as a backup linebacker for the Dallas Cowboys and Arizona Cardinals.

CLOSEST TO THE MAJORS: RHP Thomas Hackimer (4) could move quickly as a submarine righthanded reliever. He made it to low Class A last year and likely will start his first full season in high Class A.

BEST LATE-ROUND PICK: Benninghoff was a top pitching prospect with an 89-91 mph fastball and reasonably advanced changeup and breaking ball, although he threw only one inning last spring and had Tommy John surgery immediately after

the Twins signed him.

THE ONE WHO GOT AWAY: C T.J. Collett (40) was considered one of the best high school catchers in the draft class, but was known to be a tough sign away from his Kentucky commitment. The Twins also knew Louisiana State infielder Greg Deichmann (26) was going to be a tough sign as a draft-eligible sophomore.

2015

LHP Tyler Jay (1) may wind up a reliever, as the No. 6 overall pick. The Twins like the bats of 2B/3B Travis Blankenhorn (3) and OF LaMonte Wade (9), though they may both wind up tweeners.

GRADE: C

2014

SS Nick Gordon (1) finished 2016 in the Arizona Fall League and is Minnesota's top prospect. Injuries have slowed reliever RHP Nick Burdi (2), with RHPs Jake Reed (5) and Trevor Hildenberger (22) stepping forward.

GRADE: C

2013

RHP Kohl Stewart (1) has not been the power pitcher Minnesota envisioned, though he has made progress. LHP Stephen Gonsalves (4) has passed him as a prospect. C Mitch Garver (9) and OF Zack Granite (14) emerged in 2016 as potential contributors.

GRADE: C

TOP DRAFT PICKS OF THE DECADE

Year	Player, Pos.	2016 Org
2007	Ben Revere, of	Nationals
2008	Aaron Hicks, of	Yankees
2009	Kyle Gibson, rhp	Twins
2010	Alex Wimmers, rhp	Twins
2011	Levi Michael, ss	Twins
2012	Byron Buxton, of	Twins
2013	Kohl Stewart, rhp	Twins
2014	Nick Gordon, ss	Twins
2015	Tyler Jay, lhp	Twins
2016	Alex Kirilloff, of	Twins

LARGEST BONUSES IN CLUB HISTORY

Byron Buxton, 2012	$6,000,000
Joe Mauer, 2001	$5,150,000
Kohl Stewart, 2013	$4,544,400
Wander Javier, 2015	$4,000,000
Tyler Jay, 2015	$3,889,500

1 NICK GORDON, SS

Born: Oct. 24, 1995. **B-T:** L-R. **Ht.:** 6-0. **Wt.:** 160.
Drafted: HS—Orlando, 2014 (1st round).
Signed by: Brett Dowdy.

BA GRADE

55 Risk: High

SCOUTING GRADES

Batting: 50.
Power: 45.
Speed: 50.
Defense: 50.
Arm: 60.

Based on 20-80 scouting scale and future projection rather than present tools.

MIKE JANES

The son of righthander Tom Gordon—who pitched parts of 21 seasons in the big leagues—and the younger half-brother of Marlins second baseman Dee Gordon, Nick benefits from significant major league bloodlines. The Twins drafted him fifth overall in 2014 and signed him for $3.581 million, making Gordon the first high school position player selected that year. The top prep shortstop in his class, Gordon could've also followed in his father's footsteps. He showed a low-90s fastball and flashes of a curveball—Tom's signature pitch—in the summer showcase circuit. Instead, the Twins have groomed Gordon as a shortstop, and he continues to learn the nuances of the position. Gordon built on a solid 2015 season at low Class A Cedar Rapids, during which he batted .277/.336/.360, with a near identical offensive stat line at high Class A Fort Myers in 2016. However, Gordon recorded just a .530 OPS against lefthanders and made 24 errors at shortstop—two areas he'll look to improve as he moves up the ladder in the Twins organization. Gordon finished 2016 on a strong note with Surprise of the Arizona Fall League, where he made the circuit's all-star team.

Unlike his half-brother Dee, Nick doesn't boast off-the-charts speed or athleticism; he's average in both categories. As such, some scouts outside of the organization view him as more of a second baseman. The Twins believe he has the aptitude, instincts and short-area quickness to stick at short, but he'll need to continue to put in the time to learn hitters, properly position himself and refine his footwork. His success at shortstop will depend on his preparation. By most accounts, he has a strong work ethic. Gordon's plus arm strength is his greatest asset, though he did have throwing issues at times in 2016, contributing to his error total, which ranked fourth among Florida State League shortstops. Offensively, Gordon shows strength and bat speed in his lefthanded, line-drive swing as well as an ability to hit to all fields. His power is geared for the gaps at present, but he should put more balls over the fence as he develops physically. With good hand-eye coordination and barrel awareness, Gordon is generally a disciplined hitter, but he also gives away at-bats on occasion, and the Twins want him to take care of his plate appearances with a little more focus and concen-

tration. His issues against lefthanded pitchers in 2016 are worth watching, though he's shown better splits in the past and he could improve against lefties with repetition.

Gordon's game is predicated more on fundamentals than flash, and he'll need to continue to refine those fundamentals for him to stick at shortstop. Gordon's instincts and feel for the game are ahead of many players his age—thanks in part to his big league genetics—and that aptitude helps him play above his raw tools. The Twins have had 10 different starters on Opening Day at shortstop since 2005, and they will start Gordon at Double-A Chattanooga in 2017 with the hopes he'll end their revolving door at shortstop soon.

Year	Club (League)	Class	AVG	G	AB	R	H	2B	3B	HR	RBI	BB	SO	SB	CS	OBP	SLG
2014	Elizabethton (APP)	R	.294	57	235	46	69	6	4	1	28	11	45	11	7	.333	.366
2015	Cedar Rapids (MWL)	LoA	.277	120	481	79	133	23	7	1	58	39	88	25	8	.336	.360
2016	Fort Myers (FSL)	HiA	.291	116	461	56	134	23	6	3	52	23	87	19	13	.335	.386
Minor League Totals			.285	293	1177	181	336	52	17	5	138	73	220	55	28	.335	.371

2 STEPHEN GONSALVES, LHP

Born: July 8, 1994. **B-T:** L-L. **Ht.:** 6-5. **Wt.:** 213. **Drafted:** HS—San Diego, 2013 (4th round). **Signed by:** John Leavitt.

Drafted in the fourth round in 2013 and signed to an above-slot $700,000 bonus, Gonsalves has moved steadily up the Twins system. He returned to high Class A Fort Myers in 2016 after making 15 starts there at the end of 2015, and he quickly earned a promotion to Double-A Chattanooga in late June. He went 13-5, 2.06 between both levels, with his ERA ranking seventh in the minors and his .179 opponent average ranking fourth. Gonsalves' strikeout rate actually went up a tick—from 9.0 to 10.8 per nine—in Double-A. However, his walk rate nearly doubled from 2.7 per nine to 4.5. Athletic with a loose arm and easy delivery, Gonsalves' 90-91 mph fastball plays up due to his extension and the tough angle created by his low arm slot. He can touch up to 95 mph, but he's effective as long as he works the corners. The command of his fastball lacks consistency and will need to improve. A plus sinking changeup is Gonsalves' best secondary offering and gives him a weapon against righthanded hitters. The Twins had him throw more curveballs in 2016, but it's a pitch Gonsalves still needs to mix in more. While it doesn't project as a plus pitch, his curveball flashes average and should be a usable third option. Gonsalves is also toying with a slider or cutter, but he has enough of an arsenal at present to put hitters away. Gonsalves will likely pitch at Triple-A Rochester at some point in 2017 and could crack the big league rotation as soon as 2018. He has the look of a mid- to back-of-the-rotation starter.

BA GRADE
50 Risk: Medium

Year	Club (League)	Class	W	L	ERA	G	GS	CG	SV	IP	H	HR	BB	SO	K/9	WHIP	AVG
2014	Elizabethton (APP)	R	2	0	2.79	6	6	0	0	29	23	1	10	26	8.1	1.14	.225
	Cedar Rapids (MWL)	LoA	2	3	3.19	8	8	0	0	37	31	1	11	44	10.8	1.15	.228
2015	Cedar Rapids (MWL)	LoA	6	1	1.15	9	9	0	0	55	29	2	15	77	12.6	0.80	.154
	Fort Myers (FSL)	HiA	7	2	2.61	15	15	1	0	79	66	2	38	55	6.2	1.31	.225
2016	Fort Myers (FSL)	HiA	5	4	2.33	11	11	1	0	66	43	2	20	66	9.0	0.96	.188
	Chattanooga (SL)	AA	8	1	1.82	13	13	1	0	74	43	1	37	89	10.8	1.08	.171
Minor League Totals			32	12	2.13	70	67	3	0	368	253	9	142	396	9.7	1.07	.195

3 ALEX KIRILLOFF, OF/1B

Born: Nov. 9, 1997. **B-T:** L-L. **Ht.:** 6-2. **Wt.:** 195. **Drafted:** HS—Pittsburgh, 2016 (1st round). **Signed by:** Jay Weitzel.

The Twins drafted Kirilloff 15th overall in 2016 signed him away from Liberty—where he had been committed since he was a freshman in high school—with a $2,817,100 bonus. They thought the preseason first-team All-American was advanced enough to eschew the Rookie-level Gulf Coast League, where most of his fellow prep draftees went, and start at Rookie-level Elizabethton. That assignment proved prudent. Kirilloff went on to win MVP honors in the Appalachian League before being shut down late in the season with elbow inflammation. Though only 18, Kirilloff showed a college hitter's polish in his pro debut. With strong, quick wrists and a fluid, balanced lefthanded swing, Kirilloff hits the ball to all fields and has the chance to hit for both average and plus power at higher levels. Reminding some in the Twins organization of big league outfielder Max Kepler, Kirilloff could develop 20-25 home-run power, as he matures physically and learns to pull the ball more. While he played some center field in high school and is a solid-average runner, he projects best in a corner. His plus arm plays in right field, and that's likely where he'll spend the bulk of his time in the minors. Kirilloff is also an adept first baseman with good hands and could end up there as a fallback option. The Twins envision Kirilloff as a power-hitting corner outfielder or first baseman—though he has a long way to go to reach that ceiling. Riding a strong pro debut, he will play at low Class A Cedar Rapids in 2017.

BA GRADE
60 Risk: Extreme

Year	Club (League)	Class	AVG	G	AB	R	H	2B	3B	HR	RBI	BB	SO	SB	CS	OBP	SLG
2016	Elizabethton (APP)	R	.306	55	216	33	66	9	1	7	33	11	32	0	1	.341	.454
Minor League Totals			.306	55	216	33	66	9	1	7	33	11	32	0	1	.341	.454

4 FERNANDO ROMERO, RHP

Born: Dec. 24, 1994. **B-T:** R-R. **Ht.:** 6-0. **Wt.:** 215. **Signed:** Dominican Republic, 2011. **Signed by:** Fred Guerrero.

The Twins have had high hopes for Romero since they signed him as a 16-year-old. Tommy John surgery in June 2014 wiped out his last two seasons. He missed all of 2015 and made just three starts the season prior. Finally healthy, Romero took a step forward in 2016, thriving at two levels and making it through the season unscathed. The Twins were pleased with Romero's conditioning work during Tommy John rehab, and he came into 2016 leaner and stronger than he was before the surgery. Though just 6 feet tall, Romero flirts with triple digits, routinely working 94-97 mph with an electric, double-plus fastball. He pairs that fastball with a firm 86-92 mph slider—a wipeout pitch when it's working—and an average changeup that he'll need to throw more. With two potential high-end pitches, Romero might possess the best raw stuff in the Twins organization, but he needs to polish his command and his approach. Romero brings an attacking, aggressive mindset to the mound. However, he can sometimes fall into the trap of trying to strike out every hitter he faces, elevating his pitch counts. Making it through a full season healthy was an important step for Romero, and he'll pitch with few restrictions in 2017. He has No. 2 or No. 3 starter ceiling.

BA GRADE
60 Risk: Extreme

Year	Club (League)	Class	W	L	ERA	G	GS	CG	SV	IP	H	HR	BB	SO	K/9	WHIP	AVG
2014	Cedar Rapids (MWL)	LoA	0	0	3.00	3	3	0	0	12	13	1	5	9	6.8	1.50	.289
2015	Did not play—Injured																
2016	Cedar Rapids (MWL)	LoA	4	1	1.93	5	5	0	0	28	18	0	5	25	8.0	0.82	.186
	Fort Myers (FSL)	HiA	5	2	1.88	11	11	0	0	62	48	1	10	65	9.4	0.93	.211
Minor League Totals			12	7	2.37	45	31	0	0	178	137	2	47	174	8.8	1.03	.211

5 TYLER JAY, LHP

Born: April 19, 1995. **B-T:** L-L. **Ht.:** 6-1. **Wt.:** 185. **Drafted:** Illinois, 2015 (1st round). **Signed by:** Jeff Pohl.

The Twins drafted Jay sixth overall in 2015 with visions of developing him as a starter. He was a power closer and first-team All-American on a 2015 Illinois team that went to super regionals. In 71 college appearances, Jay started just twice. He made 15 starts in 2016 before moving to the bullpen in the second half at Double-A Chattanooga, and the Twins shut him down at the end of the year with neck inflammation. With his mid-90s fastball and hard, late-breaking 88-92 mph slider, Jay has two big league quality pitches that give him a high floor as a potential closer. As a starter, he features a four-pitch mix, flashing an above-average curveball and mixing in a changeup that has proven effective against righthanded hitters. Evaluators question whether the modest-framed Jay has the physicality to sustain his stuff in extended work. Though electric in short stints, he wasn't as sharp the second and third time through lineups in 2016. Whether Jay will ever build that durability is a divisive topic among scouts. The Twins remain committed to developing Jay as a starter, and he should return to Chattanooga in 2017. However, with the major league club in need of arms, he could at least begin his major league career out of the bullpen.

BA GRADE
55 Risk: High

Year	Club (League)	Class	W	L	ERA	G	GS	CG	SV	IP	H	HR	BB	SO	K/9	WHIP	AVG
2015	Fort Myers (FSL)	HiA	0	1	3.93	19	0	0	1	18	18	0	8	22	10.8	1.42	.247
2016	Fort Myers (FSL)	HiA	5	5	2.84	13	13	0	0	70	64	5	21	68	8.8	1.22	.248
	Chattanooga (SL)	AA	0	0	5.79	5	2	0	0	14	13	2	5	9	5.8	1.29	.245
Minor League Totals			5	6	3.44	37	15	0	1	102	95	7	34	99	8.7	1.26	.247

6 ADALBERTO MEJIA, LHP

Born: June 20, 1993. **B-T:** L-L. **Ht.:** 6-3. **Wt.:** 240. **Signed:** Dominican Republic, 2011. **Signed by:** Pablo Peguero (Giants).

The Twins acquired Mejia from the Giants just before the 2016 trade deadline, sending big league infielder Eduardo Nunez to the Bay. Signed by the Giants in 2011, Mejia moved quickly through the system, buoyed by his advanced pitching feel. A 50-game suspension for the stimulant Sibutramine slowed his progress in 2015, but he worked his way to Triple-A Sacramento in 2016 and continued on with Triple-A Rochester after the trade. Mejia throws strikes and keeps the ball low in the zone, fitting the Twins' pitching paradigm. The thick-bodied lefthander isn't overpowering. Mejia generally works 91-93 mph with his fastball, mixing in an average low-80s slider that can flash better and an above-average changeup, and he has command of all

BA GRADE
45 Risk: Low

three pitches. The Twins love Mejia's even-keeled makeup and mound presence, and he's shown the ability to make adjustments on the mound when necessary. Essentially a finished product, Mejia should vie for a role in the back of the Twins' rotation immediately and projects safely as a No. 5 starter.

Year	Club (League)	Class	W	L	ERA	G	GS	CG	SV	IP	H	HR	BB	SO	K/9	WHIP	AVG
2014	Richmond (EL)	AA	7	9	4.67	22	21	0	0	108	119	9	31	82	6.8	1.39	.283
2015	Richmond (EL)	AA	5	2	2.45	12	9	0	0	51	38	2	18	38	6.7	1.09	.204
2016	Richmond (EL)	AA	3	2	1.94	11	11	0	0	65	48	4	16	58	8.0	0.98	.203
	Sacramento (PCL)	AAA	4	1	4.20	7	7	0	0	41	42	5	11	43	9.5	1.30	.263
	Minnesota (AL)	MAJ	0	0	7.71	1	0	0	0	2	5	0	1	0	0.0	2.57	.455
	Rochester (IL)	AAA	2	2	3.76	4	4	0	0	26	28	3	3	25	8.5	1.18	.269
Major League Totals			0	0	7.71	1	0	0	0	2	5	0	1	0	0.0	2.57	.455
Minor League Totals			43	29	3.29	116	96	1	0	566	535	40	133	487	7.7	1.18	.247

7 KOHL STEWART, RHP

BA GRADE

50 Risk: High

Born: Oct. 7, 1994. **B-T:** R-R. **Ht.:** 6-3. **Wt.:** 195. **Drafted:** HS—Houston, 2013 (1st round). **Signed by:** Greg Runser.

A Texas A&M recruit, Stewart might have succeeded Heisman Trophy winner Johnny Manziel at quarterback. Instead, the two-sport star signed with the Twins for $4,544,400 after they drafted him fourth overall in 2013. A type 1 diabetic, Stewart battled second-half shoulder soreness his first two seasons and elbow inflammation in his third. Aside from a brief bout with biceps tendinitis, he shouldered a full workload in 2016. Drafted for his power stuff, Stewart has missed fewer bats than expected. His strikeout rate rose a tick from a subpar 4.9 per nine a year ago, but it still remained a curiously low 5.7 per nine in 2016. Stewart is behind other pitchers his age due to his football background, and the Twins believe his strikeout rate will improve as he learns sequencing and improves the command of his full arsenal. Stewart can touch 96 mph with his four-seamer, but he leans more on his 91-92 two-seamer. He throws a hard slider, up to 87-88 mph, a power 12-to-6 curveball and the occasional changeup. His above-average slider is the best of the mix, but it produces more weak contact than swings and misses. Stewart's next step is Triple-A Rochester, and 2017 could be a big season for him as he tries to establish his identity as a pitcher. He has a No. 3 starter ceiling.

Year	Club (League)	Class	W	L	ERA	G	GS	CG	SV	IP	H	HR	BB	SO	K/9	WHIP	AVG
2014	Cedar Rapids (MWL)	LoA	3	5	2.59	19	19	0	0	87	75	4	24	62	6.4	1.14	.233
2015	Fort Myers (FSL)	HiA	7	8	3.20	22	22	1	0	129	134	2	45	71	4.9	1.38	.273
2016	Fort Myers (FSL)	HiA	3	2	2.61	9	9	0	0	52	39	2	19	44	7.7	1.12	.207
	Chattanooga (SL)	AA	9	6	3.03	16	16	1	0	92	91	4	44	47	4.6	1.47	.265
Minor League Totals			22	21	2.84	73	70	2	0	380	352	12	136	248	5.9	1.28	.248

8 FELIX JORGE, RHP

BA GRADE

50 Risk: High

Born: Jan. 2, 1994. **B-T:** R-R. **Ht.:** 6-2. **Wt.:** 170. **Signed:** Dominican Republic, 2011. **Signed by:** Fred Guerrero.

Signed as a slender teenager for $400,000 out of the Dominican Republic in 2011, Jorge took a step forward in 2016 after repeating low Class A Cedar Rapids in 2015. The righthander started the season 9-3, 1.55 at high Class A Fort Myers, earning a July promotion to Double-A Chattanooga. The Southern League proved more challenging for Jorge. His strikeout rate dipped to 3.9 per nine, but he maintained his trademark control. Jorge fits the command-oriented mold of past Twins starters. He finally started to fill out his frame in 2016. Working anywhere from 86-94 mph in the past, Jorge now has the physicality to sit consistently at 90 and above. He touches 95 mph with sink and has added more action and velocity to his breaking pitches. Jorge uses an average, late-breaking slider, but his above-average sinking changeup is his main out pitch. Jorge throws with a clean, athletic delivery and fields his position well. With feel and command beyond his years, Jorge is finally developing the durability necessary to maintain his stuff deeper into outings. He projects as a back-end starter and will likely pick up where he left off at Chattanooga in 2017.

Year	Club (League)	Class	W	L	ERA	G	GS	CG	SV	IP	H	HR	BB	SO	K/9	WHIP	AVG
2014	Cedar Rapids (MWL)	LoA	2	5	9.00	12	8	0	0	39	57	9	20	23	5.3	1.97	.354
	Elizabethton (APP)	R	4	2	2.59	12	12	0	0	66	58	2	14	61	8.3	1.09	.237
2015	Cedar Rapids (MWL)	LoA	6	7	2.79	23	22	0	0	142	118	11	32	114	7.2	1.06	.225
2016	Fort Myers (FSL)	HiA	9	3	1.55	14	14	2	0	93	76	3	11	77	7.5	0.94	.226
	Chattanooga (SL)	AA	3	5	4.12	11	11	1	0	74	83	7	12	32	3.9	1.28	.290
Minor League Totals			28	28	3.17	105	91	5	2	537	497	34	128	442	7.4	1.16	.246

9 DANIEL PALKA, OF

Born: Oct. 28, 1991. **B-T:** L-L. **Ht.:** 6-2. **Wt.:** 220. **Drafted:** Georgia Tech, 2013 (3rd round). **Signed by:** T.R. Lewis (Diamondbacks).

The Diamondbacks took Palka in the third round in 2013 and dealt him in November 2015 to the Twins for catcher Chris Hermann. He opened 2016 at Double-A Chattanooga with a display of power and punchouts, and that pattern continued after a promotion to Triple-A Rochester. He finished fourth in the minors in home runs (34) and third in strikeouts (186). Palka has led the minor leagues with 63 homers since 2015. Much like former farmhand Adam Brett Walker, Palka has huge raw power and an all-or-nothing approach that leads to egregious strikeout totals. However, Palka features a more well-rounded tool set than Walker, and while he'll likely never hit for a high average, the Twins have more conviction that Palka will be able to make the necessary adjustments to hit just enough at the next level. He batted .267/.319/.527 against lefthanders in 2016—a touch better than he hit against righties. Though not an outstanding athlete, Palka is a serviceable defender in right field and his strong arm helps make up for some of his deficiencies in range. Palka is coming off his best pro season and is on the cusp of cracking the big league roster at some point in 2017, where he could provide some needed thump either off of the bench or in an outfield corner.

BA GRADE

50 Risk: High

Year	Club (League)	Class	AVG	G	AB	R	H	2B	3B	HR	RBI	BB	SO	SB	CS	OBP	SLG
2014	South Bend (MWL)	LoA	.248	118	455	63	113	23	5	22	82	56	129	9	3	.332	.466
2015	Visalia (CAL)	HiA	.279	129	512	95	143	36	3	29	90	56	164	24	7	.352	.531
2016	Chattanooga (SL)	AA	.270	79	300	42	81	12	4	21	65	38	100	7	4	.348	.547
	Rochester (IL)	AAA	.232	54	203	31	47	12	0	13	25	18	86	2	1	.296	.483
Minor League Totals			.268	448	1722	277	462	104	14	94	310	204	540	45	17	.346	.509

10 TRAVIS BLANKENHORN, 3B/2B

Born: Aug. 3, 1996. **B-T:** L-R. **Ht.:** 6-2. **Wt.:** 208. **Drafted:** HS—Pottsville, Pa., 2015 (3rd round). **Signed by:** Jay Weitzel.

An accomplished prep basketball and football player and a Kentucky baseball signee, Blankenhorn signed with the Twins for $650,0000 after they plucked him in the third round in 2015. After playing the bulk of his pro debut in the Rookie-level Appalachian League, Blankenhorn returned to Elizabethton in 2016 before forcing a promotion to low Class A Cedar Rapids in August. Primarily a shortstop in high school, he has played mostly second base since signing, with occasional starts at third. The Twins believe in Blankenhorn's lefthanded bat and envision him hitting for average and potentially 15-20 home runs per year as he physically matures. He

BA GRADE

50 Risk: High

has a quick, balanced swing, good presence in the box and an advanced offensive approach for his age. Blankenhorn's future position is up in the air, because he likely will outgrow second base, where he's a fringy defender at present. He's athletic enough to handle left field but seems destined to land at an infield corner. He has an average arm. Blankenhorn has the look of an bat-first player with some defensive versatility. He could evolve into one of the best pure hitters in the system, with the chance to hit for power. He'll likely return to Cedar Rapids to start 2017.

Year	Club (League)	Class	AVG	G	AB	R	H	2B	3B	HR	RBI	BB	SO	SB	CS	OBP	SLG
2015	Twins (GCL)	R	.245	14	49	6	12	4	2	0	3	7	11	2	0	.362	.408
	Elizabethton (APP)	R	.243	39	144	14	35	3	0	3	20	11	32	1	0	.306	.326
2016	Elizabethton (APP)	R	.297	34	138	30	41	7	1	9	29	8	33	3	0	.342	.558
	Cedar Rapids (MWL)	LoA	.286	25	91	11	26	5	2	1	12	8	28	2	1	.356	.418
Minor League Totals			.270	112	422	61	114	19	5	13	64	34	104	8	1	.335	.431

11 J.T. CHARGOIS, RHP

BA GRADE

45 Risk: Medium

Born: Dec. 3, 1990. **B-T:** B-R. **Ht.:** 6-3. **Wt.:** 200. **Drafted:** Rice, 2012 (2nd round). **Signed by:** Greg Runser.

Once teammates with fellow Twins righthander Tyler Duffey at Rice, Chargois reunited with Duffey in the major leagues in 2016. The promotion was a long time coming for Chargois, who signed for $712,600 in 2012 but didn't pitch in 2013 or 2014 after having Tommy John surgery. He finally returned to the mound in 2015, splitting time between high Class A Fort Myers and Double-A Chattanooga before earning a 40-man roster spot that November. He made a quick jump to Triple-A Rochester in May 2016 and earned a one-game cup of coffee in June. The Twins recalled Chargois again in August and he solidified a role in the big league bullpen. A power reliever, he has one of the best fastballs in the system, averaging 97 mph with sink. He threw his slider about 30 percent of the time, and it's a hard 87-88 mph pitch with excellent depth. Chargois also throws a mid-80s changeup with fade, but he uses it sparingly. He has feel for pitching and three pitches at his disposal, but his max-effort delivery points to a bullpen role. He has a closer's mentality, having closed at Rice. Chargois projects to open 2017 in the major league bullpen.

Year	Club (League)	Class	W	L	ERA	G	GS	CG	SV	IP	H	HR	BB	SO	K/9	WHIP	AVG
2014	Did not play—Injured																
2015	Fort Myers (FSL)	HiA	1	0	2.40	16	0	0	4	15	12	0	5	19	11.4	1.13	.200
	Chattanooga (SL)	AA	1	1	2.73	32	0	0	11	33	26	1	20	34	9.3	1.39	.218
2016	Chattanooga (SL)	AA	0	0	1.54	11	0	0	7	12	8	1	5	14	10.8	1.11	.190
	Rochester (IL)	AAA	2	1	1.29	28	0	0	9	35	27	1	8	41	10.5	1.00	.208
	Minnesota (AL)	MAJ	1	1	4.70	25	0	0	0	23	25	0	12	17	6.7	1.61	.291
Major League Totals			1	1	4.70	25	0	0	0	23	25	0	12	17	6.7	1.61	.291
Minor League Totals			4	2	1.95	99	0	0	36	111	83	3	43	130	10.6	1.14	.204

12 LUIS ARRAEZ, 2B

BA GRADE **50** Risk: High

Born: April 9, 1997. **B-T:** L-R. **Ht.:** 5-10. **Wt.:** 184. **Signed:** Venezuela, 2013.
Signed by: Jose Leon.

Signed for $40,000 as a 16-year-old in 2013, Arraez has done nothing but hit since joining the Twins. He owns a career .338 average as a pro and hit .347 in 2016 to claim the low Class A Midwest League batting title as a 19-year-old. Though undersized at 5-foot-10, Arraez has added about 30 pounds since signing. He's shown excellent bat control and contact ability. He hits to all fields with a line-drive, inside-out swing and lacks pull-side pop, and doesn't project to hit for much power going forward. While he is a plus hitter, Arraez's other tools are lacking. He is a fringy defender at second base, with below-average speed and a below-average arm. He makes up for deficiencies in his range with good hands and positioning, but he'll likely never be a standout defender and is limited to second base. Arraez's chance to be a major league player hinges solely on his hitting ability, making him a risky prospect. He has garnered comparisons within the organization to former Twins farmhand and current Padres third baseman Yangervis Solarte. Arraez will try to lead a new league in hitting when he moves up to high Class A Fort Myers in the Florida State League in 2017.

Year	Club (League)	Class	AVG	G	AB	R	H	2B	3B	HR	RBI	BB	SO	SB	CS	OBP	SLG
2014	Twins (DSL)	R	.348	31	115	23	40	6	0	0	15	16	9	10	5	.433	.400
2015	Twins (GCL)	R	.309	57	207	23	64	15	1	0	19	19	10	8	8	.377	.391
2016	Cedar Rapids (MWL)	LoA	.347	114	475	67	165	31	3	3	66	31	51	3	3	.386	.444
Minor League Totals			.338	202	797	113	269	52	4	3	100	66	70	21	16	.391	.424

13 WANDER JAVIER, SS

BA GRADE **55** Risk: Extreme

Born: Dec. 29, 1998. **B-T:** R-R. **Ht.:** 6-1. **Wt.:** 180. **Signed:** Dominican Republic, 2015. **Signed by:** Fred Guerrero.

The Twins pursued Javier aggressively in 2015, going slightly above their international pool to sign the Dominican shortstop for $4 million—the largest bonus the organization has awarded an international amateur. Ranked No. 9 in the 2015 international class, Javier debuted in the Dominican Summer League in 2016, but a hamstring strain limited him to just 26 at-bats. He remains exceptionally raw, but the Twins are enticed by his five-tool potential at shortstop. A plus runner with a plus arm, Javier has quick defensive actions and the potential to be an above-average defender, and most evaluators believe the wiry infielder won't outgrow the position. His explosive bat speed gives him the chance to develop above-average power, with his two home runs in nine 2016 games serving as a somewhat surprising preview. However, Javier needs to clean up his mechanics, avoid lunging at pitches and hone in on the strike zone. He spent more of his youth working out than playing games, so his game IQ has room to grow. With his first season cut short, Javier has been training in Florida and should be ready for a Rookie-level Gulf Coast League assignment in 2017.

Year	Club (League)	Class	AVG	G	AB	R	H	2B	3B	HR	RBI	BB	SO	SB	CS	OBP	SLG
2016	Twins (DSL)	R	.308	9	26	7	8	3	0	2	6	4	5	0	0	.400	.654
Minor League Totals			.308	9	26	7	8	3	0	2	6	4	5	0	0	.400	.654

14 PAT LIGHT, RHP

BA GRADE **45** Risk: High

Born: March 29, 1991. **B-T:** R-R. **Ht.:** 6-6. **Wt.:** 225. **Drafted:** Monmouth, 2012 (1st round supplemental). **Signed by:** Ray Fagnant (Red Sox).

The Twins have had their eyes on Light for some time. They originally drafted him in the 28th round in 2009 out of his New Jersey high school but Light instead went to Monmouth, and the Red Sox drafted him 37th overall three years later. The Twins finally got the hard-throwing reliever in August 2016, when they acquired him for lefthander Fernando Abad. Coming off a breakout 2015 season, Light made his major league debut in a quick, two-game April stint for the Red Sox, then appeared in 15 more games for the Twins late in the year. He showed both electric stuff and below-average command in those big league appearances, averaging 95 mph but throwing just 54 percent of his pitches for strikes and walking 8.6 per nine innings. Command has long been Light's bugaboo, and the 6-foot-6 righthander has struggled to maintain consistency in his mechanics. His heavy fastball touches 100 mph and he pairs it with a hard, diving splitter and the occasional fringy slider. If he can develop at least fringe-average control, his stuff should play in a high-leverage role, perhaps as closer. Light has a chance to earn a bullpen role in 2017.

Year	Club (League)	Class	W	L	ERA	G	GS	CG	SV	IP	H	HR	BB	SO	K/9	WHIP	AVG
2014	Greenville (SAL)	LoA	2	0	4.15	3	3	0	0	17	15	1	4	19	9.9	1.10	.231
	Salem (CAR)	HiA	6	6	4.93	22	22	1	0	115	135	10	33	57	4.5	1.46	.295
2015	Portland (EL)	AA	1	1	2.43	21	0	0	3	30	18	3	11	32	9.7	0.98	.168
	Pawtucket (IL)	AAA	2	4	5.18	26	0	0	2	33	31	2	26	35	9.5	1.73	.248
2016	Boston (AL)	MAJ	0	0	23.63	2	0	0	0	3	7	2	1	2	6.8	3.00	.438
	Pawtucket (IL)	AAA	1	1	2.32	25	0	0	7	31	21	1	17	36	10.5	1.23	.188
	Rochester (IL)	AAA	1	0	2.57	6	0	0	2	7	5	0	2	6	7.7	1.00	.200
	Minnesota (AL)	MAJ	0	1	9.00	15	0	0	0	14	15	2	15	14	9.0	2.14	.259
Major League Totals			0	1	11.34	17	0	0	0	17	22	4	16	16	8.6	2.28	.297
Minor League Totals			14	18	4.35	128	49	1	14	298	300	22	114	246	7.4	1.39	.261

15 NICK BURDI, RHP

BA GRADE
50 Risk: Extreme

Born: Jan. 19, 1993. **B-T:** R-R. **Ht.:** 6-5. **Wt.:** 220. **Drafted:** Louisville, 2014 (2nd round). **Signed by:** Alan Sandberg.

The Twins liked Burdi so much they drafted him twice. The Illinois prep passed on pro ball as a 24th-round pick in 2011 before coming to terms as the 46th overall pick out of Louisville in 2014. On the cusp of breaking through to the big leagues in 2016, Burdi began the year at Double-A Chattanooga but pitched in just three games before a bone bruise on his right humerus sent him to the disabled list and ended his season. He touched triple digits in college, where his younger brother Zack Burdi—drafted 26th overall by the White Sox in 2016—succeeded him as Louisville's closer. When healthy, Nick complements his upper-90s fastball with a wipeout 87-90 mph slider and an occasional firm changeup. His control needs improvement—he walked 6.6 per nine innings in 2015 at Chattanooga—but when he throws strikes, Burdi's stuff gives him the chance to be a late-inning reliever. In the Twins' plans in 2016 before his injury, he now probably requires more minor league seasoning after his lost season. Both Burdi and his younger brother could pitch in American League Central bullpens in 2017.

Year	Club (League)	Class	W	L	ERA	G	GS	CG	SV	IP	H	HR	BB	SO	K/9	WHIP	AVG
2014	Cedar Rapids (MWL)	LoA	0	0	4.15	13	0	0	4	13	8	0	8	26	18.0	1.23	.174
	Fort Myers (FSL)	HiA	2	0	0.00	7	0	0	1	7	5	0	2	12	14.7	0.95	.208
2015	Fort Myers (FSL)	HiA	2	2	2.25	13	0	0	2	20	12	1	3	29	13.1	0.75	.179
	Chattanooga (SL)	AA	3	4	4.53	30	0	0	2	44	40	3	32	54	11.1	1.65	.242
2016	Chattanooga (SL)	AA	1	0	9.00	3	0	0	0	3	4	0	1	1	3.0	1.67	.308
Minor League Totals			8	6	3.72	66	0	0	9	87	69	4	46	122	12.6	1.32	.219

16 AKIL BADDOO, OF

BA GRADE
50 Risk: Extreme

Born: Aug. 16, 1998. **B-T:** L-L. **Ht.:** 6-1. **Wt.:** 209. **Drafted:** HS—Conyers, Ga., 2016 (2nd round supplemental). **Signed by:** Jack Powell.

The Twins drafted Baddoo with the 74th overall pick in 2016 and signed him for $750,000 away from a Kentucky commitment, expecting the Georgia prep to flourish as a plus runner and potential top-of-the-order type. But since last summer, Baddoo expanded his 5-foot-11, 185-pound frame and was listed at 6-foot-1, 209 in instructional league. Though Baddoo had a poor debut in the Rookie-level Gulf Coast League—tallying twice as many strikeouts (36) as hits (19)—the Twins are intrigued by his physical growth. He could hit for more power than expected and project to an outfield corner in lieu of center field, though his below-average arm might push him to left. He also needs to improve his route-running and reads in the outfield. A lefthanded hitter, Baddoo can get pull-happy at times and has a raw, aggressive approach, but if he channels his above-average bat speed, he has the chance to develop into a plus hitter to go along with his speed and burgeoning power. Whether he hits at the top of the order or middle will likely hinge on his physical development. He should head to Rookie-level Elizabethton in 2017.

Year	Club (League)	Class	AVG	G	AB	R	H	2B	3B	HR	RBI	BB	SO	SB	CS	OBP	SLG
2016	Twins (GCL)	R	.178	38	107	15	19	0	2	2	15	18	36	8	1	.299	.271
Minor League Totals			.178	38	107	15	19	0	2	2	15	18	36	8	1	.299	.271

17 MITCH GARVER, C

Born: Jan. 15, 1991. **B-T:** R-R. **Ht.:** 6-1. **Wt.:** 220. **Drafted:** New Mexico, 2013 (9th round). **Signed by:** Ted Williams.

Drafted as a senior out of New Mexico in 2013, Garver signed with the Twins for $40,000 after going undrafted the year before—despite hitting 10 home runs. Scouts questioned his ability to stick at catcher as he entered pro ball. He's long been viewed as a bat-first player, though even his bat received some scrutiny in college because he played in a hitter-friendly environment in Albuquerque. Garver has been a steady offensive player in pro ball, impressing the Twins with the professional quality of his at-bats and home run power. Where he has seen the most growth is on the defensive side. In particular, Garver has made significant strides in controlling the running game, and he threw out an organization-best 48 percent of basestealers between Double-A Chattanooga and Triple-A Rochester in 2016. Though not as naturally gifted defensively as former system-mate Stuart Turner, Garver has closed the defensive gap between the two catchers. That progress, coupled with Garver's higher offensive ceiling, elevates his standing on the organization's depth chart. The Twins added Garver to the 40-man roster after the 2016 season, and he could factor in the big league team's plans in 2017.

Year	Club (League)	Class	AVG	G	AB	R	H	2B	3B	HR	RBI	BB	SO	SB	CS	OBP	SLG
2014	Cedar Rapids (MWL)	LoA	.298	120	430	65	128	29	1	16	79	61	65	7	5	.399	.481
2015	Fort Myers (FSL)	HiA	.245	127	433	46	106	24	1	4	58	69	82	5	3	.356	.333
2016	Chattanooga (SL)	AA	.257	95	358	44	92	25	0	11	66	43	86	1	3	.334	.419
	Rochester (IL)	AAA	.329	22	76	6	25	5	0	1	8	7	21	0	0	.381	.434
Minor League Totals			.267	420	1499	177	400	98	4	34	241	199	285	13	11	.359	.406

18 ZACK GRANITE, OF

Born: Sept. 17, 1992. **B-T:** L-L. **Ht.:** 5-11. **Wt.:** 167. **Drafted:** Seton Hall, 2013 (14th round). **Signed by:** John Wilson.

Drafted in the 14th round in 2013, Granite has made a steady climb through the system before enjoying a breakout 2016 season. The outfielder won the Twins' minor league player of the year award with his .295/.347/.382 season at Double-A Chattanooga in which he led the Southern League with 155 hits and the minors with 56 stolen bases (in 70 attempts). Granite made adjustments to his swing at Chattanooga to start his hands a little sooner, and he drove the ball more than in the past. He hit a career-high four home runs in 2016, but more significantly forced outfielders to play him at normal depth. Granite doesn't project to hit for much power, but he graduated from pure slap hitter in 2016. He is a plus runner and an adept basestealer with a top-of-the-order skill set. He can play all three outfield positions, and is a serviceable center fielder with an adequate arm. Granite earned a 40-man roster spot with his loud season and could be in the Twins' major league plans in the near future. Granite appears destined for Triple-A Rochester in 2017, but his versatility and speed give him the chance to be at least a fourth outfielder in the big leagues.

Year	Club (League)	Class	AVG	G	AB	R	H	2B	3B	HR	RBI	BB	SO	SB	CS	OBP	SLG
2014	Cedar Rapids (MWL)	LoA	.291	21	79	9	23	2	2	0	2	4	8	1	4	.321	.367
	Twins (GCL)	R	.214	4	14	4	3	0	0	0	0	2	4	3	0	.313	.214
2015	Cedar Rapids (MWL)	LoA	.358	19	67	17	24	5	1	0	5	12	6	7	1	.463	.463
	Fort Myers (FSL)	HiA	.249	105	381	59	95	10	4	1	26	41	63	21	12	.328	.304
2016	Chattanooga (SL)	AA	.295	127	526	86	155	18	8	4	52	42	43	56	14	.347	.382
Minor League Totals			.282	337	1309	214	369	39	20	5	109	130	149	102	38	.349	.354

19 LEWIS THORPE, LHP

Born: Nov. 23, 1995. **B-T:** R-L. **Ht.:** 6-1. **Wt.:** 160. **Signed:** Australia, 2012. **Signed by:** Howard Norsetter.

The Twins signed Thorpe out of Australia for $500,000 in 2012 and still believe in his upside, but so far they haven't gotten much return on their investment. He made a strong debut in the Rookie-level Gulf Coast League in 2013, but he was shut down late in 2014 with a sprained ulnar collateral ligament. After tearing the ligament the next spring, Thorpe missed all of 2015 while rehabbing from Tommy John surgery. His rehab hit two snags in 2016 when he tweaked his knee after dealing with a bout of mononucleosis. The result: a second consecutive lost year. When healthy, Thorpe has shown stuff the Twins believe could play in the middle of a rotation. The Australian lefthander has a four-pitch mix, fronted by a mid-90s fastball and a potentially plus changeup with sink and fade, and he's shown the feel to spin a slider and curveball, both of which could be average or better. The issue has been getting Thorpe on a mound. He will likely start throwing in the spring and begin the season in extended spring training before continuing on with a full-season club. Thorpe has No. 3 starter ceiling, but maintaining his health is imperative after he missed each of the last two seasons with injury.

Year	Club (League)	Class	W	L	ERA	G	GS	CG	SV	IP	H	HR	BB	SO	K/9	WHIP	AVG
2014	Cedar Rapids (MWL)	LoA	3	2	3.52	16	16	0	0	72	62	7	36	80	10.0	1.37	.232
2015	Did not play—Injured																
2016	Did not play—Injured																
Minor League Totals			7	3	2.96	28	24	0	0	116	94	9	42	144	11.2	1.18	.221

20 JUSTIN HALEY, RHP

Born: June 16, 1991. **B-T:** R-R. **Ht.:** 6-5. **Wt.:** 230. **Drafted:** Fresno State, 2012 (6th round). **Signed by:** Desmond Smith (Red Sox).

BA GRADE
40 Risk: Medium

A workhorse starter at Fresno State, Haley spent five seasons in the Red Sox system and advanced to Triple-A for the first time in the second half of 2016. The Twins acquired him—with Rule 5 draft restrictions—at the 2016 Winter Meetings when they traded their pick, righthander Miguel Diaz, to the Padres for Haley and cash. Owner of possibly the coolest pre-pitch setup in the minors, Haley sets up on the third-base side of the rubber, with his other foot straddling the rubber. With the ball in his glove raised in front of his face, he looks in for the sign with his pitching hand cocked at his waist, fingers dancing back and forth like Wyatt Earp ready to draw. He gets the sign for the pitch and then locks, loads and fires. As a starter, Haley's velocity ticked up in 2016 as the season warmed up. Late in the season he was sitting 90-92 mph, but his fastball plays up because he locates it well. He also has an above-average slider as well as a useable curveball and changeup. He dominated in Double-A in 2016 and was solid in Triple-A as a starter. He also looked sharp in the Dominican League in winter ball. Because he has Triple-A experience, Haley has a strong case to make the Twins' Opening Day pitching staff if he has a good spring.

Year	Club (League)	Class	W	L	ERA	G	GS	CG	SV	IP	H	HR	BB	SO	K/9	WHIP	AVG
2014	Salem (CAR)	HiA	7	4	2.82	19	11	1	1	93	77	4	23	74	7.2	1.08	.229
	Portland (EL)	AA	3	2	1.19	6	6	0	0	38	30	2	16	33	7.9	1.22	.222
2015	Portland (EL)	AA	5	16	5.15	27	27	0	0	124	142	7	50	95	6.9	1.55	.289
2016	Portland (EL)	AA	5	4	2.20	12	12	1	0	61	49	1	19	59	8.7	1.11	.219
	Pawtucket (IL)	AAA	8	6	3.59	15	14	1	0	85	70	8	26	67	7.1	1.13	.230
Minor League Totals			35	44	3.41	118	106	3	1	559	488	33	224	485	7.8	1.27	.238

21 LAMONTE WADE, OF

Born: Jan. 1, 1994. **B-T:** L-L. **Ht.:** 6-1. **Wt.:** 189. **Drafted:** Maryland, 2015 (9th round). **Signed by:** John Wilson.

BA GRADE
45 Risk: High

Wade had an up-and-down career at Maryland but finished with a flourish by leading the Terrapins to an NCAA tournament upset over No. 1 overall seed UCLA in the 2015 regionals. The Twins drafted him in the ninth round days later, and the outfielder has found consistency in pro ball. Possessing plus lefthanded bat speed and an advanced knowledge of the strike zone, Wade's bat is his asset. He sprays the ball to all fields, hits both lefties and righties and has walked more (101) than struck out (80) in his pro career. The Twins love his makeup and believe he'll grow into at least average power, and the progress of that development could determine whether he's a fourth outfielder or big league regular. While Wade has center field experience and can handle the position in the lower levels, he's best suited for a corner. He has fringy arm strength but enough speed and athleticism to make up for it. He played well after a June promotion from low Class A Cedar Rapids to high Class A Fort Myers, but a broken hand cut his season short. He'll likely see time at Double-A Chattanooga at some point in 2017.

Year	Club (League)	Class	AVG	G	AB	R	H	2B	3B	HR	RBI	BB	SO	SB	CS	OBP	SLG
2015	Elizabethton (APP)	R	.312	64	231	36	72	8	5	9	44	46	34	12	1	.428	.506
	Cedar Rapids (MWL)	LoA	.143	4	14	1	2	0	0	0	1	1	2	0	0	.250	.143
2016	Cedar Rapids (MWL)	LoA	.280	56	207	32	58	6	3	4	27	44	27	5	3	.410	.396
	Fort Myers (FSL)	HiA	.318	32	110	17	35	8	1	4	24	10	17	1	1	.386	.518
Minor League Totals			.297	156	562	86	167	22	9	17	96	101	80	18	5	.409	.459

22 GRIFFIN JAX, RHP

Born: Nov. 22, 1994. **B-T:** R-R. **Ht.:** 6-2. **Wt.:** 195. **Drafted:** Air Force, 2016 (3rd round). **Signed by:** Ted Williams.

BA GRADE
50 Risk: Extreme

The son of NFL linebacker Garth Jax—who played for the Dallas Cowboys and Arizona Cardinals—Griffin has been drafted twice. Taken in the 12th round out of high school by the Phillies in 2013, Jax instead enrolled at Air Force, where he evolved into one of the top arms in the west. The righthander went 9-2, 2.05 his junior season, striking out 90 against 20 walks in 105.1 innings to earn co-Mountain West pitcher of the year honors. Jax likely would have been drafted higher than 93rd overall if not for the uncertainty of his military commitment. Signed for $645,600, he pitched in just four games at Rookie-level Elizabethton before having to return to school in August. He will likely get his required five years of active military duty deferred, but he won't be available to the Twins until he graduates from the Academy in May. A good athlete, the 6-foot-2, 195-pound Jax touches 95 mph and routinely sits in the low 90s, working in a changeup with plus potential and an average slider that lacks consistency. The Twins love his makeup and work ethic and envision him as a starter, but his biggest question mark is his sheer lack of innings. He should resume his pro career early in the summer of 2017.

Year	Club (League)	Class	W	L	ERA	G	GS	CG	SV	IP	H	HR	BB	SO	K/9	WHIP	AVG
2016	Elizabethton (APP)	R	0	1	4.15	4	0	0	0	9	15	2	1	8	8.3	1.85	.385
Minor League Totals			0	1	4.15	4	0	0	0	9	15	2	1	8	8.3	1.85	.385

23 BEN RORTVEDT, C

BA GRADE

50 Risk: Extreme

Born: Sept. 25, 1997. **B-T:** L-R. **Ht.:** 5-10 **Wt.:** 190. **Drafted:** HS—Verona, Wis., 2016 (2nd round). **Signed by:** Mark Wilson.

Wisconsin high school draftees are a rare breed, with just 26 drafted and signed in the top 10 rounds in the 50-year history of the draft prior to 2016. Rortvedt joined that exclusive group when the Twins took him in the second round and signed him for $900,000 to forgo an Arkansas commitment. Old for his draft class—he turned 19 in September—Rortvedt earned a promotion to Rookie-level Elizabethton in July, where he joined first-rounder Alex Kirilloff. Rortvedt packs wiry strength into a compact frame and flashes above-average power potential from the left side with his short, quick swing. He is defensively raw and needs to polish his footwork and blocking behind the plate, but his mobility and above-average arm give him defensive upside. The Twins love his motor and competitiveness, and he has the makeup teams look for in catchers. Rortvedt is always going to face questions about his size, but his strength and grit give him the chance to be a regular at catcher. Rortvedt could open 2017 at low Class A Cedar Rapids.

Year	Club (League)	Class	AVG	G	AB	R	H	2B	3B	HR	RBI	BB	SO	SB	CS	OBP	SLG
2016	Twins (GCL)	R	.203	20	59	3	12	3	0	0	3	5	8	0	0	.277	.254
	Elizabethton (APP)	R	.250	13	40	2	10	0	0	0	7	5	2	0	0	.348	.250
Minor League Totals			.222	33	99	5	22	3	0	0	10	10	10	0	0	.306	.253

24 JOSE MIRANDA, SS/3B

BA GRADE

50 Risk: Extreme

Born: June 29, 1998. **B-T:** R-R. **Ht.:** 6-2. **Wt.:** 180. **Drafted:** HS—Guaynabo, P.R., 2016 (2nd round supplemental). **Signed by:** Freddie Thon.

The second Puerto Rican player taken in the 2016 draft after Cardinals first-rounder Delvin Perez, Miranda went to the Twins 73rd overall and signed for $775,000. The 18-year-old struggled offensively in his debut in the Rookie-level Gulf Coast League, but the Twins view his hit tool as one of the best in their draft class, envisioning him in a similar vein as Travis Blankenhorn. Like Blankenhorn, Miranda has a smooth swing and advanced bat-to-ball skills and the chance for average or better power as he physically develops. And also like Blankenhorn, Miranda faces a likely move off shortstop. Though Miranda showed smooth actions and hands at short in the GCL, most evaluators project him to outgrow the position and slide over to third base, where his average arm should be sufficient. His carrying tool is his bat, and he will try to rebound in 2017.

Year	Club (League)	Class	AVG	G	AB	R	H	2B	3B	HR	RBI	BB	SO	SB	CS	OBP	SLG
2016	Twins (GCL)	R	.227	55	185	14	42	7	1	1	20	19	36	4	5	.308	.292
Minor League Totals			.227	55	185	14	42	7	1	1	20	19	36	4	5	.308	.292

25 ENGELB VIELMA, SS

BA GRADE

40 Risk: Medium

Born: June 22, 1994. **B-T:** B-R. **Ht.:** 5-11. **Wt.:** 170. **Signed:** Venezuela, 2011. **Signed by:** Jose Leon.

Vielma was a slender 150-pound teen when the Twins signed him out of Venezuela for $90,000 in 2011, and there were questions whether the shortstop could develop the physicality to be an everyday player and a productive hitter. Though he has added some muscle and strength to his frame, those questions linger. A switch-hitter, Vielma has well below-average power from both sides and posted an anemic .047 isolated slugging percentage at Double-A Chattanooga in 2016. He did reach the gaps more frequently than in the past, however. An average runner, Vielma's offensive toolset is limited. His defensive prowess could be his ticket to the big leagues. A plus defender and the best pure shortstop in the system, he has soft hands, sharp instincts, quick actions and a plus arm. The Twins added Vielma to the 40-man roster after the 2016 season and put him in a strength-and-conditioning camp in the offseason to try to build his strength and stamina. He could be the first man up from Triple-A Rochester in 2017 if the Twins need defensive help in the middle infield.

Year	Club (League)	Class	AVG	G	AB	R	H	2B	3B	HR	RBI	BB	SO	SB	CS	OBP	SLG
2014	Cedar Rapids (MWL)	LoA	.266	112	418	63	111	13	4	1	33	28	71	10	6	.313	.323
2015	Fort Myers (FSL)	HiA	.270	120	441	49	119	9	2	1	29	35	71	35	12	.321	.306
2016	Fort Myers (FSL)	HiA	.200	8	25	5	5	0	0	0	0	5	8	2	0	.333	.200
	Chattanooga (SL)	AA	.271	90	314	47	85	7	4	0	21	34	62	10	8	.345	.318
Minor League Totals			.264	422	1509	215	398	36	13	2	114	136	269	81	34	.327	.309

26 LEWIN DIAZ, 1B

BA GRADE
50 Risk: Extreme

Born: Sept. 19, 1996 **B-T:** L-L. **Ht.:** 6-3. **Wt.:** 250. **Signed:** Dominican Republic, 2013. **Signed by:** Fred Guerrero.

Signed as a big-bodied 16-year-old in 2013 for $1.4 million, Diaz had an inconsistent first two seasons in pro ball, struggling at times to tap into his massive raw power. Physical conditioning could have played a role because weight management has been and will continue to be a key issue for Diaz, who has gained about 40 pounds since signing. The Twins have worked with him to steadily trim body fat and build muscle, and in 2016 he put together his best season to date, hitting for average and power at Rookie-level Elizabethton. Diaz draws 70 grades on the 20-80 scouting scale from some evaluators for his power, showing particularly impressive juice to his pull side. He uses a leg kick and a somewhat long stride, but Diaz has the ability to hit the ball to the opposite field, supplying hope he can hit for average. The lefthanded hitter has posted relatively even platoon splits in his pro career. Though he has some outfield experience and a strong throwing arm, Diaz's large frame and lack of mobility limits him to first base, where he is at least an average defender. His ceiling is tied to his bat, but he could develop into a middle-of-the-order hitter. The 20-year-old will play at low Class A Cedar Rapids in 2017.

Year	Club (League)	Class	AVG	G	AB	R	H	2B	3B	HR	RBI	BB	SO	SB	CS	OBP	SLG
2014	Twins (DSL)	R	.257	43	144	17	37	13	0	5	27	26	24	0	0	.385	.451
2015	Twins (GCL)	R	.261	33	111	12	29	7	1	1	15	14	24	2	0	.354	.369
	Elizabethton (APP)	R	.167	14	48	7	8	1	0	3	5	3	17	0	0	.245	.375
2016	Elizabethton (APP)	R	.310	46	174	26	54	15	2	9	37	12	35	0	0	.353	.575
Minor League Totals			.268	136	477	62	128	36	3	18	84	55	100	2	0	.353	.470

27 TREVOR HILDENBERGER, RHP

BA GRADE
40 Risk: Medium

Born: Dec. 15, 1990. **B-T:** R-R. **Ht.:** 6-2. **Wt.:** 211. **Drafted:** California, 2014 (22nd round). **Signed by:** Elliott Strankman.

Among a crowded class of hard-throwing righthanded relievers in the Twins system, Hildenberger stands out for his unique low three-quarters arm slot and plus command. Drafted in the 22nd round in 2014, he doesn't have the raw stuff of a Nick Burdi or J.T. Chargois, but his low-90s fastball plays up because of heavy sink and his deceptive arm action. Hildenberger commands both a slider with depth and a changeup—neither of which is better than average—but he is able to generate weak contact and swings and misses. He was surgical at Double-A Chattanooga in 2016, walking just six batters to 45 strikeouts in his 38.2 innings, and he's posted about a 9-to-1 strikeout-to-walk ratio in his pro career, earning the trust of every one of his managers. The organization has had success with low-slot relievers in the past (Pat Neshek, Michael Tonkin), so Hildenberger likely will crack into the big leagues at some point in 2017 and has the chance to thrive in a relief role.

Year	Club (League)	Class	W	L	ERA	G	GS	CG	SV	IP	H	HR	BB	SO	K/9	WHIP	AVG
2014	Twins (GCL)	R	1	4	2.57	23	0	0	10	28	27	1	5	30	9.6	1.14	.243
	Elizabethton (APP)	R	0	0	0.00	1	0	0	0	1	0	0	0	2	18.0	0.00	.000
2015	Cedar Rapids (MWL)	LoA	2	1	0.80	28	0	0	14	45	24	0	5	59	11.8	0.64	.153
	Fort Myers (FSL)	HiA	1	1	3.32	13	0	0	3	19	15	0	2	21	9.9	0.89	.231
2016	Fort Myers (FSL)	HiA	1	1	0.96	6	0	0	3	9	11	0	0	8	7.7	1.18	.282
	Chattanooga (SL)	AA	2	3	0.70	32	0	0	16	39	21	2	6	45	10.5	0.70	.157
Minor League Totals			7	10	1.47	103	0	0	46	141	98	3	18	165	10.5	0.82	.193

28 JAKE REED, RHP

BA GRADE
45 Risk: High

Born: Sept. 29, 1992. **B-T:** R-R. **Ht.:** 6-2. **Wt.:** 190. **Drafted:** Oregon, 2014 (5th round). **Signed by:** Trevor Brown.

Starting 2015 at Double-A Chattanooga proved to be too stiff a challenge for Reed, a 2014 fifthrounder from Oregon, but the righthander eventually made the appropriate adjustments in a return trip to Chattanooga in 2016. His ERA hovered around 5.00 in June, but a strong July propelled Reed to

Triple-A Rochester, where he allowed just two earned runs in nine appearances. The former Ducks closer is armed with a power mid-90s fastball with heavy boring action that touched the upper 90s and even flirted with triple digits in 2016. Reed's slider, however, is an average pitch and continual work in progress since he signed. He throws it in the mid-80s, harder than he did at Oregon, but the pitch has inconsistent break and can be slurvy at times. He also uses a changeup sparingly, and it's a pitch he could afford to work more into his arsenal, especially against lefties. Reed is one of several high-velocity righthanded relief options at the Twins' disposal, and he figures to make his big league debut in 2017.

Year	Club (League)	Class	W	L	ERA	G	GS	CG	SV	IP	H	HR	BB	SO	K/9	WHIP	AVG
2014	Elizabethton (APP)	R	0	0	0.00	4	0	0	3	6	1	0	0	8	12.0	0.17	.053
	Cedar Rapids (MWL)	LoA	3	0	0.36	16	0	0	5	25	10	0	3	31	11.2	0.52	.116
2015	Fort Myers (FSL)	HiA	1	0	0.00	9	0	0	1	12	8	0	1	7	5.1	0.73	.195
	Chattanooga (SL)	AA	4	4	6.32	35	0	0	1	47	55	3	21	39	7.5	1.62	.289
2016	Chattanooga (SL)	AA	3	3	3.90	41	0	0	3	60	51	2	22	64	9.6	1.22	.235
	Rochester (IL)	AAA	1	1	1.69	9	0	0	0	11	8	0	2	8	6.8	0.94	.211
Minor League Totals			12	8	3.47	114	0	0	13	161	133	5	49	157	8.8	1.13	.225

29 HUASCAR YNOA, RHP

BA GRADE

50 Risk: Extreme

Born: May 28, 1998. **B-T:** R-R. **Ht.:** 6-3. **Wt.:** 221. **Signed:** Dominican Republic, 2014. **Signed by:** Fred Guerrero.

The younger brother of White Sox righthander Michael Ynoa—who signed for a then-record $4.25 million as a 16-year-old with the Athletics in 2008—Huascar received an $800,000 bonus from the Twins in 2014 after an inconsistent showcase circuit raised concerns over his command. He walked 30 in 56.2 innings in an otherwise solid 2015 debut in the Dominican Summer League, and he took a step forward in the Rookie-level Gulf Coast League in 2016, walking just 12 against 51 strikeouts in 51 innings. Not nearly as tall as his 6-foot-7 brother, Ynoa is still a strong 6-foot-3, 221-pound 18-year-old without much physical projection left. He sits 92-93 mph and can reach 95, and he projects as a starter with his durable body and three-pitch arsenal. He throws an 80-82 mph slurve-like breaking ball that projects as an average offering and could evolve into a tighter slider, and he adds an average low-80s changeup. Ynoa has a better feel for pitching and spinning the ball than many pitchers his age, and if he continues to refine his command, he could develop into a mid-rotation starter. He will likely start 2017 at Rookie-level Elizabethton.

Year	Club (League)	Class	W	L	ERA	G	GS	CG	SV	IP	H	HR	BB	SO	K/9	WHIP	AVG
2015	Twins (DSL)	R	2	5	2.70	14	14	0	0	57	43	1	30	47	7.5	1.29	.207
2016	Twins (GCL)	R	3	5	3.18	11	11	0	0	51	44	1	12	51	9.0	1.10	.228
Minor League Totals			5	10	2.93	25	25	0	0	108	87	2	42	98	8.2	1.20	.217

30 MASON MELOTAKIS, LHP

BA GRADE

45 Risk: High

Born: June 28, 1991. **B-T:** R-L. **Ht.:** 6-2. **Wt.:** 220. **Drafted:** Northwestern State, 2012 (2nd round). **Signed by:** Greg Runser.

After missing the entire 2015 season while rehabbing from Tommy John surgery, Melotakis returned to action in 2016 by throwing 33.1 innings at Double-A Chattanooga. Drafted in the second round in 2012 and signing for $750,000, the lefthander began his career as a starter at low Class A Cedar Rapids but transitioned to a full-time relief role in 2014 before surgery. His pre-Tommy John mid-90s velocity remains intact, and he routinely touches 95 mph and reaches back at times for a tick or two higher. He throws with a short arm action and deceptive delivery, allowing his fastball to play up, especially against lefties. His main strikeout pitch is a hard low- to mid-80s curveball. Added to the 40-man roster after the 2015 season, Melotakis still has some rust to shake off—namely regaining his command—but he could force himself into the big league mix late in 2017. His power stuff from the left side could make him a bullpen weapon.

Year	Club (League)	Class	W	L	ERA	G	GS	CG	SV	IP	H	HR	BB	SO	K/9	WHIP	AVG
2014	Fort Myers (FSL)	HiA	3	1	3.45	25	2	0	1	47	50	3	24	45	8.6	1.57	.269
	New Britain (EL)	AA	1	0	2.25	13	0	0	2	16	17	0	3	17	9.6	1.25	.274
2015	Did not play—Injured																
2016	Chattanooga (SL)	AA	1	2	2.97	36	0	0	0	33	36	3	12	42	11.3	1.44	.277
Minor League Totals			20	9	3.00	118	20	0	5	231	226	15	84	222	8.6	1.34	.253

New York Mets

BY MATT EDDY

Giants ace Madison Bumgarner ended the Mets' season with a shutout in the National League Wild Card Game, but even the disappointing finish to 2016 did not obscure a successful season for New York. The Mets, after advancing to the 2015 World Series, qualified for the postseason in consecutive years for just the second time in franchise history.

While the Mets failed to defend their NL pennant, they overcame long odds to even make the postseason. They finished play on Aug. 19 with a 60-62 record before winning 27 of their final 40.

Before Bumgarner vanquished them, the Mets contended with an equally formidable foe: the disabled list. New York played the majority of the season without third baseman David Wright, first baseman Lucas Duda and center fielder Juan Lagares. When their farm system couldn't fill in the cracks, the Mets turned to freely available players Jose Reyes and James Loney while improvising in center field. One bright spot was 25-year-old Wilmer Flores, who enjoyed a career year as a corner-infield patch—before he suffered a wrist injury of his own and finished on the DL.

The most debilitating injuries struck the Mets' rotation. Righthander Matt Harvey succumbed to thoracic outlet surgery in July. Rookie lefthander Steven Matz made his last start on Aug. 14, then later had surgery to remove bone chips from his elbow. Ace righthander Jacob deGrom had elbow surgery to reposition the ulnar nerve in his right elbow in September.

The Mets had more success replacing lost innings, and even with myriad injuries still ranked third in the NL with a 3.58 ERA. Rookie righthanders Robert Gsellman—the system's top big league-ready arm—and Seth Lugo—owner of the highest-spin curveball of the MLB Statcast era—positioned themselves for larger roles.

Gsellman and Lugo both are products of the 2011 draft, the first under general manager Sandy Alderson as the Mets embarked on a rebuild. In those first few drafts, New York emphasized high school players with its top pick, selecting outfielder Brandon Nimmo in 2011, shortstop Gavin Cecchini in 2012, first baseman Dominic Smith in 2013 and outfielder Desmond Lindsay in 2015. Nimmo, Cecchini and Smith will integrate into the big league lineup in 2017 and 2018, where they will join 2014 top pick Michael Conforto.

The Mets deviated from their prep-heavy draft strategy in 2016, their first without scouting and player development head Paul DePodesta, who left to work for the NFL's Cleveland Browns. They

An elbow injury scuttled what had been a well-rounded rookie season by Steven Matz

ROB CUNI

TOP PROSPECTS OF THE DECADE

Year	Player, Pos.	2016 Org
2007	Mike Pelfrey, rhp	Tigers
2008	Fernando Martinez, of	Did not play
2009	Fernando Martinez, of	Did not play
2010	Jenrry Mejia, rhp	Did not play
2011	Jenrry Mejia, rhp	Did not play
2012	Zack Wheeler, rhp	Mets
2013	Zack Wheeler, rhp	Mets
2014	Noah Syndergaard, rhp	Mets
2015	Noah Syndergaard, rhp	Mets
2016	Steven Matz, lhp	Mets

selected Boston College righthander Justin Dunn, Connecticut lefthander Anthony Kay and Florida first baseman Pete Alonso in the first and second rounds.

Dunn and Alonso played well at short-season Brooklyn, while Kay did not pitch and ultimately had Tommy John surgery. That trio could advance quickly in a system that skews toward high school players and international free agents.

Though the organization's domestic winning percentage has fallen from .568 in 2014 (No. 1 in baseball) to .532 in 2015 (No. 7) to .480 in 2016 (No. 20), the Mets had several prospects take steps forward in 2016. Notably, shortstop Amed Rosario and first baseman Smith both appeared in the Futures Game and finished the year at Double-A Binghamton.

ORGANIZATION OVERVIEW

General manager: Sandy Alderson. **Farm director:** Ian Levin. **Scouting director:** Marc Tramuta.

Class	Team	League	W	L	PCT	Finish	Manager
Majors	New York Mets	National	87	75	.537	4th (15)	Terry Collins
Triple-A	Las Vegas 51s	Pacific Coast	70	74	.486	10th (16)	Wally Backman
Double-A	Binghamton Mets	Eastern	63	77	.450	8th (12)	Pedro Lopez
High Class A	St. Lucie Mets	Florida State	74	61	.548	5th (12)	Luis Rojas
Low Class A	Columbia Fireflies	South Atlantic	67	73	.479	10th (14)	Jose Leger
Short season	Brooklyn Cyclones	New York-Penn	37	39	.487	10th (14)	Tom Gamboa
Rookie	GCL Mets	Gulf Coast	26	29	.473	10th (17)	Jose Carreno
Overall 2016 Minor League Record			364	394	.480	20th (30)	

THIS YEAR'S TOP 30

No.	Player, Pos.	Grade/Risk
1.	Amed Rosario, ss	60/Medium
2.	Dominic Smith, 1b	55/High
3.	Justin Dunn, rhp	60/Extreme
4.	Desmond Lindsay, of	60/Extreme
5.	Brandon Nimmo, of	50/Medium
6.	Gavin Cecchini, ss/2b	50/Medium
7.	Robert Gsellman, rhp	50/Medium
8.	Thomas Szapucki, lhp	60/Extreme
9.	Gabriel Ynoa, rhp	50/High
10.	Tomas Nido, c	50/High
11.	Marcos Molina, rhp	55/Extreme
12.	Anthony Kay, lhp	55/Extreme
13.	Pete Alonso, 1b	50/High
14.	Merandy Gonzalez, rhp	55/Extreme
15.	Luis Guillorme, ss/2b	50/High
16.	Wuilmer Becerra, of	50/High
17.	Andres Gimenez, ss	55/Extreme
18.	Matt Reynolds, ss/3b	45/Medium
19.	P.J. Conlon, lhp	50/High
20.	Luis Carpio, ss/2b	55/Extreme
21.	Patrick Mazeika, c	50/High
22.	Chris Flexen, rhp	45/High
23.	Ricardo Cespedes, of	50/Extreme
24.	T.J. Rivera, 2b/3b	40/Medium
25.	Phillip Evans, ss/2b	45/High
26.	Corey Taylor, rhp	45/High
27.	Ali Sanchez, c	50/Extreme
28.	Harol Gonzalez, rhp	50/Extreme
29.	Gregory Guerrero, ss	50/Extreme
30.	Colby Woodmansee, ss	50/Extreme

LAST YEAR'S TOP 30

No.	Player, Pos.	Status
1.	Steven Matz, lhp	Majors
2.	Amed Rosario, ss	No. 1
3.	Dominic Smith, 1b	No. 2
4.	Gavin Cecchini, ss	No. 6
5.	Brandon Nimmo, of	No. 5
6.	Marcos Molina, rhp	No. 11
7.	Luis Carpio, ss/2b	No. 20
8.	Desmond Lindsay, of	No. 4
9.	Matt Reynolds, ss/2b	No. 18
10.	Wuilmer Becerra, of	No. 16
11.	Jhoan Urena, 3b	Dropped out
12.	Luis Guillorme, ss	No. 15
13.	Gabriel Ynoa, rhp	No. 9
14.	Robert Gsellman, rhp	No. 7
15.	Ali Sanchez, c	No. 27
16.	Andres Gimenez, ss	No. 17
17.	Max Wotell, lhp	(Reds)
18.	Logan Verrett, rhp	(Orioles)
19.	Milton Ramos, ss	Dropped out
20.	Seth Lugo, rhp	Majors
21.	Eudor Garcia, 3b	Dropped out
22.	Akeel Morris, rhp	(Braves)
23.	L.J. Mazzilli, 2b	Dropped out
24.	Josh Smoker, lhp	Dropped out
25.	Patrick Mazeika, c/1b	No. 21
26.	Chris Flexen, rhp	No. 22
27.	Jeff McNeil, 2b/ss	Dropped out
28.	John Mora, of	Dropped out
29.	Dash Winningham, 1b	Dropped out
30.	Mike Gibbons, rhp	Dropped out

BEST TOOLS

Best Hitter for Average	Dominic Smith
Best Power Hitter	Pete Alonso
Best Strike-Zone Discipline	Brandon Nimmo
Fastest Baserunner	Champ Stuart
Best Athlete	Amed Rosario
Best Fastball	Justin Dunn
Best Curveball	Thomas Szapucki
Best Slider	Justin Dunn
Best Changeup	P.J. Conlon
Best Control	P.J. Conlon
Best Defensive Catcher	Tomas Nido
Best Defensive Infielder	Luis Guillorme
Best Infield Arm	Amed Rosario
Best Defensive Outfielder	Champ Stuart
Best Outfield Arm	Travis Taijeron

2020 LINEUP

Catcher	Tomas Nido
First Base	Dominic Smith
Second Base	Gavin Cecchini
Third Base	Wilmer Flores
Shortstop	Amed Rosario
Left Field	Yoenis Cespedes
Center Field	Desmond Lindsay
Right Field	Michael Conforto
No. 1 Starter	Noah Syndergaard
No. 2 Starter	Jacob deGrom
No. 3 Starter	Steven Matz
No. 4 Starter	Zack Wheeler
No. 5 Starter	Justin Dunn
Closer	Jeurys Familia

MINOR LEAGUE DEPTH CHART

NEW YORK METS

TOP 2017 ROOKIE: Robert Gsellman, rhp. He got his foot in the door in 2016 and is ready for an expanded workload.
BREAKOUT PROSPECT: Merandy Gonzalez, rhp. The 21-year-old Dominican has the raw stuff to dominate Class A and become more of a household name.
SLEEPER: Ranfy Adon, of. The 19-year-old center fielder is 6-foot-3 and has all the raw tools to succeed—now he just needs to learn to hit.

SOURCE OF TOP 30 TALENT			
Homegrown	29	Acquired	1
College	8	Trades	1
Junior college	0	Rule 5 draft	0
High school	10	Independent leagues	0
Nondrafted free agents	1	Free agents/waivers	0
International	10		

LF
Brandon Nimmo (5)
Gene Cone
Wagner Lagrange

CF
Desmond Lindsay (4)
Ricardo Cespedes (23)
Champ Stuart
Ranfy Adon
John Mora
Raul Beracierta

RF
Wuilmer Becerra (16)
Travis Taijeron
Edinson Valdez

3B
Gregory Guerrero (29)
David Thompson
Eudor Garcia
Jhoan Urena
Blake Tiberi

SS
Amed Rosario (1)
Luis Guillorme (15)
Andres Gimenez (17)
Matt Reynolds (18)
Colby Woodmansee (30)
Milton Ramos

2B
Gavin Cecchini (6)
Luis Carpio (20)
T.J. Rivera (24)
Phillip Evans (25)
Michael Paez
L.J. Mazzilli
Jeff McNeil

1B
Dominic Smith (2)
Pete Alonso (13)
Matt Oberste
Dash Winningham

C
Tomas Nido (10)
Patrick Mazeika (21)
Ali Sanchez (27)
Carlos Sanchez
Colton Plaia
Dan Rizzie

LHP

LHSP	LHRP
Thomas Szapucki (8)	P.J. Conlon (19)
Anthony Kay (12)	Josh Smoker
Jake Simon	David Roseboom

RHP

RHSP	RHRP
Justin Dunn (3)	Corey Taylor (26)
Robert Gsellman (7)	Ty Bashlor
Gabriel Ynoa (9)	Paul Sewald
Marcos Molina (11)	Chris Viall
Merandy Gonzalez (14)	Adonis Uceta
Chris Flexen (22)	Joe Shaw
Harrol Gonzalez (28)	Mike Gibbons
Jordan Humphries	Gary Cornish
Nabil Crismatt	Chase Bradford
Corey Oswalt	
Tyler Pill	
Andrew Church	
Cameron Planck	
Luis Silva	
Luis de los Santos	
Christian James	

DRAFT ANALYSIS

2016

BEST PURE HITTER: New York selected pitchers with its two first-round picks. 1B Pete Alonso (2) proved himself offensively at Florida, then hit batted .321 in his debut at short-season Brooklyn. OF Gene Cone (10) excelled in the Southeastern Conference this spring, batting .363 and walking more often than he struck out, though his performance was lighter in pro ball.

BEST POWER: Alonso has easy plus raw power, with some evaluators grading the tool as a 70. He can drive the ball out to any part of the ballpark.

FASTEST RUNNER: New York didn't focus on acquiring speed. SS Michael Paez (4) and Cone are both average runners but don't project as game-changers on the basepaths.

BEST DEFENSIVE PLAYER: SS Colby Woodmansee (5) is a steady defender at short-stop, though he isn't the most explosive or lithe defender. Alonso receives praise for his defense at first base. C Dan Rizzie (13) has solid catch-and-throw skills.

BEST FASTBALL: RHP Justin Dunn's (1) fastball can reach as high as 98 mph in a starter's role. 6-foot-9 RHP Chris Viall (6) has size and elite velocity, though his command and control will need refinement for the pitch to play more consistently.

BEST SECONDARY PITCH: Dunn's slider earns plus grades as a hard vertical snapper. LHP Anthony Kay (1) has an outstanding changeup with late fading action, though he does throw it from a lower arm slot.

BEST PRO DEBUT: Dunn was on a tight leash in order to limit his workload, but he performed exceptionally well, striking out 35 and walking 10 in 30 innings while compiling a 1.50 ERA. Alonso also excelled before a broken finger ended his season, slashing .321/.382/.587 in more than 120 plate appearances. RHP Gary Cornish (19) posted a 44-to-3 SO-BB ratio at short-season Brooklyn.

BEST ATHLETE: Dunn has a loose, athletic delivery with explosiveness and quick-twitch ability.

MOST INTRIGUING BACKGROUND: LHP Placido Torres (8) was born in the Dominican Republic but grew up in New Jersey. He excelled at Advanced Software Analysis JC in New York before transferring to Tusculum (Tenn.), where he posted an 0.70 ERA and a strikeout-to-walk ratio of 7-to-1.

CLOSEST TO THE MAJORS: Dunn has shown the ability to command four pitches and he could move quickly. Kay seemed like a candidate to move quickly, but he had Tommy John surgery after signing. Alonso's offensive upside and polish at first base could allow him to find early success.

BEST LATE-ROUND PICK: RHP Cameron Planck (11) is strong and physical, and he's shown the ability to run his fastball into the mid-90s

while flashing a promising slider. RHP Matt Cleveland (12) has an ideal pitcher's body and has reached the mid-90s with his fastball.

THE ONE WHO GOT AWAY: New York took a shot at 2B/OF Carlos Cortes (20), one of the best pure hitters in the class, but he ultimately ended up honoring his South Carolina commitment. RHP Alex Haynes (29) has arm strength and a projectable body, as does RHP George Kirby (32). Haynes ended up at Walters State (Tenn.) CC and Kirby went to Elon.

2015

The Mets went heavy for high schoolers atop their class and already have traded LHP Max Wotell (3) to the Reds. OF Desmond Lindsay (2) and LHP Thomas Szapucki (5) have flashed big tools, while LHP P.J. Conlon (13) has performed despite fringy stuff.

GRADE: C+.

2014

The No. 10 overall pick, OF Michael Conforto (1) stumbled in his sophomore big league season. No one from the rest of the draft class made the Top 30 Prospects.

GRADE: B.

2013

1B Dominic Smith (1) developed power in 2016, but he's a divisive prospect due to his physique and low-energy approach. RHP Casey Meisner (3), was traded to Oakland. SS Luis Guillorme (10) can pick it.

GRADE: C

TOP DRAFT PICKS OF THE DECADE

Year	Player, Pos.	2016 Org
2007	Eddie Kunz, rhp (1st round supp.)	Did not play
2008	Ike Davis, 1b	Yankees
2009	Steven Matz, lhp (2nd round)	Mets
2010	Matt Harvey, rhp	Mets
2011	Brandon Nimmo, of	Mets
2012	Gavin Cecchini, ss	Mets
2013	Dominic Smith, 1b	Mets
2014	Michael Conforto, of	Mets
2015	Desmond Lindsay, of (2nd round)	Mets
2016	Justin Dunn, rhp	Mets

LARGEST BONUSES IN CLUB HISTORY

Mike Pelfrey, 2005	$3,550,000
Philip Humber, 2004	$3,000,000
Michael Conforto, 2014	$2,970,800
Dominic Smith, 2013	$2,600,000
Matt Harvey, 2010	$2,525,000

1 AMED ROSARIO, SS

Born: Nov. 20, 1995. **B-T:** R-R. **Ht.:** 6-2. **Wt.:** 190.
Signed: Dominican Republic, 2012.
Signed by: Chris Becerra/Gerardo Cabrera.

Sandy Alderson took the reins as Mets general manager after the 2010 season and promoted Chris Becerra to international scouting director in 2012. Becerra had previously worked as an area scout in Southern California— he recommended Robert Gsellman for the 2011 draft—and in his new role focused on Rosario as his first major acquisition. The Mets signed the Dominican shortstop for $1.75 million on July 2, 2012, and that bonus amount stands as a franchise record for an international amateur. Rosario, who was teammates with Rangers right fielder Nomar Mazara as a youth in Santo Domingo, graduated from high school before turning pro. His father, who was a lawyer and a judge, helped steer the signing process. Rosario wowed the Mets at instructional league after signing and made his pro debut at Rookie-level Kingsport in 2013, ranking as the No. 1 prospect in Appalachian League at age 17. After ranking as the top position prospect in the short-season New York-Penn League in 2014, he shot to high Class A St. Lucie in 2015. Rosario advanced rapidly through the minors in his teens, but he didn't begin to hit until 2016, his age-20 season, when he spent half the year at St. Lucie before moving to Double-A Binghamton in the second half. All told he hit .324/.374/.459 with 42 extra-base hits and 19 stolen bases in 120 games, and his .833 OPS ranked fourth among minor league shortstops.

Tall and lean, Rosario began to fill out his frame and swing the bat with more authority in 2016. He also improved his pitch selectivity and bat-to-ball skills, resulting a career-best .324 average and walk rate of 7.6 percent across high Class and Double-A. His bat plays best when he lets the ball travel and uses his hands, strong wrists and plus bat speed to drive the ball to all fields. Capable of turning on the ball for occasional pull power, Rosario set a new personal standard with five home runs and .135 isolated slugging percentage in 2016. While his strikeout rate crept into dangerous territory at Double-A, Rosario has all the tools to be a plus hitter with possibly fringe-average power. Plus speed and strong instincts will help him take extra bases and steal perhaps 20 bags per season. The best athlete in the Mets system, Rosario stands out most for his glove work. Managers in both the Florida State and Eastern leagues recognized him as the best defensive shortstop in those leagues in 2016, and he has the easy plus range and arm strength to profile as a true impact defender. He will improve his throwing accuracy with experience, but scouts rave about his hands, live body and infield actions.

Rosario has the potential to be an all-star shortstop with Gold Glove potential who can bat near the top of a lineup. He might begin 2017 back at Binghamton to refine his plate discipline, but he could push his way into the big league picture later in the season. The Mets have Asdrubal Cabrera under contract through 2017, meaning Rosario could be the organization's full-time shortstop at some point in 2018.

BA GRADE	
60	Risk: Medium

SCOUTING GRADES

Batting: 60.
Power: 45.
Speed: 60.
Defense: 70.
Arm: 60.

Based on 20-80 scouting scale and future projection rather than present tools.

RODGER WOOD

Year	Club (League)	Class	AVG	G	AB	R	H	2B	3B	HR	RBI	BB	SO	SB	CS	OBP	SLG
2014	Savannah (SAL)	LoA	.133	7	30	2	4	0	1	1	4	1	11	0	0	.161	.300
	Brooklyn (NYP)	SS	.289	68	266	39	77	11	5	1	23	17	47	7	3	.337	.380
2015	St. Lucie (FSL)	HiA	.257	103	385	41	99	20	5	0	25	23	73	12	4	.307	.335
	Binghamton (EL)	AA	.100	2	10	1	1	0	0	0	1	0	5	1	0	.100	.100
2016	St. Lucie (FSL)	HiA	.309	66	265	27	82	10	8	3	40	21	36	13	6	.359	.442
	Binghamton (EL)	AA	.341	54	214	38	73	14	5	2	31	19	51	6	2	.392	.481
Minor League Totals			.280	358	1382	170	387	63	28	10	147	92	266	41	21	.328	.388

2 DOMINIC SMITH, 1B

Born: June 15, 1995. **B-T:** L-L. **Ht.:** 6-0. **Wt.:** 250. **Drafted:** HS—Gardena, Calif., 2013 (1st round). **Signed by:** Drew Toussaint.

The 11th overall pick in the 2013 draft, Smith hit only one home run in his full-season debut at low Class A Savannah in 2014. He corrected course in 2015 with a Florida State League MVP season at high Class A St. Lucie and then in 2016 with a seamless transition to Double-A Binghamton, where he ranked third in the Eastern League in both hits (146) and RBIs (91). Smith strongly resembles the player he was on draft day in that he is a natural hitter—the best in the system—with strong defensive ability at first base. He hit .300 for a second straight season in 2016 while establishing career-best marks for strikeout rate (13.6 percent), home runs (14) and isolated slugging percentage (.156). Smith hit all but four of his homers in the first half, but his average surged to .345 in the second after he adjusted his swing to keep his front hip closed, his bat path direct and his hands down through the ball. He began to drive the ball consistently in 2016 and shows solid-average power to go with a plus hit tool. He is listed at 250 pounds and doesn't run well, but is nimble around first base with a quick first step and sure hands to save his infielders errors. His lack of hustle and sloppy physique turn off some evaluators. Smith will head to Triple-A Las Vegas in 2017, and by the time he is big league ready will have no one blocking his path in New York.

BA GRADE
55 Risk: High

Year	Club (League)	Class	AVG	G	AB	R	H	2B	3B	HR	RBI	BB	SO	SB	CS	OBP	SLG
2014	Savannah (SAL)	LoA	.271	126	461	52	125	26	1	1	44	51	77	5	4	.344	.338
2015	St. Lucie (FSL)	HiA	.305	118	456	58	139	33	0	6	79	35	75	2	1	.354	.417
2016	Binghamton (EL)	AA	.302	130	484	64	146	29	2	14	91	50	74	2	1	.367	.457
Minor League Totals			.294	425	1574	199	462	101	4	24	240	162	263	11	10	.360	.409

3 JUSTIN DUNN, RHP

Born: Sept. 22, 1995. **B-T:** R-R. **Ht.:** 6-2. **Wt.:** 185. **Drafted:** Boston College, 2016 (1st round). **Signed by:** Michael Pesce.

Dunn worked primarily as a reliever at Boston College—and in the 2015 Cape Cod League—and remained in that role until two months before the 2016 draft. Though he made just eight starts as a junior, he generated first-round buzz based on his impressive arm speed and athletic delivery. The Mets selected Dunn, a Long Island native, 19th overall and signed him for slot value of $2,378,800. No first-round college righthander has moved from the bullpen to the rotation in the midst of his draft-eligible season in recent draft history. Dunn, however, showed the arsenal and results to warrant first-round selection. He already has the best fastball and slider in the Mets system, using his primary weapons to strike out 10.5 per nine innings in his pro debut at short-season Brooklyn. He generates mid-90s velocity and good life on his fastball—which touched 98 mph—with a loose arm and fluid motion. His mid-80s slider already grades as above-average and should mature into a plus pitch with tight spin and late vertical break. He will need to develop his below-average curveball and changeup to give lefthanders different looks. Though Dunn is athletic, he has a lean frame and is not as physical as many starters. With two projected plus pitches, Dunn could be a No. 2 or 3 starter, though some scouts project him to the bullpen. He should spend time at both Class A levels in 2017.

BA GRADE
60 Risk: Extreme

Year	Club (League)	Class	W	L	ERA	G	GS	CG	SV	IP	H	HR	BB	SO	K/9	WHIP	AVG
2016	Brooklyn (NYP)	SS	1	1	1.50	11	8	0	0	30	25	1	10	35	10.5	1.17	.227
Minor League Totals			1	1	1.50	11	8	0	0	30	25	1	10	35	10.5	1.17	.227

4 DESMOND LINDSAY, OF

Born: Jan. 15, 1997. **B-T:** R-R. **Ht.:** 6-0. **Wt.:** 200. **Drafted:** HS—Sarasota, Fla., 2015 (2nd round). **Signed by:** Cesar Aranguren.

Lindsay fell to No. 53 overall in the 2015 draft because he missed virtually all of his senior year with a hamstring injury, but he intrigued the Mets with his power-speed potential and feel to hit. He strained the same hamstring in 2016, which precluded him from joining a full-season team. He joined short-season Brooklyn in late July and showed tantalizing ability in 32 games. A twitchy athlete, Lindsay is naturally muscled and already physically mature as a teenager. With plus bat speed and an all-fields approach, he has the chance to grade as a plus hitter with above-average power. He walked nearly as often as he struck out in the New York-Penn League and takes disciplined at-bats, which helps him get to plus raw power to his pull side. A plus runner,

BA GRADE
60 Risk: Extreme

Lindsay still looks tentative in the field and on the bases because of his injury history. A third baseman in high school, he has work to do to become average in center field. He has improved his jumps with experience and his throwing by lengthening his arm stroke. The long rehab periods and daily pre-game work have taught Lindsay self-discipline and have prepared him mentally to play every day. Lindsay has true five-tool potential if he improves his outfield play and regains confidence in his twice-injured hamstring. Low Class A Columbia will be his next step.

Year	Club (League)	Class	AVG	G	AB	R	H	2B	3B	HR	RBI	BB	SO	SB	CS	OBP	SLG
2015	Mets (GCL)	R	.304	21	69	10	21	4	2	1	6	11	21	3	2	.400	.464
	Brooklyn (NYP)	SS	.200	14	45	3	9	3	0	0	7	7	19	0	1	.308	.267
2016	Mets (GCL)	R	.364	5	11	3	4	1	0	0	0	5	5	0	0	.563	.455
	Brooklyn (NYP)	SS	.297	32	111	18	33	5	0	4	17	20	26	3	1	.418	.450
Minor League Totals			.284	72	236	34	67	13	2	5	30	43	71	6	4	.401	.419

5 BRANDON NIMMO, OF

Born: March 23, 1993. **B-T:** L-R. **Ht.:** 6-3. **Wt.:** 205. **Drafted:** HS—Cheyenne, Wyo., 2011 (1st round). **Signed by:** Jim Reeves.

The first and only high school first-rounder from the state of Wyoming, Nimmo made incremental gains through his first five pro seasons before enjoying a career year at Triple-A Las Vegas in 2016. He led the Pacific Coast League with a .423 on-base percentage, finished second with a .352 average and third with a .964 OPS. He made his big league debut in June 2016 and received three separate callups. With the best strike-zone judgment in the Mets system, Nimmo has built a career .389 OBP in the minors, and in 2016 he established career-best marks for strikeout rate (16.4 percent), home runs (11) and isolated slugging percentage (.189). He works

BA GRADE

50 Risk: Medium

deep counts, takes walks and hits the ball where it's pitched, making him a solid-average hitter with average power. With a muscular 6-foot-3 frame, Nimmo shows plus raw power in batting practice and probably could hit more home runs if he hunts fastballs early in counts. An average runner, he is no better than average defensively in center field and probably will settle on an outfield corner with his near-average arm. He won't be a stolen-base threat, though he runs the bases intelligently. Scouts love his makeup, and his infectious personality is evident by his wide smile. While Nimmo possesses all-around ability, he projects more as a table-setting corner outfielder than a masher. He is ready for a larger big league role in 2017.

Year	Club (League)	Class	AVG	G	AB	R	H	2B	3B	HR	RBI	BB	SO	SB	CS	OBP	SLG
2014	St. Lucie (FSL)	HiA	.322	62	227	59	73	9	5	4	25	50	51	9	3	.448	.458
	Binghamton (EL)	AA	.238	65	240	38	57	12	4	6	26	36	54	5	1	.339	.396
2015	St. Lucie (FSL)	HiA	.125	4	16	3	2	1	0	0	2	4	3	0	0	.300	.188
	Binghamton (EL)	AA	.279	68	269	26	75	12	3	2	16	26	55	0	2	.354	.368
	Las Vegas (PCL)	AAA	.264	32	91	19	24	3	1	3	8	18	20	5	4	.393	.418
2016	Las Vegas (PCL)	AAA	.352	97	392	72	138	25	8	11	61	46	73	7	8	.423	.541
	New York (NL)	MAJ	.274	32	73	12	20	1	0	1	6	6	20	0	0	.338	.329
Major League Totals			.274	32	73	12	20	1	0	1	6	6	20	0	0	.338	.329
Minor League Totals			.285	517	1934	325	551	98	29	36	222	303	479	37	30	.389	.421

6 GAVIN CECCHINI, SS/2B

Born: Dec. 22, 1993. **B-T:** R-R. **Ht.:** 6-2. **Wt.:** 200. **Drafted:** HS—Lake Charles, La., 2012 (1st round). **Signed by:** Tommy Jackson.

The 12th overall pick in 2012, Cecchini missed time with injuries early in his career before putting things together at Class A in 2014. He blended contact skills with strong batting eye to hit .325 at Triple-A Las Vegas in 2016 to rank third in the Pacific Coast League batting race and fifth with a .390 on-base percentage. He earned a September callup and then participated in the Arizona Fall League for a second straight year. Cecchini has hit .321 at Double-A and Triple-A in nearly 900 at-bats, experiencing more success after adding muscle mass and toning down his leg kick to catch up with velocity. His swing is geared to produce line drives and

BA GRADE

50 Risk: Medium

hard ground balls, and though he has below-average power, he can drive the left-center field gap when he works the count to his favor. He ranks consistently as one of the most difficult batters to strike out in his league and will take a walk. A fringy runner, he hardly ever attempts to steal. Cecchini lacks great range or fluidity at shortstop and also lacks throwing accuracy from his average arm, a problem compounded by a high slot and slow release. All that contributed to him leading his league in errors by a shortstop in both 2015 and 2016. Cecchini should see more time at second base in 2017 as he prepares to make the position part of his job description, either as a starter or a utility infielder. A return to Triple-A is probable.

Year	Club (League)	Class	AVG	G	AB	R	H	2B	3B	HR	RBI	BB	SO	SB	CS	OBP	SLG
2014	Savannah (SAL)	LoA	.259	57	228	42	59	17	4	3	25	25	41	7	1	.333	.408
	St. Lucie (FSL)	HiA	.236	68	233	36	55	10	1	5	31	32	40	3	3	.325	.352
	Binghamton (EL)	AA	.250	1	4	1	1	0	0	0	0	0	1	0	0	.250	.250
2015	Binghamton (EL)	AA	.317	109	439	64	139	26	4	7	51	42	55	3	4	.377	.442
2016	Las Vegas (PCL)	AAA	.325	117	446	71	145	27	2	8	55	48	55	4	1	.390	.448
	New York (NL)	MAJ	.333	4	6	2	2	2	0	0	2	0	2	0	0	.429	.667
Major League Totals			.333	4	6	2	2	2	0	0	2	0	2	0	0	.429	.667
Minor League Totals			.287	461	1740	255	499	97	13	24	198	179	266	24	16	.353	.399

7 ROBERT GSELLMAN, RHP

Born: July 18, 1993. **B-T:** R-R. **Ht.:** 6-4. **Wt.:** 205. **Drafted:** HS—Los Angeles, 2011 (13th round). **Signed by:** Chris Becerra.

Gsellman starred in both baseball and basketball in high school, and his natural athleticism and desire to learn made him a complete pitcher as a pro. He spent three years in short-season before emerging as a prospect in 2014 and breaking out in 2015, which he finished at Double-A Binghamton. He missed about a month with a quad injury at Triple-A Las Vegas in 2016 but returned in July and made his big league debut on Aug. 23, making seven effective starts for the injury-depleted Mets. An extreme groundball pitcher, Gsellman pitches at 93 mph and tops out at 96 with a fastball featuring plus sink. He consistently works ahead of opposing batters by throwing strike one and then compelling them to put his pitch in play. Gsellman's fastball is so live it generates swings and misses, while the improved quality of his secondary stuff led to a career-best strikeout rate of 7.3 per nine innings in 2016. His above-average slider in the high 80s functions as an out pitch when located down in the zone. He improved his high-80s changeup to above-average by relaxing his grip to create more velocity separation, and he also throws a fringe curveball in the low 80s. He throws plenty of strikes but needs to command the ball to the edges of the zone better. Gsellman impressed scouts during his big league debut—they see him as a No. 4 starter—and could be ready for a larger role in 2017. That's a distinct possibility given that Jacob deGrom, Matt Harvey, Steven Matz and Zack Wheeler all are returning from surgery.

BA GRADE

50 Risk: Medium

Year	Club (League)	Class	W	L	ERA	G	GS	CG	SV	IP	H	HR	BB	SO	K/9	WHIP	AVG
2014	Savannah (SAL)	LoA	10	6	2.55	20	20	4	0	116	122	2	34	92	7.1	1.34	.275
2015	St. Lucie (FSL)	HiA	6	0	1.76	8	8	0	0	51	37	1	11	37	6.5	0.94	.204
	Binghamton (EL)	AA	7	7	3.51	16	16	0	0	92	89	4	26	49	4.8	1.25	.254
2016	Binghamton (EL)	AA	3	4	2.71	11	11	0	0	66	57	2	15	48	6.5	1.09	.233
	Las Vegas (PCL)	AAA	1	5	5.73	9	9	0	0	49	56	8	16	40	7.4	1.48	.286
	New York (NL)	MAJ	4	2	2.42	8	7	0	0	45	42	1	15	42	8.5	1.28	.258
Major League Totals			4	2	2.42	8	7	0	0	45	42	1	15	42	8.5	1.28	.258
Minor League Totals			34	31	3.10	101	89	4	1	539	517	26	145	390	6.5	1.23	.252

8 THOMAS SZAPUCKI, LHP

Born: June 12, 1996. **B-T:** R-L. **Ht.:** 6-2. **Wt.:** 205. **Drafted:** HS—Palm Beach Gardens, Fla., 2015 (5th round). **Signed by:** Cesar Aranguren.

The Mets sacrificed their first-round pick in 2015 when they signed Michael Cuddyer, but still identified a pair of top prospects in Florida preps Desmond Lindsay (second round) and Szapucki (fifth). After a brief pro debut in 2015, Szapucki raised his arm slot closer to three-quarters at instructional league, granting him better fastball control and more life on his secondary pitches. In 2016 he led all short-season pitchers with 14.9 strikeouts per nine innings, while recording a 1.38 ERA in nine starts between Rookie-level Kingsport and short-season Brooklyn. Szapucki throws the best curveball in the Mets system—it's a mid-70s pitch with plus top-to-bottom action—but his slider might be even better. The pitch receives plus grades from scouts for its low-80s velocity and sweeping action and late depth. He has a track record for spinning his breaking pitches. As a prep in 2014 he recorded the highest breaking-ball spin rate at Perfect Game National, according to TrackMan data. Szapucki throws a plus fastball that sits 93 mph and touches 96. He commands a low-90s sinker to both sides of the plate, though he needs to refine a little-used, below-average changeup that features late tumbling action. He struggles to locate his changeup for strikes in part because of a hard-to-repeat delivery, which includes a stabbing arm action, recoil in his finish and a head whack. The Mets shut Szapucki down with back stiffness in August, so he has yet to prove he can hold up under a starter's workload. If he can, he has No. 2 or 3 starter upside with two plus pitches and potentially average control. A full season at low Class A Columbia would be telling.

BA GRADE

60 Risk: Extreme

Year	Club (League)	Class	W	L	ERA	G	GS	CG	SV	IP	H	HR	BB	SO	K/9	WHIP	AVG
2015	Mets (GCL)	R	0	0	15.43	3	0	0	0	2	5	0	0	3	11.6	2.14	.455
2016	Kingsport (APP)	R	2	1	0.62	5	5	0	0	29	16	2	9	47	14.6	0.86	.157
	Brooklyn (NYP)	SS	2	2	2.35	4	4	0	0	23	10	0	11	39	15.3	0.91	.130
Minor League Totals			4	3	1.99	12	9	0	0	54	31	2	20	89	14.7	0.94	.163

9 GABRIEL YNOA, RHP

Born: May 26, 1993. **B-T:** R-R. **Ht.:** 6-2. **Wt.:** 205. **Signed:** Dominican Republic, 2009. **Signed by:** Rafael Perez/Ismael Cruz/Modesto Abreu.

BA GRADE
50 Risk: High

Ynoa has attracted attention for his sharp control and smooth delivery since his days at short-season Brooklyn. He won pitcher-of-the-year honors in the low Class A South Atlantic League in 2013 and in three subsequent seasons averaged 150 innings and 1.9 walks per nine innings while climbing to Triple-A Las Vegas in 2016. He made his big league debut in August, which included three spot starts in September. Ynoa relies on pitch movement, control and changing speeds to succeed. He pitches with an average fastball at 93 mph that features heavy sinking and tailing action. He mixes two- and four-seam fastballs at velocities ranging from 85-95 mph to keep hitters off balance. Ynoa's 83-85 mph slider has developed into an above-average neutralizer that generates both swinging strikes and ground balls with its quick, late tilt. His above-average mid-80s changeup features late drop and some fading action. Ynoa exhibits focus on the mound and knows how to read opponents' swings, yet he struck out just 4.5 per nine innings at Triple-A. Some scouts project future growth for Ynoa based on his clean mechanics. Evaluators who like Ynoa see a No. 4 starter, while those who don't project him to a swingman or relief role.

Year	Club (League)	Class	W	L	ERA	G	GS	CG	SV	IP	H	HR	BB	SO	K/9	WHIP	AVG
2014	St. Lucie (FSL)	HiA	8	2	3.95	14	14	0	0	82	95	7	13	64	7.0	1.32	.288
	Binghamton (EL)	AA	3	2	4.21	11	11	2	0	66	74	9	12	42	5.7	1.30	.281
2015	Binghamton (EL)	AA	9	9	3.90	25	24	2	0	152	157	14	31	82	4.8	1.23	.265
2016	Las Vegas (PCL)	AAA	12	5	3.97	25	25	0	0	154	170	15	40	78	4.5	1.36	.285
	New York (NL)	MAJ	1	0	6.38	10	3	0	0	18	26	0	7	17	8.3	1.80	.333
Major League Totals			1	0	6.38	10	3	0	0	18	26	0	7	17	8.3	1.80	.333
Minor League Totals			59	30	3.36	136	128	6	1	796	800	61	134	498	5.6	1.17	.262

10 TOMAS NIDO, C

Born: April 12, 1994. **B-T:** R-R. **Ht.:** 6-0. **Wt.:** 205. **Drafted:** HS—Maitland, Fla., 2012 (8th round). **Signed by:** Mike Silvestri.

BA GRADE
50 Risk: High

Born in Puerto Rico, Nido moved to the Orlando area in high school and passed on Florida State when the Mets offered him $250,000 as an eighth-round pick in 2012. He spent three years in short-season and one at low Class A before breaking out at high Class A St. Lucie in 2016, when he hit .320 to claim the Florida State League batting title. Despite hitting for a high average in 2016, Nido is better known for his above-average to plus raw power. He consistently drives the ball to his pull side with a quick swing and established career highs with seven home runs and a .140 isolated slugging percentage in 2016. Nido makes contact at high rate and doesn't walk or strike out much, but in 2016 he focused on letting the ball travel deeper into the zone and using the whole field, especially with two strikes. It paid off with a career year. Pitchers like throwing to Nido, the best defensive catcher in the system. He grades as average overall because his hands and blocking ability are sound, while his arm and game-calling ability are above-average. He needs to improve the accuracy of his throws, though he did retire 42 percent of FSL basestealers. Double-A Binghamton is the next step for Nido, whom the Mets added to the 40-man roster in November. He has the tools to be the Mets' backstop of the future.

Year	Club (League)	Class	AVG	G	AB	R	H	2B	3B	HR	RBI	BB	SO	SB	CS	OBP	SLG
2014	Brooklyn (NYP)	SS	.277	58	188	20	52	6	1	1	21	14	41	2	2	.325	.335
2015	Savannah (SAL)	LoA	.259	86	317	39	82	14	2	6	40	12	86	1	1	.284	.372
2016	St. Lucie (FSL)	HiA	.320	90	344	38	110	23	2	7	46	19	42	0	1	.357	.459
Minor League Totals			.271	305	1092	115	296	55	5	17	133	61	213	4	5	.310	.377

11 MARCOS MOLINA, RHP

BA GRADE
55 Risk: Extreme

Born: March 8, 1995. **B-T:** R-R. **Ht.:** 6-3. **Wt.:** 188. **Signed:** Dominican Republic, 2012. **Signed by:** Daurys Nin/Gerardo Cabrera.

Molina jumped on the prospect radar in 2014, his third pro season, when he ranked as the No. 1

prospect in the short-season New York-Penn League. He skipped a level when he advanced to high Class A St. Lucie in 2015, where, plagued by a strained right elbow, he pitched just 41 innings and then had Tommy John surgery in September. Molina missed the entire 2016 season but returned for the Arizona Fall League—and so did the power on his fastball and breaking ball. He pitched at 94 mph with life and reached 96 with his four-seam fastball, while his slider sat in the mid-80s and flashed downer action. Both pitches can be above-average to plus weapons for him, though feel for his above-average changeup had not yet returned. Molina relies on arm speed more than extension in his delivery, tends to lose velocity during starts and throws from a low three-quarters arm slot. Those factors lead some evaluators to project him as a future reliever. The Mets added Molina to the 40-man roster after the 2016 season to shield him from the Rule 5 draft, and he should return to St. Lucie to begin 2017 with a midseason move to Double-A Binghamton probable.

Year	Club (League)	Class	W	L	ERA	G	GS	CG	SV	IP	H	HR	BB	SO	K/9	WHIP	AVG
2014	Brooklyn (NYP)	SS	7	3	1.77	12	12	0	0	76	46	2	18	91	10.7	0.84	.170
2015	Mets (GCL)	R	0	0	0.00	1	1	0	0	3	0	0	0	3	9.0	0.00	.000
	St. Lucie (FSL)	HiA	1	5	4.57	8	7	0	0	41	49	1	11	36	7.8	1.45	.295
2016	Did not play—Injured																
Minor League Totals			17	13	3.30	46	39	1	0	229	199	6	57	213	8.4	1.12	.231

12 ANTHONY KAY, LHP

BA GRADE

55 Risk: Extreme

Born: March 21, 1995. **B-T:** L-L. **Ht.:** 6-0. **Wt.:** 190. **Drafted:** Connecticut, 2016 (1st round). **Signed by:** Michael Pesce.

The Mets selected Kay with the 31st pick in the 2016 draft and signed him for $1.1 million, about $872,000 below slot after a physical turned up an elbow injury. A Long Island native, Kay attended the same high school as Mets lefthander Steven Matz and at Connecticut set a school record with 263 career strikeouts. The Mets had previously drafted Kay in the 29th round out of Melville High in 2013. As a three-pitch lefty with the ability to work both sides of the plate, he would have been a prime candidate to move rapidly in pro ball, but he had Tommy John surgery in early October and probably will not pitch in 2017. Kay improved his fastball and changeup while in college, and his changeup ranked as one of the finest in the 2016 draft class. His change is a swing-and-miss pitch because of its late fading action and could grade as plus one day, though he drops him arm slot slightly to throw it. Kay works his fastball in the low 90s and touches 95 mph with an ability to run the ball to his arm side and cut it to his glove side. His curveball shows tight spin but not consistent depth—he used it only against lefthanded batters in college—and could be an average pitch if he develops it in pro ball. Kay throws strikes and has a ceiling of No. 3 starter if he makes a full recovery from surgery.

Year	Club (League)	Class	W	L	ERA	G	GS	CG	SV	IP	H	HR	BB	SO	K/9	WHIP	AVG
2016	Did not play—Injured																

13 PETE ALONSO, 1B

BA GRADE

50 Risk: High

Born: Dec. 7, 1994. **B-T:** R-R. **Ht.:** 6-3. **Wt.:** 225. **Drafted:** Florida, 2016 (2nd round). **Signed by:** Jon Updike.

Power is Alonso's carrying tool, and he has the best in the Mets system after signing for $909,200 as a 2016 second-round pick. He showed premium power at Florida, particularly at the 2015 and 2016 College World Series, where he smashed three home runs at cavernous TD Ameritrade Park, including the two longest bombs in the six-year history of the venue. He continued to rake at short-season Brooklyn by slugging .587 to rank second among New York-Penn League batters with at least 100 plate appearances. With wide hips and a physical 6-foot-3 frame, Alonso uses his legs well to generate double-plus raw power to all fields and he can demolish mistakes, particularly on pitches low in the zone. He studies pitchers and controls the strike zone, but tends to leak out on his front side and might hit no better than .260 at higher levels. Though he is a poor runner, Alonso takes pride in his defense at first base, where he grades as solid-average thanks to his agility and soft hands that allow him to scoop throws in the dirt. He missed most of August at Brooklyn after he broke the pinky finger on his left hand while sliding into second base, though he was back at full strength for instructional league. Evaluators who like Alonso compare him with Mike Napoli or Evan Gattis as a middle-of-the-order, righthanded power source. He will likely open at high Class A St. Lucie in 2017.

Year	Club (League)	Class	AVG	G	AB	R	H	2B	3B	HR	RBI	BB	SO	SB	CS	OBP	SLG
2016	Brooklyn (NYP)	SS	.321	30	109	20	35	12	1	5	21	11	22	0	1	.382	.587
Minor League Totals			.321	30	109	20	35	12	1	5	21	11	22	0	1	.382	.587

14 MERANDY GONZALEZ, RHP

BA GRADE

55 Risk: Extreme

Born: Oct. 9, 1995. **B-T:** R-R. **Ht.:** 6-1. **Wt.:** 195. **Signed:** Dominican Republic, 2013. **Signed by:** Daurys Nin/Gerardo Cabrera.

The Mets signed Gonzalez out of the Dominican Republic as a 17-year-old in March 2013. Though he is on the short side for a righthanded starter—about 6 feet—he is strong through his core and lower body and stays in his legs well during his delivery. This allows Gonzalez to touch 97 mph with life and pitch at 93-95 with a plus fastball. He threw a seven-inning no-hitter in the Rookie-level Gulf Coast League in 2015 and then shined at short-season Brooklyn in 2016 by ranking third in the New York-Penn League with 71 strikeouts and eighth with a 2.87 ERA. Gonzalez shows the ability to spin a breaking ball at a young age, and his above-average curveball at 78-82 mph shows consistent top-to-bottom shape. He also throws a slider with shorter break. He doesn't have great feel for his below-average changeup, and his command also grades as below-average. He throws enough strikes to compete as a starter but is more a thrower than pitcher at this stage. He throws with effort, so unless he develops his changeup and command, he could fit best as a high-leverage reliever. He will play at low Class A Columbia in 2017.

Year	Club (League)	Class	W	L	ERA	G	GS	CG	SV	IP	H	HR	BB	SO	K/9	WHIP	AVG
2014	Mets2 (DSL)	R	0	2	5.48	6	5	0	0	21	24	1	8	22	9.3	1.50	.286
	Mets1 (DSL)	R	3	1	2.34	7	7	0	0	35	26	1	7	25	6.5	0.95	.210
2015	Mets (GCL)	R	2	1	2.05	4	2	1	0	22	9	1	3	25	10.2	0.55	.120
	Kingsport (APP)	R	2	2	2.82	9	7	0	0	45	40	1	19	39	7.9	1.32	.240
2016	Brooklyn (NYP)	SS	6	3	2.87	14	14	0	0	69	65	2	27	71	9.3	1.33	.254
Minor League Totals			17	10	2.93	54	37	1	1	236	203	6	80	211	8.0	1.20	.233

15 LUIS GUILLORME, SS/2B

BA GRADE

50 Risk: High

Born: Sept. 27, 1994. **B-T:** L-R. **Ht.:** 5-9. **Wt.:** 190. **Drafted:** HS—Coral Springs, Fla., 2013 (10th round). **Signed by:** Mike Silvestri.

Guillorme grew up in Venezuela but moved to the U.S. at age 12 to further his baseball development. He signed for an above-slot $200,000 as a 10th-round pick out of high school and went on to win MVP honors in the low Class A South Atlantic League in 2015 despite hitting zero home runs. Guillorme hit his first pro homer at high Class A St. Lucie in 2016, but otherwise he showed the same high-contact, opposite-field hitting approach as always. He won't have to hit much to assume a major league role, however, because he's the best defensive infielder in the Mets system, alternately referred to as a wizard or double-plus defender at shortstop by scouts outside the organization. The word "quick" best describes his infield actions, as in quick first step, quick transfer, quick feet and quick release. His throwing and running tools also grade as above-average, though a lack of physicality and lack of power raise questions about his offensive potential. He controls the strike zone and handles the bat well enough to project to a near-average or better hitter to scouts who like him. Guillorme's defensive chops and supporting tools could make him a utility infielder or better.

Year	Club (League)	Class	AVG	G	AB	R	H	2B	3B	HR	RBI	BB	SO	SB	CS	OBP	SLG
2014	Kingsport (APP)	R	.282	57	238	38	67	10	0	0	17	17	28	6	4	.337	.324
	Savannah (SAL)	LoA	.333	3	9	2	3	0	0	0	0	1	0	0	0	.400	.333
2015	Savannah (SAL)	LoA	.318	122	446	67	142	16	0	0	55	54	70	18	8	.391	.354
2016	St. Lucie (FSL)	HiA	.263	123	441	47	116	16	2	1	46	43	63	4	2	.332	.315
Minor League Totals			.285	346	1293	176	369	46	2	1	129	132	178	34	18	.355	.326

16 WUILMER BECERRA, OF

BA GRADE

50 Risk: High

Born: Oct. 1, 1994. **B-T:** R-R. **Ht.:** 6-3. **Wt.:** 225. **Signed:** Venezuela, 2011. **Signed by:** Marco Paddy/Rafael Moncada (Blue Jays).

The Blue Jays might never live down trading Noah Syndergaard to the Mets for R.A. Dickey in December 2012, but adding insult to injury is the fact Toronto also surrendered Travis d'Arnaud and Becerra in the deal. Becerra signed for $1.3 million in 2011 but has progressed slowly, in part because he suffered a broken jaw in his 2012 pro debut. Injuries also curtailed his 2016 season at high Class A St. Lucie, when Becerra hit .312 in 65 games despite a labrum tear in his right shoulder. He had season-ending surgery in July after hitting only one home run and playing the field sporadically (13 times) because he struggled to throw. When healthy, Becerra shows across-the-board ability but perhaps not a carrying tool. He has the strength, bat speed and loft to hit for at least average power. He has hit the ball hard consistently enough in the low minors to overcome ordinary walk and strikeout rates. The 6-foot-4 Becerra runs well and shows solid-average range in right field, where his above-average arm plays up because of accuracy. Some scouts think Becerra will grow into more power, and if it manifests he could be an every-day corner bat. Still just 22 in 2017, he will spend at least part of the year at Double-A Binghamton.

Year	Club (League)	Class	AVG	G	AB	R	H	2B	3B	HR	RBI	BB	SO	SB	CS	OBP	SLG
2014	Kingsport (APP)	R	.300	58	207	37	62	10	2	7	29	14	55	7	3	.351	.469
2015	Savannah (SAL)	LoA	.290	118	449	67	130	27	3	9	63	33	96	16	8	.342	.423
2016	St. Lucie (FSL)	HiA	.312	65	247	27	77	17	0	1	34	9	52	7	1	.341	.393
Minor League Totals			.288	304	1108	157	319	64	5	18	155	80	270	35	19	.345	.403

17 ANDRES GIMENEZ, SS

BA GRADE
55 Risk: Extreme

Born: Sept. 4, 1998. **B-T:** L-R. **Ht.:** 6-0. **Wt.:** 165. **Signed:** Venezuela, 2015.
Signed by: Robert Espejo/Hector Rincones.

The Mets zeroed in on Gimenez both for his talent—he ranked as the No. 2 prospect available on the 2015 international market—and also for his makeup. The 16-year-old Venezuelan signed for $1.2 million and is all business both on and off the field. Gimenez made his pro debut in the Dominican Summer League in 2016 and led the circuit in on-base percentage (.469) while ranking second in average (.350) and doubles (20). A lefthanded hitter, he shows plus bat speed, contact ability and enough latent power to suggest at least average thump down the line. He can spray the ball to all fields and could be a prototype No. 2 hitter. An above-average runner, Gimenez should be at least a solid-average defensive shortstop with good hands and a plus arm. He broke a finger on his right hand late in the DSL season but returned in time for Dominican instructional league in November. Thanks to a high baseball IQ, Gimenez should get the most out of his offensive and defensive tools to become a threat on both sides of the ball. An assignment to a domestic short-season affiliate—possibly Rookie-level Kingsport—is next.

Year	Club (League)	Class	AVG	G	AB	R	H	2B	3B	HR	RBI	BB	SO	SB	CS	OBP	SLG
2016	Mets2 (DSL)	R	.360	31	114	24	41	10	4	1	17	21	13	7	1	.461	.544
	Mets1 (DSL)	R	.340	31	100	28	34	10	0	2	21	25	9	6	7	.478	.500
Minor League Totals			.350	62	214	52	75	20	4	3	38	46	22	13	8	.469	.523

18 MATT REYNOLDS, SS/3B

BA GRADE
45 Risk: Medium

Born: Dec. 3, 1990. **B-T:** R-R. **Ht.:** 6-1. **Wt.:** 200. **Drafted:** Arkansas, 2012 (2nd round). **Signed by:** Steve Gossett.

Reynolds' performance swung dramatically from one extreme to the other early in his pro career. The 2012 second-rounder hit just .226 at high Class A St. Lucie in 2013 but followed with a .343 campaign in 2014 that got him to Triple-A Las Vegas in the second half and placed him sixth in the overall minor league batting race. Reynolds spent most of 2015 and 2016 in the Pacific Coast League, establishing himself as a near-average hitter with gap power and solid-average speed. He hits lefthanders particularly well, though he strikes out too much for a player with only modest power. Reynolds made his big league debut in 2016, receiving four different callups to New York and starting games at shortstop, second base and third base. That versatility will be Reynolds' ticket to an expanded role. While he has ordinary range, he has sound hands, a high game IQ and the plus arm to handle any infield assignment. Scouts see him as a future utility infielder or possible second-division starter at second base.

Year	Club (League)	Class	AVG	G	AB	R	H	2B	3B	HR	RBI	BB	SO	SB	CS	OBP	SLG
2014	Binghamton (EL)	AA	.355	58	211	33	75	5	3	1	21	29	41	6	3	.430	.422
	Las Vegas (PCL)	AAA	.333	68	267	54	89	16	4	5	40	21	60	14	4	.385	.479
2015	Mets (GCL)	R	.400	3	5	1	2	0	0	0	1	1	1	0	0	.500	.400
	Las Vegas (PCL)	AAA	.267	115	445	70	119	32	5	6	65	32	92	13	4	.319	.402
2016	Las Vegas (PCL)	AAA	.264	71	269	43	71	15	2	2	24	26	64	9	2	.336	.357
	New York (NL)	MAJ	.225	47	89	11	20	8	0	3	13	4	34	0	1	.266	.416
Major League Totals			.225	47	89	11	20	8	0	3	13	4	34	0	1	.266	.416
Minor League Totals			.276	475	1791	278	495	97	20	22	213	157	364	56	16	.342	.390

19 P.J. CONLON, LHP

BA GRADE
50 Risk: High

Born: Nov. 11, 1993. **B-T:** L-L. **Ht.:** 5-11. **Wt.:** 190. **Drafted:** San Diego, 2015 (13th round). **Signed by:** Fred Mazuca.

Born in Belfast, Northern Ireland, Conlon moved with his parents to Southern California at age 2 and thus does not speak with an Irish accent. A three-year starter at San Diego, he landed with the Mets as a 13th-round pick in 2015 and then logged 17 relief innings without allowing an earned run at short-season Brooklyn in his pro debut. Conlon continued to suppress runs as a starter over two Class A stops and 142 innings in 2016, recording a 1.65 ERA that led all qualified minor league starters. With above-average control—he walked 1.5 per nine innings in 2016—he mixes his four pitches, including the best changeup in the system, for maximum effect. Conlon averages about 88 mph with his fastball and hits 90 on a good night, but keeps the ball off the barrel with natural deceptiveness and feel for changing speeds. He throws an average cutter to his glove side, which keeps righthanders honest, and commands an above-average to plus changeup to his arm side. His low-70s curveball receives below-average grades but works in small doses as a means to change eye levels. Critics point to Conlon's lack of physicality and funky arm action and project him to the bullpen. Still, he has a competitive streak and a track record that will keep him in the rotation for now. The challenges at Double-A Binghamton await in 2017.

Year	Club (League)	Class	W	L	ERA	G	GS	CG	SV	IP	H	HR	BB	SO	K/9	WHIP	AVG
2015	Brooklyn (NYP)	SS	0	1	0.00	17	0	0	0	17	8	0	2	25	13.2	0.59	.136
2016	Columbia (SAL)	LoA	8	1	1.84	12	12	0	0	78	68	4	10	61	7.0	1.00	.233
	St. Lucie (FSL)	HiA	4	1	1.41	12	11	0	1	64	47	1	14	51	7.2	0.96	.203
Minor League Totals			12	3	1.47	41	23	0	1	159	123	5	26	137	7.8	0.94	.211

20 LUIS CARPIO, SS/2B

BA GRADE

55 Risk: Extreme

Born: July 11, 1997. **B-T:** R-R. **Ht.:** 6-0. **Wt.:** 165. **Signed:** Venezuela, 2013.
Signed by: Carlos Perez/Hector Rincones.

The Mets loved Carpio's mature, blue-collar approach when they signed the 16-year-old for $300,000 out of Venezuela in 2013. He raised his prospect profile when he hit .304 at Rookie-level Kingsport in 2015, but didn't get a chance to follow up in 2016 because he tore the labrum in his right shoulder in early March and had surgery. Carpio recovered quicker than expected and returned to action in mid-August, though he appeared exclusively at DH for his 20 games and didn't play the field until instructional league. Carpio's bat is his carrying tool. He lines the ball to all fields with a short swing and executes an intelligent hitting approach with advanced pitch recognition. Already bigger than his listed height and weight, he could grow into more power as his body matures and he learns to hunt for his pitch. An average runner, Carpio has ordinary quickness and a fringe-average arm that might force him to second base down the road. Three days after having labrum surgery, he reported to the Mets' complex at Port St. Lucie, Fla., asking team trainers for extra work as he rehabbed. That excited the Mets almost as much as his ability, and it's why he can probably handle a jump to low Class A Columbia in 2017.

Year	Club (League)	Class	AVG	G	AB	R	H	2B	3B	HR	RBI	BB	SO	SB	CS	OBP	SLG
2014	Mets2 (DSL)	R	.234	60	209	35	49	9	1	1	20	33	33	12	4	.347	.301
2015	Kingsport (APP)	R	.304	45	181	31	55	10	0	0	22	17	34	9	7	.372	.359
2016	Mets (GCL)	R	.290	8	31	3	9	1	1	0	2	1	11	0	0	.353	.387
	Brooklyn (NYP)	SS	.140	12	43	4	6	2	0	0	1	8	10	0	0	.288	.186
Minor League Totals			.256	125	464	73	119	22	2	1	45	59	88	21	11	.351	.319

21 PATRICK MAZEIKA, C

BA GRADE

50 Risk: High

Born: Oct. 14, 1993. **B-T:** L-R. **Ht.:** 6-3. **Wt.:** 210. **Drafted:** Stetson, 2015 (8th round). **Signed by:** Jon Updike.

Mazeika has rough edges to his game, but his advanced hitting approach make him a sleeper if he can stay at catcher. He hit .348 in three years at Stetson and .354 in his 2015 pro debut to finish runner-up in the Rookie-level Appalachian League batting race. Mazeika in 2016 spent two stints on the low Class A Columbia disabled list with a right elbow injury, but he hit .305 in 70 games when healthy, with elite strikeout (13.3 percent) and walk rates (13 percent). He spread out his stance in 2016 in order to more consistently hit behind the ball. He can be a plus hitter so long as he maintains a direct bat path and avoids becoming too rotational in his swing. Mazeika can throw his hands at the ball and pull it for home-run power, but he operates better when he drives the ball to all fields. South Atlantic League basestealers tested Mazeika frequently, and he threw out a below-average 29 percent of them. His problems stem from making the exchange from glove to hand and then staying low on his throws to second base. He fights the urge to stand all the way up when he throws, though he has average arm strength. He does a good job receiving and blocking balls in the dirt. Mazeika played first base as well as catcher in college, and it might be his fallback option if his bat forces him to the big leagues before his glove to catches up.

Year	Club (League)	Class	AVG	G	AB	R	H	2B	3B	HR	RBI	BB	SO	SB	CS	OBP	SLG
2015	Kingsport (APP)	R	.354	62	226	44	80	27	0	5	48	24	26	1	0	.451	.540
2016	Columbia (SAL)	LoA	.305	70	239	34	73	14	0	3	35	38	39	2	0	.414	.402
Minor League Totals			.329	132	465	78	153	41	0	8	83	62	65	3	0	.432	.469

22 CHRIS FLEXEN, RHP

BA GRADE

45 Risk: High

Born: July 1, 1994. **B-T:** R-R. **Ht.:** 6-3. **Wt.:** 235. **Drafted:** HS—Newark, Calif., 2012 (14th round). **Signed by:** Jim Blueberg.

The Mets under Sandy Alderson like to speculate in the draft on athletic high school pitchers after the 10th round and buy them out of college commitments. This philosophy has yielded righthander Robert Gsellman (2011) and trade chips such as John Gant (2011), Erik Manoah (2014) and Rob Whalen

(2012). Flexen would have joined that group had his inclusion in the July 2016 trade to the Reds for Jay Bruce not been nixed amid elbow concerns. Flexen had Tommy John surgery in July 2014, returned late in 2015 and made 25 starts at high Class A St. Lucie in 2016. Scouts regard him as having No. 5 starter upside because he throws strikes with three pitches and has a durable frame. He pitches at 92 mph and bumps 94 with a tailing fastball that grades as plus with its movement. He mixes in a solid-average cutter in the high 80s and a mid-70s curveball that plays as fringe-average but has potential. He struggles to repeat his stabbing arm action and command his breaking ball and below-average changeup. Flexen could come into focus as a big league option in 2018.

Year	Club (League)	Class	W	L	ERA	G	GS	CG	SV	IP	H	HR	BB	SO	K/9	WHIP	AVG
2014	Savannah (SAL)	LoA	3	5	4.83	13	13	0	0	69	75	5	37	46	6.0	1.62	.276
2015	Mets (GCL)	R	0	0	0.00	3	2	0	0	6	2	0	1	5	7.5	0.50	.100
	Brooklyn (NYP)	SS	0	2	5.11	3	2	0	0	12	15	0	8	13	9.5	1.86	.300
	Savannah (SAL)	LoA	4	0	1.87	6	5	0	0	34	28	0	7	33	8.8	1.04	.226
2016	St. Lucie (FSL)	HiA	10	9	3.56	25	25	1	0	134	125	6	51	95	6.4	1.31	.249
Minor League Totals			26	20	3.54	68	64	3	0	356	336	19	130	280	7.1	1.31	.248

23 RICARDO CESPEDES, OF

BA GRADE
50 Risk: Extreme

Born: Aug. 24, 1997. **B-T:** L-L. **Ht.:** 6-1. **Wt.:** 200. **Signed:** Dominican Republic, 2013. **Signed by:** Alexis de la Cruz/Gerardo Cabrera.

The Mets signed Cespedes for $725,000 on the day he turned 16, and because his birthday fell eight days shy of the Sept. 1 cutoff, he is one of the youngest players from the 2013 international signing class. After three pro seasons he still is just 19 and will play most of 2017 at that age. While Cespedes' tools and abilities are obvious, so too are his immaturity and lack of focus. He has an excellent first step in center field and could develop into a plus defender with an above-average arm. While not a burner, he has at least average speed and is a smart baserunner. These attributes could make Cespedes a table-setter if he can improve his hitting approach. He can turn around mid-90s heat with a loose, easy swing, and some scouts see him as a potential plus hitter. He hangs in well versus lefthanders, hits to all fields and can bunt for hits. Like many young hitters, he tends to drift out front on offspeed pitches and seldom walks. Cespedes doesn't show much power, so unless he takes a step forward in that department, he might fit best as a fourth outfielder. He could be ready for a full-season assignment at low Class A Columbia in 2017.

Year	Club (League)	Class	AVG	G	AB	R	H	2B	3B	HR	RBI	BB	SO	SB	CS	OBP	SLG
2014	Mets2 (DSL)	R	.485	8	33	8	16	3	1	0	7	3	2	3	1	.528	.636
	Mets1 (DSL)	R	.227	46	185	21	42	6	2	0	10	11	34	4	4	.271	.281
2015	Mets (GCL)	R	.224	44	165	17	37	3	2	0	15	13	29	7	3	.282	.267
2016	Kingsport (APP)	R	.322	56	227	30	73	4	3	1	16	9	36	7	7	.356	.379
Minor League Totals			.275	154	610	76	168	16	8	1	48	36	101	21	15	.319	.333

24 T.J. RIVERA, 2B/3B

BA GRADE
40 Risk: Medium

Born: Oct. 27, 1988. **B-T:** R-R. **Ht.:** 6-1. **Wt.:** 205. **Signed:** Troy, 2011 (NDFA). **Signed by:** Tommy Jackson.

Sometimes an underdog just needs a chance. Rivera, who played high school ball in the Bronx, N.Y., traveled to Alabama to play collegiately, first at Wallace CC and then for two years at Troy. He helped the Trojans make an NCAA regionals appearance as a senior in 2011, but no team drafted him. The Mets signed Rivera as a passed-over player shortly after the draft, and he proceeded to hit .318, while playing three positions regularly, through his first five seasons. Still, the Mets left Rivera, then 27, unprotected in the 2015 Rule 5 draft. Again, no team selected him. Rivera finally knocked loudly enough at Triple-A Las Vegas in 2016, when he hit .353 to win the Pacific Coast League batting title and earn a mid-August callup. He hit .333 in 105 at-bats for the Mets and even started the Wild Card Game against Madison Bumgarner. With limited power, speed and patience, Rivera would not be an ideal fit as a regular, but he makes a ton of contact and has a long track record for hitting. That combined with his capable defensive play at second and third base make him an attractive part-time option.

Year	Club (League)	Class	AVG	G	AB	R	H	2B	3B	HR	RBI	BB	SO	SB	CS	OBP	SLG
2014	St. Lucie (FSL)	HiA	.341	61	252	42	86	16	0	4	47	14	37	2	1	.383	.452
	Binghamton (EL)	AA	.358	54	201	28	72	13	0	1	28	11	27	1	0	.394	.438
2015	Las Vegas (PCL)	AAA	.306	54	183	26	56	17	1	2	21	7	25	0	0	.345	.443
	Binghamton (EL)	AA	.341	56	220	37	75	10	0	5	27	12	22	1	1	.380	.455
2016	Las Vegas (PCL)	AAA	.353	105	405	67	143	31	1	11	85	23	54	3	3	.393	.516
	New York (NL)	MAJ	.333	33	105	10	35	4	1	3	16	3	17	0	0	.345	.476
Major League Totals			.333	33	105	10	35	4	1	3	16	3	17	0	0	.345	.476
Minor League Totals			.324	625	2415	372	783	147	7	35	344	151	332	27	14	.371	.434

25 PHILLIP EVANS, SS/2B

BA GRADE
45 Risk: High

Born: Sept. 10, 1992. **B-T:** R-R. **Ht.:** 5-9. **Wt.:** 220. **Drafted:** HS—Carlsbad, Calif., 2011 (15th round). **Signed by:** Fred Mazuca.

Evans slipped to the 15th round of the 2011 draft after a poor senior year at La Costa Canyon High, but the Mets ponied up supplemental first-round money ($650,000) to sign him away from San Diego State. Evans then slipped from prospect relevancy by hitting .228/.294/.298 in more than 1,100 plate appearances in Class A ball from 2013 to 2015. Thus, he surprised even the Mets in 2016 by hitting .335 at Double-A Binghamton to claim the Eastern League batting title. Evans uses a short, compact swing and employs a middle-field approach, so he can be an average hitter. He works all fields with plus bat control and the ability to gap the ball for doubles. Though Evans seldom walks, he began to drive the ball consistently in the second half of 2016 and has the near-average power to hit about 10 home runs. He started more games at shortstop than any other position at Binghamton but is better at second or third base with average range and an above-average arm. Most evaluators see Evans as big league utility player with enough bat and flexibility to be interesting. He will begin at Triple-A Las Vegas in 2017.

Year	Club (League)	Class	AVG	G	AB	R	H	2B	3B	HR	RBI	BB	SO	SB	CS	OBP	SLG
2014	Mets (GCL)	R	.667	1	3	0	2	0	0	0	0	0	1	0	0	.667	.667
	St. Lucie (FSL)	HiA	.247	111	389	34	96	16	0	4	39	39	59	0	1	.314	.319
2015	St. Lucie (FSL)	HiA	.234	77	252	19	59	14	3	0	32	24	44	2	2	.300	.313
2016	St. Lucie (FSL)	HiA	.143	9	28	3	4	0	0	0	2	5	3	0	0	.273	.143
	Binghamton (EL)	AA	.335	96	361	50	121	30	0	8	39	19	60	1	1	.374	.485
Minor League Totals			.255	482	1711	180	437	85	5	19	170	151	280	9	7	.318	.344

26 COREY TAYLOR, RHP

BA GRADE
45 Risk: High

Born: Jan. 8, 1993. **B-T:** R-R. **Ht.:** 5-11. **Wt.:** 245. **Drafted:** Texas Tech, 2015 (7th round). **Signed by:** Max Semler.

Taylor recorded a 0.31 ERA as a reliever at Texas Tech in 2015, the same year the Mets made him a seventh-round pick and signed the senior for $20,000. He proved to be more than a bargain sign in 2016, when he jumped to high Class A St. Lucie and ranked second in the Florida State League with 20 saves, then earned a spot in the Arizona Fall League. Taylor opened eyes in the AFL by averaging 97 mph with his heavy, sinking fastball that functions as an extreme groundball pitch. His 86 mph slider features occasional above-average vertical break and generates swings and misses because batters are keyed for his fastball. Taylor lacks a usable changeup but has average control overall and keeps the ball in the park. He relies on arm speed rather than an athletic delivery and lacks fine command. A thickset, 5-foot-11 righthander, Taylor has a future in a major league bullpen based on the strength of his two primary pitches. That the Mets assigned him to the AFL after just two years in pro ball underscores his proximity to New York.

Year	Club (League)	Class	W	L	ERA	G	GS	CG	SV	IP	H	HR	BB	SO	K/9	WHIP	AVG
2015	Brooklyn (NYP)	SS	1	1	1.50	18	0	0	0	18	14	1	4	16	8.0	1.00	.212
2016	St. Lucie (FSL)	HiA	4	5	1.87	45	0	0	20	53	53	1	13	45	7.6	1.25	.252
Minor League Totals			5	6	1.77	63	0	0	20	71	67	2	17	61	7.7	1.18	.243

27 ALI SANCHEZ, C

BA GRADE
50 Risk: Extreme

Born: Jan. 20, 1997. **B-T:** R-R. **Ht.:** 6-1. **Wt.:** 200. **Signed:** Venezuela, 2013. **Signed by:** Robert Espejo/Hector Rincones.

Catchers tend to develop later than other position players, which is good news for Sanchez, who signed for $690,000 as a 16-year-old out of Venezuela in 2013. He had shown strong contact skills and an all-fields hitting approach early in his career but regressed badly at the plate at short-season Brooklyn in 2016. Sanchez recorded the second-lowest OPS (.535) among regular New York-Penn League catchers as he struggled to pull the ball in the air. The Mets believe he can develop into a fringe-average hitter with below-average power, and his raw defensive ability will buy him time to develop his bat. While Sanchez is not the most vocal catcher and plays with a quiet intensity, he has plus arm strength and the quick transfer and pinpoint accuracy to make the most of it. He threw out 48 percent of basestealers in 2016. He blocks and frames the ball well, though he can improve on both counts on pitches thrown to his glove side. Sanchez can develop into a big league catcher, but it's going to take time.

Year	Club (League)	Class	AVG	G	AB	R	H	2B	3B	HR	RBI	BB	SO	SB	CS	OBP	SLG
2014	Mets1 (DSL)	R	.303	50	175	21	53	7	0	3	24	27	31	6	6	.406	.394
2015	Mets (GCL)	R	.278	46	162	20	45	6	0	0	17	12	26	2	0	.339	.315
	Kingsport (APP)	R	.182	3	11	2	2	0	0	0	3	0	2	0	0	.182	.182
2016	Brooklyn (NYP)	SS	.216	46	171	15	37	10	0	0	11	10	26	2	0	.260	.275
Minor League Totals			.264	145	519	58	137	23	0	3	55	49	85	10	6	.335	.326

28 HAROL GONZALEZ, RHP

BA GRADE

50 Risk: Extreme

Born: March 2, 1995. **B-T:** R-R. **Ht.:** 6-0. **Wt.:** 170. **Signed:** Dominican Republic, 2014. **Signed by:** Daurys Nin.

The Mets initially scouted Gonzalez as a shortstop, but when international director Chris Becerra returned to see him play again, the Dominican teen was showcasing for teams as a pitcher. Becerra invited the 19-year-old Gonzalez to throw a bullpen session, after which the Mets signed him for just $7,500. Gonzalez lacks overpowering stuff but knows how to compete by spotting his 88-89 mph fastball, repeating his delivery and locating his two secondary pitches. He dominated New York-Penn League competition in 2016, ranking first in the circuit with a 2.01 ERA and 88 strikeouts at short-season Brooklyn. Gonzalez moves his fastball around the zone and can top out at 93 mph early in starts, but he generally pitches with a below-average fastball. He keeps hitters at bay with an above-average changeup he sells with plus arm speed. His slider plays up to average but lacks consistent power or shape, but it works so long as he stays ahead in the count. The margin for error is small for starters who lack a big fastball, but Gonzalez has a chance to develop a plus changeup with plus command, which could make him a back-end starter. He is ready for low Class A Columbia in 2017.

Year	Club (League)	Class	W	L	ERA	G	GS	CG	SV	IP	H	HR	BB	SO	K/9	WHIP	AVG
2014	Mets2 (DSL)	R	1	3	3.41	7	7	0	0	29	27	1	8	26	8.1	1.21	.239
	Mets1 (DSL)	R	1	0	3.00	8	0	0	2	21	24	0	3	27	11.6	1.29	.289
2015	Kingsport (APP)	R	2	4	4.96	13	9	1	1	65	68	12	9	56	7.7	1.18	.264
2016	Brooklyn (NYP)	SS	7	3	2.01	14	13	0	0	85	69	2	17	88	9.3	1.01	.223
Minor League Totals			11	10	3.28	42	29	1	3	200	188	15	37	197	8.9	1.12	.246

29 GREGORY GUERRERO, SS

BA GRADE

50 Risk: Extreme

Born: Jan. 20, 1999. **B-T:** R-R. **Ht.:** 6-1. **Wt.:** 180. **Signed:** Dominican Republic, 2015. **Signed by:** Daurys Nin/Gerardo Cabrera.

Guerrero's uncle Vladimir Sr. made nine big league all-star teams, while his uncle Wilton spent parts of eight years in the majors and also served as his trainer. His older brother Jose pitches in the Mets system, while his cousin Vladimir Jr. ranks as the Blue Jays' No. 1 prospect. As such, it's fair to say baseball flows in the blood of Gregory Guerrero, who signed for $1.5 million in 2015. While he hit an empty .247 in his 2016 pro debut in the Dominican Summer League, Guerrero uses a loose, athletic swing that Mets officials compare with Amed Rosario. He tends to swing uphill and needs to do a better job slowing the game down to reach his ceiling as an above-average hitter with average power. Projected to move to third base eventually, Guerrero held his own at shortstop in 2016 by showing sound footwork and a plus arm. He doesn't run well and probably will outgrow the position, which ups the ante on his power production. Guerrero should be ready to tackle an assignment in a domestic short-season league in 2017, quite possibly in the Rookie-level Gulf Coast League.

Year	Club (League)	Class	AVG	G	AB	R	H	2B	3B	HR	RBI	BB	SO	SB	CS	OBP	SLG
2016	Mets1 (DSL)	R	.247	64	247	32	61	10	0	0	20	28	51	10	2	.324	.287
Minor League Totals			.247	64	247	32	61	10	0	0	20	28	51	10	2	.324	.287

30 COLBY WOODMANSEE, SS

BA GRADE

50 Risk: Extreme

Born: Aug. 27, 1994. **B-T:** R-R. **Ht.:** 6-3. **Wt.:** 190. **Drafted:** Arizona State, 2016 (5th round). **Signed by:** Kevin Roberson.

Woodmansee started every game at shortstop for Arizona State in 2015 and 2016, and he led the Sun Devils with eight home runs and 44 RBIs as a junior in the latter season. The Mets made him a fifth-round pick in 2016, and he played well at short-season Brooklyn initially before tiring late. Woodmansee has a short, direct bat path but fell out of his mechanics as his season stretched into September. He has above-average raw power but needs to get out of his pull-heavy mentality from college and focus on the middle of the field. A 6-foot-3, physical shortstop, Woodmansee has an above-average arm and a good first step but just ordinary range and below-average speed. That should be enough to keep him at shortstop in the minors, though he's athletic enough to handle third base or the outfield if necessary. Woodmansee will be ready for a full-season assignment in 2017, though his ceiling has not yet come into focus.

Year	Club (League)	Class	AVG	G	AB	R	H	2B	3B	HR	RBI	BB	SO	SB	CS	OBP	SLG
2016	Brooklyn (NYP)	SS	.257	64	249	30	64	11	0	2	29	19	75	4	3	.305	.325
Minor League Totals			.257	64	249	30	64	11	0	2	29	19	75	4	3	.305	.325

New York Yankees

BY JOSH NORRIS

When the Yankees acquired Andrew Miller and Aroldis Chapman, they thought the duo would be used to get key outs in the middle of a run to the World Series. They were right—except that they weren't getting outs for the Yankees.

Instead, Miller was shipped to the Indians and Chapman to the Cubs as the Yankees went through their first major sell-off since the early 1990s. With those two trades, plus three more, the Yankees acquired 14 prospects, including three midseason Top 100 Prospects: shortstop Gleyber Torres (Cubs), outfielder Clint Frazier and lefthander Justus Sheffield (Indians).

Before they could get younger, however, the Yankees had to shed some of their past. They released Alex Rodriguez, while first baseman Mark Teixeira announced his retirement. The slew of changes helped create lineup space for the team's host of talented youngsters and provided a preview for 2017 and beyond.

No one took advantage of that opportunity like catcher Gary Sanchez, who positioned himself to become the face of the franchise. He scalded the ball over the final two months and hit .299/.376/.657 with 20 home runs in just 53 games.

He hit a record 11 in his first 23 games and thrust himself into the middle of the rookie-of-the-year conversation. Prospects Aaron Judge and Tyler Austin contributed moments of their own and could join Sanchez as focal points of the team's offense in 2017.

To truly move back into contention, though, the Yankees will need major pitching upgrades. Masahiro Tanaka did his job at the front of the rotation, going 14-4, 3.07 and finishing seventh in Cy Young voting, but righthanders Michael Pineda and Luis Severino took steps backward, righthander Nathan Eovaldi turned in an uneven performance before having Tommy John surgery and being released in the offseason, and Ivan Nova was traded to the Pirates.

That leaves Tanaka as the only rotation certainty entering 2017. Pineda and Severino will likely be given more chances. Righthanders Luis Cessa and Chad Green, both acquired from the Tigers for lefty reliever Justin Wilson, made a combined 17 starts and should get cracks at the back-end spots out of spring training.

The Yankees could choose other avenues to address their pitching. Armed with one of the game's top farm systems, they could try to swing a trade for an ace. They have the ammunition to pull

Gary Sanchez established himself as the new face of the Yankees by hitting 20 home runs

TOP PROSPECTS OF THE DECADE

Year	Player, Pos.	2016 Org
2007	Phil Hughes, rhp	Twins
2008	Joba Chamberlain, rhp	Indians
2009	Austin Jackson, of	White Sox
2010	Jesus Montero, c	Blue Jays
2011	Jesus Montero, c	Blue Jays
2012	Jesus Montero, c	Blue Jays
2013	Mason Williams, of	Yankees
2014	Gary Sanchez, c	Yankees
2015	Luis Severino, rhp	Yankees
2016	Jorge Mateo, ss	Yankees

off such a deal, although they balked at trading for White Sox ace Chris Sale, who went to the division rival Red Sox instead.

They also have young arms developing at the upper levels of the system. Four of their Top 10 Prospects—Sheffield and righthanders James Kaprielian, Chance Adams and Domingo Acevedo—should pitch in Double-A or higher in 2017. Lefthander Jordan Montgomery, who went 14-5, 2.13 while helping lead Scranton/Wilkes-Barre to the Triple-A championship, also could help in New York in 2017.

The Yankees missed the playoffs for the third time in four years, but finally their youth movement is under way.

This offseason will determine how quickly they return to big league relevance.

ORGANIZATION OVERVIEW

General Manager: Brian Cashman. **Farm Director:** Gary Denbo. **Scouting Director:** Damon Oppenheimer.

Class	Team	League	W	L	PCT	Finish	Manager
Majors	New York Yankees	American	84	78	.519	t-8th (15)	Joe Girardi
Triple-A	Scranton/W-B RailRiders	International	91	52	.636	1st (14)	Al Pedrique
Double-A	Trenton Thunder	Eastern	87	55	.613	2nd (12)	Bobby Mitchell
High Class A	Tampa Yankees	Florida State	77	58	.570	2nd (12)	Patrick Osborn
Low Class A	Charleston RiverDogs	South Atlantic	76	63	.547	t-2nd (14)	Luis Dorante
Short-season	Staten Island Yankees	New York-Penn	44	31	.587	4th (14)	Dave Bialas
Rookie	Pulaski Yankees	Appalachian	29	37	.439	8th (10)	Tony Franklin
Rookie	GCL Yankees East	Gulf Coast	19	36	.345	17th (17)	Raul Dominguez
Rookie	GCL Yankees West	Gulf Coast	24	31	.436	t-12th (17)	Julio Mosquera
Overall 2016 Minor League Record			447	363	.552	3rd (30)	

THIS YEAR'S TOP 30

No.	Player, Pos.	Grade/Risk
1.	Gleyber Torres, ss	60/Medium
2.	Clint Frazier, of	60/High
3.	Blake Rutherford, of	60/High
4.	Jorge Mateo, ss	55/High
5.	James Kaprielian, rhp	60/Extreme
6.	Aaron Judge, of	55/High
7.	Justus Sheffield, lhp	55/High
8.	Chance Adams, rhp	55/High
9.	Albert Abreu, rhp	55/High
10.	Dustin Fowler, of	50/Medium
11.	Domingo Acevedo, rhp	55/Extreme
12.	Miguel Andujar, 3b	50/High
13.	Jordan Montgomery, lhp	50/High
14.	Estevan Florial, of	55/Extreme
15.	Dillon Tate, rhp	50/High
16.	Tyler Austin, of/1b	45/Medium
17.	Tyler Wade, ss/of	45/Medium
18.	Nolan Martinez, rhp	50/High
19.	Nick Solak, 2b	50/High
20.	Chad Green, rhp	50/High
21.	Dermis Garcia, 3b	55/Extreme
22.	Abiatal Avelino, ss/2b	50/High
23.	Yefrey Ramirez, rhp	50/High
24.	Zack Littell, rhp	45/High
25.	Giovanny Gallegos, rhp	45/High
26.	Jorge Guzman, rhp	45/High
27.	Ronald Herrera, rhp	45/High
28.	Jonathan Holder, rhp	45/High
29.	Wilkerman Garcia, ss	50/Extreme
30.	Thairo Estrada, 2b	45/High

LAST YEAR'S TOP 30

No.	Player, Pos.	Status
1.	Jorge Mateo, ss	No. 4
2.	Gary Sanchez, c	Majors
3.	Aaron Judge, of	No. 6
4.	James Kaprielian, rhp	No. 5
5.	Domingo Acevedo, rhp	No. 11
6.	Rookie Davis, rhp	(Reds)
7.	Tyler Wade, ss	No. 17
8.	Rob Refsnyder, 2b	Majors
9.	Wilkerman Garcia, ss	No. 29
10.	Dustin Fowler, of	No. 10
11.	Bryan Mitchell, rhp	Majors
12.	Miguel Andujar, 3b	No. 12
13.	Eric Jagielo, 3b	(Reds)
14.	Jacob Lindgren, lhp	(Braves)
15.	Jhalan Jackson, of	Dropped out
16.	Ian Clarkin, lhp	Dropped out
17.	Luis Torrens, c	(Padres)
18.	Slade Heathcott, of	(White Sox)
19.	Mason Williams, of	Dropped out
20.	Vicente Campos, rhp	(Angels)
21.	Ben Gamel, of	(Mariners)
22.	Brady Lail, rhp	Dropped out
23.	Jeff Degano, lhp	Dropped out
24.	Drew Finley, rhp	Dropped out
25.	Hoy Jun Park, ss	Dropped out
26.	Carlos Vidal, of	Dropped out
27.	Kyle Holder, ss	Dropped out
28.	Austin DeCarr, rhp	Dropped out
29.	James Pazos, lhp	(Mariners)
30.	Thairo Estrada, ss	No. 30

BEST TOOLS

Best Hitter for Average	Gleyber Torres
Best Power Hitter	Aaron Judge
Best Strike-Zone Discipline	Tyler Austin
Fastest Baserunner	Jorge Mateo
Best Athlete	Jorge Mateo
Best Fastball	Domingo Acevedo
Best Curveball	James Kaprielian
Best Slider	Justus Sheffield
Best Changeup	Domingo Acevedo
Best Control	Jordan Montgomery
Best Defensive Catcher	Luis Torrens
Best Defensive Infielder	Gleyber Torres
Best Infield Arm	Gleyber Torres
Best Defensive Outfielder	Dustin Fowler
Best Outfield Arm	Aaron Judge

PROJECTED 2020 LINEUP

Catcher	Gary Sanchez
First Base	Greg Bird
Second Base	Jorge Mateo
Third Base	Didi Gregorius
Shortstop	Gleyber Torres
Left Field	Clint Frazier
Center Field	Blake Rutherford
Right Field	Aaron Judge
Designated Hitter	Jacoby Ellsbury
No. 1 Starter	Masahiro Tanaka
No. 2 Starter	James Kaprielian
No. 3 Starter	Justus Sheffield
No. 4 Starter	Chance Adams
No. 5 Starter	Michael Pineda
Closer	Dellin Betances

MINOR LEAGUE DEPTH CHART

NEW YORK YANKEES

TOP 2017 ROOKIE: Aaron Judge, of. He'll get the chance to win the starting right-field job out of spring training.

BREAKOUT PROSPECT: Estevan Florial, of. After impressing in his first season he'll bring his big-time tool package to full-season ball.

SLEEPER: Juan De Paula, rhp: The Mariners were reticent to let the big-armed righthander go in the Ben Gamel trade.

SOURCE OF TOP 30 TALENT

Homegrown	20	Acquired	10
College	6	Trades	9
Junior college	0	Rule 5 draft	1
High school	5	Independent leagues	0
Nondrafted free agents	0	Free agents/waivers	0
International	9		

LF
Clint Frazier (2)
Blake Rutherford (4)
Erick Mendez
Mason Williams

CF
Dustin Fowler (10)
Estevan Florial (14)
Jake Cave
Ricardo Ferreira
Jeff Hendrix

RF
Aaron Judge (6)
Isiah Gilliam
Jhalan Jackson
Trey Amburgey

3B
Miguel Andujar (12)
Dermis Garcia (21)
Nelson Gomez

SS
Gleyber Torres (1)
Tyler Wade (17)
Abiatal Avelino (22)
Wilkerman Garcia (29)
Kyle Holder
Hoy Jun Park

2B
Jorge Mateo (4)
Nick Solak (19)
Thairo Estrada (30)
Oswaldo Cabrera

1B
Tyler Austin (16)
Chris Gittens

C
Kyle Higashioka
Donny Sands

LHP

LHSP	LHRP
Justus Sheffield (7)	Nestor Cortes
Jordan Montgomery (13)	Caleb Frare
Daniel Camarena	James Reeves
Dietrich Enns	
Ian Clarkin	

RHP

RHSP	RHRP
James Kaprielian (5)	Giovanny Gallegos (25)
Chance Adams (8)	Jorge Guzman (26)
Albert Abreu (9)	Jonathan Holder (28)
Domingo Acevedo (11)	Ben Heller
Dillon Tate (15)	J.P. Feyereisen
Nolan Martinez (18)	Johnny Barbato
Chad Green (20)	
Yefrey Ramirez (23)	
Zack Littell (24)	
Ronald Herrera (27)	
Domingo German	
Brody Koerner	
Josh Rogers	
Stephen Tarpley	
Christian Morris	

DRAFT ANALYSIS

2016

BEST PURE HITTER: OF Blake Rutherford (1) has a loose swing and covers the plate well; he has a knack for hitting line drives from gap-to-gap. Nick Solak (2) was a consistent college performer for three years in the Atlantic Coast Conference, and the Yankees feel that his bat will carry him.

BEST POWER: Rutherford's raw power grades as at least plus, and some in the organization believe it could be better as he gets stronger and fills out his frame.

FASTEST RUNNER: OF Edel Luaces (25) has elite speed, with the ability to reach first base in less than four seconds from the right side. Luaces has run the 60-yard dash in less than 6.30 seconds, and at one workout this spring he ran it in 6.15 seconds. OF Jordan Scott (14) and OF Evan Alexander (19) are also impact runners.

BEST DEFENSIVE PLAYER: Rutherford's out-of-the-box run times don't line up with what's usually seen in premium center fielders, but the Yankees like his instincts and routes.

BEST ATHLETE: Scott is a plus runner and a graceful athlete who could have gone on to play college football. OF Dominic Thompson-Williams (5) was also recruited as a football player.

BEST FASTBALL: RHP Taylor Widener (12) is a power reliever who can bump 97 mph, and his fastball jumps on hitters from his long-limbed frame. RHP Nick Nelson (4) has reached 96 mph and projects well after being a two-way player in junior college.

BEST SECONDARY PITCH: RHP Nolan Martinez (3) has an out pitch in his curveball, a hard vertical breaker; it projects as a plus pitch long term.

BEST PRO DEBUT: Rutherford batted .351/.415/.570 across two of the lowest level minor leagues. Widener's stock erupted in his debut; he struck out nearly 14 batters per nine innings and allowed only two runs over 38 innings.

MOST INTRIGUING BACKGROUND: Luaces is Cuban-born, though he came to U.S. as an adolescent. His mother was an accomplished hurdler in Cuba. Luaces graduated high school in Hialeah, Fla., in 2013, then played at Globe Tech (N.Y.) as a freshman in 2014 before spending some time in the Dominican Republic, which caused confusion among scouts as to whether he'd be an international free agent. He didn't play in games this spring, but worked out for teams in South Florida. Yankees area scout Carlos Marti had scouted Luaces dating back to his high school days.

CLOSEST TO THE MAJORS: Widener could move through the system quickly, having already excelled in a full-season league as a power reliever. Solak also has a chance to develop quickly. The Yankees say his bat will carry him, and his makeup will allow him to improve his defense.

BEST LATE-ROUND PICK: Power relievers like Widener's typically come off the draft board much sooner than the 12th round. Luaces' combination of power, speed and athleticism make him a steal.

THE ONE WHO GOT AWAY: RHP Zach Linginfelter (16) has physicality and has shown a powerful fastball. His spring got off to a slow start due to mono, and his velocity was down as a result. Linginfelter went to Tennessee.

2015

RHP James Kaprielian (1) showed first-round stuff when he pitched but missed all but three starts before returning in the Arizona Fall League. RHP Chance Adams (5) streaked to Double-A with one of the best seasons in the minors.

GRADE: C

2014

Former Mississippi State relievers LHP Jacob Lindgren (2) and RHP Jonathan Holder (6) streaked to the majors, with Lindgren lost to the Braves after being non-tendered. LHP Jordan Montgomery (4) and RHP Matt Wotherspoon (34) have reached Triple-A.

GRADE: C

2013

OF Aaron Judge (1) has been the best of three first-round picks. A deep class also produced OF Dustin Fowler (18), SS Tyler Wade (4) and RHP Nick Rumbelow (7), plus Rule 5 picks LHPs Tyler Webb (10) and Caleb Smith (14).

GRADE: B

TOP DRAFT PICKS OF THE DECADE

Year	Player, Pos.	2016 Org
2007	Andrew Brackman, rhp	Did not play
2008	*Gerrit Cole, rhp	Pirates
2009	Slade Heathcott, of	White Sox
2010	Cito Culver, ss	Yankees
2011	Dante Bichette Jr. (1st round supp.)	Yankees
2012	Ty Hensley, rhp	Yankees
2013	Eric Jagielo, 3b	Reds
2014	Jacob Lindgren, lhp (2nd round)	Yankees
2015	James Kaprielian, rhp	Yankees
2016	Blake Rutherford, of	Yankees

* Did not sign

LARGEST BONUSES IN CLUB HISTORY

Hideki Irabu, 1997	$8,500,000
Jose Contreras, 2002	$6,000,000
Andrew Brackman, 2007	$3,350,000
Blake Rutherford, 2016	$3,282,000
Gary Sanchez, 2009	$3,000,000

1 GLEYBER TORRES, SS

Born: Dec. 13, 1996. **B-T:** R-R. **Ht.:** 6-1. **Wt.:** 175.
Signed: Venezuela, 2013.
Signed by: Louie Eljaua/Hector Ortega (Cubs).

BA GRADE

60 Risk: Medium

SCOUTING GRADES

Batting: 60.
Power: 55.
Speed: 50.
Defense: 60.
Arm: 60.

Based on 20-80 scouting scale and future projection rather than present grades.

CLIFF WELCH

As an amateur, Torres trained in Venezuela with Ciro Barrios, who also worked with Athletics shortstop prospect Franklin Barreto. The Cubs signed Torres on July 2, 2013, for a bonus of $1.7 million as part of the same international haul that brought outfielder Eloy Jimenez to the Chicago organization. Torres also worked with Cubs minor league infield coordinator Jose Flores to help him mold the skills that will help him stay at shortstop for the long term. Yankees general manager Brian Cashman reportedly was given a choice between Torres and Jimenez when negotiating the Aroldis Chapman deal with the Cubs, and he chose the shortstop. Torres joined high Class A Tampa after the trade and slotted in at shortstop despite the presence of Jorge Mateo, another of the system's cadre of shortstops and the organization's No. 1 prospect entering the season. Pushing Mateo to the other side of the bag, Torres continued to hit after the trade. He batted .270/.354/.421 with 11 home runs, 21 stolen bases and 58 walks at two high Class A stops and impressed evaluators in the Carolina (No. 4 prospect) and Florida State (No. 2) leagues.

Even with a host of talented middle-infield prospects in the system, Torres shoots to the top of the ranking. He's an excellent bet to stay at shortstop because of his soft, quick hands and smooth actions around the bag. He's also got range to both sides, and an accurate arm with enough strength to handle third base if he switches positions. He also played a little second base in the Arizona Fall League (because there are other players who need time at shortstop) and showed the same smooth actions and instincts at the keystone. Moreover, he looked comfortable turning the double play from that position. Evaluators in the FSL compared his defensive chops with the Reds' Zack Cozart. What makes Torres special, however, is his offensive potential. At just 19 years old he already has excellent pitch recognition skills and has shown the ability to sort through breaking pitches in order to get to the fastball he desires. Early in the season, Torres tried too hard to hit for power and got pull happy, but he showed the ability to adjust and got back to an all-fields approach. Evaluators believe

Torres has the ability to hit for plus average and plus power, and this season showed pop to both corners. It's evident in both games and batting practice, but Torres has an uncanny ability to put barrel of the bat on the baseball. To prove it, he opened his AFL campaign with a monster home run to the opposite field at Scottsdale Stadium. Though he has just average speed, he has enough baseball instincts, aggressiveness and intellect to make it play on the bases.

After being named MVP of the Fall League, Torres should move up to Double-A Trenton in 2017. He'll continue to be paired with Mateo in what should be a dynamic Trenton lineup. He'll play all of the 2017 season at age 20, and with a good year could position himself to make his big league debut before he turns 22.

Year	Club (League)	Class	AVG	G	AB	R	H	2B	3B	HR	RBI	BB	SO	SB	CS	OBP	SLG
2014	Cubs (AZL)	R	.279	43	154	33	43	6	3	1	29	25	33	8	7	.372	.377
	Boise (NWL)	SS	.393	7	28	4	11	2	3	1	4	4	7	2	0	.469	.786
2015	South Bend (MWL)	LoA	.290	118	459	52	133	24	5	3	61	43	106	22	12	.350	.383
	Myrtle Beach (CAR)	HiA	.174	7	23	1	4	0	0	0	2	1	7	0	1	.208	.174
2016	Myrtle Beach (CAR)	HiA	.275	94	356	62	98	23	3	9	47	42	87	19	10	.359	.433
	Tampa (FSL)	HiA	.254	31	122	19	31	6	2	2	19	16	23	2	3	.341	.385
Minor League Totals			.280	300	1142	171	320	61	16	16	162	131	263	53	33	.355	.404

2 CLINT FRAZIER, OF

DAVID MONSEUR

Born: Sept. 6, 1994. **B-T:** R-R. **Ht.:** 6-1. **Wt.:** 201. **Drafted:** HS—Loganville, Ga., 2013 (1st round). **Signed by:** Brad Tyler (Indians).

The Indians used the fifth overall selection in the 2013 draft to take Frazier, the BA High School Player of the Year, and they signed him for $3.5 million. Cleveland dealt Frazier to the Yankees in 2016 along with lefthander Justus Sheffield and relievers J.P. Feyereisen and Ben Heller in the deal that sent closer Andrew Miller to the Indians. Frazier's calling card is his elite bat speed, which is generated by a taut, muscular frame and huge forearms. That bat speed produces well above-average raw power. He has worked to quiet his pre-swing movement to help cut down on his growing strikeout totals. He's got above-average speed, which has served him well on the bases and in the field. He has worked at all three outfield positions in his career, but his above-average throwing arm would serve him well in a corner spot. His range could be helpful in left field, which evaluators have noted is more challenging than right field at Yankee Stadium. Frazier struggled at both Triple-A stops in 2016 and will return there in 2017. A student of the game, he will continue to work on pitch recognition and cutting down his strikeout rate in the hopes that he can make his debut late in the season.

BA GRADE 60 Risk: High

Year	Club (League)	Class	AVG	G	AB	R	H	2B	3B	HR	RBI	BB	SO	SB	CS	OBP	SLG
2014	Lake County (MWL)	LoA	.266	120	474	70	126	18	6	13	50	56	161	12	6	.349	.411
2015	Lynchburg (CAR)	HiA	.285	133	501	88	143	36	3	16	72	68	125	15	7	.377	.465
2016	Akron (EL)	AA	.276	89	341	56	94	25	1	13	48	41	86	13	4	.356	.469
	Columbus (IL)	AAA	.238	5	21	2	5	0	1	0	0	0	6	0	0	.238	.333
	Scranton/W-B (IL)	AAA	.228	25	101	17	23	2	3	3	7	7	30	0	0	.278	.396
Minor League Totals			.275	416	1610	265	442	92	19	50	205	189	469	43	19	.355	.448

3 BLAKE RUTHERFORD, OF

BILL MITCHELL

Born: May 2, 1997. **B-T:** L-L. **Ht.:** 6-2. **Wt.:** 192. **Drafted:** HS—Canoga Park, Calif. (1st round). **Signed by:** Bobby DeJardin.

Because he was 19 years old and had a big price tag, Rutherford fell to the Yankees with the No. 18 pick. He had the big price tag because he ranked among the best hitters available in the 2016 draft, with a long track record of success in Southern California high school ranks and with USA Baseball's 18U national team. The Yankees gladly took him and awarded him a $3,282,000 bonus, which ranks as the second-highest figure they've given a draftee. Rutherford spent most of his debut at Rookie-level Pulaski, where he dealt with a hamstring injury that cost him time and eventually ended his season on Aug. 24. Rutherford made plenty of hard contact in his pro debut and projects as a four-tool player. He's athletic and rangy and center field, but his arm is below-average and could push him to left. He also has the potential for plus power, with some scouts putting future 60 grades (on the 20-80 scouting scale) on both his hitting ability and power. Scouts laud his smooth lefthanded swing and ability to cover the plate. He's an average runner, but jumps and instincts will help him stay in center as long as possible. After his first pro offseason, Rutherford probably will start 2017 at low Class A Charleston. He'll continue to get reps in both center and left field.

BA GRADE 60 Risk: High

Year	Club (League)	Class	AVG	G	AB	R	H	2B	3B	HR	RBI	BB	SO	SB	CS	OBP	SLG
2016	Yankees2 (GCL)	R	.240	8	25	3	6	1	0	1	3	4	6	0	0	.333	.400
	Pulaski (APP)	R	.382	25	89	13	34	7	4	2	9	9	24	0	2	.440	.618
Minor League Totals			.351	33	114	16	40	8	4	3	12	13	30	0	2	.415	.570

4 JORGE MATEO, SS/2B

MIKE JANES

Born: June 23, 1995. **B-T:** R-R. **Ht.:** 6-0. **Wt.:** 179. **Signed:** Dominican Republic, 2012. **Signed by:** Juan Rosario.

After signing for $225,000 in 2012, Mateo quickly blazed a path through the lower levels of the minors. Despite playing just 15 games in 2014, Mateo jumped to low Class A Charleston in 2015, and he responded by showing off an all-around tool set and leading the minor leagues with 80 stolen bases. His performance took a step backward in 2016, and his makeup took a hit, too, when the Yankees announced a two-week suspension for insubordination. He reportedly lashed out at team officials over not receiving a promotion to Double-A Trenton. As ever, Mateo is still blessed with 80-grade speed on the 20-80 scouting scale. How the Yankees want to employ it, however, is another question. That level of speed will play in the outfield, and Mateo saw time in instructional league in center field. He plays average defense at shortstop and second base,

BA GRADE 55 Risk: High

leading multiple evaluators to project center as his best path to the big leagues. He's got plenty of bat speed to catch up to good fastballs but still has rough edges to polish at the plate. He showed a vulnerability to breaking balls, though he should be an average hitter with surprising power for his wiry frame. Mateo probably will move to Double-A Trenton in 2017, where he will pair with Gleyber Torres and see time at shortstop, second base and center field.

Year	Club (League)	Class	AVG	G	AB	R	H	2B	3B	HR	RBI	BB	SO	SB	CS	OBP	SLG
2014	Yankees1 (GCL)	R	.276	15	58	14	16	5	1	0	1	7	17	11	1	.354	.397
2015	Charleston, SC (SAL)	LoA	.268	96	365	51	98	18	8	2	33	36	80	71	15	.338	.378
	Tampa (FSL)	HiA	.321	21	84	15	27	5	3	0	7	7	18	11	2	.374	.452
2016	Tampa (FSL)	HiA	.254	113	464	65	118	16	9	8	47	33	108	36	15	.306	.379
Minor League Totals			.270	323	1284	210	347	55	28	18	122	129	286	182	44	.340	.399

5 JAMES KAPRIELIAN, RHP

MIKE JANES

Born: March 2, 1994. **B-T:** R-R. **Ht.:** 6-4. **Wt.:** 200. **Drafted:** UCLA, 2015 (1st round). **Signed by:** Bobby DeJardin.

The Yankees drafted Kaprielian with the No. 16 overall pick and signed him for $2.65 million in 2015. The team expected big things from him after a strong pro debut, and general manager Brian Cashman hinted Kaprielian had an outside chance of making his big league debut by season's end. Instead, Kaprielian dealt with a strained right flexor tendon in his elbow and made just three starts. He made it back for instructional league and performed well enough there to warrant an assignment to the Arizona Fall League. After touching 95 mph toward the end of his college career, Kaprielian added 20 pounds of muscle prior to this season and

BA GRADE

60 Risk: Extreme

saw his velocity jump again. He touched 97 mph both with Tampa and again in the AFL, and he sat between 94-96. He throws all four pitches, including a slider and curveball that have both been plus at their best, as well as a changeup that could be an average fourth pitch. Evaluators note that his delivery, featuring a plunging arm action, is high-stress and could contribute to further injury issues. Kaprielian has front-of-the-rotation makeup and stuff with a well below-average delivery. After six weeks in the AFL to make up for lost time, Kaprielian could join either high Class A Tampa or Double-A Trenton in 2017.

Year	Club (League)	Class	W	L	ERA	G	GS	CG	SV	IP	H	HR	BB	SO	K/9	WHIP	AVG
2015	Yankees2 (GCL)	R	0	0	11.57	2	0	0	0	2	2	0	2	2	7.7	1.71	.250
	Staten Island (NYP)	SS	0	1	2.00	3	3	0	0	9	8	0	2	12	12.0	1.11	.229
2016	Tampa (FSL)	HiA	2	1	1.50	3	3	0	0	18	8	1	3	22	11.0	0.61	.136
Minor League Totals			2	2	2.45	8	6	0	0	29	18	1	7	36	11.0	0.85	.176

6 AARON JUDGE, OF

Born: April 26, 1992. **B-T:** R-R. **Ht.:** 6-7. **Wt.:** 275. **Drafted:** Fresno State, 2013 (1st round). **Signed by:** Troy Afenir.

The Yankees drafted Judge with their second of three first-round selections in 2013 and awarded him a $1.8 million bonus. He found success at every stop before becoming a bit streaky when he reached Triple-A late in 2015. He missed time in July 2016 with a knee injury but made his major league debut on Aug. 13. He and Tyler Austin that day became the first teammates in history to record back-to-back home runs in their first major league at-bats. Judge continued to show the big-time power, but he also struck out in 42 of his 84 at-bats. He easily has the best raw power in the system, and the tool rates as a 70 on the 20-80 scouting scale. He

BA GRADE

55 Risk: High

won't completely access that power until he cleans up his approach and lowers his strikeout rate. He cut his strikeout percentage to 23.9 this year at Triple-A—his lowest mark since low Class A—but big league pitchers exploited holes in his swing. He's a slightly above-average runner underway and plays average defense in right field with a well above-average throwing arm. The right-field job in the Bronx is Judge's for the taking, but he'll have to continue to work to cut his strikeouts in order to seize the job in 2017.

Year	Club (League)	Class	AVG	G	AB	R	H	2B	3B	HR	RBI	BB	SO	SB	CS	OBP	SLG
2014	Charleston (SAL)	LoA	.333	65	234	36	78	15	2	9	45	39	59	1	0	.428	.530
	Tampa (FSL)	HiA	.283	66	233	44	66	9	2	8	33	50	72	0	0	.411	.442
2015	Trenton (EL)	AA	.284	63	250	44	71	16	3	12	44	24	70	1	0	.350	.516
	Scranton/W-B (IL)	AAA	.224	61	228	27	51	10	0	8	28	29	74	6	2	.308	.373
2016	Scranton/W-B (IL)	AAA	.270	93	352	62	95	18	1	19	65	47	98	5	0	.366	.489
	New York (AL)	MAJ	.179	27	84	10	15	2	0	4	10	9	42	0	1	.263	.345
Major League Totals			.179	27	84	10	15	2	0	4	10	9	42	0	1	.263	.345
Minor League Totals			.278	348	1297	205	361	68	8	56	215	189	373	13	2	.373	.473

7 JUSTUS SHEFFIELD, LHP

Born: May 13, 1996. **B-T:** L-L. **Ht.:** 5-10. **Wt.:** 195. **Drafted:** HS—Tullahoma, Tenn., 2014 (1st round). **Signed by:** Chuck Bartlett (Indians).

Sheffield was set to pitch at Vanderbilt with his brother Jordan before the Indians made him a first-round pick and signed him for $1.6 million. He blitzed the competition in the Rookie-level Arizona League in his debut but was arrested in the off-season for underage drinking and criminal trespass. He pled guilty to those charges. Cleveland traded him to the Yankees at the 2016 trade deadline, along with outfielder Clint Frazier and relievers J.P. Feyereisen and Ben Heller, in the deal that sent closer Andrew Miller to the Indians. A short lefthander, Sheffield owns three plus or potential plus pitches. His fastball, which has sinking action, sits in the 93-95 mph range and can touch 97. He complements it with a short-breaking slider in the low- to mid-80s and a changeup in the same range. His slider is his best secondary pitch, but he has good feel for his changeup, and with more reps it could be as good as the slider. Sheffield, who will open 2017 as a 20-year-old, is probably headed for Double-A Trenton with a future as a mid-rotation starter if he achieves his ceiling.

BA GRADE
55 Risk: High

Year	Club (League)	Class	W	L	ERA	G	GS	CG	SV	IP	H	HR	BB	SO	K/9	WHIP	AVG
2014	Indians (AZL)	R	3	1	4.79	8	4	0	0	21	24	0	9	29	12.6	1.60	.286
2015	Lake County (MWL)	LoA	9	4	3.31	26	26	0	0	128	135	8	38	138	9.7	1.36	.264
2016	Lynchburg (CAR)	HiA	7	5	3.59	19	19	0	0	95	91	6	40	93	8.8	1.37	.252
	Tampa (FSL)	HiA	3	1	1.73	5	5	0	0	26	14	0	10	27	9.3	0.92	.157
	Trenton (EL)	AA	0	0	0.00	1	1	0	0	4	2	0	3	9	20.3	1.25	.125
Minor League Totals			22	11	3.32	59	55	0	0	274	266	14	100	296	9.7	1.34	.251

8 CHANCE ADAMS, RHP

Born: Aug. 10, 1994. **B-T:** R-R. **Ht.:** 6-0. **Wt.:** 2015. **Drafted:** Dallas Baptist, 2015 (5th round). **Signed by:** Mike Leuzinger.

Adams started his college career at Yavapai (Ariz.) JC before transferring to Dallas Baptist as a junior. He made just 10 starts—all in his sophomore year—before the Yankees popped him in the fifth round in 2015. He moved into the rotation this year and was one of the breakout stars in the minor leagues. He went 13-1, 2.33 and led all qualified starters with a .169 opponent average. A stocky-bodied righty, Adams starts his four-pitch mix with a hard, lively fastball that sits in the mid-90s and can check in as high as 97 mph. He complements his fastball with a hard slider that he uses as his out pitch. His changeup is his third pitch, and he's worked hard to make sure he throws it from the same arm slot as his fastball. He's also got a curveball, but it's well behind his other three pitches at this point. He pitches with ferocity and has shown the ability to command the strike zone. Scouts noticed that Adams' fastball tended to flatten when left up in the zones. The Yankees shut down Adams just before Double-A Trenton began the Eastern League playoffs because he reached his innings limit. He will move to Triple-A Scranton/Wilkes-Barre in 2017 and has a ceiling of a No. 3 starter.

BA GRADE
55 Risk: High

Year	Club (League)	Class	W	L	ERA	G	GS	CG	SV	IP	H	HR	BB	SO	K/9	WHIP	AVG
2015	Staten Island (NYP)	SS	1	0	0.93	4	0	0	0	10	5	0	3	13	12.1	0.83	.147
	Charleston (SAL)	LoA	1	1	3.09	5	0	0	0	12	7	0	4	16	12.3	0.94	.163
	Tampa (FSL)	HiA	1	0	1.29	5	0	0	0	14	12	0	2	16	10.3	1.00	.226
2016	Tampa (FSL)	HiA	5	0	2.65	12	12	0	0	58	41	4	15	73	11.4	0.97	.196
	Trenton (EL)	AA	8	1	2.07	13	12	0	0	70	35	5	24	71	9.2	0.85	.145
Minor League Totals			16	2	2.21	39	24	0	0	163	100	9	48	189	10.5	0.91	.172

9 ALBERT ABREU, RHP

Born: Sept. 25, 1995. **B-T:** R-R. **Ht.:** 6-2. **Wt.:** 198. **Signed:** Dominican Republic, 2013. **Signed by:** Oz Ocampo/Rafael Belen/Francis Mojica (Astros).

The Astros signed Abreu for $185,000, and a mere two years later he had added 5 mph to his fastball, giving him a mid-90s heater that has touched 99 mph as well as a useful assortment of secondary pitches. Houston traded him to the Yankees as part of the Brian McCann deal after the 2016 season. Abreu's pure stuff allows him to succeed so far with an approach that can best be described as, "Here it is—try to hit it." He doesn't really set up hitters and finish them off as much as he overwhelms them. Abreu's plus fastball blew away hitters in the low Class A Midwest League in 2016, especially when he located it to his arm side with excellent run. His average curveball is a slower, bigger breaker that is generally best as an early-count offering, but he will flash a

BA GRADE
55 Risk: High

harder curve that flashes plus in late-count situations. His slider is even more inconsistent, but it flashes above-average potential when he stays through his delivery. His changeup will show fade and deception at times. Abreu's delivery is quite simple, but he doesn't repeat it consistently yet from either the stretch or windup, and there is some recoil in his finish. His control is below-average at this point. Abreu's four-pitch assortment screams starter, but his approach and his control lead many to think he'll end up as a high-leverage reliever.

Year	Club (League)	Class	W	L	ERA	G	GS	CG	SV	IP	H	HR	BB	SO	K/9	WHIP	AVG
2014	Astros (DSL)	R	3	2	2.78	14	14	0	0	68	48	1	29	54	7.1	1.13	.197
2015	Greeneville (APP)	R	2	3	2.51	13	7	1	1	47	35	2	21	51	9.8	1.20	.206
2016	Quad Cities (MWL)	LoA	2	8	3.50	21	14	0	4	90	62	5	49	104	10.4	1.23	.193
	Lancaster (CAL)	HiA	1	0	5.40	3	2	0	0	12	12	2	9	11	8.5	1.80	.267
Minor League Totals			8	13	3.16	51	37	1	5	216	157	10	108	220	9.2	1.22	.201

10 DUSTIN FOWLER, OF

Born: Dec. 29, 1994. **B-T:** L-L. **Ht.:** 6-0. **Wt.:** 185. **Drafted:** HS—Dexter, Ga., 2013 (18th round). **Signed by:** Darryl Monroe.

BA GRADE
50 Risk: Medium

Fowler was a Louisville commit out of high school, but the Yankees liked his all-around ability and signed him for $278,000 as an 18th-round pick in 2013. So far, they've liked what they've seen. He began to break out in 2015, when he put up dynamic numbers at two Class A stops and finished with a nice run in the Arizona Fall League. He continued that trend this year at Double-A Trenton, where he was a force on both sides of the ball for a team that made it to the Eastern League championship series. Fowler is an above-average defender in center field with range both side to side and back and forth. His arm is a little bit below-average, but he makes up for it with a quick release. He's a slashing type of hitter with above-average speed that serves him well both on the bases and on defense. Some evaluators noted that his speed will play even better once he learns to take more aggressive leads. He's got more power than other players his size. It's primarily to the gaps, but his speed helps earn him extra bases. For example, his 15 triples led the EL. His biggest weakness is that he tends to expand the zone, and he walked just 22 times all year. After a successful season in Double-A, Fowler will move to Triple-A Scranton/Wilkes-Barre in 2017 and play all season there as a 22-year-old.

Year	Club (League)	Class	AVG	G	AB	R	H	2B	3B	HR	RBI	BB	SO	SB	CS	OBP	SLG
2014	Charleston (SAL)	LoA	.257	66	257	33	66	13	6	9	41	13	53	3	2	.292	.459
2015	Charleston (SAL)	LoA	.307	58	241	35	74	9	3	4	31	11	47	18	7	.340	.419
	Tampa (FSL)	HiA	.289	65	246	29	71	11	3	1	39	15	43	12	6	.328	.370
2016	Trenton (EL)	AA	.281	132	541	67	152	30	15	12	88	22	86	25	11	.311	.458
Minor League Totals			.279	351	1397	172	390	71	31	26	208	65	252	61	27	.313	.430

11 DOMINGO ACEVEDO, RHP

BA GRADE
55 Risk: Extreme

Born: March 6, 1994. **B-T:** R-R. **Ht.:** 6-6. **Wt.:** 242. **Signed:** Dominican Republic, 2012. **Signed by:** Esteban Castillo.

Signed for just $7,500, the Yankees have already gotten more than their money's worth from Acevedo. The burly righthander cuts an imposing figure on the mound, but injuries have slowed his rise. He started last season at low Class A Charleston, but was limited to just one start after blister issues surfaced. He opened this year at Charleston again, dominated there and then was pushed to high Class A Tampa. He was limited to just eight starts there because of hamstring and right shoulder injuries and was shut down for the season on Aug. 15. With Acevedo's massive frame comes massive velocity. He can sit in the mid-90s and touches triple-digits regularly. His changeup is above-average and has the makings of a plus pitch. His low-80s slider is still a work in progress, and is a key to determining whether he ends up a starter or in the bullpen. He throws plenty of strikes with his arsenal, and finished the year with 102 punchouts against just 22 walks. Acevedo is a tantalizing prospect with some flaws who could become elite with a few key improvements. He will return to high Class A Tampa to start 2017 but should make his Double-A debut at some point.

Year	Club (League)	Class	W	L	ERA	G	GS	CG	SV	IP	H	HR	BB	SO	K/9	WHIP	AVG
2014	Yankees2 (GCL)	R	0	1	4.11	5	5	0	0	15	16	0	6	21	12.3	1.43	.271
2015	Charleston(SAL)	LoA	0	0	5.40	1	1	0	0	2	2	0	1	1	5.4	1.80	.286
	Staten Island (NYP)	SS	3	0	1.69	11	11	0	0	48	37	2	15	53	9.9	1.08	.207
2016	Charleston (SAL)	LoA	3	1	1.90	8	8	0	0	43	34	1	7	48	10.1	0.96	.221
	Tampa (FSL)	HiA	2	3	3.22	10	10	1	0	50	49	3	15	54	9.7	1.27	.261
Minor League Totals			9	7	2.53	46	45	1	0	199	180	6	55	220	9.9	1.18	.240

12 MIGUEL ANDUJAR, 3B

BA GRADE
50 Risk: High

Born: March 2, 1995. **B-T:** R-R. **Ht.:** 6-0. **Wt.:** 175. **Signed:** Dominican Republic, 2011. **Signed by:** Victor Mata/Coanabo Cosme.

Andujar signed for $750,000 in 2011 and was trained by Basilio Vizcaino, who also helped mold catcher Gary Sanchez before he signed with the Yankees. No single tool stood out as an amateur, and he continues to show an overall blend of skills as a pro. Andujar returned to high Class A Tampa to begin this season and earned a promotion to Double-A Trenton as a 21-year-old. He has a level, balanced swing that could allow him to hit for average and power if he sharpens his pitch recognition and improves his plate discipline. Despite being a free-swinger, Andujar makes a lot of contact. He struck out just 72 times in 512 at-bats last season, along with 39 walks. The raw ingredients are there for Andujar to stick at third base, but there are rough edges to be polished. Evaluators who like him see the ability to move laterally as well as in on a bunt and a plus arm as well. He needs to improve the accuracy on his throws, however, and learn when to hold onto it. After a successful stint in the Arizona Fall League, Andujar is likely to return to Double-A Trenton to start the season.

Year	Club (League)	Class	AVG	G	AB	R	H	2B	3B	HR	RBI	BB	SO	SB	CS	OBP	SLG
2014	Charleston (SAL)	LoA	.267	127	484	75	129	25	4	10	70	35	83	5	1	.318	.397
2015	Tampa (FSL)	HiA	.243	130	485	54	118	24	5	8	57	29	90	12	1	.288	.363
2016	Tampa (FSL)	HiA	.283	58	230	34	65	10	2	10	41	18	30	1	3	.343	.474
	Trenton (EL)	AA	.266	72	282	28	75	16	2	2	42	21	42	2	1	.323	.358
Minor League Totals			.263	471	1791	230	471	95	13	35	254	123	303	25	10	.315	.389

13 JORDAN MONTGOMERY, LHP

BA GRADE
50 Risk: High

Born: Dec. 27, 1992. **B-T:** L-L. **Ht.:** 6-6. **Wt.:** 225. **Drafted:** South Carolina, 2014 (4th round). **Signed by:** Billy Godwin.

After watching him go 20-7 over three years at South Carolina, the Yankees spent a fourth-round pick on Montgomery and signed him for $424,000 in 2014. Despite a pedestrian-appearing repertoire, Montgomery shows excellent control and command of all of his pitches, which has helped him zoom through the system. He reached Double-A in his second season and returned to the Eastern League in 2016 before finishing with Triple-A Scranton/Wilkes-Barre and earning the start and the win in the Triple-A Championship Game. His 2.13 ERA was ninth-best in the minor leagues. Montgomery's 88-92 mph fastball won't blow away hitters, but the angle on the pitch produced by his large frame helps mitigate the lack of velocity. Montgomery complements his fastball with a fringe-average changeup in the low-80s and an average 12-to-6 curveball in the high-70s. His 134 strikeouts ranked second in the organization behind only Chance Adams' 144 whiffs. Montgomery is likely to start back at Triple-A to begin the year, and if he can continue to throw strikes he has the future of an innings-eating starter in the big leagues.

Year	Club (League)	Class	W	L	ERA	G	GS	CG	SV	IP	H	HR	BB	SO	K/9	WHIP	AVG
2014	Yankees2 (GCL)	R	0	1	4.76	3	3	0	0	6	5	0	2	5	7.9	1.24	.227
	Staten Island (NYP)	SS	1	0	3.38	7	4	0	0	13	11	0	4	15	10.1	1.13	.220
2015	Charleston (SAL)	LoA	4	3	2.68	9	9	0	0	44	36	1	12	55	11.3	1.10	.228
	Tampa (FSL)	HiA	6	5	3.08	16	15	1	0	91	82	4	24	77	7.6	1.17	.240
2016	Trenton (EL)	AA	9	4	2.55	19	19	1	0	102	94	5	36	97	8.5	1.27	.239
	Scranton/W-B (IL)	AAA	5	1	0.97	6	6	0	0	37	28	0	9	37	9.0	1.00	.212
Minor League Totals			25	14	2.61	60	56	2	0	293	256	10	87	286	8.8	1.17	.233

14 ESTEVAN FLORIAL, OF

BA GRADE
55 Risk: Extreme

Born: Nov. 25, 1997. **B-T:** L-R. **Ht.:** 6-1. **Wt.:** 189. **Signed:** Haiti, 2015. **Signed by:** Esteban Castillo.

The owner of the perhaps the most complex background in the Yankees' system, Florial has already earned a considerable amount of fame in prospect circles. An identity snafu as an amateur led to a suspension and led to a signing bonus of just $200,000 instead of the seven-figures he could have received without complications. By any name, Florial is still among the system's most tooled-up prospects. His power, arm and speed earn 70 grades on the 20-to-80 scouting scale, and evaluators who saw him in 2016 believe he has the potential to stick in center field. Florial spent most of his time with Rookie-level Pulaski in center field, although he occasionally slid to a corner or DH to accommodate 2016 first-rounder Blake Rutherford. The biggest knock on Florial is the amount of swing-and-miss to his game. He struck out 78 times in 236 at-bats with Pulaski, one less than league leader and teammate Dermis Garcia. As one of five Pulaski players age 18 or younger, however, strikeouts were to be expected. Florial made cameos at both low Class A Charleston and high Class A Tampa during the season, and he is likely to begin the season back with Charleston.

Year	Club (League)	Class	AVG	G	AB	R	H	2B	3B	HR	RBI	BB	SO	SB	CS	OBP	SLG
2015	Yankees1 (DSL)	R	.313	57	224	51	70	11	8	7	53	30	61	15	5	.394	.527
2016	Tampa (FSL)	HiA	.125	2	8	0	1	0	0	0	0	0	2	0	0	.125	.125
	Pulaski (APP)	R	.225	60	236	36	53	10	1	7	25	28	78	10	2	.315	.364
	Charleston (SAL)	LoA	.300	5	20	4	6	0	1	1	5	2	5	0	0	.348	.550
Minor League Totals			.266	124	488	91	130	21	10	15	83	60	146	25	7	.351	.443

15 DILLON TATE, RHP

BA GRADE
50 Risk: High

Born: May 1, 1994. **B-T:** R-R. **Ht.:** 6-2. **Wt.:** 165. **Drafted:** UC Santa Barbara, 2015 (1st round). **Signed by:** Todd Guggiana (Rangers).

After pitching as UC Santa Barbara's closer as a sophomore, Tate moved into the Gauchos' rotation in his junior year and raised his stock dramatically. The Rangers took him No. 4 overall and signed him for $4.2 million. Tate suffered through hamstring injuries and poor performance throughout his first full year in pro ball, however, and the Rangers traded him away a year after drafting him as part of the Carlos Beltran deal. Tate moved to the bullpen after joining the Yankees system and returned to form at low Class A Charleston. His fastball peaked at 97 mph in the Arizona Fall League after sitting in the high 80s to low 90s in the early part of the season, while his slider and changeup each flashed above-average and garnered swings and misses but lacked consistency. After making 16 starts in 17 appearances with the Rangers, Tate was used exclusively out of the bullpen at both Charleston and in the AFL. He projects as a reliever long-term, but could be a high-leverage arm out of the pen with improved command. He is likely to start 2017 at high Class A Tampa.

Year	Club (League)	Class	W	L	ERA	G	GS	CG	SV	IP	H	HR	BB	SO	K/9	WHIP	AVG
2015	Spokane (NWL)	SS	0	0	0.00	2	2	0	0	2	0	0	3	3	13.5	1.50	.000
	Hickory (SAL)	LoA	0	0	1.29	4	4	0	0	7	3	1	0	5	6.4	0.43	.130
2016	Hickory (SAL)	LoA	3	3	5.12	17	16	0	0	65	78	5	27	55	7.6	1.62	.311
	Charleston (SAL)	LoA	1	0	3.12	7	0	0	0	17	21	1	6	15	7.8	1.56	.292
Minor League Totals			4	3	4.34	30	22	0	0	91	102	7	36	78	7.7	1.51	.291

16 TYLER AUSTIN, OF/1B

BA GRADE
45 Risk: Medium

Born: Sept. 6, 1991. **B-T:** R-R. **Ht.:** 6-2. **Wt.:** 220. **Drafted:** HS—Conyers, Ga., 2010 (13th round). **Signed by:** Darryl Monroe.

Even before he was drafted, Austin had been through a lot. He was diagnosed with testicular cancer in high school and had surgery to remove the tumor. Little more than a week after the surgery, he played in a high school showcase. The Yankees drafted Austin in the 13th round in 2010 and gave him a $130,000 bonus to forgo a Kennesaw State commitment. He rocketed through the lower levels of the system and earned a place on the 40-man roster in 2014, but injuries and struggles stalled his career and led to him being designated for assignment after the 2015 season. Finally healthy in 2016, Austin found success at Triple-A and made history in his major league debut when he and Aaron Judge became the first teammates to go back-to-back with home runs in their first big league at-bats. Austin showed all-fields power and patience in the minors, though he struck out at a 40-percent clip once he got to the majors. He is an average defender in right field and at first base, and could win a job in a utility role with the Yankees out of spring training.

Year	Club (League)	Class	AVG	G	AB	R	H	2B	3B	HR	RBI	BB	SO	SB	CS	OBP	SLG
2014	Trenton (EL)	AA	.275	105	396	56	109	20	5	9	47	36	80	3	2	.336	.419
2015	Scranton/W-B (IL)	AAA	.235	73	264	33	62	8	0	4	27	26	81	8	1	.309	.311
	Trenton (EL)	AA	.260	21	77	8	20	5	2	2	8	8	16	3	2	.337	.455
2016	Trenton (EL)	AA	.260	50	177	22	46	10	1	4	29	30	46	1	1	.367	.395
	Scranton/W-B (IL)	AAA	.323	57	201	39	65	24	0	13	49	32	59	5	0	.415	.637
	New York (AL)	MAJ	.241	31	83	7	20	3	0	5	12	7	36	1	0	.300	.458
Major League Totals			.241	31	83	7	20	3	0	5	12	7	36	1	0	.300	.458
Minor League Totals			.287	550	2033	323	584	137	17	61	316	240	499	65	8	.366	.461

17 TYLER WADE, SS/OF

BA GRADE
45 Risk: Medium

Born: Nov. 23, 1994. **B-T:** L-R. **Ht.:** 6-1. **Wt.:** 180. **Drafted:** HS—Murrieta, Calif., 2013 (4th round). **Signed by:** David Keith.

In a system with Didi Gregorius in the major leagues and new acquisition Gleyber Torres atop the depth chart, something had to give with the Yankees' glut of shortstops in the minors. With that in mind, Wade spent the Arizona Fall League beginning his conversion to the outfield. Wade returned to Double-A in 2016 and continued showing his ability to do a little bit of everything. He sprayed the ball to all fields nearly equally and his splits against righties and lefties were nearly identical. He is an above-average runner as well, and his 66 walks were the second-most in the system behind only Hoy Jun Park. Wade still has the skills to play shortstop or second base if necessary and scouts praised his range at shortstop, arm strength and willingness to hang in on double-play turns. He also gets high marks for his makeup and workmanlike effort. Wade won't wow anybody with his tools but the sum of his parts makes him an attractive candidate as a utilityman in the major leagues. That is especially true if he shows a smooth conversion to the outfield. He is likely to start 2017 in Triple-A Scranton/Wilkes-Barre.

Year	Club (League)	Class	AVG	G	AB	R	H	2B	3B	HR	RBI	BB	SO	SB	CS	OBP	SLG
2014	Charleston (SAL)	LoA	.272	129	507	77	138	24	6	1	51	57	118	22	13	.350	.349
2015	Tampa (FSL)	HiA	.280	98	368	51	103	11	5	2	28	39	65	31	15	.349	.353
	Trenton (EL)	AA	.204	29	113	6	23	4	0	1	3	2	24	2	1	.224	.265
2016	Trenton (EL)	AA	.259	133	505	90	131	16	7	5	27	66	103	27	8	.352	.349
Minor League Totals			.267	439	1668	261	446	65	18	9	122	198	356	93	38	.350	.344

18 NOLAN MARTINEZ, RHP

BA GRADE

50 Risk: High

Born: June 30, 1998. **B-T:** R-R. **Ht.:** 6-2. **Wt.:** 165. **Drafted:** HS—Culver City, Calif., 2016. (3rd round). **Signed by:** Bobby DeJardin.

Martinez was a two-way player at Culver City (Calif.) HS just outside Los Angeles throughout his career, but scouts preferred him as a pitcher. The Yankees agreed with that assessment, drafted him in the third round and gave him a $1.15 million signing bonus to sway him from a San Diego State commitment. His fastball was measured with the highest spin rate the World Wood Bat Association event in Jupiter, Fla., that typically closes the showcase season. The pitch typically sits in the 87-93 mph range but reached 95 mph the summer before he was drafted. His primary offspeed pitch is a curveball in the upper-70s that flashes plus. He can land the pitch for strikes and use it to get chases as well. He has a changeup but, like most dominant high school pitchers, didn't need it to get outs against prep competition. He will continue developing the pitch as a professional to fulfill his starter's potential. Further, the Yankees want to add strength to Martinez's frame to help him handle a starter's workload as he develops. They'll be patient, but they believe he has massive potential as he matures. Martinez will likely spend 2017 at Rookie-level Pulaski.

Year	Club (League)	Class	W	L	ERA	G	GS	CG	SV	IP	H	HR	BB	SO	K/9	WHIP	AVG
2016	Yankees1 (GCL)	R	0	1	3.86	3	3	0	0	7	6	0	4	3	3.9	1.43	.261
Minor League Totals			0	1	3.86	3	3	0	0	7	6	0	4	3	3.9	1.43	.261

19 NICK SOLAK, 2B

BA GRADE

50 Risk: High

Born: Jan. 11, 1995. **B-T:** R-R. **Ht.:** 5-11. **Wt.:** 175. **Drafted:** Louisville, 2016. (2nd round). **Signed by:** Mike Gibbons.

After shifting between second base and the outfield in the Cape Cod League between his sophomore and junior years, Solak settled in at second base on a stacked Louisville club for his junior season. He hit .376/.470/.564 as the Cardinals made a run to Super Regionals, and found enough helium along the way to earn a $950,000 signing bonus as a second-round pick. Solak is a contact-oriented hitter who struck out just 67 times over three years at Louisville while showing consistent gap power and home run juice to the opposite field. His range is limited at second base, but he has worked hard to improve and get himself playable at the position. He is an above-average runner who stole 36 bases in college and then added nine more in as many tries in his professional debut with short-season Staten Island. A polished hitter in the mold of current Yankee Rob Refsnyder, Solak has a chance to skip low Class A Charleston altogether and begin next season at high Class A Tampa.

Year	Club (League)	Class	AVG	G	AB	R	H	2B	3B	HR	RBI	BB	SO	SB	CS	OBP	SLG
2016	Staten Island (NYP)	SS	.321	64	240	48	77	13	1	3	25	30	39	8	0	.412	.421
Minor League Totals			.321	64	240	48	77	13	1	3	25	30	39	8	0	.412	.421

20 CHAD GREEN, RHP

BA GRADE

50 Risk: High

Born: May 24, 1991. **B-T:** L-R. **Ht.:** 6-3. **Wt.:** 210. **Drafted:** Louisville, 2013 (11th round). **Signed by:** Harold Zonder (Tigers).

Green was drafted in 2013 out of Louisville, where he was teammates with fellow righthanders Kyle Funkhouser and Nick Burdi, who are currently prospects in the Tigers and Twins systems, respectively. He signed for $100,000 then reached as high as Double-A with the Tigers before being dealt to New York along with righty Luis Cessa in exchange for lefty setup man Justin Wilson. He bounced up and down between Triple-A Scranton/Wilkes-Barre and the big leagues, and made eight starts with the Yankees before being shut down with a sprained ulnar collateral ligament and a strained flexor tendon in his right elbow. He did not have surgery. At his best, Green pitched with a fastball that averaged 95 mph and an above-average hard-breaking slider in the mid-80s. He also has an above-average cutter and a rarely-thrown below-average changeup. The four-pitch arsenal gives Green a chance to start, but his fastball and slider would play well out of the bullpen as well. He'll compete for a rotation spot in spring training.

Year	Club (League)	Class	W	L	ERA	G	GS	CG	SV	IP	H	HR	BB	SO	K/9	WHIP	AVG
2014	West Michigan (MWL)	LoA	6	4	3.11	23	23	0	0	130	121	8	28	125	8.6	1.14	.251
2015	Erie (EL)	AA	5	14	3.93	27	27	1	0	149	170	9	43	137	8.3	1.43	.287
2016	Scranton/W-B (IL)	AAA	7	6	1.52	16	16	0	0	95	68	3	21	100	9.5	0.94	.200
	New York (AL)	MAJ	2	4	4.73	12	8	0	1	46	49	12	15	52	10.2	1.40	.272
Major League Totals			2	4	4.73	12	8	0	1	46	49	12	15	52	10.2	1.40	.272
Minor League Totals			22	24	3.06	78	68	1	1	394	378	21	98	378	8.6	1.21	.253

21 DERMIS GARCIA, 3B

BA GRADE
55 Risk: Extreme

Born: Jan. 7, 1998. **B-T:** R-R. **Ht.:** 6-2. **Wt.:** 228. **Signed:** Dominican Republic, 2014. **Signed by:** Miguel Benitez.

Garcia was one of the jewels of the Yankees' $30 million international spending spree, and his $3 million bonus is tied with Gary Sanchez for the fifth-highest in franchise history. As an amateur Garcia was coveted for his tremendous raw power, and the same is true two years into his pro career. His 13 home runs were second in the Appalachian League and his 32 walks were the fifth-most in the league in 2016, but his 79 strikeouts were a league-worst. Scouts are split on his future hitting ability, but the consensus is he will be no better than average unless he makes major strides with his pitch recognition and plate discipline. Garcia has put on nearly 30 pounds since signing and a move off of third base over to first is considered inevitable. He has a strong arm, but his feet are clunky and he's already nearly too big for third. He is a bottom-of-the-scale runner. The Yankees will look for more development at the plate to unlock his double-plus raw power more in games. He could wind up at low Class A Charleston to start the year.

Year	Club (League)	Class	AVG	G	AB	R	H	2B	3B	HR	RBI	BB	SO	SB	CS	OBP	SLG
2015	Yankees2 (GCL)	R	.159	23	69	7	11	2	0	6	9	25	0	1	.256	.188
2016	Pulaski (APP)	R	.206	57	194	31	40	9	0	13	24	32	79	0	2	.326	.454
Minor League Totals			.194	80	263	38	51	11	0	13	30	41	104	0	3	.308	.384

22 ABIATAL AVELINO, SS/2B

BA GRADE
50 Risk: High

Born: Feb. 14, 1995. **B-T:** R-R. **Ht.:** 5-11. **Wt.:** 186. **Drafted:** Dominican Republic, 2011. **Signed by:** Jose Sabino.

The Yankees scooped up a pack of international prospects in 2011, including righthander Luis Severino, third baseman Miguel Andujar and Avelino from the Dominican Republic. Avelino's $300,000 bonus was second-highest of that group, behind only Andujar. Since signing, Avelino has shown steady production. He bounced back and forth between shortstop and second base at high Class A Tampa and Double-A Trenton, but that was mostly due to the presence of Jorge Mateo and Gleyber Torres at Tampa and Tyler Wade in Trenton. Evaluators believe Avelino still has the range, instincts and arm to play shortstop despite the shuffling. Offensively he is a contact-oriented player with a hint of power, but the Yankees would like to see him work the middle of the field more instead of seeking to pull the ball over the fence. He is an above-average runner, but he needs to work on his base-stealing technique to maximize his speed. He is likely to return to Double-A Trenton, where he'll defer at shortstop to top prospect Gleyber Torres.

Year	Club (League)	Class	AVG	G	AB	R	H	2B	3B	HR	RBI	BB	SO	SB	CS	OBP	SLG
2014	Yankees1 (GCL)	R	.355	8	31	7	11	6	0	0	3	2	4	0	0	.394	.548
	Charleston (SAL)	LoA	.232	53	220	31	51	12	1	2	12	17	44	11	5	.296	.323
2015	Charleston (SAL)	LoA	.301	20	83	16	25	8	0	0	4	5	16	16	3	.341	.398
	Tampa (FSL)	HiA	.252	103	405	64	102	12	2	4	23	32	63	38	15	.309	.321
2016	Tampa (FSL)	HiA	.266	93	357	54	95	17	2	6	34	29	63	20	13	.325	.375
	Trenton (EL)	AA	.244	33	127	15	31	11	0	0	14	10	19	1	2	.307	.331
Minor League Totals			.269	418	1643	278	442	86	11	13	138	142	260	134	44	.335	.358

23 YEFREY RAMIREZ, RHP

BA GRADE
50 Risk: High

Born: Nov. 28, 1993. **B-T:** R-R. **Ht.:** 6-2. **Wt.:** 165. **Drafted:** Dominican Republic, 2011. **Signed by:** Junior Noboa (Diamondbacks).

Ramirez was initially signed by the Diamondbacks as a position player and spent a season as a hitter in the Dominican Summer League before moving to the mound in 2012. He pitched for three more seasons in the DSL and short-season levels before the Yankees took him in the minor league phase of the 2015 Rule 5 draft. After finally making it to full-season ball, Ramirez's 132 strikeouts ranked third in the Yankees system behind only Chance Adams and Jordan Montgomery. Ramirez works primarily with three pitches—fastball, curveball and changeup—from a high three-quarters slot. His fastball sat in the low-90s for most of the season but touched 96 mph during Tampa's run to the Florida State League championship series. His changeup, which sits in the low-80s, and his curveball both rank as average pitches. He effectively used both offspeed pitches to handle both righthanders and lefthanders with nearly equal success. The Yankees thought enough of Ramirez to add him to the 40-man roster to protect him from the Rule 5 draft, and he will begin 2017 in Double-A Trenton.

Year	Club (League)	Class	W	L	ERA	G	GS	CG	SV	IP	H	HR	BB	SO	K/9	WHIP	AVG
2014	Diamondbacks (AZL)	R	4	2	1.93	7	4	0	0	37	26	0	4	48	11.6	0.80	.186
	Missoula (PIO)	R	2	1	4.45	6	6	0	0	30	32	8	7	17	5.0	1.29	.271
2015	Missoula (PIO)	R	5	5	5.35	14	13	0	0	69	68	11	21	61	8.0	1.29	.259
2016	Charleston, SC (SAL)	LoA	4	2	2.80	11	11	0	0	61	48	4	14	66	9.7	1.02	.209
	Tampa (FSL)	HiA	3	7	2.84	11	11	0	0	63	34	5	18	66	9.4	0.82	.156
Minor League Totals			20	23	3.44	80	56	0	0	346	290	31	97	338	8.8	1.12	.224

24 ZACK LITTELL, RHP

BA GRADE

45 Risk: High

Born: Oct. 5, 1995. **B-T:** R-R. **Ht.:** 6-3. **Wt.:** 190. **Drafted:** HS—Mebane, N.C., 2013 (11th round). **Signed by:** Devitt Moore (Mariners).

The Mariners drafted Littell as a 17-year old long-term project in 2013 and signed him for $100,000 to buy him out of an Appalachian State commitment. Seattle began to see the payoff three years after drafting him, but needing lefthander relief help traded him after the 2016 season to the Yankees for James Pazos. Littell's fastball sits 89-91, touching 93, and plays up because of high spin rate and advanced command. His main secondary offering is a true curveball that flashes plus, and he rounds out his three-pitch mix with an average to above-average changeup. Beyond his stuff Littell draws praise for his pre-start preparation, which includes advanced study of hitters' swings and tendencies. Littell often excelled most when pitching the final game of a series, when he had two or three days to watch an opposing team's hitters and figure out their weaknesses. His ERA has dropped every level he has climbed and his growing strength helped him hold up over 165.2 innings last season. He projects as a back-end starter and will begin 2017 in high Class A Tampa's rotation, with a strong chance to ascend to Double-A Trenton by summer.

Year	Club (League)	Class	W	L	ERA	G	GS	CG	SV	IP	H	HR	BB	SO	K/9	WHIP	AVG
2014	Pulaski (APP)	R	5	5	4.52	13	13	0	0	70	75	3	12	64	8.3	1.25	.275
2015	Clinton (MWL)	LoA	3	6	3.78	20	20	0	0	112	119	4	28	83	6.7	1.31	.272
2016	Clinton (MWL)	LoA	5	5	2.76	16	16	2	0	98	94	5	21	95	8.8	1.18	.258
	Bakersfield (CAL)	HiA	8	1	2.51	12	11	0	0	68	64	3	13	61	8.1	1.13	.246
Minor League Totals			21	23	3.62	71	67	2	1	381	391	17	87	331	7.8	1.26	.266

25 GIOVANNY GALLEGOS, RHP

BA GRADE

45 Risk: High

Born: Aug. 14, 1991. **B-T:** R-R. **Ht.:** 6-2. **Wt.:** 210. **Signed:** Mexico, 2011. **Signed by:** Lee Sigman.

A year after Yankees scout Lee Sigman plucked Manny Banuelos from Mexico, he signed Gallegos for $100,000 as one half of a package deal with righthander Luis Niebla, who was selected by the Rockies in the minor league portion of last year's Rule 5 Draft. After a brief cameo at Double-A Trenton in 2015, he returned to the level as the team's closer and turned into one of the system's most dominant relievers. He struck out 12.2 hitters per nine innings across 42 appearances at the system's upper levels. Gallegos' best pitch is his mid-90s fastball with excellent downhill angle and tailing action, but he had to be coaxed into throwing the pitch more often by Trenton pitching coach Jose Rosado. He couples the pitch with a low-80s curveball that flashes plus at times and a below-average changeup as his third pitch. The Yankees added Gallegos to the 40-man roster this offseason to protect him from the Rule 5 Draft, and he could make his big league debut at some point in 2017 in a relief role.

Year	Club (League)	Class	W	L	ERA	G	GS	CG	SV	IP	H	HR	BB	SO	K/9	WHIP	AVG
2014	Charleston, SC (SAL)	LoA	5	5	4.57	29	6	0	1	89	108	8	19	91	9.2	1.43	.298
2015	Tampa (FSL)	HiA	3	1	1.35	30	0	0	5	53	32	2	7	54	9.1	0.73	.172
	Trenton (EL)	AA	0	0	5.40	3	0	0	0	7	7	0	2	7	9.5	1.35	.259
	Scranton/W-B (IL)	AAA	0	0	0.00	2	0	0	0	3	2	0	0	3	9.0	0.67	.182
2016	Trenton (EL)	AA	2	1	1.09	17	0	0	2	33	20	1	7	53	14.5	0.82	.171
	Scranton/W-B (IL)	AAA	5	1	1.40	25	0	0	2	45	28	4	10	53	10.6	0.84	.178
Minor League Totals			17	17	2.91	134	26	0	10	322	288	25	61	326	9.1	1.08	.238

26 JORGE GUZMAN, RHP

BA GRADE
50 Risk: **Extreme**

Born: Jan. 28, 1996. **B-T:** R-R. **Ht.:** 6-2. **Wt.:** 182. **Signed:** Dominican Republic, 2014. **Signed by:** Oz Ocampo/Roman Ocumarez/Francis Mojica (Astros).

The Astros signed Guzman out of the Dominican Republic in 2014 and sent him to the Dominican Summer League to begin his first professional season. They moved him to the Rookie-level Gulf Coast League later in the season and returned him there to begin 2016. He struck out 12.2 hitters per nine innings between the GCL and the Appalachian League in 2016, and was sent to the Yankees with right-hander Albert Abreu in the offseason in the deal that sent catcher Brian McCann to Houston. Guzman's calling card is his lightning arm speed and corresponding velocity, which has peaked at 103 mph and normally sits in the high-90s. He is working on a slider to complement the fastball, but the pitch is below-average. He drops his arm slot and slows his arm down when he throws the slider. Guzman also has a changeup, but it is in its developmental stages. Despite his premium velocity, Guzman's delivery isn't particularly violent. He has a three-quarter slot and can get a little bit stiff and across his body, but it's not as high-effort as most triple-digit-throwers. Guzman is likely a reliever down the line, but he could have a big-time impact if everything develops as planned. He's likely to begin the year at low Class A Charleston.

Year	Club (League)	Class	W	L	ERA	G	GS	CG	SV	IP	H	HR	BB	SO	K/9	WHIP	AVG
2015	Astros Orange (DSL)	R	0	2	7.43	4	4	0	0	13	19	1	8	8	5.4	2.03	.322
	Astros Blue (DSL)	R	2	1	4.91	9	7	0	0	33	36	1	15	19	5.2	1.55	.255
	Astros (GCL)	R	1	1	2.00	4	1	0	0	9	8	0	7	2	2.0	1.67	.258
2016	Astros (GCL)	R	1	1	3.12	7	4	0	0	17	4	0	10	25	13.0	0.81	.071
	Greeneville (APP)	R	2	3	4.76	6	4	0	0	23	25	1	7	29	11.5	1.41	.272
Minor League Totals			6	8	4.63	30	20	0	0	95	92	3	47	83	7.8	1.46	.243

27 RONALD HERRERA, RHP

BA GRADE
45 Risk: **High**

Born: May 3, 1995. **B-T:** R-R. **Ht.:** 5-11. **Wt.:** 185. **Signed:** Venezuela, 2011. **Signed by:** Julio Franco/Juan Carlos Villanueva (Athletics).

Herrera has been traded twice since originally signing with the Athletics in 2011, first to the Padres for Kyle Blanks and then from San Diego to the Yankees for Jose Pirela after the 2015 season. The Yankees assigned Herrera to Double-A, where he spent the first portion of the season as one of the Eastern League's most dominant arms. His 131 strikeouts were fourth-most in the organization. Herrera's fastball sits in the low-90s and touched 94 mph during the season. He also throws a slider and changeup that get swings-and-misses, but he fell in love with the changeup and had to be coaxed into a more equal division of his offspeed pitches when his fastball got hit. Mechanically, Herrera's delivery is mostly sound but it has a small stab in the back and he can throw a little across his body at times. He commands his arsenal well and walked just 2.4 hitters per nine innings. The Yankees added Herrera to the 40-man roster this offseason to protect him from the Rule 5 Draft. He'll move to Triple-A Scranton/Wilkes-Barre in 2017.

Year	Club (League)	Class	W	L	ERA	G	GS	CG	SV	IP	H	HR	BB	SO	K/9	WHIP	AVG
2014	Beloit (MWL)	LoA	3	4	3.38	9	9	0	0	51	53	6	10	35	6.2	1.24	.272
	Fort Wayne (MWL)	LoA	3	5	4.26	17	16	0	0	82	93	5	15	47	5.1	1.31	.288
2015	Lake Elsinore (CAL)	HiA	5	6	3.88	18	17	0	0	102	100	6	28	69	6.1	1.25	.258
	San Antonio (TL)	AA	3	1	4.53	8	8	1	0	44	48	4	14	35	7.2	1.42	.276
2016	Scranton/W-B (IL)	AAA	0	1	9.00	1	1	0	0	5	7	1	3	8	14.4	2.00	.333
	Trenton (EL)	AA	10	7	3.75	23	23	0	0	132	131	9	35	123	8.4	1.26	.258
Minor League Totals			33	32	3.83	106	98	2	0	552	584	35	138	427	7.0	1.31	.272

28 JONATHAN HOLDER, RHP

BA GRADE
45 Risk: **High**

Born: June 9, 1993. **B-T:** R-R. **Ht.:** 6-2. **Wt.:** 235. **Drafted:** Mississippi State, 2014. (6th round). **Signed by:** Andy Cannizaro.

Holder was teammates at Mississippi State with lefthander Jacob Lindgren, whom the Yankees selected with their first choice in 2014 but has since been designated for assignment and signed by the Braves. Holder was a closer in college but was used early in his professional career as a starter. He moved back to the bullpen in 2016 and had one of the more dominant seasons in the minors, including a game in which he struck out 12 in four innings, including 11 straight. Overall, Holder went 5-1, 1.65 with 101 strikeouts against just seven walks in 65.1 minor league innings. After initially not being on the Yankees' list for September callups, the team reversed course and he made his debut Sept. 2. Unlike most reliev-ers, Holder uses a four-pitch arsenal that includes a fastball that tops out at 94 mph and a cutter in the high-80s with sharp bite. He supplements his fastballs with a mid-70s curveball he uses to get swings and misses and a seldom-thrown changeup in the mid-80s. His repertoire has given the Yankees thoughts of returning him to the rotation, but he could battle for a spot in the big league bullpen.

Year	Club (League)	Class	W	L	ERA	G	GS	CG	SV	IP	H	HR	BB	SO	K/9	WHIP	AVG
2014	Yankees2 (GCL)	R	1	1	12.27	2	1	0	0	4	7	0	3	4	9.8	2.73	.438
	Staten Island (NYP)	SS	1	2	3.03	10	7	0	0	33	35	1	10	30	8.3	1.38	.285
2015	Yankees2 (GCL)	R	0	0	1.00	3	3	0	0	9	5	0	0	8	8.0	0.56	.156
	Tampa (FSL)	HiA	7	5	2.44	19	18	1	0	103	92	3	21	78	6.8	1.09	.234
	Scranton/W-B (IL)	AAA	0	1	6.35	1	0	0	0	6	4	1	4	4	6.4	1.41	.200
2016	Tampa (FSL)	HiA	0	0	0.00	2	0	0	0	4	2	0	0	7	15.8	0.50	.154
	Trenton (EL)	AA	3	1	2.20	28	0	0	10	41	27	2	7	59	13.0	0.83	.188
	Scranton/W-B (IL)	AAA	2	0	0.89	12	0	0	6	20	7	1	0	35	15.5	0.34	.103
	New York (AL)	MAJ	0	0	5.40	8	0	0	0	8	8	1	4	5	5.4	1.44	.258
Major League Totals			0	0	5.40	8	0	0	0	8	8	1	4	5	5.4	1.44	.258
Minor League Totals			14	10	2.50	77	29	1	16	220	179	8	45	225	9.2	1.02	.221

29 WILKERMAN GARCIA, SS

BA GRADE
50 Risk: Extreme

Born: April 1, 1998. **B-T:** B-R. **Ht.:** 6-0. **Wt.:** 184. **Signed:** Venezuela, 2014.
Signed by: Esteban Castillo.

The first season away from the complex leagues did not go well for Garcia, who ranked as the No. 7 international prospect in 2014 and was part of the Yankees' $30 million haul that summer. The Yankees liked Garcia's feel to hit from both sides of the plate and his advanced discipline for his age. He missed out on a full-season assignment to begin this year because of a shoulder injury from spring training, then struggled as one of the younger players in the Rookie-level Appalachian League. He hit .198/.255/.284 with Pulaski and managed 14 extra-base hits in 54 games. Scouts inside and outside of the organization still believe in Garcia's ability to be an average hitter as he matures, albeit without much power. He's a polished defender with an arm that some rate as just average while others have seen it flash above-average. He's an average runner, and scouts who saw him this year think he might have to move to second base. The Yankees could continue with an aggressive track for Garcia and assign him to low Class A Charleston, but another year in extended spring training followed by short-season Staten Island is a likely path as well.

Year	Club (League)	Class	AVG	G	AB	R	H	2B	3B	HR	RBI	BB	SO	SB	CS	OBP	SLG
2015	Yankees1 (DSL)	R	.667	2	6	3	4	0	0	0	1	1	0	5	1	.750	.667
	Yankees1 (GCL)	R	.281	37	121	20	34	6	1	0	18	24	19	6	8	.396	.314
2016	Pulaski (APP)	R	.198	54	222	21	44	10	3	1	13	15	44	4	5	.255	.284
Minor League Totals			.235	93	349	44	82	16	4	1	32	40	63	15	14	.318	.312

30 THAIRO ESTRADA, 2B

BA GRADE
45 Risk: High

Born: Feb 22, 1996. **B-T:** R-R. **Ht.:** 5-10. **Wt.:** 155. **Signed:** Venezuela, 2012.
Signed by: Alan Atacho/Ricardo Finol.

Estrada was signed for just $49,000 in 2012 as part of a larger international class that also included shortstop Jorge Mateo and catcher Luis Torrens. Estrada has moved relatively quickly, reaching A-ball as a 20-year-old for the first time in 2016 and spending the bulk of his season at high Class A Tampa. He played mostly second and third base with Tampa in deference to shortstops Jorge Mateo and Gleyber Torres. The Yankees see Estrada as a second baseman in the long-term because he lacks the range for shortstop. He has a plus arm, however, and saw time at third base as well. He is a plus runner who can get from home to first base in 4.2 seconds, but needs to refine his base-stealing techniques. He is more of a contact hitter than a power threat, but he has improved his body as he's grown and shed fat from his teenage years. As that process continues, the Yankees believe Estrada could develop into a double-digit home run threat. He's likely to begin 2017 in Double-A Trenton with Torres, Mateo and Miguel Andujar.

Year	Club (League)	Class	AVG	G	AB	R	H	2B	3B	HR	RBI	BB	SO	SB	CS	OBP	SLG
2014	Staten Island (NYP)	SS	.271	17	59	11	16	1	0	0	2	6	7	8	1	.348	.288
	Yankees1 (GCL)	R	.273	6	22	2	6	2	0	0	4	1	4	0	0	.304	.364
2015	Staten Island (NYP)	SS	.267	63	247	37	66	17	0	2	23	23	30	8	13	.338	.360
2016	Charleston (SAL)	LoA	.286	35	140	11	40	3	1	5	19	8	21	11	3	.324	.429
	Tampa (FSL)	HiA	.292	83	315	52	92	15	1	3	30	29	46	7	5	.355	.375
Minor League Totals			.281	254	959	141	269	49	7	12	95	79	138	41	17	.344	.384

Oakland Athletics

BY VINCE LARA-CINISOMO

The Athletics knew entering 2016 they were likely not going to contend in the tough American League West. The A's did, however, expect to be competitive, but even that did not happen.

Ace righthander Sonny Gray struggled, with no obvious underlying cause, and lefthander Rich Hill missed a month because of a blister, short-circuiting the rotation.

A lineup that has lacked power and explosiveness since the trade of Josh Donaldson to the Blue Jays never picked up steam and wound up ranking last in the AL in runs.  (Two years ago, Oakland ranked third.) So when a promising 10-7 start turned into a 19-26 record in late May, it was time to start thinking about the future.

Under Billy Beane, the A's have always been aggressive when it comes to turning the page. They packaged Hill and pending free agent outfielder Josh Reddick to the Dodgers for three righthanders: Jharel Cotton, Grant Holmes and Frankie Montas. The A's have high expectations for all three, and Cotton received a September callup.

The arrival of those players accompanied other promising developments. Lefthander Sean Manaea, acquired from the Royals in 2015 for Ben Zobrist, reached the majors and more than held his own, going 7-9, 3.86 with 124 strikeouts in 144.1 innings. He was especially good in the second half, going 4-4, 2.67, and his WHIP (1.02), strikeout rate (8.0 per nine innings) and walk-to-strikeout ratio (4.1) all improved.

Cotton, Manaea, Gray (unless he's traded) and Kendall Graveman give the rotation a sturdy, young nucleus.

Oakland needs immediate offensive help and got some in the second half from Ryon Healy. While his defense at third base remains a question, he made his presence felt after being recalled from Triple-A Nashville. He won AL rookie of the month honors for September. He could form an offensive core with shortstop Marcus Semien, who had a breakout season with 27 homers, and left fielder Khris Davis, who became the first Oakland player to hit 40 homers since Jason Giambi in 2000.

Additional lineup help should be on the way. Top prospect Franklin Barreto might not remain at shortstop, but he'll hit his way to the majors, perhaps as soon as late 2017 after finishing the 2016 season at Nashville. Third baseman Matt Chapman ranked third in the minors with 36 homers in 2016.

BILL MITCHELL

Sean Manaea provides a power arm for the front of the Athletics' big league rotation

TOP PROSPECTS OF THE DECADE

Year	Player, Pos.	2016 Org
2007	Travis Buck, of	Did not play
2008	Daric Barton, 1b	Mexican League
2009	Brett Anderson, lhp	Dodgers
2010	Chris Carter, 1b/of	Brewers
2011	Grant Green, ss	Giants
2012	Jarrod Parker, rhp	Athletics
2013	Addison Russell, ss	Cubs
2014	Addison Russell, ss	Cubs
2015	Daniel Robertson, ss	Rays
2016	Franklin Barreto, ss	Athletics

The system added depth with a 2016 draft class that focused on college arms, including former Florida roommates A.J. Puk and Logan Shore as well as California righthander Daulton Jefferies. Puk ranked No. 1 in Baseball America's predraft rankings before sliding to Oakland at No. 6 overall. Jefferies (supplemental first round) and catcher Sean Murphy (third round) fell due to spring injuries.

On the international front, the A's were uncharacteristically aggressive. They signed Cuban Lazaro Armenteros for $3 million and gave seven-figure deals to Dominican shortstops Marcus Brito and Yerdel Vargas.

Who will still be in Oakland when some of those players graduate to the majors depends on which pieces the A's hold on to going forward.

ORGANIZATION OVERVIEW

President: Billy Beane. **GM:** David Forst. **Farm Director:** Keith Lieppman. **Scouting Director:** Eric Kubota.

Class	Team	League	W	L	PCT	Finish	Manager
Majors	Oakland Athletics	American	69	93	.426	13th (15)	Bob Melvin
Triple-A	Nashville Sounds	Pacific Coast	83	59	.585	1st (16)	Steve Scarsone
Double-A	Midland RockHounds	Texas	78	62	.557	2nd (8)	Ryan Christenson
High Class A	Stockton Ports	California	60	80	.429	t-8th (10)	Rick Magnante
Low Class A	Beloit Snappers	Midwest	59	80	.424	15th (16)	Fran Riordan
Short-season	Vermont Lake Monsters	New York-Penn	28	48	.368	13th (14)	Aaron Nieckula
Rookie	AZL Athletics	Arizona	29	24	.547	6th (14)	Webster Garrison
Overall 2016 Minor League Record			337	353	.488	18th (30)	

THIS YEAR'S TOP 30

No.	Player, Pos.	Grade/Risk
1	Franklin Barreto, ss/2b	60/High
2	A.J. Puk, lhp	60/High
3	Matt Chapman, 3b	55/Medium
4	Jharel Cotton, rhp	55/Medium
5	Frankie Montas, rhp	55/High
6	Grant Holmes, rhp	55/High
7	Chad Pinder, ss/2b	45/Low
8	Daniel Gossett, rhp	50/Medium
9	Richie Martin, ss	50/High
10	Bruce Maxwell, c	45/Medium
11	Lazaro Armenteros, of	55/Extreme
12	Daulton Jeffries, rhp	55/Extreme
13	Logan Shore, rhp	50/High
14	Yairo Munoz, ss/3b	50/High
15	Heath Fillmyer, rhp	50/High
16	Dakota Chalmers, rhp	50/Extreme
17	Matt Olson, of/1b	45/High
18	Renato Nunez, 3b/of	45/High
19	Raul Alcantara, rhp	45/High
20	Sean Murphy, c	45/High
21	Joey Wendle, 2b	45/High
22	Max Schrock, 2b	45/High
23	Paul Blackburn, rhp	45/High
24	Jaycob Brugman, of	40/Medium
25	Oscar Tovar, rhp	45/Extreme
26	Bobby Wahl, rhp	40/High
27	Skylar Szynski, rhp	45/Extreme
28	Yerdel Vargas, ss	45/Extreme
29	Dillon Overton, lhp	40/High
30	James Naile, rhp	40/High

LAST YEAR'S TOP 30

No.	Player, Pos.	Status
1.	Franklin Barreto, ss	No. 1
2.	Sean Manaea, lhp	Majors
3.	Matt Chapman, 3b	No. 3
4.	Renato Nunez, 3b/1b	No. 18
5.	Richie Martin, ss	No. 9
6.	Matt Olson, 1b/of	No. 17
7.	Chad Pinder, ss	No. 7
8.	Dillon Overton, lhp	No. 29
9.	Casey Meisner, rhp	Dropped out
10.	Yairo Munoz, ss	No. 14
11.	Jacob Nottingham, c	(Brewers)
12.	Bubba Derby, rhp	(Brewers)
13.	Max Muncy, 1b/3b	Majors
14.	Sean Nolin, lhp	(Brewers)
15.	Rangel Ravelo, 1b	Dropped out
16.	Dakota Chalmers, rhp	No. 16
17.	Joey Wendle, 2b	No. 21
18.	Dylan Covey, rhp	Dropped out
19.	Raul Alcantara, rhp	No. 19
20.	Arnold Leon, rhp	(Korea)
21.	Ryan Dull, rhp	Majors
22.	Ryon Healy, 3b/1b	Majors
23.	Skye Bolt, of	Dropped out
24.	Daniel Mengden, rhp	Majors
25.	Heath Fillmyer, rhp	No. 15
26.	Daniel Gossett, rhp	No. 8
27.	Mikey White, ss/3b	Dropped out
28.	Dustin Driver, rhp	Dropped out
29.	Bobby Wahl, rhp	No. 26
30.	Jhonny Rodriguez, of	Dropped out

BEST TOOLS

Best Hitter for Average	Franklin Barreto
Best Power Hitter	Matt Chapman
Best Strike-Zone Discipline	Matt Olson
Fastest Baserunner	Jeremiah McCray
Best Athlete	Lazaro Armenteros
Best Fastball	Frankie Montas
Best Curveball	Grant Holmes
Best Slider	Frankie Montas
Best Changeup	Jharel Cotton
Best Control	Daniel Gossett
Best Defensive Catcher	Sean Murphy
Best Defensive Infielder	Matt Chapman
Best Infield Arm	Matt Chapman
Best Defensive Outfielder	Skye Bolt
Best Outfield Arm	Skye Bolt

PROJECTED 2020 LINEUP

Catcher	Bruce Maxwell
First Base	Ryon Healy
Second Base	Marcus Semien
Third Base	Matt Chapman
Shortstop	Richie Martin
Left Field	Khris Davis
Center Field	Franklin Barreto
Right Field	Matt Olson
Designated Hitter	Renato Nunez
No. 1 Starter	Sonny Gray
No. 2 Starter	Sean Manaea
No. 3 Starter	A.J. Puk
No. 4 Starter	Jharel Cotton
No. 5 Starter	Grant Holmes
Closer	Frankie Montas

MINOR LEAGUE DEPTH CHART

OAKLAND ATHLETICS

TOP 2017 ROOKIE: Jharel Cotton, rhp. Cotton was outstanding in a late-season audition and figures to be in the big league rotation when the team breaks camp.

BREAKOUT PROSPECT: Lazaro Armenteros, of. The Cuban, just 17, was one of the best players on the island at the time he left. He's very raw but already the most athletic player in the system.

SOURCE OF TOP 30 TALENT			
Homegrown	22	Acquired	8
College	13	Trades	8
Junior college	1	Rule 5 draft	0
High school	3	Independent leagues	0
Nondrafted free agents	0	Free agents/waivers	0
International	5		

SLEEPER: Brandon Bailey, rhp. The sixth-round pick from Gonzaga is just 5-foot-10, but has polish, a solid delivery and projects to have above-average command.

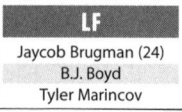

LF
Jaycob Brugman (24)
B.J. Boyd
Tyler Marincov

CF
Skye Bolt
J.P. Sportman
JaVon Shelby
Tyler Ramirez

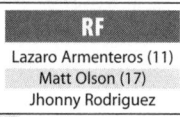

RF
Lazaro Armenteros (11)
Matt Olson (17)
Jhonny Rodriguez

3B
Matt Chapman (3)
Yairo Munoz (14)

SS
Richie Martin (9)
Yerdel Vargas (28)
Mikey White
Marcus Brito
Eli White
George Bell

2B
Franklin Barreto (1)
Chad Pinder (7)
Joey Wendle (21)
Max Schrock (22)
Trace Loehr

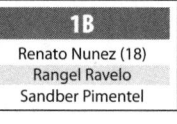

1B
Renato Nunez (18)
Rangel Ravelo
Sandber Pimentel

C
Bruce Maxwell (10)
Sean Murphy (20)
Beau Taylor
Argenis Raga

LHP

LHSP	LHRP
A.J. Puk (2)	Cody Stull
Dillon Overton (29)	Jared Lyons
Evan Manarino	Mike Fagan
Chris Kohler	Will Gilbert
Ivan Andueza	Dalton Sawyer
Kevin Duchene	

RHP

RHSP	RHRP
Jharel Cotton (4)	Frankie Montas (5)
Grant Holmes (6)	Bobby Wahl (26)
Daniel Gossett (8)	Trey Cochran-Gill
Daulton Jefferies (12)	Aaron Kurcz
Logan Shore (13)	Casey Meisner
Heath Fillmyer (15)	
Dakota Chalmers (16)	
Raul Alcantara (19)	
Paul Blackburn (23)	
Oscar Tovar (25)	
Skylar Szynski (27)	
James Naile (30)	
Brett Graves	
Boomer Biegalski	
Angel Duno	
Brandon Bailey	

DRAFT ANALYSIS

2016

BEST PURE HITTER: 2B Nate Mondou (13) has a fairly mature plate approach and present strength that helped him bat .298/.375/.364 at short-season Vermont.

BEST POWER HITTER: 2B/3B Javon Shelby (5) struggled with contact in the spring and after signing, but his plus raw power is real. He's giving center field a try in instructionalleague as well.

FASTEST RUNNER: OF Jeremiah McCray (25) is a true 70 runner; five of his 23 hits in his debut in the Rookie-level Arizona League were triples.

BEST DEFENSIVE PLAYER: C Sean Murphy (3) has plenty of strength at 6-foot-3, 220 pounds, and was the best defensive catcher in the draft. He's a potential plus defender with a plus arm, good hands and agility who just needs more polish. SS Eli White (11) has the athletic ability and arm to stick at shortstop, but his focus wanders at times.

BEST FASTBALL: LHP A.J. Puk (1) was in play to go No. 1 overall before falling to the A's at No. 6 overall. The A's didn't think he'd be there for them until draft day arrived and he started falling. His 95-97 mph fastball and the leverage he gets on it at 6-foot-7, 220 pounds, makes him tough to square up and elevate. He'll have to locate it better and more consistently as a pro.

BEST SECONDARY PITCH: RHPs Daulton Jefferies (1s) and Logan Shore (2) both have plus changeups at least, with Jefferies getting some 70 grades from scouts. Early in the year, the A's were evaluating whether he would fit at No. 6, but an injury helped push them to their second pick, No. 37.

BEST PRO DEBUT: White struck out a lot but hit .279/.348/.368 with 12 stolen bases, mostly with Vermont. RHP Brandon Bailey (6) went 3-1, 3.08 with 42-9 strikeouts-walk rate with Vermont. He's got a solid-average slider and above-average change-up to go with a low-90s fastball but stands just 5-foot-10. Already 23, 5-foot-8 2B Josh Vidales (28) hit .345/.437/.507 as he led the Rookie-level Arizona League in batting and on-base percentage.

BEST ATHLETE: McCray is smaller than White but with more speed, while White has lean, angular athleticism that will keep him in the dirt.

MOST INTRIGUING BACKGROUND: Shelby's father John spent parts of 11 seasons in the majors, and he has two older brothers who have played pro ball. RHP Mitchell Jordan (10) in 2015 tied the Cape Cod League record for lowest ERA with a 0.21 mark; he shares the record with ex-big leaguer Eric Milton. Shore and Puk were college roommates at Florida.

CLOSEST TO THE MAJORS: Puk gets the edge over the more-polished Jefferies and Shore because he could wind up moving quickly as a reliever. Oakland has no plans to put him in the bullpen at this time.

BEST LATE-ROUND PICK: White qualifies, as does RHP Nolan Blackwood (14), a low-slot reliever out of Memphis who competes with a fastball-slider combo.

THE ONE WHO GOT AWAY: Hard-throwing RHP Brigham Hill (20) returned to Texas A&M for his junior season after pitching his way into the Aggies' rotation during the spring.

2015

SS Richie Martin (1) finished the year in Double-A, but his bat needs to catch up to his glove. RHP Dakota Chalmers (3) is a long-play project, while RHP James Naile (20) finished the year in the Double-A playoffs. Oakland used RHP Bubba Derby (6) to acquire Khris Davis.

GRADE: C.

2014

3B Matt Chapman (1) has impressed with his power and defense so far. RHPs Heath Fillmyer (5) and Daniel Gossett (2) made significant strides in 2016. RHP Brandon McCurry (22) was traded for Jed Lowrie last offseason and has reached Triple-A.

GRADE: C

2013

OF Billy McKinney (1), now a Yankee, has been traded twice, in deals for Jon Lester and Aroldis Chapman. 3B Ryon Healy (3) powered his way to the big leagues, and 2B/SS Chad Pinder (2s) joined him in August. LHP Dillon Overton (2) also reached Oakland but had a terrible debut.

GRADE: B

TOP DRAFT PICKS OF THE DECADE

Year	Player, Pos.	2016 Org
2007	James Simmons, rhp	Atlantic League
2008	Jemile Weeks, 2b	Padres
2009	Grant Green, ss	Giants
2010	Michael Choice, of	Indians
2011	Sonny Gray, rhp	Athletics
2012	Addison Russell, ss	Cubs
2013	Billy McKinney, of	Yankees
2014	Matt Chapman, 3b	Athletics
2015	Richie Martin, ss	Athletics
2016	A.J. Puk,lhp	Athletics

LARGEST BONUSES IN CLUB HISTORY

Michael Ynoa, 2008	$4,250,000
A.J. Puk, 2016	$4,069,200
Mark Mulder, 1998	$3,200,000
Grant Green, 2009	$2,750,000
Addison Russell, 2012	$2,625,000

1 FRANKLIN BARRETO, SS/2B

Born: Feb. 27, 1996. **B-T:** R-R. **Ht.:** 5-9. **Wt.:** 175.
Signed: Venezuela, 2012.
Signed by: Ismael Cruz/Luis Marquez (Blue Jays)

The Athletics were long enamored of Barreto. They scouted him at age 14 when he starred for Venezuela in the Pan Am Games. They and other teams regarded him as the top international prospect in 2012, and he signed with the Blue Jays for $1.45 million. When the A's decided to move Josh Donaldson in the winter of 2014, they targeted Barreto as part of the exchange they sought from Toronto. Two years later, the Blue Jays have made consecutive trips to the playoffs with 2015 MVP Donaldson, while Barreto remains the key part of the deal for Oakland. Sean Nolin and Brett Lawrie have moved on, while Kendall Graveman led the big league club in innings and wins in 2016. The second-youngest player in the Texas League on Opening Day, Barreto ranked sixth in the TL in batting (.281) and third and steals (30), then finished the season at Triple-A Nashville, which included an 8-for-19 showing in the Pacific Coast League playoffs.

Barreto began the season slowly and turned things around in the second half. Scouts said he felt pressure to move quickly and wanted to get off to a good start, so he swung too often at pitches outside the zone. After expanding the strike zone too much in the first half, Barreto did a better job of controlling the zone and turning on pitches he can drive. A line-drive hitter with a low-maintenance swing, he has no problem catching up to high velocity. He has above-average bat speed, but his power projection might be limited because of his up-the-middle approach. His swing seems more geared for doubles and triples, though he can ride the ball out if he catches it right. Just 20, Barreto has already begun to thicken through his trunk and legs, and while he's still a plus runner, he was a burner when he signed. He matured quickly, which accounts for some strength gains, though he retains his quick-twitch ability. At shortstop, Barreto is an average defender. His arm grades as average, with some evaluators expressing concern about the firmness and accuracy of his throws from the left side. At second base, he is an above-average defender, with the shorter throw less of a concern. He also played center field in winter ball in the Venezuelan League in 2015, though he played shortstop and second base in the 2016 Arizona Fall League. His baseball instincts receive high marks.

BA GRADE

60 Risk: High

SCOUTING GRADES

Batting: 60.
Power: 50.
Defense: 50
Arm: 50
Speed: 55

Based on 20-80 scouting scale and future projection rather than present grades.

MIKE JANES

The A's have the luxury of a shortstop surplus. Major leaguer Marcus Semien is just 25 but has faced defensive challenges; Chad Pinder is a better defender than Barreto; Yairo Munoz is toolsy and fits at third base; and 2015 first-rounder Richie Martin has the best glove of the bunch. While center field remains an option, second base is Barreto's most likely short-term path to Oakland, with injury-prone incumbent Jed Lowrie entering the final season of his contract in 2017. Wherever Barreto ends up defensively, it's his bat that will do the heavy lifting. He will begin the 2017 season back at Triple-A, but he probably will make his big league debut at some point during the season.

Year	Club (League)	Class	AVG	G	AB	R	H	2B	3B	HR	RBI	BB	SO	SB	CS	OBP	SLG
2014	Vancouver (NWL)	SS	.311	73	289	65	90	23	4	6	61	26	64	29	5	.384	.481
2015	Stockton (CAL)	HiA	.302	90	338	50	102	22	3	13	47	15	67	8	3	.333	.500
2016	Midland (TL)	AA	.281	119	462	63	130	25	3	10	50	30	90	30	15	.340	.413
	Nashville (PCL)	AAA	.353	4	17	2	6	0	1	1	3	0	4	0	2	.389	.647
Minor League Totals			.293	345	1334	214	391	91	18	34	187	92	281	77	31	.349	.465

2 A.J. PUK, LHP

Born: April 25, 1995. **B-T:** L-L. **Ht.:** 6-7. **Wt.:** 220. **Drafted:** Florida, 2016 (1st round). **Signed by:** Trevor Schaffer.

Puk ranked No. 85 on the BA 500 out of an Iowa high school, but the Florida commit wasn't drafted until the 35th round by the Tigers. He ranked second in Division I as a sophomore with 12 strikeouts per nine innings and entered 2016 as the No. 1 prospect for the draft but dropped to the Athletics with the No. 6 pick after an inconsistent spring. Puk's $4,069,200 bonus is the largest for a draft pick in Oakland history. Puk leverages his size to get great extension on all of his pitches. His fastball touched 98 mph in 2016 with great downhill angle. Puk's long levers and relative lack of athleticism make it difficult at times for him to keep his torso over his front side consistently, and his inability to repeat his delivery gives him below-average command. A head-whack finish further complicates his delivery. A's coaches moved him to the first-base side of the rubber to help square him to the plate. Puk threw his changeup more often in his pro debut at short-season Vermont, but his slider lacked the bite and feel of its plus reputation in college. When he throws online to the plate, Puk is difficult to square up and shows a ceiling of a front-end starter, but he must become more efficient with his pitches and more consistent with his command. At worst, he could become a dominating high-leverage reliever.

BA GRADE
60 Risk: High

Year	Club (League)	Class	W	L	ERA	G	GS	CG	SV	IP	H	HR	BB	SO	K/9	WHIP	AVG
2016	Vermont (NYP)	SS	0	4	3.03	10	10	0	0	33	23	0	12	40	11.0	1.07	.185
Minor League Totals			0	4	3.03	10	10	0	0	33	23	0	12	40	11.0	1.07	.185

3 MATT CHAPMAN, 3B

Born: April 28, 1993. **B-T:** R-R. **Ht.:** 6-2. **Wt.:** 205. **Drafted:** Cal State Fullerton, 2014 (1st round). **Signed by:** Eric Martins.

A knee injury and then a wrist injury that eventually necessitated surgery truncated Chapman's first full season. But fully healthy in 2016, he blasted 36 homers at Double-A Midland and Triple-A Nashville, ranking third overall in the minors. In 2015, Chapman reworked his swing with high Class A Stockton hitting coach Brian McArn to tap into his power, and it has worked, with 59 homers the last two seasons. Chapman was more of a gap-to-gap hitter in college, but he has moved his hands back a little and found a consistent spot to start and trigger his swing. He has above-average raw power and can drive the ball out to all fields. His swing retains some rigidity and length, so he'll strike out a lot and is a below-average hitter. He has solid average pitch recognition and draws walks. Chapman showcases at least 70 arm strength with carry on the 20-80 scouting scale. He projects to be a plus defender at third base. While the A's have other third-base options such as Healy and Renato Nunez, Chapman is the best defender of the group. He likely will return to Triple-A Nashville to start 2017, but once ready he should push Healy off the hot corner in Oakland.

BA GRADE
55 Risk: Medium

Year	Club (League)	Class	AVG	G	AB	R	H	2B	3B	HR	RBI	BB	SO	SB	CS	OBP	SLG
2014	Athletics (AZL)	R	.429	3	14	1	6	1	1	0	0	1	1	0	0	.467	.643
	Beloit (MWL)	LoA	.237	50	190	22	45	8	3	5	20	7	46	2	1	.282	.389
	Midland (TL)	AA	.000	1	3	0	0	0	0	0	0	0	0	0	0	.000	.000
2015	Stockton (CAL)	HiA	.250	80	304	60	76	21	3	23	57	39	79	4	1	.341	.566
2016	Midland (TL)	AA	.244	117	438	78	107	26	4	29	83	59	147	7	4	.335	.521
	Nashville (PCL)	AAA	.197	18	76	14	15	1	1	7	13	9	26	0	0	.282	.513
Minor League Totals			.243	269	1025	175	249	57	12	64	173	115	299	13	6	.325	.509

4 JHAREL COTTON, RHP

Born: Jan. 19, 1992. **B-T:** R-R. **Ht.:** 5-11. **Wt.:** 190. **Drafted:** East Carolina, 2012 (20th round). **Signed by:** Clair Rierson (Dodgers).

The Virgin Islands native played high school baseball in Virginia, then played at Miami-Dade JC. He spurned the Mets in 2011 as a 28th-rounder before signing as a 20th-rounder with the Dodgers after a year at East Carolina. Oakland acquired him (with righthanders Frankie Montas and Grant Holmes) on Aug. 1 while dealing Rich Hill and Josh Reddick to the Dodgers. Cotton led the Pacific Coast League with 155 strikeouts, a 1.08 WHIP and .214 opponent average. Cotton's best weapon is his double-plus 77 mph changeup, which has screwball action. His command of his fastball improved in 2016, and the 92-93 mph pitch can touch

BA GRADE
55 Risk: Medium

96. He also throws two-seamers and cutters that give hitters different looks, and they all come out of the same release point. His delivery is not something pitching coaches would teach, but it works for him, and his athleticism belies his 5-foot-11 frame. Cotton mixes in a slider and curveball. Having succeeded as a September callup, Cotton will open spring training with a tentative spot in the big league rotation. He projects as a back-end starter if not a bit more.

Year	Club (League)	Class	W	L	ERA	G	GS	CG	SV	IP	H	HR	BB	SO	K/9	WHIP	AVG
2014	R. Cucamonga (CAL)	HiA	6	10	4.05	25	20	1	0	127	113	18	34	138	9.8	1.16	.239
2015	Great Lakes (MWL)	LoA	0	0	5.40	1	1	0	0	3	4	0	1	6	16.2	1.50	.286
	R. Cucamonga (CAL)	HiA	1	0	1.61	4	2	0	0	22	14	1	7	28	11.3	0.94	.182
	Tulsa (TL)	AA	5	2	2.30	11	8	0	0	63	49	4	21	71	10.2	1.12	.221
	Oklahoma City (PCL)	AAA	0	0	4.91	5	0	0	0	7	9	0	2	9	11.0	1.50	.321
2016	Oklahoma City (PCL)	AAA	8	5	4.90	22	16	1	0	97	80	17	32	119	11.0	1.15	.249
	Nashville (PCL)	AAA	3	1	2.82	6	6	1	0	38	28	3	7	36	8.5	0.91	.201
	Oakland (AL)	MAJ	2	0	2.15	5	5	0	0	29	20	4	4	23	7.1	0.82	.185
Major League Totals			2	0	2.15	5	5	0	0	29	20	4	4	23	7.1	0.82	.185
Minor League Totals			26	25	3.68	100	65	4	0	447	367	47	130	499	10.0	1.11	.223

5 FRANKIE MONTAS, RHP

Born: March 21, 1993. **B-T:** R-R. **Ht.:** 6-2. **Wt.:** 255. **Signed:** Dominican Republic, 2009. **Signed by:** Manny Nanita (Red Sox)

Originally signed by the Red Sox, Montas has been traded three times, twice since last December. He went from the White Sox to the Dodgers after the 2015 season as part of the three-team trade involving Todd Frazier and Trayce Thompson, then joined Oakland as part of the return for lefthander Rich Hill and outfielder Josh Reddick. A broken rib that followed offseason rib surgery curtailed Montas in 2016. Evaluators of any stripe come away impressed with Montas' easy velocity. He hit triple digits in the Arizona Fall League in 2016 and paired that with a power slider at 90 mph with good depth that projects as an above-average pitch.

BA GRADE

55 Risk: High

He uses his changeup sparingly, but evaluators believe it eventually could be an average pitch, and the A's are pushing him to throw it more. Montas is thick but surprisingly athletic for his size, and his mound presence and poise grade as plus. The A's will continue using Montas in the rotation, and 86 of his 106 pro appearances have been as a starter. His physicality, velocity and pitch mix could still succeed in the rotation if his control improves, but his career walk rate of 3.8 per nine innings and spotty fastball command could push him to a relief role as soon as 2017.

Year	Club (League)	Class	W	L	ERA	G	GS	CG	SV	IP	H	HR	BB	SO	K/9	WHIP	AVG
2014	Winston-Salem (CAR)	HiA	4	0	1.60	10	10	1	0	62	45	2	14	56	8.1	0.95	.202
	White Sox (AZL)	R	1	0	1.29	4	4	0	0	14	6	1	7	23	14.8	0.93	.128
	Birmingham (SL)	AA	0	0	0.00	1	1	0	0	5	1	0	1	1	1.8	0.40	.063
2015	Birmingham (SL)	AA	5	5	2.97	23	23	1	0	112	89	3	48	108	8.7	1.22	.219
	Chicago (AL)	MAJ	0	2	4.80	7	2	0	0	15	14	1	9	20	12.0	1.53	.246
2016	Tulsa (TL)	AA	0	0	1.93	3	1	0	0	5	2	1	1	7	13.5	0.64	.133
	Oklahoma City (PCL)	AAA	0	0	2.38	4	3	0	0	11	12	0	2	15	11.9	1.24	.279
Major League Totals			0	2	4.80	7	2	0	0	15	14	1	9	20	12.0	1.53	.246
Minor League Totals			16	25	3.79	99	84	3	0	399	343	20	166	412	9.3	1.28	.232

6 GRANT HOLMES, RHP

Born: March 22, 1996. **B-T:** R-R. **Ht.:** 6-1. **Wt.:** 215. **Drafted:** HS—Conway, S.C., 2014 (1st round). **Signed by:** Lon Joyce (Dodgers).

The highest-drafted prep righthander ever from South Carolina—22nd overall—Holmes was drafted three spots ahead of Matt Chapman, Oakland's first pick in 2014. The A's acquired Holmes from the Dodgers in the five-player deal that also yielded Jharel Cotton and Frankie Montas. Holmes pitched effectively early at high Class A Rancho Cucamonga, but after the trade he struggled with Stockton as he surpassed his previous career high for innings. Holmes has a power arm with a riding 92-95 mph fastball with tremendous sink that produces a well above-average groundball rate. His power curve at 80-83 mph gives him a strikeout pitch, and he can cut his

BA GRADE

55 Risk: High

fastball as well. His changeup has its moments and has a chance to be average but lefthanded hitters took advantage of its inconsistency, hitting .303 against him. Holmes is an above-average athlete but at times lands stiffly on his front leg and also has timing issues separating his hands and getting his arm in sync with the rest of his body. Holmes' delivery issues are correctable, and at 20 he was one of the youngest players in the California League. The A's may slow him down a bit and have him repeat high Class A in 2017, though his ceiling remains mid-rotation starter.

Year	Club (League)	Class	W	L	ERA	G	GS	CG	SV	IP	H	HR	BB	SO	K/9	WHIP	AVG
2014	Dodgers (AZL)	R	1	2	3.00	7	6	0	0	30	20	2	7	33	9.9	0.90	.187
	Ogden (PIO)	R	1	1	4.91	4	4	0	0	18	19	1	6	25	12.3	1.36	.271
2015	Great Lakes (MWL)	LoA	6	4	3.14	24	24	0	0	103	86	6	54	117	10.2	1.35	.229
2016	R. Cucamonga (CAL)	HiA	8	4	4.02	20	18	0	1	105	103	6	43	100	8.5	1.39	.254
	Stockton (CAL)	HiA	3	3	6.91	6	5	0	0	29	44	4	10	24	7.5	1.88	.355
Minor League Totals			19	14	3.94	61	57	0	1	286	272	19	120	299	9.4	1.37	.251

7 CHAD PINDER, SS/2B

Born: March 29, 1992. **B-T:** R-R. **Ht.:** 6-2. **Wt.:** 190. **Drafted:** Virginia Tech, 2013 (2nd round supplemental). **Signed by:** Neil Avent.

Pinder comes from a baseball family. His father played at Virginia Commonwealth and his younger brother Chase plays at Clemson. The Athletics have challenged Pinder since they drafted him 71st overall in 2013. They asked the former Virginia Tech third baseman to play second base in 2014, then shortstop in 2015 following the trades of Addison Russell and Daniel Robertson. Pinder held his own with each position switch and even won the Texas League MVP award at Double-A Midland in 2015. He started slowly at Triple-A Nashville in 2016, then rallied to make his major league debut. Pinder has fluid actions and an above-average arm that make

BA GRADE

50 Risk: Medium

him capable at shortstop and an asset at second or third base. His versatility is a major plus. At the plate, Pinder is an intelligent hitter with a solid plan, though his approach can be too aggressive for the Athletics' liking. He has a quick bat with average power and average feel to hit, and evaluators project he could hit 15-20 homers at his peak. He's a tick below-average runner. Pinder's defensive versatility and power potential make him a utility option in the big leagues for 2017. To be a regular, he'll have to win a battle with Joey Wendle and Jed Lowrie at second base.

Year	Club (League)	Class	AVG	G	AB	R	H	2B	3B	HR	RBI	BB	SO	SB	CS	OBP	SLG
2014	Stockton (CAL)	HiA	.288	94	403	61	116	32	5	13	55	22	99	12	9	.336	.489
2015	Midland (TL)	AA	.317	117	477	71	151	32	2	15	86	28	103	7	5	.361	.486
2016	Nashville (PCL)	AAA	.258	107	426	72	110	23	3	14	51	25	108	5	1	.310	.425
	Oakland (AL)	MAJ	.235	22	51	4	12	4	0	1	4	3	14	0	0	.273	.373
Major League Totals			.235	22	51	4	12	4	0	1	4	3	14	0	0	.273	.373
Minor League Totals			.280	360	1446	218	405	91	10	45	200	87	351	25	15	.331	.450

8 DANIEL GOSSETT, RHP

Born: Nov. 13, 1992. **B-T:** R-R. **Ht.:** 6-2. **Wt.:** 185. **Drafted:** Clemson, 2014 (2nd round). **Signed by:** Neil Avent.

A 16th-round pick out of a South Carolina high school in 2011, Gossett had high expectations at Clemson and mostly lived up to them—he went 23-9, 2.80— working with two big breaking balls and a fastball. Once the Athletics took him in the second round in 2014, they helped him develop a true slider and sharpened his curveball Gossett thrives with a four-pitch mix delivered with a short arm action and simplified delivery. His 90-95 mph fastball with glove-side run ticked up in 2016, and he locates down and away better. His soft-contact and strikeout rates improved while his walk rate stayed in line with career norms. He has worked with

BA GRADE

50 Risk: Medium

A's coaches to hone his slider, which has become a hard cutter, an 88-89 mph pitch that at times breaks straight down. His changeup drew the most swings and misses of any of his pitches, and he also mixes in a curveball. He earns high marks for his dedication, hard work and coachability. Gossett is on the fast track but should start 2017 back at Triple-A Nashville. Even with the infusion of pitching talent into the organization in 2016, Gossett ranks among the organization's best arms and could make his big league debut in 2017.

Year	Club (League)	Class	W	L	ERA	G	GS	CG	SV	IP	H	HR	BB	SO	K/9	WHIP	AVG
2014	Vermont (NYP)	SS	1	0	2.25	12	1	0	0	24	16	1	1	25	9.4	0.71	.188
2015	Beloit (MWL)	LoA	5	13	4.73	27	27	2	0	145	151	16	52	112	7.0	1.40	.270
2016	Stockton (CAL)	HiA	4	1	3.33	9	9	0	0	46	40	4	13	53	10.4	1.15	.225
	Midland (TL)	AA	5	5	2.49	16	16	0	0	94	75	4	25	94	9.0	1.06	.220
	Nashville (PCL)	AAA	1	0	1.98	2	2	0	0	14	10	0	3	4	2.6	0.95	.213
Minor League Totals			16	19	3.57	66	55	2	0	322	292	25	94	288	8.0	1.20	.241

9 RICHIE MARTIN, SS

Born: Dec. 22, 1994. **B-T:** R-R. **Ht.:** 6-0. **Wt.:** 192. **Drafted:** Florida, 2015 (1st round). **Signed by:** Trevor Schaffer.

Martin became the fourth of the record five college shortstops selected in the first round of the 2015 draft, and signed after helping Florida reach the College World Series that year. He's young for his draft class and played his first full season at age 21 in 2016, when he returned from a spring training injury that required surgery to repair a torn meniscus his left knee. Martin impressed the Athletics with his dedication and work in continuing to try and improve his all-around game. His range and quickness are quality traits, and his above-average arm is adequate for shortstop. He's athletic but not unnecessarily flashy at shortstop, with solid actions and mechanics and excellent footwork. Offensively, Martin has work to do, but the A's like his swing plane and bat speed. He has bat-to-ball skills, decent plate discipline and strength but hits for below-average power. He's an above-average runner even after the knee issue. Martin is part of a shortstop surplus for the A's, but he should be the best defender of a group that includes Franklin Barreto, Yairo Munoz and Chad Pinder. He likely will start 2017 back at Double-A Midland, and if his bat develops, he eventually could push Marcus Semien down the defensive spectrum.

BA GRADE
50 **Risk: High**

Year	Club (League)	Class	AVG	G	AB	R	H	2B	3B	HR	RBI	BB	SO	SB	CS	OBP	SLG
2015	Vermont (NYP)	SS	.237	51	190	31	45	6	4	2	16	25	47	7	7	.353	.342
2016	Stockton (CAL)	HiA	.230	86	330	46	76	14	2	3	31	36	73	12	8	.322	.312
	Midland (TL)	AA	.333	5	15	1	5	1	1	0	7	3	2	2	1	.444	.533
Minor League Totals			**.236**	**142**	**535**	**78**	**126**	**21**	**7**	**5**	**54**	**64**	**122**	**21**	**16**	**.337**	**.329**

10 BRUCE MAXWELL, C

Born: Dec. 20, 1990. **B-T:** L-R. **Ht:** 6-1. **Wt.:** 250. **Drafted:** Birmingham-Southern, 2012 (2nd round). **Signed by:** Kelcey Mucker.

When the A's took him with the 62nd overall pick in 2012, Maxwell became the highest-drafted Division III player since Jason Hirsh in 2003. Primarily a first baseman in college, Maxwell embraced catching as a pro with his characteristic enthusiasm. His improvement behind the plate prompted Oakland to call him up in July when Stephen Vogt took family medical leave. He stuck on the big league roster the rest of the season. Maxwell has an above-average throwing arm, with improved accuracy, and pitchers praise his framing skills. He threw out 39 percent of basestealers at Triple-A Nashville in 2016, though he went 0-for-8 in the majors. Maxwell has soft hands and does a good job keeping pitches in front of him—a vast improvement from 2012, when he had 18 passed balls in 38 games. At the plate, Maxwell has plenty of strength, and his lefthanded swing takes a good plane through the zone. He has enough bat speed and selectivity, and he started to produce solid power numbers in 2016. He's a below-average, base-clogging runner. Vogt has been a fine bat-first catcher at a low price for Oakland, and Maxwell could at least compete with Josh Phegley as the big league backup. He's the most likely in-house replacement option for Vogt.

BA GRADE
45 **Risk: Medium**

Year	Club (League)	Class	AVG	G	AB	R	H	2B	3B	HR	RBI	BB	SO	SB	CS	OBP	SLG
2014	Stockton (CAL)	HiA	.273	79	289	33	79	11	1	6	35	41	58	0	1	.365	.381
	Midland (TL)	AA	.141	25	85	8	12	3	0	0	2	9	32	0	1	.223	.176
2015	Midland (TL)	AA	.243	96	338	32	82	16	0	2	48	39	54	0	1	.321	.308
2016	Nashville (PCL)	AAA	.321	60	193	27	62	12	0	10	41	24	38	1	0	.393	.539
	Oakland (AL)	MAJ	.283	33	92	8	26	6	1	1	14	8	24	0	0	.337	.402
Major League Totals			**.283**	**33**	**92**	**8**	**26**	**6**	**1**	**1**	**14**	**8**	**24**	**0**	**0**	**.337**	**.402**
Minor League Totals			**.266**	**431**	**1528**	**174**	**407**	**82**	**1**	**25**	**201**	**187**	**283**	**2**	**3**	**.346**	**.370**

11 LAZARO ARMENTEROS, OF

BA GRADE
55 **Risk: Extreme**

Born: May 22, 1999. **B-T:** R-R. **Ht.:** 6-0. **Wt.:** 182. **Signed:** Cuba, 2016. **Signed by:** Juan De La Cruz.

Armenteros, one of the best players in his age group at the time he left Cuba in the spring of 2015, signed for $3 million during the July 2 signing period. He played for Cuba's youth national team in August 2014 at the 15U World Cup, where he hit .462/.611/.962 with 10 walks and eight strikeouts in 36 plate appearances. Just 17, Armenteros has a strong, physical build with a combination of plus raw power and speed. One evaluator said Armenteros had the most gifted body of any 17-year-old he'd seen. But in brief looks in instructional league, Lazarito understandably looked raw and rusty. His swing had a tendency to get uphill, and he will have to develop an offensive approach. His arm, which was called plus prior to signing, was marked as just average by scouts who saw him in instructs, although that could be attributed to rust and poor mechanics. Armenteros is a long way off, but has at least average tools across the board. He is likely to start 2017 in extended spring training before starting his pro career in the Rookie-level Arizona League.

Year	Club (League)	Class	AVG	G	AB	R	H	2B	3B	HR	RBI	BB	SO	SB	CS	OBP	SLG
2016	Did not play																

12 DAULTON JEFFERIES, RHP

BA GRADE
55 Risk: Extreme

Born: Aug. 2, 1995. **B-T:** L-R. **Ht.:** 6-0. **Wt.:** 180. **Drafted:** California, 2016 (1st round supplemental). **Signed by:** Jermaine Clark.

The Northern California native was the third pitcher in five years drafted out of Buhach Colony High in Atwater. But like Brett Mooneyham (Stanford) and Dylan Floro (Cal State Fullerton), Jefferies went to college before going pro. He was expected to be one of the first pitchers off the board in the 2016 draft, but a shoulder injury sidelined him for eight weeks and pushed him down the board and to the A's at No. 37 overall. Not particularly big, Jefferies carries durability questions as he missed time as a sophomore as well. But he is a superb athlete with a quick arm and a plus changeup that bottoms out. At its best, it earns 70 grades. His fastball sits at 90-92 with good location, has touched 96 mph in the past, and he has a knack for the bottom of the strike zone. Scouts said his slider was below average at times and looks more like a cutter than slider. Jefferies draws comparisons from Jeremy Hellickson to Sonny Gray. If he stays healthy, he'll zoom through the system and could be an impact starter, but his durability track record is a major red flag.

Year	Club (League)	Class	W	L	ERA	G	GS	CG	SV	IP	H	HR	BB	SO	K/9	WHIP	AVG
2016	Athletics (AZL)	R	0	0	2.38	5	5	0	0	11	11	0	2	17	13.5	1.15	.262
Minor League Totals			0	0	2.38	5	5	0	0	11	11	0	2	17	13.5	1.15	.262

13 LOGAN SHORE, RHP

BA GRADE
50 Risk: High

Born: Dec. 28, 1994. **B-T:** R-R. **Ht.:** 6-2. **Wt.:** 215. **Drafted:** Florida, 2016 (2nd round). **Signed by:** Trevor Schaffer.

Shore was drafted in the 29th round in 2013 by the Twins out of high school, but instead went to Florida where he teamed with now organization-mate A.J. Puk. Shore was the more consistent pitcher at Florida than Puk, leading the Gators to two College World Series appearances in 2015 and '16. Shore has a changeup that grades as a plus pitch, with the rest of his stuff average across the board to go with potentially above-average command. In college Shore lived off his changeup and four-seamer, though he's not a power pitcher, generally sitting around 90 mph with his fastball. He does a great job locating the four-seamer and the A's are confident he will throw harder with more consistent fastball use. He showed a tight cutter at 84 mph, but his slider was below average and is the pitch the A's will work on with him most. Shore is described as studious, perhaps too much so as he tried to incorporate all he was taught rather than just trust his stuff and throw. His ceiling is as a back-of-the-rotation option who could move quickly, and he should pitch in the high Class A California League in 2017.

Year	Club (League)	Class	W	L	ERA	G	GS	CG	SV	IP	H	HR	BB	SO	K/9	WHIP	AVG
2016	Vermont (NYP)	SS	0	2	2.57	7	7	0	0	21	17	1	7	21	9.0	1.14	.207
Minor League Totals			0	2	2.57	7	7	0	0	21	17	1	7	21	9.0	1.14	.207

14 YAIRO MUNOZ, SS/3B

BA GRADE
50 Risk: High

Born: Jan. 23, 1995. **B-T:** R-R. **Ht.:** 6-1. **Wt.:** 165. **Signed:** Dominican Republic, 2012. **Signed by:** Amaurys Reyes.

Munoz signed for $280,000 in January 2012 and made his full-season debut in 2015. While he hit into 26 double plays that year, he also hit 13 homers and finished with a flourish in high Class A. The Athletics aggressively pushed him to Double-A Midland in 2016 at age 21, even after he spent time on the shelf with heel and foot issues in spring training, delaying his regular-season debut in late April. Munoz split time between shortstop, third base and second base at Midland in deference to both Franklin Barreto and Richie Martin, and he played third almost exclusively in the Arizona Fall League. His arm is a plus— among the best in the system—and he has good hands and range. His speed is average to a tick above, but his inconsistent focus and aptitude lead to sloppy play defensively and keep his speed from playing consistently on the bases. Munoz's pitch recognition and plate approach are subpar and short-circuit his average raw power. Scouts can dream on his tools, and because he was one of the youngest players in the

Texas League, he could repeat that level in 2017.

Year	Club (League)	Class	AVG	G	AB	R	H	2B	3B	HR	RBI	BB	SO	SB	CS	OBP	SLG
2014	Vermont (NYP)	SS	.298	66	252	29	75	17	3	5	20	7	42	14	6	.319	.448
2015	Beloit (MWL)	LoA	.236	97	369	48	87	14	3	9	48	22	62	10	2	.278	.363
	Stockton (CAL)	HiA	.320	39	150	21	48	12	0	4	26	11	20	1	1	.372	.480
2016	Midland (TL)	AA	.240	102	387	44	93	16	3	9	39	23	76	6	7	.286	.367
Minor League Totals			.256	361	1330	163	340	69	12	28	160	80	234	36	19	.301	.389

15 HEATH FILLMYER, RHP

BA GRADE

50 Risk: High

Born: May 16, 1994. **B-T:** R-R. **Ht.:** 6-1. **Wt.:** 180. **Drafted:** Mercer County (N.J.) JC, 2014 (5th round). **Signed by:** Ron Vaughn.

As a freshman at Mercer County (N.J.) JC, Fillmyer played shortstop and pitched just 7.2 innings, but that was enough to entice the Rockies to draft him in the 28th round as a pitcher. He passed on signing and decided to return to school and took the hint, moving to the mound full-time. He went 9-0, 0.68, drawing the attention of A's area scout Ron Vaughn and signing for $305,000 after being drafted in the fifth round in 2014. Fillmyer got knocked around in 2015, but in 2016 he put stuff and results together. The athletic righthander showed a much-improved changeup that now projects above average and improved command overall. His fastball is still an above-average pitch, working in the 92-96 mph range with good sink. Fillmyer has a much cleaner delivery with improved timing and tightened up the spin on his curveball, which projects as an average pitch. Fillmyer is solidly built and a good athlete on the mound. He missed the season's final week and Double-A Midland's playoff run because he had pitched a career-high 134 innings, which Oakland believed was enough. He should begin 2017 back at Double-A, with a promotion to Triple-A possible if he continues to progress.

Year	Club (League)	Class	W	L	ERA	G	GS	CG	SV	IP	H	HR	BB	SO	K/9	WHIP	AVG
2014	Athletics (AZL)	R	1	0	2.79	6	0	0	0	10	5	0	5	10	9.3	1.03	.147
2015	Beloit (MWL)	LoA	3	13	4.98	23	22	0	0	99	112	10	56	77	7.0	1.69	.297
2016	Stockton (CAL)	HiA	5	6	3.60	18	16	0	0	95	101	4	31	89	8.4	1.39	.264
	Midland (TL)	AA	2	0	2.54	8	8	1	0	39	31	3	8	29	6.7	1.00	.223
Minor League Totals			11	19	3.96	55	46	1	0	243	249	17	100	205	7.6	1.44	.267

16 DAKOTA CHALMERS, RHP

BA GRADE

50 Risk: Extreme

Born: Oct. 8, 1996. **B-T:** R-R. **Ht.:** 6-3. **Wt.:** 170. **Drafted:** HS—Cumming, Ga., 2015 (3rd round). **Signed by:** Jemel Spearman.

Chalmers was the top prep pitcher in Georgia in the 2015 draft and fell to the A's in third round. They pounced and gave him $1.2 million—twice the slot amount—and Chalmers rejected a Georgia scholarship to go pro. He opened the year in extended spring training before joining 2016 first-rounder A.J. Puk and supplemental pick Logan Shore in short-season Vermont's rotation. Chalmers can throw his 92-94 mph fastball for strikes and needs to improve the consistency of his changeup and curveball. He got 40 percent swings-and-misses on his 1-to-7 curveball but was landing it for strikes just half the time. The A's believe repetition will sharpen it up. His changeup, while too firm at times, flashes above-average with good arm speed and downward action. Chalmers has some moving parts in his delivery, such as a head whack, that complicate his ability to stay on line to home plate. His back knee also tends to collapse, and the A's will try to improve his tempo. Chalmers just turned 20 in October, so the A's won't rush him. He is likely to start 2017 in low Class A Beloit.

Year	Club (League)	Class	W	L	ERA	G	GS	CG	SV	IP	H	HR	BB	SO	K/9	WHIP	AVG
2015	Athletics (AZL)	R	0	1	2.66	11	11	0	0	20	15	0	17	18	8.0	1.57	.205
2016	Vermont (NYP)	SS	5	4	4.70	15	13	0	0	67	55	8	37	62	8.3	1.37	.217
Minor League Totals			5	5	4.23	26	24	0	0	87	70	8	54	80	8.2	1.42	.214

17 MATT OLSON, OF/1B

BA GRADE

45 Risk: High

Born: March 29, 1994. **B-T:** L-R. **Ht.:** 6-5. **Wt.:** 230. **Drafted:** HS—Lilburn, Ga., 2012 (1st round supplemental). **Signed by:** Matt Ranson.

The Athletics went heavy with high schoolers in 2012, drafting Addison Russell, Daniel Robertson and Olson, but only Olson remains in the organization. He made his big league debut in 2016 and is a classic Moneyball-era A's player, with plus raw power and a penchant for drawing walks to go with plenty of strikeouts. Still just 22, Olson has hit 34 home runs the last two seasons after ripping 37 in the high Class A California League in 2014, and his walk rate has diminished at upper levels while his strikeout rate has risen. A below-average hitter, he's been compared to the Orioles' Chris Davis for his power and patience, though he tends to do most of his damage to the pull side. Olson hit just .167 against lefthanders with only one homer and looks like a platoon player at this point. That said, Olson has excellent pitch recognition skills and is patient, almost to a fault. An above-average first baseman, Olson played the majority of his games in right field due to Oakland's surplus of corner infielders and is an average outfielder.

Year	Club (League)	Class	AVG	G	AB	R	H	2B	3B	HR	RBI	BB	SO	SB	CS	OBP	SLG
2014	Stockton (CAL)	HiA	.262	138	512	111	134	31	1	37	97	117	137	2	0	.404	.543
2015	Midland (TL)	AA	.249	133	466	82	116	37	0	17	75	105	139	5	1	.388	.438
2016	Nashville (PCL)	AAA	.235	131	464	69	109	34	1	17	60	71	132	1	0	.335	.422
	Oakland (AL)	MAJ	.095	11	21	3	2	1	0	0	0	7	4	0	0	.321	.143
Major League Totals			.095	11	21	3	2	1	0	0	0	7	4	0	0	.321	.143
Minor League Totals			.246	586	2111	363	520	150	3	103	370	384	606	12	4	.364	.467

18 RENATO NUNEZ, 3B/OF

BA GRADE 45 Risk: High

Born: April 4, 1994. **B-T:** R-R. **Ht.:** 6-1. **Wt.:** 200. **Signed:** Venezuela, 2010. **Signed by:** Julio Franco.

Nunez reached the majors in 2016, six years after being signed for $2.2 million. This is his seventh Prospect Handbook appearance, but he regressed overall on the season and faces a crossroads in his career. After a strong year at Double-A in which he cut his strikeout rate, Nunez struggled at Triple-A, in part because of a .249 average on balls in play. Still, Nunez has plus raw power, although it's mostly to his pull side, and has impact strength in his bat. But he's a below-average hitter, doesn't hit the ball to the middle or opposite field and doesn't make consistent contact. He's a below-average fielder at third base and moved to left field at Triple-A Nashville when Matt Chapman, a vastly superior defender, joined the roster. Meanwhile, Ryon Healy leapfrogged him to the big leagues. Nunez spent some time at first base in Double-A, and first and left may be his best and only paths to big league time in 2017.

Year	Club (League)	Class	AVG	G	AB	R	H	2B	3B	HR	RBI	BB	SO	SB	CS	OBP	SLG
2014	Stockton (CAL)	HiA	.279	124	509	75	142	28	3	29	96	34	113	2	0	.336	.517
2015	Midland (TL)	AA	.278	93	381	62	106	23	0	18	61	28	66	1	0	.332	.480
2016	Nashville (PCL)	AAA	.228	128	505	61	115	20	2	23	74	31	119	2	0	.278	.412
	Oakland (AL)	MAJ	.133	9	15	0	2	0	0	0	1	0	3	0	0	.133	.133
Major League Totals			.133	9	15	0	2	0	0	0	1	0	3	0	0	.133	.133
Minor League Totals			.265	568	2257	318	598	128	8	98	386	144	508	12	4	.317	.459

19 RAUL ALCANTARA, RHP

BA GRADE 45 Risk: High

Born: Dec. 4, 1992. **B-T:** R-R. **Ht.:** 6-3. **Wt.:** 205. **Signed:** Dominican Republic, 2009. **Signed by:** Manny Nanita (Red Sox).

Acquired along with Josh Reddick from the Red Sox in 2011 for Andrew Bailey, Alcantara was on a fast track before Tommy John surgery cost him virtually all of 2014. The A's were careful with him in 2015, not allowing him to throw his slider. He was back to full health in 2016 with a full arsenal, and finished the year in the majors. Alcantara has never had trouble throwing strikes and has above-average control of a four-pitch mix. After struggling at Double-A Midland, Alcantara broke through at Triple-A Nashville, flashing 97 mph with his fastball while sitting 92-94 and showing a changeup with above-average potential. The slider was back and firm, in the upper 80s, with bottom to it at its best. He mixes in a rare curveball as well. Still, none of his pitches consistently misses bats, and opponents hit .277 against him overall on the year. Consistency of his offspeed stuff will be the key for Alcantara, who was hit hard in five starts in the majors, allowing nine homers in just 22.1 innings. He logged a career-high 158 innings, showing he's back to full strength, and will compete for a rotation spot in 2017.

Year	Club (League)	Class	W	L	ERA	G	GS	CG	SV	IP	H	HR	BB	SO	K/9	WHIP	AVG
2014	Midland (TL)	AA	2	0	2.29	3	3	0	0	20	17	0	5	10	4.6	1.12	.250
2015	Stockton (CAL)	HiA	0	2	3.88	15	15	0	0	49	54	3	8	29	5.4	1.27	.286
2016	Midland (TL)	AA	5	6	4.80	17	17	0	0	90	100	11	27	73	7.3	1.41	.284
	Nashville (PCL)	AAA	4	0	1.18	8	8	0	0	46	38	1	3	32	6.3	0.90	.229
	Oakland (AL)	MAJ	1	3	7.25	5	5	0	0	22	31	9	4	14	5.6	1.57	.333
Major League Totals			1	3	7.25	5	5	0	0	22	31	9	4	14	5.6	1.57	.333
Minor League Totals			35	32	3.52	123	113	2	0	589	594	39	125	409	6.3	1.22	.265

20 SEAN MURPHY, C

BA GRADE 45 Risk: High

Born: Oct. 10, 1994. **B-T:** R-R. **Ht.:** 6-3. **Wt.:** 215. **Drafted:** Wright State, 2016 (3rd round). **Signed by:** Rich Sparks.

Murphy was not drafted out of high school in Ohio—he was just 5-foot-9, 145 pounds as a junior—and got just one scholarship offer, from Wright State. He went on to be a two-time All-Horizon League selection, and three years and 70 pounds later, he was the highest-drafted Raiders player since Keith Gordon in 1990. Murphy had the strongest arm of the catchers in the 2016 class, with scouts pegging it as a 70 on the 20-80 scale. Despite his size, Murphy has above-average athleticism, moving well side-to-side and displaying good footwork. He is physical and durable, presents a quiet target and he blocks balls well. At the plate Murphy has average power potential due to solid bat speed and strength, but his offense lags behind his glove right now. He broke the hamate bone in his left hand while in college and contracted MRSA during the summer, which cost him about six weeks. Murphy needs more reps behind the plate and at the plate, but could move quickly for a catcher due to his advanced defense. He might skip to high Class A Stockton if the Athletics want to push him.

Year	Club (League)	Class	AVG	G	AB	R	H	2B	3B	HR	RBI	BB	SO	SB	CS	OBP	SLG
2016	Athletics (AZL)	R	.000	1	3	1	0	0	0	0	0	0	0	0	0	.000	.000
	Vermont (NYP)	SS	.237	22	76	10	18	1	0	2	7	9	12	1	0	.318	.329
Minor League Totals			.228	23	79	11	18	1	0	2	7	9	12	1	0	.307	.316

21 JOEY WENDLE, 2B

BA GRADE
45 Risk: High

Born: April, 26, 1990. **B-T:** L-R. **Ht:** 6-1. **Wt.:** 190. **Drafted:** West Chester (Pa.), 2012 (6th round). **Signed by:** Brent Urcheck (Indians).

Wendle signed for $10,000 as a sixth-round, senior sign after leading West Chester (Pa.) to its first-ever Division II national championship in 2012. Acquired from the Indians in December 2014 for Brandon Moss, Wendle hit hit .333/.376/.545 post-all-star break at Triple-A Nashville in 2016 and earned his first big league callup at the end of August, quickly becoming a favorite of Athletics manager Bob Melvin. Wendle's bat remains his best asset, though his walk and strikeout rates went backward at Triple-A. He has a short, compact swing and an advanced feel for hitting. He uses the whole field and makes good contact. He's an average defender and limited to second base, but does turn the pivot well and graded as an above-average defender at second during his small sample in the majors. Wendle worked with Triple-A Nashville manager Steve Scarsone and coach Eric Martins every day in 2016 to become a better fielder. He has average speed, but savvy on the bases allowed him to steal 16 bases in 20 tries last season, just below his 80 percent career success rate. Wendle started at second base for the A's for most of the final month of the 2016 season and will look to solidify the job in 2017 as a grinder who can do a little bit of everything.

Year	Club (League)	Class	AVG	G	AB	R	H	2B	3B	HR	RBI	BB	SO	SB	CS	OBP	SLG
2014	Indians (AZL)	R	.455	6	22	8	10	1	1	0	4	4	4	1	1	.538	.591
	Akron (EL)	AA	.253	87	336	46	85	20	5	8	50	26	56	4	2	.311	.414
2015	Nashville (PCL)	AAA	.289	137	577	80	167	42	8	10	57	22	114	12	2	.323	.442
2016	Nashville (PCL)	AAA	.279	125	491	81	137	31	9	12	61	26	112	14	4	.324	.452
	Oakland (AL)	MAJ	.260	28	96	11	25	1	0	1	11	6	16	2	0	.298	.302
Major League Totals			.260	28	96	11	25	1	0	1	11	6	16	2	0	.298	.302
Minor League Totals			.288	523	2084	320	601	141	32	50	273	137	390	45	12	.340	.459

22 MAX SCHROCK, 2B

BA GRADE
45 Risk: High

Born: Oct. 12, 1994. **B-T:** L-R. **Ht:** 5-8. **Wt.:** 180. **Drafted:** South Carolina, 2015 (13th round). **Signed by:** Paul Faulk (Nationals).

A highly-touted recruit, Schrock struggled with injuries at South Carolina but still had a .392 career on-base percentage when the Nationals drafted him in the 13th round in 2015. The Athletics acquired Schrock in July 2016 for lefthanded reliever Marc Rzepczynski. In many ways, Schrock is similar to Joey Wendle, another bat-first A's second baseman who worked his way to the majors in 2016. Schrock has a simple swing, with good bat speed and a feel for the strike zone. His pro and amateur track records are short on strikeouts and he uses the whole field with some power, with double-digit home runs not out of the question. Schrock led the minors with 177 hits in 2016, and used his average speed and sharp instincts to steal 22 bases as well. He continued to perform in the Arizona Fall League, hitting .278 with five doubles in 13 games. An offense-first player, Schrock is adequate at second base with a below-average arm, but his hands are solid and he turns the pivot well on double plays. He should start 2017 back at Double-A Midland, where he finished the year, and could hit his way to Oakland soon.

Year	Club (League)	Class	AVG	G	AB	R	H	2B	3B	HR	RBI	BB	SO	SB	CS	OBP	SLG
2015	Auburn (NYP)	SS	.308	46	172	31	53	10	4	2	14	13	16	2	1	.355	.448
2016	Hagerstown (SAL)	LoA	.326	67	270	46	88	20	2	4	39	22	20	15	3	.381	.459
	Potomac (CAR)	HiA	.341	54	232	30	79	11	0	5	29	9	22	7	2	.373	.453
	Stockton (CAL)	HiA	.111	2	9	0	1	0	0	0	0	0	0	0	0	.111	.111
	Midland (TL)	AA	.391	6	23	3	9	1	0	0	3	0	0	0	1	.375	.435
Minor League Totals			.326	175	706	110	230	42	6	11	85	44	58	24	7	.369	.449

23 PAUL BLACKBURN, RHP

BA GRADE
45 Risk: High

Born: December 4, 1993. **B-T:** R-R. **Ht.:** 6-2. **Wt.:** 185. **Drafted:** HS—Brentwood, Calif., 2012 (1st round supplemental). **Signed by:** Scott Fairbanks (Cubs).

The Cubs drafted Blackburn 56th overall out of high school in Brentwood, about 50 miles east of Oakland, and signed him away from an Arizona State commitment for $911,700. The Mariners acquired Blackburn with Dan Vogelbach at the 2016 trade deadline, and Seattle traded him to Oakland straight up for Danny Valencia that November. Blackburn's best offering is a plus upper-70s curveball he can land for a strike at any time, and he complements it with an average 90-93 mph fastball he commands well in the bottom half of the zone. Blackburn has induced more than 60 percent more groundouts than airouts in his career, a testament to his command of his top two offerings. His 82-86 mph slider ranks behind his curveball and his changeup grades below-average, but he is able to mix and match them well off his other pitches. Blackburn importantly showed durability after two disabled list stints in 2015—one for a foot injury and one for forearm soreness—by throwing 143 innings during the 2016 regular season at Double-A followed by two six-inning starts in the Southern League playoffs, including a win in the clinching game of the championship series. He will begin 2017 at Triple-A and could rise to Oakland as a groundball-oriented long man or spot starter.

Year	Club (League)	Class	W	L	ERA	G	GS	CG	SV	IP	H	HR	BB	SO	K/9	WHIP	AVG
2014	Kane County (MWL)	LoA	9	4	3.23	24	24	0	0	117	108	6	31	75	5.8	1.19	.247
2015	Myrtle Beach (CAR)	HiA	7	5	3.11	18	18	0	0	90	89	3	22	63	6.3	1.24	.264
2016	Tennessee (SL)	AA	6	4	3.17	18	18	0	0	102	96	6	26	72	6.3	1.19	.251
	Jackson (SL)	AA	3	1	3.54	8	7	0	0	41	42	2	9	27	6.0	1.25	.268
Minor League Totals			29	17	3.24	90	85	0	0	416	399	22	124	288	6.2	1.26	.255

24 JAYCOB BRUGMAN, OF

BA GRADE
40 Risk: Medium

Born: Jan. 18, 1992. **B-T:** L-L. **Ht:** 6-0. **Wt.:** 195. **Drafted:** Brigham Young, 2013 (17th round). **Signed by:** Trevor Ryan.

Brugman was the Mountain West Conference's freshman of the year in 2011 and a two-time all-conference pick. In his fourth year in the system, Brugman reached Triple-A and is poised to contribute to the big club next season after being added to the 40-man roster. Brugman is a well-rounded, fundamentally sound player and an organization favorite. He has a smooth, compact lefthanded swing with average power, most of it to the pull side. He profiles as an average hitter with gap power, and he draws enough walks to hit toward the top of a lineup. He's a solid-average outfielder who positions himself well, which overcomes his average foot speed. His arm is average but accurate. He profiles as a fourth outfielder, one who can play all three spots.

Year	Club (League)	Class	AVG	G	AB	R	H	2B	3B	HR	RBI	BB	SO	SB	CS	OBP	SLG
2014	Beloit (MWL)	LoA	.278	70	248	33	69	19	4	8	37	35	65	5	2	.371	.484
	Stockton (CAL)	HiA	.282	50	195	34	55	6	2	13	35	16	50	3	3	.332	.533
2015	Midland (TL)	AA	.260	132	500	61	130	27	8	6	63	62	89	11	7	.343	.382
2016	Midland (TL)	AA	.261	38	157	27	41	7	3	5	20	16	33	2	3	.335	.439
	Nashville (PCL)	AAA	.295	94	386	50	114	26	4	7	67	36	88	5	3	.352	.438
Minor League Totals			.274	433	1651	218	452	94	25	40	245	172	373	33	18	.343	.434

25 OSCAR TOVAR, RHP

BA GRADE
45 Risk: Extreme

Born: March 19, 1998. **B-T:** R-R. **Ht.:** 6-1. **Wt.:** 160. **Signed:** Venezuela, 2014. **Signed by:** Julio Franco.

Tovar was an under-the-radar signing from Venezuela in 2014 and made the transition to the U.S. after just one year in the Dominican Summer League, but his season started late because of a 25-game suspension for an undisclosed violation of the joint drug agreement. Tovar is slight but has a quick arm and can get his fastball up to 95 mph with late movement. He is aggressive in the strike zone, with a hard, power sinker. That helped him generate a robust groundball rate, and opponents slugged just .309 against him with no home runs in the Rookie-level Arizona League in 2016. His breaking ball is improving and his changeup is a work in progress but flashed above-average at times with good arm speed. Tovar doesn't miss many bats because he lacks separation on his pitches, but he does draw weak contact. He has a clean arm action and an easy delivery from the windup, but pitches with noticeably more effort with men on base. Tovar is likely to return to extended spring training with an assignment to short-season Vermont to follow.

Year	Club (League)	Class	W	L	ERA	G	GS	CG	SV	IP	H	HR	BB	SO	K/9	WHIP	AVG
2015	Athletics (DSL)	R	3	5	2.60	13	11	0	0	55	35	0	22	26	4.2	1.03	.184
2016	Athletics (AZL)	R	3	2	3.56	10	5	0	0	43	41	0	17	31	6.5	1.35	.253
Minor League Totals			6	7	3.02	23	16	0	0	98	76	0	39	57	5.2	1.17	.216

26 BOBBY WAHL, RHP

Born: March 21, 1992. **B-T:** R-R. **Ht.:** 6-2. **Wt.:** 210. **Drafted:** Mississippi, 2013 (5th round). **Signed by:** Kelcey Mucker.

BA GRADE

40 Risk: High

Injuries have set back Wahl, Mississippi's former Friday starter. He dealt with an oblique issue in 2014, and even after the Athletics moved him to the bullpen, he felt numbness in his right arm that turned out to be a nerve impingement in his elbow. That necessitated surgery in 2015. But 2016 was Wahl's healthiest and most consistent season. He tamped down his walk percentage—at least until he got to Triple-A—and his opponent average was a career-best .194. Wahl's big pitch is his fastball, which touched 100 mph in 2016. His curveball is his best secondary pitch and shows some bite, but is not consistent and doesn't get many swings and misses. He also throws a sparingly-used changeup. Wahl's problem, beside injuries and lack of command, is he tends to pitch up in the zone, and even with his velocity he can be hit. He needs to get his fastball down in the zone and sharpen his curveball so that he can get batters to chase. But as one evaluator said, "100 is 100," so Wahl could earn a big league bullpen role as soon as 2017.

Year	Club (League)	Class	W	L	ERA	G	GS	CG	SV	IP	H	HR	BB	SO	K/9	WHIP	AVG
2014	Beloit (MWL)	LoA	0	4	5.06	20	7	0	4	43	46	5	19	43	9.1	1.52	.267
	Stockton (CAL)	HiA	0	0	4.22	9	0	0	0	11	8	2	6	19	16.0	1.31	.190
2015	Midland (TL)	AA	2	0	4.18	24	0	0	4	32	36	2	14	36	10.0	1.55	.283
2016	Stockton (CAL)	HiA	0	0	6.75	3	0	0	0	4	3	0	5	3	6.8	2.00	.231
	Midland (TL)	AA	0	1	2.21	33	0	0	10	41	26	3	17	48	10.6	1.06	.188
	Nashville (PCL)	AAA	1	0	2.79	9	0	0	4	10	7	0	6	14	13.0	1.34	.200
Minor League Totals			3	5	3.90	108	12	0	24	162	146	15	75	191	10.6	1.37	.239

27 SKYLAR SZYNSKI, RHP

Born: July 14, 1997. **B-T:** R-R. **Ht.:** 6-2. **Wt.:** 195. **Drafted:** HS—Mishawaka, Ind., 2016 (4th round). **Signed by:** Rich Sparks.

BA GRADE

45 Risk: Extreme

An Indiana commit, Szynski jumped up draft boards with a strong showing on the showcase circuit in 2016. The Athletics liked him enough to give him a $1 million signing bonus, about double the recommended slot of the 112th overall pick. He was one of just three high school players in Oakland's 2016 draft class. Szynski's pro debut didn't go as planned, however. In his first Rookie-level Arizona League start he got one out and gave up four runs, as the Brewers put up a 15 runs in the first inning. Overall he gave up at least one run in five of his seven outings, despite pitching more than two innings only once. Szynski has a quick arm and generates 92-93 mph velocity on his fastball that touches 95. Despite his rough debut, evaluators said his fastball, curveball and changeup all flashed above-average with solid-average command of all three. The Athletics made small tweaks to his delivery, which had some effort to it. Szynski has three pitches to start and a solid pitcher's body, and he'll likely report to extended spring training before heading to short-season Vermont in 2017.

Year	Club (League)	Class	W	L	ERA	G	GS	CG	SV	IP	H	HR	BB	SO	K/9	WHIP	AVG
2016	Athletics (AZL)	R	0	3	8.10	7	7	0	0	13	16	1	4	8	5.4	1.50	.296
Minor League Totals			0	3	8.10	7	7	0	0	13	16	1	4	8	5.4	1.50	.296

28 YERDEL VARGAS, SS

Born: Feb. 17, 2000. **B-T:** R-R. **Ht.:** 5-11. **Wt.:** 170. **Signed:** Dominican Republic, 2016. **Signed by:** Juan De La Cruz.

BA GRADE

45 Risk: Extreme

Vargas, the No. 24 prospect in the 2016 international class, signed for $1.5 million, one of a handful of A's high-profile July 2 signings. Just 16, Vargas has a strong build already and quick bat speed. He cranks his back elbow and wraps his bat when he loads, creating a loop with some length and uppercut in his swing, leaving him especially vulnerable when he lunges and gets caught out front. Some scouts believed he was one of the better defensive shortstops in the class, with smooth hands and footwork to go with a strong, accurate arm. He is a quick-twitch athlete and projects to add size and strength as he matures, so the Athletics aren't sure where he'll end up on the defensive spectrum. Vargas is aggressive at the plate and had trouble recognizing pitches in the instructional league, which is not uncommon for international signees getting their first taste of organized ball. He has a high ceiling but is very far from reaching it, likely heading to the Dominican Summer League to make his pro debut in 2017.

Year	Club (League)	Class	AVG	G	AB	R	H	2B	3B	HR	RBI	BB	SO	SB	CS	OBP	SLG
2016	Did not play—Signed 2017 contract																

29 DILLON OVERTON, LHP

BA GRADE
40 Risk: High

Born: Aug. 17, 1991. **B-T:** L-L. **Ht.:** 6-2. **Wt.:** 175. **Drafted:** Oklahoma, 2013 (2nd round). **Signed by:** Yancy Ayres.

One of the top college arms in the 2013 draft, Overton had Tommy John surgery after the Athletics drafted him. Three years later, his pre-surgery velocity has not returned, but Overton has adapted to his 86-91 mph fastball. He locates his fastball, average changeup and fringe-average curveball well. He also added a cutter, but needs to pitch inside more often to righthanders. He tends to stay away with his pitches. Scouts say Overton will need to learn to come in to miss the strike zone, and then go back away to entice batters to chase. He is a flyball pitcher who gave up just six homers en route to ranking fifth in the Triple-A Pacific Coast League in ERA, but righthanded batters pounded him in his brief major league stint (.422/.455/.800) as he gave up 12 home runs in two stints lasting 24.1 innings. Overton's big league debut included the worst ERA in 20 or more innings by a big league rookie since 1994. He must adjust and make batters uncomfortable by pitching inside to fulfill his ceiling as a back-end starter.

Year	Club (League)	Class	W	L	ERA	G	GS	CG	SV	IP	H	HR	BB	SO	K/9	WHIP	AVG
2014	Athletics (AZL)	R	0	2	1.64	7	7	0	0	22	19	0	3	31	12.7	1.00	.232
	Vermont (NYP)	SS	0	1	2.40	5	5	0	0	15	11	0	1	22	13.2	0.80	.200
2015	Stockton (CAL)	HiA	2	4	3.82	14	12	0	0	61	62	7	12	59	8.7	1.21	.270
	Midland (TL)	AA	5	2	3.06	13	13	0	0	65	65	4	15	47	6.5	1.24	.260
2016	Nashville (PCL)	AAA	13	5	3.29	21	20	1	0	126	132	6	31	105	7.5	1.30	.268
	Oakland (AL)	MAJ	1	3	11.47	7	5	0	0	24	48	12	7	17	6.3	2.26	.407
Major League Totals			1	3	11.47	7	5	0	0	24	48	12	7	17	6.3	2.26	.407
Minor League Totals			20	14	3.18	60	57	1	0	289	289	17	62	264	8.2	1.22	.260

30 JAMES NAILE, RHP

BA GRADE
40 Risk: High

Born: Feb 8, 1993. **B-T:** R-R. **Ht:** 6-4. **Wt.:** 185. **Drafted:** Alabama-Birmingham, 2015 (20th round). **Signed by:** Kelcey Mucker.

Naile missed his sophomore season at Alabama-Birmingham after having Tommy John surgery in 2013, but Oakland selected him in the 20th round in 2015 after he led Conference USA in innings pitched (110) and strikeouts (92). Naile overcomes his fringe-average stuff with plus makeup and a bulldog mentality and that helped him pitch at four levels in 2016, reaching Triple-A. He tossed six scoreless innings in Game Five of the Double-A Texas League finals to pitch Midland to the title, getting 12 groundball outs with no flyouts, as is his modus operandi. Naile locates his 86-90 mph fastball well, commanding the bottom of the zone to generate an extreme groundball rate. His fastball has excellent sink and late run, and he mixes in a cutter on occasion. His slider is average at 79-83 and he has some feel for the changeup, but it's firm at 85-87. He's an excellent defender, winning a minor league gold glove, and has a strong pickoff move. Naile, who led the organization's minor leaguers with 156.2 regular-season innings, should start 2017 back at Midland.

Year	Club (League)	Class	W	L	ERA	G	GS	CG	SV	IP	H	HR	BB	SO	K/9	WHIP	AVG
2015	Athletics (AZL)	R	0	0	0.00	2	0	0	0	2	0	0	0	1	4.5	0.00	.000
	Vermont (NYP)	SS	3	0	1.93	18	0	0	6	23	19	0	6	17	6.6	1.07	.218
2016	Nashville (PCL)	AAA	1	1	5.73	2	2	0	0	11	11	1	5	4	3.3	1.45	.256
	Beloit (MWL)	LoA	3	8	2.66	15	14	0	0	88	67	2	19	64	6.5	0.98	.211
	Stockton (CAL)	HiA	4	1	3.76	8	7	0	0	41	39	5	11	46	10.2	1.23	.257
	Midland (TL)	AA	1	1	4.76	3	3	0	0	17	20	1	3	11	5.8	1.35	.303
Minor League Totals			12	11	3.16	48	26	0	6	182	156	9	44	143	7.1	1.10	.232

Philadelphia Phillies

BY BEN BADLER

After five straight seasons without a play-off appearance, the Phillies are staring ahead at another year that's unlikely to yield a postseason spot.

At least in 2017, however, there will be tangible signs of hope in Philadelphia. The Phillies have one of the game's best farm systems, with much of that talent congregated at the upper levels of the minors in the form of position prospects. That's a welcome sign for a team that scored the fewest runs in the majors in 2016.

Center fielder Odubel Herrera (an astute Rule 5 draft pick from the Rangers in 2014) second baseman Cesar Hernandez and third baseman Maikel Franco all could be a part of the next Phillies team to reach the playoffs, but they will need a lot more help. Fortunately for them, a slew of young hitters are on the way.

Shortstop J.P. Crawford, the team's top prospect, didn't take the big leap forward in 2016 the Phillies were hoping he would, but he's still a potential cornerstone player who should be in Philadelphia at some point in 2017.

Catcher Jorge Alfaro, first baseman Rhys Hoskins and outfielders Nick Williams, Roman Quinn and Dylan Cozens all played at Double-A Reading or Triple-A Lehigh Valley in 2016 and should be among the help coming to the major league club in 2017.

Center fielder Mickey Moniak, the No. 1 overall pick in the 2016 draft, is still at least a few years away, but he's a high-upside talent at a premium position with promising skills on both sides of the ball.

The team's best pitching prospects are at the lower levels. Under the watch of international scouting director Sal Agostinelli, the Phillies continue to churn out low-cost gems on the pitching side from Latin America. The latest is righthander Sixto Sanchez, a $35,000 signing out of the Dominican Republic who dazzled scouts in the Rookie-level Gulf Coast League. He has a chance to be a frontline starter.

Joining Sanchez are righthanders Franklyn Kilome ($40,000), Adonis Medina ($70,000), Jose Taveras ($5,000) and Ricardo Pinto ($15,000) and lefthander Elniery Garcia ($92,500). All are promising Latin American pitching prospects the Phillies signed for less than $100,000.

Righty Ricardo Pinto is the only one of that group who has pitched at Double-A or above. Righthanders Nick Pivetta, Mark Appel, Ben Lively and Thomas Eshelman also have upper-level experience and could help in 2017, while lefty Joely Rodriguez pitched in the Philadelphia

Second baseman Cesar Hernandez broke through with a big year in 2016

TOP PROSPECTS OF THE DECADE

Year	Player, Pos.	2016 Org
2007	Carlos Carrasco, rhp	Indians
2008	Carlos Carrasco, rhp	Indians
2009	Domonic Brown, of	Blue Jays
2010	Domonic Brown, of	Blue Jays
2011	Domonic Brown, of	Blue Jays
2012	Trevor May, rhp	Twins
2013	Jesse Biddle, lhp	Braves
2014	Maikel Franco, 3b/1b	Phillies
2015	J.P. Crawford, ss	Phillies
2016	J.P. Crawford, ss	Phillies

bullpen in September.

They mostly project as back-end starters or relievers, but they should help supplement an already young major league rotation that includes Jerad Eickhoff, Aaron Nola, Vince Velasquez, Jake Thompson and Zach Eflin as 25-and-under righthanders.

The transition to the major leagues won't be seamless for every young player the Phillies bring up in 2017, but by 2018 they should have a strong young nucleus to build around, with the resources and payroll flexibility (the club's payroll dropped to 26th in baseball in 2016) to add to their core.

While 2017 probably won't end the franchise's playoff drought, it should provide a key developmental bridge for the franchise with an eye toward contention in 2018.

ORGANIZATION OVERVIEW

General manager: Matt Klentak. **Farm director:** Joe Jordan. **Scouting director:** Johnny Almaraz.

Class	Team	League	W	L	PCT	Finish	Manager
Majors	Philadelphia Phillies	National	71	91	.438	11th (15)	Pete Mackanin
Triple-A	Lehigh Valley IronPigs	International	85	58	.594	2nd (14)	Dave Brundage
Double-A	Reading Fightin' Phils	Eastern	89	52	.631	1st (12)	Dusty Wathan
High Class A	Clearwater Threshers	Florida State	82	54	.603	1st (12)	Greg Legg
Low Class A	Lakewood BlueClaws	South Atlantic	74	65	.532	4th (14)	Shawn Williams
Short-season	Williamsport Crosscutters	New York-Penn	39	36	.520	6th (14)	Pat Borders
Rookie	GCL Phillies	Gulf Coast	43	15	.741	1st (17)	Roly De Armas
Overall 2016 Minor League Record			412	280	.595	1st (30)	

THIS YEAR'S TOP 30

No.	Player, Pos.	Grade/Risk
1.	J.P. Crawford, ss	60/Medium
2.	Mickey Moniak, of	65/High
3.	Jorge Alfaro, c	55/Medium
4.	Nick Williams, of	55/High
5.	Sixto Sanchez, rhp	60/Extreme
6.	Rhys Hoskins, 1b	55/High
7.	Franklyn Kilome, rhp	55/High
8.	Roman Quinn, of	50/Medium
9.	Scott Kingery, 2b	50/Medium
10.	Dylan Cozens, of	55/High
11.	Kevin Gowdy, rhp	55/Extreme
12.	Nick Pivetta, rhp	50/High
13.	Daniel Brito, 2b	55/Extreme
14.	Andrew Knapp, c	45/Medium
15.	Cornelius Randolph, of	50/High
16.	Adonis Medina, rhp	50/High
17.	Victor Arano, rhp	45/Medium
18.	Ben Lively, rhp	45/Medium
19.	Jonathan Guzman, ss	50/Extreme
20.	Mark Appel, rhp	40/Medium
21.	Jose Tavares, rhp	45/High
22.	Jhailyn Ortiz, of	50/Extreme
23.	Joely Rodriguez, lhp	40/Medium
24.	Ricardo Pinto, rhp	45/High
25.	Thomas Eshelman, rhp	40/Medium
26.	Alberto Tirado, rhp	50/Extreme
27.	Elniery Garcia, lhp	45/High
28.	Francisco Morales, rhp	50/Extreme
29.	Carlos Tocci, of	45/High
30.	Drew Anderson, rhp	45/High

LAST YEAR'S TOP 30

No.	Player, Pos.	Status
1.	J.P. Crawford, ss	No. 1
2.	Nick Williams, of	No. 4
3.	Jake Thompson, rhp	Majors
4.	Andrew Knapp, c	No. 14
5.	Jorge Alfaro, c	No. 3
6.	Cornelius Randolph, of	No. 15
7.	Franklyn Kilome, rhp	No. 7
8.	Roman Quinn, of	No. 8
9.	Adonis Medina, rhp	No. 16
10.	Carlos Tocci, of	No. 29
11.	Ricardo Pinto, of	No. 24
12.	Malquin Canelo, ss	Dropped out
13.	Zach Eflin, rhp	Majors
14.	Scott Kingery, 2b	No. 9
15.	Nick Pivetta, rhp	No. 12
16.	Dylan Cozens, of	No. 10
17.	Edubray Ramos, rhp	Majors
18.	Alberto Tirado, rhp	No. 26
19.	Aaron Brown, of	Dropped out
20.	Deivi Grullon, c	Dropped out
21.	Jonathan Arauz	(Astros)
22.	Elniery Garcia, lhp	No. 27
23.	Rhys Hoskins, 1b	No. 6
24.	Edgar Garcia, rhp	Dropped out
25.	Jhailyn Ortiz, of	No. 22
26.	Darnell Sweeney, of	(Dodgers)
27.	Ben Lively, rhp	No. 18
28.	Jimmy Cordero, rhp	(Nationals)
29.	Tom Windle, lhp	Dropped out
30.	Kyle Martin, 1b	Dropped out

BEST TOOLS

Best Hitter for Average	J.P. Crawford
Best Power Hitter	Dylan Cozens
Best Strike-Zone Discipline	J.P. Crawford
Fastest Baserunner	Roman Quinn
Best Athlete	Roman Quinn
Best Fastball	Alberto Tirado
Best Curveball	Nick Pivetta
Best Slider	Edgar Garcia
Best Changeup	Ricardo Pinto
Best Control	Thomas Eshelman
Best Defensive Catcher	Jorge Alfaro
Best Defensive Infielder	J.P. Crawford
Best Infield Arm	J.P. Crawford
Best Defensive Outfielder	Roman Quinn
Best Outfield Arm	Jose Pujols

PROJECTED 2020 LINEUP

Catcher	Jorge Alfaro
First Base	Rhys Hoskins
Second Base	Cesar Hernandez
Third Base	Maikel Franco
Shortstop	J.P. Crawford
Left Field	Odubel Herrera
Center Field	Mickey Moniak
Right Field	Nick Williams
No. 1 Starter	Aaron Nola
No. 2 Starter	Jerad Eickhoff
No. 3 Starter	Vince Velasquez
No. 4 Starter	Sixto Sanchez
No. 5 Starter	Franklyn Kilome
Closer	Victor Arano

MINOR LEAGUE DEPTH CHART

PHILADELPHIA PHILLIES

TOP 2016 ROOKIE: J.P. Crawford, ss. The Phillies have a wave of talent ticketed for Philadelphia in 2017, none more important than Crawford, who has all-star potential.
BREAKOUT PROSPECT: Daniel Brito, 2b. A skinny second baseman, he has superb bat control, controls the strike zone and defends his position.
SLEEPER: Brayan Gonzalez, ss. A 2016 signing out of Venezuela, he is a switch-hitter with an advanced offensive approach, quick hands and footwork at shortstop and a high overall baseball IQ.

SOURCE OF TOP 30 TALENT			
Homegrown	21	Acquired	9
College	3	Trades	9
Junior college	0	Rule 5 draft	0
High school	7	Independent leagues	0
Nondrafted free agents	0	Free agents/waivers	0
International	11		

LF
Nick Williams (4)
Cornelius Randolph (15)
Josh Stephen

CF
Mickey Moniak (2)
Roman Quinn (8)
Carlos Tocci (29)
Simon Muzziotti
Juan Luis

RF
Dylan Cozens (10)
Jhailyn Ortiz (22)
Jose Pujols
Zach Coppola

3B
Cole Stobbe
Mitch Walding

SS
J.P. Crawford (1)
Jonathan Guzman (17)
Malquin Canelo
Brayan Gonzalez
Arquimedes Gamboa

2B
Scott Kingery (9)
Daniel Brito (13)
Jesmuel Valentin
Josh Tobias
Keudy Bocio
Nicolas Torres

1B
Rhys Hoskins (6)
Kyle Martin

C
Jorge Alfaro (3)
Andrew Knapp (14)
Chance Numata
Rafael Marchan
Deivi Grullon
Juan Aparicio

LHP

LHSP	LHRP
Elniery Garcia (27)	Joely Rodriguez (23)
Cole Irvin	
Jojo Romero	
Bailey Falter	

RHP

RHSP	RHRP
Sixto Sanchez (5)	Victor Arano (18)
Franklyn Kilome (7)	Alberto Tirado (26)
Kevin Gowdy (11)	Edgar Garcia
Nick Pivetta (12)	Mauricio Llovera
Adonis Medina (16)	
Ben Lively (19)	
Mark Appel (20)	
Jose Taveras (21)	
Ricardo Pinto (24)	
Thomas Eshelman (25)	
Francisco Morales (28)	
Drew Anderson (30)	
Seranthony Dominguez	
Tyler Viza	

DRAFT ANALYSIS

2016

BEST PURE HITTER: Mickey Moniak (1) has elite pitch recognition and strike zone awareness to go along with a compact swing and plus hands in the box. Going straight from high school to the Rookie-level Gulf Coast League, Moniak batted .284/.340/.409 in his professional debut. OF Josh Stephen (11) also shows promise with the bat.

BEST POWER: 1B Darick Hall (14) has all-fields power; he swatted 20 home runs for Dallas Baptist in the spring, then posted a .236 isolated slugging percentage with nine home runs and 19 doubles in his pro debut at short-season Williamsport. SS Cole Stobbe (3) shows plus raw power and the ball comes off his bat with life even when he doesn't loft it over the fence.

FASTEST RUNNER: Moniak is a plus runner, with the ability to reach first base in 4.15 seconds from the left side.

BEST DEFENSIVE PLAYER: Moniak makes excellent reads of the ball off the bat, and has elite range and instincts in center field. OF David Martinelli (6) has the tools and instincts to excel in all three outfield positions.

BEST FASTBALL: Gowdy's fastball works in the low 90s and has reached as high as 96. He commands the pitch well and it shows late finish. LHP JoJo Romero (4) and Blake Quinn (9) have each bumped 95 with their fastballs.

BEST SECONDARY PITCH: Gowdy throws a hard and deep, late-breaking slider with power and he can command it to either side of the strike zone. RHP Grant Dyer (8) has a true top-to-bottom curveball that earns plus grades as well.

BEST PRO DEBUT: Moniak excelled in his debut, particularly in July, when he batted .346. LHP Cole Irvin never allowed more than two earned runs in a single start, and pitched to a 1.97 ERA. Dyer forced his way up to low Class A Lakewood, posting a robust 57-to-6 strikeout-to-walk ratio in 42.1 innings out of the bullpen across two levels. Quinn posted a 1.11 ERA across short-season Williamsport and low Class A Lakewood.

BEST ATHLETE: Moniak's combination of arm strength, speed and graceful actions and balance are difficult to beat. RHP Kevin Gowdy (1s) has a very athletic delivery, and has a black belt in taekwondo.

MOST INTRIGUING BACKGROUND: LHP Jonathan Hennigan (21) is the grandson of former major leaguer Phil Hennigan. Moniak's grandfather, Bill Moniak, was an early bonus baby of the Red Sox, and he is family friends with surfer Rob Machado.

CLOSEST TO THE MAJORS: There isn't an obvious fast-riser, but Romero, Irvin, Dyer and Quinn could all progress smoothly as more polished college pitchers.

BEST LATE-ROUND PICK: Stephen's loud hit tool and promising athleticism make him the top prospect of the late rounds. LHP Kyle Young is 6-foot-10 and the Phillies see an upper-90s fastball in his future to go along with extremely promising command and a curveball that works well from his angle.

THE ONE WHO GOT AWAY: SS Logan Davidson (30) was essentially unsignable and will attend Clemson. Junior college RHP Davis Agle converted to pitching; his fastball has reached the mid-90s and he has a projectable build.

2015

Aggressive 2B Scott Kingery (2) shot to Double-A in his first full season. OF Cornelius Randolph (1) can hit but has moved off shortstop and got hurt in 2016. LHP Luke Leftwich (7) finished the year at high Class A.

GRADE: C

2014

As hoped, RHP Aaron Nola (1) zipped to the majors. 1B Rhys Hoskins (5) splits scouts but has an impressive hitting track record. LHP Matt Imhof (2) lost an eye when his stretching equipment malfunctioned.

GRADE: B

2013

A hitter-heavy class started with SS J.P. Crawford (1), still the club's top prospect, and continued with C Andrew Knapp (2), who has come back from Tommy John surgery. RHP Tyler Viza (32) is an intriguing sleeper.

GRADE: B+

TOP DRAFT PICKS OF THE DECADE

Year	Player, Pos.	2016 Org
2007	Joe Savery, lhp	Did not play
2008	Anthony Hewitt, of	Atlantic League
2009	Kelly Dugan, of (2nd round)	Cubs
2010	Jesse Biddle, lhp	Braves
2011	Larry Greene, of (1st round supp.)	Did not play
2012	Shane Watson, rhp (1st round supp.)	Phillies
2013	J.P. Crawford, ss	Phillies
2014	Aaron Nola, rhp	Phillies
2015	Cornelius Randolph, of	Phillies
2016	Mickey Moniak, of	Phillies

LARGEST BONUSES IN CLUB HISTORY

Mickey Moniak, 2016	$6,100,000
Gavin Floyd, 2001	$4,200,000
Jhailyn Ortiz, 2015	$4,010,000
Kevin Gowdy, 2016	$3,500,000
Aaron Nola, 2014	$3,300,900

1 J.P. CRAWFORD, SS

Born: Jan. 11, 1995. **B-T:** L-R. **Ht.:** 6-2. **Wt.:** 180.
Drafted: HS—Lakewood, Calif., 2013 (1st round).
Signed by: Demerius Pittman.

BA GRADE

60 Risk: Medium.

SCOUTING GRADES

Batting: 60.
Power: 45.
Speed: 50.
Defense: 60.
Arm: 60.

Based on 20-80 scouting scale and future projection rather than present grades.

TOMASSO DeROSA

For the third straight season, Crawford ranks as the Phillies' top prospect. It's a ranking that comes after a season in which he didn't take the next big leap forward that was expected of him coming into the year, but he's still one of the game's elite shortstop prospects. His athleticism runs in the family—he's a cousin of Carl Crawford and his father played football at Iowa State and the Canadian Football League—but it's the combination of athleticism and polished baseball skills for his age that have made Crawford stand out since his high school days. The Phillies selected him with the No. 16 overall pick in the 2013 draft and signed him for $2,299,300. Crawford moved through the system quickly, reaching Double-A Reading as a 20-year-old in 2015 in a season that ended when he tore a ligament in his thumb in the Arizona Fall League. He opened 2016 by returning to Reading, where he spent six weeks before playing the rest of the season at Triple-A Lehigh Valley. He missed one week in August with an injured oblique. Crawford hit .250/.349/.339 with seven home runs in 123 games between the two stops.

Crawford's best offensive asset is his plate discipline. He has nearly as many walks (232) as strikeouts (243) in his career and shows a keen eye at the plate by recognizing offspeed pitches and rarely expanding the strike zone. Even as he went through growing pains upon reaching Triple-A, his strike-zone judgment remained intact. Crawford is a high-contact hitter with an efficient, compact swing from the left side, which combined with his plate discipline gives him a chance to be a high on-base threat at the top of a lineup. When Crawford struggled, he had a habit of stepping in the bucket and leaking open early with his hips, creating a longer path to the ball. His ability to keep his hands back and control the bat head still allowed him to make contact, however. When his swing is in sync, Crawford stays inside the ball well, with a chance to be an above-average hitter. Getting stronger will be critical for him because his power is mostly to the gaps, with the occasional home run to the pull side. His power hasn't developed as quickly as some evaluators expected, but between his bat speed and room to fill out his frame, Crawford could develop average pop in the future. In the field, Crawford shows plus defense, a mixture of athleticism, actions and instincts. With average speed, he isn't a burner on the basepaths, but he has a quick first step and reads the ball well off the bat, providing him with plenty of range at shortstop. Crawford is a fluid defender who can make plays to either side with his plus throwing arm, which plays up because of his fast hands and quick transfer.

Crawford isn't on the Phillies' 40-man roster yet, though he hasn't shown enough yet to merit a spot in the Opening Day lineup ahead of incumbent Freddy Galvis. Instead, he should return to Triple-A, with an opportunity to force his way to the major leagues by the all-star break. If everything clicks, the Phillies should have a franchise cornerstone at shortstop.

Year	Club (League)	Class	AVG	G	AB	R	H	2B	3B	HR	RBI	BB	SO	SB	CS	OBP	SLG
2014	Lakewood (SAL)	LoA	.295	60	227	37	67	16	0	3	19	37	37	14	7	.398	.405
	Clearwater (FSL)	HiA	.275	63	236	32	65	7	0	8	29	28	37	10	7	.352	.407
2015	Clearwater (FSL)	HiA	.392	21	79	15	31	1	0	1	8	14	9	5	2	.489	.443
	Reading (EL)	AA	.265	86	351	53	93	21	7	5	34	49	45	7	2	.354	.407
2016	Reading (EL)	AA	.265	36	136	23	36	8	0	3	13	30	21	5	3	.398	.390
	Lehigh Valley (IL)	AAA	.244	87	336	40	82	11	1	4	30	42	59	7	4	.328	.318
Minor League Totals			.278	406	1560	234	434	73	11	25	154	232	243	62	31	.372	.387

2 MICKEY MONIAK, OF

Born: May 13, 1998. **B-T:** L-R. **Ht.:** 6-2. **Wt.:** 185. **Drafted:** HS—Carlsbad, Calif., 2016 (1st round). **Signed by:** Mike Garcia.

Moniak was the center fielder and two-hole hitter for the U.S. team that won the 18U World Cup in Japan in 2015. A strong high school senior season propelled him to the top of the 2016 draft, with the Phillies signing him for a club-record $6.1 million as the No. 1 overall pick. Moniak is a premium position prospect who does a lot of things well with few glaring weaknesses. He has an easy lefthanded swing that's short, quick and fluid. His barrel awareness and pitch recognition allow him to consistently square up good fastballs and adjust to put the bat on breaking balls. He's a disciplined hitter who goes with where the ball is pitched and uses the whole field. He's still skinny with mostly gap power now, but he should hit 10-15 home runs one day with strength gains, and he added about 20 pounds in the fall after a three-week strength and conditioning camp at the Phillies' Clearwater complex. Moniak is an above-average runner with a quick first step in center field, where his good instincts and above-average arm make him a plus fielder. Moniak's balance of tools and skills on both sides of the ball make him a high-upside prospect without any major risk factors, aside from inexperience. He will make his full-season debut at low Class A Lakewood in 2017.

BA GRADE
65 Risk: High

Year	Club (League)	Class	AVG	G	AB	R	H	2B	3B	HR	RBI	BB	SO	SB	CS	OBP	SLG
2016	Phillies (GCL)	R	.284	46	176	27	50	11	4	1	28	11	35	10	4	.340	.409
Minor League Totals			.284	46	176	27	50	11	4	1	28	11	35	10	4	.340	.409

3 JORGE ALFARO, C

Born: June 11, 1993 **B-T:** R-R. **Ht.:** 6-2. **Wt.:** 225. **Signed:** Colombia, 2010. **Signed by:** Rodolfo Rosario/Don Welke (Rangers).

Dealt to the Phillies at the 2015 trade deadline in the seven-player Cole Hamels deal, Alfaro missed most of the second half in 2015 with a broken left ankle that required surgery. In 2016 he returned showing cleaned-up defense at Double-A Reading before debuting in the majors in September. Alfaro is strong, has plus bat speed and double-plus raw power. He stays through the ball well to use the middle of the field and can drive the ball out to any part of the park. Plate discipline remains a weakness, and a more selective approach will be key to tapping into his raw power more in games. He surprises people with average speed, and his athleticism is evident behind the plate. He has top-of-the-scale arm strength and gets rid of the ball quickly and accurately, resulting in elite pop times. He threw out 44 percent of basestealers in Double-A. Alfaro still has room to improve his blocking and receiving but took major steps forward in those areas in 2016. With Cameron Rupp and Andrew Knapp ahead of him, Alfaro will likely head to Triple-A to start 2017. He has the upside to be an above-average regular behind the plate.

BA GRADE
55 Risk: Medium

Year	Club (League)	Class	AVG	G	AB	R	H	2B	3B	HR	RBI	BB	SO	SB	CS	OBP	SLG
2014	Myrtle Beach (CAR)	HiA	.261	100	398	63	104	22	5	13	73	23	100	6	5	.318	.440
	Frisco (TL)	AA	.261	21	88	12	23	4	0	4	14	6	23	0	0	.343	.443
2015	Frisco (TL)	AA	.253	49	190	22	48	15	2	5	21	9	61	2	1	.314	.432
	Phillies (GCL)	R	.500	3	4	0	2	1	0	0	1	0	0	0	0	.667	.750
2016	Reading (EL)	AA	.285	97	404	68	115	21	2	15	67	22	105	3	2	.325	.458
	Philadelphia (NL)	MAJ	.125	6	16	0	2	0	0	0	0	1	8	0	0	.176	.125
Major League Totals			.125	6	16	0	2	0	0	0	0	1	8	0	0	.176	.125
Minor League Totals			.266	550	2092	313	556	122	18	67	317	117	597	38	18	.326	.437

4 NICK WILLIAMS, OF

Born: Sept. 8, 1993. **B-T:** L-L. **Ht.:** 6-3. **Wt.:** 195. **Drafted:** HS—Galveston, Texas, 2012 (2nd round). **Signed by:** Jay Heafner (Rangers).

Williams was in the middle of his finest season in 2015 at Double-A Frisco when Texas included him in the blockbuster deal for Cole Hamels at the trade deadline. Instead of continuing his upward trend, Williams went backwards in 2016 at Triple-A Lehigh Valley. Williams' tantalizing physical talent remains intact, but his hitting approach regressed in 2016 as his offensive performance cratered. He walked less (4 percent of the time) and struck out more (26 percent) in 2016 than he did the previous season. Williams must develop better plate discipline to tap into his potential. His hand speed is top notch. He whips the barrel into the hitting zone

BA GRADE
55 Risk: High

quickly with a loose, fluid swing, though it can get long. Williams uses the whole field, has good hitting actions and easy plus raw power evident in batting practice, though it hasn't translated into big home run totals yet. Though he doesn't steal many bases, Williams is a plus runner who can play all three outfield spots with a solid-average arm. Williams can still turn into an above-average regular, but his 2016 struggles add greater risk to his projection. He should return to Triple-A in 2017. Philadelphia's outfield is wide open, so a good start could get him to Citizens Bank Park quickly.

Year	Club (League)	Class	AVG	G	AB	R	H	2B	3B	HR	RBI	BB	SO	SB	CS	OBP	SLG
2014	Rangers (AZL)	R	.308	13	13	3	4	0	1	0	2	1	2	0	0	.357	.462
	Myrtle Beach (CAR)	HiA	.292	94	377	61	110	28	4	13	68	19	117	5	7	.343	.491
	Frisco (TL)	AA	.226	15	62	4	14	2	1	0	4	2	21	1	1	.250	.290
2015	Frisco (TL)	AA	.299	97	378	56	113	21	4	13	45	32	77	10	8	.357	.479
	Reading (EL)	AA	.320	22	97	21	31	5	2	4	10	3	20	3	0	.340	.536
2016	Lehigh Valley (IL)	AAA	.258	125	497	78	128	33	6	13	64	19	136	6	4	.287	.427
Minor League Totals			.286	499	2001	327	573	117	36	62	280	107	533	48	27	.331	.474

5 SIXTO SANCHEZ, RHP

BA GRADE

60 Risk: Extreme

Born: July 29, 1998. **B-T:** R-R. **Ht.:** 6-0. **Wt.:** 200. **Signed:** Dominican Republic, 2015. **Signed by:** Carlos Salas.

Phillies special assistant Bart Braun was at a workout in the Dominican Republic to scout a Cuban catcher. The player who caught his eye was Sanchez, the 16-year-old pitcher throwing to him, so the Phillies moved quickly to sign him for $35,000. When Sanchez jumped to U.S. in 2016, his stuff and stock soared as he overmatched hitters while leading the Rookie-level Gulf Coast League with a 0.50 ERA. He finished off his season with seven scoreless innings in the GCL playoffs. Prior to signing with the Phillies, Sanchez worked out for teams as an infielder, but he shows polish on the mound with an easy delivery. His explosive fastball sits at 92-96 mph and can reach 99 with good movement—a combination of sink and armside run that helps him generate weak contact. He's a good athlete who commands his fastball well for his age to all areas of the strike zone. Between his curveball and changeup, Sanchez has two offspeed pitches that flash plus and with more consistency should allow his strikeout rate to jump. He sells his changeup with good arm speed, and it runs away form lefthanded batters with good sinking action. He fields his position well. Sanchez is advanced enough to jump to low Class A Lakewood in 2017, with a chance to develop into a No. 2 or 3 starter.

Year	Club (League)	Class	W	L	ERA	G	GS	CG	SV	IP	H	HR	BB	SO	K/9	WHIP	AVG
2015	Phillies (DSL)	R	1	2	4.56	11	2	0	0	26	32	0	6	18	6.3	1.48	.291
2016	Phillies (GCL)	R	5	0	0.50	11	11	0	0	54	33	0	8	44	7.3	0.76	.181
Minor League Totals			6	2	1.81	22	13	0	0	80	65	0	14	62	7.0	0.99	.223

6 RHYS HOSKINS, 1B

BA GRADE

55 Risk: Medium

Born: March 17, 1993. **B-T:** R-R. **Ht.:** 6-4. **Wt.:** 225. **Drafted:** Sacramento State, 2014 (5th round). **Signed by:** Joey Davis.

Hoskins has skeptics, but his track record is difficult to dismiss. He hit well in the Cape Cod League and at Sacramento State, then signed with the Phillies for $349,700 as a fifth-round pick in 2014. Hoskins has hit at every level up through Double-A Reading, where he ranked fourth in the Eastern League in 2016 with a .377 on-base percentage and second in slugging (.566) and home runs (38). Scouts who like him see a hitter with plus power, a sound swing path, good timing, the bat speed to catch up to quality fastballs and a smart plan at the plate. His power comes with some strikeouts, but he doesn't swing and miss excessively and is a patient hitter who walked 12 percent of the time in 2016. While Reading is a terrific hitter's park, he still hit .270/.357/.496 on the road. Hoskins' doubters think he's more of a mistake hitter who has a longer swing with stiffness and holes that better pitchers will exploit. Hoskins is slow-footed and isn't very agile, but he has improved his defense to become an adequate defender with good hands at first base. Hoskins doesn't have the same athleticism or tools as fellow Reading masher Dylan Cozens, but he is the better pure hitter. He will start 2017 at Triple-A Lehigh Valley with a chance to get to Philadelphia by the end of the season.

Year	Club (League)	Class	AVG	G	AB	R	H	2B	3B	HR	RBI	BB	SO	SB	CS	OBP	SLG
2014	Williamsport (NYP)	SS	.237	70	245	30	58	15	0	9	40	21	54	3	3	.311	.408
2015	Lakewood (SAL)	LoA	.322	68	255	39	82	17	4	9	51	26	50	2	4	.397	.525
	Clearwater (FSL)	HiA	.317	67	243	47	77	19	2	8	39	29	49	2	0	.394	.510
2016	Reading (EL)	AA	.281	135	498	95	140	26	1	38	116	71	125	8	3	.377	.566
Minor League Totals			.288	340	1241	211	357	77	7	64	246	147	278	15	10	.372	.516

7 FRANKLYN KILOME, RHP

Born: June 25, 1995. **B-T:** R-R. **Ht.:** 6-6. **Wt.:** 215. **Signed:** Dominican Republic, 2013. **Signed by:** Koby Perez.

A gangly righthander with a quick arm when the Phillies signed him for $40,000 in 2013, Kilome has filled out, with the additional mass and delivery adjustments helping him become one of the team's top pitching prospects. In his first exposure to the cold at low Class A Lakewood in 2016, his first three starts were a disaster. He allowed 19 runs and 10 walks in 9.2 innings, but he recovered to record a 2.74 ERA with 10.5 strikeouts per nine innings the rest of the way. Kilome boasts a plus fastball with good movement that sits 91-95 mph and can touch 98. He started the season throwing a spike knuckle curveball he had trouble landing in the strike zone.

BA GRADE
55 Risk: High

After his early struggles, the Phillies gave him a more standard grip on his curveball and that helped him throw it for strikes, though he still has the spike curve in his arsenal. His curve is a swing-and-miss pitch that flashes plus. His changeup is too firm and a below-average pitch he hasn't used much, so bringing it along will be important. Kilome doesn't always keep his long limbs in sync during his delivery, which leads to spotty command. If Kilome can improve his changeup and tighten his command, he can develop into a mid-rotation starter with a chance for more. High Class A Clearwater is his next stop.

Year	Club (League)	Class	W	L	ERA	G	GS	CG	SV	IP	H	HR	BB	SO	K/9	WHIP	AVG
2014	Phillies (GCL)	R	3	1	3.12	11	8	0	0	40	36	2	11	25	5.6	1.17	.235
2015	Williamsport (NYP)	SS	3	2	3.28	11	11	0	0	49	41	1	21	36	6.6	1.26	.230
2016	Lakewood (SAL)	LoA	5	8	3.85	23	23	0	0	115	113	6	50	130	10.2	1.42	.259
Minor League Totals			11	11	3.57	45	42	0	0	204	190	9	82	191	8.4	1.33	.247

8 ROMAN QUINN, OF

Born: May 14, 1993. **B-T:** B-R. **Ht.:** 5-9. **Wt.:** 170. **Drafted:** HS—Port St. Joe, Fla., 2011 (2nd round). **Signed by:** Aaron Jersild.

In four years of pro ball, Quinn has yet to play more than 100 games in a season because of a lengthy medical file. A broken wrist and torn right Achilles heel in 2013, leg injuries in 2014 and 2015 and an oblique strain in 2016 have held him back, but he remains an explosive athlete. Quinn performed well when healthy at Double-A Reading in 2016 before making his major league debut as a September callup. Despite an array of lower-body injuries, Quinn remains a true 80 runner on the 20-80 scouting scale. Signed as a shortstop, he has played center field the last three years, where his speed gives him excellent range to go with a plus arm and

BA GRADE
50 Risk: Medium

good accuracy. Quinn isn't a pure hitter, but he has solid bat-to-ball skills from both sides of the plate with good bat speed and the sneaky pop to hit 8-12 home runs. His game has to be about getting on base, and he must develop more selectivity to have a better grasp of the strike zone. Quinn's speed and defense should make him at least a fourth outfielder, though he has the upside to become a regular in center field with more progress as a hitter. Triple-A Lehigh Valley should be his next stop.

Year	Club (League)	Class	AVG	G	AB	R	H	2B	3B	HR	RBI	BB	SO	SB	CS	OBP	SLG
2014	Clearwater (FSL)	HiA	.257	88	327	51	84	10	3	7	36	36	80	32	12	.343	.370
2015	Reading (EL)	AA	.306	58	232	44	71	6	6	4	15	18	42	29	10	.356	.435
2016	Phillies (GCL)	R	.500	6	22	6	11	2	0	0	0	1	3	5	1	.522	.591
	Reading (EL)	AA	.287	71	286	58	82	14	6	6	25	30	68	31	8	.361	.441
	Philadelphia (NL)	MAJ	.263	15	57	10	15	4	0	0	6	8	19	5	1	.373	.333
Major League Totals			.263	15	57	10	15	4	0	0	6	8	19	5	1	.373	.333
Minor League Totals			.276	356	1394	252	385	48	29	23	120	140	318	159	46	.353	.402

9 SCOTT KINGERY, 2B

Born: April 29, 1994. **B-T:** R-R. **Ht.:** 5-10. **Wt.:** 180. **Drafted:** Arizona, 2015 (2nd round). **Signed by:** Brad Holland.

Kingery was a walk-on at Arizona, where he formed a double-play combination with Pirates 2015 first-rounder Kevin Newman. Kingery showed enough for the Phillies to sign him for $1,259,600 as a second-round pick in 2015. He hit well at high Class A Clearwater in 2016, but when he got to Double-A Reading in late July he seemed run down, which carried over to the Arizona Fall League as well. Kingery seems to grow on scouts the more they see him. He has a quick righthanded stroke that's short, simple and repeatable. He has good bat control and plate coverage, and he stays through the middle of the field. He has good strike-zone judgment, though

BA GRADE
50 Risk: Medium

that came unglued when he got to Double-A when he got away from his usually disciplined approach. Kingery's power is mostly to the gaps, but he can occasionally pull a ball over the fence. His plus speed and baserunning savvy helped him steal 30 bases in 2016. Kingery can look awkward at times in the field, but he is a solid-average defender at second base who's quick on the double-play pivot with an average arm. Kingery isn't flashy, but he has a chance to grow into an average regular at second base. He appears set to return to Double-A to begin 2017.

Year	Club (League)	Class	AVG	G	AB	R	H	2B	3B	HR	RBI	BB	SO	SB	CS	OBP	SLG
2015	Lakewood (SAL)	LoA	.250	66	252	43	63	9	2	3	21	18	43	11	1	.314	.337
2016	Clearwater (FSL)	HiA	.293	94	375	60	110	29	3	3	28	33	54	26	5	.360	.411
	Reading (EL)	AA	.250	37	156	16	39	7	0	2	18	5	36	4	2	.273	.333
Minor League Totals			.271	197	783	119	212	45	5	8	67	56	133	41	8	.328	.372

10 DYLAN COZENS, OF

Born: May 31, 1994. **B-T:** L-L. **Ht.:** 6-6. **Wt.:** 235. **Drafted:** HS—Scottsdale, Ariz., 2012 (2nd round). **Signed by:** Brad Holland.

Cozens starred in both baseball and football in high school, so he entered pro ball a bit raw after the Phillies made him a second-round pick in 2012. The 6-foot-6 right fielder took giant strides at Double-A Reading in 2016, his fifth pro season, by improving his batting eye and more frequently getting to his monstrous raw power. Cozens led the minors with 40 home runs and 125 RBIs, though he hit just 11 of those bombs away from the cozy confines at Reading. Cozens is a player of extremes. He is a huge, strong, long-armed hitter who generates at least 70 raw power grades on the 20-80 scouting scale, with outstanding leverage when he's in

BA GRADE

55 Risk: High

sync, on time and able to get his hands extended. Even when he doesn't square up the ball, it flies off his bat with power to all fields. Cozens' long, uphill swing path leaves him with holes pitchers can exploit. This is particularly true when he faces lefthanders. While contact is an issue, he does show solid plate patience to go with his power. He also moves surprisingly well for his size, with average speed that helped him steal 21 bases in 22 attempts. He has worked his way into a playable defender with an average arm who played all three outfield spots in 2016. Cozens has the power to mash in the middle of the lineup, but a long list of power-hitting prospects have been stymied by contact issues. Triple-A Lehigh Valley is next.

Year	Club (League)	Class	AVG	G	AB	R	H	2B	3B	HR	RBI	BB	SO	SB	CS	OBP	SLG
2014	Lakewood (SAL)	LoA	.248	132	509	69	126	25	6	16	62	40	147	23	7	.303	.415
2015	Phillies (GCL)	R	.200	4	15	1	3	1	0	0	4	0	4	0	0	.200	.267
	Clearwater (FSL)	HiA	.282	96	365	52	103	22	5	5	46	26	79	18	5	.335	.411
	Reading (EL)	AA	.350	11	40	6	14	2	0	3	9	3	7	2	1	.386	.625
2016	Reading (EL)	AA	.276	134	521	106	144	38	3	40	125	61	186	21	1	.350	.591
Minor League Totals			.267	495	1856	308	496	118	18	78	305	179	531	83	22	.332	.476

11 KEVIN GOWDY, RHP

BA GRADE

55 Risk: Extreme

Born: Nov. 16, 1997. **B-T:** R-R. **Ht.:** 6-4. **Wt.:** 175. **Drafted:** HS—Santa Barbara, Calif., 2016 (2nd round). **Signed by:** Shane Bowers.

Gowdy and Mickey Moniak were both SoCal high school players, teammates on USA Baseball's 18U World Cup team that won the gold medal in Japan in 2015 and UCLA commits. Neither ended up on campus, but they still ended up teammates. The Phillies drafted Moniak first overall in 2016 and took Gowdy with their next pick (No. 42) in the second round, signing him for well above slot at $3.5 million. After working with Cubs scout Tom Myers as a pitching coach since he was nine, Gowdy shows polished feel for pitching for his age to go with his sharp stuff. His fastball sits in the low 90s with late movement and touches 96 mph. He throws a slider with deep, late-breaking action and power, giving him a second plus pitch at its best. He hasn't needed to use his changeup much yet, but with his clean arm action and feel for the pitch, it could become at least a solid-average third pitch. A black belt in taekwondo, Gowdy's athleticism helps him repeat his low-maintenance delivery with good fastball command. Gowdy will go to low Class A Lakewood in 2017. His feel for pitching could help him move relatively quickly with a chance to develop into a mid-rotation starter or better.

Year	Club (League)	Class	W	L	ERA	G	GS	CG	SV	IP	H	HR	BB	SO	K/9	WHiP	AVG
2016	Phillies (GCL)	R	0	1	4.00	4	4	0	0	9	9	0	2	9	9.0	1.22	.231
Minor League Totals			0	1	4.00	4	4	0	0	9	9	0	2	9	9.0	1.22	.231

12 NICK PIVETTA, RHP

Born: Feb. 14, 1993. **B-T:** R-R. **Ht.:** 6-5. **Wt.:** 210. **Drafted:** New Mexico JC, 2013 (4th round). **Signed by:** Mitch Sokol (Nationals).

BA GRADE

50 Risk: High

The Phillies traded Jonathan Papelbon to the Nationals in July 2015 to get Pivetta, who showed good stuff but struggled to throw strikes during the 2015 season in Double-A. Upon his return to the Eastern League in 2016, Pivetta showed improved command and made it to Triple-A Lehigh Valley the last month of the season. The Phillies worked on Pivetta's mechanics to get him going in a better direction to the plate, which helped him better locate his fastball. His fastball sits at 92-94 mph and can reach 97, combining good velocity, movement and downhill angle. Pivetta's out pitch is his hard curveball, which has good shape and late finish to miss bats. He throws a slider and a changeup, but neither offering is average yet. Improving his changeup to get more separation off his fastball will be key for Pivetta to give him a reliable third pitch against lefties. He projects as a back-end starter with a chance for more if his changeup matures. Pivetta should open 2017 in Triple-A but could crack Philadelphia's big league rotation by the end of the season.

Year	Club (League)	Class	W	L	ERA	G	GS	CG	SV	IP	H	HR	BB	SO	K/9	WHIP	AVG
2014	Hagerstown (SAL)	LoA	13	8	4.22	26	25	0	0	132	142	15	39	98	6.7	1.37	.277
2015	Potomac (CAR)	HiA	7	4	2.29	15	14	0	0	86	70	4	29	72	7.5	1.15	.225
	Harrisburg (EL)	AA	0	2	7.20	3	3	0	0	15	19	4	9	6	3.6	1.87	.311
	Reading (EL)	AA	2	2	7.31	7	7	0	0	28	32	4	19	25	7.9	1.80	.294
2016	Reading (AA)	AA	11	6	3.41	22	22	1	0	124	108	10	41	111	8.1	1.20	.235
	Lehigh Valley (IL)	AAA	1	2	2.55	5	5	0	0	25	20	2	10	27	9.9	1.22	.233
Minor League Totals			35	25	3.72	87	84	1	0	445	421	40	160	364	7.4	1.31	.253

13 DANIEL BRITO, 2B

Born: Jan. 23, 1998. **B-T:** L-R. **Ht.:** 6-1. **Wt.:** 160. **Signed:** Venezuela, 2014. **Signed by:** Carlos Salas.

BA GRADE

55 Risk: Extreme

The two biggest international bonuses the Phillies awarded in 2014 went to Arquimedez Gamboa ($900,000) and Brito ($650,000), a pair of Venezuelan shortstops. While the Phillies have pushed Gamboa more aggressively, Brito thus far looks like the better prospect. After a promising season in the Dominican Summer League in 2015, Brito impressed in his U.S. debut last year in the Rookie-level Gulf Coast League. Brito hasn't gained much weight since signing, so he's still a skinny, long-limbed teenager, but he has a mature hitting approach for his age. He's a disciplined hitter who tracks offspeed well and keeps his weight back, trusting his hands to put the ball in play at a high clip. He has a loose, handsy swing with good hand-eye coordination and the bat control to square up all types of pitches. Brito has minimal power right now, though he has the physical projection to grow into 8-12 home runs. An average runner, Brito moved to second base full time in 2016 and likely stays there. He's smooth turning the double play with a solid-average arm and charges the ball well, projecting as an average to slightly better fielder. Brito should compete for a spot with low Class A Lakewood in 2017.

Year	Club (League)	Class	AVG	G	AB	R	H	2B	3B	HR	RBI	BB	SO	SB	CS	OBP	SLG
2015	Phillies (DSL)	R	.269	60	212	33	57	10	3	0	19	35	22	8	9	.383	.344
2016	Phillies (GCL)	R	.284	47	190	35	54	10	5	2	25	21	27	7	2	.355	.421
Minor League Totals			.276	107	402	68	111	20	8	2	44	56	49	15	11	.370	.381

14 ANDREW KNAPP, C

Born: Nov. 9, 1991. **B-T:** B-R. **Ht.:** 6-1. **Wt.:** 195. **Drafted:** California, 2013 (2nd round). **Signed by:** Joey Davis.

BA GRADE

45 Risk: Low

The organization's minor league player of the year in 2015, Knapp's offensive performance was steady but not quite as robust in 2016 with Triple-A Lehigh Valley. Knapp is a switch-hitter with good balance at the plate, though he got himself in trouble in 2016 when he tried to do too much to force power and got big with his swing, rather staying back and trusting his hands. His strikeout rate also jumped a tick from 2015 as he started to chase more pitches out of the zone. He has a chance to develop into an average hitter who works gap to gap with enough power for 10-15 home runs. Knapp earns high praise for his intelligence and game awareness behind the plate, both in terms of his leadership and game-calling skills. He had Tommy John surgery in 2013, which has slowed his development as a catcher, particularly in terms of his blocking and receiving. He has a solid-average arm and a quick exchange, however, and threw out 38 percent of basestealers. After a full year of at-bats in Triple-A, Knapp could open 2017 in Philadelphia. He should be at least a steady backup with a chance to be a regular.

Year	Club (League)	Class	AVG	G	AB	R	H	2B	3B	HR	RBI	BB	SO	SB	CS	OBP	SLG
2014	Clearwater (FSL)	HiA	.157	23	83	7	13	1	0	1	7	5	26	1	0	.222	.205
	Lakewood (SAL)	LoA	.290	75	283	39	82	19	4	5	25	27	71	3	3	.354	.438
2015	Clearwater (FSL)	HiA	.262	63	244	38	64	14	3	2	28	29	63	0	1	.356	.369
	Reading (EL)	AA	.360	55	214	39	77	21	2	11	56	22	43	1	0	.419	.631
2016	Lehigh Valley (IL)	AAA	.266	107	403	55	107	24	1	8	46	37	107	2	2	.330	.390
Minor League Totals			.276	385	1444	208	398	99	10	31	185	142	367	14	11	.348	.422

15 CORNELIUS RANDOLPH, OF

BA GRADE
50 Risk: High

Born: June 2, 1997. **B-T:** L-R. **Ht.:** 5-11. **Wt.:** 205. **Drafted:** HS—Griffin, Ga., 2015 (1st round). **Signed by:** Aaron Jersild.

Randolph was the No. 10 overall pick in the 2015 draft, signed for $3,231,300, then showed why the Phillies were so enamored with his bat by hitting well that summer in the Rookie-level Gulf Coast League. Randolph's 2016 didn't go quite as well. He got off to a slow start in his first 12 games with low Class A Lakewood, then missed two and a half months due to shoulder and hamstring issues before returning on June 29. Drafted as an offensive-minded player, Randolph's lefthanded swing is calm, balanced and compact, with solid bat-to-ball skills and an approach geared toward shooting the ball to the opposite field. Randolph has strong hands, bat speed and average raw power in batting practice, but he shows little game power because of his approach. That power could show up once he learns to pull the ball with more authority and drive the ball in the air instead of putting it on the ground. A shortstop in high school, Randolph immediately moved to left field last season. A below-average runner with an average arm, Randolph made strides defensively, but the lack of outfield experience still shows. He will still be just 19 on Opening Day in 2017 and could return to Lakewood.

Year	Club (League)	Class	AVG	G	AB	R	H	2B	3B	HR	RBI	BB	SO	SB	CS	OBP	SLG
2015	Phillies (GCL)	R	.302	53	172	34	52	15	3	1	24	32	32	6	5	.425	.442
2016	Phillies (GCL)	R	.077	5	13	1	1	0	0	0	0	2	3	0	0	.200	.077
	Lakewood (SAL)	LoA	.274	63	241	33	66	12	1	2	27	26	57	5	4	.355	.357
Minor League Totals			.279	121	426	68	119	27	4	3	51	60	92	11	9	.380	.383

16 ADONIS MEDINA, RHP

BA GRADE
50 Risk: High

Born: Dec. 18, 1996. **B-T:** R-R. **Ht.:** 6-1. **Wt.:** 185. **Signed:** Dominican Republic, 2014. **Signed by:** Koby Perez/Carlos Salas.

When Medina was a 17-year-old in the Dominican Republic, he had an athletic, projectable build, a loose arm and a fastball that touched 90 mph, so the Phillies signed him for $70,000. His fastball has jumped since then and he's had success at every level, most recently in the short-season New York-Penn League in 2016, coming within two outs of a no-hitter in his third start with Williamsport. Medina has an easy, repeatable delivery with a wide release point and does a good job commanding his fastball to both sides of the plate for his age. His fastball sits 90-94 mph and can touch 96 with explosive late action through the zone. He's able to spin a curveball and mix in both a changeup and slider that all flash average, though none is a true out pitch at this point. Medina has a pitch-to-contact approach but needs to sharpen the finish and quality of his secondary offerings to improve his low strikeout rate of 4.7 per nine innings. He's a good athlete who does a good job of holding runners. Medina has a chance to be a back-end to mid-rotation starter, with low Class A Lakewood his next stop.

Year	Club (League)	Class	W	L	ERA	G	GS	CG	SV	IP	H	HR	BB	SO	K/9	WHIP	AVG
2014	Phillies (DSL)	R	2	3	1.37	11	2	0	1	26	22	0	4	22	7.5	0.99	.220
2015	Phillies (GCL)	R	3	2	2.98	10	8	0	0	45	42	1	12	35	6.9	1.19	.253
2016	Williamsport (NYP)	SS	5	3	2.92	13	13	0	0	65	47	5	24	34	4.7	1.10	.203
Minor League Totals			10	8	2.64	34	23	0	1	136	111	6	40	91	6.0	1.11	.223

17 VICTOR ARANO, RHP

BA GRADE
45 Risk: Medium

Born: Feb. 7, 1995. **B-T:** R-R. **Ht.:** 6-2. **Wt.:** 200. **Signed:** Mexico, 2013. **Signed by:** Mike Brito/Pat Kelly (Dodgers).

The Dodgers signed Arano from the Mexico City Red Devils in 2013, then in Aug. 2014 traded him and infielder Jesmuel Valentin to the Phillies for righthander Roberto Hernandez. The Phillies kept developing Arano as a starter in 2015, but last season they moved him to the bullpen and he flourished, racking up 10.7 strikeouts per nine innings between high Class A Clearwater and Double-A Reading. Arano has an unusual profile for a relief prospect given his diverse repertoire with good pitchability for his age, but he's looked more comfortable out of the bullpen than he did as a starter. His fastball jumped to 93-95 mph and can touch 97 with tight spin to get swings and misses up in the zone, mixing both four-seamers and two-seamers. Arano's slider is his out pitch, giving him another above-average weapon to miss bats.

His changeup has good separation off his fastball, but he doesn't use it or his curveball as much now that he's a reliever. Arano is an excellent strike-thrower who should continue to move quickly and could reach the majors in the second half of 2017, with a chance to eventually pitch high-leverage innings.

Year	Club (League)	Class	W	L	ERA	G	GS	CG	SV	IP	H	HR	BB	SO	K/9	WHIP	AVG
2014	Great Lakes (MWL)	LoA	4	7	4.08	22	15	0	3	86	88	11	20	83	8.7	1.26	.260
2015	Clearwater (FSL)	HiA	4	12	4.72	24	22	1	0	124	131	7	26	69	5.0	1.27	.276
2016	Clearwater (FSL)	HiA	4	1	2.29	35	0	0	4	63	52	4	15	71	10.1	1.06	.222
	Reading (EL)	AA	1	1	2.16	11	0	0	1	17	11	2	4	24	13.0	0.90	.177
Minor League Totals			16	23	3.90	105	45	1	8	339	334	28	78	296	7.9	1.22	.254

18 BEN LIVELY, RHP

Born: March 5, 1992. **B-T:** R-R. **Ht.:** 6-4. **Wt.:** 190. **Drafted:** Central Florida, 2013 (4th round). **Signed by:** Greg Zunino (Reds).

Traded from the Reds to the Phillies after the 2014 season for Marlon Byrd, Lively showed up early to 2016 spring training. While there, he made a mechanical adjustment with his lower half to help him create better downhill plane on his fastball. Lively's fastball trajectory had previously gotten flat and he paid for mistakes up in the zone, but now he started to generate better angle and was able to pound the bottom of the strike zone with more frequency. He moved from Double-A Reading to Triple-A Lehigh Valley at the end of May, won the organization's minor league pitcher of the year award and was added to the 40-man roster after the season. Those adjustments were key for Lively, who relies more on finesse and command than pure stuff. He's a four-pitch guy with a low-90s fastball, using a two-seamer more this year to try to get early-count grounders. Lively has a slider he throws more than his curveball and a changeup he improved in 2016, with all of his pitches earning 45-50 grades on the 20-80 scale. A polished strike-thrower, Lively is a durable starter who could stick around as a No. 5 starter, likely making his major league debut at some point in 2017.

Year	Club (League)	Class	W	L	ERA	G	GS	CG	SV	IP	H	HR	BB	SO	K/9	WHIP	AVG
2014	Bakersfield (CAL)	HiA	10	1	2.28	13	13	0	0	79	57	6	16	95	10.8	0.92	.201
	Pensacola (SL)	AA	3	6	3.88	13	13	0	0	72	60	7	36	76	9.5	1.33	.232
2015	Reading (EL)	AA	8	7	4.13	25	25	1	0	144	160	14	45	111	7.0	1.43	.290
2016	Reading (EL)	AA	7	0	1.87	9	9	0	0	53	35	1	15	49	8.3	0.94	.185
	Lehigh Valley (IL)	AAA	11	5	3.06	19	19	1	0	118	83	10	27	90	6.9	0.93	.196
Minor League Totals			39	23	3.06	92	92	2	0	506	418	38	152	477	8.5	1.13	.226

19 JONATHAN GUZMAN, SS

Born: Aug. 17, 1999. **B-T:** R-R. **Ht.:** 6-0. **Wt.:** 160. **Signed:** Dominican Republic, 2015. **Signed by:** Carlos Salas.

The focal point of the Phillies' 2015-16 international signing period was Dominican outfielder Jhailyn Ortiz, who signed for $4.01 million on July 2, 2015. Guzman signed a month later with far less attention, getting a $60,000 bonus on his 16th birthday. He has quickly looked like a bargain. Guzman played nearly the entire Dominican Summer League season as a 16-year-old and hit .300 thanks to his excellent hand-eye coordination and innate feel for the barrel. He does not possess the most conventional stroke, but he's a high-contact hitter who consistently finds the sweet spot. A line-drive hitter with a pull approach, Guzman lacks strength because he's still so young, and while he has a projectable frame, he doesn't project to be a power hitter. An average runner, Guzman is a true shortstop who fields his position well for his age and has an above-average arm. He should jump to the Rookie-level Gulf Coast League as a 17-year-old in 2017.

Year	Club (League)	Class	AVG	G	AB	R	H	2B	3B	HR	RBI	BB	SO	SB	CS	OBP	SLG
2016	Phillies (DSL)	R	.300	64	240	27	72	11	0	0	13	21	25	13	13	.370	.346
Minor League Totals			.300	64	240	27	72	11	0	0	13	21	25	13	13	.370	.346

20 MARK APPEL, RHP

Born: July 15, 1991. **B-T:** R-R. **Ht.:** 6-5. **Wt.:** 220. **Drafted:** Stanford, 2013 (1st round). **Signed by:** Brian Byrne (Astros).

Appel's decision to pass on signing with the Pirates as the No. 8 overall pick in the 2012 draft paid off, as he returned to Stanford for his senior year, went first overall to the Astros in 2013 and signed for $6.35 million. Thus far, that's been the career highlight for Appel, who had a brutal first full season and was traded to Philadelphia after the 2015 season in the seven-player deal that sent Ken Giles to Houston. Appel made eight starts for Triple-A Lehigh Valley in 2016 before having season-ending surgery to remove a bone spur from his elbow. Before he got hurt, Appel showed a fastball around 92-94 mph and reached 98, though he had trouble maintaining his velocity deep into starts. His fastball comes in on a flat plane, making it more hittable, especially since he struggles to command it down in the zone. His slider is a plus pitch, while his changeup is below-average. The Phillies intend to keep developing Appel as a starter, though an upper-90s fastball in short bursts combined with a plus slider would be intriguing out of the bullpen. He is expected to be at full strength for spring training and should return to Triple-A.

Year	Club (League)	Class	W	L	ERA	G	GS	CG	SV	IP	H	HR	BB	SO	K/9	WHIP	AVG
2014	Lancaster (CAL)	HiA	2	5	9.74	12	12	0	0	44	74	9	11	40	8.1	1.92	.372
	Corpus Christi (TL)	AA	1	2	3.69	7	6	1	0	39	35	2	13	38	8.8	1.23	.236
2015	Corpus Christi (TL)	AA	5	1	4.26	13	13	1	0	63	68	7	23	49	7.0	1.44	.279
	Fresno (PCL)	AAA	5	2	4.48	12	12	0	0	68	67	6	28	61	8.0	1.39	.255
2016	Lehigh Valley (IL)	AAA	3	3	4.46	8	8	0	0	38	40	3	20	34	8.0	1.57	.267
Minor League Totals			19	14	5.04	62	61	2	0	291	320	29	104	255	7.9	1.46	.278

21 JOSE TAVERAS, RHP

BA GRADE
45 Risk: High

Born: Nov. 6, 1993. **B-T:** R-R. **Ht.:** 6-4. **Wt.:** 210. **Signed:** Dominican Republic, 2013. **Signed by:** Koby Perez.

Taveras had just turned 20 and was looking to sign for any price when the Phillies spotted him in the Dominican Republic and liked his ability to throw strikes. They gave him $5,000 and he has developed into a pleasant surprise for the organization. He spent the first month of 2016 in the bullpen with low Class A Lakewood, moved to the rotation and led the South Atlantic League with 154 strikeouts. Taveras isn't overpowering, but he's able to leverage his size, deception and command from a crossfire delivery. His fastball sits 88-92 mph, but the ball gets on hitters faster than anticipated because of Taveras' ability to generate extension out front. Taveras keeps hitters off balance with his solid-average changeup, mixing in a fringe-average slider too. He's a smart pitcher and a prolific strike-thrower, which should help him move quickly. There's a lot of smoke-and-mirrors to Taveras' game, which is why he has his skeptics until he proves himself at higher levels, but he could develop into a back-end starter. He will start in high Class A Clearwater in 2017.

Year	Club (League)	Class	W	L	ERA	G	GS	CG	SV	IP	H	HR	BB	SO	K/9	WHIP	AVG
2014	Phillies (DSL)	R	8	4	1.05	15	13	1	0	85	61	1	8	70	7.4	0.81	.202
2015	Williamsport (NYP)	SS	7	4	3.88	13	13	0	0	63	63	3	21	59	8.5	1.34	.273
2016	Lakewood (SAL)	LoA	8	8	3.28	25	20	1	0	137	116	15	26	154	10.1	1.03	.229
Minor League Totals			23	16	2.74	53	46	2	0	285	240	19	55	283	8.9	1.03	.231

22 JHAILYN ORTIZ, OF

BA GRADE
50 Risk: Extreme

Born: Nov. 18, 1998. **B-T:** R-R. **Ht.:** 6-3 **Wt.:** 240. **Signed:** Dominican Republic, 2015. **Signed by:** Carlos Salas/Franklin Felida.

When the Phillies signed Ortiz as a 16-year-old for $4.01 million, a franchise record for an international signing, they were drawn to the player with the biggest raw power in the 2015 signing class. Other clubs considered the signing a reach, given the concerns about Ortiz's ability to hit live pitching and huge frame. While those risk factors are still valid, Ortiz showed his power translated to games in the Rookie-level Gulf Coast League, where he ranked third in home runs. Ortiz's combination of bat speed and strength allows him to put on a show in batting practice. He can punish a fastball with power to all fields and has the potential to hit 25-30 home runs, but the key will be whether he can improve his pitch recognition and hitting ability. Ortiz doesn't have a long swing, but he lacks natural rhythm and balance and doesn't stay on breaking pitches well, which throws off his timing and makes him susceptible to chasing. He has been better than expected defensively in right field with improving routes and reads and a plus arm. Short-season Williamsport or low Class A Lakewood should be his next stop.

Year	Club (League)	Class	AVG	G	AB	R	H	2B	3B	HR	RBI	BB	SO	SB	CS	OBP	SLG
2016	Phillies (GCL)	R	.231	47	173	29	40	9	1	8	27	17	53	8	2	.325	.434
Minor League Totals			.231	47	173	29	40	9	1	8	27	17	53	8	2	.325	.434

23 JOELY RODRIGUEZ, LHP

BA GRADE
40 Risk: Medium

Born: Nov. 14, 1991. **B-T:** L-L. **Ht.:** 6-1. **Wt.:** 200. **Signed:** Dominican Republic, 2009. **Signed by:** Rene Gayo/Ellis Pena (Pirates).

Through his first six seasons with the Pirates, Rodriguez barely distinguished himself as a prospect, with Pittsburgh trading him to the Phillies after the 2014 season for Antonio Bastardo. After a rough 2015 campaign with Double-A Reading and Triple-A Lehigh Valley, Rodriguez returned to Reading in 2016 as a reliever, but by the end of April the Phillies sent him down to high Class A Clearwater. The Phillies wanted to put him in a situation where he could stay calm and work on staying within his delivery with a lowered arm angle. The strategy worked, as Rodriguez took one step backward before zooming forward, getting back to Triple-A in August and making his major league debut as a September callup. Rodriguez's fastball sits at 94-96 mph and can touch 98 with sink to help him get grounders, pounding the bottom of the strike zone especially to his glove side. He throws a solid-average slider that's tough on lefthanded hitters from his arm angle. His changeup is below-average but he hasn't thrown it as much as a reliever. Rodriguez should be able to stick in the big league bullpen as a middle reliever.

Year	Club (League)	Class	W	L	ERA	G	GS	CG	SV	IP	H	HR	BB	SO	K/9	WHIP	AVG
2014	Altoona (EL)	AA	6	11	4.84	30	21	2	1	134	151	10	43	73	4.9	1.45	.289
2015	Lehigh Valley (IL)	AAA	2	6	6.32	13	13	1	0	68	89	3	37	33	4.3	1.84	.321
	Reading (EL)	AA	5	4	5.90	19	8	0	0	61	73	8	20	41	6.0	1.52	.302
2016	Clearwater (FSL)	HiA	0	0	0.00	7	0	0	3	8	3	0	1	10	10.8	0.48	.107
	Reading (EL)	AA	7	0	2.57	33	0	0	2	49	46	3	16	41	7.5	1.27	.260
	Lehigh Valley (IL)	AAA	0	0	2.79	13	0	0	0	19	16	0	6	18	8.4	1.14	.232
	Philadelphia (NL)	MAJ	0	0	2.79	12	0	0	0	10	8	0	4	7	6.5	1.24	.235
Major League Totals			0	0	2.79	12	0	0	0	10	8	0	4	7	6.5	1.24	.235
Minor League Totals			36	41	4.24	183	104	3	7	647	709	45	211	404	5.6	1.42	.283

24 RICARDO PINTO, RHP

BA GRADE
45 Risk: High

Born: Jan. 21, 1994. **B-T:** R-R. **Ht.:** 6-0. **Wt.:** 185. **Signed:** Venezuela, 2011.
Signed by: Jesus Mendez.

Just as 2011 was ending, the Phillies signed Pinto for $15,000 as a 17-year-old out of Venezuela. After two years in the Venezuelan Summer League and one in short-season Williamsport, Pinto became the organization's minor league pitcher of the year in 2015. He followed that with a solid Double-A campaign in 2016 and pitched in the Futures Game. Pinto has proven to be a durable starter, throwing 170 innings in 2016 between Double-A Reading and winter ball in Venezuela. Pinto works off his fastball-changeup combination. Both are plus pitches, with his fastball sitting at 91-95 mph and touching 97. He maintains his arm speed on his changeup, an out pitch that keeps hitters off balance. Pinto's strikeout rate is modest because he's still working to find a reliable breaking ball. He's tried a curveball and a slider, focusing more on the slider recently, but both are below-average. He has clean arm action and coordinated delivery that he repeats to throw frequent strikes, though when he elevates the ball hitters can make him pay for mistakes. If Pinto can develop an average breaking pitch, he has a chance to be a back-end starter, with Triple-A Lehigh Valley his next test.

Year	Club (League)	Class	W	L	ERA	G	GS	CG	SV	IP	H	HR	BB	SO	K/9	WHIP	AVG
2014	Williamsport (NYP)	SS	1	5	2.11	9	9	0	0	47	36	4	15	48	9.2	1.09	.203
2015	Lakewood (SAL)	LoA	6	2	3.09	11	11	0	0	67	65	4	18	60	8.1	1.24	.258
	Clearwater (FSL)	HiA	9	2	2.87	13	13	0	0	78	64	6	19	45	5.2	1.06	.231
2016	Reading (EL)	AA	7	6	4.10	27	25	0	0	156	150	20	51	101	5.8	1.29	.253
Minor League Totals			33	23	3.20	89	82	0	1	480	440	42	135	344	6.4	1.20	.244

25 THOMAS ESHELMAN, RHP

BA GRADE
40 Risk: Medium

Born: June 20, 1994. **B-T:** R-R. **Ht.:** 6-3. **Wt.:** 210. **Drafted:** Cal State Fullerton, 2015 (2nd round). **Signed by:** Brad Buzinski (Astros).

Eshelman picked apart college hitters with superior command and control, walking just 18 batters over three seasons at Cal State Fullerton and leading Div. I in walk rate each year. The Astros drafted Eshelman in the second round, No. 46 overall, in 2015 but he barely pitched for them, with the Astros shipping him to the Phillies six months later in the seven-player trade that sent Ken Giles to Houston. In his first year in the Phillies organization, Eshelman pitched well at high Class A Clearwater before seeing his ERA swell at hitter-friendly Double-A Reading. Eshelman is a finesse pitcher who is able to succeed by commanding his fastball, moving the ball around the zone and keeping hitters off balance with his pitchability as opposed to his pure stuff. His offerings are fringe-average across the board, with an 87-91 mph fastball that touches 93, a curveball and a changeup, but everything plays up because of his ability to locate and understand hitters' strengths and weaknesses. Eshelman's ceiling is limited, but he could develop into a back-end, up-and-down starter along the lines of former Twins righthander Kevin Slowey.

Year	Club (League)	Class	W	L	ERA	G	GS	CG	SV	IP	H	HR	BB	SO	K/9	WHIP	AVG
2015	Astros (GCL)	R	0	1	4.50	2	2	0	0	4	3	0	2	3	6.8	1.25	.200
	Quad Cities (MWL)	LoA	0	0	4.26	2	2	0	0	6	9	0	3	5	7.1	1.89	.346
2016	Clearwater (FSL)	HiA	4	2	3.34	11	11	0	0	59	58	7	11	64	9.7	1.16	.251
	Reading (EL)	AA	5	5	5.14	13	13	0	0	61	79	4	17	55	8.1	1.57	.307
Minor League Totals			9	8	4.26	28	28	0	0	131	149	11	33	127	8.7	1.39	.282

26 ALBERTO TIRADO, RHP

BA GRADE
50 Risk: Extreme

Born: Dec. 10, 1994. **B-T:** R-R. **Ht.:** 6-0. **Wt.:** 185. **Signed:** Dominican Republic, 2011. **Signed by:** Marco Paddy/Domingo Toribio (Blue Jays).

When the Blue Jays signed Tirado for $300,000 as a 16-year-old, his fastball topped out at 91 mph. Now, Tirado pumps triple-digit heat, though he doesn't always know where the ball will go. Tirado opened 2016 as a reliever with low Class A Lakewood, spent most of May and June in extended spring training to work on his delivery, then moved into Lakewood's rotation at the end of June. He struck out at least eight batters in each of his final six starts, including 11- and 10-strikeout performances to end the season. Tirado's fastball ranges from 95-100 mph and his plus slider can be a wipeout pitch, which is how he racked up 14.1 strikeouts per nine innings in Lakewood. He has a changeup but hasn't thrown it much yet. Wildness remains Tirado's weakness. He has to keep his delivery in sync and under control to avoid racking up walks and falling behind hitters. Putting Tirado in the rotation helped give him a more regimented, scheduled routine that helped his development, but his future is likely in relief. Added to the 40-man roster in November, Tirado should jump to high Class A Clearwater's rotation in 2017.

Year	Club (League)	Class	W	L	ERA	G	GS	CG	SV	IP	H	HR	BB	SO	K/9	WHIP	AVG
2014	Lansing (MWL)	LoA	1	2	6.30	13	7	0	1	40	45	3	39	40	9.0	2.10	.283
	Vancouver (NWL)	SS	1	0	3.53	17	3	0	0	36	25	1	28	36	9.1	1.49	.191
2015	Dunedin (FSL)	HiA	4	3	3.23	31	0	0	3	61	45	4	35	61	9.0	1.30	.213
	Clearwater (FSL)	HiA	1	0	0.56	9	0	0	0	16	6	0	18	16	9.0	1.50	.130
2016	Clearwater (FSL)	HiA	0	0	16.20	2	0	0	0	3	3	0	6	6	16.2	2.70	.273
	Lakewood (SAL)	LoA	7	1	3.23	20	11	0	0	61	48	3	36	96	14.1	1.37	.214
Minor League Totals			20	8	3.32	118	43	0	4	314	245	12	199	338	9.7	1.41	.219

27 ELNIERY GARCIA, LHP

BA GRADE
45 Risk: High

Born: Dec. 24, 1994. **B-T:** L-L. **Ht.:** 6-0. **Wt.:** 170. **Signed:** Dominican Republic, 2011. **Signed by:** Koby Perez.

Garcia is among the many hidden gems the Phillies have uncovered in Latin America and developed into quality pitching prospects. Garcia signed for $92,500 out of the Dominican Republic in 2011 and has steadily climbed up the ladder as a strike-throwing lefty with an improving fastball. His velocity jumped in 2016 to sit 90-93 mph and touch the mid-90s, with sneaky late life that allows him to get swings and misses when he pitches up in the zone. Garcia has a four-pitch mix with a curveball, changeup and slider. His curveball has good spin and shape to be an average pitch, though he's still learning how to land it for a strike. Garcia's changeup improved in 2016 and flashed as another average pitch. Garcia is athletic, pitches inside well, repeats his delivery and fills the strike zone, though his lack of a plus pitch leaves him with a modest strikeout rate. Added to the 40-man roster in November, Garcia will move to Double-A Reading in 2017 and could develop into a back-end starter.

Year	Club (League)	Class	W	L	ERA	G	GS	CG	SV	IP	H	HR	BB	SO	K/9	WHIP	AVG
2014	Williamsport (NYP)	SS	0	0	5.79	4	0	0	0	5	6	1	2	5	9.6	1.71	.273
	Phillies (GCL)	R	2	2	2.08	7	4	0	0	26	26	0	4	23	8.0	1.15	.250
2015	Lakewood (SAL)	LoA	8	9	3.23	21	21	0	0	120	125	7	36	66	5.0	1.34	.275
2016	Clearwater (FSL)	HiA	12	4	2.68	20	19	0	0	118	94	8	36	91	7.0	1.10	.219
Minor League Totals			25	19	3.26	69	56	0	0	329	317	18	100	235	6.4	1.27	.254

28 FRANCISCO MORALES, RHP

BA GRADE
50 Risk: Extreme

Born: Oct. 27, 1999. **B-T:** R-R. **Ht.:** 6-5. **Wt.:** 220. **Signed:** Venezuela, 2016. **Signed by:** Jesus Mendez.

One of the top pitchers on the 2016 international market, Morales signed with the Phillies for $750,000 as a 16-year-old out Venezuela. Morales, now 17, has an impressive combination of size and present stuff. He already has a plus fastball, sitting at 90-94 mph and reaching 96. Morales has a tendency to get underneath the ball from his three-quarters arm slot, but when he stays on top he generates good downhill angle. Scouts who followed Morales before he signed were split on his future outlook because of his shaky slider and control. Early on while Morales was working out for clubs, he had trouble keeping his delivery under control, which hurt his ability to throw strikes. He has done a better job since signing of keeping his delivery in sync and his slider has improved, showing good shape, spin and late action. Morales hasn't needed to throw a changeup much yet, but he has shown early signs of having feel for that pitch. Morales should make his pro debut in the Rookie-level Gulf Coast League in 2017

Year	Club (League)	Class	W	L	ERA	G	GS	CG	SV	IP	H	HR	BB	SO	K/9	WHIP	AVG
2016	Did not play—Signed 2017 contract																

29 CARLOS TOCCI, OF

BA GRADE
45 Risk: High

Born: Aug. 23, 1995. **B-T:** R-R. **Ht.:** 6-2. **Wt.:** 180. **Signed:** Venezuela, 2011.
Signed by: Jesus Mendez.

Tocci ranked among the team's Top 10 prospects the past four seasons, but his lack of physical development has slowed his progress. When Tocci signed with the Phillies for $759,000 out of Venezuela as a 16-year-old, he had an extremely skinny, narrow frame, and he has been slow to add weight ever since. Getting stronger has long been the key for Tocci, an instinctive player with a high baseball IQ in all phases of the game. He's a smooth, fluid defender in center field. He's a solid-average runner with a quick first step and gliding strides, getting good reads off the bat with sharp routes to go with an average, accurate arm. Tocci is a sound hitter with solid contact skills, a line-drive approach and the ability to spread the ball to all fields. He has minimal power and needs to get stronger to be able to do more damage on contact. The Phillies left Tocci off their 40-man roster after the season and he didn't get picked in the Rule 5 draft. For as long as Tocci has been on the radar, he will play nearly all of 2017 as a 21-year-old, most likely in Double-A Reading.

Year	Club (League)	Class	AVG	G	AB	R	H	2B	3B	HR	RBI	BB	SO	SB	CS	OBP	SLG
2014	Lakewood (SAL)	LoA	.242	125	487	59	118	18	8	2	30	25	96	10	11	.297	.324
2015	Lakewood (SAL)	LoA	.321	59	234	35	75	14	2	2	25	20	31	14	2	.387	.423
	Clearwater (FSL)	HiA	.258	68	275	31	71	9	0	2	18	12	52	3	9	.296	.313
2016	Clearwater (FSL)	HiA	.284	127	500	66	142	26	2	3	50	34	76	13	6	.331	.362
Minor League Totals			.259	535	2014	244	521	86	12	9	158	119	350	55	37	.310	.327

30 DREW ANDERSON, RHP

BA GRADE
45 Risk: High

Born: March 22, 1994. **B-T:** R-R. **Ht.:** 6-3. **Wt.:** 195. **Drafted:** HS—Reno, Nev., 2012 (21st round). **Signed by:** Joey Davis.

Anderson moved through the system slowly his first three years, then had Tommy John surgery that wiped out his entire 2015 campaign. He vaulted his way back to prospect status upon his return in 2016, pounding the strike zone with a plus fastball and struck out more than a batter per inning between low Class A Lakewood and high Class A Clearwater. It was compelling enough that the Phillies added him to the 40-man roster after the season to protect him from the Rule 5 draft. After showing an average fastball earlier in his career, Anderson sat at 91-95 mph and touched 97 with explosive life through the zone. He throws an average curveball that he leans on as his primary offspeed pitch. In working his way back from surgery, Anderson didn't focus much on his changeup, a below-average pitch that will be important for him to develop to remain a starter. He shows an occasional slider in his repertoire as well. Durability is a risk factor with Anderson, but he shows the stuff and control to pitch at the back of a rotation or in a big-league bullpen. Double-A Reading is his next stop.

Year	Club (League)	Class	W	L	ERA	G	GS	CG	SV	IP	H	HR	BB	SO	K/9	WHIP	AVG
2014	Lakewood (SAL)	LoA	4	4	3.68	9	9	0	0	44	46	1	15	46	9.4	1.39	.266
	Phillies (GCL)	R	1	1	3.18	2	1	0	0	6	5	1	3	6	9.5	1.41	.238
2015	Did not play—Injured																
2016	Lakewood (SAL)	LoA	1	3	3.38	7	7	0	0	37	29	3	12	41	9.9	1.10	.220
	Clearwater (FSL)	HiA	2	1	1.93	8	8	0	0	33	26	0	10	37	10.2	1.10	.217
Minor League Totals			15	13	2.88	49	42	0	0	219	190	12	70	200	8.2	1.19	.235

Pittsburgh Pirates

BY JOHN PERROTTO

The Pirates had a turn-back-the-clock season in 2016. That didn't produce a lot of warm and fuzzy feelings in Pittsburgh.

After three consecutive postseason appearances, the Pirates finished 78-83 and in third place in the National League Central. They ended up a whopping 25 games back of the division-winning Cubs.

The year was reminiscent of many of the 20 consecutive losing seasons—the record for a major North American sports franchise—that the Pirates suffered from 1993 to 2012.

A dozen players made their major league debuts with the 2016 Pirates, including eight who were drafted and signed by the organization. Four starting pitchers who ranked among the preseason Top 30 Prospects made their big league debuts: righthanders Jameson Taillon (18 starts), Chad Kuhl (14) and Tyler Glasnow (four) and lefthander Steven Brault (seven).

Ever-optimistic manager Clint Hurdle tried to look on the bright side.

"It wasn't the way we planned it, but a lot of guys got their feet wet, and they are going to be better for it," Hurdle said. "This is going to aid in their development in the long haul."

Many of those players showed well enough that the Pirates believe they can be key contributors. In addition to the starting pitchers, first baseman Josh Bell and utilityman Adam Frazier also made impressions.

Taillon's performance was particularly encouraging. The second overall pick in the 2010 draft missed all of 2014 and 2015 recovering from Tommy John surgery and a sports hernia. He showed very little rust while going 5-4, 3.38 in 104 innings.

Taillon helped offset a somewhat disappointing first taste of the major leagues by Glasnow, who ranked as the organization's No. 1 prospect heading into 2015 and 2016.

The Pirates face a steep path to return to contention in the NL Central because of the resources available to the division-rival Cubs and Cardinals.

The Cubs have more young big league talent than Pittsburgh. Both Chicago and St. Louis have far more money to spend than the smaller-market Pirates, whose reality was brought home when they gave the Blue Jays two prospects (Reese McGuire and Harold Ramirez) to take on Francisco Liriano's contract in a deal that brought only Drew Hutchison in.

Critics contend the Pirates' window of contention shut in 2016, which was especially frustrating because the club won 98 games in 2015 but lost to the Cubs in the NL Wild Card Game. However,

Jameson Taillon, who missed the last two seasons, turned in a strong rookie season in 2016

TOP PROSPECTS OF THE DECADE

Year	Player, Pos.	2016 Org
2007	Andrew McCutchen, of	Pirates
2008	Andrew McCutchen, of	Pirates
2009	Pedro Alvarez, 3b	Orioles
2010	Pedro Alvarez, 3b	Orioles
2011	Jameson Taillon, rhp	Pirates
2012	Gerrit Cole, rhp	Pirates
2013	Gerrit Cole, rhp	Pirates
2014	Gregory Polanco, of	Pirates
2015	Tyler Glasnow, rhp	Pirates
2016	Tyler Glasnow, rhp	Pirates

the Pirates believe they have a core in place who can help them return to contention without a long rebuilding process. The arrival of Taillon, Kuhl, Glasnow and Brault gives Pittsburgh a large number of low-cost pitching options.

Along with the promising 2016 debuts, right fielder Gregory Polanco, a five-tool talent, is under contract through 2023, and Gold Glove-winning left fielder Starling Marte is signed through 2021. Outfielder Austin Meadows, the organization's No. 1 prospect, will likely make his big league debut in 2017 and shortstop prospect Kevin Newman should be ready for Pittsburgh by 2018.

But for a fan base that last experienced a World Series championship in 1979, it appears the wait for another title is going to take at least a little while longer.

ORGANIZATION OVERVIEW

General manager: Neal Huntington. **Farm director:** Larry Broadway. **Scouting director:** Joe Delli Carri.

Class	Team	League	W	L	PCT	Finish	Manager
Majors	Pittsburgh Pirates	National	78	83	.484	8th (15)	Clint Hurdle
Triple-A	Indianapolis Indians	International	70	74	.486	7th (14)	Dean Treanor
Double-A	Altoona Curve	Eastern	76	64	.543	4th (12)	Joey Cora
High Class A	Bradenton Marauders	Florida State	70	66	.515	6th (12)	Michael Ryan
Low Class A	West Virginia Power	South Atlantic	71	68	.511	7th (12)	Brian Esposito
Short-season	West Virginia Black Bears	New York-Penn	38	38	.500	8th (14)	Wyatt Toregas
Rookie	Bristol Pirates	Appalachian	25	43	.368	10th (10)	Edgar Varela
Rookie	GCL Pirates	Gulf Coast	22	34	.393	15th (17)	Milver Reyes
Overall 2016 Minor League Record			372	387	.490	17th (30)	

THIS YEAR'S TOP 30

No.	Player, Pos.	Grade/Risk
1.	Austin Meadows, of	65/Medium
2.	Mitch Keller, rhp	65/High
3.	Tyler Glasgow, rhp	65/High
4.	Josh Bell, 1b/of	55/Medium
5.	Kevin Newman, ss	55High
6.	Ke'Bryan Hayes, 3b	55/High
7.	Steven Brault, lhp	50/Medium
8.	Cole Tucker, ss	50/High
9.	Will Craig, 3b	50/High
10.	Elias Diaz, c	45/Medium
11.	Nick Kingham, rhp	50/High
12.	Gage Hinsz, rhp	50/High
13.	Max Moroff, inf	45/Medium
14.	Taylor Hearn, lhp	50/High
15.	Trevor Williams	45/Medium
16.	Yeudy Garcia, rhp	50/High
17.	Brandon Waddell, lhp	50/High
18.	Tyler Eppler, rhp	45/Medium
19.	Alen Hanson, 2b/of	40/Medium
20.	Clay Holmes, rhp	45/High
21.	Kevin Kramer, 2b	45/High
22.	Travis MacGregor, rhp	50/Extreme
23.	Frank Duncan, rhp	40/Medium
24.	Dovydas Neverauskas, rhp	40/Medium
25.	Braeden Ogle, lhp	50/Extreme
26.	Jose Osuna, of/1b	40/Medium
27.	Jin-De Jhang, c	40/Medium
28.	Luis Escobar, rhp	45/High
29.	Stephen Alemais, ss	45/High
30.	Tyler Webb, lhp	45/High

LAST YEAR'S TOP 30

No.	Player, Pos.	Status
1.	Tyler Glasnow, rhp	No. 3
2.	Austin Meadows, of	No. 1
3.	Josh Bell, 1b	No. 4
4.	Jameson Taillon, rhp	Majors
5.	Harold Ramirez, of	(Blue Jays)
6.	Reese McGuire, c	(Blue Jays)
7.	Cole Tucker, ss	No. 8
8.	Kevin Newman, ss	No. 5
9.	Ke'Bryan Hayes, 3b	No. 6
10.	Elias Diaz, c	No. 10
11.	Alen Hanson, 2b	No. 19
12.	Willy Garcia, of	Dropped out
13.	Nick Kingham, rhp	No. 11
14.	Jordan Luplow, 3b	Dropped out
15.	Steven Brault, lhp	No. 7
16.	Yeudy Garcia, rhp	No. 16
17.	Stephen Tarpley, lhp	(Yankees)
18.	Mitch Keller, rhp	No. 2
19.	Clay Holmes, rhp	No. 20
20.	Trey Supak, rhp	(Brewers)
21.	Gage Hinsz, rhp	No. 12
22.	Chad Kuhl, rhp	Majors
23.	Trevor Williams, rhp	No. 15
24.	Barrett Barnes, of	Dropped out
25.	Max Moroff, 2b	No. 13
26.	Casey Hughston, of	Dropped out
27.	Adam Frazier, ss/of	Majors
28.	Kevin Kramer, 2b/ss	No. 21
29.	Jacob Taylor, rhp	Dropped out
30.	Jose Osuna, of/1b	No. 26

BEST TOOLS

Best Hitter for Average	Kevin Newman
Best Power Hitter	Eric Wood
Best Strike-Zone Discipline	Austin Meadows
Fastest Baserunner	Alen Hanson
Best Athlete	Austin Meadows
Best Fastball	Taylor Hearn
Best Curveball	Mitch Keller
Best Slider	Edgar Santana
Best Changeup	Brandon Waddell
Best Control	Nick Kingham
Best Defensive Catcher	Elias Diaz
Best Defensive Infielder	Gift Ngoepe
Best Infield Arm	Alfredo Reyes
Best Defensive Outfielder	Casey Hughston
Best Outfield Arm	Willy Garcia

PROJECTED 2020 LINEUP

Catcher	Elias Diaz
First Base	Josh Bell
Second Base	Adam Frazier
Third Base	Ke'Bryan Hayes
Shortstop	Kevin Newman
Left Field	Gregory Polanco
Center Field	Starling Marte
Right Field	Austin Meadows
No. 1 Starter	Gerrit Cole
No. 2 Starter	Jameson Taillon
No. 3 Starter	Mitch Keller
No. 4 Starter	Tyler Glasnow
No. 5 Starter	Steven Brault
Closer	Yeudy Garcia

MINOR LEAGUE DEPTH CHART

PITTSBURGH PIRATES

TOP 2017 ROOKIE: Steven Brault, lhp. He should fill the need for a lefthander in the rotation.

BREAKOUT PROSPECT: Taylor Hearn, lhp. Acquired from the Nationals in 2016 for Mark Melancon, he misses plenty of bats and should be healthy.

SLEEPER: Edgar Santana, rhp. His fastball reaches triple digits and plays well out of the bullpen.

SOURCE OF TOP 30 TALENT			
Homegrown	27	Acquired	3
College	7	Trades	3
Junior college	0	Rule 5 draft	0
High school	12	Independent leagues	0
Nondrafted free agents	0	Free agents/waivers	0
International	8		

LF
Jordan Luplow
Barrett Barnes

CF
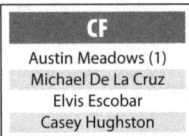
Austin Meadows (1)
Michael De La Cruz
Elvis Escobar
Casey Hughston

RF
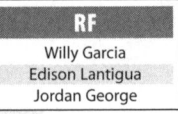
Willy Garcia
Edison Lantigua
Jordan George

3B
Ke'Bryan Hayes (6)
Will Craig (9)
Eric Wood
Connor Joe
Wyatt Mathisen

SS
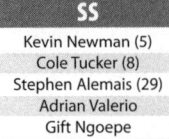
Kevin Newman (5)
Cole Tucker (8)
Stephen Alemais (29)
Adrian Valerio
Gift Ngoepe

2B

Max Moroff (13)
Alen Hanson (16)
Kevin Kramer (21)
Mitchell Tolman
Chris Bostick

1B
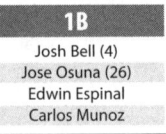
Josh Bell (4)
Jose Osuna (26)
Edwin Espinal
Carlos Munoz

C
Elias Diaz (10)
Jin-De Jhang (27)
Jacob Stallings

LHP

LHSP	LHRP
Steven Brault (7)	Tyler Webb (30)
Brandon Waddell (17)	Jared Lakind
Taylor Hearn (20)	Sean Keselica
Braeden Ogle (25)	
Ike Schlabach	
Cody Dickson	

RHP

RHSP	RHRP
Mitch Keller (2)	Dovydas Neverauskas (24)
Tyler Glasnow (3)	Edgar Santana
Nick Kingham (11)	Montana DuRupau
Gage Hinsz (12)	Tate Scioneaux
Clay Holmes (14)	
Yeudy Garcia (15)	
Tyler Eppler (18)	
Trevor Williams (19)	
Frank Duncan (22)	
Travis MacGregor (23)	
Luis Escobar (28)	
Danny Beddes	
Max Kranick	
J.T. Brubaker	
Lisalverto Bonilla	

DRAFT ANALYSIS

2016

BEST PURE HITTER: 3B Will Craig (1) hit .379 in his junior year at Wake Forest and has a lengthy track record of hitting in college. His lack of exceptional bat speed and poor speed limit him from projecting as more than an above-average hitter.

BEST POWER HITTER: The Pirates drafted only four position players in the top 10 rounds, so they didn't sign a lot of power. Craig hit 16 home runs at Wake Forest last spring and has at least average power because of plenty of strength in his swing.

FASTEST RUNNER: OF Garrett Brown (23) has plus-plus speed and already a feel for how to use it. He stole 34 bases at Western Carolina during the spring and eight in nine attempts as a pro.

BEST DEFENSIVE PLAYER: SS Stephen Alemais (3) was seen as one of the best defensive college shortstops in the draft class. He has an above-average arm, good hands and average range.

BEST FASTBALL: RHP Blake Cederlind (7) has touched 97 mph and sits in the mid-90s. RHP Max Kranick (11) doesn't throw as hard as Cederlind yet, but as a lanky, young projectable arm, it's possible his low-90s fastball that touches 95 could gain a tick or two eventually. LHP Braeden Ogle (4) has touched 96. Craig is a just hitter now, but he sat in the low 90s and touched 94-95 as a reliever at Wake Forest.

BEST SECONDARY PITCH: Ogle's curveball is average. RHP Travis McGregor (2) flashes an average changeup. LHP Cam Vieaux (7) has an average changeup.

BEST PRO DEBUT: Craig didn't hit for power, but he did post a .412 on-base percentage at short-season West Virginia. Kranick went 1-2, 2.43 with the Rookie-level GCL Pirates while walking just four in 33 innings.

BEST ATHLETE: Brown played wide receiver and quarterback at Western Carolina and at one point focused fully on football before coming back to the baseball diamond. He has plus-plus speed.

MOST INTRIGUING BACKGROUND: Brown returned to the diamond after using up his football eligibility at Western Carolina. He hit enough as a senior outfielder to become an intriguing, if a little old, senior sign as a 23-year-old who has come back to baseball later in his college career than most.

CLOSEST TO THE MAJORS: Craig (1) faces questions about his defense and athleticism, but he is a polished hitter which gives him a chance to move quickly.

BEST LATE-ROUND PICK: Kranick is the kind of late-round projectable high school arm the Pirates seem to thrive at developing. He showed advanced control but didn't miss many bats with his low-90s fastball in his Gulf Coast League debut.

THE ONE WHO GOT AWAY: RHP Nick Lodolo (2) was the only player picked in the top five rounds who did not sign. The Texas Christian signee sits in the upper 80s with his fastball, touching 92, with the lanky, projectable frame to add velocity. The Pirates get a pick in next year's draft as compensation for not signing Lodolo.

2015

SS Kevin Newman (1) reversed a recent Bucs trend with college bats, hitting from Day One and reaching Double-A in his first pro season. 3B Ke'Bryan Hayes (1) has flashed a plus bat as well. LHP Brandon Waddell (5) quickly progressed to Double-A.

GRADE: B.

2014

The Pirates spent heavily on prep talent and saw a breakthrough in 2016 from RHP Mitch Keller (2), with progress as well from RHPs Gage Hinsz (11) and college picks Tyler Eppler (6), Frank Duncan (13) and Montana DuRapau (32). A labrum injury has hampered SS Cole Tucker (1).

GRADE: B.

2013

OF Austin Meadows (1) has emerged as Pittsburgh's top prospect, while OF JaCoby Jones (3; since traded to the Tigers), 2B/OF Adam Frazier (6) and RHP Chad Kuhl (90 have reached the major leagues. Pittsburgh traded C Reese McGuire (1) in the much-maligned Francisco Liriano salary dump.

GRADE: A.

TOP DRAFT PICKS OF THE DECADE

Year	Player, Pos.	2016 Org
2007	Daniel Moskos, lhp	Padres
2008	Pedro Alvarez, 3b	Orioles
2009	Tony Sanchez, c	Giants
2010	Jameson Taillon, rhp	Pirates
2011	Gerrit Cole, rhp	Pirates
2012	*Mark Appel, rhp	Phillies
2013	Austin Meadows, of	Pirates
2014	Cole Tucker, ss	Pirates
2015	Kevin Newman, ss	Pirates
2016	Will Craig, 3b	Pirates

* Did not sign

LARGEST BONUSES IN CLUB HISTORY

Gerrit Cole, 2011	$8,000,000
Jameson Taillon, 2010	$6,500,000
Pedro Alvarez, 2008	$6,000,000
Josh Bell, 2011	$5,000,000
Bryan Bullington, 2002	$4,000,000

1 AUSTIN MEADOWS, OF

Born: May 3, 1995. **B-T:** L-L. **Ht.:** 6-3. **Wt.:** 200.
Drafted: HS—Loganville, Ga., 2013 (1st round).
Signed by: Jerry Jordan.

The Pirates selected Meadows with the first of two first-round picks in the 2013 draft, choosing him ninth overall with the compensation pick the club received for failing to sign first-rounder Mark Appel in 2012. Meadows battled back-and-forth with fellow Georgia prep outfielder Clint Frazier for the title of best high school bat in the 2013 draft class. Frazier ended up going before Meadows but both have lived up to expectations so far.

Meadows signed for $3,029,600 to forgo a Clemson commitment. He comes from an athletic background as the son of two Division I athletes. His father played baseball and football at Morehead State, while his mother was a softball player at Georgia Southern and Georgia State. Meadows also played football in high school as a running back, linebacker and punter. He ranked among the top prospects in Double-A Eastern and Triple-A International leagues in 2016, a season in which he batted .266/.333/.536 with 12 home runs and 17 stolen bases in 87 games.

Meadows has harnessed his athleticism to become a pure hitter with a short, smooth stroke who sprays line drives to all fields. He is in the process of unlocking his raw power as he continues to get comfortable turning on pitches and learning when it is wise to sell out for power. Meadows also shows a good eye at the plate, rarely chasing pitches out of the strike zone, and is willing to take a walk.

Defensively, Meadows is a fluid outfielder with outstanding instincts that allow him to get good jumps in center field and run down fly balls from gap to gap. His arm is slightly above-average, which will allow him to play right field if needed—or left field at Pittsburgh's PNC Park, where the gap in left-center field stretches to 410 feet. Meadows also runs well and has the raw speed to become a top-flight baserunner, though he still needs to improve his leads and jumps on balls off the bat while running the bases. Meadows wins high marks for his makeup as a hard worker with a great attitude and leadership capabilities. One potential drawback is durability. He missed most of the 2014 season and a month in 2016 at Triple-A Indianapolis because

BA GRADE

60 Risk: Medium

SCOUTING GRADES

Batting: 60
Power: 60
Speed: 60
Defense: 60
Arm: 55

Based on 20-80 scouting scale and future projection rather than present grades.

MIKE JANES

of hamstring injuries. The 2016 injury caused him to miss the Futures Game in San Diego.

Meadows is expected to begin 2017 back at Indianapolis, but it is not out of the question that he will make his major league debut before the all-star break or earlier if the Pirates decide to trade Andrew McCutchen. Some additional development time wouldn't hurt because Meadows did not get a full year of development in 2016, and injuries, which also included a fractured orbital bone sustained in spring training in a freak accident while playing catch, set him back slightly. He projects to be a star-caliber player and probably will follow in the footsteps of such outfielders as Andrew McCutchen, Starling Marte and Gregory Polanco, who have been developed by the Pirates over the last decade.

Year	Club (League)	Class	AVG	G	AB	R	H	2B	3B	HR	RBI	BB	SO	SB	CS	OBP	SLG
2014	Pirates (GCL)	R	1.000	2	4	1	4	2	1	0	1	2	0	0	0	1.000	2.000
	Bristol (APP)	R	.071	5	14	2	1	0	0	0	0	3	3	0	0	.235	.071
	West Virginia (SAL)	LoA	.322	38	146	18	47	13	1	3	15	14	30	2	3	.388	.486
2015	Bradenton (FSL)	HiA	.307	121	508	72	156	22	4	7	54	41	79	20	7	.357	.407
	Altoona (EL)	AA	.360	6	25	5	9	2	3	0	1	2	5	1	0	.429	.680
2016	Altoona (EL)	AA	.311	45	167	33	52	16	8	6	23	16	32	9	3	.365	.611
	West Virginia (NYP)	SS	.200	5	15	0	3	2	0	0	2	1	0	0	0	.294	.333
	Indianapolis (IL)	AAA	.214	37	126	16	27	7	3	6	24	15	34	8	2	.297	.460
Minor League Totals			.300	307	1182	184	355	75	25	29	140	124	230	43	17	.368	.480

2 MITCH KELLER, RHP

Born: April 4, 1996. **B-T:** R-R. **Ht.:** 6-3. **Wt.:** 195. **Drafted:** HS—Cedar Rapids, Iowa, 2014 (2nd round). **Signed by:** Matt Bimeal.

Keller climbed up many teams' draft boards when he added nearly 10 mph to his fastball between his junior and senior seasons of high school. The Pirates snatched him in the second round of the 2014 draft and signed him for an above-slot $1 million to forgo a North Carolina commitment. His older brother Jon is a pitcher in the Orioles system. Keller's fastball reaches 97 mph, sits at 93-95 and has the type of late life that causes plenty of swings and misses. He also has an above-average curveball with 11-to-5 shape that improved as the 2016 season progressed. He learned to take a little off his breaking ball in order to gain better control. Keller's changeup is also becoming an effective pitch. It drops just as it reaches the strike zone, generating many ground balls. Durability is a concern after Keller missed most of 2015 with forearm problems, but he stayed healthy throughout the 2016 season at low Class A West Virginia and finished strong with high Class A Bradenton, winning a pair of playoff starts to help the Marauders win the Florida State League title. He earns high marks for his maturity. For example, he immediately offered to help victims when flooding struck southern West Virginia. Keller will begin 2017 back with Bradenton and will likely end it at Double-A Altoona. He has the stuff, size and makeup to become a front-of-the-rotation stalwart and could reach the majors by late 2018 or early 2019.

BA GRADE
65 Risk: High

Year	Club (League)	Class	W	L	ERA	G	GS	CG	SV	IP	H	HR	BB	SO	K/9	WHIP	AVG
2014	Pirates (GCL)	R	0	0	1.98	9	8	0	0	27	19	0	13	29	9.5	1.17	.202
2015	Bristol (APP)	R	0	3	5.49	6	6	0	0	20	25	1	16	25	11.4	2.08	.309
2016	West Virginia (SAL)	LoA	8	5	2.46	23	23	0	0	124	96	4	18	131	9.5	0.92	.211
	Bradenton (FSL)	HiA	1	0	0.00	1	1	0	0	6	5	0	1	7	10.5	1.00	.227
Minor League Totals			9	8	2.64	39	38	0	0	177	145	5	48	192	9.7	1.09	.223

3 TYLER GLASNOW, RHP

Born: Aug. 23, 1993. **B-T:** L-R. **Ht.:** 6-8. **Wt.:** 220. **Drafted:** HS—Newhall, Calif., 2011 (5th round). **Signed by:** Rick Allen.

Glasnow threw just 83-89 mph in high school with an uncoordinated 6-foot-7 frame, but the Pirates saw potential and drafted him in the fifth round of the 2011 draft. He has added strength to his body and became one of the most dominant pitching prospects in the game as he ascended. His trek culminated in his major league debut in 2016. Glasnow's added strength gave him outstanding raw stuff, topped by a 92-95 mph fastball that hits 99 and a wipeout curveball. He also throws his changeup at 90 mph, and the pitch is showing signs of being a third plus weapon. He has allowed a career .172 opponent average in 500 minor league innings. Walks, however, have been a major problem for the now 6-foot-8 Glasnow, who like many other tall pitchers has problems repeating his mechanics. He also struggles holding runners because of his slow times to the plate and lack of an effective pickoff move. That weakness was exposed at the major league level. While some have questioned his athleticism, Glasnow answered by posting a video on social media of him dunking a basketball after pulling it between his legs. He will get a chance to win a rotation spot in spring training but will likely return to Triple-A Indianapolis. He has the ceiling of a No. 1 starter, but many evaluators outside the organization believe his futures lies as a reliever due to his poor control.

BA GRADE
65 Risk: High

Year	Club (League)	Class	W	L	ERA	G	GS	CG	SV	IP	H	HR	BB	SO	K/9	WHIP	AVG
2014	Bradenton (FSL)	HiA	12	5	1.74	23	23	0	0	124	74	3	57	157	11.4	1.05	.174
2015	West Virginia (NYP)	SS	0	1	3.38	2	2	0	0	5	3	0	2	6	10.1	0.94	.150
	Altoona (EL)	AA	5	3	2.43	12	12	0	0	63	41	2	19	82	11.7	0.95	.182
	Indianapolis (IL)	AAA	2	1	2.20	8	8	0	0	41	33	1	22	48	10.5	1.34	.220
2016	Altoona (EL)	AA	0	0	3.00	2	2	0	0	6	4	1	6	11	16.5	1.67	.190
	Indianapolis (IL)	AAA	8	3	1.87	20	20	0	0	111	65	4	62	133	10.8	1.15	.175
	Pittsburgh (NL)	MAJ	0	2	4.24	7	4	0	0	23	22	2	13	24	9.5	1.50	.250
Major League Totals			0	2	4.24	7	4	0	0	23	22	2	13	24	9.3	1.50	.250
Minor League Totals			36	19	2.03	103	102	0	0	500	297	23	246	645	11.6	1.09	.172

4 JOSH BELL, 1B/OF

Born: Aug. 14 1992. **B-T:** S-R. **Ht.:** 6-2. **Wt.:** 240. **Drafted:** HS—Dallas, 2011 (2nd round). **Signed by:** Mike Leuzinger.

Bell gained fame after signing for $5 million, a record for a second-round pick, after originally telling teams not to draft him because he wanted to attend Texas. He broke through to the majors in 2016 after a steady climb. The switch-hitter transitioned from right field to first base in 2015, allowing him to focus on hitting and letting his bat flourish. Bell has an advanced understanding of the strike zone, which allows him to work counts and get his pitch to hit. When he does, he makes hard contact to all fields, especially from the left side. He has the size and strength to be an above-average hitter with above-average power and is improving his approach and swing to be successful at the top level. Defensively, Bell has worked hard to improve his play at first base, but his range is limited and his hands are stiff. He is more comfortable in right field, where his strong arm mitigates a lack of range. He is not much of a threat on the bases. Bell is in line to be the Opening Day first baseman for the Pirates but could eventually wind up back in right field, though Pittsburgh projects to have no vacancies there for years. He has a chance to be a middle-of-the-order regular, especially if he can increase his power output.

BA GRADE
55 Risk: Medium

Year	Club (League)	Class	AVG	G	AB	R	H	2B	3B	HR	RBI	BB	SO	SB	CS	OBP	SLG
2014	Bradenton (FSL)	HiA	.335	84	331	45	111	20	4	9	53	25	43	5	4	.384	.502
	Altoona (EL)	AA	.287	24	94	13	27	2	0	0	7	8	12	4	1	.343	.309
2015	Altoona (EL)	AA	.307	96	368	47	113	17	6	5	60	44	50	7	4	.376	.427
	Indianapolis (IL)	AAA	.347	35	121	20	42	7	3	2	18	21	15	2	0	.441	.504
2016	Indianapolis (IL)	AAA	.295	114	421	57	124	23	4	14	60	57	74	3	7	.382	.468
	Pittsburgh (NL)	MAJ	.273	45	128	18	35	8	0	3	19	21	19	0	1	.368	.406
Major League Totals			.273	45	128	18	35	8	0	3	19	21	19	0	1	.368	.406
Minor League Totals			.303	487	1856	263	562	111	19	44	285	209	305	23	18	.373	.454

5 KEVIN NEWMAN, SS

Born: Aug. 4, 1993. **B-T:** R-R. **Ht.:** 6-1. **Wt.:** 180. **Drafted:** Arizona, 2015 (1st round). **Signed by:** Derrick Van Dusen.

Newman went from going undrafted following his senior year of high school in Poway, Calif., to being the 19th overall pick after three seasons at Arizona. He became the first player to win back-to-back batting titles in the Cape Cod League and followed by hitting .370 during his junior year before being drafted. He shook off a broken orbital bone in May 2016 to finish at Double-A. Newman has an advanced feel for hitting and all the earmarks of a prototype No. 2 hitter, with an ability to work counts, take walks and make consistent contact. He could add more power to his game, but it's unlikely Newman would ever hit more than 12-15 home runs a season. Regardless, he is a plus hitter who won't need substantial power to supply offensive value. He also has above-average speed and good instincts on the bases, which he could eventually turn into stolen bases. Newman's range and arm grade as merely average to slightly above-average at shortstop, but he is able to make plays in the hole and rarely misses the routine ones. Newman likely will split the 2017 season between Double-A Altoona and Triple-A Indianapolis, putting him in line to make his major league debut in 2018. He is the heir apparent to shortstop Jordy Mercer, who becomes a free agent after the 2018 season.

BA GRADE
55 Risk: High

Year	Club (League)	Class	AVG	G	AB	R	H	2B	3B	HR	RBI	BB	SO	SB	CS	OBP	SLG
2015	West Virginia (NYP)	SS	.226	38	159	25	36	10	1	2	9	10	22	7	1	.281	.340
	West Virginia (SAL)	LoA	.306	23	98	14	30	4	1	0	8	9	8	6	1	.376	.367
2016	Bradenton (FSL)	HiA	.366	41	164	24	60	10	1	3	24	17	12	4	1	.428	.494
	Altoona (EL)	AA	.288	61	233	41	67	11	2	2	28	26	24	6	3	.361	.378
Minor League Totals			.295	163	654	104	193	35	5	7	69	62	66	23	6	.362	.396

6 KE'BRYAN HAYES, 3B

BA GRADE

55 Risk: High

Born: Jan. 28, 1997. **B-T:** R-R. **Ht.:** 6-1. **Wt.:** 210. **Drafted:** HS—Tomball, Texas, 2015 (1st round). **Signed by:** Tyler Stohr.

Hayes' father Charlie played third base in the major leagues for 14 seasons from 1988-2001. That included a stint with the 1996 Pirates before they traded him to the Yankees, who he helped win a World Series that fall. The Pirates chose Hayes 32nd overall in 2015, three slots higher than his father was selected by the Giants in 1983. Hayes has the potential to be an above-average hitter for both average and power, but scouts have to project a bit to get to that point. He uses an all-fields approach to spray drives from foul line to foul line and at times reads pitches well for a young hitter. He did not do that consistently enough to dominate at low Class A West Virginia in 2016, his first taste of full-season ball. Hayes began to show his power potential before a back injury caused him to miss the entire second half. His next step in that direction is learning how to drive breaking balls and changeups. Hayes has a strong arm and some teams wanted to draft him as a pitcher. He also has good instincts and hands at third base but is a below-average runner. Hayes will return to West Virginia to start 2017 to make up for time lost time. A strong showing will cue him up for a quick promotion to high Class A Bradenton.

Year	Club (League)	Class	AVG	G	AB	R	H	2B	3B	HR	RBI	BB	SO	SB	CS	OBP	SLG
2015	Pirates (GCL)	R	.333	44	144	24	48	4	1	0	13	22	24	7	1	.434	.375
	West Virginia (NYP)	SS	.220	12	41	8	9	1	0	0	7	6	7	1	1	.320	.244
2016	West Virginia (SAL)	LoA	.263	65	247	27	65	12	1	6	37	16	51	6	5	.319	.393
	Pirates (GCL)	R	.400	2	5	0	2	1	0	0	0	1	1	0	0	.500	.600
Minor League Totals			.284	123	437	59	124	18	2	6	57	45	83	14	7	.361	.375

7 STEVEN BRAULT, LHP

BA GRADE

50 Risk: Medium

Born: April 29, 1992. **B-T:** L-L. **Ht.:** 6-0. **Wt.:** 200. **Drafted:** Regis (Colo.), 2013 (11th round). **Signed by:** Jim Gillette (Orioles).

The Pirates acquired Brault and fellow lefthander Stephen Tarpley in a trade with the Orioles for journeyman outfielder Travis Snider in 2015. While Snider spent 2016 in the minors, Brault made his major league debut with the Pirates. It was the culmination of a stunning ascent for Brault, who three years earlier was majoring in music performance as an aspiring singer and just playing baseball on the side at the Division II level. Brault does not have a wipeout pitch. He succeeds by mixing three offerings and throwing them all for strikes with a deceptive, athletic delivery that features a low three-quarters arm slot. His fastball sits 87-90 mph and touches 92 with good sinking action. Some scouts give both his secondary pitches above-average grades. After throwing two breaking pitches earlier in his career, Brault now throws only a slider, and the pitch continues to improve along with an at-times plus changeup, which is becoming a better pitch against righthanders. An above-average athlete, Brault got hit in his first shot at the majors but attributed much of that to nerves. He also was uncharacteristically wild in 2016. Brault has a shot to win a rotation spot in 2017 out of spring training. While his stuff is ordinary, he has the smarts to eventually become a reliable back-end starter.

Year	Club (League)	Class	W	L	ERA	G	GS	CG	SV	IP	H	HR	BB	SO	K/9	WHIP	AVG
2014	Delmarva (SAL)	LoA	9	8	3.05	22	21	1	0	130	107	4	28	115	8.0	1.04	.227
	Frederick (CAR)	HiA	2	0	0.55	3	3	1	0	16	7	0	2	9	5.0	0.55	.127
2015	Bradenton (FSL)	HiA	4	1	3.02	13	13	0	0	66	62	3	21	45	6.2	1.26	.252
	Altoona (EL)	AA	9	3	2.00	15	15	0	0	90	72	1	19	80	8.0	1.01	.212
2016	West Virginia (NYP)	SS	0	0	0.00	1	1	0	0	4	1	0	0	5	11.3	0.25	.077
	Indianapolis (IL)	AAA	2	7	3.91	16	15	0	0	71	66	6	35	81	10.2	1.42	.243
	Pittsburgh (NL)	MAJ	0	3	4.86	8	7	0	0	33	45	5	17	29	7.8	1.86	.313
Major League Totals			0	3	4.86	8	7	0	0	33	45	5	17	29	7.8	1.86	.313
Minor League Totals			27	21	2.74	82	80	2	0	420	350	15	117	373	8.0	1.11	.226

8 COLE TUCKER, SS

Born: July 3, 1996. **B-T:** B-R. **Ht.:** 6-3. **Wt.:** 185. **Drafted:** HS—Phoenix, 2014 (1st round). **Signed by:** Mike Steele.

The Pirates surprised many by selecting Tucker with the 24th overall pick in the 2014 draft, with the industry consensus that he was a second- to third-round talent. He signed for $1.8 million to pass up an Arizona commitment. Tucker's raw, projectable tools and off-the-charts makeup are what attracted the Pirates. They believe he has the potential to hit for above-average power because of his large frame, all while retaining the athleticism necessary to play shortstop. Tucker's potentially average hitting ability has yet to truly manifest itself in pro ball, but he has shown enough flashes for the Pirates to keep faith, especially because he puts together solid at-bats from both sides of the plate. Tucker had shoulder surgery late in the 2014 season but continues to regain arm strength while showing solid range and hands. He is an above-average runner who is still learning to translate his speed into success on the basepaths. Tucker will begin 2017 back at high Class A Bradenton after struggling as one of the younger players in the Florida State League in 2016. He still is a project, but his tools, athleticism and youth remain intriguing.

BA GRADE
50 Risk: High

Year	Club (League)	Class	AVG	G	AB	R	H	2B	3B	HR	RBI	BB	SO	SB	CS	OBP	SLG
2014	Pirates (GCL)	R	.267	48	180	39	48	6	2	2	13	26	38	13	5	.368	.356
2015	West Virginia (SAL)	LoA	.293	73	300	46	88	13	3	2	25	16	49	25	6	.322	.377
2016	West Virginia (SAL)	LoA	.262	15	61	9	16	4	2	1	2	4	9	1	1	.308	.443
	Bradenton (FSL)	HiA	.238	65	269	36	64	12	1	1	25	29	62	5	6	.312	.301
Minor League Totals			.267	201	810	130	216	35	8	6	65	75	158	44	18	.328	.352

9 WILL CRAIG, 3B

Born: Nov. 16, 1994. **B-T:** R-R. **Ht.:** 6-3. **Wt.:** 212. **Drafted:** Wake Forest, 2016 (1st round). **Signed by:** Jerry Jordan.

The Royals drafted Craig in the 37th round out of a Tennessee high school, but he went to Wake Forest and became one of the most prolific hitters in program history. He capped a historic college run by hitting .379/.520/.731 with 16 home runs as a junior and ranked third in the nation in slugging. He also served as the team's closer. The Pirates selected Craig with the 22nd overall pick in 2016 and signed him for $2,253,700. He is a thickly-built masher who many scouts compare with Billy Butler, who had a fine career, primarily as DH for the Royals. Like the young Butler, Craig is a below-average defender at third base and a slow runner. Craig does have a good blend of power and patience that give him a chance to be a successful hitter, though he has had trouble making the transition to wood bats. He struggled in the Cape Cod League in 2015 and hit just .280 with two home runs at short-season West Virginia in his pro debut. While throwing 94 mph fastballs out of the Wake Forest bullpen is testament to Craig's plus arm strength, a lack of range will likely result in him eventually landing at first base. Craig will likely jump to high Class A Bradenton to begin 2017.

BA GRADE
50 Risk: High

Year	Club (League)	Class	AVG	G	AB	R	H	2B	3B	HR	RBI	BB	SO	SB	CS	OBP	SLG
2016	West Virginia (NYP)	SS	.280	63	218	28	61	12	0	2	23	41	37	2	0	.412	.362
Minor League Totals			.280	63	218	28	61	12	0	2	23	41	37	2	0	.412	.362

10 ELIAS DIAZ, C

Born: Nov. 17, 1990. **B-T:** R-R. **Ht.:** 6-0. **Wt.:** 210. **Signed:** Venezuela, 2008. **Signed by:** Rene Gayo/Rodolfo Petit.

Diaz won the Captain's Catcher Award in 2015, which is awarded annually by Baseball America to the top defensive catcher in the minor leagues. He was felled by a right elbow injury in 2016 spring training that required surgery. Diaz returned to action in July but batted just 128 times. Diaz is a glove-first catcher who wins high marks for his mobility behind the plate, strong arm and ability to work with pitchers. The total package makes him an elite defender. The Pirates' medical staff is confident he should regain most of his strength by the beginning of spring training. Offensively Diaz is a fringe-average hitter with below-average power, but he has worked hard to become someone who can work counts, post a decent average and keep pitchers honest by popping an occasional ball into the gap. Diaz will return to Triple-A Indianapolis for a fourth season in 2017 because the Pirates are set at catcher with veterans Francisco Cervelli and Chris Stewart. .

BA GRADE
45 Risk: Medium

Year	Club (League)	Class	AVG	G	AB	R	H	2B	3B	HR	RBI	BB	SO	SB	CS	OBP	SLG
2014	Altoona (EL)	AA	.328	91	326	41	107	20	0	6	54	30	51	3	2	.378	.445
	Indianapolis (IL)	AAA	.152	10	33	4	5	1	0	0	0	3	6	0	1	.243	.182
2015	Indianapolis (IL)	AAA	.271	93	325	33	88	16	4	4	47	29	47	1	4	.330	.382
	Pittsburgh (NL)	MAJ	.000	2	2	0	0	0	0	0	0	0	1	0	0	.000	.000
2016	Bradenton (FSL)	HiA	.391	7	23	6	9	0	0	1	5	4	2	0	1	.464	.522
	Altoona (EL)	AA	.286	2	7	0	2	0	0	0	1	1	1	0	0	.375	.286
	Pittsburgh (NL)	MAJ	.000	1	4	0	0	0	0	0	1	0	1	0	0	.000	.000
	Indianapolis (IL)	AAA	.266	25	94	4	25	3	0	0	10	3	17	1	0	.289	.298
Major League Totals			.000	3	6	0	0	0	0	0	1	0	2	0	0	.000	.000
Minor League Totals			.258	572	2004	241	518	107	13	25	259	185	352	20	21	.323	.362

11 NICK KINGHAM, RHP

BA GRADE
50 Risk: High

Born: Nov. 8, 1991. **B-T:** R-R. **Ht.:** 6-6. **Wt.:** 225. **Drafted:** HS—Las Vegas, 2010 (4th round). **Signed by:** Larry Broadway.

Kingham was one of many high school pitchers the Pirates went over slot to sign before the bonus-pool system went into effect in 2012. They signed him for $485,000 to forego a scholarship to Oregon after he was high school teammates with Bryce Harper in Las Vegas. Scout Larry Broadway, now Pirates farm director, was persistent in getting Kingham to sign. Kingham's rise stalled when he injured his elbow in May 2015 while pitching at Triple-A Indianapolis, and it required Tommy John surgery. He returned to the mound in the second half of 2016 and spent the half-season working his way back to Double-A Altona. Kingham has a fastball that sits in the low 90s but appears quicker because he uses his 6-foot-6 frame to get good downhill plane in his delivery. He also has a plus changeup as well as a curveball that is a solid third pitch. Kingham has retained outstanding command of his pitches post-surgery, pounds the zone and is a good athlete for his size. After tossing 46 innings in 2016, Kingham should begin 2017 back in Triple-A and is in position to make his major league debut at during the year.

Year	Club (League)	Class	W	L	ERA	G	GS	CG	SV	IP	H	HR	BB	SO	K/9	WHIP	AVG
2014	Altoona (EL)	AA	1	7	3.04	12	12	0	0	71	71	3	25	54	6.8	1.35	.259
	Indianapolis (IL)	AAA	5	4	3.58	14	14	0	0	88	70	6	27	65	6.6	1.10	.213
2015	Indianapolis (IL)	AAA	1	2	4.31	6	6	0	0	31	34	3	7	32	9.2	1.31	.270
2016	Pirates (GCL)	R	0	4	3.00	6	6	0	0	24	23	0	1	16	6.0	1.00	.256
	Bradenton (FSL)	HiA	2	0	0.00	2	2	0	0	11	8	0	1	10	8.2	0.82	.211
	Altoona (EL)	AA	1	1	5.73	2	2	0	0	11	6	1	4	10	8.2	0.91	.162
Minor League Totals			31	34	3.32	113	109	0	0	581	518	40	160	497	7.7	1.17	.238

12 GAGE HINSZ, RHP

BA GRADE
50 Risk: High

Born: April 20, 1996. **B-T:** R-R. **Ht.:** 6-4. **Wt.:** 210. **Drafted:** HS—Billings, Mont., 2014 (11th round). **Signed by:** Max Kwan.

Hinsz didn't get as much exposure to scouts as most teenage prospects because Montana does not have high school baseball. Thus scouts got most of their looks at Hinsz while he was playing American Legion ball or with the Langley (B.C.) Blaze travel program. With no high school baseball, Hinsz spent his springs working on his prized 1967 Dodge Coronet and winters working the shot clock at Rocky Mountain College basketball games in Billings. There is more projection needed in evaluating Hinsz than most prospects his age because of his lack of experience. Regardless, his plus fastball now reaches 95 mph as he has learned to repeat his delivery more consistently since entering pro ball. His command also improved drastically as a result. His curveball and changeup both have the possibility of becoming above-average pitches but are a ways off. Hinsz is a good athlete and a willing learner. The Pirates knew he was a project when they drafted him, but he impressed by successfully making the jump to low Class A West Virginia in 2016 and is right on par with other prospects his age. Hinsz continues to make steady progress and should begin 2017 in the rotation at high Class A Bradenton.

Year	Club (League)	Class	W	L	ERA	G	GS	CG	SV	IP	H	HR	BB	SO	K/9	WHIP	AVG
2014	Pirates (GCL)	R	0	0	3.38	3	2	0	0	8	8	0	4	7	7.9	1.50	.267
2015	Bristol (APP)	R	3	4	3.79	10	9	0	0	38	37	1	23	24	5.7	1.58	.252
2016	West Virginia (SAL)	LoA	6	8	3.66	17	17	0	0	93	93	8	25	67	6.5	1.26	.266
Minor League Totals			9	12	3.68	30	28	0	0	139	138	9	52	98	6.3	1.36	.262

13 TAYLOR HEARN, LHP

BA GRADE
50 Risk: High

Born: Aug. 30, 1994. **B-T:** L-L. **Ht.:** 6-5. **Wt.:** 210. **Drafted:** Oklahoma Baptist, 2015 (5th round). **Signed by:** Ed Gustafson (Nationals).

The Pirates angered their fans and created some discord in their clubhouse when they traded all-star closer Mark Melancon to the Nationals at the 2016 trade deadline for lefthanded reliever Felipe Rivero and

Hearn despite being just 3 1/2 games out of a wild card spot. While Rivero moved immediately into the big league bullpen, Hearn continued rehabbing from a broken foot he suffered while covering first base during his second start of the 2016 season. The Pirates were familiar with Hearn after drafting him in the 22nd round in 2012 out of high school—the first of four instances he was drafted—and saw him flash a 99 mph fastball and potentially wipeout slider once he joined their system. Hearn lacks a third pitch at present, with his changeup in the rudimentary stage of development, and his command of all his pitches is spotty. He will start 2017 in the high Class A Bradenton rotation but could move to the bullpen if his changeup and command don't improve.

Year	Club (League)	Class	W	L	ERA	G	GS	CG	SV	IP	H	HR	BB	SO	K/9	WHIP	AVG
2015	Nationals (GCL)	R	0	0	0.00	2	1	0	0	5	4	0	2	7	12.6	1.20	.250
	Auburn (NYP)	SS	1	5	3.98	10	10	0	0	43	49	2	13	38	8.0	1.44	.280
2016	Nationals (GCL)	R	0	0	1.42	2	2	0	0	6	2	1	6	8	11.4	1.26	.105
	Hagerstown (SAL)	LoA	1	0	3.18	8	2	0	0	23	25	3	7	31	12.3	1.41	.278
	West Virginia (SAL)	LoA	1	1	1.99	8	3	0	0	23	15	2	10	36	14.3	1.10	.183
Minor League Totals			3	6	2.98	30	18	0	0	100	95	8	38	120	10.8	1.33	.249

14 TREVOR WILLIAMS, RHP

BA GRADE
45 Risk: Medium

Born: April 25, 1992. **B-T:** R-R. **Ht.:** 6-3. **Wt.:** 230. **Drafted:** Arizona State, 2013 (2nd round). **Signed by:** Scott Stanley (Marlins).

The Pirates officially acquired Williams from the Marlins for righthander Richard Mitchell, who was almost immediately released. The acquisition was a side deal as compensation for the Marlins hiring Pirates pitching guru Jim Benedict as their vice president of pitching development. Williams quickly took to the Pirates system and made his major league debut in 2016 with a September callup. He provided one of the most emotional moments of the season when he notched his first win with three scoreless relief innings against the Cardinals and celebrated with a long, emotional hug in the stands with his father, who was battling lymphoma. Williams is a sinker-slider pitcher who sits 90-93 mph and uses the same slider grip as Indians ace Corey Kluber. Williams' four-seam fastball, curveball and changeup all flash as potentially average pitches. The Pirates are unsure whether Williams fits as a back-end starter or long reliever, but they like his ability to induce ground balls and will have him in the rotation at Triple-A.

Year	Club (League)	Class	W	L	ERA	G	GS	CG	SV	IP	H	HR	BB	SO	K/9	WHIP	AVG
2014	Jupiter (FSL)	HiA	8	6	2.79	23	23	0	0	129	138	5	29	90	6.3	1.29	.277
	Jacksonville (SL)	AA	0	1	6.00	3	3	0	0	15	22	0	6	14	8.4	1.87	.344
2015	Jacksonville (SL)	AA	7	8	4.00	22	21	0	0	117	126	9	36	88	6.8	1.38	.275
	New Orleans (PCL)	AAA	0	2	2.57	3	3	0	0	14	15	0	7	13	8.4	1.57	.268
2016	Bradenton (FSL)	HiA	1	0	0.00	1	1	0	0	5	4	0	0	4	7.2	0.80	.235
	Indianapolis (IL)	AAA	9	6	2.53	20	19	0	0	110	103	5	30	74	6.0	1.21	.249
	Pittsburgh (NL)	MAJ	1	1	7.82	7	1	0	0	13	19	4	5	11	7.8	1.89	.339
Major League Totals			1	1	7.82	7	1	0	0	13	19	4	5	11	7.8	1.89	.339
Minor League Totals			25	25	3.10	84	82	0	0	424	439	19	116	307	6.5	1.31	.267

15 YEUDY GARCIA, RHP

BA GRADE
50 Risk: High

Born: Oct. 6, 1992. **B-T:** R-R. **Ht.:** 6-2. **Wt.:** 203. **Signed:** Dominican Republic, 2013. **Signed by:** Rene Gayo/Juan Mercado.

Garcia is the rare Latin American player who did not sign as an international free agent until he was already 20 years old. Thus the Pirates have pushed him aggressively to make up for lost time. Garcia had a breakout year at low Class A West Virginia in 2015, but while his surface statistics were fine at high Class A Bradenton in 2016 he consistently had trouble with his command, which resulted in running up high pitch counts. Garcia admitted at the end of the season he had pitched through shoulder pain. The Pirates hope offseason rest will help solve the problem. When healthy, he has a power fastball that touches 99 mph and sits in the mid-90s. He also throws a hard slider that flashes plus, but he continues to struggle to find for a consistent grip on his changeup. The Pirates plan to stick with Garcia as a starter at Double-A Altoona in 2017, but his fastball-slider combination could make him a potential late-inning reliever if he is unable to master his changeup.

Year	Club (League)	Class	W	L	ERA	G	GS	CG	SV	IP	H	HR	BB	SO	K/9	WHIP	AVG
2014	Pirates1 (DSL)	R	4	3	2.41	13	13	0	0	60	50	0	20	47	7.1	1.17	.225
2015	West Virginia (SAL)	LoA	12	5	2.10	30	21	0	1	124	92	4	41	112	8.1	1.07	.204
2016	Bradenton (FSL)	HiA	6	8	2.76	26	25	1	1	127	122	7	54	127	9.0	1.38	.248
Minor League Totals			22	16	2.43	69	59	1	2	311	264	11	115	286	8.3	1.22	.227

16 BRANDON WADDELL, LHP

BA GRADE

50 Risk: High

Born: June 3, 1994. **B-T:** L-L. **Ht.:** 6-3. **Wt.:** 180. **Drafted:** Virginia, 2015 (5th round). **Signed by:** Dan Radcliff.

Waddell was one of the best big-game college pitchers in recent years. He won all five career starts in the College World Series for Virginia, including a complete-game shutout in 2014, and helped the Cavs win the 2015 CWS. Overall he went 6-1, 2.34 in 11 NCAA Tournament starts. Waddell climbed all the way to Double-A Altoona in his first full season in 2016. Waddell's stuff grades out as just average across the board, with an 89-91 mph fastball along with a slider and a changeup. He sets himself apart by expertly mixing his pitches and his willingness to pitch inside despite subpar velocity, which dovetails with the Pirates' organizational philosophy. Waddell won't ever pitch at the top of the rotation and his inability to get Double-A hitters to chase pitches outside the strike zone is a concern. He'll start 2017 back in the Double-A rotation.

Year	Club (League)	Class	W	L	ERA	G	GS	CG	SV	IP	H	HR	BB	SO	K/9	WHIP	AVG
2015	West Virginia (NYP)	SS	1	1	5.75	6	6	0	0	20	24	0	7	18	8.0	1.52	.276
2016	Bradenton (FSL)	HiA	4	0	0.93	5	5	0	0	29	13	1	2	26	8.1	0.52	.133
	Altoona (EL)	AA	7	9	4.12	22	20	0	0	118	122	9	61	94	7.2	1.55	.271
Minor League Totals			12	10	3.76	33	31	0	0	167	159	10	70	138	7.4	1.37	.250

17 MAX MOROFF, 2B

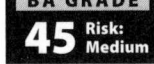

BA GRADE

45 Risk: Medium

Born: May 13, 1993. **B-T:** S-R. **Ht.:** 5-10. **Wt.:** 185. **Drafted:** HS—Winter Park, Fla., 2012 (16th round). **Signed by:** Nick Presto.

Moroff was committed to Central Florida until the Pirates enticed the 16th-round pick to reverse course and enter pro ball with a $300,000 bonus. He began his pro career as a shortstop before moving to second base and saw his first action at third base in 2016 at Triple-A Indianapolis. He is considered slightly above-average defensively at second base and average at third base and shortstop, where his fringe-average arm strength does not play as well. Moroff has moderate power but his offensive strength is getting on base. Because he works deep counts, he strikes out nearly at power-hitter rates, and he needs to use his above-average speed more effectively on the bases. If he does that, he could be an offensive weapon. The Pirates will continue shuffling him around the diamond, hoping he can become a valuable switch-hitter capable of playing three infield positions. Adam Frazier figures to be the Pirates' utility infielder in 2017, but Moroff will be at the ready at Triple-A Indianapolis if the need arises.

Year	Club (League)	Class	AVG	G	AB	R	H	2B	3B	HR	RBI	BB	SO	SB	CS	OBP	SLG
2014	Bradenton (FSL)	HiA	.244	130	467	57	114	30	6	1	50	54	129	21	15	.324	.340
2015	Altoona (EL)	AA	.293	136	523	79	153	28	6	7	51	70	111	17	13	.374	.409
2016	Pittsburgh (NL)	MAJ	.000	2	2	0	0	0	0	0	0	0	2	0	0	.000	.000
	Indianapolis (IL)	AAA	.230	133	421	61	97	18	4	8	45	90	129	9	7	.367	.349
Major League Totals			.000	2	2	0	0	0	0	0	0	0	2	0	0	.000	.000
Minor League Totals			.255	537	1907	289	487	97	19	25	201	296	482	62	46	.356	.365

18 ALEN HANSON, 2B/OF

BA GRADE

45 Risk: Medium

Born: Oct. 22, 1992. **B-T:** B-R. **Ht.:** 5-11. **Wt.:** 175. **Signed:** Dominican Republic, 2009. **Signed by:** Rene Gayo/Ellis Pena.

Once considered among the Top 100 Prospects in baseball—he ranked No. 61 prior to the 2013 season and No. 76 in 2014—Hanson's stock has dropped over the last two years as he has been converted from a middle infielder into a utility player at Triple-A Indianapolis. He made his major league debut in 2016, coming off the bench mostly as a pinch-hitter and pinch-runner. Hanson has been unable to convert his considerable tools into consistent production, though his athleticism still makes him intriguing as a potentially valuable bench piece. The switch-hitter is wiry strong and can hit the occasional home run, and he also has outstanding speed that makes him a threat on the bases. However, he does not always make solid contact. Hanson is not a strong defender and his attitude was questionable earlier in his career. However, he has embraced learning multiple positions. Hanson is out of minor league options, so he will have to fight an uphill battle against Adam Frazier for the utility infielder spot on the Pirates roster.

Year	Club (League)	Class	AVG	G	AB	R	H	2B	3B	HR	RBI	BB	SO	SB	CS	OBP	SLG
2014	Altoona (EL)	AA	.280	118	482	64	135	21	12	11	58	31	88	25	11	.326	.442
2015	Indianapolis (IL)	AAA	.263	117	475	66	125	17	12	6	43	37	91	35	12	.313	.387
2016	Indianapolis (IL)	AAA	.266	110	432	58	115	15	7	8	32	32	78	36	15	.318	.389
	Pittsburgh (NL)	MAJ	.226	27	31	5	7	1	0	0	1	2	5	2	1	.273	.258
Major League Totals			.226	27	31	5	7	1	0	0	1	2	5	2	1	.273	.258
Minor League Totals			.281	719	2834	442	797	136	71	53	316	240	531	205	87	.340	.435

19 CLAY HOLMES, RHP

BA GRADE

45 Risk: High

Born: March 27, 1993. **B-T:** R-R. **Ht.:** 6-5. **Wt.:** 230. **Drafted:** HS—Slocomb, Ala., 2011 (9th round). **Signed by:** Darren Mazeroski.

Holmes appeared solidly committed to Auburn after being his high school valedictorian with a strong interest in physics, but the Pirates swooped in with a $1.2 million signing bonus. It remains the largest bonus ever given to a ninth-round pick. Holmes' development stalled when he had Tommy John surgery in May 2014, but he was completely healthy again in 2016 and spent the entire season in the Double-A Altoona rotation. Holmes' best pitch is a fastball that sits in the low 90s with better sinking action on it since he returned from surgery. Nearly 63 percent of batted balls against him were groundballs in 2016. Holmes also throws a curveball, slider and changeup. His curveball became a strikeout pitch for him late in 2016, and the key is now turning his changeup into a third at least average pitch. He has the large frame that should allow to be a durable innings eater if he can be more pitch-efficient and reduce his walk rate. The Pirates added him to the 40-man roster after the 2016 season and spring training will determine whether he returns to Altoona or moves up to Triple-A Indianapolis.

Year	Club (League)	Class	W	L	ERA	G	GS	CG	SV	IP	H	HR	BB	SO	K/9	WHIP	AVG
2014	Did not play—Injured																
2015	Pirates (GCL)	R	1	0	2.03	3	3	0	0	13	13	0	1	10	6.8	1.05	.250
	Bradenton (FSL)	HiA	0	2	2.74	6	6	0	0	23	18	0	7	16	6.3	1.09	.222
2016	Altoona (EL)	AA	10	9	4.22	26	26	0	0	136	138	10	64	101	6.7	1.48	.272
Minor League Totals			21	20	3.67	74	73	0	0	351	310	18	170	251	6.4	1.37	.242

20 TYLER EPPLER, RHP

BA GRADE

45 Risk: Medium

Born: Jan. 5, 1993. **B-T:** R-R. **Ht.:** 6-6. **Wt.:** 220. **Drafted:** Sam Houston State, 2014 (6th round). **Signed by:** Trevor Haley.

Eppler was the second pitcher selected by the Pirates from Sam Houston State early in the 2014 draft. Pittsburgh chose him two rounds after taking lefthander Cody Dickson in the fourth round. Eppler's career got off to a delayed start after he was sidelined for the first 10 weeks of 2015 with elbow soreness, but he has still risen relatively quickly and spent all of 2016 in the Double-A Altoona rotation. Eppler has added a few ticks to his fastball velocity since college and now reaches 95 mph while sitting at 91-93. That is part of a four-pitch mix that includes an average slider and curveball along with a changeup still in its developmental changes. While Eppler has good control, the lack of strikeouts for a pitcher with his stuff is concerning. He has averaged just 6.1 strikeouts per nine innings across his career, with his total decreasing every level he ascends. He did answer questions about durability in 2016 by taking his regular turn in the Altoona rotation. Eppler is ready for a shot at Triple-A Indianapolis, but a backlog of starting pitchers in the upper minors could send him back to Altoona at least begin 2017.

Year	Club (League)	Class	W	L	ERA	G	GS	CG	SV	IP	H	HR	BB	SO	K/9	WHIP	AVG
2014	Jamestown (NYP)	SS	3	2	2.49	14	14	0	0	69	54	6	11	49	6.4	0.95	.213
2015	Bradenton (FSL)	HiA	6	1	2.58	14	12	1	1	66	58	1	14	46	6.2	1.09	.232
	Altoona (EL)	AA	0	1	10.13	1	1	0	0	5	4	1	3	3	5.1	1.31	.211
2016	Altoona (EL)	AA	9	10	3.99	27	27	1	0	162	176	14	33	106	5.9	1.29	.280
Minor League Totals			18	14	3.45	56	54	2	1	303	292	22	61	204	6.1	1.17	.253

21 KEVIN KRAMER, 2B

BA GRADE

45 Risk: High

Born: Oct. 3, 1993. **B-T:** L-R. **Ht.:** 6-1. **Wt.:** 190. **Drafted:** UCLA, 2015 (2nd round). **Signed by:** Rick Allen.

Kramer spent four years at UCLA after being a high school baseball and football star in Turlock, Calif. He missed his junior season in 2014 after surgery to repair a torn labrum in his right shoulder, but he returned the following year to lead the Bruins to the top seed in the NCAA Tournament as their starting shortstop. Kramer has the chance to be a high-average hitter with his excellent knowledge of the strike zone and ability to hit the ball to all fields. His power is only middling, but the Pirates believe he could eventually reach in 10-12 homers a season. Drafted as a shortstop, Kramer has now settled in as a second baseman. He has good range and hands for the position, and the shorter throws cover for a somewhat below-average arm. He doesn't pose much threat on the bases as an average runner. Kramer will start 2017 at Double-A Altoona and could be in position to move fairly quickly in a utility role as long as he hits.

Year	Club (League)	Class	AVG	G	AB	R	H	2B	3B	HR	RBI	BB	SO	SB	CS	OBP	SLG
2015	West Virginia (NYP)	SS	.305	46	177	34	54	7	3	0	17	25	28	9	4	.390	.379
	West Virginia (SAL)	LoA	.240	12	50	9	12	2	1	0	3	5	8	3	0	.321	.320
2016	Bradenton (FSL)	HiA	.277	118	444	56	123	29	2	4	57	48	63	3	9	.352	.378
Minor League Totals			.282	176	671	99	189	38	6	4	77	78	99	15	13	.360	.374

22 TRAVIS MACGREGOR, RHP

BA GRADE

50 Risk: Extreme

Born: Oct. 15, 1997. **B-T:** R-R. **Ht.:** 6-3. **Wt.:** 180. **Drafted:** HS—Tarpon Springs, Fla., 2016 (2nd round). **Signed by:** Nick Presto.

MacGregror was a late-riser whose draft stock rose significantly after he added a few ticks of velocity. The Pirates drafted him 68th overall in 2016, which was an overdraft in the eyes of many analysts, and signed him for a below-slot $900,000 to forgo a Clemson scholarship. MacGregor's new 94 mph fastball represented an upgrade of 5 mph from his previous high, and the Pirates believe his velocity will continue to increase as his body fills out. He has good command of his average changeup for a young pitcher, and he has shown some feel for locating his curveball, which is still in the developmental stages. The Pirates love MacGregor's athleticism and believe it will enable him to consistently repeat his delivery, which in turn should give him above-average control and command. MacGregor showed fairly well in his first taste of pro ball, though his subpar strikeout rate is a testament to the rawness of his stuff. He will likely begin 2017 in extended spring training before heading to Rookie-level Bristol.

Year	Club (League)	Class	W	L	ERA	G	GS	CG	SV	IP	H	HR	BB	SO	K/9	WHIP	AVG
2016	Pirates (GCL)	R	1	1	3.13	9	9	0	0	32	29	1	10	19	5.4	1.23	.248
Minor League Totals			1	1	3.13	9	9	0	0	32	29	1	10	19	5.4	1.23	.248

23 FRANK DUNCAN, RHP

BA GRADE

40 Risk: Medium

Born: Jan. 30, 1992. **B-T:** R-R. **Ht.:** 6-4. **Wt.:** 215. **Drafted:** Kansas, 2014 (13th round). **Signed by:** Matt Bimeal.

Duncan declined to sign with the Indians after they selected him in the 39th round of the 2013 draft, and he returned to Kansas for his senior season. The move worked. Duncan completed his civil engineering degree while also improving his draft stock significantly. By embracing the Pirates' organizational philosophy of throwing sinkers to induce groundball outs and keep the ball in the park, Duncan has quickly made his way up the system and had a fine 2016 at Triple-A Indianapolis. Duncan rarely tops 90 mph but the sinking action on his fastball and a plus slider give him a chance to either be a spot starter or a groundball-inducing middle reliever. He is especially effective against righthanders, holding them to a .214/.286/.288 line at Triple-A. Duncan wins high marks for his baseball smarts, his ability to self-evaluate and for his ability to adjust quickly on the mound. He will head back to the Indianapolis rotation to begin 2017 but is on the cusp of making his major league debut.

Year	Club (League)	Class	W	L	ERA	G	GS	CG	SV	IP	H	HR	BB	SO	K/9	WHIP	AVG
2014	Jamestown (NYP)	SS	3	3	3.58	14	14	0	0	65	75	3	11	49	6.8	1.32	.292
2015	Bradenton (FSL)	HiA	9	10	4.32	27	25	0	0	152	194	12	19	111	6.6	1.40	.311
2016	Altoona (EL)	AA	3	2	2.36	7	2	0	0	27	23	0	7	24	8.1	1.13	.228
	Indianapolis (IL)	AAA	9	6	2.33	20	20	0	0	112	106	4	29	92	7.4	1.21	.251
Minor League Totals			24	21	3.41	68	61	0	0	356	398	19	66	276	7.0	1.30	.283

24 DOVYDAS NEVERAUSKAS, RHP

BA GRADE

40 Risk: Medium

Born: Jan. 14, 1993. **B-T:** R-R. **Ht.:** 6-3. **Wt.:** 175. **Signed:** Lithuania, 2009. **Signed by:** Tom Randolph.

No players born and raised in Lithuania had signed a contract with a major league organization until Neverauskas did in 2009. He caught the Pirates' attention while attending Major League Baseball's European Academy in Italy and signed for $60,000 as a 16-year old. After stalling as a starter at low Class A West Virginia, Neverauskas' career took off in 2015 when he moved to the bullpen. Pitching in short stretches, he became more comfortable cutting loose his fastball, and it has since been clocked as high as 98 mph. He was selected to play in the 2016 Futures Game and impressed with a scoreless inning of relief. He also mixes in an occasional slider and cutter, which are both average pitches. Neverauskas' hit a speed bump when he was suspended for the final week of the 2016 season at Triple-A Indianapolis after being involved in a bar fight. The Pirates added him to the 40-man roster in November to prevent him from becoming a minor league free agent. Neverauskas will begin 2017 back at Triple-A .

Year	Club (League)	Class	W	L	ERA	G	GS	CG	SV	IP	H	HR	BB	SO	K/9	WHIP	AVG
2014	West Virginia (SAL)	LoA	6	12	5.60	27	26	1	0	124	151	12	55	88	6.4	1.67	.305
2015	West Virginia (NYP)	SS	1	0	3.86	1	0	0	0	2	4	1	3	2	7.7	3.00	.364
	West Virginia (SAL)	LoA	1	2	3.65	18	5	0	2	49	39	3	19	37	6.8	1.18	.214
	Bradenton (FSL)	HiA	0	0	1.62	12	0	0	4	17	15	0	5	10	5.4	1.20	.238
2016	Altoona (EL)	AA	1	0	2.57	22	0	0	1	28	12	0	11	32	10.3	0.82	.129
	Indianapolis (IL)	AAA	3	4	3.60	25	0	0	4	30	36	1	11	24	7.2	1.57	.308
Minor League Totals			21	24	4.21	147	58	1	11	385	387	31	165	289	6.8	1.43	.263

25 BRAEDEN OGLE, LHP

BA GRADE

50 Risk: Extreme

Born: July 30, 1997. **B-T:** L-L. **Ht.:** 6-2. **Wt.:** 170. **Drafted:** HS—Jensen Beach, Fla., 2016 (4th round). **Signed by:** Nick Presto.

Scouts began showing up in droves when Ogle hit 96 mph with his fastball in the first start of his senior high school season in 2016. His velocity eventually leveled off At 90-93 range. Though some teams cooled on him, the Pirates drafted Ogle in the fourth round and signed him for an over-slot $800,000 to pass up a Florida commitment. HE showed decent feel for his changeup during his pro debut in the Rookie-level Gulf Coast League, but he tended to try to overthrow his curveball and the velocity on the heater did not match what it was in February. Furthermore, Ogle struggled to consistently throw strikes. Even with those struggles however, he didn't give up many hits. Overall his live left arm, frame and well-regarded athleticism make him an interesting prospect. Ogle is a long way away and figures to start 2017 at extended spring training before joining Rookie-level Bristol in June.

Year	Club (League)	Class	W	L	ERA	G	GS	CG	SV	IP	H	HR	BB	SO	K/9	WHIP	AVG
2016	Pirates (GCL)	R	0	2	2.60	8	8	0	0	28	18	2	11	20	6.5	1.05	.188
Minor League Totals			0	2	2.60	8	8	0	0	28	18	2	11	20	6.5	1.05	.188

26 JOSE OSUNA, 1B/OF

BA GRADE

40 Risk: Medium

Born: Dec. 12, 1992. **B-T:** R-R. **Ht.:** 6-2. **Wt.:** 213. **Signed:** Venezuela, 2009. **Signed by:** Rene Gayo/Rodolfo Petit.

It has been a long, slow climb up the organizational ladder for Osuna, and he has yet to play in the major leagues eight years after signing. However, he is now on the cusp after being promoted from Double-A Altoona to Triple-A Indianapolis in 2016 and then being added to the 40-man roster after the season so that he would not qualify as a minor league free agent. Osuna was primarily a pitcher during his amateur days, but the Pirates were intrigued by his raw power potential as a hitter. Though his pop has yet to completely manifest, Osuna did show more power in 2016 while also maintaining his good eye at the plate. He is not very athletic and is a very slow runner. However, through hard work he has turned himself into a solid defensive first baseman. Though he has a strong arm, his lack of his range makes him a below-average fielder at both outfield corners. Osuna will head back to Indianapolis to begin the 2017 season, but he has a chance to break through to the majors as a righthanded power source off the bench.

Year	Club (League)	Class	AVG	G	AB	R	H	2B	3B	HR	RBI	BB	SO	SB	CS	OBP	SLG
2014	Bradenton (FSL)	HiA	.296	97	365	47	108	23	3	10	57	28	72	4	2	.347	.458
2015	Bradenton (FSL)	HiA	.282	44	174	23	49	12	1	4	29	14	33	1	1	.333	.431
	Altoona (EL)	AA	.288	85	323	46	93	20	2	8	52	17	61	6	3	.327	.437
2016	Altoona (EL)	AA	.269	70	253	34	68	18	3	6	38	23	44	1	1	.329	.435
	Indianapolis (IL)	AAA	.291	63	220	27	64	19	1	7	31	13	36	2	3	.333	.482
Minor League Totals			.278	722	2672	355	743	184	14	73	403	199	460	41	26	.330	.439

27 JIN-DE JHANG, C

BA GRADE

40 Risk: Medium

Born: May 17, 1993. **B-T:** L-R. **Ht.:** 5-11. **Wt.:** 220. **Signed:** Taiwan, 2011. **Signed by:** Fu Chun Chiang.

Signed for $250,000 as an 18-year old free agent out of Taiwan in 2011, Jhang has had his ups and downs during five seasons in the minor leagues. His combination of being able to hit for average and being a plus defender behind the plate makes him an interesting prospect. Jhang has not hit with the lefthanded power the Pirates hoped when they signed him, but he is willing to work the count and makes solid contact, giving him at least some offensive upside. He is a good catch-and-throw receiver with a strong arm that helps him slow down the running game. While he's shown the ability to handle a pitching staff, staying in shape has proven to be a constant battle. Jhang drew rave reviews for his defensive work in the Arizona Fall League at the end of 2016, but the Pirates did not protect him on the 40-man roster. He went unselected in the Rule 5 draft. With Reese McGuire traded, Jhang has a clear path to start at Double-A Altoona, and he profiles as a big league backup.

Year	Club (League)	Class	AVG	G	AB	R	H	2B	3B	HR	RBI	BB	SO	SB	CS	OBP	SLG
2014	Bradenton (FSL)	HiA	.219	77	269	29	59	12	2	2	35	15	36	3	0	.263	.301
2015	Bradenton (FSL)	HiA	.292	99	370	45	108	16	1	5	41	22	43	2	4	.332	.383
2016	Indianapolis (IL)	AAA	.200	6	20	2	4	1	0	0	2	1	2	0	0	.261	.250
	Altoona (EL)	AA	.298	54	188	20	56	13	0	1	21	11	12	1	0	.338	.383
Minor League Totals			.274	332	1159	130	317	55	6	14	156	80	133	7	6	.323	.368

28 LUIS ESCOBAR, RHP

BA GRADE

45 Risk: High

Born: May 30, 1996. **B-T:** R-R. **Ht.:** 6-1. **Wt.:** 155. **Signed:** Colombia, 2013.
Signed by: Rene Gayo/Orlando Covo.

The Pirates have been more heavily involved in Colombia than most other organizations during Rene Gayo's tenure as Latin American scouting director, and they believe they found a potential gem when they signed the hard-throwing Escobar for $150,000 in 2013. Though Escobar is slightly built, he generates outstanding arm speed that allows him to run his fastball up to 97 mph while sitting at 93-95. He gets good spin on his curveball, though he is still in the process of gaining better command of it, and he has a changeup that could eventually become a solid third offering. Escobar showed during his first taste of action in the U.S. in 2016 that he still needs work on the finer points of pitching, particularly when it comes to consistently throwing strikes and holding runners. He will likely begin the 2017 season at low Class A West Virginia.

Year	Club (League)	Class	W	L	ERA	G	GS	CG	SV	IP	H	HR	BB	SO	K/9	WHIP	AVG
2014	Pirates1 (DSL)	R	2	4	4.75	13	13	0	0	55	50	2	31	34	5.6	1.47	.242
2015	Pirates (GCL)	R	2	1	3.54	11	11	0	0	41	29	1	13	37	8.2	1.03	.200
	West Virginia (NYP)	SS	0	0	5.68	2	2	0	0	6	7	0	4	5	7.1	1.74	.304
2016	West Virginia (NYP)	SS	6	5	2.93	15	12	0	0	68	50	4	28	61	8.1	1.15	.208
Minor League Totals			10	10	3.77	41	38	0	0	170	136	7	76	137	7.3	1.25	.221

29 STEPHEN ALEMAIS, SS

BA GRADE

45 Risk: High

Born: April 12, 1995. **B-T:** R-R. **Ht.:** 6-0. **Wt.:** 190. **Drafted:** Tulane, 2016 (3rd round). **Signed by:** Wayne Mathis.

Alemais was considered a potential first-round pick at the beginning of 2016, but his stock dropped after he hit .311/.368/.401 in 212 at-bats for Tulane. The Pirates selected him in the third round. While Alemais has a decent eye at the plate and the speed to steal bases, he lacks strength and was overpowered most of the time in his pro debut, which he spent mostly at short-season West Virginia. The Pirates, though, are confident he came become at least a competent offensive player. Alemais' calling card is defense. He has excellent range, hands, actions and instincts. Despite having shoulder surgery during his junior year at All-Hallows High in the Bronx, N.Y., his arm is above-average and he has a quick release. Alemais is extremely athletic and was a three-year starter in basketball in high school as a point guard. The Pirates pushed him to finish 2016 at low Class A West Virginia. Thus, despite his advanced defense, Alemais will head back to the South Atlantic League in 2017 with an eye on a potential early-season promotion to high Class A Bradenton if his offense picks up.

Year	Club (League)	Class	AVG	G	AB	R	H	2B	3B	HR	RBI	BB	SO	SB	CS	OBP	SLG
2016	West Virginia (NYP)	SS	.263	39	156	23	41	5	0	1	18	5	18	9	3	.297	.314
	West Virginia (SAL)	LoA	.189	11	37	2	7	1	1	0	2	2	11	1	3	.244	.270
Minor League Totals			.249	50	193	25	48	6	1	1	20	7	29	10	6	.286	.306

30 TYLER WEBB, LHP

BA GRADE

45 Risk: High

Born: July 20, 1990. **B-T:** R-L. **Ht.:** 6-6. **Wt.:** 225. **Drafted:** South Carolina, 2013 (10th round). **Signed by:** Adam Czajkowski (Yankees).

Webb's four years at South Carolina were filled with highlights. He was a contributor as a freshman and sophomore on the Gamecocks' back-to-back national championship teams and finished his career with a dominant senior season as closer. The Yankees selected him in the 10th round in 2013 and signed him for just $30,000. Webb carved up batters in the low minors and succeeded at Double-A Trenton and Triple-A Scranton/Wilkes-Barre as well. The Pirates selected Webb in the 2016 Rule 5 draft, and he was one of four players the Yankees lost in the draft. He will be looking to make the Pirates roster as a matchup reliever after holding Triple-A lefthanders to a sub-.600 OPS in back-to-back seasons. His fringe-average 90-92 mph fastball has enough deception to be effective, and his sweepy fringe-average slider dives away from lefties effectively. His below-average changeup gives him something to toss up against righthanders, but he's best in left-on-left matchups.

Year	Club (League)	Class	W	L	ERA	G	GS	CG	SV	IP	H	HR	BB	SO	K/9	WHIP	AVG
2014	Tampa (FSL)	HiA	0	0	2.77	8	0	0	4	13	7	0	1	17	11.8	0.62	.152
	Trenton (EL)	AA	1	6	4.04	23	0	0	7	36	35	2	14	51	12.9	1.37	.255
	Scranton/W-B (IL)	AAA	2	0	4.05	17	0	0	1	20	17	3	7	26	11.7	1.20	.221
2015	Scranton/W-B (IL)	AAA	2	3	2.84	25	0	0	2	38	40	4	11	41	9.7	1.34	.261
2016	Scranton/W-B (IL)	AAA	4	3	3.59	36	5	0	1	73	67	5	23	82	10.2	1.24	.245
Minor League Totals			12	13	3.48	129	5	0	18	215	190	18	64	265	11.1	1.18	.234

St. Louis Cardinals

BY DERRICK GOOLD

As October proved it could do just fine without them and their archrival soared to heights not seen in generations, the Cardinals found comfort in something they did subtly and strategically, under the surface of the standings that turned so sour.

With an abundance of draft picks and a cap-busting spending spree on international talent in 2016, the Cardinals feel they replenished their farm system. General manager John Mozeliak referred to it as the "deepest" he had seen in his tenure. What it lacked in advanced prospects, it had in impact talent percolating the lower ranks. The Cardinals believed they could maintain their place as a contender while making the transition to a younger team, one that can close the gap on the new kings of the National League Central, the Cubs.

Mozeliak had one word for the team he imagines: "Exciting."

That was not an adjective that applied to the 2016 Cardinals as they thundered their way to an 86-76 record with a curious club. The Cardinals wanted more power and got it with an NL-leading 225 homers, the second-most in club history. But the trade-off was crippling.

A franchise known for its crisp play, coming off one of the best run-prevention seasons in history, saw its fundamentals fray. The Cardinals had one of the most unreliable defenses in the league. The pitching crumpled as a result. Both kept the team from keeping pace—they finished 17½ games behind the Cubs—and left them, for the first time since 2010, out of the postseason.

To reclaim a seat in October, Mozeliak set out to establish a more athletic lineup and a more agile defense, one that can keep clean the real engine of contention for the Cardinals, their rotation. Budding ace Carlos Martinez will be joined by future ace Alex Reyes and established ace Adam Wainwright. The Cardinals spent $82.5 million to bring center fielder Dexter Fowler from the top of the Cubs' lineup to the top of theirs. Mozeliak committed to the athletic Kolten Wong as their everyday second baseman.

For the past half-dozen years, Mozeliak has stressed athleticism in the draft, wanting to find it and pitching whenever possible to overcome the Cardinals' annually low position. With his first pick as scouting director, Randy Flores picked a caliber of player the Cardinals rarely have had a shot at: top-five talent Delvin Perez. The teenage shortstop fell to No. 23 because of a positive test for performance-enhancing drugs. The Cardinals took the risk and acquired a player a lot like what

System graduate Stephen Piscotty helped supply power to a powerful Cardinals lineup

TOP PROSPECTS OF THE DECADE

Year	Player, Pos.	2016 Org
2007	Colby Rasmus, of	Astros
2008	Colby Rasmus, of	Astros
2009	Colby Rasmus, of	Astros
2010	Shelby Miller, rhp	Diamondbacks
2011	Shelby Miller, rhp	Diamondbacks
2012	Shelby Miller, rhp	Diamondbacks
2013	Oscar Taveras, of	Deceased
2014	Oscar Taveras, of	Deceased
2015	Marco Gonzales, lhp	Cardinals
2016	Alex Reyes, rhp	Cardinals

they sought in every corner of the amateur ranks.

Through the first half of the international signing window, the Cardinals had blown past their $2 million bonus pool and signed four $1 million bonuses. Cuban center fielder Jonatan Machado ($2.3 million) alone surpassed the spending limit.

All of this was done to close what the Cardinals recognize as a "gap" in their system. With the graduation of Stephen Piscotty to the everyday lineup in 2016 and Alex Reyes to the rotation in 2017, there is a low tide before the next crest of elite talent.

That talent collected at the low minors in 2016, where the Cardinals' short-season affiliates in the Gulf Coast, Appalachian and New York-Penn leagues all won titles. That deep group of talent is the reinforcements the Cardinals believe will keep them in perpetual contention

ORGANIZATION OVERVIEW

General manager: John Mozeliak. **Farm director:** Gary LaRocque. **Scouting director:** Randy Flores.

Class	Team	League	W	L	PCT	Finish	Manager
Majors	St. Louis Cardinals	National	86	76	.531	6th (15)	Mike Matheny
Triple-A	Memphis Redbirds	Pacifc Coast	65	77	.458	14th (16)	Mike Shildt
Double-A	Springfield Cardinals	Texas	75	65	.536	3rd (8)	Dann Billardello
High Class A	Palm Beach Cardinals	Florida State	58	79	.423	11th (12)	Oliver Marmol
Low Class A	Peoria Chiefs	Midwest	73	66	.525	5th (16)	Joe Kruzel
Short-season	State College Spikes	New York-Penn	50	26	.658	1st (14)	Johnny Rodriguez
Rookie	Johnson City Cardinals	Appalachian	39	29	.574	2nd (10)	Chris Swauger
Rookie	GCL Cardinals	Gulf Coast	33	21	.611	3rd (17)	Steve Turco
Overall 2016 Minor League Record			393	363	.520	10th (30)	

THIS YEAR'S TOP 30

No.	Player, Pos.	Grade/Risk
1.	Alex Reyes, rhp	70/Medium
2.	Luke Weaver, rhp	55/Medium
3.	Delvin Perez, ss	65/Extreme
4.	Carson Kelly, c	50/Medium
5.	Magneuris Sierra, of	60/Extreme
6.	Sandy Alcantara, rhp	55/High
7.	Harrison Bader, of	50/Medium
8.	Edmundo Sosa, ss	55/High
9.	Dakota Hudson, rhp	50/High
10.	Eliezer Alvarez, 2b	50/High
11.	Jack Flaherty, rhp	50/High
12.	Randy Arozarena, of	55/Extreme
13.	Marco Gonzales, lhp	45/Medium
14.	Paul DeJong, ss/3b	50/High
15.	Austin Gomber, lhp	50/High
16.	Dylan Carlson, of	50/High
17.	Jake Woodford, rhp	55/Extreme
18.	Connor Jones, rhp	50/High
19.	Jonathan Machado, of	55/Extreme
20.	Alvaro Seijas, rhp	50/Extreme
21.	Junior Fernandez, rhp	50/Extreme
22.	Victor Garcia, of	50/Extreme
23.	Sam Tuivailala, rhp	40/Low
24.	Nick Plummer, of	50/Extreme
25.	Ronnie Williams, rhp	50/Extreme
26.	Bryce Denton, 3b/of	50/Extreme
27.	John Gant, rhp	40/Medium
28.	Jordan Hicks, rhp	50/Extreme
29.	Breyvic Valera, 2b/ss	40/Medium
30.	Johan Oviedo, rhp	50/Extreme

LAST YEAR'S TOP 30

No.	Player, Pos.	Status
1.	Alex Reyes, rhp	No. 1
2.	Tim Cooney, lhp	(Indians)
3.	Jack Flaherty, rhp	No. 11
4.	Luke Weaver, rhp	No. 2
5.	Marco Gonzales, lhp	No. 13
6.	Magneuris Sierra, of	No. 5
7.	Edmundo Sosa, ss	No. 8
8.	Nick Plummer, of	No. 23
9.	Junior Fernandez, rhp	No. 20
10.	Carson Kelly, c	No. 4
11.	Sam Tuivailala, rhp	No. 22
12.	Aledmys Diaz, ss	Majors
13.	Charlie Tilson, of	(White Sox)
14.	Austin Gomber, lhp	No. 15
15.	Harrison Bader, of	No. 7
16.	Paul DeJong, ss/3b	No. 14
17.	Jake Woodford, rhp	No. 17
18.	Bryce Denton, 3b/of	No. 26
19.	Sandy Alcantara, rhp	No. 6
20.	Greg Garcia, ss	Majors
21.	Anthony Garcia, of	Dropped out
22.	Artie Reyes, rhp	Dropped out
23.	Jacob Wilson, 2b/3b	Dropped out
24.	Luis Perdomo, rhp	(Padres)
25.	Allen Cordoba, ss	(Padres)
26.	Oscar Mercado, ss	Dropped out
27.	Derian Gonzalez, lhp	Dropped out
28.	Ronnie Williams, rhp	No. 23
29.	Dean Kiekhefer, lhp	(Mariners)
30.	Mike Ohlman, c	(Blue Jays)

BEST TOOLS

Best Hitter for Average	Eliezer Alvarez
Best Power Hitter	Paul DeJong
Best Strike-Zone Discipline	Tommy Edman
Fastest Baserunner	Magneuris Sierra
Best Athlete	Magneuris Sierra
Best Fastball	Alex Reyes
Best Curveball	Alex Reyes
Best Slider	Dakota Hudson
Best Changeup	Marco Gonzales
Best Control	Luke Weaver
Best Defensive Catcher	Carson Kelly
Best Defensive Infielder	Edmundo Sosa
Best Infield Arm	Patrick Wisdom
Best Defensive Outfielder	Magneuris Sierra
Best Outfield Arm	Magneuris Sierra

PROJECTED 2020 LINEUP

Catcher	Carson Kelly
First Base	Matt Carpenter
Second Base	Kolten Wong
Third Base	Aledmys Diaz
Shortstop	Delvin Perez
Left Field	Randal Grichuk
Center Field	Dexter Fowler
Right Field	Stephen Piscotty
No. 1 Starter	Carlos Martinez
No. 2 Starter	Alex Reyes
No. 3 Starter	Luke Weaver
No. 4 Starter	Jack Flaherty
No. 5 Starter	Mike Leake
Closer	Sandy Alcantara

MINOR LEAGUE DEPTH CHART

ST. LOUIS CARDINALS

TOP 2017 ROOKIE: Alex Reyes, rhp. The Cardinals' top pitching prospect since Rick Ankiel will ride his elite fastball to Rookie of the Year contention.

BREAKOUT PROSPECT: Randy Arozarena, of. One of the club's million-dollar Cuban players, he's the closest to the majors with athleticism that could get him to the doorstep in first year.

SOURCE OF TOP 30 TALENT			
Homegrown	29	Acquired	1
College	7	Trades	1
Junior college	0	Rule 5 draft	0
High school	10	Independent leagues	0
Draft-and-follow	0	Free agents/waivers	0
Nondrafted free agents	0	International	12

SLEEPER: Oscar Mercado, of. The 2013 second-round pick at shortstop shifted to center field, which unlocked confidence, comfort and an improved bat.

LF
Nick Plummer (23)
Bryce Denton (26)
Jose Martinez

CF
Magneuris Sierra (5)
Harrison Bader (7)
Randy Arozarena (12)
Jonathan Machado (19)
Oscar Mercado

RF
Dylan Carlson (16)
Walker Robbins
Todd Cunningham
Austin Wilson

3B
Paul DeJong (14)
Patrick Wisdom

SS
Delvin Perez (3)
Edmundo Sosa (8)
Juan Herrera
Alex Mejia
Tommy Edman

2B
Eliezer Alvarez (10)
Breyvic Valera (29)
Jacob Wilson
Luke Dykstra

1B
Victor Garcia (22)
Chad Huffman
Luke Voit

C
Carson Kelly (4)
Gabriel Lino
Brian O'Keefe
Jeremy Martinez
Steve Bean

LHP

LHSP	LHRP
Marco Gonzales (13)	Corey Littrell
Austin Gomber (15)	Ryan Sherriff
Ian Oxnevad	Zach Phillips
John Kilichowski	

RHP

RHSP	RHRP
Alex Reyes (1)	Junior Fernandez (21)
Luke Weaver (2)	Sam Tuivailala (23)
Sandy Alcantara (6)	John Gant (27)
Dakota Hudson (9)	Artie Reyes
Jack Flaherty (11)	Chris Ellis
Jake Woodford (17)	Kendry Flores
Connor Jones (18)	Rowan Wick
Alvaro Seijas (20)	Ryan Helsley
Ronnie Williams (25)	Daniel Poncedeleon
Jordan Hicks (28)	
Johan Oviedo (30)	
Mike Mayers	
Zac Gallen	
Derian Gonzalez	

DRAFT ANALYSIS

2016

BEST PURE HITTER: OF Dylan Carlson (1) is a switch-hitter with a track record of hitting in upper-level showcase events. He has an advanced understanding of what pitchers are trying to do, has a good feel for the game and projects as an above-average hitter. SS Delvin Perez (1) has greater upside as a hitter than Carlson with lots of bat speed and the speed to beat out infield hits. He could end up as a plus hitter but has further to go as far pitch recognition.

BEST POWER HITTER: Carlson could develop above-average power as he matures. He showed some of that potential with a strong finish to his pro debut. After hitting only five extra base hits in June and July, Carlson had 14 extra-base hits in August while slugging .523.

FASTEST RUNNER: Perez is a plus runner who knows how to use his speed. He swiped 12 bags in 13 tries in the Gulf Coast League. OF Shane Billings (13) is also a plus runner.

BEST DEFENSIVE PLAYER: Perez was considered by many to be the best defensive shortstop in the 2016 draft class and is a plus defender. He has a plus arm, plenty of range and the hands and actions teams look for in a shortstop.

BEST FASTBALL: RHP Dakota Hudson (1) will pitch at 92-96 mph on his best days, settling in around 92-94 regularly. He does need to improve the command of his plus fastball. RHP Connor Jones (2) likes to work in the bottom of the strike zone with an above-average 90-92 mph sinker, but has reached 96 with his four-seamer.

BEST SECONDARY PITCH: Hudson's 78-82 mph curveball regularly flashes plus. Jones does a good job of controlling his plus 82-85 mph slider.

BEST PRO DEBUT: C Jeremy Martinez (4) hit .325/.419/.433 with twice as many walks (32) as strikeouts with short-season State College. C Andrew Knizner hit .319/.423/.429 with Rookie-level Johnson City.

BEST ATHLETE: Perez was seen as one of the best all-around athletes of this year's draft class, though his positive test for performance-enhancing drugs before the draft tarnishes that reputation.

MOST INTRIGUING BACKGROUND: RHP Sam Tewes (8) missed most of the past two seasons at Wichita State with elbow injuries showed a 92-95 mph fastball when healthy.

CLOSEST TO THE MAJORS: Hudson, Jones and RHP Zac Gallen (3) should be in a race to the big leagues as a trio of aces at major Division I schools.

BEST LATE-ROUND PICK: LHP John Kilichowski (11) returned to Vanderbilt after an excellent sophomore season but struggled through an injury-plagued junior season. If he returns to form he has a chance to be a lefty reliever and possibly more. 2B J.R. Davis (15) is a power-speed second baseman who can hit. There are questions about his defense at second base, but his willingness to work gives him a chance to improve.

THE ONE WHO GOT AWAY: A wide receiver who played on back-to-back Oklahoma state championship football teams, OF Cade Cabbiness (21) has a big league body and significant raw power. He signed with Oklahoma State.

2015

Four preps picked in the first five rounds rank in the Top 30 Prospects, led by RHP Jake Woodford (12) and 3B Bryce Denton (2). Collegians OF Harrison Bader (3), who has reached Triple-A, and 3B Paul DeJong (4), who will give shortstop a try, have moved quickly.

GRADE: B

2014

A pitcher-heavy draft features three of the system's top arms, with RHP Luke Weaver (1) leaping to the majors in 2016. RHP Jack Flaherty (1) hasn't made The Leap yet, while LHP Austin Gomber (4) finished 2016 in Double-A.

GRADE: B

2013

LHP Marco Gonzales (1) started his career strong before Tommy John surgery and now may be a reliever. RHP Mike Mayers (3) reached the majors in 2016 with an inauspicious debut. The rest of the class has provided trade and organization fodder.

GRADE: D

TOP DRAFT PICKS OF THE DECADE

Year	Player, Pos.	2016 Org
2007	Pete Kozma, ss	Yankees
2008	Brett Wallace, 3b	Padres
2009	Shelby Miller, rhp	Diamondbacks
2010	Zack Cox, 3b	Marlins
2011	Kolten Wong, 2b	Cardinals
2012	Michael Wacha, rhp	Cardinals
2013	Marco Gonzales, lhp	Cardinals
2014	Luke Weaver, rhp	Cardinals
2015	Nick Plummer, of	Cardinals
2016	Delvin Perez, ss	Cardinals

LARGEST BONUSES IN CLUB HISTORY

J.D. Drew, 1998	$3,000,000
Shelby Miller, 2009	$2,875,000
Rick Ankiel, 1999	$2,500,000
Chad Hutchinson, 1998	$2,300,000
Delvin Perez, 2016	$2,222,500

1 ALEX REYES, RHP

Born: Aug. 29, 1994. **B-T:** R-R. **Ht.:** 6-3. **Wt.:** 175.
Signed: Dominican Republic, 2012.
Signed by: Rodney Jimenez/Angel Ovalles.

BA GRADE

70 Risk: Medium

SCOUTING GRADES

Fastball: 80.
Curveball: 70.
Changeup: 60.
Control: 50.

Based on 20-80 scouting scale and future projection rather than present tools.

BILL MITCHELL

When he decided to leave his home and family in New Jersey to see if baseball would take notice of him in the Dominican Republic, Reyes packed his dreams of being a third baseman, a glove, some cleats and a few bats. He wouldn't need the bats for long. Born and raised in Elizabeth, N.J., the right-hander skipped his prom and graduation to live with his grandmother and become eligible as an international amateur, if he could draw the scouts. He did with one move—to the mound. Reyes volunteered to throw when his Dominican team ran out of pitchers one day, and after flashing a power fastball a trainer gave him advice: "Stick to pitching," Reyes recalled. As his velocity increased, scouts swarmed. The Cardinals signed him for $950,000 in December 2012 after winning a bidding war against the Astros and Royals. Reyes zoomed through the minors, but late in 2015, at the Arizona Fall League, he drew a 50-game suspension for marijuana use. That delayed his 2016 debut but not his arrival in the majors. He reached St. Louis on Aug. 9 and topped out at 101 mph.

The Cardinals see Reyes as a stronger, taller, broader version of a pitcher with whom he'll share the rotation: Carlos Martinez. Reyes operates at the highest registers when it comes to velocity. He averaged 97 mph on his fastball in the majors, routinely worked from 96-100 with it, and an opposing team clocked him in the minors at 102. He can maintain that power late into his starts and spot it up in the zone. Nearly 45 percent of his outs recorded came via strikeouts in the minors. His fastball has been described as elite and a true top-of-the-scale weapon. With it, he mixes a hard, hammer curve that unnerves the first batter who sees it in every game. It too is a plus pitch, and increasingly in the majors his strikeouts came off the curve, or soon after a hitter saw it. Reyes' changeup profiles as a plus pitch, though he's had less consistency with it, and he is working on a cutter-slider hybrid that can get him access to both sides of the plate. Reyes throws across his body and his mechanics, like his command, can fluctuate. To pitch deeper into games he has to become more efficient with his pitch count (he walked 4.5

per nine innings in the majors), and a root cause coaches feel is finding a rhythm for his delivery so that he can repeat it. He has the wide shoulders and tree-trunk legs to hog innings.

If other teams' interest is any measure of a prospect, then Reyes is poised for stardom. The Cardinals had difficulty finding an impact trade for an outfielder because other teams wanted Reyes. That was a non-starter for the Cardinals, who intend to make Reyes a permanent part of the big league rotation in 2017. In the years to come could emerge as that rare, power-packed, bona fide ace.

Year	Club (League)	Class	W	L	ERA	G	GS	CG	SV	IP	H	HR	BB	SO	K/9	WHIP	AVG
2014	Peoria (MWL)	LoA	7	7	3.62	21	21	1	0	109	82	6	61	137	11.3	1.31	.207
2015	Cardinals (GCL)	R	0	0	0.00	1	1	0	0	3	0	0	0	3	9.0	0.00	.000
	Palm Beach (FSL)	HiA	2	5	2.26	13	13	0	0	64	49	0	31	96	13.6	1.26	.216
	Springfield (TL)	AA	3	2	3.12	8	8	0	0	35	21	1	18	52	13.5	1.13	.174
2016	Memphis (PCL)	AAA	2	3	4.96	14	14	0	0	65	63	6	32	93	12.8	1.45	.252
	St. Louis (NL)	MAJ	4	1	1.57	12	5	0	1	46	33	1	23	52	10.2	1.22	.201
Major League Totals			4	1	1.57	12	5	0	1	46	33	1	23	52	10.2	1.22	.201
Minor League Totals			20	21	3.50	69	69	1	0	334	269	14	170	449	12.1	1.31	.220

2 LUKE WEAVER, RHP

Born: Aug. 21, 1993. **B-T:** R-R. **Ht.:** 6-2. **Wt.:** 170. **Drafted:** Florida State, 2014 (1st round). **Signed by:** Charlie Gonzalez.

There was a time Weaver used his slight frame as a ruse. He would dial back his warmups so his stuff looked as undersized as he did, but there was no hiding his velocity from live hitters. An ace at Florida State and a member of USA Baseball's 2013 Collegiate National Team, Weaver signed for $1,843,000. He was sidelined in 2016 by a broken wrist but returned in June, emerged as a Texas League dynamo, and zoomed to majors. The elasticity and athleticism of Weaver's mechanics allow him excellent pound-for-pound velocity. His fastball sits 92-94 mph and touches 96, which he complements with an an above-average changeup. He is fearless with the pitch, throwing it to either side of the plate. In the minors, Weaver relentlessly worked the edges of the strike zone with his sinker or changeup 80 percent of the time with double-plus control. He wasn't as aggressive in the majors, groping for a precise pitch instead relying on movement. That made him less economical and prone to damage. Earmarked to be the ace of the Triple-A Memphis staff so he can sharpen his approach, a strong spring will cement Weaver as the Cardinals' next arm up when a starter is needed.

BA GRADE: 60 Risk: High

Year	Club (League)	Class	W	L	ERA	G	GS	CG	SV	IP	H	HR	BB	SO	K/9	WHIP	AVG
2014	Cardinals (GCL)	R	0	0	0.00	4	4	0	0	6	4	0	0	9	13.5	0.67	.190
	Palm Beach (FSL)	HiA	0	1	21.60	2	2	0	0	3	11	1	4	3	8.1	4.50	.550
2015	Palm Beach (FSL)	HiA	8	5	1.62	19	19	0	0	105	98	2	19	88	7.5	1.11	.247
2016	Springfield (TL)	AA	6	3	1.40	12	12	0	0	77	63	4	10	88	10.3	0.95	.214
	Memphis (PCL)	AAA	1	0	0.00	1	1	0	0	6	2	0	2	4	6.0	0.67	.100
	St. Louis (NL)	MAJ	1	4	5.70	9	8	0	0	36	46	7	12	45	11.1	1.60	.311
Major League Totals			1	4	5.70	9	8	0	0	36	46	7	12	45	11.1	1.60	.311
Minor League Totals			15	9	1.78	38	38	0	0	198	178	7	35	192	8.7	1.08	.237

3 DELVIN PEREZ, SS

Born: Nov. 24, 1998. **B-T:** R-R. **Ht.:** 6-3. **Wt.:** 175. **Drafted:** HS—Ceiba, P.R., 2016 (1st round). **Signed by:** Mike Dibiase/Juan Ramos.

Perez was a top-10 talent entering the 2016 draft and the top shortstop available, before a report surfaced that he tested positive for an undisclosed performance-enhancing drug. Perez tumbled to 23rd overall, where the Cardinals pounced for a $2,222,500 bonus. Perez draws comparisons to fellow Puerto Ricans Carlos Correa and Francisco Lindor with a lithe, quick-twitch lope that comes from high-functioning athleticism. He has 70 speed on a 20-80 scouting scale and movement in the field that match that quickness. He showed flashes of instincts, true hands, and above-average range, but also committed 17 errors because he had difficulty playing under control. Consistency will come when he syncs his raw skills. A project at the plate, Perez proved aggressive and able to drive fastballs. He was a pull hitter in his pro debut and undone by quality offspeed pitches. Scouts see strong hands and strong forearms that project for gap power, and maybe more. Encouraged by how he responded to why he dropped in the draft and how he gobbled up instruction, the Cardinals believe they may have a blue-chip stock in Perez. He'll get work in extended spring training before heading to Rookie-level Johnson City, a launch pad for prospects.

CLIFF WELCH

BA GRADE: 60 Risk: High

Year	Club (League)	Class	AVG	G	AB	R	H	2B	3B	HR	RBI	BB	SO	SB	CS	OBP	SLG
2016	Cardinals (GCL)	R	.294	43	163	19	48	8	4	0	19	12	28	12	1	.352	.393
Minor League Totals			.294	43	163	19	48	8	4	0	19	12	28	12	1	.352	.393

4 CARSON KELLY, C

Born: July 14, 1994. **B-T:** R-R. **Ht.:** 6-2. **Wt.:** 220. **Drafted:** HS—Portland, Ore., 2012 (2nd round). **Signed by:** Matt Swanson.

When Cardinals manager Mike Matheny, a former Gold Glove winner, authored the chapter on catching in 'The Cardinal Way' handbook, he listed traits any good receiver must have. Kelly memorized and tried to mimic all of them. A third baseman when the Cardinals drafted him Kelly has morphed into a Cardinals catcher straight out of central casting. He reached the majors in September and doubled off Antonio Bastardo in his first at-bat. After two seasons consumed by learning to catch, the Cardinals felt Kelly's promotion to Double-A Springfield was a chance to reveal he could hit. He took advantage. Kelly generates reasonable power with

BA GRADE: 60 Risk: High

his strength and pendulum swing. He's been more selective at each level and the gap between his bat and his glove shrank. Kelly has made himself into a double-plus backstop with smooth framing, quick transitions, a strong arm and nimbleness. He is ready to be Yadier Molina's backup if needed in 2017, but the Cardinals would prefer he start every day at Memphis instead of rusting on their bench.

Year	Club (League)	Class	AVG	G	AB	R	H	2B	3B	HR	RBI	BB	SO	SB	CS	OBP	SLG
2014	Peoria (MWL)	LoA	.248	98	363	41	90	17	4	6	49	37	54	1	0	.326	.366
2015	Palm Beach (FSL)	HiA	.219	108	389	30	85	18	1	8	51	22	64	0	0	.263	.332
2016	Springfield (TL)	AA	.287	64	216	29	62	7	0	6	18	14	46	0	1	.338	.403
	Memphis (PCL)	AAA	.292	32	113	14	33	10	0	0	14	11	17	0	0	.352	.381
	St. Louis (NL)	MAJ	.154	10	13	1	2	1	0	0	1	0	2	0	0	.214	.231
Major League Totals			.154	10	13	1	2	1	0	0	1	0	2	0	0	.214	.231
Minor League Totals			.248	471	1711	191	425	84	6	35	202	127	270	2	1	.306	.366

5 MAGNEURIS SIERRA, OF

Born: April 7, 1996. **B-T:** L-L. **Ht.:** 5-11. **Wt.:** 160. **Signed:** Dominican Republic, 2012. **Signed by:** Rodney Jimenez/Angel Ovalles.

Part of an international signing class with Alex Reyes and Edmundo Sosa, Sierra landed a $105,000 bonus and swiftly asserted himself. . In his debut season he became the first teenager to win the Cardinals' organization player of the year award, and that invited an aggressive promotion the next season that chilled his production. Given a second crack at low Class A Peoria in 2016, the live-wire athlete got his groove back. Sierra is a superior defensive center fielder with an easy gallop and wide-open range. He shows instincts beyond his level, playing shallow to steal singles and still being able to track back without a glitch. His arm plays even better than its plus strength because of his quick release and accuracy. His glove will keep him in the lineup, allowing a polarizing bat to steady. Sierra has a swift, compact swing, and he added strength that allows him to drive the ball. Better pitch recognition will help him unlock the above-average hitter he can be. He's an above-average runner still learning how to use his speed efficiently on the bases. Sierra will begin 2017 at high Class A Palm Beach, and if he hits, could surge quickly because the glove is deft.

Year	Club (League)	Class	AVG	G	AB	R	H	2B	3B	HR	RBI	BB	SO	SB	CS	OBP	SLG
2014	Cardinals (GCL)	R	.386	52	202	42	78	12	3	2	30	16	30	13	3	.434	.505
2015	Peoria (MWL)	LoA	.191	51	178	19	34	1	3	1	7	7	52	4	5	.219	.247
	Johnson City (APP)	R	.315	53	216	38	68	8	0	3	15	19	42	15	2	.371	.394
2016	Peoria (MWL)	LoA	.307	122	524	78	161	29	4	3	60	22	97	31	17	.335	.395
Minor League Totals			.299	341	1332	221	398	56	13	10	133	93	254	78	34	.346	.383

6 SANDY ALCANTARA, RHP

Born: Sept. 7, 1995. **B-T:** R-R. **Ht.:** 6-4. **Wt.:** 170. **Signed:** Dominican Republic, 2013. **Signed by:** Rodney Jimenez.

Longer than they've been pros, Alcantara and teammate Junior Fernandez have been linked, from their time with the same trainer (Felix Liriano) to 2016 in the same, power-packed Peoria rotation. For the first time, Alcantara surged ahead as a prospect. Signed for a $125,000 bonus at 17, the righthander always had a frame and untamed power that suggested robust talent. During an extended spring outing in 2015, he hit 102 mph with his fastball and he routinely touched 100 mph while sitting 95-96. At the time of his promotion to high Class A Palm Beach, he led the Midwest League with 119 strikeouts. There is still room on Alcantara's frame for strength gains, and that could help the lean, loose, wiry starter center his delivery and make it more consistent. The makings are there. At present, he can lose his feel for his mechanics and his fastball drifts up or out of the zone and the walks flow. Alcantara improved throughout the season and started showing an effective curve and above-average changeup. The righthander has packed on the innings as a pro and his three-pitch mix is enough for the Cardinals to project him as a starter, even ahead of sidekick Fernandez. Primed for a return to Palm Beach and its pitcher-friendly environs, Alcantara's climb is about to accelerate, especially if a need opens at higher levels for a 100-mph blowtorch in the bullpen.

Year	Club (League)	Class	W	L	ERA	G	GS	CG	SV	IP	H	HR	BB	SO	K/9	WHIP	AVG
2014	Cardinals (DSL)	R	1	9	3.97	12	11	1	0	57	56	1	19	55	8.7	1.32	.253
2015	Cardinals (GCL)	R	4	4	3.22	12	12	0	0	64	59	3	20	51	7.1	1.23	.244
2016	Peoria (MWL)	LoA	5	7	4.08	17	17	0	0	90	78	4	45	119	11.9	1.36	.228
	Palm Beach (FSL)	HiA	0	4	3.62	6	6	1	0	32	25	0	14	34	9.5	1.21	.216
Minor League Totals			10	24	3.77	47	46	2	0	244	218	8	98	259	9.6	1.30	.237

7 HARRISON BADER, OF

Born: June 3, 1994. **B-T:** R-R. **Ht.:** 6-0. **Wt.:** 195. **Drafted:** Florida, 2015 (3rd round). **Signed by:** Ty Boyles.

Bader shined as a three-year starter for Florida and even hit the first home run to center field at Omaha's TD Ameritrade Park, but faced persistent questions whether he would hit for enough power to fit a corner outfield spot. The Cardinals drafted and signed Bader for a $400,000 bonus, and he rewarded them with a .311/.368/.523 line in his debut. His 11 homers led all 2015 draft picks. That allowed the Cardinals to test him with advanced placement in Double-A, where before the end of May he had a 17-game hitting streak, one shy of affiliate record. Cast as a leadoff hitter to inspire a grinding approach, Bader, at heart, remains an eager hitter. Two evaluators called him "aggressively confident" at the plate and his ambush power has grown as a result. He is a coiled, broad-shouldered athlete that has above-average speed and a rising aptitude to take an extra base. A solid-average swing and a seasoned feel for the strike zone served him well in the Arizona Fall League to go with his average power potential. Bader showed capable range and a good arm for center, where his bat profiles as an asset. A taste of Triple-A in 2016 will become a priority starting role there in 2017. If he sticks at center, Bader will increase his imminent value to the Cardinals as a fourth outfielder or muscle his way into a trade.

BA GRADE
60 Risk: High

Year	Club (League)	Class	AVG	G	AB	R	H	2B	3B	HR	RBI	BB	SO	SB	CS	OBP	SLG
2015	State College (NYP)	SS	.379	7	29	6	11	2	0	2	4	0	5	2	0	.400	.655
	Peoria (MWL)	LoA	.301	54	206	34	62	11	2	9	28	15	44	15	6	.364	.505
2016	Memphis (PCL)	AAA	.231	49	147	22	34	7	1	3	17	11	38	2	3	.298	.354
	Springfield (TL)	AA	.283	82	318	48	90	12	4	16	41	25	93	11	10	.351	.497
Minor League Totals			.281	192	700	110	197	32	7	30	90	51	180	30	19	.346	.476

8 EDMUNDO SOSA, SS

Born: March 6, 1996. **B-T:** R-R. **Ht.:** 5-11. **Wt.:** 170. **Signed:** Panama, 2012. **Signed by:** Arquimedes Nieto.

The third headliner from the 2012 international class, Sosa's climb through the system has been more deliberate. Sosa received a $425,000 bonus, the largest for any Panamanian in 2012 and debuted in 2013. He's been called a bat-first infielder, the finest glove in his league, and, most recently, the club's best all-around prospect at shortstop. Sosa has above-average actions at shortstop, from his range to his arm and especially his superb hands. He plays with a natural levity that can sometimes be misread as laissez faire. He has a flair—and a knack for making plays that cannot be taught. A .300/.369/.485 hitter at short-season, Sosa's approach came undone with low class A Peoria. He lost track of his zone and as a result his ability to get on base flagged. He did not start hitting to the level until the Cardinals promoted him out of need, and then a left wrist injury (tendinitis) ended his season in late July. Sosa is likely headed back to high Class A Palm Beach, and a good showing in the challenging Florida State League should result in a promotion to Double-A Springfield.

BA GRADE
60 Risk: High

Year	Club (League)	Class	AVG	G	AB	R	H	2B	3B	HR	RBI	BB	SO	SB	CS	OBP	SLG
2014	Cardinals (GCL)	R	.275	52	207	37	57	8	5	1	23	18	29	8	5	.341	.377
	State College (NYP)	SS	.200	3	5	0	1	0	0	0	0	0	2	0	0	.200	.200
2015	Johnson City (APP)	R	.300	49	200	30	60	8	4	7	16	16	38	6	2	.369	.485
2016	Peoria (MWL)	LoA	.268	88	351	42	94	13	1	3	30	19	71	5	4	.307	.336
	Palm Beach (FSL)	HiA	.294	9	34	3	10	0	2	0	4	1	8	0	0	.314	.412
Minor League Totals			.285	248	966	145	275	37	15	14	100	76	163	26	16	.343	.398

9 DAKOTA HUDSON, RHP

Born: Sept. 15, 1994. **B-T:** R-R. **Ht.:** 6-5. **Wt.:** 215. **Drafted:** Mississippi State, 2016 (1st round). **Signed by:** Clint Brown.

Few college arms had as much buoyancy as Hudson, who added 25 pounds through college and via the Cape Cod League (54 strikeouts in 56 2/3 innings) emerged as an intriguing, four-pitch power collegian. He threw in the upper-90s coming out of a Tennessee high school but had an uncomfortable relationship with control. Strength and experience brought command. He cut his walk rate in half as a junior and had a 9.2 strikeouts per nine rate. A balloon rising in teams' evaluations, Hudson went 34th overall to the Cardinals and became a rocket, finishing the year in the Double-A Texas League playoffs. Hudson has a fastball that rises to 96-97

BA GRADE
60 Risk: High

CLIFF WELCH

mph and sits 94 mph. He offsets it with a biting 78-82 mph curveball and a slider that sizzles around 87 mph and is already the best of its ilk in the organization. An improved changeup will defy lefthanded hitters. One crosschecker called Hudson's arsenal the most-advanced blend of pitches in college this past year, and what brought it all together for was a simplification of his delivery that can be more repeatable. His velocity and feel faltered with career-high innings and stiffer SEC competition, but it snapped back as a pro. After a promotion to Double-A Springfield to get playoff experience, Hudson has the organization seeing its next quantum-leap college starter, following the jet streams of Michael Wacha, Marco Gonzales, and Luke Weaver.

Year	Club (League)	Class	W	L	ERA	G	GS	CG	SV	IP	H	HR	BB	SO	K/9	WHIP	AVG
2016	Cardinals (GCL)	R	1	0	0.00	4	1	0	0	4	4	0	0	9	20.3	1.00	.235
	Palm Beach (FSL)	HiA	1	1	0.96	8	0	0	3	9	6	0	7	10	9.6	1.39	.188
Minor League Totals			2	1	0.68	12	1	0	3	13	10	0	7	19	12.8	1.28	.204

10 ELIEZER ALVAREZ, 2B

Born: Oct. 15, 1994. **B-T:** L-R. **Ht.:** 5-11. **Wt.:** 165. **Signed:** Dominican Republic, 2011. **Signed by:** Rene Rojas/Juan Mercado.

An Appalachian League all-star in 2015 like teammates Magneuris Sierra and Edmundo Sosa, Alvarez hardly had the name recognition or shine of his peers. Four summers spent as a short-season denizen and several injuries gave him the look of an idle infielder. Dubbed a "five-tool player" early in his career, his career took a sharp turn with his first full-season assignment. Alvarez's .879 OPS ranked behind only heralded prospect Eloy Jimenez (Cubs) in the low Class A Midwest League,

BA GRADE

60 Risk: High

his 36 steals led the league, and no other Cardinals infielder had a slash line like his .323/.404/.476. A simple swing from the left side gives Alvarez a balanced sweep through the strike zone and ability to dart pitches to all fields. He rarely lunges or gets caught with a silly swing. Alvarez inflated his slugging percentage with smart baserunning, racing for 36 doubles. That same headiness is sometimes lacking in the field. Alvarez can ease back on grounders, invite a bad hop, and that contributed to 27 errors. He has an above-average arm for second and Cardinals feel keener attention could make him an adequate fielder at several infield positions. The manifest of Alvarez's talent was so assertive that the Cardinals added him to the 40-man roster and are leaning toward pushing him straight to Double-A.

Year	Club (League)	Class	AVG	G	AB	R	H	2B	3B	HR	RBI	BB	SO	SB	CS	OBP	SLG
2012	Cardinals (DSL)	R	.205	53	176	33	36	5	2	2	15	27	35	10	7	.324	.290
2013	Cardinals (GCL)	R	.209	20	67	12	14	2	3	1	7	4	14	6	2	.264	.373
2014	Cardinals (GCL)	R	.353	21	68	11	24	6	5	1	15	6	7	3	1	.413	.632
2015	Johnson City (APP)	R	.314	52	204	32	64	20	1	2	31	11	32	9	4	.353	.451
2016	Peoria (MWL)	LoA	.323	116	433	70	140	36	6	6	59	53	96	36	15	.404	.476
Minor League Totals			.293	262	948	158	278	69	17	12	127	101	184	64	29	.369	.440

11 JACK FLAHERTY, RHP

BA GRADE

50 Risk: High

Born: Oct. 15, 1995. **B-T:** R-R. **Ht.:** 6-4. **Wt.:** 205. **Drafted:** HS—Los Angeles, 2014 (1st round). **Signed by:** Mike Garciaparra.

As a sophomore at Harvard-Westlake High, Flaherty was a teammate with two first-round pitchers, Lucas Giolito (now White Sox) and Max Fried (Padres). No wonder he played third base. The Cardinals wooed the 34th overall pick in 2014 with a $2 million bonus, convinced his future was on the mound. He showed a polish beyond his age and a feel for four pitches, any or all of which could, given some nurturing, be above-average. Although he has the look of a pitcher with more velocity to reveal, Flaherty operates at 90-92 mph with his fastball and has yet to fulfill projections. He's persistent with throwing strikes. Flaherty mixes the fastball with a solid changeup that was projected to be a plus-plus pitch for him but hasn't reached that point yet. He also has a rolling curve and a slider that get muddled. With agility and reliable mechanics, he's getting good gas mileage in third gear and could reach the upper levels on reliability alone, but if he can find fourth and redline to fifth he'll move swifter. A return to high Class A Palm Beach is possible, at least to start the season, and if Flaherty's velocity continues to creep up so will he, with a chance be a front-line starter.

Year	Club (League)	Class	W	L	ERA	G	GS	CG	SV	IP	H	HR	BB	SO	K/9	WHIP	AVG
2014	Cardinals (GCL)	R	1	1	1.59	8	6	0	0	23	18	1	4	28	11.1	0.97	.209
2015	Peoria (MWL)	LoA	9	3	2.84	18	18	0	0	95	92	2	31	97	9.2	1.29	.251
2016	Palm Beach (FSL)	HiA	5	9	3.56	24	23	0	0	134	129	8	45	126	8.5	1.30	.254
Minor League Totals			15	13	3.11	50	47	0	0	252	239	11	80	251	9.0	1.27	.249

12 RANDY AROZARENA, OF

BA GRADE
50 Risk: High

Born: Feb. 28, 1995. **B-T:** R-R. **Ht.:** 5-11. **Wt.:** 170. **Signed:** Cuba, 2016. **Signed by:** Ramon Garcia.

One of the Cuban talents the Cardinals signed later in spending spree on international talent, Arozarena could arrive sooner than any of them. The 21-year-old athlete has all of the traits of a player who could speed toward the majors and enough rawness that some think he'll need some nurturing at a lower level before, in a year or so, being unleashed upon a higher level. Arozarena (which has also been spelled "Arrozarena") starred in Cuba's junior leagues, batting .375/.510/.500 in 154 plate appearances. That earned him a spot on the Cuban 18U national team in 2013 that appeared in Taiwan, and by tournament's end he ranked second on the team in on-base percentage behind uber-prospect Yoan Moncada. The Cardinals went to Mexico to sign Arozarena, who briefly played in the Mexican League for Tijuana in April, for a $1.25 million bonus, and they are open to pushing Arozarena in 2017. He is a plus athlete with good speed and above range at either second or center field. He gets a good jolt from his bat, but is swing is built for liners not lofting. The Cardinals had him focus on center field in winter ball in Mexico, where he slumped after a fast start and hit .289/.382/.347 through 51 games. Because his experience outside of Cuba is so limited, there is an unknown about Arozarena. The Cardinals see untapped, raw talent. He has the look of a leadoff type with a vibrant style in the field, and swift move toward Double-A or Triple-A is possible.

Year	Club (League)	Class	AVG	G	AB	R	H	2B	3B	HR	RBI	BB	SO	SB	CS	OBP	SLG
2014	Pinar del Rio (CNS)	CNS	.291	74	227	49	66	12	4	3	24	36	37	15	6	.412	.419
2015	Did not play																
2016	Tijuana (MEX)	AAA	.100	5	20	3	2	1	0	0	0	2	3	0	0	.182	.150
Minor League Totals			.100	5	20	3	2	1	0	0	0	2	3	0	0	.182	.150

13 MARCO GONZALES, LHP

BA GRADE
50 Risk: High

Born: Feb. 16, 1992. **B-T:** L-L. **Ht.:** 6-1. **Wt.:** 195. **Drafted:** Gonzaga, 2013 (1st round). **Signed by:** Matt Swanson.

Between the breakout of Michael Wacha and the advent of Alex Reyes, Gonzales stood out as the team's top prospect. He moved as swiftly to the majors as Wacha and had as prominent a late-season role as Reyes, making six relief appearances in the 2014 playoffs. But before Gonzales cemented himself in the majors, his elbow betrayed him. The lefty missed all of the 2016 season recovering from Tommy John and he'll return to a uncertain place, first as a starter at Triple-A Memphis. A prep star in Colorado who won four consecutive state championships, Gonzales was also a two-way star at Gonzaga. The 19th overall pick in 2013, he made his major league debut at Coors Field less than 12 months later. At his peak, he throws 88-91 mph, and he uses a precision fastball to setup his best pitch, a superior changeup that he once said he knows as well as a handshake. In 2015, the zip on some of his pitches slipped and his changeup became less effective. He pitched through some soreness and eventually surrendered to surgery in the spring. In Gonzales, the Cardinals see a reliable starter but perhaps a more effective, devilish multi-inning reliever. He'll have the first half of this season to prove his health before they determine his role.

Year	Club (League)	Class	W	L	ERA	G	GS	CG	SV	IP	H	HR	BB	SO	K/9	WHIP	AVG
2014	Palm Beach (FSL)	HiA	2	2	1.43	6	6	0	0	38	34	1	8	32	7.6	1.12	.239
	Springfield (TL)	AA	3	2	2.33	7	7	0	0	39	33	2	10	46	10.7	1.11	.220
	Memphis (PCL)	AAA	4	1	3.35	8	8	0	0	46	43	7	9	39	7.7	1.14	.251
	St. Louis (NL)	MAJ	4	2	4.15	10	5	0	0	35	32	4	21	31	8.0	1.53	.241
2015	Palm Beach (FSL)	HiA	0	0	0.00	2	2	0	0	5	5	0	0	4	7.7	1.07	.250
	Springfield (TL)	AA	0	0	0.00	2	2	0	0	7	6	0	0	6	8.1	0.90	.231
	St. Louis (NL)	MAJ	0	0	13.50	1	1	0	0	3	7	1	1	1	3.4	3.00	.500
	Memphis (PCL)	AAA	1	5	5.45	14	14	0	0	69	91	10	24	51	6.6	1.66	.323
2016	Did not play—Injured																
Major League Totals			4	2	4.82	11	6	0	0	37	39	5	22	32	7.7	1.63	.265
Minor League Totals			10	10	3.27	47	45	0	0	226	230	21	59	201	8.0	1.28	.263

14 PAUL DeJONG, 3B/SS

BA GRADE
50 Risk: High

Born: Aug. 2, 1993. **B-T:** R-R. **Ht.:** 6-1. **Wt.:** 195. **Drafted:** Illinois State, 2015 (4th round). **Signed by:** Tom Lipari.

When DeJong took the field for his first workout at the Arizona Fall League, he began taking grounders at third base before doing a quick head count. He was one of three at the corner. There was only one at shortstop. That's because, his manager Aaron Rowand later revealed, the Cardinals wanted him to play shortstop after seeing him handle it in 11 games with Double-A Springfield. DeJong played mostly third with some second base and catcher mixed in for Illinois State, and the Cardinals are intent to see if he can be an everyday shortstop at Triple-A Memphis in 2017. Power plays. Where is the only question. DeJong received a $200,000 bonus in 2015 and instantly became one of the Cardinals' top power prospects. They were intrigued by the exit velocity off his bat, the paws and forearms that generate bat speed and thus distance, and of course an eagerness to swing big. DeJong does not get cheated and will trade strikeouts for homers; he ranked fifth in the Texas League in homers (22) but second in strikeouts (144). He has improved his sense for the difference between pitches to drive and pitches to survive. DeJong has playable footwork for shortstop and a strong, true arm. He's expanding his range with positioning and experience. If he can stick at a premium position, he'll follow Allen Craig's route as a bat with a variety of gloves.

Year	Club (League)	Class	AVG	G	AB	R	H	2B	3B	HR	RBI	BB	SO	SB	CS	OBP	SLG
2015	Johnson City (APP)	R	.486	10	37	10	18	6	0	4	15	6	9	0	0	.578	.973
	Peoria (MWL)	LoA	.288	56	219	32	63	12	3	5	26	23	43	13	4	.360	.438
2016	Springfield (TL)	AA	.260	132	496	62	129	29	2	22	73	40	144	3	2	.324	.460
Minor League Totals			.279	198	752	104	210	47	5	31	114	69	196	16	6	.348	.479

15 AUSTIN GOMBER, LHP

BA GRADE
50 Risk: High

Born: Nov. 23, 1993. **B-T:** L-L. **Ht.:** 6-5. **Wt.:** 215. **Drafted:** Florida Atlantic, 2014 (3rd round). **Signed by:** Charlie Gonzalez.

At the end of his pro debut with short-season State College, Gomber headed back to school with an offseason project assigned by the Cardinals. They wanted him to get a curveball, one that he could throw with force to make movement happen, rather than the one he threw at Florida Atlantic, one he tried to force and saw nothing happen. That downward-diving pitch sent his production soaring. Gomber went 15-3, 2.67 the next summer and came to major league spring training as its youngest pitcher, 22. He reached Double-A Springfield in 2016 and finished in the Arizona Fall League as one of its most impressive and economical starters. A hulking lefty, Gomber pitches with an unusual angle, pace and guile. He doesn't have one overwhelming pitch, but the command and sequence he can use throws off top-shelf hitters. His fastball sits from 89-92 mph, and when it's on it helps set up his average changeup; quick outs follow and he flourishes. He spent most of spring observing the major league starters between their appearances, memorizing with an intent to mimic their routines so improve his own conditioning and strength. Gomber has a seasoned feel for how he intends to pitch and, thanks to the upper-70s curveball, a confidence in pitches at three different speeds. He'll advance as a starter, first to Double-A and then wherever needed.

Year	Club (League)	Class	W	L	ERA	G	GS	CG	SV	IP	H	HR	BB	SO	K/9	WHIP	AVG
2014	State College (NYP)	SS	2	2	2.30	11	11	0	0	47	55	3	18	36	6.9	1.55	.297
2015	Peoria (MWL)	LoA	15	3	2.67	22	22	1	0	135	97	10	34	140	9.3	0.97	.196
2016	Palm Beach (FSL)	HiA	6	8	2.93	17	17	1	0	108	91	5	24	101	8.4	1.07	.229
	Springfield (TL)	AA	1	0	1.40	4	4	0	0	19	11	0	9	15	7.0	1.03	.167
Minor League Totals			24	13	2.62	54	54	2	0	309	254	18	85	292	8.5	1.10	.222

16 DYLAN CARLSON, OF

BA GRADE
50 Risk: High

Born: Oct. 23, 1998. **B-T:** B-L. **Ht.:** 6-3. **Wt.:** 195. **Drafted:** HS—Elk Grove, Calif., 2016 (1st round). **Signed by:** Zach Mortimer.

One of the youngest players available in the draft, Carlson also had some of the deepest roots in the game. His father, Jeff, has been the coach at Elk Grove High for more than a decade, and his son was well known as a cage rat on the elite showcase circuits. He was a surprise first-round pick for the Cardinals, who convinced him to step out of a commitment to Cal State Fullerton and into a $1,350,000 bonus as the 33rd overall pick. Carlson had a .718 OPS in his first 183 at-bats, but he got better, more thunderous with each month. Carlson had 14 extra-base hits and slugged .523 in August. As he grows into his frame and balances his swing, Carlson could have above-average power from both sides. He flattened his swing during the season to be less of a flick and more of a sweep through the zone. At 17, he saw offspeed pitches at rates and proficiencies he hadn't before, so some trouble was expected. He's better from the left side now, but shows the same steady approach from both boxes. He'll play center field for as long as he can, but with a fringy arm and corner-outfield speed he'll gravitate to left or right or become a plus first baseman as he strides toward Rookie-level Johnson City.

Year	Club (League)	Class	AVG	G	AB	R	H	2B	3B	HR	RBI	BB	SO	SB	CS	OBP	SLG
2016	Cardinals (GCL)	R	.251	50	183	30	46	13	3	3	22	16	52	4	2	.313	.404
Minor League Totals			.251	50	183	30	46	13	3	3	22	16	52	4	2	.313	.404

17 JAKE WOODFORD, RHP

BA GRADE

50 Risk: High

Born: Oct. 28, 1996. **B-T:** R-R. **Ht.:** 6-4. **Wt.:** 210. **Drafted:** HS—Tampa, 2015 (1st round supplemental). **Signed by:** Mike Dibiase.

Outshined by hitters like Paul DeJong and Harrison Bader in his draft class and overshadowed by the power arms he shared a rotation with in low Class A Peoria, Woodford still has a ceiling as high as any because of his frame and the pitches he flashes. Woodford made the most of his time in front of scouts who came to see his high school teammate and first-round pick Kyle Tucker, the 2015 High School Player of the Year. Woodford has a projectable body, a competitive poise, and he proved to be a quick study in his pro debut. Within his first 12 months, Woodford's changeup and breaking ball both improved. He has games where all his pitches are average to above, though consistency isn't always at his fingertips. Peoria's opening day starter, at 19, Woodford builds his game around a sinking two-seamer that has a steep downhill angle and hitters have difficulty elevating. He doesn't have the high-octane arm of Sandy Alcantara, but Woodford is expected to see a spike from his 90-92 mph fastball as he builds strength and stamina. He and Jack Flaherty are similar enough that they're jockeying for advancement, and either could see Double-A.

Year	Club (League)	Class	W	L	ERA	G	GS	CG	SV	IP	H	HR	BB	SO	K/9	WHIP	AVG
2015	Cardinals (GCL)	R	1	0	2.39	8	5	0	1	26	26	1	7	21	7.2	1.25	.260
2016	Peoria (MWL)	LoA	5	5	3.31	21	21	0	0	109	104	7	37	82	6.8	1.30	.254
Minor League Totals			6	5	3.13	29	26	0	1	135	130	8	44	103	6.9	1.29	.255

18 CONNOR JONES, RHP

BA GRADE

50 Risk: High

Born: Oct. 10, 1994. **B-T:** R-R. **Ht.:** 6-3. **Wt.:** 200. **Drafted:** Virginia, 2016 (2nd round). **Signed by:** Sean Moran.

If the Cardinals could design, trait by trait, the type of player they would like to find in every draft it would be Jones. Not since Michael Wacha has there been a more Cardinal-type pitcher available to them. Billed as one of the safest pitching picks in the 2016 draft, Jones led Virginia's rotation to a national championship as a sophomore and was the Friday-night ace as a junior, when his stuff backed up across the board, dropping him in the draft. He harmonizes with all of the things the Cardinals value. His stats satisfied the analytics, his athleticism satisfied the front office, his pitches satisfied the scouts, and even his sinker satisfies the organization's groundball-greedy approach. Jones' fastball runs heavy at 90-92 mph, and he can gear up for 96 mph. Jones has toyed with a splitter grip instead of a changeup. Both his breaking balls, a curve and a slider, are viable, and the slider has flashed plus in the past. Jones has some flaws in his mechanics, typical of Virginia pitchers, that complicate his command. The Cardinals believe they're easy to correct and may refresh after Jones has a break from a long season. He could see high Class A in 2017 because safe is a synonym for predictable and predictable gets promoted.

Year	Club (League)	Class	W	L	ERA	G	GS	CG	SV	IP	H	HR	BB	SO	K/9	WHIP	AVG
2016	Cardinals (GCL)	R	0	0	2.25	4	0	0	0	4	3	0	1	3	6.8	1.00	.231
	State College (NYP)	SS	0	0	4.22	7	0	0	1	11	15	0	2	8	6.8	1.59	.341
Minor League Totals			0	0	3.68	11	0	0	1	15	18	0	3	11	6.8	1.43	.316

19 JONATHAN MACHADO, OF

BA GRADE

50 Risk: High

Born: Jan. 21, 1999. **B-T:** L-L. **Ht.:** 5-9. **Wt.:** 160. **Signed:** Cuba, 2016. **Signed by:** Angel Ovalles.

As the Cardinals geared up for a record spending spree on international talent, one of the youngest and littlest players they intended to sign was also one of the hardest to scout and set to receive one of the highest bonuses they have ever offered. Machado (whose first name is sometimes spelled "Jonatan") received a $2.35 million deal from the Cardinals, the largest international bonus in club history. Machado's bonus alone eclipsed the Cardinals' cap, something they knew in 2016-17 they'd blown past—by a lot. Machado is a contact-oriented hitter who rarely struck out and showed a keen ability to barrel all kinds of pitches. For Havana in Cuba's 15-and-under league, Machado hit .336/.387/.451 and had as many steals (five) as strikeouts (five). He's a fleet-footed runner and that gives him excellent range in center. While he's deft enough to drop a bunt for a hit, he also has ambush power. He's described as a prototypical leadoff-type with potential for gap-to-gap power and 70 speed to invent doubles, plus he can handle a premium position. He'll get a run in those roles in the Rookie-level Gulf Coast League in 2017.

Year	Club (League)	Class	AVG	G	AB	R	H	2B	3B	HR	RBI	BB	SO	SB	CS	OBP	SLG
2016	Cardinals (DSL)	R	.209	17	67	10	14	4	1	0	7	7	10	2	1	.284	.299
Minor League Totals			.209	17	67	10	14	4	1	0	7	7	10	2	1	.284	.299

20 ALVARO SEIJAS, RHP

BA GRADE **55** Risk: High

Born: Oct. 10, 1998. **B-T:** R-R. **Ht.:** 5-8. **Wt.:** 175. **Signed:** Venezuela, 2015. **Signed by:** Jose Gonzalez Maestre.

Seijas had a good showing when he reached the Rookie-level Gulf Coast League for his first domestic innings since turning pro. Only 17, Seijas displayed a three-pitch mix, and scouts saw flashes of above-average from each for his level and age. Despite his 5-foot-8 stature, one GCL manager said he looks like a basketball player on the mound— and his father was a superb basketball player—and then the leg lifts, the torso rotates, and the velocity flows. Seijas threw 91-95 mph and that is expected to skyrocket as he matures. His composure is expected to settle at the same time, as familiarity and confidence replace the agitation of youth that came with tricky situations. Seijas has strong start to a changeup and a curveball with natural, tight spin that has the trappings of a plus pitch. He'll start at-bats with it, showing his precociousness. He could earn time at Rookie-level Johnson City in 2017.

Year	Club (League)	Class	W	L	ERA	G	GS	CG	SV	IP	H	HR	BB	SO	K/9	WHIP	AVG
2016	Cardinals (DSL)	R	2	0	4.19	4	4	0	0	19	20	0	6	22	10.2	1.34	.260
	Cardinals (GCL)	R	3	2	3.06	10	9	0	0	50	48	4	13	33	5.9	1.22	.249
Minor League Totals			5	2	3.38	14	13	0	0	69	68	4	19	55	7.1	1.25	.252

21 JUNIOR FERNANDEZ, RHP

BA GRADE **50** Risk: High

Born: March 2, 1997. **B-T:** R-R. **Ht.:** 6-1. **Wt.:** 180. **Signed:** Dominican Republic, 2014. **Signed by:** Rodney Jimenez.

Fernandez played for Miami's Varela High before his family moved back to the Dominican in April 2013, freeing him from the amateur draft and allowing him to land a $400,000 bonus from the Cardinals. Fernandez blazed into the top 10 a year ago with a fastball that delighted radar guns, chugging at 94-99 mph and touching 100 mph. He complemented it with a sinker, an advanced and tumbling changeup, and a peripheral slider with improved tilt. The pitches alone did equal success at high Class A. While carved from the same athletic mold as other Cardinals power pitchers, Fernandez has a violent delivery that rattles loose. Scouts see a pitcher who would respond to trouble by throwing harder, then hardest, and rarely more accurately. He can overpower hitters, but must improve on doing so with pitches in the zone. Fernandez pitches with a reliever's assertiveness, a reliever's speed-slider combo, and he could see late-inning work at Double-A this summer.

Year	Club (League)	Class	W	L	ERA	G	GS	CG	SV	IP	H	HR	BB	SO	K/9	WHIP	AVG
2014	Cardinals (DSL)	R	0	5	5.79	7	6	0	0	28	29	1	12	13	4.2	1.46	.276
2015	Cardinals (GCL)	R	3	2	3.88	11	9	0	0	51	54	0	15	58	10.2	1.35	.274
	Palm Beach (FSL)	HiA	0	0	1.35	2	1	0	0	7	8	0	2	5	6.8	1.50	.308
2016	Peoria (MWL)	LoA	6	5	3.33	14	14	0	0	78	71	3	34	63	7.2	1.34	.244
	Palm Beach (FSL)	HiA	2	2	5.36	10	6	0	0	44	48	4	20	25	5.2	1.56	.271
Minor League Totals			11	14	4.16	44	36	0	0	208	210	8	83	164	7.1	1.41	.264

22 VICTOR GARCIA, OF

BA GRADE **50** Risk: High

Born: Sept. 16, 1999. **B-T:** R-R. **Ht.:** 6-3. **Wt.:** 215. **Signed:** Venezuela, 2016. **Signed by:** Estuar Ruiz.

Eight months before bidding could truly begin, Garcia was a one-man jubilee at Major League Baseball's national showcase in Venezuela. That show of force had scouts convinced he had the most raw power of his class, and BA ranked him 10th in the 2016 international class. The Cardinals had favorable evaluations before Garcia's power went public and signed him to a $1.5 million bonus. Garcia has the bat and body type built for power. He can hit with it to all fields and gets good carry on his hits without the need of loft. True to his age, he needs more time in the box to develop pitch recognition and better off-speed understanding so that his power translates more consistently into games. When he connects against live pitching, it's loud, and that has the Cardinals believing he has a tool that cannot be taught but will benefit from an approach that can be. Garcia hasn't show much arm strength and has limited range. He'll start as a corner outfielder, but the possibility of adding on strength and weight as he grows could lead him to first base. His position is hitter. As he moves toward the Rookie-level Gulf Coast League, how he bats is more essential than where he plays.

Year	Club (League)	Class	AVG	G	AB	R	H	2B	3B	HR	RBI	BB	SO	SB	CS	OBP	SLG
2016	Did not play—Signed 2017 contract																

23 SAM TUIVAILALA, RHP

BA GRADE

50 Risk: High

Born: Oct. 19, 1992. **B-T:** R-R. **Ht.:** 6-3. **Wt.:** 195. **Drafted:** HS—San Mateo, Calif., 2010 (3rd round). **Signed by:** Matt Swanson.

When the Cardinals returned Tuivailala to Triple-A in 2016 and a late-inning role for the highest affiliate, they did so with a clear assignment: Master the cutter. Manager Mike Matheny was one of the loudest advocates of the pitch, which he believed would turn Tuivailala into a power arm that could be counted on for the seventh inning, or later. The pitch was relatively new for Tuivailala, who was only in his fourth season as a pitcher. Back in 2011, as an infielder, Tuivailala homered and his coaches already knew what awaited him later that day. A team official had come to Johnson City to tell Tuivailala he was moving to the mound. With little idea how to actually deliver a pitch, Tuivailala threw a bullpen—and touched high-90s mph. That power has been good enough to get him to the majors, but he'll need more to stick there. The intriguing cutter works at 87 mph, a needed tick down from his 97 mph heater. He has toyed with a power curve and a loopier curve, but lefthanded hitters at Triple-A torched him for a .939 OPS. Quality strikes is what he must get with the fastball and either secondary if he's to seize anything more than a recurring cameo in St. Louis.

Year	Club (League)	Class	W	L	ERA	G	GS	CG	SV	IP	H	HR	BB	SO	K/9	WHIP	AVG
2014	Palm Beach (FSL)	HiA	0	1	3.58	29	0	0	3	38	29	1	18	64	15.3	1.25	.207
	Springfield (TL)	AA	2	1	2.57	17	0	0	1	21	18	0	9	30	12.9	1.29	.234
	Memphis (PCL)	AAA	0	0	0.00	2	0	0	1	1	1	0	0	3	20.3	0.75	.200
	St. Louis (NL)	MAJ	0	0	36.00	2	0	0	0	1	5	2	2	1	9.0	7.00	.625
2015	Memphis (PCL)	AAA	3	1	1.60	43	0	0	17	45	28	2	26	43	8.6	1.20	.176
	St. Louis (NL)	MAJ	0	1	3.07	14	0	0	0	15	13	2	8	20	12.3	1.43	.228
2016	Memphis (PCL)	AAA	3	2	5.21	42	0	0	17	47	47	3	22	72	13.9	1.48	.254
	St. Louis (NL)	MAJ	0	0	6.00	12	0	0	0	9	12	0	6	7	7.0	2.00	.308
Major League Totals			0	1	5.47	28	0	0	0	25	30	4	16	28	10.2	1.86	.288
Minor League Totals			8	8	3.74	172	0	0	40	200	166	7	108	285	12.8	1.37	.221

24 RONNIE WILLIAMS, RHP

BA GRADE

50 Risk: High

Born: Jan. 6, 1996. **B-T:** R-R. **Ht.:** 6-0. **Wt.:** 170. **Drafted:** HS—Hialeah, Fla., 2014 (2nd round). **Signed by:** Charlie Gonzalez.

The Cardinals selected six consecutive pitchers to open the 2014 draft. They grabbed the surefire college righthander (Luke Weaver), the upside high schooler (Jack Flaherty), and even the high-performance college lefty (Austin Gomber). In the middle of all that polish, the Cardinals also picked a project. Small, athletic and gifted with a spring-loaded right arm, Williams had far less experience as a pitcher than his contemporaries. An eager student of the position, Williams proved to be as quick to learn as he was quick to throw. The righthander builds his game around a fastball that sits in the low 90s mph and touches 97. He sometimes loses velocity to gain command and needs more consistency with the fastball to use his secondary pitches. Williams has a changeup that will play at higher levels and a wipeout breaking ball that will play if he can throw it for a strike. His stuff has been described as "electric," but it's not always efficient. He got better later in the season—no surprise because he's also getting stronger—earning a promotion from short-season State College to low Class A Peoria. The ingredients are all there awaiting the catalyst that only comes from experience, which he's set to get as a priority starter at Peoria in 2017.

Year	Club (League)	Class	W	L	ERA	G	GS	CG	SV	IP	H	HR	BB	SO	K/9	WHIP	AVG
2014	Cardinals (GCL)	R	0	5	4.71	10	8	0	1	36	39	1	9	30	7.4	1.32	.279
2015	Johnson City (APP)	R	3	3	3.70	12	12	0	0	56	45	5	25	43	6.9	1.25	.223
2016	State College (NYP)	SS	4	2	2.72	7	7	0	0	46	37	1	7	33	6.4	0.95	.213
	Peoria (MWL)	LoA	1	3	4.29	6	6	0	0	36	31	7	17	36	9.1	1.35	.231
Minor League Totals			8	13	3.77	35	33	0	1	174	152	14	58	142	7.3	1.20	.234

25 NICK PLUMMER, OF

BA GRADE

50 Risk: High

Born: July 31, 1996. **B-T:** L-L. **Ht.:** 5-10. **Wt.:** 200. **Drafted:** HS—Bloomfield Hills, Mich., 2015 (1st round). **Signed by:** Jason Bryans.

Before the teen's first full professional year could begin, it was over. In June, Plummer had a second surgery on his hand to address an injury that had twice kept him from playing. During spring he had the hamate bone removed, and later a tear within the hand had to be repaired. Those surgeries meant he would spend all of 2016 rehabbing and building strength so that he could start back at the same spot for 2017. The Cardinals hope the injury is just a delay, not a sidetrack. Plummer became the first Michigan prep player drafted in the first round since 1997 (Ryan Anderson) and only the second since Derek Jeter (1992). He signed for a $2,124,000 bonus, one of the top six in club history, and the Cardinals realized he would also require an investment of time. Plummer had 39 walks in his pro debut, carrying over a studious, patient reputation he earned in a high school league that started hitters with a 1-1 count. He's got a short swing and solid pitch recognition that does well against even the velocity monsters he faced in Rookie ball. Set for a short-season club, he's got the build and bat to fit at center and will get a run there; it's just getting a slower start.

Year	Club (League)	Class	AVG	G	AB	R	H	2B	3B	HR	RBI	BB	SO	SB	CS	OBP	SLG
2015	Cardinals (GCL)	R	.228	51	180	43	41	8	5	1	22	39	56	8	6	.379	.344
2016	Did not play—Injured																
Minor League Totals			.228	51	180	43	41	8	5	1	22	39	56	8	6	.379	.344

26 BRYCE DENTON, 3B/OF

BA GRADE
50 Risk: High

Born: Aug. 1, 1997. **B-T:** R-R. **Ht.:** 6-0. **Wt.:** 190. **Drafted:** HS—Brentwood, Tenn., 2015 (2nd round). **Signed by:** Jason Bryans.

Whatever frustrations Denton had offensively in his early games as a pro a coach said he never let on, never wore them on his sleeve. The success he had in his final games of 2016 means he can wear them on his finger. Denton slugged a three-run homer and had a career-best five RBIs in the clinching game as Rookie-level Johnson City swept its way to the Appalachian League title. Denton muscled the JC-Cards into the playoffs with a .287/.362/.404 August and 19 RBIs in 25 games. It was the punctuation on a learning-curve season. Denton landed a $1.2 million bonus from the team for his power potential, which some evaluators peg as average. The Cardinals believe there's more locked within a projectable frame and quick, belting swing. As he matures—he was only 17 when drafted—and sees more higher-level pitching, the belief is his power will perk. Denton has a liveliness on the field, especially in the field, where whatever rough edges he has at third base he smooths with high energy. He has the arm and range to remain at third base as he reaches a full-season club, but he could move to a corner outfield spot or first base, depending on how the bat plays at low Class A Peoria in 2017.

Year	Club (League)	Class	AVG	G	AB	R	H	2B	3B	HR	RBI	BB	SO	SB	CS	OBP	SLG
2015	Cardinals (GCL)	R	.194	44	155	21	30	1	2	1	14	11	32	3	0	.254	.245
2016	Johnson City (APP)	R	.282	54	202	34	57	7	0	4	26	20	37	2	1	.356	.376
Minor League Totals			.244	98	357	55	87	8	2	5	40	31	69	5	1	.312	.319

27 JOHN GANT, RHP

BA GRADE
50 Risk: High

Born: Aug. 6, 1992. **B-T:** R-R. **Ht.:** 6-5. **Wt.:** 205. **Drafted:** HS—Wesley Chapel, Fla., 2011 (21st round). **Signed by:** Les Parker (Mets).

Gant and Rob Whalen joined the Braves when Atlanta sent journeymen Juan Uribe and Kelly Johnson to New York near the trading deadline in 2015. Less than a year later he was on the move again, this time as part of a three-player package, St. Louis-bound for lefty Jaime Garcia. After pitching well at the end of 2015 at Double-A Mississippi, the righthander spent most of 2016 bouncing between the big leagues and Triple-A Gwinnett while missing nearly a month at midseason due to a left oblique strain. Gant averaged 8.8 strikeouts per nine innings with Atlanta. His funky delivery begins with him scraping his left foot on the ground, pausing and then pitching. Gant can repeat the two-tap mechanics and has solid command, generating lots of grounders by throwing on a downhill plane with his 6-foot-5 frame. Gant's strength is his ability to set up hitters. He throws his low-90s fastball about 58 percent of the time and splits his remaining offerings between an above-average changeup and a tight curveball with a sharp break. Gant has the toolset to be a No. 4 or 5 starter or a situational reliever, and is likely to pitch for multiple teams before his career concludes. He'll provide the Cardinals a long reliever or sub-starter when needed in 2017.

Year	Club (League)	Class	W	L	ERA	G	GS	CG	SV	IP	H	HR	BB	SO	K/9	WHIP	AVG
2014	Savannah (SAL)	LoA	11	5	2.56	21	21	2	0	123	107	5	40	114	8.3	1.20	.231
2015	St. Lucie (FSL)	HiA	2	0	1.79	6	6	0	0	40	27	4	10	48	10.7	0.92	.180
	Binghamton (EL)	AA	4	5	4.70	11	11	0	0	59	67	2	26	43	6.5	1.57	.289
	Mississippi (SL)	AA	4	0	1.99	7	7	0	0	41	28	1	14	43	9.5	1.03	.201
2016	Rome (SAL)	LoA	1	0	0.00	1	0	0	0	3	1	0	1	2	6.0	0.67	.111
	Gwinnett (IL)	AAA	3	3	4.18	12	10	0	0	56	58	5	22	57	9.2	1.43	.262
	Atlanta (NL)	MAJ	1	4	4.86	20	7	0	0	50	54	7	21	49	8.8	1.50	.278
Major League Totals			1	4	4.86	20	7	0	0	50	54	7	21	49	8.8	1.50	.278
Minor League Totals			33	22	3.33	87	81	3	0	462	421	26	163	445	8.7	1.26	.241

28 JORDAN HICKS, RHP

BA GRADE
50 Risk: High

Born: Sept. 6, 1996. **B-T:** R-R. **Ht.:** 6-2. **Wt.:** 185. **Drafted:** HS—Houston, 2015 (3rd round supplemental). **Signed by:** Ralph Garr Jr.

If there is one true referendum on a club's farm system and the talent inside, it's what other teams ask for in trades. As the Cardinals sought a reliever around the non-waiver trade deadline in 2016, one of the

players deep in the system that clubs coveted was Hicks, an otherwise unheralded and quietly intriguing talent who had a delayed debut. Hicks did not pitch in a game until 2016 because of shoulder inflammation, and the Cardinals played ultra-conservative with his workload. When they unleashed him on the Rookie-level Appalachian League and later the short-season New York-Penn League, he rated as one of the best pitching prospects in each. Hicks, a Tulane commit who received a $600,000 bonus, is a standout athlete with the stuff that inspires dreams. His fastball has sink and zips at 92-97 mph. His changeup is firm and effective against lefthanded batters. He's got a tightly-wound, biting 78-83 mph curve that earns plus grades, with one scout giving it a future 70. "It's sick," was a report. His delivery adds some deception and some concern. It has been difficult for him to repeat or maintain deep into games; as it goes so does command. His pitches will get him to low Class Peoria's rotation; command will accelerate his rise.

Year	Club (League)	Class	W	L	ERA	G	GS	CG	SV	IP	H	HR	BB	SO	K/9	WHIP	AVG
2016	Johnson City (APP)	R	2	1	4.20	6	6	0	0	30	33	1	13	20	6.0	1.53	.292
	State College (NYP)	SS	4	1	1.76	6	6	0	0	31	25	0	16	22	6.5	1.34	.217
Minor League Totals			6	2	2.97	12	12	0	0	61	58	1	29	42	6.2	1.43	.254

29 BREYVIC VALERA, SS/2B

BA GRADE
50 Risk: High

Born: Jan. 8, 1992. **B-T:** B-R. **Ht.:** 5-11. **Wt.:** 160. **Signed:** Venezuela, 2010. **Signed by:** Jose Gregorio Gonzalez.

Perhaps because he's spent parts of four seasons at Double-A Springfield and seemed to bump his head against a ceiling there, some prospect fatigue set in for Valera. He moved around the infield as much as he didn't move up in the system, all despite a steady, switch-hitting bat that in 2,524 minor-league at-bats has a .302/.358/.375 slash line. When the Cardinals faced the prospect of losing him as a six-year free agent they rushed to add him to the 40-man roster. General manager John Mozeliak said the team saw "a maturing curve" with Valera in 2016 and became convinced that no other player on the open market was "an elite performer" like him. Valera isn't flashy or toolsy. What he is is baseball smart and compellingly average at everything. He's a patient singles hitter who is savvy running the bases if not stealing them. Primarily a second baseman as he advanced, Valera has sneaky range, good hands and excellent instincts. He can play third, handle shortstop, and doesn't look out of place in the outfield. Bumped to Triple-A for the first time in 2016, Valera thrived with a .832 OPS in half a season and had more walks (31) than strikeouts (22). He was thriving in winter ball in Venezuela, even hitting six homers in his first 185 at-bats. That has the Cardinals thinking that Valera, after years of seasoning, is poised to contribute to the majors as a utility infielder.

Year	Club (League)	Class	AVG	G	AB	R	H	2B	3B	HR	RBI	BB	SO	SB	CS	OBP	SLG
2014	Palm Beach (FSL)	HiA	.333	73	294	35	98	8	4	0	37	25	13	13	10	.385	.388
	Springfield (TL)	AA	.286	59	227	31	65	8	2	0	20	15	22	4	5	.329	.339
2015	Palm Beach (FSL)	HiA	.353	14	51	9	18	3	1	0	7	11	2	0	3	.468	.451
	Springfield (TL)	AA	.236	105	360	37	85	9	2	3	31	34	27	2	4	.301	.297
2016	Springfield (TL)	AA	.258	52	178	16	46	5	1	0	12	9	18	3	1	.289	.298
	Memphis (PCL)	AAA	.341	73	217	32	74	14	1	0	31	31	22	8	4	.417	.415
Minor League Totals			.302	683	2524	351	761	108	30	6	263	222	202	77	49	.358	.375

30 JOHAN OVIEDO, RHP

BA GRADE
50 Risk: High

Born: March 2, 1998. **B-T:** R-R. **Ht.:** 6-6. **Wt.:** 210. **Signed:** Cuba, 2016. **Signed by:** Angel Ovalles.

The two headliners for the Cardinals' first significant lunge into the market for Cuban teens couldn't be more different. One is nearly a foot taller than the other, who was far more heralded as a prospect entering the signing period. What Jonathan Machado and Oviedo share however is important: $1 million bonuses and a game built for speed. Oviedo wowed scouts with a hulking frame for an 18-year-old and a heavy 94-96 mph fastball that touched 98. Described as "physically impressive" by one evaluator, Oviedo has a fluidity to his movements, an athleticism that guides his mechanics. The Cardinals' scouts harmonized their early reports on him and the club insisted on being aggressive, signing him for a $1.9 million bonus. In seven starts at the Dominican Summer League he struck out 29 in 21.2 innings. His fastball is overpowering and he has a wipeout curve that will have to be tightened and used for a strike as he advances. He'll get some scrutinized innings in extended, a turn in the GCL, and be a "jump the fence" candidate at high Class A Palm Beach as the Cardinals attempt to nurture an arm with impact-starter potential.

Year	Club (League)	Class	W	L	ERA	G	GS	CG	SV	IP	H	HR	BB	SO	K/9	WHIP	AVG
2016	Cardinals (DSL)	R	0	1	1.66	7	7	0	0	22	19	0	6	29	12.0	1.15	.238
Minor League Totals			0	1	1.66	7	7	0	0	22	19	0	6	29	12.0	1.15	.238

San Diego Padres

BY KYLE GLASER

Everything that could go wrong for the Padres did go wrong at the major league level in 2016, with any hope of a successful season dashed in a matter of days. San Diego's season-opening home series against the Dodgers served as a harbinger of things to come when Los Angeles swept all three games by a combined score of 25-0.

The Padres not only suffered their sixth straight losing season, but posted their worst record in that time with a 68-94 mark. First-year manager Andy Green injected relentless energy and optimism into the clubhouse, but it wasn't enough to overcome the calamities that struck the franchise.

A series of routine injuries had devastated the club by the end of April. Ace Tyson Ross did not pitch after Opening Day with shoulder problems. Second baseman Cory Spangenberg never reappeared after straining his left quad a week later.

After a 16-4 shellacking at the hands of the Mariners on May 31 that dropped the Padres' record to 20-33, executive chairman Ron Fowler publicly called the team "miserable failures" on their flagship radio station.

And so began a fire sale, with veterans James Shields, Matt Kemp, Fernando Rodney, Melvin Upton, Andrew Cashner and Drew Pomeranz all traded by August, starting the latest rebuilding process in a franchise history full of them.

Even the fire sale didn't go smoothly. Major League Baseball suspended general manager A.J. Preller in September for 30 days after ruling he did not properly disclose relevant medical information to the Red Sox in their July trade of Pomeranz. Another trade with the Marlins was modified after righthander Colin Rea, one of the players the Padres traded, suffered a torn UCL in his first start with Miami. The two parties reworked the deal to return Rea to the Padres and promising righthander Luis Castillo to the Marlins.

Things got even worse after the season, when team president and CEO Mike Dee was fired without explanation.

With the front office in disarray and the major league product delivering its worst performance, the season's lone positives could be found on the farm. Homegrown prospect such as outfielders Hunter Renfroe and Michael Gettys, second baseman Luis Urias and righthanders Jacob Nix and Dinelson Lamet all took significant steps forward in their development. Offseason acquisitions such as outfielder Manuel Margot, second baseman Carlos Asuaje, lefthander Logan Allen and righthander Enyel de los Santos showed promise.

Most critically, the midseason trades of veterans

Colin Rea's elbow injury nixed a trade and focused scrutiny on the Padres' front office

TOP PROSPECTS OF THE DECADE

Year	Player, Pos.	2016 Org
2007	Cedric Hunter, of	Phillies
2008	Chase Headley, 3b	Yankees
2009	Kyle Blanks, 1b	Giants
2010	Donovan Tate, of	Dodgers
2011	Casey Kelly, rhp	Braves
2012	Anthony Rizzo, 1b	Cubs
2013	Casey Kelly, rhp	Braves
2014	Austin Hedges, c	Padres
2015	Matt Wisler, rhp	Braves
2016	Javier Guerra, ss	Padres

yielded an intriguing haul of prospect talent, led by righthander Anderson Espinoza, first baseman Josh Naylor, righthander Chris Paddack and shortstop Fernando Tatis Jr.

The Padres furthered bolstered their system with three of the 2016 draft's top 25 picks, and then shattered spending records during the international signing period. San Diego spent upwards of $60 million signing international amateur talent, including penalties for overages, and brought in eight of the top 50 international prospects in the class, including three of the top six.

The injection of talent from all avenues turned the Padres system into one of the game's deepest. Now, the team must develop it to end years of poor performance and reverse the entrenched skepticism in San Diego.

ORGANIZATION OVERVIEW

General manager: A.J. Preller. **Farm director:** Sam Geaney. **Scouting director:** Mark Connor.

Class	Team	League	W	L	PCT	Finish	Manager
Majors	San Diego Padres	National	68	94	.420	15th (15)	Bud Black
Triple-A	El Paso Chihuahuas	Pacific Coast	73	70	.510	5th (16)	Rod Barajas
Double-A	San Antonio Missions	Texas	58	82	.414	8th (10)	Phil Wellman
High Class A	Lake Elsinore Storm	California	69	71	.493	6th (10)	Francisco Morales
Low Class A	Fort Wayne Tincaps	Midwest	62	78	.443	13th (16)	Anthony Contreras
Short-season	Tri-City Dust Devils	Northwest	34	42	.447	4th (8)	Ben Fritz
Rookie	AZL Padres	Arizona	25	30	.455	11th (14)	Michael Collins
Overall 2016 Minor League Record			321	373	.463	24th (30)	

THIS YEAR'S TOP 30

No.	Player, Pos.	Grade/Risk
1.	Anderson Espinoza, rhp	65/High
2.	Manuel Margot, of	60/Medium
3.	Hunter Renfroe, of	55/Medium
4.	Cal Quantrill, rhp	60/Extreme
5.	Adrian Morejon, lhp	60/Extreme
6.	Luis Urias, 2b/ss	55/High
7.	Jacob Nix, rhp	55/High
8.	Michael Gettys, of	55/High
9.	Dinelson Lamet, rhp	50/Medium
10.	Josh Naylor, 1b	55/High
11.	Carlos Asuaje, 2b	45/Low
12.	Jorge Ona, of	55/Extreme
13.	Eric Lauer, lhp	50/High
14.	Hudson Potts, 3b/ss	55/Extreme
15.	Chris Paddack, rhp	55/Extreme
16.	Enyel de los Santos, rhp	50/High
17.	Fernando Tatis Jr., ss	55/Extreme
18.	Phil Maton, rhp	45/Medium
19.	Logan Allen, lhp	50/High
20.	Luis Almanzar, ss	55/Extreme
21.	Jose Torres, lhp	45/Medium
22.	Jose Rondon, ss	45/Medium
23.	Franchy Cordero, of	45/Medium
24.	Joey Lucchesi, lhp	50/High
25.	Javier Guerra, ss	50/Extreme
26.	Mason Thompson, rhp	50/Extreme
27.	Ruddy Giron, ss	45/High
28.	Walker Lockett, rhp	40/Medium
29.	Allen Cordoba, ss	50/Extreme
30.	Austin Allen, c	45/High

LAST YEAR'S TOP 30

No.	Player, Pos.	Status
1.	Javier Guerra, ss	No. 25
2.	Manuel Margot, of	No. 2
3.	Hunter Renfroe, of	No. 3
4.	Ruddy Giron, ss	No. 27
5.	Jose Rondon, ss	No. 22
6.	Travis Jankowski, of	Majors
7.	Colin Rea, rhp	Majors
8.	Logan Allen, lhp	No. 19
9.	Austin Smith, rhp	Dropped out
10.	Michael Gettys, of	No. 8
11.	Jacob Nix, rhp	No. 7
12.	Cory Mazzoni, rhp	Dropped out
13.	Carlos Asuaje, 2b	No. 11
14.	Ryan Butler, rhp	Dropped out
15.	Enyel de los Santos, rhp	No. 16
16.	Tayron Guerrero, rhp	(Marlins)
17.	Dinelson Lamet, rhp	No. 9
18.	Nick Torres, of	Dropped out
19.	Yimmi Brasoban, rhp	Dropped out
20.	Fernando Perez, 2b	Dropped out
21.	Jose Pirela, 2b/of	Majors
22.	Alex Dickerson, of	Majors
23.	Rymer Liriano, of	(White Sox)
24.	Jose Urena, of	Dropped out
25.	Justin Hancock, rhp	Dropped out
26.	Phil Maton, rhp	No. 18
27.	Jose Castillo, lhp	Dropped out
28.	Jose Torres, lhp	No. 21
29.	Luis Urias, 2b/ss	No. 6
30.	Emmanuel Ramirez, rhp	Dropped out

BEST TOOLS

Best Hitter for Average	Luis Urias
Best Power Hitter	Hunter Renfroe
Best Strike-Zone Discipline	Luis Urias
Fastest Baserunner	Manuel Margot
Best Athlete	Michael Gettys
Best Fastball	Anderson Espinoza
Best Curveball	Jacob Nix
Best Slider	Dinelson Lamet
Best Changeup	Cal Quantrill
Best Control	Joey Lucchesi
Best Defensive Catcher	A.J. Kennedy
Best Defensive Infielder	Javier Guerra
Best Infield Arm	Javier Guerra
Best Defensive Outfielder	Manuel Margot
Best Outfield Arm	Hunter Renfroe

PROJECTED 2020 LINEUP

Catcher	Austin Hedges
First Base	Wil Myers
Second Base	Luis Urias
Third Base	Yangervis Solarte
Shortstop	Fernando Tatis Jr.
Left Field	Michael Gettys
Center Field	Manuel Margot
Right Field	Hunter Renfroe
No. 1 Starter	Anderson Espinoza
No. 2 Starter	Cal Quantrill
No. 3 Starter	Jacob Nix
No. 4 Starter	Dinelson Lamet
No. 5 Starter	Eric Lauer
Closer	Phil Maton

MINOR LEAGUE DEPTH CHART

SAN DIEGO PADRES

TOP 2017 ROOKIE: Hunter Renfroe, of. He will be the Opening Day right fielder and immediately provide a middle-of-the-order power source.

BREAKOUT PROSPECT: Enyel de los Santos, rhp. With youth and electric arm strength, he has serious helium potential if he successfully jumps to Double-A.

SLEEPER: Brad Wieck, lhp. The 6-foot-9 southpaw reliever boasts a vicious fastball-slider combo and uses his size well to deceive opponents.

SOURCE OF TOP 30 TALENT			
Homegrown	18	Acquired	12
College	6	Trades	11
Junior college	0	Rule 5 draft	1
High school	5	Independent leagues	0
Nondrafted free agents	0	Free agents/waivers	0
International	7		

LF
Jorge Ona (12)
Nick Torres
Tirso Ornelas

CF
Manuel Margot (2)
Michael Gettys (8)
Franchy Cordero (23)
Buddy Reed
Jeisson Rosario

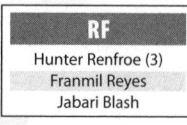

RF
Hunter Renfroe (3)
Franmil Reyes
Jabari Blash

3B
Hudson Potts (14)
Carlos Belen

SS
Fernando Tatis Jr. (17)
Luis Almanzar (20)
Jose Rondon (22)
Javier Guerra (25)
Ruddy Giron (27)
Allen Cordoba (29)
Gabrial Arias
Chris Baker

2B
Luis Urias (6)
Carlos Asuaje (11)
Eguy Rosario

1B
Josh Naylor (10)
Ty France
Brad Zunica

C
Austin Allen (30)
Luis Torrens
A.J. Kennedy

LHP

LHSP	LHRP
Adrian Morejon (5)	Jose Torres (21)
Eric Lauer (13)	Brad Wieck
Logan Allen (19)	Jose Castillo
Joey Lucchesi (24)	Kyle McGrath

RHP

RHSP	RHRP
Anderson Espinoza (1)	Phil Maton (18)
Cal Quantrill (4)	Miguel Diaz
Jacob Nix (7)	Yimmi Brasoban
Dinelson Lamet (9)	Trey Wingenter
Chris Paddack (15)	Rafael De Paula
Enyel de los Santos (16)	Will Stillman
Mason Thompson (26)	Jose Ruiz
Walker Lockett (28)	Starlin Cordero
Reggie Lawson	Andres Munoz
Henry Henry	
Lake Bachar	
Ronald Bolanos	
Hansel Rodriguez	
Michael Kelly	
Jean Cosme	
Brett Kennedy	
Austin Smith	

DRAFT ANALYSIS

2016

BEST PURE HITTER: SS/3B Hudson Potts (1) wasn't a consensus first-rounder, but the Padres believed in his bat. He has timing, bat-to-ball skills and an ease of operation that gives the club's scouts conviction in his hitting tool.

BEST POWER HITTER: Potts' average future power stands out in a pitcher-heavy draft class.

FASTEST RUNNER: OF Buddy Reed (2) has a high waist, long legs and easy gliding strides that play on the bases. He's shy of a true 70 runner, mainly because of his big swing at the plate.

BEST DEFENSIVE PLAYER: Reed's speed plays better in center field, where he lets his athleticism play and has plus range and has at least an above-average arm.

BEST FASTBALL: RHP Cal Quantrill (1), the first of the Padres' three first-rounders, has come back from Tommy John surgery throwing 93-96 mph. He has plus control, though his command is still coming back. RHPs Reggie Lawson (2s) and Mason Thompson (3) both have low-90s heaters with projection for more. LHP Eric Lauer (1) throws 88-92 mph but pitches off his fastball extremely well with angle and location.

BEST SECONDARY PITCH: Quantrill throws three variations of his plus changeup, with a feel for manipulating the ball and locating it. He has the confidence to throw it in any count, to any hitter.

BEST PRO DEBUT: LHP Joey Lucchesi (4) showed his deception, 90-94 mph fastball with late life and downer curveball will play in pro ball. He went 0-2, 1.29 in 42 overall innings with a 56-3 strikeout-walk ratio. Lauer struck out 37 in 31 innings while posting a 2.03 ERA over three levels. SS Chris Baker (17) hit .295/.380/.428 with 14 stolen bases between short-season Tri-City and low Class A Fort Wayne.

BEST ATHLETE: Reed was a three-sport prep star in Rhode Island, thriving at soccer and hockey. OF A.J. Brown (19), a physical specimen at 6-foot-1, 225 pounds, is playing wide receiver at Mississippi, with 14 catches and two touchdowns in his first five games.

MOST INTRIGUING BACKGROUND: Quantrill (father Paul) and 2B Nate Easley (23) (father Damion) have fathers who played more than 12 years in the big leagues apiece. RHP Lake Bachar (5) went to Division III Wisconsin-Whitewater as a punter/kicker but wound up reaching 95 mph on the mound.

CLOSEST TO THE MAJORS: Lauer has built up stamina, throwing 135 innings between college and pro ball in 2016, and has the fastball command to get on the fast track. Lucchesi (153 IP in 2016) shares similar traits.

BEST LATE-ROUND PICK: OF Tre Carter (11) was a second-team preseason All-American, with athleticism to rival Reed and Brown. He signed for $100,000. The Padres went higher in bonuses for strong OF Jack Suwinski (15, $550,000) and SS/OF Ethan Skender (28), who has feel for hitting.

THE ONE WHO GOT AWAY: SS Grae Kessinger (26), grandson of ex-big leaguer Don Kessinger, flirted with signing before heading to Mississippi, where his father played and grandfather coached.

2015

With no first-round pick, the Padres still found upside with RHP Jacob Nix (3), their second pick. RHP Phil Maton (20) has reached Triple-A with a 14.5 SO/9 ratio as a pro, while C Austin Allen (4) has hit his way to prospect status.

GRADE: C

2014

SS Trea Turner (1) has become a dynamic big leaguer in Washington after being traded in the Wil Myers deal. OFs Michael Gettys (2) and Nick Torres (4) had strong 2016 seasons, with Gettys the better prospect. OF Austin Bousfield (5) and RHP Jason Jester (23) joined Torres in Triple-A.

GRADE: A

2013

OF Hunter Renfroe (1) was MVP of the Triple-A Pacific Coast League in 2016. RHP Trevor Gott (6) sped to the majors after being traded to the Angels. 1B/OF Jake Bauers (7) and OF Dustin Peterson (2) have thrived but were traded to the Rays and Braves, respectively.

GRADE: B

TOP DRAFT PICKS OF THE DECADE

Year	Player, Pos.	2016 Org
2007	Nick Schmidt, lhp	Did not play
2008	Allan Dykstra, 1b	Did not play
2009	Donovan Tate, of	Dodgers
2010	*Karsten Whitson, rhp	Did not play
2011	Cory Spangenberg, 2b	Padres
2012	Max Fried, lhp	Braves
2013	Hunter Renfroe, of	Padres
2014	Trea Turner, ss	Nationals
2015	Austin Smith, rhp (2nd round)	Padres
2016	Cal Quantrill, rhp	Padres

*Did not sign.

LARGEST BONUSES IN CLUB HISTORY

Adrian Morejon, 2016	$11,000,000
Jorge Ona, 2016	$7,000,000
Donovan Tate, 2009	$6,250,000
Luis Almanzar, 2016	$4,050,000
Cal Quantrill, 2016	$3,963,045

1 ANDERSON ESPINOZA, RHP

Born: March 9, 1998. **B-T:** R-R. **Ht.:** 6-0. **Wt.:** 160.
Signed: Venezuela, 2014.
Signed by: Eddie Romero/Manny Padron (Red Sox).

BA GRADE

65 Risk: High

SCOUTING GRADES

Fastball: 70.
Changeup: 70.
Curveball: 60.
Control: 55.

Based on 20-80 scouting scale and future projection rather than present tools.

BILL MITCHELL

While some teenage international stand-outs fly under the radar, Espinoza is one whose promise has been evident for some time. Considered the top available pitcher by a wide margin in the 2014 international class, he signed with the Red Sox for $1.8 million. If Espinoza felt any pressure from the lofty expectations he never showed it, zooming all the way from the Dominican Summer League to low Class A in 2015, his age-17 season, and ranking as one of baseball's top prospects one year after signing. The Red Sox were reluctant to part with him but ultimately did in a one-for-one swap for Drew Pomeranz two days after Pomeranz pitched in the 2016 All-Star Game as a member of the host Padres.

The lean Espinoza is not physically intimidating but possesses a strong lower half and electric arm speed that allows him to nonetheless pitch with elite velocity. He is not dissimilar from fellow 6-foot flamethrower Yordano Ventura in that regard. Espinoza's 95-98 mph four-seam fastball possesses so much late tail away from lefthanded batters that Padres broadcaster and former major league pitcher Mark Grant confused it for a two-seamer—a mistake made by others before him—and Espinoza commands it masterfully to both sides of the plate. His main secondary pitch is a mid-80s changeup that is above-average on a bad day and "simply fantastic" in the words of one opposing scout on a good one. His upper-70s curveball lacks consistency but still flashes plus with 11-to-5 movement. Spotty command of his breaking pitches led to Espinoza getting hit more often at low Class A in 2016 than his pure stuff indicates he should, and he also struggled with trying to be too fine at times rather than attacking hitters. He admitted being a bit shell-shocked after being traded and struggled in his first few outings in the Padres system, but he adjusted and finished strong with 10 strikeouts and just two runs allowed in his final two starts at Fort Wayne. He continued that with a dominant 1-2-3 inning in the Padres' futures game at Petco Park on Oct. 7, where he struck out two Rangers batters. His exceptional performance on a big stage at Petco was nothing new for Espinoza, who draws raves for his ability to reach back and find something extra in big moments. He possesses exceptional makeup and intelligence, signified both by his poise on the mound and the fact he learned English almost fluently by age 18, less than two years after first coming to the U.S.

Ventura is a common comparison for Espinoza in terms of size and raw stuff, but Espinoza does it easier and possesses superior makeup and maturity that should help him surpass the Royals righthander. He has all the tools to become a front-of-the-rotation ace and will look to solidify that profile atop high Class A Lake Elsinore's rotation in 2017.

Year	Club (League)	Class	W	L	ERA	G	GS	CG	SV	IP	H	HR	BB	SO	K/9	WHIP	AVG
2015	Red Sox2 (DSL)	R	0	0	1.20	4	4	0	0	15	13	0	3	21	12.6	1.07	.232
	Red Sox (GCL)	R	0	1	0.68	10	10	0	0	40	24	0	9	40	9.0	0.83	.170
	Greenville (SAL)	LoA	0	1	8.10	1	1	0	0	3	4	0	2	4	10.8	1.80	.267
2016	Greenville (SAL)	LoA	5	8	4.38	17	17	0	0	76	77	2	27	72	8.5	1.37	.269
	Fort Wayne (MWL)	LoA	1	3	4.73	8	7	0	0	32	38	1	8	28	7.8	1.42	.290
Minor League Totals			6	13	3.35	40	39	0	0	167	156	3	49	165	8.9	1.23	.248

2 MANUEL MARGOT, OF

Born: Sept. 18, 1994. **B-T:** R-R. **Ht.:** 5-11. **Wt.:** 180. **Signed:** Dominican Republic, 2011. **Signed by:** Manny Nanita/Craig Shipley (Red Sox).

The Red Sox signed Margot for $800,000 as a 16-year old international free agent in 2011 and watched him stand out at every level as he ascended their system. He was a consensus Top 100 Prospect when the Padres acquired him and three other well-regarded minor leaguers in exchange for closer Craig Kimbrel after the 2015 season. Margot possesses strong wrists and exceptional feel for the barrel, allowing him to make consistent hard contact. His plus speed helps his bat play up, turning singles into doubles and doubles into triples, and his control of the strike zone was uncanny for a player his age at Triple-A. The sum of all of that profiles Margot as a plus offensive player, even with fringe-average power. The Padres were surprised at Margot's lack of defensive polish when he first arrived, but he dramatically improved his reads and routes throughout 2016, which combined with his raw speed and athleticism, turned him into one of the top defensive outfielders in the upper minors. His above-average arm also took a huge leap forward in 2016, with corrected footwork leading to more strength behind his throws to the point he led the Pacific Coast League with 18 assists. Margot has everything you want in a top-of-the-order center fielder. His superior offensive profile to Travis Jankowski makes Margot the Padres' center fielder of the future, beginning in 2017.

BA GRADE
60 Risk: Medium

Year	Club (League)	Class	AVG	G	AB	R	H	2B	3B	HR	RBI	BB	SO	SB	CS	OBP	SLG
2014	Greenville (SAL)	LoA	.286	99	370	61	106	20	5	10	45	37	49	39	13	.355	.449
	Salem (CAR)	HiA	.340	16	50	4	17	5	0	2	14	2	5	3	2	.364	.560
2015	Salem (CAR)	HiA	.282	46	181	35	51	6	5	3	17	11	15	20	5	.321	.420
	Portland (EL)	AA	.271	64	258	38	70	21	4	3	33	21	36	19	8	.326	.419
2016	El Paso (PCL)	AAA	.304	124	517	98	157	21	12	6	55	36	64	30	11	.351	.426
	San Diego (NL)	MAJ	.243	10	37	4	9	4	1	0	3	0	7	2	0	.243	.405
Major League Totals			.243	10	37	4	9	4	1	0	3	0	7	2	0	.243	.405
Minor League Totals			.288	466	1821	314	525	91	35	29	230	165	234	162	56	.350	.424

3 HUNTER RENFROE, OF

Born: Jan. 28, 1992. **B-T:** R-R. **Ht.:** 6-1. **Wt.:** 220. **Drafted:** Mississippi State, 2013 (1st round). **Signed by:** Andrew Salvo.

Renfroe was a star prep athlete in small-town Mississippi and was drafted by the Red Sox in the 31st round out of high school in 2010. He instead attended Mississippi State, where he anchored the middle of the Bulldogs' lineup and led them to the College World Series as junior. He was drafted 13th overall after that season in 2013 by the Padres and signed for $2.678 million. Renfroe's carrying tool has long been his double-plus raw power, but up until 2016 it was largely to his pull side and came with a 25 percent career strikeout rate. He closed his stance and shortened his stroke in 2016 at Triple-A El Paso and had his best season yet, hitting 10 of his Pacific Coast League-leading 30 home runs the opposite way and cutting his strikeout rate to 20 percent as he rolled to the circuit's MVP award. He continued to mash after his first big league callup in September with four home runs in 11 games—including a titanic blast onto the roof of the Western Metal Supply Co. building, beyond the left-field wall at Petco Park. He was named the National League Player of the Week for the final week of the regular season. Renfroe's improved feel to hit and massive power comes with a double-plus arm in right field and the athleticism to hold down the position ably. His aggressiveness swinging in early counts will keep his strikeouts high and his walks low, but the swing adjustments he has made give him a better chance to make conisistent contact and annually reach his 30-homer potential. He will be the Padres' Opening Day right fielder in 2017 and represents the franchise's best hope to be its first impactful first-round draft selection since Derrek Lee in 1993.

BA GRADE
55 Risk: Medium

Year	Club (League)	Class	AVG	G	AB	R	H	2B	3B	HR	RBI	BB	SO	SB	CS	OBP	SLG
2014	Lake Elsinore (CAL)	HiA	.295	69	278	46	82	21	3	16	52	28	81	9	3	.370	.565
	San Antonio (TL)	AA	.232	60	224	17	52	12	0	5	23	25	53	2	1	.307	.353
2015	San Antonio (TL)	AA	.259	112	421	50	109	22	3	14	54	33	112	4	1	.313	.425
	El Paso (PCL)	AAA	.333	21	90	15	30	5	2	6	24	4	20	1	0	.358	.633
2016	El Paso (PCL)	AAA	.306	133	533	95	163	34	5	30	105	22	115	5	2	.336	.557
	San Diego (NL)	MAJ	.371	11	35	8	13	3	0	4	14	1	5	0	0	.389	.800
Major League Totals			.371	11	35	8	13	3	0	4	14	1	5	0	0	.389	.800
Minor League Totals			.281	438	1716	249	482	108	13	77	283	121	430	23	7	.330	.494

4 CAL QUANTRILL, RHP

BILL MITCHELL

Born: Feb. 10, 1995. **B-T:** L-R. **Ht.:** 6-2. **Wt.:** 165. **Drafted:** Stanford, 2016 (1st round).
Signed by: Sam Ray.

The son of former Blue Jays all-star reliever Paul Quantrill starred on Canada's 18U national team growing up in Port Hope, Ontario, and was drafted by the Yankees in the 26th round out of high school. He instead went to Stanford, where he became the first freshman pitcher to start Opening Day since Mike Mussina in 1988. Quantrill pitched just three games as a sophomore before requiring Tommy John surgery, which kept him out all of his junior season as well. Undeterred, the Padres drafted him eighth overall and signed him for $3,963,045. Quantrill displayed no ill effects from surgery once he got into the Padres system, showing a 92-96 mph fastball and diving 81-84 mph changeup that was considered the best in the 2016 draft class. His slider is his third pitch but showed vast improvement by sitting 83-84 mph with late bite and generating swings and misses to become an above-average offering. Quantrill's command remains shaky post-surgery, but he was around the strike zone with all of his pitches during his pro debut, which he spent primarily at short-season Tri-City. He possesses the poise and pitchability expected from the son of a former major leaguer, and his competitiveness earns raves. Because Quantrill hasn't pitched a full season since 2014, the Padres will manage his workload carefully in 2017 at low Class A Fort Wayne.

BA GRADE
60 Risk: Extreme

Year	Club (League)	Class	W	L	ERA	G	GS	CG	SV	IP	H	HR	BB	SO	K/9	WHIP	AVG
2016	Padres (AZL)	R	0	2	5.27	5	5	0	0	14	12	0	2	16	10.5	1.02	.231
	Tri-City (NWL)	SS	0	2	1.93	5	5	0	0	19	15	0	2	28	13.5	0.91	.205
	Fort Wayne (MWL)	LoA	0	1	17.36	2	2	0	0	5	12	1	4	2	3.9	3.43	.522
Minor League Totals			0	5	5.11	12	12	0	0	37	39	1	8	46	11.2	1.27	.264

5 ADRIAN MOREJON, LHP

Born: Feb. 27, 1999. **B-T:** L-L. **Ht.:** 6-1. **Wt.:** 195. **Signed:** Cuba, 2016.

Morejon jumped on the international radar when he was named MVP of the 15U World Cup in 2014 while pitching for the Cuban national team. His biggest moment came in the gold-medal game, when he threw 124 pitches in a complete-game, 6-3 victory against the U.S. with 12 strikeouts and one walk. Morejon became a talent considered on par with any top-10 draft pick, and the Padres signed him for an eye-popping $11 million in July 2016. Morejon throws a 91-93 mph fastball that touches 96 with an athletic, easy delivery that portends more velocity as the teen southpaw's body matures. His ability to spin a future plus curveball draws the highest praise from scouts, and he throws two different changeups—one a knuckle-change with late diving action and the other a more traditional changeup with sink and run. Both project above-average. Morejon's above-average command, stuff, arm action and feel for pitching are all advanced for his age and make few opposing evaluators doubt the wisdom of signing him, though some shied away from the price tag. The Padres compare Morejon with the Dodgers' Julio Urias, while scouts outside the organization compare his delivery and stuff with Padres 2012 first-rounder Max Fried. Morejon is targeted for 100 innings in 2017 and will begin the year in extended spring training.

BA GRADE
60 Risk: Extreme

Year	Club (League)	Class	W	L	ERA	G	GS	CG	SV	IP	H	HR	BB	SO	K/9	WHIP	AVG
2016	Did not play—Signed 2017 contract																

6 LUIS URIAS, 2B/SS

Born: June 3, 1997. **B-T:** R-R. **Ht.:** 5-9. **Wt.:** 160. **Signed:** Mexico, 2013. **Signed by:** Chad MacDonald/Robert Rowley.

The Padres purchased Urias from the Mexican League's Mexico City franchise when he 16, intrigued by his bat control and plate discipline. He has rewarded that interest by posting a career .317 career average in the minors with more walks than strikeouts. Urias' foundation for success is his approach. He rarely swings at anything outside the strike zone, forcing pitchers to come to him. When they do, his quick hands and elite hand-eye coordination allow him to barrel any velocity, while those same tools allow him to track breaking balls and square them up as well. Using those attributes as his base, Urias hit .330 at high Class A Lake Elsinore in 2016 to win the California League batting title and MVP award despite being the circuit's youngest player on Opening Day. He faces questions about his below-average speed and power, though he showed progress on the latter front by slugging .505 in the second half of 2016 by staying back and driving the

BA GRADE
55 Risk: High

ball rather than settling for line-drive singles. Defensively he is above-average at second base with soft hands and excellent footwork, with an above-average arm strong enough to make throws from deep in the hole at shortstop. His range is best suited for second base. Urias resembles 16-year big league vet Placido Polanco in terms of size and skill set, and he has perennial .300-hitting ability to match. He will begin 2017 at Double-A San Antonio.

Year	Club (League)	Class	AVG	G	AB	R	H	2B	3B	HR	RBI	BB	SO	SB	CS	OBP	SLG
2014	Padres (DSL)	R	.100	2	10	1	1	0	0	0	0	1	1	0	0	.182	.100
	Padres (AZL)	R	.310	43	155	29	48	5	1	0	14	18	13	10	6	.393	.355
2015	Tri-City (NWL)	SS	.355	10	31	6	11	1	0	0	1	5	1	3	3	.487	.387
	Fort Wayne (MWL)	LoA	.290	51	193	28	56	5	1	0	16	16	18	5	10	.370	.326
2016	El Paso (PCL)	AAA	.444	3	9	6	4	0	0	1	3	5	1	1	0	.667	.778
	Lake Elsinore (CAL)	HiA	.330	120	466	71	154	26	5	5	52	40	36	7	13	.397	.440
Minor League Totals			.317	229	864	141	274	37	7	6	86	85	70	26	32	.395	.397

7 JACOB NIX, RHP

Born: Jan. 9, 1996. **B-T:** R-R. **Ht.:** 6-3. **Wt.:** 200. **Drafted:** HS—Bradenton, Fla., 2015 (3rd round). **Signed by:** Chris Kelly.

The Astros drafted Nix in the fifth round out of Los Alamitos (Calif.) High in 2014 but failed to sign him after the Brady Aiken debacle curtailed their bonus-pool amount. Nix, a UCLA commit, instead went to postgrad IMG Academy in Florida and went to the Padres a year later in the third round. He signed for $900,000. Long described as physical, athletic and projectable, Nix found a consistent, repeatable delivery in 2016 and saw his stuff take off at low Class A Fort Wayne in 2016. He recorded one of the highest average velocities in the Padres system with a 93-95 mph fastball that touched 97. His curveball shows improved depth thanks to a consistent release point and now projects to plus. It has 12-to-6 action and earned recognition as the best breaking pitch in the Midwest League. Nix's above-average changeup also began getting swings and misses in the bottom of the zone with his improved delivery. His control leapt forward as well. He cut his walk rate nearly in half from 2015 to 2016, highlighted by a midsummer stretch where he walked only one batter in six starts. Everything is trending up for Nix, who will begin 2017 at high Class A Lake Elsinore and projects as a quality mid-rotation starter.

BA GRADE

55 Risk: High

Year	Club (League)	Class	W	L	ERA	G	GS	CG	SV	IP	H	HR	BB	SO	K/9	WHIP	AVG
2015	Padres (AZL)	R	0	2	5.49	7	3	0	0	20	23	1	7	19	8.7	1.53	.284
2016	Fort Wayne (MWL)	LoA	3	7	3.93	25	25	0	0	105	115	5	20	90	7.7	1.28	.280
Minor League Totals			3	9	4.18	32	28	0	0	125	138	6	27	109	7.8	1.32	.280

8 MICHAEL GETTYS, OF

Born: Oct. 22, 1995. **B-T:** R-R. **Ht.:** 6-1. **Wt.:** 2013. **Drafted:** HS—Gainesville, Ga., 2014 (2nd round). **Signed by:** Andrew Salvo.

Gettys was an enigmatic talent in high school who posted off-the-charts measurables at showcases but often disappointed in game action. The Padres gambled on his raw upside and drafted him 51st overall in 2014 and signed him for $1.3 million to forgo a Georgia commitment. Gettys' primary problem had always been a lack of hitting instincts, pitch recognition and balance in the box, which led to high strikeout rates and poor quality contact in the early part of his career. He made major strides on those fronts in 2016, adding a back stretch to the start of his swing to improve his rhythm and timing, while also giving him a better look at the pitches as they approach the palte. The result was a more athletic swing with less chasing and harder contact, albeit with a poor contact rate and just average power. Center field is where Gettys really shines, using his plus speed and elite defensive instincts to track down fly balls in every direction, with double-plus arm strength to boot. His speed is limited out of the batter's box but ticks up on the basepaths to make him a dangerous basestealing threat. Gettys is starting to turn his loud tools into baseball skills but needs to continue improving as a hitter to reach his everyday potential. He will jump to Double-A San Antonio in 2017.

BA GRADE

55 Risk: High

Year	Club (League)	Class	AVG	G	AB	R	H	2B	3B	HR	RBI	BB	SO	SB	CS	OBP	SLG
2014	Padres (AZL)	R	.310	52	213	29	66	8	5	3	38	15	66	14	2	.353	.437
2015	Fort Wayne (MWL)	LoA	.231	122	494	62	114	27	6	6	44	28	162	20	10	.271	.346
2016	Fort Wayne (MWL)	LoA	.304	68	257	37	78	10	5	3	27	18	69	24	10	.369	.416
	Lake Elsinore (CAL)	HiA	.306	60	248	40	76	13	0	9	33	17	77	9	6	.356	.468
Minor League Totals			.276	302	1212	168	334	58	16	21	142	78	374	67	28	.324	.402

9 DINELSON LAMET, RHP

Born: July 18, 1992. **B-T:** R-R. **Ht.:** 6-4. **Wt.:** 187. **Signed:** Dominican Republic, 2014. **Signed by:** Randy Smith/Felix Feliz/Emenegildo Diaz/Jose Salado.

The Padres signed Lamet for $100,000 as a rare 21-year old international signee, but despite the late sign he has used his experience to climb the minor league ladder rapidly. He skipped short-season ball and went straight to low Class A Fort Wayne in 2015, and then in 2016 rose through three levels to finish the year at Triple-A El Paso. Lamet possesses a strong, durable, athletic build, allowing him to repeat his delivery and hold his stuff deep into starts. His mid-90s fastball and upper-80s slider both possess sharp, late movement and grade above-average to plus. He added an 85-88 mph changeup during 2016 spring training under the tutelage of high Class A Lake Elsinore pitching coach Glendon Rusch that evaluators project to average. The addition of the change allowed Lamet to better neutralize lefthanded batters and make it through the order a third time. The result was he led the Padres system in wins (12) and strikeouts (158) while ranking second in innings (150) and ERA (3.00). Lamet's control is fringe-average, but the overall quality of his stuff generates plenty of swings and misses and limits hard contact. Lamet can be a No. 4 or 5 starter with further changeup development or a high-leverage reliever if the pitch stagnates. He will begin 2017 at El Paso with a strong chance to join the Padres by midsummer.

BA GRADE
50 Risk: Medium

Year	Club (League)	Class	W	L	ERA	G	GS	CG	SV	IP	H	HR	BB	SO	K/9	WHIP	AVG
2014	Padres (DSL)	R	0	0	0.00	2	0	0	0	4	2	0	0	8	18.0	0.50	.143
2015	Fort Wayne (MWL)	LoA	5	8	2.99	26	24	0	0	105	82	9	44	120	10.3	1.20	.214
2016	Lake Elsinore (CAL)	HiA	7	1	2.35	12	12	0	0	65	56	4	26	54	7.5	1.26	.241
	San Antonio (TL)	AA	5	7	3.39	14	14	0	0	74	57	2	31	91	11.0	1.18	.207
	El Paso (PCL)	AAA	0	2	4.22	2	2	0	0	11	13	2	4	13	11.0	1.59	.302
Minor League Totals			17	18	2.95	56	52	0	0	259	210	17	105	286	9.9	1.21	.221

10 JOSH NAYLOR, 1B

Born: June 22, 1997. **B-T:** L-L. **Ht.:** 6-0. **Wt.:** 225. **Drafted:** HS—Mississauga, Ontario, 2015 (1st round). **Signed by:** Steve Payne (Marlins).

The Marlins drafted Naylor 12th overall in 2015, making him the highest-drafted Canadian position player ever, and Miami signed him for $2.2 million. He wowed during Futures Game batting practice in 2016 with long home runs deep to right-center field at Petco Park, and three weeks later the Padres acquired him and two others from the Marlins for Andrew Cashner. Plus raw power is Naylor's carrying tool and will have to be because he is a thick-bodied lefthanded batter limited to first base. He generates his power using a strong lower half and quick hands, creating elite bat speed to drive the ball with authority. Naylor is presently able to tap into his power on fastballs but has trouble with offspeed pitches, especially against lefthanders, limiting his ability to get to his power in games. Defensively he is below-average and prone to errors because his focus wavers, but in short bursts will show unexpected athleticism. He is an average runner who is faster than his body might indicate but projects to slow down as he ages. Naylor faced questions about his maturity when he was drafted, and questions still linger after he injured Marlins minor league teammate Stone Garrett with a knife in what team officials described as a "prank gone bad." Naylor will begin 2017 at high Class A Lake Elsinore as he tries to live up to his middle-of-the order potential.

BA GRADE
55 Risk: High

Year	Club (League)	Class	AVG	G	AB	R	H	2B	3B	HR	RBI	BB	SO	SB	CS	OBP	SLG
2015	Marlins (GCL)	R	.327	25	98	8	32	4	1	1	16	4	11	1	0	.352	.418
2016	Greensboro (SAL)	LoA	.269	89	342	42	92	24	2	9	54	22	62	10	3	.317	.430
	Lake Elsinore (CAL)	HiA	.252	33	139	17	35	5	0	3	21	3	22	1	1	.264	.353
Minor League Totals			.275	147	579	67	159	33	3	13	91	29	95	12	4	.311	.409

11 CARLOS ASUAJE, 2B

BA GRADE
45 Risk: Low

Born: Nov. 2, 1991. **B-T:** L-R. **Ht.:** 5-9. **Wt.:** 160. **Drafted:** Nova Southeastern (Fla.), 2013 (11th round). **Signed by:** Willie Romay (Red Sox).

Asuaje was born in Venezuela but raised in South Florida and attended Division II power Nova Southeastern (Fla.) before the Red Sox drafted him in the 11th round in 2013. He was one of four prospects the Padres acquired for Craig Kimbrel after the 2015 season. Asuaje is an above-average hitter who combines excellent strike-zone discipline with a picturesque load and line-drive stroke to spray base hits all over the field and into both gaps. He led the Pacific Coast League with 172 hits in 2016. Asuaje's power grades as below-average, but he showed at Triple-A El Paso he is capable of driving the ball on a line over the fence on occasion. He is an average runner but a fringe-average defender at second base, which complicates his upside. He has steady hands and a reliable arm but lacks the range or reflexes for the position, which is also true at third base. He has experimented in left field as well. Asuaje's bat has everyday upside, but his defensive limitations will likely limit him to a bench role, much as they have for the Cubs' Tommy La Stella. Asuaje is in position to break camp with the Padres in 2017 and be an oft-used and valuable reserve.

Year	Club (League)	Class	AVG	G	AB	R	H	2B	3B	HR	RBI	BB	SO	SB	CS	OBP	SLG
2014	Greenville (SAL)	LoA	.305	90	325	59	99	24	10	11	73	41	56	7	4	.391	.542
	Salem (CAR)	HiA	.323	39	155	27	50	14	2	4	28	18	34	1	3	.398	.516
2015	Portland (EL)	AA	.251	131	495	60	124	23	7	8	61	56	88	9	6	.334	.374
2016	El Paso (PCL)	AAA	.321	134	535	98	172	32	11	9	69	49	82	10	5	.378	.473
	San Diego (NL)	MAJ	.208	7	24	2	5	2	0	0	2	1	4	0	0	.240	.292
Major League Totals			.208	7	24	2	5	2	0	0	2	1	4	0	0	.240	.292
Minor League Totals			.292	446	1681	263	491	105	31	33	251	191	293	31	21	.368	.450

12 JORGE ONA, OF

BA GRADE
55 Risk: Extreme

Born: Dec. 31, 1996. **B-T:** R-R. **Ht.:** 6-0. **Wt.:** 220. **Signed:** Cuba, 2016.

Ona first made waves at the 2014 COPABE 18U Pan American Championship in Mexico, when he hit .636 (14-for-22) with four homers and a 1.364 slugging percentage in eight games. He left Cuba in July 2015 and trained in the Dominican Republic for a year before the Padres signed him for $7 million in July 2016. Ona is a muscular specimen with plus power to all fields, both present and projectable. His bat speed is above-average and his hand-eye coordination earns positive reviews, giving him a promising foundation as a hitter. Some evaluators, however, note stiff actions and poor timing in his swing, raising concerns he won't ever be more than a fringe-average hitter. The Padres acknowledge these shortcomings but believe they can be fixed with mechanical adjustments. Ona is a fringe-average runner and fringe-average defender limited to a corner, likely left field, though his above-average arm gives him a chance to stick in right. He hasn't played competitive game situations since leaving Cuba, so rust was a factor in his early evaluations. Ona's bat will be what carries him, with the potential to be an annual 25-home run threat. He will begin his career at low Class A Fort Wayne in 2017.

Year	Club (League)	Class	AVG	G	AB	R	H	2B	3B	HR	RBI	BB	SO	SB	CS	OBP	SLG
2016	Did not play—Signed 2017 contract																

13 ERIC LAUER, LHP

BA GRADE
50 Risk: High

Born: June 3, 1995. **B-T:** R-L. **Ht.:** 6-3. **Wt.:** 205. **Drafted:** Kent State, 2016 (1st round). **Signed by:** Matt Maloney.

Lauer was a first-team All-American as a junior at Kent State in 2016 after he went 10-2, 0.69 with 125 strikeouts in 104 innings. His ERA was not only the best in the nation but the lowest in Division I since 1979. The Padres drafted Lauer 25th overall and signed him for $2 million. He pounds the strike zone with a four-pitch mix, topped by an 89-92 mph fastball with downward angle that he locates well. His 82-86 mph slider flashes above-average but has such short break it looks like a cutter at times, while his mid-70s curveball showed good shape but not much finish in his pro debut, registering as an average-at-best pitch. He also has a rarely-used changeup. Scouts worry about Lauer's future command of his breaking pitches because of his cross-body delivery and lower arm slot, though his fastball command is above-average. While his stuff doesn't stand out on the surface, deception in his delivery helps it play up, while his loose, athletic body creates optimism his stuff will improve. Lauer's poise, pitchability, and well-rounded mix have him poised to move quickly as a back-end starter. He will begin 2017 at low Class A Fort Wayne.

Year	Club (League)	Class	W	L	ERA	G	GS	CG	SV	IP	H	HR	BB	SO	K/9	WHIP	AVG
2016	Padres (AZL)	R	0	1	6.75	2	2	0	0	4	7	1	1	7	15.8	2.00	.368
	Tri-City (NWL)	SS	1	0	1.44	7	7	0	0	25	17	0	7	28	10.1	0.96	.191
	Fort Wayne (MWL)	LoA	0	0	0.00	1	1	0	0	2	0	0	1	2	9.0	0.50	.000
Minor League Totals			1	1	2.03	10	10	0	0	31	24	1	9	37	10.7	1.06	.211

14 HUDSON POTTS, 3B/SS

BA GRADE
55 Risk: Extreme

Born: Oct. 28, 1998. **B-T:** R-R. **Ht.:** 6-2. **Wt.:** 180. **Drafted:** HS—Southlake, Texas, 2016 (1st round). **Signed by:** Matt Schaffner.

Potts, who went by Hudson Sanchez before adopting his stepfather's surname, wasn't considered a first-round talent entering the 2016 draft, but the Padres took him 24th overall and gave him $1 million to forgo a Texas A&M commitment. Potts made the Padres look prescient for drafting him above industry consensus in his pro debut, which he spent primarily in the Rookie-level Arizona League. He showed such advanced feel for the barrel, pitch recognition and poise in the batter's box that he projects as a plus hitter with above-average power as he fills out. He was so advanced at the plate the Padres felt comfortable bumping him to short-season Tri-City, where he hit third in the lineup as a 17-year old and got on base at a .352 clip. Potts was drafted as a shortstop, but his average lateral range and stiff throwing motion have most evaluators projecting a move to third base, where his plus arm strength will play. Potts' bat is his carrying tool, but his average speed and potential to be an above-average defender at third give him a chance to be a well-rounded everyday player. He is advanced enough to begin 2017 at low Class A Fort Wayne as an 18-year old.

Year	Club (League)	Class	AVG	G	AB	R	H	2B	3B	HR	RBI	BB	SO	SB	CS	OBP	SLG
2016	Padres (AZL)	R	.295	43	183	35	54	12	2	1	21	9	34	8	4	.333	.399
	Tri-City (NWL)	SS	.233	16	60	7	14	0	1	0	6	9	13	2	1	.352	.267
Minor League Totals			.280	59	243	42	68	12	3	1	27	18	47	10	5	.338	.366

15 CHRIS PADDACK, RHP

BA GRADE

55 Risk: Extreme

Born: Jan. 8, 1996. **B-T:** R-R. **Ht.:** 6-4. **Wt.:** 195. **Drafted:** HS—Cedar Park, Texas, 2015 (8th round). **Signed by:** Ryan Wardinsky (Marlins).

The Marlins made Paddack the first player ever drafted out of Cedar Park (Texas) High in 2015 and signed him away from a Texas A&M commitment for $400,000. Almost one year to the day after drafting him, the Marlins sent him to the Padres in a one-for-one swap for Fernando Rodney. Paddack used his darting 90-95 mph fastball and double-plus mid-80s changeup to put up video-game numbers at low Class A Greensboro in 2016, where he recorded an 0.85 ERA with 71 strikeouts to just five walks in 42.1 innings. His fastball-changeup combo has been evident since high school, but he also made strides with his mid-70s curveball by finding a consistent release point and giving it increased depth, making it project now as a possibly average pitch. Health concerns overshadow Paddack's pitch mix and strong control. He missed the first six weeks of 2016 with biceps tendinitis and then had Tommy John surgery in August after just three starts in the Padres system, which will keep him out all of 2017. Paddack is a potential mid-rotation starter with room in his projectable body to still add velocity, but he must prove he can stay healthy to reach that ceiling.

Year	Club (League)	Class	W	L	ERA	G	GS	CG	SV	IP	H	HR	BB	SO	K/9	WHIP	AVG
2015	Marlins (GCL)	R	4	3	2.18	11	7	0	0	45	37	1	7	39	7.7	0.97	.219
2016	Greensboro (SAL)	LoA	2	0	0.95	6	6	0	0	28	9	2	2	48	15.2	0.39	.098
	Fort Wayne (MWL)	LoA	0	0	0.64	3	3	0	0	14	11	0	3	23	14.8	1.00	.212
Minor League Totals			6	3	1.54	20	16	0	0	88	57	3	12	110	11.3	0.79	.182

16 ENYEL DE LOS SANTOS, RHP

BA GRADE

50 Risk: High

Born: Dec. 25, 1995. **B-T:** R-R. **Ht.:** 6-3. **Wt.:** 170. **Signed:** Dominican Republic, 2014. **Signed by:** Eddy Romero/Domingo Toribio (Mariners).

The Mariners signed de los Santos for just $15,000 as an international free agent in 2014, but he blossomed quickly as he went from upper-80s fastball velocity when they signed him to mid-90s less than a year later. The Padres acquired him for Joaquin Benoit after the 2015 season, a trade that dismayed some in the Mariners organization who felt de los Santos was the most promising starter in their system. De los Santos made good on some of that promise in 2016, showing a 92-95 mph fastball that frequently touched 97, with room in his frame to add even more velocity. He experienced less success after a midseason promotion to high Class A Lake Elsinore because of inconsistent feel for his breaking pitches, but still held his own as a 20-year-old playing against older competition in the hitter-friendly California League. His curveball projects average and his changeup above-average as he gets better command of them, but he presently has fringe-average control overall. De los Santos projects as a No. 4 or 5 starter, but his youth and room for physical growth raise the possibility he could grow into more. He will begin 2017 back at Lake Elsinore.

Year	Club (League)	Class	W	L	ERA	G	GS	CG	SV	IP	H	HR	BB	SO	K/9	WHIP	AVG
2015	Mariners (AZL)	R	3	0	2.55	5	5	0	0	25	24	1	5	29	10.6	1.18	.250
	Everett (NWL)	SS	3	0	4.06	8	8	0	0	38	37	2	13	42	10.0	1.33	.270
2016	Fort Wayne (MWL)	LoA	3	2	2.91	11	7	0	0	53	38	2	14	45	7.7	0.99	.199
	Lake Elsinore (CAL)	HiA	5	3	4.35	15	15	0	0	68	70	11	24	52	6.8	1.38	.267
Minor League Totals			14	5	3.63	39	35	0	0	183	169	16	56	168	8.2	1.23	.246

17 FERNANDO TATIS JR., SS

BA GRADE
55 Risk: Extreme

Born: Jan. 2, 1999. **B-T:** R-R. **Ht.:** 6-3. **Wt.:** 185. **Signed:** Dominican Republic, 2015. **Signed by:** Miguel Peguero (White Sox).

The son of former big league third baseman Fernando Tatis split scouts as an international amateur because of what some felt was a weak physical frame. The White Sox went against the grain in 2015 and signed him for $700,000, then used him as the main prospect in a trade to the Padres for James Shields a year later. Tatis showed the White Sox were on to something. He grew two inches and improved his strength and coordination after signing. He now shows plus arm strength and impressive lateral range for his size at shortstop with reliable hands, combined with above-average feel for the barrel and power potential at the plate. Tatis has a lot of moving parts to his swing and struggles swinging at pitches outside the zone, most notably on breaking balls, but he showed he was capable of driving anything in the strike zone with good leverage. Big and strong at the plate and free and easy with his movements at shortstop, Tatis projects as an above-average everyday shortstop as long as he tightens up his strike-zone discipline. He will begin 2017 at low Class A Fort Wayne as an 18-year-old.

Year	Club (League)	Class	AVG	G	AB	R	H	2B	3B	HR	RBI	BB	SO	SB	CS	OBP	SLG
2016	Padres (AZL)	R	.273	43	176	35	48	13	1	4	20	10	44	14	2	.312	.426
	Tri-City (NWL)	SS	.273	12	44	4	12	4	2	0	5	3	13	1	1	.306	.455
Minor League Totals			.273	55	220	39	60	17	3	4	25	13	57	15	3	.311	.432

18 PHIL MATON, RHP

BA GRADE
45 Risk: Medium

Born: March 25, 1993. **B-T:** R-R. **Ht.:** 6-3. **Wt.:** 220. **Drafted:** Louisiana Tech, 2015 (20th round). **Signed by:** Eddie Ciafardini/Matt Schaffner.

Maton was an all-Conference USA starter at Louisiana Tech but shifted to the bullpen after the Padres drafted him in 2015. He missed most of the first month of 2016 with an oblique injury, but still zoomed through the system to reach Triple-A El Paso only a year after being drafted. Maton operates with a heavy 93-96 mph fastball, a low-80s curveball with one of the highest spin rates in the organization, a low-90s cutter that saws bats off and plus control. He began the year at low Class A Fort Wayne but ended it as closer for the Pacific Coast League champions, notching three saves in as many chances in the postseason. He continued his run of dominance with a 2.92 ERA and 15-to-1 strikeout-to-walk ratio in the Arizona Fall League. With a repeatable delivery, a good pitcher's body and elite stuff, Maton profiles as a high-leverage reliever or possible closer. Multiple scouts reported they had already written him up as a trade target by the end of 2016. Maton is in position to make his major league debut in 2017 and stay there.

Year	Club (League)	Class	W	L	ERA	G	GS	CG	SV	IP	H	HR	BB	SO	K/9	WHIP	AVG
2015	Tri-City (NWL)	SS	4	2	1.38	23	0	0	6	33	23	0	5	58	16.0	0.86	.192
2016	Fort Wayne (MWL)	LoA	1	1	1.42	8	0	0	1	13	14	0	1	19	13.5	1.18	.269
	Lake Elsinore (CAL)	HiA	3	2	1.91	25	0	0	9	33	17	2	8	47	12.8	0.76	.149
	El Paso (PCL)	AAA	1	0	1.50	5	0	0	1	6	1	1	2	12	18.0	0.50	.053
Minor League Totals			9	5	1.60	61	0	0	17	84	55	3	16	136	14.5	0.84	.180

19 LOGAN ALLEN, LHP

BA GRADE
50 Risk: High

Born: May 23, 1997. **B-T:** L-L. **Ht.:** 6-3. **Wt.:** 200. **Drafted:** HS—Bradenton, Fla., 2015 (8th round). **Signed by:** Stephen Hargett (Red Sox).

The Red Sox made Allen a 2015 eighth-round pick out of IMG Academy and signed him for an above-slot $725,000—third-round money—to forgo a South Carolina commitment. The Padres acquired Allen as part of the four-player package for Craig Kimbrel after the 2015 season. Allen's first season in the Padres system was limited by elbow soreness that shelved him for two months in the middle of the year, but he returned to make three starts at low Class A Fort Wayne at the end. Allen works at 90-92 mph with his fastball and touches 94, and he commands it well with a repeatable delivery. He also possesses advanced command of his breaking pitches for a 19-year-old, spinning an above-average curveball and average changeup he can land for strikes. Overall, Allen's solid-average command, deep pitch mix and good tempo on the mound portend a reliable back-of-the-rotation starter. A full season without elbow trouble could help his stuff tick up and go beyond that projection. He will begin 2017 at high Class A Lake Elsinore.

Year	Club (League)	Class	W	L	ERA	G	GS	CG	SV	IP	H	HR	BB	SO	K/9	WHIP	AVG
2015	Red Sox (GCL)	R	0	0	0.90	7	7	0	0	20	12	0	1	24	10.8	0.65	.171
	Lowell (NYP)	SS	0	0	2.08	1	1	0	0	4	6	0	0	2	4.2	1.38	.300
2016	Padres (AZL)	R	0	0	3.00	3	3	0	0	6	5	0	1	8	12.0	1.00	.217
	Tri-City (NWL)	SS	0	1	7.71	1	1	0	0	2	4	0	1	4	15.4	2.14	.364
	Fort Wayne (MWL)	LoA	3	4	3.33	15	11	0	0	54	48	2	22	47	7.8	1.30	.242
Minor League Totals			3	5	2.80	27	23	0	0	87	75	2	25	85	8.8	1.15	.233

20 LUIS ALMANZAR, SS

BA GRADE
55 Risk: Extreme

Born: Nov. 1, 1999. **B-T:** R-R. **Ht.:** 6-0. **Wt.:** 180. **Signed:** Dominican Republic, 2016. **Signed by:** Felix Feliz.

Almanzar was born and raised in the Dominican Republic, came to the U.S. and played high school baseball at prep power American Heritage High in Plantation, Fla., for one year, then moved back to the Dominican to take advantage of the less-restrictive bonus pools available to international amateurs. He emerged as arguably the top hitter in the 2016 international class and the Padres signed him for $4 million. Almanzar has excellent bat speed and takes a short, direct path to the ball that produces a vast amount of hard line drives, combined with a discerning batting eye that allows him to work counts and get his pitch to hit. He uses the whole field and projects as a plus hitter with above-average power as he matures physically. Defensively, Almanzar has an above-average arm, though scouts are split whether he will stay at shortstop or have to move to third base as he fills out. His speed is average. Almanzar's bat will carry him, with a ceiling as a potent offensive shortstop. He is many years away from that, however, and will begin his pro career in the Dominican Summer League in 2017.

Year	Club (League)	Class	AVG	G	AB	R	H	2B	3B	HR	RBI	BB	SO	SB	CS	OBP	SLG
2016	Did not play—Signed 2017 contract																

21 JOSE TORRES, LHP

BA GRADE
45 Risk: Medium

Born: Sept. 24, 1993. **B-T:** L-L. **Ht.:** 6-2. **Wt.:** 175. **Signed:** Venezuela, 2010. **Signed by:** Julio Franco/Oswaldo Troconis (Athletics).

The Athletics signed Torres for $150,000 as a 16-year old international free agent out of Venezuela in 2010 and traded him in the five-player deal that sent Drew Pomeranz to the Padres after the 2015 season. Pomeranz blossomed into an all-star, but the Padres also received a great return on Torres in 2016. The starter-turned-reliever began the season at high Class A Lake Elsinore and finished in the majors, posting a 2.14 ERA and strikeout rate of 8.8 per nine innings across four levels. Torres' main weapon is his 94-96 mph fastball, which touched 98 in the Arizona Fall League. He uses a three-quarters arm slot that produces cut action on his fastball, helping it play against batters on both sides of the plate. He deploys an above-average power curveball as his main secondary pitch, and it shows tilt and downward action at 83-86 mph. He rarely uses a fringy upper-80s changeup. Near-average control led to high walk rates and less strikeouts than his pure stuff would indicate, but he limits damage by keeping the ball on the ground about half the time. Torres is ready to compete for a spot in the Padres bullpen in 2017.

Year	Club (League)	Class	W	L	ERA	G	GS	CG	SV	IP	H	HR	BB	SO	K/9	WHIP	AVG
2014	Vermont (NYP)	SS	0	6	4.38	14	9	0	2	62	62	4	22	47	6.9	1.36	.267
2015	Beloit (MWL)	LoA	4	5	2.69	44	0	0	8	74	55	4	23	80	9.8	1.06	.212
	Stockton (CAL)	HiA	0	0	0.00	3	0	0	0	4	0	0	1	4	9.8	0.27	.000
2016	Lake Elsinore (CAL)	HiA	0	2	3.55	20	0	0	1	25	21	2	10	25	8.9	1.22	.223
	San Antonio (TL)	AA	1	2	1.24	25	0	0	2	36	20	1	12	36	8.9	0.88	.165
	El Paso (PCL)	AAA	0	0	3.38	3	0	0	0	3	4	0	1	2	6.8	1.88	.333
	San Diego (NL)	MAJ	0	0	0.00	4	0	0	0	3	3	0	2	3	9.0	1.67	.250
Major League Totals			0	0	0.00	4	0	0	0	3	3	0	2	3	9.0	1.67	.250
Minor League Totals			12	23	3.24	147	39	0	13	344	293	16	137	296	7.7	1.25	.231

22 JOSE RONDON, SS

BA GRADE
45 Risk: Medium

Born: March 3, 1994. **B-T:** R-R. **Ht.:** 6-1. **Wt.:** 195. **Signed:** Venezuela, 2011. **Signed by:** Lebi Ochoa/Carlos Ramirez (Angels).

Rondon signed with the Angels for $70,000 out of Venezuela as a 16-year old international free agent and was traded to the Padres three years later as the centerpiece prospect in a deal for closer Huston Street. Rondon owns a career .290 average in the minors despite being roughly two years younger than average at every level. A fractured elbow on a slide ended his 2015 season prematurely, but he returned in 2016 and hit .279 at Double-A San Antonio to earn his first big league callup. He hit .300 at Triple-A El Paso after returning to the minors. Rondon's barrel control is his one above-average offensive skill. His bat stays through the hitting zone, allowing him to make consistent contact and use the whole field, making him an average hitter. He is an average defender at shortstop with suitable lateral range, reliable hands and an above-average arm, but he is a fringe-average runner with below-average power, limiting his overall upside. Rondon rarely does anything flashy but is the lone shortstop in the Padres system with a track record of consistent offensive production and defensive reliability. He will start 2017 at Triple-A El Paso.

Year	Club (League)	Class	AVG	G	AB	R	H	2B	3B	HR	RBI	BB	SO	SB	CS	OBP	SLG
2014	Angels (AZL)	R	.125	2	8	3	1	0	0	0	0	1	0	2	1	.300	.125
	Inland Empire (CAL)	HiA	.327	72	297	40	97	17	5	0	24	17	50	8	6	.362	.418
	Lake Elsinore (CAL)	HiA	.301	37	136	18	41	9	0	1	12	13	23	3	1	.371	.390
2015	Lake Elsinore (CAL)	HiA	.300	57	237	50	71	12	3	3	22	21	38	17	6	.360	.414
	San Antonio (TL)	AA	.190	28	100	6	19	2	1	0	9	4	15	1	3	.219	.230
2016	San Antonio (TL)	AA	.279	96	376	45	105	21	2	5	44	15	66	13	4	.310	.386
	San Diego (NL)	MAJ	.120	8	25	1	3	0	0	0	1	1	4	0	0	.154	.120
	El Paso (PCL)	AAA	.300	24	80	8	24	4	0	1	9	1	12	0	1	.305	.388
Major League Totals			.120	8	25	1	3	0	0	0	1	1	4	0	0	.154	.120
Minor League Totals			.290	487	1887	273	547	112	18	12	212	135	278	72	39	.338	.387

23 FRANCHY CORDERO, OF

BA GRADE

45 Risk: Medium

Born: Sept. 22, 1994. **B-T:** L-R. **Ht.:** 6-3. **Wt.:** 175. **Signed:** Dominican Republic, 2011. **Signed by:** Randy Smith/Felix Feliz/Martin Jose.

The Padres signed Cordero for $175,000 as a 17-year old international free agent with the idea of making him a shortstop, but they moved him to the outfield after he made 126 errors in 165 career games at short. In his first full year in the outfield in 2016, Cordero showed exceptional first-step quickness and range, plus speed and an above-average arm, making him an above-average defender almost immediately. Freed from the burden of his infield mistakes, Cordero also eased up at the plate and had his best season yet, with 24 doubles, 16 triples, 11 home runs and 23 stolen bases as he moved from high Class A Lake Elsinore all the way to Triple-A El Paso. Cordero's struggles controlling the strike zone make him a fringe-average hitter in the eyes of evaluators, but as an above-average defender hitting from the left side with plus speed has a chance to be a valuable fourth outfielder in the majors—if not more. He will begin 2017 at Triple-A and could join San Diego before long.

Year	Club (League)	Class	AVG	G	AB	R	H	2B	3B	HR	RBI	BB	SO	SB	CS	OBP	SLG
2014	Fort Wayne (MWL)	LoA	.188	22	85	5	16	2	1	0	9	4	36	3	3	.237	.235
	Eugene (NWL)	SS	.279	61	240	40	67	8	4	9	35	14	75	13	5	.329	.458
2015	Fort Wayne (MWL)	LoA	.243	126	481	59	117	13	1	5	34	31	121	22	11	.293	.306
2016	Lake Elsinore (CAL)	HiA	.286	74	297	47	85	16	8	5	35	19	83	11	8	.339	.444
	San Antonio (TL)	AA	.306	59	245	31	75	8	8	6	19	17	67	12	6	.356	.478
	El Paso (PCL)	AAA	.077	4	13	1	1	0	0	0	0	3	4	0	0	.250	.077
Minor League Totals			.271	442	1732	245	470	60	34	29	187	135	492	86	37	.330	.395

24 JOEY LUCCHESI, LHP

BA GRADE

50 Risk: High

Born: June 6, 1993. **B-T:** L-L. **Ht.:** 6-5. **Wt.:** 204. **Drafted:** Southeast Missouri State, 2016 (4th round). **Signed by:** Troy Hoerner.

Lucchesi went undrafted after his junior season at Southeast Missouri State but added a tick to his fastball velocity as a senior to sit 91-94 mph with deception and late movement. He went 10-5, 2.19 and led all of Division I with 149 strikeouts as a senior and became the highest player ever drafted out of SEMO, signing for $100,000. Lucchesi continued to show his improved stuff in pro ball, with his fastball velocity holding steady and peaking at 96. He complemented it with an above-average curveball with 12-to-6 action and an above-average changeup, all with plus command that led to an astounding 56-to-3 strikeout-to-walk ratio in his pro debut. Lucchesi's stuff plays up with a funky delivery that includes a high leg kick and a pause mid-windup, not dissimilar from Clayton Kershaw. His delivery also makes baserunners freeze and allows him to hold them close. Lucchesi's dominant showing came as a 23-year-old playing against younger competition, giving some evaluators pause. Still, with three usable pitches and plus control, Lucchesi fits the profile of a solid back-end starter. He will start 2017 at low Class A Fort Wayne with a chance to move quickly.

Year	Club (League)	Class	W	L	ERA	G	GS	CG	SV	IP	H	HR	BB	SO	K/9	WHIP	AVG
2016	Tri-City (NWL)	SS	0	2	1.35	14	10	0	1	40	27	0	2	53	11.9	0.73	.189
	Fort Wayne (MWL)	LoA	0	0	0.00	1	0	0	0	2	4	0	1	3	13.5	2.50	.444
Minor League Totals			0	2	1.29	15	10	0	1	42	31	0	3	56	12.0	0.81	.204

25 JAVIER GUERRA, SS

BA GRADE

50 Risk: Extreme

Born: Sept. 29, 1995. **B-T:** L-R. **Ht.:** 5-11. **Wt.:** 155. **Signed:** Panama, 2012. **Signed by:** Eddie Romero/Cris Garibaldo (Red Sox).

The Red Sox signed Guerra for $250,000 as an international amateur and the Padres acquired him along with three others in exchange for Craig Kimbrel after the 2015 season. Wiry, athletic and rangy, Guerra looks the part at shortstop but regressed at the plate at high Class A Lake Elsinore in 2016 so much it affected his play on defense, dropping him from the system's No. 1 prospect to, in the eyes of some evaluators, a non-prospect. Guerra struck out 141 times in 105 games with swings so out of line with incoming pitches that some scouts questioned his eyesight. Others saw an abrupt load, swing that didn't stay in the zone and persistent inability to adjust, grading him a poor hitter overall. Guerra visibly appeared defeated in the box by mid-June and brought it onto the field with him, committing an organization-worst 30 errors. He showed exceptional lateral range and double-plus arm strength but frequently booted routine grounders, while inconsistent footwork and arm action resulted in wild throws. Guerra was placed on the disabled list for the final month of the season with an unspecified, non-baseball-related ailment. He will repeat the California League in 2017 to try and re-establish his everyday potential.

Year	Club (League)	Class	AVG	G	AB	R	H	2B	3B	HR	RBI	BB	SO	SB	CS	OBP	SLG
2014	Red Sox (GCL)	R	.269	51	201	21	54	14	4	2	26	5	42	1	5	.286	.408
2015	Greenville (SAL)	LoA	.279	116	434	64	121	23	3	15	68	30	112	7	9	.329	.449
2016	Lake Elsinore (CAL)	HiA	.202	105	391	49	79	19	1	9	41	34	141	4	4	.264	.325
Minor League Totals			.248	332	1236	161	306	65	8	26	158	102	335	19	22	.307	.376

26 MASON THOMPSON, RHP

BA GRADE
50 Risk: **Extreme**

Born: Feb. 20, 1998. **B-T:** R-R. **Ht.:** 6-7. **Wt.:** 186. **Drafted:** HS—Round Rock, Texas, 2016 (3rd round). **Signed by:** Matt Schaffner.

Thompson was considered a first-round talent as a prep underclassman but blew out his elbow as a junior and had Tommy John surgery in March 2015. He pitched only one inning as a senior, but the Padres liked his upside enough to draft him 85th overall and sign him away from a Texas commitment for $1.75 million. Thompson impressed in his five outings in the Rookie-level Arizona League, sitting in the low 90s with his fastball and touching 94 mph. He also showed feel for an above-average power curveball and a potentially plus changeup with fade and deception. He also added a slider to his repertoire the Padres feel can eventually be an average pitch. Thompson is long-levered at 6-foot-7 and not expected to have better than average control, but the overall quality of his stuff should generate swings and misses regardless. He also has plenty of room to add strength to his ultra-lean frame to add more velocity. Thompson must prove he can stay healthy to reach his mid-rotation ceiling. He will begin 2017 in extended spring training as the Padres monitor his workload.

Year	Club (League)	Class	W	L	ERA	G	GS	CG	SV	IP	H	HR	BB	SO	K/9	WHIP	AVG
2016	Padres (AZL)	R	0	0	2.25	5	5	0	0	12	8	0	5	12	9.0	1.08	.186
Minor League Totals			0	0	2.25	5	5	0	0	12	8	0	5	12	9.0	1.08	.186

27 RUDDY GIRON, SS

BA GRADE
45 Risk: **High**

Born: Jan. 4, 1997. **B-T:** R-R. **Ht.:** 5-11. **Wt.:** 175. **Signed:** Dominican Republic, 2013. **Signed by:** Randy Smith/Felix Feliz/Ysrael Rojas/Martin Jose.

The Padres signed Giron for $600,000 as an international free agent in 2013 and he impressed quickly, reaching low Class A Fort Wayne as an 18-year old and excelling in a partial season there. Sent back to Fort Wayne to begin 2016, Giron suffered a groin strain early that threw off his lower-half mechanics and timing at the plate. The result was a swing that got too long with no power, and at the end of June he was hitting .189 with no home runs. Giron earned plaudits for staying mentally strong through his slump and finally broke out of it in July, hitting .305 with 24 extra-base hits the rest of the season. When right, Giron is an above-average hitter, though he struggles with good breaking pitches, and his power potential remains fringe-average. Defensively, he is a question mark at shortstop, with rigid movements and inconsistent glove work, which overshadows his plus arm. Giron's defensive shortcomings limit his upside, but his bat can carry him if he stays mechanically sound. He will begin 2017 at high class A Lake Elsinore.

Year	Club (League)	Class	AVG	G	AB	R	H	2B	3B	HR	RBI	BB	SO	SB	CS	OBP	SLG
2014	Padres (AZL)	R	.168	48	185	23	31	10	0	0	13	8	42	1	2	.205	.222
2015	Fort Wayne (MWL)	LoA	.285	96	386	58	110	12	4	9	49	29	68	15	14	.335	.407
2016	Fort Wayne (MWL)	LoA	.222	106	401	49	89	23	2	2	20	34	74	8	7	.284	.304
	Lake Elsinore (CAL)	HiA	.426	14	47	7	20	7	1	1	5	3	13	1	0	.460	.681
Minor League Totals			.245	264	1019	137	250	52	7	12	87	74	197	25	23	.298	.345

28 WALKER LOCKETT, RHP

BA GRADE
40 Risk: **Medium**

Born: May 3, 1994. **B-T:** R-R. **Ht.:** 6-5. **Wt.:** 225. **Drafted:** HS—Jacksonville, 2012 (4th round). **Signed by:** Chris Kelly.

The Padres drafted Lockett in 2012 after he led Providence High to the Florida state 3A championship with a shutout in the title game. He signed for $393,000 to forgo a South Florida commitment. Injuries to his finger and shoulder limited Lockett to just 31 pro innings entering 2015, and then he was demoted twice during that season, first for poor performance and second for missing curfew, all the way down to Rookie ball. Written off as a bust, Lockett re-emerged in 2016. He increased usage of his 91-94 mph sinker and made huge leaps in the development of his slider and changeup, both of which now project to average. Working out of a three-quarters arm slot, Lockett excels at pounding the bottom of the strike zone with all three pitches, keeping his walks low and his ground ball rate high. Finally healthy and matured, Lockett began 2016 at low Class A Fort Wayne and rose all the way to Triple-A El Paso, ultimately leading the Padres system in ERA (2.96) and innings (164). While he doesn't have supreme stuff, Lockett's strike-throwing ability and groundball tendency bode well for him, especially now that he's a member of the 40-man roster, to see innings in 2017 in a Padres rotation short on able bodies.

Year	Club (League)	Class	W	L	ERA	G	GS	CG	SV	IP	H	HR	BB	SO	K/9	WHIP	AVG
2014	Fort Wayne (MWL)	LoA	0	0	0.00	1	1	0	0	5	3	0	1	1	1.8	0.80	.150
	Eugene (NWL)	SS	0	2	21.94	4	2	0	0	5	13	0	12	1	1.7	4.69	.481
2015	Fort Wayne (MWL)	LoA	0	3	7.98	4	4	0	0	15	20	2	4	10	6.1	1.64	.308
	Tri-City (NWL)	SS	3	0	2.83	11	11	0	0	57	50	3	10	47	7.4	1.05	.230
	Padres (AZL)	R	1	1	5.40	3	2	0	0	15	19	2	6	13	7.8	1.67	.317
2016	Fort Wayne (MWL)	LoA	1	3	3.00	8	8	0	0	45	43	0	8	29	5.8	1.13	.244
	Lake Elsinore (CAL)	HiA	4	3	2.98	11	10	0	0	66	57	3	12	56	7.6	1.04	.225
	San Antonio (TL)	AA	4	1	2.08	6	4	0	0	35	27	2	2	26	6.8	0.84	.216
	El Paso (PCL)	AAA	1	2	4.50	3	3	0	0	18	23	2	2	12	6.0	1.39	.319
Minor League Totals			14	16	3.79	64	48	0	0	282	285	16	63	210	6.7	1.23	.259

29 ALLEN CORDOBA, SS

BA GRADE
50 Risk: Extreme

Born: Dec. 6, 1995. **B-T:** R-R. **Ht.:** 6-1. **Wt.:** 175. **Signed:** Panama, 2013. **Signed by:** Arquimedes Nieto/Angel Ovalles (Cardinals).

Cordoba signed for just $7,500 as part of the Cardinals' 2013 international class and was more raw than many of his fellow Panamanians after growing up in the remote northwestern part of the country near the Costa Rica border. He needed more development time as a result but busted out in his third year in Rookie ball, winning Gulf Coast League MVP honors in 2015. Cordoba followed up by winning the Appalachian League batting title (.362) at Rookie-level Johnson City in 2016. The Padres selected him with the third pick of the Rule 5 draft at the 2016 Winter Meetings. He had been Rule 5 eligible only because his initial contract with St. Louis had been voided. Cordoba controls the barrel well and shows exceptional strike-zone discipline, allowing him to wait for a hittable pitch and drive it to the gaps. His offensive game is enhanced with above-average speed that allows him to leg out infield hits and steal bases efficiently. He has no power present or projectable, however. Defensively he can stick at shortstop with good short-range quickness and plus arm strength, though he struggles with accuracy. Cordoba is nowhere near ready for the majors, but the Padres will try to hide him at the end of their bench until they can send him down to the minors for further development in 2018.

Year	Club (League)	Class	AVG	G	AB	R	H	2B	3B	HR	RBI	BB	SO	SB	CS	OBP	SLG
2014	Cardinals (DSL)	R	.258	62	244	41	63	9	1	2	18	15	46	14	4	.301	.328
2015	Cardinals (GCL)	R	.342	53	202	40	69	6	2	2	20	15	20	11	3	.401	.421
2016	Johnson City (APP)	R	.362	50	196	49	71	16	5	0	18	21	19	22	4	.427	.495
Minor League Totals			.309	206	767	150	237	36	9	4	63	70	109	52	14	.375	.395

30 AUSTIN ALLEN, C

BA GRADE
45 Risk: High

Born: Jan. 16, 1994. **B-T:** L-R. **Ht.:** 6-4. **Wt.:** 225. **Drafted:** Florida Tech, 2015 (4th round). **Signed by:** Willie Bosque.

Allen was arguably the top Division II hitter available in the 2015 draft, and the Padres took him in the fourth round, making him the highest player ever drafted from Florida Tech. He signed for $484,000. Allen lived up to that offensive profile in 2016 by using his above-average bat speed and natural strength to hit .320/.364/.425 at low Class A Fort Wayne to rank sixth in the Midwest League batting race. Behind the plate is where Allen needs the most work. Evaluators consider him a well below-average defender, and his average arm strength is nullified by a hitch that costs him valuable time throwing to bases. Opponents successfully stole 119 bases in 150 attempts against him in 2016. Allen has made strides to improve his blocking, receiving and framing, and optimistic reports indicate he has fringe-average potential overall. Allen has a chance to be an offensively-driven, lefthanded-hitting platoon catcher. He will begin 2017 at high Class A Lake Elsinore.

Year	Club (League)	Class	AVG	G	AB	R	H	2B	3B	HR	RBI	BB	SO	SB	CS	OBP	SLG
2015	Tri-City (NWL)	SS	.240	53	196	23	47	10	1	2	34	21	38	1	2	.315	.332
2016	Fort Wayne (MWL)	LoA	.320	109	409	52	131	22	0	7	61	29	69	0	0	.364	.425
	San Antonio (TL)	AA	.273	3	11	1	3	0	0	1	1	0	0	0	0	.273	.545
Minor League Totals			.294	165	616	76	181	32	1	10	96	50	107	1	2	.347	.398

San Francisco Giants

BY J.J. COOPER

As the 2017 season draws near, the Giants sit in the same position they occupied in each of the past five seasons. If they can just beat the Dodgers, the National League West should be theirs.

The Diamondbacks, Padres and Rockies (who have never won the division) seem stuck in a perpetual rebuild. Not one of those three teams has posted a winning record since the Arizona won the division in 2011. Since then, it's been the Giants and Dodgers battling for supremacy each year.

Eventually that duopoly will have to end, though it may not change in 2017.

But the most stable organization in baseball enters 2017 with the realization its current window of contention is closing slowly. The Dodgers are younger than the Giants. They have a better farm system and more money to spend. Also, Los Angeles has topped 90 wins and claimed the NL West title in each of the past four seasons. San Francisco hasn't reached 90 wins since 2012.

A team with catcher Buster Posey, lefthander Madison Bumgarner, shortstop Brandon Crawford and three World Series titles in the past seven seasons has no need to panic. Bruce Bochy is still a Hall of Fame manager. The front office is still in place with decades of experience and success. The Giants have enviable stability, and their scouting and player-development departments work together seamlessly in a way many organizations struggle to emulate.

But the same players who have given the Giants their most successful stretch since John McGraw was the club's manager are getting older. More than half of the Giants' projected everyday starters will play most of 2017 at age 30 or older. If righthander Matt Cain is in the rotation, three-fifths of the starting five will be 30 or older, as will imported free agent closer Mark Melancon.

That doesn't mean San Francisco has incentive or reason to change direction until the current stalwarts show significant signs of decline. The team's homegrown core—first baseman Brandon Belt, Bumgarner, Crawford and Posey—is under contract for the next three seasons. All but Bumgarner are signed through 2021.

The Giants lack elite prospects, but the system features a number of players in the upper levels of the minors who aren't far from being big league ready, namely a group of starting pitchers headed for Triple-A Sacramento, fronted by No. 1 prospect and 2014 first-rounder Tyler Beede. San Francisco also has a number of close-to-the-majors bullpen arms to call upon as well as 2013 first-rounder Christian Arroyo, the club's potential

The Giants leverage their prospect depth to trade for big leaguers like Matt Moore

TOP PROSPECTS OF THE DECADE

Year	Player, Pos.	2016 Org
2007	Tim Lincecum, rhp	Angels
2008	Angel Villalona, 1b	Giants
2009	Madison Bumgarner, lhp	Giants
2010	Buster Posey, c	Giants
2011	Brandon Belt, 1b	Giants
2012	Gary Brown, of	Atlantic League
2013	Kyle Crick, rhp	Giants
2014	Kyle Crick, rhp	Giants
2015	Andrew Susac, c	Giants
2016	Christian Arroyo, ss	Giants

third baseman of the future.

But the Giants' stable lineup and rotation also create plenty of opportunities for the organization to trade prospects to fill holes at the big league level. San Francisco has dealt young players such as shortstop Lucius Fox, third baseman Matt Duffy, outfielder Adam Duvall and righthander Keury Mella to reinforce the big league rotation with like Mike Leake (2015) and Matt Moore (2016). More prospects could be moving on in 2017.

Luckily for the Giants, they don't have to top the Dodgers in the standings, not with two NL wild cards available. They merely have to be the best of the second-place teams, and that's an attainable goal for 2017, when the D-backs and Padres look like rebuilders and the young Rockies appear a year away from contention.

ORGANIZATION OVERVIEW

President: Brian Sabean. **GM:** Bobby Evans. **Farm director:** Shane Turner. **Scouting director:** John Barr.

Class	Team	League	W	L	PCT	Finish	Manager
Majors	San Francisco Giants	National	87	75	.537	5th (15)	Bruce Bochy
Triple-A	Sacramento River Cats	Pacific Coast	69	75	.479	12th (16)	Jose Alguacil
Double-A	Richmond Flying Squirrels	Eastern	62	79	.440	10th (12)	Miguel Ojeda
High Class A	San Jose Giants	California	68	72	.486	9th (12)	Lipso Nava
Low Class A	Augusta Greenjackets	South Atlantic	76	63	.547	2nd (14)	Nestor Rojas
Short-season	Salem-Keizer Volcanoes	Northwest	32	42	.432	6th (8)	Kyle Haines
Rookie	AZL Giants	Arizona	28	27	.509	8th (14)	Henry Cotto
Overall 2016 Minor League Record			335	358	.483	19th (30)	

THIS YEAR'S TOP 30

No.	Player, Pos.	Grade/Risk
1.	Tyler Beede, rhp	55/Medium
2.	Christian Arroyo, ss	50/Medium
3.	Chris Shaw, 1b	50/High
4.	Bryan Reynolds, of	50/High
5.	Andrew Suarez, lhp	50/High
6.	Ty Blach, lhp	45/Medium
7.	Joan Gregorio, rhp	45/Medium
8.	Sandro Fabian, of	50/High
9.	Aramis Garcia, c	50/High
10.	Steven Duggar, of	50/High
11.	Sam Coonrod, rhp	45/Medium
12.	Reyes Moronta, rhp	50/High
13.	Steven Okert, lhp	40/Low
14.	Heath Quinn, of	50/High
15.	Rodolfo Martinez, rhp	50/High
16.	C.J. Hinojosa, ss	45/Medium
17.	Melvin Adon, rhp	55/Extreme
18.	Dan Slania, rhp	45/Medium
19.	Austin Slater, of	45/Medium
20.	Matt Krook, lhp	50/Extreme
21.	Cory Taylor, rhp	45/High
22.	Chris Stratton, rhp	45/High
23.	Clayton Blackburn, rhp	40/Low
24.	Garrett Williams, lhp	50/Extreme
25.	Chase Johnson, rhp	45/High
26.	Kelvin Beltre, 3b	50/Extreme
27.	Jalen Miller, 2b	50/Extreme
28.	Matt Gage, lhp	40/Low
29.	Orlando Calixte, ss/of	40/Low
30.	Miguel Gomez, 3b	45/High

LAST YEAR'S TOP 30

No.	Player, Pos.	Status
1.	Christian Arroyo, ss	No. 2
2.	Tyler Beede, rhp	No. 1
3.	Phil Bickford, rhp	(Brewers)
4.	Lucius Fox, ss	(Rays)
5.	Chris Shaw, 1b	No. 3
6.	Sam Conrood, rhp	No. 11
7.	Aramis Garcia, c	No. 9
8.	Clayton Blackburn, rhp	No. 23
9.	Jarrett Parker, of	Majors
10.	Adalberto Mejia, lhp	(Twins)
11.	Mac Williamson, of	Majors
12.	Andrew Suarez, lhp	No. 5
13.	Ray Black, rhp	Dropped out
14.	Chase Johnson, rhp	No. 25
15.	Jordan Johnson, rhp	Dropped out
16.	Jalen Miller, ss	No. 27
17.	Ian Gardeck, rhp	Dropped out
18.	Joan Gregorio, rhp	Dropped out
19.	Michael Santos, rhp	(Rays)
20.	Ty Blach, lhp	No. 6
21.	Ronnie Jebavy, of	Dropped out
22.	Jake Smith, rhp	(Padres)
23.	Derek Law, rhp	Majors
24.	Steven Okert, lhp	No. 13
25.	Steven Duggar, of	No. 10
26.	Chris Stratton, rhp	No. 22
27.	Kyle Crick, rhp	Dropped out
28.	Mac Marshall, lhp	Dropped out
29.	Cody Hall, rhp	Free Agent
30.	Hunter Cole, of	Dropped out

BEST TOOLS

Best Hitter for Average	Christian Arroyo
Best Power Hitter	Chris Shaw
Best Strike-Zone Discipline	Steven Duggar
Fastest Baserunner	Ronnie Jebavy
Best Athlete	Steven Duggar
Best Fastball	Ray Black
Best Curveball	Tyler Beede
Best Slider	Andrew Suarez
Best Changeup	Tyler Beede
Best Control	Ty Blach
Best Defensive Catcher	Aramis Garcia
Best Defensive Infielder	Christian Arroyo
Best Infield Arm	Ryder Jones
Best Defensive Outfielder	Ronnie Jebavy
Best Outfield Arm	Sandro Fabian

PROJECTED 2020 LINEUP

Catcher	Buster Posey
First Base	Brandon Belt
Second Base	Joe Panik
Third Base	Christian Arroyo
Shortstop	Brandon Crawford
Left Field	Bryan Reynolds
Center Field	Steven Duggar
Right Field	Heath Quinn
No. 1 Starter	Madison Bumgarner
No. 2 Starter	Johnny Cueto
No. 3 Starter	Jeff Samardzija
No. 4 Starter	Tyler Beede
No. 5 Starter	Andrew Suarez
Closer	Mark Melancon

MINOR LEAGUE DEPTH CHART

SAN FRANCISCO GIANTS

TOP 2017 ROOKIE: Ty Blach, lhp: His strong finish in 2016 gives him a shot to be the No. 5 starter. His control and just-good-enough stuff would play at AT&T Park.

BREAKOUT PROSPECT: Matt Krook, lhp: His fastball could be one of the best in baseball if he could locate it consistently. A full season of work could help him refine his control.

SLEEPER: Ricardo Genoves, c: He could quickly become the system's best defender behind the plate. After all, he caught Anderson Espinoza in Venezuela.

SOURCE OF TOP 30 TALENT			
Homegrown	29	Acquired	1
College	19	Trades	0
Junior college	0	Rule 5 draft	0
High school	3	Independent leagues	0
Nondrafted free agents	0	Free agents/waivers	1
International	7		

LF
Austin Slater (19)
Hunter Cole
Jacob Heyward
Dylan Davis

CF
Bryan Reynolds (4)
Steven Duggar (10)
Ronnie Jebavy
Johneshwy Fargas
Ashford Fulmer

RF
Sandro Fabian (8)
Heath Quinn (16)
Gio Brusa

3B
Christian Arroyo (2)
Kelvin Beltre (26)
Miguel Gomez (30)
Ryder Jones

SS
C.J. Hinojosa (15)
Orlando Calixte (29)
Ryan Howard
Brandon Van Horn
Rando Moreno
Manuel Geraldo
Jose Rivero

2B
Jalen Miller (27)
Kevin Rivera
Michael Bernal
Nishell Gutierrez

1B
Chris Shaw (3)
Beicker Mendoza
Jonah Arenado

C
Aramis Garcia (9)
Matt Winn
Ricardo Genoves
Ty Ross

LHP

LHSP	LHRP
Andrew Suarez (5)	Steven Okert (13)
Ty Blach (6)	Mac Marshall
Matt Krook (23)	Christian Jones
Garrett Williams (24)	
Matt Gage (28)	
Alex Bostic	
Matt Lujan	

RHP

RHSP	RHRP
Tyler Beede (1)	Sam Coonrod (11)
Joan Gregorio (7)	Reyes Moronta (12)
Chris Stratton (21)	Rodolfo Martinez (14)
Clayton Blackburn (22)	Melvin Adon (17)
Jaiser Herrera	Dan Slania (18)
	Cory Taylor (20)
	Chase Johnson (25)
	Ian Gardeck
	Ray Black
	Stephen Woods
	Jordan Johnson

DRAFT ANALYSIS

2016

BEST PURE HITTER: OF Bryan Reynolds (2) is a switch-hitter who drives the ball from both sides with gap power. His free-swinging ways could catch up to him eventually, but he was a .329 career hitter in three years at Vanderbilt. He hit with Team USA's College National Team and in the Cape Cod League and he hit .313 in his debut.

BEST POWER HITTER: OF Heath Quinn (3) hit 21 home runs for Samford and nine more in his pro debut. He projects to have plus power. OF Gio Brusa (6) has similar raw power, though he gets to it less consistently. He hit 10 home runs for short-season Salem-Keizer and 14 at Pacific this spring.

FASTEST RUNNER: OF Nick Hill (26) is an athletic speedster who grades out as a 70 runner on the 20-to-80 scouting scale. OF Malique Ziegler (22) has turned in plus-plus run times himself in the past although a nagging injury slowed him down to a plus runner in his pro debut.

BEST DEFENSIVE PLAYER: SS Brandon Van Horn (19) faces plenty of question about his bat, but he's a true shortstop who can stay at the position with quick hands and plenty of range. SS Ryan Howard (5) is a bigger, more physical defender than Van Horn with less range and quickness. He projects as at least an average defender at second base with an above-average arm.

BEST FASTBALL: RHP Stephen Woods (8) showed the most consistent velocity as a pro by sitting 93-96 mph. LHP Garrett Williams (7) and LHP Matt Krook (4) both have fastballs that are above-average to plus. Krook's fastball has exceptional life, sometimes too much.

BEST SECONDARY PITCH: Williams' curveball and Krook's slider will both grade at plus on their better nights, although their control issues have kept both of them from getting to use them as much as they would like.

BEST PRO DEBUT: Quinn made it up to high Class A in his first half season and hit .344/.434/.564 between three stops. Reynolds hit .313/.363/.484 combined at short-season Salem-Keizer and low Class A Augusta.

BEST ATHLETE: Reynolds has a nice combination of speed and power. OF Jose Layer (13) is a center fielder with plus speed and some quick-twitch burst.

MOST INTRIGUING BACKGROUND: OF Jacob Heyward (18) is the younger brother of Cubs outfielder Jason Heyward. Heyward impressed the Giants' coaches with his work ethic and all-out playing style.

CLOSEST TO THE MAJORS: Reynolds and Quinn should be ready for high Class A in 2017 and could reach the majors by 2018 or 2019 if they progress on schedule.

BEST LATE-ROUND PICK: C Jeffery Parra (24) is a well-rounded catcher with hitting potential. He handled velocity well for a young New Jersey high school draftee. RHP C.J. Gettman (34) is an arm-strength reliever who gets good downhill plane on his 92-95 mph fastball.

THE ONE WHO GOT AWAY: LHP Adam Laskey (31) is a cold-weather loose-armed lefty with room to grow and develop. His slider and changeup give him a chance to have three average or better pitches. The Giants would have loved to have signed him, but he's pitching for Duke.

2015

RHP Phil Bickford (1) was traded to Milwaukee for lefty Will Smith, then suspended for drug-of-abuse issues. 1B Chris Shaw (1) is the system's best power hitter. LHP Andrew Suarez (2), OF Steven Duggar (6) and SS C.J. Hinojosa (11) have quickly reached Double-A.

GRADE: B

2014

A college-heavy draft has seen significant progress from RHP Tyler Beede (1), now the system's top prospect. C Aramis Garcia (2), RHP Sam Coonrod (5), OFs Austin Slater (8) and LHP Matt Gage (10) all made real progress in 2016.

GRADE: B

2013

The rare prep-heavy Giants draft started with SS Christian Arroyo (1), a steady middle infielder, while 1B/OF Ryder Jones (2) has improved offensively while moving down the defensive spectrum.

GRADE: C

TOP DRAFT PICKS OF THE DECADE

Year	Player, Pos.	2016 Org
2007	Madison Bumgarner, lhp	Giants
2008	Buster Posey, rhp	Giants
2009	Zack Wheeler, rhp	Mets
2010	Gary Brown, of	Atlantic League
2011	Joe Panik, ss	Giants
2012	Chris Stratton, rhp	Giants
2013	Christian Arroyo, ss	Giants
2014	Tyler Beede, rhp	Giants
2015	Phil Bickford, rhp	Brewers
2016	Bryan Reynolds (2nd round)	Giants

LARGEST BONUSES IN CLUB HISTORY

Buster Posey, 2008	$6,200,000
Lucius Fox, 2015	$6,000,000
Zack Wheeler, 2009	$3,300,000
Rafael Rodriguez, 2008	$2,550,000
Phil Bickford, 2015	$2,333,800

1 TYLER BEEDE, RHP

Born: May 23, 1993. **B-T:** R-R. **Ht.:** 6-4. **Wt.:** 210.
Drafted: Vanderbilt, 2013 (1st round).
Signed by: Andrew Jefferson.

A two-time first-round pick, Beede turned down the Blue Jays out of high school as the 21st overall pick in 2011. He went to Vanderbilt and dominated as a sophomore, going 14-1, 2.32 and leading Division I in wins. He also ranked inside the top 10 in the nation for hit rate per nine innings (5.7) despite plenty of wildness (5.6 walks per nine, 14 wild pitches). He threw more strikes as a junior, but wasn't as effective. The Giants selected Beede 14th overall in the 2014 draft and signed him for a shade more than $2.6 million. After letting him go out and pitch like he had at Vanderbilt in his short first pro season, San Francisco reworked his delivery in 2015 by slowing down his tempo and simplifying his windup. Beede said he models his deliver now on that of Zack Greinke. He starts his delivery slowly, but the tempo builds as he gathers on the rubber. The Giants also asked him to focus on throwing more two-seam fastballs and cutters and relying less on his power four-seamer. The approach helped him thrive at high Class A San Jose in 2015, but he hit a wall following a promotion to Double-A Richmond, in part because his stuff backed up. He started throwing more in the high-80s to low-90s instead of showing the mid-90s velocity he'd shown in the past. Back in the Eastern League in 2016, Beede more consistently got to the mid-90s velocity he showed in college, which helped his entire repertoire play better. On his best nights he'd touch 96-97 in his final inning of work. He led the EL in ERA (2.81), finished second in strikeouts (135) and fifth in opponent average (.248).

One of the keys to Beede's big step forward in 2016 was his emphasis on conditioning. In a January camp that included several big leaguers, Beede won the Giants award for the hardest worker. That hard work paid off when his fastball returned to the 92-94 mph range he had showed at Vanderbilt. His heater sat 90-92 mph in 2015. Now he touches 97 mph deep in games when needed. Beede has quickly grown to enjoy manipulating his two-seamer, but the higher-velocity four-seamer is always in his back pocket. As important as his fastball is, he succeeds because he has a varied assortment of pitches. Beede's curveball is a plus

BA GRADE
55 Risk: Medium

SCOUTING GRADES
Fastball: 55.
Curveball: 60.
Cutter: 55.
Changeup: 50.
Control: 50.

Based on 20-80 scouting scale and future projection rather than present tools.

KEN BABBITT

pitch at its best. He still needs to command it better, but if he can land it more consistently, it could be his best secondary pitch. His above-average 87-90 mph cutter is more consistent—though sometimes he throws it too much. It plays well off his sinker with consistent running action. His changeup took a slight step back in 2016, but it has been above-average in the past and was average in 2016. Beede has come a long way from the all-power, all-the-time approach he once used, but he's no soft-tosser after regaining the power he seemed to lose in 2015 in his first full pro season. He now can pitch—or he can overpower. His body control still wavers enough to make it hard to see him ever having plus control, but he has refined his delivery to the point where average control is possible.

Beede could be a future mid-rotation starter with enough stuff and control to thrive in the big leagues. He will head to Triple-A Sacramento in 2017 for further refinement, but the Giants believe he has come far enough that he would be able to handle the big leagues in 2017.

Year	Club (League)	Class	W	L	ERA	G	GS	CG	SV	IP	H	HR	BB	SO	K/9	WHIP	AVG
2014	Giants (AZL)	R	0	1	3.12	4	4	0	0	9	8	0	4	11	11.4	1.38	.242
	Salem-Keizer (NWL)	SS	0	0	2.70	2	2	0	0	7	8	0	3	7	9.5	1.65	.308
2015	San Jose (CAL)	HiA	2	2	2.24	9	9	0	0	52	51	2	9	37	6.4	1.15	.254
	Richmond (EL)	AA	3	8	5.23	13	13	0	0	72	62	4	35	49	6.1	1.34	.234
2016	Richmond (EL)	AA	8	7	2.81	24	24	1	0	147	136	9	53	135	8.2	1.28	.248
Minor League Totals			13	18	3.32	52	52	1	0	287	265	15	104	239	7.5	1.28	.247

2 CHRISTIAN ARROYO, SS/3B

BA GRADE

50 Risk: Medium

Born: May 30, 1995. **B-T:** R-R. **Ht.:** 6-1. **Wt.:** 180. **Drafted:** HS—Brooksville, Fla., 2013 (1st round). **Signed by:** Mike Metcalf.

Scouts have long loved Arroyo's hitting ability and his confident, aggressive style of play dating back to his amateur days, including a star turn for of USA Baseball's 18U team in 2012. The 25th pick in the 2013 draft, he owns a career .294 average in pro ball but faces questions about his impact potential after hitting just three home runs at Double-A Richmond in 2016. The Giants had Arroyo split time between shortstop and third base for the first time in 2016. He projects as a plus defender at third with above-average instincts, an ability to throw accurately from multiple arm angles, soft hands and an excellent internal clock. His throws generally seem to have just enough to nab the baserunner. At shortstop, Arroyo is reliably fringe-average but has limited range, especially to his left, thanks to his fringe-average speed and short-range quickness. He runs the bases better than his speed would indicate because he has excellent anticipation and awareness. At the plate, Arroyo has a very short swing and excellent hand-eye coordination. It's easy to find scouts who project him as a plus hitter capable of hitting .280 or higher, but they see 10-home run potential to go with 35 doubles. Arroyo's aggressive approach and ability to make a lot of contact limits his walk rate. Giants incumbent third baseman Eduardo Nunez is a free agent after the 2017 season, which syncs up nearly perfectly with Arroyo's timetable. He projects along the lines of former Giant Matt Duffy as a bat-first third baseman with a good glove.

Year	Club (League)	Class	AVG	G	AB	R	H	2B	3B	HR	RBI	BB	SO	SB	CS	OBP	SLG
2014	Augusta (SAL)	LoA	.203	31	118	10	24	3	1	1	14	4	22	1	2	.226	.271
	Salem-Keizer (NWL)	SS	.333	58	243	39	81	14	2	5	48	18	31	6	1	.378	.469
2015	San Jose (CAL)	HiA	.304	90	381	48	116	28	2	9	42	19	73	5	3	.344	.459
2016	Richmond (EL)	AA	.274	119	474	57	130	36	1	3	49	29	72	1	1	.316	.373
Minor League Totals			.294	343	1400	201	411	99	11	20	192	89	230	16	9	.337	.423

3 CHRIS SHAW, 1B

BA GRADE

55 Risk: High

Born: Oct. 20, 1993. **B-T:** L-R. **Ht.:** 6-4. **Wt.:** 255. **Drafted:** Boston College, 2015 (1st round). **Signed by:** Mark O'Sullivan.

During his sophomore and junior years at Boston College, Shaw hit 17 of the Eagles' 39 home runs, many of which were titanic shots. The Giants selected him 31st overall in the 2015 draft and signed him for $1.4 million. Shaw led the short-season Northwest League with 12 home runs in his 2015 pro debut, then launched 16 more at high Class A San Jose in 2016 prior to a promotion to Double-A Richmond, where Eastern League pitchers gave him his first pro challenge. Shaw has plus-plus raw power, and EL pitchers worked hard to prevent him getting his arms extended on pitches in the zone. No part of the ballpark can contain a pitch Shaw gets hold of. Even with a below-average hit tool, he has the potential to hit 20-plus home runs on an annual basis. His swing has some length and has a tendency to be a little too grooved. Pitchers who fail to locate are bound to get hurt, but Shaw doesn't have the quick hands to adjust his swing quickly on pitches in his cold zone. He does have a solid understanding of the strike zone and will collect his share of walks and strikeouts. Shaw spent much of the 2016 season putting in plenty of early work on defense. He also spent 10 days at instructional league working on his footwork around first. He's still below-average defensively but has improved his range and footwork. Shaw has an above-average arm, but it doesn't come into play much at first base. Shaw's power potential gives him a chance to be a first-division first baseman, but he'll need to improve his defense and hit tool to reach his ceiling. He will head back to Richmond in 2017.

Year	Club (League)	Class	AVG	G	AB	R	H	2B	3B	HR	RBI	BB	SO	SB	CS	OBP	SLG
2015	Salem-Keizer (NWL)	SS	.287	46	178	22	51	11	0	12	30	19	41	0	0	.360	.551
2016	San Jose (CAL)	HiA	.285	72	270	47	77	22	0	16	55	28	70	0	0	.357	.544
	Richmond (EL)	AA	.246	60	232	26	57	16	4	5	30	20	55	0	0	.309	.414
Minor League Totals			.272	178	680	95	185	49	4	33	115	67	166	0	0	.342	.501

4 BRYAN REYNOLDS, OF

BILL MITCHELL

Born: Jan. 27, 1995. **B-T:** B-R. **Ht.:** 6-3. **Wt.:** 200. **Drafted:** Vanderbilt, 2016 (2nd round). **Signed by:** Jeff Wood.

After giving up their 2016 first-round pick to sign free agent Jeff Samardzija, the Giants were thrilled to see Reynolds, a late first-round talent, slide to the second round. He hit .329 in a three-year career at Vanderbilt and .346 in the 2015 Cape Cod League. After signing with the Giants he quickly advanced to low Class A Augusta and hit .313 in his pro debut. Reynolds may not have a true plus tool, but nor does he have a below-average one. His feel for the game enhances his raw ability. He's a switch-hitter with quick hands and a loose swing. He gets too passive at times with two strikes and carries a high strikeout rate. Still, he uses a controlled swing, understands pitch sequencing and works counts to the point he is beginning to tap into his average power. Defensively, Reynolds is a plus defender in the corners and is playable in center field because of his average speed. His arm is average but plays because he's accurate. As a switch-hitter who can hit and play all three outfield spots, Reynolds has a high floor as at least a big league contributor. His ability to stay in center and rein in his strikeout rate will determine whether he can be an everyday impact player.

BA GRADE
50 Risk: High

Year	Club (League)	Class	AVG	G	AB	R	H	2B	3B	HR	RBI	BB	SO	SB	CS	OBP	SLG
2016	Salem-Keizer (NWL)	SS	.312	40	154	28	48	12	1	5	30	11	41	2	0	.368	.500
	Augusta (SAL)	LoA	.317	16	63	11	20	5	0	1	8	3	20	1	0	.348	.444
Minor League Totals			.313	56	217	39	68	17	1	6	38	14	61	3	0	.363	.484

5 ANDREW SUAREZ, LHP

Born: Sept. 11, 1992. **B-T:** L-L. **Ht.:** 6-2. **Wt.:** 210. **Drafted:** Miami, 2015 (2nd round). **Signed by:** Jose Alou.

Three times Suarez has been selected with a draft pick in the first 10 rounds. He turned down the Blue Jays (ninth round) out of high school and survived shoulder surgery to become a key part of Miami's rotation. The two-time second-round pick spurned the Nationals in 2014 to return to the Hurricanes. The Giants signed him for a touch more than $1 million in 2015. Suarez is yet another creative Giants starter. He mixes his pitches, changes speeds, works in and out, elevates and sinks and manipulates the ball around the strike zone like a veteran. And he does it with legitimate stuff. Suarez pitches with an 89-93 mph fastball that touches 95 with late life. It plays as an above-average pitch because his slinging, low three-quarters arm slot presents a tough angle. His slider is an above-average pitch and his changeup is average. He also uses a fringe-average curveball and cutter. All Suarez's pitches play up because of his plus control (strikes with 70 percent of pitches, according to the Giants) and above-average command, though he would benefit by making hitters chase a pitch more often. Suarez's feel and control are reminiscent of fellow Giants lefthander Ty Blach, but he pitches with firmer stuff. He should slot in as a No. 4 starter and is ready for Triple-A Sacramento in 2017.

BA GRADE
50 Risk: High

Year	Club (League)	Class	W	L	ERA	G	GS	CG	SV	IP	H	HR	BB	SO	K/9	WHIP	AVG
2015	Giants (AZL)	R	0	0	1.80	3	0	0	0	5	2	0	1	6	10.8	0.60	.118
	Salem-Keizer (NWL)	SS	1	0	1.40	5	5	0	0	19	17	2	2	15	7.0	0.98	.236
	San Jose (CAL)	HiA	1	0	1.80	3	3	0	0	15	13	2	2	16	9.6	1.00	.236
2016	San Jose (CAL)	HiA	2	1	2.43	5	5	0	0	30	25	2	5	34	10.3	1.01	.225
	Richmond (EL)	AA	7	7	3.95	19	19	0	0	114	129	11	24	90	7.1	1.34	.292
Minor League Totals			11	8	3.20	35	32	0	0	183	186	17	34	161	7.9	1.20	.267

6 TY BLACH, LHP

Born: Oct. 20, 1990. **B-T:** R-L. **Ht.:** 6-2. **Wt.:** 200. **Drafted:** Creighton, 2012 (5th round). **Signed by:** Lou Colletti.

One of the more durable starters in the minors, Blach has exceeded 100 innings in each of his past six seasons, stretching back to his sophomore year at Creighton. He topped 160 in both 2015 and 2016 at Triple-A Sacramento. A September callup, Blach provided a 2016 season highlight when he outdueled the Dodgers' Clayton Kershaw on Oct. 1 with eight scoreless innings to sew up the Giants' playoff spot. Blach repeated the Pacific Coast League in 2016 and improved across the board, notably by inducing batters to chase out of the zone more frequently and sequencing better to allow less hard contact. He has long been a favorite of Giants coaches for his intelligent approach to pitching and his excellent work ethic. He lacks a plus pitch, but his changeup is above-average and his control allows him to keep hitters off balance. He hits his spots with

BA GRADE
45 Risk: Medium

average stuff, has above-average control, keeps the ball in the park, holds baserunners and is an excellent fielder. Blach has also gained strength to the point where his fastball is now an average 91-92 mph rather than the 89-90 he showed when he signed. He tightened his curveball in 2016, making the formerly loopy pitch sharper, albeit still fringe-average. His slider is a fringe-average pitch without the bite to be an out pitch. Blach profiles as a No. 5 starter and will compete in 2017 with more tenured pitchers for a spot in the big league rotation.

Year	Club (League)	Class	W	L	ERA	G	GS	CG	SV	IP	H	HR	BB	SO	K/9	WHIP	AVG
2014	Richmond (EL)	AA	8	8	3.13	25	25	1	0	141	142	8	39	91	5.8	1.28	.261
2015	Sacramento (PCL)	AAA	11	12	4.46	27	27	2	0	165	189	16	31	93	5.1	1.33	.290
2016	Sacramento (PCL)	AAA	14	7	3.43	26	26	3	0	163	147	9	38	113	6.3	1.14	.244
	San Francisco (NL)	MAJ	1	0	1.06	4	2	0	0	17	8	1	5	10	5.3	0.76	.143
Major League Totals			1	0	1.06	4	2	0	0	17	8	1	5	10	5.3	0.76	.143
Minor League Totals			45	31	3.53	100	98	6	0	599	602	41	126	414	6.2	1.21	.262

7 JOAN GREGORIO, RHP

Born: Jan. 12, 1992. **B-T:** R-R. **Ht.:** 6-7. **Wt.:** 230. **Signed:** Dominican Republic, 2010. **Signed by:** Pablo Peguero.

Gregorio signed as an "older" 18-year-old out of the Dominican Republic in 2010, yet Giants had to be patient as he filled out his massive 6-foot-7 frame and learned how to repeat his delivery. He cruised through an assignment at Double-A Richmond in 2016 to earn a May promotion to Triple-A Sacramento, where he ran up a 5.28 ERA in 21 starts at age 24. Even as he struggled every fifth day, Gregorio impressed at times. He ranges from 90-93 mph as he mixes two- and four-seam fastball. He struggles to locate to his glove side but is comfortable locating arm side.

BA GRADE

45 Risk: Medium

Gregorio has shown improved feel, and he creates plenty of angle on his fastball with his long limbs. His best secondary pitch is an average 82-85 mph slider. His below-average 85-86 mph changeup took a big step forward in 2016 when he started to show conviction in throwing it. He showed improved maturity in his pitch selection by sticking with a pitch even if it's getting hit and sharpening it during the game. Scouts are split on Gregorio's future role. His age, wavering control and the Giants' crowded Triple-A rotation all hint at a move to the bullpen.

Year	Club (League)	Class	W	L	ERA	G	GS	CG	SV	IP	H	HR	BB	SO	K/9	WHIP	AVG
2014	San Jose (CAL)	HiA	2	2	6.75	6	5	0	0	23	27	2	13	27	10.7	1.76	.303
	Augusta (SAL)	LoA	2	7	3.57	13	12	0	1	68	50	2	27	65	8.6	1.13	.204
2015	Richmond (EL)	AA	3	2	3.09	37	9	0	1	79	64	6	32	72	8.2	1.22	.225
2016	Richmond (EL)	AA	0	2	2.33	5	5	0	0	27	15	1	6	30	10.0	0.78	.165
	Sacramento (PCL)	AAA	6	8	5.28	21	21	0	0	107	112	13	43	122	10.2	1.44	.267
Minor League Totals			35	34	4.00	138	107	0	2	574	526	38	194	553	8.7	1.25	.244

8 SANDRO FABIAN, OF

Born: March 6, 1998. **B-T:** R-R. **Ht.:** 6-1. **Wt.:** 180. **Signed:** Dominican Republic, 2014. **Signed by:** Pablo Peguero/Felix Peguero/Jonathan Bautista.

Fabian was the Giants' top target on the 2014 international market, and they signed him for $500,000. He helped lead the his Dominican Summer League team to the league title in 2015 and followed it up by being one of the best hitters in the Rookie-level Arizona League in 2016. The 18-year-old ranked among the league's best in many offensive categories, including average (.340), extra-base hits (20) and slugging (.522). Fabian is an advanced hitter for his age, and he loves the challenge of catching up to quality fastballs. He has a significant leg lift to begin his swing, using it to load and explode into the pitch. He does a good job of using his lower

BILL MITCHELL

BA GRADE

50 Risk: High

half in his swing, but his lack of current pitch awareness makes him vulnerable to offspeed pitches. His hand-eye coordination allowed him to survive against AZL pitchers despite his aggressiveness. Fabian is a plus defender in right field with excellent routes and a good first step. He has a plus arm with accuracy. Fabian is a below-average runner and faces questions about his power potential. He shows fringe-average raw power now, but his lean frame limits his growth potential. Fabian lacks physical projection and is a fringe athlete who succeeds more because of hard work and feel for the game. He will attempt to keep exceeding expectations in 2017, possibly at low Class A Augusta.

Year	Club (League)	Class	AVG	G	AB	R	H	2B	3B	HR	RBI	BB	SO	SB	CS	OBP	SLG
2015	Giants (DSL)	R	.269	65	242	47	65	10	2	3	37	15	47	2	0	.348	.364
2016	Giants (AZL)	R	.340	42	159	30	54	13	5	2	35	7	28	3	1	.364	.522
Minor League Totals			.297	107	401	77	119	23	7	5	72	22	75	5	1	.354	.426

9 ARAMIS GARCIA, C

Born: Jan. 12, 1993. **B-T:** R-R. **Ht.:** 6-2. **Wt.:** 220. **Drafted:** Florida International, 2014 (2nd round). **Signed by:** Jose Alou.

One of the better hitting catchers available in the 2014 draft, Garcia walked more than he struck out as a Florida International junior and led Conference USA in average (.368) and slugging (.626). He popped 15 home runs at low Class A Augusta in 2015, but his timing never returned in 2016 after he missed two months with a facial fracture that required surgery. He injured himself in a collision at second base as he slid to break up a double play. He then hit just .191 in the Arizona Fall League. Garcia has focused attention on his defense in pro ball as a result of being labeled a bat-first catcher in high school and college. A fringe-average defender with a plus arm, he is more than playable behind the plate. He will rip off above-average pop times of 1.85-1.9 seconds on throws to second base. Garcia's blocking and the smoothness of his receiving is limited by his size and by a little stiffness, but he has worked to improve. But his performance at the plate in 2016 disappointed because he didn't show his trademark power or consistent approach. If he can get back to pre-injury form, Garcia is a .250 hitter with line-drive power and about 10 home run potential. Even in a lost season, Garcia didn't carry his offensive struggles into the field, where he has only improved. He will attempt to rebound in 2017, possibly with a return to San Jose.

BA GRADE
50 Risk: High

Year	Club (League)	Class	AVG	G	AB	R	H	2B	3B	HR	RBI	BB	SO	SB	CS	OBP	SLG
2014	Giants (AZL)	R	.219	8	32	6	7	3	0	0	3	5	6	0	0	.324	.313
	Salem-Keizer (NWL)	SS	.229	20	70	5	16	3	0	2	12	5	19	0	0	.289	.357
2015	Augusta (SAL)	LoA	.273	83	319	42	87	15	1	15	61	35	77	0	1	.350	.467
	San Jose (CAL)	HiA	.227	20	75	10	17	4	0	0	5	9	22	1	0	.310	.280
2016	Giants (AZL)	R	.227	6	22	1	5	1	0	0	4	0	1	0	0	.217	.273
	San Jose (CAL)	HiA	.257	41	144	20	37	6	0	2	20	14	42	1	0	.323	.340
Minor League Totals			**.255**	**178**	**662**	**84**	**169**	**32**	**1**	**19**	**105**	**68**	**167**	**2**	**1**	**.328**	**.393**

10 STEVEN DUGGAR, OF

Born: Nov. 4, 1993. **B-T:** L-R. **Ht.:** 6-2. **Wt.:** 195. **Drafted:** Clemson, 2015 (6th round). **Signed by:** Donnie Suttles.

A right fielder at Clemson and early in his pro career, Duggar slid over to center field and blossomed in 2016. He spent the second half at Double-A Richmond and combined to hit .302 at two stops while showing wide-ranging ability, including 10 home runs, 72 walks and 15 stolen bases (albeit with 14 failed attempts). Thanks to plenty of extra work, Duggar turned himself into a potentially above-average defender in center with lots of range thanks to his plus speed. That and his plus arm will be essential if he is to man San Francisco's spacious right field. A lefthanded batter, Duggar also made strides at the plate as he worked to flatten the angle his bat takes as it enters the hitting zone. The flatter path led to more consistent hard contact, which helped him spray the ball to all fields, particularly at Richmond, where he hit .321. Duggar's strike-zone discipline enhances his above-average hit tool and drives his high on-base percentage. His speed hasn't translated into basestealing success. The strength in his swing could allow him to hit 15 home runs or more if he is willing to trade average for power. Duggar is a premium athlete who is proving he can hit. Unless he develops more power, he profiles best as a potential top-of-the-order batter.

BA GRADE
50 Risk: High

Year	Club (League)	Class	AVG	G	AB	R	H	2B	3B	HR	RBI	BB	SO	SB	CS	OBP	SLG
2015	Salem-Keizer (NWL)	SS	.293	58	229	40	67	12	1	1	27	35	52	6	3	.390	.367
2016	San Jose (CAL)	HiA	.284	70	264	43	75	12	4	9	30	44	66	6	7	.386	.462
	Richmond (EL)	AA	.321	60	243	35	78	16	4	1	24	28	51	9	7	.391	.432
Minor League Totals			**.299**	**188**	**736**	**118**	**220**	**40**	**9**	**11**	**81**	**107**	**169**	**21**	**17**	**.389**	**.423**

11 SAM COONROD, RHP

BA GRADE
45 Risk: Medium

Born: Sept. 22, 1992. **B-T:** R-R. **Ht.:** 6-2. **Wt.:** 225. **Drafted:** Southern Illinois, 2014 (5th round). **Signed by:** James Gabella.

Coonrod can handle the pressure of a big game. He led Carrollton High to an Illinois state title in 2011, and in his final college game for Southern Illinois he outdueled Rockies 2014 first-rounder Kyle Freeland in the Missouri Valley Conference tournament. Coonrod's intense, hypercompetitive approach has carried over to pro ball. He has no qualms about pitching inside, and even when he gets hit, he shows no visible discomfort. His point of emphasis in 2016 was to improve his control and be more efficient. That paid off in lengthier outings, but it also led to slips in strikeout (6.0) and walk (3.8) rates per nine innings. Coonrod comes after hitters with a power-heavy approach. He sits 90-94 mph and touches higher with a heavy fastball that can break bats, and he also tosses in an above-average mid-80s slider that can be a little slurvy, but he tightens and loosens it depending on situation. His changeup is a fringe-average third pitch with some deception, but he doesn't use it very much. Coonrod's high-effort delivery limits his control, while he needs to command the ball to the corners better. His temperament would suit an eventual move to the bullpen, and that may fit the Giants' needs as well.

Year	Club (League)	Class	W	L	ERA	G	GS	CG	SV	IP	H	HR	BB	SO	K/9	WHIP	AVG
2014	Giants (AZL)	R	1	0	3.90	15	5	0	0	28	32	0	6	25	8.1	1.37	.291
2015	Augusta (SAL)	LoA	7	5	3.14	23	22	0	0	112	103	3	34	114	9.2	1.23	.243
2016	San Jose (CAL)	HiA	5	3	1.98	11	11	0	0	64	46	3	22	42	5.9	1.07	.204
	Richmond (EL)	AA	4	3	3.03	13	13	0	0	77	59	7	38	52	6.1	1.25	.214
Minor League Totals			17	11	2.92	62	51	0	0	280	240	13	100	233	7.5	1.21	.232

12 REYES MORONTA, RHP

BA GRADE **50** Risk: High

Born: Jan. 6, 1993. **B-T:** R-R. **Ht.:** 6-0. **Wt.:** 175. **Signed:** Dominican Republic, 2010. **Signed by:** Pablo Peguero/Felix Peguero/Jonathan Bautista.

Moronta began the 2016 season as Rodolfo Martinez's setup man at high Class A San Jose before ascending to the closer job when the Giants promoted Martinez to Double-A Richmond. In his first week in the job, Moronta struck out eight in five scoreless innings while allowing only one hit and one walk. He is more advanced than Martinez with better control and a better slider. Moronta sits 95-97 mph with his heater and touches triple digits at his best. He does a good job of locating his fastball down in the strike zone. His hard slider has a short, late bite and can be a plus pitch as well. He can loosen his breaking ball to throw it in the zone early in counts. He even throws a changeup sporadically to take advantage of the element of surprise. Moronta is at least 50 pounds heavier than his listed weight of 175 pounds and conditioning is a concern, but so far his weight has not inhibited his ability to find the strike zone. He has at least average control for a reliever already and locates better than most Class A relievers. The Giants added Moronta to the 40-man roster after the 2016 season and he's ready for Richmond.

Year	Club (League)	Class	W	L	ERA	G	GS	CG	SV	IP	H	HR	BB	SO	K/9	WHIP	AVG
2014	Giants (AZL)	R	0	1	4.66	20	0	0	5	19	16	1	11	30	14.0	1.40	.222
2015	Augusta (SAL)	LoA	1	7	5.73	42	0	0	12	49	56	1	23	64	11.8	1.62	.281
2016	San Jose (CAL)	HiA	0	3	2.59	60	0	0	14	59	43	7	20	93	14.2	1.07	.195
Minor League Totals			7	14	3.71	159	6	0	37	209	185	16	84	263	11.3	1.29	.232

13 STEVEN OKERT, LHP

BA GRADE **40** Risk: Low

Born: July 9, 1991. **B-T:** L-L. **Ht.:** 6-3. **Wt.:** 210. **Drafted:** Oklahoma, 2012 (4th round). **Signed by:** Dan Murray.

After spending two seasons at Triple-A Sacramento, Okert probably won't return to the Pacific Coast League in 2017. Called up three separate times to San Francisco in 2016, he has demonstrated that he's ready to handle a lefthanded reliever role. Okert has some funkiness to his delivery. He sets up on the first-base side of the rubber with his back to the hitter and throws across his body. His arm stroke is very long in the back, but his approach is simple. Okert throws 92-94 mph fastballs, 88-91 mph cutters and mid-80s sliders. None is truly a plus pitch, but all can play that way against lefthanded batters, who don't track the ball well against him. Okert hasn't proven that his stuff plays as well against righthanders. The same could be said for the changeup he barely throws. Okert's fringe-average control and stuff is enough to get big league lefties out right now, but that might be his ceiling unless he finds a way to retire righthanders.

Year	Club (League)	Class	W	L	ERA	G	GS	CG	SV	IP	H	HR	BB	SO	K/9	WHIP	AVG
2014	San Jose (CAL)	HiA	1	2	1.53	33	0	0	19	35	33	2	11	54	13.8	1.25	.241
	Richmond (EL)	AA	2	0	2.73	24	0	0	5	33	24	3	11	38	10.4	1.06	.207
2015	Sacramento (PCL)	AAA	5	3	3.82	52	0	0	3	61	62	7	29	69	10.1	1.48	.265
2016	Sacramento (PCL)	AAA	4	3	3.80	41	0	0	3	47	53	2	11	60	11.4	1.35	.270
	San Francisco (NL)	MAJ	0	0	3.21	16	0	0	0	14	14	2	4	14	9.0	1.29	.259
Major League Totals			0	0	3.21	16	0	0	0	14	14	2	4	14	9.0	1.29	.259
Minor League Totals			15	10	3.01	211	0	0	32	266	255	17	98	308	10.4	1.33	.250

14 RODOLFO MARTINEZ, RHP

BA GRADE **50** Risk: High

Born: April 4, 1994. **B-T:** R-R. **Ht.:** 6-2. **Wt.:** 178. **Signed:** Dominican Republic, 2013. **Signed by:** Pablo Peguero/Felix Peguero/Jesus Stephens.

Martinez served as closer in a dominant one-two combo with Reyes Moronta in the high Class A San Jose bullpen during the first half of 2016. Martinez was so dominant that the Giants bumped him to

Double-A Richmond, but that proved to be a step too far. He struggled immediately after his promotion, then got into the bad habit of trying to do more to get out of trouble. He started overthrowing, and his delivery fell apart. Martinez composed himself in instructional league but fell into the same bad habits during a brief Arizona Fall League stint and was shut down. Martinez's fastball is exceptional. He has touched 102 mph, but he's most effective when he looks like he's lobbing the ball to the plate at 98-99. With Martinez, increased effort in his delivery usually comes with less movement and control. His 86-88 mph slider and his 86-88 mph changeup are both below-average pitches that need further refinement, but with his arm speed he has closer potential. He returns to Double-A in 2017.

Year	Club (League)	Class	W	L	ERA	G	GS	CG	SV	IP	H	HR	BB	SO	K/9	WHIP	AVG
2014	Giants (AZL)	R	1	5	8.78	15	7	0	0	28	45	1	16	35	11.4	2.20	.375
2015	Augusta (SAL)	LoA	1	2	2.54	35	0	0	0	46	41	1	14	44	8.6	1.20	.232
2016	San Jose (CAL)	HiA	1	1	0.88	32	0	0	21	31	23	1	10	33	9.7	1.08	.205
	Richmond (EL)	AA	0	3	6.65	25	0	0	3	23	29	1	15	17	6.7	1.91	.315
Minor League Totals			3	11	4.24	107	7	0	24	127	138	4	55	129	9.1	1.52	.275

15 C.J. HINOJOSA, SS

BA GRADE **45** Risk: Medium

Born: July 15, 1994. **B-T:** R-R. **Ht.:** 5-10. **Wt.:** 180. **Drafted:** Texas, 2015 (11th round). **Signed by:** Todd Thomas.

The Giants marry analytics and scouting and have for some time, but when it comes to drafting college players, San Francisco never has been scared to take a toolsy college player with mediocre statistics. Hinojosa was one of the top high school talents from the 2012 draft to make it to campus in 2013. He starred for Texas on its College World Series team in 2014, but slumped badly as a junior. As a pro, Hinojosa quickly hit his way to Double-A Richmond in 2016, where he held his own. He swings with a flat bat path through the hitting zone that gives him a chance to be a solid-average hitter who sprays line drives. Hinojosa has well below-average power, but he can yank a ball over the fence if a pitcher gets careless. That power gets him in trouble when he chases fastballs up and out of the zone that he's better off taking. Defensively, he's capable of being an average defender at shortstop with solid hands and instincts to go with an above-average arm. Hinojosa projects as a utility infielder who can play short, second base and third base, but if he keeps improving at the plate, he could be a second-division regular.

Year	Club (League)	Class	AVG	G	AB	R	H	2B	3B	HR	RBI	BB	SO	SB	CS	OBP	SLG
2015	Salem-Keizer (NWL)	SS	.296	48	189	24	56	18	1	5	19	8	15	2	3	.328	.481
2016	San Jose (CAL)	HiA	.296	69	260	45	77	14	3	6	34	36	46	1	4	.378	.442
	Richmond (EL)	AA	.248	57	226	27	56	7	2	3	19	20	43	1	0	.312	.336
Minor League Totals			.280	174	675	96	189	39	6	14	72	64	104	4	7	.343	.418

16 HEATH QUINN, OF

BA GRADE **50** Risk: High

Born: June 7, 1995. **B-T:** R-R. **Ht.:** 6-2. **Wt.:** 190. **Drafted:** Samford, 2016 (3rd round). **Signed by:** Jeff Wood.

Quinn ranked among the Division I home run leaders in 2015 when he hit 21 for Samford. A Giants third-round pick in 2016, he hit nine more in an outstanding pro debut at short-season Salem-Keizer. Despite all his power exploits, Quinn is a better hitter than slugger. He likes to let the ball travel deep into the hitting zone and drive it to right-center field for singles and doubles rather than trying to yank home runs. It's a wise approach because Quinn lacks exceptional raw power and the plus raw power he shows in batting practice plays well with a patient approach. His hard-hit line drives sometimes have enough carry to clear the wall. Quinn possesses the batting eye and patience to produce an above-average batting average and on-base percentage. His swing has some holes and he's susceptible to breaking balls, but he makes adjustments and gets into hitter's counts. He projects to have average power. Defensively, Quinn is an average defender in the outfield corners with average speed. His above-average arm makes right field an option. Quinn is advanced enough to skip to high Class A San Jose in 2017.

Year	Club (League)	Class	AVG	G	AB	R	H	2B	3B	HR	RBI	BB	SO	SB	CS	OBP	SLG
2016	Giants (AZL)	R	.600	2	5	4	3	1	0	0	0	2	1	0	0	.778	.800
	Salem-Keizer (NWL)	SS	.337	54	205	37	69	19	1	9	34	26	50	3	0	.423	.571
	San Jose (CAL)	HiA	.353	4	17	2	6	1	0	0	0	2	7	0	0	.421	.412
Minor League Totals			.344	60	227	43	78	21	1	9	34	30	58	3	0	.434	.564

17 MELVIN ADON, RHP

BA GRADE **55** Risk: Extreme

Born: June 9, 1994. **B-T:** R-R. **Ht.:** 6-3. **Wt.:** 195. **Signed:** Dominican Republic, 2015. **Signed by:** Pablo Peguero/Felix Peguero/Jesus Stephens.

The Giants have had no problem with signing late bloomers in Latin America like Adon, who didn't sign his first pro contract until he was nearly 21. He is way behind his peers when it comes to development, but he did survive an aggressive jump from the Dominican Summer League in 2015 to short-season Salem-Keizer in 2016. Adon has a special arm but has struggled to pick up the nuances of the game, such as holding runners and fielding his position. He sits 94-98 mph and touches 100 in most every outing with average life. Sometimes he sinks his fastball and other times it will run, but none of it is really by design yet. His slider has made big strides, and he flashes a plus breaking ball on occasion. Adon's hard 88-90 mph changeup improved as well, but all three pitches need refinement. He loses his release point at times, so he's not consistent with how he uses his front side. Given his power arm and late start, Adon probably fits best as a future power reliever, though he will continue to get innings in the rotation.

Year	Club (League)	Class	W	L	ERA	G	GS	CG	SV	IP	H	HR	BB	SO	K/9	WHIP	AVG
2015	Giants (DSL)	R	4	0	2.48	14	14	0	0	69	57	2	21	54	7.0	1.13	.223
2016	Salem-Keizer (NWL)	SS	5	5	5.48	14	14	0	0	67	85	3	34	55	7.4	1.77	.317
Minor League Totals			9	5	3.96	28	28	0	0	136	142	5	55	109	7.2	1.44	.271

18 DAN SLANIA, RHP

Born: May 24, 1992. **B-T:** R-R. **Ht.:** 6-5. **Wt.:** 275. **Drafted:** Notre Dame, 2013 (5th round). **Signed by:** Kevin Christman.

BA GRADE
45 Risk: Medium

Slania did a little bit of everything in 2016. He pitched at three levels—including two appearances at Triple-A Sacramento—and became a starting pitcher for the first time since high school. As a reward for an impressive season, the Giants added Slania to the 40-man roster after the season. A massive 6-foot-5 righthander, he doesn't use all his height to generate extension because he has a short stride in his delivery and doesn't explode off the rubber. Instead, he finishes somewhat closed off, with a crossfire delivery. Slania sits 90-94 mph with his fastball. It plays as above-average because of its run and the way he hides it in his delivery. His splitter is potentially above-average. When he starts he also uses a fringy changeup, slider and a slow curve, but as a reliever he relies on his fastball and splitter. Slania could fill a middle relief role in the big leagues as soon as 2017.

Year	Club (League)	Class	W	L	ERA	G	GS	CG	SV	IP	H	HR	BB	SO	K/9	WHIP	AVG
2014	Augusta (SAL)	LoA	2	5	3.99	43	0	0	12	59	56	5	21	46	7.1	1.31	.253
	Richmond (EL)	AA	0	0	0.79	10	0	0	0	11	10	0	3	4	1.15	.244
2015	San Jose (CAL)	HiA	4	5	3.53	59	0	0	16	71	70	7	15	90	11.4	1.19	.253
2016	Richmond (EL)	AA	7	6	2.50	27	10	0	0	83	68	6	22	79	8.6	1.09	.223
	San Jose (CAL)	HiA	2	2	5.25	5	4	0	0	24	27	3	9	18	6.8	1.50	.284
	Sacramento (PCL)	AAA	2	0	1.38	2	2	0	0	13	8	0	4	14	9.7	0.92	.170
Minor League Totals			18	19	3.28	158	16	0	31	275	252	22	77	264	8.7	1.20	.243

19 AUSTIN SLATER, OF

Born: Dec. 13, 1992. **B-T:** R-R. **Ht.:** 6-2. **Wt.:** 205. **Drafted:** Stanford, 2014 (8th round). **Signed by:** Keith Snider.

BA GRADE
45 Risk: Medium

A high school shortstop who played outfield at Stanford, Slater moved back into the infield in 2015 but discovered he fit better in the outfield. He celebrated his move back to the outfield in 2016 by hitting for more power than ever and advancing to Triple-A Sacramento. Slater's natural approach has always been to let the ball travel deep in the strike zone before spraying it around the field. But he got more aggressive and started to get the bat head out front more often. The results were dramatic. Slater hit 10 total home runs in his three years at Stanford plus his first two in pro ball. He hit 18 in 2016. Slater's newfound power keeps him alive as a corner prospect because he's a left fielder who is below-average in center field. He doesn't have the first step or the speed (he's a fringe-average runner) to handle center field. He does have an average arm that can slide over to right field in a pinch. A righthanded batter, Slater produced against Triple-A lefthanders (1.200 OPS), but will need to keep producing power to profile as a big league regular in left field.

Year	Club (League)	Class	AVG	G	AB	R	H	2B	3B	HR	RBI	BB	SO	SB	CS	OBP	SLG
2014	Giants (AZL)	R	.333	2	9	2	3	0	1	0	2	0	2	0	0	.333	.556
	Salem-Keizer (NWL)	SS	.347	29	118	21	41	6	0	2	23	10	17	7	1	.417	.449
2015	San Jose (CAL)	HiA	.292	60	250	25	73	15	1	3	34	10	44	4	3	.321	.396
	Richmond (EL)	AA	.296	54	199	21	59	11	1	0	13	14	48	1	1	.350	.362
2016	Richmond (EL)	AA	.317	41	145	20	46	8	1	5	25	24	36	6	1	.413	.490
	Sacramento (PCL)	AAA	.298	68	245	36	73	12	0	13	42	33	53	2	6	.381	.506
Minor League Totals			.305	254	966	125	295	52	4	23	139	91	200	20	12	.369	.439

20 CORY TAYLOR, RHP

Born: Dec. 14, 1993. **B-T:** R-R. **Ht.:** 6-2. **Wt.:** 252. **Drafted:** Dallas Baptist, 2015 (8th round). **Signed by:** Todd Thomas.

A three-year starter at Dallas Baptist, Taylor moved quickly in 2016, his first full pro season, by reaching Double-A Richmond. The Giants were comfortable that his heavy sinker would play against more advanced hitters. A barrel-chested righthander with two above-average pitches, Taylor attacks hitters with his sinker-slider combo. Both come out of his hand looking the same, but the 80-82 mph slider dives away from righthanded batters while the 90-95 mph sinker runs in on them. Taylor's fastball velocity is often average at best, but the sink and run makes it play up. His changeup is an infrequently used and below-average. Because of that he is much more effective against righthanded batters (.551 OPS in 2016) than lefthanders (.745 OPS). That's why many scouts see his future as a groundball-generating middle reliever. The Giants see starter potential because of his strike-throwing ability and extreme groundball profile.

Year	Club (League)	Class	W	L	ERA	G	GS	CG	SV	IP	H	HR	BB	SO	K/9	WHIP	AVG
2015	Salem-Keizer (NWL)	SS	2	0	2.45	18	0	0	1	33	36	1	12	50	13.6	1.45	.286
2016	Augusta (SAL)	LoA	9	5	2.58	18	18	0	0	98	99	4	25	100	9.2	1.27	.261
	Richmond (EL)	AA	1	0	0.75	2	2	0	0	12	10	0	5	10	7.5	1.25	.227
	San Jose (CAL)	HiA	1	1	6.75	3	3	0	0	9	12	0	4	11	10.6	1.71	.300
Minor League Totals			13	6	2.66	41	23	0	1	152	157	5	46	171	10.1	1.34	.266

21 CHRIS STRATTON, RHP

Born: Aug. 22, 1990. **B-T:** R-R. **Ht.:** 6-3. **Wt.:** 190. **Drafted:** Mississippi State, 2012 (1st round). **Signed by:** Hugh Walker.

Stratton dominated the Southeastern Conference as a Mississippi State junior, but the stuff that made him a first-round pick seemed to quickly diminish once he was asked to start every fifth day. A concussion he suffered when hit by a line drive in 2012 didn't help because it took him time to get comfortable again on the mound. But in 2016, Stratton regained half a tick of velocity and showed a consistent 92-94 mph fastball again, which was up from the 88-92 he showed in the previous two seasons. That velocity bump helped his other pitches play up. His changeup, slider and curveball are all fringe-average offerings, with his changeup sometimes playing as an average pitch. Stratton has made himself into a strike-throwing back-end starter who succeeds based on mixing pitches and working in and out to hitters. Stratton made his big league debut in 2016. He's slated to return to Triple-A Sacramento to start 2017, but he's now a viable depth starter option.

Year	Club (League)	Class	W	L	ERA	G	GS	CG	SV	IP	H	HR	BB	SO	K/9	WHIP	AVG
2014	San Jose (CAL)	HiA	7	8	5.07	19	18	0	0	99	103	13	36	102	9.2	1.40	.270
	Richmond (EL)	AA	1	1	3.52	5	5	0	0	23	29	2	12	18	7.0	1.78	.315
2015	Richmond (EL)	AA	1	5	4.14	9	9	0	0	50	40	3	22	39	7.0	1.24	.215
	Sacramento (PCL)	AAA	4	5	3.86	17	17	1	0	98	88	6	40	72	6.6	1.31	.242
2016	San Francisco (NL)	MAJ	1	0	3.60	7	0	0	0	10	11	1	5	6	5.4	1.60	.289
	Sacramento (PCL)	AAA	12	6	3.87	21	20	1	0	126	120	6	39	103	7.4	1.27	.254
Major League Totals			1	0	3.60	7	0	0	0	10	11	1	5	6	5.4	1.60	.289
Minor League Totals			34	29	3.92	101	96	3	0	544	522	36	206	473	7.8	1.34	.255

22 CLAYTON BLACKBURN, RHP

Born: Jan. 6, 1993. **B-T:** L-R. **Ht.:** 6-3. **Wt.:** 230. **Drafted:** HS—Edmond, Okla., 2011 (16th round). **Signed by:** Daniel Murray.

Blackburn has been on the cusp of a big league callup for two years, but that opportunity seems to be receding. He pitched well at Triple-A Sacramento in 2015 by avoiding the heart of the plate while dotting the corners with below-average stuff. Blackburn knows how to sink, run and cut his fastball, but as an 89-92 mph righthander, he's doing so with a below-average fastball. His slider is an average pitch, and he mixes in a fringe-average changeup. Blackburn succeeds with above-average command and by staying one pitch ahead of the hitter, but he has a very small margin for error. If he falls behind in the count, he has nothing to scare the hitter, and Pacific Coast League batters teed off in those situations in 2016 (.972 OPS). Blackburn will return to Triple-A in 2017, but now he has plenty of company in the rotation.

Year	Club (League)	Class	W	L	ERA	G	GS	CG	SV	IP	H	HR	BB	SO	K/9	WHIP	AVG
2014	Giants (AZL)	R	0	1	3.60	2	2	0	0	5	4	0	0	9	16.2	0.80	.222
	Richmond (EL)	AA	5	6	3.29	18	18	0	0	93	94	1	20	85	8.2	1.23	.268
2015	Sacramento (PCL)	AAA	10	4	2.85	23	20	0	0	123	127	6	32	99	7.2	1.29	.269
2016	Sacramento (PCL)	AAA	7	10	4.36	25	23	0	0	136	142	18	35	101	6.7	1.30	.266
Minor League Totals			40	31	3.24	125	114	0	0	655	610	42	143	605	8.3	1.15	.245

23 MATT KROOK, LHP

BA GRADE

50 Risk: Extreme

Born: Oct. 21, 1994. **B-T:** L-L. **Ht.:** 6-4. **Wt.:** 195. **Drafted:** Oregon, 2016 (4th round). **Signed by:** Larry Casian.

A Marlins supplemental first-round pick in 2013, Krook was the second-highest drafted player that year to not sign. A post-draft physical revealed injury concerns that caused Miami to drop its bonus offer. So Krook went to Oregon and was on his way to a dominating freshman year when he suffered an elbow injury that required Tommy John surgery. Back on the mound as a junior his control deserted him. Krook has been unable to consistently repeat his release point since he returned from surgery. He spins off to third base too often and fails to stay online to the plate. But his 93-94 mph fastball has some of the best sink and life evaluators have ever seen. The pitch has been compared with Orioles closer Zach Britton's turbo sinker. One evaluator described it as having split-finger action. When Krook is locating his fastball, he succeeds with that one pitch. He actually flashes a plus curveball and a usable changeup as well, but he has thrown so few strikes that they rarely make an appearance. Krook's control has been bottom-of-the-scale for the past year, but he retains a ceiling of power reliever or possibly mid-rotation starter based on his incredible fastball. He will jump to low Class A Augusta in 2017.

Year	Club (League)	Class	W	L	ERA	G	GS	CG	SV	IP	H	HR	BB	SO	K/9	WHIP	AVG
2016	Giants (AZL)	R	0	1	1.59	2	1	0	0	6	6	0	2	2	3.2	1.41	.261
	Salem-Keizer (NWL)	SS	1	3	6.17	11	10	0	0	35	35	2	33	39	10.0	1.94	.263
Minor League Totals			1	4	5.53	13	11	0	0	41	41	2	35	41	9.1	1.87	.263

24 GARRETT WILLIAMS, LHP

BA GRADE

50 Risk: Extreme

Born: Sept. 15, 1994. **B-T:** L-L. **Ht.:** 6-1. **Wt.:** 205. **Drafted:** Oklahoma State, 2016 (7th round). **Signed by:** Daniel Murray.

Few pitchers have succeeded to a greater extent than Williams in the Little League World Series. He struck out 42, allowed five hits and walked two in 16.2 scoreless innings in Williamsport. For a while, that looked like Williams' career highlight. He missed part of his senior year in high school when he suffered thoracic outlet syndrome, and he actually threw more innings at the LLWS than he did as a junior at Oklahoma State the year the Giants made him a seventh-round pick. Wildness relegated him to the OSU bullpen, and he threw 73 innings and walked 61 as a Cowboy. But for all his control problems, Williams has dominating stuff and a loose arm. His short takeaway doesn't seem to indicate long-term control problems. The Giants had Williams work on two delivery flaws. He too often collapses his back leg and gets underneath the ball, and he also needs to be more direct to the plate. He works with a plus 93-97 mph fastball as well as a plus curveball that is now showing tighter spin and later break than it did in college. He also has a fringe-average changeup. If Williams can refine his well below-average control—a very big if—everything is place for him to become a mid-rotation starter.

Year	Club (League)	Class	W	L	ERA	G	GS	CG	SV	IP	H	HR	BB	SO	K/9	WHIP	AVG
2016	Giants (AZL)	R	1	0	2.57	3	1	0	0	7	4	0	3	5	6.4	1.00	.174
	Salem-Keizer (NWL)	SS	1	2	5.68	7	7	0	0	25	28	1	14	22	7.8	1.66	.275
Minor League Totals			2	2	5.01	10	8	0	0	32	32	1	17	27	7.5	1.52	.256

25 CHASE JOHNSON, RHP

BA GRADE

45 Risk: High

Born: Jan. 9, 1992. **B-T:** R-R. **Ht.:** 6-3. **Wt.:** 185. **Drafted:** Cal Poly, 2013 (3rd round). **Signed by:** Gil Kubski.

The Giants had to shut Johnson down before the 2016 season ended with shoulder fatigue, but before that he had thrived after moving back to the bullpen. He worked as a reliever at Cal Poly, but the Giants shifted him to the rotation to get more innings. Ultimately he fits best in relief because he struggles against lefthanded batters. Johnson's plus fastball sits 93-96 mph and touches 98. When he's throwing his two-seamer it has quality sink. He pairs it with an average curve that varies from loopy to hard but has good 12-to-6 break at its best. As a starter, Johnson relied on generating weak contact, but his pitches miss more bats in shorter stints. Johnson's control is still below-average, and he is prone to throwing wild pitches. He throws a below-average changeup when starting. Johnson's shoulder fatigue is not expected to be a lingering issue. He will jump to Triple-A Sacramento after being added to the 40-man roster after the 2016 season. He is a viable emergency relief option in 2017.

Year	Club (League)	Class	W	L	ERA	G	GS	CG	SV	IP	H	HR	BB	SO	K/9	WHIP	AVG
2014	Augusta (SAL)	LoA	4	7	4.57	23	22	0	0	110	111	5	40	94	7.7	1.37	.260
2015	San Jose (CAL)	HiA	8	3	2.43	20	18	0	0	111	95	5	34	111	9.0	1.16	.235
	Richmond (EL)	AA	1	1	5.93	3	3	0	0	14	16	0	8	18	11.9	1.76	.281
2016	Richmond (EL)	AA	1	4	3.27	24	7	0	5	52	47	2	18	37	6.4	1.24	.242
Minor League Totals			18	17	3.61	83	60	0	5	334	310	15	113	304	8.2	1.27	.248

26 KELVIN BELTRE, 3B

Born: Sept. 25, 1996. **B-T:** R-R. **Ht.:** 5-11. **Wt.:** 170. **Signed:** Dominican Republic, 2013. **Signed by:** Pablo Peguero/Felix Peguero/Jesus Stephens.

BA GRADE
50 Risk: Extreme

More than anything, Beltre needs a season of good health. After a hamstring injury ruined his 2015 season, he missed nearly two months in 2016 after breaking his left arm when hit by a pitch. He missed all of June and July and got back to low Class A Augusta just before the season ended. The Giants moved Beltre from shortstop to third base to help his defense catch up to his bat. He has shown outstanding bat speed and plus raw power, but he will have to tone everything down a notch because his high-energy approach contributes to a tendency to chase pitches out of the zone. Belte's move to third base looks promising. A step shy at shortstop, he has plenty of arm strength and range for third base—with the power potential to match. Beltre missed enough time in 2016 that he might repeat the South Atlantic League.

Year	Club (League)	Class	AVG	G	AB	R	H	2B	3B	HR	RBI	BB	SO	SB	CS	OBP	SLG
2014	Giants (DSL)	R	.235	22	68	21	16	5	0	3	10	22	11	7	4	.430	.441
2015	Giants (AZL)	R	.239	14	46	5	11	2	0	1	3	8	17	3	2	.375	.348
2016	Giants (AZL)	R	.333	7	24	3	8	4	1	0	5	1	4	1	0	.360	.583
	Augusta (SAL)	LoA	.250	55	192	29	48	14	2	4	22	16	63	7	4	.329	.406
Minor League Totals			.252	98	330	58	83	25	3	8	40	47	95	18	10	.362	.418

27 JALEN MILLER, 2B

Born: Dec. 19, 1996. **B-T:** R-R. **Ht.:** 5-11. **Wt.:** 175. **Drafted:** HS—Sandy Springs, Ga., 2015 (3rd round). **Signed by:** Andrew Jefferson.

BA GRADE
50 Risk: Extreme

When the Giants assigned shortstop Lucius Fox and second baseman Jalen Miller to low Class A Augusta in 2016, they expected growing pains. They weren't disappointed. Fox and Miller both struggled to survive against more advanced pitchers. Eventually the Giants traded Fox to the Rays for Matt Moore, but Miller kept on muddling in the South Atlantic League. Pitchers feasted on his over-aggressiveness from April to September. With a quick bat, Miller can catch up to any fastball, but he struggles to hang in on breaking balls and changeups and is too impatient to lay off fastballs. He could get to 10 home run eventually, but he must swing at better pitches. Miller's below-average arm keeps him from being an everyday shortstop, but his soft hands, above-average range and improved internal clock makes him a potentially above-average second baseman. He's also an above-average runner. Miller will try Augusta again in 2017.

Year	Club (League)	Class	AVG	G	AB	R	H	2B	3B	HR	RBI	BB	SO	SB	CS	OBP	SLG
2015	Giants (AZL)	R	.218	44	174	28	38	5	1	0	13	17	42	11	2	.292	.259
2016	Augusta (SAL)	LoA	.223	112	457	65	102	20	5	5	44	26	107	11	5	.271	.322
Minor League Totals			.222	156	631	93	140	25	6	5	57	43	149	22	7	.277	.304

28 MATT GAGE, LHP

Born: Feb. 11, 1993. **B-T:** R-L:. **Ht.:** 6-4. **Wt.:** 240. **Drafted:** Siena, 2014 (10th round). **Signed by:** Ray Callari.

BA GRADE
40 Risk: Low

There's nothing flashy about Gage, but he has a long track record of durability and strike throwing. Gage impressed scouts in the leadup to the 2014 draft as he allowed one run in a 10-inning start in the Metro Atlantic Athletic Conference, then held Texas Christian to one run in nine innings in the NCAA tournament. As a pro, Gage has moved quickly. He made it to Double-A in his first full season and impressed with his consistency in Richmond in 2016. Gage fills the strike zone with a wide array of pitches. Much like fellow Giants' Ty Blach or Clayton Blackburn, his stuff is less notable for its firmness than his ability to spot his pitches and mess with hitters' heads. Gage mixes an 88-92 mph fastball, a high 80s cutter, a low 80s slider and changeup and a mid-70s curveball. None is plus, but Gage's control is at least above-average and he gets good sink on his fastball, helping to keep the ball in the ballpark and rarely catching the middle of the plate. Gage looks to be a fifth starter at best, but the Giants have full big league rotation and a very crowded Triple-A rotation as well.

Year	Club (League)	Class	W	L	ERA	G	GS	CG	SV	IP	H	HR	BB	SO	K/9	WHIP	AVG
2014	Giants (AZL)	R	2	0	1.89	13	6	0	0	33	27	1	8	32	8.6	1.05	.225
2015	Augusta (SAL)	LoA	4	4	4.07	15	15	0	0	77	87	3	13	71	8.3	1.29	.290
	Richmond (EL)	AA	2	3	4.66	9	7	0	0	39	39	2	10	30	7.0	1.27	.262
2016	Richmond (EL)	AA	9	7	3.38	23	23	1	0	136	130	2	34	106	7.0	1.21	.248
Minor League Totals			17	14	3.56	60	51	1	0	285	283	8	65	239	7.5	1.22	.259

29 ORLANDO CALIXTE, SS/OF

BA GRADE
40 Risk: Low

Born: Feb. 3, 1992. **B-T:** R-R. **Ht.:** 5-11. **Wt.:** 180. **Signed:** Dominican Republic, 2010. **Signed by:** Alvin Cuevas/Hector Pineda (Royals).

A long-time Royals prospect who ranked among that organization's Top 30 Prospects in five different seasons, Calixte came to the Giants as a minor league free agent after the 2016 season and was added to the 40-man roster to shield him from the Rule 5 draft. He may end up filling a utility role in San Francisco. Calixte is a fringe-average defender at shortstop, but he is playable there and he has experience at every other position other than first base and catcher. His best positions are second base and third base, where he has above-average range and an above-average arm. With average speed, he also is capable in the outfield. At the plate, Calixte's above-average bat speed gives him average power potential and he is a good baserunner. He is prone to chase pitches out of the zone too often, limiting his potential to hit for average.

Year	Club (League)	Class	AVG	G	AB	R	H	2B	3B	HR	RBI	BB	SO	SB	CS	OBP	SLG
2014	NW Arkansas (TL)	AA	.241	96	374	43	90	15	1	11	37	27	92	9	5	.288	.374
2015	Kansas City (AL)	MAJ	.000	2	3	1	0	0	0	0	0	0	0	0	0	.000	.000
	Omaha (PCL)	AAA	.229	107	354	38	81	11	2	8	27	27	84	22	3	.287	.339
2016	NW Arkansas (TL)	AA	.295	38	139	26	41	9	0	2	14	9	31	14	3	.333	.403
	Omaha (PCL)	AAA	.265	88	332	48	88	17	5	9	29	28	68	5	6	.320	.428
Major League Totals			.000	2	3	1	0	0	0	0	0	0	0	0	0	.000	.000
Minor League Totals			.247	678	2522	312	623	118	21	55	248	202	598	88	41	.303	.376

30 MIGUEL GOMEZ, 3B

BA GRADE
45 Risk: High

Born: Dec. 17, 1992. **B-T:** B-R. **Ht.:** 5-10. **Wt.:** 185. **Signed:** Dominican Republic, 2011. **Signed by:** Pablo Peguero/Felix Peguero/Jonathan Bautista.

If Gomez had a clear position, he would rank significantly higher. But the late-blooming switch-hitter can really hit, and pure hitters usually find some path to the big leagues. A career .314 hitter, Gomez stayed behind in the Dominican Summer League for three seasons as he sought a full-time position. A catcher when he signed, he has never embraced the position even though it's where his tools profile best. Gomez was lighter and stronger in 2016, which helped his range, but he's a below-average defender at second or third base because of limited range. At 5-foot-10 he's too short to play first base. His well below-average speed would make him a below-average corner outfielder, though his average arm gives him survival skills. The Giants added Gomez to the 40-man roster after the 2016 season. His bat will have to carry him to the big leagues, but as a plus hitter with at least average power he has intriguing upside.

Year	Club (League)	Class	AVG	G	AB	R	H	2B	3B	HR	RBI	BB	SO	SB	CS	OBP	SLG
2014	Giants (DSL)	R	.318	65	258	35	82	18	1	5	60	17	37	3	0	.367	.453
2015	Salem-Keizer (NWL)	SS	.319	66	276	30	88	14	1	6	52	5	24	0	1	.331	.442
2016	Augusta (SAL)	LoA	.371	66	267	41	99	17	1	8	43	12	25	3	2	.401	.532
	San Jose (CAL)	HiA	.267	43	172	25	46	9	2	9	24	8	28	1	0	.302	.500
Minor League Totals			.314	312	1205	164	378	76	8	31	219	63	166	10	4	.353	.467

Seattle Mariners

BY KYLE GLASER

Everything changed for the Mariners in 2016. For an organization that has often struggled to win at the major league level or develop frontline homegrown talent, that was a good thing.

Jerry Dipoto took over as general manager after the 2015 season and cleaned house. Dipoto replaced Jack Zdurencik, who was fired after seven seasons without a playoff berth, and brought in Scott Servais as manager, hired Andy McKay as farm director and made 12 trades before the season began.

The result was the Mariners' most successful season in years. They went 86-76 and remained in the hunt for an American League wild card until the season's final weekend, while their second-place finish in the AL West was the franchise's best since 2007.

The Mariners' success was even more pronounced at the minor league level. All six of Seattle's domestic affiliates made the playoffs, with Double-A Jackson and the Rookie-level Arizona League club winning championships. All in all, Mariners domestic affiliates combined for a .581 winning percentage, the third-best rate by any organization in the last eight years.

Dipoto and McKay instituted a hitting summit for their minor leaguers in their first season at the helm, gathering their offensive prospects in Arizona for a week in January to impart an organization-wide hitting philosophy focused on reducing strikeouts.

A system-wide improvement in contact rate yielded major improvements in performance from many of the organization's top prospects. Noted power hitters Tyler O'Neill, D.J. Peterson and others cut their strikeout rates from the previous year and saw jumps in production as a result of better pitch selection.

That, plus steps forward from righthanders Nick Neidert and Andrew Moore and lefthanders Luiz Gohara and Ryan Yarbrough, gave the Mariners a large group of quality prospects who performed, a welcome development for a front office emphasizing players' need to "earn their promotions" with measurable on-field performance.

The positive results from the initial round of change led to even more change after the season. Dipoto made five trades in a span of 16 days in November, with previous regime holdovers Taijuan Walker, Alex Jackson, Ketel Marte and Zack Littell highlighting a cavalcade of players sent away and Jean Segura, Danny Valencia, Mitch Haniger and Max Povse leading the group of players heading to Seattle.

The new players brought in strengthened the

General manager Jerry Dipoto produced immediate results after an overhaul in Seattle

TOP PROSPECTS OF THE DECADE

Year	Player, Pos.	2016 Org
2007	Adam Jones, of	Orioles
2008	Jeff Clement, c	Did not play
2009	Greg Halman, of	Deceased
2010	Dustin Ackley, of/1b	Yankees
2011	Dustin Ackley, 2b	Yankees
2012	Taijuan Walker, rhp	Mariners
2013	Mike Zunino, c	Mariners
2014	Taijuan Walker, rhp	Mariners
2015	Alex Jackson, of	Mariners
2016	Alex Jackson, of	Mariners

Mariners both at the major league level and in their farm system, which already received a boost over the summer when Kyle Lewis, the 2016 Golden Spikes Award winner and BA College Player of the Year, fell to them with the No. 11 overall pick in the draft. They also snagged well-regarded prep third baseman Joe Rizzo, college middle infielders Bryson Brigman and Donnie Walton, and a number of later picks who had impressive pro debuts, topped by righthander Brandon Miller (sixth round), third baseman Nick Zammarelli (eighth) and outfielder Eric Filia (20th).

Coming off their most successful season in years at the major league level and with the farm system in better shape than any time in recent memory, optimism abounds in Seattle with the Dipoto-led regime at the helm.

ORGANIZATION OVERVIEW

General manager: Jerry Dipoto. **Farm director:** Andy McKay. **Scouting director:** Scott Hunter

Class	Team	League	W	L	PCT	Finish	Manager
Majors	Seattle Mariners	American	86	76	.531	7th (15)	Scott Servais
Triple-A	Tacoma Rainiers	Pacific Coast	81	62	.566	3rd (16)	Pat Listach
Double-A	* Jackson Generals	Southern	84	55	.604	1st (10)	Daren Brown
High Class A	** Bakersfield Blaze	California	76	64	.543	5th (10)	Eddie Menchaca
Low Class A	Clinton LumberKings	Midwest	86	54	.614	1st (16)	Mitch Canham
Short-season	Everett AquaSox	Northwest	45	31	.592	2nd (8)	Rob Mummau
Rookie	AZL Mariners	Arizona	31	25	.554	t-4th (14)	Zac Livingston
Overall 2016 Minor League Record			403	291	.581	2nd (30)	

* Affiliate moves to Arkansas (Texas) in 2017. ** Affiliate moves to Modesto (California) in 2017.

THIS YEAR'S TOP 30

No.	Player, Pos.	Grade/Risk
1.	Kyle Lewis, of	60/High
2.	Tyler O'Neill, of	55/Medium
3.	Luiz Gohara, lhp	55/High
4.	Nick Neidert, rhp	50/High
5.	Mitch Haniger, of	50/High
6.	Andrew Moore, rhp	45/Medium
7.	Drew Jackson, ss	50/High
8.	Max Povse, rhp	50/High
9.	Dan Altavilla, rhp	45/Medium
10.	Dan Vogelbach, 1b	45/Medium
11.	Joe Rizzo, 3b	55/Extreme
12.	Ryan Yarbrough, lhp	50/High
13.	D.J. Peterson, 1b	45/Medium
14.	Thyago Vieira, rhp	55/Extreme
15.	Braden Bishop, of	50/High
16.	Brayan Hernandez, of	55/Extreme
17.	Rob Whalen, rhp	45/Medium
18.	Guillermo Heredia, of	40/Low
19.	Tony Zych, rhp	45/High
20.	Ben Gamel, of	40/Medium
21.	Christopher Torres, ss	50/Extreme
22.	Bryson Brigman, 2b/ss	45/High
23.	Thomas Burrows, lhp	45/High
24.	Luis Liberato, of	45/High
25.	Brandon Miller, rhp	45/High
26.	Carlos Vargas, ss	50/Extreme
27.	Taylor Motter, ss/of	40/Low
28.	James Pazos, lhp	40/Medium
29.	Tyler Marlette, c	40/High
30.	Donnie Walton, 2b	40/High

LAST YEAR'S TOP 30

No.	Player, Pos.	Status
1.	Alex Jackson, of	(Braves)
2.	Edwin Diaz, rhp	Majors
3.	Drew Jackson, ss	No. 7
4.	Tyler O'Neill, of	No. 2
5.	Nick Neidert, rhp	No. 4
6.	Luiz Gohara, lhp	No. 3
7.	Braden Bishop, of	No. 15
8.	Andrew Moore, rhp	No. 6
9.	Boog Powell, of	Dropped out
10.	D.J. Peterson, 1b	No. 13
11.	Jabari Blash, of	(Padres)
12.	Dylan Thompson, rhp	(Rays)
13.	Luis Liberato, of	No. 24
14.	Ryan Yarbrough, lhp	No. 12
15.	Freddy Peralta, rhp	(Brewers)
16.	Brayan Hernandez, of	No. 16
17.	Gareth Morgan, of	Dropped out
18.	Christopher Torres, ss	No. 22
19.	Tony Zych, rhp	No. 19
20.	Rayder Ascanio, ss	Dropped out
21.	Nick Wells, lhp	Dropped out
22.	Kyle Wilcox, rhp	Dropped out
23.	Dan Altavilla, rhp	No. 9
24.	Jio Orozco, rhp	(Yankees)
25.	Jake Brentz, lhp	(Pirates)
26.	Dario Pizzano, of	Dropped out
27.	Mayckol Guaipe, rhp	Dropped out
28.	Cody Mobley, rhp	Dropped out
29.	Juan De Paula, rhp	(Yankees)
30.	Daniel Missaki, rhp	(Brewers)

BEST TOOLS

Best Hitter for Average	Joe Rizzo
Best Power Hitter	Tyler O'Neill
Best Strike-Zone Discipline	Eric Filia
Fastest Baserunner	Drew Jackson
Best Athlete	Kyle Lewis
Best Fastball	Thyago Vieira
Best Curveball	Nick Wells
Best Slider	Dan Altavilla
Best Changeup	Nick Neidert
Best Control	Andrew Moore
Best Defensive Catcher	Steve Baron
Best Defensive Infielder	Rayder Ascanio
Best Infield Arm	Drew Jackson
Best Defensive Outfielder	Braden Bishop
Best Outfield Arm	Tyler O'Neill

PROJECTED 2020 LINEUP

Catcher	Mike Zunino
First Base	Dan Vogelbach
Second Base	Jean Segura
Third Base	Kyle Seager
Shortstop	Drew Jackson
Left Field	Mitch Haniger
Center Field	Kyle Lewis
Right Field	Tyler O'Neill
Designated Hitter	Robinson Cano
No. 1 Starter	Felix Hernandez
No. 2 Starter	James Paxton
No. 3 Starter	Luiz Gohara
No. 4 Starter	Nick Neidert
No. 5 Starter	Andrew Moore
Closer	Edwin Diaz

MINOR LEAGUE DEPTH CHART

SEATTLE MARINERS

TOP 2017 ROOKIE: Dan Altavilla, rhp: His upper-90s heat and low-90s slider confound hitters and have him primed to be a bridge to Edwin Diaz.
BREAKOUT PROSPECT: Christopher Torres, ss: The teen switch-hitter has speed, plate discipline, a strong arm and plus range.
SLEEPER: Ian Miller, of: Speedy center fielder was 49-for-52 in stolen bases at Double-A in 2016, one year after swiping 50 bags.

SOURCE OF TOP 30 TALENT

Homegrown	22	Acquired	8
College	11	Trades	8
Junior college	0	Rule 5 draft	0
High school	5	Independent leagues	0
Nondrafted free agents	0	Free agents/waivers	0
International	7		

LF
Mitch Haniger (5)
Ben Gamel (20)
DeAires Moses

CF
Kyle Lewis (1)
Braden Bishop (15)
Brayan Hernandez (16)
Guillermo Heredia (18)
Luis Liberato (24)
Anthony Jimenez
Ian Miller

RF
Tyler O'Neill (2)
Eric Filia

3B
Joe Rizzo (11)
Joe DeCarlo
Nick Zammarelli
Logan Taylor

SS
Drew Jackson (7)
Christopher Torres (21)
Bryson Brigman (22)
Carlos Vargas (26)
Taylor Motter (27)
Rayder Ascanio

2B
Donnie Walton (30)
Greifer Andrade
Tyler Smith

1B
Dan Vogelbach (10)
D.J. Peterson (13)
Richie Shaffer

C
Tyler Marlette (29)
Steve Baron
Marcus Littlewood

LHP

LHSP	LHRP
Luiz Gohara (3)	Thomas Burrows (23)
Ryan Yarbrough (12)	James Pazos (28)
Nick Wells	Zac Curtis
Anthony Misiewicz	Paul Fry
	Joe Pistorese
	Elliot Surrey
	Tim Viehoff

RHP

RHSP	RHRP
Nick Neidert (4)	Dan Altavilla (9)
Andrew Moore (6)	Thyago Vieira (14)
Max Povse (8)	Tony Zych (19)
Rob Whalen (17)	Darin Gillies
Brandon Miller (25)	Ronald Dominguez
Pablo Lopez	Emilio Pagan
Dylan Unsworth	Matt Walker
Tyler Herb	Art Warren
Matt Festa	
Ryne Inman	
Reggie McClain	

DRAFT ANALYSIS

2016

BEST PURE HITTER: 3B Joe Rizzo (2) has a stocky 5-foot-9, 194-pound frame with present strength and short, strong lefthanded swing. OF Kyle Lewis (1) has a longer, more athletic body but also has shown a potential plus hit tool, including hitting 300 in the Cape Cod League last summer.

BEST POWER HITTER: Lewis ranked sixth in the country with 20 homers in the spring en route to College Player of the Year honors. He's earned 70 grades for his raw power and was showing that power in pro ball before a knee injury ended his season July 19.

FASTEST RUNNER: Seattle drafted OF DeAires Moses (19) out of a Nashville high school but only signed him after two junior-college seasons. He's an 80 runner.

BEST DEFENSIVE PLAYER: The Mariners know SS/2B Bryson Brigman (3) can handle second base and be above-average there, but they think he can handle short, particularly if his fringy arm strength bounces back after a sports hernia affected him in the spring. Lewis impressed in center field before his injury and falls back to being an above-average right fielder if his knee costs him some speed.

BEST FASTBALL: The Mariners saw RHP Matt Festa (7) sit 93-95 mph in a college playoff game against RHP Brandon Miller (6) over an eight-inning start. Shortly thereafter, they drafted and signed him for just $5,000. LHP Thomas Burrows (4) sits 93-94 out of the bullpen.

BEST SECONDARY PITCH: Burrows has a short, hard slider that helped him limit lefthanded hitters to a 3-for-27 mark (all singles) in his pro debut.

BEST PRO DEBUT: OF Eric Filia (20) earned short-season Northwest League MVP honors, batting .362/.450/.496 with a 39-19 walk-strikeout ratio. 3B Nick Zammarelli (8) ranked third in the NWL to Filia in batting during a .329/.391/.467 campaign.

BEST ATHLETE: Lewis' athleticism will be tested as he tries to return from a home-plate collision that resulted in a torn ACL and torn cartilage in his right knee, though his rehabilitation is off to an encouraging start.

MOST INTRIGUING BACKGROUND: OF Trey Griffey (24) is a wide receiver at Arizona and son of Hall of Famer Ken Griffey Jr. If he plays baseball, it will be for the Mariners. OF Austin Grebeck (21) is the son of ex-big league infielder Craig, while SS/2B Donnie Walton (5) is son of Oklahoma State pitching coach Rob Walton.

CLOSEST TO THE MAJORS: Walton, a senior draft, could fit a utility profile quickly as a middle infielder whose hands work well.

BEST LATE-ROUND PICK: Filia, a hero of UCLA's 2013 College World Series champs, has a long hitting track record interrupted by shoulder and off-field woes in college. Already 24, he's an above-average hitter.

THE ONE WHO GOT AWAY: The Mariners drafted many of the top preps in the Pacific Northwest who were tough signs, such as C Adley Rutschman (40), who's kicking off for Oregon State's football team. They made a stronger effort to sign C Lyle Lin (16), who instead is attending Arizona State.

2015

RHPs Nick Neidert (2) and Andrew Moore (2s) have made progress, with Moore racing to Double-A despite modest stuff. SS Drew Jackson (5) came back to earth a bit after an amazing debut. OF Braden Bishop (3) has a great glove and iffy bat.

GRADE: C

2014

LHP Ryan Yarbrough (4), when healthy, has pitched well while RHP Dan Altavilla (5) raced to the majors as a reliever. Top picks OFs Alex Jackson (1), Gareth Morgan (2s) and Austin Cousino (3) all have disappointed. The Mariners traded Jackson and have released Cousino.

GRADE: C

2013

OF Tyler O'Neill (3) looks like a steal and was MVP of the Double-A Southern League. 1B D.J. Peterson (1) looks like a platoon option in 2017. Unsigned OF Corey Ray (33) became the No. 5 overall pick in 2016.

GRADE: C

TOP DRAFT PICKS OF THE DECADE

Year	Player, Pos.	2016 Org
2007	Phillippe Aumont, rhp	White Sox
2008	Josh Fields, rhp	Dodgers
2009	Dustin Ackley, of	Yankees
2010	Taijuan Walker, rhp (1st round supp.)	Mariners
2011	Danny Hultzen, lhp	Mariners
2012	Mike Zunino, c	Mariners
2013	D.J. Peterson, 3b	Mariners
2014	Alex Jackson, of	Mariners
2015	Nick Neidert, rhp (2nd round)	Mariners
2016	Kyle Lewis, of	Mariners

LARGEST BONUSES IN CLUB HISTORY

Danny Hultzen, 2011	$6,350,000
Dustin Ackley, 2009	$6,000,000
Ichiro Suzuki, 2000	$5,000,000
Alex Jackson, 2014	$4,200,000
Mike Zunino, 2012	$4,000,000

1 KYLE LEWIS, OF

Born: July 13, 1995. **B-T:** R-R. **Ht.:** 6-4. **Wt.:** 210.
Drafted: Mercer, 2016 (1st round).
Signed by: John Wiedenbauer.

BA GRADE

60 Risk: High

SCOUTING GRADES

Batting: 55
Power: 60
Speed: 50
Defense: 55
Arm: 60

Based on 20-80 scouting scale and future projection rather than present tools.

TOM PRIDDY

In the age of never-ending prospect showcases and 14-year-old class rankings, Lewis was somewhat of a late bloomer. He played varsity all four years at Shiloh High in Snellville, Ga., but never won anything more than regional honors and went undrafted out of high school. No Southeastern Conference school offered him a scholarship—including Georgia less than an hour away—and he ended up at Mercer, which had just two NCAA tournament appearances in its 65-year history when Lewis arrived on campus. He split time playing baseball and basketball growing up, but once he began focusing solely on baseball in college, he flourished. With his elite athleticism and intelligence, Lewis adapted quickly and made the Atlantic Sun Conference all-freshman team. He became a middle-of-the-order impact regular as a sophomore, thrived in the Cape Cod League (.300/.344/.500) and emerged as one of the most potent forces in college baseball as a junior, hitting .395/.535/.731 with 20 home runs and winning the Golden Spikes Award and the BA College Player of the Year. The Mariners had him ranked as one of the top three players on their board, and they were shocked and ecstatic when he fell to them at No. 11. He signed for $3,286,700. Lewis got off to a blazing start as a pro before he tore the ACL and medial and lateral meniscus in his right knee in a grisly collision at home plate just 30 games into his pro career at short-season Everett Lewis is an offense-first center fielder with plus power to all fields and a patient approach that allows him to control the strike zone and punish mistakes. He has some swing-and-miss to his game, like most power hitters, but he has enough feel for the barrel and understanding of what to do at the plate that he still is regarded as an solid-average hitter. He is a below-average runner out of the box but ticks up to average underway. His instincts, reflexes and efficient routes make up for whatever he lacks in terms of raw speed in the outfield and make him an above-average defender. His plus arm, combined with average speed, have some evaluators predicting he ends up in right field. However, the Mariners will leave him in center for now. There is concern about how his knee injury will affect his power base and already suspect speed, but Lewis is a hard worker who plays the game with passion and a big smile. There is little doubt among observers Lewis will put in the work to get back to the diamond as quickly and strongly as possible His makeup, aptitude and work ethic draw raves, with his combination of talent and personality making him a potential face-of-the-franchise type player.

Lewis draws comparisons with his childhood hero Adam Jones, another former Mariners top prospect. He had surgery on his knee in August and is not expected to begin baseball activities until April. He will continue his rehab at the team complex in Arizona until then, with an eye on reporting to a full-season affiliate by mid-summer. Low Class A Clinton is his likely destination, but high Class A Modesto is a possibility with its drier climate making for a better playing environment post-surgery. If Lewis returns to full health, an accelerated track up the minors and to the majors by 2018 is very much in the cards.

Year	Club (League)	Class	AVG	G	AB	R	H	2B	3B	HR	RBI	BB	SO	SB	CS	OBP	SLG
2016	Everett (NWL)	SS	.299	30	117	26	35	8	5	3	26	16	22	3	0	.385	.530
Minor League Totals			.299	30	117	26	35	8	5	3	26	16	22	3	0	.385	.530

2 TYLER O'NEILL, OF

Born: June 22, 1995. **B-T:** R-R. **Ht.:** 5-11. **Wt.:** 210. **Drafted:** HS—Maple Ridge, B.C,
2013 (3rd round). **Signed by:** Wayne Norton.

The Mariners drafted O'Neill 85th overall in 2013 and signed him for $650,000 because of his powerful build and power projection. The son of former Mr. Canada bodybuilder Terry O'Neill was so square and bulky that he played catcher in high school, but his underrated athleticism has allowed him to transition to the outfield. O'Neill has grown even stronger since his prep days, with muscles that bulge out of his arms, thighs and backside so much he is nicknamed "Wreck-It-Ralph" after the cartoonishly muscular animated character. Combining that muscle-driven power

BA GRADE

55 Risk: Medium

with exceptional bat speed, O'Neill creates double-plus power to all fields and draws raves for hitting jaw-dropping home runs. His power plays in all parks, with tales of his longballs retold in awe. O'Neill adapted to the new Mariners' dedication to reducing strikeouts and cut his rate from 31 percent in 2015 to 26 percent in 2016. His adjustment propelled him to triple-crown contention in the Double-A Southern League and the league's MVP award, as well as upgraded him to an average to above-average hitter in scouts' eyes. He is at times succeptible to fastballs inside and changeups out front, but anything in the strike zone he crushes. O'Neill's bulky build doesn't prevent him from tapping into his athleticism and showing average speed, which he uses efficiently on the basepaths to make him double-digit stolen-base threat. His above-average arm and improving reads have evaluators projecting him as an average defensive right fielder. O'Neill has held his own among the game's top prospects as one of the better performers in the Arizona Fall League two years in a row now, and will begin 2017 at Triple-A Tacoma with a chance to make his major league debut by the end of the season.

Year	Club (League)	Class	AVG	G	AB	R	H	2B	3B	HR	RBI	BB	SO	SB	CS	OBP	SLG
2014	Mariners (AZL)	R	.000	1	2	0	0	0	0	0	0	0	1	0	0	.000	.000
	Everett (NWL)	SS	.400	3	10	2	4	2	0	0	2	1	5	0	0	.455	.600
	Clinton (MWL)	LoA	.247	57	219	31	54	9	0	13	38	20	79	5	0	.322	.466
2015	Bakersfield (CAL)	HiA	.260	106	407	68	106	21	2	32	87	29	137	16	5	.316	.558
2016	Jackson (SL)	AA	.293	130	492	68	144	26	4	24	102	62	150	12	2	.374	.508
Minor League Totals			.276	325	1230	181	339	63	9	70	244	124	399	35	11	.349	.512

3 LUIZ GOHARA, LHP

Born: July 31, 1996. **B-T:** L-L. **Ht.:** 6-3. **Wt.:** 215. **Signed:** Brazil, 2012. **Signed by:**
Emilio Carrasquel/Hide Sueyoshi.

The Mariners signed Gohara for $880,000 as a 16-year international free agent out of Brazil in 2012 based on a fastball that could already reach 94 mph, but in succeeding years he frustrated the organization as his weight ballooned to 250 pounds and he showed little work ethic or dedication to competing on the mound. He finally had a breakthrough and shed 30 pounds in 2016 after being ticketed for extended spring training for the fourth straight year. Gohara's rededication to his fitness led to a jump in his stuff across the board. His fastball now sits 95-98 mph and gets up to 100 after he previously struggled to maintain those velocities. His slurvy slider

BA GRADE

55 Risk: High

became a mid-80s swing-and-miss pitch with increased velocity and depth, in large part because of added strength and stability in his lower half after cutting weight from his upper body. His three-quarters arm slot and improved stuff made him difficult to square up even after a midseason promotion to low Class A Clinton. Lefties in particular had a tough time with Gohara, hitting .227/.261/.295 off him. His fastball-slider combo gives him two future plus to double-plus pitches, and his changeup progressed to fringe-average as learned to take velocity off while keeping the same arm speed. His control comes and goes, though it improved with his newfound focus on repeating his delivery and mechanics. His total package was on display in the Arizona Fall League, where Gohara posted a 3.86 ERA with 19 strikeouts and just three walks in 11.2 innings despite being on the youngest pitchers in the league. Gohara is finally moving in the right direction to reach his No. 2 or 3 starter potential. He will begin 2017 at high Class A Modesto.

Year	Club (League)	Class	W	L	ERA	G	GS	CG	SV	IP	H	HR	BB	SO	K/9	WHIP	AVG
2014	Mariners (AZL)	R	1	1	2.13	2	2	0	0	13	11	0	2	16	11.4	1.03	.234
	Everett (NWL)	SS	0	6	8.20	11	11	0	0	37	46	6	24	37	8.9	1.88	.293
2015	Clinton (MWL)	LoA	0	1	1.86	2	2	0	0	10	10	0	6	5	4.7	1.66	.294
	Everett (NWL)	SS	3	7	6.20	14	14	0	0	54	67	4	32	62	10.4	1.84	.305
2016	Everett (NWL)	SS	2	0	1.76	3	3	0	0	15	13	1	3	21	12.3	1.04	.224
	Clinton (MWL)	LoA	5	2	1.82	10	10	0	0	54	44	1	20	60	9.9	1.18	.223
Minor League Totals			12	19	4.40	48	48	0	0	205	213	13	96	228	10.0	1.51	.267

4 NICK NEIDERT, RHP

Born: Nov. 20, 1996. **B-T:** R-R. **Ht.:** 6-1. **Wt.:** 180. **Drafted:** HS—Suwanee, Ga., 2015 (2nd round). **Signed by:** Dustin Evans.

The Mariners made Neidert their first selection in 2015 and signed the Georgia prep for an above-slot $1.2 million. His slight frame but competitive nature draws comparisons with Tim Hudson. Neidert added velocity after a full offseason in the Mariners system, with a fastball frequently hitting 94 mph now after previously registering 90-92. He locates his fastball in every quadrant and excels at using it to get ahead immediately as a first-pitch strike. His low-80s changeup shows deception and fade, and he is developing feel for his slider, now a low-80s offering increasingly becoming a swing-and-miss pitch. What separates Neidert is exceptional command and an aggressive approach that keeps his pitch counts low and hitters on their heels. Neidert posted the third-lowest WHIP in the league from the time he debuted and throwing 69 percent of his pitches for strikes. He also made major strides holding runners and fielding his position. Neidert's increased velocity and stuff ups his ceiling to a No. 3 or 4 starter. He will begin 2017 at high Class A Modesto.

BA GRADE
50 Risk: High

Year	Club (League)	Class	W	L	ERA	G	GS	CG	SV	IP	H	HR	BB	SO	K/9	WHIP	AVG
2015	Mariners (AZL)	R	0	2	1.53	11	11	0	0	35	25	1	9	23	5.9	0.96	.198
2016	Clinton (MWL)	LoA	7	3	2.57	19	19	0	0	91	75	7	13	69	6.8	0.97	.225
Minor League Totals			7	5	2.28	30	30	0	0	126	100	8	22	92	6.6	0.97	.218

5 MITCH HANIGER, OF

Born: Dec. 23, 1990. **B-T:** R-R. **Ht.:** 6-2. **Wt.:** 215. **Drafted:** Cal Poly, 2012 (1st round supplemental). **Signed by:** Dan Huston (Brewers).

Originally drafted 38th overall by the Brewers in 2012, Haniger moved to the Diamondbacks in a deal for Gerardo Parra in July 2014 and then to the Mariners after the 2016 season (with two others) for Taijuan Walker and Jean Segura. He led the minors with a .999 OPS in 2016 and received his first major league callup. Haniger overhauled his swing mechanics after he was demoted from Double-A to high Class A in 2015, using D-backs all-star A.J. Pollock as a template. He changed his load and swing path, added a leg kick and continued his revisions throughout 2016. The result was improved pitch recognition and the ability to use all fields by keeping the bat in the zone longer. With plenty of raw power and good bat speed, Haniger makes consistent hard contact. Observers believe more in-game power could come when he gets the timing on his new leg kick down. He's a good athlete who is a tick above-average runner, with good range, and his above-average arm allows him to play all three outfield positions effectively. Haniger is in good shape to crack the Mariners' Opening Day roster and help give them a righthanded power threat in the outfield.

BA GRADE
50 Risk: High

Year	Club (League)	Class	AVG	G	AB	R	H	2B	3B	HR	RBI	BB	SO	SB	CS	OBP	SLG
2014	Huntsville (SL)	AA	.255	67	243	41	62	7	1	10	34	19	41	4	0	.316	.416
	Diamondbacks (AZL)	R	.200	4	15	4	3	1	0	1	4	1	6	0	0	.250	.467
	Mobile (SL)	AA	.333	8	24	5	8	3	0	0	5	3	4	0	0	.433	.458
2015	Mobile (SL)	AA	.281	55	153	23	43	10	1	1	19	16	32	4	4	.351	.379
	Visalia (CAL)	HiA	.332	49	202	40	67	16	3	12	36	17	39	8	2	.381	.619
2016	Mobile (SL)	AA	.294	55	197	21	58	14	2	5	30	30	37	4	3	.407	.462
	Reno (PCL)	AAA	.341	74	261	58	89	20	3	20	64	39	62	8	1	.428	.670
	Arizona (NL)	MAJ	.229	34	109	9	25	2	1	5	17	12	27	0	0	.309	.404
Major League Totals			.229	34	109	9	25	2	1	5	17	12	27	0	0	.309	.404
Minor League Totals			.290	455	1617	277	469	111	15	61	268	189	326	38	12	.370	.490

6 ANDREW MOORE, RHP

Born: Jan. 2, 1994. **B-T:** R-R. **Ht.:** 6-0. **Wt.:** 185. **Drafted:** Oregon State, 2015 (2nd round supplemental). **Signed by:** Jeff Sakamoto.

Moore was a two-time All-American at Oregon State who routinely confounded Pacific-12 Conference hitters despite subpar velocity. The Mariners made him supplemental second-round pick in 2015 and signed him for $800,000. Moore possesses an uncanny ability to read swings and put any of his four pitches where he wants them, working quickly and drawing early weak contact to mow through batting orders. His fastball sits 90-91 mph but has one of the highest spin rates in the organization, making it appear faster than it actually is. His breaking pitches are average to fringe-average because his feel for them comes and goes, and his changeup grades as merely solid-average. Despite pedestrian stuff on the surface, Moore dominated hit-

BA GRADE
45 Risk: Medium

ters and held up deep into games all year at high Class A Bakersfield and Double-A Jackson, highlighted by a nine-inning, one-hit, no walk, eight-strikeout performance in Game One of the Southern League semifinals. "Cerebral" is a word often used to describe Moore, with double-plus command and control at his disposal. Moore projects as a reliable back-of-the-rotation option and will either begin 2017 back at Double-A or Triple-A Tacoma depending on his spring-training performance.

Year	Club (League)	Class	W	L	ERA	G	GS	CG	SV	IP	H	HR	BB	SO	K/9	WHIP	AVG
2015	Everett (NWL)	SS	1	1	2.08	14	8	0	0	39	37	2	2	43	9.9	1.00	.250
2016	Bakersfield (CAL)	HiA	3	1	1.65	9	9	0	0	55	36	2	13	47	7.7	0.90	.188
	Jackson (SL)	AA	9	3	3.16	19	19	1	0	108	112	9	18	86	7.1	1.20	.274
Minor League Totals			13	5	2.54	42	36	1	0	202	185	13	33	176	7.8	1.08	.247

7 DREW JACKSON, SS

Born: July 28, 1993. **B-T:** R-R. **Ht.:** 6-2. **Wt.:** 200. **Drafted:** Stanford, 2015 (5th round). **Signed by:** Stacey Pettis.

The younger brother of ex-big leaguer Brett Jackson, Drew hit .184 with a 37 percent strikeout rate his first two seasons at Stanford but got contact lenses before his junior year. With his vision fixed he hit .320 as a junior and the Mariners were convinced enough to make him a fifth-round pick in 2015 and sign him for $335,400. Jackson's double-plus arm strength and speed are the foremost attributes that attract clubs to him. His arm alone makes him a potentially above-average defender despite inconsistent footwork and body positioning. His speed is elite out of the batter's box and often turns routine grounders into singles, but he is still learning to improve his jumps and reads on the basepaths. After stealing 47 bases at short-season Everett in 2015, he stole just 16 at high Class A Bakersfield in 2016 as pitchers paid closer attention to him. Jackson's offensive upside is his biggest question mark, with evaluators routinely grading him a fringe-average hitter with below-average power. His timing and feel for the barrel have been questioned since college, and he got out of his approach repeatedly in 2016, swinging for the fences rather than keeping the ball on the ground and letting his speed work. Jackson has all the tools but needs to prove he can hit to reach his everyday potential. He will start 2017 at Double-A Arkansas as he tries to do just that.

BA GRADE
50 Risk: High

Year	Club (League)	Class	AVG	G	AB	R	H	2B	3B	HR	RBI	BB	SO	SB	CS	OBP	SLG
2015	Everett (NWL)	SS	.358	59	226	64	81	12	1	2	26	30	35	47	4	.432	.447
2016	Bakersfield (CAL)	HiA	.258	124	524	87	135	24	2	6	47	50	105	16	8	.332	.345
Minor League Totals			.288	183	750	151	216	36	3	8	73	80	140	63	12	.363	.376

8 MAX POVSE, RHP

Born: Aug. 23, 1993. **B-T:** R-R. **Ht.:** 6-8. **Wt.:** 220. **Drafted:** UNC Greensboro, 2014 (3rd round). **Signed by:** Billy Best (Braves).

Like many tall pitchers, the 6-foot-8 Povse struggled with his mechanics when he was younger and slumped to a 5.38 career ERA in college. Undeterred, the Braves saw promise and drafted Povse 102nd overall in 2014, signing him for $425,000. The Mariners acquired Povse and fellow righthander Rob Whalen from Atlanta after the 2016 season when they parted ways with struggling 2014 first-rounder Alex Jackson. Povse has grown into his long limbs and earned midseason promotions in each of his first two full seasons. He has learned to repeat his delivery and uses his height to generate a good downhill plane on his pitches, which leads to an above-average ground ball rate. His fastball sits 89-92 mph and can get up to 94, while his big overhand curveball and changeup both project with improving depth to average or slightly above. He throws all of his pitches for strikes and uses his long limbs to hide the ball well, helping his stuff play up and limiting hard contact. Povse evokes comparisons with Doug Fister as a 6-foot-8, strike-throwing ground-ball aficionado. He will begin 2017 at Double-A Arkansas with a chance to rise quickly.

BA GRADE
50 Risk: High

BILL MITCHELL

Year	Club (League)	Class	W	L	ERA	G	GS	CG	SV	IP	H	HR	BB	SO	K/9	WHIP	AVG
2014	Danville (APP)	R	4	2	3.42	12	11	0	0	47	42	1	11	37	7.0	1.12	.235
2015	Rome (SAL)	LoA	4	2	2.56	12	12	0	0	60	50	2	16	50	7.5	1.11	.226
	Carolina (CAR)	HiA	1	3	9.33	5	5	0	0	18	24	0	7	10	4.9	1.69	.316
2016	Carolina (CAR)	HiA	5	5	3.71	15	15	0	0	87	89	5	17	91	9.4	1.21	.262
	Mississippi (SL)	AA	4	1	2.93	11	11	0	0	71	61	4	12	48	6.1	1.03	.236
Minor League Totals			18	13	3.59	55	54	0	0	283	266	12	63	236	7.5	1.16	.247

9 DAN ALTAVILLA, RHP

Born: Sept. 8, 1992. **B-T:** R-R. **Ht.:** 5-11. **Wt.:** 200. **Drafted:** Mercyhurst (Pa.), 2014 (5th round). **Signed by:** Mike Moriarty.

The Mariners drafted Altavilla and signed him for $250,000 after he was named the 2014 Division II pitcher of the year at Mercyhurst (Pa.). After progressing through the low minors as a starter, Altavilla converted to relief in 2016. Altavilla's move to the bullpen went even better than expected. He began pitching from the stretch full-time to simplify his delivery and saw his velocity spike. His fastball improved from 93-95 mph as a starter to 96-98 and touching 100 as a reliever, with a devastating plus-plus 89-92 mph slider as his putaway pitch. Altavilla rode his fastball-slider combo to become a Southern League all-star closer at Double-A Jackson and jumped straight to the majors in August, where he allowed only one run in 15 outings. He occasionally flashed a hard, below-average 89-93 mph changeup, but rarely needed it with his other two pitches consistently generating swings and misses and weak contact. Altavilla also earned plaudits for his composure pitching during the Mariners' playoff push. His control is just average, but his elite velocity and movement induces batters to swing through his stuff. Altavilla has a spot in the Mariners' 2017 bullpen and projects long-term as an elite setup man for closer Edwin Diaz.

BA GRADE
45 Risk: Medium

Year	Club (League)	Class	W	L	ERA	G	GS	CG	SV	IP	H	HR	BB	SO	K/9	WHIP	AVG
2014	Everett (NWL)	SS	5	3	4.36	14	14	0	0	66	74	7	32	66	9.0	1.61	.288
2015	Bakersfield (CAL)	HiA	6	12	4.07	28	28	1	0	148	138	11	53	134	8.1	1.29	.246
2016	Jackson (SL)	AA	7	3	1.91	43	0	0	16	57	40	3	22	65	10.3	1.09	.196
	Seattle (AL)	MAJ	0	0	0.73	15	0	0	0	12	11	0	1	10	7.3	0.97	.244
Major League Totals			0	0	0.73	15	0	0	0	12	11	0	1	10	7.3	0.97	.244
Minor League Totals			18	18	3.69	85	42	1	16	271	252	21	107	265	8.8	1.32	.247

10 DAN VOGELBACH, 1B

Born: Dec. 17, 1992. **B-T:** L-R. **Ht.:** 6-0. **Wt.:** 250. **Drafted:** HS—Fort Myers, Fla., 2011 (2nd round). **Signed by:** Lukas McKnight (Cubs).

The Cubs drafted Vogelbach 68th overall in 2011 after he showed prodigious power as a prep. The Mariners acquired him and righthander Paul Blackburn from Chicago in exchange for lefthander Mike Montgomery and righty Jordan Pries in July 2016. Vogelbach has battled injuries but produced in the minors when healthy, posting a career .871 OPS. He controls the strike zone well enough to project as an average hitter and is increasingly tapping into his above-average power. He hit 20 home runs for the first time in 2016 and Seattle rewarded him with his first major league callup in September. He struggles to make contact against lefthanders but is still able to get on base against them with his advanced, patient approach, making him more than just a platoon option. He is a well below-average defender and runner due to his hefty 6-foot frame, but the Mariners believe he can play a suitable first base with the offense he provides. With the probable free agent departures of Adam Lind and Dae-Ho Lee, Vogelbach will contend for a platoon share of the Mariners' first-base job in 2017.

BA GRADE
45 Risk: Medium

Year	Club (League)	Class	AVG	G	AB	R	H	2B	3B	HR	RBI	BB	SO	SB	CS	OBP	SLG
2014	Daytona (FSL)	HiA	.268	132	482	71	129	28	1	16	76	66	91	4	4	.357	.429
2015	Cubs (AZL)	R	.455	5	11	4	5	2	0	0	0	6	1	0	0	.647	.636
	Tennessee (SL)	AA	.272	76	254	41	69	16	1	7	39	57	61	1	1	.403	.425
2016	Iowa (PCL)	AAA	.318	89	305	53	97	18	2	16	64	55	67	0	0	.425	.548
	Tacoma (PCL)	AAA	.240	44	154	26	37	7	0	7	32	42	34	0	0	.404	.422
	Seattle (AL)	MAJ	.083	8	12	0	1	0	0	0	0	1	6	0	0	.154	.083
Major League Totals			.083	8	12	0	1	0	0	0	0	1	6	0	0	.154	.083
Minor League Totals			.286	544	1958	306	560	118	7	83	355	336	393	12	10	.391	.481

11 JOE RIZZO, 3B

BA GRADE
55 Risk: Extreme

Born: March 31, 1998. **B-T:** L-R. **Ht.:** 5-9. **Wt.:** 194. **Drafted:** HS—Vienna, Va., 2016 (2nd round). **Signed by:** Ross Vecchio.

Rizzo was considered one of the best pure high school hitters in the 2016 draft with exceptional feel for the barrel and a strong swing that played against any velocity. The Mariners drafted him 50th overall and signed him for $1.5 million to forgo a South Carolina commitment. Rizzo combines his natural knack for hitting with a patient approach that helps him work counts and get his pitch to hit, which he rarely misses. He is a plus hitter in the eyes of scouts both inside and outside the organization. He shows above-average to plus raw power in batting practice that plays average in games, although he should develop more power with natural physical maturity over time. Defensively, Rizzo is a question mark at third base with a thick build that made some teams want to try him at catcher. The Mariners have been happy with his early performance at third, including better-than-expected range and an average arm. He has a grinder personality and strong work ethic, so there is belief he will put the work in to become an average third baseman. Regardless of how his defense develops, Rizzo's bat will be what carries him. He will start 2017 in extended spring training before reporting to short-season Everett.

Year	Club (League)	Class	AVG	G	AB	R	H	2B	3B	HR	RBI	BB	SO	SB	CS	OBP	SLG
2016	Mariners (AZL)	R	.291	39	148	21	43	7	1	2	21	17	36	2	1	.355	.392
Minor League Totals			.291	39	148	21	43	7	1	2	21	17	36	2	1	.355	.392

12 RYAN YARBROUGH, LHP

BA GRADE
45 Risk: Medium

Born: Dec. 31, 1992. **B-T:** R-L. **Ht.:** 6-5. **Wt.:** 205. **Drafted:** Old Dominion, 2014 (4th round). **Signed by:** Devitt Moore.

The Mariners selected Yarbrough as a senior sign in 2014 and inked him for a below-slot $40,000, and the polished lefty has proven a good value. He keeps damage to a minimum with an array of ground-ball-oriented pitches. Yarbrough's 90-93 mph fastball has downward angle out of his 6-foot-5 frame and plays like a sinker, and he is continually developing feel for a changeup that flashes plus. His slider upgraded to average and he keeps it down and mixes it well off his other two pitches. His ability to keep pitches down in the zone helped him flourish in the hitter-friendly California League in 2015 and successfully make the jump to Double-A in 2016, where he earned Southern League pitcher-of-the-year honors after leading the circuit in wins (12) and ranking second in both ERA (3.16) and WHIP (1.11). He missed the final two weeks of 2016 while on the disabled list with a strained groin. Yarbrough is especially tough on lefthanders, who struggled to a .183/.250/.275 line against him in 2016. He will begin 2017 at Triple-A Tacoma and could reach the majors quickly as a reliever with his sinker-changeup combination and strong splits against lefties. If he continues to develop his slider, he becomes a back-of-the-rotation option.

Year	Club (League)	Class	W	L	ERA	G	GS	CG	SV	IP	H	HR	BB	SO	K/9	WHIP	AVG
2014	Pulaski (APP)	R	0	0	0.00	2	0	0	1	4	1	0	1	5	11.3	0.50	.071
	Everett (NWL)	SS	0	1	1.40	12	10	0	0	39	25	1	4	53	12.3	0.75	.180
2015	Mariners (AZL)	R	0	0	1.80	4	4	0	0	10	11	0	1	13	11.7	1.20	.282
	Clinton (MWL)	LoA	0	1	13.50	2	2	0	0	5	12	0	4	1	1.7	3.00	.462
	Bakersfield (CAL)	HiA	4	7	3.76	16	16	0	0	81	86	7	18	74	8.2	1.28	.266
2016	Jackson (SL)	AA	12	4	2.95	25	25	1	0	128	112	7	31	99	6.9	1.11	.232
Minor League Totals			16	13	3.09	61	57	1	1	268	247	15	59	245	8.2	1.14	.241

13 D.J. PETERSON, 1B

BA GRADE
45 Risk: Medium

Born: Dec. 31, 1991. **B-T:** R-R. **Ht.:** 6-1. **Wt.:** 210. **Drafted:** New Mexico, 2013 (1st round). **Signed by:** Chris Pelekoudas.

Peterson led the nation with a 1.327 OPS his junior season at New Mexico and was drafted 12th overall by the Mariners in 2013. He was derailed after being hit by a pitch that broke his jaw in eight places in his pro debut. Afterward Peterson became noticeably skittish in the box and bailed out against inside fastballs. Despite that, his quick wrists and natural strength helped him produce in the low minors. He hit 31 home runs in 2014, his first full season, but that total shrunk to seven homers at Double-A in 2015 as advanced pitchers began to exploit him. Back at Jackson for a third straight season in 2016, Peterson took heed of an organization-wide emphasis on cutting down strikeouts. With a refined approach focused on selectivity, his natural bat speed and strength flourished, and he visibly appeared more confident, resulting in a promotion to Triple-A Tacoma and 19 homers. He remains a fringe-average hitter, but possesses above-average power and is showing he can once again get to it. That has become especially important after he moved from third base to first base exclusively. Peterson's 2016 season ended after breaking his left pinky finger fielding a ground ball on Aug. 22, and he will start 2017 back at Triple-A Tacoma.

Year	Club (League)	Class	AVG	G	AB	R	H	2B	3B	HR	RBI	BB	SO	SB	CS	OBP	SLG
2014	High Desert (CAL)	HiA	.326	65	273	51	89	23	1	18	73	23	65	6	0	.381	.615
	Jackson (SL)	AA	.261	58	222	32	58	8	0	13	38	22	51	1	1	.335	.473
2015	Jackson (SL)	AA	.223	93	358	39	80	19	2	7	44	31	90	5	0	.290	.346
	Tacoma (PCL)	AAA	.214	4	14	0	3	1	0	0	0	0	3	0	1	.214	.286
2016	Jackson (SL)	AA	.271	73	277	31	75	21	0	11	43	27	68	1	1	.340	.466
	Tacoma (PCL)	AAA	.253	46	178	26	45	7	1	8	35	11	51	0	1	.307	.438
Minor League Totals			.270	394	1530	215	413	90	5	70	280	134	370	14	5	.334	.473

14 THYAGO VIEIRA, RHP

BA GRADE
55 Risk: Extreme

Born: July 1, 1993. **B-T:** R-R. **Ht.:** 6-2. **Wt.:** 210. **Signed:** Brazil, 2010. **Signed by:** Emilio Carrasquel/Hide Sueyoshi.

Vieira signed with the Mariners for $65,000 as a raw 17-year-old international free agent in 2010. Early in his career he showed arm strength and not much else, and he was best known for closing for Brazil's 2012-2013 World Baseball Classic teams. He finally made a developmental leap in 2016 under high Class A Bakersfield pitching coach Ethan Katz. Katz streamlined Vieira's delivery to allow his arm to power through free of moving parts, and the result was a consistent 96-100 mph fastball that hit 102 at the end of the season. His command also improved dramatically to average, and his 89-92 mph slider sharpened to become an above-average pitch. The result was the highest strikeout rate (10.8 per nine innings), lowest walk rate (3.7), fewest hit batters (two) and lowest ERA (2.84) of Vieira's career in 2016. He had one midsummer stretch where he didn't allow an earned run for six weeks as Bakersfield's closer, and overall he allowed only one home run all season. The Mariners rewarded him with an assignment to the Arizona Fall League, where he touched 104 mph with his fastball and began flashing a promising curveball as well. Vieira has to prove he can maintain his delivery and command, but his raw stuff is that of a dominant late-inning reliever or closer. He will start 2017 at Double-A Arkansas.

Year	Club (League)	Class	W	L	ERA	G	GS	CG	SV	IP	H	HR	BB	SO	K/9	WHIP	AVG
2014	Clinton (MWL)	LoA	1	1	5.23	13	0	0	1	21	16	1	14	23	10.0	1.45	.232
2015	Clinton (MWL)	LoA	1	4	6.97	22	0	0	0	31	35	2	20	22	6.4	1.77	.287
2016	Bakersfield (CAL)	HiA	1	0	2.84	34	0	0	8	44	37	1	18	53	10.8	1.24	.222
Minor League Totals			12	15	4.71	108	28	0	9	237	235	8	125	192	7.3	1.52	.265

15 BRADEN BISHOP, OF

BA GRADE
50 Risk: High

Born: Aug. 22, 1993. **B-T:** R-R. **Ht.:** 6-1. **Wt.:** 190. **Drafted:** Washington, 2015 (3rd round). **Signed by:** Jeff Sakamoto.

Bishop was a premium athlete recruited in football as a Division I wide receiver out of high school but ultimately took the baseball route at Washington. The premier athleticism, speed and reflexes that made him a successful receiver show up consistently in center field, where he gets to every ball in every direction and is consistently regarded as the top defensive outfielder in the Mariners system. His double-plus speed and plus arm round him into a defender so complete evaluators believe his defense alone can make him a game-changing everyday center fielder in the majors. Bishop's development as a hitter has not progressed as quickly. The Mariners adjusted his load to get him in a better position to strike the ball after drafting him and saw progress in his ability to make contact. He will show himself to be an average hitter at times with little power, but with his plus speed and elite defensive ability projects to possibly be a major leaguer in the mold of Kevin Pillar on the high end. Bishop will start 2017 at high Class A Modesto.

Year	Club (League)	Class	AVG	G	AB	R	H	2B	3B	HR	RBI	BB	SO	SB	CS	OBP	SLG
2015	Everett (NWL)	SS	.320	56	219	34	70	8	1	2	22	5	33	13	3	.367	.393
2016	Clinton (MWL)	LoA	.290	63	248	38	72	5	1	1	21	25	48	6	1	.363	.331
	Bakersfield (CAL)	HiA	.247	41	166	19	41	6	0	2	22	11	39	2	0	.300	.319
Minor League Totals			.289	160	633	91	183	19	2	5	65	41	120	21	4	.348	.349

16 BRAYAN HERNANDEZ, OF

BA GRADE
55 Risk: Extreme

Born: Sept. 11, 1997. **B-T:** R-R. **Ht.:** 6-2. **Wt.:** 175. **Signed:** Venezuela, 2014. **Signed by:** Tim Kissner/Emilio Carrasquel/Illitch Salazar.

The Mariners signed Hernandez for $1.85 million as a 17-year old in 2014 but received disappointing early returns in 2015. As such, the Mariners ended his switch-hitting and had him bat only from his natural right side starting in 2016 and saw an uptick in performance and confidence. Hernandez ranked among the Dominican Summer League leaders in extra-base hits and steals when the Mariners moved him to the Rookie-level Arizona League. He continued to perform in the AZL, hitting .285 and starting in right field for the Mariners team that won the league title. Hernandez has a pure swing from the right side that allows him to make solid, consistent contact, though he doesn't generate much power. He is a plus runner with a plus arm, allowing him to play either center field or right if necessary. He has a chance to be a plus defender in center. Opposing scouts doubt Hernandez will hit for enough power to stick in a corner, but the Mariners believe he may develop average power over time as he matures physically. He sometimes gets too pull-happy in his approach and has trouble with offspeed pitches but could grow out of those traits with experience. Hernandez will begin 2017 in extended spring training before heading to short-season Everett.

Year	Club (League)	Class	AVG	G	AB	R	H	2B	3B	HR	RBI	BB	SO	SB	CS	OBP	SLG
2015	Mariners2 (DSL)	R	.224	50	174	32	39	8	2	2	22	18	44	9	6	.295	.328
2016	Mariners (DSL)	R	.278	31	133	30	37	6	2	5	15	10	23	12	2	.331	.466
	Mariners (AZL)	R	.285	33	130	13	37	8	2	1	19	7	36	9	3	.324	.400
Minor League Totals			.259	114	437	75	113	22	6	8	56	35	103	30	11	.314	.391

17 ROB WHALEN, RHP

BA GRADE
45 Risk: Medium

Born: Jan. 31, 1994. **B-T:** R-R. **Ht.:** 6-2. **Wt.:** 200. **Drafted:** HS—Haines City, Fla. (12th round). **Signed by:** Mike Silvestri (Mets).

The Mets were intrigued by Whalen's pitchability as a prep and signed him away from a Florida Atlantic commitment for $100,000, and Whalen has shown they were onto something. The Braves acquired him from the Mets at the 2015 trade deadline, and he made his major league debut with Atlanta in 2016 before the Mariners acquired him after the season with Max Povse in exchange for Alex Jackson. Whalen succumbed to severe patellar tendinitis in both knees shortly after joining the Braves in 2015, but returned to health and led the Braves system with a 2.40 ERA across Double-A and Triple-A before making five starts in the majors at the end of the season. He has a deep six-pitch repotoire, including both four-seam and two-seam fastballs in the low 90s with sink, two different curveballs with one harder than the other, a solid-average slider and a changeup. He is a cerebral pitcher who relies more on his guile than stuff, but the sinking action on his fastballs gives him a chance to stick as a ground-ball oriented spot starter or long reliever. He will likely begin 2017 in Triple-A Tacoma's rotation and see time in Seattle during the season.

Year	Club (League)	Class	W	L	ERA	G	GS	CG	SV	IP	H	HR	BB	SO	K/9	WHIP	AVG
2014	Mets (GCL)	R	0	1	1.29	3	2	0	0	7	4	0	2	10	12.9	0.86	.160
	Savannah (SAL)	LoA	9	1	2.01	11	10	0	0	63	44	2	19	53	7.6	1.01	.192
2015	St. Lucie (FSL)	HiA	4	5	3.36	15	14	0	0	83	72	4	34	61	6.6	1.28	.231
	Carolina (CAR)	HiA	1	2	3.29	3	3	0	0	14	11	2	4	7	4.6	1.10	.224
2016	Mississippi (SL)	AA	7	5	2.49	18	18	0	0	101	87	4	37	94	8.3	1.22	.232
	Gwinnett (IL)	AAA	0	1	1.93	3	3	0	0	19	12	0	7	18	8.7	1.02	.188
	Atlanta (NL)	MAJ	1	2	6.57	5	5	0	0	25	20	4	12	25	9.1	1.30	.217
Major League Totals			1	2	6.57	5	5	0	0	25	20	4	12	25	9.1	1.30	.217
Minor League Totals			24	17	2.45	66	62	0	0	360	281	13	120	320	8.0	1.11	.212

18 GUILLERMO HEREDIA, OF

BA GRADE
40 Risk: Low

Born: Jan. 30, 1991. **B-T:** R-R. **Ht.:** 5-10. **Wt.:** 180. **Signed:** Cuba, 2016. **Signed by:** Tim Kissner.

Heredia made his name as a two-time gold-glove center fielder in Cuba's Serie Nacional and was the starting center fielder for the Cuban national team in the 2013 World Baseball Classic. He left Cuba in January 2015 and signed with the Mariners in February 2016. Heredia is a defense-first outfielder with an explosive first step and the ability to make both routine plays and spectacular ones. After beginning the year at Double-A Jackson, Heredia received a callup to Seattle for good in August and served as a late-game defensive replacement at both corner-outfield spots down the stretch. His plus defense and above-average arm allow him to play all three outfield spots, though center is where he can best use his speed, superb instincts and extensive range to maximum effect. He is an average hitter with little power who works counts and controls the strike zone well enough to consistently get on base. Heredia profiles as a valuable glove-first fourth outfielder and will fill that role for the Mariners in 2017.

Year	Club (League)	Class	AVG	G	AB	R	H	2B	3B	HR	RBI	BB	SO	SB	CS	OBP	SLG
2014	Matanzas (CNS)	CNS	1.000	1	1	0	1	0	0	0	1	0	0	0	0	1.000	1.000
2015	Did not play																
2016	Jackson (SL)	AA	.293	58	205	39	60	7	2	2	34	36	32	2	5	.405	.376
	Tacoma (PCL)	AAA	.312	35	138	27	43	6	1	2	13	12	15	3	0	.378	.413
	Seattle (AL)	MAJ	.250	45	92	12	23	3	0	1	12	12	15	1	1	.349	.315
Major League Totals			.250	45	92	12	23	3	0	1	12	12	15	1	1	.349	.315
Minor League Totals			.300	93	343	66	103	13	3	4	47	48	47	5	5	.395	.391

19 TONY ZYCH, RHP

BA GRADE
45 Risk: High

Born: Aug. 7, 1990. **B-T:** R-R. **Ht.:** 6-3. **Wt.:** 190. **Drafted:** Louisville, 2011 (4th round). **Signed by:** Tim Adkins (Cubs).

The former Louisville closer was named the Cape Cod League's top prospect in 2010 and signed with the Cubs for $400,000 after being drafted one year later as a junior. He stalled at Double-A after five seasons in the Chicago system and was sold to the Mariners for $1 at the end of spring training in 2015. The fresh start did wonders for Zych, who loosened his delivery and simplified his pitch mix to just his fastball and slider after joining Seattle. The adjustments helped him reach the majors in 2015 and 2016 and record a 2.81 ERA and 12.7 strikeouts per nine innings in 25 appearances. Zych possesses an electric 95-98 mph fastball and a plus 83-86 slider that generated a swinging strike 17 percent of the time it was thrown in the majors in 2016. Zych has the stuff to work as a set-up man, but injuries have held him back from reaching that ceiling. He made the Mariners' Opening Day roster in 2016 but went down with shoulder tendinitis May 1, missed the next three months and made two appearances in August before being shut down again. He had offseason shoulder surgery and is expected to be ready for spring training.

Year	Club (League)	Class	W	L	ERA	G	GS	CG	SV	IP	H	HR	BB	SO	K/9	WHIP	AVG
2014	Tennessee (SL)	AA	4	5	5.09	45	0	0	2	58	75	3	18	35	5.4	1.59	.329
2015	Jackson (SL)	AA	0	0	2.16	15	0	0	5	17	11	0	0	18	9.7	0.66	.186
	Tacoma (PCL)	AAA	1	2	3.41	25	0	0	4	32	34	2	9	37	10.5	1.36	.276
	Seattle (AL)	MAJ	0	0	2.45	13	1	0	0	18	17	1	3	24	11.8	1.09	.239
2016	Mariners (AZL)	R	0	0	0.00	1	1	0	0	1	0	0	1	0	0.0	1.00	.000
	Jackson (SL)	AA	0	0	0.00	1	1	0	0	1	0	0	1	2	18.0	1.00	.000
	Seattle (AL)	MAJ	1	0	3.29	12	0	0	0	14	10	0	10	21	13.8	1.46	.208
	Tacoma (PCL)	AAA	0	0	0.00	3	0	0	0	3	0	0	0	6	18.0	0.00	.000
Major League Totals			1	0	2.81	25	1	0	0	32	27	1	13	45	12.7	1.25	.227
Minor League Totals			15	16	3.63	188	2	0	20	233	231	8	71	207	8.0	1.30	.261

20 BEN GAMEL, OF

BA GRADE

40 Risk: Medium

Born: May 17, 1992. **B-T:** L-L. **Ht.:** 5-11. **Wt.:** 185. **Drafted:** HS—Jacksonville, 2010 (10th round) Signed by: Jeff Deardorff (Yankees).

Gamel, the younger brother of former big leaguer Mat, was drafted by the Yankees in 2010 and signed away from a Florida State commitment for $500,000. He earned the Triple-A International League MVP award in 2016 while playing for the Yankees' affiliate in Scranton-Wilkes Barre and was traded one day after winning the award to the Mariners for promising Rookie-level righthanders Jio Orozco and Juan De Paula. Gamel is undersized but makes hard contact from the left side and drives the ball into the gaps, allowing him to use his above-average speed to generate a high number of doubles and triples. His athleticism, solid-average arm and all-out style of play allow him to play all three outfield spots with above-average ability, but he has spent most of his time in center and left field. He played 24 games in right field for the Mariners after a September callup. Gamel doesn't have enough power to profile as a corner regular, but he is well-rounded enough in his skillset to stick on a major league roster as an oft-used backup. He will be in the mix for that role with the Mariners in 2017.

Year	Club (League)	Class	AVG	G	AB	R	H	2B	3B	HR	RBI	BB	SO	SB	CS	OBP	SLG
2014	Trenton (EL)	AA	.261	131	544	58	142	31	3	2	51	36	88	13	5	.308	.340
2015	Scranton/W-B (IL)	AAA	.300	129	500	77	150	28	14	10	64	46	108	13	5	.358	.472
2016	New York (AL)	MAJ	.125	6	8	1	1	0	0	0	0	1	1	0	0	.222	.125
	Scranton/W-B (IL)	AAA	.308	116	483	80	149	26	5	6	51	43	94	19	8	.365	.420
	Seattle (AL)	MAJ	.200	27	40	8	8	2	0	1	5	5	15	0	0	.289	.325
Major League Totals			.188	33	48	9	9	2	0	1	5	6	16	0	0	.278	.292
Minor League Totals			.288	660	2617	349	754	160	32	26	311	227	514	94	37	.345	.404

21 CHRISTOPHER TORRES, SS

BA GRADE

50 Risk: Extreme

Born: Feb. 6, 1998. **B-T:** B-R. **Ht.:** 5-11. **Wt.:** 170. **Signed:** Dominican Republic, 2014. **Signed by:** Tim Kissner/Eddy Toledo/Kelvin Dominguez.

Torres signed with the Mariners for $375,000 as a 17-year-old. After spending 2015 in the Dominican Summer League, he made his U.S. debut in 2016 and lived up to his reputation as a defense-first shortstop with impressive range and intriguing defensive tools. He is a smart defender who positions himself well and has tremendous instincts, which is amplified by his athleticism to go get anything hit in his zone. He has a plus arm as well that makes him a true shortstop. Offensively he is further behind, with a singles-oriented stroke from the right side and a poor one from the left that led to a .178 average and .467 OPS in 2016. As a below-average hitter with little power potential and above-average speed, Torres fits the mold of a potential utility infielder but has youth and time on his side to grow into more offense. He will begin 2017 in extended spring training before heading to short-season Everett.

Year	Club (League)	Class	AVG	G	AB	R	H	2B	3B	HR	RBI	BB	SO	SB	CS	OBP	SLG
2015	Mariners2 (DSL)	R	.251	64	215	40	54	8	3	2	30	51	56	20	9	.399	.344
2016	Mariners (AZL)	R	.257	44	167	31	43	9	4	0	17	19	44	12	4	.337	.359
Minor League Totals			.254	108	382	71	97	17	7	2	47	70	100	32	13	.373	.351

22 BRYSON BRIGMAN, 2B/SS

Born: June 19, 1995. **B-T:** R-R. **Ht.:** 5-11. **Wt.:** 180. **Drafted:** San Diego, 2016 (3rd round). **Signed by:** Gary Patchett.

Brigman boasts an athletic track record few can compete with. He was a standout hockey player in his youth and his father Vince was a pitcher at Pacific. Brigman chose baseball over hockey in high school and became the first player to play for three different USA Baseball championship teams. That athletic track record led to a decorated college career at San Diego and a $700,000 bonus after being taken as a draft-eligible sophomore in 2016. Brigman's athleticism helps him seamlessly play both second base and shortstop and profile as an above-average defender at both. He compensates for a near-average arm with a tremendous internal clock that ensures he makes his throws in time. Offensively he has below-average power but controls the zone well, makes solid contact and draws enough walks to let his above-average speed play on the bases. The Mariners plan to rotate Brigman between second base, shortstop and center field to prepare him for a future utility role. He will begin 2017 at low Class A Clinton.

Year	Club (League)	Class	AVG	G	AB	R	H	2B	3B	HR	RBI	BB	SO	SB	CS	OBP	SLG
2016	Everett (NWL)	SS	.260	68	265	51	69	6	1	0	19	41	43	17	12	.369	.291
Minor League Totals			.260	68	265	51	69	6	1	0	19	41	43	17	12	.369	.291

23 THOMAS BURROWS, LHP

Born: Sept. 14, 1994. **B-T:** L-L. **Ht.:** 6-1. **Wt.:** 205. **Drafted:** Alabama, 2016 (4th round). **Signed by:** Jay Catalano.

Burrows became Alabama's all-time saves leader as a junior in 2016 and finished a decorated three-year college career with a 2.20 ERA, 30 saves and 113 strikeouts in 102.1 innings before signing for $450,000. He showed a 94 mph fastball and hard-biting slider with the Crimson Tide but struggled with fatigue once in pro ball and saw his velocity decrease to 87-90 mph. His slider, more of a low-80s hard slurve, also lost some bite and velocity but is an above-average pitch when at full strength. Burrows still recorded a 2.55 ERA in 20 games in his pro debut at short-season Everett. He pitches from the first-base side of the rubber, making him exceptionally difficult for lefthanders, and his average changeup helps neutralize righthanders. His overall command needs work, but his track record of success makes the Mariners optimistic he can rise quickly and eventually be a bullpen option. He will begin 2017 at low Class A Clinton.

Year	Club (League)	Class	W	L	ERA	G	GS	CG	SV	IP	H	HR	BB	SO	K/9	WHIP	AVG
2016	Everett (NWL)	SS	0	1	2.55	20	0	0	6	25	23	1	11	37	13.5	1.38	.240
Minor League Totals			0	1	2.55	20	0	0	6	25	23	1	11	37	13.5	1.38	.240

24 LUIS LIBERATO, OF

Born: Dec. 18, 1995. **B-T:** L-L. **Ht.:** 6-1. **Wt.:** 175. **Signed:** Dominican Republic, 2012. **Signed by:** Tim Kissner/Franklin Tavares Jr.

Liberato signed for $140,000 as a 17-year-old international free agent in 2012 and climbed the minor league ladder since. He shows flashes of multi-tool potential and has developed into a plus defender in center field with above-average speed and instincts, but his bat continues to develop slowly while injuries hamper him. Liberato missed 40 games in 2016 because of two separate disabled-list stints for pulled hamstrings, which followed a leg injury that cost him a month in 2015. Liberato possesses a pure lefthanded swing he uses to drive the ball into the gaps for doubles and triples, but he struggles to make consistent contact. His power grades as below-average, and his raw speed generated just four stolen bases in 2016. Liberato is increasingly starting to profile as defense-driven fourth or fifth outfielder, but he has a chance to give his offense a jolt in the California League at high Class A Modesto in 2016.

Year	Club (League)	Class	AVG	G	AB	R	H	2B	3B	HR	RBI	BB	SO	SB	CS	OBP	SLG
2014	Mariners (AZL)	R	.211	49	175	28	37	6	3	2	14	29	47	14	2	.325	.314
2015	Clinton (MWL)	LoA	.133	8	30	3	4	1	1	0	0	2	10	1	0	.188	.233
	Jackson (SL)	AA	.000	3	10	0	0	0	0	0	0	0	2	0	0	.000	.000
	Everett (NWL)	SS	.260	53	181	34	47	10	5	5	31	24	47	10	3	.341	.453
2016	Clinton (MWL)	LoA	.258	100	372	65	96	19	8	2	29	47	100	4	2	.340	.368
Minor League Totals			.243	270	972	169	236	44	20	11	91	125	256	43	15	.330	.363

25 BRANDON MILLER, RHP

BA GRADE
45 Risk: High

Born: June 16, 1995. **B-T:** R-R. **Ht.:** 6-4. **Wt.:** 210. **Drafted:** Millersville (Pa.), 2016 (6th round). **Signed by:** Ross Vecchio.

The Mariners discovered Miller because they had kept an eye on the Division II Pennsylvania State Athletics Conference after successfully finding Mercyhurst (Pa.) righthander Dan Altavilla in 2014. Miller went 12-2, 1.42 with 115 strikeouts and 13 walks in 107.2 innings in 2016 to lead Millersville (Pa.) to a No. 1 ranking in D-II and a national runner-up finish. He tossed a complete game with five hits and one earned run and seven strikeouts in the opener of the D-II World Series and was drafted by the Mariners a week later, signing for $250,000. He kept up his dominance in pro ball, recording a 2.72 ERA and 51-to-7 strikeout-to-walk ratio in 56.1 innings at short-season Everett. Miller works off an 89-91 mph fastball that gets up to 93 with an elite spin rate, while his 80-83 mph slider grades as a plus pitch that also features excellent spin and a high whiff percentage. His curveball and changeup are currently below-average but project to average with further development. Miller's balanced four-pitch mix, poise and durability project him to a back-of-the-rotation starter, and he has a chance to skip low Class A Clinton altogether and begin 2017 at high Class A Modesto.

Year	Club (League)	Class	W	L	ERA	G	GS	CG	SV	IP	H	HR	BB	SO	K/9	WHIP	AVG
2016	Everett (NWL)	SS	4	2	2.72	14	13	0	0	56	47	3	7	51	8.1	0.96	.226
Minor League Totals			4	2	2.72	14	13	0	0	56	47	3	7	51	8.1	0.96	.226

26 CARLOS VARGAS, SS

BA GRADE
50 Risk: Extreme

Born: March 18, 1999. **B-T:** R-R. **Ht.:** 6-3. **Wt.:** 190. **Signed:** Dominican Republic, 2015. **Signed by:** Tim Kissner/Scott Hunter/Eddy Toledo.

The Mariners made Vargas the gem of their 2015 international class when they signed him for $1.625 million as a 16-year-old. Vargas, the younger brother of Diamondbacks minor league righthander Emilio Vargas, has a broad-shouldered build with strong wrists that help him generate exceptional raw power, which projects to plus and shows up in games. He hit two home runs in the MLB international showcase prior to signing, finished tied for third in home runs in the Dominican Summer League in his pro debut and was the MVP of the DSL all-star game after hitting a two-run triple. He did that while playing a better-than-expected shortstop that included highlight-reel plays on par with the system's top defenders. Vargas' below-average speed and sizable frame make him a probable third baseman once he fills out, but his power and excellent plate discipline should allow him to project at acorner. Vargas could face another season in the DSL in 2017 before moving to the Rookie-level Arizona League, though he could follow the path of Brayan Hernandez and Christopher Torres and head to the U.S.

Year	Club (League)	Class	AVG	G	AB	R	H	2B	3B	HR	RBI	BB	SO	SB	CS	OBP	SLG
2016	Mariners (DSL)	R	.242	62	215	41	52	11	0	7	35	32	35	2	0	.344	.391
Minor League Totals			.242	62	215	41	52	11	0	7	35	32	35	2	0	.344	.391

27 TAYLOR MOTTER, SS/OF

BA GRADE
40 Risk: Low

Born: Sept. 18, 1989. **B-T:** R-R. **Ht.:** 6-1. **Wt.:** 195. **Drafted:** Coastal Carolina, 2011 (17th round). **Signed by:** Brad Matthews (Rays).

Motter partnered with Tommy La Stella in the middle of Coastal Carolina's infield in college before the Rays signed him as a junior. They moved him all over the diamond defensively, moving him into a utility role, and he started coming into his power when he got to Double-A. Added to the 40-man roster after a boffo 2015 that included 43 doubles with Triple-A Durham, Motter flopped in 2016, even though he made his major league debut. Tampa traded him and Richie Shaffer to the Mariners in a November deal for non-40-man righties Andrew Kittredge and Dylan Thompson and first baseman Dalton Kelly. Motter's athleticism and versatility are his best traits. He has a plus arm that plays on the left side of the infield or in right field, and the above-average speed to play up the middle. Motter has average power but his swing and approach get too big. Always noted for playing with some flair, Motter had scouts questioned his effort in 2016. That won't fly if he wants to seize a big league utility spot in 2017.

Year	Club (League)	Class	AVG	G	AB	R	H	2B	3B	HR	RBI	BB	SO	SB	CS	OBP	SLG
2014	Montgomery (SL)	AA	.274	119	452	60	124	19	3	16	61	34	71	15	7	.326	.436
2015	Durham (IL)	AAA	.292	127	486	74	142	43	1	14	72	57	95	26	8	.366	.471
2016	Tampa Bay (AL)	MAJ	.188	33	80	11	15	3	0	2	9	11	19	0	1	.290	.300
	Durham (IL)	AAA	.229	88	350	44	80	17	0	13	46	33	65	19	4	.297	.389
Major League Totals			.188	33	80	11	15	3	0	2	9	11	19	0	1	.290	.300
Minor League Totals			.272	552	1981	284	538	125	8	56	263	232	351	127	41	.349	.428

28 JAMES PAZOS, LHP

BA GRADE
40 Risk: Medium

Born: May 5, 1991. **B-T:** R-L. **Ht.:** 6-3. **Wt.:** 230. **Drafted:** San Diego, 2012 (13th round). **Signed by:** David Keith (Yankees).

The Yankees drafted and signed Pazos for $100,000 out of San Diego in 2012 and he quickly rose through their system in the bullpen, reaching the majors in 2015 and again in 2016, when he struggled. The Mariners traded for Pazos after the 2016 season giving up righy Zack Littell. Pazos sits 95-98 mph with his fastball and 81-84 with his slider, but both have proven hittable to major league batters due to lack of command. Pazos has struggled with deep pitch counts and has to improve his below-average fastball command. Still, the Mariners see promise in Pazos' raw stuff and the .152/.250/.217 line to which he held lefthanded batters at Triple-A. He will have every chance to win a spot in the 2017 big league bullpen as a matchup reliever.

Year	Club (League)	Class	W	L	ERA	G	GS	CG	SV	IP	H	HR	BB	SO	K/9	WHIP	AVG
2014	Tampa (FSL)	HiA	0	2	3.96	18	1	0	4	25	23	0	6	33	11.9	1.16	.237
	Trenton (EL)	AA	0	1	1.50	28	0	0	6	42	28	0	19	42	9.0	1.12	.190
2015	Trenton (EL)	AA	0	0	1.86	6	0	0	1	10	4	1	0	12	11.2	0.41	.129
	Scranton/W-B (IL)	AAA	3	1	1.09	21	0	0	2	33	25	0	15	37	10.1	1.21	.208
	New York (AL)	MAJ	0	0	0.00	11	0	0	0	5	3	0	3	3	5.4	1.20	.176
2016	Scranton/W-B (IL)	AAA	2	2	2.63	23	0	0	1	27	19	1	19	41	13.5	1.39	.194
	New York (AL)	MAJ	1	0	13.50	7	0	0	0	3	7	2	1	3	8.1	2.40	.438
Major League Totals			1	0	5.40	18	0	0	0	8	10	2	4	6	6.5	1.68	.303
Minor League Totals			10	9	2.30	151	1	0	18	215	159	5	88	243	10.2	1.15	.204

29 TYLER MARLETTE, C

BA GRADE
40 Risk: High

Born: Jan. 23, 1993. **B-T:** R-R. **Ht.:** 5-11. **Wt.:** 195. **Drafted:** HS—Oviedo, Fla., 2011 (5th round). **Signed by:** Rob Mummau.

Marlette was a high school showcase standout as a power-hitting catcher, and the Mariners drafted and signed him away from a Central Florida commitment for $650,000. After a strong start to his pro career, he hit a wall as he ballooned out of shape and his 5-foot-11 frame became pudgy. Assigned back to high Class A for the third straight season in 2016, Marlette got into visibly better shape with improved core strength and demonstrated better emotional and mental maturity in all parts of his game. He made strides in his game-calling while showing an above-average arm and improved blocking. At the plate he showed a more disciplined plate approach, which led to a new career high in walks and continued offensive success after an August promotion to Double-A Jackson. Marlette possesses plus raw power to go with improving defensive tools. He still needs to improve his below-average receiving but is trending back up and will begin 2017 at Double-A Arkansas.

Year	Club (League)	Class	AVG	G	AB	R	H	2B	3B	HR	RBI	BB	SO	SB	CS	OBP	SLG
2014	High Desert (CAL)	HiA	.301	81	312	51	94	23	0	15	49	24	61	9	2	.351	.519
	Jackson (SL)	AA	.250	9	32	3	8	2	0	2	2	4	10	0	1	.333	.500
2015	Bakersfield (CAL)	HiA	.216	39	148	17	32	5	1	5	20	12	35	2	1	.284	.365
	Jackson (SL)	AA	.258	50	178	15	46	13	1	3	12	10	31	0	0	.298	.393
2016	Bakersfield (CAL)	HiA	.273	83	326	42	89	21	1	14	53	30	82	5	3	.335	.472
	Jackson (SL)	AA	.300	15	50	4	15	2	0	1	6	3	11	1	0	.333	.400
Minor League Totals			.276	422	1574	195	434	100	5	51	204	113	343	30	13	.326	.443

30 DONNIE WALTON, 2B/SS

BA GRADE
40 Risk: High

Born: May 25, 1994. **B-T:** B-R. **Ht.:** 5-10. **Wt.:** 184. **Drafted:** Oklahoma State, 2016 (5th round). **Signed by:** Ty Bowman.

Walton was a two-time all-Big 12 Conference shortstop for the Cowboys as well as a multi-year team captain and academic all-conference honoree. The Mariners drafted him as a senior and signed him for $125,000 after he helped lead the Cowboys back to the College World Series for the first time since 1999. He earns raves for his tremendous instincts that help his average tools play up. He has above-average bat speed and surprising strength in his wiry frame—particularly from the left side. He is a patient hitter who doesn't miss his pitch. Walton's speed is also average, but excellent baserunning ability makes him an efficient stolen-base threat. He positions himself well defensively and effectively handles both shortstop and second base, though his fringe-average arm fits better at second. The Mariners plan to develop Walton as versatile, switch-hitting utility infielder. He will begin 2017 at low Class A Clinton.

Year	Club (League)	Class	AVG	G	AB	R	H	2B	3B	HR	RBI	BB	SO	SB	CS	OBP	SLG
2016	Everett (NWL)	SS	.281	43	178	43	50	8	1	5	23	22	24	6	0	.361	.421
Minor League Totals			.281	43	178	43	50	8	1	5	23	22	24	6	0	.361	.421

Tampa Bay Rays

BY HUDSON BELINSKY

The 2016 season continued the Rays' downward trajectory. They held their own for most of the first half, but Tampa Bay lost 24 of 27 games in a disastrous monthlong midseason slump.

The Rays finished in a three-way tie for the second-worst record in baseball at 68-94, their worst mark since 2007.

Tampa Bay's pitching staff has been its biggest strength in recent years because the Rays have had success identifying young pitchers. As major league home run totals spiked, however, the Rays have not adjusted. The team's six starters in 2016 each posted career-worst home run rates.

Chris Archer, who had established himself as the ace of the staff, saw his home run rate jump from 0.8 per nine inning in 2015 to 1.3 in 2016. Archer's performance bounced back somewhat in the second half, but long after the Rays' postseason hopes evaporated.

The Rays weren't the only team affected by baseball's increased home run rate, but its effect on the team was as damning for them as it was for any team in the game.

On the bright side, Tampa Bay's core remains intact. It traded Matt Moore to the Giants in July in a deal that netted shortstop Matt Duffy and two prospects, but the Rays still have a deep pitching staff, their clearest path to contention. Archer should improve his home run rate, rookie lefthander Blake Snell shows promise, and the Rays can round out their rotation with veterans Jake Odorizzi, Drew Smyly and Alex Cobb.

The offense had bright spots, including a bounce-back year by Evan Longoria, but the Rays still finished 14th in the American League in runs in 2016.

Perhaps most encouraging is the help that's on the way. The Rays have a growing group of potential contributors in the upper minors. Shortstop Willy Adames, first baseman Casey Gillaspie and outfielder/first baseman Jake Bauers all project as above-average or better offensive players in the near future, while righthander Brent Honeywell could provide a significant jolt to the front of the rotation in short order.

Righthanders Chih-Wei Hu, Jacob Faria, Jaime Schultz and Ryne Stanek could all reach major league readiness in 2017. Versatile infielder Daniel Robertson could contribute as well.

The lower levels of the organization also offer plenty of promise, led by high-ceiling high school prospects in 2015 first-rounder Garrett Whitley, an outfielder, and third baseman Josh Lowe, their

CLIFF WELCH

Rookie Blake Snell struck out 98 batters in 89 innings with a plus changeup and curveball

TOP PROSPECTS OF THE DECADE

Year	Player, Pos.	2016 Org
2007	Delmon Young, of	Did not play
2008	Evan Longoria, 3b	Rays
2009	David Price, lhp	Red Sox
2010	Desmond Jennings, of	Rays
2011	Matt Moore, lhp	Giants
2012	Matt Moore, lhp	Giants
2013	Wil Myers, of/3b	Padres
2014	Jake Odorizzi, rhp	Rays
2015	Willy Adames, ss	Rays
2016	Blake Snell, lhp	Rays

2016 first-rounder. Internationally, the Rays have added slugging shortstop Adrian Rondon and tooled-up outfielder Jesus Sanchez to a system that now boasts significant upside. Lucius Fox, a shortstop acquired in the Moore deal, also brings an explosive toolset to the table.

The Rays retooled their front office as well, with Erik Neander, now the general manager, and Chaim Bloom promoted to oversee baseball operations, with team president Matt Silverman focusing on "long-term priorities." Their work is cut out for them because they compete in the rugged AL East. The Rays must shrewdly acquire talent in the amateur markets and successfully navigate the trade market. The foundation appears to be in place for the Rays to succeed, especially if some of their high-risk, high-reward prospects pan out.

ORGANIZATION OVERVIEW

President: Matt Silverman. **GM:** Erik Neander. **Farm director:** Mitch Lukevics. **Scouting director:** Rob Metzler.

Class	Team	League	W	L	PCT	Finish	Manager
Majors	Tampa Bay Rays	American	68	94	.420	14th (15)	Kevin Cash
Triple-A	Durham Bulls	International	64	80	.444	12th (14)	Jared Sandberg
Double-A	Montgomery Biscuits	Southern	76	64	.543	3rd (10)	Brady Williams
High Class A	Charlotte Stone Crabs	Florida State	64	71	.474	9th (12)	Michael Johns
Low Class A	Bowling Green Hot Rods	Midwest	84	55	.604	t-2nd (16)	Reinaldo Ruiz
Short-season	Hudson Valley Renegades	New York-Penn	47	27	.635	2nd (14)	Tim Parenton
Rookie	Princeton Rays	Appalachian	38	29	.567	3rd (10)	Danny Sheaffer
Rookie	GCL Rays	Gulf Coast	28	31	.475	9th (17)	Jim Morrison
Overall 2016 Minor League Record			401	357	.529	7th (30)	

THIS YEAR'S TOP 30

No.	Player, Pos.	Grade/Risk
1.	Willy Adames, ss	60/Medium
2.	Brent Honeywell, rhp	60/Medium
3.	Casey Gillaspie, 1b	55/Medium
4.	Jake Bauers, of/1b	55/Medium
5.	Chih-Wei Hu, rhp	55/Medium
6.	Josh Lowe, 3b/of	65/Extreme
7.	Jesus Sanchez, of	60/Extreme
8.	Jacob Faria, rhp	50/Low
9.	Justin Williams, of	55/High
10.	Garrett Whitley, of	55/Extreme
11.	Austin Franklin, rhp	55/Extreme
12.	Jaime Schultz, rhp	45/Medium
13.	Ryne Stanek, rhp	45/Medium
14.	Adrian Rondon, ss/3b	55/Extreme
15.	Daniel Robertson, ss/3b	40/Low
16.	Lucius Fox, ss	55/Extreme
17.	Taylor Guerrieri, rhp	45/Medium
18.	Greg Harris, rhp	50/High
19.	Kevin Padlo, 3b	50/High
20.	Joe McCarthy, of/1b	45/High
21.	Nick Ciuffo, c	45/High
22.	Ryan Boldt, of	45/High
23.	Jake Fraley, of	45/High
24.	David Rodriguez, c	45/High
25.	Kevin Gadea, rhp	50/Extreme
26.	Chris Betts, c	50/Extreme
27.	Hunter Wood, rhp	45/High
28.	Jose Alvarado, lhp	50/Extreme
29.	Austin Pruitt, rhp	40/Medium
30.	Resly Linares, lhp	50/Extreme

LAST YEAR'S TOP 30

No.	Player, Pos.	Status
1.	Blake Snell, lhp	Majors
2.	Willy Adames, ss	No. 1
3.	Brent Honeywell, rhp	No. 2
4.	Jake Bauers, of/1b	No. 4
5.	Garrett Whitley, of	No. 10
6.	Mikie Mahtook, of	Majors
7.	Taylor Guerrieri, rhp	No. 17
8.	Jacob Faria, rhp	No. 8
9.	Casey Gillaspie, 1b	No. 3
10.	Daniel Robertson, ss	No. 15
11.	Richie Shaffer, 3b/of	(Mariners)
12.	Ryan Brett, 2b	Dropped out
13.	Justin O'Conner, c	Dropped out
14.	German Marquez, rhp	(Rockies)
15.	Chris Betts, c	No. 26
16.	Chih-Wei Hu, rhp	No. 5
17.	Justin Williams, of	No. 9
18.	Adrian Rondon, ss	No. 14
19.	Brandon Koch, rhp	Dropped out
20.	Andrew Bellati, rhp	Dropped out
21.	Taylor Motter, inf/of	(Mariners)
22.	Tyler Goeddel, of	(Phillies)
23.	Jaime Schultz, rhp	No. 12
24.	Hunter Wood, rhp	No. 27
25.	Jake Hager, ss	Dropped out
26.	Nick Ciuffo, c	No. 21
27.	Luke Maile, c	Majors
28.	Thomas Milone, of	Dropped out
29.	Enny Romero, lhp	Majors
30.	Jose Mujica, rhp	Dropped out

BEST TOOLS

Best Hitter for Average	Jake Bauers
Best Power Hitter	Casey Gillaspie
Best Strike-Zone Discipline	Casey Gillaspie
Fastest Baserunner	Jake Fraley
Best Athlete	Josh Lowe
Best Fastball	Ryne Stanek
Best Curveball	Austin Franklin
Best Slider	Jaime Schultz
Best Changeup	Chih-Wei Hu
Best Control	Austin Pruitt
Best Defensive Catcher	Nick Ciuffo
Best Defensive Infielder	Willy Adames
Best Infield Arm	Josh Lowe
Best Defensive Outfielder	Jake Fraley
Best Outfield Arm	Eleardo Cabrera

PROJECTED 2020 LINEUP

Catcher	Nick Ciuffo
First Base	Jake Bauers
Second Base	Brad Miller
Third Base	Evan Longoria
Shortstop	Willy Adames
Left Field	Justin Williams
Center Field	Kevin Kiermaier
Right Field	Josh Lowe
Designated Hitter	Casey Gillaspie
No. 1 Starter	Chris Archer
No. 2 Starter	Blake Snell
No. 3 Starter	Brent Honeywell
No. 4 Starter	Jake Odorizzi
No. 5 Starter	Chih-Wei Hu
Closer	Jaime Schultz

MINOR LEAGUE DEPTH CHART

TAMPA BAY RAYS

TOP 2017 ROOKIE: Casey Gillaspie, 1b. Big power and a patient approach should enable the 2014 fist-rounder to claim a share of the first-base job during the season.
BREAKOUT PROSPECT: Lucius Fox, ss: Acquired from the Giants at the 2016 trade deadline, Fox comes armed with explosive tools.
SLEEPER: Benton Moss, rhp. His well-rounded arsenal allowed him to jump from the 2015 draft to high Class A in 2016.

SOURCE OF TOP 30 TALENT			
Homegrown	22	Acquired	8
College	7	Trades	8
Junior college	2	Rule 5 draft	0
High school	7	Independent leagues	0
Nondrafted free agents	0	Free agents/waivers	0
International	6		

LF
Jake Bauers (4)
Justin Williams (9)
Nathan Lukes

CF
Jesus Sanchez (7)
Garrett Whitley (10)
Ryan Boldt (22)
Jake Fraley (23)
Johnny Field
Thomas Milone

RF
Josh Lowe (6)
Eleardo Cabrera
Moises Gomez
Diego Infante

3B
Adrian Rondon (14)
Kevin Padlo (19)
Cristian Toribio

SS
Willy Adames (1)
Lucius Fox (16)
Andrew Velazquez
Michael Russell

2B
Daniel Robertson (15)
Kean Wong
Jake Cronenworth
Riley Unroe

1B
Casey Gillaspie (3)
Joe McCarthy (20)
Nathaniel Lowe

C
Nick Ciuffo (21)
David Rodriguez (24)
Chris Betts (26)
Jonah Heim

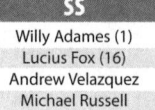

LHP

LHSP	LHRP
Resly Linares (30)	Jose Alvarado (28)
Genesis Cabrera	Kyle Bird
Chris Kirsch	Travis Ott
Brock Burke	Steve Ascher
Luis Moncada	

RHP

RHSP	RHRP
Brent Honeywell (2)	Jaime Schultz (12)
Chih-Wei Hu (5)	Ryne Stanek (13)
Jacob Faria (8)	Hunter Wood (27)
Austin Franklin (11)	Diego Castillo
Taylor Guerrieri (17)	Ryan Garton
Greg Harris (18)	Dylan Floro
Kevin Gadea (25)	Jhonleider Salinas
Austin Pruitt (29)	Ian Gibaut
Yonny Chirinos	Brandon Koch
Jose Mujica	Angel Felipe
Easton McGee	Deivy Mendez
Zach Trageton	
Adrian Navas	

DRAFT ANALYSIS

2016

BEST PURE HITTER: The Rays feel that 3B Josh Lowe (1) has a chance to develop into a strong hitter as he matures, given his strike zone awareness and the looseness of his swing, though he will have to make more consistent contact. OF Ryan Boldt (2) has a steady offensive track record, and OF Jake Fraley (3) has shown the ability to make contact despite moving parts in his swing.

BEST POWER: Lowe shows plus raw power, with fast hands and long arms that allow him to generate exceptional torque when he makes contact. He has the ability to drive the ball over the fence or hit hard line drives from gap to gap. His older brother, 1B Nathan Lowe (12) is strong-bodied and can also show impressive power.

FASTEST RUNNER: Fraley runs very well, both on the basepaths and in the outfield. He can reach first in 4.1 seconds and he recognizes opportunities to steal bases and capitalizes on them. Lowe is also a plus runner.

BEST DEFENSIVE PLAYER: Fraley's defensive instincts and ability to close gaps give him a chance to be a plus defender in center field. SS Kevin Santiago (20) stands out for his defensive actions at shortstop.

BEST ATHLETE: Lowe is high-waisted with bat speed, arm strength, power and speed. Fraley is also quick-twitch. Boldt is strong and fast as well.

BEST FASTBALL: RHP Austin Franklin (4) can reach 95 with his heater. RHP J.D. Busfield (7) has reached as high as 96, but pitches lower than that and has excellent sink and downhill angle to make the pitch effective. RHP Peter Bayer (9) has fastball life and gets lots of swings and misses at 91-94. RHP Matt Vogel (25) can reach 95 as well.

BEST SECONDARY PITCH: Franklin's curveball has deep vertical snap, and it showed improved power during his debut, when he ran it up to the upper 70s. RHP Zach Trageton (6) and LHP Kenny Rosenberg (8) both earn praise for their changeups.

BEST PRO DEBUT: Bayer's performance in the Rookie-level Appalachian League was outstanding; he struck out 45 and walked just three batters in 32 innings. Bayer allowed 18 hits and three earned runs. Also in Princeton, RHP Brian McAfee (38) had an ERA under 2.00 and struck out 12 batters per walk. RHP Joe Serrapica (24) didn't allow a single run in 22 innings out of the bullpen for Hudson Valley.

MOST INTRIGUING BACKGROUND: OF Isaac Benard (23) is the son of former major leaguer Marvin Benard.

CLOSEST TO THE MAJORS: The Rays don't draft with major league proximity in mind, and they tend to take a slow-and-steady approach to development. Fraley's advanced defensive package would make him the closest to ready on paper.

BEST LATE-ROUND PICK: Santiago's impressive defense sticks out from the group. The Rays like the offensive potential of Nathan Lowe, 2B Miles Mastrobuoni (14) and 3B Jim Haley (19)

THE ONE WHO GOT AWAY: LHP Zack Thompson (11) has athleticism, arm strength and the ability to spin his breaking ball. He could develop into a very good player at Kentucky.

2015

Top picks OF Garrett Whitley (1) and C Chris Betts (2) will need long development paths because both are raw offensively. College picks such as RHP Benton Moss (6) and SS/2B Jake Cronenworth (7) have lower ceilings but are potential big league role players.

GRADE: D

2014

RHP Brent Honeywell (2s) immediately jumped to the head of this class, but 1B Casey Gillaspie (1) got in gear in 2016 and finished in Triple-A. SS Michael Russell (5) is an intriguing utility option.

GRADE: B

2013

Top pick C Nick Ciuffo (1) is a fine defender who needs time to develop. RHPs Ryne Stanek (1), Austin Pruitt (9) and Jaime Schultz (14) all have reached Triple-A, as has OF Johnny Field (5).

GRADE: C

TOP DRAFT PICKS OF THE DECADE

Year	Player, Pos.	2016 Org
2007	David Price, lhp	Red Sox
2008	Tim Beckham, ss	Rays
2009	*LeVon Washington, of	American Association
2010	Josh Sale, of	Did not play
2011	Taylor Guerrieri, rhp	Rays
2012	Richie Shaffer, 3b	Rays
2013	Nick Ciuffo, c	Rays
2014	Casey Gillaspie, 1b	Rays
2015	Garrett Whitley, of	Rays
2016	Josh Lowe, 3b	Rays

* Did not sign

LARGEST BONUSES IN CLUB HISTORY

Matt White, 1996	$10,200,000
Rolando Arrojo, 1997	$7,000,000
Tim Beckham, 2008	$6,150,000
David Price, 2007	$5,600,000
B.J. Upton, 2002	$4,600,000

1 WILLY ADAMES, SS

Born: Sept. 2, 1995. **B-T:** R-R. **Ht.:** 6-1. **Wt.:** 180.
Signed: Dominican Republic, 2012.
Signed by: Aldo Perez/Ramon Perez/Miguel Garcia (Tigers).

BA GRADE
60 Risk Medium

SCOUTING GRADES

Batting: 60.
Power: 55.
Speed: 50.
Defense: 55.
Arm: 55.

Based on 20-80 scouting scale and future projection rather than present grades.

MIKE JANES

The Rays' 2014 trade of David Price signaled a transition from one era to another, as the organization soon saw a change of management and leadership in the baseball operations department. Adames, the lone prospect acquired in the Price trade, has since established himself as the Rays' top prospect, and he's put himself in the discussion among the best position prospects in baseball. Signed as an international free agent by the Tigers for $420,000 in 2012, Adames advanced through the low minors rapidly. The Tigers skipped him past their domestic Rookie-level affiliates and assigned him to low Class A West Michigan for his U.S. debut as an 18-year-old in 2014. After heading to the Rays as the centerpiece of the Price trade, Adames hit the ground running, and he's made steady progress and adjustments as he's climbed the minor league ladder. He reached Double-A Montgomery in 2016 and led the Southern League with 74 walks and ranked third with 31 doubles. He led all SL shortstops with 11 home runs and earned a spot in the Futures Game.

In 2014, Adames showed power to his pull side and the ability to drive the ball to the wall in center field. His power has steadily developed as he's matured physically, and in 2016 he showed the ability to drive the ball out to the opposite field in game situations. Offensively, Adames earns plus grades for his hit tool and raw power, though scouts see his power playing more in the way of hard line drives, with annual home run total projections ranging from 15-25. He has above-average bat speed and the loose wrists to control the barrel, make late adjustments and square up pitches with late movement. He shows both the ability to stay inside the ball and to turn on inside pitches. He works deep counts and isn't afraid of hitting with two strikes. Adames' timing at the plate has improved from year to year, and his strikeout rate declined to 21 percent in 2016, down from 27 percent in 2015. Defensively, he continued to endear himself to scouts in 2016. Adames has plus hands and a well-timed internal clock, and he doesn't rush plays or play nervously in the field. He lacks exceptional range and explosive foot speed, and he's more of an average runner on the basepaths,

but his pure arm strength typically plays above-average. He has an ability to get his feet set and make accurate throws consistently, though he can flash plus arm strength when needed. In addition to his well-rounded assortment of tools, Adames has exceptional makeup, both in terms of his work ethic and character. He quickly achieved fluency in English and connects well with American players as well as other Latin Americans. Rays officials laud his leadership ability and enthusiasm for game-day preparation.

Overall, Adames has the total package that teams look for in top prospects, with impact tools on both sides of the ball and the personality to become a marketable franchise player. In 2017, Adames figures to spend the season at Triple-A Durham. He projects as the Rays' shortstop of the future, with the ability to hit somewhere in the middle of the lineup.

Year	Club (League)	Class	AVG	G	AB	R	H	2B	3B	HR	RBI	BB	SO	SB	CS	OBP	SLG
2014	West Michigan (MWL)	LoA	.269	98	353	40	95	14	12	6	50	39	96	3	6	.346	.428
	Bowling Green (MWL)	LoA	.278	27	97	15	27	5	2	2	11	15	30	3	0	.377	.433
2015	Charlotte, FL (FSL)	HiA	.258	106	396	51	102	24	6	4	46	54	123	10	1	.342	.379
2016	Montgomery (SL)	AA	.274	132	486	89	133	31	6	11	57	74	121	13	6	.372	.430
Minor League Totals			.265	423	1532	243	406	86	31	24	185	238	414	38	25	.366	.409

2 BRENT HONEYWELL, RHP

Born: March 31, 1995. **B-T:** R-R. **Ht.:** 6-2. **Wt.:** 180. **Drafted:** Walters State (Tenn.) CC, 2014 (2nd round supplemental). **Signed by:** Brian Hickman.

Undrafted out of high school, Honeywell established himself as a prospect as a junior college freshman in 2014. He built his legend with his screwball, a pitch he learned from his father, who learned it from his cousin, former Dodgers reliever Mike Marshall. Honeywell's velocity jumped in junior college, and the Rays selected him in the supplemental second round. Honeywell has a well-rounded arsenal, with five pitches he can throw for strikes. His plus fastball works in the mid-90s and shows late life to induce weak contact. He has shown feel for his plus changeup and screwball, with the latter showing more fade and horizontal movement. His average curveball shows occasional bite and his cutter was a developmental focus in 2016. He missed six weeks in the middle of the summer with forearm soreness, but his fastball reached 97 mph in his first start back. Honeywell succeeded at Double-A Montgomery to close 2016, and will probably repeat that level to start 2017 before heading to Triple-A Durham.

BA GRADE 60 Risk: Medium

Year	Club (League)	Class	W	L	ERA	G	GS	CG	SV	IP	H	HR	BB	SO	K/9	WHIP	AVG
2014	Princeton (APP)	R	2	1	1.07	9	8	0	0	34	19	1	6	40	10.7	0.74	.161
2015	Bowling Green (MWL)	LoA	4	4	2.91	12	12	0	0	65	53	3	12	76	10.5	1.00	.221
	Charlotte (FSL)	HiA	5	2	3.44	12	12	1	0	65	57	2	15	53	7.3	1.10	.235
2016	Charlotte (FSL)	HiA	4	1	2.41	10	10	0	0	56	43	5	11	64	10.3	0.96	.211
	Montgomery (SL)	AA	3	2	2.28	10	10	0	0	59	51	4	14	53	8.0	1.10	.231
Minor League Totals			18	10	2.58	53	52	1	0	279	223	15	58	286	9.2	1.01	.217

3 CASEY GILLASPIE, 1B

Born: Jan. 25, 1993. **B-T:** B-R. **Ht.:** 6-4. **Wt.:** 240. **Drafted:** Wichita State, 2014 (1st round). **Signed by:** J.D. Elliby.

The younger brother of Giants third baseman Conor Gillaspie, Casey batted .389 as a Wichita State junior in 2014 while hitting 15 home runs. The Rays selected him 20th overall and signed him for a tick more than $2 million. A midseason hand injury interrupted his first full season, and he struggled after returning. Fully healthy in 2016, Gillaspie hit 18 home runs and drew 80 walks in a season split between Double-A Montgomery and Triple-A Durham. Gillaspie has a chance to impact the game offensively, with a blend of power and plate discipline as a switch-hitter with plus power potential. Gillaspie lacks elite bat speed from either side, but he is exceptionally strong and recognizes pitches that he's able to drive. In spite of his average bat speed, Gillaspie has shown the ability to turn on upper-90s fastballs. Offensively, he projects to have a high on-base and slugging percentages. While he's a modest athlete, Gillaspie has sound footwork at first base and creates a big target for infielders. He is an inferior runner. The Rays see Gillasie as a long-term solution at first base, with the ability hit in the middle of the lineup. He will have to hit his way out of Durham first.

BA GRADE 55 Risk: Medium

Year	Club (League)	Class	AVG	G	AB	R	H	2B	3B	HR	RBI	BB	SO	SB	CS	OBP	SLG
2014	Hudson Valley (NYP)	SS	.262	71	263	27	69	16	1	7	42	42	65	2	3	.364	.411
2015	Bowling Green (MWL)	LoA	.278	64	234	37	65	11	0	16	44	28	43	4	0	.358	.530
	Rays (GCL)	R	.000	2	6	0	0	0	0	0	0	0	2	0	0	.143	.000
	Charlotte (FSL)	HiA	.146	13	41	3	6	0	1	1	4	4	9	0	0	.222	.268
2016	Montgomery (SL)	AA	.270	85	293	51	79	21	0	11	41	58	79	5	1	.387	.454
	Durham (IL)	AAA	.307	47	179	27	55	13	2	7	23	22	38	0	1	.389	.520
Minor League Totals			.270	282	1016	145	274	61	4	42	154	154	236	11	5	.367	.462

4 JAKE BAUERS, OF/1B

Born: Oct. 6, 1995. **B-T:** L-L. **Ht.:** 6-1. **Wt.:** 195. **Drafted:** HS—Huntington Beach, Calif., 2013 (7th round). **Signed by:** Josh Emmerick (Padres).

Bauers excelled as a Southern California prep hitter in 2013, coming out of the same Marina High program that produced Daric Barton. The Padres drafted Bauers then challenged him with an assignment to the low Class A Midwest League in 2014. He held his own and was one of the headline prospects of the three-team trade that sent Wil Myers to San Diego. Bauers' plus lefthanded bat is his best asset. He has loose wrists, a knack for making hard contact and he consistently takes competitive at-bats. Bauers has plus bat control and has posted low strikeout rates throughout his career. Despite his routine hard contact, he has yet to show plus

BA GRADE 55 Risk: Medium

over-the-fence power in games. He has a stout, compact build with shorter levers, and his bat path is geared more for line drives. He has plus raw power that must play plus to fit his corner profile. Bauers is an excellent defensive first baseman, but he played right field while he and Casey Gillaspie were teammates in 2016. His sound baseball instincts and solid-average speed play well in the outfield corners. Bauers proved himself as a 20-year-old at Double-A Montgomery, and he should advance to Triple-A Durham in 2017. He will challenge for an everyday corner-outfield spot in Tampa Bay by 2017.

Year	Club (League)	Class	AVG	G	AB	R	H	2B	3B	HR	RBI	BB	SO	SB	CS	OBP	SLG
2014	Fort Wayne (MWL)	LoA	.296	112	406	59	120	18	3	8	64	51	80	5	6	.376	.414
2015	Charlotte (FSL)	HiA	.267	59	217	33	58	14	2	6	38	29	33	2	3	.357	.433
	Montgomery (SL)	AA	.276	69	257	36	71	18	0	5	36	21	41	6	3	.329	.405
2016	Montgomery (SL)	AA	.274	135	493	79	135	28	1	14	78	73	89	10	6	.370	.420
Minor League Totals			.280	422	1536	229	430	86	8	34	241	188	274	25	18	.360	.413

5 CHIH-WEI HU, RHP

Born: Nov. 4, 1993. **B-T:** R-R. **Ht.:** 6-1. **Wt.:** 230. **Signed:** Taiwan, 2012. **Signed by:** Cary Broder (Twins).

Signed by the Twins out of Taiwan for $220,000 in 2012, Hu progressed through the low minors on schedule. The Rays acquired him in a July 2015 trade for Kevin Jepsen. He excelled at Double-A Montgomery in 2016, leading the Southern League in ERA (2.59) and pitching in the Futures Game. In short spurts, Hu can show upper-90s fastball velocity and a changeup that humiliates both righthanded and lefthanded batters. His stuff plays a closer to average when he works as a starter. Hu competes and locates in the strike zone with his low- to mid-90s fastball while his mid-80s changeup is thrown with identical arm speed and

BA GRADE

50 Risk: Medium

generates late tumbling action. He also throws a palmball that checks in slightly softer than his changeup, acting as a second change-of-pace. He throws two average breaking pitches: an 11-to-5 curveball with average depth that he throws for strikes and a more horizontal breaking pitch that can be classified as a slider or cutter. Hu should advance to Triple-A Durham in 2017, and he is part of the Rays' long-term plan, possibly as a No. 4 type starter or high-leverage reliever.

Year	Club (League)	Class	W	L	ERA	G	GS	CG	SV	IP	H	HR	BB	SO	K/9	WHIP	AVG
2014	Elizabethton (APP)	R	1	0	1.69	3	3	0	0	16	7	0	2	16	9.0	0.56	.127
	Cedar Rapids (MWL)	LoA	7	2	2.29	10	9	0	0	55	40	0	13	48	7.9	0.96	.201
2015	Rochester (IL)	AAA	1	0	1.50	1	1	0	0	6	2	0	4	6	9.0	1.00	.105
	Fort Myers (FSL)	HiA	5	3	2.44	15	15	0	0	85	79	5	19	73	7.8	1.16	.249
	Charlotte (FSL)	HiA	0	3	7.36	5	4	0	1	18	23	1	8	20	9.8	1.69	.315
2016	Durham (IL)	AAA	0	1	7.71	1	1	0	0	5	7	1	2	7	13.5	1.93	.350
	Montgomery (SL)	AA	7	8	2.59	24	24	0	0	143	128	7	36	107	6.8	1.15	.241
Minor League Totals			23	17	2.74	71	62	0	1	364	314	14	92	316	7.8	1.12	.233

6 JOSH LOWE, 3B/OF

Born: Feb. 2, 1998. **B-T:** L-R. **Ht.:** 6-4. **Wt.:** 190. **Drafted:** HS—Marietta, Ga., 2016 (1st round). **Signed by:** Milt Hill.

Lowe comes from a baseball family. His father David was a fifth-round pick in 1986 and his older brother Nathan, a first baseman, was the Rays' 13th-round pick in 2016 out of Mississippi State. Josh was a prospect as both a hitter and pitcher, offering promising projection with three pitches. The Rays, enamored of Lowe's upside as a position player, selected him 13th overall in June. Lowe has a high-waisted, athletic look with wide, sloped shoulders. He's a lefthanded hitter with plus bat speed and the leverage to generate his raw power. His hands work well and he has shown the ability to generate hard line drives to the gaps or pull high-trajectory

BA GRADE

60 Risk: Extreme

flies over the fence. His long arms and aggressive swings come with swings and misses, but he showed promising strike-zone awareness in his pro debut. Lowe is a plus runner who takes long, graceful strides. He also has plus arm strength. His defense at third base was one of his biggest weaknesses as an amateur, so the Rays tried him in center field in instructional league. While third base may not be out of the question for Lowe, he has excellent tools for the outfield and figures to spend significant time there. His polished offensive skill set could allow him to start at low Class A Bowling Green in 2017.

Year	Club (League)	Class	AVG	G	AB	R	H	2B	3B	HR	RBI	BB	SO	SB	CS	OBP	SLG
2016	Rays (GCL)	R	.258	28	93	14	24	6	1	2	15	20	27	1	1	.386	.409
	Princeton (APP)	R	.238	26	80	11	19	0	2	3	11	17	32	1	1	.360	.400
Minor League Totals			.249	54	173	25	43	6	3	5	26	37	59	2	2	.374	.405

7 JESUS SANCHEZ, OF

Born: Oct. 7, 1997. **B-T:** L-R. **Ht.:** 6-2. **Wt.:** 190. **Signed:** Dominican Republic, 2014. **Signed by:** Danny Santana.

As an amateur, Sanchez originally showcased as a frail switch-hitter. Later in the process he showed improved strength and began hitting exclusively lefthanded. He improved his stock quickly and continued to do so after the Rays signed him for $400,000 in 2014. He hit .329/.351/.549 in 56 games in 2016 at two Rookie levels. Sanchez has an array of tools, but his offensive potential is his most exciting asset. He has a compact swing with balance and rhythm and a well-timed load. He has loose wrists and covers the plate exceptionally well. Sanchez shows rare ability to use the whole field. He has grown into power because he is physically mature, and he projects for plus power. The Rays are impressed with Sanchez's strike-zone awareness and his ability to execute an approach. He is an above-average runner underway, though his first step can be a bit awkward and he'll need to refine his center-field routes and baserunning technique. He has above-average arm strength that he is still learning how to use. Sanchez's loud tools could be refined enough for him to handle an assignment to low Class A Bowling Green at age 19 in 2017.

BA GRADE
60 **Risk:** Extreme

Year	Club (League)	Class	AVG	G	AB	R	H	2B	3B	HR	RBI	BB	SO	SB	CS	OBP	SLG
2015	Rays (DSL)	R	.335	61	239	36	80	13	7	4	45	20	32	8	1	.382	.498
2016	Rays (GCL)	R	.323	42	164	25	53	6	8	4	31	6	31	1	5	.341	.530
	Princeton (APP)	R	.347	14	49	8	17	4	0	3	8	3	12	1	0	.385	.612
Minor League Totals			.332	117	452	69	150	23	15	11	84	29	75	10	6	.368	.522

8 JACOB FARIA, RHP

Born: July 30, 1993. **B-T:** R-R. **Ht.:** 6-4. **Wt.:** 200. **Drafted:** HS—Cerritos, Calif., 2011 (10th round). **Signed by:** Jake Wilson.

The Rays took a shot on Faria as a projectable Southern California prep righthander in 2011, selecting him in the 10th round and signing him away from Cal State Fullerton. He broke out with an excellent 2015 season, when he ranked second in the minors with a 1.92 ERA. Faria didn't dominate in 2016 but still progressed to Triple-A and ranked eighth in the minors with 157 strikeouts. Faria's stuff isn't explosive. His game is founded upon his deception and downhill angle. His fastball works at 89-92 mph and will occasionally reach as high as 94. Faria throws his plus changeup with identical arm speed, and he's able to take off quite a bit of velocity and throw the pitch at 79-81 mph. He isn't afraid to throw his changeup in fastball counts or start hitters off with it. Faria throws two distinct, below-average breaking pitches. He has a curveball that shows longer and deeper break. It works as more of a get-me-over pitch to change hitters' eye levels and set up the rest of his arsenal. He also throws a firmer, fringy breaking ball with low-80s velocity and shorter 12-to-6 break. Faria's delivery isn't smooth but he repeats it and has passable control. Faria's advanced pitchability and deep arsenal are nearly major league ready. He projects to begin 2017 back at Triple-A Durham but could join the Rays in-season.

BA GRADE
50 **Risk:** Medium

Year	Club (League)	Class	W	L	ERA	G	GS	CG	SV	IP	H	HR	BB	SO	K/9	WHIP	AVG
2014	Bowling Green (MWL)	LoA	7	9	3.46	23	23	1	0	120	113	9	32	107	8.0	1.21	.248
2015	Charlotte (FSL)	HiA	10	1	1.33	12	10	0	0	74	51	1	22	63	7.6	0.98	.199
	Montgomery (SL)	AA	7	3	2.51	13	13	0	0	75	52	5	30	96	11.5	1.09	.194
2016	Montgomery (SL)	AA	1	6	4.21	14	14	0	0	83	64	5	36	93	10.0	1.20	.211
	Durham (IL)	AAA	4	4	3.72	13	13	0	0	68	46	7	32	64	8.5	1.15	.190
Minor League Totals			35	31	3.13	106	92	1	0	540	438	36	171	542	9.0	1.13	.221

9 JUSTIN WILLIAMS, OF

Born: Aug. 20, 1995. **B-T:** L-R. **Ht.:** 6-2. **Wt.:** 215. **Drafted:** HS—Houma, La., 2013 (2nd round). **Signed by:** Rusty Pendergrass (Diamondbacks).

The Diamondbacks took a shot on Williams' exceptional raw power in 2013, selecting him 52nd overall and signing him for $1.05 million. The Rays sent Jeremy Hellickson to Arizona to acquire both Williams and Andrew Velazquez after the 2014 season. Williams held his own at low Class A in 2015, then broke out in the Australian Baseball League that winter. That success carried over to 2016, when Williams reached Double-A and hit .295/.318/.447 in 90 games at two stops. Williams is a natural lefthanded hitter with a compact stroke and a knack for barreling the ball. He's shown an aggressive, if not raw, approach and doesn't always

BA GRADE
55 **Risk:** High

wait for pitches that he can drive, but he makes as much hard contact as any Rays prospect. His batting-practice sessions encourage evaluators that he eventually will develop plus power in games. Evaluators credited improved timing for Williams' jump in batting average in 2016, noting that he was able to pull the ball more often. Defensively, he has the tools to be a capable corner outfielder. He is a near-average runner and has average arm strength. Williams' bat proved too potent for the high Class A Florida State League in 2016, and he showed power in a cameo at Double-A Montgomery, where he will begin 2017.

Year	Club (League)	Class	AVG	G	AB	R	H	2B	3B	HR	RBI	BB	SO	SB	CS	OBP	SLG
2014	Missoula (PIO)	R	.386	46	189	31	73	6	2	2	23	17	44	1	1	.433	.471
	South Bend (MWL)	LoA	.284	28	102	16	29	6	3	2	23	7	23	0	1	.348	.461
2015	Bowling Green (MWL)	LoA	.284	99	387	43	110	25	2	7	42	13	76	3	1	.308	.413
	Charlotte (FSL)	HiA	.241	23	83	8	20	5	0	0	6	1	14	3	1	.250	.301
2016	Charlotte (FSL)	HiA	.330	51	194	23	64	11	0	4	31	6	26	0	1	.350	.448
	Montgomery (SL)	AA	.250	39	148	20	37	7	2	6	28	5	30	0	1	.277	.446
Minor League Totals			.310	337	1311	173	406	78	9	22	190	60	257	7	7	.343	.433

10 GARRETT WHITLEY, OF

Born: March 13, 1997. **B-T:** R-R. **Ht.:** 6-1. **Wt.:** 205. **Drafted:** HS—Niskayuna, N.Y., 2015 (1st round). **Signed by:** Tim Alexander.

BA GRADE

55 Risk: Extreme

Whitley wasn't a huge name on the amateur showcase circuit, but he broke out late in the summer as a rising senior, then showed clubs enough in 2015 to put himself in first-round consideration, where the Rays popped him 13th overall. Tampa Bay in 2016 held Whitley back in extended spring training after a hamstring injury, and he reported to short-season Hudson Valley when healthy. Whitley's exposure to high-level competition was extremely limited before he turned pro. He has elite bat speed, with scouts grading it as plus or plus-plus, so he is able to generate plus raw power, though he still is learning how to use it in games. Whitley tinkered with his mechanics at points in 2016, beginning the season with a wide-open stance as he focused on recognizing pitches and tracking the ball deeper into the hitting zone. He is prone to swinging and missing and will sometimes expand his strike zone, though he seemed to have made progress as he got into the routine of playing daily. In his final 30 games, Whitley hit .314/.394/.479. He is a plus runner who runs very well underway, and he showed improved arm strength this summer, with his arm and range in center field grading as above-average. Whitley appears poised for an assignment to low Class A Bowling Green in 2017. He shapes up as a classic boom-or-bust toolsy outfielder.

Year	Club (League)	Class	AVG	G	AB	R	H	2B	3B	HR	RBI	BB	SO	SB	CS	OBP	SLG
2015	Rays (GCL)	R	.188	30	96	12	18	4	2	3	13	16	25	5	4	.310	.365
	Hudson Valley (NYP)	SS	.143	12	42	6	6	0	1	0	4	5	12	3	1	.250	.190
2016	Hudson Valley (NYP)	SS	.266	65	256	38	68	12	7	1	31	30	75	21	5	.356	.379
Minor League Totals			.234	107	394	53	92	16	10	4	48	51	112	29	10	.333	.355

11 AUSTIN FRANKLIN, RHP

BA GRADE

55 Risk: Extreme

Born: Oct. 2, 1997. **B-T:** R-R. **Ht.:** 6-3. **Wt.:** 215. **Drafted:** HS—Paxton, Fla., 2016 (3rd round). **Signed by:** Brett Foley.

After working more in the upper 80s as a rising senior, Franklin became one of the fastest risers in the 2016 draft class after he improved his fastball velocity, sitting in the low 90s and consistently peaking at 95 mph. Franklin's upward trajectory resulted in the Rays drafting him in the third round and signing him for $597,500 to forgo a Samford commitment. He continued his progress after the draft as well, with his curveball adding velocity and power. Franklin has a very short arm action and a sturdy pitcher's frame with wide shoulders and a high waist. He has a tendency to rush off the rubber and swing his front side open, a correctable problem that he has already shown progress toward solving. When Franklin's delivery is timed up, he can pitch downhill with a plus fastball and a plus curveball, and he has shown flashes of a changeup Rays officials are excited about. Franklin headlines the next wave of young pitching prospects coming up through the lower ranks of the Rays' system. Given Tampa's slow-and-steady approach to developing pitchers, Franklin is likely to be brought along slowly, with an assignment to a short-season affiliate likely the next step in his development.

Year	Club (League)	Class	W	L	ERA	G	GS	CG	SV	IP	H	HR	BB	SO	K/9	WHIP	AVG
2016	Rays (GCL)	R	1	2	2.70	11	9	0	1	43	30	0	16	40	8.3	1.06	.192
Minor League Totals			1	2	2.70	11	9	0	1	43	30	0	16	40	8.3	1.06	.192

12 JAIME SCHULTZ, RHP

BA GRADE

45 Risk: Medium

Born: June 20, 1991. **B-T:** R-R. **Ht.:** 5-10. **Wt.:** 200. **Drafted:** High Point, 2013 (14th round). **Signed by:** Brian Hickman.

Schultz wasn't an elite draft prospect when the Rays took a shot at him in the 14th round in 2013, but he has slowly and surely progressed into one of the organization's top arms. His stature may be small, but his stuff is huge. Schultz throws a mid-90s fastball and an exceptionally tight breaking ball, both of which grade as plus. His fastball plays in the strike zone, and his curveball shape varies from 11-to-5 to a more slurvy 10-to-4, consistently showing the late snapping motion to project as a bat-missing offering against even the best breaking ball hitters. Schultz has a fast arm and relatively long arm action and he struggles to repeat the mechanics of his lower half, which results in bouts of wildness. He did, however, reduce his walk rate by more than a batter per inning when he reached Triple-A in 2016, encouraging some evaluators that he could eventually develop the control necessary to be a starter long term. If Schultz's control doesn't continue to improve, his stuff is still good enough for him to find a role as an effectively wild late-inning reliever.

Year	Club (League)	Class	W	L	ERA	G	GS	CG	SV	IP	H	HR	BB	SO	K/9	WHIP	AVG
2014	Bowling Green (MWL)	LoA	2	1	1.95	9	9	0	0	37	27	2	14	58	14.1	1.11	.203
	Charlotte (FSL)	HiA	2	0	3.13	5	5	0	0	23	19	0	15	21	8.2	1.48	.226
2015	Montgomery (SL)	AA	9	5	3.67	27	27	0	0	135	105	11	90	168	11.2	1.44	.218
2016	Durham (IL)	AAA	5	7	3.58	27	27	0	0	131	113	12	68	163	11.2	1.39	.236
Minor League Totals			19	15	3.36	85	78	0	0	370	296	28	216	465	11.3	1.38	.222

13 RYNE STANEK, RHP

BA GRADE

45 Risk: Medium

Born: July 26, 1991. **B-T:** R-R. **Ht.:** 6-4. **Wt.:** 190. **Drafted:** Arkansas, 2013 (1st round). **Signed by:** Rickey Drexler.

Stanek has been on the prospect scene for some time now. He was a third round pick out of high school before choosing to enroll at Arkansas, where he helped the Razorbacks reach the College World Series as a rotation stalwart as a sophomore. The Rays took Stanek in 2013 and aimed to develop him as a starter, taking a chance on his potent fastball-slider combo. Stanek struggled with command in the minors, however, and made the transition to the bullpen in 2016. As a reliever, Stanek pitches in the upper 90s with his fastball and he's touched triple digits. He also throws a vertical slider at 87-90 mph evaluators grade as an above-average to plus pitch, and he's continued to work on his low-90s changeup, though that doesn't project as a significant part of his arsenal going forward. Stanek has a long arm swing and his timing isn't always quite right, but when his stuff is at its best, it's good enough to get the best hitters out. The righthander's performance wasn't overwhelmingly positive in his first exposure to the bullpen, but he still projects as a late-inning reliever who could break into the majors in 2017.

Year	Club (League)	Class	W	L	ERA	G	GS	CG	SV	IP	H	HR	BB	SO	K/9	WHIP	AVG
2014	Bowling Green (MWL)	LoA	3	4	3.63	9	9	0	0	45	47	2	13	46	9.3	1.34	.275
	Rays (GCL)	R	0	0	0.00	1	1	0	0	1	0	0	0	0	0.0	0.00	.000
	Charlotte (FSL)	HiA	1	1	5.54	3	3	0	0	13	13	0	5	4	2.8	1.38	.277
2015	Charlotte (FSL)	HiA	4	2	1.78	9	9	0	0	51	33	2	15	38	6.8	0.95	.189
	Montgomery (SL)	AA	4	3	4.09	16	8	0	1	62	52	7	31	41	6.0	1.35	.232
2016	Montgomery (SL)	AA	2	6	3.79	18	11	0	2	78	64	6	35	91	10.5	1.26	.227
	Durham (IL)	AAA	2	4	5.92	16	0	0	1	24	22	3	13	22	8.1	1.44	.242
Minor League Totals			16	20	3.72	72	41	0	4	274	231	20	112	242	8.0	1.25	.233

14 ADRIAN RONDON, SS/3B

BA GRADE

55 Risk: Extreme

Born: July 7, 1998. **B-T:** R-R. **Ht.:** 6-1. **Wt.:** 190. **Signed:** Dominican Republic, 2014. **Signed by:** Danny Santana.

Rondon was the top-rated prospect in the 2014 international class and signed with the Rays for $2.95 million when he turned 16. He hit under .200 in the Rookie-level Gulf Coast League in a disappointing 2015 debut, but made significant progress in 2016. He worked out with Willy Adames before the season began, and Rays officials believe Rondon's exposure to Adames' work ethic and enthusiasm had a profound impact. Rondon advanced to the Rookie-level Appalachian League and flashed explosive tools if not standout performance. His best attribute is his plus raw power, which allows him to drive the ball out to any part of the ballpark. He has loose wrists and life in his bat, though his bat path has length from a high hand set that's geared for powerful contact. Rondon consistently impacts the ball when he makes contact, though he has a tendency to expand the strike zone and chase breaking pitches. Defensively, he has sound hands and an above-average arm, and he appears likely to end up at third base as he continues to bulk up. Scouts believe Rondon can be a quality defender at the hot corner, but he needs to continue improving offensively.

Year	Club (League)	Class	AVG	G	AB	R	H	2B	3B	HR	RBI	BB	SO	SB	CS	OBP	SLG
2015	Rays (GCL)	R	.166	43	145	3	24	8	1	0	11	17	57	0	2	.256	.234
2016	Princeton (APP)	R	.249	52	193	29	48	10	2	7	36	13	58	1	5	.301	.430
Minor League Totals			.213	95	338	32	72	18	3	7	47	30	115	1	7	.282	.346

15 DANIEL ROBERTSON, SS/3B

BA GRADE

40 Risk: Low

Born: March 22, 1994. **B-T:** R-R. **Ht.:** 6-1. **Wt.:** 205. **Drafted:** HS—Upland, Calif., 2012 (1st round supplemental). **Signed by:** Eric Martins (Athletics).

The 34th overall pick in 2012 by the A's out of high school, Robertson quickly established himself among Oakland's best prospects and was one of the key players the Rays acquired in the Ben Zobrist trade after the 2014 season. Robertson is a solid-but-unspectacular infielder who does a lot of things well and has few weaknesses, though his statistical performance did not indicate that when he reached Triple-A Durham in 2016. Robertson's best asset remains his righthanded bat, which projects as average to slightly above. He has a compact swing and shows the ability to make consistent hard contact, though he rarely lofts the ball over the fence. Defensively, Robertson shows smooth hands and above-average arm strength, though he lacks optimal range and pure foot speed for shortstop. He is also a below-average runner. Robertson appears as somewhat of a tweener, with no plus tools, but evaluators who like him note his all-around ability and believe his bat will play at the highest level. He was added to the Rays' 40-man roster in the offseason and is likely to see big league time in 2017 as a utilityman.

Year	Club (League)	Class	AVG	G	AB	R	H	2B	3B	HR	RBI	BB	SO	SB	CS	OBP	SLG
2014	Stockton (CAL)	HiA	.310	132	548	110	170	37	3	15	60	72	94	4	4	.402	.471
2015	Rays (GCL)	R	.125	4	8	2	1	0	0	0	0	3	2	1	0	.417	.125
	Montgomery (SL)	AA	.274	78	299	49	82	20	5	4	41	33	58	2	3	.363	.415
2016	Durham (IL)	AAA	.259	118	436	50	113	21	3	5	43	58	100	2	1	.358	.356
Minor League Totals			.278	488	1887	304	524	111	14	38	220	230	379	13	16	.368	.412

16 LUCIUS FOX, SS

BA GRADE

55 Risk: Extreme

Born: July 2, 1997. **B-T:** B-R. **Ht.:** 6-1. **Wt.:** 175. **Signed:** Bahamas, 2015. **Signed by:** Jose Alou/Joe Salermo (Giants).

Fox played high school baseball in Florida, but moved back to the Bahamas prior to his senior year and established himself as an international free agent. He signed with the Giants in 2015 for $6 million bonus and began his professional debut at low Class A in 2016. At the trade deadline, the Rays acquired Fox as part of the trade that sent Matt Moore to the Giants. Fox didn't play in a game after joining the Rays organization, instead resting after a rough first pro season in which he batted just above the Mendoza line and made 32 errors in 75 games. The Rays are still intrigued by Fox's loud pure tools. He is a double-plus runner with explosive strides, though his feet can get tangled in the infield and some scouts question his body control. Fox is a switch-hitter with fluid, quick hands and long arms. He struggled to time his swing in 2016, often getting caught swinging ahead of pitches and losing balance. Fox remains a quick-twitch athlete with a high ceiling, but he has a long way to go for his tools to translate into game skills and production.

Year	Club (League)	Class	AVG	G	AB	R	H	2B	3B	HR	RBI	BB	SO	SB	CS	OBP	SLG
2016	Augusta (SAL)	LoA	.207	75	285	46	59	6	4	2	16	37	76	25	7	.305	.277
Minor League Totals			.207	75	285	46	59	6	4	2	16	37	76	25	7	.305	.277

17 TAYLOR GUERRIERI, RHP

BA GRADE

45 Risk: Medium

Born: Dec. 1, 1992. **B-T:** R-R. **Ht.:** 6-3. **Wt.:** 195. **Drafted:** HS—Columbia, S.C., 2011 (1st round). **Signed by:** Brad Matthews.

Guerrieri has taken a circuitous route through the Rays system. He was a first-round pick on the strength of his upper 90s fastball in high school but has never shown that velocity as a professional, and he's endured both Tommy John surgery and a 50-game suspension for a drug of abuse on his way to the upper minors. Now, Guerrieri is more of a pitch-to-contact type coming off a successful year but not overwhelming year at Double-A, with only 89 strikeouts in 146 innings. His fastball operates mostly at 89-93 with late sinking action, allowing him to become an effective groundball pitcher. His best offspeed pitch is his curveball, which shows late depth to induce poor contact even when hitters recognize it. Scouts are split on his ultimate role. Some are encouraged by Guerrieri's changeup and control to project him as a back-of-the-rotation starter, while others are curious how Guerrieri's stuff would play in the bullpen. While he hasn't been the front-of-the-rotation cornerstone the Rays thought they were drafting, Guerrieri is still on the 40-man roster and will be on the cusp of the majors with Triple-A Durham in 2017.

Year	Club (League)	Class	W	L	ERA	G	GS	CG	SV	IP	H	HR	BB	SO	K/9	WHIP	AVG
2014	Rays (GCL)	R	0	0	0.00	5	5	0	0	9	7	0	2	10	9.6	0.96	.194
2015	Charlotte (FSL)	HiA	2	2	2.14	12	10	0	0	42	37	0	11	44	9.4	1.14	.237
	Montgomery (SL)	AA	3	1	1.50	8	8	0	0	36	28	2	8	28	7.0	1.00	.206
2016	Montgomery (SL)	AA	12	6	3.76	28	26	0	1	146	130	11	46	89	5.5	1.21	.239
Minor League Totals			24	13	2.50	79	75	0	1	352	291	18	84	267	6.8	1.06	.224

18 GREG HARRIS, RHP

BA GRADE
50 Risk: High

Born: Aug. 17, 1994. **B-T:** R-R. **Ht.:** 6-2. **Wt.:** 170. **Drafted:** HS—Los Alamitos, Calif., 2013 (17th round). **Signed by:** Bobby Darwin (Dodgers).

The son of the longtime major league righthander of the same name, Harris has made steady progress since joining the Rays in the offseason trade that sent Joel Peralta to the Dodgers in 2014. Harris pitched well in high Class A in 2016, showing additional velocity and more confidence in his stuff. He pitches comfortably in the low 90s and can reach as high as 95 mph, with some evaluators noting even more velocity than that. His fastball plays even at the lower end of its velocity range because Harris is able to generate late sinking action or arm-side run on the pitch. His best offspeed pitch is his changeup, which he is able to locate against lefthanded hitters with similar movement to his fastball. He throws an upper-80s cutter and a more vertical curveball in the upper 70s. Detractors question Harris' fastball command and don't believe his stuff is quite good enough for him to overcome erratic stretches. Evaluators who like him see a potential starter who has made quick progress and could still improve yet, given his projectable frame and steady strength gains. He is likely to advance to Double-A in 2017.

Year	Club (League)	Class	W	L	ERA	G	GS	CG	SV	IP	H	HR	BB	SO	K/9	WHIP	AVG
2014	Great Lakes (MWL)	LoA	7	6	4.45	22	16	0	0	87	88	7	28	92	9.5	1.33	.258
2015	Bowling Green (MWL)	LoA	7	5	2.17	16	16	0	0	83	74	1	28	84	9.1	1.23	.236
	Charlotte (FSL)	HiA	1	4	3.40	9	8	0	0	40	40	1	14	24	5.4	1.36	.274
2016	Charlotte (FSL)	HiA	10	6	3.12	26	23	2	0	147	119	10	58	134	8.2	1.20	.228
	Durham (IL)	AAA	0	0	9.00	1	1	0	0	3	5	0	3	6	18.0	2.67	.357
Minor League Totals			27	24	3.48	84	71	2	0	394	359	23	140	362	8.3	1.27	.245

19 KEVIN PADLO, 3B

BA GRADE
50 Risk: High

Born: July 15, 1996. **B-T:** R-R. **Ht.:** 6-2. **Wt.:** 200. **Drafted:** HS—Murrieta, Calif., 2014 (5th round). **Signed by:** Jon Lukens (Rockies).

Padlo was an all-league basketball and baseball player in high school who passed up a San Diego commitment to sign with the Rockies as a fifth-round pick in 2014. The Rays acquired him and Corey Dickerson for Jake McGee and German Marquez following the 2015 season. Padlo batted just .229 in low Class A in his first year with the Rays but reached base at a .364 clip and showed promising corner infield tools. He has plus raw power, which comes from a deep load and long, explosive swing, with plus bat speed and good leverage. He has a tendency to get rotational and pull off the ball early, leading to questions about his natural timing. Padlo works counts and draws some criticism from scouts for being too passive and not always recognizing mistakes he could potentially drive. Defensively, Padlo has above-average to plus arm strength at third and projects to be a useful defender there with his underrated athleticism. He is also an average runner. Padlo has to improve his pure hitting ability, but he has a variety of tools at his disposal and profiles well if he can make the necessary adjustments.

Year	Club (League)	Class	AVG	G	AB	R	H	2B	3B	HR	RBI	BB	SO	SB	CS	OBP	SLG
2014	Grand Junction (PIO)	R	.300	48	160	32	48	15	4	8	44	31	38	6	1	.421	.594
2015	Asheville (SAL)	LoA	.145	27	83	11	12	5	0	2	7	14	26	2	1	.273	.277
	Boise (NWL)	SS	.294	70	255	44	75	22	2	9	46	45	62	33	5	.404	.502
2016	Bowling Green (MWL)	LoA	.229	115	414	71	95	22	3	16	66	79	134	14	9	.358	.413
Minor League Totals			.252	260	912	158	230	64	9	35	163	169	260	55	16	.374	.457

20 JOE McCARTHY, OF/1B

BA GRADE
45 Risk: High

Born: February 23, 1994. **B-T:** L-L. **Ht.:** 6-3. **Wt.:** 225. **Drafted:** Virginia, 2015 (5th round). **Signed by:** Lou Wieben.

Undrafted out of high school, McCarthy made an immediate impact when he arrived at college, batting .336 as a freshman at Virginia. He developed a reputation as a sound college hitter, but missed most of his junior spring with a back injury and wasn't quite himself when he returned down the stretch and helped the Cavaliers win their first national championship in 2015. The Rays took a chance on McCarthy, and in his first full professional season, the Pennsylvania native proved himself worthy. McCarthy's best tools are on offense. He has a compact lefthanded swing and controls the bat well. Despite his muscular, long-limbed frame, McCarthy has never quite profiled as a traditional slugger, though he began to fulfill some of his power projection in 2016 with a .145 isolated slugging percentage across low- and high Class A. McCarthy shows sound strike zone awareness and puts himself in favorable counts often. He has solid-average speed and runs the bases well. McCarthy doesn't quite profile as a center fielder but has the tools to be an effective corner outfielder if he can stay healthy. He also added first base to his repertoire, giving him value as a versatile lefthanded bat moving forward.

Year	Club (League)	Class	AVG	G	AB	R	H	2B	3B	HR	RBI	BB	SO	SB	CS	OBP	SLG
2015	Hudson Valley (NYP)	SS	.277	49	184	24	51	7	2	0	21	18	23	18	3	.362	.337
2016	Bowling Green (MWL)	LoA	.288	43	153	31	44	12	0	3	29	33	30	11	2	.425	.425
	Charlotte (FSL)	HiA	.283	61	198	20	56	9	3	5	31	28	38	8	3	.376	.434
Minor League Totals			.282	153	535	75	151	28	5	8	81	79	91	37	8	.386	.398

21 NICK CIUFFO, C

BA GRADE 45 Risk: High

Born: March 7, 1995. **B-T:** L-R. **Ht.:** 6-1. **Wt.:** 205. **Drafted:** HS—Lexington, S.C., 2013 (1st round). **Signed by:** Brian Hickman.

The Rays were drawn to Ciuffo as a lefthanded-hitting catcher with promising power potential, even though high school catchers are a notoriously risky draft demographic. Ciuffo has progressed through the low minors but redefined his profile over the years, now figuring to have more of an impact defensively than offensively. Ciuffo's offense did show signs of life in 2016, however. He advanced to the high Class A Florida State League, a notoriously pitcher-friendly league. After a routine April, Ciuffo broke out in May, batting .340. His progress was derailed by a midseason hand injury, but he remains an intriguing defense-first prospect now with some offensive success to note. Ciuffo shows impressive receiving skills and some evaluators graded him as a plus defender in 2016, noting his soft hands, rapport with pitchers and framing technique. He also has above-average arm strength and accuracy. His defense is advanced enough for him to profile as a backup, but he continues to show promise in batting practice and he has the bat speed to catch up to quality velocity. Ciuffo's hitting has been light for most of his pro career, but he is headed in the right direction.

Year	Club (League)	Class	AVG	G	AB	R	H	2B	3B	HR	RBI	BB	SO	SB	CS	OBP	SLG
2014	Princeton (APP)	R	.224	52	192	25	43	7	1	4	20	17	45	2	1	.289	.333
2015	Bowling Green (MWL)	LoA	.258	94	356	30	92	21	0	1	32	7	55	2	3	.269	.326
2016	Rays (GCL)	R	.067	5	15	1	1	0	0	0	0	2	2	0	0	.176	.067
	Charlotte (FSL)	HiA	.262	59	229	16	60	8	0	0	15	9	45	2	3	.288	.297
Minor League Totals			.249	253	951	83	237	42	2	5	92	44	187	6	7	.281	.313

22 RYAN BOLDT, OF

BA GRADE 45 Risk: High

Born: Nov. 22, 1994. **B-T:** L-R. **Ht.:** 6-2. **Wt.:** 210. **Drafted:** Nebraska, 2016 (2nd round). **Signed by:** Matt Alison.

Boldt was a decorated high school player who starred at many top showcases and for Team USA's 18-and-under national team. He was considered a candidate to be taken in the first round, but an was injured the spring of his senior year and enrolled at Nebraska instead of signing with the Red Sox as a 22nd-round pick out of high school. Boldt was a solid performer in college but never quite proved himself worthy of first-round status, and the Rays took him 53rd overall in 2016 and signed him for $997,500. He added strength to his frame as his junior year approached, and hit for more power as a junior than he did as an underclassman. That did not translate to his first taste of pro ball, as he hit just .218 with one home run at short-season Hudson Valley after signing. Boldt is a mature defender in the outfield, with excellent first-step reactions and route efficiency, though his speed is more above-average than plus. He has a playable outfield arm. Boldt will need to prove he can stay healthy and hit in pro ball, neither of which are given, and will look to do just that at low Class A in 2017.

Year	Club (League)	Class	AVG	G	AB	R	H	2B	3B	HR	RBI	BB	SO	SB	CS	OBP	SLG
2016	Hudson Valley (NYP)	SS	.218	43	170	17	37	5	1	1	15	10	24	8	9	.280	.276
Minor League Totals			.218	43	170	17	37	5	1	1	15	10	24	8	9	.280	.276

23 JAKE FRALEY, OF

BA GRADE 45 Risk: High

Born: May 25, 1995. **B-T:** L-L. **Ht.:** 6-0. **Wt.:** 195. **Drafted:** Louisiana State, 2016 (2nd round supplemental). **Signed by:** Rickey Drexler.

Tasked with replacing Nationals prospect Andrew Stevenson as Louisiana State's center fielder in 2016, Fraley immediately stepped up and excelled for the Tigers as a junior in 2016. The Rays picked Fraley

No. 77 overall and gave him a $797,500 signing bonus based on his performance and impact defense and speed. He is a lefthanded hitter with a wide open stance and a high hand set that gives his swing length, but also enables him to generate hard contact. Fraley has average bat speed and doesn't project as an offensive force, though he was a key contributor at LSU, batting .326 as a junior. Fraley's best asset is his plus speed, which he shows the ability to use on the base paths and in center field. In his professional debut, Fraley lead the Rookie-level New York-Penn League in stolen bases, swiping 33 in 42 attempts. Fraley takes efficient routes in the outfield and has a near-average arm. His defensive upside and lefthanded bat alone could allow him to carve out a solid career as an extra outfielder, though he'll have a chance to prove himself as more if he proves himself offensively. He will begin 2017 at low Class A Bowling Green.

Year	Club (League)	Class	AVG	G	AB	R	H	2B	3B	HR	RBI	BB	SO	SB	CS	OBP	SLG
2016	Hudson Valley (NYP)	SS	.238	55	206	34	49	9	7	1	18	26	34	33	9	.339	.364
Minor League Totals			.238	55	206	34	49	9	7	1	18	26	34	33	9	.339	.364

24 DAVID RODRIGUEZ, C

BA GRADE 45 Risk: High

Born: Feb. 25, 1996. **B-T:** R-R. **Ht.:** 6-1. **Wt.:** 215. **Signed:** Venezuela, 2012.
Signed by: Ronnie Blanco.

Rodriguez trained with Carlos Guillen as an amateur before signing with the Rays for $600,000 in 2012. He's had the Rays excited ever since. In his professional debut, Rodriguez swatted 12 home runs in the Venezuelan Summer League in 2013. He made his full-season league debut in 2016, reaching low Class A Bowling Green. There, Rodriguez endeared himself to evaluators with his excellent defensive tools. He is an athletic, quick-twitch receiver who blocks well and has excellent hands to go with plus arm strength. He threw out 56 percent of basestealers in 2016, and he also receives positive marks for his rapport with pitchers. Rodriguez is less advanced offensively but shows plus raw power. His swing can get long though and he is prone to swinging and missing. His defensive upside alone gives him a chance to develop into a major leaguer, with a backup role in sight even if his pure hitting ability doesn't improve. If Rodriguez is able to improve his contact ability and enable his power to play, he could develop into an everyday player. He is likely to advance to high Class A Charlotte in 2017.

Year	Club (League)	Class	AVG	G	AB	R	H	2B	3B	HR	RBI	BB	SO	SB	CS	OBP	SLG
2014	Rays (GCL)	R	.273	38	128	15	35	10	2	0	23	9	31	3	0	.342	.383
2015	Princeton (APP)	R	.258	45	178	20	46	7	1	4	27	15	39	1	1	.327	.376
2016	Bowling Green (MWL)	LoA	.240	112	416	54	100	16	1	9	62	44	88	4	3	.321	.349
Minor League Totals			.270	259	959	133	259	47	4	25	141	92	220	13	6	.347	.406

25 KEVIN GADEA, RHP

BA GRADE 50 Risk: Extreme

Born: Dec. 6, 1994. **B-T:** R-R. **Ht.:** 6-5. **Wt.:** 188. **Signed:** Nicaragua, 2012.
Signed by: Nemesio Porras/Luis Molina (Mariners).

Gadea was eligible to sign during the 2011 international signing period as a third baseman, but converted to pitching and delayed signing for a year. The Mariners ultimately signed him for $42,000 in November 2012 out of Dennis Martinez's academy. Gadea took time to develop but progressively grew bigger and stronger with two above-average pitches out of his 6-foot-5 frame and at least plus control. Despite the fact Gadea had never pitched above low Class A, the Rays loved his total package and took him with the fourth pick in the 2016 Rule 5 draft. Gadea's fastball sits 91-94 mph and touches 95, and it plays exceptionally well with his mid-80s changeup that presently grades above-average and flashes plus. He also mixes in an upper-70s curveball that is a work in progress. Lean and athletic, Gadea repeats his delivery well and pounds the strike zone. His 95-to-14 strikeout-to-walk ratio in 2016 is indicative of his pinpoint control. The Rays will try to keep him as the last man in their bullpen in 2017 before sending him back to the minors to develop as a possible mid-rotation starter in 2018.

Year	Club (League)	Class	W	L	ERA	G	GS	CG	SV	IP	H	HR	BB	SO	K/9	WHIP	AVG
2014	Mariners (AZL)	R	0	0	7.71	3	1	0	0	9	13	0	9	11	10.6	2.36	.342
2015	Mariners2 (DSL)	R	4	4	2.25	13	13	1	0	76	61	5	16	74	8.8	1.01	.216
2016	Mariners (AZL)	R	1	1	2.95	5	2	0	1	18	15	1	3	23	11.3	0.98	.214
	Clinton (MWL)	LoA	3	0	2.15	10	6	0	1	50	41	4	11	72	12.9	1.03	.218
Minor League Totals			17	6	2.64	45	36	1	2	225	201	13	62	228	9.1	1.17	.237

26 CHRIS BETTS, C

BA GRADE 50 Risk: Extreme

Born: March 10, 1997. **B-T:** L-R. **Ht.:** 6-1. **Wt.:** 215. **Drafted:** HS—Long Beach, Calif. 2015 (2nd round). **Signed by:** Greg Whitworth.

Seen as one of the best offensive prospects in the 2015 draft class, Betts slid to the second round due to concerns about his long-term profile. The Rays, who remain aggressive drafting high school catchers (Justin O'Connor, Nick Ciuffo and Betts in the last six drafts) despite the risky history of the demographic, signed him for $1,482,500. He needed Tommy John surgery after the draft and couldn't begin swinging a bat until after Jan. 1. Betts's debut performance in 2016 didn't live up to his pre-draft hype, but the physical tools remain in place for him to bounce back. He is a lefthanded hitter with plus bat speed and line-drive oriented swing. Scouts note his plus raw power in batting practice, even though he did not hit a home run in his professional debut. Betts has made progress defensively, becoming lighter on his feet and gaining mobility with his improved conditioning. His arm strength has come back fine, and the Rays don't expect him to suffer long-term effects. Betts remains a high-ceiling prospect with his middle-of-the-diamond position and power potential. He appears likely to spend 2017 at another short-season affiliate.

Year	Club (League)	Class	AVG	G	AB	R	H	2B	3B	HR	RBI	BB	SO	SB	CS	OBP	SLG
2015	Did not play—Injured																
2016	Rays (GCL)	R	.214	16	42	5	9	2	1	0	6	10	13	2	0	.364	.310
	Hudson Valley (NYP)	SS	.157	23	70	2	11	4	0	0	7	17	23	0	0	.333	.214
Minor League Totals			.179	39	112	7	20	6	1	0	13	27	36	2	0	.345	.250

27 HUNTER WOOD, RHP

BA GRADE
45 Risk: High

Born: Aug. 12, 1993. **B-T:** R-R. **Ht.:** 6-1. **Wt.:** 175. **Drafted:** Howard (Texas) JC, 2013 (29th round). **Signed by:** Pat Murphy.

The Rays took a flyer Wood after he showed promising arm strength as a junior college freshman in 2013, and he's steadily established himself as a legitimate starting pitching prospect. After performing well in full-season leagues in 2015, Wood earned innings in the Arizona Fall League. He took another step forward in 2016, earning a mid-season promotion to Double-A. Evaluators are intrigued by Wood's promising stuff. He shows the potential for a plus fastball, consistently sitting at 91-93 and getting up to 94-95 when he needs to, though he has touched as high as 97. The pitch also earns praise for getting on hitters quickly with explosive life as it enters the hitting zone. Wood's curveball earned solid-average grades in 2016 because of its late vertical break and tight spin. The biggest criticism against Wood is that he has a thin-shouldered frame that doesn't fit the starter prototype, though he could be an effective reliever. He has shown flashes with his changeup, and some evaluators came away impressed with his cutter, though he doesn't use either offering frequently. Wood will aim to continue proving himself in the upper minors in 2017.

Year	Club (League)	Class	W	L	ERA	G	GS	CG	SV	IP	H	HR	BB	SO	K/9	WHIP	AVG
2014	Bowling Green (MWL)	LoA	1	0	4.07	6	6	0	0	24	22	4	12	21	7.8	1.40	.244
	Hudson Valley (NYP)	SS	3	4	3.08	13	13	0	0	64	53	3	16	57	8.0	1.07	.219
2015	Bowling Green (MWL)	LoA	1	4	1.82	20	3	0	4	64	36	3	16	81	11.3	1.00	.164
	Charlotte (FSL)	HiA	1	3	2.79	9	7	0	0	42	32	1	9	32	6.9	0.98	.208
2016	Charlotte (FSL)	HiA	3	3	1.70	11	9	0	0	64	34	2	24	56	7.9	0.91	.155
	Montgomery (SL)	AA	6	2	3.28	10	9	0	0	49	36	5	20	49	8.9	1.14	.206
Minor League Totals			18	19	2.75	85	53	0	6	353	251	23	108	355	9.1	1.02	.198

28 JOSE ALVARADO, LHP

BA GRADE
45 Risk: High

Born: May 21, 1995. **B-T:** L-L. **Ht.:** 6-0. **Wt.:** 240. **Signed:** Venezuela, 2012. **Signed by:** Ronnie Blanco.

When the Rays signed Alvarado for $50,000 in 2012, he was a skinny lefthander with a mid-80s fastball. He's gained velocity as he's added weight, and he was pitching in the mid-90s by the time he made his stateside debut in the Rookie-level Gulf Coast League in 2014. After struggling to command his pitches as a starter, Alvarado transitioned to the bullpen in 2016. Starting the year in low Class A, Alvarado was unhittable and he quickly earned a promotion to high Class A. His fastball routinely sits at 94-98 and touches 100 mph, and his downer curveball has plus depth with late snap. Alvarado throws from a slightly higher three-quarters slot and has a tendency to rush his delivery. As he's gained weight, he has struggled to maintain balance over the rubber and he is a below-average athlete, causing him trouble controlling his body and repeating his release point. That leads to well below-average command and control. His elite stuff from the left side prompted the Rays to add him to the 40-man roster to protect him from the Rule 5 draft, and he'll aim to gain more control in 2017 as he works towards his late-inning reliever ceiling.

Year	Club (League)	Class	W	L	ERA	G	GS	CG	SV	IP	H	HR	BB	SO	K/9	WHIP	AVG
2014	Rays (GCL)	R	3	5	3.79	12	11	0	0	40	28	1	29	46	10.3	1.41	.190
2015	Princeton (APP)	R	0	2	9.53	5	5	0	0	17	18	1	13	18	9.5	1.82	.300
2016	Bowling Green (MWL)	LoA	2	0	1.46	10	0	0	2	25	12	0	17	34	12.4	1.18	.150
	Charlotte (FSL)	HiA	2	1	3.91	27	0	0	0	46	38	1	38	51	10.0	1.65	.222
Minor League Totals			8	19	3.61	79	29	0	2	200	157	5	135	223	10.1	1.46	.217

29 AUSTIN PRUITT, RHP

BA GRADE

40 Risk: Medium

Born: Aug. 31, 1989. **B-T:** R-R. **Ht.:** 5-11. **Wt.:** 165. **Drafted:** Houston, 2013 (9th round). **Signed by:** Pat Murphy.

Pruitt is a sub-six foot righthander with below-average fastball velocity. As a result, he's had to prove himself at every single level. He proved himself in junior college, then transferred to Houston, where he had an immediate impact on the rotation before developing into an ace as a senior. The Rays took a shot on him, signing him for $5,000 as a low-cost lottery ticket. Since signing, Pruitt has done nothing but prove himself. He's inched his way through the upper minors and earned a 40-man roster spot after a promising season at Triple-A in 2016. Pruitt pitches at 88-90 mph and will touch 92, showing solid-average life on his fastball and the ability to command the pitch. His curveball is an above-average pitch, with 12-to-6 shape, late snap and upper 70s velocity, and his changeup is also effective, showing late tumble. His poor fastball velocity leaves him vulnerable when his command or offspeed offerings aren't at their best, so he needs to be fine to succeed as a starter. Some evaluators believe he could be an effective reliever, with the ability to pitch backwards and enough deception and command to get by. He has a chance to reach the majors in 2017.

Year	Club (League)	Class	W	L	ERA	G	GS	CG	SV	IP	H	HR	BB	SO	K/9	WHIP	AVG
2014	Charlotte (FSL)	HiA	9	7	3.73	26	25	0	0	147	144	12	31	106	6.5	1.19	.255
2015	Montgomery (SL)	AA	10	7	3.09	26	26	2	0	160	160	3	38	122	6.9	1.24	.263
2016	Durham (IL)	AAA	8	11	3.76	28	28	2	0	163	166	21	27	149	8.2	1.19	.267
Minor League Totals			27	28	3.33	94	86	4	1	520	506	39	101	416	7.2	1.17	.257

30 RESLY LINARES, LHP

BA GRADE

50 Risk: Extreme

Born: Dec. 11, 1997. **B-T:** L-L. **Ht.:** 6-2. **Wt.:** 170. **Signed:** Dominican Republic, 2014. **Signed by:** Danny Santana.

Signed for $275,000, Linares established himself as a prospect to watch with an excellent professional debut in the Dominican Summer League in 2015. He skipped past the Rookie-level Gulf Coast League and advanced to Rookie-level Princeton after extended spring training in 2016. Linares had mixed results in the Appalachian League but showed flashes, and his lithe frame offers significant projection. He has a wide-shouldered frame and a loose, fast arm that accelerates well. Linares pitches mostly at 89-92 mph and touches 94, but he projects to add velocity as he matures physically. His best offspeed pitch is his curveball, which shows tight rotation and hard 1-to-7 break. Linares's changeup is in its nascent stages and will be a developmental point of emphasis going forward. He is a promising athlete with a repeatable delivery, though his skin-and-bones body holds him back from being a truly elite prospect. Linares is a candidate to advance to a full-season league in 2017, though he could have another stop short-season ball to gain strength and reps.

Year	Club (League)	Class	W	L	ERA	G	GS	CG	SV	IP	H	HR	BB	SO	K/9	WHIP	AVG
2015	Rays (DSL)	R	0	3	1.11	14	14	0	0	49	29	0	15	59	10.9	0.90	.178
2016	Princeton (APP)	R	2	3	5.34	8	7	0	0	32	40	6	8	30	8.4	1.50	.305
Minor League Totals			2	6	2.79	22	21	0	0	81	69	6	23	89	9.9	1.14	.235

Texas Rangers

BY BEN BADLER

For the fourth time in seven years, the Rangers won the American League West. They went 95-67 despite scoring just eight more runs than they allowed, pulling ahead in the division by pummeling the Astros (15-4) and going 12-7 against the Mariners.

Yet the team that led the AL in wins exited the postseason quickly. The Blue Jays swept the Rangers 3-0 in the AL Division Series, the second year in a row that Toronto ended Texas' season in the ALDS.

In building the team, the Rangers have dipped heavily into the farm system. In three 2016 trade-deadline moves to bring back Jonathan Lucroy, Jeremy Jeffress, Carlos Beltran and Dario Alvarez, the Rangers shipped out righthanders Luis Ortiz and Dillon Tate, outfielders Lewis Brinson and Ryan Cordell and second baseman Travis Demeritte. That group includes four first-round picks: Brinson (2012), Demeritte (2013), Ortiz (2014) and Tate (2015).

Those deals came the year after the Rangers made a pair of trades—for the Phillies' Cole Hamels and the Brewers' Yovani Gallardo—that surrendered outfielder Nick Williams, catcher Jorge Alfaro, shortstop Luis Sardinas and righthanders Alec Asher, Marcos Diplan, Jared Eickhoff and Jake Thompson.

With the huge exodus of young talent from the organization, the farm system isn't as robust as it once was, but the Rangers are still positioned to contend in 2017. Hamels and Yu Darvish give them two frontline starters, while a full season of Lucroy will help the pitching staff as well as the offense.

Third baseman Adrian Beltre is a future Hall of Famer and still one of the elite players in baseball entering his age-38 season. Rougned Odor and Nomar Mazara are young building blocks in the lineup. Third baseman Joey Gallo exhausted his prospect eligibility in 2016, and while strikeouts remain a red flag, he has 40-homer power. A hamstring strain cut short his time in the Venezuelan League after the 2016 season.

On the farm, international scouting remains an organizational strength. The Rangers signed center fielder Leody Taveras for $2.1 million as a 16-year-old out of the Dominican Republic in 2015. He has emerged as the organization's top prospect with a well-rounded set of tools and advanced baseball skills for his age.

Venezuelan lefthander Yohander Mendez and Panamanian righthander Ariel Jurado give the Rangers two upper-level pitchers who could help

Nomar Mazara slammed 20 homers as a 21-year-old rookie fill-in for Shin-Soo Choo

CLIFF WELCH

TOP PROSPECTS OF THE DECADE

Year	Player, Pos.	2016 Org
2007	John Danks, lhp	White Sox
2008	Elvis Andrus, ss	Rangers
2009	Neftali Feliz, rhp	Pirates
2010	Neftali Feliz, rhp	Pirates
2011	Martin Perez, lhp	Rangers
2012	Jurickson Profar, ss	Rangers
2013	Jurickson Profar, ss	Rangers
2014	Rougned Odor, 2b	Rangers
2015	Joey Gallo, 3b	Rangers
2016	Joey Gallo, 3b	Rangers

in 2017.

Beyond them, the Rangers system features more depth than impact talent, with many of their top prospects having yet to reach Double-A and unlikely to see major league time in 2017. From that lower-level wave, however, breakout talents could emerge.

The 2016 draft yielded a pair of promising prep pitchers in lefty Cole Ragans and righthander Alex Speas, while third-round infielder Kole Enright got off to a strong start in the Rookie-level Arizona League.

Internationally, the Rangers added Venezuela's David Garcia, the top-ranked catcher on the international market, while Miguel Aparicio had a promising debut in the Dominican Summer League.

ORGANIZATION OVERVIEW

General manager: Jon Daniels. **Farm director:** Mike Daly. **Scouting director:** Kip Fagg.

Class	Team	League	W	L	PCT	Finish	Manager
Majors	Texas Rangers	American	95	67	.586	1st (15)	Jeff Banister
Triple-A	Round Rock Express	Pacific Coast	71	72	.497	t-7th (16)	Jason Wood
Double-A	Frisco RoughRiders	Texas	63	76	.453	7th (8)	Joe Mikulik
High Class A	* High Desert Mavericks	California	82	58	.586	1st (10)	Howard Johnson
Low Class A	Hickory Crawdads	South Atlantic	74	66	.529	5th (14)	Spike Owen
Short-season	Spokane Indians	Northwest	32	43	.427	7th (8)	Tim Hulett
Rookie	AZL Rangers	Arizona	18	37	.327	14th (14)	Matt Siegel
Overall 2016 Minor League Record			340	352	.491	16th (30)	

*Affiliate moves to Kinston, N.C., to become Down East Wood Ducks (Carolina) 2017

THIS YEAR'S TOP 30

No.	Player, Pos.	Grade/Risk
1.	Leody Taveras, of	65/Extreme
2.	Yohander Mendez, lhp	50/Medium
3.	Ariel Jurado, rhp	50/Medium
4.	Cole Ragans, lhp	55/High
5.	Andy Ibanez, 2b/3b	50/High
6.	Josh Morgan, 3b/ss/2b/c	50/High
7.	Ronald Guzman, 1b	50/High
8.	Alex Speas, rhp	55/Extreme
9.	Joe Palumbo, lhp	50/High
10.	Brett Martin, lhp	50/High
11.	Michael De Leon, ss	50/High
12.	Jose Trevino, c	45/High
13.	David Garcia, c	50/Extreme
14.	Miguel Aparicio, of	50/Extreme
15.	Connor Sadzeck, rhp	45/High
16.	Anderson Tejeda, ss	50/Extreme
17.	Jonathan Hernandez, rhp	45/High
18.	Kole Enright, 2b/2b	50/Extreme
19.	Michael Matuella, rhp	50/Extreme
20.	Jairo Beras, of	50/Extreme
21.	Jose Cardona, of	45/High
22.	Jose LeClerc, rhp	40/Medium
23.	Drew Robinson, of/2b/3b/1b	40/Medium
24.	Andrew Faulkner, lhp	40/Medium
25.	Mike Hauschild, rhp	40/Medium
26.	Eric Jenkins, of	45/Extreme
27.	Yanio Perez, of/3b	45/Extreme
28.	Juremi Profar, 3b/1b/2b	40/High
29.	Pedro Payano, rhp	40/High
30.	Tyler Ferguson, rhp	45/Extreme

LAST YEAR'S TOP 30

No.	Player, Pos.	Status
1.	Joey Gallo, 3b/of	Majors
2.	Lewis Brinson, of	(Brewers)
3.	Nomar Mazara, of	Majors
4.	Luis Ortiz, rhp	(Brewers)
5.	Dillon Tate, rhp	(Yankees)
6.	Eric Jenkins, of	No. 26
7.	Josh Morgan, ss/3b	No. 6
8.	Andy Ibanez, 2b	No. 5
9.	Leody Taveras, of	No. 1
10.	Ryan Cordell, of/3b	(Brewers)
11.	Michael Matuella, rhp	No. 19
12.	Andrew Faulkner, lhp	No. 24
13.	Luke Jackson, rhp	(Braves)
14.	Michael De Leon, ss	No. 11
15.	Miguel Aparicio, of	No. 14
16.	Jairo Beras, of	No. 20
17.	Hanser Alberto, ss/2b/3b	Majors
18.	Brett Martin, lhp	No. 10
19.	Ariel Jurado, rhp	No. 3
20.	Jonathan Hernandez, rhp	No. 17
21.	Jose LeClerc, rhp	No. 22
22.	Evan Van Hoosier, 2b/of	Dropped out
23.	Yohander Mendez, lhp	No. 2
24.	Patrick Kivlehan, of/1b/3b	(Reds)
25.	Jose Trevino, c	No. 12
26.	Connor Sadzeck, rhp	No. 15
27.	Yeyson Yrizarri, ss	Dropped out
28.	Travis Demeritte, 2b	(Braves)
29.	Ronald Guzman, 1b	No. 7
30.	Israel Cruz, rhp	Dropped out

BEST TOOLS

Best Hitter for Average	Leody Taveras
Best Power Hitter	Jairo Beras
Best Strike-Zone Discipline	Josh Morgan
Fastest Baserunner	Eric Jenkins
Best Athlete	Eric Jenkins
Best Fastball	Connor Sadzeck
Best Curveball	Brett Martin
Best Slider	Tyler Ferguson
Best Changeup	Yohander Mendez
Best Control	Ariel Jurado
Best Defensive Catcher	Jose Trevino
Best Defensive Infielder	Michael De Leon
Best Infield Arm	Yeyson Yrizarri
Best Defensive Outfielder	Leody Taveras
Best Outfield Arm	Jairo Beras

PROJECTED 2020 LINEUP

Catcher	Jonathan Lucroy
First Base	Ronald Guzman
Second Base	Rougned Odor
Third Base	Joey Gallo
Shortstop	Elvis Andrus
Left Field	Jurickson Profar
Center Field	Leody Taveras
Right Field	Nomar Mazara
Designated Hitter	Andy Ibanez
No. 1 Starter	Yu Darvish
No. 2 Starter	Cole Hamels
No. 3 Starter	Martin Perez
No. 4 Starter	Yohander Mendez
No. 5 Starter	Ariel Jurado
Closer	Keone Kela

MINOR LEAGUE DEPTH CHART

TEXAS RANGERS

TOP 2017 ROOKIE: Yohander Mendez, lhp. He could claim a larger role on the big league staff after rocketing from high Class A to the majors in 2016.

BREAKOUT PROSPECT: Miguel Aparicio, of. Overshadowed by fellow 2015 international signee Leody Taveras, Aparicio doesn't have the same explosive tools but he has a knack for hitting with good instincts in center field.

SLEEPER: Tyler Phillips, rhp. His 6.44 ERA at short-season Spokane wasn't pretty, but he was an 18-year-old with good size (6-foot-5, 200 pounds) and a lively, high-spin fastball at 91-95 mph.

SOURCE OF TOP 30 TALENT			
Homegrown	29	Acquired	1
College	3	Trades	0
Junior college	2	Rule 5 draft	1
High school	8	Independent leagues	0
Draft-and-follow	0	Free agents/waivers	0
Nondrafted free agents	0	International	16

LF
Scott Heineman
Eduard Pinto
Joe Jackson

CF
Leodys Taveras (1)
Miguel Aparicio (14)
Jose Cardona (21)
Eric Jenkins (26)
LeDarious Clark
Kobie Taylor

RF
Jairo Beras (20)
Drew Robinson (23)
Yanio Perez (27)
Jared Hoying
Luke Tendler

3B
Josh Morgan (6)
Juremi Profar (28)
Ti'Quan Forbes

SS
Michael De Leon (11)
Anderson Tejeda (16)
Yeyson Yrizarri
Charles LeBlanc
Luis Marte
Alberto Triunfel

2B
Andy Ibanez (5)
Kole Enright (18)
Evan Van Hoosier
Blaine Prescott

1B
Ronald Guzman (7)

C
Jose Trevino (12)
David Garcia (13)
Brett Nicholas
Yohel Pozo
Francisco Ventura

LHP

LHSP
Yohander Mendez (2)
Cole Ragans (4)
Joe Palumbo (9)
Brett Martin (10)
Frank Lopez

LHRP
Andrew Faulkner (24)
Brady Feigl
Kyle Roberts

RHP

RHSP
Ariel Jurado (3)
Alex Speas (8)
Connor Sadzeck (15)
Jonathan Hernandez (17)
Mike Hauschild (25)
Pedro Payano (29)
Kyle Cody
Tyler Phillips
Israel Cruz
Demarcus Evans
Argenis Rodriguez
Collin Wiles
David Ledbetter
Edgar Arredondo

RHRP
Michael Matuella (19)
Jose LeClerc (22)
Tyler Ferguson (30)
John Fasola
Adam Parks

DRAFT ANALYSIS

2016

BEST PURE HITTER: After a slow start in the Rookie-level Arizona League, 3B Kole Enright (3) showed why the Rangers believed in him more than much of the industry. He's a switch-hitter with a short-swing from both sides who already has showed he can make adjustments.

BEST POWER HITTER: C Sam Huff (7) showed pop to the gaps in his debut in Arizona, and the Phoenix native has power-hitter size at 6-foot-4 and close to 230 pounds.

FASTEST RUNNER: Texas signed OF Kobie Taylor (15) away from Vanderbilt for $350,000. He's at least a plus runner with instincts and athleticism who has a chance to fit the center field profile.

BEST DEFENSIVE PLAYER: SS/3B Charles LeBlanc (4) and Huff are both tall for their positions but have requisite arm strength for their jobs. The Canadian LeBlanc probably fits better at third base long-term at 6-foot-4.

BEST FASTBALL: Athletic and wiry, RHP Alex Speas (2) had one of the liveliest arms in the 2016 draft class, sitting 95-96 mph with his fastball and touching 99. LHP Kyle Roberts (5), as raw as Speas if not moreso as a junior college draftee, also has hit 99.

BEST SECONDARY: LHP Cole Ragans has a firm fastball at 92-93 mph, but his feel for his curveball and changeup, as well as pitchability, made him Texas' top pick. His changeup is more advanced and close to consistently above-average now, but both have plus potential.

BEST PRO DEBUT: Enright wound up hitting .313/.378/.420, ranking sixth in the AZL in batting. Huff lacked the plate appearances to qualify but batting .330/.436/.485 in 97 at-bats.

BEST ATHLETE: Speas' athleticism has allowed him to address some flaws in his amateur delivery in short order. RHP Tyree Thompson (26) may top him with a similarly loose, lean, athletic frame at a listed 6-foot-4, 165 pounds. The Louisiana prep product was committed to play basketball and baseball at Northwestern State.

MOST INTRIGUING BACKGROUND: Thompson rivals fellow RHP Tai Tiedemann, who was the quarterback at famed Long Beach Poly High before switching more to baseball after he was beaten out for the signal-caller job. The 6-foot-6 Roberts didn't pitch as a high school senior and never had a pitching coach as an amateur.

CLOSEST TO THE MAJORS: RHP Kyle Cody (6), an unsigned second-round pick in 2015 (Twins), has added maturity and has a big arm, capable of pitching at 93-95 mph with sink. The Rangers hope to keep his front shoulder closed more and to lengthen his stride in his delivery to help the enigmatic righty find his footing.

BEST LATE-ROUND PICK: Taylor and Thompson both have the athleticism and twitchy bodies the Rangers covet and have had success at developing.

THE ONE WHO GOT AWAY: The Rangers weren't able to corral RHP Herbie Good (36), who spent the spring working out at Driveline Baseball in Puyallup, Wash., where he's trained for at least four years. The 6-foot-8 righty can sit 92-94 mph with his fastball and headed to JC of Southern Nevada.

2015

Texas already traded RHP Dillon Tate (1) to the Yankees for Carlos Beltran. Injured RHPs Michael Matuella (3) and Jake Lemoine (4) have barely gotten on the mound. Sleepers include wild but electric RHP Tyler Ferguson (6) and OF Scott Heineman (10).

GRADE: D

2014

RHP Luis Ortiz (1) was progressing well before being traded to the Brewers for Jonathan Lucroy. 2B/3B Josh Morgan (3) and C Jose Trevino (6) lack star potential but could be regulars, while LHP Brett Martin (4) is one of the system's top pitching prospects.

GRADE: C

2013

RHP Chi Chi Gonzalez (1) reached the majors quickly but spent most of 2016 in Triple-A. Athletic OF Ryan Cordell (11) was included in the Jonathan Lucroy trade to Milwaukee. Emerging 2B Travis Demeritte (1) was dealt to Atlanta.

GRADE: C

TOP DRAFT PICKS OF THE DECADE

Year	Player, Pos.	2016 Org
2007	Blake Beavan, rhp	Atlantic League
2008	Justin Smoak, 1b	Blue Jays
2009	*Matt Purke, lhp	White Sox
2010	Jake Skole, of	Yankees
2011	Kevin Matthews, lhp	Did not play
2012	Lewis Brinson, of	Brewers
2013	Chi Chi Gonzalez, rhp	Rangers
2014	Luis Ortiz, rhp	Brewers
2015	Dillon Tate, rhp	Yankees
2016	Cole Ragans, lhp	Rangers

*Did not sign.

LARGEST BONUSES IN CLUB HISTORY

Leonys Martin, 2011	$5,000,000
Nomar Mazara, 2011	$4,950,000
Mark Teixeira, 2001	$4,500,000
Jairo Beras, 2012	$4,500,000
Dillon Tate, 2015	$4,200,000

1 LEODY TAVERAS, OF

Born: Sept. 8, 1998. **B-T:** B-R. **Ht.:** 6-2. **Wt.:** 185.
Signed: Dominican Republic, 2015.
Signed by: Willy Espinal/Gil Kim/Thad Levine.

The Rangers have had one of the most productive international pipelines in baseball over the last decade, with one of the most aggressive contingents of scouts in Latin America. They had their sights set on Taveras from an early age, then officially signed him as a 16-year-old for $2.1 million when he became eligible on July 2, 2015. Taveras is a younger cousin of Willy Taveras, the former outfielder who stood out for his speed and defense during his seven-year major league career, including 2008 when he led the majors with 68 stolen bases. Before Taveras made his official pro debut, the Rangers brought him over from the minor league back fields in 2016 and put him in three spring-training games with the major league club, and he went 1-for-4 with a double. He opened the 2016 season back home in the Dominican Summer League but didn't spend much time there before the Rangers brought him to the U.S. for the Rookie-level Arizona League. He ranked as the league's No. 1 prospect, got promoted to the short-season Northwest League in August and also ranked as that league's No. 1 prospect.

Taveras is a smooth, well-rounded player with an exciting blend of tools and skills for his age, and he draws comparisons with a young Carlos Beltran. Lean and athletic, Taveras has a short, simple swing from both sides of the plate. He's a balanced hitter who uses his hands well in connection with his lower half. He's a high-contact hitter with good feel for the barrel who unleashes a fluid swing with whippy bat speed and a clean path to the ball. He is adept at hitting fastballs, and while he's still learning to recognize offspeed pitches, he has solid strike-zone awareness and improved his ability to manage the zone since signing, showing the ability to make adjustments within an at-bat. He uses the whole field with a line-drive approach, showing mostly gap power in games with the ability to drive the ball over the fence occasionally during batting practice. With his bat speed, strong hands and room to fill out his projectable frame, Taveras could eventually grow into average power. He makes the game look easy at the plate and in center field. He's a plus runner with long, gliding strides. He looks natural and instinctive in center field, where he gets sharp reads and jumps off the bat to give him good range. Even when Taveras

does take a false step, he has the speed to compensate and cover plenty of ground. He also has a plus arm with good accuracy.

Taveras has yet to reach full-season ball, but he has the highest ceiling and most exciting skill set in the Rangers system, with five tools that could all grade out average to plus.

Mature beyond his years, he should open 2017 at low Class A Hickory. Between his ability and the Rangers' track record of hitting the accelerator with their most talented young international prospects, he could move quickly through the farm system.

BA GRADE
65 Risk: Extreme.

SCOUTING GRADES
Batting: 60.
Power: 50.
Speed: 60.
Defense: 60.
Arm: 60.

Based on 20-80 scouting scale and future projection rather than present grades.

BILL MITCHELL

Year	Club (League)	Class	AVG	G	AB	R	H	2B	3B	HR	RBI	BB	SO	SB	CS	OBP	SLG
2016	Rangers2 (DSL)	R	.385	11	39	6	15	2	2	0	9	6	5	4	3	.467	.538
	Rangers (AZL)	R	.278	33	144	22	40	6	3	1	15	11	24	11	4	.329	.382
	Spokane (NWL)	SS	.228	29	123	14	28	6	1	0	9	8	26	3	1	.271	.293
Minor League Totals			.271	73	306	42	83	14	6	1	33	25	55	18	8	.324	.366

2 YOHANDER MENDEZ, LHP

Born: Jan. 17, 1995. **B-T:** L-L. **Ht.:** 6-5. **Wt.:** 200. **Signed:** Venezuela, 2011. **Signed by:** Rafic Saab/Pedro Avila/Mike Daly.

The Rangers signed Mendez for $1.5 million as a tall, frail 16-year-old throwing in the mid- to upper 80s. He earned three in-season promotions in 2016 and made his major league debut as a September callup. Staying healthy helped Mendez pitch more than 100 innings for the first time in his career. His fastball crept up to sit in the low 90s and touch 95 mph. His calling card is his changeup, which he sells well with good separation off his fastball. It's a plus pitch that consistently fools hitters with empty swings or off balance ones for weak contact. His slider has improved but it's still fringe-average, while he mixes in an occasional get-me-over curveball early in the count. Mendez has smooth arm action, an easy delivery and throws strikes, but he needs to tighten his fastball command, particularly glove side so hitters can't key in on one side of the plate. The Rangers want to keep Mendez in the rotation, so he likely will start the year back at Triple-A Round Rock. He should be back in Texas at some point in 2017, possibly before the all-star break.

BA GRADE
50 Risk: Medium

Year	Club (League)	Class	W	L	ERA	G	GS	CG	SV	IP	H	HR	BB	SO	K/9	WHIP	AVG
2014	Rangers (AZL)	R	0	1	4.76	3	3	0	0	6	8	0	2	7	11.1	1.76	.320
	Hickory (SAL)	LoA	3	0	2.32	7	6	0	0	31	26	4	2	28	8.1	0.90	.232
2015	Hickory (SAL)	LoA	3	3	2.44	21	8	0	3	66	57	2	15	74	10.0	1.09	.230
2016	High Desert (CAL)	HiA	4	1	2.45	7	7	0	0	33	21	2	11	45	12.3	0.97	.176
	Frisco (TL)	AA	4	1	3.09	10	10	0	0	47	39	2	14	46	8.9	1.14	.228
	Round Rock (PCL)	AAA	4	1	0.57	7	4	0	0	31	12	0	16	22	6.3	0.89	.119
	Texas (AL)	MAJ	0	0	18.00	2	0	0	0	3	5	0	2	0	0.0	2.33	.333
Major League Totals			0	0	18.00	2	0	0	0	3	5	0	2	0	0.0	2.33	.333
Minor League Totals			21	10	2.46	77	59	0	3	293	230	15	90	280	8.6	1.09	.216

3 ARIEL JURADO, RHP

Born: Jan. 30, 1996. **B-T:** R-R. **Ht.:** 6-1. **Wt.:** 237. **Signed:** Panama, 2012. **Signed by:** Eduardo Thomas.

Jurado was a skinny 16-year-old who threw a lot of strikes with mid- to upper-80s fastballs when the Rangers signed him out of Panama. While he throws harder now that he's nearly 60 pounds heavier, it's his feel for pitching that stands out more than his pure stuff. Jurado throws all three of his pitches for strikes. Everything works off his two-seam fastball, which sits 88-92 mph and touches 94. It's more notable for its hard, heavy sink—he led the high Class A California League in groundout-to-airout ratio—with excellent movement and a high spin rate. He generates a lot of weak contact and more swing-and-miss than other pitchers with his two-seamer. He has good fastball command to both sides down in the zone. Jurado doesn't have a true out pitch, which will test him at higher levels. His changeup is better than his slider, with both pitches having a chance to be average and play up because he locates them. He could return to Double-A Frisco, where he ended last season, but should be in Triple-A quickly and make his major league debut by the end of 2017. He projects as a No. 4 starter with a chance for more because of his command, movement and pitchability.

BA GRADE
50 Risk: Medium

Year	Club (League)	Class	W	L	ERA	G	GS	CG	SV	IP	H	HR	BB	SO	K/9	WHIP	AVG
2014	Rangers (AZL)	R	2	1	1.63	14	3	0	0	39	35	1	8	35	8.1	1.11	.233
2015	Hickory (SAL)	LoA	12	1	2.45	22	15	0	0	99	92	5	12	95	8.6	1.05	.246
2016	High Desert (CAL)	HiA	7	2	3.86	16	16	0	0	79	83	4	24	71	8.1	1.35	.272
	Frisco (TL)	AA	1	4	3.30	8	6	0	0	44	44	3	10	35	7.2	1.24	.263
Minor League Totals			28	8	2.82	69	49	0	0	310	302	14	57	283	8.2	1.16	.255

4 COLE RAGANS, LHP

Born: Dec. 12, 1997. **B-T:** L-L. **Ht.:** 6-4. **Wt.:** 197. **Drafted:** HS—Tallahassee, Fla., (1st round). **Signed by:** Brett Campbell.

Aside from sharing a first name and the same employer, Ragans is physically similar to a young Cole Hamels, whom Ragans models his game after. The Rangers drafted Ragans with the 30th overall pick in 2016 and signed him for $2,003,400 after a decorated career at North Florida Christian High, which he helped lead to a Florida state 3A title in 2014. He passes up a Florida State commitment in the process. Tall and athletic, Ragans has a simple delivery and advanced feel for a three-pitch mix. His fastball sits at 89-93 mph and has touched 95. His changeup made rapid progress over the past year, to the point where it's his best offspeed pitch.

BA GRADE
55 Risk: High

It's an above-average offering he sells with the same arm speed as his fastball, so it's just a matter of him learning how and when to use it more in games. His curveball flashes average and could grade higher down the road once he stays on top if it more consistently and does a better job repeating his arm slot. Ragans needs to improve his fastball command, but he has the delivery and athleticism that bode well for his ability to improve. He earns praise for his maturity and being a student of the game. Ragans has the talent to develop into a mid-rotation starter. He should pitch in the low Class A Hickory rotation in 2017.

Year	Club (League)	Class	W	L	ERA	G	GS	CG	SV	IP	H	HR	BB	SO	K/9	WHIP	AVG
2016	Rangers (AZL)	R	0	0	4.70	4	2	0	0	8	11	0	6	9	10.6	2.22	.344
Minor League Totals			0	0	4.70	4	2	0	0	8	11	0	6	9	10.6	2.22	.344

5 ANDY IBANEZ, 2B/3B

Born: April 3, 1993. **B-T:** R-R. **Ht.:** 5-10. **Wt.:** 170. **Signed:** Cuba, 2015. **Signed by:** Jose Fernandez/Roberto Aquino/Gil Kim/Thad Levine.

Ibanez was a standout in Cuba's junior leagues and even played in the 2013 World Baseball Classic, where he was Cuba's youngest player. After leaving Cuba, he signed with the Rangers for $1.6 million in July 2015. The Rangers took things slowly with Ibanez and started him at low Class A Hickory for his first season, then skipped him a level to Double-A Frisco in June. Ibanez is a similar player to Josh Morgan, with Ibanez having more power but less defensive versatility. He has a short, quick stroke with good bat-to-ball skills. He stays within the strike zone, puts the ball in play at a high clip and uses the middle of the field. Ibanez is mostly

BA GRADE

50 Risk: High

a doubles hitter who focuses on line drives, but he has the power to hit 10-15 home runs. With a thick lower half and below-average speed, he doesn't stand out for his athleticism. He's a slightly below-average defender at second base with a fringy arm and doesn't have the versatility to fill in at shortstop. Getting quicker first-step reactions off the bat will be key for him. Ibanez is a second baseman blocked at that position in Texas by Rougned Odor. His profile doesn't typically fetch much in trades, but his hitting potential could carry him as an everyday second baseman.

Year	Club (League)	Class	AVG	G	AB	R	H	2B	3B	HR	RBI	BB	SO	SB	CS	OBP	SLG
2016	Hickory (SAL)	LoA	.324	49	185	28	60	18	1	7	35	29	28	10	8	.413	.546
	Frisco (TL)	AA	.261	81	307	39	80	18	2	6	31	25	47	5	2	.318	.391
Minor League Totals			.285	130	492	67	140	36	3	13	66	54	75	15	10	.355	.449

6 JOSH MORGAN, 3B/SS

Born: Nov. 16, 1995. **B-T:** R-R. **Ht.:** 5-11. **Wt.:** 195. **Drafted:** HS—Orange, Calif., 2014 (3rd round). **Signed by:** Steve Flores.

Morgan's polished feel for hitting and gamer mentality stood out since he signed for $800,000 as a third-round pick in 2014. He finished the 2016 season strong at high Class A High Desert, batting .324/.386/.437 in the second half. After experimenting at catcher at 2015 instructional league, Morgan went behind the plate again at 2016 instructs, with the plan to have him catch and play the infield in 2017. Morgan's game is built around his ability to get on base. He's a disciplined hitter who recognizes breaking balls and doesn't chase much outside the strike zone. With quick hands and a short, simple stroke, Morgan is a high-contact hitter who

BA GRADE

50 Risk: High

uses the whole field with a line-drive approach but well below-average power. Morgan's swing has minimal movement but he could grow into more sock if he learns to load and generate more separation when he starts his swing. Primarily a shortstop in 2015, he spent most of his 2016 at third base and played the position well, though he got reps at shortstop and second base, too. He has the instincts, hands and feet to play second or third, with a tick above-average arm. If Morgan is able to catch, that would significantly enhance his value. Just 21, he may yet add catching and still move up to Double-A Frisco thanks to his polished approach.

Year	Club (League)	Class	AVG	G	AB	R	H	2B	3B	HR	RBI	BB	SO	SB	CS	OBP	SLG
2014	Rangers (AZL)	R	.336	33	113	26	38	2	1	0	10	19	13	2	2	.468	.372
	Spokane (NWL)	SS	.303	23	89	11	27	1	0	0	9	10	10	1	1	.392	.315
2015	Hickory (SAL)	LoA	.288	98	351	59	101	15	1	3	36	45	53	9	4	.385	.362
2016	High Desert (CAL)	HiA	.300	128	470	74	141	19	2	7	64	44	61	4	2	.367	.394
Minor League Totals			.300	282	1023	170	307	37	4	10	119	118	137	16	9	.388	.373

7 RONALD GUZMAN, 1B

Born: Oct. 20, 1994. **B-T:** L-L. **Ht.:** 6-6. **Wt.:** 220. **Signed:** Dominican Republic, 2011. **Signed by:** Willy Espinal/Mike Daly.

The Rangers' two big 16-year-old Dominican signings in 2011 were Nomar Mazara ($4.95 million) and Guzman, who got $3.45 million. Guzman got off to a strong start to his pro career, but stalled when he spent parts of three seasons at low Class A Hickory. He rebounded in 2016, playing in the Futures Game and reaching Triple-A Round Rock as a 21-year-old. Guzman signed with a hit-over-power profile, but the last two years got caught up trying to focus on home runs. He did a better job of calming his hitting actions to keep his body under control at Double-A Frisco in 2016. That enabled him to have a more repeatable swing and recognize pitches better because his head wasn't moving as much. The results showed with improved walk and strikeout rates. Guzman's long levers add length and some stiffness to his swing, but he doesn't strike out excessively. He doesn't have traditional first-base power but could hit 15-20 home runs per year. A limited athlete and runner without great range, he showed much-improved defensive actions to go with being an already big target. Guzman, whom the Rangers added to the 40-man roster in November, should return to Triple-A to open 2017 with a chance to make his major league debut by the end of the year.

BA GRADE
50 Risk: High

Year	Club (League)	Class	AVG	G	AB	R	H	2B	3B	HR	RBI	BB	SO	SB	CS	OBP	SLG
2014	Hickory (SAL)	LoA	.218	118	445	46	97	32	0	6	63	37	107	6	3	.283	.330
2015	Hickory (SAL)	LoA	.309	24	97	10	30	3	0	3	14	6	15	2	0	.346	.433
	High Desert (CAL)	HiA	.277	107	422	54	117	25	7	9	73	27	101	3	0	.319	.434
2016	Frisco (TL)	AA	.288	102	375	51	108	16	5	15	56	33	82	2	1	.348	.477
	Round Rock (PCL)	AAA	.216	25	88	9	19	5	1	1	11	6	23	0	1	.266	.330
Minor League Totals			.268	477	1812	216	486	104	16	39	276	139	397	20	6	.322	.408

8 ALEX SPEAS, RHP

BILL MITCHELL

Born: March 4, 1998. **B-T:** R-R. **Ht.:** 6-4. **Wt.:** 190. **Drafted:** HS—Powder Springs, Ga. 2016 (2nd round). **Signed by:** Derrick Tucker.

Speas showed his high-risk, high-reward potential in high school, flashing explosive arm speed and athleticism but looking raw at times. The Rangers, who have drafted aggressively from the Georgia prep ranks under scouting director Kip Fagg since 2010, selected him in the second round in 2016 and signed him for $1,024,900 as the No. 63 overall pick. A quick-twitch athlete with an extremely fast arm, Speas sits at 93-96 mph and can reach back for 99. His arm action is clean and the ball explodes out of his hand, finishing at the plate with good movement. He throws a power slider in the mid-80s that has the highest probability of developing into an out pitch. He's still learning to throw his changeup because he didn't need it much in high school. Getting Speas to make the mechanical adjustments to throw more strikes will be key. He tends to rush out on his front side and is still learning how to use his legs more in his delivery. His athleticism should help him make those adjustments, and he's already shown the ability to stay more online to the plate instead of spinning off since he signed. Speas likely won't move as quickly as fellow 2016 draft pick Cole Ragans, but the two should anchor the low Class A Hickory rotation in 2017.

BA GRADE
55 Risk: Extreme

Year	Club (League)	Class	W	L	ERA	G	GS	CG	SV	IP	H	HR	BB	SO	K/9	WHIP	AVG
2016	Rangers (AZL)	R	0	0	0.00	4	3	0	0	8	4	0	7	11	11.9	1.32	.138
Minor League Totals			0	0	0.00	4	3	0	0	8	4	0	7	11	11.9	1.32	.138

9 JOE PALUMBO, LHP

Born: Oct. 26, 1994. **B-T:** L-L. **Ht.:** 6-1. **Wt.:** 170. **Drafted:** HS—West Islip, NY, 2013 (30th round). **Signed by:** Takeshi Sakurayama.

Palumbo has transformed himself from organizational filler to become one of the system's best pitching prospects. Signed for $32,000 as a 30th-rounder out of a Long Island high school, he never generated much attention during his first three pro seasons. He opened 2016 as the low Class A Hickory closer, often working two to three inning stints. He was so effective that he moved to the rotation at the end of July. Getting stronger and improving his command helped Palumbo significantly in 2016, when he showed the three-pitch mix to start. He pitches off a low-90s fastball that touches 96 mph with the ability to hold his velocity even after he moved into the rotation. He has a short arm stroke that makes his fastball sneak up on hitters faster than

BA GRADE
50 Risk: High

they expect, while his cross-body mechanics further enhance his deception. Palumbo has improved his ability to command his plus curveball, a tight-spinning pitch with late break that is a big reason for his high strikeout rate. Palumbo's changeup flashes average, and he isn't afraid to mix it in against lefthanded hitters. His delivery is fairly simple and he's a solid strike-thrower. Palumbo will move on to the high Class A rotation in 2017, where he needs to prove he has the stuff to remain a starter over a full workload and isn't just a one-year fluke.

Year	Club (League)	Class	W	L	ERA	G	GS	CG	SV	IP	H	HR	BB	SO	K/9	WHIP	AVG
2014	Rangers (AZL)	R	4	4	2.32	14	7	0	0	43	29	0	15	49	10.3	1.03	.190
2015	Spokane (NWL)	SS	3	3	2.82	12	9	0	0	54	52	3	22	42	7.0	1.36	.250
	Hickory (SAL)	LoA	0	0	6.23	1	0	0	0	4	5	0	3	1	2.1	1.85	.294
2016	Hickory (SAL)	LoA	7	5	2.24	33	7	0	8	96	71	5	36	122	11.4	1.11	.202
Minor League Totals			15	13	2.73	73	23	0	8	217	176	8	90	236	9.8	1.22	.218

10 BRETT MARTIN, LHP

Born: April 28, 1995. **B-T:** L-L. **Ht.:** 6-5. **Wt.:** 215. **Drafted:** Walters State (Tenn.) CC, 2014 (4th round). **Signed by:** Chris Kemp.

Martin opened 2016 by repeating low Class A Hickory, then spent June and July on the disabled list with a sprained elbow ligament. When healthy in August he jumped to high Class A High Desert. He saved his best start for last, pitching seven scoreless, no-hit innings with 15 strikeouts and one walk on 95 pitches in the California League playoffs. Over the last two years, Martin has bulked up into a strong, physical pitcher. His fastball sits at 90-92 mph and touches 94. His curveball is his putaway pitch when it's on, and it was at its best in the Cal League playoffs. He's still learning how to land it, especially early in the count, but it can be an above-average pitch with good spin, shape and power. Martin throws a firm changeup in the mid-80s, a below-average pitch that could use more separation off his fastball. He's added a short, hard cutter to give him a four-pitch mix. With long arm action and long limbs, Martin has cleaned up his mechanics by lowering his leg kick to help sync his upper and lower halves in his delivery. He's a solid strike-thrower who did a better job last season of maintaining his body control instead of overthrowing. A healthy 2017 will be key for Martin, who also was limited in 2015 by hip issues. He probably is destined for the high Class A rotation in 2017.

BA GRADE 50 Risk: High

Year	Club (League)	Class	W	L	ERA	G	GS	CG	SV	IP	H	HR	BB	SO	K/9	WHIP	AVG
2014	Rangers (AZL)	R	1	4	5.40	15	6	0	1	35	36	3	12	39	10.0	1.37	.261
2015	Hickory (SAL)	LoA	5	6	3.49	20	18	0	0	95	92	6	26	72	6.8	1.24	.265
2016	Hickory (SAL)	LoA	2	3	4.53	9	9	0	0	44	58	3	14	48	9.9	1.65	.317
	Rangers (AZL)	R	0	0	3.86	2	2	0	0	2	3	0	0	6	23.1	1.29	.273
	High Desert (CAL)	HiA	2	1	4.24	6	6	0	0	23	24	3	7	16	6.2	1.33	.270
Minor League Totals			10	14	4.15	52	41	0	1	200	213	15	59	181	8.2	1.36	.277

11 MICHAEL DE LEON, SS

BA GRADE 50 Risk: High

Born: Jan. 14, 1997. **B-T:** B-R. **Ht.:** 6-1. **Wt.:** 185. **Signed:** Dominican Republic, 2013. **Signed by:** Danilo Troncoso.

De Leon signed for $550,000 in 2013, then made his pro debut the next year at Double-A when Frisco needed a fill-in for a few days. While the Rangers slowed him down in 2016, he was still one of the youngest players in the high Class A California League as a 19-year-old. Skinny and underweight when he signed, De Leon gained 20 pounds since the end of the 2015 season. The additional strength helped him repeat his swing more frequently and allowed him to drive the ball with more authority. He's not a power hitter, though, and he relies more on excellent hand-eye coordination and a quick, short stroke from both sides of the plate to spray line drives around the field. He is a below-average runner who makes up for a lack of foot speed with a quick first step at shortstop, excellent instincts, fundamentals and a knack for being in the right place at the right time. He has a good internal clock with smooth hands and an average, accurate arm. De Leon's defense carries him right now, but his contact skills could be enough for him to develop into an everyday shortstop. He should be one of the youngest players in the Texas League in 2017.

Year	Club (League)	Class	AVG	G	AB	R	H	2B	3B	HR	RBI	BB	SO	SB	CS	OBP	SLG
2014	Frisco (TL)	AA	.333	1	3	1	1	1	0	0	0	0	1	0	0	.333	.667
	Hickory (SAL)	LoA	.244	85	336	42	82	10	2	1	26	28	40	3	4	.302	.295
	Myrtle Beach (CAR)	HiA	.292	7	24	5	7	3	0	1	6	3	4	0	0	.370	.542
2015	Hickory (SAL)	LoA	.222	81	306	29	68	11	2	1	29	23	47	1	1	.277	.281
2016	High Desert (CAL)	HiA	.267	128	454	54	121	25	1	9	54	24	57	7	5	.308	.385
Minor League Totals			.248	302	1123	131	279	50	5	12	115	78	149	11	9	.299	.334

12 JOSE TREVINO, C

BA GRADE

45 Risk: High

Born: Nov. 28, 1992. **B-T:** R-R. **Ht.:** 5-11. **Wt.:** 195. **Drafted:** Oral Roberts, 2014 (6th round). **Signed by:** Bobby Crook.

After playing catcher as a sophomore at Oral Roberts, Trevino moved to third base the next year, while seeing some time at shortstop and catcher as well. That positional uncertainty played in a role in his availability in the sixth round in the 2014 draft, where the Rangers took him and put him behind the plate. He has transformed himself into an elite defender. Trevino takes pride in running the pitching staff and draws rave reviews for his leadership skills. Pitchers love throwing to him not only because he calls a good game but because he's adept at receiving and blocking balls in the dirt. His arm is a tick above average and plays up because of his footwork, quick release and accuracy, which helped him lead the high Class A California League by throwing out 48 percent of basestealers. Trevino doesn't have the prettiest swing, but he has good bat control so he doesn't strike out much., although his tendency to swing at pitches he can't drive limits his quality of contact sometimes. Trevino is a premium defender, but how much he improves as a hitter will dictate whether he can be more than a backup. He should head to Double-A Frisco to start 2017.

Year	Club (League)	Class	AVG	G	AB	R	H	2B	3B	HR	RBI	BB	SO	SB	CS	OBP	SLG
2014	Spokane (NWL)	SS	.257	72	288	58	74	22	3	9	49	23	50	2	0	.313	.448
2015	Hickory (SAL)	LoA	.262	112	424	62	111	19	2	14	63	18	60	1	4	.291	.415
2016	High Desert (CAL)	HiA	.303	109	433	67	131	30	0	9	68	26	49	2	1	.342	.434
Minor League Totals			.276	293	1145	187	316	71	5	32	180	67	159	5	5	.316	.431

13 DAVID GARCIA, C

BA GRADE

50 Risk: Extreme

Born: Feb. 6, 2000. **B-T:** B-R. **Ht.:** 5-11. **Wt.:** 170. **Signed:** Venezuela, 2016. **Signed by:** Johnny Gomez.

The year before he was eligible to sign, Garcia was a small, frail 15-year-old at 5-foot-9, 145 pounds, but as he grew taller, gained weight and improved both as a hitter and a defender, he developed into the player many clubs had ranked as the top catching prospect on the 2016 international market. The Rangers signed him for $800,000. Garcia has a simple, compact swing from both sides. His lefty stroke used to get long but he shortened that up before signing to the point some scouts now think he is more advanced from that side. Garcia has good plate coverage and a sound hitting mindset, working the middle of the field with a line-drive approach. He has a medium frame with gap power and doesn't project to be a big home run threat. Garcia originally was a shortstop but committed to catching a year and a half before he signed. He projects to stay there because he's a smooth receiver for his age with quick feet and soft hands. His arm was average when he signed with good arm action and has already improved to flashing plus, with a quick release and good accuracy. Garcia probably will make his pro debut in the Dominican Summer League.

Year	Club (League)	Class	AVG	G	AB	R	H	2B	3B	HR	RBI	BB	SO	SB	CS	OBP	SLG
2016	Did not play—Signed 2017 contract																

14 MIGUEL APARICIO, OF

BA GRADE

50 Risk: Extreme

Born: March 7, 1999. **B-T:** L-L. **Ht.:** 6-0. **Wt.:** 180. **Signed:** Venezuela, 2015. **Signed by:** Jhonny Gomez/Rafic Saab.

The Rangers signed two of the best center fielders on the international market in 2015, adding Leody Taveras out of the Dominican Republic and Aparicio from Venezuela for $500,000. Aparicio doesn't match Taveras in terms of athleticism or explosiveness or tools, but he is a well-rounded player whose instincts and overall game awareness are advanced for his age. He's a high-contact hitter with a short, simple swing and manages his at-bats well with a good approach. He's at his best when he stays back and trusts his hands, though he can get caught out front and off balance at times, particularly when he gets too pull-conscious. Aparicio is a good hitter overall with a line-drive approach who can drill one over the fence occasionally and should grow into more power with a chance to hit 10-15 homers. Aparicio's pure speed and arm strength are both slightly below-average, but his defense might be what stands out the most. He makes up for his lack of burner speed with a quick first step, reading swings well to get excellent jumps off the bat and taking good routes. His baserunning acumen is advanced as well. Aparicio is ticketed for the Rookie-level Arizona League in 2017.

Year	Club (League)	Class	AVG	G	AB	R	H	2B	3B	HR	RBI	BB	SO	SB	CS	OBP	SLG
2016	Rangers2 (DSL)	R	.274	58	219	32	60	10	4	3	36	18	36	15	7	.337	.397
Minor League Totals			.274	58	219	32	60	10	4	3	36	18	36	15	7	.337	.397

15 CONNOR SADZECK, RHP

BA GRADE

45 Risk: High

Born: Oct. 1, 1991. **B-T:** R-R. **Ht.:** 6-7. **Wt.:** 240. **Drafted:** Howard (Texas) JC, 2011 (11th round). **Signed by:** Jay Eddings.

After missing the 2014 season due to Tommy John surgery, Sadzeck saw his velocity soar back into the triple-digits in 2015, though with little feel for where his fastball would land. His control leaped forward in 2016 at Double-A as he trimmed his walk rate from 6.1 per nine innings to 3.3. Sadzeck is a hefty 6-foot-7 with an enormous fastball that sits in the mid-90s and peaks at 101 mph. His fastball has a touch of sink but is more notable for its velocity than its life. He improved his ability to throw his slider and changeup for strikes, though neither one is a true out pitch. His slider is more advanced, flashing average but needing improvement to give him a better weapon off his fastball. The development of his slider and improving his fastball command will be crucial for Sadzeck. He will go to Triple-A Round Rock and continue his development as a starter, but given his repertoire, command, medical history and potential for more frequent 100 mph readings in short stints, there's a good chance his future lies in relief.

Year	Club (League)	Class	W	L	ERA	G	GS	CG	SV	IP	H	HR	BB	SO	K/9	WHIP	AVG
2014	Did not play—Injured																
2015	High Desert (CAL)	HiA	2	1	3.98	11	8	0	0	41	32	4	24	48	10.6	1.38	.213
	Frisco (TL)	AA	1	1	9.61	7	6	0	0	20	22	1	17	16	7.3	1.98	.293
2016	Frisco (TL)	AA	10	8	4.16	25	23	2	0	141	127	18	52	133	8.5	1.27	.244
Minor League Totals			26	18	3.76	82	76	2	0	395	327	29	191	333	7.6	1.31	.227

16 ANDERSON TEJEDA, SS

BA GRADE

50 Risk: Extreme

Born: May 1, 1998. **B-T:** L-R. **Ht.:** 5-11. **Wt.:** 175. **Signed:** Dominican Republic, 2014. **Signed by:** Rodolfo Rosario/Roberto Aquino.

The Rangers liked Tejeda's hitting ability when they signed him for $100,000 as a 16-year-old out of the Dominican Republic. After a strong pro debut in the Dominican Summer League in 2015, he built upon that in 2016 in the Rookie-level Arizona League and earned a late promotion to short-season Spokane, where he ranked fifth in the Northwest League with eight home runs despite playing just 23 games there. Tejeda has quick, whippy bat speed and a lot of moving parts in his swing—from a leg kick to the way he loads his hands. He has the power to hit 20 home runs and shows natural feel to hit, but he's a free-swinger who struck out 25 percent of the time in 2016. Tejeda has good hand-eye coordination but he has to calm his swing and get better at recognizing breaking pitches. Some scouts think he can stay at shortstop, where he has a plus arm, but his offensive game is ahead of his defense. An average runner, Tejeda made 17 errors in 45 games at shortstop and is still learning to slow the game down. He is ready for low Class A Hickory next in 2017.

Year	Club (League)	Class	AVG	G	AB	R	H	2B	3B	HR	RBI	BB	SO	SB	CS	OBP	SLG
2015	Rangers1 (DSL)	R	.277	14	47	4	13	2	2	0	8	8	11	2	4	.382	.404
	Rangers2 (DSL)	R	.323	41	158	32	51	17	4	4	32	17	38	7	5	.397	.557
2016	Rangers1 (DSL)	R	.262	11	42	9	11	2	3	1	7	5	4	5	0	.340	.524
	Rangers (AZL)	R	.293	32	133	22	39	12	6	1	21	8	36	1	0	.331	.496
	Spokane (NWL)	SS	.277	23	94	15	26	0	1	8	19	5	33	1	0	.313	.553
Minor League Totals			.295	121	474	82	140	33	16	14	87	43	122	16	7	.356	.521

17 JONATHAN HERNANDEZ, RHP

BA GRADE

45 Risk: High

Born: July 6, 1996. **B-T:** R-R. **Ht.:** 6-2. **Wt.:** 180. **Signed:** Dominican Republic, 2013. **Signed by:** Willy Espinal/Mike Daly.

Hernandez's father is former Tigers reliever Fernando Hernandez. Fernando pitched for Double-A Memphis in 1996, and that's where Jonathan was born, though he grew up in the Dominican Republic and signed with the Rangers for $300,000 in January 2013. Hernandez has a lean, skinny frame and will need to get stronger, but his fastball has steadily ticked up since signing. He now sits in the low 90s and can hit 97 mph with easy, explosive arm action and a crossfire delivery. His changeup is an average pitch with good deception. His slider has its moments, but he needs to define it with better shape because he tends to get wide with it and hitters are able to lay off as a result. Hernandez has produced ordinary strikeout rates, but he's a solid strike-thrower for his age who is ready to make the jump to the Rangers' new high Class A affiliate in the Carolina League with a chance to develop into a back-end starter.

Year	Club (League)	Class	W	L	ERA	G	GS	CG	SV	IP	H	HR	BB	SO	K/9	WHIP	AVG
2014	Rangers (DSL)	R	5	2	2.85	14	14	0	0	76	72	6	17	57	6.8	1.18	.246
2015	Rangers (AZL)	R	1	1	3.00	11	9	0	0	45	45	0	12	33	6.6	1.27	.250
2016	Hickory (SAL)	LoA	10	9	4.56	24	22	1	0	116	110	14	49	85	6.6	1.37	.252
Minor League Totals			19	13	3.32	62	53	1	0	282	255	22	100	213	6.8	1.26	.239

18 KOLE ENRIGHT, 2B/3B

BA GRADE

50 Risk: Extreme

Born: Jan. 1, 1998. **B-T:** B-R. **Ht.:** 6-2. **Wt.:** 188. **Drafted:** HS—Winter Garden, Fla., 2016 (3rd round). **Signed by:** Brett Campbell.

The Rangers had Enright ranked higher on their draft board than other clubs when they took him in the third round in 2016 and signed him away from a Stetson commitment for $675,000. The early returns were promising. Enright made a smooth transition to pro ball in the Rookie-level Arizona League despite missing two weeks early on with a hamstring injury. He has a mature swing that is simple and contact-oriented. At times it can get big, but when he stays back and uses his hands, he puts the ball in play with a line-drive approach. His pop is mostly to the gaps with enough strength projection where he could develop 10-15 home-run power. An offensive-minded prospect, Enright spent most of his time at third base and shortstop in the AZL, then at instructional league focused on second base. He probably will split time between second and third base in 2017, with most of his reps probably coming at second. He has the tools to be at least an average defender at second base with an average arm. Enright should head to low Class A Hickory in 2017.

Year	Club (League)	Class	AVG	G	AB	R	H	2B	3B	HR	RBI	BB	SO	SB	CS	OBP	SLG
2016	Rangers (AZL)	R	.313	42	150	22	47	13	0	1	17	14	33	3	1	.378	.420
Minor League Totals			.313	42	150	22	47	13	0	1	17	14	33	3	1	.378	.420

19 MICHAEL MATUELLA, RHP

BA GRADE

50 Risk: Extreme

Born: June 3, 1994. **B-T:** R-R. **Ht.:** 6-6. **Wt.:** 220. **Drafted:** Duke, 2015 (3rd round). **Signed by:** Jay Heafner.

Matuella is following Tanner Scheppers' path as a Rangers draft pick with electric stuff but durability issues that have hampered him since college. After his sophomore year at Duke, Matuella projected to be a potential No. 1 overall pick for the 2015 draft, but in the summer of 2014 he was diagnosed with spondylosis, a chronic back condition. He was back on the mound his junior year in 2015, but his stuff wasn't quite as crisp, and he had Tommy John surgery that April. Even with the injury and Matuella having never thrown more than 60 innings in college, the Rangers drafted him in the third round in 2015 and signed him for $2 million. He rehabbed and made his pro debut at short-season Spokane in 2016, but after one start felt elbow discomfort and was shut down the rest of the season. At his best, Matuella has good control and a frontline starter's repertoire, sitting 92-96 mph with his two-seamer and touching 98 with plus life. His power curveball and slider were both plus pitches, and while he didn't need his changeup much, it showed signs it could develop into an average pitch. Matuella's makeup will be an asset during the rehab, so the Rangers hold out hope that he can remain a starter.

Year	Club (League)	Class	W	L	ERA	G	GS	CG	SV	IP	H	HR	BB	SO	K/9	WHIP	AVG
2015	Did not play—Injured																
2016	Spokane (NWL)	SS	0	0	0.00	1	1	0	0	3	1	0	2	1	3.0	1.00	.111
Minor League Totals			0	0	0.00	1	1	0	0	3	1	0	2	1	3.0	1.00	.111

20 JAIRO BERAS, OF

BA GRADE

50 Risk: Extreme

Born: Dec. 25, 1994. **B-T:** R-R. **Ht.:** 6-6. **Wt.:** 195. **Signed:** Dominican Republic, 2012. **Signed by:** Danilo Troncoso/Roberto Aquino/Paul Kruger/Mike Daly.

When the Collective Bargaining Agreement went into place in December 2011, it included new international bonus pools designed to limit spending that would begin on July 2, 2012. Beras originally presented himself as a 16-year-old eligible to sign in 2012, but instead he signed with the Rangers for $4.5 million in February 2012, claiming he was really 17 and thus eligible to sign immediately. Shortly after July 2, Major League Baseball ruled Beras' age as "undetermined," but allowed the contract to stand. Beras struggled at high Class A High Desert for most of 2016, until he caught fire late and hit .308/.361/.692 in his final 29 games. Tall and lanky, he has plus raw power but gets himself out by swinging through breaking balls and expanding the strike zone. At the end of the season, Beras made an adjustment to put his hands and his body in better position, starting with a more upright stance instead of bending over from the top, allowing him to track pitches better. A below-average runner, he has a plus arm in right field but doesn't defend his position well because of a mix of puzzling routes and mental miscues. He should advance to Double-A Frisco in 2017.

Year	Club (League)	Class	AVG	G	AB	R	H	2B	3B	HR	RBI	BB	SO	SB	CS	OBP	SLG
2014	Hickory (SAL)	LoA	.242	110	389	38	94	18	0	7	33	33	133	5	4	.305	.342
2015	Hickory (SAL)	LoA	.291	88	327	45	95	18	2	9	43	19	88	9	4	.332	.440
2016	High Desert (CAL)	HiA	.262	107	409	71	107	28	4	22	78	24	121	5	5	.306	.511
Minor League Totals			.262	322	1189	165	312	66	8	40	169	81	361	20	13	.313	.432

21 JOSE CARDONA, OF

BA GRADE

45 Risk: High

Born: March 16, 1994. **B-T:** B-R. **Ht.:** 6-1. **Wt.:** 190. **Signed:** Mexico, 2011.
Signed by: Gil Kim/Bill McLaughlin.

Cardona has flown under the radar for most of his career. He hit only one home run in his first four pro seasons, but as he got stronger and matured as a hitter he started to drive the ball with more authority in 2015. He built upon that with his best offensive season in 2016 at high Class A High Desert. Cardona's tools don't immediately grab attention—and some of what he does is unorthodox—but he finds ways to contribute in all phases of the game. His best attribute is his defense, which grades as above-average in center field. He's a slightly above-average runner with a nose for the ball, good range and a strong arm in the outfield. At the plate, Cardona is short to the ball and he makes frequent contact with a line-drive approach and the ability to use the whole field. He tracks pitches well, puts together quality at-bats and has the power to hit 10-15 home runs, though he's more of a doubles threat than a power hitter. The jump to Double-A Frisco in 2017 will be a key test for Cardona's prospect status in his first taste of the upper minors.

Year	Club (League)	Class	AVG	G	AB	R	H	2B	3B	HR	RBI	BB	SO	SB	CS	OBP	SLG
2014	Myrtle Beach (CAR)	HiA	.182	7	22	2	4	0	0	0	0	0	1	0	0	.182	.182
	Rangers (AZL)	R	.316	20	76	9	24	4	2	0	11	4	14	8	0	.350	.421
	Spokane (NWL)	SS	.333	20	75	8	25	5	1	0	10	6	9	3	1	.378	.427
2015	Hickory (SAL)	LoA	.254	128	469	64	119	19	5	10	59	40	73	30	18	.317	.380
2016	High Desert (CAL)	HiA	.300	101	397	81	119	23	0	14	48	42	66	13	4	.371	.463
Minor League Totals			.276	447	1661	263	459	78	18	25	218	184	287	78	33	.353	.390

22 JOSE LECLERC, RHP

BA GRADE

40 Risk: Medium

Born: Dec. 19, 1993. **B-T:** R-R. **Ht.:** 6-0. **Wt.:** 190. **Signed:** Dominican Republic,
2010. **Signed by:** Willy Espinal.

A reliever his first four seasons, LeClerc moved to the rotation in 2015 at Double-A Frisco but had the worst season of his career. He returned to the bullpen in 2016 and made his major league debut with three appearances in July before returning to Triple-A Round Rock and then returning as a September callup. LeClerc has the stuff to be a quality reliever, but has to improve his control to stay in the big leagues. His quick arm delivers fastballs that sit 94-96 mph and can peak at 98. LeClerc has one of the most unusual changeups in baseball, with cutter-like action instead of armside fade, to the point some scouts think it's a slider. It's an above-average pitch, and he also has a straight changeup he uses as well. He mainly relies on his fastball-changeup combination, though he will mix in an occasional fringe-average curveball to give hitters another look. Fastball command and general wildness have long been an issue. At Triple-A, he got more swings and misses out of the strike zone, but major league hitters were able to resist. LeClerc should have a chance to win a job in the Rangers' bullpen in 2017 and could stay there if his location improves.

Year	Club (League)	Class	W	L	ERA	G	GS	CG	SV	IP	H	HR	BB	SO	K/9	WHIP	AVG
2014	Myrtle Beach (CAR)	HiA	4	1	3.30	42	0	0	14	57	39	8	37	78	12.2	1.33	.193
2015	Frisco (TL)	AA	6	8	5.77	26	22	0	0	103	97	8	73	98	8.6	1.65	.249
2016	Frisco (TL)	AA	5	0	3.52	10	2	0	1	23	17	1	10	28	11.0	1.17	.210
	Round Rock (PCL)	AAA	2	2	2.72	29	0	0	1	43	23	3	28	50	10.5	1.19	.160
	Texas (AL)	MAJ	0	0	1.80	12	0	0	0	15	11	0	13	15	9.0	1.60	.212
Major League Totals			0	0	1.80	12	0	0	0	15	11	0	13	15	9.0	1.60	.212
Minor League Totals			21	22	3.64	185	25	0	23	366	286	24	205	399	9.8	1.34	.216

23 DREW ROBINSON, 2B/3B

BA GRADE

40 Risk: Medium

Born: April 20, 1992. **B-T:** L-R. **Ht.:** 6-1. **Wt.:** 200. **Drafted:** HS—Las Vegas, 2010
(4th round). **Signed by:** Todd Guggiana.

Bryce Harper was the talk of Nevada when he went No. 1 overall in the 2010 draft. It has been a slower climb for Robinson, a fellow Las Vegas native who signed with the Rangers for $198,000 out of the draft that year. He would have become a minor league free agent after the 2016 season, but the Rangers added him to the 40-man roster. Robinson doesn't have one plus tool, but he does a bit of everything, bats lefthanded and plays nearly every position. He has a loose, smooth swing with strong hands to drive the ball for a tick above-average power. He walked 13 percent of the time at Triple-A Round Rock but also struck out 28 percent of his plate appearances. His patience borders on passivity, putting him in bad counts sometimes. He is an average runner with good baserunning instincts and the speed to play the outfield in addition to his natural infield spots. That versatility is key for Robinson, who projects as an offensive-minded utility man. He likely will return to Triple-A but should make his major league debut in 2017.

Year	Club (League)	Class	AVG	G	AB	R	H	2B	3B	HR	RBI	BB	SO	SB	CS	OBP	SLG
2014	Frisco (TL)	AA	.190	96	331	41	63	15	5	11	40	37	125	6	5	.273	.366
	Round Rock (PCL)	AAA	.304	8	23	3	7	2	0	1	5	6	7	3	0	.467	.522
2015	Frisco (TL)	AA	.231	126	432	78	100	23	5	21	64	83	139	14	8	.360	.454
	Round Rock (PCL)	AAA	.304	7	23	4	7	2	0	0	2	4	4	2	1	.407	.391
2016	Round Rock (PCL)	AAA	.257	125	467	76	120	24	10	20	67	66	148	17	5	.350	.480
Minor League Totals			.245	702	2427	389	594	129	33	78	356	408	761	75	33	.358	.422

24 ANDREW FAULKNER, LHP

BA GRADE

40 Risk: Medium

Born: Sept. 12, 1992. **B-T:** R-L. **Ht.:** 6-3. **Wt.:** 205. **Drafted:** HS—South Aiken, S.C., 2011 (14th round). **Signed by:** Chris Kemp.

Faulkner made his major league debut at the end of the 2015 season and pitched well for the Rangers over 11 relief outings. He made the Opening Day roster in 2016, but it ended up being a disappointing season for Faulkner. He stayed in Texas for two weeks, went down to Triple-A Round Rock for a month, returned to the major leagues for three appearances in May before going back to Triple-A the rest of the season, aside from one final scoreless inning in Oakland on Sept. 25. Faulkner's stuff backed up a bit from 2015, which resulted in less swing-and-miss and a lower strikeout rate. His fastball sits at 91-93 mph and touches 95. His crossfire delivery makes it difficult for lefties to pick up that pitch out of his hand. His slider and changeup—which he throws with a split-like grip—were both fringy pitches that didn't miss many bats, so he will have to sharpen his offspeed stuff. If Faulkner can do that, he has a future in middle relief, though he probably returns to Triple-A to begin 2017.

Year	Club (League)	Class	W	L	ERA	G	GS	CG	SV	IP	H	HR	BB	SO	K/9	WHIP	AVG
2014	Myrtle Beach (CAR)	HiA	10	1	2.07	21	18	0	1	104	86	1	31	100	8.6	1.12	.228
	Frisco (TL)	AA	2	4	4.99	7	6	0	0	31	28	3	14	33	9.7	1.37	.237
2015	Frisco (TL)	AA	7	4	4.19	28	15	0	1	92	84	9	47	90	8.8	1.42	.243
	Round Rock (PCL)	AAA	0	0	0.00	6	0	0	0	8	2	0	1	13	14.6	0.38	.080
	Texas (AL)	MAJ	0	0	2.79	11	0	0	0	10	8	2	3	10	9.3	1.14	.216
2016	Round Rock (PCL)	AAA	5	3	3.97	41	1	0	4	45	39	3	20	39	7.7	1.30	.234
	Texas (AL)	MAJ	0	0	6.75	9	0	0	0	7	8	3	4	1	1.4	1.80	.286
Major League Totals			0	0	4.41	20	0	0	0	16	16	5	7	11	6.1	1.41	.246
Minor League Totals			35	24	3.49	165	76	0	6	511	476	27	198	460	8.1	1.32	.246

25 MIKE HAUSCHILD, RHP

BA GRADE

40 Risk: Medium

Born: Jan. 22, 1990. **B-T:** R-R. **Ht.:** 6-3. **Wt.:** 210. **Drafted:** Dayton, 2012 (33rd round). **Signed by:** Nick Venuto (Astros).

Hauschild has been around sports all his life. His father Doug is the long-time media relations director at Dayton, the same school where Michael starred from 2010 to 2012. Another in the long line of Astros late-round, senior signs, Hauschild steadily progressed up the minor league ladder but rarely impressed in the Houston system. He reached Triple-A Fresno in both 2015 and 2016, and he ranked fourth in the Pacific Coast League with a 3.22 ERA in the latter season. The Rangers selected Hauschild in the Rule 5 draft at the 2016 Winter Meetings. He has above-average control to go with his 89-93 mph fastball and an effective forkball-like changeup. He also snaps off a cutter and an occasional slider. As a starter, Hauschild succeeds by keeping the ball down, generating ground balls and avoiding walks that lead to big innings. The Rangers plan to let him battle for either their No. 5 starter job or a role in the bullpen.

Year	Club (League)	Class	W	L	ERA	G	GS	CG	SV	IP	H	HR	BB	SO	K/9	WHIP	AVG
2014	Lancaster (CAL)	HiA	2	1	4.41	8	4	0	0	35	40	3	9	31	8.0	1.41	.310
	Corpus Christi (TL)	AA	2	9	4.29	20	16	0	1	99	95	5	25	87	7.9	1.22	.258
2015	Corpus Christi (TL)	AA	5	1	3.20	10	8	0	1	51	53	2	8	35	6.2	1.20	.272
	Fresno (PCL)	AAA	7	5	3.49	15	15	0	0	88	86	6	27	81	8.3	1.29	.253
2016	Fresno (PCL)	AAA	9	10	3.22	24	24	0	0	140	138	7	40	119	7.7	1.27	.259
Minor League Totals			36	32	3.50	124	87	0	5	565	563	31	148	480	7.6	1.26	.262

26 ERIC JENKINS, OF

BA GRADE

45 Risk: Extreme

Born: Jan. 30, 1997. **B-T:** L-R. **Ht.:** 6-1. **Wt.:** 175. **Drafted:** HS—Cerro Gordo, N.C., 2015 (2nd round). **Signed by:** Jay Heafner.

Signed for $2 million as the No. 45 overall pick in 2015, Jenkins piled up strikeouts in 2016 at low Class A Hickory and generally had a tough time. He still showcased double-plus speed by stealing 51 bases, most in the South Atlantic League and third overall in the minors. Jenkins has extremely quick hands and strong wrists, but his barrel doesn't stay in the hitting zone very long. He is still learning to trust his hands by keeping them back and repeating his load and separation rather than getting caught out front. Jenkins has trouble recognizing changeups, which further contributed to him getting off balance. He has more power that his lean 6-foot-1 frame suggests and could hit 10-15 home runs, though his swing path isn't geared to hit the ball in the air. Jenkins is an outstanding athlete with the speed to cover plenty of ground in center field along with an average arm. The Rangers have had other tooled-up outfielders like Lewis Brinson and Nomar Mazara repeat Hickory before, so Jenkins could follow that path unless the Rangers push him to high Class A in 2017.

Year	Club (League)	Class	AVG	G	AB	R	H	2B	3B	HR	RBI	BB	SO	SB	CS	OBP	SLG
2015	Rangers (AZL)	R	.249	51	177	35	44	4	6	0	13	23	57	27	3	.342	.339
	Hickory (SAL)	LoA	.389	5	18	3	7	1	0	0	1	1	4	1	0	.421	.444
2016	Hickory (SAL)	LoA	.221	126	506	72	112	13	9	8	40	40	154	51	15	.279	.330
	High Desert (CAL)	HiA	.000	1	4	0	0	0	0	0	0	0	3	0	0	.000	.000
Minor League Totals			.231	183	705	110	163	18	15	8	54	64	218	79	18	.297	.333

27 YANIO PEREZ, OF/3B

BA GRADE
45 Risk: Extreme

Born: Aug. 10, 1995. **B-T:** R-R. **Ht.:** 6-2. **Wt.:** 205. **Signed:** Cuba, 2016. **Signed by:** Jose Fernandez/Chu Halabe/Rafic Saab.

Perez hit well in Cuba's junior national leagues, batting .351/.448/.523 in 135 plate appearances in the country's 18U national league and earning a spot on the Cuban team that went to the 18U World Cup in Taiwan. Perez batted .265/.333/.347 in 514 plate appearances over two seasons with Artemisa in Cuba's top league, Serie Nacional, then left the country and signed with the Rangers in September 2016 for $1.1 million. He didn't stand out much when he was in Cuba, but his tools jumped after he left. During workouts in Mexico before he signed, he showed above-average raw power, and while he was a fringe-average runner in Cuba, he showed plus speed in the 60-yard dash. Those tools are intriguing, though his pure hitting ability remains a question mark. In Cuba, Perez mostly played third base but also got time at second base, right field and first base. He's expected to get most of his playing time rotating between all three outfield spots with the Rangers. His first action should come with low Class A Hickory in 2017 as he makes his U.S. professional debut.

Year	Club (League)	Class	AVG	G	AB	R	H	2B	3B	HR	RBI	BB	SO	SB	CS	OBP	SLG
2014	Artemisa (CNS)	CNS	.265	80	268	32	71	12	2	2	33	21	42	0	3	.333	.347
2015	Did not play																
2016	Did not play																

28 JUREMI PROFAR, 3B/1B

BA GRADE
40 Risk: High

Born: Jan. 30, 1996. **B-T:** R-R. **Ht.:** 6-1. **Wt.:** 215. **Signed:** Curacao, 2012. **Signed by:** Jose Felomonia/Chu Halabi/Mike Daly.

When Profar signed with the Rangers for $150,000 in September 2012, it appeared a token signing from the organization that knew him since he was 12. At the time Juremi signed, older brother Jurickson was 19 years old and already in the majors. While Juremi was known mostly as Jurickson's younger brother his first few years in the system, he made his own name with a strong offensive campaign at high Class A High Desert in 2016. None of Profar's tools grade out better than average, but he has outstanding game awareness and a knack for squaring up the ball. He controls the strike zone with good plate discipline and plate coverage, resulting just an 11 percent strikeout rate in 2016. The power spike he showed was mostly a product of High Desert, but he can be a 10-15 home run hitter. Profar is an offensive-oriented player who mostly split time at third base and first base, with sporadic time at second base. He doesn't run well, but he has good hands and an average arm. Profar doesn't have a true position, but his bat has a chance to carry him to the majors, with Double-A Frisco his next step.

Year	Club (League)	Class	AVG	G	AB	R	H	2B	3B	HR	RBI	BB	SO	SB	CS	OBP	SLG
2014	Hickory (SAL)	LoA	.269	7	26	3	7	0	0	1	4	2	3	1	0	.321	.385
	Round Rock (PCL)	AAA	.333	2	6	1	2	0	0	0	0	0	0	0	0	.333	.333
	Spokane (NWL)	SS	.247	67	251	26	62	10	0	1	36	22	47	1	1	.307	.299
2015	High Desert (CAL)	HiA	.240	13	50	7	12	2	1	1	7	4	9	0	0	.304	.380
	Hickory (SAL)	LoA	.272	64	243	26	66	17	1	3	26	14	27	1	1	.313	.387
2016	High Desert (CAL)	HiA	.300	103	383	66	115	23	2	13	58	33	47	1	3	.355	.473
Minor League Totals			.276	319	1176	167	325	65	5	19	175	97	146	5	9	.334	.389

29 PEDRO PAYANO, RHP

BA GRADE
40 Risk: High

Born: Sept. 27, 1994. **B-T:** R-R. **Ht.:** 6-2. **Wt.:** 210. **Signed:** Dominican Republic, 2011. **Signed by:** Rodolfo Rosario.

The Rangers signed Nomar Mazara on July 2, 2011, for $4.95 million out of Ivan Noboa's program. At the same time, Texas landed Payano, who also trained with Noboa, for $650,000. Payano, who was born in New York but grew up in the Dominican Republic, pitched three full seasons in the Dominican Summer League, with the Rangers leaving him there in part due to maturity issues. He was in the midst of his best season in 2016 when a comebacker fractured his right arm on July 7, ending his season. Payano kept low Class A South Atlantic League hitters off balance with one of the best changeups in the league. His fastball grades as below-average and sits 88-91 mph and touches 93, but he gets whiffs because he uses his changeup liberally, to the point some scouts would like to see him pitch more off his fastball. His curveball and slider both grade as below-average. Payano needs to tighten his fastball command, but he is generally a solid strike-thrower. He has a high-slot delivery that helps him stay on top of the baseball, generate downhill plane and keep the ball in the bottom of the strike zone. He should be ready to jump to high Class A in 2017.

Year	Club (League)	Class	W	L	ERA	G	GS	CG	SV	IP	H	HR	BB	SO	K/9	WHIP	AVG
2014	Rangers (DSL)	R	7	2	2.95	14	14	1	0	76	68	3	17	65	7.7	1.11	.241
2015	Rangers1 (DSL)	R	1	1	0.00	3	3	1	0	16	9	0	3	24	13.8	0.77	.164
	Rangers (AZL)	R	6	0	1.55	8	4	0	0	41	33	0	9	46	10.2	1.03	.226
	Hickory (SAL)	LoA	3	1	1.10	6	5	0	0	33	27	1	10	31	8.5	1.13	.229
2016	Hickory (SAL)	LoA	3	3	2.08	15	13	1	0	74	59	2	29	82	10.0	1.19	.219
Minor League Totals			27	15	2.68	72	60	3	0	349	306	13	97	330	8.5	1.16	.239

30 TYLER FERGUSON, RHP

BA GRADE
45 Risk: Extreme

Born: Oct. 5, 1993. **B-T:** R-R. **Ht.:** 6-4. **Wt.:** 225. **Drafted:** Vanderbilt, 2015 (6th round). **Signed by:** Jay Heafner.

As a sophomore at Vanderbilt, Ferguson pitched in the Commodores rotation and started a game in Omaha during their College World Series title run. Ferguson's control escaped him as a junior in 2015—he walked 35 in 20 innings—but his stuff was tantalizing enough for the Rangers to take him in the sixth round and sign him for $200,000. Strictly a relief prospect in 2016, Ferguson overpowered short-season Northwest League hitters in June and July, but when he got moved up to low Class A Hickory in August, his control vanished again. No pitcher in the Rangers system has a wider gap between his pure stuff and his feel for pitching than Ferguson. His fastball rides at 93-97 mph with plus movement, and his plus slider has sharp bite. Ferguson has the ability to generate swings and misses with both pitches, but his wildness makes him extremely risky. He should open 2017 either back at Hickory or at high Class A Down East, with a chance to develop into a quality reliever—though he might not escape Class A if he can't harness his control.

Year	Club (League)	Class	W	L	ERA	G	GS	CG	SV	IP	H	HR	BB	SO	K/9	WHIP	AVG
2015	Rangers (AZL)	R	0	0	13.50	5	0	0	0	5	3	0	9	5	9.6	2.57	.167
2016	Spokane (NWL)	SS	2	0	1.78	13	0	0	2	30	18	1	10	46	13.6	0.92	.161
	Hickory (SAL)	LoA	0	1	8.78	10	0	0	1	13	12	1	18	10	6.8	2.25	.261
Minor League Totals			2	1	4.84	28	0	0	3	48	33	2	37	61	11.4	1.45	.188

Toronto Blue Jays

BY JOHN MANUEL

The first year of the Mark Shapiro era in Toronto looked a lot like the previous era.

For the first time since 1992-93, when the Blue Jays won consecutive World Series championships, the club made the playoffs in consecutive seasons. Toronto rallied late in September to earn a wild-card spot, then beat the Orioles in the Wild Card Game. The Jays won a playoff series for the second straight year, beating the Rangers before losing to the Indians in the American League Championship Series.

The cast of characters was familiar for Jays fans, most of the big league roster having been assembled  by Alex Anthopoulos, the team's general manager from 2010-15. But Shapiro took over as team president in September 2015, and two months later Anthopoulos and the Jays split.

Shapiro hired Ross Atkins as the new GM. When Shapiro was GM of the Indians, Atkins worked under him in scouting and player development roles. The duo tweaked the big league rotation with moves such as signing free agent J.A. Happ to replace David Price. Happ won 20 of his 32 starts, helping a rotation bolstered by a breakout year from 2010 supplemental first-rounder Aaron Sanchez. Toronto also brought back free agent Marco Estrada, who returned to the rotation and pitched well in the postseason again.

Bigger changes are coming. Longtime right-handed power plants Jose Bautista, who has averaged nearly 30 homers per year over nine seasons with Toronto, and Edwin Encarnacion, who has averaged 39 homers annually the last five years, became free agents after the season. Neither was likely to be back, particularly after Toronto struck quickly and signed Kendrys Morales to be its new DH. The Blue Jays probably will try to hold payroll in the $119-137 million range it has held in the last four seasons.

A farm system that had a strong development year looks primed to provide low-cost reinforcements soon. While no Blue Jays full-season team had a winning record, most of the organization's top prospects from a year ago took a step forward in 2016, none more so than Vladimir Guerrero Jr. The son of the ex-big leaguer debuted impressively in the Rookie-level Appalachian League, showing a polished hitting approach for his age and prodigious power potential.

While the Jays have talent even after last year's flurry of prospect trades, Shapiro has started overhauling scouting and player development in

Aaron Sanchez emerged as an impact starter as the Blue Jays reached the ALCS again

TOP PROSPECTS OF THE DECADE

Year	Player, Pos.	2016 Org
2007	Adam Lind, of	Mariners
2008	Travis Snider, of	Royals
2009	Travis Snider, of	Royals
2010	Zach Stewart, rhp	(Korea)
2011	Kyle Drabek, rhp	Giants
2012	Travis d'Arnaud, c	Mets
2013	Aaron Sanchez, rhp	Blue Jays
2014	Daniel Norris, lhp	Tigers
2015	Daniel Norris, lhp	Tigers
2016	Anthony Alford, of	Blue Jays

Toronto. He didn't renew the contract of scouting director Brian Parker, eventually replacing him with former Red Sox assistant director Steve Sanders. The Jays also fired minor league field coordinator Doug Davis and pitching coordinator Sal Fasano.

Shapiro has added to player development, bringing in a high-performance team to coordinate strength and conditioning, mental training and nutrition, as well as former Indians manager Eric Wedge as a player development advisor. Speculation dogged the Jays all season that Wedge was sizing up minor league talent so he could later manage as John Gibbons' replacement in the Toronto dugout.

That would be the most tangible sign yet that indeed these are Shapiro's Blue Jays.

ORGANIZATION OVERVIEW

President: Mark Shapiro. **GM:** Ross Atkins. **Farm director:** Gil Kim. **Scouting director:** Steve Sanders.

Class	Team	League	W	L	PCT	Finish	Manager
Majors	Toronto Blue Jays	American	89	73	.549	t-4th (15)	John Gibbons
Triple-A	Buffalo Bisons	International	66	78	.458	10th (14)	Gary Allenson
Double-A	New Hampshire Fisher Cats	Eastern	69	73	.486	7th (12)	Bobby Meacham
High Class A	Dunedin Blue Jays	Florida State	76	59	.563	3rd (12)	Ken Huckaby
Low Class A	Lansing Lugnuts	Midwest	69	71	.493	9th (16)	John Schneider
Short-season	Vancouver Canadians	Northwest	29	45	.392	8th (8)	John Tamargo Jr.
Rookie	Bluefield Blue Jays	Appalachian	37	31	.544	4th (10)	Dennis Holmberg
Rookie	GCL Blue Jays	Gulf Coast	39	17	.696	2nd (17)	Cesar Martin
Overall 2016 Minor League Record			385	374	.507	13th (30)	

THIS YEAR'S TOP 30

No.	Player, Pos.	Grade/Risk
1	Vladimir Guerrero Jr., 3b	65/High
2	Anthony Alford, of	60/High
3	Loudres Gurriel, of/inf	55/High
4	Sean Reid-Foley, rhp	55/High
5	Conner Greene, rhp	55/High
6	Richard Urena, ss	55/High
7	Rowdy Tellez, 1b	55/High
8	T.J. Zeuch, rhp	55/High
9	Bo Bichette, ss/2b	55/Extreme
10	Jon Harris, rhp	50/High
11	Justin Maese, rhp	50/High
12	Max Pentecost, c/1b	55/Extreme
13	Reese McGuire, c	45/Medium
14	Harold Ramirez, of	50/High
15	J.B. Woodman, of	50/High
16	Ryan Borucki, lhp	50/Extreme
17	Francisco Rios, rhp	45/High
18	Angel Perdomo, lhp	50/Extreme
19	Josh Palacios, of	45/High
20	Patrick Murphy, rhp	50/Extreme
21	Zach Jackson, rhp	50/Extreme
22	Dan Jansen, c	45/High
23	Danny Barnes, rhp	40/Medium
24	Jordan Romano, rhp	45/High
25	Cavan Biggio, 2b	45/High
26	Osman Gutierrez, rhp	50/Extreme
27	Yeltsin Gudino, ss	45/Extreme
28	Yennsy Diaz, rhp	45/Extreme
29	Matt Dermody, lhp	40/Medium
30	Travis Hosterman, lhp	45/Extreme

LAST YEAR'S TOP 30

No.	Player, Pos.	Status
1.	Anthony Alford, of	No. 2
2.	Conner Greene, rhp	No. 5
3.	Vladimir Guerrero Jr., 3b/of	No. 1
4.	Richard Urena, ss	No. 6
5.	Sean Reid-Foley, rhp	No. 4
6.	Jon Harris, rhp	No. 10
7.	Rowdy Tellez, 1b	No. 7
8.	Max Pentecost, c	No. 12
9.	Justin Maese, rhp	No. 11
10.	D.J. Davis, of	Dropped out
11.	Reggie Pruitt, of	Dropped out
12.	Clint Hollon, rhp	Dropped out
13.	Roemon Fields, of	Dropped out
14.	Ryan Borucki, lhp	No. 16
15.	Jose Espada, rhp	Dropped out
16.	Brady Dragmire, rhp	(Rangers)
17.	Chad Girodo, lhp	Dropped out
18.	Hansel Rodriguez, rhp	(Padres)
19.	Yennsy Diaz, rhp	No. 28
20.	Lupe Chavez, rhp	(Astros)
21.	Tom Robson, rhp	Dropped out
22.	Dan Jansen, c	No. 22
23.	Mitch Nay, 3b	Dropped out
24.	Matt Dean, 1b/3b	Dropped out
25.	Carl Wise, 3b	Dropped out
26.	Angel Perdomo, lhp	No. 18
27.	Andy Burns, 2b/of	Dropped out
28.	Dwight Smith Jr., of	Dropped out
29.	Tyler Burden, rhp	Dropped out
30.	Evan Smith, lhp	Dropped out

BEST TOOLS

Best Hitter for Average	Bo Bichette
Best Power Hitter	Vladimir Guerrero Jr.
Best Strike-Zone Discipline	Cavan Biggio
Fastest Baserunner	Roemon Fields
Best Athlete	Anthony Alford
Best Fastball	Conner Greene
Best Curveball	Zach Jackson
Best Slider	Sean Reid-Foley
Best Changeup	Ryan Borucki
Best Control	Ryan Borucki
Best Defensive Catcher	Javier Hernandez
Best Defensive Infielder	Richard Urena
Best Infield Arm	Richard Urena
Best Defensive Outfielder	Reggie Pruitt
Best Outfield Arm	Reggie Pruitt

PROJECTED 2020 LINEUP

Catcher	Reese McGuire
First Base	Rowdy Tellez
Second Base	Devon Travis
Third Base	Josh Donaldson
Shortstop	Richard Urena
Left Field	Bo Bichette
Center Field	Anthony Alford
Right Field	Vladimir Guerrero Jr.
Designated Hitter	Troy Tulowitzki
No. 1 Starter	Aaron Sanchez
No. 2 Starter	Marcus Stroman
No. 3 Starter	Sean Reid-Foley
No. 4 Starter	Conner Greene
No. 5 Starter	T.J. Zeuch
Closer	Roberto Osuna

MINOR LEAGUE DEPTH CHART

TORONTO BLUE JAYS

TOP 2017 ROOKIE: Lourdes Gurriel, of: The easiest path for the Cuban import to big league playing time is in left field, which he should be able to handle.
BREAKOUT PROSPECT: Patrick Murphy, rhp: He has the raw tools and now the health to become one of the system's best pitching prospects.
SLEEPER: Bradley Jones, 1b/of: The 2016 draftee has big power potential and should settle in at a corner.

SOURCE OF TOP 30 TALENT			
Homegrown	28	**Acquired**	2
College	10	Trades	2
Junior college	0	Rule 5 draft	0
High school	10	Independent leagues	0
Nondrafted free agents	0	Free agents/waivers	0
International	8		

LF
Lourdes Gurriel (3)
D.J. Davis
D.J. Daniels
Jonathan Davis

CF
Antony Alford (2)
Josh Palacios (19)
Darrell Ceciliani
Reggie Pruitt
Roemon Fields
Dom Abadessa

RF
Harold Ramirez (13)
J.B. Woodman (14)
Chavez Young

3B
Vladimir Guerrero Jr. (1)
Bryan Lizardo
Andy Burns

SS
Richard Urena (6)
Bo Bichette (9)
Yeltsin Gudino (27)
Kevin Vicuna

2B
Cavan Biggio (25)
Christian Lopes
Tim Lopes
John La Prise
Jason Leblebijian

1B
Rowdy Tellez (7)
Max Pentecost (15)
Ryan McBroom
Bradley Jones

C
Reese McGuire (12)
Danny Jansen (22)
A.J. Jimenez
Javier Hernandez
Ryan Hissey
Ryan Gold

LHP

LHSP	LHRP
Ryan Borucki (16)	Matt Dermody (29)
Angel Perdomo (18)	Tim Mayza
Travis Hosterman (30)	Chad Girodo
Wilfri Aleton	Kirby Snead
	Travis Bergen

RHP

RHSP	RHRP
Sean Reid-Foley (4)	Zack Jackson (21)
Conner Greene (5)	Danny Barnes (23)
T.J. Zeuch (8)	Chris Smith
Jon Harris (10)	Griffin Glaude
Justin Maese (11)	
Francisco Rios (17)	
Patrick Murphy (20)	
Jordan Romano (24)	
Osman Gutierrez (26)	
Yennsy Diaz (28)	
Glenn Sparkman	
Jose Espada	
Justin Shafer	
Casey Lawrence	

DRAFT ANALYSIS

2016

BEST PURE HITTER: OF Josh Palacios (4) has natural rhythm, timing at the plate and a track record of hitting. It's doubtful Toronto would have been able to wait so long to draft him had he not broken his left wrist on April 7 playing for Auburn. SS Bo Bichette (2) has good strike zone awareness and shows the ability to make adjustments with two strikes.

BEST POWER HITTER: Bichette has an unorthodox swing but isn't afraid to let the bat fly, producing plus raw power that played in his pro debut. Toronto will try to keep him at shortstop as long as possible, but he could end up at second or third base.

FASTEST RUNNER: OF Dom Abbadessa (23) is a plus runner with some defensive polish; OF Chavez Young (39) is similarly a plus runner with much more rawness to his game.

BEST DEFENSIVE PLAYER: Palacios and OF J.B. Woodman (2) shared time in center field and right after signing; both have a chance to be above-average center fielders, and Woodman's arm makes him a potentially above-average right fielder as well.

BEST FASTBALL: RHP T.J. Zeuch (1) rode his fastball into the first round. It sits in the 92-94 mph range and plays up with sinking life down in the zone. RHP Kyle Weatherly (8) has touched 95 mph and has the best velocity in the class.

BEST SECONDARY PITCH: RHP Zach Jackson (3) has a hard breaking ball, a tight 12-to-6 curve thrown with power that has 70-grade potential on the 20-80 scouting scale.

BEST PRO DEBUT: Bichette ranked second in the Rookie-level Gulf Coast League in RBIs (36) even though he missed a month with appendicitis; he hit .427/.451/.732 in just 82 at-bats. 1B/3B Bradley Jones (18) led the Rookie-level Appalachian League in home runs (16) and slugging (.578) while hitting .291. Palacios hit .330/.397/.426 in three stops, spending most of his time at short-season Vancouver.

BEST ATHLETE: Palacios has baseball athleticism, while Young is twitchier, faster and a bit more explosive. OF D.J. Daniels (6) has power and speed befitting his three-sport high school background and James Madison football scholarship offer.

MOST INTRIGUING BACKGROUND: Bichette's dad Dante hit 274 home runs in 14 big league seasons; older brother Dante Jr. played Double-A in the Yankees' system the last two years. 2B Cavan Biggio (5) is the son of Hall of Famer Craig. LHP Luke Gillingham (37) is one of Navy's most decorated pitchers ever and is stationed in his native San Diego, assigned to the USS Stockdale, a guided missile destroyer.

CLOSEST TO THE MAJORS: Jackson's path in a bullpen role will depend on his ability to throw strikes. LHP Kirby Snead (10) could move faster with a three-pitch mix and left-on-left experience out of Florida's bullpen.

BEST LATE-ROUND PICK: Young stands out. LHP Travis Hosterman (11), who got a $400,000 bonus, is further away but has projection in his 6-foot-3, 190-pound frame and three pitches with potential.

THE ONE WHO GOT AWAY: RHP Chris Lincoln (13) has a clean arm and projectable 6-foot-4, 175-pound frame, but the Jays couldn't sign him away from UC Santa Barbara.

2015

RHPs Jon Harris (1) and Justin Maese (3) are good athletes with back-of-the-rotation upside. No other draftee made this year's Top 30.

GRADE: C.

2014

RHP Jeff Hoffman (1) was the key to the Troy Tulowitzki trade. RHP Sean Reid-Foley (2) made significant progress in 2016, as did RHP Jordan Romano (10). Shoulder surgeries have left C Max Pentecost (1) a significant wild card.

GRADE: B.

2013

The Jays didn't sign RHP Phil Bickford (1) and traded LHP Matt Boyd (6) and RHP Kendall Graveman (8). RHP Conner Greene (7) and 1B Rowdy Tellez (30) have first-division upside.

GRADE: B

TOP DRAFT PICKS OF THE DECADE

Year	Player, Pos.	2016 Org
2007	Kevin Ahrens, 3b	Did not play
2008	David Cooper, 1b	Did not play
2009	Chad Jenkins, rhp	Blue Jays
2010	Deck McGuire, rhp	Cardinals
2011	*Tyler Beede, rhp	Giants
2012	D.J. Davis, of	Blue Jays
2013	*Phil Bickford, rhp	Brewers
2014	Jeff Hoffman, rhp	Rockies
2015	Jon Harris, rhp	Blue Jays
2016	T.J. Zeuch, rhp	Blue Jays
*Did not sign.		

LARGEST BONUSES IN CLUB HISTORY

Adeiny Hechavarria, 2010	$4,000,000
Vladimir Guerrero Jr., 2015	$3,900,000
Jeff Hoffman, 2014	$3,080,000
Max Pentecost, 2014	$2,888,300
Adonys Cardona, 2010	$2,800,000

1 VLADIMIR GUERRERO JR., 3B

Born: March 16, 1999. **B-T:** R-R. **Ht.:** 6-1. **Wt.:** 200.
Signed: Dominican Republic, 2015.
Signed by: Ismael Cruz/Sandy Rosario/Luciano Del Rosario.

Vladimir Guerrero signed with the Expos in March 1993, reached the majors in 1996 and became American League MVP with the Angels in 2004, one of his nine all-star seasons. In spring training before his first all-star campaign, in 1999, his son Vladimir Jr. was born in Montreal. He grew into a hitting prospect with some of his father's mannerisms (such as a lack of batting gloves), a strong facial resemblance and plenty more fanfare. The father signed for a $2,100 bonus, while Vladimir Jr. signed for $3.9 million. In fact, the Blue Jays traded minor leaguers Tim Locastro and Chase De Jong to the Dodgers for three international bonus slots, raising their international pool high enough just to sign the junior Guerrero. The Blue Jays first saw Guerrero take swings in their Dominican complex when he was 14 years old, after he'd already been training with his uncle Wilton, also a former major leaguer. He shifted from outfield to third base in instructional league after signing, went through his first spring training in 2016 and had a strong pro debut in the Rookie-level Appalachian League, finishing third in total bases while being the league's youngest player.

Guerrero does just about everything evaluators want to see in a teenage hitter. He has tremendous hand-eye coordination and bat-to-ball skills, to the point he seems to have been born to hit. His special hands allow him to manipulate the barrel and square up pitches of all types. He has excellent strike-zone judgment for a 17-year-old, walking nearly as often as he struck out and showing an ability to lay off breaking balls that will be further tested at higher levels. He has tremendous raw power and showed the ability to drive the ball to all fields at an advanced rate for his age. Guerrero covers the plate well and should be an above-average hitter with 30-plus homer potential down the line. Some club officials have compared his overall offensive profile to that of Edwin Encarnacion, though with more speed, as he's actually an average runner. Like Encarnacion, Guerrero has a chance to be a third baseman early in his career. Defense was rarely a focus of his as an amateur, and moving to third base from outfield has prompted Guerrero to work harder on all aspects of that side of the ball. He has improved his short-area quickness and arm strength the most. If he keeps working on

BA GRADE

65 Risk High

SCOUTING GRADES

Batting: 60.
Power: 70.
Speed: 50.
Defense: 45.
Arm: 55.

Based on 20-80 scouting scale and future projection rather than present grades.

BRIAN WELSTERHOLT

his defense, he should have average range. Once owner of a below-average arm, he now flirts with a plus tool. His footwork has improved as well, and he made the routine play with some reliability in his debut. Guerrero has gotten his stocky body in better shape since signing, but it will always be a concern and is his biggest weakness as a prospect.

The Blue Jays' high-performance team, which focuses on mental and physical training, will continue to work with Guerrero to maintain his looseness while improving his body fitness. His potential may not match his father's, but he won't shame his dad's name as a ballplayer. He figures to reach low Class A Lansing in 2017, and he could make it hard for the Jays to keep him from getting to the big leagues by the time he's 20.

Year	Club (League)	Class	AVG	G	AB	R	H	2B	3B	HR	RBI	BB	SO	SB	CS	OBP	SLG
2016	Bluefield (APP)	R	.271	62	236	32	64	12	3	8	46	33	35	15	5	.359	.449
Minor League Totals			.271	62	236	32	64	12	3	8	46	33	35	15	5	.359	.449

2 ANTHONY ALFORD, OF

Born: July 20, 1994. **B-T:** R-R. **Ht.:** 6-1. **Wt.:** 215. **Drafted:** HS—Petal, Miss., 2012 (3rd round). **Signed by:** Brian Johnston.

A two-sport prep star in Mississippi, Alford signed for $750,000 on a contract that allowed him to play college football, first at Southern Mississippi as a quarterback, then at Mississippi as a defensive back. He had 94 pro at-bats in three seasons before giving up football and breaking out in 2015, but injuries slowed him in 2016. He wrenched his right knee on Opening Day, then suffered a concussion in an outfield collision in mid-June. Alford struggled immediately after both injuries. Back to full strength in July and August, he showed the same tools and similar production he had in 2015, with a power-speed combination buoyed by good plate discipline. He lost a step with his knee injury (he was forced to wear a bulky brace), making him merely a plus runner instead of a true burner, and scouts want to see if he gets it back this offseason. He still has athleticism, strength in his swing and improving power as he's tamed his swing a bit, giving him better bat control. Alford could still add polish in center field but has plenty of range that helps make up for a below-average arm. The Blue Jays were pleased with Alford's big finish and maturity handling his injuries. He is ready for Double-A in 2017 and could push for a regular role in 2018.

BA GRADE

60 Risk: High

Year	Club (League)	Class	AVG	G	AB	R	H	2B	3B	HR	RBI	BB	SO	SB	CS	OBP	SLG
2014	Bluefield (APP)	R	.207	9	29	5	6	0	0	1	2	5	13	1	0	.343	.310
	Lansing (MWL)	LoA	.320	5	25	3	8	1	0	1	3	0	8	4	0	.320	.480
2015	Lansing (MWL)	LoA	.293	50	188	49	55	14	1	1	16	39	60	12	1	.418	.394
	Dunedin (FSL)	HiA	.302	57	225	42	68	11	6	3	19	28	49	15	6	.380	.444
2016	Dunedin (FSL)	HiA	.236	92	339	53	80	17	2	9	44	53	117	18	6	.344	.378
Minor League Totals			.266	224	846	157	225	45	10	16	87	133	257	56	13	.370	.400

3 LOURDES GURRIEL, OF/3B

BA GRADE

55 Risk: High

Born: Oct. 19, 1993. **B-T:** R-R. **Ht.:** 6-3. **Wt.:** 185. **Signed:** Cuba, 2016. **Signed by:** Andrew Tinnish.

Gurriel's father, with the same name, starred for Cuban national teams (winning Olympic gold in 1992) for more than a decade, as did his older brother Yulieski. The brothers came to the U.S. in early 2016, with Yulieski signing with the Astros for a $47.5 million major league deal. Lourdes waited to sign until he turned 23 in October to get out from under the international bonus pools and signed a seven-year, $22 million contract with the Blue Jays in November. Scouts often have compared Gurriel to his father and brother, but he's a prospect on his own, with a lean, athletic frame. He has a fairly polished offensive approach, knows the strike zone and has the bat speed to catch up to good fastballs, even though his swing has some length. It also features some loft and leverage, giving him above-average power potential. Gurriel has run better in recent years, rating from average to above-average. He played shortstop, third base and left field in Cuba and profiles best at third or in left field. He has a solid-average arm. The Blue Jays are fairly set on the left side of the infield with Troy Tulowitzki and Josh Donaldson, so the outfield looks like Gurriel's best path to helping Toronto in the short term. He's expected to open his pro career at Double-A New Hampshire, likely giving third base a try before a move to the outfield.

Year	Club (League)	Class	AVG	G	AB	R	H	2B	3B	HR	RBI	BB	SO	SB	CS	OBP	SLG
2014	Industriales (CNS)	CNS	.308	63	221	36	68	11	0	8	42	28	28	7	4	.388	.854
2015	Industriales (CNS)	CNS	.344	59	218	43	75	17	0	10	53	21	23	8	3	.407	.560
2016	Did not play																

4 SEAN REID-FOLEY, RHP

Born: Aug. 30, 1995. **B-T:** R-R. **Ht.:** 6-3. **Wt.:** 220. **Drafted:** HS—Jacksonville, 2014 (2nd round). **Signed by:** Matt Bishoff.

Reid-Foley is close to becoming the second big leaguer ever born in Guam. He would join John Hattig, who got 24 at-bats in 2006 for Toronto. Reid-Foley's older brother David, a converted catcher, pitched in the Dodgers system and taught his younger brother a curveball last offseason, helping him have a breakout 2016 season. The only flaw was an elbow flare-up in August that prompted the Jays to shut him down. The Jays knew Reid-Foley had power stuff, which he maintained and improved in 2016 with the strides he made with his upper-70s curveball, which now rivals his slider as his best secondary pitch. At times both play as plus, though his

BA GRADE

55 Risk: High

mid-80s slider was less consistent than it had been in the past. Sent back to low Class A to start the season, Reid-Foley streamlined his leg kick in his delivery, which improved his direction to the plate, resulting in more command of his 92-94 mph fastball that touches 97. He threw harder in 2015 but has better command now while retaining good angle to the plate and solid life. His changeup, his fourth pitch, shows average potential if he can commit to it. Reid-Foley and Conner Greene should front the rotation at Double-A New Hampshire at some point in 2017. Greene's stuff is more electric, but Reid-Foley's strides in commanding his plus stuff gives him the edge as a potential future No. 2 starter.

Year	Club (League)	Class	W	L	ERA	G	GS	CG	SV	IP	H	HR	BB	SO	K/9	WHIP	AVG
2014	Blue Jays (GCL)	R	1	2	4.76	9	6	0	0	23	21	0	10	25	9.9	1.37	.244
2015	Dunedin (FSL)	HiA	1	5	5.23	8	8	0	0	33	25	1	24	35	9.6	1.50	.210
	Lansing (MWL)	LoA	3	5	3.69	17	17	0	0	63	57	3	43	90	12.8	1.58	.239
2016	Lansing (MWL)	LoA	4	3	2.95	11	11	0	0	58	43	2	22	59	9.2	1.12	.208
	Dunedin (FSL)	HiA	6	2	2.67	10	10	0	0	57	35	2	16	71	11.1	0.89	.172
Minor League Totals			15	17	3.58	55	52	0	0	234	181	8	115	280	10.8	1.26	.212

5 CONNER GREENE, RHP

Born: April 4, 1995. **B-T:** R-R. **Ht.:** 6-3. **Wt.:** 185. **Drafted:** HS—Santa Monica, Calif., 2013 (7th round). **Signed by:** Jim Lentine.

Greene broke out in 2015, finishing the year in Double-A. He didn't respond well when sent back to high Class A to start 2016 and struggled with his control, ranking 13th in the minors with 71 walks. In terms of stuff, no Blue Jays farmhand can match Greene, who has the system's most explosive fastball for a starter. He can reach 98 mph and pitches in the 93-97 range at his best with his four-seamer, at times mixing in an 89-92 two-seamer. He's very athletic, lean and loose. His changeup remains his best secondary pitch, an above-average pitch thrown with good arm speed and featuring late fade. His 83-87 mph slider flashes above-average

BA GRADE
55 Risk: High

with depth, but it lacks consistency, while his curveball gets slow and loopy. Scouts outside the organization question Greene's dedication to learning pitch sequencing and attention to detail, both on and off the mound. Greene tinkered with his delivery to sync up his body and fast arm and had an inconsistent between-starts routine, which contributed to his below-average control. If his control clicks, Greene has front-of-the-rotation potential, but he has to throw quality strikes above Class A. He will likely return to Double-A in 2017.

Year	Club (League)	Class	W	L	ERA	G	GS	CG	SV	IP	H	HR	BB	SO	K/9	WHIP	AVG
2014	Blue Jays (GCL)	R	2	2	1.99	7	4	0	0	32	25	2	6	30	8.5	0.98	.216
	Bluefield (APP)	R	1	2	4.23	6	5	0	0	28	26	1	12	21	6.8	1.37	.250
2015	Lansing (MWL)	LoA	7	3	3.88	14	14	0	0	67	75	4	19	65	8.7	1.40	.285
	Dunedin (FSL)	HiA	2	3	2.25	7	7	0	0	40	36	1	8	35	7.9	1.10	.238
	New Hampshire (EL)	AA	3	1	4.68	5	5	0	0	25	25	1	12	15	5.4	1.48	.269
2016	Dunedin (FSL)	HiA	4	4	2.90	15	15	0	0	78	74	5	38	51	5.9	1.44	.252
	New Hampshire (EL)	AA	6	5	4.19	12	12	1	0	69	57	5	33	48	6.3	1.31	.224
Minor League Totals			26	21	3.59	77	66	1	0	369	355	20	143	285	7.0	1.35	.254

6 RICHARD URENA, SS

Born: Feb. 26, 1996. **B-T:** B-R. **Ht.:** 6-0. **Wt.:** 185. **Signed:** Dominican Republic, 2012. **Signed by:** Ismael Cruz/Sandy Rosario/Luciano del Rosario.

The Blue Jays signed Urena for $725,000 in 2012 and have kept him after trading other top international shortstops, such as Franklin Barreto (Athletics) or Dawel Lugo (Diamondbacks). Urena reached Double-A New Hampshire but wore out at the end of the season, finishing 4-for-37. When he first got to Double-A, Urena showed his ceiling, which could be an above-average offensive player with average defense at shortstop. He has a feel for hitting with an aggressive approach, quick wrists and solid strength that produces solid-average power from the left side. He hasn't shown much righthanded pop in games the last two seasons, with just 12

BA GRADE
55 Risk: High

extra-base hits from that side in 250 at-bats. Urena slightly improved his walk rate and cut his strikeouts while maintaining solid power production, though he still gives away at-bats swinging at pitchers' pitches. He also makes careless errors too often at short, flipping throws instead of setting his feet and flashing his arm, which is plus at its best. Urena flashes above-average tools in every area but speed but lacks polish and consistency at the plate and in the field. He'll open 2017 back at Double-A, where he finished the 2016 season, and may mix in some second base time with Troy Tulowitzki, signed through 2020, blocking his big league path to shortstop.

Year	Club (League)	Class	AVG	G	AB	R	H	2B	3B	HR	RBI	BB	SO	SB	CS	OBP	SLG
2014	Bluefield (APP)	R	.318	53	217	35	69	15	2	2	20	16	51	5	4	.363	.433
	Vancouver (NWL)	SS	.242	9	33	3	8	2	1	0	5	3	5	1	0	.297	.364
2015	Dunedin (FSL)	HiA	.250	30	124	9	31	3	1	1	8	3	26	3	1	.268	.315
	Lansing (MWL)	LoA	.266	91	384	62	102	13	4	15	58	13	84	5	5	.289	.438
2016	Dunedin (FSL)	HiA	.305	97	394	52	120	18	7	8	41	25	64	9	6	.351	.447
	New Hampshire (EL)	AA	.266	30	124	14	33	6	5	0	18	4	19	0	2	.282	.395
Minor League Totals			.287	381	1546	223	444	78	22	27	188	97	298	32	23	.331	.418

7 ROWDY TELLEZ, 1B

Born: March 16, 1995. **B-T:** L-L. **Ht.:** 6-4. **Wt.:** 220. **Drafted:** HS—Elk Grove, Calif., 2013 (30th round). **Signed by:** Darold Brown.

Tellez played with future pros J.D. Davis (Astros), Dom Nunez (Rockies), Derek Hill (Tigers 2014 first-rounder) and Dylan Carlson (Cardinals 2016 first-rounder) at Elk Grove High before signing for $850,000, the largest bonus in the Blue Jays' 2013 draft class. He had a strong 2016, ranking second in the Double-A Eastern League in on-base percentage (.387) and third in slugging (.530). A slow start (.164 in April) tested Tellez's confidence, but he turned up his aggressiveness and rallied, hitting .318 the rest of the way. He has improved his body significantly since signing, losing 15 pounds. Scouts laud his makeup for his dedication to his fitness, which also has helped improve his power production. Tellez always has shown feel for hitting and good control for the strike zone, and he's got plus power to punish mistakes when pitchers miss. He chased plenty of breaking balls early but adjusted and started laying off them, and he has enough bat speed to catch up to good fastballs. Tellez is a fringy defender with good enough footwork to improve to average. Tellez is the most advanced hitter among top Toronto farmhands and could hit his way to the majors in 2017, depending on how the Blue Jays' offseason shapes up. More likely, he'll head to Triple-A Buffalo.

CLIFF WELCH

BA GRADE

55 Risk: High

Year	Club (League)	Class	AVG	G	AB	R	H	2B	3B	HR	RBI	BB	SO	SB	CS	OBP	SLG
2014	Bluefield (APP)	R	.293	53	191	26	56	11	1	4	36	19	27	3	2	.358	.424
	Lansing (MWL)	LoA	.357	12	42	6	15	0	0	2	7	7	10	0	0	.449	.500
2015	Lansing (MWL)	LoA	.296	68	270	36	80	19	0	7	49	24	56	2	2	.351	.444
	Dunedin (FSL)	HiA	.275	35	131	17	36	5	0	7	28	14	28	3	0	.338	.473
2016	New Hampshire (EL)	AA	.297	124	438	71	130	29	2	23	81	63	92	4	3	.387	.530
Minor League Totals			.289	326	1196	166	346	69	6	45	221	142	239	13	7	.364	.470

8 T.J. ZEUCH, RHP

Born: Aug. 1, 1995. **B-T:** R-R. **Ht.:** 6-7. **Wt.:** 225. **Drafted:** Pittsburgh, 2016 (1st round). **Signed by:** Doug Witt.

The Royals drafted Zeuch in 2013 out of an Ohio high school in the 31st round, and he became the highest draft pick in the history of Pittsburgh's program. He signed for $2.175 million as the 21st overall pick. Zeuch's father Tim pitched two games in 1980 for the independent Victoria (B.C.) Mussels. Zeuch had one of the best fastballs in the draft class. He pitches off his plus fastball, which has armside run as well as heavy sinking life at its best. He'll touch 97 mph but usually sits in the 93-94 range. He uses his size well, leveraging his 6-foot-7 frame to drive the ball downhill and get solid extension out in front. He repeats his delivery well for a tall pitcher and should have average major league command. He throws a solid-average curveball with 12-to-6 shape from his high three-quarters release point that's his preferred secondary pitch, but he also can throw strikes with his average slider and fringe-average changeup. Toronto again landed one of the top college starters in the draft while picking in the 20s. A potential No. 3 starter, Zeuch has a higher ceiling and more power than 2015 first-rounder Jon Harris and should join Harris in high Class A Dunedin's rotation in 2017.

BA GRADE

55 Risk: High

Year	Club (League)	Class	W	L	ERA	G	GS	CG	SV	IP	H	HR	BB	SO	K/9	WHIP	AVG
2016	Blue Jays (GCL)	R	0	0	0.00	1	1	0	0	3	0	0	0	2	6.0	0.00	.000
	Vancouver (NWL)	SS	0	1	3.52	6	6	0	0	23	21	1	5	22	8.6	1.13	.247
	Lansing (MWL)	LoA	0	1	9.00	2	2	0	0	8	10	1	2	14	15.8	1.50	.294
Minor League Totals			0	2	4.50	9	9	0	0	34	31	2	7	38	10.1	1.12	.242

9 BO BICHETTE, SS/2B

MIKE JANES

Born: March 5, 1998. **B-T:** R-R. **Ht.:** 6-0. **Wt.:** 200. **Drafted:** HS—St. Petersburg, Fla., 2016 (2nd round). **Signed by:** Matt Bishoff.

Bichette's father and brother paved his way into baseball. Dante Sr. hit 274 home runs in 14 big league seasons, while Dante Jr., a supplemental first-round pick of the Yankees in 2011, has reached Double-A. The brothers played together for Brazil's World Baseball Classic qualifier team in September in Brooklyn; their mother is Brazilian. He hit .427 and ranked second in the Rookie-level Gulf Coast League with 36 RBIs in just 22 games. He missed a month with appendicitis but didn't require surgery. Bichette uses a somewhat unconventional swing with an exaggerated, deep load in his swing, but it worked throughout his amateur career and worked extremely well in his pro debut. He makes in-at-bat adjustments with an advanced approach for a prep, and scouts who believe his hand and bat speed will make his approach work see him as an above-average hitter with at least plus power. Bichette has solid athleticism, average range and speed and an above-average arm. The Blue Jays will keep him at shortstop as long as he can play it. From his exaggerated swing to defensive future, which is likely at third base, Bichette shares similarities with Josh Donaldson. He's headed to low Class A Lansing, where he'll play short next to third baseman Vladimir Guerrero Jr. in 2017.

BA GRADE
55 Risk: Extreme

Year	Club (League)	Class	AVG	G	AB	R	H	2B	3B	HR	RBI	BB	SO	SB	CS	OBP	SLG
2016	Blue Jays (GCL)	R	.427	22	82	21	35	9	2	4	36	6	17	3	0	.451	.732
Minor League Totals			.427	22	82	21	35	9	2	4	36	6	17	3	0	.451	.732

10 JON HARRIS, RHP

Born: Oct. 16, 1993. **B-T:** R-R. **Ht.:** 6-4. **Wt.:** 175. **Drafted:** Missouri State, 2015 (1st round). **Signed by:** Dallas Black.

Harris flirted with being a top-10 pick in a soft crop of college starting pitchers in the 2015 draft. As it turned out, he wasn't a team's first choice until the 29th overall pick, where Toronto snatched him and signed him for just less than $2 million. The Blue Jays had picked him out of high school as well in the 33rd round. Harris had a poor pro debut (6.75 ERA) but finished 2016 in high Class A after adopting several changes to his delivery. The Blue Jays simplified Harris' leg kick and got him to lengthen his stride out front, giving him a bit more effective velocity and allowing him to better repeat his delivery. He has better plane to his fastball and still has the same clean arm action as before, and he threw more quality strikes this year with all four of his pitches. Harris will pop a 97 mph fastball at times but sits 90-94. His changeup and upper-70s curveball flash above-average, as the curve has some depth and the changeup has good life, while his cutter-type slider lacks consistent tilt but has solid mid-80s power. His lack of a true plus pitch makes it hard for him to rack up swings-and-misses; increased strength could help the quality of his stuff. Harris needs a plus pitch to be a potential No. 3 starter and innings-eater. More realistically, he profiles as a solid No. 4 who could reach Double-A in 2017.

BA GRADE
50 Risk: High

Year	Club (League)	Class	W	L	ERA	G	GS	CG	SV	IP	H	HR	BB	SO	K/9	WHIP	AVG
2015	Vancouver (NWL)	SS	0	5	6.75	12	11	0	0	36	48	1	21	32	8.0	1.92	.318
2016	Lansing (MWL)	LoA	8	2	2.23	16	16	0	0	85	74	1	24	73	7.8	1.16	.232
	Dunedin (FSL)	HiA	3	2	3.60	8	8	1	0	45	37	2	14	26	5.2	1.13	.224
Minor League Totals			11	9	3.59	36	35	1	0	166	159	4	59	131	7.1	1.32	.250

11 JUSTIN MAESE, RHP

BA GRADE
50 Risk: High

Born: Oct. 24, 1996. **B-T:** R-R. **Ht.:** 6-3. **Wt.:** 190. **Drafted:** HS—El Paso, 2015 (3rd round). **Signed by:** Gerald Turner.

The Blue Jays signed Maese for just $300,000, less than half the bonus slot for the 91st overall pick. Held back in extended spring training in 2016, he earned the first start of the season for short-season Vancouver, then got a promotion to low Class A Lansing. Maese has a fine pitcher's frame at 6-foot-3, 190 pounds with the athleticism and present strength to repeat his delivery. He attacks hitters seeking early-count contact and gets it, usually on the ground. He generated more than two groundouts for every out in the air in 2016. He averaged right around 13 pitches per inning, making him one of the organization's most efficient pitchers. His sinking fastball touches 96 mph and resides in the 90-94 range with the best fastball life in the organization. Maese picked up a new slider grip this year to give him a solid-average secondary pitch. It's hard, reaching the upper 80s. He's still learning some feel for the pitch and learning a changeup. He needs to refine his defense. The Jays have had success developing power sinkerballers of late, including Henderson Alvarez and Aaron Sanchez. Maese has similar sink with a bit less velocity than those two and profiles as a back-of-the-rotation starter. He could start 2017 at high Class A Dunedin and should finish the season there.

Year	Club (League)	Class	W	L	ERA	G	GS	CG	SV	IP	H	HR	BB	SO	K/9	WHIP	AVG
2015	Blue Jays (GCL)	R	5	0	1.01	8	4	1	0	36	32	0	6	19	4.8	1.07	.241
2016	Vancouver (NWL)	SS	2	2	2.05	5	5	0	0	26	20	1	1	20	6.8	0.80	.204
	Lansing (MWL)	LoA	2	4	3.36	10	10	0	0	56	59	2	14	44	7.0	1.30	.272
Minor League Totals			9	6	2.36	23	19	1	0	118	111	3	21	83	6.3	1.12	.248

12 MAX PENTECOST, C/1B

BA GRADE

55 Risk: Extreme

Born: March 10, 1993. **B-T:** R-R. **Ht.:** 6-2. **Wt.:** 191. **Drafted:** Kennesaw State, 2014 (1st round). **Signed by:** Mike Tidick.

Pentecost got back on the field in 2016, and the Blue Jays will take what they can get from the second of their two first-round picks in 2014 (11th overall). He went 3-for-4 with a home run in his season debut in May with low Class A Lansing, his first game since 2014. Pentecost, who didn't sign as a seventh-round pick by the Rangers out of high school in 2011 due to an elbow issue, has had at least two labrum surgeries since signing for $2,888,300. That caused him to miss all of '15 and limited him to DH duty only in 2016. Pentecost knocked off the rust offensively, showing excellent power and solid contact ability in his righthanded swing. He's still short to the ball with his swing, can use the whole field and has shown power the opposite way. He's a fringe-average runner and solid athlete who should be able to handle a move to first base or left field. However, the Blue Jays intend to try him back behind the plate in 2017. If he can handle catching, Pentecost could re-emerge as an elite two-way talent, but he has work to do to show he can be an everyday catcher.

Year	Club (League)	Class	AVG	G	AB	R	H	2B	3B	HR	RBI	BB	SO	SB	CS	OBP	SLG
2014	Blue Jays (GCL)	R	.364	6	22	2	8	2	0	0	3	0	3	0	1	.364	.455
	Vancouver (NWL)	SS	.313	19	83	15	26	2	3	0	9	2	18	2	1	.322	.410
2015	Did not play—Injured																
2016	Lansing (MWL)	LoA	.314	62	239	36	75	15	3	7	34	21	51	4	2	.375	.490
	Dunedin (FSL)	HiA	.245	12	49	6	12	2	0	3	7	3	17	1	1	.288	.469
Minor League Totals			.308	99	393	59	121	21	6	10	53	26	89	7	5	.353	.468

13 REESE MCGUIRE, C

BA GRADE

45 Risk: Medium

Born: March 2, 1995. **B-T:** L-R. **Ht.:** 5-11. **Wt.:** 215. **Drafted:** HS—Covington, Wash., 2013 (1st round). **Signed by:** Greg Hopkins (Pirates).

The Pirates drafted McGuire with the second of their two first-round picks in 2013, No. 14 overall, and the Blue Jays acquired him in a deadline deal that also brought lefty Francisco Liriano and outfielder Harold Ramirez to the Jays. Only one prep catcher has been drafted as highly since McGuire's selection (Reds, Tyler Stephenson, 11th overall in 2015), and high school catcher is a notoriously risky demographic. McGuire's risk is with his bat. He is a solid catch-and-throw backstop with has soft hands, good agility and an average arm that plays up with a quick transfer and plus accuracy. He threw out 37 percent of baserunners, third-best in the Double-A Eastern League. He opened the season as one of the youngest players in the EL, and it has caught up to him offensively. McGuire has drawn walks and made contact in full-season ball but has just 54 extra-base hits, including only four home runs, the last three seasons. McGuire's short swing path is flat and helps him make consistent contact, but he doesn't have the bat speed or strength to consistently drive the ball. The Jays lacked upper-level catching prospects until acquiring McGuire, who needs offensive development but could be Russell Martin's heir if it happens.

Year	Club (League)	Class	AVG	G	AB	R	H	2B	3B	HR	RBI	BB	SO	SB	CS	OBP	SLG
2014	West Virginia (SAL)	LoA	.262	98	389	46	102	11	4	3	45	24	44	7	2	.307	.334
2015	Bradenton (FSL)	HiA	.254	98	374	32	95	15	0	0	34	26	39	14	7	.301	.294
2016	Altoona (EL)	AA	.259	77	266	29	69	16	2	1	37	29	26	4	3	.337	.346
	New Hampshire (EL)	AA	.226	15	53	5	12	2	0	0	5	7	8	2	2	.328	.264
Minor League Totals			.267	338	1274	145	340	55	6	4	142	102	136	33	16	.324	.329

14 HAROLD RAMIREZ, OF

BA GRADE

50 Risk: High

Born: Sept. 6, 1994. **B-T:** R-R. **Ht.:** 5-10. **Wt.:** 220. **Signed:** Colombia, 2011. **Signed by:** Rene Gayo/Orlando Covo (Pirates).

The Blue Jays acquired Ramirez, a career .306 hitter in the minors, along with catcher Reese McGuire and lefty Francisco Liriano exchange for Drew Hutchison at the 2016 trade deadline. Ramirez had a mixed season, starting with a stint helping Colombia win its World Baseball Classic qualifier in March. He played more regular-season games than ever in his injury-plagued career, but backed up offensively and moved down the defensive spectrum. Ramirez always has shown hitting ability and has the bat speed and barrel ability to hit good fastballs. His raw power doesn't translate to games, in part because he isn't selective and because he often gets fooled by breaking balls. He is an above-average runner whose instincts haven't parlayed his speed into stolen bases or the ability to stay in center field. He has a fringe-average arm and fits better in left field if he can't stick in center. Ramirez has not been durable as a pro, and a left knee injury ended his season in early August. He still has yet to play 100 games in a season. Conditioning has never been a strong suit, but Ramirez is in a new organization and has a chance to change his reputation in 2017, which likely will start at Triple-A Buffalo.

Year	Club (League)	Class	AVG	G	AB	R	H	2B	3B	HR	RBI	BB	SO	SB	CS	OBP	SLG
2014	West Virginia (SAL)	LoA	.309	49	204	30	63	14	1	1	24	11	35	12	3	.364	.402
2015	Bradenton (FSL)	HiA	.337	80	306	45	103	13	6	4	47	25	48	22	15	.399	.458
2016	Altoona (EL)	AA	.306	98	379	58	116	16	7	2	49	21	66	7	10	.354	.401
	New Hampshire (EL)	AA	.750	1	4	2	3	1	0	0	1	1	0	0	0	.800	1.000
Minor League Totals			.306	338	1302	195	398	60	19	13	173	87	221	73	44	.364	.411

15 J.B. WOODMAN, OF

BA GRADE

50 Risk: High

Born: Dec. 13, 1994. **B-T:** L-R. **Ht.:** 6-2. **Wt.:** 195. **Drafted:** Mississippi, 2016 (2nd round). **Signed by:** Don Norris.

A 40th-round pick out of high school by the Mets, Woodman instead headed to Mississippi and helped the Rebels reach the College World Series as a freshman. A prep quarterback, Woodman loosened up physically and lost some of his football physique, and it helped him have his best college season as a junior. He tied for the Southeastern Conference lead with 14 home runs and the Blue Jays took him 57th overall, signing him for $975,000. His debut was mixed. After slumping through a 4-for-32 start, Woodman showed above-average power and ranked fifth in the short-season Northwest League in doubles, but also ranked fifth in strikeouts before a late promotion to low Class A Lansing. Woodman split his time between center field and right after signing, and the Jays believe he will be a plus defender in right who could also handle center. He is an above-average runner underway who can steal a base as well. Woodman struck out in nearly 32 percent of his plate appearances, a consequence of his willingness to work deep counts and his own pitch recognition issues. The tradeoff may be worth it if he can be a power-speed center fielder, and he may have enough polish to jump to high Class A Dunedin in 2017.

Year	Club (League)	Class	AVG	G	AB	R	H	2B	3B	HR	RBI	BB	SO	SB	CS	OBP	SLG
2016	Vancouver (NWL)	SS	.272	54	195	28	53	18	1	3	24	30	72	10	2	.375	.421
	Lansing (MWL)	LoA	.441	9	34	5	15	2	0	1	5	4	13	0	1	.487	.588
Minor League Totals			.297	63	229	33	68	20	1	4	29	34	85	10	3	.391	.445

16 RYAN BORUCKI, LHP

BA GRADE

50 Risk: Extreme

Born: March 31, 1994. **B-T:** L-L. **Ht.:** 6-4. **Wt.:** 175. **Drafted:** HS—Mundelein, Ill., 2012 (15th round). **Signed by:** Mike Medici.

Borucki finally returned at full strength in 2016 after three injury-filled seasons, including Tommy John surgery as a prep senior and shoulder issues that shut him down in July 2015. The Blue Jays started him in the high Class A Florida State League, but Borucki wasn't ready. He gave up 10 home runs in just 20 innings before being reassigned to low Class A Lansing, where he thrived. He ranked second in the Midwest League in ERA, first in winning percentage (.714) and fourth in WHIP (1.13). Borucki's best pitch is an above-average changeup that's the best in the organization, thrown with confidence and good arm speed that is a plus pitch at its best. He can still get more consistent with the change, and it would play up if his fastball improved. It's an average pitch at 88-92 mph, touching 94, with modest life that he needs to spot with precision. Borucki's slider has its moments as a pitch to induce groundouts but needs tighter shape to get swings and misses. Borucki earns plaudits for his work ethic and answered questions about his durability. He's a potential No. 4 starter who will headed back to high Class A Dunedin for 2017.

Year	Club (League)	Class	W	L	ERA	G	GS	CG	SV	IP	H	HR	BB	SO	K/9	WHIP	AVG
2014	Bluefield (APP)	R	2	1	2.70	8	6	0	0	33	26	2	6	30	8.1	0.96	.211
	Vancouver (NWL)	SS	1	1	1.90	5	4	0	1	24	13	1	3	22	8.4	0.68	.159
2015	Blue Jays (GCL)	R	0	0	0.00	1	0	0	0	1	1	0	0	1	9.0	1.00	.250
	Vancouver (NWL)	SS	0	1	3.86	2	2	0	0	5	6	0	3	6	11.6	1.93	.300
2016	Dunedin (FSL)	HiA	1	4	14.40	6	6	0	0	20	40	10	12	10	4.5	2.60	.421
	Lansing (MWL)	LoA	10	4	2.41	20	20	1	0	116	105	1	26	107	8.3	1.13	.247
Minor League Totals			15	11	3.61	46	38	1	1	204	195	15	50	186	8.2	1.20	.253

17 FRANCISCO RIOS, RHP

BA GRADE

45 Risk: High

Born: May 6, 1995. **B-T:** R-R. **Ht.:** 6-1. **Wt.:** 180. **Signed:** Mexico, 2012. **Signed by:** Ismael Cruz/Sandy Rosario.

Rios had unremarkable career since signing in July 2012 out of Monclova, Mexico, until 2016. In his first shot at full-season ball, the 21-year-old shot out of the gate at low Class A Lansing to earn a promotion to high Class A Dunedin, with a spot in the Futures Game interrupting his season. He gave up a home run to Orioles top prospect Chance Sisco in San Diego and struggled a bit down the stretch as he tired while pitching more than 120 innings. Rios had always impressed club officials with his ability to spin a breaking ball, and he throws both a curveball and a slider that are both at least solid-average, with the curve at times giving him an above-average pitch. His fastball also is average, having reached 96-97 mph but usually sitting 91-92. He learned to pitch off it more in 2016 and improved his fastball command as a result, throwing it more and learning to maintain his compact delivery with a three-quarters release point. His below-average changeup hasn't hindered him so far against lefthanded hitters. Rios lacks prototype physicality but has a chance to be a four-pitch starter with good control, making him a back-end rotation option. He should reach Double-A in 2017.

Year	Club (League)	Class	W	L	ERA	G	GS	CG	SV	IP	H	HR	BB	SO	K/9	WHIP	AVG
2014	Bluefield (APP)	R	3	2	5.91	13	9	0	0	53	79	5	18	38	6.4	1.82	.351
2015	Vancouver (NWL)	SS	3	6	4.27	15	12	0	0	65	72	1	25	59	8.1	1.48	.279
2016	Lansing (MWL)	LoA	2	0	1.20	6	6	0	0	30	21	0	8	43	12.9	0.97	.193
	Dunedin (FSL)	HiA	5	6	3.47	19	15	2	0	91	88	5	21	65	6.5	1.20	.257
Minor League Totals			17	20	4.04	68	51	2	1	292	311	12	91	253	7.8	1.38	.274

18 ANGEL PERDOMO, LHP

BA GRADE

50 Risk: Extreme

Born: May 7, 1994. **B-T:** L-L. **Ht.:** 6-6. **Wt.:** 200. **Signed:** Dominican Republic, 2011. **Signed by:** Ismael Cruz/Marino Tejada/Jose Rosario.

Acquired as part of the Blue Jays' impressive 2011 international class, Perdomo blossomed in 2016 in his first try at full-season ball. He led the low Class A Midwest League with 156 strikeouts and 10.8 strikeouts per nine innings, ranked second in the league in opponents average (.219) and was named to several all-star teams, from the Futures Game to the MWL midseason and postseason teams. Perdomo has a big frame with long levers, leading to bouts of wildness and inconsistent command that must improve for him to remain a starter. His fringy control prompted the Blue Jays to leave him off the 40-man roster, exposing him to the Rule 5 draft. When his delivery is in sync, though, Perdomo can dominate, getting good angle on his fastball that sits 92-94 mph at its best, more often sitting 88-92. His delivery gives the pitch some deception and his fastball plays as plus, eliciting awkward swings. His inconsistent slider has tilt and low-80s power when it's right, but most scouts still grade both of his secondary pitches, a slider and changeup, as below average. Perdomo needs at least one consistent secondary pitch to continue to succeed at higher levels. He'll head to high Class A in 2017.

Year	Club (League)	Class	W	L	ERA	G	GS	CG	SV	IP	H	HR	BB	SO	K/9	WHIP	AVG
2014	Blue Jays (GCL)	R	3	2	2.54	13	3	0	1	46	36	1	21	57	11.2	1.24	.209
2015	Bluefield (APP)	R	4	1	2.63	9	9	0	0	48	42	3	14	36	6.8	1.17	.231
	Vancouver (NWL)	SS	2	0	2.53	5	3	0	0	21	10	1	16	31	13.1	1.22	.152
2016	Lansing (MWL)	LoA	5	7	3.19	27	25	0	1	127	101	4	54	156	11.1	1.22	.219
Minor League Totals			14	11	3.01	73	42	0	4	281	207	10	136	336	10.8	1.22	.205

19 JOSH PALACIOS, OF

BA GRADE

45 Risk: High

Born: July 30, 1995. **B-T:** L-R. **Ht.:** 6-2. **Wt.:** 183. **Drafted:** Auburn, 2016 (4th round). **Signed by:** Don Norris.

The nephew of ex-Royals catcher Rey Palacios, Josh grew up in Brooklyn and wound up at San Jacinto (Texas) JC for two seasons, getting drafted by the Reds in 2014. He didn't sign and transferred to Auburn for 2016 before a broken left wrist ended his season in April. Blue Jays officials doubt they would have gotten Palacios as late as they got him if not for his injury. Palacios is one of the best pure hitters in the Jays' system thanks to his natural rhythm and timing at the plate, smooth lefthanded swing, present strength and the speed to leg out infield hits from time to time. He hit .330 in his debut, albeit with no home runs, and he controls the strike zone while providing decent gap power. He's a slightly above-average runner who played left field at Auburn in deference to Diamondbacks supplemental first-rounder Anfernee Grier, but the Jays intend to try him in center field for 2017. He may have to share time with J.B. Woodman, another Southeastern Conference outfielder whom the Jays drafted with thei rsecond pick. Palacios doesn't have the arm for right field but could hit his way into being a regular eventually, with fourth outfielder a more likely career path. He's likely to lead off at low Class A Lansing in 2017.

Year	Club (League)	Class	AVG	G	AB	R	H	2B	3B	HR	RBI	BB	SO	SB	CS	OBP	SLG
2016	Blue Jays (GCL)	R	.265	13	49	10	13	3	0	0	4	3	6	4	1	.321	.327
	Vancouver (NWL)	SS	.355	28	110	15	39	7	3	0	13	14	17	4	2	.437	.473
	Lansing (MWL)	LoA	.342	9	38	2	13	3	0	0	1	1	3	0	2	.375	.421
Minor League Totals			.330	50	197	27	65	13	3	0	18	18	26	8	5	.397	.426

20 PATRICK MURPHY, RHP

BA GRADE

50 Risk: Extreme

Born: June 10, 1995. **B-T:** R-R. **Ht.:** 6-4. **Wt.:** 220. **Drafted:** HS—Chandler, Ariz., 2013 (3rd round). **Signed by:** Blake Crosby.

Murphy prepped at Arizona's famed Hamilton High, where he teamed with Jays 2012 draftee Mitch Nay and current Dodgers prospect Cody Bellinger. Murphy missed his senior season with an elbow injury that required Tommy John surgery, but the Blue Jays drafted him in the third round anyway and signed him for $500,000. While Murphy returned to limited action in 2014, he struggled in his rehabilitation and eventually had surgery for thoracic outlet syndrome that cost him 2015. He entered his fourth pro season in 2016 with four professional innings under his belt, joined low Class A Lansing in May and finished the season in the short-season Vancouver rotation. Murphy is put together with a good pitcher's body and improved strength—he can deadlift 500 pounds—that he uses in his delivery. His fastball reaches 95-96 mph, often sitting there, and some see him as a future candidate to throw 100 mph. He had the ability to spin a breaking ball in high school and still flashes plus with his biting curveball even after the missed development time. Murphy's changeup gives him a chance to have three pitches that grade at least average, and he bought into using it this year with zeal. He will join a Class A rotation in 2017.

Year	Club (League)	Class	W	L	ERA	G	GS	CG	SV	IP	H	HR	BB	SO	K/9	WHIP	AVG
2014	Blue Jays (GCL)	R	0	1	11.25	3	2	0	0	4	8	0	2	4	9.0	2.50	.400
2015	Did not play—Injured																
2016	Lansing (MWL)	LoA	0	1	4.29	8	2	0	2	21	24	3	14	20	8.6	1.81	.286
	Vancouver (NWL)	SS	4	5	2.84	13	13	0	0	70	71	0	23	48	6.2	1.35	.264
Minor League Totals			4	7	3.52	24	17	0	2	95	103	3	39	72	6.8	1.50	.276

21 ZACH JACKSON, RHP

BA GRADE

50 Risk: Extreme

Born: Dec. 25, 1994. **B-T:** R-R. **Ht.:** 6-4. **Wt.:** 215. **Drafted:** Arkansas, 2016 (3rd round). **Signed by:** Dallas Black.

Jackson was an extremely successful reliever for Arkansas during his college career, often pitching multiple innings and helping the Razorbacks reach the 2015 College World Series despite an injury-ravaged rotation. He averaged 13.3 strikeouts per nine that season, but when the Razorbacks needed starters in 2016, they gave Jackson a try for five Southeastern Conference games, and it didn't go well. Jackson has a long arm action with a deep stab in the back that makes it hard for him to find his release point consistently. The result is well-below-average fastball command with poor control that limits him to a relief role. He averaged 5.5 walks-per-nine as a collegian and 5.8 per-nine in his pro debut. He throws hard, sitting 92-96 mph in short relief bursts, but his 12-to-6 curveball is his real calling card. It's a tight, hard downer in the low-80s that grades as plus if not better. He's often had a better feel for locating the curve than the fastball or his rarely thrown changeup. Jackson will move as quickly as the Jays can get him to locate his fastball with some consistency, and it will be in a bullpen role.

Year	Club (League)	Class	W	L	ERA	G	GS	CG	SV	IP	H	HR	BB	SO	K/9	WHIP	AVG
2016	Blue Jays (GCL)	R	0	0	0.00	1	0	0	0	1	1	0	0	0	0.0	1.00	.333
	Vancouver (NWL)	SS	1	1	3.57	13	0	0	0	18	13	0	12	23	11.7	1.42	.206
Minor League Totals			1	1	3.38	14	0	0	0	19	14	0	12	23	11.1	1.39	.212

22 DAN JANSEN, C

BA GRADE

45 Risk: High

Born: April 15, 1995. **B-T:** R-R. **Ht.:** 6-2. **Wt.:** 230. **Drafted:** HS—Appleton, Wis., 2013 (16th round). **Signed by:** Wes Penick.

For the second straight year, an injury to his left hand cost Jansen significant playing time. In 2015 his left hand was hit by a bat during a swing, breaking a bone and costing him three months. In 2016, he missed two months after breaking the hook of the hamate bone in his left hand while swinging the bat. This time, Jansen returned early enough to get some second-half reps and to play in the Arizona Fall League, where he played his way onto the 40-man roster. His injuries robbed him of some power, but he still has good strength and average power when healthy. He makes contact and isn't afraid to work a count. Defensively, Jansen needs development time to work on his game-calling and pitch-framing, but is adept at blocking balls in the dirt and is a sound receiver. He has a quick transfer with fringe-average arm strength. With Reese McGuire now in the system, Jansen must stay healthy and put together a solid 2017 season at Double-A to remain part of the Blue Jays' plans.

Year	Club (League)	Class	AVG	G	AB	R	H	2B	3B	HR	RBI	BB	SO	SB	CS	OBP	SLG
2014	Bluefield (APP)	R	.282	38	124	22	35	10	0	5	17	16	17	2	1	.390	.484
2015	Blue Jays (GCL)	R	.238	7	21	4	5	1	0	1	3	2	5	0	0	.304	.429
	Lansing (MWL)	LoA	.206	46	160	19	33	8	0	4	27	19	22	2	0	.299	.331
2016	Blue Jays (GCL)	R	.222	3	9	0	2	0	0	0	2	1	2	0	0	.364	.222
	Dunedin (FSL)	HiA	.218	54	188	18	41	7	0	1	23	22	40	7	1	.313	.271
Minor League Totals			.234	184	616	82	144	30	0	11	90	81	96	11	2	.336	.336

23 DANNY BARNES, RHP

BA GRADE **40** Risk: Medium

Born: Oct. 21, 1989. **B-T:** R-R. **Ht.:** 6-1. **Wt.:** 195. **Drafted:** Princeton, 2010 (35th round). **Signed by:** Bobby Gandolfo.

Barnes was the first player ever signed by area scout Bobby Gandolfo, an interesting choice considering he was an Ivy Leaguer at Princeton who had pitched 95 innings in three seasons. Barnes impressed Gandolfo enough to get turned in, signed as a 35th-rounder, and in 2016, he reached the major leagues. He's one of the few big leaguers with a degree and wrote his senior thesis (on MLB free agents) while riding buses with low Class A Lansing in 2013. Barnes has consistently missed bats out of the bullpen as a pro, averaging 11.86 K/9 IP over 320 minor league innings. He had his best season in 2016 with a 77-6 strikeout-walk ratio between Double-A and Triple-A. Barnes locates his 91-94 mph fastball well and has improved the plane on the pitch, though it still tends to flatten out. He pitches up and down in the zone with his fastball and solid-average changeup with late sink, and he locked down lefthanded hitters in 2016, including a 1-for-42 mark with 20 strikeouts in Triple-A. A firm 82-84 mph slider gives him a third average pitch. Barnes is older, having missed most of 2013 with a shoulder injury, but has been durable in recent years and pitches with poise. He's a middle relief option for 2017 and beyond.

Year	Club (League)	Class	W	L	ERA	G	GS	CG	SV	IP	H	HR	BB	SO	K/9	WHIP	AVG
2014	Dunedin (FSL)	HiA	0	5	4.19	36	0	0	7	39	36	4	12	49	11.4	1.24	.245
2015	New Hampshire (EL)	AA	3	2	2.97	40	1	0	4	61	64	5	19	74	11.0	1.37	.270
2016	New Hampshire (EL)	AA	2	1	1.01	24	0	0	1	36	17	3	4	40	10.1	0.59	.139
	Buffalo (IL)	AAA	1	0	0.35	17	0	0	5	26	6	0	2	37	13.0	0.31	.071
	Toronto (AL)	MAJ	0	0	3.95	12	0	0	0	14	14	0	5	14	9.2	1.39	.275
Major League Totals			0	0	3.95	12	0	0	0	14	14	0	5	14	9.2	1.39	.275
Minor League Totals			14	14	2.39	238	3	0	65	320	245	20	89	422	11.9	1.04	.207

24 JORDAN ROMANO, RHP

BA GRADE **45** Risk: High

Born: Dec. 22, 1992. **B-T:** R-R. **Ht.:** 6-3. **Wt.:** 210. **Drafted:** Oral Roberts, 2014 (10th round). **Signed by:** Dallas Black.

The Blue Jays always are on the lookout for Canadian talent such as Romano, an Ontario prep product who went to two Oklahoma colleges—Connors State JC and then Oral Roberts. He closed there in 2014 and likely will return to a relief role eventually due to a violent delivery, but it works for him in short bursts. The most encouraging sign for Romano in 2016 was his return to form from Tommy John surgery that caused him to miss all of 2015. The Jays, who signed him for $25,000 as a money-saver in the 10th round, built him up slowly in extended spring training and put him in low Class A Lansing's rotation to improve his stamina and get him needed innings. Romano thrived despite his inexperience, throwing plenty of strikes with a fastball that sits 92-93 but can ramp up to 95-96 mph with armside life. Romano has proved adept at pitching up and down with his heater, elevating for strikeouts but using his size to pitch downhill and get groundballs early in the count. His slider is his best secondary pitch and flashes plus with power. His changeup doesn't stand out. If Romero returns to the bullpen, as is likely, he could move quickly in 2017 with his fastball-slider combination.

Year	Club (League)	Class	W	L	ERA	G	GS	CG	SV	IP	H	HR	BB	SO	K/9	WHIP	AVG
2014	Blue Jays (GCL)	R	0	0	0.00	2	0	0	0	3	2	0	4	1	3.0	2.00	.182
	Bluefield (APP)	R	1	1	2.16	11	0	0	0	25	19	0	9	33	11.9	1.12	.209
2015	Did not play—Injured																
2016	Lansing (MWL)	LoA	3	2	2.11	15	14	1	0	73	49	3	27	72	8.9	1.05	.191
Minor League Totals			4	3	2.06	28	14	1	0	101	70	3	40	106	9.5	1.09	.195

25 CAVAN BIGGIO, 2B

BA GRADE **45** Risk: High

Born: April 11, 1995. **B-T:** L-R. **Ht.:** 6-1. **Wt.:** 189. **Drafted:** Notre Dame, 2016 (5th round). **Signed by:** Jeff Johnson.

To be clear, Biggio does not have the upside of his Hall of Fame father Craig, with significantly less athleticism. That said, the younger Biggio has a solid hitting track record, established on his own as an amateur and in his pro debut. A lefthanded hitter with a high-handed setup similar to fellow ex-Notre

Dame infielder Craig Counsell, Biggio controls the strike zone well and is selective enough to grade out as a solid-average hitter. A preseason first-team All-American, he cut his strikeout rate and increased his batting average as a junior for the Fighting Irish, though on a offensively-challenged club he was rarely challenged and hit just four home runs. Biggio's best attribute is his batting eye, and he walked more than he struck out at short-season Vancouver. He profiles best as a leadoff hitter, and while he's just an average runner at best, he's a savvy baserunner and basestealer. Biggio's fringy athleticism limits his defensive upside. He is limited to second base or perhaps left field, and he lacks the power to fit a corner profile. He will have to hit to be a regular but has the savvy to maximize his tools.

Year	Club (League)	Class	AVG	G	AB	R	H	2B	3B	HR	RBI	BB	SO	SB	CS	OBP	SLG
2016	Vancouver (NWL)	SS	.282	53	202	24	57	11	3	0	21	29	28	9	3	.382	.366
	Lansing (MWL)	LoA	.222	9	36	3	8	1	0	0	5	4	7	2	0	.310	.250
Minor League Totals			.273	62	238	27	65	12	3	0	26	33	35	11	3	.371	.349

26 OSMAN GUTIERREZ, RHP

BA GRADE
50 Risk: Extreme

Born: Dec. 15, 1995. **B-T:** R-R. **Ht.:** 6-4. **Wt.:** 226. **Signed:** Nicaragua, 2011.
Signed by: Marco Paddy/Daniel Sotelo.

Gutierrez still has yet to reach full-season ball since signing out of Nicaragua in 2011 for $210,000, the largest bonus out of that country that year. He needed three years in the Dominican Summer League before getting to the U.S. in 2015, but he has big arm strength and has made solid strides the last two years. He's physical, having gained about 30 pounds since signing, and a power pitcher who holds his velocity well. With the added strength, Gutierrez pushed his fastball up to 97 mph and sits in the 94-96 range. He came into pro ball with a curveball but has converted it to a slider, which is generally above-average and flashes plus, giving him a weapon for swings-and-misses and helping produce groundball outs. He throws a decent changeup as well which, with more consistency, could give him a third pitch that is at least average. He has a longer arm action that hinders his command, but he has shown solid control to this point. Gutierrez has started moving in the right direction and will finally get his full-season shot in 2017 at low Class A Lansing.

Year	Club (League)	Class	W	L	ERA	G	GS	CG	SV	IP	H	HR	BB	SO	K/9	WHIP	AVG
2014	Blue Jays (DSL)	R	0	1	1.91	12	10	0	0	47	44	0	25	42	8.0	1.47	.256
2015	Blue Jays (GCL)	R	4	3	4.66	11	9	0	0	46	50	3	15	41	8.0	1.40	.273
2016	Bluefield (APP)	R	4	3	3.88	12	11	1	0	65	69	5	21	66	9.1	1.38	.264
Minor League Totals			9	8	3.62	50	34	1	0	184	197	8	76	166	8.1	1.48	.273

27 YELTSIN GUDINO, SS

BA GRADE
45 Risk: Extreme

Born: Jan. 17, 1997. **B-T:** R-R. **Ht.:** 6-0. **Wt.:** 180. **Signed:** Venezuela, 2013.
Signed by: Ismael Cruz/Luis Marquez/Jose Contreras.

Gudino was the No. 8 prospect in the 2013 international class, which included Eloy Jimenez, Gleyber Torres and Rafael Devers. Gudino received a $1.29 million bonus after signing out of Carlos Guillen's Venezuelan academy. He has a long, lean frame he is growing into, having gained about 30 pounds since signing. Gudino's best attribute is his hands, which play at the plate in terms of basic bat-to-ball skills, and in the field, where he's smooth with the glove. While he has an average arm, he has good footwork and instincts. He's shown infield actions and adjusted to the speed of the game at short-season Vancouver after a slow start both in the field and at the plate. Overwhelmed early with a 5-for-36 start, Gudino settled in and showed contact ability as well as patience. His swing is geared for contact, and he has well below-average power. He is an average runner. Gudino's impact will have to come with his glove, as the second half of the Northwest League season was the first time he's shown life at the plate. He could play shortstop for low Class A Lansing in 2017, but if the Jays stick with Bo Bichette there, Gudino will defer as the lesser prospect.

Year	Club (League)	Class	AVG	G	AB	R	H	2B	3B	HR	RBI	BB	SO	SB	CS	OBP	SLG
2014	Blue Jays (GCL)	R	.145	40	138	17	20	3	0	0	12	13	28	0	1	.219	.167
2015	Bluefield (APP)	R	.185	56	211	21	39	12	1	1	13	17	36	2	2	.251	.265
2016	Vancouver (NWL)	SS	.226	54	186	18	42	4	1	0	15	29	43	0	1	.338	.258
Minor League Totals			.189	150	535	56	101	19	2	1	40	59	107	2	4	.275	.237

28 YENNSY DIAZ, RHP

BA GRADE
45 Risk: Extreme

Born: Nov. 15, 1996. **B-T:** R-R. **Ht.:** 6-1. **Wt.:** 191. **Signed:** Dominican Republic, 2014. **Signed by:** Ismael Cruz/Sandy Rosario/Luciano Del Rosario.

Diaz accelerated his development in 2015 with a strong pro debut, pushing his way to the Rookie-level Gulf Coast League to end the season. The Jays thought he had enough fastball command to make the leap to Rookie-level Bluefield, and Diaz held his own there for half of the Appalachian League season. However, he struggled with control down the stretch en route to a 5.79 ERA, giving up seven home runs in his final five starts. Diaz still excited the organization with his raw stuff, including a 92-95 mph four-seamer he struggled to locate much of the season despite a balanced delivery and easy, clean arm action. Evaluators said he got on the side of the ball when he overthrew, flattening out his four-seamer and leaving him vulnerable to home runs. Diaz may have to lean on his 89-91 mph sinker more going forward. His curveball and changeup remain fringy to below-average pitches, though the curve has its moments. Still a plus raw arm, Diaz should graduate to short-season Vancouver in 2017 as a 20-year-old.

Year	Club (League)	Class	W	L	ERA	G	GS	CG	SV	IP	H	HR	BB	SO	K/9	WHIP	AVG
2015	Blue Jays (DSL)	R	3	3	1.93	10	6	0	0	37	30	0	16	39	9.4	1.23	.217
	Blue Jays (GCL)	R	1	1	4.74	5	3	0	1	19	24	0	7	19	9.0	1.63	.316
2016	Bluefield (APP)	R	4	6	5.79	12	10	0	0	56	59	9	27	48	7.7	1.54	.267
Minor League Totals			8	10	4.33	27	19	0	1	112	113	9	50	106	8.5	1.45	.260

29 MATT DERMODY, LHP

BA GRADE 40 Risk: Medium

Born: July 4, 1990. **B-T:** R-L. **Ht.:** 6-5. **Wt.:** 190. **Drafted:** Iowa, 2013 (28th round). **Signed by:** Wes Penick.

The long road to the 40-man roster for Dermody included plenty of twists. The Iowa native wound up being drafted four times—once out of high school and three times with the Hawkeyes. He was set to sign in 2012 with Arizona before a physical showed an elbow injury. He recovered with rehab rather than surgery, pitched 94 innings the next spring and has stayed healthy as a pro. The Blue Jays shifted him to the bullpen in 2014, and he took off in 2016, walking just eight in 54.1 innings. Dermody commands a fastball in the 88-92 mph range, notable more for its high spin rate and armside sink. He gets good extension out of his 6-foot-5 frame and generally keeps the ball down, giving up just three homers in the last two minor league seasons, spanning more than 130 innings. Dermody's short low-80s slider, an average pitch, generates more groundballs than swings-and-misses. Dermody will battle low-slot lefty Chad Girodo and hard-throwing but wild Tim Mayza for a lefty relief spot in Toronto in 2017.

Year	Club (League)	Class	W	L	ERA	G	GS	CG	SV	IP	H	HR	BB	SO	K/9	WHIP	AVG
2014	Lansing (MWL)	LoA	4	6	4.67	27	12	0	0	96	113	5	36	65	6.1	1.55	.294
2015	Dunedin (FSL)	HiA	4	1	4.21	35	1	0	1	77	98	2	13	62	7.2	1.44	.308
2016	Dunedin (FSL)	HiA	1	1	1.96	16	0	0	3	18	21	0	1	20	9.8	1.20	.296
	New Hampshire (EL)	AA	2	0	0.92	16	0	0	0	20	12	1	2	21	9.6	0.71	.174
	Buffalo (IL)	AAA	0	0	2.76	15	0	0	0	16	22	0	5	6	3.3	1.65	.324
	Toronto (AL)	MAJ	0	0	12.00	5	0	0	0	3	6	1	0	5	15.0	2.00	.400
Major League Totals			0	0	12.00	5	0	0	0	3	6	1	0	5	15.0	2.00	.400
Minor League Totals			16	9	3.49	125	16	0	4	271	312	8	61	225	7.5	1.38	.289

30 TRAVIS HOSTERMAN, LHP

BA GRADE 45 Risk: Extreme

Born: Aug. 19, 1998. **B-T:** L-L. **Ht.:** 6-3. **Wt.:** 190. **Drafted:** HS—Oviedo, Fla., 2016 (11th round). **Signed by:** Matt O'Brien.

A Central Florida recruit, Hosterman was young for the draft class and was just 17 when the Blue Jays signed him for $400,000. That was the fifth-largest bonus in the club's 2016 draft class. The organization lacks lefthanded starting pitching depth and sees Hosterman as a potential back-of-the-rotation piece. He is still filling out physically and needs to add strength to firm up a fastball that presently sits 87-88 mph. Scouts like his chances to add weight in his frame. Hosterman's ability to pitch off his fastball belies his present velocity, as he locates it to his glove side well and can pitch to both sides of the plate. He is able to throw his changeup with similar arm speed as his fastball. It's more consistent than his curveball, which has 1-to-7 shape and above-average potential, but he locates both secondary pitches down in the zone. A projection pick who will have to add velocity, Hosterman will likely be ticketed for extended spring training before an assignment to either Rookie-level Bluefield or short-season Vancouver in 2017.

Year	Club (League)	Class	W	L	ERA	G	GS	CG	SV	IP	H	HR	BB	SO	K/9	WHIP	AVG
2016	Blue Jays (GCL)	R	0	0	4.91	8	5	0	0	18	19	2	10	14	6.9	1.58	.250
Minor League Totals			0	0	4.91	8	5	0	0	18	19	2	10	14	6.9	1.58	.250

Washington Nationals

BY TEDDY CAHILL

After a disappointing 2015 season that ended with them missing the playoffs and firing manager Matt Williams, the Nationals bounced back strong in 2016. With Dusty Baker at the helm, they won 95 games and topped the National League East for the third time in five years.

But the Nationals again lost in the Division Series, felled this time by the Dodgers.

Though Washington again exited the playoffs early, it has maintained an impressive standard of success over the last five years under general manager Mike Rizzo. The Nationals have posted winning records for five straight seasons, the longest streak in the franchise's 48-year history, and finished no worse than second place in the division.

Washington benefitted from key acquisitions by Rizzo. In the offseason, the Nationals signed second baseman Daniel Murphy, who led the team with 25 home runs and finished second in MVP voting. At the trade deadline, Rizzo dipped into the system's pitching depth to acquire closer Mark Melancon from the Pirates.

The Nationals also got key contributions from their own prospects. Trea Turner provided a spark to the lineup after he was promoted in July. He eventually took over as the everyday center fielder and finished second in NL Rookie of the Year balloting.

Much-anticipated righthanders Lucas Giolito and Reynaldo Lopez also arrived in Washington in 2016. Giolito, the club's 2012 first-round pick, wasn't quite ready for the big leagues and stumbled. Lopez pitched well enough in the bullpen in September to make the playoff roster.

Rizzo bundled both Giolito and Lopez with 2016 first-rounder Dane Dunning to acquire White Sox outfielder Adam Eaton at the Winter Meetings. The trade signifies Washington's confidence in its farm system, which continued to churn out big leaguers in 2016, while also remaining strong at the lower levels.

Center fielder Victor Robles built on his breakout 2015 season as he advanced to full-season ball, and 17-year-old outfielder Juan Soto excelled in his pro debut in the Rookie-level Gulf Coast League.

Lopez, Robles and Soto are just a few examples of the Nationals' recent successes in the international amateur market, and that group could soon be growing larger. Washington has not been a major player in the market since the scandal surrounding the 2006 signing of the Dominican prospect then known as Esmailyn Gonzalez, who was revealed three years later to be Carlos Alvarez

ED WOLFSTEIN

Trea Turner moved from shortstop to center field and had an outstanding rookie year

TOP PROSPECTS OF THE DECADE

Year	Player, Pos.	2016 Org
2007	Collin Balester, rhp	Korea
2008	Chris Marrero, 1b	Red Sox
2009	Jordan Zimmermann, rhp	Tigers
2010	Stephen Strasburg, rhp	Nationals
2011	Bryce Harper, of	Nationals
2012	Anthony Rendon, 3b	Nationals
2013	Lucas Giolito, rhp	Nationals
2014	Lucas Giolito, rhp	Nationals
2015	Lucas Giolito, rhp	Nationals
2016	Lucas Giolito, rhp	Nationals

and four years older than he originally presented himself. The fallout cost then-GM Jim Bowden his job and the Nationals slimmed down their international operations.

After beginning to spend more money internationally in recent years, Washington made its biggest move yet in 2016. The Nationals surpassed their international bonus pool to sign three shortstops ranked among the top 15 players in the class.

With its robust international class and draft class that featured two first-rounders—Dunning and prep shortstop Carter Kieboom—the Nationals were able to add depth to a system that had been more top heavy in recent years. In so doing, the organization underlined its commitment to scouting and player development under Rizzo and his front office staff.

ORGANIZATION OVERVIEW

General manager: Mike Rizzo. **Farm director:** Mark Scialabba. **Scouting director:** Kris Kline.

Class	Team	League	W	L	PCT	Finish	Manager
Majors	Washington Nationals	National	95	67	.586	2nd (15)	Dusty Baker
Triple-A	Syracuse Chiefs	International	61	82	.427	14th (14)	Billy Gardner Jr.
Double-A	Harrisburg Senators	Eastern	76	66	.535	5th (12)	Matthew Lecroy
High Class A	Potomac Nationals	Carolina	73	65	.529	4th (8)	Tripp Keister
Low Class A	Hagerstown Suns	South Atlantic	83	57	.593	1st (14)	Patrick Anderson
Short-season	Auburn Doubledays	New York-Penn	28	47	.373	12th (14)	Jerad Head
Rookie	GCL Nationals	Gulf Coast	30	23	.566	4th (17)	Josh Johnson
Overall 2016 Minor League Record			351	340	.508	12th (30)	

THIS YEAR'S TOP 30

No.	Player, Pos.	Grade/Risk
1.	Victor Robles, of	65/High
2.	Erick Fedde, rhp	60/High
3.	Juan Soto, of	60/Extreme
4.	Wilmer Difo, ss/2b	45/Low
5.	Andrew Stevenson, of	45/Medium
6.	Koda Glover, rhp	50/High
7.	Luis Garcia, ss	55/Extreme
8.	Carter Kieboom, ss	55/Extreme
9.	Pedro Severino, c	45/Medium
10.	Austin Voth, rhp	45/Medium
11.	Rafael Bautista, of	45/Medium
12.	Drew Ward, 3b	50/High
13.	A.J. Cole, rhp	45/Medium
14.	Anderson Franco, 3b	50/High
15.	Jesus Luzardo, lhp	55/Extreme
16.	Kelvin Gutierrez, 3b	50/High
17.	Sheldon Neuse, 3b	50/High
18.	Jakson Reetz, c	50/High
19.	Brian Goodwin, of	45/Medium
20.	Blake Perkins, of	50/Extreme
21.	Osvaldo Abreu, ss	45/High
22.	Raudy Read, c	45/High
23.	Edwin Lora, ss	50/Extreme
24.	Jose Sanchez, ss	50/Extreme
25.	Yasel Antuna, ss	50/Extreme
26.	Jose Marmolejos, 1b	40/Medium
27.	Tyler Watson, lhp	50/Extreme
28.	Telmito Agustin, of	50/Extreme
29.	Joan Baez, rhp	50/Extreme
30.	Matt Skole, 1b/3b	40/Medium

LAST YEAR'S TOP 30

No.	Player, Pos.	Status
1.	Lucas Giolito, rhp	(White Sox)
2.	Trea Turner, ss	Majors
3.	Victor Robles, of	No. 1
4.	Erick Fedde, rhp	No. 2
5.	Reynaldo Lopez, rhp	(White Sox)
6.	Wilmer Difo, ss/2b	No. 4
7.	A.J. Cole, rhp	No. 13
8.	Andrew Stevenson, of	No. 5
9.	Austin Voth, rhp	No. 10
10.	Anderson Franco, 3b	No. 14
11.	Pedro Severino, c	No. 9
12.	Blake Perkins, of	No. 20
13.	Rafael Bautista, of	No. 11
14.	Jakson Reetz, c	No. 18
15.	Osvaldo Abreu, ss	No. 21
16.	Drew Ward, 3b	No. 12
17.	Sammy Solis, lhp	Majors
18.	Joan Baez, rhp	No. 29
19.	Austen Williams, rhp	Dropped out
20.	Abel de los Santos, rhp	(Angels)
21.	Rhett Wiseman, of	Dropped out
22.	Edwin Lora, ss	No. 23
23.	Raudy Read, c	No. 22
24.	Juan Soto, of	No. 3
25.	Chris Bostick, 2b/of	(Pirates)
26.	Phillips Valdez, rhp	Dropped out
27.	Nick Lee, lhp	Dropped out
28.	Taylor Hearn, lhp	(Pirates)
29.	Mariano Rivera, rhp	Dropped out
30.	Koda Glover, rhp	No. 6

BEST TOOLS

Best Hitter for Average	Victor Robles
Best Power Hitter	Matt Skole
Best Strike-Zone Discipline	Austin Davidson
Fastest Baserunner	Rafael Bautista
Best Athlete	Victor Robles
Best Fastball	Koda Glover
Best Curveball	Joan Baez
Best Slider	Erick Fedde
Best Changeup	A.J. Cole
Best Control	Jaron Long
Best Defensive Catcher	Pedro Severino
Best Defensive Infielder	Jose Sanchez
Best Infield Arm	Kelvin Gutierrez
Best Defensive Outfielder	Victor Robles
Best Outfield Arm	Victor Robles

PROJECTED 2020 LINEUP

Catcher	Pedro Severino
First Base	Daniel Murphy
Second Base	Wilmer Difo
Third Base	Anthony Rendon
Shortstop	Trea Turner
Left Field	Adam Eaton
Center Field	Victor Robles
Right Field	Bryce Harper
No. 1 Starter	Max Scherzer
No. 2 Starter	Stephen Strasburg
No. 3 Starter	Erick Fedde
No. 4 Starter	Joe Ross
No. 5 Starter	Austin Voth
Closer	Koda Glover

MINOR LEAGUE DEPTH CHART

WASHINGTON NATIONALS

TOP 2017 ROOKIE: Pedro Severino, c. He isn't as offensive as newly acquired catcher Derek Norris, but he's more than ready defensively to share duties.

BREAKOUT PROSPECT: Tyler Watson, lhp. After taking a step forward in 2016, he could make an even bigger jump as the projectable lefty continues to mature.

SLEEPER: Jake Noll, 2b. He established a track record of hitting in college and should keep hitting in pro ball thanks to his simple swing and above-average bat speed.

SOURCE OF TOP 30 TALENT			
Homegrown	30	Acquired	0
College	6	Trades	0
Junior college	1	Rule 5 draft	0
High school	7	Independent leagues	0
Nondrafted free agents	0	Free agents/waivers	0
International	16		

LF
Telmito Agustin (28)
Isaac Ballou

CF
Victor Robles (1)
Andrew Stevenson (5)
Rafael Bautista (11)
Brian Goodwin (19)
Blake Perkins (20)
Yadiel Hernandez
Daniel Johnson
Armond Upshaw

RF
Juan Soto (3)
Nick Banks
Rhett Wiseman

3B
Drew Ward (12)
Anderson Franco (14)
Kelvin Gutierrez (16)
Sheldon Neuse (17)

SS
Wilmer Difo (4)
Luis Garcia (7)
Carter Kieboom (8)
Osvaldo Abreu (21)
Edwin Lora (23)
Jose Sanchez (24)
Yasel Antuna (25)

2B
Jake Noll
Bryan Mejia

1B
Jose Marmolejos (26)
Matt Skole (30)
Ryan Ripken

C
Pedro Severino (9)
Jakson Reetz (18)
Raudy Read (22)
Spencer Kieboom
Tres Barrera

LHP

LHSP	LHRP
Jesus Luzardo (15)	Nick Lee
Tyler Watson (27)	Taylor Guilbeau
Matt Crownover	

RHP

RHSP	RHRP
Erick Fedde (2)	Koda Glover (6)
Austin Voth (10)	Ryan Brinley
A.J. Cole (13)	Jimmy Cordero
Joan Baez (29)	Francys Peguero
Luis Reyes	Mariano Rivera
Phillips Valdez	Jefry Rodriguez
Weston Davis	Tommy Peterson
Austen Williams	Jake Johansen
Andrew Lee	Dakota Bacus
Jaron Long	Taylor Hill

DRAFT ANALYSIS

2016

BEST PURE HITTER: SS Carter Kieboom (1s) has excellent timing and bat speed. The Nationals believe he could develop a plus hit tool down the line. Kieboom is an aggressive hitter and has some swing and miss to his game as a result, but he knows the strike zone well and understands which pitches he can drive.

BEST POWER: 3B Sheldon Neuse (3) has the best raw power of the group, but he doesn't always get his hips cleared to turn on the ball and use his power. Kieboom's power showed well in his pro debut and during fall instructional league. Kieboom has the ability to drive the ball more than 400 feet, and he's shown the ability to hit the ball over the fence to the opposite field.

FASTEST RUNNER: OF Armond Upshaw (11) and OF Daniel Johnson (5) show elite foot speed. Upshaw is an 80-runner and has run the 60-yard dash in 6.3 seconds.

BEST DEFENSIVE PLAYER: Kieboom's improved actions and footwork this spring stand out from the group. He shows range to both sides and he shows average to above-average arm strength. Even if he eventually needs to move off of shortstop in deference to a superior big leaguer, he could be an outstanding defender at third base.

BEST FASTBALL: RHP Dane Dunning (1s) excellent command of his two-seam fastball, which shows late movement and life, and he can run his four-seamer up to 97 in short bursts. RHP Phil Morse (16) lacks Dunning's movement or array of secondary pitches, but his fastball can also reach 97 out of the bullpen.

BEST SECONDARY PITCH: The Nationals have seen LHP Jesus Luzardo (3) show the ability to manipulate his curveball and they see it as a plus pitch. Luzardo's changeup is also a weapon, among the best of the prep class in 2016. Dunning's slider could be a plus pitch, and he began using his curveball more in pro ball, and the Nationals believe that could be a plus pitch as well.

BEST PRO DEBUT: Dunning hit the ground running, posting a 2.02 ERA in the low minors.

BEST ATHLETE: Johnson has freakish athleticism, with explosive quick-twitch ability. He has fast hands and generates pull power, giving him a chance to develop into a five-tool talent because of his plus-plus arm strength and speed. Upshaw is also highly athletic.

MOST INTRIGUING BACKGROUND: Kieboom is the brother of Spencer, another Nationals prospect who reached the big leagues in 2016.

CLOSEST TO THE MAJORS: Dunning's athleticism and four-pitch mix could allow him to move relatively quickly.

BEST LATE-ROUND PICK: The Nationals are enamored with Upshaw's all-around tools.

THE ONE WHO GOT AWAY: RHP Noah Murdock (38) had a firm commitment to Virginia and stuck to it. He's 6-foot-7 and shows flashes of velocity and a potentially devastating breaking ball from a low slot. RHP Morgan Cooper (34) was still relatively fresh off of Tommy John surgery, and he has already boosted his stock since returning to college, with his fastball reaching 95 and his breaking ball regaining some of its oomph.

2015

OF Andrew Stevenson (2), the club's top pick, has excellent defensive ability in center field. RHP Koda Glover (7) was one of the first 2015 draftees to reach the majors. LHP Taylor Hearn (5) and 2B Max Schrock (13) were traded for Mark Melancon and Marc Rzepczynski.

GRADE: B

2014

RHP Erick Fedde (1) has recovered from Tommy John surgery. C Jakson Reetz (3) has breakout potential in 2017. Unsigned C Evan Skoug (34, now at Texas Christian) is a potential 2017 first-rounder.

GRADE: C

2013

RHPs Nick Pivetta (4) and Austin Voth (5) emerged as the class' top prospects, with Pivetta dealt to the Phillies for Jonathan Papelbon. LHP Travis Ott (25) was used in the Trea Turner deal, and there's hope for 3B Drew Ward (3).

GRADE: C

TOP DRAFT PICKS OF THE DECADE

Year	Player, Pos.	2016 Org
2007	Ross Detwiler, lhp	Athletics
2008	*Aaron Crow, rhp	Cubs
2009	Stephen Strasburg, rhp	Nationals
2010	Bryce Harper, of	Nationals
2011	Anthony Rendon, 3b	Nationals
2012	Lucas Giolito, rhp	Nationals
2013	Jake Johansen, rhp (2nd round)	Nationals
2014	Erick Fedde, rhp	Nationals
2015	Andrew Stevenson, of (2nd round)	Nationals
2016	Carter Kieboom, ss	Nationals

* Did not sign

LARGEST BONUSES IN CLUB HISTORY

Stephen Strasburg, 2009	$7,500,000
Bryce Harper, 2010	$6,250,000
Anthony Rendon, 2011	$6,000,000
Yasel Antuna, 2016	$3,850,000
Brian Goodwin, 2011	$3,000,000

1 VICTOR ROBLES, OF

Born: May 19, 1997. **B-T:** R-R. **Ht.:** 6-0. **Wt.:** 185.
Signed: Dominican Republic, 2013.
Signed by: Modesto Ulloa.

BA GRADE

65 Risk: High

SCOUTING GRADES

Hitting: 60.
Power: 50.
Speed: 70.
Defense: 60.
Arm: 60.

Based on 20-80 scouting scale and future projection rather than present grades.

TONY FARLOW

Robles had impressed Nationals evaluators for years before breaking out in 2015 during his U.S. debut. He signed with Washington for $225,000 in 2013 and impressed in the Dominican Summer League the following year. He wowed the Nationals during extended spring training in 2015, then carried that performance over to the regular season in the Rookie-level Gulf Coast League and short-season Auburn. He ranked as the No. 2 prospect in both leagues while hitting a combined .352/.445/.507 with 24 stolen bases in 61 games. Robles advanced to full-season ball in 2016 for the first time, beginning the season at low Class A Hagerstown. After earning a spot in the South Atlantic League all-star game, he was promoted to high Class A Potomac, where the 19-year-old was the youngest player in the Carolina League. He again ranked as a top prospect in two leagues—No. 1 in the South Atlantic and No. 3 in the Carolina. Robles was sidelined for about three weeks in the second half of the season by a thumb injury he suffered after being hit in the hand by a fastball, one of 34 times he was hit by a pitch in 2016. Even as he has raced through the minor leagues, Robles has continued to hit and earn praise for his baseball IQ and willingness to learn.

Robles has excellent quick-twitch athleticism and true five-tool potential. He is advanced for his age, displaying a good feel for hitting. He has strong, quick hands that help him to produce impressive bat speed. Presently, his power results mostly in hard line drives to the gaps, but as he physically matures, those balls should start going over the fence. He sometimes gets big in his swing as he tries to drive the ball with more authority. He has a good feel for the barrel and is difficult to strike out, though he does not often walk. He sets up very close to the plate, which allows him to cover the outer half of the plate well, but also results in him often being hit by pitches. He is confident in his ability to turn on inside pitches, but after his stint on the disabled list he is also starting to learn about the importance of getting out of the way of inside pitches. Robles is a plus runner and makes good use of his speed on both the basepaths and in the outfield. He tracks down balls well in center field and has plus arm strength. His defensive ability and speed enable him to impact the game in many different ways. He plays with lots of energy in all facets of the game, a trait that endears him to teammates, coaches and scouts alike.

Robles has proven to be capable of moving quickly in the minors and will likely return to Potomac to open 2017. Because he won't turn 20 until May, he will likely again be among the youngest players in the Carolina League. It will be a challenging assignment for the precocious outfielder, but his makeup and dynamic skill set should help him continue to find success against older competition. He has all-star potential and could arrive in Washington late in the 2018 season and be a regular player at age 22 in 2019.

Year	Club (League)	Class	AVG	G	AB	R	H	2B	3B	HR	RBI	BB	SO	SB	CS	OBP	SLG
2014	Nationals (DSL)	R	.313	47	182	46	57	14	4	3	25	16	26	22	9	.408	.484
2015	Nationals (GCL)	R	.370	23	73	19	27	6	1	2	11	10	12	12	1	.484	.562
	Auburn (NYP)	SS	.343	38	140	29	48	5	4	2	16	8	21	12	4	.424	.479
2016	Hagerstown (SAL)	LoA	.305	64	233	48	71	9	6	5	30	18	38	19	8	.405	.459
	Nationals (GCL)	R	.150	5	20	3	3	0	0	1	1	0	7	0	1	.190	.300
	Potomac (CAR)	HiA	.262	41	168	24	44	8	2	3	11	14	32	18	5	.354	.387
Minor League Totals			.306	218	816	169	250	42	17	16	94	66	136	83	28	.401	.458

2 ERICK FEDDE, RHP

BA GRADE
60 Risk: High

Born: Feb. 25, 1993. **B-T:** R-R. **Ht.:** 6-4. **Wt.:** 180. **Drafted:** Nevada-Las Vegas, 2014 (1st round). **Signed by:** Mitch Sokol.

A 24th-round pick by the Padres coming out of Las Vegas High, Fedde stayed close to home and attended Nevada-Las Vegas. After his sophomore season at college, Fedde had a strong showing with USA Baseball's Collegiate National Team and carried that into his junior year back at school, where he went 8-2, 1.76 with 82 strikeouts in 77 innings. He appeared to be on his way to becoming a top-10 pick in the 2014 draft until he had Tommy John surgery that May. Despite the injury, he didn't fall far on draft day and the Nationals selected him 18th overall. Fedde made his pro debut a year later and reached Double-A Harrisburg in 2016. As more time has passed since Fedde's surgery, he has gotten stronger and seen his stuff return. His fastball has reached 97 mph, but he more typically pitches in the low 90s. It plays up because of excellent sinking action, and he pounds the strike zone with it. His low-80s slider is a plus offering and generates swings and misses. He made strides with his changeup in 2016, and it could become an average pitch. Fedde throws a lot of strikes but still has room to refine his command to more consistently locate all his pitches. He is an excellent athlete, helping him to both repeat his delivery and field his position well. Now that he's fully healthy, Fedde could make quick work of the upper minors. He will return to Harrisburg to start 2017 and is closing in on his big league debut. He has a No. 2 starter ceiling with a high floor based on his wide-ranging ability.

Year	Club (League)	Class	W	L	ERA	G	GS	CG	SV	IP	H	HR	BB	SO	K/9	WHIP	AVG
2014	Did not play—Injured																
2015	Auburn (NYP)	SS	4	1	2.57	8	8	0	0	35	38	1	8	36	9.3	1.31	.264
	Hagerstown (SAL)	LoA	1	2	4.34	6	6	0	0	29	24	1	8	23	7.1	1.10	.224
2016	Potomac (CAR)	HiA	6	4	2.85	18	17	0	0	92	85	7	19	95	9.3	1.13	.244
	Harrisburg (EL)	AA	2	1	3.99	5	5	1	0	29	33	1	10	28	8.6	1.47	.284
Minor League Totals			13	8	3.21	37	36	1	0	185	180	10	45	182	8.9	1.22	.252

3 JUAN SOTO, OF

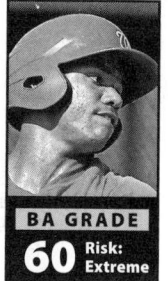

BA GRADE
60 Risk: Extreme

Born: Oct. 25, 1998. **B-T:** L-L. **Ht.:** 6-1. **Wt.:** 185. **Signed:** Dominican Republic, 2015. **Signed by:** Modesto Ulloa.

The Nationals established a new franchise bonus record for an international teen when they signed Soto for $1.5 million in 2015, though it wsa shattered a year later in their international spending spree. He skipped the Dominican Summer League in 2016 to make made his pro debut as a 17-year-old in the Rookie-level Gulf Coast League, where he won MVP honors after leading the circuit in batting (.361) and slugging (.550) and ranking second in on-base percentage (.410). He earned a late-season promotion to short-season Auburn and continued to succeed against older competition. Soto ranked No. 13 in the 2015 international class largely because of his hitting ability, which translated well to pro ball. He is an advanced hitter for his age, showing a feel for the barrel and good pitch-recognition skills. He has a short, easy, lefthanded swing and uses the whole field to hit. He makes good adjustments at the plate thanks to his impressive understanding of hitting. His power is still developing, and he could have above-average pop by the time he is done physically maturing. Soto has average speed and arm strength, and he profiles in right field. Soto earns priase for his makeup, maturity and confidence. He will play the entire 2017 season as an 18-year-old, and is probably advanced enough to handle an assignment to low Class A Hagerstown. But the Nationals could opt for a more conservative approach and send him back to Auburn, where he would still be one of the youngest players in the league.

Year	Club (League)	Class	AVG	G	AB	R	H	2B	3B	HR	RBI	BB	SO	SB	CS	OBP	SLG
2016	Nationals (GCL)	R	.361	45	169	25	61	11	3	5	31	14	25	5	2	.410	.550
	Auburn (NYP)	SS	.429	6	21	3	9	3	0	0	1	3	4	0	0	.500	.571
Minor League Totals			.368	51	190	28	70	14	3	5	32	17	29	5	2	.420	.553

4 WILMER DIFO, SS/2B

Born: April 2, 1992. **B-T:** B-R. **Ht.:** 5-11. **Wt.:** 200. **Signed:** Dominican Republic, 2011.
Signed by: Modesto Ulloa.

A late bloomer, Difo struggled in the low minors before breaking out in 2014, when he won the South Atlantic League MVP award as a 22-year-old at low Class A Hagerstown. He has built on that progress, making his major league debut in 2015 and returning to Washington for much of the second half in 2016. He also earned a spot on the postseason roster thanks to his versatility and speed. Difo is a well above-average runner and has an aggressive approach on the basepaths and at the plate. A switch-hitter, he has a short, quick swing. He has some wiry strength and can drive the ball into the gaps for extra-base hits but has produced below-average power in the upper levels. After moving around the infield early in his career, Difo has settled at shortstop, where he has made strides as a defender. He is still improving his consistency in the field, but he has above-average arm strength and the hands necessary to play shortstop. He also played second and third base in the major leagues. Because Difo has played only one game at Triple-A, the Nationals could send him to Syracuse to play every day at shortstop and continue to work on his defense. He also could return to Washington to reprise his role as a utility infielder.

BA GRADE
45 Risk: Low

Year	Club (League)	Class	AVG	G	AB	R	H	2B	3B	HR	RBI	BB	SO	SB	CS	OBP	SLG
2014	Hagerstown (SAL)	LoA	.315	136	559	91	176	31	7	14	90	37	65	49	9	.360	.470
2015	Potomac (CAR)	HiA	.320	19	75	13	24	7	0	3	14	8	13	4	1	.386	.533
	Harrisburg (EL)	AA	.279	87	359	48	100	21	6	2	39	12	79	26	1	.312	.387
	Washington (NL)	MAJ	.182	15	11	1	2	0	0	0	0	0	2	0	0	.182	.182
2016	Harrisburg (EL)	AA	.259	104	410	59	106	15	3	6	41	34	59	28	11	.318	.354
	Syracuse (IL)	AAA	.200	1	5	0	1	0	0	0	0	0	2	0	0	.200	.200
	Washington (NL)	MAJ	.276	31	58	14	16	3	0	1	7	8	12	3	0	.364	.379
Major League Totals			.261	46	69	15	18	3	0	1	7	8	14	3	0	.338	.348
Minor League Totals			.274	571	2194	333	602	98	35	30	244	199	344	178	46	.340	.392

5 ANDREW STEVENSON, OF

Born: June 1, 1994. **B-T:** L-L. **Ht.:** 6-0. **Wt.:** 185. **Drafted:** Louisiana State, 2015 (2nd round). **Signed by:** Ed Gustafson.

Signing Max Scherzer cost the Nationals their first-round pick in 2015, making Stevenson their top selection in the second round. He ranked as one of the best defensive outfielders in NCAA Division I and helped Louisiana State reach the College World Series in 2015. He then hit the ground running in pro ball, quickly advancing to low Class A Hagerstown in his debut. He carried that momentum into 2016, which began at high Class A Potomac, included a midseason promotion to Double-A Harrisburg and ended with a strong showing in the Arizona Fall League. He led the AFL in hits (30) and finished second in the batting race with a .353 mark. Stevenson employed an unconventional set-up at the plate at LSU that forced him to slash at the ball. The Nationals worked with him to adjust his hands and give him a better chance to drive the ball. His swing is still geared to hit the ball on the ground to take advantage of his well above-average speed, but he is now more likely to line the ball into gaps for extra-base hits. His speed and feel for the barrel are good enough to make him a top-of-the-order candidate. Stevenson is a plus defender in center field with exceptional range thanks to his speed and instincts. His below-average arm strength is his only defensive deficiency. Stevenson earns praise for his high-energy play and makeup. He likely will return to Harrisburg to start 2017, looking to build on his strong finish to the season.

BA GRADE
45 Risk: Medium

WILL BENTZEL-HARRISBURG SENATORS

Year	Club (League)	Class	AVG	G	AB	R	H	2B	3B	HR	RBI	BB	SO	SB	CS	OBP	SLG
2015	Auburn (NYP)	SS	.361	18	72	11	26	1	2	0	9	7	12	7	3	.413	.431
	Nationals (GCL)	R	.200	2	5	1	1	0	0	0	0	1	2	0	0	.333	.200
	Hagerstown (SAL)	LoA	.285	35	137	28	39	3	2	1	16	8	16	16	4	.338	.358
2016	Potomac (CAR)	HiA	.304	68	273	37	83	12	8	1	18	24	44	27	9	.359	.418
	Harrisburg (EL)	AA	.246	65	256	38	63	11	2	2	16	20	51	12	5	.302	.328
Minor League Totals			.285	188	743	115	212	27	14	4	59	60	125	62	21	.341	.376

6 KODA GLOVER, RHP

Born: April 13, 1993. **B-T:** R-R. **Ht.:** 6-5. **Wt.:** 225. **Drafted:** Oklahoma State, 2015 (8th round). **Signed by:** Ed Gustafson.

Glover established himself as a weapon out of the bullpen in 2015, first at Oklahoma State and then in his pro debut after the Nationals made him an eighth-round pick. He built on that momentum in 2016 by pitching his way from high Class A Potomac to the big leagues. He made his major league debut in July, almost 13 months to the day after signing with the Nationals. After a strong debut, Glover recorded a 7.27 ERA in September before being shut down late in the season with a hip injury. He has a physical 6-foot-5 frame and the power arm to match. His fastball touched 100 mph in the big leagues and sat 97-98 with heavy sinking action. He complements it with a hard slider that sits in the low 90s. Glover also throws both a curveball and changeup but seldom throws either. He isn't afraid to come after hitters and throws plenty of strikes. Glover earns praise for his poise and mound presence, and he has the tools to be a big league closer. He probably won't fill that role in 2017 but should go to spring training with a chance to win a spot in the Washington bullpen.

BA GRADE
50 Risk: High

Year	Club (League)	Class	W	L	ERA	G	GS	CG	SV	IP	H	HR	BB	SO	K/9	WHIP	AVG
2015	Auburn (NYP)	SS	0	0	0.00	3	0	0	1	6	1	0	1	11	16.5	0.33	.053
	Hagerstown (SAL)	LoA	1	1	2.25	16	0	0	4	24	21	2	1	27	10.1	0.92	.231
2016	Potomac (CAR)	HiA	0	0	0.00	7	0	0	2	10	3	0	4	15	14.0	0.72	.094
	Harrisburg (EL)	AA	2	0	3.22	17	0	0	4	22	20	1	7	29	11.7	1.21	.238
	Syracuse (IL)	AAA	1	1	2.25	16	0	0	2	24	16	2	3	22	8.3	0.79	.195
	Washington (NL)	MAJ	2	0	5.03	19	0	0	0	20	15	3	7	16	7.3	1.12	.200
Major League Totals			2	0	5.03	19	0	0	0	20	15	3	7	16	7.3	1.12	.200
Minor League Totals			4	2	2.09	59	0	0	13	86	61	5	16	104	10.9	0.90	.198

7 LUIS GARCIA, SS

Born: May 16, 2000. **B-T:** L-R. **Ht.:** 5-11. **Wt.:** 170. **Signed:** Dominican Republic, 2016. **Signed by:** Carlos Ulloa.

The Nationals busted their international bonus pool in 2016 by signing three of the top 15 prospects in the class. Garcia, whose father Luis Garcia reached the big leagues in 1999 with the Tigers, was the No. 3 prospect in the class and headlined Washington's haul, though his bonus of $1.3 million was not the largest the Nationals handed out in 2016. Garcia has impressive all-around tools and evolved as a prospect in the year leading up to his signing. He has good bat-to-ball skills and a simple lefthanded swing that is geared for hitting line drives to the middle of the diamond. He makes loud contact and shows signs that he will develop more power as he physically matures. He is an excellent athlete with well above-average speed and plays with a hard-nosed, high-energy style. Garcia has above-average arm strength and good hands, giving scouts reason to believe he will be able to stay at shortstop. He will need to improve his infield actions, but even if he does move, his tools will play well at second base or in center field. Garcia is far from a finished product but earns praise for his baseball IQ and work ethic. Those traits will serve him well as he tries to become a big leaguer like his father. He will likely begin his pro career in the Dominican Summer League.

BA GRADE
55 Risk: Extreme

BILL MITCHELL

Year	Club (League)	Class	AVG	G	AB	R	H	2B	3B	HR	RBI	BB	SO	SB	CS	OBP	SLG
2016	Did not play—Signed 2017 contract																

8 CARTER KIEBOOM, SS

Born: Sept. 3, 1997. **B-T:** R-R. **Ht.:** 6-2. **Wt.:** 190. **Drafted:** HS—Marietta, Ga., 2016 (1st round). **Signed by:** Eric Robinson.

Kieboom helped lead Walton High to a 2016 state championship and scored the winning run in the decisive game. A few weeks later he joined his older brother Spencer in the Nationals organization after they selected him 28th overall. He dealt with minor injuries after signing but still held his own in the Rookie-level Gulf Coast League during his pro debut and was fully healthy in time to participate in instructional league. Kieboom is a steady, solid all-around player. He stands out for his bat speed and timing at the plate, though he struck out in nearly 28 percent of his plate appearances in the GCL. He employs a gap-to-gap approach at the plate, and projects to hit for average power as he physically matures and learns to drive the ball more consis-

BA GRADE
55 Risk: Extreme

MIKE JANES

tently. Kieboom is a solid runner and has good first-step quickness on defense. He has above-average arm strength and good infield actions, giving him the tools necessary to continue to develop as a shortstop. Spencer Kieboom made his major league debut in 2016, and Carter should one day join him in the big league fraternity. The younger Kieboom has the potential to deliver more impact than his brother, who has a backup catcher profile. He should be ready for low Class A Hagerstown in 2017.

Year	Club (League)	Class	AVG	G	AB	R	H	2B	3B	HR	RBI	BB	SO	SB	CS	OBP	SLG
2016	Nationals (GCL)	R	.244	36	135	22	33	8	4	4	25	12	43	1	2	.323	.452
Minor League Totals			.244	36	135	22	33	8	4	4	25	12	43	1	2	.323	.452

9 PEDRO SEVERINO, C

Born: July 20, 1993. **B-T:** R-R. **Ht.:** 6-0. **Wt.:** 215. **Signed:** Dominican Republic, 2010. **Signed by:** Moises de la Mota.

Severino has built a reputation as an excellent defensive catcher, and his glove has carried him through the minor leagues. He made a his major league debut in September 2015 and returned in 2016, taking over as the Nationals' everyday catcher down the stretch and in the postseason when Wilson Ramos was injured. Severino stands out for his catch-and-throw ability, leaving no doubt he has the skills necessary to catch in the big leagues. He has plus arm strength and has thrown out 35 percent of basestealers in his pro career. He is a good athlete and game-caller, he blocks balls in the dirt well and he quickly developed a rapport with the big league pitching staff. He receives well thanks to his soft hands and has excellent footwork. Though Severino held his own in the big leagues, his bat has long lagged behind his glove. He is best offensively when his swing is short and compact and he works the middle of the field. But he has hit just .251 in four years of full-season ball and has below-average power. Ramos' season-ending injury as he headed for free agency left the Nationals in an uncertain position behind the plate. They traded for Derek Norris in early December, and Severino could work with the veteran behind the plate as a superior defensive option.

BA GRADE 45 Risk: Medium

Year	Club (League)	Class	AVG	G	AB	R	H	2B	3B	HR	RBI	BB	SO	SB	CS	OBP	SLG
2014	Potomac (CAR)	HiA	.247	94	291	41	72	15	1	9	36	21	57	2	0	.306	.399
2015	Harrisburg (EL)	AA	.246	91	329	33	81	13	0	5	34	19	51	1	2	.288	.331
	Washington (NL)	MAJ	.250	2	4	1	1	0	0	0	0	0	1	0	0	.250	.500
2016	Syracuse (IL)	AAA	.271	82	291	25	79	13	0	2	21	19	45	3	4	.316	.337
	Washington (NL)	MAJ	.321	16	28	6	9	2	0	2	4	5	3	0	0	.441	.607
Major League Totals			.313	18	32	7	10	3	0	2	4	5	4	0	0	.421	.594
Minor League Totals			.243	421	1417	152	345	67	5	19	153	91	243	7	6	.294	.338

10 AUSTIN VOTH, RHP

Born: June 26, 1992. **B-T:** R-R. **Ht.:** 6-2. **Wt.:** 215. **Drafted:** Washington, 2013 (5th round). **Signed by:** Fred Costello.

Voth's stuff doesn't match up with other top pitchers in the Nationals system, but he has become the organization's strikeout king. He led the system in strikeouts for three straight seasons, 2014-16, amassing 414 whiffs in that time. He spent all of 2016 with Triple-A Syracuse and joined the 40-man roster in November after finishing the season in the Arizona Fall League, where he closed the year on a 16-inning scoreless streak. Voth pounds the zone with all three of his pitches. His fastball sits around 90 mph and can reach the mid-90s. He has a good feel for his changeup, which has late sinking action. The consistency of his breaking ball has improved, giving him a solid third pitch. Though his stuff isn't electric, Voth has a good understanding of his craft and mixes his pitches well. That in addition to his above-average control helps him accumulate strikeouts. Built like an innings-eater, he often gets better the deeper he works into games and has thrown more than 150 innings in back-to-back years. The Nationals have a deep pitching staff, but now that Voth is on the 40-man roster, he is in line to make his major league debut in 2017. He lacks a plus pitch and has a small margin for error, but his control and above-average changeup give him a ceiling as a possible No. 4 starter.

BA GRADE 45 Risk: Medium

Year	Club (League)	Class	W	L	ERA	G	GS	CG	SV	IP	H	HR	BB	SO	K/9	WHIP	AVG
2014	Hagerstown (SAL)	LoA	4	3	2.45	13	13	0	0	70	51	1	22	74	9.6	1.05	.206
	Potomac (CAR)	HiA	2	1	1.43	6	6	0	0	38	16	2	7	40	9.6	0.61	.126
	Harrisburg (EL)	AA	1	3	6.52	5	5	0	0	19	22	4	9	19	8.8	1.60	.286
2015	Harrisburg (EL)	AA	6	7	2.92	28	27	0	0	157	134	10	40	148	8.5	1.11	.230
2016	Syracuse (IL)	AAA	7	9	3.15	27	25	0	0	157	138	11	57	133	7.6	1.24	.232
Minor League Totals			23	23	2.84	90	87	0	0	487	394	28	141	469	8.7	1.10	.219

11 RAFAEL BAUTISTA, OF

BA GRADE

45 Risk: Medium

Born: March 8, 1993. **B-T:** R-R. **Ht.:** 6-2. **Wt.:** 165. **Signed:** Dominican Republic, 2012. **Signed by:** Pablo Arias.

Bautista ranked second in the minor leagues with 69 stolen bases in 2014, but a broken finger sidelined him for three months the following season and prevented him from racing to the top of the leaderboard again. After a solid winter ball campaign in his native Dominican Republic, Bautista swiped 56 bases in 2016 with Double-A Harrisburg, tying him for the most in the minors. Bautista's well above-average speed is his best tool, but his success on the bases is a result of more than just raw speed. He has good instincts, reads pitchers well and doesn't run indiscriminately. He has geared his approach at the plate to making contact and hitting the ball on the ground to use his speed to get on base. He has below-average power as a result, but when he does hit a ball into the gaps, he can turn it into extra bases. Defensively, Bautista takes good routes and tracks down an impressive number of fly balls in center field. He has an average arm. Bautista was added to the 40-man roster in November and will advance to Triple-A Syracuse in 2017. He has a chance to develop into an everyday center fielder. At worst, his speed and defense should play as a fourth outfielder.

Year	Club (League)	Class	AVG	G	AB	R	H	2B	3B	HR	RBI	BB	SO	SB	CS	OBP	SLG
2012	Nationals (DSL)	R	.329	67	210	38	69	8	3	0	25	27	39	47	7	.419	.395
2013	Nationals (GCL)	R	.322	52	202	44	65	7	2	1	27	18	34	26	7	.400	.391
2014	Hagerstown (SAL)	LoA	.290	134	487	97	141	20	5	5	54	33	72	69	15	.341	.382
2015	Nationals (GCL)	R	.313	6	16	3	5	0	0	1	2	0	1	0	0	.313	.500
	Auburn (NYP)	SS	.273	8	33	6	9	3	0	0	4	1	7	3	0	.294	.364
	Potomac (CAR)	HiA	.272	52	206	23	56	7	2	0	8	11	22	23	4	.318	.325
2016	Harrisburg (EL)	AA	.282	135	542	76	153	12	4	4	39	42	94	55	10	.341	.341
Minor League Totals			.294	454	1696	287	498	57	16	11	159	132	269	223	43	.355	.366

12 DREW WARD, 3B

BA GRADE

50 Risk: High

Born: Nov. 25, 1994. **B-T:** R-R. **Ht.:** 6-3. **Wt.:** 215. **Drafted:** HS—Leedey, Okla., 2013 (3rd round). **Signed by:** Ed Gustafson.

Originally on track to finish high school in 2014, Ward sped up his graduation timetable and entered the 2013 draft. Since reclassifying, he has been young at every level and held his own, reaching Double-A Harrisburg in 2016 as a 21-year-old and finishing with a strong showing in the Arizona Fall League. As an amateur Ward was known mostly for his power. While it took him a while to start tapping into it in the minor leagues, he began to find his power stroke in 2016 and hit a career-high 14 home runs. With his power comes a fair amount of swing-and-miss, and he has struck out in 25 percent of his plate appearances as a professional. Ward balances that with an ability to work his way into hitter's counts and has enough feel for the barrel to eventually cut his strikeout rate to a more palatable level. He has made strides defensively at third base, increasing his chances of staying at the hot corner in the long run. His below-average speed limits his range, but he has the arm strength and hands for the position. Ward will return to Harrisburg to begin 2017, looking to build on his AFL performance.

Year	Club (League)	Class	AVG	G	AB	R	H	2B	3B	HR	RBI	BB	SO	SB	CS	OBP	SLG
2014	Hagerstown (SAL)	LoA	.269	115	431	45	116	26	3	10	73	42	121	2	2	.341	.413
2015	Nationals (GCL)	R	.154	4	13	2	2	0	0	1	2	3	8	0	0	.313	.385
	Potomac (CAR)	HiA	.249	111	377	47	94	19	2	6	47	39	110	2	1	.327	.358
2016	Potomac (CAR)	HiA	.278	64	230	36	64	16	0	11	32	34	70	0	1	.377	.491
	Harrisburg (EL)	AA	.219	53	178	19	39	7	0	3	24	22	51	0	1	.310	.309
Minor League Totals			.261	396	1397	173	364	81	5	32	206	165	404	6	9	.347	.394

13 A.J. COLE, RHP

BA GRADE

45 Risk: Medium

Born: Jan. 5, 1992. **B-T:** R-R. **Ht.:** 6-5. **Wt.:** 215. **Drafted:** HS—Oviedo, Fla., 2010 (4th round). **Signed by:** Paul Tinnell.

The Nationals originally signed Cole for $2 million as a fourth-round pick in 2010 before trading him to the Athletics for Gio Gonzalez in November 2011. After a disappointing 2012 season, Washington reacquired Cole in March 2013, and he made his big league debut two years later. He returned to the majors in 2016, starting eight games with middling results. He showed swing-and-miss stuff in the majors with 39 strikeouts in 38.1 innings, but also showed he can get hit hard when he doesn't locate precisely, with 16 of his 37 hits allowed going for extra bases, including seven home runs. Cole's fastball sits in the low 90s, and he commands it effectively to both sides of the plate. He has good feel for his changeup, which is his best secondary pitch. He throws both a slider and a curveball, with the slider being the better of the two fringy-to-average breaking balls. Cole repeats his simple, clean delivery well, and he has average control. The Nationals' crowded rotation has proven difficult for Cole to break into, so he will likely start 2017 back in Triple-A Syracuse's rotation as he awaits another chance in the big leagues.

Year	Club (League)	Class	W	L	ERA	G	GS	CG	SV	IP	H	HR	BB	SO	K/9	WHIP	AVG
2014	Harrisburg (EL)	AA	6	3	2.92	14	14	1	0	71	79	1	15	61	7.7	1.32	.273
	Syracuse (IL)	AAA	7	0	3.43	11	11	0	0	63	69	9	17	50	7.1	1.37	.283
2015	Washington (NL)	MAJ	0	0	5.79	3	1	0	0	9	14	1	1	9	8.7	1.61	.341
	Syracuse (IL)	AAA	5	6	3.15	21	19	0	0	106	91	9	34	76	6.5	1.18	.227
2016	Syracuse (IL)	AAA	8	8	4.26	22	22	2	0	125	131	16	35	109	7.9	1.33	.266
	Washington (NL)	MAJ	1	2	5.17	8	8	0	0	38	37	7	14	39	9.2	1.33	.248
Major League Totals			1	2	5.29	11	9	0	1	48	51	8	15	48	9.1	1.38	.268
Minor League Totals			46	39	3.63	141	136	3	0	731	723	70	188	689	8.5	1.25	.255

14 ANDERSON FRANCO, 3B

BA GRADE
50 Risk: High

Born: Aug. 15, 1997. **B-T:** R-R. **Ht.:** 6-3. **Wt.:** 190. **Signed:** Dominican Republic, 2013. **Signed by:** Pablo Arias.

Franco was one of the youngest players in the 2013 international class, and he was still 17 when he made his U.S. debut in 2015 in the Gulf Coast League. He earned a late-summer promotion to short-season Auburn, but was unable to capitalize on that momentum in 2016 as a back injury sidelined him until late July. When healthy, Franco generates good bat speed and raw power, which he should get to more consistently as he matures physically and improves his pitch recognition. In particular, he needs to learn to lay off breaking balls away, but he has shown a willingness to work a walk and has a decent offensive approach for a young player. Franco profiles well at third base. He has plus arm strength, and his range and athleticism make him a good defender at the hot corner who will be able to stay at the position. He has four tools that have a chance to be above-average, with the exception being his speed. Franco's upside is considerable, but he first needs to prove his injuries are behind him. After a lost year, he likely will head back to Auburn in 2017.

Year	Club (League)	Class	AVG	G	AB	R	H	2B	3B	HR	RBI	BB	SO	SB	CS	OBP	SLG
2014	Nationals (DSL)	R	.272	57	206	26	56	8	1	4	35	26	46	4	2	.346	.379
2015	Nationals (GCL)	R	.281	46	153	19	43	6	1	4	19	14	26	2	3	.347	.412
	Auburn (NYP)	SS	.225	11	40	0	9	1	1	0	4	7	2	0	0	.340	.300
2016	Nationals (GCL)	R	.277	24	83	9	23	3	0	1	9	4	11	1	0	.307	.349
Minor League Totals			.272	138	482	54	131	18	3	9	67	51	85	7	5	.339	.378

15 JESUS LUZARDO, LHP

BA GRADE
55 Risk: Extreme

Born: Sept. 30, 1997. **B-T:** L-L. **Ht.:** 5-11. **Wt.:** 209. **Drafted:** HS—Parkland, Fla., 2016 (3rd round). **Signed by:** Alex Morales.

Luzardo started his senior season of high school strong and appeared to be pitching himself into the first round. His momentum was halted, however, when he got injured four starts into the season and required Tommy John surgery in March. The Nationals, who have not shied away from drafting prominent pitchers with health concerns, made the Miami commit the 94th overall pick and signed him for $1.4 million, happy to add another premium arm to their system. Luzardo first stood out as an underclassman for his pitchability and offspeed stuff. But in 2016, before his injury, he showed improved velocity, running his fastball up to 97 mph. He more typically threw the pitch in the low 90s with good sinking action. He has a good feel for his changeup, which projects as a plus pitch, and shows multiple looks with his breaking ball. He commands his whole arsenal well, and has an advanced understanding of his craft. The Nationals have had success helping young pitchers through Tommy John rehab, including Lucas Giolito, Stephen Strasburg and Jordan Zimmermann. Luzardo will look to follow in their footsteps and should be ready to make his pro debut when the Rookie-level Gulf Coast League opens in 2017.

Year	Club (League)	Class	W	L	ERA	G	GS	CG	SV	IP	H	HR	BB	SO	K/9	WHIP	AVG
2016	Did not play—Injured																

16 KELVIN GUTIERREZ, 3B

BA GRADE
50 Risk: High

Born: Aug. 28, 1994. **B-T:** R-R. **Ht.:** 6-3. **Wt.:** 185. **Signed:** Dominican Republic, 2013. **Signed by:** Modesto Ulloa.

Signed for $30,000 in 2013 as a shortstop, Gutierrez has since outgrown the position but impressed evaluators as he's moved to third base and improved offensively. He advanced to full-season ball for the first time in 2016, spending most of the year with low Class A Hagerstown before being promoted to high Class A Potomac for a playoff push. Gutierrez has a short, balanced swing and makes consistent contact, resulting in a .288 batting average so far in his young career. His power mostly manifests itself as doubles pop, but as he physically matures he should start driving the ball over the fence more often and could develop average power. He also became a threat on the bases for the first time in 2016, swiping 25 bags in 34 tries as an average runner. Gutierrez has adjusted well defensively to the hot corner. He has plus arm strength and has the hands and range to make highlight-reel plays. He is prone to making errors, but as he matures and continues to learn his new position, he can be an above-average defender. Gutierrez earns praise for his makeup and baseball IQ and is set to return to Potomac in 2017.

Year	Club (League)	Class	AVG	G	AB	R	H	2B	3B	HR	RBI	BB	SO	SB	CS	OBP	SLG
2014	Nationals (GCL)	R	.286	53	192	27	55	6	3	0	25	23	29	4	6	.362	.349
2015	Auburn (NYP)	SS	.305	62	239	31	73	21	1	1	30	16	52	2	0	.358	.414
2016	Auburn (NYP)	SS	.323	9	31	5	10	3	0	0	6	3	5	4	0	.371	.419
	Hagerstown (SAL)	LoA	.300	96	377	58	113	19	6	3	48	29	65	19	7	.349	.406
	Potomac (CAR)	HiA	.237	10	38	7	9	1	0	1	2	3	5	2	2	.326	.342
Minor League Totals			.288	290	1085	163	313	63	12	5	134	97	192	40	17	.350	.382

17 SHELDON NEUSE, 3B

BA GRADE
50 Risk: High

Born: Dec. 10, 1994. **B-T:** R-R. **Ht.:** 6-0. **Wt.:** 195. **Drafted:** Oklahoma, 2016 (2nd round). **Signed by:** Ed Gustafson.

Neuse was a two-way player at Oklahoma and scouting directors twice voted him a Preseason All-American. While his big arm worked out of the bullpen, he impressed at the plate in 2016 and led the Big 12 Conference in slugging percentage (.646). The Nationals drafted him in the second round (No. 58 overall) as a third baseman, signed him for a $900,000 bonus and sent him to short-season Auburn for his professional debut. Neuse has a short, compact swing and uses the whole field to hit. He has average power potential, but at times sells out his approach to drive the ball. Neuse was a shortstop in college, but is a fringy runner and has range better suited for third base. His plus strength and hands give him a chance to become an average defender at his new position. Third base is a deep position in the Nationals' system, enabling them to start Neuse out slowly. He will likely begin his first full professional season with low Class A Hagerstown in 2017.

Year	Club (League)	Class	AVG	G	AB	R	H	2B	3B	HR	RBI	BB	SO	SB	CS	OBP	SLG
2016	Auburn (NYP)	SS	.230	36	126	16	29	5	3	1	11	13	26	2	2	.305	.341
Minor League Totals			.230	36	126	16	29	5	3	1	11	13	26	2	2	.305	.341

18 JAKSON REETZ, C

BA GRADE
50 Risk: High

Born: Jan. 3, 1996. **B-T:** R-R. **Ht.:** 6-1. **Wt.:** 195. **Drafted:** HS—Firth, Neb., 2014 (3rd round). **Signed by:** Ed Gustafson.

After an impressive showing in the summer of 2013, including leading USA Baseball's 18U national team in hitting at the World Cup in Taiwan, Reetz became the first high school player from Nebraska to be drafted in the top five rounds since 1996 when the Nats took him 93rd overall is 2014. He was slowed by injuries during his first full professional season, but advanced to full-season ball in 2016. He got off to a slow start with low Class A Hagerstown, but improved as the season went on. Reetz is still raw, but has a dynamic set of tools. He worked to adjust his setup offensively to allow him to more consistently barrel balls. He is best when he hits line drives from gap to gap, and has the potential to develop average power in time. Defensively, Reetz has the athleticism and hands to become a solid receiver. He has above-average arm strength and threw out 33 percent of base-stealers in 2016. Having acclimated to full-season ball, Reetz will look to improve on his performance as he advances to high Class A Potomac in 2017.

Year	Club (League)	Class	AVG	G	AB	R	H	2B	3B	HR	RBI	BB	SO	SB	CS	OBP	SLG
2014	Nationals (GCL)	R	.274	43	117	20	32	6	1	1	15	26	30	6	3	.429	.368
2015	Auburn (NYP)	SS	.212	36	113	18	24	4	0	0	5	13	37	3	0	.326	.248
2016	Hagerstown (SAL)	LoA	.230	88	283	41	65	24	0	4	38	38	79	4	1	.346	.357
Minor League Totals			.236	167	513	79	121	34	1	5	58	77	146	13	4	.362	.335

19 BRIAN GOODWIN, OF

BA GRADE
45 Risk: Medium

Born: Nov. 2, 1990. **B-T:** L-R. **Ht.:** 6-0. **Wt.:** 205. **Drafted:** Miami-Dade JC (1st round supplemental). **Signed by:** Alex Morales.

After an impressive professional debut in 2012, Goodwin struggled to find traction over the next three seasons in the upper minors. He began to get back on track with a strong showing in winter ball in Venezuela after the 2015 season and carried that performance into 2016. He earned a spot in the Triple-A All-Star Game and made his major league debut in August. Goodwin never lost the tools and athleticism that made him the 34th overall pick in 2011, and was able to harness them more consistently in 2016. He worked to simplify his swing and improved his approach at the plate. Those adjustments allowed his fast hands and bat speed to play, and he did a better job of driving the ball. An above-average runner, his speed and instincts make him a solid defender in center field. He has solid-average arm strength and appeared at all three outfield positions during his time in the big leagues. Goodwin's tools give him a chance to be an everyday player, but he is more likely to find a role as a fourth outfielder. He could earn a spot on the Nationals' bench in 2017, or return to Triple-A Syracuse to start the season.

Year	Club (League)	Class	AVG	G	AB	R	H	2B	3B	HR	RBI	BB	SO	SB	CS	OBP	SLG
2014	Syracuse (IL)	AAA	.219	81	274	31	60	10	4	4	32	50	95	6	4	.342	.328
2015	Harrisburg (EL)	AA	.226	114	429	58	97	17	4	8	46	38	93	15	7	.290	.340
2016	Syracuse (IL)	AAA	.278	119	436	51	121	25	1	14	67	46	106	15	3	.347	.436
	Washington (NL)	MAJ	.286	22	42	1	12	4	1	0	5	2	14	0	0	.318	.429
Major League Totals			.286	22	42	1	12	4	1	0	5	2	14	0	0	.318	.429
Minor League Totals			.253	536	1978	286	500	97	22	50	237	261	504	73	32	.344	.400

20 BLAKE PERKINS, OF

BA GRADE
50 Risk: Extreme

Born: Sept. 10, 1996. **B-T:** B-R. **Ht.:** 6-1. **Wt.:** 165. **Drafted:** HS—Buckeye, Ariz., 2015 (2nd round). **Signed by:** Mitch Sokol.

The Nationals doubled up on toolsy, athletic outfielders in the second round of the 2015 draft, selecting Perkins 11 picks after Andrew Stevenson. Perkins spent most of his first full professional campaign with short-season Auburn before moving up to low Class A Hagerstown near the end of the year. Perkins is still raw, but has five-tool potential and a habit of making the game look easy. He was a natural right-handed hitter most of his life, but the Nationals have helped him become a switch-hitter. He is still learning to hit lefthanded, but the early returns have been promising. He has more of a line-drive approach now, but should grow into more power as he physical matures. Perkins is a plus runner and takes good routes in the outfield, helping him cover center field with ease. He has played all three outfield positions as a pro, and with his athleticism and speed, he should be able to stick in center. He earns praise for his makeup and aptitude and will return to Hagerstown to open 2017.

Year	Club (League)	Class	AVG	G	AB	R	H	2B	3B	HR	RBI	BB	SO	SB	CS	OBP	SLG
2015	Nationals (GCL)	R	.211	49	166	21	35	5	2	1	12	13	36	4	5	.265	.283
2016	Auburn (NYP)	SS	.233	56	210	31	49	5	1	1	16	25	39	10	3	.318	.281
	Hagerstown (SAL)	LoA	.200	7	25	4	5	0	0	0	2	5	6	0	1	.333	.200
Minor League Totals			.222	112	401	56	89	10	3	2	30	43	81	14	9	.297	.277

21 OSVALDO ABREU, SS

BA GRADE
45 Risk: High

Born: June 13, 1994. **B-T:** R-R. **Ht.:** 6-0. **Wt.:** 170. **Signed:** Dominican Republic, 2012. **Signed by:** Modesto Ulloa.

Abreu has advanced steadily in the minor leagues since the Nationals signed him out of the Dominican Republic in 2012. After a tough first half in 2016 with high Class A Potomac, he improved in the second half and finished the year with a solid showing in the Arizona Fall League. Much of Abreu's improvement at the plate was as a result of a more consistent approach. He isn't a power hitter, but produces good bat speed and has some pop when turns on the ball. He is patient at the plate and has drawn a good amount of walks at every level, boosting his on-base percentage to above-average levels even when his batting average is low. He's an above-average runner and a threat to steal. Earlier in his career, Abreu split his time between second base and shortstop, but he played shortstop exclusively with Potomac. His athleticism, hands and arm strength give him a chance to become a solid defender at the position. Abreu will try to build on his late-season momentum as he advances to Double-A Harrisburg in 2017.

Year	Club (League)	Class	AVG	G	AB	R	H	2B	3B	HR	RBI	BB	SO	SB	CS	OBP	SLG
2014	Auburn (NYP)	SS	.229	58	210	31	48	7	3	1	15	9	41	10	6	.279	.305
2015	Hagerstown (SAL)	LoA	.274	123	442	74	121	35	4	6	47	50	89	30	11	.357	.412
2016	Potomac (CAR)	HiA	.247	126	497	86	123	23	4	6	52	55	108	18	10	.328	.346
Minor League Totals			.261	410	1511	253	394	91	14	13	164	160	311	96	47	.342	.365

22 RAUDY READ, C

BA GRADE
45 Risk: High

Born: Oct. 29, 1993. **B-T:** R-R. **Ht.:** 6-0. **Wt.:** 170. **Signed:** Dominican Republic, 2011. **Signed by:** Modesto Ulloa.

Read finished the 2015 season strong, earning a late-summer promotion to high Class A Potomac. He built on that performance the following year in his return to the Carolina League, and again played well down the stretch and in the playoffs. He impressed the Nationals enough to be added to the 40-man roster in November. Read has a solid approach at the plate, showing a good understanding of the strike zone and a knack for hitting. The righthanded hitter has solid raw power thanks to his strength, particularly to his pull side. Read has improved behind the plate, and was voted best defensive catcher in the Carolina League in 2016. He has above-average arm strength, but will need further refinement defensively to become an everyday catcher in the big leagues. He will reach the upper minors for the first time in 2017 as he advances to Double-A Harrisburg.

Year	Club (League)	Class	AVG	G	AB	R	H	2B	3B	HR	RBI	BB	SO	SB	CS	OBP	SLG
2014	Auburn (NYP)	SS	.281	57	210	27	59	20	0	6	35	14	37	0	3	.332	.462
2015	Hagerstown (SAL)	LoA	.244	82	295	38	72	20	1	5	36	25	50	4	3	.307	.369
	Potomac (CAR)	HiA	.389	5	18	1	7	2	0	0	5	2	3	0	0	.450	.500
2016	Potomac (CAR)	HiA	.262	101	386	54	101	30	1	9	51	31	53	6	3	.324	.415
Minor League Totals			.249	389	1423	175	355	98	3	35	213	100	213	16	19	.308	.396

23 EDWIN LORA, SS

BA GRADE
50 Risk: Extreme

Born: Sept. 14, 1995. **B-T:** R-R. **Ht.:** 6-1. **Wt.:** 150. **Signed:** Dominican Republic, 2012. **Signed by:** Moises de la Mota.

Lora has steadily advanced in the minor leagues since signing with the Nationals in 2012. He reached full-season ball in 2016 as a 20-year old, where he continued to show quick-twitch actions on both side of the ball. He produces above-average bat speed that gives him surprising power, particularly when he can turn on the ball. That mostly results in doubles now, but as he gets stronger, he could develop average power. He has some feel for the barrel, but needs to improve his approach at the plate. South Atlantic League pitchers took advantage of this shortcoming, giving Lora 113 strikeouts in 118 games. He is a plus runner and is improving on the basepaths. Thanks to his speed and athleticism, Lora has good range at shortstop. He has a strong arm and soft hands, but like the rest of his game, needs to develop more consistency in the field after committing 29 errors last season. He will continue to work on the rough edges of his game in 2017 as he advances to high Class A Potomac.

Year	Club (League)	Class	AVG	G	AB	R	H	2B	3B	HR	RBI	BB	SO	SB	CS	OBP	SLG
2014	Nationals (GCL)	R	.293	52	181	27	53	8	0	0	15	11	37	13	6	.333	.337
2015	Auburn (NYP)	SS	.259	38	116	19	30	8	2	2	17	6	33	7	0	.298	.414
2016	Hagerstown (SAL)	LoA	.231	118	386	56	89	32	5	4	42	30	113	23	4	.297	.370
Minor League Totals			.242	263	868	131	210	56	7	8	87	65	227	49	14	.302	.350

24 JOSE SANCHEZ, SS

BA GRADE
50 Risk: Extreme

Born: July 12, 2000. **B-T:** R-R. **Ht.:** 6-0. **Wt.:** 165. **Signed:** Venezuela, 2016. **Signed by:** German Robles.

A part of the Nationals' bonus-pool busting 2016 international signing class, Sanchez was the ninth-ranked player on the market. Washington signed him to a deal for a $950,000 bonus on his 16th birthday. Sanchez stands out most for his ability to stay at shortstop and advanced feel for the game. His hands and footwork were among the best in the international class and he has good infield actions. He is an average runner with the athleticism and arm strength necessary for shortstop. At the plate, Sanchez has a short swing and a good feel for the barrel. His approach is more geared to contact and hitting line drives, but he is expected to add power as he physically matures. Importantly, Sanchez separated himself as someone who performed at the plate in games rather than just in batting practice and workouts. He sprays the ball to all fields and is able to drive pitches on the outer third of the plate the other way, a rare skill for someone so young. Sanchez will need to get stronger as he develops, but his all-around skill set sets him up for success. He will make his professional debut in the Dominican Summer League in 2017.

Year	Club (League)	Class	AVG	G	AB	R	H	2B	3B	HR	RBI	BB	SO	SB	CS	OBP	SLG
2016	Did not play—Signed 2017 contract

25 YASEL ANTUNA, SS

BA GRADE
50 Risk: Extreme

Born: Oct. 26, 1999. **B-T:** B-R. **Ht.:** 6-0. **Wt.:** 173. **Signed:** Dominican Republic, 2016. **Signed by:** Pablo Arias.

Attracted by his bat, scouts have followed Antuna since he was 13, and he ranked No. 14 in the 2016 international signing class. He signed with the Nationals for a $3.85 million bonus, a franchise-record for an international signee. Antuna has a calm approach at the plate and solid bat-to-ball skills. His swing is more geared for line drives, but he could develop average power in time. He started switch-hitting as a 16-year-old and is more advanced from his natural left side. Antuna showed good athleticism and above-average run times early in the scouting process, but he has grown more physical and may end up moving off shortsop position as a result. His arm strength is good enough for third base if he does have to move, but the Nationals will give him a chance to develop at short. One concern is Antuna rarely dominated in games in a way scouts would have liked to see, but the overall components for success are present. He will start his professional career in 2017 in the Dominican Summer League.

Year	Club (League)	Class	AVG	G	AB	R	H	2B	3B	HR	RBI	BB	SO	SB	CS	OBP	SLG
2016	Did not play—Signed 2017 contract																

26 JOSE MARMOLEJOS, 1B

BA GRADE
40 Risk: Medium

Born: Jan. 2, 1993. **B-T:** L-L. **Ht.:** 6-1. **Wt.:** 185. **Signed:** Dominican Republic, 2011. **Signed by:** Johnny DiPuglia.

Born in New Jersey, Marmolejos moved between the U.S. and the Dominican Republic a few times while growing up, eventually finishing high school in Florida. After going undrafted in 2010, he returned to the Dominican Republic and signed as an international free agent a year later for $55,000. Marmolejos broke out over the last two years, and the Nationals named him their Minor League Player of the Year in both 2015 and '16. After he reached Double-A Harrisburg in the second half of 2016, Washington added him to the 40-man roster in November. Marmolejos has a simple, repeatable swing and has a patient, disciplined approach at the plate. His swing is geared to produce line drives and, as a result, his power mostly results in doubles into the gaps. While Marmolejos has occasionally played left field as a professional, he is best suited to first base, where he is a capable defender. His hitability as a lefthander makes him a solid candidate to carve out a role as a platoon player or pinch hitter. For now, however, he'll return to Harrisburg in 2017 to continue to play every day.

Year	Club (League)	Class	AVG	G	AB	R	H	2B	3B	HR	RBI	BB	SO	SB	CS	OBP	SLG
2014	Auburn (NYP)	SS	.265	65	234	30	62	19	3	1	31	28	50	0	1	.341	.385
2015	Hagerstown (SAL)	LoA	.310	124	468	63	145	39	5	11	87	35	89	3	1	.363	.485
2016	Potomac (CAR)	HiA	.286	103	378	72	108	36	5	11	59	59	84	2	3	.381	.495
	Harrisburg (EL)	AA	.299	33	127	15	38	9	0	2	15	5	29	0	0	.333	.417
Minor League Totals			.288	491	1787	262	514	141	24	32	273	187	345	8	9	.359	.447

27 TYLER WATSON, LHP

BA GRADE
50 Risk: Extreme

Born: May 22, 1997. **B-T:** R-L. **Ht.:** 6-5. **Wt.:** 200. **Drafted:** HS—Gilbert, Ariz., 2015 (34th round). **Signed by:** Mitch Sokol.

The Nationals drafted Watson in the 34th round in 2015 and signed him away from a Loyola Marymount commitment for $400,000, fifth-round money. He excelled as a 19-year-old with short-season Auburn the next year, and finished the season with low Class A Hagerstown. Watson is advanced for his age and takes advantage of his large 6-foot-5 frame to throw from a steep downhill angle. His fastball sits in the upper 80s and he locates the pitch well. He still has some projectability, and his fastball could eventually sit in the low 90s. His curveball has the potential to be an above-average offering and his he has good feel for his changeup. Watson throws all three of his pitches for strikes and earns praise for his poise and confidence on the mound. Watson has the tools and pitchability to develop as a starter, but his ceiling will depend on how much he physically matures and adds strength to his frame. He will return to Hagerstown to begin 2017.

Year	Club (League)	Class	W	L	ERA	G	GS	CG	SV	IP	H	HR	BB	SO	K/9	WHIP	AVG
2015	Nationals (GCL)	R	1	1	0.00	5	4	0	0	13	7	0	4	16	10.8	0.83	.149
2016	Auburn (NYP)	SS	1	2	1.88	9	9	0	0	43	30	1	9	48	10.0	0.91	.189
	Hagerstown (SAL)	LoA	1	1	4.80	3	3	0	0	15	16	0	6	16	9.6	1.47	.296
Minor League Totals			3	4	2.14	17	16	0	0	71	53	1	19	80	10.1	1.01	.204

28 TELMITO AGUSTIN, OF

BA GRADE
50 Risk: Extreme

Born: Oct. 9, 1996. **B-T:** L-L. **Ht.:** 5-10. **Wt.:** 160. **Signed:** Dominican Republic, 2013. **Signed by:** Virgilio DeLeon.

Born in the U.S. Virgin Islands, Agustin moved to the Dominican Republic prior to signing with the Nationals for $50,000 in October 2013. After an impressive showing in 2015 in the Gulf Coast League and with short-season Auburn, he advanced to full-season ball in 2016. He was limited to 76 games by injuries, including an ankle injury that sidelined him for six weeks in the first half, but he held his own as a 19-year-old with low Class A Hagerstown. Agustin is an athletic, toolsy outfielder. He has well above-average speed and has built his game around it. He has good feel for the barrel and his approach at the plate is geared toward hitting the ball on the ground to take advantage of his speed. His pitch recognition skills are still developing, however, and he will need to cut down on his swing-and-miss after striking out in 27 percent of his plate appearances. His approach does not lend itself to power. His speed plays well in the outfield, and he has made strides as a defender. He has primarily played left field, but if he continues to improve his reads and routes, his tools would play well in center. Agustin will likely return to Hagerstown to start 2017 as he makes up for lost time.

Year	Club (League)	Class	AVG	G	AB	R	H	2B	3B	HR	RBI	BB	SO	SB	CS	OBP	SLG
2014	Nationals (DSL)	R	.300	60	220	56	66	14	10	3	41	40	47	25	7	.413	.495
2015	Nationals (GCL)	R	.331	38	130	13	43	8	2	1	18	9	17	9	2	.371	.446
	Auburn (NYP)	SS	.400	7	30	5	12	1	2	0	4	1	5	1	1	.419	.567
2016	Nationals (GCL)	R	.000	1	4	0	0	0	0	0	0	0	2	0	0	.000	.000
	Hagerstown (SAL)	LoA	.265	72	238	35	63	12	1	5	30	16	71	14	9	.309	.387
Minor League Totals			.296	178	622	109	184	35	15	9	93	66	142	49	19	.365	.444

29 JOAN BAEZ, RHP

BA GRADE
50 Risk: **Extreme**

Born: Dec. 26, 1994. **B-T:** R-R. **Ht.:** 6-3. **Wt.:** 190. **Signed:** Dominican Republic, 2014. **Signed by:** Modesto Ulloa.

The Nationals signed Baez for $7,500 in 2014 and he broke out a year later in his first full season in the U.S. when his fastball velocity spiked and he touched 100 mph. He spent the 2016 season with low Class A Hagerstown, where he again impressed with his arm strength. Baez's fastball sits in the mid 90s and regularly reaches the upper 90s. He pairs that with a curveball that is an above-average offering and a developing changeup. Like many young power pitchers, Baez's control will need improvement. He is still working to consistently repeat his delivery, as well as learning to refine his approach to become more of a pitcher and less of a thrower. Baez remains raw, but offers plenty of upside. He will advance to high Class A Potomac in 2017 as he continues to work to harness his considerable arm strength.

Year	Club (League)	Class	W	L	ERA	G	GS	CG	SV	IP	H	HR	BB	SO	K/9	WHIP	AVG
2014	Nationals (DSL)	R	4	1	1.15	11	11	0	0	55	33	1	17	49	8.1	0.91	.168
	Nationals (GCL)	R	1	3	3.78	4	3	0	0	17	18	2	3	12	6.5	1.26	.254
2015	Hagerstown (SAL)	LoA	0	1	11.32	3	3	0	0	10	13	1	6	5.2	1.84	.295
	Nationals (GCL)	R	1	3	2.13	9	9	0	0	42	31	0	19	42	8.9	1.18	.211
	Auburn (NYP)	SS	2	2	7.13	5	5	0	0	18	21	0	14	17	8.7	1.98	.313
2016	Hagerstown (SAL)	LoA	9	7	3.94	27	27	0	0	126	120	5	64	119	8.5	1.46	.258
Minor League Totals			17	17	3.57	59	58	0	0	267	236	9	123	245	8.2	1.34	.238

30 MATT SKOLE, 1B/3B

BA GRADE
40 Risk: **Medium**

Born: July 30, 1989. **B-T:** L-R. **Ht.:** 6-4. **Wt.:** 220. **Drafted:** Georgia Tech, 2011 (5th round). **Signed by:** Eric Robinson.

Skole made waves in his first full professional season in in 2012 when he hit 27 home runs. His ensuing campaign was brought to an abrupt halt by a collision in the second game of the season that forced him to have Tommy John surgery and a procedure to repair a microfracture in his wrist. Skole struggled in 2014 in his return to the field, but rebounded to lead all Nationals' minor leaguers in home runs in each of the last two seasons. Skole's best tool is his above-average power and he knows how to work a walk. There is still a lot of swing-and-miss in his game, but he has worked to consistently repeat his swing and has decreased his strikeout rate every year he's been healthy in the minors. Skole began his professional career as a third baseman, but has primarily played first base since his injuries. He is capable of playing either corner, and is an above-average defender at first. Skole was added to the 40-man roster in November, and his lefthanded power and defensive versatility give him a chance to carve out a role on a big league bench. He could fill that spot in Washington as soon as 2017.

Year	Club (League)	Class	AVG	G	AB	R	H	2B	3B	HR	RBI	BB	SO	SB	CS	OBP	SLG
2014	Harrisburg (EL)	AA	.241	132	461	58	111	29	1	14	68	78	127	3	1	.352	.399
2015	Harrisburg (EL)	AA	.232	90	314	34	73	14	1	12	56	44	92	3	1	.332	.398
	Syracuse (IL)	AAA	.238	42	151	21	36	9	0	8	26	28	35	0	1	.357	.457
2016	Syracuse (IL)	AAA	.244	140	499	67	122	22	1	24	78	66	119	2	0	.337	.437
Minor League Totals			.256	597	2115	308	542	126	5	90	382	359	560	21	4	.365	.448

B aseball America national writer Ben Badler reports on international players who were free agents as the Prospect Handbook went to press but are expected to sign with major league teams.

NORGE RUIZ, RHP

BA GRADE
50 Risk: High

Born: March 15, 1994. **B-T:** r-R. **Ht.:** 5-10. **Wt.:** 195.

In the summer of 2013, Ruiz dazzled in front of scouts in Omaha against a U.S. college national team that included Kyle Schwarber, Trea Turner, Michael Conforto, Alex Bregman and Bradley Zimmer, striking out 11 over 7.1 innings with one run, two walks and three hits allowed. Ruiz had just won the Serie Nacional rookie of the year award and went on to become a top starter on the Cuban national team before leaving to pursue a contract with a major league team in May 2015. Ruiz has had difficulty getting signed, standing out more in games than he does in a workout. He has excellent feel for pitching, operating off a fastball that, when he's at his best, sits 89-92 mph and touches 94 with sink and tail. He doesn't overpower hitters but mixes his stuff well and gets groundballs. He throws a plus changeup, a slider that flashes above-average but can flatten out on him and mixes in an effective splitter as well. Ruiz's smaller stature and recoil in his delivery gives some scouts concern about his durability. Ruiz made three starts for Aguilas in the Dominican League in October and November, but otherwise it's been a long layoff for him from competitive baseball. Once he signs, he should be ready for a Double-A assignment, with the upside to be a No. 4 starter.

CIONEL PEREZ, LHP

BA GRADE
45 Risk: High

Born: April 21, 1996. **B-T:** L-L. **Ht.:** 5-10. **Wt.:** 170.

As a teenager in a pitching-depleted Serie Nacional league in Cuba, Perez quickly developed into one of the league's better starting pitchers. Pitching for Matanzas in his final season in Serie Nacional (2014-15), Perez posted a 2.06 ERA in 87.1 innings over 17 starts with 76 strikeouts and 32 walks. After Perez left Cuba, he originally signed with the Astros for $5.15 million in October 2016, but the Astros voided that contract after his physical due to an issue they saw in his left elbow, though Perez claims to be asymptomatic. He re-signed with the Astros in December for $2 million. A small, athletic lefty with a quick arm, Perez in Cuba threw a fastball that mostly ranged from 88-93 mph and touched 94, often sitting around 88-91 mph as a starter and touching the higher end out of relief. After leaving Cuba, he has hit 96 mph. He lacked a true out pitch in Cuba, leaning on a fringy, three-quarters breaking ball at 74-80 mph that blended between a slider and a curveball. Reports from scouts who saw Perez after leaving Cuba were more encouraging, with his slider flashing average. He didn't throw a changeup in Cuba but has added that to his repertoire, so the development of that pitch will be key for him. He should be ready for an assignment to a low or high Class A affiliate, with a chance to be a back-end starter but a good chance he ends up a reliever.

JOSE ADOLIS GARCIA, OF

BA GRADE

45 Risk: High

Born: March 2, 1992. **B-T:** R-R. **Ht.:** 6-1. **Wt.:** 175.

Garcia's older brother Adonis signed with the Yankees for $400,000 in 2012 and became the everyday third baseman for the Braves in 2016. Meanwhile in Cuba, Jose Adolis Garcia won the Serie Nacional MVP award in the 2015-16 season, batting .315/.395/.517 in 380 plate appearances with 14 home runs, 39 walks and 59 strikeouts to go with 11 stolen bases in 17 attempts. After the season, he went to Japan to play for the farm team of the Yomiuri Giants, but they released him after he hit .234/.274/.396 with six walks and 37 strikeouts in 117 plate appearances. Garcia had some of the best raw tools in Cuba, though despite his performance in Serie Nacional, the emphasis there is on raw. He's a good athlete with a lean frame, plus speed and a 70 arm. While he played a lot of right field in Cuba, he has looked comfortable during his time in center field and should play center in pro ball. Garcia has good bat speed and the raw power to hit 20 home runs, but his long stroke and free-swinging approach hold him back, as he struggles to recognize offspeed pitches and frequently expands the strike zone. Garcia is a free agent exempt from the international bonus pools who should be ready for an assignment to Double-A or Triple-A.

2016 INTERNATIONAL TOP 50 PROSPECTS

Pos.	Country	Team	Video	
1.	Kevin Maitan	ss	Venezuela	Braves
2.	Luis Almanzar	ss	Dominican Republic	Padres
3.	Luis Garcia	ss	Dominican Republic	Nationals
4.	Gabriel Arias	ss	Venezuela	Padres
5.	Freudis Nova	ss	Dominican Republic	Astros
6.	Jeisson Rosario	of	Dominican Republic	Padres
7.	David Garcia	c	Venezuela	Rangers
8.	Yunior Severino	ss	Dominican Republic	Braves
9.	Jose Sanchez	ss	Venezuela	Nationals
10.	Victor Garcia	of	Venezuela	Cardinals
11.	Yorbin Ceuta	ss	Venezuela	Astros
12.	Francisco Morales	rhp	Venezuela	Phillies
13.	Marcos Brito	ss	Dominican Republic	Athletics
14.	Yasel Antuna	ss	Dominican Republic	Nationals
15.	Abrahan Gutierrez	c	Venezuela	Braves
16.	Livan Soto	ss	Venezuela	Braves
17.	Luis Noguera	lhp	Venezuela	Rockies
18.	Diego Infante	of	Venezuela	Rays
19.	Brayan Gonzalez	ss	Venezuela	Phillies
20.	Jean Carlos Carmona	ss	Dominican Republic	Brewers
21.	Yeikel Blandin	of	Dominican Republic	Rockies
22.	Alison Quintero	c	Venezuela	Padres
23.	Wenceel Perez	ss	Dominican Republic	Tigers
24.	Yerdel Vargas	ss	Dominican Republic	Athletics
25.	Roansy Contreras	rhp	Dominican Republic	Yankees
26.	Yefri Del Rosario	rhp	Dominican Republic	Braves
27.	Marcos Gonzalez	ss	Dominican Republic	Indians
28.	Justin Lopez	ss	Venezuela	Padres
29.	Luis Veloz	of	Dominican Republic	Mariners
30.	Ricardo Mendez	of	Venezuela	Nationals
31.	Roimer Bolivar	of	Venezuela	Rays
32.	Yenci Pena	ss	Dominican Republic	Braves
33.	Josue Guerrero	of	Dominican Republic	White Sox
34.	Tirso Ornelas	of	Mexico	Padres
35.	Carlos Soler	of	Dominican Republic	Cardinals
36.	Luis Mieses	of	Dominican Republic	White Sox
37.	Anderson Comas	of	Dominican Republic	White Sox
38.	Leuri Mejia	of	Dominican Republic	
39.	Kevin Richards	of	Dominican Republic	Athletics
40.	Angel Macuare	rhp	Venezuela	Astros
41.	Juan Contreras	rhp	Dominican Republic	Braves
42.	Diego Blanco	rhp	Venezuela	Rockies
43.	Nerio Rodriguez	c	Dominican Republic	Astros
44.	Pablo Abreu	of	Dominican Republic	Brewers
45.	Nicolas Torres	ss	Venezuela	Phillies
46.	Deurys Carrasco	ss	Dominican Republic	Astros
47.	Juan Aparicio	c	Venezuela	Phillies
48.	Michell Miliano	rhp	Dominican Republic	Padres
49.	Alexander Campos	ss	Venezuela	Mariners
50.	Yordy Barley	ss	Dominican Republic	Padres

Some scouts think Kevin Maitan has future 70 power

Luis Almanzar projects as a plus hitter at the next level

2016 INTERNATIONAL PROSPECTS BEST TOOLS

For the best tools in the 2016 international signing class, we're limiting it to the players who ranked in our Top 50 international prospects list.

BEST POWER: There are scouts who grade out Venezuelan shortstop Kevin Maitan with plus raw power right now, with a chance to grow into 70 power in his prime. In terms of the combination of hitting ability and power, Maitan is the top player in the class, which is part of what makes him the No. 1 player overall in the class. In terms of pure raw power, the edge goes to Venezuelan outfielder Victor Garcia. Garcia is already 6-foot-2, 225 pounds and will probably get even bigger over the next few years, so he's likely limited to left field or first base. While Maitan wasn't at the MLB international showcase in February, it was clear that Garcia had the biggest raw power there. It's at least 60 raw power and it could be 70 future power.

BEST HITTER: The top three players on the Top 50—Maitan and Dominican shortstops Luis Almanzar and Luis Garcia—could all get the nod here, while Venezuelan shortstop Yorbin Ceuta has also demonstrated excellent bat-to-ball skills. The best performer at the MLB international showcase was Garcia, who went 4-for-6, drew two walks and didn't strike out, impressing scouts with his bat speed, swing and in-game approach. Almanzar went to American Heritage (Plantation, Fla.) and showed the ability to hit in games there. Almanzar and Garcia could both develop into plus hitters, but Kevin Maitan has the greatest probability of developing into an impact hitter. Other players might end up with lower strikeout rates, but nobody combines the ability to hit and do damage on contact the way Maitan does, performing in games and doing it with plenty of extra-base thump.

BEST SPEED: Several players in the Top 50 have high-end speed. Ricardo Mendez and Leuri Mejia are two of the fastest outfielders in the class. Dominican outfielder Kevin Richards and Dominican shortstop Yordy Barley have both been clocked at 6.4-6.5 seconds in the 60. Barley and Richards are both raw athletes who are still learning to translate their speed into game situations. As a tiebreaker, the player with the best speed who knows how to use that speed in games is Venezuelan shortstop Nicolas Torres. He shows plus-plus speed, running the 60-yard dash in 6.4 seconds.

BEST FASTBALL: Righthander Angel Macuare could develop into a power arm, with a fastball that already reaches 93-94 mph. Dominican righthander Yefri Del Rosario has hit 94, as has Dominican righthander Juan Contreras. In the next few years, Contreras could be throwing in the upper-90s. Right now, nobody throws harder than Venezuelan righthander Francisco Morales, who has seen his fastball go from touching 94 earlier in 2016 to 96 later in the year. There's good movement on his fastball too, and at 6-foot-5, 200 pounds, there could be another velo jump in his future.

BEST BREAKING BALL: With most pitchers at this level, scouts are just looking for pitchers who show feel to spin a breaking ball. It doesn't have to be consistent and it doesn't have to flash plus. Most of the time, it's going to be a slurvy, three-quarters breaking ball. One pitcher who separated himself from the pack was Dominican righthander Roansy Contreras, whose curveball flashes true top-to-bottom action and could develop into an out pitch. His breaking ball is slightly behind Dominican righthander Yefri Del Rosario's. For Del Rosario, his curveball has tight spin and hard, sharp bite to miss plenty of bats.

BEST DEFENSIVE SHORTSTOP: Picking a winner here is tricky. The shortstop on Venezuela's COPABE 15U Pan American Championship team last year was Justin Lopez. He might have the softest hands of anyone in the class, with sweet actions, footwork, a strong arm and good instincts too. Some scouts thought Yerdel Vargas out of the Dominican Republic was one of the best defensive shortstops in the class with the ability to make flashy plays, though others thought he too might end up at another position. There's also a case for Venezuelan shortstop Livan Soto, who has good hands, runs better than Lopez and is an instinctive defender with a high baseball IQ. The shortstop who earned the most consistent praise for both his present defensive ability and future projection to remain at the position was Venezuelan shortstop Jose Sanchez. Other players have louder tools, but multiple scouts said Sanchez had some of the best hands and footwork in the class, with good actions, fluid body control and instincts for the position.

BEST DEFENSIVE OUTFIELDER: Ricardo Mendez has the speed and quick reactions off the bat to develop into an above-average defender in center. The one liability for Mendez in the outfield right now is his arm, which is why we will give the edge here to speedy Dominican center fielder Leuri Mejia, who had yet to sign.

BEST ATHLETE: Freudis Nova and fellow Dominican shortstop Luis Garcia are both premium athletes who combined tools and the ability to perform in games. In terms of raw athleticism, Yordy Barley, another Dominican shortstop, stood out as well and earned nods from some as the best athlete in the class, even if his game skills will need time to catch up. This one goes to Dominican outfielder Kevin Richards for his combination of athleticism, tools and body type. He has top-end speed, bursting with quick-twitch from his lean, wiry frame (6-foot-1, 160 pounds) with graceful strides. Richards has a long ways to go at the plate, but the athleticism is impossible to miss.

MOST EXCITING PLAYER: There's a lot of subjectivity here. For pure offensive excitement, it doesn't get better than Kevin Maitan, who has a special combination of hitting ability and power. Freudis Nova has the loudest all-around tool package. If you want a player who has a chance to do something exciting in nearly every aspect of the game, it doesn't get better than Dominican shortstop Luis Garcia. He's one of the best hitters in the class. He can't match Maitan's raw power, but he makes consistent hard, loud contact with line drives all over the field. When he gets on base, he's always a threat to use his plus-plus speed to steal second. He's a quick-twitch athlete with a strong arm in the field too.

2016 DRAFT

TOP 100 PICKS

FIRST ROUND

Pick. Team: Player, Pos.	Bonus
1. Phillies: Mickey Moniak, of	$6,100,000
2. Reds: Nick Senzel, 3b	$6,200,000
3. Braves: Ian Anderson, rhp	$4,000,000
4. Rockies: Riley Pint, rhp	$4,800,000
5. Brewers: Corey Ray, of	$4,125,000
6. Athletics: A.J. Puk, lhp	$4,069,200
7. Marlins: Braxton Garrett, lhp	$4,145,900
8. Padres: Cal Quantrill, rhp	$3,963,045
9. Tigers: Matt Manning, rhp	$3,505,800
10. White Sox: Zack Collins, c	$3,380,600
11. Mariners: Kyle Lewis, of	$3,286,700
12. Red Sox: Jason Groome, lhp	$3,650,000
13. Rays: Josh Lowe, 3b	$2,597,500
14. Indians: Will Benson, of	$2,500,000
15. Twins: Alex Kirilloff, of	$2,817,100
16. Angels: Matt Thaiss, c	$2,150,000
17. Astros: Forrest Whitley, rhp	$3,148,000
18. Yankees: Blake Rutherford, of	$3,282,000
19. Mets: Justin Dunn, rhp	$2,378,800
20. Dodgers: Gavin Lux, ss	$2,314,500
21. Blue Jays: T.J. Zeuch, rhp	$2,175,000
22. Pirates: Will Craig, 3b	$2,253,700
23. Cardinals: Delvin Perez, ss	$2,222,500
24. Padres: Hudson Potts, ss	$1,000,000
25. Padres: Eric Lauer, lhp	$2,000,000
26. White Sox: Zack Burdi, rhp	$2,128,500
27. Orioles: Cody Sedlock, rhp	$2,097,200
28. Nationals: Carter Kieboom, ss	$2,000,000
29. Nationals: Dane Dunning, rhp	$2,000,000
30. Rangers: Cole Ragans, lhp	$2,003,400
31. Mets: Anthony Kay, lhp	$1,100,000
32. Dodgers: Will Smith, c	$1,772,500
33. Cardinals: Dylan Carson, of	$1,350,000
34. Cardinals: Dakota Hudson, rhp	$2,000,000

SUPPLEMENTAL FIRST ROUND

Pick. Team: Player, Pos.	Bonus
35. Reds: Taylor Trammell, of	$3,200,000
36. Dodgers: Jordan Sheffield, rhp	$1,847,500
37. Athletics: Daulton Jefferies, rhp	$1,600,000
38. Rockies: Robert Tyler, rhp	$1,701,600
39. D-backs: Anfernee Grier, of	$1,500,000
40. Braves: Joey Wentz, lhp	$3,050,000
41. Pirates: Nick Lodolo, lhp	Did not sign

SECOND ROUND

Pick. Team: Player, Pos.	Bonus
42. Phillies: Kevin Gowdy, rhp	$3,500,000
43. Reds: Chris Okey, c	$2,000,000
44. Braves: Kyle Muller, lhp	$2,500,000
45. Rockies: Ben Bowden, lhp	$1,600,000
46. Brewers: Lucas Erceg, 3b	$1,150,000
47. Athletics: Logan Shore, rhp	$1,500,000
48. Padres: Buddy Reed, of	$1,075,000
49. White Sox: Alec Hansen, rhp	$1,284,500

Pick. Team: Player, Pos.	Bonus
50. Mariners: Joe Rizzo, 3b	$1,750,000
51. Red Sox: C.J. Chatham, ss	$1,100,000
52. D-backs: Andy Yerzy, c	$1,214,100
53. Rays: Ryan Boldt, of	$997,500
54. Orioles: Keegan Akin, lhp	$1,177,200
55. Indians: Nolan Jones, ss	$2,250,000
56. Twins: Ben Rortvedt, c	$900,000
57. Blue Jays: J.B. Woodman, of	$975,000
58. Nationals: Sheldon Neuse, 3b	$900,000
59. Giants: Bryan Reynolds, of	$1,350,000
60. Angels: Brandon Marsh, of	$1,073,300
61. Astros: Ronnie Dawson, of	$1,056,800
62. Yankees: Nick Solak, 2b	$950,000
63. Rangers: Alex Speas, rhp	$1,024,900
64. Mets: Peter Alonso, 1b	$909,200
65. Dodgers: Mitchell White, rhp	$588,300
66. Blue Jays: Bo Bichette, ss	$1,100,000
67. Royals: A.J. Puckett, rhp	$1,200,000
68. Pirates: Travis MacGregor, rhp	$900,000
69. Orioles: Matthias Dietz, rhp	$1,300,000
70. Cardinals: Connor Jones, rhp	$1,100,000

SUPPLEMENTAL SECOND ROUND

Pick. Team: Player, Pos.	Bonus
71. Padres: Reggie Lawson, rhp	$1,900,000
72. Indians: Logan Ice, c	$850,000
73. Twins: Jose Miranda, ss	$775,000
74. Twins: Akil Baddoo, of	$750,000
75. Brewers: Mario Feliciano, c	$800,000
76. Braves: Brett Cumberland, c	$1,500,000
77. Rays: Jake Fraley, of	$797,500

THIRD ROUND

Pick. Team: Player, Pos.	Bonus
78. Phillies: Cole Stobbe, ss	$1,100,000
79. Reds: Nick Hanson, rhp	$925,000
80. Braves: Drew Harrington, lhp	$900,000
81. Rockies: Garrett Hampson, ss	$750,000
82. Brewers: Braden Webb, rhp	$700,000
83. Athletics: Sean Murphy, c	$753,100
84. Marlins: Thomas Jones, of	$1,000,000
85. Padres: Mason Thompson, rhp	$1,750,000
86. White Sox: Alex Call, of	$719,100
87. Mariners: Bryson Brigman, ss	$700,000
88. Red Sox: Shaun Anderson, rhp	$700,000
89. D-backs: Jon Duplantier, rhp	$686,600
90. Rays: Austin Franklin, rhp	$597,500
91. Orioles: Austin Hays, of	$665,800
92. Indians: Aaron Civale, rhp	$625,000
93. Twins: Griffin Jax, rhp	$645,600
94. Nationals: Jesus Luzardo, lhp	$1,400,000
95. Giants: Heath Quinn, of	$625,900
96. Angels: Nonnie Williams, ss	$950,000
97. Astros: Jake Rogers, c	$614,000
98. Yankees: Nolan Martinez, rhp	$1,150,000
99. Rangers: Kole Enright, 3b	$675,000
100. Mets: Blake Tiberi, 3b	$500,000

SIGNING BONUSES

2015 DRAFT

TOP 100 PICKS

FIRST ROUND

Pick Team: Player, Pos.	Bonus
1. Diamondbacks: Dansby Swanson, ss	$6,500,000
2. Astros: Alex Bregman, ss	$5,900,000
3. Rockies: Brendan Rodgers, ss	$5,500,000
4. Rangers: Dillon Tate, rhp	$4,200,000
5. Astros: Kyle Tucker, of	$4,000,000
6. Minnesota Twins: Tyler Jay, lhp	$3,889,500
7. Red Sox: Andrew Benintendi, of	$3,590,400
8. White Sox: Carson Fulmer, rhp	$3,470,600
9. Cubs: Ian Happ, of	$3,000,000
10. Phillies: Cornelius Randolph, ss	$3,231,300
11. Reds: Tyler Stephenson, c	$3,141,600
12. Marlins: Josh Naylor, 1b	$2,200,000
13. Rays: Garrett Whitley, of	$2,959,600
14. Braves: Kolby Allard, lhp	$3,042,400
15. Brewers: Trent Clark, of	$2,700,000
16. Yankees: James Kaprielian, rhp	$2,650,000
17. Indians: Brady Aiken, lhp	$2,513,280
18. Giants: Phil Bickford, rhp	$2,333,800
19. Pirates: Kevin Newman, ss	$2,175,000
20. Athletics: Richie Martin, ss	$1,950,000
21. Royals: Ashe Russell, rhp	$2,190,200
22. Tigers: Beau Burrows, rhp	$2,154,200
23. Cardinals: Nick Plummer, of	$2,124,400
24. Dodgers: Walker Buehler, rhp	$1,777,500
25. Orioles: D.J. Stewart, of	$2,064,500
26. Angels: Taylor Ward, c	$1,670,000
27. Rockies: Mike Nikorak, rhp	$2,300,000
28. Braves: Mike Soroka, rhp	$1,974,700
29. Toronto Blue Jays: Jon Harris, rhp	$1,944,800
30. Yankees: Kyle Holder, ss	$1,800,000
31. Giants: Chris Shaw, 1b	$1,400,000
32. Pirates: Ke'Bryan Hayes, 3b	$1,855,000
33. Royals: Nolan Watson, rhp	$1,825,200
34. Tigers: Christin Stewart, of	$1,795,100
35. Dodgers: Kyle Funkhouser, rhp	Unsigned
36. Orioles: Ryan Mountcastle, ss	$1,300,000

SUPPLEMENTAL FIRST ROUND

Pick.Team: Player, Pos.	Bonus
37. Astros: Daz Cameron, of	$4,000,000
38. Rockies: Tyler Nevin, 3b	$2,000,000
39. Cardinals: Jake Woodford, rhp	$1,800,000
40. Brewers: Nathan Kirby, lhp	$1,250,000
41. Braves: Austin Riley, 3b	$1,600,000
42. Indians: Triston McKenzie, rhp	$2,302,500

SECOND ROUND

Pick.Team: Player, Pos.Pick Value	Bonus
43. Diamondbacks, Alex Young, lhp	$1,431,400
44. Rockies: Peter Lambert, lhp	$1,495,000
45. Rangers: Eric Jenkins, rhp, of	$2,000,000
46. Astros: Thomas Eshelman, rhp	$1,100,000
47. Cubs: Donnie Dewees, of	$1,700,000
48. Phillies: Scott Kingery, 2b	$1,259,600
49. Reds: Antonio Santillan, rhp	$1,350,000
50. Marlins: Brett Lilek, lhp	$1,000,000

Pick.Team: Player, Pos.	Bonus
51. Padres: Austin Smith, rhp	$1,200,000
52. Rays: Chris Betts, c	$1,482,500
53. Mets: Desmond Lindsay, of	$1,142,700
54. Braves: Lucas Herbert, c	$1,125,200
55. Brewers: Cody Ponce, rhp	$1,108,000
56. Blue Jays: Brady Singer, rhp	Unsigned
57. Yankees: Jeff Degano, lhp	$650,000
58. Nationals: Andrew Stevenson, of	$750,000
59. Indians: Juan Hillman, lhp	$825,000
60. Mariners: Nick Neidert, rhp	$1,200,000
61. Giants: Andrew Suarez, lhp	$1,010,100
62. Pirates: Kevin Kramer, ss	$850,000
63. Athletics: Mikey White, ss	$900,000
64. Royals: Josh Staumont, rhp	$964,600
65. Tigers: Tyler Alexander, lhp	$1,000,000
66. Cardinals: Bryce Denton, 3b	$1,200,000
67. Dodgers: Mitch Hansen, of	$997,500
68. Orioles: Jonathan Hughes, rhp	Unsigned
69. Nationals: Blake Perkins, of	$800,000
70. Angels: Jahmai Jones, of	$1,100,000

SUPPLEMENTAL SECOND ROUND

Pick.Team: Player, Pos.	Bonus
71. Cincinnati Reds: Tanner Rainey, rhp	$432,950
72. Seattle Mariners: Andrew Moore, rhp	$800,000
73. Minnesota Twins: Kyle Cody, rhp	Unsigned
74. Los Angeles Dodgers: Josh Sborz, rhp	$722,500
75. Atlanta Braves: A.J. Minter, lhp	$814,300

THIRD ROUND

Pick.Team: Player, Pos.Pick Value	Bonus
76. Diamondbacks: Taylor Clarke, rhp	$801,900
77. Rockies: Javier Medina, rhp	$740,000
78. Rangers: Michael Matuella, rhp	$2,000,000
79. Astros: Riley Ferrell, rhp	$1,000,000
80. Twins: Travis Blankenhorn, 3b	$650,000
81. Red Sox: Austin Rei, c	$742,400
82. Cubs: Bryan Hudson, lhp	$1,100,000
83. Phillies: Lucas Williams, ss	$719,800
84. Reds: Blake Trahan, ss	$708,900
85. Marlins: Isaiah White, of	$698,100
86. Padres: Jacob Nix, rhp	$900,000
87. Rays: Brandon Lowe, 2b	$697,500
88. Mets: Max Wotell, lhp	$775,000
89. Braves: Anthony Guardado, rhp	$550,000
90. Brewers: Nash Walters, rhp	$800,000
91. Blue Jays: Justin Maese, rhp	$300,000
92. Yankees: Drew Finley, rhp	$950,000
93. Indians: Mark Mathias, 2b	$550,000
94. Mariners: Braden Bishop, of	$607,700
95. Giants: Jalen Miller, ss	$1,100,000
96. Pirates: Casey Hughston, of	$700,000
97. Athletics: Dakota Chalmers, rhp	$1,200,000
98. Royals: Anderson Miller, of	$581,300
99. Tigers: Drew Smith, rhp	$575,800
100. Cardinals: Harrison Bader, of	$400,000

SIGNING BONUSES

2014 DRAFT

FIRST ROUND

Pick Team: Player, Pos.	Bonus
1. Astros: Brady Aiken, lhp	Unsigned
2. Marlins: Tyler Kolek, rhp	$6,000,000
3. White Sox: Carlos Rodon, lhp	$6,582,000
4. Cubs: Kyle Schwarber, c	$3,125,000
5. Twins: Nick Gordon, ss	$3,851,000
6. Mariners: Alex Jackson, of	$4,200,000
7. Phillies: Aaron Nola, rhp	$3,300,900
8. Rockies: Kyle Freeland, lhp	$2,300,000
9. Blue Jays: Jeff Hoffman, rhp	$3,080,800
10. Mets: Michael Conforto, of	$2,970,800
11. Blue Jays: Max Pentecost, C	$2,888,300
12. Brewers: Kodi Medeiros, shp	$2,500,000
13. Padres: Trea Turner, ss	$2,900,000
14. Giants: Tyler Beede, rhp	$2,613,200
15. L.A. Angels: Sean Newcomb, lhp	$2,518,400
16. D'Backs: Touki Toussaint, rhp	$2,700,000
17. Royals: Brandon Finnegan, lhp	$2,200,600
18. Nationals: Erick Fedde, rhp	$2,511,100
19. Reds: Nick Howard, rhp	$1,990,500
20. Rays: Casey Gillaspie, 1b	$2,035,500
21. Indians: Bradley Zimmer, of	$1,900,000
22. Dodger: Grant Holmes, rhp	$2,500,000
23. Tigers: Derek Hill, of	$2,000,000
24. Pirates: Cole Tucker, ss	$1,800,000
25. Athletics: Matt Chapman, 3b	$1,750,000
26. Red Sox: Michael Chavis, ss	$1,870,500
27. Cardinals: Luke Weaver, rhp	$1,843,000
28. Royals: Foster Griffin, lhp	$1,925,000
29. Reds: Alex Blandino, ss	$1,788,000
30. Rangers: Luis Ortiz, rhp	$1,750,000
31. Indians: Justus Sheffield, lhp	$1,600,000
32. Braves: Braxton Davidson, Of	$1,705,000
33. Red Sox: Michael Kopech, rhp	$1,500,000
34. Cardinals: Jack Flaherty, rhp	$2,000,000

SUPPLEMENTAL FIRST ROUND

Pick. Team: Player, Pos.	Bonus
35. Rockies: Forrest Wall, 2b	$2,000,000
36. Marlins: Blake Anderson, C	$1,170,000
37. Astros: Derek Fisher, of	$1,534,100
38. Indians: Mike Papi, of	$1,250,000
39. Pirates: Connor Joe, of	$1,250,000
40. Royals: Chase Vallot, c	$1,350,000
41. Brewers: Jake Gatewood, ss	$1,830,000

SECOND ROUND

Pick. Team: Player, Pos.	Pick Value	Bonus
42. Astros: A.J. Reed, 1b		$1,350,000
43. Marlins: Justin Twine, ss		$1,316,000
44. White Sox: Spencer Adams, rhp		$1,282,700
45. Cubs: Jake Stinnett, Rhp		$1,000,000
46. Twins: Nick Burdi, Rhp		$1,218,800
47. Phillies: Matt Imhof, lhp		$1,187,900
48. Rockies: Ryan Castellani, rhp		$1,100,000
49. Blue Jays: Sean Reid-Foley, rhp		$1,128,800
50. Brewers: Monte Harrison, Of		$1,800,000

51. Padres: Michael Gettys, of	$1,300,000
52. Giants: Aramis Garcia, c	$1,100,000
53. Angels: Joe Gatto, rhp	$1,200,000
54. Diamondbacks: Cody Reed, lhp	$1,034,500
55. Yankees: Jacob Lindgren, lhp	$1,018,700
56. Royals: Scott Blewett, rhp	$1,800,000
57. Nationals: Andrew Suarez, lhp	Unsigned
58. Reds: Taylor Sparks, 3b	$972,800
59. Rangers: Ti'quan Forbes, ss	$1,200,000
60. Rays: Cameron Varga, rhp	$1,097,500
61. Indians: Grant Hockin, rhp	$1,100,000
62. Dodgers: Alex Verdugo, of	$914,600
63. Tigers: Spencer Turnbull, rhp	$900,000
64. Pirates: Mitch Keller, rhp	$1,000,000
65. Athletics: Daniel Gossett, rhp	$750,000
66. Braves: Garrett Fulenchek, rhp	$1,000,000
67. Red Sox: Sam Travis, 1b	$846,800
68. Cardinals: Ronnie Williams, rhp	$833,900

SUPPLEMENTAL SECOND ROUND

Pick. Team: Player, Pos.	Bonus
69. Diamondbacks: Marcus Wilson, of	$1,000,000
70. Diamondbacks: Isan Diaz, ss	$750,000
71. Cardinals: Andrew Morales, rhp	$546,100
72. Rays: Brent Honeywell, rhp	$800,000
73. Pirates: Trey Supak, rhp	$1,000,000
74. Mariners: Gareth Morgan, of	$2,000,000

THIRD ROUND

Pick. Team: Player, Pos.	Pick Value	Bonus
75. Astros: J.D. Davis, 3b		$748,600
76. Marlins: Brian Anderson, 2b		$600,000
77. White Sox: Jace Fry, lhp		$760,000
78. Cubs: Mark Zagunis, s		$615,000
79. Twins: Michael Cederoth, rhp		$703,900
80. Mariners: Austin Cousino, of		$400,000
81. Phillies: Aaron Brown, Of		$750,000
82. Rockies: Sam Howard, lhp		$672,100
83. Blue Jays: Nick Wells, lhp		$661,800
84. Mets: Milton Ramos, ss		$750,000
85. Brewers: Cy Sneed, rhp		$400,000
86. Padres: Zech Lemond, rhp		$600,000
87. Giants: Dylan Davis, of		$650,000
88. Angels: Chris Ellis, rhp		$575,000
89. Diamondbacks: Matt Railey, of		$600,000
90. Orioles: Brian Gonzalez, lhp		$700,000
91. Yankees: Austin DeCarr, rhp		$1,000,000
92. Royals: Eric Skoglund, lhp		$576,100
93. Nationals: Jakson Reetz, c		$800,000
94. Reds: Wyatt Strahan, rhp		$558,700
95. Rangers: Josh Morgan, ss		$800,000
96. Rays: Brock Burke, lhp		$897,500
97. Indians: Bobby Bradley, 1b		$912,500
98. Dodgers: John Richy, rhp		$534,400
99. Tigers: Grayson Greiner, C		$529,400
100. Pirates: Jordan Luplow, of		$500,000

COLLEGE TOP 100

Rank. Name, Pos., School	B-T	Ht.	Wt.	Previously Drafted
1. Alex Faedo, rhp, Florida	R-R	6-5	220	Tigers '14 (40)
2. Jeren Kendall, of, Vanderbilt	L-R	6-0	190	Red Sox '14 (30)
3. J.B. Bukauskas, rhp, North Carolina	R-R	6-0	196	D-backs '14 (20)
4. Brendan McKay, lhp/1b, Louisville	L-L	6-2	212	Padres '14 (34)
5. Kyle Wright, rhp, Vanderbilt	R-R	6-4	220	Never drafted
6. Tristan Beck, rhp, Stanford	R-R	6-4	190	Brewers '15 (34)
7. Alex Lange, rhp, Louisiana State	R-R	6-3	201	Never drafted
8. Tanner Houck, rhp, Missouri	R-R	6-5	218	Blue Jays '14 (12)
9. Pavin Smith, of/1b, Virginia	L-L	6-2	210	Rockies '14 (32)
10. Seth Romero, lhp, Houston	L-L	6-3	240	Never drafted
11. Wil Crowe, rhp, South Carolina	R-R	6-2	250	Indians '16 (21)
12. Brendon Little, lhp, State JC of Florida	L-L	6-2	215	Giants '15 (36)
13. Colton Hock, rhp, Stanford	R-R	6-5	220	Never drafted
14. Michael Gigliotti, of, Lipscomb	L-L	6-1	176	Never drafted
15. J.J. Schwarz, c, Florida	R-R	6-2	215	Brewers '14 (17)
16. Griffin Canning, rhp, UCLA	R-R	6-1	170	Rockies '14 (38)
17. Clarke Schmidt, rhp, South Carolina	R-R	6-1	205	Never drafted
18. Dalton Guthrie, ss, Florida	R-R	5-11	175	Twins '14 (40)
19. Peter Solomon, rhp, Notre Dame	R-R	6-4	191	Padres '14 (21)
20. Keston Hiura, of/2b, UC Irvine	R-R	6-0	188	Never drafted
21. Kevin Smith, ss, Maryland	R-R	6-0	188	Never drafted
22. Evan Skoug, c, Texas Christian	L-R	5-11	200	Nationals '14 (34)
23. Corbin Martin, rhp, Texas A&M	R-R	6-2	200	Never drafted
24. Taylor Walls, ss, Florida State	B-R	5-10	180	Never drafted
25. Dylan Busby, 3b/1b, Florida State	R-R	6-3	190	Never drafted
26. Joe Dunand, ss/3b, North Carolina State	R-R	6-2	205	Indians '14 (35)
27. Jake Burger, 3b, Misssouri State	R-R	6-2	210	Never drafted
28. Mike Rivera, c, Florida	R-R	5-10	205	Athletics '14 (33)
29. Jake Mangum, of, Mississippi State	B-L	6-0	185	Never drafted
30. David Peterson, lhp, Oregon	L-L	6-6	242	Red Sox '14 (28)
31. Zach Rutherford, ss, Old Dominion	R-R	6-2	180	Never drafted
32. Deon Stafford, c, St. Joseph's	R-R	6-0	202	Never drafted
33. Evan White, of/1b, Kentucky	B-L	6-3	200	Never drafted
34. Drew Rasmussen, rhp, Oregon State	R-R	6-1	226	D-backs '14 (39)
35. Tyler Johnson, rhp, South Carolina	R-R	6-2	205	Never drafted
36. Carl Chester, of, Miami	R-R	6-0	205	Brewers '14 (38)
37. Riley Adams, c, San Diego	R-R	6-4	210	Cubs '14 (37)
38. Morgan Cooper, rhp, Texas	R-R	6-4	220	Nationals '16 (34)
39. Will Gaddis, rhp, Furman	R-R	6-1	185	Yankees '14 (36)
40. Zac Lowther, lhp, Xavier	L-L	6-2	235	Never drafted
41. Nate Pearson, rhp, JC of Central Florida	R-R	6-6	245	Never drafted
42. Kade McClure, rhp, Louisville	R-R	6-7	235	Never drafted
43. Jayson Rose, rhp, Utah	R-R	6-0	180	Never drafted
44. Ricky Tyler Thomas, lhp, Fresno State	R-L	6-1	175	Never drafted
45. Keegan Thompson, rhp, Auburn	R-R	6-2	209	Tigers '16 (33)
46. Devin Hairston, ss, Louisville	R-R	5-7	162	Never drafted
47. Clay Fisher, ss, UC Santa Barbara	R-R	6-1	175	Never drafted
48. K.J. Harrison, 1b, Oregon State	R-R	6-0	208	Indians '14 (25)
49. Brock Deatherage, of, North Carolina State	L-L	6-1	186	Never drafted
50. Logan Warmoth, ss, North Carolina	R-R	6-0	189	Never drafted

COLLEGE TOP 100, CONTINUED

51. Connor Seabold, rhp, Cal State Fullerton	R-R	6-2	185	Orioles '14 (19)
52. Matt Whatley, c, Oral Roberts	R-R	5-10	190	Never drafted
53. J.J. Matijevic, of/1b, Arizona	L-R	6-0	206	Red Sox '14 (22)
54. Kyle Johnston, rhp, Texas	R-R	6-0	220	Never drafted
55. Glenn Otto, rhp, Rice	R-R	6-5	240	Never drafted
56. Garrett Cave, rhp, Tampa	R-R	6-4	205	Yankees '14 (17)
57. Tarik Skubal, lhp, Seattle	L-L	6-3	218	Never drafted
58. Hunter Williams, lhp, North Carolina	L-L	6-3	225	Giants '14 (32)
59. Ernie Clement, 2b/of, Virginia	R-R	6-0	165	Never drafted
60. Michael Baumann, rhp, Jacksonville	R-R	6-4	225	Twins '14 (34)
61. Josh Anthony, 3b, Auburn	R-R	5-10	195	Braves '16 (16)
62. Mitch Hart, rhp, Southern California	R-R	6-4	195	Giants '14 (35)
63. Adam Haseley, of, Virginia	L-L	6-1	195	Never drafted
64. Zach Warren, lhp, Tennessee	L-L	6-5	200	Pirates '14 (23)
65. Tyler Wilson, lhp, Rhode Island	L-L	6-4	225	Never drafted
66. James Karinchak, rhp, Bryant	R-R	6-3	230	Never drafted
67. Kyle Nelson, lhp, UC Santa Barbara	L-L	6-1	180	Never drafted
68. Jake Bird, rhp, UCLA	R-R	6-3	205	Never drafted
69. Evan Steele, lhp, Chipola (Fla.) JC	R-L	6-5	210	Never drafted
70. Tommy Doyle, rhp, Virginia	R-R	6-6	235	Nationals '14 (35)
71. Patrick Mathis, of, Texas	L-L	6-1	215	Never drafted
72. Brian Miller, of, North Carolina	L-R	6-0	186	Never drafted
73. Erich Uelmen, rhp, Cal Poly	R-R	6-3	195	Never drafted
74. Zach Pop, rhp, Kentucky	R-R	6-4	225	Blue Jays '14 (23)
75. Brigham Hill, rhp, Texas A&M	R-R	6-0	185	Athletics '16 (20)
76. Zack Gahagan, 2b/3b, North Carolina	R-R	6-2	197	D-backs '14 (40)
77. Jake Latz, lhp, Kent State	R-L	6-2	196	Blue Jays '14 (11)
78. Quinn Brodey, of, Stanford	L-L	6-1	195	Nationals '14 (37)
79. Mike Papierski, c, Louisiana State	B-R	6-3	210	Blue Jays '14 (16)
80. Will Toffey, 3b, Vanderbilt	L-R	6-2	205	Orioles '16 (25)
81. Stuart Fairchild, of, Wake Forest	R-R	6-0	195	Nationals '14 (38)
82. Charlie Barnes, lhp, Clemson	L-L	6-1	170	Never drafted
83. Greg Deichmann, of/1b, Louisiana State	L-R	6-2	191	Twins '16 (26)
84. Zach Willeman, rhp, Kent State	R-R	6-3	200	Never drafted
85. Logan Sowers, of, Indiana	R-R	6-4	220	Padres '14 (31)
86. Alex Destino, of, South Carolina	L-L	6-2	225	Never drafted
87. Evan Mendoza, 3b, North Carolina State	R-R	6-2	200	Never drafted
88. Connor Wong, c, Houston	R-R	6-0	181	Never drafted
89. Zach Schellenger, rhp, Seton Hall	R-R	6-5	210	Never drafted
90. Deacon Liput, 2b, Florida	R-R	5-10	190	Yankees '16 (39)
91. Luis Gonzalez, of/lhp, New Mexico	L-L	6-0	185	Never drafted
92. Brandon Bielak, rhp, Notre Dame	L-R	6-1	209	Never drafted
93. Kyle Serrano, rhp, Tennessee	R-R	6-3	200	Brewers '16 (40)
94. Gunnar Troutwine, c, Wichita State	R-R	6-2	222	Never drafted
95. Brady Puckett, rhp, Lipscomb	R-R	6-9	242	Mets' 14 (33)
96. Ryan Noda, of/1b, Cincinnati	L-L	6-3	216	Never drafted
97. Nick Feight, c, UNC Wilmington	R-R	5-11	200	Never drafted
98. Daulton Varsho, c, Wisconsin-Milwaukee	L-R	5-10	200	Never drafted
99. Tyler Buffett, rhp, Oklahoma State	R-R	6-2	197	Astros '16 (7)
100. Bryce Montes de Oca, rhp, Missouri	R-R	6-7	261	White Sox '14 (14)

HIGH SCHOOL TOP 100

Rank. Player	Position	High School, City	Commitment
1. Hunter Greene	ss/rhp	Notre Dame High, Sherman Oaks, Calif.	UCLA
2. Royce Lewis	ss/of	JSerra Catholic High, San Juan Capistrano, Calif.	UC Irvine
3. Jordon Adell	of/rhp	Ballard High, Louisville, Ky.	Louisville
4. DL Hall	lhp	Valdosta (Ga.) High	Florida State
5. Hans Crouse	rhp	Dana Hills High, Dana Point, Calif.	Southern California
6. Jacob Heatherly	lhp	Cullman (Ala.) High	Alabama
7. Blayne Enlow	rhp	St. Amant (La.) High	Louisiana State
8. Garrett Mitchell	of	Orange (Calif.) Lutheran High	UCLA
9. Trevor Rogers	lhp	Carlsbad (N.M) High	Texas Tech
10. Nick Storz	rhp	Poly Prep Country Day School, Brooklyn, N.Y.	Louisiana State
11. Quentin Holmes	of	McClancy Memorial High, E. Elmhurst, N.Y.	Mississippi State
12. Calvin Mitchell	of	Rancho Bernardo High, San Diego	San Diego
13. Nick Allen	ss	Francis Parker School, San Diego	Southern California
14. Mark Vientos	ss/3b	American Heritage School, Plantation, Fla.	Miami
15. M.J. Melendez	c	Westminster Christian School, Palmetto Bay, Fla.	Florida International
16. Adam Hall	ss/2b	A.B. Lucas Secondary School, London, Ont.	Texas A&M
17. Cole Brannen	of	The Westfield School, Perry, Ga.	Georgia Southern
18. Jeremiah Estrada	rhp	Palm Desert (Calif.) High	UCLA
19. Brady McConnell	ss	Merritt Island (Fla.) High	Florida
20. Jake Eder	lhp	Atlantic High, Delray Beach, Fla.	Vanderbilt
21. Alex Scherff	rhp	Colleyville (Texas) Heritage High	Texas A&M
22. Mitchell Stone	lhp	Deer Creek High, Edmond, Okla.	Oklahoma State
23. Chris McMahon	rhp	West Chester (Pa.) Rustin High	Miami
24. Heliot Ramos	of	Leadership Christian Academy, Guaynabo, P.R.	Florida International
25. Kyle Hurt	rhp	Torrey Pines High, San Diego	Southern California
26. Shane Baz	rhp/3b	Concordia Lutheran High, Tomball, Texas	Texas Christian
27. Nick Pratto	1b/lhp	Huntington Beach (Calif.) High	Southern California
28. Drew Waters	of	Etowah High, Woodstock, Ga.	Georgia
29. Garrett Hunter Ruth	rhp	Buchholz High, Gainesville, Fla.	Florida
30. Hagen Danner	rhp/c	Huntington Beach (Calif.) High	UCLA
31. Tim Elko	1b	Hillsborough High, Tampa	Mississippi
32. Conner Uselton	of	Southmoore High, Moore, Okla.	Oklahoma State
33. Brandon McCabe	rhp	Forest Hill High, West Palm Beach, Fla.	Louisiana State
34. Jordan Anderson	of	James Clemens High, Madison, Ala.	Mississippi State
35. Austin Martin	ss	Trinity Christian Academy, Jacksonville, Fla.	Uncommited
36. Nick Egnatuk	3b	Immaculata High, Somerville, N.J.	Pittsburgh
37. Cole Turney	of	Travis High, Richmond, Texas	Arkansas
38. MacKenzie Gore	lhp	Whiteville (N.C.) High	East Carolina
39. Jacob Pearson	of	West Monroe (La.) High	Louisiana State
40. Wilberto Rivera	rhp	Carlos Beltran Baseball Academy, Florida, P.R.	Florida International
41. Sam Carlson	rhp/of	Burnsville (Minn.) High	Florida
42. Landon Leach	rhp	Pickering High, Ajax, Ont.	Texas
43. Brad Dobzanski	rhp	Delsea (N.J.) High	Kentucky
44. Steven Williams	c/of	Deerfield-Windsor High, Albany, Ga.	Auburn
45. Ricardo De La Torre	ss	Puerto Rico Baseball Academy, Gurabo, P.R.	Auburn
46. Alex Toral	1b	Archbishop McCarthy High, Southwest Ranches, Fla.	Miami
47. Seth Corry	lhp	Lone Peak High, Highland, Utah	Brigham Young
48. Christian Robinson	of	Viera High, Melbourne, Fla.	Stanford
49. Jason Willow	3b	Lambrick Park Secondary School, Victoria, B.C.	UC Santa Barbara
50. Tanner Burns	rhp	Decatur (Ala.) High Auburn	

HIGH SCHOOL TOP 100, CONTINUED

51.	Daniel Ritcheson	rhp	Bishop Alemany High, Los Angeles	San Diego State
52.	Joe Boyle	rhp	North Oldham High, Goshen, Ky.	Notre Dame
53.	Kier Meredith	of	Glenn High, Winston-Salem, N.C.	Clemson
54.	CJ Van Eyk	rhp	Steinbrenner High, Lutz, Fla.	Florida State
55.	Spencer Strider	rhp	Christian Academy of Knoxville	Clemson
56.	Calvin Greenfield	c	Jensen Beach (Fla.) High	Florida
57.	Joe Perez	rhp/1b	Archbishop McCarthy High, Southwest Ranches, Fla.	Miami
58.	Matt Tabor	rhp	Milton (Mass.) Academy	Elon
59.	Philip Clarke	c	Christ Presbyterian Academy, Nashville	Vanderbilt
60.	Tristen Lutz	of	Martin High, Arlington, Texas	Texas
61.	Joe Lancellotti	rhp	Archbishop Wood High, Warminster, Pa.	North Carolina
62.	Jeter Downs	ss	Monsignor Edward Pace High, Miami	Miami
63.	Chris Seise	ss	West Orange High, Winter Garden, Fla.	Central Florida
64.	Jeff Criswell	rhp	Portage (Mich.) Central High	Michigan
65.	Mason Hickman	rhp	Pope John Paul II High, Hendersonville, Tenn.	Vanderbilt
66.	Zach Daniels	of	Eagle's Landing Christian Academy, McDonough, Ga.	Tennessee
67.	Baron Radcliff	of	Norcross (Ga.) High	Georgia Tech
68.	Jamal O'Guinn	ss	Buchanan High, Clovis, Calif.	Southern California
69.	Kyle Jacobsen	of	Allatoona High, Acworth, Ga.	South Carolina
70.	Matthew Golda	ss	Inspiration Academy, Bradenton, Fla.	Florida Atlantic
71.	Daniel Cabrera	of	Parkview Baptist High, Baton Rouge, La.	Louisiana State
72.	Brady Smith	c	TNXL Academy, Longwood, Fla.	Florida
73.	Logan Allen	lhp	University High, Orange City, Fla.	Florida International
74.	Andrew Papantonis	ss	Delbarton High, Morristown, N.J.	Virginia
75.	Isaiah Smith	of	Battle Ground (Wash.) High	Washington State
76.	Bubba Thompson	of	McGill-Toolen Catholic High, Mobile, Ala.	Auburn
77.	Cooper Davis	of	St. Aloysius Gonzaga SS, Mississauga, Ont.	Vanderbilt
78.	Tanner Morris	ss/2b	Miller School, Charlottesville, Va.	Virginia
79.	Cody Bolton	rhp	Tracy (Calif.) High	Michigan
80.	Sam McMillan	c	Suwannee High, Live Oak, Fla.	Florida
81.	Matthew Sauer	rhp	Ernest Righetti High, Santa Maria, Calif.	Arizona
82.	Andres Santana	ss/3b	Doral (Fla.) Academy	Florida International
83.	Ryan Vilade	3b	Stillwater (Okla.) High	Oklahoma State
84.	Oscar Serratos	ss/rhp	Grayson High, Ga.	Georgia Tech
85.	Caleb Sloan	rhp	Regis Jesuit High, Aurora, Colo.	Texas Christian
86.	Tyler Freeman	ss/2b	Etiwanda High, Rancho Cucamonga, Calif.	Texas Christian
87.	Christian Santana	rhp	American Heritage School, Plantation, Fla.	Florida International
88.	Jacob Gonzalez	3b	Chaparral High, Scottsdale, Ariz.	Texas Christian
89.	Hugh Fisher	lhp	Briarcrest Christian School, Eads, Tenn.	Vanderbilt
90.	Trevor Hauver	ss	Perry High, Gilbert, Ariz.	Arizona State
91.	A.J. Gardner	of	Whitewater High, Fayetteville, Ga.	Alabama State
92.	Tylor Fischer	rhp	Langham Creek High, Houston	Texas A&M
93.	Devin Ortiz	rhp/ss	St. Joseph Regional High, Montvale, N.J.	Virginia
94.	Buddy Kennedy	3b	Millville (N.J.) Senior High	North Carolina
95.	Roman Phansalkar	rhp	Heritage Hall, Oklahoma City	Arizona
96.	Steve Mann	of	Detroit Country Day	Duke
97.	Gavin Williams	rhp	Cape Fear High, Fayetteville, N.C.	East Carolina
98.	Bryce Hutchinson	rhp	Spruce Creek High, Port Orange, Fla.	Mississippi State
99.	Luis Campusano	c	Cross Creek High, Augusta, Ga.	South Carolina
100.	Kyler McMahan	ss	Lynwood (Wash.) High	Oregon State

TOP 20 PROSPECTS

FROM EVERY MINOR LEAGUE

TRIPLE-A

International League

1. Trea Turner, ss, Syracuse (Nationals)
2. Byron Buxton of, Rochester (Twins)
3. Gary Sanchez c, Scranton/Wilkes-Barre (Yankees)
4. J.P.Crawford ss, Lehigh Valley (Phillies)
5. Tyler Glasnow rhp, Indianapolis (Pirates)
6. Blake Snell lhp, Durham (Rays)
7. Austin Meadows of, Indianapolis (Pirates)
8. Jameson Taillon rhp, Indianapolis (Pirates)
9. Tim Anderson SS, Charlotte (White Sox)
10. Josh Bell 1b, Indianapolis (Pirates)
11. Ozzie Albies, ss/2b, Gwinnett (Braves)
12. Bradley Zimmer, of, Columbus (Indians)
13. Nick Williams, of, Lehigh Valley (Phillies)
14. Mike Clevinger, rhp, Columbus (Indians)
15. Jose Berrios, rhp, Rochester (Twins)
16. Amir Garrett, lhp, Louisville (Reds)
17. Jose Peraza, ss, Louisville (Reds)
18. Cody Reed, lhp, Louisville (Reds)
19. Aaron Judge, of, Scranton/Wilkes-Barre (Yankees)
20. A.J. Cole, rhp, Syracuse (Nationals)

Pacific Coast League

1. Alex Reyes, rhp Memphis (Cardinals)
2. Willson Contreras, c, Iowa (Cubs)
3. Jose De Leon, rhp, Oklahoma City (Dodgers)
4. Orlando Arcia, ss, Colorado Springs (Brewers)
5. Jeff Hoffman, rhp, Albuquerque (Rockies)
6. Joey Gallo, 3b/1b, Round Rock (Rangers)
7. Hunter Renfroe, of, El Paso (Padres)
8. A.J. Reed, 1b, Fresno (Astros)
9. Joe Musgrove, rhp, Fresno (Astros)
10. Jharel Cotton, rhp, Oklahoma City (Dodgers) /Nashville (Athletics)
11. Josh Hader, lhp, Colorado Springs (Brewers)
12. Albert Almora, of, Iowa (Cubs)
13. Manuel Margot, of, El Paso (Padres)
14. Teoscar Hernandez, of, Fresno (Astros)
15. Hunter Dozier, 3b, Omaha (Royals)
16. Brock Stewart, rhp, Oklahoma City (Dodgers)
17. Jeimer Candelario, 3b, Iowa (Cubs)
18. Daniel Mengden, rhp, Nashville (Athletics)
19. Brandon Nimmo, of, Las Vegas (Mets)
20. Anthony Banda, lhp, Reno (Diamondbacks)

DOUBLE-A

Eastern League

1. Yoan Moncada, 2b/3b, Portland (Red Sox)
2. Andrew Benintendi, of, Portland (Red Sox)
3. Austin Meadows, of, Altoona (Pirates)
4. David Dahl, of, Hartford (Rockies)
5. Lucas Giolito, rhp, Harrisburg (Nationals)
6. J.P. Crawford, ss, Reading (Phillies)
7. Amed Rosario, ss, Binghamton (Mets)
8. Clint Frazier, of, Akron (Indians)
9. German Marquez, rhp, Hartford (Rockies)
10. Reynaldo Lopez, rhp, Harrisburg (Nationals)

11. Raimel Tapia, of, Hartford (Rockies)
12. Jorge Alfaro, c, Reading (Phillies)
13. Dylan Cozens, of, Reading (Phillies)
14. Bradley Zimmer, of, Akron (Indians)
15. Dominic Smith, 1b, Binghamton (Mets)
16. Chance Sisco, c, Bowie (Orioles)
17. Tyler Beede, rhp, Richmond (Giants)
18. Chance Adams, rhp, Trenton (Yankees)
19. Kevin Newman, ss, Altoona (Pirates)
20. Dustin Fowler, of, Trenton (Yankees)

Southern League

1. Dansby Swanson, ss, Mississippi (Braves)
2. Willy Adames, ss, Montgomery (Rays)
3. Ozzie Albies, 2b/ss, Mississippi (Braves)
4. Tyler O'Neill, of, Jackson (Mariners)
5. Jake Bauers, of/1b, Montgomery (Rays)
6. Josh Hader, lhp, Biloxi (Brewers)
7. Brent Honeywell, rhp, Montgomery (Rays)
8. Sean Newcomb, lhp, Mississippi (Braves)
9. Ian Happ, 2b/of, Tennessee (Cubs)
10. Anthony Banda, lhp, Mobile (Diamondbacks)
11. Amir Garrett, lhp, Pensacola (Reds)
12. Dustin Peterson, of, Mississippi (Braves)
13. Stephen Gonsalves, lhp, Chattanooga (Twins)
14. Chih-Wei Hu, rhp, rhp, Montgomery (Rays)
15. Casey Gillaspie, 1b, Montgomery (Rays)
16. Brandon Woodruff, rhp, Biloxi (Brewers)
17. Zach Granite, of, Chattanooga (Twins)
18. Lucas Sims, rhp, Mississippi (Braves)
19. Domingo Leyba, ss, Mobile (Diamondbacks)
20. Carson Fulmer, rhp, Birmingham (White Sox)

Texas League

1. Alex Bregman ss/3b, Corpus Christi (Astros)
2. Cody Bellinger 1b/of, Tulsa (Dodgers)
3. Francis Martes rhp, Corpus Christi (Astros)
4. Luke Weaver rhp, Springfield (Cardinals)
5. David Paulino rhp, Corpus Christi (Astros)
6. Matt Chapman 3b, Midland (Athletics)
7. Franklin Barreto ss/2b, Midland (Athletics)
8. Ryon Healy, 1b/3b, Midland (Athletics)
9. Teoscar Hernandez of, Corpus Christi (Astros)
10. Lewis Brinson of, Frisco (Rangers)
11. Carson Kelly, c, Springfield (Cardinals)
12. Andrew Toles, of, Tulsa (Dodgers)
13. Alex Verdugo, of, Tulsa (Dodgers)
14. Franchy Cordero, of, San Antonio (Padres)
15. Brock Stewart, rhp, Tulsa (Dodgers)
16. Willie Calhoun, 2b, Tulsa (Dodgers)
17. Matt Strahm, lhp, Northwest Arkansas (Royals)
18. Derek Fisher, of, Corpus Christi (Astros)
19. Yohander Mendez, lhp, Frisco (Rangers)
20. Harrison Bader, of, Springfield (Cardinals)

HIGH CLASS A

California League

1. Ryan Castellani, rhp, Modesto (Rockies)
2. Chris Shaw, 1b, San Jose (Giants)
3. Luis Urias, 2b/ss, Lake Elsinore (Padres)

4. Grant Holmes, rhp, Rancho Cucamonga/
   Stockton (Dodgers/Athletics)
5. Yusniel Diaz, of, Rancho Cucamonga (Dodgers)
6. Michael Gettys, of, Lake Elsinore (Padres)
7. Domingo Leyba, ss/2b, Visalia (Diamondbacks)
8. Travis Demeritte, 2b, High Desert (Rangers)
9. Dinelson Lamet, rhp, Lake Elsinore (Padres)
10. Ariel Jurado, rhp, High Desert (Rangers)
11. Andrew Moore, rhp, Bakersfield (Mariners)
12. Dawel Lugo, 3b, Visalia (Diamondbacks)
13. Johan Mieses, of, Rancho Cucamonga (Dodgers)
14. Yency Almonte, rhp, Modesto (Rockies)
15. Drew Jackson, ss, Bakersfield (Mariners)
16. Josh Sborz, rhp, Rancho Cucamonga (Dodgers)
17. Franchy Cordero, of, Lake Elsinore (Padres)
18. Jose Trevino, c, High Desert (Rangers)
19. Rodolfo Martinez, rhp, San Jose (Giants)
20. Ramon Laureano, of, Lancaster (Astros)

Carolina League

1. Yoan Moncada, 2b, Salem (Red Sox)
2. Andrew Benintendi, of, Salem (Red Sox)
3. Victor Robles, of, Potomac (Nationals)
4. Gleyber Torres, ss, Myrtle Beach (Cubs)
5. Francisco Mejia, c, Lynchburg (Indians)
6. Rafael Devers, 3b, Salem (Red Sox)
7. Bobby Bradley, 1b, Lynchburg (Indians)
8. Michael Kopech, rhp, Salem (Red Sox)
9. Erick Fedde, rhp, Potomac (Nationals)
10. Ian Happ, 2b, Myrtle Beach (Cubs)
11. Justus Sheffield, lhp, Lynchburg (Indians)
12. Trevor Clifton, rhp, Myrtle Beach (Cubs)
13. Zack Collins, c, Winston-Salem (White Sox)
14. Mauricio Dubon, ss, Salem (Red Sox)
15. Yu-Cheng Chang, ss, Lynchburg (Indians)
16. Anthony Santander, of, Lynchburg (Indians)
17. Max Povse, rhp, Carolina (Braves)
18. Josh Staumont, rhp, Wilmington (Royals)
19. Travis Demeritte, 2b, Carolina (Braves)
20. Max Schrock, 2b, Potomac (Nationals)

Florida State League

1. Amed Rosario, ss, St. Lucie (Mets)
2. Gleyber Torres, ss, Tampa (Yankees)
3. Kevin Newman, ss, Bradenton (Pirates)
4. Nick Gordon, ss, Fort Myers (Twins)
5. Jorge Mateo, ss/2b, Tampa (Yankees)
6. Corey Ray, of, Brevard County (Brewers)
7. Anthony Alford, of, Dunedin (Blue Jays)
8. Sean Reid-Foley, rhp, Dunedin (Blue Jays)
9. Aristedes Aquino, of, Daytona (Reds)
10. Stephen Gonsalves, lhp, Fort Myers (Twins)
11. Luis Castillo, rhp, Jupiter (Marlins)
12. Brent Honeywell, rhp, Charlotte (Rays)
13. Fernando Romero, rhp, Fort Myers (Twins)
14. Scott Kingery, 2b, Clearwater (Phillies)
15. Christin Stewart, of, Lakeland (Tigers)
16. Brandon Woodruff, rhp, Brevard County (Brewers)
17. Conner Greene, rhp, Dunedin (Blue Jays)
18. Chance Adams, rhp, Tampa (Yankees)
19. Justin Williams, of, Charlotte (Rays)
20. Tomas Nido, c, St. Lucie (Mets)

LOW CLASS A

Midwest League

1. Nick Senzel, 3b, Dayton (Reds)
2. Eloy Jimenez, of, South Bend (Cubs)
3. Francisco Mejia, c, Lake County (Indians)
4. Kyle Tucker, of, Quad Cities (Astros)
5. Sandy Alcantara, rhp, Peoria (Cardinals)
6. Marcos Diplan, rhp, Wisconsin (Brewers)
7. Isan Diaz, ss/2b, Wisconsin (Brewers)
8. Michael Gettys, of, Fort Wayne (Padres)
9. Sean Reid-Foley, rhp, Lansing (Blue Jays)
10. Franklin Perez, rhp, Quad Cities (Astros)
11. Luiz Gohara, lhp, Clinton (Mariners)
12. Magneuris Sierra, of, Peoria (Cardinals)
13. Jon Harris, rhp, Lansing (Blue Jays)
14. Albert Abreu, rhp, Quad Cities (Astros)
15. Matt Thaiss, 1b, Burlington (Angels)
16. Beau Burrows, rhp, West Michigan (Tigers)
17. Trent Clark, of, Wisconsin (Brewers)
18. Jake Cronenworth, ss, Bowling Green (Rays)
19. Eli Alvarez, 2b, Peoria (Cardinals)
20. Lucas Erceg, 3b, Wisconsin (Brewers)

South Atlantic League

1. Victor Robles, of, Hagerstown (Nationals)
2. Mitch Keller, rhp, West Virginia (Pirates)
3. Brendan Rodgers, ss/2b, Asheville (Rockies)
4. Anderson Espinoza, rhp, Greenville (Red Sox)
5. Kolby Allard, lhp, Rome (Braves)
6. Max Fried, lhp, Rome (Braves)
7. Mike Soroka, rhp, Rome (Braves)
8. Franklyn Kilome, rhp, Lakewood (Phillies)
9. Luis Alexander Basabe, of, Greenville (Red Sox)
10. Patrick Weigel, rhp, Rome (Braves)
11. Phil Bickford, rhp, Augusta (Giants)
12. Ronald Acuna, of, Rome (Braves)
13. Austin Riley, 3b, Rome (Braves)
14. Ke'Bryan Hayes, 3b, West Virginia (Pirates)
15. Touki Toussaint, rhp, Rome (Braves)
16. Max Schrock, 2b, Hagerstown (Nationals)
17. Gage Hinsz, rhp, West Virginia (Pirates)
18. Luis Alejando Basabe, 2b/ss, Greenville (Red Sox)
19. Jose Taveras, rhp, Lakewood (Phillies)
20. Joe Palumbo, lhp, Hickory (Rangers)

SHORT-SEASON

New York-Penn League

1. A.J. Puk, lhp, Vermont (Athletics)
2. Triston McKenzie, rhp, Mahoning Valley (Indians)
3. Justin Dunn rhp, Brooklyn (Mets)
4. Desmond Lindsay, of, Brooklyn (Mets)
5. Cody Sedlock, rhp, Aberdeen (Orioles)
6. Dane Dunning, rhp, Auburn (Nationals)
7. Will Craig, 3b, West Virginia (Pirates)
8. Peter Alonso, 1b, Brooklyn (Mets)
9. Bobby Dalbec, 3b, Lowell (Red Sox)
10. Jordan Hicks, rhp, State College (Cardinals)
11. Adonis Medina, rhp, Williamsport (Phillies)
12. Keegan Akin, lhp, Aberdeen (Orioles)
13. C.J. Chatham, ss, Lowell (Red Sox)

14. Austin Hays, of, Aberdeen (Orioles)
15. Tyler Hill, of, Lowell (Red Sox)
16. Josh Pennington, rhp, Lowell (Red Sox)
17. Aaron Civale, rhp, Mahoning Valley (Indians)
18. Garrett Whitley, of, Hudson Valley (Rays)
19. Daz Cameron, of, Tri-City (Astros)
20. Alex Wells, lhp, Aberdeen (Orioles)

Northwest League

1. Leody Taveras, of, Spokane (Rangers)
2. Kyle Lewis, of, Everett (Mariners)
3. Dylan Cease, rhp, Eugene (Cubs)
4. Anderson Tejeda, ss, Spokane (Rangers)
5. Bryan Reynolds, of, Salem-Keizer (Giants)
6. J.B.Woodman, of, Vancouver (Blue Jays)
7. Garrett Hampson, ss, Boise (Rockies)
8. Justin Maese, rhp, Vancouver (Blue Jays)
9. Heath Quinn, of, Salem-Keizer (Giants)
10. Wladimir Galindo, 3b, Eugene (Cubs)
11. Joey Lucchesi, lhp, Tri-City (Padres)
12. Patrick Murphy, rhp, Vancouver (Blue Jays)
13. D.J. Wilson, of, Eugene (Cubs)
14. Gio Brusa, of, Salem-Keizer (Giants)
15. Bryson Brigman, ss/2b, Everett (Mariners)
16. Chris Pieters, 1b/of, Eugene (Cubs)
17. Matt Krook, lhp, Salem-Keizer (Giants)
18. Melvin Adon, rhp, Salem-Keizer (Giants)
19. Tyler Ferguson, rhp, Spokane (Rangers)
20. Buddy Reed, of, Tri-City (Padres)

ROOKIE

Appalachian League

1. Vladimir Guerrero Jr., 3b, Bluefield (Blue Jays)
2. Blake Rutherford, of, Pulaski (Yankees)
3. Estevan Florial, of, Pulaski (Yankees)
4. Kolby Allard, lhp, Danville (Braves)
5. Jordan Hicks, rhp, Johnson City (Cardinals)
6. Alex Kirilloff, of, Elizabethton (Twins)
7. Adrian Rondon, ss, Princeton (Rays)
8. Thomas Szapucki, lhp, Kingsport (Mets)
9. Cristian Pache, of, Danville (Braves)
10. Joey Wentz, lhp, Danville (Braves)
11. Josh Lowe, 3b, Princeton (Rays)
12. Derian Cruz, ss, Danville (Braves)
13. Allen Cordoba, ss, Johnson City (Cardinals)
14. Miguelangel Sierra, ss, Greeneville (Astros)
15. Ian Oxnevad, lhp, Johnson City (Cardinals)
16. Garrett Davila, lhp, Burlington (Royals)
17. Yennsy Diaz, rhp, Bluefield (Blue Jays)
18. Travis Blankenhorn, 2b, Elizabethton (Twins)
19. Nicky Lopez, ss, Burlington (Royals)
20. Brett Cumberland, c, Danville (Braves)

Arizona League

1. Leody Taveras, of, Rangers
2. Yadier Alvarez, rhp, Dodgers
3. Will Benson, of, Indians
4. Khalil Lee, of, Royals
5. Brady Aiken, lhp, Indians
6. Nolan Jones, 3b/ss, Indians
7. Hudson Potts, ss, Padres

8. Seuly Matias, of, Royals
9. Gavin Lux, ss, Dodgers
10. Fernando Tatis Jr., ss, Padres
11. Anderson Tejeda, ss, Rangers
12. Dustin May, rhp, Dodgers
13. Oscar Gonzalez, of, Indians
14. Sandro Fabian, of, Giants
15. Mario Feliciano, c, Brewers
16. Kole Enright, 3b/ss, Rangers
17. Joe Rizzo, 3b, Mariners
18. Gabriel Garcia, 1b, Brewers
19. Amado Nunez, ss, White Sox
20. Sebastian Rivero, c, Royals

Gulf Coast League

1. Mickey Moniak of, Phillies
2. Matt Manning, rhp, Tigers
3. Juan Soto, of, Nationals
4. Bo Bichette, ss, Blue Jays
5. Delvin Perez, ss, Cardinals
6. Jesus Sanchez, of, Rays
7. Sixto Sanchez, rhp, Phillies
8. Josh Lowe, 3b, Rays
9. Alvaro Seijas, rhp, Cardinals
10. Cristian Pache, of, Braves
11. Kyle Muller, lhp, Braves
12. Daniel Brito, 2b, Phillies
13. Derian Cruz, ss, Braves
14. Carter Kieboom, ss, Nationals
15. Jhailyn Ortiz, of, Phillies
16. Dylan Carlson, of, Cardinals
17. Austin Franklin, rhp, Rays
18. Lorenzo Cedrola, of, Red Sox
19. Diego Castillo, ss, Yankees
20. Lupe Chavez, rhp, Astros

Pioneer League

1. Riley Pint, rhp, Grand Junction (Rockies)
2. Alec Hansen, rhp, Great Falls (White Sox)
3. Taylor Trammell, of, Billings (Reds)
4. Lucas Erceg, 3b, Helena (Brewers)
5. Jahmai Jones, of, Orem (Angels)
6. Tony Santillan, rhp, Billings (Reds)
7. D.J. Peters, of, Ogden (Dodgers)
8. Gilbert Lara, ss, Helena (Brewers)
9. Jasrado Chisholm, ss, Missoula (Diamondbacks)
10. T.J. Friedl, of, Billings (Reds)
11. Pedro Gonzalez, of, Grand Junction (Rockies)
12. Meibrys Viloria, c, Idaho Falls (Royals)
13. Mitch Hansen, of, Ogden (Dodgers)
14. Cody Thomas, of, Ogden (Dodgers)
15. Colton Welker, 3b, Grand Junction (Rockies)
16. Keibert Ruiz, c, Ogden (Dodgers)
17. Jose Gomez, ss, Grand Junction (Rockies)
18. Ian Kahaloa, rhp, Billings (Reds)
19. Demi Orimoloye, of, Helena (Brewers)
20. Bernardo Flores, lhp, Great Falls (White Sox)

Diaz, Yandy (Indians)	134	Gallegos, Giovanny (Yankees)	315	Guzman, Jonathan (Phillies)	345
Diaz, Yennsy (Blue Jays)	476	Gamel, Ben (Mariners)	426	Guzman, Jorge (Yankees)	316
Diaz, Yusniel (Dodgers)	229	Gant, John (Cardinals)	380	Guzman, Ronald (Rangers)	453
Didder, Ray-Patrick (Braves)	44	Garabito, Gerson (Royals)	202		
Dietz, Matthias (Orioles)	55	Garcia, Aramis (Giants)	406		

H

Difo, Wilmer (Nationals)	484	Garcia, Bryan (Tigers)	170		
Diplan, Marcos (Brewers)	262	Garcia, David (Rangers)	455	Hader, Josh (Brewers)	259
Dozier, Hunter (Royals)	195	Garcia, Dermis (Yankees)	314	Haley, Justin (Twins)	282
Dubon, Mauricio (Brewers)	262	Garcia, Elniery (Phillies)	348	Hall, Matt (Tigers)	172
Duenez, Samir (Royals)	201	Garcia, Jarlin (Marlins)	245	Hamilton, Ian (White Sox)	108
Duensing, Cole (Angels)	217	Garcia, Jason (Orioles)	61	Hampson, Garrett (Rockies)	151
Duggar, Steven (Giants)	406	Garcia, Luis (Nationals)	485	Haniger, Mitch (Mariners)	420
Duncan, Frank (Pirates)	363	Garcia, Victor (Cardinals)	378	Hannemann, Jacob (Cubs)	91
Dunn, Justin (Mets)	291	Garcia, Wilkerman (Yankees)	317	Hansen, Alec (White Sox)	102
Dunning, Dane (White Sox)	102	Garcia, Yeudy (Pirates)	360	Hansen, Mitch (Dodgers)	237
Duplantier, Jon (Diamondbacks)	21	Garrett, Amir (Reds)	115	Hanson, Alen (Pirates)	361
Duran, Jhoan (Diamondbacks)	24	Garrett, Braxton (Marlins)	242	Hanson, Nick (Reds)	125
		Garrett, Stone (Marlins)	246	Happ, Ian (Cubs)	83

E

		Garver, Mitch (Twins)	281	Harrington, Drew (Braves)	43
		Gasparini, Marten (Royals)	202	Harris, Greg (Rays)	441
Ecker, Mark (Tigers)	168	Gassaway, Randolph (Orioles)	59	Harris, Jon (Blue Jays)	470
Edwards, Andrew (Royals)	202	Gatewood, Jake (Brewers)	267	Harrison, Monte (Brewers)	266
Engel, Adam (White Sox)	105	Gatto, Joe (Angels)	221	Hart, Donnie (Orioles)	56
Enright, Kole (Rangers)	457	Gerber, Mike (Tigers)	165	Harvey, Hunter (Orioles)	51
Eppler, Tyler (Pirates)	362	Gettys, Michael (Padres)	389	Hatch, Thomas (Cubs)	87
Erceg, Lucas (Brewers)	262	Gillaspie, Casey (Rays)	435	Hathaway, Steve (Diamondbacks)	27
Ervin, Phillip (Reds)	121	Gimenez, Andres (Mets)	297	Hauschild, Mike (Rangers)	459
Esch, Jake (Marlins)	247	Giolito, Lucas (White Sox)	99	Hayes, Ke'Bryan (Pirates)	357
Escobar, Luis (Pirates)	365	Giron, Ruddy (Padres)	396	Hays, Austin (Orioles)	53
Eshelman, Thomas (Phillies)	347	Glasnow, Tyler (Pirates)	355	Hearn, Taylor (Pirates)	359
Espinoza, Anderson (Padres)	386	Glover, Koda (Nationals)	485	Hendrix, Ryan (Reds)	123
Estevez, Omar (Dodgers)	235	Gohara, Luiz (Mariners)	419	Herbert, Lucas (Braves)	45
Estrada, Thairo (Yankees)	317	Gomber, Austin (Cardinals)	376	Heredia, Guillermo (Mariners)	425
Evans, Phillip (Mets)	300	Gomez, Miguel (Giants)	413	Herget, Jimmy (Reds)	119
Eveld, Tommy (Diamondbacks)	29	Gonsalves, Stephen (Twins)	275	Hermosillo, Michael (Angels)	216
		Gonzales, Marco (Cardinals)	375	Hernandez, Ariel (Reds)	122

F

		Gonzalez, Brian (Orioles)	56	Hernandez, Brayan (Mariners)	424
		Gonzalez, Erik (Indians)	134	Hernandez, Darwinzon (Red Sox)	77
Fabian, Sandro (Giants)	405	Gonzalez, Harol (Mets)	301	Hernandez, Jonathan (Rangers)	456
Faria, Jacob (Rays)	437	Gonzalez, Marcos (Indians)	141	Hernandez, Jose Luis (Astros)	189
Faulkner, Andrew (Rangers)	459	Gonzalez, Merandy (Mets)	296	Hernandez, Marco (Red Sox)	69
Fedde, Erick (Nationals)	483	Gonzalez, Oscar (Indians)	140	Hernandez, Teoscar (Astros)	181
Feliciano, Mariano (Brewers)	269	Gonzalez, Pedro (Rockies)	155	Herrera, Jose (Diamondbacks)	27
Ferguson, Tyler (Rangers)	461	Goodwin, Brian (Nationals)	489	Herrera, Ronald (Yankees)	316
Fermin, Jose (Indians)	141	Gordon, Nick (Twins)	274	Hicks, Jordan (Cardinals)	380
Fernandez, Junior (Cardinals)	378	Gossett, Daniel (Athletics)	325	Higgins, P.J. (Cubs)	90
Fillmyer, Heath (Athletics)	328	Gowdy, Kevin (Phillies)	342	Hildenberger, Trevor (Twins)	284
Fisher, Derek (Astros)	182	Granite, Zack (Twins)	281	Hill, David (Rockies)	153
Fisher, Jameson (White Sox)	103	Green, Chad (Yankees)	313	Hill, Derek (Tigers)	166
Flaherty, Jack (Cardinals)	374	Greene, Conner (Blue Jays)	468	Hillman, Juan (Indians)	135
Fletcher, David (Angels)	215	Gregorio, Joan (Giants)	405	Hinojosa, C.J. (Giants)	408
Flexen, Chris (Mets)	298	Greiner, Grayson (Tigers)	169	Hinsz, Gage (Pirates)	359
Flores, Bernardo (White Sox)	107	Grier, Anfernee (Diamondbacks)	20	Hofacket, Adam (Angels)	218
Florial, Estevan (Yankees)	311	Griffin, Foster (Royals)	205	Hoffman, Jeff (Rockies)	147
Foster, Jared (Angels)	217	Groome, Jason (Red Sox)	67	Holder, Jonathan (Yankees)	316
Fowler, Dustin (Yankees)	310	Gsellman, Robert (Mets)	293	Holloway, Thomas (Marlins)	248
Fox, Lucius (Rays)	440	Guaimaro, Albert (Marlins)	249	Holmes, Clay (Pirates)	362
Fraley, Jake (Rays)	442	Gudino, Yeltsin (Blue Jays)	476	Holmes, Grant (Athletics)	324
Franco, Anderson (Nationals)	488	Guerra, Javier (Padres)	395	Honeywell, Brent (Rays)	435
Franklin, Austin (Rays)	438	Guerrero Jr., Vladimir (Blue Jays)	466	Hoskins, Rhys (Phillies)	340
Frazier, Clint (Yankees)	307	Guerrero, Gregory (Mets)	301	Hosterman, Travis (Blue Jays)	477
Freeland, Kyle (Rockies)	149	Guerrero, Tayron (Marlins)	248	Houston, Zac (Tigers)	170
French, Parker (Rockies)	155	Guerrieri, Taylor (Rays)	440	Howard, Sam (Rockies)	153
Fried, Max (Braves)	38	Guillon, Ismael (Reds)	125	Hoyt, James (Astros)	187
Friedl, T.J. (Reds)	120	Guillorme, Luis (Mets)	296	Hu, Chih-Wei (Rays)	436
Fulmer, Carson (White Sox)	101	Gunkel, Joe (Orioles)	57	Huang, Wei-Chieh (Diamondbacks)	26
Funkhouser, Kyle (Tigers)	164	Gurriel, Loudres (Blue Jays)	467	Hudson, Bryan (Cubs)	91
		Gurriel, Yulieski (Astros)	181	Hudson, Dakota (Cardinals)	373

G

		Gustave, Jandel (Astros)	185		
		Gutierrez, Abrahan (Braves)	44		

I

Gadea, Kevin (Rays)	443	Gutierrez, Kelvin (Nationals)	488		
Gage, Matt (Giants)	412	Gutierrez, Osman (Blue Jays)	476	Ibanez, Andy (Rangers)	452
Galindo, Wladimir (Cubs)	89	Gutierrez, Vladimir (Reds)	118	Ice, Logan (Indians)	135
Gallagher, Cam (Royals)	200	Guzman, Jeison (Royals)	204		

J

Name	Page
Jackson, Alex (Braves)	45
Jackson, Drew (Mariners)	421
Jackson, Luke (Braves)	44
Jackson, Zach (Blue Jays)	474
Jansen, Dan (Blue Jays)	474
January, Ryan (Diamondbacks)	29
Javier, Wander (Twins)	279
Jax, Griffin (Twins)	282
Jay, Tyler (Twins)	276
Jaye, Myles (Tigers)	168
Jeffries, Daulton (Athletics)	327
Jenkins, Eric (Rangers)	459
Jewell, Jake (Angels)	221
Jhang, Jin-De (Pirates)	364
Jimenez, Eloy (Cubs)	82
Jimenez, Joe (Tigers)	166
Johnson, Brian (Red Sox)	69
Johnson, Chase (Giants)	411
Johnson, Micah (Dodgers)	235
Johnson, Pierce (Cubs)	89
Jones, Connor (Cardinals)	377
Jones, JaCoby (Tigers)	164
Jones, Jahmai (Angels)	210
Jones, Nolan (Indians)	133
Jones, Thomas (Marlins)	246
Jorge, Felix (Twins)	277
Judge, Aaron (Yankees)	308
Junis, Jake (Royals)	200
Jurado, Ariel (Rangers)	451
Justus, Connor (Angels)	215

K

Name	Page
Kahaloa, Ian (Reds)	124
Kaminsky, Rob (Indians)	140
Kaprielian, James (Yankees)	308
Kay, Anthony (Mets)	295
Keller, Brad (Diamondbacks)	21
Keller, Mitch (Pirates)	355
Kelly, Carson (Cardinals)	371
Kemp, Tony (Astros)	188
Kieboom, Carter (Nationals)	485
Kilome, Franklyn (Phillies)	341
Kingery, Scott (Phillies)	341
Kingham, Nick (Pirates)	359
Kirby, Nathan (Brewers)	268
Kiriloff, Alex (Twins)	275
Knapp, Andrew (Phillies)	343
Koch, Matt (Diamondbacks)	22
Kolek, Tyler (Marlins)	243
Kopech, Michael (White Sox)	100
Kramer, Kevin (Pirates)	362
Krieger, Tyler (Indians)	137
Krook, Matt (Giants)	411

L

Name	Page
Labourt, Jairo (Tigers)	172
Lakins, Travis (Red Sox)	71
Lambert, Peter (Rockies)	150
Lamet, Dinelson (Padres)	390
Lara, Gilbert (Brewers)	262
Lauer, Eric (Padres)	391
Laureano, Ramon (Astros)	183
Leathersich, Jack (Cubs)	93
LeClerc, Jose (Rangers)	458
Lee, Chris (Orioles)	54
Lee, Khalil (Royals)	199
Lemieux, Mack (Diamondbacks)	24
Lewis, Kyle (Mariners)	418
Leyba, Domingo (Diamondbacks)	19
Liberato, Luis (Mariners)	427

Name	Page
Light, Pat (Twins)	279
Lilek, Brett (Marlins)	252
Linares, Resly (Rays)	445
Lindsay, Desmond (Mets)	291
Liranzo, Jesus (Orioles)	55
Littell, Zack (Yankees)	315
Lively, Ben (Phillies)	345
Lockett, Walker (Padres)	396
Long, Grayson (Angels)	213
Long, Shed (Reds)	120
Longhi, Nick (Red Sox)	71
Lopez, Jorge (Brewers)	264
Lopez, Nicky (Royals)	199
Lopez, Reynaldo (White Sox)	99
Lora, Edwin (Nationals)	491
Lowe, Josh (Rays)	436
Lucchesi, Joey (Padres)	395
Lugo, Dawel (Diamondbacks)	19
Lund, Brennon (Angels)	220
Lux, Gavin (Dodgers)	230
Luzardo, Jesus (Nationals)	488

M

Name	Page
MacGregor, Travis (Pirates)	363
Machado, Dixon (Tigers)	167
Machado, Jonathan (Cardinals)	377
Maese, Justin (Blue Jays)	470
Mahle, Tyler (Reds)	119
Maitan, Kevin (Braves)	37
Mancini, Trey (Orioles)	52
Manning, Matt (Tigers)	162
Margot, Manuel (Padres)	387
Marlette, Tyler (Mariners)	429
Marmolejos, Jose (Nationals)	492
Marquez, German (Rockies)	148
Marsh, Brandon (Angels)	211
Martes, Francis (Astros)	178
Martin, Brett (Rangers)	454
Martin, Kyle (Red Sox)	73
Martin, Richie (Athletics)	326
Martinez, Eddy (Cubs)	86
Martinez, Nolan (Yankees)	313
Martinez, Rodolfo (Giants)	407
Mata, Bryan (Red Sox)	76
Mateo, Jorge (Yankees)	307
Mathias, Mark (Indians)	135
Matias, Seuly (Royals)	198
Maton, Phil (Padres)	393
Matuella, Michael (Rangers)	457
Maxwell, Bruce (Athletics)	326
May, Dustin (Dodgers)	231
May, Jacob (White Sox)	106
Mazeika, Patrick (Mets)	298
McCarthy, Joe (Rays)	441
McCarthy, Kevin (Royals)	204
McClanahan, Chad (Brewers)	269
McGowin, Kyle (Angels)	218
McGuire, Reese (Blue Jays)	471
McKenzie, Triston (Indians)	131
McMahon, Ryan (Rockies)	150
Meadows, Austin (Pirates)	354
Medeiros, Kodi (Brewers)	265
Medina, Adonis (Phillies)	344
Mejia, Adalberto (Twins)	276
Mejia, Francisco (Indians)	130
Melendez, Manuel (Rockies)	157
Mella, Keury (Reds)	121
Melotakis, Mason (Twins)	285
Mendez, Yohander (Rangers)	451
Merritt, Ryan (Indians)	138
Merryweather, Julian (Indians)	139
Meyer, Alex (Angels)	211
Michalczewski, Trey (White Sox)	103

Name	Page
Middleton, Keynan (Angels)	213
Mieses, Johan (Dodgers)	232
Miller, Brandon (Mariners)	428
Miller, Jalen (Giants)	412
Miller, Jared (Diamondbacks)	25
Mills, Alec (Royals)	199
Milner, Hoby (Indians)	139
Miniard, Micah (Indians)	141
Minter, A.J. (Braves)	41
Miranda, Jose (Twins)	283
Molina, Marcos (Mets)	294
Moll, Sam (Rockies)	156
Moncada, Yoan (White Sox)	98
Moniak, Mickey (Phillies)	339
Montas, Frankie (Athletics)	324
Montgomery, Jordan (Yankees)	311
Moore, Andrew (Mariners)	420
Morales, Francisco (Phillies)	348
Morales, Roy (Marlins)	250
Moran, Colin (Astros)	189
Morejon, Adrian (Padres)	388
Moreno, Erling (Cubs)	90
Morgan, Josh (Rangers)	452
Morimando, Shawn (Indians)	137
Moroff, Max (Pirates)	361
Moronta, Reyes (Giants)	407
Motter, Taylor (Mariners)	428
Mountcastle, Ryan (Orioles)	51
Moya, Steven (Tigers)	165
Muckenhirn, Zack (Orioles)	60
Mullens, Cedric (Orioles)	60
Muller, Kyle (Braves)	40
Mundell, Brian (Rockies)	156
Munoz, Yairo (Athletics)	327
Murphy, Patrick (Blue Jays)	474
Murphy, Sean (Athletics)	329
Murphy, Tom (Rockies)	149
Musgrave, Harrison (Rockies)	155

N

Name	Page
Naile, James (Athletics)	333
Narvaez, Omar (White Sox)	109
Naylor, Josh (Padres)	390
Neidert, Nick (Mariners)	420
Nelson, James (Marlins)	249
Neuse, Sheldon (Nationals)	489
Neverauskas, Dovydas (Pirates)	363
Nevin, Tyler (Rockies)	153
Newcomb, Sean (Braves)	37
Newman, Kevin (Pirates)	356
Nido, Tomas (Mets)	294
Nikorak, Mike (Rockies)	154
Nimmo, Brandon (Mets)	292
Nix, Jacob (Padres)	389
Nogosek, Stephen (Red Sox)	75
Norwood, John (Marlins)	253
Nottingham, Jacob (Brewers)	263
Nova, Freudis (Astros)	188
Nunez, Dom (Rockies)	151
Nunez, Renato (Athletics)	329

O

Name	Page
O'Hearn, Ryan (Royals)	197
O'Neill, Tyler (Mariners)	419
Oaks, Trevor (Dodgers)	231
Ockimey, Josh (Red Sox)	70
Ogle, Braeden (Pirates)	364
Okert, Steven (Giants)	407
Okey, Chris (Reds)	120
Olson, Matt (Athletics)	328
Ona, Jorge (Padres)	391
Orimoloye, Demi (Brewers)	268

Ortiz, Jhailyn (Phillies)	346
Ortiz, Luis (Brewers)	259
Osuna, Jose (Pirates)	364
Overton, Dillon (Athletics)	333
Oviedo, Johan (Cardinals)	381

P

Pache, Christian (Braves)	39
Paddack, Chris (Padres)	392
Padlo, Kevin (Rays)	441
Palacios, Josh (Blue Jays)	473
Palka, Daniel (Twins)	278
Palumbo, Joe (Rangers)	453
Paredes, Isaac (Cubs)	93
Pastrone, Sam (Angels)	216
Patterson, Jordan (Rockies)	151
Paulino, David (Astros)	179
Paulino, Jose (Cubs)	90
Payano, Pedro (Rangers)	460
Pazos, James (Mariners)	429
Pennington, Josh (Brewers)	265
Pentecost, Max (Blue Jays)	471
Peralta, Freddy (Brewers)	266
Peralta, Ofelky (Orioles)	55
Perdomo, Angel (Blue Jays)	473
Perez, Arvicent (Tigers)	171
Perez, Delvin (Cardinals)	371
Perez, Franklin (Astros)	180
Perez, Hector (Astros)	184
Perez, Sam (Marlins)	251
Perez, Yanio (Rangers)	460
Perez, Yefri (Marlins)	253
Perkins, Blake (Nationals)	490
Peter, Jake (White Sox)	104
Peters, D.J. (Dodgers)	234
Peters, Dillon (Marlins)	244
Peterson, D.J. (Mariners)	423
Peterson, Dustin (Braves)	40
Phillips, Brett (Brewers)	262
Pieters, Chris (Cubs)	93
Pinder, Chad (Athletics)	325
Pint, Riley (Rockies)	147
Pinto, Ricardo (Phillies)	347
Pinto, Wladimir (Tigers)	170
Pivetta, Nick (Phillies)	343
Plummer, Nick (Cardinals)	379
Plutko, Adam (Indians)	136
Ponce, Cody (Brewers)	264
Poteet, Cody (Marlins)	248
Potts, Hudson (Padres)	391
Pounders, Brooks (Angels)	217
Povse, Max (Mariners)	421
Profar, Juremi (Rangers)	460
Pruitt, Austin (Rays)	445
Puckett, A.J. (Royals)	196
Puk, A.J. (Athletics)	323

Q

Quantrill, Cal (Padres)	388
Quinn, Heath (Giants)	408
Quinn, Roman (Phillies)	341

R

Ragans, Cole (Rangers)	451
Rainey, Tanner (Reds)	124
Ramirez, Harold (Blue Jays)	471
Ramirez, Yefrey (Yankees)	314
Randolph, Cornelius (Phillies)	344
Raudes, Roniel (Red Sox)	68
Ravenelle, Adam (Tigers)	165
Ray, Corey (Brewers)	260

Reed, A.J. (Astros)	180
Reed, Cody (Reds)	115
Reed, Jake (Twins)	284
Reed, Michael (Brewers)	269
Reed, Raudy (Nationals)	490
Reed, Remey (Marlins)	252
Reetz, Jackson (Nationals)	489
Reid-Foley, Sean (Blue Jays)	467
Reinheimer, Jack (Diamondbacks)	24
Renfroe, Hunter (Padres)	387
Reyes, Alex (Cardinals)	370
Reyes, Jomar (Orioles)	53
Reyes, Victor (Diamondbacks)	26
Reynolds, Bryan (Giants)	404
Reynolds, Matt (Mets)	297
Riddle, J.T. (Marlins)	250
Riley, Austin (Braves)	38
Rios, Francisco (Blue Jays)	473
Rivera, T.J. (Mets)	299
Rivero, Sebastian (Royals)	204
Rizzo, Joe (Mariners)	422
Robertson, Daniel (Rays)	440
Robinson, Drew (Rangers)	458
Robles, Victor (Nationals)	482
Robson, Jacob (Tigers)	171
Rodgers, Brady (Astros)	186
Rodgers, Brendan (Rockies)	146
Rodriguez, Alfredo (Reds)	123
Rodriguez, Chris (Angels)	213
Rodriguez, David (Rays)	443
Rodriguez, Joely (Phillies)	346
Rodriguez, Nellie (Indians)	139
Rogers, Jake (Astros)	186
Romano, Jordan (Blue Jays)	475
Romano, Sal (Reds)	118
Romero, Fernando (Twins)	276
Rondon, Adrian (Rays)	439
Rondon, Jose (Padres)	394
Rortvedt, Ben (Twins)	283
Rosario, Amed (Mets)	290
Rose, Joey (Diamondbacks)	28
Ruiz, Keibert (Dodgers)	234
Ruiz, Rio (Braves)	42
Russell, Ashe (Royals)	203
Rutherford, Blake (Yankees)	307

S

Sadzeck, Connor (Rangers)	456
Sanchez, Ali (Mets)	300
Sanchez, Jesus (Rays)	437
Sanchez, Jose (Nationals)	491
Sanchez, Sixto (Phillies)	340
Santander, Anthony (Orioles)	53
Santillan, Tony (Reds)	119
Sborz, Josh (Dodgers)	233
Scavuzzo, Jacob (Dodgers)	237
Schnurbusch, Aaron (White Sox)	106
Schrock, Max (Athletics)	330
Schultz, Jamie (Rays)	439
Scott, Robby (Red Sox)	72
Scott, Tanner (Orioles)	54
Sedlock, Cody (Orioles)	51
Seijas, Alvaro (Cardinals)	377
Senzatela, Antonio (Rockies)	150
Senzel, Nick (Reds)	114
Severino, Pedro (Nationals)	486
Shaw, Chris (Giants)	403
Shawaryn, Mike (Red Sox)	71
Sheffield, Jordan (Dodgers)	231
Sheffield, Justus (Yankees)	309
Shepherd, Chandler (Red Sox)	74
Sherfy, Jimmy (Diamondbacks)	23
Shore, Logan (Athletics)	327

Sierra, Magneuris (Cardinals)	372
Sierra, Miguelangel (Astros)	183
Sierra, Yaisel (Dodgers)	234
Simcox, A.J. (Tigers)	168
Sims, Lucas (Braves)	39
Sisco, Chance (Orioles)	50
Skoglund, Eric (Royals)	196
Skole, Matt (Nationals)	493
Slania, Dan (Giants)	409
Slater, Austin (Giants)	409
Smith, Dominic (Mets)	291
Smith, Drew (Tigers)	170
Smith, Nate (Angels)	212
Smith, Will (Dodgers)	232
Sodders, Austin (Tigers)	168
Solak, Nick (Yankees)	313
Sopko, Andrew (Dodgers)	236
Soroka, Mike (Braves)	35
Sosa, Edmundo (Cardinals)	373
Soto, Gregory (Tigers)	173
Soto, Isael (Marlins)	247
Soto, Juan (Nationals)	483
Speas, Alex (Rangers)	453
Stanek, Ryne (Rays)	439
Starling, Bubba (Royals)	205
Staumont, Josh (Royals)	194
Steckenrider, Drew (Marlins)	251
Steele, Justin (Cubs)	91
Stephens, Jordan (White Sox)	103
Stephenson, Robert (Reds)	116
Stephenson, Tyler (Reds)	118
Stevenson, Andrew (Nationals)	484
Stewart, Brock (Dodgers)	229
Stewart, Christin (Tigers)	163
Stewart, D.J. (Orioles)	57
Stewart, Kohl (Twins)	277
Strahm, Matt (Royals)	195
Stratton, Chris (Giants)	410
Stubbs, Garrett (Astros)	182
Suarez, Andrew (Giants)	404
Suarez, Jose (Angels)	216
Swanson, Dansby (Braves)	34
Szapucki, Thomas (Mets)	293
Szynski, Skylar (Athletics)	332

T

Tapia, Raimel (Rockies)	147
Tate, Dillon (Yankees)	312
Tatis Jr., Fernando (Padres)	393
Tavares, Jose (Phillies)	346
Tavarez, Aneury (Orioles)	56
Taveras, Leody (Rangers)	450
Taylor, Ben (Red Sox)	74
Taylor, Corey (Mets)	300
Taylor, Cory (Giants)	410
Taylor, Curtis (Diamondbacks)	22
Taylor, Josh (Diamondbacks)	27
Tejeda, Anderson (Rangers)	456
Tellez, Rowdy (Blue Jays)	469
Thaiss, Matt (Angels)	211
Thomas, Cody (Dodgers)	237
Thompson, Mason (Padres)	396
Thompson, Zach (White Sox)	107
Thornton, Trent (Astros)	186
Thorpe, Lewis (Twins)	281
Tilson, Charlie (White Sox)	105
Tirado, Alberto (Phillies)	348
Tocci, Carlos (Phillies)	349
Toles, Andrew (Dodgers)	228
Torres, Christopher (Mariners)	426
Torres, Gleyber (Yankees)	306
Torres, Jose (Padres)	394
Torres, Ramon (Royals)	203

Tortosa, Cristhian (Tigers)	171	Wilson, Bryse (Braves)	43
Toussaint, Touki (Braves)	39	Wilson, D.J. (Cubs)	86
Tovar, Oscar (Athletics)	331	Wilson, Marcus (Diamondbacks)	26
Trahan, Blake (Reds)	125	Winker, Jesse (Reds)	117
Trammell, Taylor (Reds)	116	Wood, Hunter (Rays)	444
Travieso, Nick (Reds)	121	Woodford, Jake (Cardinals)	376
Travis, Sam (Red Sox)	67	Woodman, J.B. (Blue Jays)	472
Trevino, Jose (Rangers)	455	Woodmansee, Colby (Mets)	301
Tucker, Cole (Pirates)	358	Woodruff, Brandon (Brewers)	261
Tucker, Kyle (Astros)	179		

Waddell, Brandon (Pirates) — 361
Wade, LaMonte (Twins) — 282
Wade, Tyler (Yankees) — 312
Wahl, Bobby (Athletics) — 332
Walker, Adam Brett (Orioles) — 57
Walker, Christian (Orioles) — 59
Wall, Forrest (Rockies) — 152
Walsh, Connor (White Sox) — 108
Walton, Donnie (Mariners) — 429
Ward, Drew (Nationals) — 487
Ward, Taylor (Angels) — 212
Watson, Nolan (Royals) — 200
Watson, Tyler (Nationals) — 492
Weaver, Luke (Cardinals) — 371
Webb, Tyler (Pirates) — 365
Weigel, Patrick (Braves) — 37
Weiss, Zack (Reds) — 124
Welker, Colton (Rockies) — 152
Wells, Alex (Orioles) — 59
Wendle, Joey (Athletics) — 330
Wentz, Joey (Braves) — 40
Whalen, Rob (Mariners) — 425
White, Isaiah (Marlins) — 251
White, Mitchell (Dodgers) — 233
Whitley, Forrest (Astros) — 181
Whitley, Garrett (Rays) — 438
Williams, Devin (Brewers) — 268
Williams, Garrett (Giants) — 411
Williams, Justin (Rays) — 437
Williams, Nick (Phillies) — 339
Williams, Nonie (Angels) — 214
Williams, Ronnie (Cardinals) — 379
Williams, Trevor (Pirates) — 360

Tuivailala, Sam (Cardinals) — 378
Turnbull, Spencer (Tigers) — 169
Twine, Justin (Marlins) — 253
Tyler, Robert (Rockies) — 154

U

Underwood, Duane (Cubs) — 88
Urena, Richard (Blue Jays) — 468
Urias, Luis (Padres) — 388

V

Valera, Breyvic (Cardinals) — 381
Vallot, Chase (Royals) — 197
Vargas, Carlos (Mariners) — 428
Vargas, Ildemaro (Diamondbacks) — 28
Vargas, Yerdel (Athletics) — 332
Vasto, Jerry (Rockies) — 157
Verdugo, Alex (Dodgers) — 227
Vieira, Thyago (Mariners) — 424
Vielma, Engelb (Twins) — 283
Viloria, Meibrys (Royals) — 201
Vogelbach, Dan (Mariners) — 422
Voth, Austin (Nationals) — 486

W

Y

Yacabonis, Jimmy (Orioles) — 58
Yarbrough, Ryan (Mariners) — 423
Yerzy, Andy (Diamondbacks) — 23
Ynoa, Gabriel (Mets) — 294
Ynoa, Huascar (Twins) — 285
Young, Alex (Diamondbacks) — 22
Young, Chesny (Cubs) — 88
Ysla, Luis (Red Sox) — 74

Z

Zagunis, Mark (Cubs) — 84
Zastryzny, Rob (Cubs) — 87
Zeuch, T.J. (Blue Jays) — 469
Zimmer, Bradley (Indians) — 131
Zimmer, Kyle (Royals) — 198
Zimmerman, Jordan (Angels) — 220
Zych, Tony (Mariners) — 425